THE ROUGH GUIDE TO
THAILAND

This tenth edition updated by
Ron Emmons, Marco Ferrarese and Paul Gray

ROUGH
GUIDES

Contents

Introduction to
Thailand

With over thirty million foreigners flying into the country each year, Thailand is Asia's primary holiday destination. Yet despite this vast influx of visitors, Thailand's cultural integrity remains largely undamaged – a country that adroitly avoided colonization has been able to absorb Western influences while maintaining its own rich heritage. Though the high-rises and neon lights occupy the foreground of the tourist picture, the typical Thai community is still the farming village, and you need not venture far to encounter a more traditional scene of fishing communities, rubber plantations and Buddhist temples. Around forty percent of Thais earn their living from the land, based around the staple rice, which forms the foundation of the country's unique and famously sophisticated cuisine.

Tourism has been just one factor in the country's development which, since the deep-seated uncertainties surrounding the Vietnam War faded, has been free, for the most part, to proceed at death-defying pace – for a time in the 1980s and early 1990s, Thailand boasted the fastest-expanding economy in the world. Politics in Thailand, however, has not been able to keep pace. Since World War II, coups d'état have been as common a method of changing government as general elections; the malnourished democratic system – when the armed forces allow it to operate – is characterized by corruption and cronyism.

Through all the changes of the last seventy years, the much-revered constitutional monarch, King Bhumibol, sitting at the pinnacle of an elaborate hierarchical system of deference covering the whole of Thai society, lent a measure of stability. Furthermore, some 85 percent of the population are still practising Theravada Buddhists, a unifying faith that colours all aspects of daily life – from the tiered temple rooftops that dominate every skyline, to the omnipresent saffron-robed monks and the packed calendar of festivals.

Where to go

The clash of tradition and modernity is most intense in **Bangkok**, the first stop on almost any itinerary. Within its historic core you'll find resplendent temples, canalside markets and the opulent indulgence of the eighteenth-century **Grand Palace**, while downtown's forest of skyscrapers shelters cutting-edge fashion and decor boutiques, as well as cool bars and clubs. After touchdown in Bangkok, much of the package-holiday traffic flows east to **Pattaya**, the country's seediest resort, but for prettier beaches you're better off venturing just a little further, to the islands of **Ko Samet** and the **Ko Chang archipelago**, with their squeaky white sand and shorefront bungalows.

Few tourists visit **Isaan**, the poorest and in some ways the most traditionally Thai region. Here, a trip through the gently modulating landscapes of the **Mekong River** valley, which defines Thailand's northeastern extremities, takes in archetypal agricultural villages and a fascinating array of religious sites, while the southern reaches of Isaan hold some of Thailand's best-kept secrets – the magnificent stone temple complexes of **Phimai**, **Phanom Rung** and **Khao Phra Viharn**, all built by the Khmers of Cambodia almost ten centuries ago. Closer to the capital, **Khao Yai National Park** encapsulates the phenomenal diversity of Thailand's flora and fauna, which here range from wild orchids to strangling figs, elephants to hornbills.

At the heart of the northern uplands, **Chiang Mai** is both an attractive historic city and a vibrant cultural centre, with a strong tradition of arts, crafts and festivals, and a burgeoning line in self-improvement courses – from ascetic meditation to the more earthly pleasures of Thai cookery classes. Plenty of outdoor activities and courses, as well as hot springs and massages, can also be enjoyed at **Pai**, a surprisingly cosmopolitan hill station for travellers. **Chiang Rai**'s array of museums and temples is almost as fascinating as Chiang Mai's, while the ancient cities of Lampang, Nan and Chiang Saen provide further excuses for travelling through the glorious mountainscapes.

With Chiang Mai and the north so firmly planted on the independent tourist trail, the intervening **central plains** tend to get short shrift. Yet there is rewarding trekking

FACT FILE

- Divided into 76 provinces or *changwat* and one special administrative area (Bangkok), Thailand was known as **Siam** until 1939 (and again from 1945 to 1949); some academics suggest changing the name back again, to better reflect the country's Thai and non-Thai diversity.
- The **population** of 69 million is made up of ethnic Thais (75 percent) and Chinese (14 percent), with the rest comprising mainly immigrants from neighbouring countries as well as hill-tribespeople.
- Buddhism is the national **religion**, Islam the largest minority religion, but nearly all Thais also practise some form of animism (spirit worship).
- Since 1932 the country has been a **constitutional** monarchy. At the time of his death in 2016, King Bhumibol, also known as Rama IX (being the ninth ruler of the Chakri dynasty), was the world's longest-ruling head of state, having been on the throne since 1946; he was succeeded by his son, who became King Vajiralongkorn (Rama X), though at the time of writing the coronation had yet to be held.
- The world record for **nonstop kissing** was set in Pattaya on Valentine's Day, 2013, at a gobsmacking 58 hours, 35 minutes and 58 seconds.

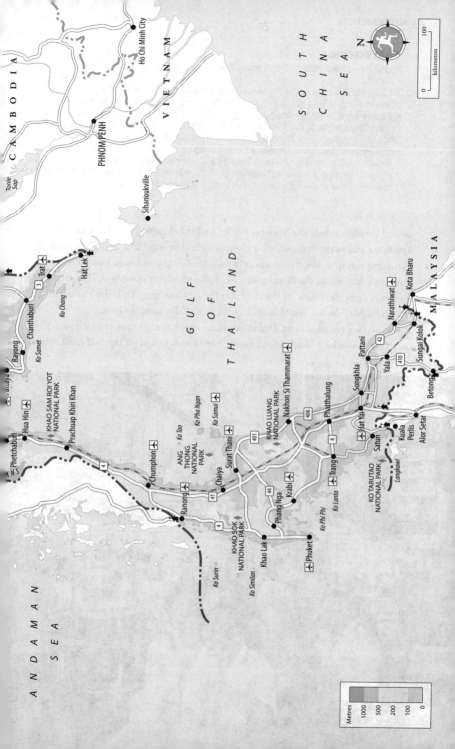

THAI BOXING

Such is the national obsession with **muay thai**, or Thai boxing, that when Wijan Ponlid returned home from the Sydney 2000 Olympics with the country's only gold medal (for international flyweight boxing), he was paraded through town at the head of a procession of 49 elephants, given a new house and over 20 million baht, and offered a promotion in the police force. Belatedly perhaps, *muay thai* has recently entered the canon of martial-arts cinema: *Ong Bak* (2003), *Tom Yum Goong* (2005) and their various sequels were global box-office hits, and their all-punching, all-kicking star, Tony Jaa, who performed all his own stunts, has been appointed Cultural Ambassador for Thailand.

Though there are boxing venues all around the country, the very best fights are staged at Bangkok's two biggest stadiums, Rajdamnoen and Lumphini, and are well worth attending as a cultural experience even if you have no interest in the sport itself (see pages 50 and 164).

around **Umphang**, near the Burmese border, and the elegant ruins of former capitals **Ayutthaya** and **Sukhothai** embody a glorious artistic heritage, displaying Thailand's distinctive ability to absorb influences from quite different cultures. **Kanchanaburi**, stunningly located on the **River Kwai**, tells of a much darker episode in Thailand's past, for it was along the course of this river that the Japanese army built the Thailand–Burma Railway during World War II, at the cost of thousands of lives.

Sand and sea are what most Thai holidays are about, though, and the pick of the coasts are in southern Thailand, where the Samui archipelago off the **Gulf coast** is one

STREET RESTAURANTS IN BANGKOK

of the highlights. **Ko Samui** itself has the most sweeping white-sand beaches, and the greatest variety of accommodation and facilities to go with them. **Ko Pha Ngan** next door is still largely backpacker territory, where you have a stark choice between desolate coves and **Hat Rin**, Thailand's party capital. The remotest island, rocky **Ko Tao**, is acquiring increasing sophistication as Southeast Asia's largest dive-training centre.

Across on the other side of the peninsula, the **Andaman coast** boasts even more exhilarating scenery and the finest coral reefs in the country, in particular around the **Ko Similan** island chain, which ranks among the best dive sites in the world. The largest Andaman coast island, **Phuket**, is one of Thailand's top tourist destinations and graced with a dozen fine beaches, though several have been overdeveloped with a glut of high-rises and tacky nightlife. Beautiful little **Ko Phi Phi** is a major party hub, surrounded by the turquoise seas and dramatic limestone cliffs that characterize the coastline throughout **Krabi province**. Large, forested **Ko Lanta Yai** is, for the moment at least, a calmer alternative for families, but for genuine jungle you'll need to head inland, to the rainforests of **Khao Sok National Park**.

Further down the Thai peninsula, in the provinces of the **deep south**, the teeming sea life and unfrequented sands of the **Trang islands** and **Ko Tarutao National Marine Park** are the main draws. There's now the intriguing possibility of **island-hopping** your way down through them – in fact, all the way from Phuket to Penang in Malaysia – without setting foot on the mainland.

When to go

The **climate** of most of Thailand is governed by three seasons: rainy (roughly May–Oct), caused by the southwest monsoon dumping moisture gathered from the Andaman Sea and the Gulf of Thailand; cool (Nov–Feb); and hot (March–May). The **rainy season** is the least predictable of the three, varying in length and intensity from year to year, but it's never a case of the heavens opening in May and not closing again till October: there'll be rain most days, but often only for a few hours in the afternoon or at night. The rains usually gather force between June and August, coming to a peak in September and October, when unpaved roads are reduced to mud troughs. The **cool season** is the pleasantest time to visit, although temperatures can still reach a broiling

---

SPIRIT HOUSES

Although the vast majority of Thais are Buddhist, nearly everyone also believes that the physical world is inhabited by **spirits**. These spirits can cause trouble if not given enough care and attention, and are apt to wreak havoc when made homeless. Therefore, whenever a new building is constructed – be it a traditional village house or a multistorey office block – the owners will also construct a home for the spirits who previously occupied that land. Crucially, these spirit houses must be given the best spot on the site – which in Bangkok often means on the roof – and must also reflect the status of the building in question, so their architecture can range from the simplest wooden structure to an elaborate scale model of a particularly ornate temple or even a sleek little icon of modernism. Daily **offerings** of flowers, incense and candles are set inside the spirit house, sometimes with morsels of food.

RAT OR RAJA?

There's no standard system of **transliterating** Thai script into Roman, so you're sure to find that the Thai words in this book don't always match the versions you'll see elsewhere. Maps and street signs are the biggest sources of confusion, so we've generally gone for the transliteration that's most common on the spot; where it's a toss-up between two equally popular versions, we've used the one that helps best with pronunciation. However, sometimes you'll need to do a bit of lateral thinking, bearing in mind that a classic variant for the town of Ayutthaya is Ayudhia, while among street names, Thanon Rajavithi could come out as Thanon Ratwithi – and it's not unheard of to find one spelling posted at one end of a road, with another at the opposite end.

30°C in the middle of the day. In the **hot season**, when temperatures often rise to 35°C in Bangkok, the best thing to do is to hit the beach.

Within this scheme, slight variations are found from region to region (see page 61). The upland, less humid **north** experiences the greatest range of temperatures: at night in the cool season the thermometer dips markedly, occasionally approaching zero on the higher slopes, and this region is often hotter than the central plains between March and May. It's the **northeast** that gets the very worst of the hot season, with clouds of dust gathering above the parched fields, and humid air too. In **southern Thailand**, temperatures are more consistent throughout the year, with less variation the closer you get to the equator. The rainy season hits the **Andaman coast** of the southern peninsula harder than anywhere else in the country: rainfall can start in April and usually persists until November.

One area of the country, the **Gulf coast** of the southern peninsula, lies outside this general pattern. With the sea immediately to the east, this coast and its offshore islands feel the effects of the northeast monsoon, which brings rain between October and January, especially in November, but suffers less than the Andaman coast from the southwest monsoon.

Overall, the cool season is the **best time** to come to Thailand: as well as having more manageable temperatures and less rain, it offers waterfalls in full spate and the best of the upland flowers in bloom. Bear in mind, however, that it's also the busiest season, so forward planning is essential.

Author picks

Having finally settled down in Thailand after twenty years of toing and froing, our author, Paul, has plenty to write home about. Here are some of his personal favourites.

Kneads must A good pummelling at the massage pavilions amid the historic, kaleidoscopic architecture of Wat Pho (see page 90) is one of Bangkok's unbeatable experiences.

Road trips You'll get to know the mighty Mekong River up close and personal along the Chiang Khan–Nong Khai road in Isaan (see page 486), while the three thousand bends of the Mae Hong Son loop reveal the pick of Thailand's upland scenery (see page 328).

Islands ahoy Messing about in boats is a big part of island life, and it's hard to beat a short, richly diverse circuit of Ko Tao and the causeway beaches of Ko Nang Yuan (see page 569).

Lam te te "Delicious" food is never far away in Chiang Mai, be it pork-belly curry or *khao soi* (curry soup with egg noodles) – sign up for a guided food walk to make the most of it (see page 293).

Let yourself go Mad, bad and bawdy carousing at Yasothon's Rocket Festival (see page 467) and Phi Ta Kon in Dan Sai (see page 480).

Simply celadon Among dozens of highly skilled, good-value handicrafts in Thailand, one that's especially appealing is celadon, elegant stoneware subtly glazed in green (see page 298).

Khon It's hard to catch these days, but if you come across a performance, sit down and soak up the haunting music, beautiful costumes and exquisite gestures of Thailand's highest dramatic art (see page 49).

Best view? You decide: a godlike panorama of the concrete jungle from Bangkok's *Sky Bar* (see page 162), wave after wave of forested mountains from Doi Chang Moob (see page 364), or the implausible limestone turrets in Phang Nga bay (see page 646)?

> Our author recommendations don't end here. We've flagged up our favourite places – a perfectly sited hotel, an atmospheric café, a special restaurant – throughout the Guide, highlighted with the ★ symbol.

KO NANG YUAN

PHI TA KON PERFORMER; LOEI PROVINCE

30

things not to miss

It's not possible to see everything that Thailand has to offer in one trip – and we don't suggest you try. What follows, in no particular order, is a selective taste of the country's highlights: beautiful beaches, outstanding national parks, magnificent temples and thrilling activities. All entries have a page reference to take you straight into the Guide, where you can find out more.

1 KO KOOD
See page 425

An untamed beauty, fringed by very pretty beaches.

2 AYUTTHAYA
See page 213

River boats and bicycles are the perfect way to explore the scattered temple ruins of this former capital.

3 NAKHON SI THAMMARAT
See page 572

Home to superb food and the chief religious and cultural riches of the south.

4 KHAO YAI NATIONAL PARK
See page 435

Easy trails and tours, night safaris and a healthy cast of hornbills and gibbons.

5 VEGETARIAN FESTIVAL, PHUKET
See page 620

During Taoist Lent, fasting Chinese devotees test their spiritual resolve with acts of gruesome self-mortification.

6 CHATUCHAK WEEKEND MARKET
See page 128
Thailand's top shopping experience features over ten thousand stalls selling everything from cooking pots to designer lamps.

7 FOLK MUSEUM, PHITSANULOK
See page 234
One of Thailand's best ethnology museums, complete with a reconstructed village home.

8 KHAO SOK NATIONAL PARK
See page 601
Mist-clad outcrops, jungle trails serenaded by whooping gibbons, and the vast Cheow Lan Lake all make Khao Sok a rewarding place to explore.

9 WAT PHRA THAT DOI SUTHEP, CHIANG MAI
See page 301
One of the most harmonious ensembles of temple architecture in the country.

10 SONGKHRAN
See page 48
Thai New Year is the excuse for a national waterfight.

11 JIM THOMPSON'S HOUSE
See page 118
The house of the legendary American adventurer, entrepreneur and art collector is a small, personal museum of Thai crafts and architecture

12 KHMER RUINS
See pages 444 and 458
The Khmers of neighbouring Angkor left a chain of magnificent temple complexes across the northeast, including this one at Phimai.

13 NIGHT MARKETS
See page 40
Evening gatherings of pushcart kitchens, which are usually the best-value places to eat.

14 TRADITIONAL MASSAGE
See page 51
Combining elements of acupressure and yoga, a pleasantly brutal way to end the day.

15 FULL MOON PARTY AT HAT RIN, KO PHA NGAN
See page 558
Apocalypse Now without the war.

11

12

13

14

15

17

21

22

23

18

19

20

21 THAI COOKERY CLASSES IN CHIANG MAI
See page 281
Of the many courses on offer in the town, cookery classes are the most instantly gratifying and popular.

22 THE MAE HONG SON LOOP
See page 328
A spectacular 600km trip, winding over steep forested mountains.

23 AO PHANG NGA
See page 646
Boat or kayak your way through the bizarre and beautiful rock formations rising out of the Andaman Sea.

24 ROCK-CLIMBING
See page 55
Even novice climbers can scale the cliffs at Ko Yao Noi, Phi Phi or the Railay peninsula for an unbeatable perspective on the Andaman seascape.

25 LOY KRATHONG
See page 49
At this festival in honour of the water spirits, Thais float baskets of flowers and lighted candles on rivers, ponds and seashores.

26

27

28

26 KO LANTA YAI
See page 679

A popular choice for families, with its many long beaches and plentiful but low-key resort facilities.

27 SUKHOTHAI
See page 237

Rent a bicycle to explore the elegant ruins of Thailand's thirteenth-century capital.

28 TREKKING
See page 56

Walking through the beautiful, rainforested scenery of northern Thailand's mountains comes with the bonus of getting to know the fascinating hill tribes.

29 WAT PHU TOK
See page 495

A uniquely atmospheric meditation temple on a steep, wooded outcrop.

30 NAN
See page 320

Set in rich mountain scenery, with a strong handicraft tradition and some intriguing temples.

Itineraries

The following itineraries cover Thailand in all its diversity, from running the rapids in the northern mountains to beach-bumming your way through the Andaman archipelagos. Whether you want to feel the buzz of adventure in the great outdoors, feast on the never-ending variety of Thai cuisine, or find the nearest thing to a desert island paradise, these will point the way.

THE GREAT OUTDOORS

Thailand now offers an astonishing range of good-value active pursuits, both on land and in the teeming tropical seas.

❶ **Khao Yai National Park** One of the very few national parks to maintain a network of hiking trails that visitors can explore by themselves, passing dramatic waterfalls, orchids and an abundance of wildlife. See page 435

❷ **Chiang Mai** The best single base for outdoor activities, offering cycling day-trips and multi-day tours, mountain biking, trekking, rafting, rock-climbing and many others. See page 275

❸ **Pai rafting** A good place for trekking, but the real highlight here is the two-day whitewater rafting trip down the Pai River, taking in waterfalls, hot springs and a night in a jungle camp. See page 346

❹ **Umphang trekking** The best way to reach the 200m-high Thi Law Su Falls is by rafting and hiking your way through the jungle on a three-day trip. See page 264

❺ **Diving and snorkelling off Ko Similan** The underwater scenery at this remote chain of national park islands is world-class and can be explored on appealing, small-scale live-aboards. See page 612

❻ **Sea-canoeing in Ao Phang Nga** Low-impact paddling on day, night or multi-day trips is the best way to explore the secret caves and mangrove swamps of this extraordinary bay. See page 648

❼ **Ko Yao Noi** This relaxing island on the edge of Phang Nga bay is a low-key hub for active visitors, who kayak, snorkel, dive and climb rocks. See page 641

❽ **Rock-climbing on the Railay peninsula** Offering courses for beginners, as well as equipment rental and guides, this is Thailand's premier site for climbers, with over seven hundred bolted routes amid awesome scenery. See page 664

THE FOODIE TRAIL

We're not daring to claim that the restaurants mentioned below are the very best in Thailand, but they're all locally famous places serving regional specialities where you can eat extremely well.

❶ **Chiang Rai** Not a town renowned for its gastronomy, but *Salungkham* always stops the traffic and delivers the goods – and you might well want to take away some of its home-smoked pork. See page 359

❷ **Chiang Mai** The nearest thing to nirvana for foodies: loads of Thai cooking classes, culinary walking tours and a choice between Burmese-influenced northern Thai food at restaurants such as *Huen Phen* and an innovative contemporary Thai food experience at *Blackitch Artisan Kitchen*. See pages 294 and 293

❸ Bangkok Among fifty thousand places to eat in the capital, a couple of restaurants can be singled out for special mention: *Taling Pling*, with a long list of dishes from the four corners of the country praised by Thai food critics; and *Bolan*, for its meticulous commitment to traditional recipes and the "Slow Food" philosophy. See pages 159 and 155

❹ Hua Hin Long the favourite seaside retreat of Bangkok's food-loving middle classes, Hua Hin has built up a thriving culinary scene – the super-fresh, reasonably priced seafood at *Sopa Seafood* and *Baan Itsara*'s creative dishes stand out. See page 512

❺ Phuket Town A good place to sample Phuket and southern Thai specialities, such as pork with Chinese herbs at *Kopitiam* by *Wilai* at Aaron. See page 617

❻ Krabi You may have to queue for a table at *Ko Tung*, but it's worth the wait for the fresh, southern-style seafood such as delicious sweet mussels and baked crab. See page 649

❼ Nakhon Si Thammarat *Krua Thale* is almost reason in itself to go to Nakhon – don't miss the chunky mussels in herb soup. See page 572

ISLAND-HOPPING ON THE QUIET

Ferries now join up the karst islands of the southern Andaman coast, so it's possible to get from Phuket to Penang in Malaysia without setting foot on the mainland. You can avoid the crowds, and save yourself money and hassle, by bypassing the kiss-me-quick resorts of Phuket, Ko Phi Phi and Ko Lipe in favour of these island beauties.

❶ Phuket Town Base yourself among the Sino-Portuguese architecture of the island capital, which has better-value and more interesting places to stay and eat than the big-name beaches, and much better transport links. See page 617

❷ With around 20km of west-facing sands and a laidback, family-friendly atmosphere, **Ko Lanta Yai** offers a wide range of affordable accommodation and an almost endless choice of beach bars for sundowners. See page 679

❸ A short detour from Lanta brings you to **Ko Jum**'s half-dozen wild and lonely beaches facing the sunset, with boat trips to enjoy and a small mountain to climb. See page 675

❹ There's a variety of good resorts for all budgets on **Ko Hai** and a gorgeous panorama of jagged limestone islands. See page 701

❺ A quick hop from Ko Hai, **Ko Mook**'s main draw is the stunning Emerald Cave, with its inland beach of fine sand at the base of a spectacular natural chimney. See page 703

❻ Just southwest of Ko Mook, **Ko Kradan** is a remote island that's uninhabited apart from its half-dozen resorts, with a long, powdery, east-facing strand, crystal-clear waters and a reef for snorkellers to explore. See page 704

❼ Ko Tarutao Huge national park island with mangroves and jungle tracks to explore, and the most unspoilt beaches in the area. See page 708

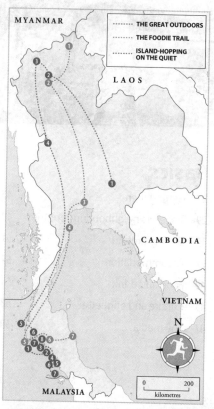

THANON KHAO SAN, BANGKOK

Basics

Getting there

Thailand currently has nine main international airports: in Bangkok (Suvarnabhumi and Don Muang), Chiang Mai, Chiang Rai, Hat Yai (see page 716), Krabi, Phuket, Ko Samui and Pattaya (U-Tapao). The vast majority of travellers fly into Suvarnabhumi Airport (see page 132).

Air fares to Thailand generally depend on the **season**, with the highest being approximately mid-November to mid-February, when the weather is best (with premium rates charged for flights between mid-Dec and New Year), and in July and August to coincide with school holidays. You will need to book several months in advance to get reasonably priced tickets during these peak periods.

The cheapest way of getting to most **regional Thai airports** is usually to buy a flight to Bangkok and then a separate domestic ticket. However, there are dozens of potentially useful, mostly seasonal, international routes into **Phuket**, including direct flights with several airlines from Australia. Most international flights into Chiang Mai, Chiang Rai, Krabi, Ko Samui, Pattaya and Don Muang are from Malaysia, Singapore and China (including Hong Kong and Macau). Krabi also handles seasonal, mostly charter flights from Scandinavia, while Korean Airlines from Seoul is a popular route for North American visitors into Chiang Mai Airport, which has links with Myanmar and Laos too. Qatar Airways has recently started nonstop flights from Doha to Chiang Mai, Krabi and Pattaya airports.

Flights from the UK and Ireland

The fastest and most comfortable way of reaching Thailand **from the UK** is to fly nonstop from London to Bangkok with Thai Airways (Ⓦthaiairways.com), British Airways (Ⓦba.com) or Eva Airways (Ⓦevaair.com), a journey of about eleven and a half hours. These airlines sometimes have special promotions, but a typical fare in high season might come in at around £800–900. Fares on indirect scheduled flights to Bangkok are always cheaper than nonstop flights –

starting at about £450 in high season if booked many months in advance with Qatar Airways (Ⓦqatarairways.com), for example – though these journeys can take anything from two to twelve hours longer.

There are no nonstop flights from any **regional airports** in Britain or from any **Irish airports**, but rather than routing via London, you may find it convenient to fly to another hub such as Frankfurt (with Lufthansa; Ⓦlufthansa.com), Doha (Qatar Airways), Abu Dhabi (with Etihad; Ⓦetihadairways.com) or Istanbul (with Turkish Airlines; Ⓦturkishairlines.com), and take a connecting flight from there. Return flights from Newcastle upon Tyne with Emirates (Ⓦemirates.com), for example, currently start at around £500 in high season if booked far in advance, from Dublin with Qatar, at around €550.

Flights from the US and Canada

At the moment, Thai Airways is no longer offering non-stop flights from the West Coast to Bangkok, though it's considering restarting them, either from Seattle or, possibly, San Francisco. Plenty of other airlines run to Bangkok from East and West Coast cities with one stop en route; it's generally easier to find a reasonable fare on flights via Asia than via Europe, even if you're departing from the East Coast – if you book far in advance, you can get a flight from LA or New York for as little as US$700 return in high season, including taxes. Air Canada (Ⓦaircanada.com) has the most convenient service to Bangkok from the largest number of Canadian cities; from Vancouver, expect to pay around Can$1250 in high season if booked in advance; from Toronto, Can$1500. Cheaper rates are often available if you're prepared to make two or three stops and take more time.

Minimum **flying times** are around twenty hours from New York or Toronto (westbound or eastbound), including stopovers, twenty hours from LA, and eighteen hours from Vancouver.

Flights from Australia and New Zealand

There's no shortage of **scheduled flights** to Bangkok and Phuket **from Australia**, with direct services from

---

A BETTER KIND OF TRAVEL

At Rough Guides we are passionately committed to travel. We believe it helps us understand the world we live in and the people we share it with – and of course tourism is vital to many developing economies. But the scale of modern tourism has also damaged some places irreparably, and climate change is accelerated by most forms of transport, especially flying. All Rough Guides' flights are carbon-offset, and every year we donate money to a variety of environmental charities.

major cities operated by Thai Airways (🌐thaiairways. com), Qantas (🌐qantas.com) and half a dozen others (around 9hr from Sydney, Melbourne and Perth), and plenty of indirect flights via Asian hubs, which take at least eleven and a half hours. There's often not much difference between the fares on nonstop and indirect flights with the major carriers, nor between the fares from the major eastern cities. From Melbourne, if you book far in advance, you can get a ticket to Bangkok in high season for as little as Aus$450, on a low-cost carrier such as Jetstar; nonstop flights with the major airlines from the east coast more typically cost from Aus$900 if booked ahead. Fares from Perth and Darwin can be up to Aus$200 cheaper.

From **New Zealand**, Thai Airways runs nonstop twelve-hour flights between Auckland and Bangkok, costing from around NZ$1300 (including taxes) in high season with advanced booking. Qantas flights from Auckland make brief stops in Sydney, adding about three hours to the trip, and other major Asian airlines offer indirect flights via their hubs (from 13hr, but more typically 17hr); fares for indirect flights booked far in advance can start as low as NZ$1000 in high season.

Flights from South Africa

Thai Airways' nonstop code-sharing flights with South African Airways (🌐flysaa.com) from Johannesburg to Bangkok have been discontinued, so you'll be making a stop in East Africa, the Middle East, Singapore or Hong Kong, with fares starting at around ZAR7000 for an advance booking in high season, and a journey time of fourteen hours (via Singapore) or more.

AGENTS AND OPERATORS

All Points East UK ☎ 023 9225 8859, Thailand ☎ 081 885 9490; 🌐 allpointseast.com. Southeast Asia specialist operating small-group adventure holidays with off-the-beaten-track itineraries.

Andaman Discoveries Thailand 🌐 andamandiscoveries.com. Award-winning village-based homestay community tourism programmes around Khuraburi on the north Andaman coast, which allow visitors to experience daily activities such as cooking and batik-making, cultural activities and the local flora and fauna. Other tours include trips to Ko Surin National Park to snorkel and learn about Moken life and to Khao Sok.

Asian Trails Thailand 🌐 asiantrails.travel. Western-run company that offers cycling adventures, inland cruises on the River Kwai in Kanchanaburi, plus more typical package tours.

Backpackers Thailand Travel Thailand 🌐 backpackersthailandtravel.com. Activities and accommodation packages in Ko Pha Ngan and the south, as well as homestays and volunteer programmes in Singburi in the Central Plains and cultural and food tours in Chiang Mai.

Eastern & Oriental Express UK ☎ 0845 077 2222, US ☎ 800 524 2420; 🌐 belmond.com/eastern-and-oriental-express. Tours by luxury train between Bangkok and Singapore.

Grasshopper Adventures Australia ☎ 03 9016 3172, Thailand ☎ 02 280 0832, UK ☎ 020 8123 8144, US ☎ 818 921 7101; 🌐 grasshopperadventures.com. Cycling half-day and one-day trips around Bangkok and Chiang Mai, as well as three- to eleven-day tours to the north, west and south of Thailand.

Hivesters Thailand 🌐 hivesters.com. This social enterprise and sustainable travel company offers interesting tours mostly in Bangkok, but also with the chance to be a fisherman for a day on Ko Yao Noi, and runs a project, APPEAR, to revivify six of the capital's neighbourhoods.

Local Alike Thailand 🌐 localalike.com. Online marketplace that gives access to responsible tourism activities in communities from Chiang Mai to Surin, and from Trat to Trang.

North South Travel UK ☎ 01245 608 291, 🌐 northsouthtravel. co.uk. Friendly, competitive travel agency, offering discounted fares worldwide. Profits are used to support projects in the developing world, especially the promotion of sustainable tourism.

Nutty's Adventures Thailand 🌐 nutty-adventures.com. Fascinating, multi-day, community-based-tourism trips going off the beaten track all over the country, many with homestays and farmstays, including island-hopping on the Andaman Coast and cycling and boating from Kanchanaburi to Ayutthaya.

Origin Asia Thailand 🌐 alex-kerr.com. Cultural programmes that teach and explain living Thai arts such as dance, music, martial arts, textiles, flower offerings and cooking. Courses last from a day to a week and are held in Bangkok and Chiang Mai.

Responsible Travel UK ☎ 01273 823700, 🌐 responsibletravel. com. One-stop shop for scores of fair-trade, ethically inclined holidays in Thailand, including trips that focus on cycling, cuisine and family activities.

Spice Roads Thailand 🌐 spiceroads.com. Escorted day and multi-day bike tours – including mountain biking – through all regions of Thailand.

STA Travel UK ☎ 0333 321 0099, US ☎ 800 781 4040, Australia ☎ 134 782, New Zealand ☎ 0800 474 400, South Africa ☎ 0861 781 781, Thailand ☎ 02 236 0262; 🌐 statravel.co.uk. Worldwide specialists in independent travel (with branches in Bangkok and Chiang Mai); also student IDs, travel insurance, car rental and more. Good discounts for students and under-26s.

Take Me Tour Thailand 🌐 takemetour.com. Online marketplace for one-day tours with local guides all over Thailand, from boating through Tha Kha floating market to being an organic farmer in the north.

Telltale Travel UK ☎ 0800 011 2571, US ☎ 866 211 5972, 🌐 telltaletravel.co.uk. Tailor-made, upscale company that offers off-the-beaten-track wildlife, cultural, family, homestay and cooking tours.

Thailand Birdwatching Thailand 🌐 thailandbirdwatching.com. Specialist birdwatching tours in national parks and nature reserves.

Trailfinders UK ☎ 0207 368 1200, Ireland ☎ 0167 77888, ⓦ trailfinders.com. One of the best-informed and most efficient agents for independent travellers.

Travel CUTS Canada ☎ 800 667 2887, ⓦ travelcuts.com. Canadian youth and student travel firm.

USIT Ireland ☎ 01 602 1906, Australia ☎ 1800 092 499, ⓦ usit.ie. Ireland's main student and youth travel specialists, with a branch in Sydney.

Travel via neighbouring countries

Sharing land borders with Myanmar, Laos, Cambodia and Malaysia, Thailand works well as part of many overland itineraries, both across Asia and between Europe and Australia. Bangkok is also one of the major regional flight hubs for Southeast Asia. Cross-border links in Southeast Asia have improved considerably recently and are likely to continue to do so in the next few years.

The main restrictions on overland routes in and out of Thailand are determined by where the permitted land crossings lie and by **visas**. All **Asian embassies** are located in Bangkok (see page 170), but waiting times can be shorter at visa-issuing -consulates outside the capital: China and India run consulates in Chiang Mai (see page 299), and Laos and Vietnam have consulates in Khon Kaen (see page 473). In Bangkok, many Khao San tour agents offer to get your visa for you, but beware: some are reportedly **faking the stamps**, which could get you into pretty serious trouble, so it's safer to go to the embassy yourself.

The right paperwork is also crucial if you're planning to **drive your own car or motorbike** into Thailand; see the Golden Triangle Rider website (ⓦ gt-rider. com) for advice.

Looking beyond the country's immediate borders, it's possible to get **from Vietnam** into Thailand, via Savannakhet on the Lao–Thai border, in a matter of hours; you'll need to use Vietnam's Lao Bao border crossing, west of Dong Ha, where you can catch a bus to Savannakhet and then another bus across the Mekong bridge to Mukdahan. Coming **from China**, the much-improved Route 3 and the Fourth Thai–Lao Friendship Bridge over the Mekong at Chiang Khong now form a popular link between Yunnan and northern Thailand; this has made the passenger route by speedboat or cargo boat

down the Mekong from Yunnan to Chiang Saen redundant.

Myanmar (Burma)

There are now four overland access points between **Myanmar (Burma)** and Thailand that are open to non-Thais: at Thachileik opposite Mae Sai; at Myawaddy near Mae Sot; at remote Htee Khee opposite Phu Nam Ron in Kanchanaburi province, a crossing that's being developed to facilitate transport between the major new port at Dawei on the Bay of Bengal and Bangkok; and at Kaw Thaung (Victoria Point) near Ranong. At these borders Western tourists forearmed with a Burmese tourist visa can enter Myanmar, and at most of them you can get a temporary US$10 (or B500) **border pass**, which will allow you to make limited-distance trips into Myanmar, usually just for the day (see relevant accounts for details). The crossings at Three Pagodas Pass near Kanchanaburi and at Dan Singkhon near Prachuap Khiri Khan are currently open only to Thai tourists.

Cambodia

At the time of writing, six overland crossings on the **Thai–Cambodia border** are open to non-Thais; see the relevant town accounts for specific details on all the border crossings.

Most travellers use the crossing at Poipet, which has transport connections with Sisophon, Siem Reap and Phnom Penh and lies just across the border from the Thai town of Aranyaprathet (see page 379), with its transport to Bangkok and to Chanthaburi; there are now also direct public buses that run all the way between Bangkok and Siem Reap and between Bangkok and Phnom Penh, which should help you dodge the scams and touts at this frontier post. The second most popular route is from Sihanoukville in Cambodia via Koh Kong (Cham Yeam) and Hat Lek to Trat, which is near Ko Chang on Thailand's east coast.

The crossings in northeast Thailand include the Chong Chom–O'Smach border pass, near Kap Choeng in Thailand's Surin province, and the Chong Sa Ngam–Choam border in Thailand's Si Saket province; from both these borders there's transport to Anlong Veng and on to Siem Reap. There are also two little-used crossings in Chanthaburi province, with transport to and from Pailin in Cambodia.

Tourist **visas** for Cambodia are issued to travellers on arrival at all the above-listed overland border crossings. If you want to buy an advance thirty-day visa, you can do so online at ⓦ evisa.gov.kh. Of the land borders discussed here, these "e-visas" can be used only at Poipet and Koh Kong, but they should help you to avoid the more excessive scams at these two frontier posts.

Laos

There are seven main points along the **Lao border** where tourists can cross into Thailand: Houayxai (for Chiang Khong); between Nam Ngeun and Huai Kon in Thailand's Nan province; on the Nam Heuang River at the Thai settlement of Tha Li (Loei province); Vientiane (for Nong Khai); Khammouan (aka Thakhek, for Nakhon Phanom); Savannakhet (for Mukdahan); and Pakse (for Chong Mek). Increasing numbers of direct, long-distance public buses, such as those between Loei and Luang Prabang via Tha Li and between Nan and Luang Prabang via Huai Kon, use these crossings to link major towns in the two countries. There's a remoter frontier post, where transport is a little more difficult, between Paksan and Bueng Kan. All these borders can also be used as exits into Laos; tourist **visas** are available **on arrival** at all of the above-listed land borders except Paksan, or you can buy one in advance from either the Lao Embassy in Bangkok or the Lao Consulate in Khon Kaen.

Malaysia

Travelling between Thailand and **Malaysia** has in the past been a straightforward and very commonly used overland route, with plentiful connections by bus, minibus, share-taxi and train, most of them routed through the southern Thai city and transport hub of Hat Yai. However, because of the ongoing **violence in Thailand's deep south** (see page 696), all major Western governments are currently advising people not to travel to or through Songkhla, Pattani, Yala and Narathiwat provinces, unless essential (and consequently most insurance companies are not covering travel there). This encompasses Hat Yai and the following border crossings to and from Malaysia: at Padang Besar, on the main rail line connecting Malaysia (and, ultimately, Singapore) with Hat Yai and Bangkok; at Sungai Kolok, terminus of a railway line from Hat Yai and Bangkok, and at adjacent Ban Taba, both of which are connected by road to nearby Kota Bharu in Malaysia; and at the road crossings at Sadao, south of Hat Yai, and at Betong, south of Yala. (The routes towards Kota Bharu and Betong pass through particularly volatile territory, with martial law declared in Pattani, Yala and Narathiwat provinces; however, martial law is not in effect in Hat Yai itself.)

Nevertheless, the provinces of Trang and Satun on the west coast are not affected, and it's still perfectly possible to travel **overland via Satun**: by ferry between Satun's Thammalang pier and the island of Langkawi, or overland between Satun and Kangar (see page 715); or by boat between Ko Lipe and Langkawi (see page 711). For up-to-the-minute advice, consult your government travel advisory (see page 63).

Most Western tourists can spend thirty days in Malaysia without having bought a visa beforehand, and there are Thai embassies or consulates in Kuala Lumpur, Kota Bharu and Penang (see page 65).

Getting around

Travel in Thailand is inexpensive and comparatively efficient, if not always speedy. Unless you travel by plane, long-distance journeys in Thailand can be arduous, especially if a shoestring budget restricts you to hard seats and no air conditioning.

Nonetheless, the wide range of transport options makes travelling around Thailand easier than elsewhere in Southeast Asia. **Buses** are fast, cheap and frequent, and can be quite luxurious. **Trains** are slower but safer and offer more chance of sleeping during overnight trips; moreover, if travelling by day you're likely to follow a more scenic route by rail than by road. Inter-town **songthaews** and **air-conditioned minibuses** are handy, and **ferries** provide easy access to all major islands. Local transport comes in all sorts of permutations, both public and chartered.

Online bookings in English on trains, private "join" buses (see below) and ferries in Thailand are now offered by ⓦ busonlineticket.co.th and ⓦ 12go.asia, which seems to have a wider choice of ferries and buses.

Inter-town buses

Buses, overall the most convenient way of getting around the country, generally come in four main categories. In ascending order of comfort, speed and cost, they are **ordinary** buses (*rot thammadaa*; not air-conditioned, often orange-coloured) and three overall types of **air-conditioned** bus (*rot ae – "air"* – or *rot thua*; often blue or partly blue): second-class, first-class and VIP first-class. Many ordinary and air-conditioned buses are operated by the government-controlled Baw Khaw Saw (*borisat khon song*), known in English as the Transport Company; fairly up-to-date schedules and fares to and from Bangkok can be seen in English at ⓦ transport.co.th, while the English-language pages on its official booking site, ⓦ pns-allthai.com, may reappear – you should still be able to book tickets in English over the phone on ☎02 872 1777. Privately owned buses that are licensed by the Baw Khaw Saw (*rot ruam*, usually translated as "join buses"), some of which operate from Baw Khaw Saw terminals, also ply most routes; on many short-distance routes, air-conditioned minibuses (see page 32) are replacing buses. Be warned that long-distance overnight buses, on which some drivers are rumoured to take ampheta-mines to stay awake, seem to be involved in more than their fair share of accidents; because of this, some travellers prefer to do the overnight journeys by train and then make a shorter bus connection to their destination.

Ordinary and second-class

On most routes, **second-class** (*baw sawng*; often with a "2" on the side of the vehicle) air-conditioned buses have now replaced **ordinary buses** as the main workhorses of the Thai bus system, though you'll still see plenty of the latter on shorter routes in more remote parts of the country, especially in the north and northeast. Whether air-conditioned or not, these basic buses are incredibly inexpensive, generally run frequently during daylight hours, pack as many people in as possible and stop often, which slows them down considerably.

It's best to ask locally where to catch your bus. Failing that, designated **bus stops** are often marked by **sala**, small, open-sided wooden structures with bench seats, located at intervals along the main long-distance bus route through town or on the fringes of any decent-sized settlement, for example on the main highway that skirts the edge of town. Where there is only a bus shelter on the "wrong" side of the road, you can be sure that buses travelling in both directions will stop there for any waiting passen-gers; simply leave your bag on the right side of the road to alert the bus driver and wait in the shade. But if you're in the middle of nowhere with no *sala* in sight, any ordinary or second-class bus should stop for you if you flag it down.

First-class and VIP

Express services, with fewer stops, are mostly operated by **first-class** (*baw neung*; often with a "1" on the side of the vehicle) and **VIP** (usually written in English on the side) buses. These are your best option for long-distance journeys: you'll generally be allotted specific seats, there'll be a toilet, and on the longest journeys you may get blankets, snacks and nonstop DVDs, though you might want a sweater to cope with excessive air conditioning. The first-class services have fewer seats than second-class and

more leg room for reclining, VIP services fewer seats again. Other nomenclature for the top-of-the-range services is also used, especially by the **private "join" companies**: "999", "super VIP" (with even fewer seats), "Gold Class" and, confusingly, sometimes even "First Class" (in imitation of airlines, with just eighteen huge, well-equipped seats).

On a lot of long-distance routes private "join" buses are indistinguishable from government ones and operate out of the same Baw Khaw Saw bus terminals. The major private companies, such as Nakhon Chai Air (☎1624, ⓦnakhonchaiair.com with an English-language booking facility), Sombat Tour (☎02 792 1456 at Mo Chit Terminal in Bangkok, ⓦsombattour.com – which shows timetables in English, with English-language booking facility "coming soon") and, operating out of Chiang Mai, Green Bus (☎053 241933, ⓦgreenbusthailand.com, with English-language timetables), have roughly similar fares, though naturally with more scope for price variation, and offer comparable facilities and standards of service. The opposite is unfortunately true of a number of the smaller, private, unlicensed companies, which have a poor reputation for service and comfort, but gear themselves towards foreign travellers with bargain fares and convenient timeta-bles. The long-distance tour buses that run **from Thanon Khao San** in Banglamphu to Chiang Mai and Surat Thani are a case in point; though promised VIP buses, travellers on these routes frequently complain about shabby furnishings, ineffective air conditioning, unhelpful (even aggressive) drivers, lateness and a frightening lack of safety awareness – and there are frequent reports of theft from luggage on these routes, too, and even the spraying of "sleeping gas" so that hand luggage can be rifled without interruption. Generally it's best to travel with the government or licensed private bus companies from the main bus terminals (who have a reputation with their regular Thai customers to maintain and now operate a handy ticket office near Bangkok's Thanon Khao San) or to go by train instead – the extra comfort and peace of mind are well worth the extra baht.

Tickets and timetables

Tickets for all buses can be bought from the departure terminals, but for ordinary and second-class air-conditioned buses it's normal to buy them on board. First-class and VIP buses may operate from a separate station or office, and it's best to book tickets for the more popular routes at least a day in advance. As a rough indication of **fares**, a trip from Bangkok to Chiang Mai, a distance of 700km, on the Baw Khaw Saw's own buses costs B778 for VIP, B500 for first-class air-conditioned and B389 for second-class air-conditioned.

Long-distance buses often depart in clusters around the same time (early morning or late at night, for example), leaving a gap of five or more hours during the day with no services at all. Local TAT offices occasionally keep up-to-date bus **timetables**, and there are useful downtown information and booking offices in Banglamphu in Bangkok (see page 135) and in Chiang Mai (Green Bus – see page 287). Bus company websites and general transport booking sites are detailed above. Thai Ticket Major's website (Ⓦ thaiticketmajor.com) offers timetables and booking in English for many Baw Khaw Saw and "join" company routes. Ticketing options include buying them online by credit card through the site; reserving them online or by phone on ☎ 02 262 3456, then making your payment at designated outlets around the country, including banks, supermarkets, cinemas and scores of affiliated major post offices (as listed on the site), including the Ratchadamnoen post office just north of Thanon Rajdamnoen Klang in Banglamphu and the Thanon Na Phra Lan post office opposite the entrance to the Grand Palace in Ratanakosin.

Songthaews, share-taxis and air-conditioned minibuses

In rural areas, the bus network is often supplemented by **songthaews** (literally "two rows"), which are open-ended vans (or occasionally cattle-trucks) onto which the drivers squash as many passengers as possible on two facing benches, leaving late-comers to swing off the running board at the back. As well as their essential role within towns (see page 34), songthaews ply set routes from larger towns out to their surrounding suburbs and villages, and occasionally, where there's no call for a regular bus service, between small towns: some have destinations written on in Thai, but few are numbered. In most towns you'll find the songthaew "terminal" near the market; to pick one up between destinations just flag it down. To indicate to the driver that you want to get out, the normal practice is to rap hard with a coin on the metal railings as you approach the spot (or press the bell if there is one).

In the deep south (see page 694) they have traditionally done things in a little more style, with **share-taxis** – sometimes antique Mercedes – connecting the major towns, but they are now being inexorably replaced by more comfortable **air-conditioned minibuses** (*rot tuu*, meaning "cupboard cars"). Scores of similar private air-conditioned minibus services are now cropping up all over the country, either operating out of small offices or pavement desks in town centres or from the bus terminals or even their own *rot tuu* terminals. Some of these services have a timetable, but many just aim to leave when they have a full complement of passengers; then again, some companies publish a timetable but depart when they're full – whether before or after the published time. They cover the distance faster than buses, but often at breakneck speed, and they can be uncomfortably cramped when full – they're not ideal for travellers with huge rucksacks, who may be required to pay extra. In some areas, GPS devices are now used to regulate the driver's speed, sometimes with a "GPS" sticker on the back of the vehicle. *Rot tuu* services are usually licensed and need to keep up their reputation with their regular Thai passengers but, as with full-sized buses (see page 30), you should be wary of unlicensed private companies that offer minibuses solely for farangs from Bangkok's Thanon Khao San.

In many cases, long-distance songthaews and air-conditioned minibuses will drop you at an exact address (for example, a particular guesthouse) if you warn them far enough in advance. As a rule, the **cost** of inter-town songthaews is comparable to that of air-conditioned buses, that of air-conditioned minibuses perhaps a shade more.

Trains

Managed by the State Railway of Thailand (SRT), the **rail** network consists of four main lines and a few branch lines, mostly radiating out of Bangkok's Hualamphong Station. The **Northern Line** connects Bangkok with Chiang Mai via Ayutthaya, Lopburi, Phitsanulok and Lampang. The **Northeastern Line** splits into two just beyond Ayutthaya, the lower branch running eastwards to Ubon Ratchathani via Khorat and Surin, the more northerly branch linking the capital with Nong Khai (with a very short extension over the Mekong into Laos via Khon Kaen and Udon Thani; a high-speed line on this branch, financed by the Chinese government, is in the pipeline. The **Eastern Line** (slow, third-class only) also has two branches, one of which runs from Bangkok to Aranyaprathet on the Cambodian border, the other of which connects Bangkok with Si Racha and Pattaya. The **Southern Line** (which also carries a few slow trains from Bangkok's Thonburi Station, as far as Nam Tok and Chumphon) extends via Hua Hin, Chumphon and Surat Thani, with spurs off to Trang and Nakhon Si Thammarat, to Hat Yai, where it branches: one line continues to Padang Besar on the Malaysian border, where you can change trains for Butterworth (for Penang) and the west coast of Malaysia; the other heads down the eastern side of the

TRAIN INFORMATION

The State Railway of Thailand (SRT) offers 24hr **train information and booking in English** on its free hotline ☎1690 and publishes free **timetables** in English, detailing types of trains available on each route (the best place to get hold of them is over the counter at Bangkok's Hualamphong Station). Its main website (Ⓦrailway.co.th) carries English-language timetables, while its Ⓦthairailwayticket.com now accepts bookings by credit card in English. For more comprehensive information and advice, go to Ⓦseat61.com/thailand.htm, which includes a link to download Dave Bernstein's compendious Thailand Rail Guide.

peninsula to Sungai Kolok on the Thailand–Malaysia border (20km from Pasir Mas on Malaysia's interior railway). At Nakhon Pathom a branch of this line veers off to Nam Tok via Kanchanaburi – this is all that's left of the Death Railway, of *Bridge on the River Kwai* notoriety (see page 190).

Fares depend on the class of seat, whether or not you want air conditioning, and on the speed of the train; those quoted here include the supplements for the various "speed" types of train (see below). Hard, wooden or thinly padded third-class seats are much cheaper than buses (Bangkok–Chiang Mai B231 on the Rapid train), and are fine for about three hours, after which numbness sets in; a few trains have air-conditioned third-class carriages. For longer journeys you'd be wise to opt for the padded and usually reclining seats in second class (Bangkok–Chiang Mai B391 on the Rapid train, or B641 on the daytime Special Express with a/c for example). On long-distance trains, you also usually have the option of second-class berths (Bangkok–Chiang Mai B531–581, or B751–821 with a/c, on the Express service, for example), with pairs of day seats facing each other that convert into comfortable curtained-off bunks in the evening; lower bunks, which are more expensive than upper, have a few cubic centimetres more of space, a little more shade from the lights in the carriage, and a window. Travelling first class (Bangkok–Chiang Mai B1253–1653 per person on the Special Express) generally means a two-person sleeping compartment (occasionally a one-person compartment), complete with washbasin and fierce air conditioning.

There are several different types of train, most of which incur various **"speed"** supplements: slowest of all is the third-class-only Ordinary service, which is generally (but not always) available only on short and medium-length journeys, including Bangkok commuter trains, and has no speed supplement. Next comes the misleadingly named Rapid train, a trip on which from Bangkok to Chiang Mai, for example, takes fourteen hours twenty minutes; the equally euphemistic Express, which does the Chiang Mai route in about the same time; and the Special Express which covers the ground in around eleven to thirteen hours. The fastest services are usually the daytime Special

Express trains, which can usually be relied on to run roughly on time (most other services pay only lip service to their time-tables and are sometimes an hour or two late). Nearly all long-distance trains have **dining cars**, and rail staff will also bring meals to your seat.

Booking at least one day in advance – longer if possible, especially in high season and over national holidays – is strongly recommended for second- and first-class seats on all lengthy journeys, while sleepers should be booked as far in advance as you can (reservations open sixty days before departure). You can make bookings for any journey in Thailand in person (bring your passport) at Hualamphong Station in Bangkok (see page 134) or at the train station in any major town. You can now book online and print your ticket (tickets on mobile phones not acceptable) through the SRT's Ⓦthairailwayticket.com or through general Thai transport booking sites.

Ferries

Regular **ferries** connect all major islands with the mainland, and for the vast majority of crossings you simply buy your ticket on board. Safety standards are generally just about adequate but there have been a small number of sinkings in recent years – avoid travelling on boats that are clearly overloaded or in poor condition. In tourist areas competition ensures that prices are kept low, and fares tend to vary with the speed of the crossing: thus Surat Thani–Ko Pha Ngan costs between B350 (around 4hr) and B700 (2hr 30min).

On the east coast and the Andaman coast boats generally operate a reduced service during the monsoon season (May–Oct), when the more remote spots may become inaccessible. Ferries in the Samui archipelago are fairly constant year-round. Details on island connections are given in the relevant chapters.

Flights

Thai Airways (Ⓦthaiairways.com) now concentrates more on international routes, leaving Bangkok Airways (Ⓦbangkokair.com) as the major full-service airline on the internal **flight** network, which extends to all parts of the country, using some two-dozen airports. Air Asia (🌐airasia.com), Nok Air (🌐nokair.com), which is part-owned by Thai Airways, Thai Smile (🌐thaismileair. com), a subsidiary of Thai Airways, Thai Lion Air (🌐lion-airthai.com) and Viet Jet (🌐vietjetair.com) provide the main "low-cost" competition. In a recently deregulated but ever-expanding market, other smaller airlines come and go with surprising frequency – and while they are operating, schedules tend to be erratic and flights are sometimes cancelled. Kan Airlines, which operated some useful routes out of Chiang Mai Airport, has gone under but may resurface as Wisdom Airways.

In some instances a flight can save you days of travelling: a flight from Chiang Mai to Phuket with Bangkok Airways, Thai Smile or Air Asia, for example, takes two hours, as against a couple of days by meandering train and/or bus. Book early if possible – you can reserve online with all companies – as fares fluctuate wildly. For a fully flexible economy ticket, Bangkok to Chiang Mai costs around B3000 with Thai Airways, but you'll find flights on the same route with the "low-cost" carriers for under B1000 (with restrictions on changes), if you book online far enough in advance.

Local transport

Most sizeable towns have some kind of **local transport system**, comprising a network of buses, songthaews or even longtail boats, usually with set fares and routes but not rigid timetabling – in many cases vehicles wait until they're full before they leave.

Buses and songthaews

A few larger cities such as Bangkok and Khorat have a **local bus** network that usually extends to the suburbs and operates from dawn till dusk (through the night in Bangkok). Most vehicles display route numbers in Western numerals – see the relevant accounts for further details.

Within medium-sized and large towns, the main transport role is often played by **songthaews**. The size and shape of vehicle used varies from town to town – and in some places they're known as "tuk-tuks" from the noise they make, not to be confused with the smaller tuk-tuks, described below, that operate as private taxis – but all have the tell-tale two benches (*sawng thaew*) facing each other in the back. In some towns, especially in the northeast, songthaews follow fixed routes; in others, such as Chiang Mai, they act as communal taxis, picking up a number of people who are going in roughly the same direction and taking each of them right to their destination. To hail a songthaew just flag it down, and to indicate that you want to get out, either rap hard with a coin on the metal railings, or ring the bell if there is one.

Fares within towns are B10–30, depending on distance, usually payable when you disembark.

Taxi services

Taxis also come in many guises, and in bigger towns you can sometimes choose between taking a tuk-tuk, a samlor and a motorbike taxi. The one thing common to all modes of chartered transport, bar metered and app-based taxis such as Uber and Grab in Bangkok and one or two cities in the northeast and the north, is that you must establish the **fare** beforehand: although drivers nearly always pitch their first offers too high, they do calculate with traffic and time of day in mind, as well as according to distance – if successive drivers scoff at your price, you know you've got it wrong.

Tuk-tuks

Named after the noise of its excruciatingly unsilenced engine, the three-wheeled, open-sided **tuk-tuk** is the classic Thai vehicle. Painted in primary colours, tuk-tuks blast their way round towns and cities on two-stroke engines, zipping around faster than any car and taking corners on two wheels. They aren't as dangerous as they look though, and can be an exhilarating way to get around, as long as you're not too fussy about exhaust fumes. Fares come in at around B60 for a short city journey (over B100 in Bangkok) regardless of the number of passengers – three is the safe maximum, though six is not uncommon. It's worth paying attention to advice on how to avoid getting ripped off by Bangkok tuk-tuk drivers (see page 141).

Samlors

Tuk-tuks are also sometimes known as samlors (literally "three wheels"), but the original **samlors** are tricycle rickshaws propelled by pedal power alone. Slower and a great deal more stately than tuk-tuks, samlors still operate in one or two towns around the country.

A further permutation is the motorized samlors (often called "skylabs" in northeastern Thailand), where the driver relies on a motorbike rather than a bicycle to propel passengers to their destination. They look much the same as cycle samlors, but often sound as noisy as tuk-tuks.

Motorbike taxis

Even faster and more precarious than tuk-tuks, **motorbike taxis** feature both in towns and in out-of-the-way places. In towns – where the drivers are identified by coloured, numbered vests – they have the advantage of being able to dodge traffic jams, but are obviously only really suitable for the single traveller, and motorbike taxis aren't the easiest mode of transport if you're carrying luggage. In remote spots, on the other hand, they're often the only alternative to hitching or walking, and are especially useful for getting between bus stops on main roads, around car-free islands and to national parks or ancient ruins.

Within towns motorbike-taxi fares can start at B10 for very short journeys, but for trips to the outskirts the cost rises steeply – reckon on around B300 for a 20km round trip.

Longtail boats

Wherever there's a decent public waterway, there'll be a **longtail boat** ready to ferry you along it. Another great Thai trademark, these elegant, streamlined boats are powered by deafening diesel engines – sometimes custom-built, more often adapted from cars or trucks – which drive a propeller mounted on a long shaft that is swivelled for steering. Longtails carry a maximum of between eight and twenty passengers: generally you'll have to charter the whole boat, but on popular fixed routes, for example between small, inshore islands and the mainland, it's cheaper to wait until the boatman gets his quorum.

Vehicle rental

Despite first impressions, a high accident fatality rate, especially involving motorcycles, and the obvious mayhem that characterizes Bangkok's roads, **driving** yourself around Thailand can be fairly straightforward. Many roads, particularly in the northeast and the south, are remarkably uncongested. Major routes are clearly signed in English, though this only applies to some minor roads.

Outside the capital, the eastern seaboard and the major tourist resorts of Ko Samui and Phuket, local drivers are generally considerate and unaggressive; they very rarely use their horns for example, and will often indicate left and even swerve away when it's safe for you to overtake. The most inconsiderate and dangerous road-users in Thailand are bus drivers and lorry drivers, many of whom drive ludicrously fast, hog the road, race round bends on the wrong side of the road and use their horns remorselessly; worse still, many of them are tanked up on amphetamines, which makes them quite literally fearless.

Bus and lorry drivers are at their worst after dark (many of them only drive then), so it's best **not to drive at night** – a further hazard being the inevitable stream of unlit bicycles and mopeds in and around built-up areas (often driving on the wrong side of the road), as well as poorly signed roadworks, which are often not made safe or blocked off from unsuspecting traffic. Orange signs, or sometimes just a couple of tree branches or a pile of stones on the road, warn of hazards ahead.

As for local **rules of the road**, Thais drive on the left, and the speed limit is usually 60km/h within built-up areas and 90km/h outside them. Beyond that, there are few rules that are generally followed – smaller vehicles usually have to give way to larger ones, and you'll need to keep your concentration up and expect the unexpected from fellow road-users. Watch out especially for vehicles pulling straight out of minor roads, when you might expect them to give way. An oncoming vehicle flashing its lights or beeping its horn means it's coming through no matter what; a right indicator signal from the car in front usually means it's not safe for you to overtake, while a left indicator signal usually means that it is safe to do so.

Theoretically, foreigners need an international **driver's licence** to rent any kind of vehicle, but most car-rental companies accept national licences, and the smaller operations have been known not to ask for any kind of proof whatsoever; motorbike renters very rarely bother. However, if you don't have the correct licence, your travel insurance may not cover you if there's an accident. (There have been occasional reports of particularly brazen police asking motorcyclists for international driving licences at roadblocks, in an attempt to extort money.) A popular rip-off on islands such as Ko Pha Ngan is for small agents to charge renters exorbitant amounts for any minor damage to a jeep or motorbike, even paint chips, that they find on return – they'll claim that it's very expensive to get a new part shipped over from the mainland. Be sure to check out any vehicle carefully before renting.

For **petrol** (nam man, which can also mean oil), most Thais use gasohol, which can generally be used in rental cars (though it's worth checking) and currently costs around B27 a litre. The big fuel stations (pam nam man) are the least costly places to fill up (hai tem), and many of these also have toilets, minimarts and restaurants, though some of the more decrepit-looking fuel stations on the main highways only sell diesel. Most small villages have easy-to-spot roadside huts where the fuel is pumped out of a large barrel or sold in litre bottles.

Renting a car

If you decide to **rent a car**, go to a reputable dealer, such as Avis, Budget or National, or a rental company recommended by TAT, and make sure you get insurance from them (and check the level of insurance included). There are international car-rental places at many airports, including Bangkok's Suvarnabhumi, which is not a bad place to kick off, as you're on the edge of the city and within fairly easy, signposted reach of the major regional highways.

Car-rental places in provincial capitals and resorts are listed in the relevant accounts in this book. The price of a small car at a reputable company can start as low as B900 per day if booked online. In some parts of the country, including Chiang Mai, you'll still be able to rent a car or air-conditioned minibus with driver, which will cost from around B1200 for a local day-trip, more for a longer day-trip, up to about B3000 per day for a multi-day trip, including the driver's keep and petrol.

Jeeps or basic 4WDs are a lot more popular with farangs, especially on beach resorts and islands like Pattaya, Phuket and Ko Samui, but they're notoriously dangerous; a huge number of tourists manage to roll their jeeps on steep hillsides and sharp bends. Jeep rental usually works out somewhere around B1000–1200 per day.

International companies will accept your credit-card details as surety, but smaller agents will usually want to hold on to your passport.

CAR RENTAL AGENCIES

Avis Ⓦ avisthailand.com
Budget Ⓦ budget.co.th
Master Ⓦ mastercarrental.com
National Ⓦ nationalcarthailand.com
Thai Rentacar Ⓦ thairentacar.com

Renting a motorbike

One of the best ways of exploring the countryside is to **rent a motorbike**, an especially popular option in the north of the country. You'll almost never be asked for a driving licence, but take it easy out there – Thailand's roads are not really the place to learn to ride a motorbike from scratch. Bikes of around 100cc, either fully automatic or with step-through gears, are best for inexperienced riders, but aren't really suited for long slogs. If you're going to hit the dirt roads you'll certainly need something more powerful, like a 125–250cc trail bike. These have the edge in gear choice and are the best bikes for steep slopes, though an inexperienced rider may find these machines a handful; the less widely available 125–250cc road bikes are easier to control and much cheaper on fuel.

Rental **prices** for the day usually work out at somewhere around B150–200 for a small bike and B500 for a good trail bike, though you can bargain for a discount on a long rental. Renters will usually ask to hold on to your passport as surety but will generally accept a deposit instead; vehicle insurance is not often available (and some travel insurance policies won't cover you for motorcycle mishaps).

Before signing anything, **check the bike** thoroughly – test the brakes, look for oil leaks, check the treads and the odometer, and make sure the chain isn't stretched too tight (a tight chain is more likely to break) – and

preferably take it for a test run. As you will have to pay an inflated price for any damage when you get back, make a note on the contract of any defects such as broken mirrors, indicators and so on. Make sure you know what kind of fuel the bike takes as well.

As far as **equipment** goes, a helmet is essential – most rental places provide poorly made ones, but they're better than nothing. Helmets are obligatory on all motorbike journeys, and the law is often rigidly enforced with on-the-spot fines in major tourist resorts. You'll need sunglasses if your helmet doesn't have a visor. Long trousers, a long-sleeved top and decent shoes will provide a second skin if you go over, which most people do at some stage. Pillions should wear long trousers to avoid getting nasty burns from the exhaust. For the sake of stability, leave most of your luggage in baggage storage and pack as small a bag as possible, strapping it tightly to the bike with bungy cords – these can usually be provided. Bag snatches from the front baskets of small motorbikes have recently been reported in some tourist resorts, so try to keep any valuables on your person. Once on the road, oil the chain at least every other day, keep the radiator topped up and fill up with oil every 300km or so. Be especially careful when there's water or loose gravel on the roads.

For expert **advice** on motorbike travel in Thailand, check out David Unkovich's website (Ⓦ gt-rider.com).

Cycling

The options for **cycling** in Thailand are numerous, whether you choose to ride the length of the country from the Malaysian border to Chiang Rai, or opt for a dirt-road adventure in the mountains around Chiang Mai. Most Thai roads are in good condition and clearly signposted; although the western and northern borders are mountainous, most of the rest of the country is surprisingly flat. The secondary **roads** (distinguished by their three- or four-digit numbers) are paved but carry far less traffic than the main arteries and are the preferred cycling option. Traffic is reasonably well behaved but the largest vehicles unofficially have – or take – the right of way and there are a fair number of accidents involving cyclists, so you'll need to "ride to survive"; dogs can also be a nuisance on minor roads so it's probably worth having rabies shots before your trip. There are bike shops in nearly every town, and basic equipment and repairs are cheap. Unless you head into the remotest regions around the Burmese border you are rarely more than 25km from food, water and accommodation. Overall, the best time to cycle is during the cool, dry season from November to February.

The traffic into and out of Bangkok is dense so it's worth hopping on a bus or train for the first

50–100km to your starting point. Intercity buses (though sometimes there's a small charge), taxis and some Thai domestic planes will **carry your bike** free of charge. Intercity trains will generally transport your bike for a cargo fare (about the price of a person), either in the luggage carriage, if there is one, or tucked out of the way at the end of your passenger carriage – or, of course, you can dismantle it and carry it as luggage in the compartment with you. Songthaews will carry your bike on the roof for a fare (about the price of a person).

Local one-day cycle tours and **bike-rental outlets** (from around B50/day for a sit-up-and-beg) are listed throughout this book. There are also a number of longer organized **cycle tours**, both nationwide (see page 28) and from Bangkok (see page 136) and Chiang Mai (see page 278). A very helpful English-language resource, dealing with all aspects of cycling in Thailand, is the **website** ⓦbicyclethailand. com, while ⓦchiangmaicycling.org is very useful for the Chiang Mai area.

Cycling practicalities

Strong, light, quality **mountain bikes** are the most versatile choice; 26-inch wheels are standard throughout Thailand and are strongly recommended, with dual-use (combined road and off-road) tyres best for touring. As regards panniers and **equipment**, the most important thing is to travel light. Carry a few spare spokes, but don't overdo it with too many tools and spares; parts are cheap in Thailand and most problems can be fixed quickly at any bike shop.

Bringing your bike from home is the best option as you are riding a known quantity. **Importing** it by plane should be straightforward, but check with the airlines for details. Most Asian airlines do not charge extra.

Buying in Thailand is also a possibility: ⓦbicy-clethailand.com and ⓦchiangmaicycling.org give plenty of advice and listings.

Hitching

Public transport being so inexpensive, you should only have to resort to **hitching** in the most remote areas, in which case you'll probably get a lift to the nearest bus or songthaew stop quite quickly. On routes served by buses and trains, hitching is very rare, but in other places locals do rely on regular passers-by (such as national park officials), and you can make use of this "service" too. As with hitching anywhere in the world, think twice about hitching solo or at night, especially if you're female. Like bus drivers, truck drivers are notorious users of amphetamines, so you may want to wait for a safer offer.

Accommodation

For the very simplest double room, prices start at a bargain B200 in the outlying regions, around B300 in Bangkok, and B400–500 in the pricier resorts. Tourist centres invariably offer a tempting range of more upmarket choices but in these areas rates fluctuate according to demand, plummeting during the off-season, peaking over the Christmas and New Year fortnight and, in some places, rising at weekends throughout the year.

Guesthouses, bungalows and hostels

Most of Thailand's **budget accommodation** is in **guesthouses** and **bungalows**. These are small, traveller-friendly hotels whose services nearly always include an inexpensive restaurant, wi-fi and safe storage for valuables and left luggage, and often a tour desk. The difference between guesthouses and bungalows is mostly in their design, with "bungalows" – which are generally found on the beach and in rural areas – mostly comprising detached or semi-detached rooms in huts, villas, chalets or indeed bungalows, and "guesthouses" being either a purpose-built mini-hotel or a converted home. Showers and flush toilets, whether en-suite or shared, are common in both, but at the cheapest up-country places you might be bathing with a bowl dipped into a large water jar, and using squat toilets.

Many guesthouses and bungalows offer a spread of options to cater for all budgets: their **cheapest rooms** will often be furnished with nothing more than a double bed, a blanket and a fan (window optional, private bathroom extra) and might cost anything from B200–400 for two people, depending on the location and the competition. A similar room with **en-suite** bathroom, and possibly more stylish furnishings, generally comes in at B300–700, while for a room with **air conditioning**, and perhaps a TV and fridge as well, you're looking at B400/500 and up. In the north of Thailand in the cool season, air condi-tioning is more or less redundant, but you might want to check that your room has a hot shower.

In the most popular tourist centres at the busiest times of year, the best-known guesthouses are often full night after night. Some will take **bookings** and advance payment via their websites, but for those that don't it's usually a question of turning up and waiting for a vacancy. At most guesthouses **checkout time** is either 11am or noon.

Generally you should be wary of taking accommodation advice from a **tout** or tuk-tuk driver, as they demand commission from guesthouse owners, which, if not passed directly on to you via a higher room price, can have a crippling effect on the smaller guesthouses. If a tout claims your intended accommodation is "full" or "no good" or has "burnt down", it's always worth phoning to check yourself. Touts can come into their own, however, on islands such as Ko Lanta where it can be a long and expensive ride to your chosen beach, and frustrating if you then discover your bungalow is full; island touts may sweet-talk you on the boat and then transport you for free to view their accommodation, ideally with no obligation to stay.

With only a dozen or so registered **youth hostels** in the country, bookable via ⓦtyha.org, it's not worth becoming a Hostelling International member just for your trip to Thailand, especially as card-holders get only a small discount and room rates work out the same as or more expensive than guesthouse equivalents. In addition, there are a growing number of smart, modern, non-affiliated **hostels**, especially in Bangkok. They usually work out more expensive than budget guesthouses but are good places to meet other travellers.

Budget hotels

Thai sales reps and other people travelling for business rather than pleasure rarely use guest-houses, opting instead for **budget hotels**, which offer rooms for around B200–600. Usually run by Chinese-Thais, these functional three- or four-storey places are found in every sizeable town, often near the bus station or central market. Beds are large enough for a couple, so it's quite acceptable for two people to ask and pay for a "single" room (*hawng thiang diaw*, literally a "one-bedded room"). Though the rooms are generally clean, en suite and furnished with either a fan or air conditioning, there's rarely an on-site restaurant and the atmosphere is generally less convivial than at guesthouses. A number of budget hotels also double as brothels, though as a farang you're unlikely to be offered this sideline, and you might not even notice the goings-on.

Advance reservations are accepted over the phone, but this is rarely necessary, as such hotels rarely fill up. The only time you may have difficulty finding a budget hotel room is during Chinese New Year (a moveable three-day period in late Jan or Feb), when many Chinese-run hotels close and others get booked up fast.

Tourist hotels

The rest of the accommodation picture is all about **tourist hotels**, which, like anywhere in the world, come in all sizes and qualities and are often best booked via online accommodation booking services such as local outfit ⓦsawadee.com. Other useful booking sites that specialize in Thailand include ⓦtrue-beachfront.com, which carries all kinds of accommodation as long as there's no road between it and the strand; and ⓦsecret-retreats.com, a curated collection of independent accommodation, including some lovely boutique hotels, resorts and villas. One way or another, it's a good idea to **reserve ahead** in popular tourist areas during peak season.

Rates for **middle-ranking hotels** fall between B600 and B2000. For this you can expect many of the trimmings of a top-end hotel – air conditioning, TV and mini-bar in the room, plus an on-site pool, restaurant and perhaps nightclub – but with dated and possibly faded furnishings and little of the style of the famous big names; they're often the kind of places that once stood at the top of the range, but were outclassed when the multinational luxury hotels muscled in. At these places, breakfast – often referred to as "**ABF**", short for "American Breakfast" – is usually included, as noted in our listings.

Many of Thailand's **expensive hotels** belong to the big international chains: Hilton, Marriott and

---

ACCOMMODATION PRICES

Throughout this guide, the prices given for guesthouses, bungalows and hotels represent the **minimum** you can expect to pay in each establishment in the **high season** (roughly July, Aug and Nov–Feb in most parts of the country) for a typical **double room**, booked via the hotel website where available; there may however be an extra "peak" supplement for the Christmas–New Year period. If travelling on your own, expect to pay between sixty and one hundred percent of the rates quoted for a double room. Where a hostel or guesthouse also offers **dormitory beds**, the minimum price per bed is also given; where a place has both fan-cooled and air-conditioned rooms, we've given the minimum price for a double in each category. Top-end hotels will add **seven percent tax** (though this may increase to ten percent) and **ten percent service charge** to your bill; the prices given in the Guide are net rates after these taxes (usually referred to as "plus plus") have been added.

BATHROOM ETIQUETTE

Although modern, Western-style bathrooms are commonplace throughout Thailand, it's as well to be forewarned about local bathroom etiquette.

Sit-down **toilets** are now the norm but at public amenities in bus and train stations, and in some homes and old-style guesthouses and hotels, you'll still find squat toilets. Thais traditionally don't use **paper** but wash rather than wipe themselves after going to the toilet. Modern bathrooms are fitted with a special squirting hose by the toilet for this purpose, while more primitive bathrooms just provide a **bucket of water and a dipper**. Thais always use their left hand for washing – and their right hand for eating (see page 42). As Thai plumbing is notoriously sluggish, where toilet paper is provided, you're often asked to throw it in the wastebasket and not down the U-bend. If a toilet is not plumbed in, you flush it yourself with water from the bucket. In really basic hotel bathrooms with no **shower** facilities, you also use the bucket and dipper for scoop-and-slosh bathing.

Sofitel (and the rest of the Accor group) all have a strong presence in the country, alongside upmarket home-grown groups such as Amari, Anantara and Dusit. Between them they maintain premium standards in Bangkok and major resorts at prices of B3000 and upward for a double – far less than you'd pay for equivalent accommodation in the West.

Thailand also boasts an increasing number of deliciously stylish, independent **luxury hotels**, many of them designed as intimate, small-scale **boutique** hotels, with chic, minimalist décor and exceptional personal service and excellent facilities that often include private plunge pools and a spa. A night in one of these places may start at as little as B2500, rising rapidly if indulgences such as private plunge pools and spas are laid on.

Homestays

As guesthouses have become increasingly hotel-like and commercial in their facilities and approach, many tourists looking for old-style local hospitality are choosing **homestay accommodation** instead. Homestay facilities are often simple, and cheap at around B300 per person per night, with guests staying in a spare room and eating with the family. Homestays give an unparalleled insight into typical Thai (usually rural) life and can often be incorporated into a programme that includes experiencing village activities such as rice farming, squid fishing, rubber tapping or silk weaving. They are also a positive way of supporting small communities, as all your money will feed right back into the village. Many of Thailand's homestays are geared towards Bangkokians, so language might be a barrier for overseas visitors. However, as well as the listed homestays that are used to dealing with farangs in Mae Hong Son province (see pages 338 and 344), Chiang Rai (see page 353), Ban Prasat (see page 444), Mukdahan (see page 496), Ban Khiriwong and Khuraburi (see page 597), there are many others bookable through tour operators (see page 28).

National parks and camping

Nearly all the **national parks** have accommodation facilities, usually comprising a series of simple concrete bungalows that cost at least B600 for two or more beds plus a basic bathroom. Because most of their custom comes from Thai families and student groups, park officials are sometimes loath to discount them for lone travellers, though a few parks do offer dorm-style accommodation from around B150 a bed. In most parks, advance booking is unnecessary except at weekends and national holidays.

If you do want to pre-book, you'll have to take on the parks departments' new but cumbersome, uninformative and deeply frustrating website, Ⓦ nps.dnp.go.th. Bookings open sixty days ahead of a proposed stay, though hopefully it won't take quite that long to navigate through the maze to the payment page. If you turn up without booking, check in at the park headquarters, which is usually adjacent to the visitor centre. In a few parks, private operators have set up low-cost guesthouses on the outskirts, and these generally make more attractive and economical places to stay.

Camping

You can usually **camp** in a national park for a nominal fee of B60 per two-person tent, and some national parks also rent out fully equipped tents from B150, though the condition of the equipment is sometimes poor. Unless you're planning an extensive tour of national parks, though, there's little point in lugging a tent around Thailand: accommodation everywhere else is very inexpensive, and there are no campsites inside town perimeters, though camping is allowed on nearly all islands and beaches, many of which are national parks in their own right.

Food and drink

Bangkok and Chiang Mai are the country's big culinary centres, boasting the cream of Thai restaurants and the best international cuisines. The rest of the country is by no means a gastronomic wasteland, however, and you can eat well and cheaply in even the smallest provincial towns, many of which offer the additional attraction of regional specialities. In fact you could eat more than adequately without ever entering a restaurant, as itinerant food vendors hawking hot and cold snacks materialize in even the most remote spots, as well as on trains and buses – and night markets often serve customers from dusk until dawn.

Hygiene is a consideration when eating anywhere in Thailand, but being too cautious means you'll end up spending a lot of money and missing out on some real local treats. Wean your stomach gently by avoiding excessive amounts of chillies and too much fresh fruit in the first few days.

You can be pretty sure that any noodle stall or curry shop that's permanently packed with customers is a safe bet. Furthermore, because most Thai dishes can be cooked in under five minutes, you'll rarely have to contend with stuff that's been left to smoulder and stew. Foods that are generally considered high risk include salads, ice cream, shellfish and raw or under-cooked meat, fish or eggs.

Most restaurants in Thailand are open every day for lunch and dinner; we've given full opening hours throughout the Guide. In a few of the country's most expensive restaurants, mostly in Bangkok, a ten percent service charge and possibly even VAT (currently seven percent, but may be increased to ten percent) might be added to your bill.

For those interested in **learning to cook Thai food**, short courses designed for visitors are held in Bangkok (see page 153), Chiang Mai (see page 281) and dozens of other tourist centres around the country, while Chiang Mai offers fascinating **food walking tours** (see page 293).

Where to eat

A lot of tourists eschew the huge range of Thai **places to eat**, despite their obvious attractions, and opt instead for the much "safer" restaurants in guest-houses and hotels. Almost all tourist accommodation has a kitchen, and while some are excellent, the vast majority serve up bland imitations of Western fare alongside equally pale versions of common Thai dishes. Having said that, it can be a relief to get your teeth into a processed-cheese sandwich after five days' trekking in the jungle, and guesthouses do serve comfortingly familiar Western breakfasts.

Throughout the country most **inexpensive Thai restaurants** and cafés specialize in one general food type or preparation method, charging around B40–50 a dish – a "noodle shop", for example, will do fried noodles and/or noodle soups, plus maybe a basic fried rice, but they won't have curries or meat or fish dishes. Similarly, a restaurant displaying whole roast chickens and ducks in its window will offer these sliced, usually with chillies and sauces and served over rice, but their menu probably won't extend to noodles or fish, while in "curry shops" your options are limited to the vats of curries stewing away in the hot cabinet.

To get a wider array of low-cost food, it's better to head for the local **night market** (*talaat yen*), a term for the gatherings of open-air night-time kitchens found in every town. Sometimes operating from 6pm to 6am, they are typically to be found on permanent patches close to the fruit and vegetable market or the bus station, and as often as not they're the best and most entertaining places to eat, not to mention the least expensive – after a lip-smacking feast of savoury dishes, a fruit drink and a dessert you'll come away no more than B150 poorer.

A typical night market has maybe thirty-odd "specialist" pushcart kitchens (*rot khen*) jumbled together, each fronted by several sets of tables and stools. Noodle and fried-rice vendors always feature prominently, as do sweets stalls, heaped high with sticky rice cakes wrapped in banana leaves or thick with bags of tiny sweetcorn pancakes hot from the griddle – and no night market is complete without its fruit-drink stall, offering banana shakes and freshly squeezed orange, lemon and tomato juices. In the best setups you'll find a lot more besides: curries, barbecued sweetcorn, satay sticks of pork and chicken, deep-fried insects, fresh pineapple, water-melon and mango and – if the town's by a river or near the sea – heaps of fresh fish. Having decided what you want, you order from the cook (or the cook's assistant) and sit down at the nearest table; there is no territorialism about night markets, so it's normal to eat several dishes from separate stalls and rely on the nearest cook to sort out the bill.

Some large markets, particularly in Bangkok, have separate **food court** areas where you buy coupons

FRUITS OF THAILAND

You'll find **fruit** (*phonlamai*) offered everywhere in Thailand – neatly sliced in glass boxes on hawker carts, blended into delicious shakes and served as a dessert in restaurants. The fruits described here can be found in all parts of Thailand; with enhanced agricultural techniques – and imports – many of them can now be found year-round, but we've given the traditional seasons where applicable below, which is when they should be at their best and cheapest. The country's more familiar fruits include forty varieties of **banana** (*kluay*), dozens of different **mangoes** (*mamuang*), several types of **pineapple** (*sapparot*), **coconuts** (*maprao*), **oranges** (*som*), **limes** (*manao*) and **watermelons** (*taeng moh*). Thailand's most prized and expensive fruit is the **durian** (*thurian*; see page 130).

To avoid stomach trouble, **peel all fruit** before eating it, and use common sense if you're tempted to buy it pre-peeled on the street, avoiding anything that looks fly-blown or seems to have been sitting in the sun for hours.

Custard apple (*noina*; July–Sept). Inside the knobbly, muddy green skin is a creamy, almond-coloured blancmange-like flesh, with a strong flavour of strawberries and pears, and a hint of cinnamon, and many seeds.

Guava (*farang*; year-round). The apple of the tropics has green textured skin and sweet, crisp pink or white flesh, studded with tiny edible seeds. Has five times the vitamin C content of an orange and is sometimes eaten cut into strips and sprinkled with sugar and chilli.

Jackfruit (*khanun*; year-round). This large, pear-shaped fruit can weigh up to 20kg and has a thick, bobbly, greeny-yellow shell protecting sweet yellow flesh. Green, unripe jackfruit is sometimes cooked in curries or pounded in salads, especially in the north.

Longan (*lamyai*; July–Oct). A close relative of the lychee, with succulent white flesh covered in thin, brittle skin.

Lychee (*linjii*; April–May). Under rough, reddish-brown skin, the lychee has sweet, richly flavoured white flesh, rose scented and with plenty of vitamin C.

Mangosteen (*mangkut*; April–Sept). The size of a small apple, with smooth, purple skin and a fleshy inside that divides into succulent white segments that are sweet though slightly acidic.

Papaya (paw-paw; *malakaw*; year-round). Looks like an elongated watermelon, with smooth green skin and yellowy-orange flesh that's a rich source of vitamins A and C. It's a favourite in fruit salads and shakes, and sometimes appears in its green, unripe form in salads, notably *som tam*.

Pomelo (*som oh*; Oct–Dec). The largest of all the citrus fruits, it looks rather like a grapefruit, though it is sweeter; sometimes used in delicious salads.

Rambutan (*ngaw*; May–Sept). The bright red rambutan's soft, spiny exterior has given it its name – *rambut* means "hair" in Malay. Usually about the size of a golf ball, it has a white, opaque flesh of delicate flavour, similar to a lychee.

Rose apple (*chomphuu*; year-round). Linked in myth with the golden fruit of immortality; small and pear-shaped, with white, rose-scented flesh.

Sapodilla (sapota; *lamut*; Sept–Dec). These small, brown, rough-skinned ovals look a bit like kiwi fruit and conceal a grainy, yellowish pulp that tastes almost honey-sweet.

Tamarind (*makhaam*; Dec–Jan). A Thai favourite and a pricey delicacy – carrying the seeds is said to make you safe from wounding by knives or bullets. Comes in rough, brown pods containing up to ten seeds, each surrounded by a sticky, dry pulp which has a lemony taste; generally sour, but some parts of the country, notably Phetchabun, produce sweet tamarinds.

first and select food and drink to their value at the stalls of your choice. This is also usually the modus operandi in the food courts found in department stores and shopping centres across the country, though some of the more modern ones issue each diner with a plastic card, on which is recorded their expenditure, for payment at the end.

For a more relaxing ambience, Bangkok and the larger towns have a range of more upmarket **restaurants**, many of which serve regional specialities. Some specialize in **"royal" Thai cuisine**, which is differentiated mainly by the quality of the ingredients, the complexity of preparation and the way the food is presented. Great care is taken over how individual dishes look: they are served in small portions and decorated with carved fruit and vegetables in a way that used to be the prerogative of royal cooks, but has now filtered down to the common folk. The cost of such delights is not prohibitive, either – a meal in one of these places is unlikely to cost more than B500 per person.

VEGETARIANS AND VEGANS

Very few Thais are **vegetarian** (*mangsawirat*) but, if you can make yourself understood, you can often get a non-meat or fish alternative to what's on the menu; simply ask the cook to exclude meat and fish: *mai sai neua, mai sai plaa*. You may end up eating a lot of unexciting vegetable fried rice and *phat thai* minus the shrimps, but in better restaurants you should be able to get veggie versions of most curries; the mushroom version of chicken and coconut soup is also a good standby: ask for *tom kha hed*. Browsing food stalls also expands your options, with barbecued sweetcorn, nuts, fruit and other non-meaty goodies all common. The two ingredients that you will have to consider compromising on are the fermented **fish sauce** and **shrimp paste** that are fundamental to most Thai dishes; only in the vegan Thai restaurants described below, and in tourist spots serving specially concocted Thai and Western veggie dishes, can you be sure of avoiding them.

If you're **vegan** (*jay*, sometimes spelt "*jeh*") you'll need to stress when you order that you don't want egg, as they get used a lot; cheese and other dairy produce, however, don't feature at all in Thai cuisine. Many towns will have one or more **vegan restaurants** (*raan ahaan jay*), which are usually run by members of a temple or Buddhist sect and operate from unadorned premises off the main streets; because strict Buddhists prefer not to eat late in the day, most of the restaurants open early, at around 6 or 7am, and close by 2pm. Most of these places have a yellow and red sign, though few display an English-language name. Nor is there ever a menu: customers simply choose from the trays of veggie stir-fries and curries, nearly all of them made with soya products, that are laid out canteen-style. Most places charge around B40 for a couple of helpings served over a plate of brown rice.

How to eat

Thai food is eaten with a **fork** (left hand) and a **spoon** (right hand); there is no need for a knife as food is served in bite-sized chunks, which are forked onto the spoon and fed into the mouth. Cutlery is often delivered to the table wrapped in a perplexingly tiny pink napkin: Thais use this, not for their lap, but to give their fork, spoon and plate an extra wipe-down before they eat. Steamed **rice** (*khao*) is taken with most meals, and indeed the most commonly heard phrase for "to eat" is *kin khao* (literally, "eat rice"). **Chopsticks** are provided only for noodle dishes, and northeastern and northern sticky-rice dishes are usually eaten with the **fingers of your right hand**. Never eat with the fingers of your left hand, which is used for washing after going to the toilet.

So that complementary taste combinations can be enjoyed, the dishes in a Thai meal are served all at once, even the soup, and shared communally. The more people, the more taste and texture sensations; if there are only two of you, it's normal to order three dishes, plus your own individual plates of steamed rice, while three diners would order four dishes, and so on. Only put a serving of one dish on the side of your rice plate each time, and then only one or two spoonfuls.

Bland food is anathema to Thais, and restaurant tables everywhere come decked out with **condiment sets** featuring the four most basic flavours (salty, sour, sweet and spicy): usually fish sauce with chopped chillies; vinegar with chopped chillies; sugar; and dried chillies – and often extra bowls of ground peanuts and a bottle of chilli ketchup as well. Similarly, many individual Thai dishes are served with their own specific, usually spicy, condiment dip (*nam jim*). If you do bite into a **chilli**, the way to combat the searing heat is to take a mouthful of plain rice and/or beer: swigging water just exacerbates the sensation.

What to eat

Five core tastes are identified in Thai cuisine – spiciness, sourness, bitterness, saltiness and sweetness – and diners aim to share a variety of dishes that impart a balance of these flavours, along with complementary textures. Lemon grass, basil, coriander, galangal, chilli, garlic, lime juice, coconut milk and fermented fish sauce are just some of the distinctive components that bring these tastes to life. A detailed food and drink glossary can be found at the end of "Contexts" (see page 786).

Curries and soups

Thai **curries** (*kaeng*) have a variety of curry pastes as their foundation: elaborate blends of herbs, spices, garlic, shallots and chilli peppers ground together with pestle and mortar. The use of some of these spices, as well as coconut cream, was imported from India long ago; curries that don't use coconut cream are naturally less sweet, spicier and thinner, with the consistency of soups. While some curries, such as *kaeng karii* (mild and yellow) and *kaeng matsaman* ("Muslim curry", with potatoes, peanuts and usually beef), still show their roots, others have been adapted into quintessentially Thai dishes, notably *kaeng khiaw wan* (sweet and green), *kaeng phet* (red and hot) and *kaeng phanaeng* (thick and savoury, with peanuts). *Kaeng som* generally contains fish and takes its distinctive sourness from the addition of tamarind or, in the northeast, okra leaves. Traditionally eaten during the cool season, *kaeng liang* uses up bland vegetables, but is made aromatic with hot peppercorns.

Eaten simultaneously with other dishes, not as a starter, Thai **soups** often have the tang of lemon grass, kaffir lime leaves and galangal, and are sometimes made extremely spicy with chillies. Two favourites are *tom kha kai*, a creamy coconut chicken soup; and *tom yam kung*, a hot and sour prawn soup without coconut milk. *Khao tom* and *jok*, starchy rice soups that are generally eaten for breakfast, meet the approval of few Westerners, except as a traditional hangover cure.

Salads

One of the lesser-known delights of Thai cuisine is the *yam* or **salad**, which imparts most of the -fundamental flavours in an unusual and refreshing harmony. *Yam* come in many permutations – with noodles, meat, seafood or vegetables – but at the heart of most varieties is a liberal squirt of lime juice and a fiery sprinkling of chillies. Salads to look out for include *yam som oh* (pomelo), *yam hua plee* (banana flowers) and *yam plaa duk foo* (fluffy deep-fried catfish).

Noodle and rice dishes

Sold on street stalls everywhere, **noodles** come in assorted varieties – including *kway tiaw* (made with rice flour) and *ba mii* (egg noodles) – and get boiled up as soups (*nam*), doused in gravy (*rat na*) or stir-fried (*haeng*, "dry", or *phat*, "fried"). Most famous of all is *phat thai* ("Thai fry-up"), a delicious combination of noodles (usually *kway tiaw*), egg, tofu and spring onions, sprinkled with ground peanuts and lime, and often spiked with tiny dried shrimps. Other faithful standbys include fried rice (*khao phat*) and cheap, one-dish meals served on a bed of steamed rice, notably *khao kaeng* (with curry).

Regional dishes

Many of the specialities of **northern Thailand** -originated in Myanmar, including *khao soi*, featuring both boiled and crispy egg noodles plus beef, chicken or pork in a curried coconut soup; and *kaeng hang lay*, a pork curry with ginger, turmeric and tamarind. Also look out for spicy dipping sauces such as *nam phrik ong*, made with minced pork, roast tomatoes and lemon grass, and served with *khep muu* (deep-fried pork rind), crisp cucumber slices and other raw or blanched vegetables.

The crop most suited to the infertile lands of **Isaan** is sticky rice (*khao niaw*), which replaces the standard grain as the staple for northeasterners. Served in a rattan basket, it's usually eaten with the fingers, rolled up into small balls and dipped into chilli sauces. It's perfect with such spicy local -delicacies as *som tam*, a green-papaya salad with raw chillies, green beans, tomatoes, peanuts and dried shrimps (or fresh crab). Although you'll find basted barbecued chicken on a stick (*kai yaang*) all over Thailand, it originated in Isaan and is especially tasty in its home region. Raw minced pork, beef or chicken is the basis of another popular Isaan and northern dish, *laap*, a salad that's subtly flavoured with mint and lime. A similar northeastern salad is *nam tok*, featuring grilled beef or pork and roasted rice powder, which takes its name, "waterfall", from its refreshing blend of complex tastes.

Aside from putting a greater emphasis on seafood, **southern Thai** cuisine displays a marked Malaysian and Muslim aspect as you near the border, notably in *khao mok kai*, the local version of a biryani: chicken and rice cooked with turmeric and other Indian spices, and served with chicken soup. Southern markets often serve *khao yam* for breakfast or lunch, a delicious salad of dried cooked rice, dried shrimp and grated coconut served with a sweet sauce. You'll also find many types of *roti*, a flatbread sold from pushcart griddles and, in its plain form, rolled with condensed milk. Other versions include savoury *mataba*, with minced chicken or beef, and *roti kaeng*, served with curry sauce for breakfast. A huge variety of very spicy curries are also dished up in the south, many substituting shrimp paste for fish sauce. Two of the most distinctive are *kaeng luang*, "yellow curry", featuring fish, turmeric, pineapple, squash, beans and green papaya; and *kaeng tai plaa*, a powerful combination of fish stomach with potatoes, beans, pickled bamboo shoots and turmeric.

Desserts

Desserts (*khanom*) don't really figure on most restaurant menus, but a few places offer bowls of *luk taan cheum*, a jellied concoction of lotus or palm seeds floating in a syrup scented with jasmine or other aromatic flowers. Coconut milk is a feature of most other desserts, notably delicious coconut ice cream, *khao niaw mamuang* (sticky rice with mango), and a royal Thai cuisine special of coconut custard (*sangkhayaa*) cooked inside a small pumpkin, whose flesh you can also eat.

Drinks

Thais don't drink water straight from the tap, and nor should you; plastic bottles of drinking **water** (*nam* plao) are sold countrywide, in even the smallest villages, for around B10. Cheap restaurants and hotels generally serve free jugs of boiled water, which should be fine to drink, though they are not as foolproof as the bottles. In some large towns, notably Chiang Mai, you'll come across blue-and-white roadside machines that dispense purified water for B1 for 1–2 litres (bring your own bottle); however, a recent survey found that half of these machines did not meet hygiene standards.

Night markets, guesthouses and restaurants do a good line in freshly squeezed **fruit juices** such as lime (*nam manao*) and orange (*nam som*), which often come with salt and sugar already added, particularly upcountry. The same places will usually do **fruit shakes** as well, blending bananas (*nam kluay*), papayas (*nam malakaw*), pineapples (*nam sapparot*) and others with liquid sugar or condensed milk (or yoghurt, to make lassi). Fresh **coconut water** (*nam maprao*) is another great thirst-quencher – you buy the whole fruit dehusked, decapitated and chilled – as is **pandanus-leaf juice** (*bai toey*); Thais are also very partial to freshly squeezed **sugar-cane juice** (*nam awy*), which is sickeningly sweet.

Bottled and canned brand-name **soft drinks** are sold all over the place, with a particularly wide range in the ubiquitous 7-Eleven chain stores. Glass soft-drink bottles are returnable, so some drink stalls have a system of pouring the contents into a small plastic bag (fastened with an elastic band and with a straw inserted) rather than charging you the extra for taking away the bottle. The larger restaurants keep their soft drinks refrigerated, but smaller cafés and shops add **ice** (*nam khaeng*) to glasses and bags. Most ice is produced commercially under hygienic conditions, but it might become less pure in transit so be wary (ice cubes are generally a better bet than shaved ice) – and don't take ice if you have diarrhoea. For those travelling with children, or just partial themselves to **dairy products**, UHT-preserved milk and chilled yoghurt drinks are widely available (especially at 7-Eleven stores), as are a variety of soya drinks.

Weak Chinese **tea** (*nam chaa*) makes a refreshing alternative to water and often gets served in Chinese restaurants and roadside cafés, while posher restaurants keep stronger Chinese and Western-style teas. Instant Nescafé is the most widespread form of **coffee** (*kaafae*), even though fresh Thai-grown coffee – notably several excellent kinds of arabica coffee from the mountains of the north – is now easily available. If you would like to try traditional Thai coffee, most commonly found at Chinese-style cafés in the south of the country or at outdoor markets, and prepared through filtering the grounds through a cloth, ask for *kaafae thung* (literally, "bag coffee";

sometimes known as *kaafae boran* – "traditional coffee" – or *kopii*), normally served very bitter with sugar as well as sweetened condensed milk alongside a glass of black or Chinese tea to wash it down with. Fresh Western-style coffee (*kaafae sot*) in the form of Italian espresso, cappuccino and other derivatives has recently become popular among Thais, so you'll now come across espresso machines in large towns all over the country (though some of these new coffee bars, frustratingly, don't open for breakfast, as locals tend to get their fix later in the day).

Alcoholic drinks

The two most famous local **beers** (*bia*) are Singha (ask for "*bia sing*") and Chang, though many travellers find Singha's weaker brew, Leo, more palatable than either. In shops you can expect to pay around B35–40 for a 330ml bottle of these beers, B70 for a 660ml bottle. All manner of slightly pricier foreign beers are now brewed in Thailand, including Heineken and Asahi, and in the most touristy areas you'll find expensive imported bottles from all over the world.

Wine is now found on plenty of upmarket and tourist-oriented restaurant menus, but expect to be disappointed by both quality and price, which is jacked up by heavy taxation. Thai wine is now produced at several vineyards, including by the family behind Red Bull at the Monsoon Valley Vineyard near Hua Hin, which produces an especially tasty rosé.

At about B100 for a hip-flask-sized 375ml bottle, the local **whisky** is a lot better value, and Thais think nothing of consuming a bottle a night, heavily diluted with ice and soda or Coke. The most palatable and widely available of these is Mekong, which is very pleasant once you've stopped expecting it to taste like Scotch; distilled from rice, Mekong is 35 percent proof, deep gold in colour and tastes slightly sweet. If that's not to your taste, a pricier Thai **rum** is also available, Sang Som, made from sugar cane, and even stronger than the whisky at forty percent proof. Check the menu carefully when ordering a bottle of Mekong from a bar in a tourist area, as they sometimes ask up to five times more than you'd pay in a guesthouse or shop. A hugely popular way to enjoy whisky or rum at beach resorts is to pick up a bucket, containing a quarter-bottle of spirit, a mixer, Red Bull, ice and several straws, for around B200–300: that way you get to share with your friends and build a sandcastle afterwards.

You can **buy** beer and whisky in food stores, guesthouses and most restaurants (by a law that's spottily enforced, it's not meant to be for sale between 2pm and 5pm, when schools are finishing for the day); **bars** aren't strictly an indigenous feature as Thais traditionally don't drink out without eating, but you'll find plenty of Western-style drinking holes in Bangkok and larger centres elsewhere in the country, ranging from ultra-cool haunts in the capital to basic, open-to-the-elements "**bar-beers**".

Culture and etiquette

Tourist literature has marketed Thailand as the "Land of Smiles" so successfully that a lot of farangs arrive in the country expecting to be forgiven any outrageous behaviour. This is just not the case: there are some things so universally sacred in Thailand that even a hint of disrespect will cause deep offence.

The monarchy

It is both socially unacceptable to many Thais and a criminal offence to make critical or defamatory remarks about the **royal family**. Thailand's monarchy is technically a constitutional one, but pictures of King Vajiralongkorn, who acceded to the throne on the death of his much-loved father King Bhumibol in 2016, are displayed in many public places and submissive crowds mass whenever the royals make a public appearance. When addressing or speaking about royalty, Thais use a special language full of deference, called *rajasap* (literally "royal language").

Thailand's **lese-majeste laws** are among the most strictly applied in the world and have been increasingly invoked since the 2014 coup. Accusations of lese-majeste can be levelled by and against anyone, Thai national or farang, and must be investigated by the police. As a few high-profile cases involving foreigners have demonstrated, they can be raised for seemingly minor infractions, such as defacing a poster or being less than respectful in a work of fiction. Article 112 of the Thai criminal code specifies insults to the king, the queen, the heir-apparent and the regent, but the law has been wielded against supposed slights to the king's dog and to kings who have been dead for four centuries. Transgressions are met with jail sentences of up to fifteen years for each offence.

Aside from keeping any anti-monarchy sentiments to yourself, you should be prepared to stand when the **king's anthem** is played at the beginning of every cinema programme, and to stop in your tracks if the town you're in plays the **national anthem** over its public address system – many small towns do this twice a day at 8am and again at 6pm, as do some train stations and airports. A less obvious point: as the king's head features on all Thai currency, you should never step on a coin or banknote, which is tantamount to kicking the king in the face.

Religion

Almost equally insensitive would be to disregard certain **religious** precepts. **Buddhism** plays a fundamental role in Thai culture, and Buddhist monuments should be treated with respect – which basically means wearing long trousers or knee-length skirts, covering your arms and removing your shoes whenever you visit one.

All **Buddha images** are sacred, however small, tacky or ruined, and should never be used as a backdrop for a portrait photo, clambered over, placed in a position of inferiority or treated in any manner that could be construed as disrespectful. In an attempt to prevent foreigners from committing any kind of transgression the government requires a special licence for all Buddha statues exported from the country (see page 64).

Monks come only a little beneath the monarchy in the social hierarchy, and they too are addressed and discussed in a special language. If there's a monk around, he'll always get a seat on the bus, usually right at the back. Theoretically, monks are forbidden to have any close contact with women, which means that, as a female, you mustn't sit or stand next to a monk, or even brush against his robes; if it's essential to pass him something, put the object down so that he can then pick it up – never hand it over directly. Nuns, however, get treated like ordinary women.

See "Contexts" for more on religious practices in Thailand (see page 738).

The body

The Western liberalism embraced by the Thai sex industry is very unrepresentative of the majority Thai attitude to the body. **Clothing** – or the lack of it – is what bothers Thais most about tourist behaviour. You need to dress modestly when entering temples (see page 84), but the same also applies to other important buildings and all public places. Stuffy and sweaty as it sounds, you should keep short shorts and vests for the real tourist resorts, and be especially diligent about covering up and, for women, wearing bras in rural areas. Baring your flesh on beaches is very much a Western practice: when Thais go swimming they often do so fully clothed, and they find topless and nude bathing offensive.

According to ancient Hindu belief, the **head** is the most sacred part of the body and the **feet** are the most unclean. This belief, imported into Thailand, means that it's very rude to touch another person's head or to point your feet either at a human being or at a sacred image – when sitting on a temple floor, for example, you should **tuck your legs beneath you** rather than stretch them out towards the Buddha. These hierarchies also forbid people from wearing **shoes** (which are even more unclean than feet) inside temples and most private homes, and – by extension – Thais take offence when they see someone sitting on the "head", or prow, of a boat. **Putting your feet up** on a table, a chair or a pillow is also considered very uncouth, and Thais will always take their shoes off if they need to stand on a train or bus seat to get to the luggage rack, for example. On a more practical note, the **left hand** is used for washing after going to the toilet (see page 39), so Thais never use it to put food in their mouth, pass things or shake hands – as a farang, though, you'll be assumed to have different customs, so left-handers shouldn't worry unduly.

Social conventions

Thais rarely shake hands, instead using the **wai** to greet and say goodbye and to acknowledge respect, gratitude or apology. A prayer-like gesture made with raised hands, the *wai* changes according to the relative status of the two people involved: Thais can instantaneously assess which *wai* to use, but as a farang your safest bet is to raise your hands close to your chest, bow your head and place your fingertips just below your nose. If someone makes a *wai* at you, you should generally *wai* back, but it's safer not to initiate.

Public displays of **physical affection** in Thailand are more common between friends of the same sex than between lovers, whether hetero- or homosexual. Holding hands and hugging is as common among male friends as with females, so if you're caressed by a Thai acquaintance of the same sex, don't necessarily assume you're being propositioned.

Finally, there are three specifically Thai **concepts** you're bound to come across, which may help you comprehend a sometimes laissez-faire attitude to delayed buses and other inconveniences. The first, **jai yen**, translates literally as "cool heart" and is something everyone tries to maintain: most Thais hate raised voices, visible irritation and confrontations of any kind, so losing one's cool can have a much more inflammatory effect than in more combative cultures. Related to this is the oft-quoted response to a difficulty, **mai pen rai** – "never mind", "no problem" or "it can't be helped" – the verbal equivalent of an open-handed shoulder shrug, which has its basis in the Buddhist notion of karma (see page 739). And then there's **sanuk**, the wide-reaching philosophy of "fun", which, crass as it sounds, Thais do their best to inject into any situation, even work. Hence the crowds of inebriated Thais who congregate at waterfalls and other beauty spots on public holidays (travelling solo is definitely not *sanuk*), the reluctance to do almost anything without high-volume musical accompaniment, and the national waterfight which takes place during Songkhran every April on streets right across Thailand.

Thai names

Although all Thais have a first **name** and a family name, everyone is addressed by their first name – even when meeting strangers – prefixed by the title "**Khun**" (Mr/Ms); no one is ever addressed as Khun Surname, and even the phone book lists people by their given name. In Thailand you will often be addressed in an anglicized version of this convention, as "Mr Paul" or "Miss Lucy" for example. Bear in mind, though, that when a man is introduced to you as Khun Pirom, his wife will definitely not be Khun Pirom as well (that would be like calling them, for instance, "Mr and Mrs Paul"). Among friends and relatives, **Phii** ("older brother/sister") is often used instead of Khun when addressing older familiars (though as a tourist you're on surer ground with Khun), and **Nong** ("younger brother/sister") is used for younger ones.

Many Thai **first names** come from ancient Sanskrit and have an auspicious meaning; for example, Boon means good deeds, Porn means blessings, Siri means glory and Thawee means to increase. However, Thais of all ages are commonly known by the **nickname** given them soon after birth rather than by their official first name. This tradition arises out of a deep-rooted superstition that once a child has been officially named the spirits will begin to take an unhealthy interest in them, so a nickname is used instead to confuse the spirits. Common nicknames – which often bear no resemblance to the adult's personality or physique – include Yai (Big), Uan (Fat) and Muu (Pig); Lek or Noi (Little), Nok (Bird), Nuu (Mouse) and Kung (Shrimp); and English nicknames like Apple, Joy or even Pepsi.

Family names were only introduced in 1913 (by Rama VI, who invented many of the aristocracy's surnames himself), and are used only in very formal situations, always in conjunction with the first name. It's quite usual for good friends never to know each other's surname. Ethnic Thais generally have short surnames like Somboon or Srisai, while the long, convoluted family names – such as Sonthanasumpun – usually indicate Chinese origin, not because they are phonetically Chinese but because many Chinese immigrants have chosen to adopt Thai surnames and Thai law states that every newly created surname must be unique. Thus anyone who wants to change their surname must submit a shortlist of five unique Thai names – each to a maximum length of ten Thai characters – to be checked against a database of existing names. As more and more names are taken, Chinese family names get increasingly unwieldy, and more easily distinguishable from the pithy old Thai names.

The media

To keep you abreast of world affairs, there are several English-language newspapers in Thailand, though various forms of censorship (and self-censorship) affect all newspapers and the predominantly state-controlled media.

Newspapers and magazines

Of the hundreds of **Thai-language newspapers and magazines** published every week, the sensationalist daily tabloid *Thai Rath* attracts the widest readership, with circulation of around a million, while the moderately progressive *Matichon* is the leading quality daily, with an estimated circulation of 600,000.

Alongside these, the two main daily **English-language papers** are the *Bangkok Post* (W bangkokpost. com) and the *Nation* (W nationmultimedia.com), but you'll get a more balanced idea of what's going on in Thailand at W khaosodenglish.com, which is owned by *Matichon*. Both the *Post* and *Nation* are still sold at many newsstands in the capital as well as in major provincial towns and tourist resorts; the more isolated places receive their few copies one day late. Details of local English-language newspapers, magazines and listings publications and websites are given in the relevant Guide accounts.

You can also pick up **foreign** magazines such as *Newsweek* and *Time* in Bangkok, Chiang Mai and the major resorts. English-language bookshops such as Bookazine and some expensive hotels carry air-freighted, or sometimes locally printed and stapled, copies of foreign national newspapers for at least B50 a copy; the latter are also sold in tourist-oriented minimarkets in the big resorts.

Television

There are six government-controlled, terrestrial **TV channels** in Thailand: channels 3, 5 (owned and

operated by the army), 7 (operated under license from the army) and 9 transmit a blend of news, soaps, sports, talk, quiz, reality and game shows, while the more serious-minded public-service channels are NBT, owned and operated by the government's public relations department, and the state-funded but more independent PBS. **Cable** networks – available in many guesthouse and hotel rooms – carry channels from all around the world, including CNN from the US, BBC World News from the UK and sometimes ABC from Australia, as well as English-language movie channels and various sports, music and documentary channels.

Radio

Thailand boasts over five hundred **radio stations**, mostly music-oriented, ranging from Eazy (105.5 FM), which serves up Western pop, through *luk thung* (see page 764) on Rak Thai (90FM), to Cat (formerly Fat) Radio, which streams Thai indie sounds 24hr on its website (W thisiscat.com) and app. Met 107 on 107 FM is one of several stations that include English-language news bulletins.

By going **online** or with a **shortwave radio (BBC only)**, you can listen to the BBC World Service (W bbc.co.uk/worldserviceradio), Radio Australia (W radioaustralia.net.au), Voice of America (W voanews.com), Radio Canada (W rcinet.ca) and other international stations.

Festivals

Nearly all Thai festivals have a religious aspect. The most theatrical are generally Brahmin (Hindu) or animistic in origin, honouring elemental spirits and deities with ancient rites and ceremonial costumed parades. Buddhist celebrations usually revolve round the local temple, and while merit-making is a significant feature, a light-hearted atmosphere prevails, as the wat grounds are swamped with food and trinket vendors and makeshift stages are set up to show *likay* folk theatre, singing stars and beauty contests.

Many of the **secular festivals** (like the elephant roundups and the Bridge over the River Kwai spectacle) are outdoor local culture shows, geared specifically towards Thai and farang tourists. Others are thinly veiled but lively trade fairs held in provincial capitals to show off the local speciality, be it exquisite silk weaving or especially tasty rambutans.

Few of the **dates** for religious festivals are fixed, so check with TAT for specifics (W tourismthailand.org).

The names of the most touristy celebrations are given here in English; the more low-key festivals are more usually known by their Thai name (*ngan* – usually religious – and *tetsagaan* – usually organized by the municipality – are the words for "festival"). See the relevant town accounts for fuller details of the festivals below; some of them are designated as national holidays (see page 71).

A festival calendar

JANUARY–MARCH

Chinese New Year Nakhon Sawan (Truut Jiin; three days between mid-Jan and late Feb). In Nakhon Sawan, the new Chinese year is welcomed in with particularly exuberant parades of dragons and lion dancers, Chinese opera performances, an international lion-dance competition and a fireworks display. Also celebrated in Chinatowns across the country, especially in Bangkok and Phuket.

Flower Festival Chiang Mai (usually first weekend in Feb). Enormous floral sculptures are paraded through the streets.

Makha Puja Nationwide (particularly Wat Benjamabophit in Bangkok, Wat Phra That Doi Suthep in Chiang Mai and Wat Mahathat in Nakhon Si Thammarat; full-moon day usually in Feb). A day of merit-making marks the occasion when 1250 disciples gathered spontaneously to hear the Buddha preach, and culminates with a candlelit procession round the local temple's bot.

Ngan Phrabat Phra Phutthabat, near Lopburi (early Feb and early March). Pilgrimages to the Holy Footprint attract food and handicraft vendors and travelling players.

King Narai Reign Fair Lopburi (Feb). Costumed processions and a *son et lumière* show at Narai's palace.

Ngan Phra That Phanom That Phanom (Feb). Thousands come to pay homage at the holiest shrine in Isaan, which houses relics of the Buddha.

Kite fights and flying contests Nationwide, including a three-day festival in Hua Hin (late Feb to mid-April).

APRIL AND MAY

Poy Sang Long Mae Hong Son and Chiang Mai (early April). Young Thai Yai boys precede their ordination into monkhood by parading the streets in floral headdresses and festive garb.

Songkhran Nationwide (particularly Chiang Mai, and Bangkok's Thanon Khao San; usually April 13–15). The most exuberant of the national festivals welcomes the Thai New Year with massive waterfights, sandcastle building in temple compounds and the inevitable parades and "Miss Songkhran" beauty contests.

Ngan Phanom Rung Prasat Hin Khao Phanom Rung (usually April). The three-day period when the sunrise is perfectly aligned through fifteen doorways at these magnificent eleventh-century Khmer ruins is celebrated with daytime processions and nightly *son et lumière*.

Visakha Puja Nationwide (particularly Bangkok's Wat Benjamabophit, Wat Phra That Doi Suthep in Chiang Mai and Nakhon Si Thammarat's

Wat Mahathat; full-moon day usually in May). The holiest day of the Buddhist year, commemorating the birth, enlightenment and death of the Buddha all in one go; the most public and photogenic part is the candlelit evening procession around the wat.

Raek Na Sanam Luang, Bangkok (early May). The royal ploughing ceremony to mark the beginning of the rice-planting season; ceremonially clad Brahmin leaders parade sacred oxen and the royal plough, and interpret omens to forecast the year's rice yield.

Rocket Festival Yasothon (Bun Bang Fai; weekend in mid-May). Beautifully crafted, painted wooden rockets are paraded and fired to ensure plentiful rains; celebrated all over Isaan, but especially raucous and raunchy in Yasothon.

JUNE–SEPTEMBER

Phi Ta Kon Dan Sai, near Loei (end June or beginning July). A re-enactment of the Buddha's penultimate incarnation provides the excuse for bawdy, masked merry-making.

Candle Festival Ubon Ratchathani (Asanha Puja; usually July, three days around the full moon). This nationwide festival marking the Buddha's first sermon and the subsequent beginning of the annual Buddhist retreat period (Khao Pansa) is celebrated across the northeast with parades of enormous wax sculptures, most spectacularly in Ubon Ratchathani.

Tamboon Deuan Sip Nakhon Si Thammarat (Sept or Oct). Merit-making ceremonies to honour dead relatives accompanied by a ten-day fair.

OCTOBER–DECEMBER

Vegetarian Festival Phuket and Trang (Tetsagaan Kin Jeh; Oct or Nov). Chinese devotees become vegetarian for a nine-day period and then parade through town performing acts of self-mortification such as pushing skewers through their cheeks. Celebrated in Bangkok's Chinatown by most food vendors and restaurants turning vegetarian for about a fortnight.

Bang Fai Phaya Nak Nong Khai and around (usually Oct). The strange appearance of pink balls of fire above the Mekong River draws sightseers from all over Thailand.

Tak Bat Devo and Awk Pansa Nationwide (especially Ubon Ratchathani and Nakhon Phanom; full-moon day usually in Oct). Offerings to monks and general merrymaking to celebrate the Buddha's descent to earth from Tavatimsa heaven and the end of the Khao Pansa retreat. Celebrated in Ubon with a procession of illuminated boats along the rivers, and in Nakhon Phanom with another illuminated boat procession and Thailand–Laos dragon-boat races along the Mekong.

Chak Phra Surat Thani (mid-Oct). The town's chief Buddha images are paraded on floats down the streets and on barges along the river.

Boat Races Nan, Nong Khai, Phimai and elsewhere (Oct to mid-Nov). Longboat races and barge parades along town rivers.

Thawt Kathin Nationwide (the month between Awk Pansa and Loy Krathong, generally Oct–Nov). During the month following the end of the monks' rainy-season retreat, it's traditional for the laity to donate new robes to the monkhood and this is celebrated in most towns with parades and a festival, and occasionally, when it coincides with a kingly anniversary, with a spectacular Royal Barge Procession down the Chao Phraya River in Bangkok.

Cat Expo Bangkok (over a weekend in Nov; details on Facebook near the time). Formerly Fat Festival, this is Thailand's biggest indie music event, featuring over a hundred established and emerging bands on several stages, meet-the-bands booths and film screenings.

Loy Krathong Nationwide (particularly Sukhothai and Chiang Mai; full moon in Nov). Baskets (*krathong*) of flowers and lighted candles are floated on any available body of water (such as ponds, rivers, lakes, canals and seashores) to honour water spirits and celebrate the end of the rainy season, and paper hot-air balloons are released into the night sky. Nearly every town puts on a big show, with bazaars, public entertainments and fireworks; in Sukhothai it is the climax of a *son et lumière* festival that's held over several nights.

Ngan Wat Saket Wat Saket, Bangkok (nine days around Loy Krathong, Nov). Probably Thailand's biggest temple fair, held around the Golden Mount, with all the usual festival trappings.

Elephant Roundup Surin (third weekend of Nov). Two hundred elephants play team games, perform complex tasks and parade in battle dress.

River Kwai Bridge Festival Kanchanaburi (ten nights from the last week of Nov into the first week of Dec). Spectacular *son et lumière* at the infamous bridge.

Silk and Phuk Siao Festival Khon Kaen (Nov 29–Dec 10). Weavers from around the province come to town to sell their lengths of silk.

World Heritage Site Festival Ayutthaya (mid-Dec). Week-long celebration, including a nightly historical *son et lumière* romp, to commemorate the town's UNESCO designation.

New Year's Eve Countdown Nationwide (Dec 31). Most cities and tourist destinations welcome in the new year with fireworks, often backed up by food festivals, beauty contests and outdoor performances.

Entertainment and sport

Bangkok is the best place to catch authentic performances of classical Thai dance, though more easily digestible tourist-oriented shows are staged in some of the big tourist centres as well as in Bangkok. The country's two main Thai boxing stadia are also in the capital, but you'll come across local matches in the provinces too.

Drama and dance

Drama pretty much equals **dance** in classical Thai theatre, and many of the traditional dance-dramas are based on the *Ramakien*, the Thai version of the Hindu epic the *Ramayana*, an adventure tale of good versus evil that is taught in all schools. Not understanding the plots can be a major dis-advantage, so try reading an abridged version -beforehand (see pages 781 and 88) and check out the wonderfully imaginative murals at Wat Phra Kaeo in Bangkok. There are three broad categories of traditional Thai dance-drama – *khon, lakhon* and *likay* – described below in descending order of refinement.

Khon

The most spectacular form of traditional Thai theatre is **khon**, a stylized drama performed in masks and elaborate costumes by a troupe of highly trained classical dancers. There's little room for individual interpretation in these dances, as all the movements follow a strict choreography that's been passed down through generations: each graceful, angular gesture depicts a precise event, action or emotion which will be familiar to educated *khon* audiences. The dancers don't speak, and the story is chanted and sung by a chorus who stand at the side of the stage, accompanied by a classical *phipat* orchestra.

A typical *khon* performance features several of the best-known **Ramakien** episodes, in which the main characters are recognized by their masks, headdresses and heavily brocaded costumes. Gods and humans don't wear masks, but the hero Rama and heroine Sita always wear tall gilded headdresses and often appear as a trio with Rama's brother Lakshaman. Monkey **masks** are wide-mouthed: monkey army chief Hanuman always wears white, and his two right-hand men – Nilanol, the god of fire, and Nilapat, the god of death – wear red and black respectively. In contrast, the demons have grim mouths, clamped shut or snarling; Totsagan, king of the demons, wears a green face in battle and a gold one during peace, but always sports a two-tier headdress carved with two rows of faces.

Khon is performed with English subtitles at Bangkok's Sala Chalermkrung (see page 163) and is also featured within the various cultural **shows** staged by tourist restaurants in Bangkok, Phuket and Pattaya. Even if you don't see a show, you're bound to come across finely crafted real and replica *khon* masks both in museums and in souvenir shops all over the country.

Lakhon

Serious and refined, **lakhon** is derived from *khon* but is used to dramatize a greater range of stories, including Buddhist *Jataka* tales, local folk dramas and of course the *Ramakien*.

The form you're most likely to come across is *lakhon chatri*, which is performed at shrines like Bangkok's

Erawan and at a city's *lak muang* as entertainment for the spirits and a token of gratitude from worshippers. Usually female, the *lakhon chatri* dancers perform as an ensemble, executing sequences that, like *khon* movements, all have minute and particular symbolism. They also wear ornate costumes, but no masks, and dance to the music of a *phipat* orchestra. Unfortunately, as resident shrine troupes tend to repeat the same dances a dozen times a day, it's rarely the sublime display it's cracked up to be. Bangkok's National Theatre stages the more elegantly executed *lakhon nai*, a dance form that used to be performed at the Thai court and often re-tells the *Ramakien*.

Likay

Likay is a much more popular and dynamic derivative of *khon* – more light-hearted, with lots of comic interludes, bawdy jokes and panto-style over-the-top acting and singing. Some *likay* troupes perform *Ramakien* excerpts, but a lot of them adapt pot-boiler romances or write their own, and most will ham things up with improvisations and up-to-the-minute topical satire. Costumes might be traditional as in *khon* and *lakhon*, modern and Western as on TV, or a mixture of both.

Likay troupes travel around the country doing shows on makeshift outdoor stages wherever they think they'll get an audience, most commonly at temple fairs. Performances are often free and generally last for about five hours, with the audience strolling in and out of the show, cheering and joking with the cast throughout. Televised *likay* dramas get huge audiences and always follow romantic soap-opera-style plot-lines. Short *likay* dramas are also a staple of Bangkok's National Theatre, but for more radical and internationally minded *likay*, look out for performances by **Makhampom** (Ⓦmakhampom.org), a famous, long-established troupe with bases in Bangkok and Chiang Dao that pushes *likay* in new directions to promote social causes and involve minority communities.

Nang

Nang, or shadow plays (see page 577), are said to have been the earliest dramas performed in Thailand, but now are rarely seen except in the far south, where the Malaysian influence ensures an appreciative audience for *nang thalung*. Crafted from buffalo hide, the two-dimensional *nang thalung* puppets play out scenes from popular dramas against a backlit screen, while the storyline is told through songs, chants and musical interludes. An even rarer *nang* form is the *nang yai*, which uses enormous cut-outs of whole scenes rather than just individual characters, so the play becomes something like an animated film.

Film

All sizeable towns have a **cinema** or two – Bangkok has over fifty – and tickets generally start at around B100. Several websites give showtimes of movies around the country, including Ⓦmoveedoo.com/th. In some rural areas, villagers still have to make do with the travelling cinema, or *nang klarng plaeng*, which sets up a mobile screen in wat compounds or other public spaces, and often entertains the whole village in one sitting (in larger towns, you might catch a travelling cinema at a temple festival). However makeshift the cinema, the **king's anthem** is always played before every screening, during which the audience is expected to stand up.

Fast-paced Chinese and Korean blockbusters have long dominated the programmes at Thai cinemas, serving up a low-grade cocktail of sex, spooks, violence and comedy. Not understanding the dialogue is rarely a drawback, as the storylines tend to be simple and the visuals more entertaining than the words. In the cities, **Western films** are also popular, and new releases often get subtitled rather than dubbed.

In recent years Thailand's own film industry (see page 775) has been enjoying a boom, and in the larger cities and resorts you may be lucky enough to come across one of the bigger Thai hits showing with English subtitles.

Thai boxing

Thai boxing (*muay thai*) enjoys a following similar to football or baseball in the West: every province has a stadium and whenever a big fight is shown on TV you can be sure that large, noisy crowds will gather round the sets in streetside restaurants. The best place to see Thai boxing is at one of Bangkok's two main stadia, which between them hold bouts every night of the week (see page 164), but many tourist resorts also stage regular matches.

There's a strong spiritual and **ritualistic** dimension to *muay thai*, adding grace to an otherwise brutal sport. Each boxer enters the ring to the wailing music of a three-piece *phipat* orchestra, wearing the statutory red or blue shorts and, on his head, a sacred rope headband or *mongkhon*. Tied around his biceps are *phra jiat*, pieces of cloth that are often decorated with cabalistic symbols and may contain Buddhist tablets. The fighter then bows, first in the direction of his birthplace and then to the north, south, east and west, honouring both his teachers and the spirit of the ring. Next he performs a slow dance, claiming the audience's attention and demonstrating his prowess as a performer.

Any part of the body except the head may be used as an **offensive weapon** in *muay thai*, and all parts except the groin are fair targets. Kicks to the head are the blows that cause most knockouts. As the action hots up, so the orchestra speeds up its tempo and the betting in the audience becomes more frenetic. It can be a gruesome business, but it was far bloodier before modern boxing gloves were introduced in the 1930s, when the Queensbury Rules were adapted for *muay* – combatants used to wrap their fists with hemp impregnated with a face-lacerating dosage of ground glass.

A number of *muay thai* gyms and camps offer training **courses** for foreigners, including several in Bangkok, as well as Chiang Mai, Hua Hin, Ko Pha Ngan, Ko Tao and Ko Yao Noi – see the relevant accounts for details or go to ⓦmuaycampsthailand.com for advice and a fuller list of camps.

Takraw

Whether in Bangkok or upcountry, you're quite likely to come across some form of **takraw** game being played in a public park, a school, a wat compound or just in a backstreet alley. Played with a very light rattan ball (or one made of plastic to look like rattan), the basic aim of the game is to keep the ball off the ground. To do this you can use any part of your body except your hands, so a well-played *takraw* game looks extremely balletic, with players leaping and arching to get a good strike.

There are at least five versions of **competitive takraw**, based on the same principles. Sepak takraw, the version featured in the Southeast Asian Games and most frequently in school tournaments, is played over a volleyball net and involves two teams of three; the other most popular competitive version has a team ranged round a basketball-type hoop trying to score as many goals as possible within a limited time period before the next team replaces them and tries to outscore them.

Other *takraw* games introduce more complex rules (like kicking the ball backwards with your heels through a ring made with your arms behind your back) and many assign points according to the skill displayed by individual players rather than per goal or dropped ball.

Spas and traditional massage

With their focus on indulgent self-pampering, spas are usually associated with high-spending tourists, but the treatments on offer at Thailand's five-star hotels are often little different from those used by traditional medical practitioners, who have long held that massage and herbs are the best way to restore physical and mental well-being.

Thai massage (*nuad boran*) is based on the principle that many physical and emotional problems are caused by the blocking of vital energy channels within the body. The masseur uses his or her feet, heels, knees and elbows, as well as hands, to exert pressure on these channels, supplementing this acupressure-style technique by pulling and pushing the limbs into yogic stretches. This distinguishes Thai massage from most other massage styles, which are more concerned with tissue manipulation. One is supposed to emerge from a Thai massage feeling both relaxed and energized, and it is said that regular massages produce long-term benefits in muscles as well as stimulating the circulation and aiding natural detoxification.

Thais will visit a masseur for many conditions, including fevers, colds and muscle strain, but bodies that are not sick are also considered to benefit from the restorative powers of a massage, and nearly every hotel and guesthouse will be able to put you in touch with a **masseur**. On the more popular beaches, it can be hard to walk a few hundred metres without being offered a massage – something Thai tourists are just as enthusiastic about as foreigners. Thai masseurs do not traditionally use oils or lotions and the client is treated on a mat or mattress; you'll often be given a pair of loose-fitting trousers and perhaps a loose top to change into. English-speaking masseurs will often ask if there are any areas of your body that you would like them to concentrate on, or if you have any problem areas that you want them to avoid; if your masseur doesn't speak English, the simplest way to signal the latter is to point at the offending area while saying *mai sabai* ("not well"). If you're in pain during a massage, wincing usually does the trick, perhaps adding *jep* ("it hurts"); if your masseur is pressing too hard for your liking, say *bao bao na khrap/kha* ("gently please").

The best places for a basic massage are usually the government-accredited clinics and hospitals that are found in large towns all over the country. A session should ideally last at least one and a half hours and will cost from around B300. If you're a bit wary of submitting to the full works, try a **foot massage** first, which will apply the same techniques of acupressure and stretching to just your feet and lower legs. Most places also offer **herbal massages**, in which the masseur will knead you with a ball of herbs (*phrakop*) wrapped in a cloth and steam-heated; they're said to be particularly good for stiffness of the neck, shoulders and back.

The **science** behind Thai massage has its roots in Indian Ayurvedic medicine, which classifies each component of the body according to one of the four elements (earth, water, fire and air), and holds that balancing these elements within the body is crucial to good health. Many of the stretches and manipulations fundamental to Thai massage are thought to have derived from yogic practices introduced to Thailand from India by Buddhist missionaries in about the second century BC; Chinese acupuncture and reflexology have also had a strong influence. In the nineteenth century, King Rama III ordered a series of murals illustrating the principles of Thai massage to be painted around the courtyard of Bangkok's Wat Pho, and they are still in place today, along with statues of ascetics depicted in typical massage poses.

Wat Pho has been the leading school of Thai massage for hundreds of years, and it is possible to take courses there as well as to receive a massage (see page 91); it also has several satellite health centres scattered around Bangkok. Masseurs who trained at Wat Pho are considered to be the best in the country and masseurs all across Thailand advertise this as a credential, whether or not it is true. Many Thais consider blind masseurs to be especially sensitive practitioners.

While Wat Pho is the most famous place to take a **course** in Thai massage, many foreigners interested in learning this ancient science head for Chiang Mai, which offers the biggest concentration of massage schools (including another satellite branch of the Wat Pho school), though you will find others all over Thailand, including in Bangkok and at southern beach resorts.

All **spas** in Thailand feature traditional Thai massage and herbal therapies in their programmes, but most also offer dozens of other international treatments, including facials, aromatherapy, Swedish massage and various body wraps. Spa centres in upmarket hotels and resorts are usually open to non-guests but generally need to be booked in advance. Day-spas that are not attached to hotels are generally cheaper and are found in some of the bigger cities and resorts – some of these may not require reservations.

Meditation centres and retreats

Of the hundreds of meditation temples in Thailand, a few cater specifically for foreigners by holding meditation sessions and retreats in English. Novices as well as practised meditators are generally welcome at these wats, but absolute beginners might like to consider the regular retreats at Wat Suan Dork in Chiang Mai or Wat Suan Mokkh on Ko Samui and in Chaiya, which are conducted by supportive and experienced Thai and Western teachers and include talks and interviews on Buddhist teachings and practice. The meditation taught is mostly Vipassana, or "insight", which emphasizes the minute observation of internal sensations; the other main technique you'll come across is Samatha, which aims to calm the mind and develop concentration (these two techniques are not entirely separate, since you cannot have insight without some degree of concentration).

Longer **retreats** are for the serious-minded only. All the temples listed below welcome both male and female English-speakers, but strict segregation of the sexes is enforced and many places observe a vow of silence. Reading and writing are also discouraged, and you'll not be allowed to leave the retreat complex unless absolutely necessary, so try to bring whatever you'll need in with you. All retreats expect you to wear modest clothing, and some require you to wear white – check ahead whether there is a shop at the retreat complex or whether you are expected to bring this with you.

An average day at any one of these monasteries starts with a **wake-up call** at around 4am and includes several hours of **group meditation** and chanting, as well as time put aside for chores and personal reflection. However long their stay, visitors are expected to keep the eight main Buddhist precepts, the most restrictive of these being the abstention from food after midday and from alcohol, tobacco, drugs and sex at all times. Most wats ask for a minimal daily **donation** (around B200) to cover the costs of the simple accommodation and food.

Further details about many of the temples listed below – including how to get there – are given in the relevant sections in the Guide chapters. Little Bangkok Sangha (Ⓦlittlebang.org) is a handy blog maintained by a British-born monk, Phra Pandit, which gives details of group meditation sessions and talks in Bangkok and retreats. Also in Bangkok, keep an eye out for events for English-speakers at the Buddhadasa Indapanno Archives in Chatuchak Park in the north of the city (Ⓦbia.or.th), a recently built centre in honour of the founder of Wat Suan Mokkh (see page 530).

MEDITATION CENTRES AND RETREAT TEMPLES

In addition to those listed below, additional meditation centres and retreat temples are listed in the Guide chapters, including **Wat Mahathat** in Bangkok (see page 93), several retreats and sessions in **Chiang Mai** (see page 285), and **Wat Suan Mokkh** on Ko Samui (see page 530) and in Chaiya (see page 529).

House of Dhamma Insight Meditation Centre 26/9 Soi Lardprao 15, Chatuchak, Bangkok ☎ 02 511 0439, ⓦ houseofdhamma.com. Regular one- and two-day courses in Vipassana, as well as workshops in Metta (Loving Kindness) meditation for experienced practitioners upon request. Courses in reiki and other subjects available.

Thailand Vipassana Centres ⓦ dhamma.org. Frequent courses in a Burmese Vipassana tradition (ten days), in Phitsanulok and eight other centres around Thailand.

Wat Pah Nanachat Ban Bung Wai, Amphoe Warinchamrab, Ubon Ratchathani 34310 ⓦ watpahnanachat.org. The famous monk, Ajahn Chah, established this forest monastery, 17km west of Ubon Ratchathani, in 1975 specifically to provide monastic training for non-Thais, with English the primary language. Visitors who want to join the practice of the resident community are welcome, but the atmosphere is serious and intense and not for beginners or curious sightseers, and accommodation for students is limited, so you should write to the monastery before visiting, allowing several weeks to receive a written response.

Wat Phra Si Chom Thong Insight Meditation Centre ☎ 053 342184 or 053 826869. Located in Chom Thong (see page 329), 58km south of Chiang Mai, this is the centre of the Northern Insight Meditation School developed by the well-known Phra Ajarn Tong Sirimangalo (the meditation teachers at Chiang Mai's Wat Ram Poeng and Wat Doi Suthep are all students of Phra Tong). The basic course is a tough 21 days of Vipassana meditation taught in English and Thai. By donation.

World Fellowship of Buddhists (WFB) 616 Benjasiri Park, Soi Medhinivet off Soi 24, Thanon Sukhumvit, Bangkok ☎ 02 661 1284–7, ⓦ wfbhq.org. Headquarters of an influential worldwide organization of (mostly Theravada) Buddhists, founded in Sri Lanka in 1950, which holds occasional dhamma talks.

Outdoor activities

Many travellers' itineraries take in a few days' trekking in the hills and a stint snorkelling or diving off the beaches of the south. Trekking is concentrated in the north, but there are smaller, less touristy trekking operations in Kanchanaburi and Umphang. There are also plenty of national parks to explore and opportunities for rock climbing and kayaking.

Diving and snorkelling

Clear, warm waters (averaging 28°C), prolific marine life and affordable prices make Thailand a very rewarding place for **diving** and **snorkelling**. Most islands and beach resorts have at least one dive centre that organizes trips to outlying islands, teaches novice divers and rents out equipment, and in the bigger resorts there are dozens to choose from.

Thailand's three coasts are subject to different monsoon **seasons**, so you can dive all year round; the seasons run from November to April along the Andaman coast (though there is sometimes good diving here up until late Aug), and all year round on the Gulf and east coasts. Though every diver has their favourite reef, Thailand's **premier diving destinations** are generally considered to be Ko Similan, Ko Surin, Richelieu Rock and Hin Muang and Hin Daeng – all of them off the Andaman coast (see page 634). As an accessible base for diving, Ko Tao off the Gulf coast is hard to beat, with deep, clear inshore water and a wide variety of dive sites in very close proximity.

Whether you're snorkelling or diving, try to minimize your impact on the fragile reef structures by **not touching the reefs** and by asking your boatman not to anchor in the middle of one; **don't buy coral souvenirs**, as tourist demand only encourages local entrepreneurs to dynamite reefs.

Should you scrape your skin on coral, wash the wound thoroughly with boiled water, apply antiseptic and keep protected until healed. Wearing a T-shirt is a good idea when snorkelling to stop your back from getting sunburnt.

Diving

It's usually worth having a look at several **dive centres** before committing yourself to a trip or a course. Always verify the dive instructors' and dive shops' PADI (Professional Association of Diving Instructors) or equivalent accreditations as this guarantees a certain level of professionalism. You can view a list of PADI dive shops and resorts in Thailand at ⓦ padi.com.

We've highlighted dive shops that are accredited Five-Star centres, as these are considered by PADI to offer very high standards, but you should always consult other divers first if possible. Some dive operators do fake their PADI credentials. Avoid booking ahead over the internet without knowing anything else about the dive centre, and be wary of any operation offering extremely cheap courses: maintaining diving equipment is an expensive business in Thailand so any place offering unusually good rates will probably be cutting corners and compromising your safety. Ask to **meet your instructor** or dive leader, find out how many people

THAILAND'S MAIN DIVE RESORTS

THE EAST COAST

Ko Chang (see page 405)
Pattaya (see page 382)

THE GULF COAST

Ko Pha Ngan (see page 550)
Ko Samui (see page 533)
Ko Tao (see page 562)

THE ANDAMAN COAST

Ao Nang (see page 657)
Khao Lak (see page 606)
Ko Lanta (see page 679)
Ko Phi Phi (see page 666)
Phuket (see page 613)

THE DEEP SOUTH

Ko Lipe (see page 710)

there'll be in your group, check out the kind of instruction given (some courses are over-reliant on videos) and look over the equipment, checking the quality of the air in the tanks yourself and also ensuring there's an oxygen cylinder on board. Most divers prefer to travel to the dive site in a decent-sized **boat** equipped with a radio and emergency medical equipment rather than in a longtail. If this concerns you, ask the dive company about their boat before you sign up; firms that use longtails generally charge less.

Insurance should be included in the price of courses and introductory dives; for qualified divers, you're better off checking that your general travel insurance covers diving, though some diving shops can organize cover for you. There are **recompression chambers** in Pattaya, on Ko Samui and on Phuket and it's a good idea to check whether your dive centre is a member of one of these outfits, as recompression services are extremely expensive for anyone who's not.

Trips and courses

All dive centres run programmes of day and night **dives starting at around** B1000/dive (with reductions for subsequent dives and if you bring your own gear), and many of the Andaman-coast dive centres also do three- to seven-day **live-aboards** to the exceptional reefs off the remote Similan and Surin islands (from B12,000). Most dive centres can rent **underwater cameras** for about B1500 per day.

All dive centres offer a range of **courses** from beginner to advanced level, with equipment rental usually included in the cost; Ko Tao is now the largest, and most competitive, dive-training centre

in Southeast Asia, with around fifty dive companies including plenty of PADI Five-Star centres. The most popular courses are the one-day **introductory** or resort dive (a pep talk and escorted shallow dive, open to anyone aged 10 or over), which costs anything from B2000 for a very local dive to B7000 for an all-inclusive day-trip to the Similan Islands; and the four-day **open-water course**, which entitles you to dive without an instructor (around B9800 on Ko Tao in high season). Kids' Bubblemaker courses, for children aged 8 and up, cost around B2000.

Snorkelling

Boatmen and tour agents on most beaches offer **snorkelling** trips to nearby reefs and many dive operators welcome snorkellers to tag along for discounts of thirty percent or more; not all diving destinations are rewarding for snorkellers, though, so check carefully with the dive shop first. As far as snorkelling **equipment** goes, the most important thing is that you buy or rent a mask that fits. To check the fit, hold the mask against your face, then breathe in and remove your hands – if it falls off, it'll leak water. If you're buying equipment, you should be able to kit yourself out with a mask, snorkel and fins for about B1500, available from most dive centres. Few places rent fins, but a mask and snorkel set usually costs about B150 a day to rent, and if you're going on a snorkelling day-trip they are often included in the price.

National parks and wildlife observation

Thailand's hundred-plus **national parks**, which are administered by the National Park, Wildlife and Plant Conservation Department, are generally the best places to **observe wildlife**. Though you're highly unlikely to encounter tigers or sun bears, you have a good chance of spotting gibbons, civets, mouse deer and hornbills and may even get to see a wild elephant. A number of wetlands also host a rewarding variety of birdlife. Most parks charge an **entrance fee**, which for foreigners is usually B200 (B100 for children), though some charge B100 and a few charge B300, B400 or B500. Cars are usually B30 each, motorbikes B20. The parks department has a website of sorts (ⓦ nps.dnp.go.th) but you'll find ⓦ thainationalparks. com much more helpful, covering thirty or so of the most popular parks, with useful species lists.

Waymarked hiking **trails** in most parks are generally limited and rarely very challenging, and decent park maps are hard to come by, so for serious national park treks you'll need to hire a guide and venture beyond the public routes. Nearly all parks provide **accom-**

modation and/or campsites (see page 39). Some national parks **close** for several weeks or months every year for conservation, safety or environmental reasons, as noted in the Guide.

A detailed guide to Thailand's wildlife and their habitats, a look at the environmental issues, and a list of Thai wildlife charities and volunteer projects are provided in "Contexts" (see page 753).

Rock climbing

The limestone karsts that pepper southern Thailand's Andaman coast make ideal playgrounds for **rock-climbers**, and the sport has really taken off here in the past twenty years. Most climbing is centred round **East Railay** and **Ton Sai** beaches on Laem Phra Nang in Krabi province (see page 664), where there are dozens of routes within easy walking distance of tourist bungalows, restaurants and beaches. **Offshore Deep Water Soloing** – climbing a rock face out at sea, with no ropes, partner or bolts and just the water to break your fall – is also huge round here. Several **climbing schools** at East Railay and Ton Sai provide instruction (from B1000/half-day), as well as equipment rental (about B2400/day for two people) and guides. Ko Phi Phi (see page 666) also offers a few routes and a couple of climbing schools, as does the quieter and potentially more interesting Ko Yao Noi (see page 641) and Ko Lao Liang (see page 707). Climbing is also popular near Chiang Mai (see page

278), and there are less developed climbing areas on Ko Tao (see page 562) and in Lopburi province (see page 225). For an introduction to climbing on Railay and elsewhere in south Thailand, see ⓦ railay.com, which features interactive route maps, while *King Climbers: Thailand Route Guide Book* is a fairly regularly updated guidebook that concentrates on Railay, Ton Sai and the islands.

Sea kayaking and whitewater rafting

Sea kayaking is also centred around Thailand's Andaman coast, where the limestone outcrops, sea caves, *hongs* (hidden lagoons), mangrove swamps and picturesque shorelines of Ao Phang Nga in particular (see page 646) make for rewarding paddling. Kayaking day-trips around Ao Phang Nga can be arranged from any resort in Phuket, at Khao Lak, at all Krabi beaches and islands, and on Ko Yao Noi; multi-day kayaking expeditions are also possible. Over on Ko Samui, Blue Stars (see page 550) organize kayaking trips around the -picturesque islands of the Ang Thong National Marine Park, while Kayak Chang (see page 410) offers one- to twelve-day trips around Ko Chang. Many bungalows at other beach resorts have free kayaks or rent them out (from B100/hr) for casual, independent coastal exploration.

You can go **river kayaking** and **whitewater rafting** on several rivers in north, west and south

---

TOP NATIONAL PARKS

Ang Thong (see page 549). Spectacular archipelago in the Gulf of Thailand, generally visited on a day-trip from Ko Samui or Ko Pha Ngan.

Doi Inthanon (see page 329). Waterfalls, hill tribes, orchids, around four hundred bird species and the country's highest peak.

Erawan (see page 198). An exceptionally pretty, seven-tiered waterfall that extends deep into the forest. Hugely popular as a day-trip from Kanchanaburi.

Khao Sam Roi Yot (see page 520). Coastal flats on the Gulf coast known for their rich birdlife plus an extensive stalactite-filled cave system.

Khao Sok (see page 601). Southern Thailand's most visited park has rainforest trails and caves plus a flooded river system with eerie outcrops and raft-house accommodation.

Khao Yai (see page 435). Thailand's most popular national park, three hours from Bangkok, features half a dozen upland trails plus organized treks and night safaris.

Ko Similan (see page 612). Remote group of Andaman Sea islands with famously fabulous reefs and fine above-water scenery. Mostly visited by dive boat but limited national park accommodation is provided.

Ko Surin (see page 599). National marine park archipelago of beautiful coastal waters in the Andaman Sea, though much of its coral became severely bleached in 2010. Good snorkelling and national park campsites.

Ko Tarutao (see page 708). Beautiful and wildly varied land- and seascapes on the main 26km-long island and fifty other smaller islands on its western side.

Phu Kradung (see page 481). Dramatic and strange 1300m-high plateau, probably best avoided at weekends.

Thailand. Some stretches of these rivers can run quite fast, particularly during the rainy season from July to November, but there are plenty of options for novices too. The best time is from October through February; during the hot season (March–June), many rivers run too low. The most popular white-water-rafting rivers include the Umphang and Mae Khlong rivers near Umphang (see page 263) and the Pai River near Pai (see page 344). Gentler rafting excursions take place as part of organized treks in the north, as well as on the River Kwai and its tributaries near Kanchanaburi (see page 187), at Mae Hong Son (see page 335) and Pai (see page 344). Southwest of Chiang Mai, raft trips can be arranged at the adjacent national park headquarters for trips in Ob Luang Gorge (see page 332).

Trekking

Trekking in the mountains of north Thailand differs from trekking in most other parts of the world in that the emphasis is not primarily on the scenery but on the region's inhabitants. Northern Thailand's **hill tribes**, now numbering over 800,000 people living in around 3500 villages, have preserved their subsistence-oriented way of life with comparatively little change over thousands of years (see page 769). In recent years, the term **mountain people** (a translation of the Thai *chao khao*) is increasingly used as a less condescending way to describe them; since these groups have no chief, they are technically not tribes. While some of the villages are near enough to a main road to be reached on a day-trip from a major town, to get to the other, more traditional, villages usually entails joining a guided party for a few days, roughing it in a different place each night. For most visitors, however, these hardships are far outweighed by the experience of encountering peoples of so different a culture, travelling through beautiful tropical countryside and tasting the excitement of elephant riding and river rafting.

On any trek you are necessarily confronted by the **ethics** of your role. About a hundred thousand travellers now go trekking in Thailand each year, the majority heading to certain well-trodden areas such as the Mae Taeng valley, 40km northwest of Chiang Mai, and the hills around the Kok River west of Chiang Rai. Beyond the basic level of disturbance caused by any tourism, this steady flow of trekkers creates pressures for the traditionally insular hill tribes. Foreigners unfamiliar with hill-tribe customs can easily cause grave offence, especially those who go looking for drugs. Though tourism acts as a distraction from their traditional way of life, most tribespeople are genuinely welcoming and hospitable to foreigners, appreciating the contact with Westerners and the minimal material benefits which trekking brings them. Nonetheless, to minimize disruption, it's important to take a responsible attitude when trekking. While it's possible to trek independently from one or two spots such as *Cave Lodge* near Soppong (see page 344), the lone trekker will learn very little without a guide as intermediary, and is far more likely to commit an unwitting offence against the local customs; it's best to go with a sensitive and knowledgeable **guide** who has the welfare of the local people in mind, and follow the basic guidelines on etiquette outlined below. If you don't fancy an organized trek in a group, it's possible to hire a personal guide from an agent, at a cost of about B1000–1500 per day.

The hill tribes are big business in northern Thailand: in **Chiang Mai** there are dozens of agencies, which between them cover just about all the trekkable areas in the north. **Chiang Rai** is the second-biggest trekking centre, and agencies can also be found in Nan, Mae Sariang, Mae Hong Son, Pai, Chiang Dao and Mae Salong, which usually arrange treks only to the villages in their immediate area. Guided trekking on a smaller scale than in the north is available in Umphang and Kanchanaburi.

The basics

The cool, dry season from November to February is the best time for treks, which can be as short as one day or as long as ten, but are typically of three or four days' duration. The standard size of a group is between five and twelve people; being part of a small group is preferable, enabling you to strike a more informative relationship with your guides and with the villagers. Everybody in the group usually sleeps on a mattress in the village's guest hut, with a guide cooking communal meals, for which some ingredients are brought from outside and others are found locally.

Each trek usually follows a regular **itinerary** established by the agency, although they can sometimes be customized, especially for smaller groups and with agencies in the smaller towns. Some itineraries are geared towards serious hikers while others go at a much gentler pace, but on all treks much of the walking will be up and down steep forested hills, often under a burning sun, so a reasonable level of fitness is required. Many treks now include a ride on an elephant and a trip on a bamboo raft – exciting to the point of being dangerous if the river is running fast. The typical three-day, two-night trek **costs** about B1600–3000 in Chiang Mai (including transport, accommodation, food and guide), sometimes less in other towns, much less without rafting and elephant riding.

HILL-TRIBE TREKKING ETIQUETTE

As the guests, it's up to farangs to adapt to the customs of the hill tribes and not to make a nuisance of themselves. Apart from keeping an open mind and not demanding too much of your hosts, a few **simple rules** should be observed.

• Dress modestly, in long trousers or skirt (or at least knee-length shorts if you must) and a T-shirt or shirt. Getting dressed or changing your clothes in front of villagers is also offensive.

• Loud voices and **boisterous behaviour** are out of place. Smiling and nodding establishes good intent. A few hill-tribe phrasebooks and dictionaries are available from local bookshops and you'll be a big hit if you learn some words of the relevant language.

• If travelling with a loved one, avoid **displays of public affection** such as kissing, which are extremely distasteful, and disrespectful, to local people.

• Look out for **taboo signs** (*ta-laew*), woven bamboo strips, on the ground outside the entrance to a village, on the roof above a house entrance or on a fresh tree branch; these mean a special ceremony is taking place and that you should not enter. Be careful about what you touch; in Akha villages, keep your hands off cult structures like the entrance gates and the giant swing. Ask first before entering a house, and do not step or sit on the doorsill, which is often considered the domain of the house spirits. If the house has a raised floor on stilts, take off your shoes. Most hill-tribe houses contain a religious shrine: do not touch or photograph this shrine, or sit underneath it. If you are permitted to watch a ceremony, this is not an invitation to participate unless asked. Like the villagers themselves, you'll be expected to pay a fine for any violation of local customs.

• Some villagers like to be photographed, most do not. Point at your **camera** and nod if you want to take a photograph. Never insist if the answer is an obvious "no". Be particularly careful with the sick and the old, and with pregnant women and babies – most tribes believe cameras affect the soul of the foetus or newborn.

• Taking **gifts** can be dubious practice. If you want to take something, writing materials for children and clothing are welcome, as well as sewing tools (such as needles) for women – ask your guide to pass any gifts to the village headman for fair distribution. However, money, sweets and cigarettes may encourage begging and create unhealthy tastes.

• Do not ask for **opium**, as this will offend your hosts.

Choosing a trek

There are several features to look out for when **choosing a trek**. If you want to trek with a small group, get an assurance from your agency that you won't be tagged onto a larger group. Make sure the trek has at least two guides – a leader and a back-marker; some trekkers have been known to get lost for days after becoming separated from the rest of the group. Check exactly when the trek starts and ends and ask about transport to and from base; most treks begin with a pick-up ride out of town, but on rare occasions the trip can entail a long public bus ride. If at all possible, meet and chat with the other trekkers in advance, as well as the guides, who should speak reasonable English and know about hill-tribe culture, especially the details of etiquette in each village. Finally, ask what meals will be included, check how much walking is involved per day and get a copy of the route map to gauge the terrain.

While everybody and their grandmother act as **agents**, only a few know their guides personally, so choose a reputable agent or guesthouse. When picking an agent, you should check whether they and their guides have licences and certificates from the Tourist Authority of Thailand, which they should be able to show you: this ensures at least a minimum level of training, and provides some comeback in case of problems. Word of mouth is often the best recommendation, so if you hear of a good outfit, try it. Each trek should be **registered** with the tourist police, stating the itinerary, the duration and the participants, in case the party encounters any trouble – it's worth checking with the agency that the trek has been registered with the tourist police before departure.

What to take

The right **clothing** is the first essential on any trek. Strong boots with ankle protection are the best footwear, although in the dry season training shoes are adequate. Wear thin, loose clothes – long trousers should be worn to protect against thorns and, in the wet season, leeches – and a hat, and cover your arms if you're prone to sunburn. Antiseptic, antihistamine cream, anti-diarrhoea **medicine** and insect repellent are essential, as is a mosquito net – check if one will be provided where you're staying. At least two changes of clothing are needed, plus a sarong or towel (women in particular should bring a sarong to wash or change underneath).

If you're going on an organized trek, **water** is usually provided by the guide, as well as a small backpack. **Blankets** or, preferably, a **sleeping bag** are also supplied, but might not be warm enough in the cool season, when night-time temperatures can dip to freezing; you should bring at least a sweater, and perhaps buy a cheap, locally made balaclava to be sure of keeping the chill off.

It's wise not to take anything valuable with you; most guesthouses in trekking-oriented places like Chiang Mai have safes and left-luggage rooms.

Travelling with children

Despite the relative lack of child-centred attractions in Thailand, there's plenty to appeal to families, both on the beach and inland, and Thais are famously welcoming to young visitors.

Of all the **beach resorts** in the country, two of the most family friendly are the islands of Ko Samui and Ko Lanta. Both have plenty of on-the-beach accommodation for mid- and upper-range budgets, and lots of easy-going open-air shorefront restaurants so that adults can eat in relative peace while kids play within view. Both islands also offer many day-tripping activities, from elephant riding to snorkelling. Phuket is another family favourite, though shorefront accommodation here is at a premium; there are also scores of less mainstream alternatives. In many beach resorts older kids will be able to go kayaking or learn rock climbing, and many dive centres will teach the PADI children's scuba courses on request: the Bubblemaker programme is designed for kids of 8 and over, and the Discover Scuba Diving day is open to anyone 10 and over.

Inland, the many **national parks** and their waterfalls and caves are good for days out, and there are lots of opportunities to go **rafting** and **elephant riding**. Kanchanaburi is a rewarding centre for all these, with the added plus that many of the town's guesthouses are set round decent-sized lawns. Chiang Mai is another great hub for all the above and also offers boat trips, an attractive, modern zoo and aquarium, the chance to watch umbrella-makers and other craftspeople at work, and, in the Mae Sa valley, many family-oriented attractions, such as the botanical gardens and **an insect zoo**. Bangkok has several child-friendly **theme parks** and activity centres.

Should you be in Thailand in January, your kids will be able to join in the free entertainments and activities staged all over the country on **National Children's Day** (Wan Dek), which is held on the second Saturday of January. They also get free entry to zoos that day, and free rides on public buses.

Hotels and transport

Many of the expensive **hotels** listed in this guide allow one or two under-12s to share their parents' room for free, as long as no extra bedding is required. It's often possible to cram two adults and two children into the double rooms in budget and mid-range hotels (as opposed to guesthouses), as beds in these places are usually big enough for two. An increasing number of guesthouses now offer three-person rooms, and may even provide special family accommodation. Decent cots are available free in the bigger hotels, and in some smaller ones (though cots in these places can be a bit grotty), and top- and mid-range rooms often come with a small fridge. Many hotels can also provide a **babysitting** service.

Few museums or transport companies offer student reductions, but in some cases children get **discounts**. One of the more bizarre provisos is the State Railway's regulation that a child aged 3 to 12 qualifies for half-fare only if under 150cm tall; some stations have a measuring scale painted onto the ticket-hall wall. Most domestic airlines charge ten percent of the full fare, or are free, for under-2s, but only Thai Airways and Thai Smile offer reduced fares for under-12s.

Other practicalities

Although most Thai babies don't wear them, **disposable nappies** (diapers) are sold at convenience stores, pharmacies and supermarkets in big resorts and sizeable towns – Mamy Poko is a reliable Japanese brand, available in supermarkets; for stays on lonely islands, consider bringing some washable ones as back-up. A **changing mat** is another necessity as there are few public toilets in Thailand, let alone ones with baby facilities (though posh hotels are always a useful option). International brands of powdered milk are available throughout the country, and brand-name baby food is sold in big towns and resorts, though some parents find restaurant-cooked rice and bananas go down just as well. Thai women do not **breastfeed** in public.

For touring, child-carrier backpacks are ideal (though make sure that the child's head extends no higher than yours, as there are countless low-hanging obstacles on Thai streets). Opinions are divided on whether or not it's worth bringing a **buggy** or three-wheeled **stroller**. Where they exist, Thailand's pavements are bumpy at best, and there's an almost total absence of ramps; sand is especially difficult for buggies, though less so for three-wheelers. Buggies and strollers do, however, come in handy for feeding small children (and even for daytime naps), as highchairs are provided only in some restaurants (and then often without restraints for smaller toddlers). You can buy buggies fairly cheaply in most towns, but if you bring your own and then wish you hadn't, most hotels and guesthouses will keep it for you until you leave. Bring an appropriately sized **mosquito net** if necessary or buy one locally in any department store; a mini **sun tent** for the beach is also useful. Taxis almost never provide baby **car seats**, and even if you bring your own you'll often find there are no seatbelts to strap them in with; branches of inter-national car-rental companies should be able to provide car seats. Most department stores have dedicated kids' sections selling everything from bottles to dummies. There are even several Mothercare outlets in Bangkok.

Hazards

Even more than their parents, children need protecting from the sun, unsafe drinking water, heat and unfamiliar **food**. Consider packing a jar of a favourite spread so that you can always rely on toast if all else fails to please. As with adults, you should be careful about unwashed fruit and salads and about dishes that have been left uncovered for a long time. As diarrhoea could be dangerous for a child, rehydration solutions (see page 68) are vital if your child goes down with it; sachets formulated specially for children are available in local pharmacies. Other significant **hazards** include thundering traffic; huge waves, strong currents and jellyfish; and the **sun** – not least because many beaches offer only limited shade, if at all. Sunhats, sunblock and waterproof suntan lotions are essential, and can be bought in the major resorts. Avoiding mosquitoes is difficult, but low-strength DEET lotions should do the trick. You should also make sure, if possible, that your child is aware of the dangers of **rabies**; keep children away from **animals**, especially dogs and monkeys, and ask your medical advisor about rabies jabs.

INFORMATION AND ADVICE

Bangkok Mothers and Babies International Ⓦ bambiweb.org. For expat mothers and kids, but some of the information and advice on the website should be useful.
Bkk Kids Ⓦ bkkkids.com. Especially good on activities for kids in Bangkok, but also covers health matters and other services thoroughly.

Thailand 4 Kids Ⓦ thailand4kids.com. Lots of advice on the practicalities of family holidays in Thailand.

Travel essentials

Charities and volunteer projects

Reassured by the plethora of well-stocked shopping plazas, efficient services and apparent abundance in the rice fields, it is easy to forget that life is extremely hard for many people in Thailand. Countless **charities** work with Thailand's many poor and disadvantaged communities: listed below are a few that would welcome help in some way from visitors. Longer-term placements, volunteer jobs on charitable wildlife projects and organized holidays that feature community-based programmes are also available (see pages 70, 759 and 28 respectively).

Andaman Discoveries Khuraburi Ⓦ andamandiscoveries.com. As well as community-based tourism programmes, this organization offers the chance to volunteer in rural schools, an orphanage, a Burmese learning centre or a special education centre.
Baan Unrak, Home of Joy Sangkhlaburi Ⓦ baanunrak.org. Works with ethnic-minority refugee women and children from Myanmar. Volunteers and donations welcome. See page 209.
Foundation to Encourage the Potential of Disabled Persons Chiang Mai Ⓦ assistdisabled.org. This foundation provides, among other things, free wheelchairs and home visits for disabled people. Donations and sponsorships for wheelchairs are sought.
Children's World Academy Kapong, near Khao Lak Ⓦ yaowawit. com. Set in quiet countryside on the Takua Pa–Phang Nga road, Yaowawit School was set up for tsunami orphans and socially disadvantaged children. It accepts donations, sponsorships, volunteer teachers and guests who wish to stay at its lodge, a hospitality training centre.
Hill Area and Community Development Foundation Chiang Rai Ⓦ naturalfocus-cbt.com. Aiming to help hill tribes in dealing with problems such as environmental management, HIV/AIDS, child and drug abuse, the foundation has set up a community-based tourism company, Natural Focus (see page 355), to offer mountain-life tours and volunteer opportunities.
Human Development Foundation Mercy Centre Klong Toey, Bangkok Ⓦ mercycentre.org. Founded in 1973, Father Joe Maier's organization provides education and support for Bangkok's street kids and slum-dwellers. It now runs two dozen kindergartens in the slums, as well as one in Ranong for sea-gypsy children, among many other projects. Contact the centre for information about donations, sponsoring and volunteering. Father Joe's books, *Welcome to the Bangkok Slaughterhouse* and *The Open Gate of Mercy*, give eye-opening insights into this often invisible side of Thai life.
Koh Yao Children's Community Center Ko Yao Noi Ⓦ koyao-ccc. com. Aims to improve the English-language and lifelong learning

ADDRESSES IN THAILAND

Thai **addresses** can be immensely confusing, mainly because property is often numbered twice, first to show which real-estate lot it stands in, and then to distinguish where it is on that lot. Thus 154/7–10 Thanon Rajdamnoen means the building is on lot 154 and occupies numbers 7–10. However, neither of these numbers will necessarily help you to find a particular building on a long street; when asking for directions or talking to taxi drivers, it's best to be able to quote a nearby temple, big hotel or other landmark. There's an additional idiosyncrasy in the way Thai roads are sometimes named: in large cities a minor road running off a major road is often numbered as a soi ("lane" or "alley", though it may be a sizeable thoroughfare), rather than given its own street name. Thanon Sukhumvit for example – Bangkok's longest – has minor roads numbered Soi 1 to Soi 103, with odd numbers on one side of the road and even on the other; so a Thanon Sukhumvit address could read something like 27/9–11 Soi 15, Thanon Sukhumvit, which would mean the property occupies numbers 9–11 on lot 27 on minor road number 15 running off Thanon Sukhumvit.

skills of islanders on Ko Yao Noi. Visitors, volunteers and donations welcome. See page 643.

Mae Tao Clinic Mae Sot ⓦ maetaoclinic.org. Award-winning health centre providing free care to Burmese refugees. Donations and long-term volunteer health-workers welcome. See page 259.

The Mirror Foundation Chiang Rai and Bangkok ⓦ themirrorfoundation.org. NGO working with the hill tribes in Chiang Rai province to help combat such issues as drug abuse, lack of citizenship and trafficking of women and children, with a branch in Bangkok dealing with urban problems. It offers a guesthouse, trekking and homestays in Chiang Rai (see page 355); volunteers and donations sought.

The Students' Education Trust (SET) ⓦ thaistudentcharity. org. High-school and further education in Thailand is a luxury that the poorest kids cannot afford so many are sent to live in temples instead. The SET helps such kids pursue their education and escape from the poverty trap. Some of their stories are told in *Little Angels: The Real-Life Stories of Twelve Thai Novice Monks*. SET welcomes donations.

Thai Child Development Foundation Pha To ⓦ thaichilddevelopment.org. This small Thai-Dutch-run village project near Ranong helps educate and look after needy local children. The foundation welcomes donations, takes on volunteers, and has an ecotourism arm.

Tour de Thailand ⓦ tourdethailand.com. Join a long-distance cycle tour through one of Thailand's five regions and raise money for Hua Hin Rotary Club's local projects and End Polio Now.

Climate

There are three main **seasons** in most of Thailand: rainy, caused by the southwest monsoon (the least predictable, but roughly May–Oct); cool (Nov–Feb; felt most distinctly in the far north, but hardly at all in the south); and hot (March–May). The Gulf coast's climate is slightly different: it suffers less from the southwest monsoon, but is then hit by the northeast monsoon, making November its rainiest month.

Costs

Thailand can be a very cheap place to travel. At the bottom of the scale, you can manage on a **budget** of about B650 (£15/US$20) per day if you're willing to opt for basic accommodation, eat, drink and travel as the locals do, and stay away from the more expensive resorts like Phuket, Ko Samui and Ko Phi Phi – and you'd have to work hard to stick to this daily allowance in Bangkok. On this budget, you'll be spending around B200–250 for a dorm or shared room (more for a single room), around B200 on three meals (eating mainly at night markets and simple noodle shops, and eschewing beer), and the rest on travel (sticking to the cheaper buses and third-class trains where possible) and incidentals. With extras like air conditioning in rooms, taking the various forms of taxi rather than buses or shared songthaews for cross-town journeys, and a meal and beer in a more touristy restaurant, a day's outlay would be at least B1000 (£23/US$32). Staying in well-equipped, mid-range hotels and eating in more upmarket restaurants, you should be able to live comfortably for around B2000 a day (£46/US$64).

Travellers soon get so used to the low cost of living in Thailand that they start **bargaining** at every available opportunity, much as Thai people do. Although it's expected practice for a lot of commercial transactions, particularly at markets and when hiring tuk-tuks and unmetered taxis (though not in supermarkets or department stores), bargaining is a delicate art that requires humour, tact and patience. If your price is way out of line, the vendor's vehement refusal should be enough to make you increase your offer: never forget that the few pennies or cents you're making such a fuss over will go a lot further in a Thai person's hands than in your own.

It's rare that foreigners can bargain a price down as low as a Thai could, anyway, while **two-tier pricing** has been made official at government-run sights, as a kind of informal tourist tax: at national parks, for example, foreigners pay up to B500 entry while Thais pay just B20–100. A number of privately owned tourist attractions follow a similar two-tier system, posting an inflated price in English for foreigners and a lower price in Thai for locals.

Shoppers who are departing via an international airport can save some money by claiming a **Value Added Tax refund** (🌐 vrtweb.rd.go.th/index.php/en), though it's a bit of a palaver for seven percent (the current rate of VAT, though this may increase to ten percent). The total amount of your purchases from participating shops needs to be at least B2000 per person. You'll need to show your passport and fill in an application form (to which original tax invoices need to be attached) at the shop. At the relevant airport, you'll need to show your form and purchases to customs officers before checking in, then make your claim from VAT refund officers – from which fees of at least B60 are deducted.

Crime and personal safety

As long as you keep your wits about you, you shouldn't encounter much trouble in Thailand. **Pickpocketing** and **bag-snatching** are two of the main problems – not surprising considering that a huge percentage of the local population scrape by on under US$10 per day – but the most common cause for concern is the number of con-artists who dupe gullible tourists into parting with their cash. There are various Thai laws that tourists need to be aware of, particularly regarding passports, the age of consent and smoking in public.

Theft

To **prevent theft**, most travellers prefer to carry their valuables with them at all times, but it's often possible to use a safe in a hotel or a locker in a guesthouse – the safest are those that require your own padlock, as there are occasional reports of valuables being stolen by guesthouse staff. **Padlock your luggage** when leaving it in storage or taking it on public transport. Padlocks also come in handy as extra security on your room, particularly on the doors of beachfront bamboo huts.

Theft from some long-distance **buses** is also a problem, with the majority of reported incidents taking place on the temptingly cheap overnight buses run by private companies direct from Bangkok's Thanon Khao San (as opposed to those that depart from the government bus stations) to destinations such as Chiang Mai and southern beach resorts. The best solution is to go direct from the bus stations.

Personal safety

On any bus, private or government, and on any train journey, never keep anything of value in luggage that is stored out of your sight and be wary of accepting food and drink from fellow passengers as it may be drugged. This might sound paranoid, but there have been enough **drug-muggings** for TAT to publish a specific warning about the problem. Drinks can also

AVERAGE MAXIMUM DAILY TEMPERATURES AND MONTHLY RAINFALL

	Jan	Feb	Mar	Apr	May	Jun	Jul	Aug	Sep	Oct	Nov	Dec
BANGKOK												
Max temp (°C)	26	28	29	30	30	29	29	28	28	28	27	26
Rainfall (mm)	11	28	31	72	190	152	158	187	320	231	57	9
CHIANG MAI												
Max temp (°C)	21	23	26	29	29	28	27	27	27	26	24	22
Rainfall (mm)	8	6	15	45	153	136	167	227	251	132	44	15
PATTAYA												
Max temp (°C)	26	28	29	30	30	29	29	28	28	28	27	26
Rainfall (mm)	12	23	41	79	165	120	166	166	302	229	66	10
KO SAMUI												
Max temp (°C)	26	26	28	29	29	28	28	28	28	27	26	25
Rainfall (mm)	38	8	12	63	186	113	143	123	209	260	302	98
PHUKET												
Max temp (°C)	27	28	28	29	28	28	28	28	27	27	27	27
Rainfall (mm)	35	31	39	163	348	213	263	263	419	305	207	52

be spiked in bars and clubs; at full moon parties on Ko Pha Ngan this has led to sexual assaults against farang women, while prostitutes sometimes spike drinks so they can steal from their victim's room.

Violent crime against tourists is not common, but it does occur, and there have been several serious attacks on travellers in recent years, notably on Ko Pha Ngan and Ko Tao. However, bearing in mind that thirty million foreigners visit Thailand every year, the statistical likelihood of becoming a victim is extremely small. **Obvious precautions** for travellers of either sex include locking accessible windows and doors – preferably with your own padlock (doors in many of the simpler guesthouses and beach bungalows are designed for this) – and taking care at night, especially around bars. You should not risk jumping into an unlicensed taxi at the airport in Bangkok at any time of day: there have been some very violent robberies in these, so take the well-marked licensed, metered taxis instead.

Among hazards to watch out for in the natural world, **riptides** claim a number of tourist lives every year, particularly off Phuket, Ko Chang (Trat), Hua Hin, Cha-am, Rayong, Pattaya and the Ko Samui archipelago during stormy periods of the monsoon season, so always pay attention to warning signs and red flags, and always ask locally if unsure. **Jellyfish** can be a problem on any coast, especially just after a storm (see page 67).

Unfortunately, it is also necessary for female tourists to think twice about spending time alone with a **monk**, as not all men of the cloth uphold the Buddhist precepts and there have been rapes and murders committed by men wearing the saffron robes of the monkhood.

Though unpalatable and distressing, Thailand's high-profile **sex industry** is relatively unthreatening for Western women, with its energy focused exclusively on farang men; it's also quite easily avoided, being contained within certain pockets of the cities and beach resorts.

As for **harassment** from men, it's hard to generalize, but most Western women find it less of a problem in Thailand than they do back home. Outside the main tourist spots, you're more likely to be of interest as a foreigner rather than a woman and, if travelling alone, as an object of concern rather than of sexual aggression.

Regional issues

It's advisable to travel with a guide if you're going off the roads in a few **border areas** or, at the very least, to take advice before setting off. As these regions are generally covered in dense unmapped jungle, you shouldn't find yourself alone in the area anyway. In the immediate vicinity of the Burmese border, fighting on the other side of the frontier very occasionally spills over and there are rare clashes between Thai security forces and illegal traffickers. Certain areas of the border between Cambodia and southern Isaan are littered with unexploded mines, and there have been recent clashes between the Thai and Cambodian armies over the disputed line of the border, especially at Khao Phra Viharn (Preah Vihear).

Because of the **violence in the deep south**, all Western governments are currently advising against travel to or through the border provinces of Songkhla, Yala, Pattani and Narathiwat, unless essential (see page 696). For up-to-the-minute advice on current political trouble-spots, consult your government's travel advisory (see page 63).

Scams

Despite the best efforts of guidebook writers, TAT and the Thai tourist police, countless travellers to Thailand get scammed every year. Nearly all **scams** are easily avoided if you're on your guard against anyone who makes an unnatural effort to befriend you. We have outlined the main scams in the relevant sections of this guide, but con-artists are nothing if not creative, so if in doubt walk away at the earliest opportunity. The worst areas for scammers are the busy tourist centres, including many parts of Bangkok and the main beach resorts.

Many **tuk-tuk drivers** earn most of their living through securing **commissions** from tourist-oriented shops; this is especially true in Bangkok, where they will do their damnedest to get you to go to a gem

---

REPORTING A CRIME OR EMERGENCY

In the event of a crime, contact the English-speaking **tourist police** who maintain a 24-hour toll-free nationwide line (☎ 1155) and have offices in the main tourist centres; getting in touch with the tourist police first is invariably more efficient than directly contacting the local police. The tourist police's job is to offer advice and tell you what to do next, but they do not file crime reports, which must be done at the nearest police station. In a medical emergency, call either the tourist police or the nationwide ambulance hotline (☎ 1669), which is likely to be quicker than calling an individual hospital for an ambulance.

GOVERNMENTAL TRAVEL ADVISORIES

Australian Department of Foreign Affairs Ⓦ smarttraveller.gov.au.
British Foreign & Commonwealth Office Ⓦ gov.uk/foreign-travel-advice/thailand
Canadian Department of Foreign Affairs Ⓦ travel.gc.ca.
Irish Department of Foreign Affairs Ⓦ dfa.ie/travel.
New Zealand Ministry of Foreign Affairs Ⓦ safetravel.govt.nz.
South African Department of Foreign Affairs Ⓦ dirco.gov.za.
US State Department Ⓦ travel.state.gov.

shop (see page 169). The most common tactic is for drivers to pretend that the Grand Palace or other major sight you intended to visit is closed for the day (see page 79), and to then offer to take you on a round-city tour instead, perhaps even for free. The tour will invariably include a visit to a gem shop. The easiest way to avoid all this is to take a **metered taxi**; if you're fixed on taking a tuk-tuk, ignore any tuk-tuk that is parked up or loitering and be firm about where you want to go.

Self-styled **tourist guides**, **touts** and anyone else who might introduce themselves as **students** or **business people** and offer to take you somewhere of interest, or invite you to meet their family, are often the first piece of bait in a well-honed chain of con-artists. If you bite, chances are you'll end up either at a gem shop or in a gambling den, or, at best, at a tour operator or hotel that you had not planned to patronize. This is not to say that you should never accept an invitation from a local person, but be extremely wary of doing so following a street encounter in Bangkok or the resorts. Tourist guides' ID cards are easily faked.

For many of these characters, the goal is to get you inside a dodgy **gem shop**, nearly all of which are located in Bangkok (see page 169), but the bottom line is that if you are not experienced at buying and trading in valuable gems you will definitely be ripped off, possibly even to the tune of several thousand dollars.

A less common but potentially more frightening scam involves a similar cast of warm-up artists leading tourists into a **gambling** game. The scammers invite their victim home on an innocent-sounding pretext, get out a pack of cards, and then set about fleecing the incomer in any number of subtle or unsubtle ways. Often this can be especially scary as the venue is likely to be far from hotels or recognizable landmarks, and there have been stories of visitors being forced to withdraw large amounts of money from ATMs. You're unlikely to get any sympathy from police, as gambling is **illegal** in Thailand.

An increasing number of travel agents in tourist centres all over the country are trying to pass themselves off as official government tourist information offices, displaying nothing but "**Tourist Information**" on their shop signs or calling themselves names like "TAD" (note that the actual TAT, the Tourism Authority of Thailand, does not book hotels or sell any kind of travel ticket). Fakers like this are more likely to sell you tickets for services that turn out to be sub-standard or even not to exist. A word of warning also about **jet skis**: operators, who usually ask for a passport as guarantee, will often try to charge renters exorbitant amounts of money for any minor damage they claim to find on return.

Age restrictions and other laws

Thai law requires that tourists **carry their original passports** at all times, though sometimes it's more practical to carry a photocopy and keep the original locked in a safety deposit. The **age of consent** is 15, but the law allows anyone under the age of 18, or their parents, to file charges in retrospect even if they consented to sex at the time. It is against the law to have sex with a prostitute who is under 18. It is illegal for **under-18s** to buy cigarettes or to drive and you must be 20 or over to **buy alcohol** or be allowed into a **bar or club** (ID checks are sometimes enforced in Bangkok). It is illegal for anyone to **gamble** in Thailand (though many do).

Smoking in public is widely prohibited. The ban covers all public buildings (including restaurants, bars and clubs) and trains, buses, planes and popular beaches and can even be extended to parks and the street; violators may be subject to a B2000–5000 fine. Possession of e-cigarettes is currently illegal, and several foreign nationals have been arrested. Dropping cigarette butts, **littering** and spitting in public places can also earn you a B2000–5000 fine. There are fines for **overstaying your visa** (see page 64), **working without a permit**, **not wearing a motorcycle helmet** and violating other **traffic laws**.

Drugs

Drug-smuggling carries a maximum penalty in Thailand of death, and **dealing drugs** will get you anything from four years to life in a Thai prison; penalties depend on the drug and the amount involved. Travellers caught with even the smallest amount of drugs at airports and international borders are prosecuted for trafficking, and no one charged with trafficking offences gets bail. Heroin, amphetamines, LSD and ecstasy are classed as Category 1 drugs and carry the most severe penalties: even **possession** of Category 1 drugs for personal use can result in a **life sentence**. Away from international borders, most foreigners arrested in possession of small amounts of cannabis are released on bail, then fined and deported, but the law is complex and prison sentences are possible.

Despite occasional royal pardons, don't expect special treatment as a farang: you only need to read one of the first-hand accounts by foreign former prisoners (see page 779) or read the blogs at Ⓦthaiprisonlife.com to get the picture. The **police** actively look for tourists doing drugs, reportedly searching people regularly and randomly on Thanon Khao San, for example. They have the power to order a urine test if they have reasonable grounds for suspicion, and even a positive result for marijuana consumption could lead to a year's imprisonment. Be wary also of **being shopped** by a farang or local dealer keen to earn a financial reward for a successful bust (there are setups at the Ko Pha Ngan full moon parties, for example), or having substances slipped into your luggage (simple enough to perpetrate unless all fastenings are secured with padlocks).

If you are arrested, ask for your embassy to be contacted immediately (see page 170), which is your right under Thai law, and embassy staff will talk you through procedures; the website of the British government even includes a Prisoner Pack for Thailand (Ⓦgov.uk/government/publications/thailand-prisoner-pack). The British charity Prisoners Abroad (Ⓦprisonersabroad.org.uk) carries lots of useful information on its website, and may be able to offer direct support to a British citizen (and their family) facing imprisonment in a Thai jail.

Customs regulations

The **duty-free** allowance on entry to Thailand is 200 cigarettes (or 250g of tobacco or cigars) and a litre of spirits or wine (see Ⓦen.customs.go.th for more information).

To **export antiques** or newly cast **Buddha images** from Thailand, you need to have a licence granted by the Fine Arts Department (the export of religious antiques, especially Buddha images, is forbidden). Licences can be obtained for example through the Office of Archeology and National Museums, 81/1 Thanon Si Ayutthaya (near the National Library),

Bangkok (☎02 628 5032), or through the national museum in Chiang Mai. Applications take at least three working days in Bangkok, generally more in the provinces, and need to be accompanied by the object itself, some evidence of its rightful possession, two postcard-sized colour photos of it, taken face-on and against a white background, and photocopies of the applicant's passport; furthermore, if the object is a Buddha image, the passport photocopies need to be certified by your embassy in Bangkok. Some antiques shops can organize all this for you.

Electricity

Mains **electricity** is supplied at 220 volts AC and is available at all but the most remote villages and basic beach huts. Where electricity is supplied by generators and/or solar power, for example on the smaller, less populated islands, it is often rationed to evenings only. If you're packing phone and camera chargers, a hair dryer, laptop or other appliance, you'll need to take a set of travel-plug adapters with you as several plug types are commonly in use, most usually with two round pins, but also with two flat-blade pins or three round pins.

Entry requirements

There are three main entry categories for visitors to Thailand; for all of them, your passport should be valid for at least six months. As visa requirements are subject to frequent change, you should always consult before departure a Thai embassy or consulate, a reliable travel agent, or the Thai Ministry of Foreign Affairs' website at Ⓦmfa.go.th. For further, unofficial but usually reliable, details on all visa matters – especially as the rules are not consistently enforced across all Thai border checkpoints and immigration offices – go to the moderated forums on Ⓦthaivisa.com.

Most Western passport holders (that includes citizens of the UK, Ireland, the US, Canada, Australia, New Zealand and South Africa) are allowed to enter the country for thirty days without having to apply for a visa – officially termed the **tourist visa exemption** (not to be confused with "visas on arrival", another category of entry that's not available to citizens of the countries listed above); the period of stay will be stamped into your passport by immigration officials upon entry. You're supposed to be able to show proof of means of living while in the country (B10,000 per person, B20,000 per family), and you are also required to show proof of tickets to leave Thailand again within the allotted time, and in theory you may be put back on the next plane or sent back to get a sixty-day tourist visa from the nearest Thai embassy. However, the Thai immigration authorities do not appear to be consistent about checking these requirements (it seems to be more likely at land borders, especially Aranyaprathet). However, if you have a one-way air ticket to Thailand and no evidence of onward travel arrangements, it's best to buy a tourist visa in advance: many airlines will stop you boarding the plane without one, as they would be liable for flying you back to your point of origin if you did happen to be stopped.

If you're fairly certain you may want to stay longer than thirty days, then from the outset you should apply for a **sixty-day tourist visa** from a Thai embassy or consulate, accompanying your application – which generally takes several days to process – with your passport and one or two photos. The sixty-day visa currently costs B1000 or rough equivalent; multiple-entry versions are available, with more stringent requirements. Ordinary tourist visas are valid for three months; ie you must enter Thailand within three months of the visa being issued by the Thai embassy or consulate. Visa application forms can be downloaded from, for example, the Thai Ministry of Foreign Affairs' website.

Thai embassies also consider applications for **ninety-day non-immigrant visas** (B2000 or rough equivalent for single entry, B5000 for multiple-entry) as long as you can offer a reason for your visit, such as study, business or visiting family (there are different categories of non-immigrant visa for which different levels of proof are needed). As it can be a hassle to organize a ninety-day visa, it's generally easier to apply for a thirty-day extension to your sixty-day visa once inside Thai borders.

It's not a good idea to **overstay** your visa limits. Once you're at the airport or the border, you'll have to pay a fine of B500 per day before you can leave Thailand. More importantly, however, if you're in the country with an expired visa and you get involved with police or immigration officials for any reason, however trivial, they are obliged to take you to court, possibly imprison you, and deport you.

Extensions, border runs and re-entry permits

Tourist visa exemptions, as well as sixty-day tourist visas, can be **extended** within Thailand for a further thirty days, at the discretion of immigration officials; extensions cost B1900 and are issued over the counter at immigration offices (*kaan khao muang* or *taw maw*; ☏1178 for information, ⦿immigration. go.th) in nearly every provincial capital. You'll need to bring one or two photos, one or two photocopies of the main pages of your passport including your Thai departure card, arrival stamp and visa; you may be asked for proof of tickets to leave Thailand again within the proposed time and evidence of where you're staying, and it's possible that you'll be asked for proof of means of living while in Thailand. Many Khao San tour agents offer to get your visa extension for you, but beware: some are reportedly faking the stamps, which could get you into serious trouble. The Thai immigration authorities have recently clamped down on foreigners who stay in Thailand long-term by doing back-to-back **border runs** for tourist visa exemptions; however, it's still possible for ordinary travellers to get one new thirty-day tourist visa exemption by hopping **across the border** into a neighbouring country and back (the limit seems to be two tourist visa exemptions using a land border within a year). Immigration offices also issue **re-entry permits** (B1000 single re-entry, B3800 multiple) if you want to leave the country and come back again while maintaining the validity of your existing visa.

THAI EMBASSIES AND CONSULATES ABROAD

For a full listing of Thai diplomatic missions abroad, consult the Thai Ministry of Foreign Affairs' website at ⦿ mfa.go.th/web/2712.php; its other site, ⦿ thaiembassy.org, has links to the websites of most of the offices below.

Australia 111 Empire Circuit, Yarralumla, Canberra ACT 2600 ☏ 02 6206 0100; plus consulate at 131 Macquarrie St, Sydney, NSW 2000 ☏ 02 9241 2542–3.

Cambodia 196 Preah Norodom Blvd, Sangkat Tonle Bassac, Khan Chamcar Mon, Phnom Penh ☏ 023 726306–8.

Canada 180 Island Park Drive, Ottawa, ON, K1Y 0A2 ☏ 613 722 4444; plus consulate at 1040 Burrard St, Vancouver, BC, V6Z 2R9 ☏ 604 687 1143.

Laos Vientiane: embassy at Avenue Kaysone Phomvihane, Saysettha District ☏ 021 214581–2, consular section at Unit 15 Bourichane Rd, Ban Phone Si Nuan, Muang Si Sattanak ☏ 021 453916; plus consulate at Khanthabouly District, Savannakhet Province, PO Box 513 ☏ 041 212373.

Malaysia 206 Jalan Ampang, 50450 Kuala Lumpur ☏ 03 2148 8222; plus consulates at 4426 Jalan Pengkalan Chepa, 15400 Kota Bharu ☏ 09 748 2545; and 1 Jalan Tunku Abdul Rahman, 10350 Penang ☏ 04 226 9484.

Myanmar 94 Pyay Rd, Dagon Township, Rangoon ☏ 01 226721.

New Zealand 110 Molesworth St, Thorndon, Wellington ☏ 04 476 8616.

Singapore 370 Orchard Rd, Singapore 238870 ☏ 6737 2158.

South Africa 248 Pretorius/Hill St, Arcadia, Pretoria 0083 ☏ 012 342 5470.

UK and Ireland 29–30 Queens Gate, London SW7 5JB ☏ 020 7589 2944. In Ireland, visa applications by post can be sent to the consulate in Dublin (⦿ thaiconsulateireland.com).

US 1024 Wisconsin Ave NW, Suite 401, Washington, DC 20007 ☎ 202 944 3600; plus consulates at 700 North Rush St, Chicago, IL 60611 ☎ 312 664 3129; 611 North Larchmont Blvd, 2nd Floor, Los Angeles, CA 90004 ☎ 323 962 9574; and 351 E 52nd St, New York, NY 10022 ☎ 212 754 1770.

Vietnam 26 Phan Boi Chau St, Hanoi ☎ 04 3823 5092–4; plus consulate at 77 Tran Quoc Thao St, District 3, Ho Chi Minh City ☎ 08 3932 7637–8.

Health

Although Thailand's climate, wildlife and cuisine present Western travellers with fewer health worries than in many Asian destinations, it's as well to know in advance what the risks might be, and what preventive or curative measures you should take.

For a start, there's no need to bring huge supplies of non-prescription medicines with you, as Thai **pharmacies** (*raan khai yaa*; typically open daily 8.30am–8pm) are well stocked with local and inter-national branded medicaments, and they are generally much less expensive than at home. Nearly all pharmacies are run by trained English-speaking pharmacists, who are usually the best people to talk to if your symptoms aren't acute enough to warrant seeing a doctor. The British pharmacy chain, Boots, now has branches in many big cities (see ⓦ th.boots. com for locations). These are the best place to stock up on some Western products such as **tampons** (which Thai women do not use).

Hospital (*rong phayabaan*) cleanliness and efficiency vary, but generally hygiene and health-care standards are good and the ratio of medical staff to patients is considerably higher than in most parts of the West. As with head pharmacists, doctors speak English. Several Bangkok hospitals are highly regarded (see page 170), and all provincial capitals have at least one hospital: if you need to get to one, ask at your accommodation for advice on, and possibly transport to, the nearest or most suitable. For emergency numbers in Thailand, see page 62. In the event of a major health crisis, get someone to contact your embassy (see page 170) and insurance company – it may be best to get yourself transported to Bangkok or even home.

Inoculations

There are no compulsory **inoculation** requirements for people travelling to Thailand from the West, but you should consult a doctor or other health profes-sional, preferably at least four weeks in advance of your trip, for the latest information on recommended immunizations. In addition to making sure that your recommended immunizations for life in your home country are up to date, most doctors strongly advise vaccinations or boosters against tetanus, diphtheria, hepatitis A and, in many cases, typhoid, and in some cases they might also recommend protecting yourself against Japanese encephalitis, rabies and hepatitis B. There is currently no vaccine against malaria. If you forget to have all your inoculations before leaving home, or don't leave yourself sufficient time, you can get them in Bangkok at, for example, the Thai Red Cross Society's Queen Saovabha Institute or Global Doctor (see page 170).

Mosquito-borne diseases

Mosquitoes in Thailand can spread not only malaria, but also diseases such as dengue fever and the very similar chikungunya fever, especially during the rainy season. There is also a risk of Zika virus transmission, a mild infection which may be more serious to pregnant women as it can cause birth defects. The main message, therefore, is to **avoid being bitten** by mosquitoes. You should smother yourself and your clothes in **mosquito repellent** containing the chemical compound DEET, reapplying regularly (shops, guesthouses and department stores all over Thailand stock it, but if you want the highest-strength repellent, or convenient roll-ons or sprays, do your shopping before you leave home, or at a branch of Boots in Thailand). DEET is strong stuff, and if you have sensitive skin, a natural alternative is citronella (available in the UK as Mosi-guard), made from a blend of eucalyptus oils; the Thai version is made with lemon grass.

At night you should sleep either under a **mosquito net** sprayed with DEET or in a bedroom with **mosquito screens** across the windows (or in an enclosed a/c room). Accommodation in tourist spots nearly always provides screens or a net (check both for holes), but if you're planning to go way off the beaten track or want the security of having your own mosquito net just in case, wait until you get to Bangkok to buy one, where department stores sell them for much less than you'd pay in the West. Plug-in insecticide vaporizers, insect room sprays and mosquito coils – also widely available in Thailand – help keep the insects at bay; electronic "buzzers" are useless. If you are bitten, applying locally made yellow oil (see page 402) is effective at reducing the itch.

Malaria

Thailand is **malarial**, with the disease being carried by mosquitoes that bite from dusk to dawn, but the risks involved vary across the country.

There is a significant risk of malaria, mainly in rural and forested areas, in a narrow strip along the borders with **Cambodia** (excluding Ko Chang), **Laos** and **Myanmar** (the highest-risk area, including the countryside around Mae Hong Son, but excluding, for example, Chiang Mai, Chiang Rai and Kanchanaburi towns, and resorts and road and rail routes along the Gulf coast). Discuss with your travel health adviser which anti-malarial drugs are currently likely to be effective in these areas, as prophylaxis advice can change from year to year.

Elsewhere in Thailand the risk of malaria is considered to be so low that anti-malarial tablets are not advised.

The **signs of malaria** are often similar to flu, but are very variable. The incubation period for malignant malaria, which can be fatal, is usually 7–28 days, but it can take up to a year for symptoms of the benign form to occur. The most important symptom is a raised temperature of at least 38°C beginning a week or more after the first potential exposure to malaria: if you suspect anything, go to a hospital or clinic immediately.

Dengue fever

Dengue fever, a debilitating and occasionally fatal viral disease that is particularly prevalent during and just after the rainy season, is on the increase throughout tropical Asia, and is endemic to many areas of Thailand, with around 200,000 reported cases a year. Unlike malaria, dengue fever is spread by mosquitoes that can bite during daylight hours, so you should also use mosquito repellent during the day. Symptoms may include fever, headaches, fierce joint and muscle pain ("breakbone fever" is another name for dengue), and possibly a rash, and usually develop between five and eight days after being bitten.

If you think you may have contracted the disease, you should see a doctor: the treatment is lots of rest, liquids and paracetamol (or any other acetaminophen painkiller, not aspirin or ibuprofen), and more serious cases may require hospitalization.

Rabies

Rabies is widespread in Thailand, mainly carried by dogs (between four and seven percent of stray dogs in Bangkok are reported to be rabid), but also cats and monkeys. It is transmitted by bites, scratches or even occasionally licks. Dogs are everywhere in Thailand, and even if kept as pets they're often not very well cared for; hopefully their mangy appearance will discourage the urge to pat them, as you should steer well clear of them. Rabies is invariably fatal if the patient waits until symptoms begin, though modern vaccines and treatments are very effective and deaths

are rare. The important thing is, if you are bitten, licked or scratched by an animal, to vigorously clean the wound with soap and disinfect it, preferably with something containing iodine, and to seek medical advice regarding treatment right away.

Other bites and stings

Thailand's seas are home to a few dangerous creatures that you should look out for, notably **jellyfish**, which tend to be washed towards the beach by rough seas during the monsoon season but can appear at any time of year. All manner of stinging and non-stinging jellyfish can be found in Thailand – as a general rule, those with the longest tentacles tend to have the worst stings – but reports of serious incidents are uncommon; ask around at your resort or at a local dive shop to see if there have been any sightings of venomous varieties. You also need to be wary of venomous **sea snakes**, **sea urchins** and a couple of less conspicuous species – **stingrays**, which often lie buried in the sand, and **stonefish**, whose potentially lethal venomous spikes are easily stepped on because the fish look like stones and lie motionless on the sea bed.

If **stung or bitten**, you should always seek medical advice as soon as possible, but there are a few ways of alleviating the pain or administering your own first aid in the meantime. If you're stung by a jellyfish, wash the affected area with salt water (not fresh water) and, if possible, with vinegar (failing that, ammonia, citrus fruit juice or even urine may do the trick), and try to remove the fragments of tentacles from the skin with a gloved hand, forceps, thick cloth or credit card. The best way to minimize the risk of stepping on the toxic spines of sea urchins, stingrays and stonefish is to wear thick-soled shoes, though these cannot provide total protection; sea urchin spikes should be removed after softening the skin with ointment, though some people recommend applying urine to help dissolve the spines; for stingray and stonefish stings, alleviate the pain by immersing the wound in hot water while awaiting help.

In the case of a **venomous snake bite**, don't try sucking out the venom or applying a tourniquet: wrap up and immobilize the bitten limb and try to stay still and calm until medical help arrives; all provincial hospitals in Thailand carry supplies of antivenins.

Some of Thailand's beaches are plagued by **sandflies**, tiny, barely visible midges whose bites can trigger an allergic response, leaving big red weals and an unbearable itch, and possible infection if scratched too vigorously. Many islanders say that slathering yourself in (widely available) coconut oil is the best deterrent as sandflies apparently don't like the smell. Applying locally made camphor-based yellow oil (see page 402) quells the itch, but you may need to resort to antihistamines for the inflammation. **Leeches** aren't dangerous but can be a bother when walking in forested areas, especially during and just after the rainy season. The most effective way to get leeches off your skin is to burn them with a lighted cigarette, or douse them in salt; oily suntan lotion or insect repellent sometimes makes them lose their grip and fall off.

Worms and flukes

Worms can be picked up through the soles of your feet, so avoid going barefoot. They can also be ingested by eating undercooked meat, and liver **flukes** by eating raw or undercooked freshwater fish. Worms which cause schistosomiasis (bilhar-ziasis) by attaching themselves to your bladder or intestines can be found in freshwater rivers and lakes. The risk of contracting this disease is low, but you should avoid swimming in the southern reaches of the Mekong River and in most fresh-water lakes.

Digestive problems

By far the most common travellers' complaint in Thailand, **digestive troubles** are often caused by contaminated food and water, or sometimes just by an overdose of unfamiliar foodstuffs (see page 40).

Stomach trouble usually manifests itself as simple **diarrhoea**, which should clear up without medical treatment within three to seven days and is best combated by drinking lots of fluids. If this doesn't work, you're in danger of getting **dehydrated** and should take some kind of rehydration solution, either a commercial sachet of ORS (oral rehydration solution), sold in all Thai pharmacies, or a do-it-yourself version, which can be made by adding a handful of sugar and a pinch of salt to every litre of boiled or bottled water (soft drinks are not a viable alternative). If you can eat, avoid fatty foods.

Anti-diarrhoeal agents such as Imodium are useful for blocking you up on long bus journeys, but only attack the symptoms and may prolong infections; an antibiotic such as ciprofloxacin, however, can often reduce a typical attack of traveller's diarrhoea to one day. If the diarrhoea persists for a week or more, or if you have blood or mucus in your stools, or an accompanying fever, go to a doctor or hospital.

HIV and AIDS

HIV infection is widespread in Thailand, primarily because of the sex trade (see page 125). **Condoms** (*meechai*) are sold in pharmacies, convenience stores, department stores, hairdressers and even street markets. Due to rigorous screening methods, Thailand's medical blood supply is now considered safe from HIV/AIDS infection.

MEDICAL RESOURCES

Canadian Society for International Health ☎ 613 241 5785, ⓦ csih.org. Extensive list of travel health centres.
CDC ☎ 800 232 4636, ⓦ cdc.gov/travel. Official US government travel health site.
Hospital for Tropical Diseases Travel Clinic UK ⓦ thehtd.org/travelclinic.aspx.
International Society for Travel Medicine US ☎ 404 373 8282, ⓦ istm.org. Has a full list of travel health clinics.
MASTA (Medical Advisory Service for Travellers Abroad) UK ⓦ masta-travel-health.com.
The Travel Doctor ⓦ traveldoctor.com.au. Lists travel clinics in Australia, New Zealand and South Africa.
Tropical Medical Bureau Ireland ☎ 01 271 5200, ⓦ tmb.ie.

Insurance

Most visitors to Thailand will need to take out **specialist travel insurance**, though you should check exactly what's covered. Insurers will generally not cover travel in Songkhla, Yala, Pattani and Narathiwat provinces in the deep south, as Western governments are currently advising against going to these areas unless it's essential (see page 696). Policies generally also exclude so-called **dangerous sports** unless an extra premium is paid: in Thailand this can mean such things as scuba diving, white-water rafting and trekking, sometimes even riding a motorbike.

Internet

Internet access is now almost ubiquitous in Thailand. The country is covered by 3G networks and wi-fi is available free in nearly all guesthouses, bungalow resorts and hotels; in cheaper places, the signal may not stretch to all bedrooms. Loads of cafés, restaurants, bars and other locations across the country, especially in big towns and tourist resorts, also provide wi-fi free of charge. Given all this, internet cafés are inexorably disappearing. If you're travelling without a mobile device, ask at your accommodation for advice or keep an eye out for online games centres, favourite after-school haunts that are easily spotted from the piles of orange schoolboy pumps outside the door.

Laundry

Guesthouses and cheap hotels all over the country offer low-cost, same- or next-day **laundry** services, though in luxury hotels it'll cost an arm and a leg. In some places you pay per item, in others you're charged by the kilo (generally around B30–50/kg); ironing is often included in the price.

ROUGH GUIDES TRAVEL INSURANCE

Rough Guides has teamed up with WorldNomads.com to offer great travel insurance deals. Policies are available to residents of over 150 countries, with cover for a wide range of adventure sports, 24hr emergency assistance, high levels of medical and evacuation cover and a stream of travel safety information. Roughguides.com users can take advantage of their policies online 24/7, from anywhere in the world – even if you're already travelling. And since plans often change when you're on the road, you can extend your policy and even claim online. Roughguides.com users who buy travel insurance with WorldNomads.com can also leave a positive footprint and donate to a community development project. For more information, go to ⓦ roughguides.com/travel-insurance.

Left luggage

Most major train stations have **left-luggage** -facilities (around B30–80 per item per day); at bus stations you can usually persuade someone official to look after your stuff for a few hours. Many guesthouses and basic hotels also offer an inexpensive and usually reliable service, while upmarket hotels should be able to look after your luggage for free. There's also left luggage at Chiang Mai, Phuket and both Bangkok airports (B75–200/day).

LGBTQ Thailand

Buddhist tolerance and a national abhorrence of confrontation and victimization combine to make Thai society relatively tolerant of **homosexuality**, if not exactly positive about same-sex relationships. Most Thais are extremely private and discreet about being gay, generally pursuing a "don't ask, don't tell" understanding with their family. The majority of people are horrified by the idea of gay-bashing and generally regard it as unthinkable to spurn a child or relative for being gay.

Hardly any Thai celebrities are out, yet the predilections of several respected social, political and entertainment figures are widely known and accepted. There is no mention of homosexuality at all in Thai law, which means that the **age of consent** for gay sex is fifteen, the same as for heterosexuals. However, this also means that gay rights are not protected under Thai law.

Although excessively physical displays of affection are frowned upon for both heterosexuals and homosexuals, Western gay couples should get no hassle about being seen together in public – it's much more acceptable, and common, in fact, for friends of the same sex (gay or not) to walk hand-in-hand, than for heterosexual couples to do so.

Katoey (which can refer both to transgender women and to effeminate gay men, so often translated as "ladyboys") are also a lot more visible in Thailand than in the West. You'll find transgender women doing ordinary jobs, even in small upcountry towns, and there are a number of *katoey* in the public eye – including national volleyball stars and champion *muay thai* boxers. The government tourist office vigorously promotes the transgender cabarets in Pattaya, Phuket and Bangkok, all of which are advertised as family entertainment. *Katoey* also regularly appear as characters in soap operas, TV comedies and films, where they are depicted as stereotyped but harmless figures of fun. Richard Totman's *The Third Sex* offers an interesting insight into Thai *katoey*, their experiences in society and public attitudes towards them.

The scene

Thailand's gay scene is mainly focused on **mainstream venues** like karaoke bars, restaurants, massage parlours, gyms, saunas and escort agencies. For the sake of discretion, gay venues are often intermingled with straight ones. Bangkok, Phuket and Pattaya have the biggest concentrations of farang-friendly gay bars and clubs, and Chiang Mai has an established bar scene. For a detailed though slightly outdated guide to the gay and lesbian scene throughout the country, see the *Utopia Guide to Thailand* by John Goss.

Thai **lesbians** generally eschew the word lesbian, which in Thailand is associated with male fantasies, instead referring to themselves as either *tom* (for tomboy) or *dee* (for lady). There are hardly any dedicated *tom-dee* venues in Thailand, but we've listed established ones where possible; unless otherwise specified, gay means male throughout this Guide.

The farang-oriented gay **sex industry** is a tiny but highly visible part of Thailand's gay scene. With its tawdry floor shows and host services, it bears a dispiriting resemblance to the straight sex trade, and is similarly most active in Bangkok, Pattaya, Patong (on Phuket) and Chiang Mai. Like their female counterparts in the heterosexual fleshpots, many of the boys working in the gay sex bars that dominate these districts are underage; note that anyone caught having sex with a prostitute below the age of 18 faces imprisonment. A significant number of gay prostitutes are gay by economic necessity rather than by inclination. As with the straight sex scene, we do not list commercial gay sex bars in the Guide.

INFORMATION AND CONTACTS FOR GAY TRAVELLERS

Bangkok Lesbian Ⓦ bangkoklesbian.com. Organized by foreign lesbians living in Thailand, Bangkok Lesbian posts general info and listings of the capital's few lesbian-friendly hangouts on its website.

The Gay Passport Ⓦ thegaypassport.com. Regularly updated listings for the main tourist centres.

Gay People in Thailand Ⓦ thaivisa.com/forum/forum/27-gay-people-in-thailand. Popular forum for gay expats.

Travel Gay Asia Ⓦ travelgayasia.com/destination/gay-thailand. Active, frequently updated site that covers listings and events all over the country.

Utopia Ⓦ utopia-asia.com. Lists clubs, bars, restaurants, accommodation, tour operators, organizations and resources for gays and lesbians.

Living in Thailand

The most common source of **employment** in Thailand is **teaching English**, and Bangkok and Chiang Mai are the most fruitful places to look for jobs. You can search for openings at schools all over Thailand on Ⓦ ajarn.com (*ajarn* means "teacher"), which also features extensive general advice on teaching and living in Thailand. Another useful resource is the excellent Ⓦ thaivisa.com, whose scores of well-used forums focus on specific topics that range from employment in Thailand to legal issues and cultural and practical topics.

If you're a qualified **dive instructor**, you might be able to get seasonal work at one of the major resorts – in Phuket, Khao Lak and Ao Nang and on Ko Chang, Ko Phi Phi, Ko Lanta, Ko Samui and Ko Tao, for example. Guesthouse noticeboards occasionally carry adverts for more unusual jobs, such as playing extras in Thai movies. A tourist visa does not entitle you to work in Thailand, so, legally, you'll need to apply for a **work permit**.

STUDY, WORK AND VOLUNTEER PROGRAMMES

In addition to the programmes listed below, voluntary opportunities with smaller grassroots projects (see page 59) and wildlife charity projects (see page 759) are available.

AFS Intercultural Programs Australia ☎ 1300 131736, Canada ☎ 800 361 7248, NZ ☎ 0800 600 300, South Africa ☎ 11 431 0113, US ☎ AFS INFO; Ⓦ afs.org. Intercultural exchange organization with programmes in over fifty countries.

Council on International Educational Exchange (CIEE) US ☎ 207 553 4000, Ⓦ ciee.org. Leading NGO that organizes paid

placements for a semester or more as English teachers in schools in Thailand, for US citizens, among other programmes.

Phuket Has Been Good To Us Ⓦ phukethasbeengoodtous. org. Has voluntary and paid positions teaching and assisting on its English-language programmes and after-schools clubs at schools on Phuket, as well as welcoming donations and sponsors. The aim of this non-profit foundation is to improve kids' standards of English so that they can get jobs in Phuket's tourist industry.

Volunteer Teacher Thailand Ⓦ volunteerteacherthailand.org. Continuing the good work begun by the thousands of volunteers who came to Khao Lak to help rebuild lives and homes following the 2004 tsunami, this non-profit organization teaches English to kids in and around Khao Lak to enhance their future prospects. Teaching experience is appreciated but not essential.

Volunthai Ⓦ volunthai.com. Invites volunteers to teach English in rural schools mostly in northeast Thailand. The minimal fees help to cover homestay accommodation.

Thai language classes

The most popular places to **study Thai** are Chiang Mai and Bangkok, where there's plenty of choice, including private and group lessons for both tourists and expats; note, however, that some schools' main reason for existence is to provide educational visas for long-staying foreigners. The longest-running and best-regarded courses and private lessons are provided by AUA (American University Alumni; Ⓦ auathailand.org), which has outlets in Bangkok, Pattaya and Chiang Mai (see page 275).

Maps

For most major destinations, the **maps** in this book should be all you need, though you may want to supplement them with larger-scale hard-copy maps of Bangkok and the whole country. Bangkok bookshops are the best source of these; where appropriate, detailed local maps and their stockists are recommended throughout the Guide. Decent maps of the whole country include the 1:1,500,000 versions produced by Nelles and Bartholomew, and the bilingual 1:550,000 *Thailand Deluxe Atlas* published by thinknet (Ⓦ thinknet.co.th). **Trekking maps** are hard to come by, except in the most popular national parks where you can usually pick up a free handout showing the main trails.

Money and banks

Thailand's unit of currency is the **baht** (abbreviated in this guide to "B"), divided into 100 satang – which are rarely seen these days. Coins come in B1 (silver), B2 (golden), B5 (silver) and B10 (mostly golden, encircled by a silver ring) denominations, notes in B20, B50, B100, B500 and B1000 denominations, inscribed with Western as well as Thai numerals, and generally increasing in size according to value.

At the time of writing, **exchange rates** were around B31 to US$1 and B44 to £1. A good site for current exchange rates is ⓦ xe.com. Note that Thailand has no black market in foreign currency.

Banking hours are generally Monday to Friday from 8.30am to 3.30 or 4.30pm, though branches in out-of-town shopping centres and supermarkets are often open longer hours and at weekends. Streetside exchange kiosks run by the banks in the main tourist centres are always open till at least 5pm, sometimes 10pm, and upmarket hotels change money (at poor rates) 24 hours a day. The Suvarnabhumi Airport exchange counters also operate 24 hours, while exchange kiosks at overseas airports with flights to Thailand usually keep Thai currency. Note that Scottish and Northern Irish sterling notes may not be accepted in some places.

Visa and MasterCard **credit and debit cards** are accepted at upmarket guesthouses and hotels as well as in posh restaurants, department stores, tourist shops and travel agents; American Express is less widely accepted. It's common for smaller businesses to add on a surcharge of three percent, which amounts to the fee that Visa and Mastercard charge them for the privilege. Beware theft and forgery – try not to let the card out of your sight, and never leave cards in baggage storage. With a debit or credit card and personal identification number (PIN), you can also withdraw cash from hundreds of 24hr **ATMs** around the country. Almost every town now has at least one bank with an ATM outside that accepts overseas cards (all the banks marked on our maps throughout the Guide have ATMs), and there is a huge number of standalone ATMs, in shopping malls and on the streets, often outside supermarkets and post offices. However, Thai banks now make a charge of B150–200 per ATM withdrawal (on top of whatever your bank at home will be charging you); to get around this, go into a bank with your card and passport instead and ask for a cash advance, or check with your bank before you come to Thailand – some overseas banks will not pass on to customers the B150–200 levied at Thai ATMs.

Opening hours and public holidays

Most shops **open** long hours, usually Monday to Saturday or Sunday from about 8am to 8pm, while department stores and shopping malls operate daily

from around 10am to 9pm. Private office hours are generally Monday to Friday 8am to 5pm, plus perhaps Saturday 8am to noon, though in tourist areas these hours are longer, with weekends worked like any other day. Government offices work Monday to Friday 8.30am to 4.30pm (often closing for lunch between noon and 1pm), and national museums tend to stick to these hours too, but some close on Mondays and Tuesdays rather than at weekends. Temples generally open their gates every day from dawn to dusk.

Many tourists only register **national holidays** because trains and buses suddenly get extra-ordinarily crowded, especially if the holiday is moved from a Saturday or a Sunday to a Monday or a Friday as a substitution day, thus creating a long weekend: although government offices shut on these days, most shops and tourist-oriented businesses carry on regardless, and TAT branches continue to hand out free maps. (Bank holidays vary slightly from the government office holidays given below: banks close on May 1 and July 1, but not for the Royal Ploughing Ceremony nor for Khao Pansa.) Some national holidays are celebrated with -theatrical festivals (see page 47). The only time an inconvenient number of shops, restaurants and hotels do close is during **Chinese New Year**, which, though not marked as an official national holiday, brings many businesses to a standstill for several days in late January or February. You'll notice it particularly in the south, where many service industries are Chinese-managed.

Thais use both the Western Gregorian **calendar** and a Buddhist calendar – the Buddha is said to have died (or entered Nirvana) in the year 543 BC, so Thai dates start from that point: thus 2019 AD becomes 2562 BE (Buddhist Era).

NATIONAL HOLIDAYS

Jan 1 Western New Year's Day.

Feb (day of full moon) Makha Puja. Commemorates the Buddha preaching to a spontaneously assembled crowd of 1250.

April 6 Chakri Day. The founding of the Chakri dynasty, the current royal family.

April (usually 13–15) Songkhran. Thai New Year.

May 5 Coronation Day.

May (early in the month) Royal Ploughing Ceremony. Marks the traditional start of the rice-planting season.

May (day of full moon) Visakha Puja. The holiest of all Buddhist holidays, which celebrates the birth, enlightenment and death of the Buddha.

July (day of full moon) Asanha Puja. The anniversary of the Buddha's first sermon.

July (day after Asanha Puja) Khao Pansa. The start of the annual three-month Buddhist rains retreat, when new monks are ordained.

July 28 King Vajiralongkorn's birthday.

Aug 12 Queen Mother's birthday and Mothers' Day.
Oct 23 Chulalongkorn Day. The anniversary of Rama V's death.
Dec 5 The late King Bhumibol's birthday and Fathers' Day. Also now celebrated as National Day (instead of Constitution Day).
Dec 10 Constitution Day.
Dec 31 Western New Year's Eve.

Phones

Most foreign **mobile-phone** networks have links with Thai networks but you need to check on roaming rates, which are often exorbitant, before you leave home. To get round this, most travellers purchase a Thai pre-paid SIM card (providers include AIS, DTAC and True Move) either for their mobile phone (*moe thoe*), for an old phone brought from home or for a new set cheaply purchased in Thailand (which can most easily be done in a shopping centre, especially Mah Boon Krong opposite Siam Square in Bangkok – see page 154). Available for as little as B50 (sometimes free at airports) and refillable at 7-Elevens around the country, Thai SIM cards offer very cheap calls, both domestically and inter-na-tionally (especially if you use low-cost inter-national prefixes such as 008, 009 or DTAC's 004, rather than the standard 001 or 007 prefixes). They also offer data packages (4G is now available in most places), very cheap texting and are, of course, free of charge for all incoming calls. A data package or wi-fi on your own mobile device will also allow you to make free or very cheap video or voice calls via Skype or a similar service.

When **dialling** any number in Thailand, you must now always preface it with what used to be the area code, even when dialling from the same area. Where we've given several line numbers – eg ☎02 431 1802–9 – you can substitute the last digit, 2, with any digit between 3 and 9.

Mobile-phone numbers in Thailand have ten digits, beginning "06", "08" or "09". Note, however, that Thais tend to change mobile-phone providers – and

therefore numbers – comparatively frequently, in search of a better deal.

One final local idiosyncrasy: Thai phone books list people by their first name, not their family name.

Photography

Most towns and all resorts have at least one **camera shop** where you will be able to get your digital pictures downloaded from your memory card for around B150; new cards can be bought in electronic shops in shopping centres or in dedicated IT malls such as Panthip Plaza in Bangkok or Chiang Mai.

Post

Overseas airmail usually takes around seven days from Bangkok, a little longer from the more isolated areas (it's worth asking at the post office about its express EMS services, which can cut this down to about three days and aren't prohibitively expensive). **Post offices** in Thailand (ⓦthailandpost.com) have recently become quite successfully privatized, and many now offer money-wiring facilities (in association with Western Union), parcel boxes, long-distance bus tickets, amulets, whitening cream, you name it. They're generally open Monday to Friday 8.30am to 4.30pm, Saturday 9am to noon; some close Monday to Friday noon to 1pm and may stay open until 6pm, and a few open 9am to noon on Sundays and public holidays. Almost all main post offices across the country operate a **poste restante** service and will hold letters for one to three months. Mail should be addressed: *Name* (family name underlined or capitalized), Poste Restante, GPO, *Town or City*, Thailand. It will be filed by surname, though it's always wise to check under your first and middle names as well. The smaller post offices pay scant attention to who takes what, but in the busier GPOs you need to show your passport. Post offices are the best places to buy **stamps**, though hotels and guesthouses often sell them too.

CALLING HOME FROM ABROAD

To make an international call, dial the international access code (in Thailand 001 and 007 are two standard prefixes; see page 72 for more information), then the destination's country code, before the rest of the number. Note that the initial zero is omitted from the area code when dialling the UK, Ireland, Australia and New Zealand from abroad.

Australia International access code + 61
New Zealand International access code + 64
UK International access code + 44
US and Canada International access code + 1
Ireland International access code + 353
South Africa International access code + 27

Time

Thailand is in the same time zone year-round, with no daylight savings period. It's five hours ahead of South Africa, seven hours ahead of GMT, twelve hours ahead of US Eastern Standard Time, three hours behind Australian Eastern Standard Time and five hours behind New Zealand Standard Time.

Tipping

It is usual to **tip** hotel bellboys and porters B20–40, and to round up taxi fares to the nearest B10. Most guides, drivers, masseurs and waiters also depend on tips. Some upmarket hotels and restaurants will add an automatic ten percent service charge to your bill, though this is not always shared out.

Tourist information

The **Tourism Authority of Thailand**, or **TAT** (W tourismthailand.org), maintains offices in several cities abroad and has dozens of branches within Thailand (all open daily 8.30am–4.30pm, though a few close noon–1pm). Regional offices should have up-to-date information on local festival dates and perhaps transport schedules, but service varies widely; none of them offers accommodation, tour or transport booking. You can contact the helpful TAT tourist assistance phoneline from anywhere in the country for free on T 1672 (daily 8am–8pm). In Bangkok, the Bangkok Tourism Division is a better source of information on the capital (see page 141). In some smaller towns that don't qualify for a local TAT office, the information gap is filled by a **municipal tourist assistance office**; some of these are very helpful, but at others you may find it hard to locate a fluent English-speaker.

TAT OFFICES ABROAD

Australia and New Zealand Suite 2002, Level 20, 56 Pitt St, Sydney, NSW 2000 T 02 9247 7549, E info@thailand.net.au. **South Africa** Contact the UK office.

UK and Ireland 1st Floor, 17–19 Cockspur St, London SW1Y 5BL T 020 7925 2511, E info@tourismthailand.co.uk. **US and Canada** 61 Broadway, Suite 2810, New York, NY 10006 T 212 432 0433, E info@tatny.com; 611 North Larchmont Blvd, 1st Floor, Los Angeles, CA 90004 T 323 461 9814, E tatla@tat.or.th.

Travellers with disabilities

Thailand makes few provisions for its disabled citizens and this obviously affects **travellers with disabilities**, but taxis, comfortable hotels and personal tour guides are all more affordable than in the West and most travellers with disabilities find Thais only too happy to offer assistance where they can. Hiring a local tour guide to accompany you on a day's sightseeing is particularly recommended: government-licensed tour guides can be arranged through any TAT office.

Most **wheelchair-users** end up driving on the roads because it's too hard to negotiate the uneven pavements, which are high to allow for flooding, poorly maintained and invariably lack dropped kerbs. Crossing the road can be a trial, particularly in Bangkok and other big cities, where it's usually a question of climbing steps up to a bridge rather than taking a ramped underpass. Few buildings, buses and trains have ramps, but in Bangkok some Skytrain stations and all subway stations have lifts (though you might have to ask someone to unlock them).

Several **tour companies** in Thailand specialize in organizing trips featuring adapted facilities, accessible transport and escorts. The Bangkok-based Help and Care Travel Company (T 081 375 0792, W wheelchairtours.com) designs **accessible holidays** in Thailand for slow walkers and wheelchair-users, as well as offering accessible taxis, vans and hotels, personal assistants, medical equipment and many other services. Mermaids Dive Centre in Pattaya runs Disabled Divers International programmes and certifications for **disabled divers** and instructors (T 038 303333, W mermaidsdivecenter.com).

Bangkok

WAT PHRA KAEO

1

Bangkok

The headlong pace and flawed modernity of Bangkok match few people's visions of the capital of exotic Siam. Spiked with scores of high-rise buildings of concrete and glass, it's a vast flatness that holds an estimated population of nearly fifteen million, and feels even bigger. Yet under the shadow of the skyscrapers you'll find a heady mix of chaos and refinement, of frenetic markets, snail's-pace traffic jams and hushed golden temples, of dispiriting, zombie-like sex shows and early-morning alms-giving ceremonies. Plenty of visitors enjoy the challenge of taking on the "Big Mango", but one way or another, the place is sure to get under your skin.

Most budget travellers head for the **Banglamphu** district, where if you're not careful you could end up watching movies all day long and selling your shoes when you run out of money. The district is far from having a monopoly on Bangkok accommodation, but it does have the advantage of being just a short walk from the major sights in the **Ratanakosin** area: the dazzling ostentation of the **Grand Palace** and **Wat Phra Kaeo**, lively and grandiose **Wat Pho** and the **National Museum**'s hoard of exquisite works of art. Once those cultural essentials have been seen, you can choose from a whole bevy of lesser sights, including **Wat Benjamabophit** (the "Marble Temple"), especially at festival time, and **Jim Thompson's House**, a small, personal museum of Thai design.

For livelier scenes, explore the dark alleys of **Chinatown**'s bazaars or head for the water: the great **Chao Phraya River**, which breaks up and adds zest to the city's landscape, is the backbone of a network of **canals** that remains fundamentally intact in the west-bank Thonburi district. Inevitably the waterways have earned Bangkok the title of "Venice of the East", a tag that seems all too apt when you're wading through flooded streets in the rainy season. Back on dry land, **shopping** varies from touristic outlets pushing silks, handicrafts and counterfeit watches, through home-grown boutiques selling street-wise fashions and stunning contemporary decor, to thronging local markets where half the fun is watching the crowds. Thailand's long calendar of festivals (see page 47)

ORIENTATION

Bangkok ("Krung Thep" in Thai) can be a tricky place to get your bearings as it's huge and ridiculously congested, with largely featureless modern buildings and no obvious centre. The boldest line on the map is the **Chao Phraya River**, which divides the city into Bangkok proper on the east bank and **Thonburi**, part of Greater Bangkok, on the west.

The historical core of Bangkok proper, site of the original royal palace, is **Ratanakosin**, cradled in a bend in the river. Three concentric canals radiate eastwards around Ratanakosin: the southern part of the area between the canals is the old-style trading enclave of **Chinatown** and Indian **Pahurat**, connected to the old palace by Thanon Charoen Krung (aka New Road); the northern part is characterized by old temples and the **Democracy Monument**, west of which is the backpackers' ghetto of **Banglamphu**. Beyond the canals to the north, **Dusit** is the site of many government buildings and the nineteenth-century Vimanmek Palace, and is linked to Ratanakosin by the three stately avenues, Thanon Rajdamnoen Nok, Thanon Rajdamnoen Klang and Thanon Rajdamnoen Nai.

"New" Bangkok begins to the east of the canals and beyond the main rail line and Hualamphong Station, and stretches as far as the eye can see to the east and north. The main business district is south of **Thanon Rama IV**, with the port of Khlong Toey at its eastern edge. The diverse area north of Thanon Rama IV includes the sprawling campus of Chulalongkorn University and huge shopping centres around **Siam Square**. To the east lies the swish residential quarter of **Thanon Sukhumvit**.

THE SKY BAR AT SIROCCO

Highlights

HIGHLIGHTS ARE MARKED ON THE MAP ON PAGE 78

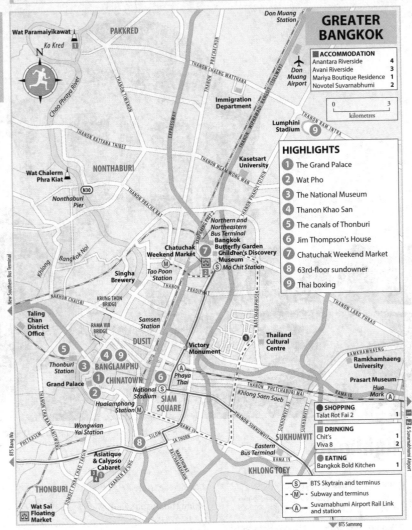

GREATER BANGKOK

■ ACCOMMODATION
Anantara Riverside	4
Avani Riverside	3
Mariya Boutique Residence	1
Novotel Suvarnbhumi	2

HIGHLIGHTS
1 The Grand Palace
2 Wat Pho
3 The National Museum
4 Thanon Khao San
5 The canals of Thonburi
6 Jim Thompson's House
7 Chatuchak Weekend Market
8 63rd-floor sundowner
9 Thai boxing

● SHOPPING
Talat Rot Fai 2	1

■ DRINKING
Chit's	1
Viva 8	2

● EATING
Bangkok Bold Kitchen	1

(S) BTS Skytrain and terminus
(M) Subway and terminus
(A) Suvarnabhumi Airport Rail Link and station

is one of the few things that has been largely decentralized away from the capital, but Bangkok does offer the country's most varied **entertainment**, ranging from traditional dancing and the orchestrated bedlam of Thai boxing, to cool bars, clubs, cafés and microbreweries, and beyond to the farang-only sex bars of the notorious Patpong district, a tinseltown Babylon that's the tip of a dangerous iceberg. Even if the above doesn't appeal, you'll almost certainly pass through Bangkok once, if not several times – not only is it Thailand's main port of entry, it's also the obvious place to sort out onward travel, with a convenient menu of embassies for visas to neighbouring countries.

Brief history

Bangkok is a relatively young capital, established in 1782 after the Burmese sacked Ayutthaya, the former capital. A temporary base was set up on the western bank of

A WORD OF WARNING

When you're heading for the Grand Palace or Wat Pho, you may well be approached by someone, possibly pretending to be a student or an official, who will tell you that the sight is closed when it's not, or some other lies to try to lead you away from the entrance, because they want to take you on a shopping trip for souvenirs, tailored clothes or, if you seem really gullible, gems (see page 169). The opening hours of the Grand Palace – but not Wat Pho – are indeed sometimes erratic because of state occasions, but you can check the details out on its website, ⓦpalaces.thai.net (click on "Annual Calendar for Visitor") – and even if it's closed on the day you want to visit, that's no reason to throw yourself at the mercy of these shysters.

the Chao Phraya River, in what is now **Thonburi**, before work started on the more defensible east bank, where the French had built a grand, but short-lived, fort in the 1660s. The first king of the new dynasty, Rama I (1782–1809), built his palace at **Ratanakosin**, within a defensive ring of two (later expanded to three) canals, and this remains the city's spiritual heart.

Initially, the city was largely **amphibious**: only the temples and royal palaces were built on dry land, while ordinary residences floated on thick bamboo rafts on the river and canals; even shops and warehouses were moored to the river bank. A major shift in emphasis came in the second half of the nineteenth century, first under Rama IV (1851–68), who as part of his effort to restyle the capital along European lines built Bangkok's first roads, and then under Rama V (1868–1910), who constructed a new residential palace in **Dusit**, north of Ratanakosin, and laid out that area's grand boulevards.

The modern metropolis

Since World War II, and especially from the mid-1960s onwards, Bangkok has seen an explosion of **modernization**, which has blown away earlier attempts at orderly planning and left the city without an obvious centre. Most of the canals have been

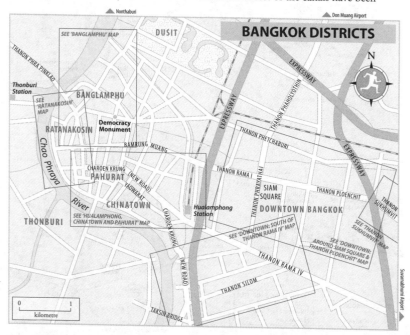

1

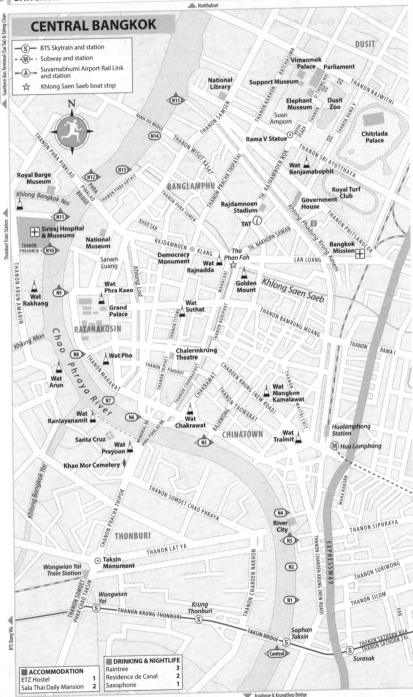

CENTRAL BANGKOK

- Ⓢ — BTS Skytrain and station
- Ⓜ -- Subway and station
- Ⓐ — Suvarnabhumi Airport Rail Link and station
- ☆ Khlong Saen Saeb boat stop

N

Nonthaburi

DUSIT

National Library

Vimanmek Palace   Parliament

Support Museum

THANON RAJWITHI

Elephant Museum   Dusit Zoo

Suan Amporn

Rama V Statue

Chitrlada Palace

THANON SRI AYUTTHAYA

Wat Benjamabophit

Royal Turf Club

RAMA VIII BRIDGE

THANON PHRA PINKLAO

Royal Barge Museum

Khlong Bangkok Noi

N15

N14

N13

N12

PHRA PINKLAO BRIDGE

THANON PHRA ARTHIT

THANON WISUT KASAT

THANON SAMSEN

THANON PRACHA THIPATAI

BANGLAMPHU

THANON PHRA SUMEN

Government House

THANON PHITSANULOK

Khlong Phadung Krung Kasem

N11

Siriraj Hospital & Museums

THANON PHRANNOK N10

KHAO SAN

Rajdamnoen Stadium

TAT ⓘ

Bangkok Mission

National Museum

Sanam Luang

RAJDAMNOEN   KLANG

Democracy Monument

Wat Rajnadda

Tha Phan Fah ☆

TH. NAKHORN SAWAN

LAN LUANG

THANON ARUN AMARIN

Khlong Lod

Wat Phra Kaeo

N9

Golden Mount

MAHACHAI

Khlong Saen Saeb

Wat Rakhang

Grand Palace

Wat Suthat

THANON TITONG

THANON DINSO

THANON BURIPHAT

THANON BAMRUNG MUANG

THANON   RAMA I

RATANAKOSIN

Khlong Mon

N8   THANON MAHARAT

Wat Pho

Chalermkrung Theatre

THANON TRIPHET

THANON PAHURAT

THANON CHAKRAPHET

CHAROEN KRUNG (NEW ROAD)

THANON YAOWARAT

Wat Mangkon Kamalawat

THANON MITRI CHIT

Chao Phraya River

Wat Arun

N7

Wat Kanlayanamit

N6

BUDDHA YODFA BR.

PHRA POKKLAO BR.

CHAKRAWAT

Wat Chakrawat

RAJAWONG

N5

CHINATOWN

Wat Traimit

Hualamphong Station

Ⓜ Hua Lamphong

Santa Cruz

Khlong Bangkok Yai

Wat Prayoon

Khao Mor Cemetery

THANON PRACHA THIPOK

THANON SOMDET CHAO PHRAYA

N4

River City

N3

THANON SIPHRAYA

MAHA NAKORN

THONBURI

THANON LAT YA

THANON CHAROEN NAKHON

N2

THANON CHAROEN KRUNG (NEW ROAD)

EXPRESSWAY

THANON SURIWONG

Wongwian Yai Train Station

Taksin Monument

Wongwian Yai

THANON SOMDET PHRA CHAO TAKSIN

N1

THANON SILOM

THANON KRUNG THONBURI

Krung Thonburi

THANON CHAROEN NAKHON

Saphan Taksin

TAKSIN BRIDGE

Central

THANON SATHORN NUA
THANON SATHORN TAI

Surasak

PAN

Asiatique & Krungthep Bridge

■ ACCOMMODATION
ETZ Hostel	1
Sala Thai Daily Mansion	2

■ DRINKING & NIGHTLIFE
Raintree	3
Residence de Canal	2
Saxophone	1

Southern Bus Terminal (Sai Tai) & Taling Chan

Thonburi Train Station

BTS Bang Wa

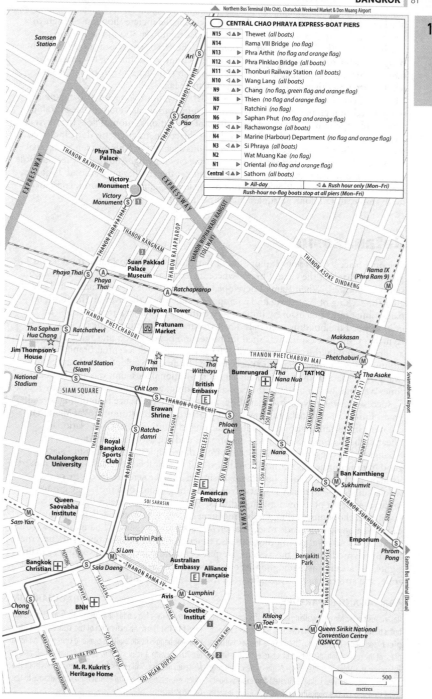

Northern Bus Terminal (Mo Chit), Chatuchak Weekend Market & Don Muang Airport

CENTRAL CHAO PHRAYA EXPRESS-BOAT PIERS

N15	◁ ▲ ▷	Thewet	(all boats)
N14	▷	Rama VIII Bridge	(no flag)
N13	▷	Phra Arthit	(no flag and orange flag)
N12	◁ ▲ ▷	Phra Pinklao Bridge	(all boats)
N11	◁ ▲ ▷	Thonburi Railway Station	(all boats)
N10	◁ ▲ ▷	Wang Lang	(all boats)
N9	▲ ▷	Chang	(no flag, green flag and orange flag)
N8	▷	Thien	(no flag and orange flag)
N7		Ratchini	(no flag)
N6	▷	Saphan Phut	(no flag and orange flag)
N5	◁ ▲ ▷	Rachawongse	(all boats)
N4		Marine (Harbour) Department	(no flag and orange flag)
N3	◁ ▲ ▷	Si Phraya	(all boats)
N2		Wat Muang Kae	(no flag)
N1	▷	Oriental	(no flag and orange flag)
Central	◁ ▲ ▷	Sathorn	(all boats)

▷ All-day	◁ ▲ Rush hour only (Mon–Fri)

Rush-hour no-flag boats stop at all piers (Mon–Fri)

1

filled in, replaced by endless rows of cheap, functional concrete shophouses, high-rises and housing estates, sprawling across a built-up area of over 300 square kilometres. The benefits of Thailand's **economic boom** since the 1980s have been concentrated in Bangkok, attracting migration from all over the country and making the capital ever more dominant: the population, over half of which is under 30 years of age, is now nearly forty times that of the second city, Chiang Mai.

Every aspect of national life is centralized in the city, but the mayor of Bangkok is not granted enough power to deal with the ensuing problems, notably that of **traffic** – which in Bangkok now comprises four-fifths of the nation's automobiles. The Skytrain and the subway have undoubtedly helped, but the competing systems don't intersect properly, and it's left to ingenious, local solutions such as the Khlong Saen Saeb canal boats and side-street motorbike taxis to keep the city moving. And there's precious little chance to escape from the pollution in green space: the city has only around 3 square metres of open space per inhabitant, one of the lowest figure in the world, compared, for example, to London's 38 square metres per person.

Ratanakosin

The only place to start your exploration of Bangkok is **Ratanakosin**, the royal island on the east bank of the Chao Phraya, where the city's most important and extravagant sights are located. When Rama I developed Ratanakosin for his new capital in 1782, after the sacking of Ayutthaya and a temporary stay across the river in Thonburi, he paid tribute to its precursor by imitating Ayutthaya's layout and architecture – he even shipped the building materials downstream from the ruins of the old city. Like Ayutthaya, the new capital was sited for protection beside a river and turned into an artificial island by the construction of defensive canals, with a central **Grand Palace** and adjoining royal temple, **Wat Phra Kaeo**, fronted by an open field, **Sanam Luang**; the Wang Na (Palace of the Second King), now the **National Museum**, was also built at this time. **Wat Pho**, which predates the capital's founding, was further embellished by Rama I's successors, who have consolidated Ratanakosin's pre-eminence by building several grand European-style palaces (now housing government institutions); **Wat Mahathat**, the most important centre of Buddhist learning in Southeast Asia; the National Theatre; the National Gallery; and Thammasat and Silpakorn universities.

Bangkok has expanded eastwards away from the river, leaving the Grand Palace a good 5km from the city's commercial heart, and the royal family has long since moved its main residence to Dusit, but Ratanakosin remains the ceremonial centre of the whole kingdom – so much so that it feels as if it might sink into the boggy ground under the weight of its own mighty edifices. The heavy, stately feel is lightened by traditional shophouses selling herbal medicines, pavement amulet-sellers and student canteens along the riverside road, **Thanon Maharat**; and by Sanam Luang, still used for cremations and royal ceremonies, but also functioning as a popular open park and the hub of the modern city's bus system. Despite containing several of the country's main sights, the area is busy enough in its own right not to have become a swarming tourist zone, and strikes a neat balance between liveliness and grandeur.

ARRIVAL AND DEPARTURE   **RATANAKOSIN**

Ratanakosin is within easy walking distance of Banglamphu, but is best approached from the river, via the **express-boat piers** (see page 137) of Tha Chang (the former bathing place of the royal elephants, which gives access to the Grand Palace) or Tha Thien (for Wat Pho). At the time of writing, however, Tha Thien was being renovated and express boats were stopping on the opposite bank at Wat Arun, leaving you a cross-river ferry ride (or a 5min walk from Tha Chang) to get to Tha Thien. An extension of the **subway** line from Hualamphong is being built (its opening currently proposed for 2019), with a new station, called Sanam Chai, at the Museum of Siam, 5min walk from Wat Pho, 10min from Tha Thien express boat pier and 15min from the entrance to the Grand Palace.

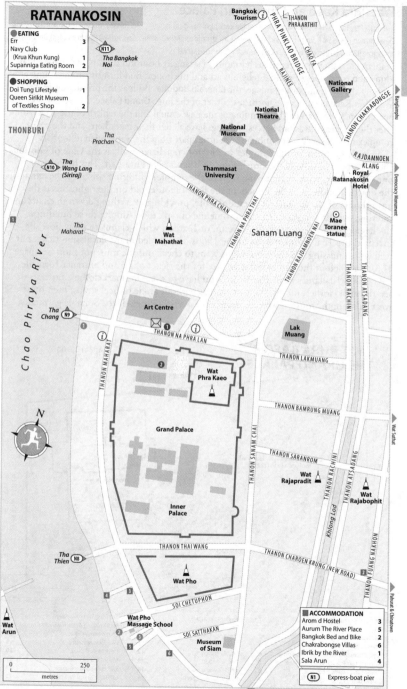

RATANAKOSIN

● EATING

Err	3
Navy Club (Krua Khun Kung)	1
Supanniga Eating Room	2

● SHOPPING

Doi Tung Lifestyle	1
Queen Sirikit Museum of Textiles Shop	2

ACCOMMODATION

Arom d Hostel	3
Aurum The River Place	5
Bangkok Bed and Bike	2
Chakrabongse Villas	6
Ibrik by the River	1
Sala Arun	4

N1 Express-boat pier

Bangkok Tourism

THANON PHRA ARTHIT

PHRA PINKLAO BRIDGE

CHAO FA

RAJINEE

National Gallery

THANON CHAKRABONGSE

Banglamphu

National Theatre

RAJDAMNOEN KLANG

Royal Ratanakosin Hotel

Democracy Monument

N11 Tha Bangkok Noi

THONBURI

Tha Prachan

National Museum

Thammasat University

THANON PHRA CHAN

THANON NA PHRA THAT

Sanam Luang

Mae Toranee statue

THANON RAJDAMNOEN NAI

THANON ATSADANG

THANON RACHINI

N10 Tha Wang Lang (Siriraj)

Tha Maharat

Wat Mahathat

Chao Phraya River

Tha Chang N9

Art Centre

THANON NA PHRA LAN

THANON MAHARAT

Lak Muang

THANON LAKMUANG

Wat Phra Kaeo

Grand Palace

THANON BAMRUNG MUANG

THANON SANAM CHAI

THANON SARANROM

Wat Rajapradit

THANON RACHINI

THANON ATSADANG

Khlong Lod

Wat Rajabophit

Wat Suthat

Inner Palace

THANON THAI WANG

THANON CHAROEN KRUNG (NEW ROAD)

THANON FUANG NAKHON

Pahurat & Chinatown

Tha Thien N8

Wat Pho

SOI CHETUPHON

Wat Pho Massage School

SOI SATTHAKAN

Museum of Siam

Wat Arun

N

0   250
metres

N7 Tha Ratchini

1

Wat Phra Kaeo and the Grand Palace

Thanon Na Phra Lan • Daily 8.30am–4.30pm, last admission 3.30pm (weapons museum, Phra Thinang Amarin Winichai and Dusit Maha Prasat interiors closed Sat & Sun) • B500, including a guide booklet and admission, within 7 days, to Dusit Park (if it's open); 2hr personal audioguide B200, with passport or credit card as deposit • ⦿ palaces.thai.net

Hanging together in a precarious harmony of strangely beautiful colours and shapes, **Wat Phra Kaeo** is the apogee of Thai religious art and the holiest Buddhist site in the country, housing the most important image, the **Emerald Buddha**. Built as the private royal temple, Wat Phra Kaeo occupies the northeast corner of the huge **Grand Palace**, whose official opening in 1785 marked the founding of the new capital and the rebirth of the Thai nation after the Burmese invasion. Successive kings have all left their mark here, and the palace complex now covers 2 acres, though very little apart from the wat is open to tourists.

The only **entrance** to the complex in 2km of crenellated walls is the Gate of Glorious Victory in the middle of the north side, on Thanon Na Phra Lan. This brings you onto a driveway with a tantalizing view of the temple's glittering spires on the left and the dowdy buildings of the Offices of the Royal Household on the right: this is the powerhouse of the kingdom's ceremonial life, providing everything down to chairs and catering, even lending an urn when someone of rank dies. Among these buildings, the hagiographic Queen Sirikit Museum of Textiles, which claims to show how she invented the Thai national dress in the 1960s, is included in the admission ticket but well worth missing, though you might want to check out the museum shop (see page 166). Turn left at the end of the driveway for the ticket office and entrance turnstiles.

As this is Thailand's most sacred site, you have to **dress in smart clothes**: no vests or see-through clothes; no flip-flops or sandals without ankle or heel straps; men must wear full-length trousers, women trousers or over-the-knee skirts. Suitable garments

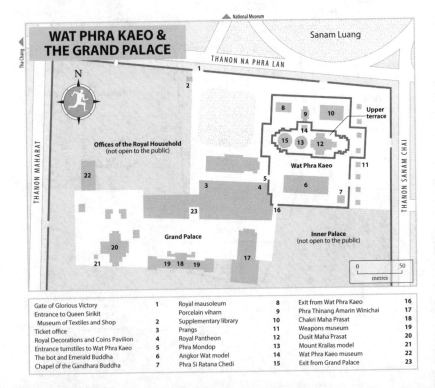

Gate of Glorious Victory	1	Royal mausoleum	8	Exit from Wat Phra Kaeo	16
Entrance to Queen Sirikit Museum of Textiles and Shop	2	Porcelain viharn	9	Phra Thinang Amarin Winichai	17
Ticket office		Supplementary library	10	Chakri Maha Prasat	18
Royal Decorations and Coins Pavilion	4	Prangs	11	Weapons museum	19
Entrance turnstiles to Wat Phra Kaeo	5	Royal Pantheon	12	Dusit Maha Prasat	20
The bot and Emerald Buddha	6	Phra Mondop	13	Mount Krailas model	21
Chapel of the Gandhara Buddha	7	Angkor Wat model	14	Wat Phra Kaeo museum	22
		Phra Si Ratana Chedi	15	Exit from Grand Palace	23

CITY OF ANGELS

When **Rama I** was crowned in 1782, he gave his new capital a grand 43-syllable name to match his ambitious plans for the building of the city. Since then, 21 more syllables have been added. Krungthepmahanakhornbowornrattanakosinmahintarayutthayamahadilokpopnoppar-atratchathaniburiromudomratchaniwetmahasathanamornpimanavatarnsathitsakkathattiyavis-nukamprasit is certified by the *Guinness Book of Records* as the longest place-name in the world, roughly translating as "Great city of angels, the supreme repository of divine jewels, the great land unconquerable, the grand and prominent realm, the royal and delightful capital city full of nine noble gems, the highest royal dwelling and grand palace, the divine shelter and living place of the reincarnated spirits". Fortunately, all Thais refer to the city simply as **Krung Thep**, "City of Angels", though plenty can recite the full name at the drop of a hat. **Bangkok** – "Village of the Plum Olive" – was the name of the original village on the Thonburi side; with remarkable persistence, it has remained in use by foreigners since the time of the French garrison.

can be borrowed from the office to the right just inside the Gate of Glorious Victory (free, deposit of B200 per item).

Wat Phra Kaeo

It makes you laugh with delight to think that anything so fantastic could exist on this sombre earth.
W. Somerset Maugham, The Gentlemen in the Parlour

Entering the temple is like stepping onto a lavishly detailed stage set, from the immaculate flagstones right up to the gaudy roofs. Reinforcing the sense of unreality, the whole compound is surrounded by arcaded walls, decorated with extraordinary murals of scenes from the *Ramayana*. Although it receives hundreds of foreign sightseers and at least as many Thai pilgrims every day, the temple, which has no monks in residence, maintains an unnervingly sanitized look, as if it were built only yesterday.

The approach to the bot

Inside the entrance turnstiles, you're confronted by 6m-tall **yaksha**, gaudy demons from the *Ramayana*, who watch over the Emerald Buddha from every gate of the temple and ward off evil spirits; the king of the demons, green, ten-faced Totsagan (labelled "Tosakanth"), stands to the left of the entrance by the southwest corner of the golden Phra Si Ratana Chedi. Less threatening is the toothless old codger, cast in bronze and sitting on a plinth immediately inside the turnstiles by the back wall of the bot, who represents a Hindu **hermit** credited with inventing yoga and herbal medicine. In front of him is a large grinding stone where previously herbal practitioners could come to grind their ingredients – with enhanced powers, of course. Skirting around the bot, you'll reach its **main entrance** on the eastern side, in front of which stands a cluster of grey **statues**, which have a strong Chinese feel: next to Kuan Im, the Chinese *bodhisattva* of mercy shown holding a bottle of *amritsa* (sacred elixir), are a sturdy pillar topped by a lotus flower, which Bangkok's Chinese community presented to Rama IV during his 27 years as a monk, and two handsome cows which commemorate Rama I's birth in the Year of the Cow. Worshippers make their offerings to the Emerald Buddha at two small, stand-in Buddhas here, where they can look at the main image through the open doors of the bot without messing up its pristine interior with gold leaf, candle wax and joss-stick ash.

The bot and the Emerald Buddha

The **bot**, the largest building of the temple, is one of the few original structures left at Wat Phra Kaeo, though it has been augmented so often it looks like the work of a wildly inspired child. Eight *sema* stones mark the boundary of the consecrated area around the bot, each sheltering in a psychedelic fairy castle, joined by a low wall decorated with Chinese porcelain tiles, which depict delicate landscapes. The walls

1

of the bot itself, sparkling with gilt and coloured glass, are supported by 112 golden garudas (birdmen) holding nagas (serpents), representing the god Indra saving the world by slaying the serpent-cloud that had swallowed up all the water. The symbolism reflects the king's traditional role as a rainmaker.

Of the bot's three doorways, the largest, in the middle, is reserved for the king himself. Inside, a 9m-high pedestal supports the tiny **Emerald Buddha**, a figure whose mystique draws pilgrims from all over Thailand – as well as politicians accused of corruption, who traditionally come here to publicly swear their innocence. Here especially you must act with respect, sitting with your feet pointing away from the Buddha. The spiritual power of the 60cm jadeite image derives from its legendary past. Reputed to have been created by the gods in India, it was discovered when lightning cracked open an ancient chedi in Chiang Rai in the early fifteenth century. The image was then moved around the north, dispensing miracles wherever it went, before being taken to Laos for two hundred years. As it was believed to bring great fortune to its possessor, the future Rama I snatched it back when he captured Vientiane in 1779, installing it at the heart of his new capital as a talisman for king and country.

Seated in the *Dhyana Mudra* (meditation), the Emerald Buddha has three **costumes**, one for each season: the crown and ornaments of an Ayutthayan king for the hot season; a gilt monastic robe for the rainy season, when the monks retreat into the temples; this is augmented with a full-length gold shawl in the cool season. To this day it's the job of the king himself to ceremonially change the Buddha's costumes. The Buddha was granted a new set of these three costumes in 1997: the old set is now in the Wat Phra Kaeo Museum (see page 89) while the two costumes of the new set that are not in use are on display among the blinding glitter of crowns and jewels in the Royal Decorations and Coins Pavilion, which lies between the ticket office and the entrance to Wat Phra Kaeo.

Among the paraphernalia in front of the pedestal sits the tiny, silver **Phra Chai Lang Chang** (Victory Buddha), which Rama I always carried into battle on the back of his elephant for luck and which still plays an important part in coronation ceremonies. Recently covered in gold, it occupies a prestigious spot dead centre, but is obscured by the umbrella of a larger gold Buddha in front. The tallest pair of a dozen standing Buddha images, all made of bronze but encased in gold and raising both hands to dispel fear, are at the front: Rama III dedicated the one on the Emerald Buddha's left to Rama I, the one on his right to Rama II, and Rama IV enshrined relics of the Buddha in their crowns.

The Chapel of the Gandhara Buddha

Near the entrance to the bot, in the southeastern corner of the temple precinct, look out for the exquisite scenes of rice sheaves, fish and turtles painted in gold on blue glass on the doors and windows of the **Chapel of the Gandhara Buddha** (labelled "Hor Phra Kanthara Rat"). The decorations allude to the fertility of the rice fields, as this building was crucial to the old royal rainmaking ritual and is still used during the Royal Ploughing Ceremony (see page 93). Adorning the roof are thousands of nagas, symbolizing water; inside the locked chapel, among the paraphernalia used in the ritual, is kept the Gandhara Buddha, a bronze image in the gesture of calling down the rain with its right hand, while cupping the left to catch it. In times of drought the king would order a week-long rainmaking ceremony to be conducted, during which he was bathed regularly and kept away from the opposite sex while Buddhist monks and Hindu Brahmins chanted continuously.

The Royal Pantheon and minor buildings

On the north side of the bot, the eastern end of the **upper terrace** is taken up with the **Prasat Phra Thep Bidorn**, known as the **Royal Pantheon**, a splendid hash of styles. The pantheon has its roots in the Khmer concept of *devaraja*, or the divinity of kings: inside are bronze and gold statues, precisely life-size, of all the kings since Bangkok became the Thai capital. Constructed by Rama IV, the building is open only on special occasions, such as Chakri Day (April 6), when the dynasty is commemorated, and Coronation Day (May 5).

From here you get the best view of the **royal mausoleum**, the **porcelain viharn** and the **supplementary library** to the north (all of which are closed to tourists, though you can sometimes glimpse Thai Buddhists worshipping in the library), and, running along the east side of the temple, a row of eight bullet-like **prangs**, each of which has a different nasty ceramic colour. Described as "monstrous vegetables" by Somerset Maugham, they represent, from north to south, the Buddha, Buddhist scripture, the monkhood, the nunhood, the Buddhas who attained enlightenment but did not preach, previous emperors, the Buddha in his previous lives and the future Buddha.

The Phra Mondop and Phra Si Ratana Chedi

In the middle of the terrace, dressed in deep-green glass mosaics, the **Phra Mondop** was built by Rama I to house the *Tripitaka*, or Buddhist scripture, which the king had rewritten at Wat Mahathat in 1788, the previous versions having all been lost in the sacking of Ayutthaya. It's famous for the mother-of-pearl cabinet and solid-silver mats inside, but is never open. Four tiny **memorials** at each corner of the mondop show the symbols of each of the nine Chakri kings, from the ancient crown representing Rama I to the present king's discus, while the bronze statues surrounding the memorials portray each king's lucky white elephants, labelled by name and pedigree. A contribution of Rama IV, on the north side of the mondop, is a **scale model of Angkor Wat**, the prodigious Cambodian temple, which during his reign (1851–68) was under Thai rule (apparently, the king had wanted to shift a whole Khmer temple to Bangkok but, fortunately, was dissuaded by his officials). At the western end of the terrace, you can't miss the golden dazzle of the **Phra Si Ratana Chedi**, which Rama IV erected, in imitation of the famous bell-shaped chedis at Ayutthaya's Wat Phra Si Sanphet (see page 218), to enshrine a piece of the Buddha's breastbone.

The murals

Extending for about a kilometre in the arcades that run inside the wat walls, the **murals of the Ramayana** depict every blow of this ancient story of the triumph of good over evil, using the vibrant buildings of the temple itself as backdrops, and setting them off against the subdued colours of richly detailed landscapes. Because of the damaging humidity, none of the original work of Rama I's time survives: maintenance is a never-ending process, so you'll always find an artist working on one of the scenes. The story is told in 178 panels, labelled and numbered in Thai only, starting in the middle of the northern side opposite the porcelain viharn: in the first episode, a hermit, while out ploughing, finds the baby Sita, the heroine, floating in a gold urn on a lotus leaf and brings her to the city. Panel 109 near the gate leading to the palace buildings shows the climax of the story, when Rama, the hero, kills the ten-headed demon Totsagan (Ravana), and the ladies of the enemy city weep at the demon's death. Panel 110 depicts his elaborate funeral procession, and in 113 you can see the funeral fair, with acrobats, sword-jugglers and tightrope-walkers. In between, Sita – Rama's wife – has to walk on fire to prove that she has been faithful during her fourteen years of imprisonment by Totsagan. If you haven't the stamina for the long walk round, you could sneak a look at the end of the story, to the left of the first panel, where Rama holds a victory parade and distributes thank-you gifts.

The palace buildings

The exit in the southwest corner of Wat Phra Kaeo brings you to the palace proper, a vast area of buildings and gardens, of which only the northern edge is on show to the public. Though the king now lives elsewhere, the **Grand Palace** is still used for state receptions and official ceremonies, during which there is no public access to any part of the palace.

1

Phra Maha Monthien

Coming out of the temple compound, you'll first of all see to your right a beautiful Chinese gate covered in innumerable tiny porcelain tiles. Extending in a straight line behind the gate is the **Phra Maha Monthien**, which was the grand residential complex of earlier kings.

Only the **Phra Thinang Amarin Winichai**, the main audience hall at the front of the complex, is open to the public. The supreme court in the era of the absolute monarchy, it nowadays serves as the venue for ceremonies such as the king's birthday speech. Dominating the hall are two gleaming, intricately carved thrones that date from the reign of Rama I: a white umbrella with the full nine tiers owing to a king shelters the front seat, while the unusual *busbok* behind is topped with a spired roof and floats on a boat-shaped base. The rear buildings are still used for the most important part of the elaborate coronation ceremony, and each new king is supposed to spend a night there to show solidarity with his forefathers.

Chakri Maha Prasat

Next door you can admire the facade of the "farang with a Thai crown", as the **Chakri Maha Prasat** is nicknamed. Rama V, whose portrait you can see over its entrance, employed an English architect to design a purely Neoclassical residence, but other members of the royal family prevailed on the king to add the three Thai spires. This used to be the site of the elephant stables: the large red tethering posts are still there and the bronze elephants were installed as a reminder. The building displays the

---

THE RAMAYANA/RAMAKIEN

The **Ramayana** is generally thought to have originated as an oral epic in India, where it appears in numerous dialects. The most famous version is that of the sage Valmiki, who is said to have drawn together the collection of stories as a tribute to his king over two thousand years ago. From India, the *Ramayana* spread to all the Hindu-influenced countries of Southeast Asia and was passed down through the Khmers to Thailand, where as the **Ramakien** it has become the national epic, acting as an affirmation of the Thai monarchy and its divine Hindu links. As a source of inspiration for literature, painting, sculpture and dance-drama, it has acquired the authority of holy writ, providing Thais with moral and practical lessons, while its appearance in the form of films and comic strips shows its huge popular appeal. The version current in Thailand was composed by a committee of poets sponsored by Rama I (all previous Thai texts were lost in the sacking of Ayutthaya in 1767), and runs to three thousand pages – available in an abridged English translation by M.L. Manich Jumsai (see page 781).

The central story of the *Ramayana* concerns **Rama** (in Thai, Phra Ram), son of the king of Ayodhya, and his beautiful wife **Sita**, whose hand he wins by lifting, stringing – and breaking – a magic bow. The couple's adventures begin when they are exiled to the forest, along with Rama's good brother, **Lakshaman** (Phra Lak), by the hero's father under the influence of his evil stepmother. Meanwhile, in the city of Lanka (Longka), the demon king **Ravana** (Totsagan) has conceived a passionate desire for Sita and, disguised as a hermit, sets out to kidnap her. By transforming one of his demon subjects into a beautiful deer, which Rama and Lakshaman go off to hunt, Ravana catches Sita alone and takes her back to Lanka. Rama then wages a long war against the demons of Lanka, into which are woven many battles, spy scenes and diversionary episodes, and eventually kills Ravana and rescues Sita.

The Thai version shows some characteristic differences from the Indian, emphasizing the typically Buddhist virtues of filial obedience and willing renunciation. In addition, Hanuman, the loyal monkey general, is given a much more playful role in the *Ramakien*, with the addition of many episodes which display his cunning and talent for mischief, not to mention his promiscuity. However, the major alteration comes at the end of the story, when Phra Ram doubts Sita's faithfulness after rescuing her from Totsagan. In the Indian story, this ends with Sita being swallowed up by the earth so that she doesn't have to suffer Rama's doubts any more; in the *Ramakien* the ending is a happy one, with Phra Ram and Sita living together happily ever after.

1

THE ROYAL TONSURE CEREMONY

To the right and behind the Dusit Maha Prasat rises a strange model mountain, decorated with fabulous animals and topped by a castle and prang. It represents **Mount Krailas**, the Himalayan home of the Hindu god Shiva (Phra Isuan in Thai), and was built by Rama IV as the site of the **royal tonsure ceremony**, last held here in 1932, just three months before the end of the absolute monarchy. In former times, Thai children generally had shaved heads, except for a tuft or topknot on the crown, which, between the age of eleven and thirteen, was cut in a Hindu initiation rite to welcome adolescence. For the royal children, the rite was an elaborate ceremony that sometimes lasted seven days, culminating with the king's cutting of the hair knot, which was then floated away on the Chao Phraya River. The child was then bathed at the model Krailas, in water representing the original river of the universe flowing down the central mountain.

emblem of the Chakri dynasty on its gable, which has a trident (*ri*) coming out of a *chak* (a discus with a sharpened rim). The only part of the Chakri Maha Prasat open to the public is the ground-floor **weapons museum**, which houses a forgettable display of hooks, pikes and guns.

The Inner Palace

The **Inner Palace** (closed to the public), which used to be the king's harem, lies behind the gate on the left-hand side of the Chakri Maha Prasat. Vividly described in M.R. Kukrit Pramoj's *Si Phaendin* (see page 781), the harem was a town in itself, with shops, law courts and an all-female police force for the huge population: as well as the current queens, the minor wives and their children (including pre-pubescent boys) and servants, this was home to the daughters and consorts of former kings, and the daughters of the aristocracy who attended the harem's finishing school. Today, the Inner Palace houses a school of cooking, fruit-carving and other domestic sciences for well-bred young Thais.

Dusit Maha Prasat

On the western side of the courtyard, the delicately proportioned **Dusit Maha Prasat**, an audience hall built by Rama I, epitomizes traditional Thai architecture. Outside, the soaring tiers of its red, gold and green roof culminate in a gilded *mongkut*, a spire shaped like the king's crown, which symbolizes the 33 Buddhist levels of perfection. Each tier of the roof bears a typical *chofa*, a slender, stylized bird's-head finial, and several *hang hong* (swans' tails), which represent three-headed nagas. Inside, you can still see the original throne, the **Phra Ratcha Banlang Pradap Muk**, a masterpiece of mother-of-pearl inlaid work. When a senior member of the royal family dies, the hall is used for the lying-in-state: the body, embalmed and seated in a huge sealed urn, is placed in the west transept, waiting up to two years for an auspicious day to be cremated.

The Wat Phra Kaeo Museum

In the nineteenth-century Royal Mint in front of the Dusit Maha Prasat, the **Wat Phra Kaeo Museum** houses a mildly interesting collection of artefacts donated to the Emerald Buddha, along with architectural elements rescued from the Grand Palace grounds during restoration in the 1980s. Highlights include the bones of various kings' white elephants, Bronze Age pottery from Ban Chiang (see page 477) and upstairs, the Emerald Buddha's original costumes and two useful scale models of the Grand Palace, one as it is now, the other as it was when first built. Also on the first floor stands the grey stone slab of the Manangasila Seat, where Ramkhamhaeng, the great thirteenth-century king of Sukhothai, is said to have sat and taught his subjects. It was discovered in 1833 by Rama IV during his monkhood and brought to Bangkok, where Rama VI used it as the throne for his coronation.

1

Wat Pho (Wat Phra Chetuphon)

Soi Chetuphon, to the south of the Grand Palace • Daily 8am–6.30pm • B100 • ⓦ watpho.com

Where Wat Phra Kaeo may seem too perfect and shrink-wrapped for some, **Wat Pho** is lively and shambolic, a complex arrangement of lavish structures which jostle with classrooms, basketball courts and a turtle pond. Busloads of tourists shuffle in and out of the **north entrance**, stopping only to gawp at the colossal Reclining Buddha, but you can avoid the worst of the crowds by using the **main entrance** on Soi Chetuphon to explore the huge compound.

Wat Pho is the oldest temple in Bangkok and is older than the city itself, having been founded in the seventeenth century under the name Wat Photaram. Foreigners have stuck to the contraction of this old name, even though Rama I, after enlarging the temple, changed the name in 1801 to **Wat Phra Chetuphon**, which is how it is generally known to Thais. The temple had another major overhaul in 1832, when Rama III built the chapel of the Reclining Buddha, and turned the temple into a public centre of learning by decorating the walls and pillars with inscriptions and diagrams on subjects such as history, literature, animal husbandry and astrology. Dubbed Thailand's first university, the wat is still an important centre for traditional medicine, notably **Thai massage** (see page 91), which is used against all kinds of illnesses, from backaches to viruses.

The eastern courtyard

The main entrance on Soi Chetuphon is one of a series of sixteen monumental gates around the main compound, each guarded by stone **giants**, many of them comic Westerners in wide-brimmed hats – ships that exported rice to China would bring these statues back as ballast.

The entrance brings you into the eastern half of the main complex, where a courtyard of structures radiates from the bot in a disorientating symmetry. To get to the bot, the principal congregation and ordination hall, turn right and cut through the two surrounding cloisters, which are lined with hundreds of Buddha images. The elegant **bot** has beautiful teak doors decorated with mother-of-pearl, showing stories from the *Ramayana* (see page 88) in minute detail. Look out also for the stone bas-reliefs around the base of the bot, which narrate the story of the capture and rescue of Sita from the *Ramayana* in 152 action-packed panels. The plush interior has a well-proportioned altar with ten statues of disciples framing a graceful, Ayutthayan Buddha image, whose base contains some of the remains of Rama I, the founder of Bangkok

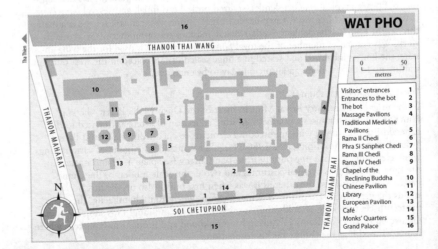

WAT PHO

THANON THAI WANG

Thai Thien

THANON MAHARAT

SOI CHETUPHON

THANON SANAM CHAI

N

Visitors' entrances	1
Entrances to the bot	2
The bot	3
Massage Pavilions	4
Traditional Medicine Pavilions	5
Rama II Chedi	6
Phra Si Sanphet Chedi	7
Rama III Chedi	8
Rama IV Chedi	9
Chapel of the Reclining Buddha	10
Chinese Pavilion	11
Library	12
European Pavilion	13
Café	14
Monks' Quarters	15
Grand Palace	16

0   50
metres

TRADITIONAL MASSAGE AND SPAS IN BANGKOK

Thai massage sessions and courses are held most famously at Wat Pho, while luxurious and indulgent spa and massage treatments are available at many posh hotels across the city, as well as at the following stand-alone places.

Asia Herb Association 20 Soi 4 (Soi Nana Tai), Thanon Sukhumvit ☏ 02 254 8631, ⓦ asiaherb association.com. The speciality here is massage with hot herbal balls (phrakop), which are freshly made each day with ingredients from their organic farm in Khao Yai (B1100/1hr 30min). Also on offer are regular Thai massages, aromatherapy oil massages, foot massages and body scrubs, with several other locations, mostly around Sukhumvit. Daily 9am–2am (last bookings midnight).

Divana Massage and Spa 7 Soi 25, Thanon Sukhumvit ☏ 02 661 6784–5, ⓦ divanaspa.com. Delightful spa serving up Thai massages (B1100/1hr 10min), foot, aromatherapy and herbal massages, as well as facials, body scrubs and other treatments, with several other locations around Bangkok. Mon–Fri 11am–11pm, Sat & Sun 10am–11pm (last bookings 9pm).

Health Land 55/5 Soi 1, Thanon Asok Montri (Sukhumvit Soi 21) ☏ 02 261 1110, ⓦ healthlandspa. com. Excellent Thai (B500/2hr) and other massages, Ayurvedic treatments, facials and body polishes, in swish surroundings, with several other locations around Bangkok. Daily 9am–11pm.

Pimmalai Thanon Sukhumvit, 50m east of BTS On Nut, exit 1, between sois 81 and 83 ☏ 02 742 6452, ⓦ pimmalai.com. In a nice old wooden house, Thai massages (B300/1hr), plus foot, herbal and oil massages, herbal steam treatments, body scrubs, masks and facials. Mon–Fri 9.30am–10pm, Sat & Sun 9.30am–10.30pm.

Ruen Nuad 42 Thanon Convent, near Thanon Sathon Nua ☏ 02 632 2662. Excellent Thai massages (B350/1hr, B650/2hr), as well as aromatherapy and foot massages and packages featuring herbal-ball massages and body scrubs, in an a/c, characterful wooden house, down an alley opposite the BNH Hospital and behind *Naj* restaurant. Daily 10am–9pm.

Wat Pho (see page 90). Excellent massages are available in two a/c buildings on the east side of Wat Pho's main compound; allow 2hr for the full works (B420/hr; foot reflexology massage B420/hr). There are often long queues here, however, so you might be better off heading over to the massage centre's other premises just outside the temple, at 392/33–4 Soi Pen Phat 1, Thanon Maharat (the soi is unmarked but look for signs for the *Riva Arun* hotel; ☏ 02 622 3533 or ☏ 02 622 3550–1, ⓦ watpomassage.com). Here you can also enrol on a 30hr massage training course in English, over five days (B9500), and foot-massage courses for B7500. Daily 8am–6pm.

(Rama IV placed them there so that the public could worship him at the same time as the Buddha).

Back outside the entrance to the double cloister, keep your eyes open for a miniature mountain covered in statues of naked men in tall hats who appear to be gesturing rudely: they are *rishis* (hermits), demonstrating various positions of healing massage. Skirting the southwestern corner of the cloisters, you'll come to two pavilions between the eastern and western courtyards, which display plaques inscribed with the precepts of traditional medicine, as well as anatomical pictures showing the different pressure points and the illnesses that can be cured by massaging them.

The western courtyard

Among the 99 chedis strewn about the grounds, the four **great chedis** in the western courtyard stand out as much for their covering of garish tiles as for their size. The central chedi is the oldest, erected by Rama I to hold the remains of the most sacred Buddha image of Ayutthaya, the Phra Si Sanphet. Later, Rama III built the chedi to the north for the ashes of Rama II and the chedi to the south to hold his own remains; Rama IV built the fourth, with bright blue tiles, though its purpose is uncertain.

In the northwest corner of the courtyard stands the chapel of the **Reclining Buddha**, a 45m-long gilded statue of plaster-covered brick which depicts the Buddha entering Nirvana, a common motif in Buddhist iconography. The chapel is only slightly bigger than the statue – you can't get far enough away to take in anything but a surreal close-up view of the beaming 5m smile. As for the feet, the vast black soles are beautifully

1

inlaid with delicate mother-of-pearl showing the 108 *lakshanas*, or auspicious signs, which distinguish the true Buddha. Along one side of the statue are 108 bowls: putting a coin in each will bring you good luck and a long life.

Museum of Siam

Thanon Sanam Chai • Tues–Sun 10am–6pm • B200 • ☎ 02 225 2777

The excellent **Museum of Siam** is a high-tech, mostly bilingual attraction that occupies the century-old, European-style, former Ministry of Commerce. It looks at what it is to be Thai, with lots of humorous short films and imaginative touches such as shadow-puppet cartoons and war video games. In addition, the museum stages playful temporary exhibitions, which in the past have, for example, let visitors have a go at rice-growing or explored the minds of Thai inventors. Generally, it's great fun for adults and kids, and there's a nice little indoor-outdoor **café-bakery-restaurant** in the grounds. The museum hosts the annual **Noise Market Festival** , usually over a weekend in November (⊕ facebook.com/noisemarketfest), a great little free festival-cum-market of indie music, handicrafts and food.

The museum exhibition kicks off with the prehistory of Southeast Asia, or Suvarnabhumi (Land of Gold) as ancient Indian documents refer to it, and the legendary arrival of Buddhism via missionaries sent by the great Indian emperor, Ashoka (Asoke). Much space is devoted to Ayutthaya, where we learn that during that kingdom's four-hundred-year history, there were no fewer than twenty outbreaks of war with the Burmese states, before the final annihilation in 1767. Beyond this, look out for a fascinating map of Thonburi, King Taksin's new capital between 1768 and 1782, as drawn by a Burmese spy. In the Bangkok period, under the banner of westernization, visitors can wind up cartoon peep-shows and dress up in colonial-style uniform shirts.

Sanam Luang

Sprawling across 30 acres north of the Grand Palace, **Sanam Luang** is one of the last open spaces left in Bangkok, a bare field where residents of the capital gather in the early evening to meet, eat and play. On its western side, spreading around Thammasat University and Wat Mahathat, especially on Sundays, scores of small-time hawkers sell amulets (see page 104), taking advantage of the spiritually auspicious location. In the

---

KITE FLYING

Flying intricate and colourful **kites** is now done mostly for fun in Thailand, but it has its roots in more serious activities. Filled with gunpowder and fitted with long fuses, kites were deployed in the first Thai kingdom at Sukhothai (1240–1438) as machines of war. In the same era, special *ngao* kites, with heads in the shape of bamboo bows, were used in Brahmin rituals: the string of the bow would vibrate in the wind and make a noise to frighten away evil spirits (nowadays noisy kites are still used, though only by farmers, to scare the birds). By the height of the Ayutthayan period (1351–1767) kites had become largely decorative: royal ceremonies were enhanced by fantastically shaped kites, adorned with jingling bells and ornamental lamps.

In the nineteenth century, Rama V, by his enthusiastic lead, popularized kite flying as a wholesome and fashionable recreation. **Contests** are now held all over the country between February and April, when winds are strong enough and farmers traditionally have free time after harvesting the rice. These contests fall into two broad categories: those involving manoeuvrable flat kites, often in the shapes of animals; and those in which the beauty of static display kites is judged. The most popular contest of all, which comes under the first category, matches two teams, one flying star-shaped *chulas*, 2m-high "male" kites, the other flying the smaller, more agile *pakpaos*, diamond-shaped "females". Each team uses its skill and teamwork to ensnare the other's kites and drag them back across a dividing line.

early part of the year, especially in March, the sky is filled with **kite-fighting** contests (see page 92).

The field is also the venue for national ceremonies, such as **royal cremations**, when huge, intricate, wooden *meru* or *phra mane* (funeral pyres) are constructed, representing Mount Meru, the Himalayan centre of the Hindu-Buddhist universe; and the **Ploughing Ceremony**, held in May at a time selected by astrologers to bring good fortune and rain to the coming rice harvest. Revived in 1960 to boost the status of the monarchy during the Cold War, the elaborate Brahmin ceremony is led by an official from the Ministry of Agriculture, who stands in for the king in case the royal power were to be reduced by any failure in the ritual. At the designated time, the official cuts a series of circular furrows with a plough drawn by two white oxen, and scatters rice from the royal experimental crop station at Chitrlada Palace, which has been sprinkled with lustral water by the Brahmin priests of the court. When the ritual is over, spectators rush in to grab handfuls of the rice, which they then plant in their own paddies for good luck.

The lak muang

Thanon Rajdamnoen Nai, southeast corner of Sanam Luang

At 6.54am on April 21, 1782 – the astrologically determined time for the auspicious founding of Bangkok – a pillar containing the city's horoscope was ceremonially driven into the ground opposite the northeast corner of the Grand Palace. This phallic pillar, the **lak muang** – all Thai cities have one, to provide a home for their guardian spirits – was made from a 4m tree trunk carved with a lotus-shaped crown. In the nineteenth century, Rama IV had a new, shorter *lak muang* made, and the two pillars now amicably cohabit in an elegant shrine surrounded by immaculate gardens.

Hundreds of worshippers come every day to pray and offer flowers, particularly childless couples seeking the gift of fertility. In one corner of the gardens you can often see short performances of **classical dancing**, paid for by well-off families when they have a piece of good fortune to celebrate.

Silpakorn University Art Centre

Thanon Na Phra Lan, directly across the road from the entrance to the Grand Palace • Mon–Fri 9am–7pm, Sat 9am–4pm • Free • ☎ 02 623 6115 ext 11418 or 11419, ⓦ www.art-centre.su.ac.th

Housed partly in the throne hall of a palace built during the reign of Rama I, the **Silpakorn University Art Centre** stages regular exhibitions of contemporary art, mostly by former students, teachers, artists-in-residence and national artists. The country's first art school, Silpakorn was founded in 1935 by Professor Silpa Bhirasri, the much-revered, naturalized Italian sculptor; a charming, shady garden along the east wall of the art centre is dotted with his sculptures.

Wat Mahathat

Main entrance on Thanon Maharat, plus a back entrance on Thanon Na Phra That on Sanam Luang

Eighteenth-century **Wat Mahathat** provides a welcome respite from the surrounding tourist hype, and a chance to engage with the eager monks studying at **Mahachulalongkorn Buddhist University** here. As the nation's centre for the Mahanikai monastic sect (where Rama IV spent many years as a monk before becoming king in 1851), and housing one of the two Buddhist universities in Bangkok, the wat buzzes with purpose. It's this activity, and the chance of interaction and participation, rather than any special architectural features, that make a visit so rewarding. The many university-attending monks at the wat are friendly and keen to practise their English, and are more than likely to approach you: diverting topics might range from the poetry of Dylan Thomas to English football results.

1

Vipassana Meditation Centre

Section Five, Wat Mahathat • Practice daily 1–4pm & 6–8pm • Donations welcome • ☎ 02 222 6011 or ☎ 02 222 4981

At the wat's **Vipassana Meditation Centre**, where the monk teachers speak some English, sitting and walking meditation practice, with chanting and dhamma talks, is available to drop-in visitors (there's now a competing "Meditation Study and Retreat Center", nearby in Section One of the wat, but this is less geared towards foreign meditators).

The National Museum

Thanon Na Phra That, northwest corner of Sanam Luang • Wed–Sun 9am–4pm; free guided tours in English, French, German and Japanese Wed & Thurs 9.30am • Currently free due to renovations, usually B200 • ☎ 02 224 1333

The **National Museum** houses a colossal hoard of Thailand's chief artistic riches, ranging from sculptural treasures in the north and south wings, to outlandish funeral chariots and the exquisite Buddhaisawan chapel, as well as sometimes staging worthwhile temporary exhibitions. However, it's currently undergoing a massive, rolling **renovation**: at the time of research, all the decorative objects in the Wang Na and the first floor of the main collection's northern building were inaccessible due to refurbishment, while the Gallery of Thai History was closed for a temporary exhibition.

There's still more than enough on display to make a visit worthwhile, especially if you take one of the free guided tours run by the National Museum Volunteers: they're generally entertaining and their explication of the choicest exhibits provides a good introduction to Thai religion and culture. (The NMV organize interesting lectures and excursions, too; ⊚ mynmv.com.) There's also a museum shop and a café by the ticket office, as well as a simple outdoor restaurant inside the museum grounds, near the west end of the main collection's northern building, which dishes up decent, inexpensive Thai food.

Gallery of Thai History

The first building you come to near the ticket office houses an overview of the authorized history of Thailand, illustrated by some choice artworks plucked from the main collection. Among them is the most famous piece of Srivijaya art, a bronze **Bodhisattva Padmapani** from around the twelfth century found at Chaiya (according to Mahayana Buddhism, a *bodhisattva* is a saint who has postponed his passage into Nirvana to help ordinary believers gain enlightenment). With its pouting face and lithe torso, this image has become the ubiquitous emblem of southern Thailand. Look out also for an elaborate eighth-century **lintel** from Ku Suan Tang, Buriram, which depicts Vishnu (aka Narayana) reclining on the dragon Ananta in the sea of eternity, dreaming up a new universe after the old one has been annihilated in the Hindu cycle of creation and destruction. Out of his navel comes a lotus, and out of this emerges four-headed Brahma, who will put the dream into practice.

This gallery houses a fascinating little archeological gem, too: a black stone **inscription** (see also page 239), credited to King Ramkhamhaeng of Sukhothai, which became the first capital of the Thai nation (c.1278–99) under his rule. Discovered in 1833 by the future Rama IV, Mongkut, it's the oldest extant inscription using the Thai alphabet. This, combined with the description it records of prosperity and piety in Sukhothai's Golden Age, has made the stone a symbol of Thai nationhood. There's recently been much controversy over the stone's origins, arising from the suggestion that it was a fake made by Mongkut, but it seems most likely that it is indeed genuine, and was written partly as a kind of prospectus for Sukhothai, to attract traders and settlers to the underpopulated kingdom.

The main collection: southern building

At the back of the compound, two large modern buildings, flanking an old converted palace, house the museum's **main collection**, kicking off on the ground floor of the **southern building**. Look out here for some historic sculptures from the rest of Asia

RECLINING BUDDHA AT WAT PHO

1

(Room 301), including one of the earliest representations of the Buddha, in the Gandhara style (first to fourth centuries AD). Alexander the Great left a garrison at Gandhara (in modern-day Pakistan), which explains why the image is in the style of Classical Greek sculpture: for example, the *ushnisha*, the supernatural bump on the top of the head, which symbolizes the Buddha's intellectual and spiritual power, is rationalized into a bun of thick, wavy hair.

Upstairs, the **prehistory** room (302) displays axe heads and spear points from Ban Chiang in the northeast of Thailand (see page 477), one of the earliest Bronze Age cultures ever discovered. Alongside are many roughly contemporaneous metal artefacts from Kanchanaburi province, as well as some excellent examples of the developments of Ban Chiang's famous pottery. In the adjacent **Dvaravati** room (303; sixth to eleventh centuries), there are several fine dharmachakras, while the pick of the stone and terracotta Buddhas is a small head in smooth, pink clay from Wat Phra Ngam, Nakhon Pathom, whose downcast eyes and faintly smiling full lips typify the serene look of this era. At the far end of the first floor, you can't miss a voluptuous Javanese statue of elephant-headed Ganesh, Hindu god of wisdom and the arts, which, being the symbol of the Fine Arts Department, is always freshly garlanded. As Ganesh is known as the clearer of obstacles, Hindus always worship him before other gods, so by tradition he has grown fat through getting first choice of the offerings – witness his trunk jammed into a bowl of food in this sculpture.

Room 305 next door is devoted to **Srivijaya** art (roughly seventh to thirteenth centuries), including an interesting *ekamukhalinga* from Nong Wai, Chaiya, a phallic stone lingam, carved with a sweet, almost plaintive bust of Shiva. The rough chronological order of the collection continues back downstairs with an exhibition of **Khmer** and **Lopburi** sculpture (seventh to fourteenth centuries), most notably some dynamic bronze statuettes and stone lintels. Look out for an elaborate eleventh- or twelfth-century lintel from Phanom Rung (Room 308), which depicts Krishna subduing the poisonous serpent, Galiya.

The main collection: northern building

The second half of the survey, in the northern building, begins upstairs with the **Sukhothai** collection (thirteenth to fifteenth centuries; rooms 404–405), which features some typically elegant and sinuous Buddha images, as well as chunky bronzes of Hindu gods and a wide range of ceramics. An ungainly but serene Buddha head, carved from grainy, pink sandstone, represents the **Ayutthaya** style of sculpture (fourteenth to eighteenth centuries; rooms 405–406): the faintest incision of a moustache above the lips betrays the Khmer influences that came to Ayutthaya after its conquest of Angkor. A sumptuous scripture cabinet, showing a cityscape of old Ayutthaya, is a more unusual piece, one of a surviving handful of such carved and painted items of furniture.

Downstairs in the section on **Bangkok** or **Ratanakosin** art (eighteenth century onwards; 407), a small, stiffly realistic standing bronze in the posture of calling down the rain brings you full circle. In his zeal for Western naturalism, Rama V had the statue made in the Gandhara style of the earliest Buddha image displayed in the first room of the museum.

The funeral chariots

To the east of the northern building stands a large garage containing the royal family's fantastically elaborate **funeral chariots**, which are constructed of teak and decorated with lacquer, gold leaf and mirrored glass. Pre-eminent among these is Phra Maha Pichai Ratcharot (the Royal Chariot of Great Victory), built by Rama I in 1796 for carrying the urn at his father's funeral. The 11m-high structure symbolizes heaven on Mount Meru, while the dragons and divinities around the sides – piled in five golden tiers to suggest the flames of the cremation – represent the mythological inhabitants of the mountain's forests. Weighing fourteen tonnes and requiring the pulling power of over two hundred soldiers, the chariot last had an outing in 2017, for the funeral of King Bhumibol (Rama IX).

Wang Na (Palace of the Second King)

The sprawling central building of the compound was originally part of the **Wang Na**, a huge palace stretching across Sanam Luang to Khlong Lod, which housed the "second king", appointed by the reigning monarch as his heir and deputy. When Rama V did away with the office in 1887, he turned the palace into a museum, which now contains a fascinating array of Thai objets d'art and richly decorated musical instruments. The display of rare gold pieces includes a well-preserved armlet taken from the ruined prang of fifteenth-century Wat Ratburana in Ayutthaya, while an intricately carved ivory seat turns out, with gruesome irony, to be a *howdah*, for use on an elephant's back. Among the masks worn by *khon* actors, look out especially for a fierce Hanuman, the white monkey-warrior in the *Ramayana* epic, gleaming with mother-of-pearl. The huge and varied ceramic collection includes some sophisticated pieces from Sukhothai, and nearby there's a riot of mother-of-pearl items, whose flaming rainbow of colours comes from the shell of the turbo snail from the Gulf of Thailand.

The Buddhaisawan chapel

The second-holiest image in Thailand, after the Emerald Buddha, is housed in the **Buddhaisawan chapel**, the vast hall in front of the eastern entrance to the Wang Na. Inside, the fine proportions of the hall, with its ornate coffered ceiling and lacquered window shutters, are enhanced by painted rows of divinities and converted demons, all turned to face the chubby, glowing **Phra Sihing Buddha**, which according to legend was magically created in Sri Lanka in the second century and sent to Sukhothai in the thirteenth century. Like the Emerald Buddha, the image was believed to bring good luck to its owner and was frequently snatched from one northern town to another, until Rama I brought it down from Chiang Mai in 1795 and installed it here in the second king's private chapel. Two other images (in Nakhon Si Thammarat and Chiang Mai) now claim to be the authentic Phra Sihing Buddha, but all three are in fact derived from a lost original – this one is in a fifteenth-century Sukhothai style. It's still much loved by ordinary people and at Thai New Year in April is carried out to the nearby City Hall, where it sits for three days while worshippers sprinkle it with water as a merit-making gesture.

The careful detail and rich, soothing colours of the surrounding two-hundred-year-old **murals** are surprisingly well preserved; the bottom row between the windows narrates the life of the Buddha, beginning in the far right-hand corner with his parents' wedding.

Tamnak Daeng

On the south side of the Buddhaisawan chapel, the gaudily restored **Tamnak Daeng** (Red House) stands out, a large, airy Ayutthaya-style house made of rare golden teak, surmounted by a multi-tiered roof decorated with swan's-tail finials. Originally part of the private quarters of Princess Sri Sudarak, elder sister of Rama I, it was moved from the Grand Palace to the old palace in Thonburi for Queen Sri Suriyen, wife of Rama II; when her son became second king to Rama IV, he dismantled the edifice again and shipped it here to the Wang Na compound. Inside, it's furnished in the style of the early Bangkok period, with some of the beautiful objects that once belonged to Sri Suriyen, a huge, ornately carved box-bed, and the uncommon luxury of an indoor bathroom.

The National Gallery

4 Thanon Chao Fa, across from the National Theatre on the north side of Sanam Luang • Wed–Sun 9am–4pm • B200 • ☎ 02 281 2224, Ⓦ facebook.com/thenationalgallerythailand

If wandering around Bangkok's National Museum doesn't finish you off, the **National Gallery** nearby probably will. In its upstairs gallery, it displays some rather beautiful

1

early twentieth-century temple banners depicting Buddhist subjects, but the permanent collection of modern Thai art downstairs is largely uninspiring and derivative. Its temporary exhibitions can be pretty good, however. The fine old building that houses the gallery is also worth more than a cursory glance – it was constructed in typical early twentieth-century, Neoclassical style, by Carlo Allegri, Rama V's court architect, as the Royal Mint.

Banglamphu and the Democracy Monument area

Immediately north of Ratanakosin, **Banglamphu**'s most notorious attraction is **Thanon Khao San**, a tiny sliver of a road built over a canal in 1892, whose multiple guesthouses and buzzing, budget-minded nightlife have made it an unmissable way-station for travellers through Southeast Asia. There is plenty of cultural interest too, in a medley of idiosyncratic temples within a few blocks of nearby landmark **Democracy Monument**, and in the typical Bangkok neighbourhoods that connect them, many of which still feel charmingly old-fashioned.

ARRIVAL AND DEPARTURE   BANGLAMPHU AND THE DEMOCRACY MONUMENT AREA

By boat Chao Phraya express-boat stops N13 (Phra Arthit), N14 (Rama VIII bridge) and N15 (Thewet) are nearby (see page 139). Banglamphu is also served by public boats along Khlong Saen Saeb to and from their Phan Fah terminus, which are useful for Siam Square and the Skytrain, while Thewet to the north is connected by boat along Khlong Phadung Krung Kasem to Hualamphong Station.

By Skytrain In addition to connecting to the Skytrain via Khlong Saen Saeb boat, the other fast way to get on to the BTS system is to take a taxi from Banglamphu to BTS National Stadium.

By bus Dozens of useful buses serve Banglamphu (see page 98).

Thanon Khao San

At the heart of Banglamphu is the legendary **Thanon Khao San**, almost a caricature of a travellers' centre, its pavements lined with cheap backpackers' fashions, tattooists and hair-braiders. It's a lively, high-energy base: great for shopping and making travel

BANGLAMPHU'S BUS STOPS AND ROUTES

The main bus stops serving Banglamphu are on Thanon Rajdamnoen Klang: with nearly thirty westbound and eastbound routes, you can get just about anywhere in the city from here. But there are some other useful pick-up points in Banglamphu for routes running out of the area. To make things simpler, we've assigned numbers to these **bus stops**, though they are not numbered on the ground. Where there are two stops served by the same buses they share a number. Bus stops are marked on the Banglamphu map (see page 100).

Bus stop 1: Thanon Krung Kasem, north side
#53 (clockwise) to Hualamphong train station
Bus stop 2: Thanon Phra Sumen, south side; and Thanon Phra Arthit, east side
#53 (anticlockwise) to the Grand Palace and Chinatown
Bus stop 3: Thanon Phra Arthit, west side; and Thanon Phra Sumen, north side
#3 to Chatuchak Weekend Market and Northern Bus Terminal
#15 to Jim Thompson's House, Siam Square and Thanon Silom
#53 (clockwise) to Hualamphong train station (change at Bus Stop 1, but same ticket)
Bus stop 4: Thanon Chakrabongse
#3 to Wat Pho, the Museum of Siam and Wongwian Yai train station
#15 to Jim Thompson's House, Siam Square and Thanon Silom

arrangements – though beware the innumerable Khao San scams (see page 62) – and a good place to meet other travellers. It's especially fun at night when young Thais from all over the city gather here to browse the clothes stalls, mingle with the crowds of foreigners and squash into the bars and clubs that have made Khao San a great place to party. Even if you're staying elsewhere, the Khao San area is a cultural curiosity in its own right, a unique and continually evolving expression of global youth culture fuelled by Thai entrepreneurship.

Thanon Phra Arthit and the riverside walkway

Students from nearby Thammasat University inject an arty vibe into the Banglamphu mix, particularly along **Thanon Phra Arthit**, which borders the Chao Phraya River. There's an attractive **riverside walkway** here too, which begins at Phra Pinklao Bridge and takes you past a couple of beautifully restored century-old mansions, currently occupied by Unicef and the UN's FAO; they show their most elegant faces to the river since in their heyday most visitors would have arrived by boat. There are plans to extend the walkway for 6km to the Rama VII Bridge (with a parallel promenade along the Thonburi bank), but for the moment it ends at the whitewashed, renovated hexagonal tower of **Phra Sumen Fortress**, one of fourteen built by Rama I in 1783 to protect the royal island of Ratanakosin – the only other surviving tower, also renovated, is Phra Mahakhan Fortress, next to the Golden Mount. Nowadays there's nothing to see inside the fort, but the area around it has been remodelled as grassy riverside **Santichaiprakarn Park**.

Wat Indraviharn

Thanon Wisut Kasat, about 20min walk north of Thanon Khao San • 10min walk from Chao Phraya express-boat stops N14 and N15

Though it can't match the graceful serenity of Ratanakosin's enormous Reclining Buddha at Wat Pho, Banglamphu has its own super-sized Standing Buddha at **Wat Indraviharn** (also spelt Wat Intharawihan or Wat In), a glittering 32m-high mirror-plated statue of the Buddha bearing an alms bowl. Commissioned by Rama IV in the mid-nineteenth century to enshrine a Buddha relic from Sri Lanka (in the topknot), it's hardly the most elegant of images, but the 30cm-long toenails peep out beneath offertory garlands of fragrant jasmine, and you can get reasonable views of the neighbourhood by climbing the stairways of the supporting tower; when unlocked, the doorways in the upper tower give access to the statue's hollow interior, affording vistas from shoulder level. The rest of the temple compound features the usual amalgam of architectural and spiritual styles, including a Chinese shrine and statues of Ramas IV and V.

Unfortunately, Wat In is an established hangout for **con-artists** (see page 62) offering tourists a tuk-tuk tour of Bangkok for a bargain B20, which invariably features a hard-sell visit to a jewellery shop (see page 169). Avoid all these hassles by hailing a passing metered taxi instead, or by catching one of the dozens of buses that run along Thanon Samsen.

Democracy Monument

The megalithic yellow-tinged wings of **Democracy Monument** (*Anu Sawari Pracha Tippatai*) loom provocatively over Thanon Rajdamnoen Klang, the avenue that connects the Grand Palace and the new royal district of Dusit, and have since their erection in 1939 acted as a focus for pro-democracy rallies. Conceived as a testimony to the ideals that fuelled the 1932 revolution and the changeover to a constitutional monarchy, the monument's positioning between the royal residences is significant, as are its dimensions, which allude to June 24, 2475 BE (1932 AD), the date the system was changed. In the decades since, Thailand's leaders have promulgated numerous

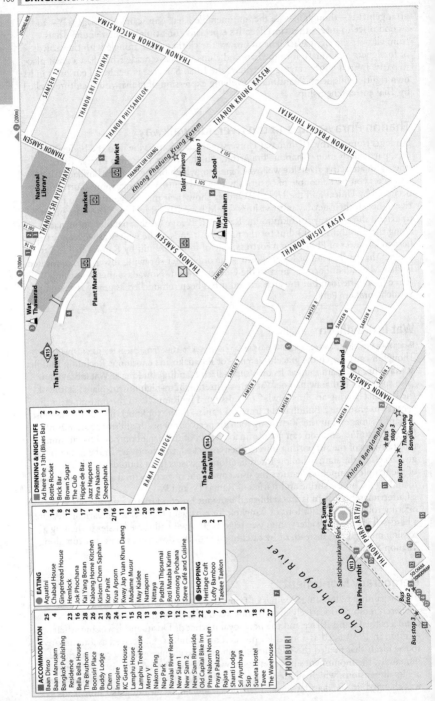

■ ACCOMMODATION	
Baan Dinso	25
Baan Manusarn	4
Bangkok Publishing Residence	23
Bella Bella House	16
The Bhuthorn	28
Boonsiri Place	1
Buddy Lodge	26
Chern	21
Innspire	29
KC Guest House	24
Lamphu House	11
Lamphu Treehouse	15
Merry V	20
Nakorn Ping	13
Nap Park	8
Navalai River Resort	19
New Siam 1	10
New Siam 2	7
New Siam Riverside	14
Old Capital Bike Inn	22
Phra Nakorn Norn Len	6
Praya Palazzo	9
Rajata	3
Shanti Lodge	1
Sri Ayutthaya	5
Ssip	18
Suneta Hostel	2
Tavee	2
The Warehouse	27

● EATING	
Aquatini	9
Chabad House	14
Gingerbread House	8
Hemlock	12
Jok Phochana	6
Kai Yang Boran	17
Kaloong Home Kitchen	1
Kinlom Chom Saphan	4
Kor Panit	2/16
Krua Apsorn	11
Kway Jap Yuan Khun Daeng	15
Madame Musur	10
May Kaidee	20
Nattaporn	13
Nittaya	18
Padthai Thipsamai	19
Roti Mataba Karim	7
Somsong Pochana	5
Steve Café and Cuisine	3

■ DRINKING & NIGHTLIFE	
Ad here the 13th (Blues Bar)	2
Bottle Rocket	3
Brick Bar	7
Brown Sugar	8
The Club	6
Hippie de Bar	5
Jazz Happens	4
Phra Nakorn	9
Sheepshank	1

■ SHOPPING	
Heritage Craft	3
Lofty Bamboo	2
Taekee Taekon	1

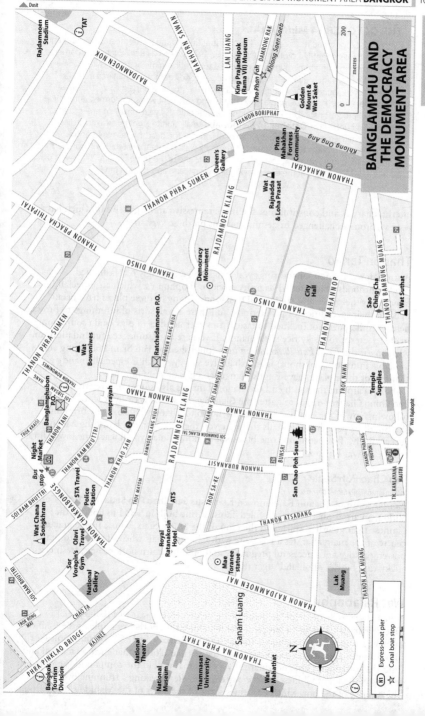

BANGLAMPHU AND THE DEMOCRACY MONUMENT AREA

1

0 ____ 200
metres

Dusit

Rajdamnoen Stadium

TAT

RAJDAMNOEN NOK

NAKHORN SAWAN

LAN LUANG

King Prajadhipok (Rama VII) Museum

DAMRONG RAK

Tha Phan Fah

Golden Mount & Wat Saket

Khlong Saen Saeb

THANON BORIPHAT

Phra Mahakhan Fortress Community

Khlong Ong Ang

THANON PRACHA THIPATAI

THANON PHRA SUMEN

Queen's Gallery

RAJDAMNOEN KLANG

Wat Rajnadda & Loha Prasat

THANON MAHACHAI

Democracy Monument

THANON DINSO

RAJDAMNOEN KLANG

THANON DINSO

City Hall

THANON MAHANNOP

Sao Ching Cha

THANON BAMRUNG MUANG

Wat Suthat

Ratchadamnoen P.O.

DAMNOEN KLANG NEUA

Wat Bowoniwes

THANON PHRA SUMEN

SOI SISAN HANG

THANON BOWONIWES

Banglamphubon P.O.

THANON TANI

TROK KRASI

THANON KHAO SAN

THANON RAM BHUTTRI

Lomprayah

THANON TANAO

THANON TANAO

THANON SOI DAMNOEN KLANG TAI

TROK SIN

Temple Supplies

TROK NAWA

Night Market

Bus stop 4

SOI RAM BHUTTRI

STA Travel

Police Station

THANON CHAKRABONGSE

DAMNOEN KLANG NEUA

RAJDAMNOEN KLANG

SOI DAMNOEN KLANG TAI

THANON BURANASIT

BUNSRI

San Chao Poh Seua

THANON PHRAENG PHUTON

TH. KANLAYANA MAITRI

Wat Rajobolit

Wat Chana Songkhram

Sor Vorapin's Gym

Olavi Travel

National Gallery

TROK MAYOM

ATS

TROK SA-KE

THANON ATSADANG

Royal Ratanakosin Hotel

PHRA PINKLAO BRIDGE

Bangkok Tourism Division

SOI RAM BHUTRI

TROK RONG MAI

CHAO FA

RAJINEE

National Theatre

National Museum

THANON NA PHRA THAT

Thammasat University

Wat Mahathat

Sanam Luang

THANON RAJDAMNOEN NAI

Mae Toranee statue

Lak Muang

THANON LAK MUANG

N

Express-boat pier

Canal boat stop

1

THE OCTOBER 14 MEMORIAL

One of the biggest and most notorious demonstrations around the Democracy Monument was the fateful student-led protest of October 14, 1973, when half a million people gathered on Rajdamnoen Klang to demand an end to the autocratic regime of the so-called "Three Tyrants". It was savagely quashed and turned into a bloody riot that culminated in the death of several hundred protesters at the hands of the police and the military; the Three Tyrants were forced into exile and a new coalition government was soon formed. After three decades of procrastination, the events of this catastrophic day were finally commemorated with the erection of the **October 14 Memorial**, a small granite amphitheatre encircling an elegant modern chedi bearing the names of some of the dead; photographs and a bilingual account of the ten-day protest fill the back wall. The memorial stands in front of the former headquarters of Colonel Narong Kittikachorn, one of the Three Tyrants, 200m west of Democracy Monument, at the corner of Rajdamnoen Klang and Thanon Tanao.

interim charters and constitutions, the more repressive and regressive of which have been vigorously challenged in demonstrations on these very streets.

Thanon Tanao

A stroll down **Thanon Tanao** brings you into some engagingly old-fashioned neighbourhoods of nineteenth-century wooden shophouses, which are especially famous for their specialist **traditional Thai foods**. Many of these places have been making their specialities for generations, and there are all sorts of fun things to browse here, even if you're not inclined to taste, from beef noodles to pigs' brain soup, home-made ice cream to sticky rice with mango. If you are after some recommendations on what to eat the *Good Eats Ratanakosin* map (published by Pan Siam Publishing and available in major bookshops) is an exhaustive survey, which is especially handy given that few of these places have English-language signs or shop numbers.

The area around the south end of Thanon Tanao is also sometimes referred to as **Sao Ching Cha** (see opposite), after the **Giant Swing**, which is easily reached either by following any of the east-bound lanes off Tanao to Thanon Dinso, or by browsing the Buddhist paraphernalia stalls that take you there via Thanon Bamrung Muang. Alternatively, if you continue one block south along Tanao you'll reach the lovely little temple of Wat Rajabophit.

San Chao Poh Seua

Thanon Tanao • Daily 6am–5pm • Free

Not far south of Thanon Rajdamnoen Klang sits **San Chao Poh Seua**, the **Tiger God Shrine**, an atmospheric, incense-filled Taoist shrine built in 1834 to honour the Chinese tiger guardian spirit and the God of the North Stars, whose image graces the centre of the main altar. It's a favourite with Chinese-Thais who come here to pray for power, prestige and successful pregnancy and offer in return pork rashers, fresh eggs, sticky rice, bottles of oil and sugar tigers.

Wat Rajabophit

Thanon Rajabophit, one block south of the Tanao/Bamrung Muang intersection, just to the east of Khlong Lod (see page 83)

One of Bangkok's prettiest temples, **Wat Rajabophit** is another example of the Chinese influence in this neighbourhood. It was built by Rama V in 1869–70 and, typical of him, is unusual in its design, particularly the circular cloister that encloses a chedi and links the rectangular bot and viharn. Every external wall in the compound is covered in the pastel shades of Chinese *bencharong* ceramic tiles, creating a stunning overall effect. The interior of the bot, which enshrines some of the ashes of the Mahidols, the current royal family, looks like a tiny banqueting hall, with gilded Gothic vaults and intricate mother-of-pearl doors.

Thanon Bamrung Muang

Thanon Bamrung Muang, which runs east from Thanon Tanao to Sao Ching Cha and Wat Suthat, was an old elephant trail that, a hundred years ago, became one of the first paved streets in Bangkok. It's famous as the best place in Thailand to buy **Buddhist paraphernalia**, or *sanghapan*, and is well worth a browse. The road is lined with shops selling everything a good Buddhist might need, from household offertory tables to temple umbrellas and cellophane-wrapped Buddha images up to 2m high. They also sell special alms packs for donating to monks, which typically come in saffron-coloured plastic buckets (used by monks for washing their robes, or themselves), and include such necessities as soap, toothpaste, soap powder, toilet roll, candles and incense.

Sao Ching Cha
Midway along Thanon Bamrung Muang, just in front of Wat Suthat

You can't miss the towering, red-painted teak posts of **Sao Ching Cha**, otherwise known as the **Giant Swing**, though it's likely to be swathed in scaffolding until the end of 2018 or so during renovation. Built in 1784, this strange contraption used to be the focal point of a ceremony to honour the Hindu god Shiva's annual visit to earth at Brahmin New Year, in which teams of young men competed to swing up to a height of 25m and grab a suspended bag of gold with their teeth. The act of swinging probably symbolized the rising and setting of the sun, though legend also has it that Shiva and his consort Uma were banned from swinging in heaven because doing so caused cataclysmic floods on earth – prompting Shiva to demand that the practice be continued on earth to ensure moderate rains and bountiful harvests. Accidents were so common with the terrestrial version that it was outlawed in the 1930s.

Wat Suthat
Thanon Bamrung Muang • Daily 9am–4pm • B20

Wat Suthat is one of Thailand's six most important temples, built in the early nineteenth century to house the 8m-high statue of the meditating **Phra Sri Sakyamuni Buddha**, which is said to date from 1361 and was brought all the way down from Wat Mahathat in Sukhothai (see page 241) by river. It now sits on a glittering mosaic dais, which contains some of the ashes of Rama VIII, surrounded with surreal murals that depict the last 24 lives of the Buddha rather than the more usual ten. The encircling galleries contain 156 serenely posed Buddha images, making a nice contrast to the **Chinese statues** dotted around the temple courtyards, most of which were brought over from China during Rama I's reign, as ballast in rice boats; there are some fun character studies among them, including gormless Western sailors and pompous Chinese scholars.

Wat Rajnadda
5min walk east of Democracy Monument, at the point where Rajdamnoen Klang meets Thanon Mahachai • **Loha Prasat** Daily 9am–5pm • B20

Among the assortment of religious buildings known collectively as **Wat Rajnadda**, the most striking is the multi-tiered, castle-like, early nineteenth-century **Loha Prasat**, or "Iron Monastery", whose 37 golden spires represent the 37 virtues necessary for attaining enlightenment. Modelled on a now-defunct Sri Lankan monastery, its tiers are pierced by passageways running north–south and east–west (fifteen in each direction at ground level) with small meditation cells at each point of intersection.

1

AMULETS

To invite good fortune, ward off malevolent spirits and gain protection from physical harm, many Thais wear or carry at least one **amulet** at all times. The most popular images are copies of sacred statues from famous wats, while others show revered monks, kings (Rama V is a favourite) or healers. On the reverse side, a yantra is often inscribed, a combination of letters and figures also designed to deflect evil, sometimes of a very specific nature: protecting your durian orchards from gales, for example, or your tuk-tuk from oncoming traffic. Individually hand-crafted or mass-produced, amulets can be made from bronze, clay, plaster or gold, and some even have sacred ingredients added, such as special herbs, or the ashes of burnt holy texts. But what really determines an amulet's efficacy is its history: where and by whom it was made, who or what it represents and who consecrated it. Stories of miracle cures and lucky escapes also prompt a rush on whatever amulet the survivor was wearing. Monks are often involved in the making of the images and are always called upon to consecrate them – the more charismatic the monk, the more powerful the amulet. Religious authorities take a relaxed view of the amulet industry, despite its anomalous and commercial functions, and proceeds contribute to wat funds and good causes.

The **belief in amulets** is thought to have originated in India, where tiny images were sold to pilgrims who visited the four holy sites associated with the Buddha's life. But not all amulets are Buddhist-related; there's a whole range of other enchanted objects to wear for protection, including tigers' teeth, rose quartz, tamarind seeds, coloured threads and miniature phalluses. Worn around the waist rather than the neck, the phallus amulets provide protection for the genitals as well as being associated with fertility, and are of Hindu origin.

For some people, amulets are not only a vital form of spiritual protection, but valuable **collectors' items** as well. Amulet-collecting mania is something akin to stamp collecting and there are at least half a dozen Thai magazines for collectors, which give histories of certain types, tips on distinguishing between genuine items and fakes, and personal accounts of particularly powerful amulet experiences. The most rewarding places to watch the collectors and browse the wares yourself are at Wat Rajnadda Buddha Centre (see page 104), the biggest amulet market and probably the best place in Bangkok; along "Amulet Alley" on Trok Mahathat, between Wat Mahathat (see page 241) and the river, where streetside vendors will have cheaper examples; and at Chatuchak Weekend Market (see page 128). Prices start as low as B50 and rise into the thousands.

Wat Rajnadda Buddha Centre

In the southeast (Thanon Mahachai) corner of the temple compound, Bangkok's biggest **amulet market**, the **Wat Rajnadda Buddha Centre**, shelters dozens of stalls selling tiny Buddha images of all designs. Alongside these miniature charms are statues of Hindu deities, dolls and carved wooden phalluses, also bought to placate or ward off disgruntled spirits, as well as love potions.

Phra Mahakhan Fortress community

Thanon Mahachai

The **Phra Mahakhan Fortress community**, across the road from Wat Rajnadda, occupies the land between the whitewashed crenellations of the renovated eighteenth-century city walls and Khlong Ong Ang. It's a historic, working-class neighbourhood where some of the fifty or so wooden houses date from the early nineteenth century. It welcomes visitors with informative signboards describing some of its traditions, including massage therapy, fish bladder soup and *likay* popular theatre. The community, however, is campaigning against a redevelopment plan by the Bangkok Metropolitan Administration, who have already knocked down a few of the houses. The land here was granted by Rama III to some of his servants, but as there were no accompanying title deeds, the BMA regards the residents as illegal occupants. In the block of shops on Thanon Mahachai, immediately south of the crenellations, is a famous shop selling *nam op*, a traditional wet-powder fragrance that originated in the royal palace.

Wat Saket

Easiest access is along Thanon Boriphat (the specialist street for custom-carved wooden doors), 5min walk south from the khlong bridge and Phan Fah canal-boat stop at the eastern end of Rajdamnoen Klang

Beautifully illuminated at night, when it seems to float unsupported above the neighbourhood, the gleaming gold chedi of late eighteenth-century **Wat Saket** actually sits atop a structure known as the Golden Mount. Being outside the capital's city walls, the wat initially served as a crematorium and then a dumping ground for sixty thousand plague victims left to the vultures because they couldn't afford funeral pyres. There's no sign of this grim episode at modern-day Wat Saket of course, which these days is a smart, buzzing hive of religious activity at the base of the golden hilltop chedi. Wat Saket hosts an enormous annual **temple fair** in the first week of November, when the mount is illuminated with lanterns and the compound seethes with funfair rides and travelling theatre shows.

The Golden Mount

Daily 7.30am–7pm • B20

The **Golden Mount**, or **Phu Khao Tong**, dates back to the early nineteenth century, when Rama III commissioned a huge chedi to be constructed here, using building materials from the ruined fortresses and walls of the former capital, Ayutthaya. However, the ground proved too soft to support the chedi. The whole thing collapsed into a hill of rubble, but as Buddhist law states that a religious building can never be destroyed, however tumbledown, fifty years later Rama V simply crowned it with the more sensibly sized chedi we see today, in which he placed some relics of the Buddha's teeth from India, donated by the British government. These days the old rubbly base is picturesquely planted with shrubs and shady trees and dotted with memorials and cooling waterfalls. Winding stairways take you up to the chedi terrace and a fine view over Banglamphu and Ratanakosin landmarks, including the golden spires of the Grand Palace, the finely proportioned prangs of Wat Arun across the river beyond and, further upriver, the striking superstructure of the Rama VIII bridge.

The Queen's Gallery

North across Rajdamnoen Klang from Wat Rajnadda, on the corner of Thanon Phra Sumen • Mon, Tues & Thurs–Sun 10am–7pm • B50 • ☎ 02 281 5360–1, ⓦ www.queengallery.org

The privately funded, five-storey **Queen's Gallery** hosts temporary shows of contemporary Thai art, plus the occasional exhibition by foreign artists. It makes a more stimulating alternative to the rather staid National Gallery down the other end of Rajdamnoen Klang, and shelters a bookshop and café.

Chinatown and Pahurat

When the newly crowned Rama I decided to move his capital across to the east bank of the river in 1782, the Chinese community living on the proposed site of his palace was obliged to relocate downriver, to the **Sampeng** area. Two centuries on, **Chinatown** has grown into the country's largest Chinese district, a sprawl of narrow alleyways, temples and shophouses packed between Charoen Krung (New Road) and the river, separated from Ratanakosin by the Indian area of **Pahurat** – famous for its cloth and dressmakers' trimmings – and bordered to the east by **Hualamphong** train station.

The **Chinese influence** on Thai culture and commerce has been significant ever since the first Chinese merchants gained a toehold in Ayutthaya in the fourteenth century. Following centuries of immigration and intermarriage, there is now some Chinese blood in almost every Thai citizen, including the king, and Chinese-Thai business interests play an enormous role in the Thai economy. This is played out

1

at its most frantic in Chinatown, whose real estate is said to be among the most valuable in the country; there are over a hundred gold and jewellery shops along Thanon Yaowarat alone.

For the tourist, Chinatown is chiefly interesting for its **markets**, shophouses, open-fronted warehouses and remnants of colonial-style architecture, though it also harbours a few noteworthy **temples**. A meander through its most interesting neighbourhoods could easily fill up a whole day, allowing for frequent breaks from the thundering traffic and choking fumes. For the most authentic Chinatown experience, it's best to come during the week (before 5pm), as some shops and stalls shut at weekends.

ARRIVAL AND GETTING AROUND   CHINATOWN AND PAHURAT

Arrival The easiest way to reach Chinatown is either by subway to Hualamphong Station, or by Chao Phraya express boat to Tha Rachawongse (Rajawong; N5) at the southern end of Thanon Rajawong. A westward extension of the subway is being built (with a proposed opening in 2019), with new stations at Wat Mangkon Kamalawat and near Pahurat. This part of the city is also well served by buses, with Hualamphong a useful and easily recognized place to disembark. Be warned that buses and taxis may take an unexpectedly circuitous route due to the many and complex one-way systems in Chinatown.

Getting around Orientation in Chinatown can be tricky: the alleys (often known as trok rather than the more usual soi) are extremely narrow, their turn-offs and other road signs often obscured by mounds of merchandise and thronging crowds, and the longer ones can change their names several times. For a detailed tour of the alleys and markets, use *Nancy Chandler's Map of Bangkok* (see page 142); alternatively, ask for help at one of the BMA tourist information booths, either just northwest of the Chinese Arch at the beginning of Thanon Yaowarat, beside Soi 5, or in front of Hualamphong Station (both Mon–Sat 9am–5pm).

Wat Traimit

Thanon Mittaphap Thai-China, just west of Hualamphong train and subway stations (exit 1) • Daily 8am–5pm; exhibitions closed Mon • Golden Buddha only B40; Golden Buddha and exhibitions B100 • ⓦ wattraimitr-withayaram.com

The obvious place to start a Chinatown tour is on its eastern perimeter, with **Wat Traimit** and its famous Golden Buddha. You can see the temple mondop's golden spire from quite a distance, a fitting beacon for the gleaming treasure housed on its third floor, the world's largest solid-gold Buddha. It's an apt attraction for a community so closely linked with the gold trade, even if the image has nothing to do with China's spiritual heritage. A recent attempt has been made to bridge this gap, with the installation of exhibitions of varying interest on the mondop's first and second floors, covering the history of Chinatown and of the iconic Buddha image.

The Golden Buddha

Over 3m tall and weighing five tonnes, the **Golden Buddha** gleams as if coated in liquid metal, seated on a white marble lotus-pad pedestal and surrounded with offerings of lotus flowers. It's a fine example of the curvaceous grace of Sukhothai art, slim-waisted and beautifully proportioned. Cast in the thirteenth century, the image was brought to Bangkok by Rama III, completely encased in stucco – a common ruse to conceal valuable statues from would-be thieves. The disguise was so good that no one guessed what was underneath until 1955 when the image was accidentally knocked in the process of being moved to Wat Traimit, and the stucco cracked to reveal a patch of gold. Just in time for Buddhism's 2500th anniversary, the discovery launched a country-wide craze for tapping away at plaster Buddhas in search of hidden precious metals, but Wat Traimit's is still the most valuable – it is valued, by weight alone, at around US$250 million.

The exhibitions

The exhibition on the making and history of the Golden Buddha, on the second floor of the mondop, is fairly missable, but the **Yaowarat Chinatown Heritage Centre** on the floor below is rather more compelling. Interesting though sanitized, its display boards

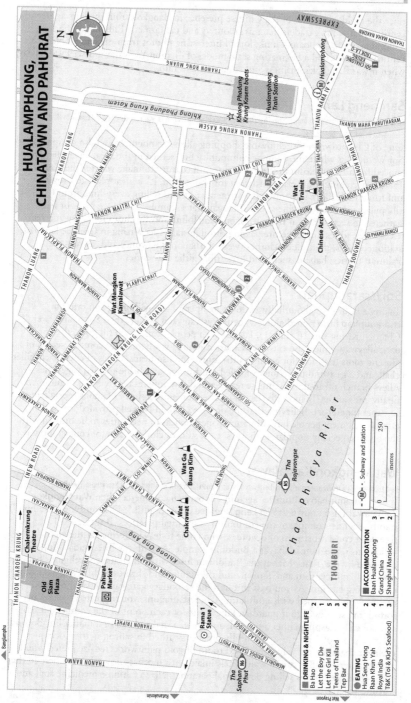

HUALAMPHONG, CHINATOWN AND PAHURAT

THANON LUANG

THANON MANGKON

EXPRESSWAY

THANON MAHA NAKORN

THANON KONG MUANG

SOI CHALONG KRUNG

TRON LA-O

Khlong Phadung Krung Kasem boats

Hualamphong Train Station

☆ Khlong Phadung Krung Kasem

THANON KRUNG KASEM

Hualamphong ⓜ ① Hualamphong

THANON RAMA IV

THANON MAHA PHRUTHARAM

THANON KHAO LAM

THANON MITTAPHAP THAI-CHINA

SOI SUKON 1

THANON MANGKON

THANON MAITRI CHIT

SOI KANA

THANON MAITRI CHIT

JULY 22 CIRCLE

THANON SANTI PHAP

THANON MITRAPHAN

THANON RAMA IV

THANON CHAROEN KRUNG

Wat Traimit

THANON MITTAPHAP THAI-CHINA

SOI CHAROEN PHANIT

THANON TRI MIT

THANON CHAROEN KRUNG

SOI PHANU RANGSI

THANON LUANG

THANON MANGKON

THANON PLAPLACHAI

THANON MANGKON

Wat Mangkon Kamalawat

PLABPLACHAIT

SOI 21

SOI PRADU (TEXAS)

THANON PLAENGNAM

Chinese Arch ①

THANON YAOWARAT

THANON SONGSAWAT

THANON SONGWAT

THANON CHAKRAWAT

THANON CHAOKHAMROP

THANON YAMMARAT SUKHUM

THANON CHAROEN KRUNG (NEW ROAD)

SOI 16

SOI 8

THANON PHADUNGDAO

THANON YAOWAPHANIT

THANON YAOWARAT

SAMPENG LANE (SOI WANIT 1)

THANON SAN (CHAO MAI)

THANON KWANG HIM PAENG

SOI ISSARANUPHAP (SOI 11)

THANON SONGWAT

THANON MAHACHAK

BAMRUNG RAT

THANON CHAROEN KRUNG (NEW ROAD)

THANON RAJAWONG

Chao Phraya River

THANON YAOWARAT

THANON MAHACHAK

SAMPENG LANE (CHAKRAWAT)

THANON

AMA WONG

Wat Ga Buang Kim

NS ◈ Tha Rajavongse

THANON CHAKRAWAT (NEW ROAD)

THANON BOBPHRAT

THANON MAHACHAI

SAMPENG LANE (SOI WANIT 1)

Wat Chakrawat

Khlong Ong Ang

THONBURI

-- ⓜ -- Subway and station

0   250
    metres

THANON CHAROEN KRUNG

Chalermkrung Theatre

THANON BURAPHA

THANON PAHURAT

Old Siam Plaza

Pahurat Market

THANON TRIPHET

THANON BANMO

Rama 1 Statue ⊙

MEMORIAL BRIDGE (SAPHAN PHUT)

PHRA POKLAO BRIDGE (RAMA I)

N6 Tha Saphan Phut

Banglamphu ▲

Rattanakosin ▼

Wat Prayoon ▼

1

trace the rapid expansion of the Chinese presence in Bangkok from the late eighteenth century, first as junk traders, later as labourers and tax farmers. Enhancing the story are a diorama of life on board a junk, lots of interesting photos from the late nineteenth century onwards and a fascinating scale model of Thanon Yaowarat in its 1950s heyday, when it was Bangkok's business and entertainment hub.

Sampeng Lane

From Wat Traimit, walk northwest from the big China Gate roundabout along Thanon Yaowarat, and make a left turn onto Thanon Songsawat to reach Sampeng Lane

One of Chinatown's most enjoyable shopping alleys, **Sampeng Lane** (also signposted as Soi Wanit 1) is where the Chinese community first settled in the area, when they were moved from Ratanakosin in the late eighteenth century to make way for the Grand Palace. Stretching southeast–northwest for about 1km, it's a great place to browse, unfurling itself like a serpentine department store and selling everything from Chinese silk pyjama trousers to selfie sticks at bargain rates. Similar goods are more or less gathered in sections, so at the eastern end you'll find mostly cheap jewellery and hair accessories, for example, before passing through stalls specializing in Chinese lanterns, stationery, toys, then shoes, clothes (west of Thanon Rajawong) and, as you near Pahurat, fabrics, haberdashery and irresistibly girlie accessories.

Soi Issaranuphap

Taking a right turn about halfway down Sampeng Lane will bring you into **Soi Issaranuphap** (also signed along its course as Yaowarat Soi 11, then Soi 6, and later Charoen Krung sois 16 and 21). Packed with people from dawn till dusk, this long, dark alleyway, which also traverses Charoen Krung, is where locals come in search of ginseng roots (essential for good health), quivering fish heads, cubes of cockroach-killer chalk and a gastronome's choice of dried mushrooms and brine-pickled vegetables. Alleys branch off to florid Chinese temples and tiny squares before Soi Issaranuphap finally ends at the Thanon Plaplachai intersection amid a flurry of shops specializing in paper **funeral art**. Believing that the deceased should be well provided for in their afterlife, Chinese people buy miniature paper replicas of necessities to be burned with the body: especially popular are houses, cars, suits of clothing and, of course, money.

Wat Mangkon Kamalawat

Best approached via its dramatic multi-tiered gateway 10m up Thanon Charoen Krung from the Soi Issaranuphap junction

If Soi Issaranuphap epitomizes age-old Chinatown commerce, then **Wat Mangkon Kamalawat** (also known as **Wat Leng Noei Yee** or, in English, "Dragon Flower Temple") stands as a fine example of the community's spiritual practices. Built in 1871, it receives a constant stream of devotees, who come to leave offerings at the altars inside this important Mahayana Buddhist temple. As with the Theravada Buddhism espoused by the Thais, Mahayana Buddhism fuses with other ancient religious beliefs, notably Confucianism and Taoism, and the statues and shrines within Wat Mangkon cover the spectrum. As you pass through the secondary gateway, under the glazed ceramic gables topped with undulating Chinese dragons, you're greeted by a set of forbidding statues of four guardian kings (one for each point of the compass), each symbolically clasping either a parasol, a pagoda, a snake's head or a mandolin. Beyond them, a series of Chinese-style Buddha images swathed in saffron netting occupies the next chamber, a lovely open-sided room of gold paintwork, red-lacquered wood, lattice lanterns and pictorial wall panels inlaid with mother-of-pearl. Elsewhere in the compound are booths selling devotional paraphernalia, a Chinese medicine stall and a fortune-teller.

Wat Ga Buang Kim

From Thanon Rajawong, take a right turn into Thanon Anawong and a further right turn into the narrow, two-pronged Soi Krai

The typical neighbourhood temple of **Wat Ga Buang Kim** is set around a tiny, enclosed courtyard. This particular wat is remarkable for its exquisitely ornamented "vegetarian hall", a one-room shrine with altar centrepiece framed by intricately carved wooden tableaux of gold-painted miniatures arranged as if in sequence, with recognizable characters reappearing in new positions and in different moods. The hall's outer wall is adorned with small tableaux, too, the area around the doorway at the top of the stairs peopled with finely crafted ceramic figurines drawn from Chinese opera stories. The other building in the wat compound is a stage used for Chinese opera performances.

Pahurat

West of Khlong Ong Ang, in the small square south of the intersection of Chakraphet and Pahurat roads, is the area known as **Pahurat**, where Bangkok's sizeable Indian community congregates. Unless you're looking for *bidi* cigarettes or Punjabi sweets, curiosity-shopping is not as rewarding here as in Chinatown, but it's good for all sorts of **fabrics**, from shirting to curtain materials and saree lengths.

Also here, at the Charoen Krung/Thanon Triphet intersection, is **Old Siam Plaza**, a colonial-look shopping centre whose nostalgia theme continues in part inside, with its ground-floor concourse given over to stalls selling traditional, handmade Thai snacks, sweets and sticky desserts. The adjacent Sala Chalermkrung Theatre sometimes stages classical Thai drama for non-Thai speakers (see page 49).

Thonburi

For fifteen years between the fall of Ayutthaya in 1767 and the founding of Bangkok in 1782, the west-bank town of **Thonburi**, across the Chao Phraya from modern-day Bangkok, stood in as the Thai capital, under the rule of General Phraya Taksin. Its time in the spotlight was too brief for the building of the fine monuments and temples that graced earlier capitals at Sukhothai and Ayutthaya, but some of its centuries-old **canals**, which once transported everyone and everything, have endured; it is these and the ways of life that depend on them that constitute Thonburi's main attractions. In some quarters, life on this side of the river still revolves around these khlongs: vendors of food and household goods paddle their boats along the canals that crisscross the residential areas, and canalside factories use them to ferry their wares to the Chao Phraya River artery. Venture onto the backroads just three or four kilometres west of the river and you find yourself surrounded by market gardens and rural homes, with no hint of the throbbing metropolis across on the other bank. The most popular way to explore these old neighbourhoods is by **boat**, but joining a bicycle tour of the older neighbourhoods is also very rewarding (see page 136). Most boat trips also encompass Thonburi's imposing riverside Temple of the Dawn, **Wat Arun**, and often the **Royal Barge Museum** as well, though both are easily visited independently, as are the small but historic temple of **Wat Rakhang** and the surprisingly intriguing and child-friendly cemetery at **Wat Prayoon**.

ARRIVAL AND GETTING AROUND   THONBURI

Arrival Getting to Thonburi is generally just a matter of crossing the river. Either use Phra Pinklao or Memorial/Phra Pokklao bridge, take a cross-river ferry, or hop on one of the express boats, which make several stops on the Thonburi bank. The planned subway extension from Hualamphong, currently scheduled to open in 2019, will include a station near Wat Arun. **Getting around** If you're not exploring Thonburi on a boat tour (see page 110), getting around the district can be complicated as the lack of footbridges over canals means that walking between sights often involves using the heavily trafficked Thanon Arun Amarin. A more convoluted alternative would be to leapfrog your way up or down the river by boat, using the various cross-river ferries that connect the Thonburi bank with the Chao Phraya express-boat stops on the other side.

1

Royal Barge Museum

Soi Wat Dusitaram, north bank of Khlong Bangkok Noi • Daily 9am–5pm • B100, plus B100 for a camera permit • Take the Chao Phraya express boat to Tha Phra Pinklao (N12), or cross-river ferry from under Pinklao Bridge in Banglamphu to Tha Phra Pinklao, then walk up the road 100m and take the first left down Soi Wat Dusitaram; if coming by bus from the Bangkok side (#507, #509 and #511 all cross the river here), get off at the first stop on the Thonburi side, which is at the mouth of Soi Wat Dusitaram – signs from Soi Wat Dusitaram lead you through a jumble of walkways and stilt-houses to the museum (10min)

Since the Ayutthaya era, kings of Thailand have been conveyed along their country's waterways in royal barges. For centuries, these slender, exquisitely elegant, black-and-gold wooden vessels were used on all important royal outings, and even up until 1967 the current king would process down the Chao Phraya to Wat Arun in a flotilla of royal barges at least once a year, on the occasion of Kathin, the annual donation of robes by the laity to the temple at the end of the rainy season. But the boats, some of which are a hundred years old, are becoming quite frail, so **royal barge processions** are now held only every few years to mark special anniversaries. However, if your trip happens to coincide with one of these magnificent events, you shouldn't miss it (see ⓦtourismthailand.org). Fifty or more barges fill the width of the river and stretch for almost 1km, drifting slowly to the measured beat of a drum and the hypnotic strains of ancient boating hymns, chanted by over two thousand oarsmen dressed in luscious brocades.

The most important vessels at the heart of the ceremony are suspended above their docks in the **Royal Barge Museum**, which often features on longtail-boat tours. Up to 50m long and intricately lacquered and gilded all over, they taper at the prow into imposing mythical figures after a design first used by the kings of Ayutthaya. Rama I had the boats copied and, when those fell into disrepair, Rama VI commissioned exact reconstructions, some of which are still in use today. The most important is

EXPLORING THONBURI BY BOAT

The most popular way to explore the sights of Thonburi is by **boat**, taking in Wat Arun and the Royal Barge Museum, then continuing along Thonburi's network of small canals. We've detailed some interesting, fixed-price tours below, but generally it's just a question of turning up at a pier on the Bangkok side of the Chao Phraya and chartering a longtail. At the pier underneath Phra Pinklao Bridge behind the Bangkok Tourism Division head office in Banglamphu, a kiss-me-quick hour-long ride will cost from B700 for two people, while a two-hour trip, taking in an orchid farm deep among the Thonburi canals, costs from B1200. You can also charter your own longtail from Tha Phra Athit, River City shopping centre, Tha Sathorn and other piers.

Many tours include visits to one of Thonburi's two main **floating markets**, both of which are heavily touristed and rather contrived. **Wat Sai** floating market is very small, very commercialized and worth avoiding; **Taling Chan** floating market is also fairly manufactured but more fun, though it only operates on Saturdays and Sundays (roughly 8am–4pm). For a more authentic floating-market experience, consider heading out of Bangkok to Amphawa (see page 184) or Tha Ka (see page 187), in Samut Songkhram province.

Arguably more photogenic, and certainly a lot more genuine than the floating markets, are the individual **floating vendors** who continue to paddle from house to house in Thonburi, touting anything from hot food to plastic buckets. You've a good chance of seeing some of them in action on almost any longtail boat tour on any day of the week, particularly in the morning.

Mitchaopaya Travel Service Tha Chang – on the left at the start of the pier, as you walk in from Thanon Na Phra Lan ☎02 225 6179. Licensed by TAT, offering fixed-price trips along the Thonburi canals of varying durations: in 1hr (B1000/boat, maximum 6 people, or B450/person if you can join in with other people), you'll pass Wat Arun and the Royal Barge Museum without stopping; in 1hr 30min (B1300), you'd have time to stop at either; while in 2hr (B1500)

you'll have time to go right down the back canals on the Thonburi side and visit an orchid farm. On Saturday and Sunday, the 2hr trip takes in Taling Chan floating market. **Pandan Tour** 780/488 Thanon Charoen Krung ☎087 109 8873, ⓦthaicanaltour.com. A selection of full-day tours of the Thonburi canals, the floating markets and beyond on an eco-friendly, natural-gas-powered teak boat, in small groups with a good English-speaking guide, starting from B2300/person, including lunch.

Sri Suphanahongse, which bears the king and is graced by a glittering 5m-high prow representing the golden swan Hamsa, mount of the Hindu god Brahma; constructed from a single piece of timber, it's said to be the largest dugout boat in the world. In front of it floats *Anantanagaraj*, fronted by a magnificent seven-headed naga and bearing a Buddha image. The newest addition to the fleet is *Narai Song Suban*, which was commissioned by King Bhumibol (Rama IX) for his golden jubilee in 1996; it is a copy of the mid-nineteenth-century original and is crowned with a black Vishnu (Narai) astride a garuda figurehead. A display of miniaturized royal barges at the back of the museum re-creates the exact formation of a traditional procession.

Wat Rakhang

Take a cross-river ferry from Tha Chang express-boat pier (near the Grand Palace) to Wat Rakhang's pier, or walk 5min from the Tha Wang Lang express-boat pier, south (left) through the Phrannok pierside market

The charming riverside temple of **Wat Rakhang** (Temple of the Bells) gets its name from the five large bells donated by King Rama I and is notable for the hundreds of smaller chimes that tinkle away under the eaves of the main bot and, more accessibly, in the temple courtyard, where devotees come to strike them and hope for a run of good luck. To be extra certain of having their wishes granted, visitors also buy loaves of bread from the temple stalls and feed the frenzy of fat fish in the Chao Phraya River below. Behind the bot stands an attractive eighteenth-century wooden *ho trai* (scripture library) that still boasts some original murals on the wooden panels inside, as well as exquisitely renovated gold-leaf paintwork on the window shutters and pillars.

Walking to Wat Rakhang from the Tha Wang Lang express-boat pier, you'll pass through the enjoyable **Phrannok pierside market**, which is good for cheap clothes and tempting home-made snacks, especially sweet ones.

Wat Arun

Daily 8am–6pm • B50 • ⓦ watarun.org • Take the cross-river ferry from the pier adjacent to the Chao Phraya express-boat pier at Tha Thien (at the time of research, the Chao Phraya express-boat pier at Tha Thien was under renovation – for how long, it's not clear – and orange- and no-flag express boats were stopping instead at Wat Arun itself, across the river)

Almost directly across the river from Wat Pho rises the enormous, gleamingly restored five-spired prang of **Wat Arun**, the Temple of Dawn, probably Bangkok's most memorable landmark and familiar as the silhouette used in the TAT logo. It looks particularly impressive from the river as you head downstream from the Grand Palace towards the *Oriental Hotel*, but is ornate enough to be well worth stopping off for a closer look.

A wat has occupied this site since the Ayutthaya period, but only in 1768 did it become known as the Temple of Dawn – when General Phraya Taksin reputedly reached his new capital at the break of day. The temple served as his royal chapel and housed the recaptured Emerald Buddha for several years until the image was moved to Wat Phra Kaeo in 1785. Despite losing its special status after the relocation, Wat Arun continued to be revered, and its corncob prang was reconstructed and enlarged to its present height of 81m by Rama II and Rama III.

The prang that you see today is classic Ayutthayan style, built as a representation of Mount Meru, the home of the gods in Khmer cosmology. Both the **central prang** and the four minor ones that encircle it are studded all over with bits of broken porcelain, ceramic shards and tiny bowls that have been fashioned into an amazing array of polychromatic flowers. The statues of mythical *yaksha* demons and half-bird, half-human *kinnari* that support the different levels are similarly decorated. The crockery probably came from China, possibly from commercial shipments that were damaged at sea or used as ballast, and the overall effect is highly decorative and far more subtle than the dazzling glass mosaics that clad most wat buildings. On the first terrace, the

1

mondops at each cardinal point contain statues of the Buddha at birth (north), in meditation (east), preaching his first sermon (south) and entering Nirvana (west). The second platform surrounds the base of the prang proper, whose closed entranceways are guarded by four statues of the Hindu god Indra on his three-headed elephant Erawan. In the niches of the smaller prangs stand statues of Phra Pai, the god of the wind, on horseback.

Wat Prayoon

Off Thanon Pracha Thipok, 3min walk from Memorial Bridge; though on the Thonburi bank, it's easiest to reach from the Bangkok side, by walking over Memorial Bridge from the express ferry stop at Tha Saphan Phut (N6)

Just west of the Thonburi approach to Memorial Bridge, the unusual **Khao Mor cemetery** makes an unexpectedly enjoyable place to take the kids, with its miniaturized shrines and resident turtles. Its dollshouse-sized chedis and shrines are set on an artificial hillock, which was constructed by Rama III to replicate the pleasing shapes made by dripping candle wax; it's the most famous *khao mor* (miniature mountain) in Bangkok, an art form that's been practised in Thailand since the early eighteenth century. Wedged in among the grottoes, caverns and ledges of this uneven mass are numerous memorials to the departed, forming a not-at-all sombre gallery of different styles, from traditional Thai chedis, bots and prangs to more foreign designs like the tiny Wild West house complete with cacti at the front door. Turtles fill the pond surrounding the mound and you can feed them with the bags of fruit and bread sold nearby. The cemetery is part of **Wat Prayoon** (officially Wat Prayurawongsawat) but located in a separate compound on the southeast side of the wat.

Memorial Bridge

It wasn't until 1932 that Thonburi was linked to Bangkok proper by the **Memorial Bridge**, or **Saphan Phut**, constructed by English company Dorman Long who also built the Sydney Harbour Bridge and Newcastle upon Tyne's Tyne Bridge. It commemorates the hundred and fiftieth anniversary of the foundation of the Chakri dynasty and of Bangkok, and is dedicated to Rama I (or Phra Buddha Yodfa, to give him his official title), whose bronze statue sits at the Bangkok approach. It proved to be such a crucial river-crossing that the bridge has since been supplemented by the adjacent twin-track **Saphan Phra Pokklao**.

Dusit

Connected to Ratanakosin via the boulevards of Rajdamnoen Klang and Rajdamnoen Nok, the spacious, leafy area known as **Dusit** has been a royal district since the reign of Rama V, King Chulalongkorn (1860–1910). The first Thai monarch to visit Europe, Rama V returned with radical plans for the modernization of his capital, the fruits of which are most visible in Dusit, notably at **Vimanmek Palace** and **Wat Benjamabophit**, the so-called "Marble Temple". Even now, **Rama V** still commands a loyal following and the statue of him, helmeted and on horseback, which stands in Royal Plaza at the Thanon U-Thong Nai/Thanon Sri Ayutthaya crossroads, is presented with offerings every week and is also the focus of celebrations on Chulalongkorn Day (Oct 23). On December 2, Dusit is also the venue for the spectacular annual **Trooping the Colour**, when hundreds of magnificently uniformed Royal Guards demonstrate their allegiance to the king by parading around Royal Plaza. Across from Chitrlada Palace, **Dusit Zoo** makes a pleasant enough place to take the kids.

Today, the Dusit area retains its European feel, and much of the country's decision-making goes on behind the high fences and impressive facades along its tree-lined avenues:

the building that houses the National Parliament is here, as is Government House and the king's residence, Amporn Palace, while the Queen Mother's home, Chitrlada Palace, occupies the eastern edge of the area. Normally a calm, stately district, in both 2008 and 2013 Dusit became the focus of **mass anti-government protests** by royalist yellow-shirts, who occupied Thanon Rajdamnoen Nok for several months on both occasions, creating a heavily defended temporary village in this most refined of neighbourhoods.

ARRIVAL AND DEPARTURE DUSIT

By bus From Banglamphu, you can get to Dusit by taking the #70 (non-expressway) bus from Rajdamnoen Klang and getting off near the Rama V statue for Wat Benjamabophit, or outside the zoo and Elephant Museum on Thanon U-Thong Nai. From downtown Bangkok, easiest access is by bus from the Skytrain stop at Victory Monument; there are many services from here, including #28.

By boat From the express-boat pier at Tha Thewet, it's about a 30min walk to Dusit Park, the zoo or Wat Benjamabophit. There's also a pier near the Thanon Nakhorn Sawan bridge on the Khlong Phadung Krung Kasem boat line that's handy for Wat Benjamabophit.

Dusit Park

Main entrance on Thanon Rajwithi, with another ticket gate opposite Dusit Zoo on Thanon U-Thong Nai • Closed for renovation at the time of writing

The outstanding feature of what's known as **Dusit Park** is the breezy, elegant **Vimanmek Palace**, which was originally built by Rama V as a summer retreat on Ko Si Chang in 1868; however, he realized that the palace was strategically too vulnerable, after the French briefly invaded the island in the 1890s, and had it transported here bit by bit in 1901. Among a dozen other specialist collections in Dusit Park, which include antique textiles, royal photographs, royal ceremonial paraphernalia and antique clocks, housed in handsome, pastel-painted, former royal residences, the most interesting are the Support Museum and Elephant Museum. Note that the same **dress rules** apply here as to the Grand Palace (see page 84), though T-shirts and sarongs are for sale for those who do not pass muster.

Vimanmek Palace

Built almost entirely of golden teak without a single nail, the coffee-coloured, L-shaped **Vimanmek Palace** is encircled by delicate latticework verandas that look out onto well-kept lawns, flower gardens and lotus ponds. Not surprisingly, this "Celestial Residence" soon became Rama V's favourite palace, and he and his enormous retinue of officials, concubines and children stayed here for lengthy periods between 1902 and 1906. All of Vimanmek's 81 rooms were out of bounds to male visitors, except for the king's own apartments in the octagonal tower, which were entered by a separate staircase.

On display inside is Rama V's collection of **artefacts** from all over the world, including *bencharong* ceramics, European furniture and bejewelled Thai betel-nut sets. Considered progressive in his day, Rama V introduced many newfangled ideas to Thailand: the country's first indoor bathroom is here, as is the earliest typewriter with Thai characters, and some of the first portrait paintings – portraiture had until then been seen as a way of stealing part of the sitter's soul.

The Support Museum

Immediately behind (to the east of) Vimanmek Palace, Dusit Park

The **Support Museum** is housed in a very pretty hundred-year-old building, the Abhisek Dusit Throne Hall, which was formerly used for meetings and banquets. It showcases the exquisite handicrafts produced under the Queen Mother's charity project, Support, which works to revitalize traditional Thai arts and crafts. Outstanding exhibits include a collection of handbags, baskets and pots woven from the *lipao* fern that grows wild in southern Thailand; jewellery and figurines inlaid with the iridescent wings of beetles; gold and silver nielloware; and lengths of intricately woven silk from the northeast.

1

THE ROYAL WHITE ELEPHANTS

In Thailand, the most revered of all elephants are the so-called **white elephants** – actually tawny brown albinos – which are considered so sacred that they all, whether wild or captive, belong to the king by law. Their special status originates from Buddhist mythology, which tells how the previously barren Queen Maya became pregnant with the future Buddha after dreaming one night that a white elephant had entered her womb. The thirteenth-century King Ramkhamhaeng of Sukhothai adopted the beast as a symbol of the great and the divine, decreeing that a Thai king's greatness should be measured by the number of white elephants he owns. A white elephant appeared on the Thai national flag until 1917, and the last king, Rama IX, had eleven white elephants, the largest royal collection to date.

Before an elephant can be granted official "white elephant" status, it has to pass a stringent assessment of its physical and behavioural **characteristics**. Key qualities include a paleness of seven crucial areas – eyes, nails, palate, hair, outer edges of the ears, tail and testicles – and an all-round genteel demeanour, manifested, for instance, in the way in which it cleans its food before eating, or in a tendency to sleep in a kneeling position. Tradition holds that an elaborate ceremony should take place every time a new white elephant is presented to the king, with the animal paraded with great pomp from its place of capture to Bangkok, before being anointed with holy water in front of an audience of priests and dignitaries. Rama IX, however, called time on this exorbitantly expensive ritual, and the royal white elephants now live in less luxurious, rural accommodation under the care of the Thai Elephant Conservation Centre (see page 313).

The expression "white elephant" probably derives from the legend that the kings used to present certain troublesome noblemen with one of these exotic creatures. The animal required expensive attention but, being royal, could not be put to work in order to pay for its upkeep.

Chang Ton Royal Elephant National Museum

Just behind (to the east of) the Support Museum, inside the Thanon U-Thong Nai entrance to Dusit Park

These two whitewashed buildings once served as the stables for the king's white elephants. Now that the sacred pachyderms have been relocated, the stables have been turned into the **Royal Elephant National Museum**. Inside you'll find some interesting pieces of elephant paraphernalia, including sacred ropes, mahouts' amulets and magic formulae, as well as photos of the all-important ceremony in which a white elephant is granted royal status (see page 114).

Dusit Zoo (Khao Din)

Entrances on Thanon Rajwithi, on Thanon U-Thong Nai across from the Elephant Museum in Dusit Park, and on Thanon Rama V, within walking distance of Wat Benjamabophit • Daily 8am–6pm • B150 • ⓦ dusitzoo.org

Dusit Zoo, also known as **Khao Din**, was once part of the Chitrlada Palace gardens (and may become so again, with tentative plans to move the zoo much further out into the suburbs recently revealed). All the usual suspects are here in the zoo, including big cats, elephants, orang-utans, chimpanzees and a reptile house, but the enclosures are pretty basic. However, it's a reasonable place for kids to let off steam, with plenty of shade, a full complement of English-language signs, a lake with pedalos, tram rides and lots of food stalls and cafés.

Wat Benjamabophit

Corner of Thanon Sri Ayutthaya and Thanon Rama V: 200m south of the zoo's east entrance, or about 600m from Vimanmek's U-Thong Nai gate • Daily 7am–6pm • B20 • ⓦ facebook.com/watbencha

Wat Benjamabophit (aka Wat Ben) is a fascinating fusion of classical Thai and nineteenth-century European design, which features on the front of five-baht coins. The Carrara-marble walls of its bot – hence the tourist tag "**The Marble Temple**" – are pierced by unusual stained-glass windows, neo-Gothic in style but depicting figures from Thai mythology. Rama V commissioned the temple in 1899, at a time when he was keen to show the major regional powers, Britain and France, that Thailand was *siwilai* (civilized), in order to baulk their usual excuse for colonizing. The temple's sema stones are a telling example of the compromises involved: they're usually prominent markers of the bot's sacred area, but here they're hard to spot, decorative and almost apologetic – look for the two small, stone lotus buds at the front of the bot on top of the white, Italianate balustrade. Inside the unusually cruciform bot, a fine replica of the highly revered Phra Buddha Chinnarat image of Phitsanulok contains some of Rama V's bones. The courtyard behind the bot houses a gallery of Buddha images from all over Asia, set up by Rama V as an overview of different representations of the Buddha.

Wat Benjamabophit is one of the best temples in Bangkok to see religious **festivals** and rituals. Whereas monks elsewhere tend to go out on the streets every morning in search of alms, at the Marble Temple the ritual is reversed, and merit-makers come to them. Between about 5.30 and 7 or 7.30am, the monks line up on Thanon Nakhon Pathom, their bowls ready to receive donations of curry and rice, lotus buds, incense, even toilet paper and Coca-Cola; the demure row of saffron-robed monks is a sight that's well worth getting up early for. The evening candlelight processions around the bot during the Buddhist festivals of Maha Puja (in Feb) and Visakha Puja (in May) are among the most entrancing in the country.

Museum of Floral Culture

315 Yaek Soi Ongkarak 13 (continuation northwards of Thanon Nakhon Ratchasima), Soi 28, Thanon Samsen • Tues–Sun 10am–6pm • B150 including 1hr guided tour • ☎ 02 669 3633–4, ⓦ floralmuseum.com • 20min walk (northeast), or a motorcycle-taxi ride, from Tha Payap (N18) express-boat pier, served by orange- and no-flag boats

Said to be the only one of its kind in the world, the **Museum of Floral Culture** has been recently opened by the renowned floral artist, Sakul Intakul. The terms are deliberately generalized here, as this is about not only flower arranging, but so much more: floral designs and uses in Thailand and other Asian cultures. Guides will lead you around the beautiful garden and the century-old, colonial-style, teak mansion, where the diverse exhibits cover temple offerings of flowers, sketches of some of Khun Sakul's most famous designs and floral artefacts from his travels around Asia. There's a lovely tea shop on one of the verandas (which opens as a restaurant on weekend evenings, serving flower-inspired seven-course menus), and the museum holds occasional floral workshops for adults and children.

Downtown Bangkok

Extending east from the main rail line and south to Thanon Sathorn and beyond, **downtown Bangkok** is central to the colossal expanse of Bangkok as a whole, but rather peripheral in a sightseer's perception of the city. In this modern high-rise area, you'll find the main shopping centres around **Siam Square**, though don't come looking for an elegant commercial piazza here: the "square" is in fact a grid of small streets, sheltering trendy fashion shops, cinemas and inexpensive restaurants. It lies to the southeast of **Pathumwan intersection**, the junction of Thanon Rama I (in Thai, "Thanon Phra Ram Neung") and Thanon Phrayathai, and the name is applied freely to the surrounding area. Further east, you'll find yet more shopping malls around the noisy and glittering **Erawan Shrine**, where Rama I becomes Thanon Ploenchit, an intersection known as **Ratchaprasong**. It was here that the opposition redshirts set up a fortified camp for several months in early 2010, before the Democrat Party government sent in the troops, leading to the deaths of 91 people. It's possible to stroll in peace above the cracked pavements, noise and fumes of Thanon Rama I, by using the elevated **walkway** that runs beneath the Skytrain lines all the way from the Siam Paragon shopping centre to the Erawan Shrine (further progress is blocked by Central and Chitlom Skytrain stations). East of Ratchaprasong, you pass under the expressway flyover and enter the farang hotel, shopping and entertainment quarter of **Thanon Sukhumvit**.

1

The area south of Thanon Rama I is dominated by Thailand's most prestigious centre of higher learning, Chulalongkorn University, and the green expanse of **Lumphini Park**. Thanon Rama IV (in Thai "Thanon Phra Ram Sii") then marks another change of character, with the high-rise, American-style boulevard of **Thanon Silom**, the heart of the financial district, extending from here to the river. Alongside the smoked-glass banks and offices, and opposite Convent Road, site of Bangkok's Carmelite nunnery, lies the dark heart of Bangkok nightlife, **Patpong**.

Surprisingly, among downtown's vast expanse of skyscraping concrete, the main attractions for visitors are four attractive museums housed in historic teak houses: **Jim Thompson's House**, the **Ban Kamthieng**, the **Suan Pakkad Palace Museum** and **M.R. Kukrit's Heritage Home**. The area's other tourist highlight is **Siam Ocean World**, a high-tech aquarium that both kids and adults can enjoy.

ARRIVAL AND DEPARTURE   **DOWNTOWN BANGKOK**

By Skytrain and subway All of the sights reviewed here are within walking range of a Skytrain station; some are also served by the subway.

By boat The fastest way to head downtown from Banglamphu is by public boat along Khlong Saen Saeb,

beginning near Democracy Monument. A slower but much more scenic route (and during rush hours, possibly quicker than a bus from Banglamphu downtown) is to take an express boat downriver, then change onto the Skytrain at BTS Saphan Taksin.

Victory Monument

Northern downtown is traversed by several major thoroughfares, including the original road to the north, Thanon Phaholyothin, which runs past the weekend market and doesn't stop until it gets to the border with Myanmar at Mae Sai, 1005km away – though it's now more commonly known as Highway 1, at least in between towns. The start of Phaholyothin is marked by the stone obelisk of **Victory Monument** (*Anu Sawari Chaisamoraphum*, or just *Anu Sawari*), which can be seen most spectacularly from Skytrains as they snake their way round it. It was erected after the Indo-Chinese War of 1940–41, when Thailand pinched back some territory in Laos and Cambodia while the French government was otherwise occupied in World War II, but nowadays it commemorates all of Thailand's past military glories.

Suan Pakkad Palace Museum

352–4 Thanon Sri Ayutthaya • Daily 9am–4pm • B100 • ☎ 02 246 1775–6 ext 229, ⊕ suanpakkad.com • 5min walk from BTS Phaya Thai

The **Suan Pakkad Palace Museum** stands on what was once a cabbage patch (*suan pakkad*) but is now one of the finest gardens in Bangkok. Most of this private collection of beautiful Thai objects from all periods is displayed in lovely traditional wooden houses on stilts, which were transported to Bangkok from various parts of the country.

In House no. 5, as well as in the modern Chumbhot-Pantip Center of Arts in the palace grounds, you'll find a very good collection of elegant, whorled pottery and bronze jewellery, axe- and spearheads, which the former owner of Suan Pakkad Palace, Princess Chumbhot, excavated from tombs at Ban Chiang, the major Bronze Age settlement in the northeast (see page 477). Scattered around the rest of the museum are some fine ceramics, notably celadon and bencharong; attractive Thai and Khmer religious sculptures; an extensive collection of colourful papier-mâché *khon* masks; beautiful betel-nut sets (see page 322); an impressive display of traditional musical instruments including beautiful xylophones (*ranat ek*) inlaid with mother-of-pearl and ivory; and monks' elegant ceremonial fans.

The Lacquer Pavilion

The highlight of Suan Pakkad is the **Lacquer Pavilion**, across the reedy pond at the back of the grounds. Set on stilts, the pavilion is actually an amalgam of two eighteenth-

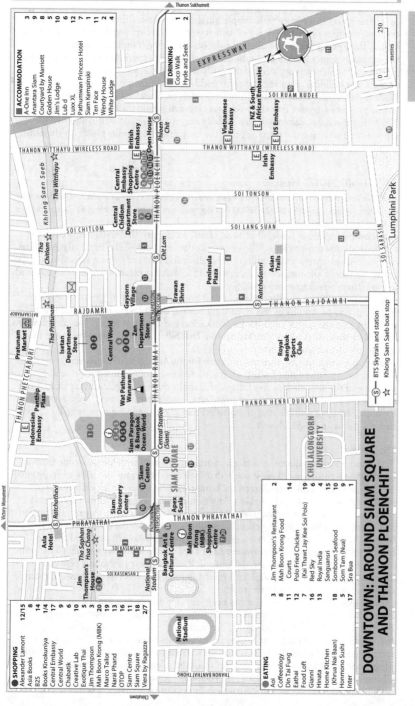

DOWNTOWN: AROUND SIAM SQUARE AND THANON PLOENCHIT

1

or late seventeenth-century teak temple buildings, a *ho trai* (library) and a *ho khien* (writing room), one inside the other, which were found between Ayutthaya and Bang Pa-In. The interior walls are beautifully decorated with gilt on black lacquer: the upper panels depict the life of the Buddha while the lower ones show scenes from the *Ramayana*. Look out especially for the grisly details in the tableau on the back wall of the inner building, showing the earth goddess drowning the evil forces of Mara. Underneath are depicted some European dandies on horseback, probably merchants, whose presence suggests that the work was executed before the fall of Ayutthaya in 1767. The carefully observed details of daily life and nature are skilful and lively, especially considering the restraints that the lacquering technique places on the artist, who has no opportunity for corrections or touching up.

Jim Thompson's House

Just off Siam Square at the north end of Soi Kasemsan 2, Thanon Rama I • Daily from 9am, viewing on frequent 30–40min guided tours, last tour 6pm; shop 9am–8pm • B150 • ☎ 02 216 7368, ⓦ jimthompsonhouse.com • BTS National Stadium, or via a canalside path from the Khlong Saen Saeb pier at Saphan Hua Chang

Jim Thompson's House is a kind of Ideal Home in elegant Thai style, and a peaceful refuge from downtown chaos. The house was the residence of the legendary American adventurer, entrepreneur, art collector and all-round character whose mysterious disappearance in the jungles of Malaysia in 1967 has made him even more of a legend among Thailand's farang community.

Apart from putting together this beautiful home, completed in 1959, Thompson's most concrete contribution was to turn traditional silk-weaving in Thailand from a dying art into the highly successful international industry it is today. The complex now includes a **shop**, part of the Jim Thompson Thai Silk Company chain (see page 119), and an excellent **bar-restaurant** (see page 154).

Above the shop, the **Jim Thompson Center for the Arts** (ⓦ jimthompsonartcenter.org) is a fascinating gallery that hosts both traditional and modern temporary exhibitions on textiles and the arts, such as royal maps of Siam in the nineteenth century or *mor lam*, the folk music of the northeast (see page 765). Ignore any con-men at the entrance to the soi looking for gullible tourists to escort on rip-off shopping trips, who'll tell you that the house is closed when it isn't.

The house

The grand, rambling **house** is in fact a combination of six teak houses, some from as far afield as Ayutthaya and most more than two hundred years old. Like all traditional houses, they were built in wall sections hung together without nails on a frame of wooden pillars, which made it easy to dismantle them, pile them onto a barge and float them to their new location. Although he had trained as an architect, Thompson had more difficulty in putting them back together again; in the end, he had to go back to Ayutthaya to hunt down a group of carpenters who still practised the old house-building methods. Thompson added a few unconventional touches of his own, incorporating the elaborately carved front wall of a Chinese pawnshop between the drawing room and the bedroom, and reversing the other walls in the drawing room so that their carvings faced into the room.

The impeccably tasteful **interior** has been left as it was during Jim Thompson's life, even down to the place settings on the dining table – Thompson entertained guests most nights and to that end designed the house like a stage set. Complementing the fine artefacts from throughout Southeast Asia is a stunning array of Thai arts and crafts, including one of the best collections of traditional Thai paintings in the world. Thompson picked up plenty of bargains from the Thieves' Quarter (Nakhon Kasem) in Chinatown, before collecting Thai art became fashionable and expensive. Other pieces were liberated from decay and destruction in upcountry temples, while many of the

THE LEGEND OF JIM THOMPSON

Thai silk-weavers, art dealers and conspiracy theorists all owe a debt to **Jim Thompson**, who even now, fifty years after his disappearance, remains Thailand's most famous farang. An architect by trade, Thompson left his New York practice in 1940 to join the Office of Strategic Services (later to become the CIA), a tour of duty that was to see him involved in clandestine operations in North Africa, Europe and, in 1945, the Far East, where he was detailed to a unit preparing for the invasion of Thailand. When the mission was pre-empted by the Japanese surrender, he served for a year as OSS station chief in Bangkok, forming links that were later to provide grist for endless speculation.

After an unhappy and short-lived stint as part-owner of the *Oriental Hotel*, Thompson found his calling with the struggling **silk-weavers** of the area near the present Jim Thompson House, whose traditional product was unknown in the West and had been all but abandoned by Thais in favour of less costly imported textiles. Encouragement from society friends and an enthusiastic write-up in *Vogue* convinced him there was a foreign market for Thai silk, and by 1948 he had founded the Thai Silk Company Ltd. Success was assured when, two years later, the company was commissioned to make the costumes for the Broadway run of *The King and I*. Thompson's celebrated eye for colour combinations and his tireless promotion – in the early days, he could often be seen in the lobby of the *Oriental* with bolts of silk slung over his shoulder, waiting to pounce on any remotely curious tourist – quickly made his name synonymous with Thai silk.

Like a character in a Somerset Maugham novel, Thompson played the role of Western exile to the hilt. Though he spoke no Thai, he made it his personal mission to preserve traditional arts and architecture (at a time when most Thais were more keen to emulate the West), assembling his famous Thai house and stuffing it with all manner of Oriental objets d'art. At the same time he held firmly to his farang roots and society connections: no foreign gathering in Bangkok was complete without Jim Thompson, and virtually every Western luminary passing through Bangkok – from Truman Capote to Ethel Merman – dined at his table (even though the food was notoriously bad).

If Thompson's life was the stuff of legend, his disappearance and presumed death only added to the mystique. On Easter Sunday, 1967, Thompson, while staying with friends in a cottage in Malaysia's Cameron Highlands, went out for a stroll and never came back. A massive search of the area, employing local guides, tracker dogs and even shamans, turned up no clues, provoking a rash of fascinating but entirely unsubstantiated theories. The grandfather of them all, advanced by a Dutch psychic, held that Thompson had been lured into an ambush by the disgraced former prime minister of Thailand, Pridi Panomyong, and spirited off to Cambodia for indeterminate purposes; later versions, supposing that Thompson had remained a covert CIA operative all his life, proposed that he was abducted by Vietnamese Communists and brainwashed to be displayed as a high-profile defector to Communism. More recently, an amateur sleuth claims to have found evidence that Thompson met a more mundane fate, having been killed by a careless truck driver and hastily buried.

Buddha images were turned over by ploughs, especially around Ayutthaya. Some of the exhibits are very rare, such as a headless but elegant seventh-century Dvaravati Buddha and a seventeenth-century Ayutthayan teak Buddha.

After the guided tour, you're free to look again, at your leisure, at the former rice barn and gardener's and maid's houses in the small, jungly **garden**, which display some gorgeous traditional Thai paintings and drawings, as well as small-scale statues and Chinese ceramics.

Bangkok Art and Cultural Centre

Junction of Rama I and Phrayathai roads • Tues–Sun 10am–9pm • Free • ☎ 02 214 6630–8, ⓦ bacc.or.th • BTS National Stadium

A striking, white hunk of modernity, the prestigious **Bangkok Art and Cultural Centre** houses several galleries on its upper floors, connected by spiralling ramps like New York's Guggenheim, as well as performance spaces, cafés, boutiques and private art

1

galleries on the lower floors. It hosts temporary shows by contemporary artists from Thailand and abroad across all media, from the visual arts to music and design, and there's usually something interesting on here – coming in from BTS National Stadium, there's a blackboard inside the entrance where the day's events and shows are chalked up in English. BACC will be one of the main venues for the first **Bangkok Art Biennale** in late 2018 and early 2019 (ⓦbkkartbiennale.com), featuring over seventy Thai and international artists, cinema, music and performing arts.

Sea Life Bangkok Ocean World

Basement of Siam Paragon shopping centre (east end), Thanon Rama I • Daily 10am–9pm, last admission 8pm; shark feeds 1pm & 4pm, as well as many other timed feedings (detailed on the website) • B990 (online, evening and weekday early-bird discounts available); B2000 including "Ocean Walker"; behind-the-scenes tour B350; glass-bottomed boat ride B350; shark dive from B5300; 4D films B350 • ⓣ 02 687 2000, ⓦ sealifebangkok.com • BTS Siam

Spread over two spacious floors, **Bangkok Ocean World** is an impressive, Australian-built aquarium. Despite the high admission price, it gets crowded at weekends and during holidays, and can be busy with school groups on weekday afternoons. Among outstanding features of this US$30-million development are an 8m-deep glass-walled tank, which displays the multicoloured variety of a coral reef drop-off to great effect, and a long, under-ocean tunnel where you can watch sharks and rays swimming over your head. In this global piscatorial display of around four hundred species, locals such as the Mekong giant catfish are not forgotten, while regularly spaced touch-screen

---

BANGKOK FOR KIDS

The following places are all designed for kids, the main drawbacks being that many are located a long way from the city centre. Other attractions kids might enjoy include the Museum of Siam (see page 92), feeding the turtles at Wat Prayoon (see page 112), Dusit Zoo (see page 114), Sea Life Bangkok Ocean World aquarium (see page 120), the Snake Farm (see page 122), cycling around Muang Boran Ancient City (see page 132), taking a canal boat through Thonburi (see page 110) and pedal-boating in Lumphini Park (see page 123). A useful resource for tips on travelling with kids (see page 58) in Bangkok is ⓦbkkkids.com.

Bangkok Butterfly Garden and Insectarium Suan Rotfai (Railway Park), just north of Chatuchak Weekend Market; Tues–Sun 8.30am–4.30pm; free; ⓣ02 272 4359. Over five hundred butterflies flutter within an enormous landscaped dome. There's also a study centre, plus family-oriented cycle routes and bikes (with infant seats) for rent in the adjacent park. The park is walkable from BTS Mo Chit or Chatuchak Park subway.

Children's Discovery Museum Queen Sirikit Park, just north of Chatuchak Weekend Market; Tues–Sun 10am–4pm; free; ⓣ 02 246 6144. With different zones for different ages, ranging from babies to 12-year-olds, this recently renovated museum lets kids excavate in the sand for dinosaur bones, do hands-on experiments and frolic in the outdoor water-play park. The BTS Mo Chit or Chatuchak Park subway are handy for the museum.

Dream World Ten minutes' drive north of Don Muang Airport at kilometre-stone 7 Thanon Rangsit–Ongkarak; Mon–Fri 10am–5pm, Sat & Sun 10am–7pm; B1200/person including transfers; ⓦdreamworld.co.th. Theme park with different areas

such as Snow Town and Fantasy Land, including water rides, a hanging roller coaster and other amusements.

Funarium Soi 26, Thanon Sukhumvit, down towards Thanon Rama IV; Mon–Thurs 9am–6pm, Fri–Sun 9am–7pm; B110–330, depending on height/age of visitor; ⓦfunarium.co.th. Huge age-segregated indoor playground that's very popular with expats, with story-telling and other activities at weekends, a restaurant and a branch of Mothercare.

KidZania Floor 5, Siam Paragon shopping centre, Thanon Rama I; Mon–Fri 10am–5pm, Sat & Sun 10.30am–8.30pm; B570–950, depending on age, more at weekends; ⓦbangkok.kidzania.com. Imaginative and varied activities centre, where kids can play at being doctors and nurses, Japanese chefs, and even fortune tellers.

Siam Park City On the far eastern edge of town at 101 Thanon Sukhapiban 2; daily 10am–6pm; B900, children 100–130cm B120, under 100cm free; ⓦsiamparkcity.com. Waterslides, wave pool and artificial beach, plus roller coasters and other rides.

terminals provide information in English about the creatures on view. It's even possible to walk in an underwater tunnel wearing a diving helmet (the "Ocean Walker"), or dive with the sharks, whether you're a licensed diver or not. You can also take a behind-the-scenes tour, see sharks and stingrays on a glass-bottomed boat ride and watch – through 3D glasses – underwater cartoons in the "4D Cinema".

The Erawan Shrine

Corner of Thanon Ploenchit and Thanon Rajdamri • Daily 24hr • Free • BTS Chit Lom

For a glimpse of the variety and ubiquity of Thai religion, drop in on the **Erawan Shrine** (*Saan Phra Prom* in Thai). Remarkable as much for its setting as anything else, this shrine to Brahma, the Hindu creation god, squeezes in on one of the busiest and noisiest intersections in modern Bangkok. And it's not the only one: half a dozen other Hindu shrines and spirit houses are dotted around Ratchaphrasong intersection, most notably **Trimurti**, who combines the three main gods, Brahma, Vishnu and Shiva, on Thanon Rajdamri outside Central World near the intersection's opposite corner. Modern Bangkokians see Trimurti as a sort of Cupid figure, and those looking for love bring red offerings.

The *Grand Hyatt Erawan Hotel*, towering over the Erawan Shrine, is the reason for its existence and its name. When a string of calamities held up the building of the original hotel in the 1950s, spirit doctors were called in, who instructed the owners to build a new home for the offended local spirits, in the form of a shrine to Brahma (who had created the many-headed elephant, Erawan, as a vehicle for the god Indra): the hotel was then finished without further mishap. Ill fortune, however, has struck the shrine itself twice in recent years. In 2006, a young, mentally ill Muslim man smashed the Brahma statue to pieces with a hammer – and was then brutally beaten to death by an angry mob. An exact replica of the statue was quickly installed, incorporating the remains of the old statue to preserve the spirit of the deity. Then in 2015, a bomb exploded on the grounds of the shrine (which was largely undamaged), killing twenty people, the most deadly act of terrorism in Thailand's history. It seems likely that the device was planted by Uighur separatists, in retaliation for Thailand's forced repatriation of a planeload of their kinsmen to China.

Be prepared for sensory overload here: the main structure shines with lurid glass of all colours and the overcrowded precinct around it is almost buried under scented garlands and incense candles. You might also catch a group of traditional dancers performing here to the strains of a small classical orchestra to entertain Brahma – worshippers hire them to give thanks for a stroke of good fortune. People set on less abstract rewards will invest in a lottery ticket from one of the physically disabled sellers: they're thought to be the luckiest you can buy.

Ban Kamthieng (Kamthieng House)

131 Thanon Asok Montri (Soi 21 off Thanon Sukhumvit) • Tues–Sat 9am–5pm • B100 • ⓦ siam-society.org • BTS Asok or Sukhumvit subway

A traditional northern Thai residence, **Ban Kamthieng** was moved in the 1960s from Chiang Mai to Thanon Sukhumvit and set up as an ethnological museum by the Siam Society, an august academic institution that was founded in 1904 to promote knowledge of Thailand. The delightful complex of polished teak buildings makes a pleasing oasis beneath the towering glass skyscrapers that dominate Sukhumvit. It differs from Suan Pakkad, Jim Thompson's House and M.R. Kukrit's Heritage Home in being the home of a rural family, and the objects on display give a fair insight into country life for the well-heeled in northern Thailand. In a traditional central Thai house at the front of the grounds, there's a nice little **café-restaurant** run by the Black Canyon chain.

1

The house was built on the banks of the Ping River in the mid-nineteenth century for local bigwigs, the Nimmanhaemins, and the ground-floor video will show you how to build your own northern Thai house. Also here are assorted looms and fish traps, which evoke the upcountry practice of fishing in flooded rice paddies to augment the supply from the rivers. Upstairs, the main display focuses on the ritual life of a typical Lanna household, explaining the role of the spirits, the practice of making offerings, and the belief in amulets, talismans, magic shirts and male tattoos. The rectangular lintel above the door is a *hum yon*, carved in floral patterns that represent testicles and are designed to ward off evil spirits. Walk along the open veranda to the authentically equipped kitchen, and to the granary to find an interesting exhibition on the ritual practices associated with rice farming.

The Queen Saovabha Memorial Institute (Snake Farm)

Corner of Thanon Rama IV and Thanon Henri Dunant • Live shows Mon–Fri 2.30pm, Sat, Sun & hols 11am; displays of venom extraction Mon–Fri 11am • B200 • ⓦ saovabha.com • 10min walk from BTS Sala Daeng, or from Sam Yan or Si Lom subway stations

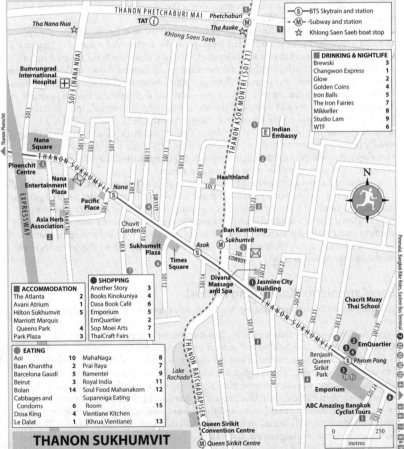

The **Queen Saovabha Memorial Institute** (*Sathan Saovapha*) is a bit of a circus act, but an entertaining, informative and worthy one at that. Taking its formal name from one of Rama V's wives, it's often simply known as the **Snake Farm**, though it's not to be confused with other, more exploitative snake shows around Bangkok. Run by the Thai Red Cross, the institute has a double function: to produce snake-bite serums, and to educate the public on the dangers of Thai snakes. The latter mission involves putting on live shows of snake handling and feeding. Well presented and safe, these displays gain a perverse fascination from the knowledge that the strongest venoms of the snakes on show can kill in only three minutes. If you're still not herpetologically sated, you can look round the attached exhibition space, where dozens of Thai snakes live in cages.

Lumphini Park

Thanon Rama IV • Daily roughly 4.30am–9pm • Free • BTS Saladaeng or Si Lom or Lumphini subway stations

If you're sick of cars and concrete, head for **Lumphini Park** (*Suan Lum*), where the air is almost fresh and the traffic noise dies down to a low murmur. Named after the town in Nepal where the Buddha was born, it was the country's first public park, donated by Rama VI in the 1920s, whose statue by Silpa Bhirasri (see page 751) stands at the main, southwest entrance. The park is arrayed around two lakes, where you can join the locals in feeding the turtles and fish with bread or take out a pedalo or rowing boat, and is landscaped with a wide variety of local trees and numerous pagodas and pavilions, usually occupied by chess-players. In the early morning and at dusk, people hit the outdoor gym on the southwest side of the park, play takraw, or en masse do aerobics, balletic t'ai chi or jogging along the yellow-marked circuit, stopping for the twice-daily broadcast of the national anthem. On late Sunday afternoons in the cool season (usually mid-Dec to mid-Feb), free classical concerts by the Bangkok Symphony Orchestra (⊕bangkoksymphony.org) draw in scores of urban picnickers.

Patpong

Concentrated into two lanes running between the eastern ends of Thanon Silom and Thanon Suriwong, the neon-lit go-go bars of the **Patpong** district loom like rides in a tawdry sexual Disneyland. In front of each bar, girls cajole passers-by with a lifeless sensuality while insistent touts proffer printed menus and photographs detailing the degradations on show. Inside, bikini-clad women gyrate to Western music and play hostess to the (almost exclusively male) spectators; upstairs, live shows feature women who, to use Spalding Gray's phrase in *Swimming to Cambodia*, "do everything with their vaginas except have babies".

Patpong was no more than a sea of mud when the capital was founded on the marshy river bank to the west, but by the 1960s it had grown into a flash district of dance halls for rich Thais, owned by a Chinese millionaire godfather, educated at the London School of Economics and by the OSS (forerunner of the CIA), who gave his name to the area. In 1969, an American entrepreneur turned an existing teahouse into a luxurious nightclub to satisfy the tastes of soldiers on R&R trips from Vietnam, and so Patpong's transformation into a Western sex reservation began. At first, the area was rough and violent, but over the years it has wised up to the desires of the affluent farang, and now markets itself as a packaged concept of Oriental decadence.

The centre of the skin trade lies along the interconnected sois of **Patpong 1 and 2**, where lines of go-go bars share their patch with respectable restaurants, a 24-hour supermarket and an overabundance of pharmacies. Even the most demure tourists – of both sexes – turn out to do some shopping at the night market down the middle of Patpong 1, where hawkers sell fake watches, bags and designer T-shirts. By day, a relaxed hangover descends on the place. Farang men slump at the open-air bars on Patpong 2, drinking and watching videos, unable to find anything else to do in the

1

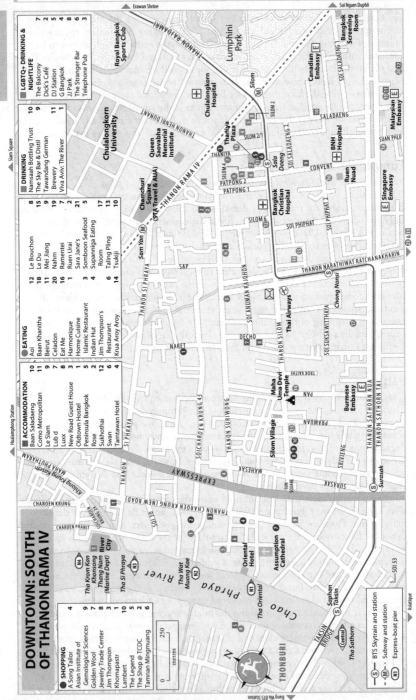

DOWNTOWN: SOUTH OF THANON RAMA IV

● SHOPPING

A Song Tailor	4
Asian Institute of Gemological Sciences	9
Golden Wool	8
Jewelry Trade Center	3
Jim Thompson	1
Khomapastr	10
Lambert	5
The Legend	2
The Shop @ TCDC	6
Tamnan Mingmuang	6

■ ACCOMMODATION

Baan Saladaeng	10
Como Metropolitan	11
Le Siam	7
Lub·d	8
Luxx	3
New Road Guest House	5
Oldtown Hostel	2
Peninsula Bangkok	12
Rose	9
Sukhothai	6
Swan	1
Tamtawan Hotel	4

● EATING

Aoi	10	Le Bouchon	12
Baan Khanitha	11	Le Du	18
Beirut	7	Mei Jiang	11
Celadon	8	Nahm	20
Eat Me	6	Ramentei	16
Harmonique	3	Ruen Urai	1
Home Cuisine	5	Sara Jane's	21
Islamic Restaurant	2	Somboon Seafood	3
Indian Hut		Supanniga Eating Room	4
Jim Thompson's Restaurant	12	Taling Pling	17
Krua Aroy Aroy	4	Tsukiji	6
			14

■ DRINKING

Namsaah Bottling Trust	10
The Sky Bar & Distil	15
Tawandang German Brewery	9
Viva Aviv: The River	19
	7
	1

■ LGBTQ+ DRINKING & NIGHTLIFE

The Balcony	7
Dick's Café	2
DJ Station	5
G Bangkok	4
JJ Park	8
The Stranger Bar	6
Telephone Pub	3

KEY

(S) —	BTS Skytrain and station
(M) ---	Subway and station
N1	Express-boat pier

THAILAND'S SEX INDUSTRY

Bangkok owes its reputation as the carnal capital of the world to a **sex industry** adept at peddling fantasies of cheap thrills on tap. More than a thousand sex-related businesses operate in the city, but the gaudy neon fleshpots of Patpong and Sukhumvit's Soi Nana and Soi Cowboy give a misleading impression of an activity that is deeply rooted in Thai culture: the overwhelming majority of Thailand's prostitutes of both sexes (estimated at anywhere between 200,000 and 700,000) work with Thai men, not farangs.

Prostitution and polygamy have long been intrinsic to the Thai way of life. Apart from a few recent exceptions, Thai kings have always kept concubines, only a few of whom would be elevated to royal mothers. The practice was aped by the nobility and, from the early nineteenth century, by newly rich merchants keen to have lots of sons. Many men of all classes still keep **mistresses**, known as *mia noi* (minor wives), or have casual girlfriends (*gig*); the common view is that an official wife (*mia luang*) should be treated like the temple's main Buddha image – respected and elevated upon the altar – whereas the minor wife is like an amulet, to be taken along wherever you go. For less wealthy men, prostitution is a far cheaper option: at least two-fifths of sexually active Thai men are thought to visit brothels twice a month.

The **farang sex industry** is a relatively new development, having started during the Vietnam War, when the American military set up seven bases around Thailand. The GIs' appetite for "entertainment" attracted women from surrounding rural areas to cash in on the boom, and Bangkok joined the fray in the late 1960s. By the mid-1970s, the GIs had left, but tourists replaced them, lured by advertising that diverted most of the traffic to Bangkok and Pattaya. Sex tourism has since grown to become an established part of the Thai economy and has spread to Phuket, Hat Yai, Ko Samui and Chiang Mai.

The majority of the women who work in the country's go-go bars and "bar-beers" (outdoor hostess bars) come from the poorest areas of north and northeast Thailand. **Economic refugees**, they're easily drawn into an industry in which they can make in a single night what would take a month to earn in the rice fields. Many women opt for a couple of years in the sex bars to help pay off family debts and improve the living conditions of parents stuck in the poverty trap.

Many bar girls, and male prostitutes too, are looking for longer-term **relationships** with their farang customers, bringing a temporary respite from bar work and perhaps even a ticket out. A surprising number of one-night transactions do develop into some sort of holiday romance, with the young woman accompanying her farang "boyfriend" (often twice her age) around the country and maintaining contact after he's returned home. An entire sub-genre of novels and confessional memoirs (among them the classic *Hello, My Big Big Honey!: Letters to Bangkok Bar Girls and Their Revealing Interviews*) testifies to the role money plays in all this, and highlights the delusions common to both parties, not to mention the cross-cultural incomprehension.

Despite its ubiquity, prostitution has been **illegal** in Thailand since 1960, but sex-industry bosses easily circumvent the law by registering their establishments as clubs, karaoke bars or massage parlours, and making payoffs to the police and politicians. Sex workers, on the other hand, often endure exploitation and violence from pimps and customers rather than face fines and long rehabilitation sentences. Hardly surprising that many prefer to go freelance, working the clubs and bars in non-red-light zones such as Thanon Khao San. Life is made even more difficult because abortion is illegal in Thailand. The **anti-prostitution law**, however, does attempt to treat sex workers as victims rather than criminals and penalizes parents who sell their children. A high-profile voice in the struggle to improve the **rights of sex workers** is the Empower Foundation (Ⓦempowerfoundation.org), which not only organizes campaigns and runs education centres for bar workers but also manages its own bar in Chiang Mai.

Inevitably, **child prostitution** is a significant issue in Thailand, but NGOs such as ECPAT (Ⓦecpat.net) say numbers have declined over the last decade, due to zero-tolerance and awareness campaigns. The government has also strengthened legislation against hiring a prostitute under the age of 18, and anyone caught having sex with an under-15 can now be charged with rape. The disadvantaged are still targeted by traffickers however, who "buy" children from desperately poor hill tribe and other minority families and keep them as bonded slaves until the debt has been repaid.

1

whole of Bangkok. Running parallel to the east, **Soi Thaniya** is Patpong's Japanese counterpart, lined with hostess bars and some good restaurants, while the focus of Bangkok's gay scene, **Silom 2** (ie Soi 2, Thanon Silom) and the more mixed **Silom 4**, flank Thaniya.

M.R. Kukrit's Heritage Home

19 Soi Phra Pinit (Soi 7, Thanon Narathiwat Ratchanakharin) • Daily 10am–4pm, though it's sometimes closed for social engagements, so worth phoning ahead to check • B50 • ☎ 02 286 8185 • 10min walk south then east from Thanon Sathorn; 20min walk from BTS Chong Nonsi

M.R. Kukrit's Heritage Home (*Baan Mom Kukrit*) is the beautiful traditional house and gardens of one of Thailand's leading figures of the twentieth century. M.R. (*Mom Rajawongse*, a princely title) **Kukrit Pramoj** (1911–95) was a remarkable all-rounder, descended from Rama II on his father's side and, on his mother's side, from the influential ministerial family, the Bunnags. Kukrit graduated in Philosophy, Politics and Economics from Oxford University and went on to become a university lecturer back in Thailand, but his greatest claim to fame is probably as a writer: he founded, owned and penned a daily column for *Siam Rath*, the most influential Thai-language newspaper, and wrote short stories, novels, plays and poetry. He was also a respected performer in classical dance-drama (*khon*), and he starred as an Asian prime minister, opposite Marlon Brando, in the Hollywood film, *The Ugly American*. In 1974, during an especially turbulent period for Thailand, life imitated art, when Kukrit was called on to become Thailand's prime minister at the head of a coalition of seventeen parties. However, just four hundred days into his premiership, the Thai military leadership dismissed him for being too anti-American.

The **residence**, which has been left just as it was when Kukrit was alive, reflects his complex character. In the large, open-sided *sala* (pavilion) for public functions, near the entrance, is an attractive display of *khon* masks, including a gold one that Kukrit wore when he played the demon king, Totsagan (Ravana). In and around the adjoining Khmer-styled garden, keep your eyes peeled for the *mai dut*, sculpted miniature trees similar to bonsai, some of which Kukrit worked on for decades. The living quarters beyond are made up of five teak houses on stilts, assembled from various parts of central Thailand and joined by an open veranda. The bedroom, study and various sitting rooms are decked out with beautiful objets d'art; look out especially for the carved bed that belonged to Rama II and the very delicate, two-hundred-year-old nielloware (gold inlay) from Nakhon Si Thammarat in the formal reception room. In the small family prayer room, Kukrit Pramoj's ashes are enshrined in the base of a reproduction of the Emerald Buddha.

The west end of Thanon Silom

Further west along **Thanon Silom** from Patpong, in a still-thriving South Indian enclave, lies the colourful landmark of the **Maha Uma Devi Temple**. Also known as **Sri Mahamariamman** or **Wat Khaek**, this vibrant, gaudy Hindu shrine was built by Tamils in 1895 in honour of Shiva's consort, Uma. Carrying on to the river, the strip west of Charoen Krung (New Road) around Thanon Silom reveals some of the history of Bangkok's early dealings with foreigners in the fading grandeur of the old trading quarter. Here you'll find the only place in Bangkok where you might be able to eke out an architectural walk, though it's hardly compelling. Incongruous churches and "colonial" buildings – the best being the Authors' Wing of the *Oriental Hotel*, where nostalgic afternoon teas are served – are hemmed in by the spice shops and *halal* canteens of the Muslim area around Thanon Charoen Krung.

1

Thailand Creative and Design Centre (TCDC)

Grand Postal Building, Thanon Charoen Krung • Tues–Sun 10.30am–9pm • Free • ⓦ web.tcdc.or.th • BTS Saphan Taksin, then a 20min walk, or Chao Phraya express boat to Tha Wat Muang Kae or Tha Si Phraya

Relocated in 2017, the **Thailand Creative and Design Centre** seeks to celebrate, promote and inspire innovative design through a resource centre, talks, a shop (see page 167), a café and often fascinating temporary exhibitions. It's now housed in the former General Post Office, which was built in 1940 under the quasi-fascist government of Field Marshal Phibun (on the former site of the British Embassy), in a brutal modernist style that's hard to love.

TCDC is planned to become the hub of a new **Charoenkrung Creative District** (ⓦfacebook.com/CharoenkrungCD). Already opened is **Warehouse 30** (ⓦfacebook. com/TheWarehouse30), a prestigious but hard-to-categorize redevelopment of seven 1940s warehouses around the corner from TCDC off Soi 30. It encompasses a co-working space, boutiques and stalls selling clothes, furniture and flowers, a variety of food and drink outlets, and spaces for art exhibitions and frequent documentary film screenings (ⓦdocumentaryclubthailand.com).

The city outskirts

The amorphous clutter of Greater Bangkok doesn't harbour many attractions, but there are a handful of places that make pleasant half-day escapes, principally **Chatuchak Weekend Market**, the cultural theme-park of **Muang Boran**, the upstream town of **Nonthaburi** and the tranquil artificial island of **Ko Kred** (see page 78).

Chatuchak Weekend Market (JJ)

Occupies a huge patch of ground extending northwest from the corner of Phaholyothin and Kamphaeng Phet roads • Sat & Sun roughly 9am–6/7pm, though many stalls open earlier and some close later • ⓦ chatuchak.org

With over ten thousand open-air stalls to peruse, 200,000 visitors each day and wares as diverse as Lao silk, Siamese kittens and designer lamps, the enormous **Chatuchak Weekend Market** (or **JJ** as it's usually abbreviated, from "Jatu Jak") is Bangkok's most enjoyable – not to mention hot and exhausting – shopping experience.

The market also contains a controversial **pets** section. In the past this has doubled as a clearing house for protected and endangered species such as gibbons, palm cockatoos and Indian pied hornbills, many of them smuggled in from Laos and Cambodia and sold to private animal collectors and foreign zoos. Crackdowns by the authorities, however, now seem to have driven this trade underground.

Where to shop

Chatuchak is divided into 27 numbered **sections**, plus half a dozen unnumbered ones, each of them more or less dedicated to a particular genre, for example household items, plants and secondhand books. The demarcation is nothing like as clear-cut as the market's website would have you believe, but if you have several hours to spare, it's fun just to browse at whim. The market's primary customers are Bangkok residents in search of idiosyncratic fashions (try sections 2, 3 and 4), including second-hand clothing (sections 5 and 6), and homewares (especially in sections A, B and C, behind the market's head office and information centre), but Chatuchak also has plenty of collector- and tourist-oriented **stalls**; best buys include antique lacquerware, unusual sarongs, traditional cotton clothing and crafts from the north, silver jewellery, and ceramics, particularly the five-coloured *bencharong*. For handicrafts (including musical instruments) and traditional textiles, you should start with sections 22, 24, 25 (which features textiles from northern Thailand) and 26, which are all in a cluster at the southwest (Kamphaeng Phet subway) end of the market. Section 7, meanwhile at the north end of the market, is full of art galleries, which are often staffed by the artists themselves.

There are dozens of food stalls at Chatuchak, but foodies will want to check out **Talat Or Tor Khor** (the Agricultural Marketing Organization), a covered market that sells a fantastic array of fruit, veg and other produce from around the country, as well as prepared dishes to take away or to eat at the food court; it's on the south side of Thanon Kamphaeng Phet, next to Kamphaeng Phet subway station. The modern building next door to Talat Or Tor Khor, the **Siam Orchid Centre**, is a lovely market for orchids and other plants. The best place in Chatuchak Market to get a drink, and perhaps a plate of paella, is *Viva* (see page 162).

ARRIVAL AND GETTING AROUND

Arrival Kamphaeng Phet subway station exits right into the most interesting, southwestern, corner of the market; on the northeast side of the market are Chatuchak Park subway and Mochit BTS stations. Coming from Banglamphu, either get a bus to BTS National Stadium or BTS Ratchathewi, or take the #503 (non-expressway version) or #509 bus all the way (about 1hr) from Thanon Rajdamnoen Klang; once the

MRT extension has opened, it should be possible to catch an express-boat to Tha Tien, then walk 5min to Sanam Chai station, for subway trains to Chatuchak Park or Kamphaeng Phet stations.

Getting around A few very small electric trams circulate around the market's main inner ring road, transporting weary shoppers for free, though they always seem to be full.

INFORMATION

Maps *Nancy Chandler's Map of Bangkok* has a fabulously detailed and informatively annotated map of all the sections in the market. Maps are also posted at various points around the market, including in the subway stations,

or go to the more in-depth ⊕ www.jjmarketmap.com. For specific help you can ask at the market office, on the main inner ring road near Gate 1 off Thanon Kamphaeng Phet 2, which also has ATMs and currency exchange booths.

The Prasart Museum

9 Soi 4A, Soi Krungthep Kreetha, Thanon Krungthep Kreetha • Tues–Sun 9.30am–2pm • B1000 for 1 person; for 2 people or more, B500 per person • Call ☎ 02 379 3601 or 02 379 3607 in advance to book the compulsory tour

Located on the far eastern edge of the city, the **Prasart Museum** is an unusual open-air exhibition of traditional Asian buildings, put together by wealthy entrepreneur and art-lover Khun Prasart. The museum is rarely visited – partly because of the intentionally limited opening hours and inflated admission price, and partly because it takes a long time to get there by public transport – but it makes a pleasant day out and is worth the effort.

Set in a gorgeously lush tropical garden, the museum comprises about a dozen beautifully crafted replicas of **traditional buildings**, including a golden teak palace inspired by the Tamnak Daeng at the National Museum, a Chinese temple and water garden, a Khmer shrine and a Sukhothai-era teak library set over a lotus pond. Some have been pieced together from ruined originals, while others were constructed from scratch. Many are filled with antique **artefacts**, including Burmese woodcarvings, prehistoric pottery from Ban Chiang and Lopburi-era statuettes. There's also an exquisite collection of *bencharong* ceramics.

ARRIVAL AND DEPARTURE

By bus Ordinary and a/c bus #93 runs almost to the door: pick it up near its starting point on Thanon Si Phraya near River City and TCDC, or anywhere along its route on Phetchaburi and Phetchaburi Mai roads (both the Khlong Saen Saeb canal boats and the subway have potentially useful stops at the Thanon Asok Montri/Sukhumvit Soi 21 junction with Thanon Phetchaburi Mai). The #93 terminates on Thanon Krungthep Kreetha, but you should get off a

couple of stops before the terminus, at the first stop on Thanon Krungthep Kreetha, as soon as you see the sign for the Prasart Museum (about 1hr 15min by bus from Si Phraya). Follow the sign down Soi Krungthep Kreetha, go past the golf course and, after about a 15min walk, turn off down Soi 4A.

By boat To speed things up, instead of a bus ride, you could take the Khlong Saen Saeb canal boat all the way to

1

The Mall Bangkapi pier (about 40min from Phan Fah, seven stops after the confusingly similar The Mall Ram pier). It is then a very short taxi ride to the museum.

By train Another time saver is to take the Suvarnabhumi Airport Rail Link from Phaya Thai to Hua Mark station, which leaves you within a very short taxi ride of the museum.

Nonthaburi

Chao Phraya Express Boat to Nonthaburi, the last stop upriver for most (N30), under 1hr from Central Pier (Sathorn) on an orange-flag boat

A trip to **NONTHABURI**, the first town and province beyond the northern boundary of Bangkok, is the easiest excursion you can make from the centre of the city and affords a perfect opportunity to recharge your batteries. Nonthaburi is the last stop upriver for most express boats and the ride itself is most of the fun, weaving round huge, crawling sand barges and tiny canoes. The slow pace of the boat gives you plenty of time to take in the sights on the way. On the north side of Banglamphu, beyond the elegant, modern **Rama VIII Bridge**, which shelters the Mekong whisky distillery on the west bank, you'll pass in turn, on the east bank: the Bangkhunprom Palace and the adjacent Devaves Palace, two gleamingly restored former princely residences in the Bank of Thailand compound; the royal boathouse at Tha Wasukri in front of the National Library, where you can glimpse the minor ceremonial boats that escort the grand royal barges; the city's first Catholic church, Holy Conception, founded in the seventeenth century during King Narai of Ayutthaya's reign and rebuilt in the early nineteenth; and, beyond Krungthon Bridge, the Singha brewery. Along the route are dazzling Buddhist temples and drably painted mosques, catering for Bangkok's growing Muslim population, as well as a few remaining communities who still live in houses on stilts or houseboats.

Disembarking at suburban Nonthaburi, on the east bank of the river, you won't find a great deal to do, in truth. There's a market that's famous for the quality of its fruit, while the attractive, old Provincial Office across the road is covered in wooden latticework. To break up your trip with a slow, scenic drink or lunch, you'll find a floating seafood restaurant, *Rim Fang*, to the right at the end of the prom.

DURIANS

The naturalist Alfred Russel Wallace, eulogizing the taste of the **durian**, compared it to "rich butter-like custard highly flavoured with almonds, but intermingled with wafts of flavour that call to mind cream cheese, onion sauce, brown sherry and other incongruities". He neglected to discuss the smell of the fruit's skin, which is so bad – somewhere between detergent and dog excrement – that durians are barred from Thai hotels and aeroplanes. The different **varieties** bear strange names that do nothing to make them more appetizing: "frog", "golden pillow", "gibbon" and so on. However, the durian has fervent admirers, perhaps because it's such an acquired taste, and because it's considered a strong aphrodisiac. Aficionados discuss the varieties with as much subtlety as if they were vintage Champagnes, and treat the durian as a social fruit, to be shared around, despite a price tag of up to B3000 each. They also pour scorn on the Thai government scientists who have recently genetically developed an odourless variety, the Chanthaburi 1 durian.

The most famous durian orchards are around Nonthaburi, where the fruits are said to have an incomparably rich and nutty flavour due to the fine clay soil. To see these and other plantations such as mango, pomelo and jackfruit, your best bet is to hire a longtail from Nonthaburi pier to take you west along Khlong Om Non. If you don't smell them first, you can recognize durians by their sci-fi appearance: the shape and size of a rugby ball, but slightly deflated, they're covered in a thick, pale-green shell which is heavily armoured with short, sharp spikes (*duri* means "thorn" in Malay). By cutting along one of the faint seams with a good knife, you'll reveal a white pith in which are set a handful of yellow blobs with the texture of a wrinkled soufflé: this is what you eat. The taste is best when the smell is at its highest, about three days after the fruit has dropped. Be careful when out walking near the trees: because of its great weight and sharp spikes, a falling durian can lead to serious injury, or even an ignominious death.

Wat Chalerm Phra Kiat

1km north of Nonthaburi pier on the west bank of the river • From the express-boat pier take the ferry straight across the Chao Phraya and then catch a motorbike taxi or walk

Set in relaxing grounds on the west bank of the river, elegant **Wat Chalerm Phra Kiat** injects a splash of urban refinement among a grove of breadfruit trees. The beautifully proportioned temple, which has been lavishly restored, was built by Rama III in memory of his mother, whose family lived and presided over vast orchards in the area. Inside the walls of the temple compound, you feel as if you've come upon a stately folly in a secret garden, and a strong Chinese influence shows itself in the unusual ribbed roofs and elegantly curved gables, decorated with pastel ceramics. The restorers have done their best work inside: look out especially for the simple, delicate landscapes on the shutters.

Ko Kred

The tiny island of **KO KRED** lies in a particularly sharp bend in the Chao Phraya, about 7km north of Nonthaburi pier, cut off from the east bank by a waterway created in the eighteenth century to make the cargo route from Ayutthaya to the Gulf of Thailand just that little bit faster. Although it get busy with day-trippers from Bangkok at weekends, when there's a lively market near Wat Paramaiyikawat, this artificial island remains something of a time capsule, a little oasis of village life completely at odds with the metropolitan chaos downriver. Roughly 10 square kilometres in all, Ko Kred has no roads, just a concrete track that follows its circumference, with a few arterial walkways branching off towards the interior. Villagers, the majority of whom are Mon (see page 210), descendants of refugees from Myanmar during the reigns of Taksin and Rama II, use a small fleet of motorbike taxis to cross their island, but as a sightseer you're much better off on a rental bicycle or just on foot: a round-island walk takes about an hour and a half.

There are few sights as such on Ko Kred, but its lushness and comparative emptiness make it a perfect place in which to wander, perhaps rounded off with a craft beer at *Chit's* (see page 162). You'll no doubt come across one of the island's potteries and kilns, which churn out the regionally famous earthenware flowerpots and small water-storage jars and employ a large percentage of the village workforce. The island's clay is very rich in nutrients and therefore excellent for fruit-growing, and banana trees, coconut palms, pomelo, papaya, mango and durian trees all grow in abundance on Ko Kred, fed by an intricate network of irrigation channels that crisscross the interior. In among the orchards, the Mons have built their wooden houses, mostly in traditional style and raised high above the marshy ground on stilts.

Wat Paramaiyikawat

Ko Kred boasts a handful of attractive riverside wats, most notably **Wat Paramaiyikawat** (also called **Wat Poramai**), at the main pier at the northeast tip of the island. This engagingly ramshackle eighteenth-century temple was restored by Rama V in honour of his grandmother, with a Buddha relic placed in its leaning, white, riverside chedi, which is a replica of the Mutao Pagoda in Hanthawadi (now Bago), capital of the Mon kingdom in Myanmar. Among an open-air scattering of Burmese-style alabaster Buddha images, the tall bot shelters some fascinating nineteenth-century murals, depicting scenes from temple life at ground level and the life of the Buddha above, all set in delicate imaginary landscapes.

ARRIVAL AND DEPARTURE
KO KRED

The easiest but busiest time to visit Ko Kred is at the weekend, when you can take a boat tour from central Bangkok. At other times, getting there by public transport is a bit of a chore.

By boat tour The Mitchaopaya Travel Service (see page 110; B500) runs boat tours to Ko Kred on Saturdays, Sundays and public holidays (if there are enough takers), leaving Tha Chang

1

in Ratanakosin at 9am, returning at about 3.30–4pm. On the way, you'll cruise along Khlong Bangkok Noi and Khlong Om, and call in at the Royal Barge Museum (see page 110), Wat Chalerm Phra Kiat in Nonthaburi (see page 130) and Wat Poramai on Ko Kred and nearby Ban Khanom Thai, where you can buy traditional sweets and watch them being made.

By public transport Your best option is to take a Chao Phraya Express Boat to Nonthaburi, then bus #32 (ordinary, coming from Wat Pho via Banglamphu) or a taxi (about B100) to Pakkred or a chartered longtail boat direct to Ko Kred (about B400–500). From Pakkred, the easiest way of getting across to the island is to hire a longtail boat, although shuttle boats cross at the river's narrowest point to Wat Poramai from Wat Sanam Neua, about 1km walk or motorbike-taxi ride south of the main Pakkred pier (getting off the bus at Tesco Lotus in Pakkred will cut down the walk to Wat Sanam Neua).

Muang Boran Ancient City

33km southeast of central Bangkok in Samut Prakan • Daily 9am–7pm • B700 9am–4pm, B350 4–7pm, including free audioguide in English • ⓦ ancientcitygroup.net • A/c bus #511 from Samrong Skytrain station (or from Thanon Rama I or Banglamphu) to the end of the line in Pak Nam, then songthaew #36 to Muang Boran; otherwise, Muang Boran operates a free pick-up once a day at weekends (11am) from Bearing Skytrain station, via Erawan Museum (an overblown exercise in spiritual psychedelia under the same ownership); the opening of the Skytrain's Sukhumvit Line extension to Kheha station in Samut Prakan, currently scheduled for 2019, should make access easier

A day-trip out to the **Muang Boran Ancient City** open-air museum is a great way to enjoy the best of Thailand's architectural heritage in relative peace and without much effort. Occupying a huge park shaped like Thailand itself, the museum comprises more than a hundred traditional Thai buildings scattered around pleasantly landscaped grounds and is best toured by free **bicycle** (or the free tram service), though doing it on foot is just about possible. Many of the buildings are copies of the country's most famous monuments, and are located in the appropriate "region" of the park, including Bangkok's Grand Palace (central region) and the spectacularly sited, hilltop Khmer Khao Phra Viharn sanctuary (northeast; make the most of it – the real temple is currently inaccessible from Thailand due to a border dispute with Cambodia). There are also some original structures, including a rare scripture library rescued from Samut Songkhram (south), and some painstaking reconstructions from contemporary documents of long-vanished gems, of which the Sanphet Prasat royal palace from Ayutthaya (central) is a particularly fine example, as well as recreated traditional villages and some purely imaginary designs. A sizeable team of restorers and skilled craftspeople maintains the buildings and helps keep some of the traditional techniques alive; if you come here during the week you can watch them at work.

ARRIVAL AND DEPARTURE
BANGKOK

Unless you arrive in Bangkok by train, be prepared for a long trip into the city centre. Suvarnabhumi and Don Muang airports are both 25km out and the three bus stations are not much closer in, though at least the Eastern Terminal is next to a Skytrain stop.

BY PLANE
When departing from Bangkok, leave plenty of time to get to Suvarnabhumi or Don Muang, as getting there by road can be severely hampered by traffic jams.

SUVARNABHUMI
Bangkok's main airport (coded "BKK" and pronounced "soo-wanna-poom"; ⓦ bangkokairportonline.com) is situated 25km east of central Bangkok between highways 7 and 34. The large airport is well stocked with 24hr exchange booths, ATMs, places to eat, pharmacies and a post office. In the arrivals hall on Floor 2, TAT operates an official 24hr tourist information counter (near landside Gate 3) and the tourist

police have an office; 24hr left-luggage depots (B100/item/day) can be found in arrivals and in the departures hall on Floor 4. There are a number of accommodation options near Suvarnabhumi (see page 149).

Suvarnabhumi Airport Rail Link The high-speed rail link (SARL; ⓦ srtet.co.th; daily 6am–midnight; B15–45) from the basement of the Suvarnabhumi terminal is generally the quickest means of getting downtown, though it also serves as an important link for commuters and can get very crowded. There's only one set of elevated tracks, ending at Phaya Thai station, with trains running roughly every 12–15min (26min), stopping at Makkasan, Ratchaprarop and four other stations. Makkasan is handy for Phetchaburi subway station and for Khlong Saen Saeb canal boats (see page 138) at Tha Asoke (Petchaburi) pier, while Phaya Thai is an interchange with the Skytrain system, and is served by #59 buses (heading south on Thanon Phrayathai) to Thanon Rajadamnoen Klang, for Banglamphu.

Taxis Taxis to the centre are comfortable, a/c and

reasonably priced, although the driving can be hairy. Walk past the pricey taxis and limousines on offer within the baggage hall and arrivals hall, and ignore any tout who may offer a cheap ride in an unlicensed and unmetered vehicle, as newly arrived travellers are seen as easy prey for robbery and the cabs are untraceable. Licensed and metered public taxis are operated from clearly signposted and well-regulated counters, outside Floor 1's landside Gates 4 and 7. Including the B50 airport pick-up fee and around B70 tolls for the overhead expressways, a journey to Thanon Silom downtown, for example, should set you back around B400, depending on the traffic. Heading back to the airport, drivers will nearly always try to leave their meters off and agree an inflated price with you – say "*poet meter, dai mai khrap/kha?*" to get them to switch the meter on. If you leave the downtown areas before 7am or after 9pm you can get to the airport in half an hour, but at other times it's best to set off at least an hour and a half before you have to check in.

Public Transportation Centre Situated on the other side of the huge airport complex from the terminal building, the Public Transportation Centre is reached by a free 10min ride on an "Express" shuttle bus (every 10min) from Gate 5 outside arrivals or Gate 5 outside departures – be sure not to confuse these with the much slower "Ordinary" shuttle buses, which ferry airport staff around the complex.

City buses and minibuses The Bangkok Mass Transit Authority operates the S1 service to Thanon Khao San from outside Gate 7 of the terminal building's Floor 1 roughly every 45min (B60). The BMTA also runs other public a/c buses and minibuses out of the Public Transportation Centre, but they're really designed for airport staff. The route that's most likely to appeal to visitors is the #551 a/c minibus to Victory Monument (every 5–20min; B40), which starts at the Public Transportation Centre and picks up outside the terminal's Floor 1 (Gates 1 and 8); however, if they fill up at the Public Transportation Centre, there'll be no pick-up at the terminal. On departure, many travellers opt for one of the private minibus services to Suvarnabhumi (B130–150) organized through guesthouses and travel agents in Banglamphu and elsewhere around the city.

Long-distance buses From the Public Transportation Centre, there are public (Baw Khaw Saw) long-distance buses and minibuses to Hua Hin, Pattaya, Chanthaburi, Trat, Ko Chang, Aranyaprathet, Khorat, Khon Kaen, Udon Thani and Nong Khai. Because of the inconvenience involved, many of these services also stop at Gate 8, Floor 1 of the terminal building (with information counters just inside the terminal); in the opposite direction, some of these buses continue to Bangkok's Eastern or Northern (Mo Chit) Bus Terminals.

Car rental companies The car-rental companies in the arrivals hall (Floor 2) near Gate 8 include Avis and Budget (see page 141).

DON MUANG
The old Don Muang Airport (coded "DMK"; ⊚donmueang airportthai.com), 25km north of the city, is now Bangkok's main base for low-cost airlines (though some still use Suvarnabhumi – check your booking carefully); its two interconnected buildings effectively form one very long terminal. It shelters currency exchange booths, ATMs, car-rental outlets, a left-luggage depot (B75/item/day), a post office and plenty of places to eat.

By taxi The easiest way to get into the city centre is by licensed, metered taxi from outside the arrivals hall on Floor 1, costing about B400, including B50 airport fee and expressway fees (B110 to Banglamphu, for instance).

By shuttle bus to/from Suvarnabhumi Airport Operating between every 12min and every 30min (see ⊚bangkokairportonline.com for times), an a/c shuttle bus that's free to passengers runs between the airports; at Suvarnabhumi, it picks up outside Gate 3, Floor 2, and drops off outside Gate 5, Floor 4. Allow at least 50min for the journey.

By Limobus These small, a/c, wifi-enabled buses (⊚limobus.co.th) operate two circular routes from outside the arrivals hall on Floor 1 (both roughly every 30min–1hr; B150), one to Thanon Khao San and one to Silom.

By public bus The Bangkok Mass Transit Authority offers several special services from outside the arrivals hall (all a/c): A1 (every 5min; B30) to Mo Chit Skytrain and Chatuchak Park subway stations and the nearby Northern Bus Terminal (Mo Chit); A2 (every 10min; B30) to Victory Monument; A3 (every 30min; B50) to Lumpini Park; and A4 (every 30min; B50) to Thanon Khao San. You could also chance your arm on the regular city buses that stop on the main highway running north–south in front of the airport buildings: the a/c and non-a/c #59 bus, for example, will drop you off on Thanon Rajdamnoen Klang near Banglamphu.

By minibus from the centre On departure, many travellers opt for one of the private minibus services to Don Muang (B130–150) organized through guesthouses and travel agents in Banglamphu and elsewhere around the city.

By train You can spare yourself the trip into Bangkok if you're planning to head north or northeast by train, as all services to these parts stop at Don Muang station. To reach the station, which is near the *Amari Airport Hotel* across the main highway, follow the signs from Arrivals.

Destinations Chiang Mai (25 daily; 1hr); Chiang Rai (14 daily; 1hr 15min); Chumphon (2 daily; 1hr); Khon Kaen (21 daily; 55min); Ko Samui (25 daily; 1hr–1hr 30min); Krabi (15 daily; 1hr 20min); Lampang (7 daily; 1hr 15min); Loei (4 daily; 1hr); Mae Sot (4 daily; 1hr 15min); Nakhon Phanom (3 daily; 1hr 15min); Nakhon Si Thammarat (12 daily; 1hr 10min); Nan (5 daily; 1hr 20min–1hr 30min); Phitsanulok (5–10 daily; 1hr); Phrae (2 daily; 1hr 30min); Phuket (30 daily; 1hr 20min); Ranong (2 daily; 1hr 30min); Sukhothai (3 daily; 1hr 20min); Surat Thani (17 daily; 1hr 15min);

Trang (5 daily; 1hr 30min); Trat (3 daily; 50min); Ubon Ratchathani (12 daily; 1hr 5min); Udon Thani (26 daily; 1hr).

BY TRAIN

Travelling to Bangkok by train from Malaysia and most parts of Thailand, you arrive at the main Hualamphong Station (note that an old plan to make Bang Sue to the north Bangkok's main station has recently resurfaced in the Thai news). Trains from Kanchanaburi, however, plus a handful from Nakhon Pathom, Hua Hin and other slow, local trains on the Southern line, pull in at Thonburi Station, while Samut Sakhon trains use Wongwian Yai Station (see page 182), also in Thonburi.

HUALAMPHONG STATION

Centrally located at the edge of Chinatown, Hualamphong Station is on the subway line and is connected to Banglamphu by bus #53. Station facilities include an exchange booth, several ATMs and a left-luggage office at the front of the main concourse (daily 4am–11pm; B20–80/day). The State Railways (SRT) information booth in the main concourse, on the right (daily 4am–11pm), keeps English-language timetables, while tickets can be bought at nearby, clearly signed ticket counters (daily 4am–11pm). Train tickets can also be bought online or through almost any travel agent and some hotels and guesthouses for a booking fee of about B50. See "Basics" for more information on tickets and timetables (see page 32). The station area used to be known as fertile ground for con-artists with fake IDs, but seems to have cleaned up its act; all the same, as at most major train stations across the world, it's as well to keep your wits about you.

Destinations Aranyaprathet (2 daily; 6hr); Ayutthaya (23–32 daily; 1hr 30min–2hr); Cha-am (3 daily; 3hr 10min–3hr 50min); Chiang Mai (5 daily; 12–14hr); Chumphon (10 daily; 7hr–9hr 30min); Hua Hin (11 daily; 3hr 30min–5hr); Khon Kaen (4 daily; 8hr 30min–9hr 45min); Khorat (11 daily; 4hr 30min–6hr 40min); Lampang (5 daily; 10–12hr); Lamphun (5 daily; 12–14hr); Lopburi (16 daily; 2hr 30min–3hr); Nakhon Pathom (12 daily; 1hr 30min); Nakhon Si Thammarat (2 daily; 15hr 30min–16hr 30min); Nong Khai (3 daily; 11–13hr); Padang Besar (for Malaysia; 1 daily; 17hr 45min); Pak Chong (for Khao Yai National Park; 11 daily; 3hr 30min–4hr 45min); Pattaya (1 daily; 4hr); Phetchaburi (11 daily; 2hr 45min–3hr 45min); Phitsanulok (11 daily; 5hr 30min–8hr); Prachuap Khiri Khan (8 daily; 5–7hr); Pranburi (1 daily; 5hr); Si Racha (1 daily; 3hr 30min); Si Saket (8 daily; 8–11hr); Surat Thani (10 daily; 9–12hr); Surin (10 daily; 6hr 30min–9hr 30min); Trang (2 daily; 15–16hr); Ubon Ratchathani (7 daily; 8hr 35min–12hr 15min); Udon Thani (4 daily; 10–12hr).

THONBURI STATION

Thonburi Station (sometimes still referred to by its former name, Bangkok Noi Station) is a short ride in a public songthaew or an 850m walk west from the N11 express-boat pier, just across the Chao Phraya River from Banglamphu and Ratanakosin.

OVERLAND TO OTHER COUNTRIES IN ASIA

Most travellers who choose to make their way **overland from Thailand** to one of its neighbours (see page 29) do so slowly, but it is possible to do many of the border-hops in one swoop from Bangkok. To get **from Bangkok to Laos**, there are public (Baw Khaw Saw) buses direct from Mo Chit to Vientiane (1 daily; 10hr) and Pakse (2 daily; 11hr 30min), or you can take a bus to the border at Chiang Khong, Nong Khai (which also has a train service from the capital), Nakhon Phanom, Mukdahan or Chong Mek. For transport **to Cambodia**, there are public buses direct from Mo Chit to Siem Reap (2 daily; 7hr 30min) and Phnom Penh (1 daily; 11hr) or you can take a bus from Bangkok to Trat (for Sihanoukville) or a train or bus from Bangkok to Aranyaprathet (for Siem Reap). Khao San travel agents offer cheap direct buses to Siem Reap, but scams and discomfort on these services are common (see page 379). The easiest way of travelling from Bangkok **to Malaysia** is by train to the west coast of the peninsula. There is one train a day from Bangkok's Hualamphong Station to Padang Besar on the border (18hr), which costs about B900 in a second-class sleeper; it's possible to make onward train connections to Butterworth (for Penang), Kuala Lumpur and Singapore. For **Myanmar**, there are direct buses from Bangkok to Mae Sai, Mae Sot and Ranong (though the quickest way to set foot on Burmese soil would be to catch a bus to Kanchanaburi, then an a/c minibus to Phu Nam Ron).

All the **foreign embassies and consulates** in Bangkok are located in the downtown area (see page 170). Phone ahead to check the opening hours (usually very limited) and documentation required. Some travellers prefer to avoid the hassle of trudging out to the relevant embassy by paying one of the Khao San travel agencies to get their visa for them; beware of doing this, however, as some agencies are reportedly **faking the stamps**, which causes serious problems at immigration.

Destinations Cha-am (2 daily; 3hr 30min–4hr 30min); Chumphon (1 daily; 9hr 30min); Hua Hin (2 daily; 4–5hr); Kanchanaburi (2 daily; 2hr 35min); Nakhon Pathom (5 daily; 1hr 10min); Nam Tok (2 daily; 4hr 35min); Phetchaburi (2 daily; 2hr 45min–3hr 45min); Prachuap Khiri Khan (2 daily; 6–7hr); Pranburi (2 daily; 5hr–5hr 30min).

BY BUS

Bangkok's three main bus terminals, all of which have left-luggage facilities of some kind, are distributed around the outskirts of town. On departure, leave plenty of time to reach them, especially if setting off from Banglamphu, from where you should allow at least 1hr 30min (outside rush hour) to get to the Eastern Bus Terminal, and a good hour to get to the Northern or Southern terminals. On many shorter routes, buses have been wholly or partly replaced by *rot tuu* (a/c minibuses), which now depart from the same three terminals. Seats on the most popular long-distance a/c bus services (such as to Chiang Mai, Krabi, Phuket and Surat Thani) should be reserved ahead of time, most easily at the ATS (Advanced Technology Systems; Mon–Fri 8.30am–5pm) office near the *Royal Ratanakosin Hotel* on Thanon Rajdamnoen Klang in Banglamphu, the official seller of government bus tickets. Otherwise, go to the relevant bus station or use any of the ways described in Basics (see page 31), as guesthouses may book you on to one of the dodgy tourist services (see page 136).

NORTHERN AND NORTHEASTERN BUS TERMINAL (MO CHIT)

All services from the north and northeast terminate at Bangkok's biggest bus station, the Northern and Northeastern Bus Terminal (Mo Chit) on Thanon Kamphaeng Phet 2; some buses from the south and the east coast also use Mo Chit (there are plans to move Mo Chit to another site that's closer to the Skytrain and subway within the next few years, reportedly by 2023). The quickest way to get into the city centre from Mo Chit is to hop onto the Skytrain at Mo Chit Station on Thanon Phaholyothin, or the subway at the adjacent Chatuchak Park Station or at Kamphaeng Phet Station (at the bottom of Thanon Kamphaeng Phet 2), all of which are about a 15min walk from the bus terminal, and then change onto a city bus if necessary. Otherwise, it's a long bus or taxi ride into town: city buses from the Northern Bus Terminal include ordinary #3, and a/c #509 to Banglamphu. A/c minibuses for the Southern Bus Terminal depart every 20min.

Destinations Aranyaprathet (at least hourly; 4hr 30min); Ayutthaya (every 20min; 1hr 30min–2hr); Chanthaburi (9 daily; 4hr); Chiang Khan (6 daily; 9–11hr); Chiang Khong (9 daily; 13–14hr); Chiang Mai (30 daily; 10–11hr); Chiang Rai (24 daily; 11–12hr); Chong Mek (5 daily; 10hr); Kamphaeng Phet (hourly; 6hr 30min); Kanchanaburi (roughly hourly; 3hr); Khon Kaen (every 30min; 6–7hr); Khorat (every 40min; 3–4hr); Khong Chiam (2 daily; 12hr); Lampang (at least hourly; 8–9hr); Loei (hourly; 8–10hr); Lopburi (every 20min; 2–3hr); Mae Hong Son (3 daily; 15hr); Mae Sai (12 daily; 13hr); Mae Sariang (5 daily; 12hr); Mae Sot (13 daily; 8hr 30min); Mukdahan (20 daily; 10–11hr); Nakhon Phanom (24 daily; 12hr); Nan (20 daily; 10–11hr); Nong Khai (18 daily; 11hr); Pak Chong (for Khao Yai National Park; hourly; 2–3hr); Pakse (Laos; 2 daily; 12hr); Pattaya (every 30min; 2hr 30min–3hr 30min); Phitsanulok (over 40 daily; 5–6hr); Phnom Penh (Cambodia; 1 daily; 11hr); Phrae (13 daily; 8hr); Sangkhlaburi (2 daily; 7hr 30min); Siem Reap (Cambodia; 2 daily; 7hr); Si Racha (every 40min; 2hr); Si Saket (9 daily; 7–9hr); Sukhothai (over 30 daily; 6–7hr); Surin (at least hourly; 7hr); That Phanom (6 daily; 12hr); Trat (hourly; 4hr 30min); Ubon Ratchathani (20 daily; 8hr 30min–10hr); Udon Thani (every 30min; 9hr); Vientiane (Laos; 1 daily; 11hr).

EASTERN BUS TERMINAL (EKAMAI)

Most buses to and from east-coast destinations such as Pattaya, Ban Phe (for Ko Samet) and Trat (for Ko Chang) use the Eastern Bus Terminal (Ekamai) between sois 40 and 42 on Thanon Sukhumvit. This bus station is right beside the Ekamai Skytrain stop and is also served by lots of city buses, including a/c #511 to and from Banglamphu and the Southern Bus Terminal. Alternatively, you can use the Khlong Saen Saeb canal-boat service, which runs westwards almost as far as Banglamphu (see page 138); there's a pier called Tha Charn Issara, near the northern end of Sukhumvit Soi 63 (Soi Ekamai), which is easiest reached from the bus station by taxi.

Destinations Ban Phe (for Ko Samet; 14 daily; 3hr–3hr 30min); Chanthaburi (at least hourly; 4–5hr); Laem Ngop (for Ko Chang; 3–4 daily; 5hr 15min–6hr); Pattaya (every 30min; 2hr 30min–3hr 30min); Si Racha (every 40min; 1hr 30min–2hr 30min); Trat (6 daily; 4hr 30min–6hr).

SOUTHERN BUS TERMINAL (SATHAANII SAI TAI)

The huge, airport-like New Southern Bus Terminal, or Sathaanii Sai Tai Mai, handles transport to and from all points south of the capital, including Hua Hin, Chumphon (for Ko Tao), Surat Thani (for Ko Samui), Phuket and Krabi, as well as buses for destinations west of Bangkok, such as Amphawa, Nakhon Pathom and Kanchanaburi. The terminal lies at the junction of Thanon Borom Ratchanani and Thanon Phutthamonthon Sai 1 in Taling Chan, an interminable 11km west of the Chao Phraya River and Banglamphu, so access to and from city accommodation can take an age, even in a taxi. City buses serving the Southern Bus Terminal include #124 for Banglamphu and #511 for Banglamphu, Thanon Sukhumvit and Ekamai, while a/c minibuses between the Southern and Northern Bus Terminals depart every 20min. Note that when arriving in Bangkok many long-distance bus services make a more

1

convenient stop before reaching the terminus (via a time-consuming U-turn), towards the eastern end of Thanon Borom Ratchanoni, much nearer Phra Pinklao Bridge and the river; the majority of passengers get off here and it's highly recommended to do the same rather than continue to the terminal. The above-listed city buses also cross the river from this bus drop, as do many additional services, and this is also a faster and cheaper place to grab a taxi into town. Nearly all a/c minibuses to points west and south of Bangkok now use the New Southern Bus Terminal, but when Bangkok's a/c minibuses were suddenly expelled from Victory Monument in 2016, a few companies set up shop (possibly temporarily) in the Old Southern Bus Terminal (Sathaanii Sai Tai Kao, aka Pinklao). On arrival in Bangkok, you may find yourself being deposited at the Old, rather than the New Southern Bus Terminal – handy, as it's much closer to the centre of town.

Destinations Amphawa (at least hourly, from the Old Southern Bus Terminal; 2hr); Cha-am (at least hourly; 2hr 45min–3hr 15min); Chumphon (roughly hourly; 7–9hr); Damnoen Saduak (every 30min; 2hr); Hua Hin (at least hourly; 3–4hr); Kanchanaburi (every 20min; 2hr 30min); Khao Lak (3 daily; 12hr); Ko Pha Ngan (3 daily; 13hr–15hr 30min); Ko Samui (8–10 daily; 12–13hr); Krabi (12 daily; 12–14hr); Nakhon Pathom (every 30min; 40min–1hr 20min); Nakhon Si Thammarat (20 daily; 13hr); Phang Nga (5 daily; 13hr); Phetchaburi (at least every 30min; 2hr 15min); Phuket (21 daily; 12hr); Prachuap Khiri Khan (roughly every 30min; 4–5hr); Pranburi (every 30min; 3hr 30min); Ranong (15 daily; 9hr); Samut Songkhram (every 20min; 1hr 30min); Satun (4 daily; 16hr); Surat Thani (20 daily; 9–12hr); Trang (5 daily; 12hr).

BY TOURIST BUS

Many Bangkok tour operators sell tickets for unlicensed budget tourist buses and minibuses to popular long-distance destinations such as Chiang Mai, Surat Thani (for Ko Samui) and Krabi (for Ko Phi Phi), and to places closer at hand such as Kanchanaburi, Ko Samet and Ko Chang. Their only advantage is convenience, as they mostly leave from the Khao San area in Banglamphu. Prices, however, can vary considerably but rarely work out cheaper than licensed buses or a/c minibuses from the public terminals. The big drawbacks, however, are the lack of comfort and poor safety, which particularly applies to the long-distance overnight services. It is standard practice for budget tour operators, especially those on Thanon Khao San, to assure you that overnight transport will be in a large, luxury VIP bus despite knowing it's actually a clapped-out old banger. Security on overnight tourist buses is a serious problem, and because they're run by unlicensed private companies there is no insurance against loss or theft of baggage: don't keep anything of value in luggage that's stored out of sight, even if it's padlocked, as luggage sometimes gets slashed and rifled in the roomy baggage compartment. In addition, passengers sometimes find themselves

TOURS OF THE CITY

Unlikely as it sounds, the most popular organized **tours** in Bangkok for independent travellers are by bicycle, heading to the city's outer neighbourhoods and beyond; these are an excellent way to gain a different perspective on Thai life and offer a unique chance to see traditional communities close up. In addition to those listed below, other tour options include Thonburi canal tours (see page 110), Chao Phraya Express tourist boats (see page 137), boat tours to Ko Kred (see page 131) and dinner cruises along the Chao Phraya River (see page 150).

ABC Amazing Bangkok Cyclist Tours 10/5–7 Soi Aree, Soi 26, Thanon Sukhumvit ☎ 02 665 6364, ⓦ realasia.net. ABC's popular, long-running and child-friendly bicycle tours last half a day or a full day, starting in the Sukhumvit area and taking you across the river to surprisingly rural khlong- and riverside communities (including a floating market at weekends); they also offer cycle-and-dine tours in the evening. Tours operate every day year-round, cover up to 24km depending on the itinerary, and need to be reserved in advance (B1300–2400 including bicycle).

Bangkok Bike Rides (Spice Roads) 45 Soi Pannee, Soi Pridi Banomyong 26, Soi 71, Thanon Sukhumvit ☎ 02 381 7490, ⓦ bangkokbikerides. com or ⓦ spiceroads.com. Bangkok Bike Rides runs a programme of half a dozen day and half-day tours

within Greater Bangkok (from B1450/person), including Ko Kred, as well as to the floating markets and canalside neighbourhoods of Damnoen Saduak and to Ayutthaya. Also offers multi-day trips, mountain biking and road biking out of the city.

Bangkok Vanguards Based at Innspire (see page 145) ⓦ bangkokvanguards.com. Fun, educational and unconventional tours (from B1700), with a focus on social entrepreneurism, including walking tours of Chinatown and evening bike tours.

Velo Thailand Soi 4, Thanon Samsen ☎ 02 628 8628, ⓦ velothailand.com. Velo Thailand runs half a dozen different bike tours of the capital (and further afield) out of its cycle shop on the edge of Banglamphu, including an after-dark tour (6–10pm; B1100) that takes in floodlit sights including Wat Pho and Wat Arun.

dumped on the outskirts of their destination city, at the mercy of unscrupulous touts. Bear in mind that Khao San tour operators open up and go bust all the time; never hand over any money until you see the ticket. One tourist company that is licensed and reliable is Lomprayah, who operate catamarans to Ko Tao, Ko Pha Ngan and Ko Samui and connecting buses from Banglamphu to Chumphon. They have an office at 154 Thanon Ram Buttri (☎02 629 2569–70, ⓦlomprayah.com). Recommended travel agents are listed in the Directory (see page 170).

GETTING AROUND

Getting around can undoubtedly be a headache in a city where it's not unusual for residents to spend 3hr getting to work. The main form of transport is **buses**, with a labyrinth of routes that reaches every part of the city, albeit slowly. Catching the various kinds of **taxi** is more expensive, and you'll still get held up by the daytime traffic jams. **Boats** are obviously more limited in their range, but they're regular and as cheap as buses, and you'll save a lot of time by using them whenever possible – a journey between Banglamphu and Saphan Taksin, for instance, will take around 30min by water, half what it would usually take on land. The **Skytrain** and **subway** each have a similarly limited range but are also worth using whenever suitable for all or part of your journey; their networks roughly coincide with each other at the east end of Thanon Silom, at the corner of Soi Asoke and Thanon Sukhumvit, and on Thanon Phaholyothin by Chatuchak Park (Mo Chit), while the Skytrain joins up with the Chao Phraya River express boats at the vital hub of Sathorn/Saphan Taksin (Taksin Bridge). At each Skytrain and subway station, you'll find a useful map of the immediate neighbourhood. Also under construction in the north of the city is the elevated metro line known as the SRT Dark Red Line from Bang Sue (to connect with the subway), which will (eventually) stop at the Northern Bus Terminal (Mo Chit) and Don Muang airport.

BY BUS

Bangkok has reputedly the world's largest bus network (see page 138), on which operate two main types of bus service. On ordinary (non-a/c) buses, which are mostly red and white or blue and white, fares range from B6.50 to B9.50; most routes operate from about 5am to 11pm, but some maintain a 24hr service. Air-conditioned buses are mostly either blue, orange or yellow and charge between B10 and B23 according to distance travelled; most stop in the late evening, but a few of the more popular routes run 24hr services. As buses can only go as fast as the car in front, which at the moment is averaging 4km/h, you'll probably be spending a long time on each journey, so you'd be well advised to pay the extra for cool air – and the a/c buses are usually less crowded, too. The main problem with using Bangkok's buses is getting reliable, up-to-date information. The Bangkok Mass Transit Authority keeps the Thai-language pages of its website (ⓦbmta.co.th) current, but the English-language route descriptions haven't been updated for a while, and in any case are difficult to follow. Easier-to-use maps are available in bookshops – Thinknet's

Bangkok Bus Guide – and online on ⓦtransitbangkok.com, but neither had been updated for a few years at the time of research.

BY BOAT

Bangkok was built as an amphibious city around a network of canals (khlongs) and the first streets were constructed only in the second half of the nineteenth century. Many canals remain on the Thonburi side of the river, but most of those on the Bangkok side have been turned into roads. Longtail boats (*reua hang yao*) ply the canals of Thonburi like commuter buses, stopping at designated shelters (fares are in line with those of express boats), and are available for individual rental here and on the river (see page 110). The Chao Phraya River itself is still a major transport route for residents and non-residents alike, forming more of a link than a barrier between the two halves of the city.

EXPRESS BOATS

The Chao Phraya Express Boat Company operates the vital express-boat (*reua duan*; ⓦchaophrayaexpressboat.com) services, using large water buses to plough up and down the river, between clearly signed piers (*tha*), which appear on all Bangkok maps. Tha Sathorn, which gives access to the Skytrain network, has been designated "Central Pier", with piers to the south of here numbered S1, S2, etc, those to the north N1, N2 and so on. Boats do not necessarily stop at every landing – they only pull in if people want to get on or off, and when they do stop, it's not for long – so when you want to get off, be ready at the back of the boat in good time for your pier. No-flag, local-line boats call at every pier between Nonthaburi and Wat Rajsingkorn, 90min away to the south beyond Sathorn, but only operate during rush hour (Mon–Fri, departing roughly 6.45–7.30am & 4–4.30pm; B10–14). The only boats to run all day, every day, are on the limited-stop orange-flag service (Nonthaburi to Wat Rajsingkorn in about 1hr; departing roughly 6am–7pm or later, every 5–20min; B15). Other limited-stop services run during rush hour, flying either a yellow flag (between Nonthaburi and Tha Sathorn, in about 40min; Mon–Fri, departing Nonthaburi roughly 6.15–8.20am, and returning from Tha Sathorn roughly 4.45–8pm; B20) or a green flag (Pakkred to Tha Sathorn Mon–Fri 6.10–8.10am, Tha Sathorn to Pakkred Mon–Fri 4.05–6.05pm; about 50min; B13–32). Tickets can be bought on board; don't discard your ticket until you're off the boat, as the staff at some piers impose a B1 fine on anyone disembarking without one.

USEFUL BUS ROUTES

In addition to those listed below, there are also bus routes from Suvarnabhumi Airport (see page 132) and Don Muang (see page 133). In Banglamphu, finding the right bus stop can sometimes be tricky (see page 98).

#3 (ordinary)
Northern Bus Terminal–Chatuchak Weekend Market–Thanon Phaholyothin–Thanon Samsen–Thanon Chakrabongse/Thanon Phra Arthit (for Banglamphu guesthouses)–Thanon Sanam Chai (for Museum of Siam)– Memorial Bridge–Taksin Monument (for Wongwian Yai) –Krung Thonburi Skytrain station.

#15 (ordinary)
Sanam Luang–Thanon Phra Arthit–Thanon Chakrabongse (for Banglamphu guesthouses)–Democracy Monument–Siam Square–Thanon Rajdamri–Thanon Silom–Thanon Charoen Krung (for Saphan Taksin and Asiatique).

#16 (ordinary and a/c)
Northern Bus Terminal–Chatuchak Weekend Market–Thanon Samsen–Thewet (for guesthouses)–Thanon Phitsanulok–Thanon Phrayathai–Siam Square–Thanon Suriwong.

#25 (ordinary)
Pak Nam (for Ancient City buses)–Thanon Sukhumvit–Eastern Bus Terminal–Siam Square–Hualamphong Station–Thanon Yaowarat (for Chinatown)–Pahurat–Wat Pho–Tha Chang (for the Grand Palace).

#53 circular (also anticlockwise; ordinary)
Thewet–Thanon Krung Kasem– Hualamphong Station–Thanon Yaowarat (for Chinatown)–Pahurat–Thanon Maharat (for Wat Pho and the Grand Palace)–Sanam Luang (for National Museum)–Thanon Phra Arthit and Thanon Samsen (for Banglamphu guesthouses)–Thewet.

#124 (ordinary and a/c)
Sanam Luang–Phra Pinklao Bridge–Southern Bus Terminal.

#503 (a/c)
Sanam Luang–Democracy Monument (for Banglamphu guesthouses)–Thanon Rajdamnoen Nok (for TAT and boxing stadium)–Wat Benjamabophit–Thanon Sri Ayutthaya–Victory Monument–Chatuchak Weekend Market–Rangsit.

#508 (ordinary and a/c)
Sanam Luang–Grand Palace–Siam Square–Thanon Sukhumvit–Eastern Bus Terminal–Pak Nam (for Ancient City buses).

#509 (a/c)
Northern Bus Terminal–Chatuchak Weekend Market–Victory Monument–Thanon Rajdamnoen Nok (for TAT and boxing stadium)–Democracy Monument–Thanon Rajdamnoen Klang (for Banglamphu guesthouses)–Phra Pinklao Bridge–Thonburi.

#511 (a/c)
Southern Bus Terminal–Phra Pinklao Bridge (for Banglamphu guesthouses)–Democracy Monument–Thanon Sukhumvit–Eastern Bus Terminal–Pak Nam (for Ancient City buses).

CHAO PHRAYA TOURIST BOATS

The Chao Phraya Express Boat Company also runs tourist boats (ⓦchaophrayatouristboat.com), distinguished by their light-blue flags, between Sathorn (departing every 30min, 9am–5.30pm) and Phra Arthit piers (departing every 30min, 9.30am–6pm). In between (in both directions), these boats call in at River City, Rachawongse, Yodpiman (adjacent to Memorial Bridge), Thien (under renovation at the time of writing, so boats were stopping at Wat Arun instead), Maharat (near Wat Mahathat, the National Museum and the Grand Palace) and Thonburi Railway Station pier. Boats departing Phra Arthit between 4pm and 6pm extend their journey southwards beyond Sathorn to Asiatique (see page 165). On-board guides provide running commentaries, and a one-day ticket for unlimited trips costs B180; one-way tickets are also available, costing B50.

CROSS-RIVER FERRIES

Smaller than express boats are the slow cross-river ferries (*reua kham fak*), which shuttle back and forth between the same two points. Found at or beside every express-boat stop and plenty of other piers in between, they are especially useful for exploring Thonburi. Fares are generally B3–4, payable at the entrance to the pier.

KHLONG SAEN SAEB BOATS

On the Bangkok side, Khlong Saen Saeb is well served by passenger boats, which run at least every 20min during daylight hours (eastbound services start and end a little later; ⓦ khlongsaensaep.com). They start from the Phan Fah pier (Panfa Leelard) at the Golden Mount (handy for Banglamphu, Ratanakosin and Chinatown), and head way out east to Wat Sribunruang, with useful stops at Thanon Phrayathai, aka Saphan Hua Chang (for Jim Thompson's House and Ratchathevi Skytrain stop); Pratunam (for the Erawan Shrine); Soi Chitlom; Thanon Witthayu (Wireless Road); and Soi Nana Nua (Soi 3), Thanon Asok Montri (Soi 21, for TAT headquarters and Phetchaburi subway stop), Soi Thonglor (Soi 55) and Charn Issara, near Soi Ekamai (Soi 63), all off Thanon Sukhumvit. This is your quickest and most interesting way of getting between the west and east parts of town, if you can stand the stench of the canal. You may have trouble actually locating the piers as few are signed in English and they all look very unassuming and rickety (see page 80); keep your eyes peeled for a plain wooden jetty – most jetties serve boats running in both directions. Once you've jumped on the boat, state your destination to the conductor when he collects your fare, which will be between B9 and B19. Due to the construction of some low bridges, all passengers change onto a different boat at Tha Pratunam – just follow the crowd. There's now also a tourist boat service (ⓦ bangkokcanal.com) on part of Khlong Saen Saeb and Khlong Banglamphu, running every 30min (10am–6pm) from Pratunam, via Saphan Hua Chang and Phan Fah, to Tha Khlong Banglamphu, which is near Thanon Samsen and handy for Thanon Khao San; the cost is B200 for a day-pass with unlimited rides.

KHLONG PADUNG KRUNG KASEM BOATS
This new, little-publicized and possibly experimental service (Mon–Fri 6–9am & 4–8pm every 20min, daytime services may be added; Sat & Sun 8am–8pm every 30min; free) runs along the canal between Hualamphong Station and the pier at Talat Dhevaraj (Thewet Market), which is 10min walk from the Thewet guesthouses and the express-boat pier at Tha Thewet. The only intermediate stops that may be of interest to visitors are at Thanon Nakhorn Sawan and Thanon Rajdamnoen Nok, though there is talk of adding a pier that connects with Khlong Saen Saeb boats in the future.

BY SKYTRAIN
Although its network is limited, the BTS Skytrain, or *rot fai faa* (ⓦ bts.co.th), provides a much faster alternative to the bus, and is clean, efficient and over-vigorously air-conditioned. There are only two Skytrain lines, which interconnect at Siam Square (Central Station). Both run every few minutes from around 6am to midnight, with fares of B15–59/trip depending on distance travelled (you'd really have to be motoring to justify buying a day pass at B140). Most of the ticket machines accept only coins, but you can change notes at staffed counters. The Sukhumvit Line runs from Mo Chit (stop N8) in the northern part of the city, via the interchange at Phayathai (N2) with the airport rail link, to Samrong way out on Thanon Sukhumvit (E15) in around 40min. This line is being extended southeast beyond Samrong towards Kheha station in Samut Prakan (currently scheduled for opening in 2019) and – more slowly – north

CENTRAL STOPS FOR THE CHAO PHRAYA EXPRESS BOATS

N15 Thewet (all express boats) – for Thewet guesthouses.
N14 Rama VIII Bridge (no flag) – for Samsen Soi 5.
N13 Phra Arthit (no flag and orange flag) – for Thanon Phra Arthit, Thanon Khao San and Banglamphu guesthouses.
N12 Phra Pinklao Bridge (all boats) – for Royal Barge Museum.
N11 Thonburi Railway Station (or Bangkok Noi; all boats) – for trains to Kanchanaburi.
N10 Wang Lang (aka Siriraj or Prannok; all boats) – for Wat Rakhang.
N9 Chang (no flag, green flag and orange flag) – for the Grand Palace, Sanam Luang and the National Museum.
N8 Thien (no flag and orange flag) – for Wat Pho, and the cross-river ferry to Wat Arun (at the time of research, Thien express-boat pier was under renovation and express boats were stopping across the river at Wat Arun instead)
N7 Ratchini (aka Rajinee; no flag).
N6 Saphan Phut (Memorial Bridge; no flag and orange flag; boats sometimes stop at the adjacent Yodpiman pier, N6/1, instead) – for Pahurat and Wat Prayoon.
N5 Rachawongse (aka Rajawong; all boats) – for Chinatown.
N4 Harbour (Marine) Department (no flag and orange flag).
N3 Si Phraya (all boats) – walk north past the *Sheraton Royal Orchid Hotel* for River City shopping complex; also for TCDC.
N2 Wat Muang Kae (no flag) – for TCDC.
N1 Oriental (no flag and orange flag) – for Thanon Silom.
Central Sathorn (all boats) – for the Skytrain and Thanon Sathorn.

1

beyond Mo Chit up Thanon Phaholyothin, running along the back of Don Muang Airport (currently slated for 2020). The Silom Line runs from the National Stadium (W1) via Saphan Taksin (Taksin, or Sathorn, Bridge; S6), to link up with the full gamut of express boats on the Chao Phraya River, to Bang Wa (S12) in Thonburi (on Thanon Phetkasem, Highway 4).

BY SUBWAY

Bangkok's underground rail system, the MRT subway (or metro; in Thai, *rot fai tai din*; ⓦ transitbangkok.com), has similar advantages to the Skytrain, though its main Blue Line goes to fewer places of interest for visitors (its other Purple Line running northwest from Tao Poon connects nothing of touristic interest). The Blue Line runs every few minutes between around 6am and midnight from Hualamphong train station, via Silom (near Sala Daeng

Skytrain station), Sukhumvit (near Asoke Skytrain), Phetchaburi (near Makkasan station on the Suvarnabhumi Airport Rail Link), Chatuchak Park (near Mo Chit Skytrain) and Bang Sue train station, to Tao Poon in the north of the city. Building work is under way to continue the Blue Line westwards from Hualamphong to Wat Mangkon Kamalawat in Chinatown, Pahurat, Thanon Sanam Chai in Ratanakosin, then across to Thonburi, with a loop back to Tao Poon (currently due for completion in 2019). Pay your fare (B16–42) at a staffed counter or machine, where you'll receive a token to tap on the entrance gate and insert into your exit gate (the various stored-value cards available are unlikely to be worthwhile for visitors).

BY TAXI

Bangkok taxis come in three main forms and are so plentiful that you rarely have to wait more than a couple of minutes

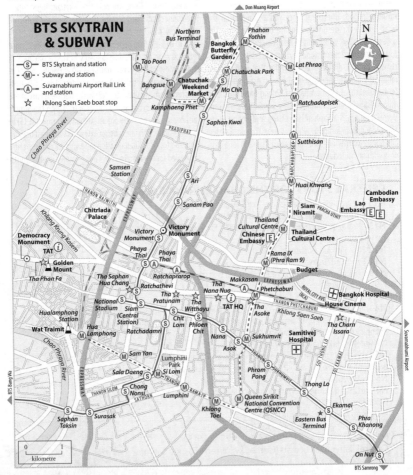

before spotting an empty one of some description. Neither tuk-tuks nor motorbike taxis have meters, so you should agree on a price before setting off, and expect to do a fair amount of haggling. App-based taxi services have recently come to Bangkok, of which the most popular are Grab (which recently took over Uber's Southeast Asian operations) and, in association with the Siam Taxi Co-operative, Line Man (Line is East Asia's equivalent to WhatsApp).

METERED TAXIS

For nearly all journeys, the best and most comfortable option is to flag down one of Bangkok's metered, a/c taxi cabs; look out for the "TAXI METER" sign on the roof, and a red light in the windscreen in front of the passenger seat, which means the cab is available for hire. Starting at B35, fares are displayed on a clearly visible meter that the driver should reset at the start of each trip (say "*poet meter, dai mai khrap/kha?*" to ask him to switch it on), and increase in stages on a combined distance/time formula; as an example, a medium-range journey from Thanon Ploenchit to Thanon Sathorn will cost around B60 at a quiet time of day. Try to have change with you as cabs tend not to carry a lot of money; tipping of up to ten percent is common, though occasionally a cabbie will round down the fare on the meter. If a driver tries to quote a flat fare (often the case with taxis that park outside tourist hotels waiting for business, or with any taxi for journeys to the airports) rather than using the meter, let him go, and avoid the now-rare unmetered cabs (denoted by a "TAXI" sign on the roof). Getting a metered taxi in the middle of the afternoon when the cars return to base for a change of drivers can sometimes be a problem. If you want to book a metered taxi by phone (B20–50 surcharge), try Siam Taxi Co-operative on ☎ 1661.

TUK-TUKS

Somewhat less stable though typically Thai, tuk-tuks in Bangkok have very little to recommend them. These noisy, three-wheeled, open-sided buggies, which can carry three medium-sized passengers comfortably, fully expose you to the worst of Bangkok's pollution and weather. You'll have to bargain very hard to get a fare lower than in a metered taxi; for a longer trip, for example from Thanon Convent to Siam Square, drivers will ask for as much as B200. Be aware,

also, that tuk-tuk drivers tend to speak less English than taxi drivers – and there have been cases of robberies and attacks on women passengers late at night. During the day it's quite common for tuk-tuk drivers to try and con their passengers into visiting a jewellery, tailor's or expensive souvenir shop with them (see page 62).

MOTORBIKE TAXIS

Motorbike taxis generally congregate at the entrances to long sois – pick the riders out by their numbered, coloured vests – and charge from B10 for short trips down into the side streets. If you're short on time and have nerves of steel, it's also possible to charter them for hairy journeys out on the main roads (a short trip from Sanam Luang to Thanon Samsen will cost around B40). Crash helmets are compulsory on all main roads in the capital (traffic police fine non-wearers on the spot), though they're rarely worn on trips down the sois.

CAR RENTAL

You'd be mad to rent a self-drive car for getting around Bangkok, especially as taxis are so cheap, but you may want to start a driving tour around the country here.

Avis Branches are at 13 Soi 1, Thanon Sathorn (delivery and collection anywhere in Bangkok), as well as Suvarnabhumi and Don Muang airports (☎ 02 251 1131–2, ⓦ avisthailand. com).

Budget Branches can be found at the following locations: 19/23 Building A, Royal City Avenue, Thanon Phetchaburi Mai; Suvarnabhumi Airport; and Don Muang Airport (☎ 02 203 9222, ⓦ budget.co.th).

BICYCLE RENTAL

Velo Thailand Soi 4, Thanon Samsen ☎ 02 628 8628, ⓦ velothailand.com. Offers good-quality bikes for B300/ day to brave/foolhardy souls.

MOTORBIKE RENTAL

Rent A Scooter Bangkok, 39/4 Soi Atthakrawi 1, Soi 26, Thanon Sukhumvit ☎ 090 542 3035, ⓦ renta scooterbangkok.com. From B250/day. Not recommended unless you know the Bangkok road system inside out. And even then, accidents are frequent.

INFORMATION

Bangkok Tourism Division The official source of information on the capital, whose head office is next to Phra Pinklao Bridge at 17/1 Thanon Phra Arthit in Banglamphu (Mon–Fri 8am–7pm, Sat & Sun 9am–5pm; ☎ 02 225 7612–4, ⓦ bangkoktourist.com). The head office is supported by about twenty strategically placed satellite booths around the capital; most open Mon–Sat 9am–5pm, though some open Sun too, including in front of the Grand Palace, on Thanon Maharat near Tha Chang, at Paragon

and Mah Boon Krong shopping centres, and in front of Banglamphu's Wat Bowoniwes.

Tourism Authority of Thailand TAT (freephone tourist assistance 8am–8pm ☎ 1672; ⓦ tourismthailand.org) maintains tourist information counters at Suvarnabhumi Airport (see page 132); at its head office, which is rather inconveniently located at 1600 Thanon Phetchaburi Mai (daily 8.30am–4.30pm); and, within walking distance of Banglamphu, at the Ministry of Tourism and Sports, 4

1

Rajdamnoen Nok (daily 8.30am–4.30pm) – it's a 20min stroll from Thanon Khao San, or a short ride in a/c bus #503. Note, however, that the many other travel agents, shops and private offices across the capital displaying "TAT Tourist Information" signs or similar are not official Tourism Authority of Thailand information centres and will not be dispensing impartial advice (they may be licensed by TAT to run their business, but that doesn't make them government information offices). The Tourism Authority of Thailand never uses the acronym TAT on its office-fronts or in its logo, and doesn't book hotels or sell transport tickets.

Useful websites The best of the current websites is *BK*

(Ⓦ bk.asia-city.com), which gives a decent rundown of the art and drama scenes, live music and club nights. If you're interested in Bangkok's contemporary art scene, go to Ⓦ facebook.com/bangkokartmap for exhibition listings.

City maps For a personal guide to Bangkok's most interesting shops, markets, restaurants and backstreets, look for the famously idiosyncratic hand-drawn *Nancy Chandler's Map of Bangkok*. It carries a mass of annotated recommendations, is impressively accurate and regularly reissued; it's sold in most tourist areas, and paper and digital copies and interim updates are also available at Ⓦ nancychandler.net.

ACCOMMODATION

If your time in Bangkok is limited, you should think especially carefully about what you want to do in the city before deciding which part of town to stay in. Traffic jams are so appalling here that easy access to Skytrain, subway or river transport can be crucial. Advance reservations are recommended where possible during high season (Nov–Feb), though some guesthouses will only take cash deposits. For cheap sleeps, your widest choice lies on and around **Banglamphu's** Thanon Khao San. The most inexpensive rooms here are no-frills crash-pads – small and often windowless, with fans, thin walls and shared bathrooms – but Banglamphu also offers plenty of modern-style hostels and well-appointed mid-priced small hotels with a/c and swimming pools. Other, far smaller and less interesting travellers' ghettoes that might be worth bearing in mind are the generally dingy **Soi Ngam Duphli**, off the south side of Thanon Rama IV, which nevertheless harbours a couple of decent shoestring options; and **Soi Kasemsan I**, which is very handily placed next to Siam Square and firmly occupies the moderate range, though with a few rooms for around B700. Otherwise, the majority of the city's moderate and expensive rooms are scattered widely across the **downtown areas**, around Siam Square and Thanon Ploenchit, to the south of Thanon Rama IV and along **Thanon Sukhumvit**, and to a lesser extent in **Chinatown**. As well as easy access to transport links and shops, the downtown views from accommodation in these areas are a real plus, especially from the deluxe hotels that are scenically sited along the banks of the Chao Phraya River. In the reviews that follow, accommodation is a/c, unless specified.

RATANAKOSIN

Several small, upmarket hotels and hostels have recently opened on the west side of Ratanakosin, which put you in a peerless location, in a quiet, traditional, heavily Chinese neighbourhood of low-rise shophouses, overlooking the river and on the doorsteps of Wat Pho and the Grand Palace. The restaurants and nightlife of Banglamphu are within walking distance if you fancy a bit more of a buzz, while

the sights of Thonburi and Chinatown, and Saphan Taksin Skytrain station are just a public boat ride away. It's also well worth considering *Ibrik by the River*, a small, appealing hotel directly opposite Ratanakosin on the Thonburi bank of the Chao Phraya, whose main link with the rest of the city is by cross-river boat.

Arom d Hostel 336 Thanon Maharat ☏ 02 622 1055, Ⓦ aromdhostel.com; map p.83. Meaning "good mood", this hostel and café overlooks Wat Pho from a century-old listed building with balconies and a roof terrace. The stylish, compact rooms include twins, doubles and mixed and women-only dorms with four bunk beds. Breakfast included. Dorms B800, twins B2250

Aurum The River Place 394/27–29 Soi Pansook, Thanon Maharat ☏ 02 622 2248, Ⓦ aurum-bangkok. com; map p.83. Modelled on a French townhouse, with wooden shutters and wrought-iron balconies, this spruce, four-storey hotel is set back very slightly from the river and four of the rooms are "City View" only, but the other eight offer at least partial views of the water. Splashed with colourful Thai fabrics and sporting heavily varnished wooden floors, the well-equipped rooms are a little on the small side, apart from those on the top floor. There's a daytime riverside café, *Vivi: The Coffee Place*, where complimentary breakfast is served. B3500

★ **Bangkok Bed and Bike** 19/6 Th Charoen Krung ☏ 094 487 8058, Ⓦ bangkokbedandbike.com; map p.83. Excellent hostel with a smart urban look, close to Wat Pho and the Grand Palace. Women's and mixed dorms are a/c with hot showers, and there are bicycle tours, bikes for rent (with great hand-drawn maps of the area) and an impressive array of amenities, including a washing machine and drier. Good breakfast included. Dorms B600, doubles B1600

Chakrabongse Villas 396 Thanon Maharat ☏ 02 222 1290, Ⓦ chakrabongsevillas.com; map p.83. Upmarket riverside accommodation with a difference: seven tranquil suites, villas and compact rooms beautifully furnished in a choice of Thai, Chinese and Moroccan styles, set in luxuriant gardens of hundred-year-old Chakrabongse House overlooking Wat Arun. All have cable TV, and there's a small, attractive swimming pool and a riverfront terrace restaurant for dinner (reservations required). B5620

★ **Ibrik by the River** 256 Soi Wat Rakhang ☎086 008 5589, ⓦibrikresort.com; map p.83. With just three rooms, this is the most bijou of boutique resorts. Each room is beautifully appointed in boho-chic style, with traditional wood floors, modernist white walls, mosquito nets over the beds and sparkling silk accessories – and two of them have balconies right over the Chao Phraya River. It's just like staying at a trendy friend's home, in a neighbourhood that sees hardly any other tourists. Located next door to *Supatra River House* restaurant and 5min walk from either express-boat stop Tha Wang Lang or the cross-river pier at Wat Rakhang (for Tha Chang and the Grand Palace). Big discounts outside of peak season. Breakfast included. B4000

Sala Arun 47 Soi Tha Thien, Thanon Maharat ☎02 622 2932–3, ⓦsalaarun.com; map p.83. At this riverside inn, the nine teak-floored rooms feature objets d'art from the owners' worldwide travels, DVDs, iPod docks and balconies (in most), while complimentary breakfast is served in the boldly coloured ground-floor café, which has a small terrace with armchairs facing Wat Arun (to get a view of the river and temple from your room, you'll have to pay B3800). B3200

BANGLAMPHU AND DEMOCRACY MONUMENT AREA

Nearly all backpackers head straight for Banglamphu, Bangkok's long-established travellers' ghetto just north of the Grand Palace, location of the cheapest accommodation, the best traveller-oriented facilities and some of the most enjoyable bars and restaurants in the city. A growing number of Banglamphu guesthouses are reinventing themselves as good-value mini-hotels boasting chic decor, swimming pools, and even views from the windows, and have recently been joined by twenty-first-century hostels, which throw in a measure of style and sociability with your wifi-enabled bunk. The cheap guesthouses are still there, particularly immediately west of Khao San, around the neighbourhood temple Wat Chana Songkhram, and along riverside Thanon Phra Arthit – where you'll also find some upscale places offering prime views over the Chao Phraya. About a 10min walk north from Thanon Khao San, the handful of guesthouses and small hotels scattered among the shophouses of the Thanon Samsen sois enjoy a more authentically Thai environment, while the Thewet area, a further 15min walk in the same direction or a 7min walk from the Thewet express-boat stop, is more local still. Heading south from Khao San, across multi-laned Rajdamnoen Klang, to the upscale places in the area immediately south of Democracy also puts you plumb in the middle of an interesting old neighbourhood, famous for its traditional shophouse restaurants. Theft is a problem in Banglamphu, particularly at the cheaper guesthouses, so don't leave anything valuable in your room and heed the guesthouses' notices about padlocks and safety lockers.

THANON KHAO SAN AND AROUND

Buddy Lodge 265 Thanon Khao San ☎02 629 4477, ⓦbuddylodge.com; map p.100. Stylish hotel right in the thick of the action, whose charming, colonial-style rooms are done out in cream, with louvred shutters, balconies, marble bathrooms and polished dark-wood floors. There's a beautiful rooftop pool, a gym, a sauna and several bars downstairs in the *Buddy Village* complex. Specify an upper-floor location away from Khao San to ensure a quieter night's sleep. B2300

Nap Park 5 Thanon Tani ☎02 282 2324, ⓦnappark.com; map p.100. On a surprisingly untouristed street just north of Thanon Khao San, this lively hostel shelters smart dorm beds with lockers and hot showers (some with personal TVs), as well as plenty of space for lounging, either inside in front of the TV or outside in the tamarind-shaded front yard. Women-only dorm and laundry available. Dorms B399

Suneta Hostel 209–11 Trok Kraisi T02 629 0150, Wsunetahostel.com; map p.100. Welcoming, well-equipped place, 5min walk from Thanon Khao San, done out with acres of wood to give a retro look, offering wide, souped-up bunk beds. Light breakfast included. Free weekly walking tours. Dorms B380, doubles B1180

AROUND WAT CHANA SONGKHRAM AND PHRA ARTHIT

Bella Bella House Soi Ram Bhuttri ☎02 629 3090; map p.100. Above a plant-strewn café, the pastel-coloured rooms here are no frills but well priced, and a few boast lovely views over Wat Chana Songkhram. The cheapest share cold-water bathrooms, a notch up gets you an en-suite hot shower, while the most expensive have a/c. Good prices for single rooms, especially the en-suite ones. Fan B320, a/c B530

KC Guest House 64 Trok Kai Chae, corner of Thanon Phra Sumen ☎02 282 0618, ⓦkc64guesthouse.com; map p.100. Friendly, family-run guesthouse offering exceptionally clean bedrooms, with either en-suite or shared, hot-water bathrooms; try to get a room away from the noisy street. There's also a rooftop terrace and a decked eating area on the soi next to 7-Eleven. B500

Lamphu House 75 Soi Ram Bhuttri ☎02 629 5861–2, ⓦlamphuhouse.com; map p.100. With smart bamboo beds, coconut-wood furniture and elegant rattan lamps in nearly all the rooms, this travellers' hotel set round a quiet courtyard has a calm, modern feel. Cheaper options share facilities (including good-value singles) and the cheapest fan rooms have no outside view; the more expensive options have balconies overlooking the courtyard and the triples and four-person rooms are popular with families. Fan B480, a/c B600

1

Merry V Soi Ram Bhuttri ☎02 282 9267; map p.100. Large, utterly plain but efficiently run guesthouse offering some of the cheapest accommodation in Banglamphu. Bottom-end rooms are basic and small, many share bathrooms and it's pot luck whether you get a window or not. Better en-suites with hot showers and a/c versions are also available. Good rates for singles. Fan B300, a/c B550

Navalai River Resort 45/1 Thanon Phra Arthit ☎02 280 9955, ⓦnavalai.com; map p.100. Style-conscious riverfront hotel, with an elegant rooftop pool, tastefully furnished bedrooms, and river views from the most desirable rooms. There's DVDs, bathtubs and private balconies, and the riverside *Aquatini* restaurant is at ground level (see page 151). B2700

New Siam 1 21 Soi Chana Songkhram ☎02 629 4844, ⓦnewsiam.net; map p.100. Above a pleasant terrace restaurant, the cheaper options here are well-kept tiled-floor rooms (doubles, twins and singles), all with windows and shared cold showers, while the a/c rooms boast en-suite hot showers. Fan B400, a/c B690

★ **New Siam 2** 50 Trok Rong Mai ☎02 282 2795, ⓦnewsiam.net; map p.100. Very pleasant and well-run small hotel whose en-suite rooms with fan and cold shower or a/c and hot shower stand out for their thoughtfully designed extras such as in-room safes, cable TV and drying rails on the balconies. Occupies a quiet but convenient location and has a small pool. Popular with families, and triple rooms are also available. Fan B790, a/c B890

New Siam Riverside 21 Thanon Phra Arthit ☎02 629 3535, ⓦnewsiam.net; map p.100. Occupying a prime spot on the Chao Phraya, the riverside branch of the *New Siam* empire offers well-designed, good-value rooms. Even the cheapest have a/c and full amenities, while the best of them boast fabulous river views from windows or private balconies. Also has a large riverside swimming pool and terrace restaurant. Breakfast included. B1590

★ **Praya Palazzo** 757/1 Soi 2, Thanon Somdet Phra Pinklao ☎02 883 2998, ⓦprayapalazzo.com; map p.100. A peaceful riverside sanctuary right opposite Banglamphu, this large, graceful, Italianate palace has been lovingly restored by an architecture professor, with great attention to detail – right down to the wallpaper and lampshades – to give the feel of its 1920s origins. Twenty-first-century luxuries have been overlaid, of course, such as DVDs and, in the bathrooms, big-head showers to go alongside the brass taps and swathes of coloured marble. There's a lovely pool in the lush waterfront garden, too. Access is by the free hotel boat, which shuttles across to Phra Arthit express-boat pier. No children under 13. Breakfast included. B3955

SAMSEN SOIS AND THEWET

Baan Manusarn 8/11 Thanon Krung Kasem, Thewet ☎02 281 2976, ⓦbaanmanusarn.com; map p.100.

A genuine B&B, friendly and helpful, in a pleasant white building near the pier, offering large rooms with lovely polished wooden floors, some sharing hot showers, and access to a kitchen. Free showers after checkout. Breakfast included. B1330

Lamphu Treehouse 155 Saphan Wanchat, Thanon Phracha Thipatai ☎02 282 0991–2, ⓦlamphutreehotel. com; map p.100. Named after the *lamphu* trees that line the adjacent canal, after which Banglamphu ("the riverside village with mangrove apple trees") is named, this attractively turned-out guesthouse offers a pool and smart rooms, with plenty of polished wood fittings made of recycled golden teak, among other traditional Thai decorative elements; most have balconies, though the cheapest in the nearby annexe are windowless. It's in a quiet neighbourhood but just a few minutes' walk from Democracy. Breakfast included. B1300

Nakorn Ping 9/1 Soi 6, Thanon Samsen ☎02 281 6574, ⓦnakornpinghotel.com; map p.100. In a low-rise, orange building dotted with plants on a fairly quiet soi, this place sports some classic elements of a Thai-Chinese hotel: spittoons for waste baskets, gnarly wooden furniture and little natural light. However, it's very clean, efficiently run and good value, offering fridges, cable TV and bathrooms in all rooms, and hot showers for an extra B100/room/day. Fan B530, a/c B630

★ **Phra Nakorn Norn Len** 46 Thewet Soi 1, Thanon Krung Kasem, Thewet ☎02 628 8188–90, ⓦphranakorn-nornlen.com; map p.100. What was once a seedy short-time motel has been transformed into a leafy bohemian haven with genuine eco-conscious and socially engaged sensibilities and a tangible fair-trade philosophy. Every one of the comfortable, though not luxurious, rooms has been cheerily hand-painted to a different retro Thai design, and each has a cute bathroom and balcony. All kinds of workshops, such as soap-making and cooking, are offered to guests. Mostly organic vegetarian breakfast included. B2600

Rajata Soi 6, Thanon Samsen ☎02 281 8977–8, ⓦrajatahotel.com; map p.100. This traditional motel of large bedrooms and bathrooms around a quiet courtyard café has been subtly transformed with retro furniture, hundreds of plants and a friendly welcome. All of the shining white, spotlessly clean accommodation has satellite TV, hot showers and mini-bars. B1000

Shanti Lodge 37 Thanon Sri Ayutthaya (at Soi 16), Thewet ☎02 281 2497, ⓦshantilodge.com; map p.100. Colourful, old-school-hippy guesthouse with a yoga balcony and a mostly vegetarian restaurant festooned with pot plants. The cheapest "traditional" rooms (fan or a/c) are in a wooden building at the back with shared hot-water bathrooms, but it's worth paying a bit extra for a bright en-suite room in the main building with more space – or splash out B1990 for the penthouse with its big, leafy roof terrace. Dorms B250, fan doubles B500, a/c doubles B600

Sri Ayutthaya 23/11 Thanon Sri Ayutthaya (at Soi 14), Thewet ☎02 282 5942, ⓦfacebook.com/sriayuttaya; map p.100. The most attractive guesthouse in Thewet, where most of the good-sized rooms (choose between fan rooms without private bathroom and en suites with a/c) are elegantly done out with wood-panelled walls and beautiful polished wood floors; these have been augmented by a few modern, "Superior" rooms (B1200) done out in bright, fetching colours. Hot showers throughout. Fan B500, a/c B700

Ssip 42 Thanon Phitsanulok, Thewet ☎02 282 1899, ⓦssiphotelthailand.com; map p.100. Genteel and helpful upmarket B&B where guests are served delicious and beautifully presented breakfasts. It's in a new building on busy Thanon Phitsanulok, but fitted with antique furniture and fixtures and polished-wood floors, as well as hot showers, TVs and fridges. No children under 8. B2200

★ **Tavee** 83 Soi 14, Thanon Sri Ayutthaya, Thewet ☎02 280 1447, ⓦfacebook.com/taveeguesthouse; map p.100. *Tavee* is located down a pedestrian alley behind *Sri Ayutthaya* and is owned by the same family, but is the quieter and friendlier of the two options. Behind the stylish little café, the fan rooms sport attractive wood floors and share chic hot-water bathrooms, while the en-suite a/c options are larger and enjoy a few more decorative touches. Fan B500, a/c B750

SOUTH AND EAST OF DEMOCRACY

Baan Dinso 113 Trok Sin, Thanon Dinso ☎096 565 9795, ⓦbaandinso.com; map p.100. This tasteful, upmarket little guesthouse occupies an elegant, carefully restored 1920s Thai house all done out in cool buttermilk paintwork and polished teak floors. Prices are a little steep considering that all but the deluxe rooms have to use shared ground-floor, hot-water bathrooms, but they all have mini-bars and DVD players. Hostelling International members get a ten percent discount. Breakfast is included. Very good single rates. B1800

★ **Bangkok Publishing Residence** 31/1 Thanon Lan Luang ☎02 282 0288, ⓦbpresidence.com; map p.100. Luxurious, friendly B&B in a beautifully converted printing house, which is also something of a museum to its most famous publication, the Bangkok Weekly magazine, scattered with old typewriters and printing blocks. The eight very comfortable rooms evoke a gentleman's club, with leather armchairs and acres of polished wood, and there's a rooftop garden and Jacuzzi. B4800

★ **The Bhuthorn** 96 Thanon Phraeng Phuthon, just off Thanon Kanlayana Maitri ☎02 622 2270, ⓦthebhuthorn.com; map p.100. The architect-owners have beautifully converted this hundred-year-old shophouse into a B&B. Behind the small lobby lie just three elegant rooms (including a junior suite with a mezzanine for B5600), fitted with Chinese, Thai and Western dark-wood antique furniture, chandeliers, *khon* masks and other

objets d'art, as well as modern comforts. Breakfast included. B4500

Boonsiri Place 55 Thanon Buranasart ☎02 622 2189–91, ⓦboonsiriplace.com; map p.100. Run by two charming sisters, this mid-sized hotel is notable for its good value, environmentally conscious policies and location in a lively, seedy old neighbourhood, just a 10min walk from the Grand Palace. Each of its 48 large rooms with hot showers (an extra B300 buys you considerably more space in a "Deluxe" room) is painted in vibrant colours and hung with a different artwork commissioned from the late Thai traditional temple artist Chanok Chunchob. Buffet breakfast included. B1400

Chern 17 Soi Ratchasak, Thanon Bamrung Muang ☎02 621 1133, ⓦchernbangkok.com; map p.100. This friendly boutique hostel "invites" (chern) you to stay in its sleek, minimalist accommodation, done out in gleaming whites, light wood and quirky murals illustrating Thai proverbs. Choose between eight-bed dorms and good-value, large private rooms with desks, fridges, safes and TVs. Dorms B400, doubles B1400

★ **Innspire** 4/4 Trok Sin, Thanon Dinso ☎097 103 3836, ⓦinnspirebangkok.com; map p.100. Describing itself as a homestay and community space that aims to connect people to Thailand on a deeper level, Innspire is also home to unconventional tour company, Bangkok Vanguards (with discounts for guests; see page 136). Set in an attractive building in a quiet, very traditional neighbourhood, the bright en-suite rooms, some with balconies, overlook a large, leafy courtyard. B1250

★ **Old Capital Bike Inn** 607 Thanon Phra Sumen ☎02 629 1787, ⓦoldcapitalbkk.com; map p.100. Formerly the Old Bangkok Inn, this chic little boutique guesthouse with an eco-friendly philosophy and a vintage bike theme has just ten rooms, each of them individually styled in dark wood, with nostalgic murals, ironwork lamps and elegant contemporary-accented bathrooms. Most of the suites are split-level and some also have a tiny private garden. The guesthouse is located a 10min walk from Khao San. Sit-up-and-beg bicycles and thrice-weekly evening bike tours are free to guests. Breakfast included. B3690

The Warehouse 120 Thanon Bunsri ☎02 622 2935, ⓦthewarehousebangkok.com; map p.100. Just down the road from Boonsiri Place, this new low-rise hotel offers an appealing version of industrial chic, reinforced by its punningly named Forklift Café. Emblazoned with playful health and safety slogans, the good-sized en-suite rooms sport balconies, polished concrete floors, blonde-wood furniture made from palettes and crisp white linens. Breakfast included. B2280

HUALAMPHONG, CHINATOWN AND PAHURAT

Set between the Ratanakosin sights and downtown, Chinatown is among the most frantic and fume-choked

1

parts of Bangkok – and there's quite some competition. If you're in the mood, however, it's got plenty of interest, sees barely any Western overnighters, and is handy for Hualamphong Station and the subway system. Another accommodation option that's handy for Hualamphong is the Oldtown Hostel (see page 149).

Baan Hualamphong 336/20 Soi Chalong Krung ☎ 02 639 8054, ☮ baanhualampong.com; map p.107. Just 5min from Hualamphong, this wooden guesthouse offers a modicum of style and is the most welcoming of several similar places in the soi, with a traveller-friendly vibe. There are big, bright, twin rooms plus five-person dorms, but most bedrooms share bathrooms. It also has kitchen and laundry facilities and inviting lounging areas, and is open 24hr. Very good single rates. Dorms B250, fan doubles B590, a/c doubles B700

Grand China 215 Thanon Yaowarat ☎ 02 224 9977, ☮ grandchina.com; map p.107. The poshest hotel in Chinatown boasts fairly luxurious accommodation in a richly coloured, contemporary style, in its 25-storey tower close to the heart of the bustle, with stunning views over all the city landmarks (the best take in the river), a spa, a pool and a panoramic rooftop restaurant. B3200

★**Shanghai Mansion** 479 Thanon Yaowarat, next to Scala shark's fin restaurant ☎ 02 221 2121, ☮ shanghai mansion.com; map p.107. The most design-conscious accommodation in Chinatown has embraced the modern Chinoiserie look with gusto. It's not actually an historic mansion, but has been purpose-built on the site of a former Beijing opera house, with most bedrooms (and their windows and private terraces) facing onto an appealing, four-storey atrium, and thus cosily isolated from the Chinatown frenzy. Rooms are prettily done out in silks, lacquer-look furniture and lanterns, featuring a lot of sumptuous reds and purples, as well as hot showers, DVD players and complimentary mini-bars. B2670

DOWNTOWN: AROUND SIAM SQUARE AND THANON PLOENCHIT

Siam Square and nearby Thanon Ploenchit are as central as Bangkok gets: all the accommodation listed here is within walking distance of a Skytrain or subway station. On hand are the city's best shopping possibilities – notably the phalanx of malls along Thanon Rama I – and a wide choice of Thai and international restaurants and food courts. There's no ultra-cheap accommodation around here, but a few scaled-up guesthouses complement the hotels. Concentrated in their own small "ghetto" on Soi Kasemsan 1, which runs north off Thanon Rama I, between the Bangkok Art and Cultural Centre and Jim Thompson's House, these offer typical travellers' facilities and basic hotel comforts – a/c and en-suite hot-water bathrooms – at moderate prices; the Khlong Saen Saeb canal-boat pier, Tha Saphan Hua Chang (easily accessed via Thanon Phrayathai), is especially

handy for heading west to the Golden Mount and beyond, to Ratanakosin.

A-One Inn 25/13 Soi Kasemsan 1, Thanon Rama I ☎ 02 215 3029 or ☎ 02 216 4770, ☮ www.aoneinn.com; map p.117. The original upmarket guesthouse on this soi, and still justifiably popular, with plenty of facilities including a reliable left-luggage room. All bedrooms have fridges and cable TV and come in a variety of sizes, including triples; breakfast included. B1750

★**Anantara Siam** 155 Thanon Rajdamri ☎ 02 126 8866, ☮ anantara.com; map p.117. The stately home of Bangkok's top hotels, formerly the *Regent*. Afternoon tea is still served in the monumental lobby, which is adorned with magnificent, vibrant eighteenth-century-style murals depicting the Thai cosmology, and flanked by acclaimed Thai, Italian and Japanese restaurants, a steakhouse, an opulent spa and lovely gardens. The large and luxurious rooms are decorated in warm Thai colours and dark wood and come with complementary smartphones, and there's an excellent concierge service. B7680

Courtyard by Marriott 155/1 Soi Mahadlekluang 1, Thanon Rajdamri ☎ 02 690 1888, ☮ marriott.com; map p.117. On a quiet but very handy soi, this hotel offers most of the facilities of a five-star, but at more manageable prices. The modern design is seductive, gleaming white outside, candy colours and plenty of natural light inside, and there's a long, narrow, infinity pool, a fitness centre and a spa. B4240

Golden House 1025/5–9 Thanon Ploenchit ☎ 02 252 9535–7, ☮ goldenhousebangkok.com; map p.117. A very clean and welcoming small hotel in a peerless location, situated down a short soi by Chit Lom BTS. The colourful, parquet-floored bedrooms are equipped with hot water, cable TV and mini-bar – ask for one of the larger front rooms with bay windows, which leave just enough space for an armchair or two. B1400

Jim's Lodge 125/7 Soi Ruam Rudee, Thanon Ploenchit ☎ 02 255 3100, book through ☮ booking.com; map p.117. In a relatively peaceful residential area, with friendly and helpful staff, this long-running inn offers international-standard facilities, including hot showers, satellite TV and mini-bars, at bargain prices. B1020

Lub d 925/9 Thanon Rama I ☎ 02 612 4999, ☮ lubd. com; map p.117. Branch of the popular, well-run Silom hostel (see page 148), with similar style and facilities (including women-only dorms). It's right on Thanon Rama I, under BTS National Stadium, so handy for just about everything but rather noisy. Dorms B300, doubles B1300

Luxx XL 82/8 Soi Lang Suan ☎ 02 684 1111, ☮ staywithluxx.com; map p.117. Quietly set back behind *Thang Long* restaurant, this boutique hotel is the younger, but bigger, sister of the original Silom *Luxx*. It shelters large, balconied "Studio" rooms and suites in a seductive contemporary style, all red wood and grey stone, as well as a 13m, infinity-edge, slate pool in the leafy garden. B2100

Pathumwan Princess Hotel 444 Thanon Phrayathai ☎02 216 3700, ⓦpprincess.com; map p.117. Central luxury hotel in a crisp, modern style, at the southern end of MBK Shopping Centre. Service is of a high standard, and the facilities include a very good Italian restaurant, overlooking a large, saltwater swimming pool on the eighth floor, a spa and a huge, popular fitness club, The Olympic, that encompasses squash and tennis courts and a 400m jogging track. B4100

Siam Kempinski 991/9 Thanon Rama I ☎02 162 9000, ⓦkempinski.com/bangkok; map p.117. Though it's in downtown's throbbing heart, right behind Paragon shopping centre, this top-of-the-range offering from Europe's oldest luxury hotel group styles itself as a resort: all rooms turn in on an artfully landscaped triangular garden with three pools (some ground-floor rooms even have direct access to one of the pools). As the site used to be part of the "lotus-pond palace", Wang Sra Pathum, the interior designers have made subtle but striking use of lotus motifs, complemented by over two hundred specially commissioned paintings and sculptures by Thai artists, amid the Art Deco-inspired architecture. There's also a beautiful spa and an excellent contemporary Thai restaurant, Sra Bua (see page 155). B8400

Ten Face 81 Soi 2, Soi Ruam Rudee ☎02 695 4242, ⓦtenfacebangkok.com; map p.117. The name comes from Totsagan, the ten-faced demon of the Ramakien, and this place ingeniously combines sleek, contemporary design with striking artworks inspired by the national myth, without being gimmicky. All the rooms are spacious suites with espresso machines and iPods, some with small kitchens; ask for a room at the back if you're worried about noise from the nearby expressway. There's a fusion restaurant, fitness centre, long, narrow "dipping" pool and shuttle service to Ploen Chit Skytrain, plus a special concierge, who DJs in the ultra-stylish Sita Bar and dispenses the lowdown on Bangkok parties and happenings. B2080

Wendy House 36/2 Soi Kasemsan 1, Thanon Rama I ☎02 214 1149, ⓦwendyguesthouse.com; map p.117. Friendly and well-run guesthouse, with smart, clean and comfortable rooms, all with fridge and cable TV, most with queen-size double beds. Breakfast (included in the price) is available in the ground-floor café, and there's reliable luggage storage among a host of useful facilities. B1500

White Lodge 36/8 Soi Kasemsan 1, Thanon Rama I ☎02 216 8867, ⓔwhitelodgebangkok@gmail.com; map p.117. The cheapest guesthouse on the soi, and not always the cleanest, with plain white cubicles and a lively, welcoming atmosphere – the best rooms, bright and quiet, are on the upper floors. B700

THANON SUKHUMVIT

Thanon Sukhumvit is Bangkok's longest road – it keeps going east all the way to Cambodia – but for such an important artery it's far too narrow for the volume of traffic that needs to use it, and is further hemmed in by the Skytrain line that runs above it. Packed with high-rise office blocks and business hotels (though very little budget accommodation), an impressive array of specialist restaurants (from Lebanese to Lao), and stall after stall selling cheap souvenirs and T-shirts, it's a lively place that attracts a high proportion of single male tourists to its enclaves of girlie bars on Soi Nana Tai and Soi Cowboy. But for the most part it's not a seedy area, and is home to many expats and middle-class Thais. Even at the west end of Sukhumvit, many of the sois are refreshingly quiet, even leafy; transport down the longer sois is provided by motorbike-taxi (mohtoesai) drivers who wait at the soi's mouth, clad in numbered waistcoats. Odd-numbered sois run off the north side of Thanon Sukhumvit, even-numbered off the south side; some of the sois have become important enough to earn their own names, which are often used in preference to their numbers; many sois are long enough to have sub-sois running off them, which usually have their own numbers (or names).

The Atlanta At the far southern end of Soi 2 ☎02 252 1650, ⓦtheatlantahotelbangkok.com; map p.122. A Bangkok institution, this classic, five-storey budget hotel was built in 1952 around a famously photogenic Art Deco-style lobby and continues to emphasize an old-fashioned, conservative style of hospitality. It offers some of the cheapest accommodation on Sukhumvit: rooms are plain and simple, though they are all en suite and some have a/c and hot water; many have small balconies. There's a swimming pool and kids' pool in the garden, a good restaurant and a free left-luggage facility. Fan B950, a/c B1050

Avani Atrium 1880 Thanon Phetchaburi Mai ☎02 718 2000–1, ⓦminorhotels.com; map p.122. Good-value, 600-room luxury hotel that's a little to the north of the Sukhumvit strip, but handy for the subway (Phetchaburi), the airport rail link (Makkasan) and Khlong Saen Saeb boats. Well-equipped, tasteful rooms enjoy great views of downtown, and there's a delicious and theatrical Japanese teppanyaki restaurant, Benihana. B2090

Hilton Sukhumvit 11 Soi 24 ☎02 620 6666, ⓦhilton. com; map p.122. This high-rise luxury hotel cleverly links the skyscraper cities of New York and Bangkok, with an Art Deco-influenced contemporary design that's intended to suggest 1920s Manhattan. The design continues in the excellent Italian restaurant, Scalini, and in the capacious bedrooms and their opulent bathrooms; on the rooftop are an infinity pool and a gym. B4680

Marriott Marquis Queens Park 199 Soi 22 ☎02 059 5555, ⓦmarriott.com; map p.122. This new 1400-room hotel overlooks and has direct access to Benjasiri Park (and its jogging track). Luxurious rooms offer subtly appealing hints of Thai style in their contemporary decor, and there are two pools and a lovely spa. A wide choice of eating outlets

1

includes a Thai–Western tea room, a Chinese restaurant, a Japanese soba canteen and, on the rooftop, a clubby cocktail bar and a spectacular contemporary Asian restaurant that fuses Japanese, Korean and Western influences. B5530 **Park Plaza** 9 Soi 18 ☎02 658 7000, ⓦparkplaza.com; map p.122. The quieter and newer of two nearby Park Plazas, this small hotel is topped by an appealing, open-air 20m pool, gym and bar-restaurant on the eighth floor. Fitted with DVD players, the rooms sport a perky contemporary look, with bright colours set against businessman's black. B2880

DOWNTOWN: SOUTH OF THANON RAMA IV
South of Thanon Rama IV, the area sometimes known as Bangrak contains a full cross-section of accommodation. Tucked away at its eastern edge, there are a few cheap places that are worth recommending in the small travellers' haunt of Soi Ngam Duphli and adjacent Soi Sri Bamphen and Soi Saphan Khu. The neighbourhood is often traffic-clogged and occasionally seedy, but is close to Lumphini Park and subway station and fairly handy for Suvarnabhumi Airport. As well as a fair scattering of medium-range places, the arc between Thanon Rama IV and the river also lays claim to the capital's biggest selection of top hotels, which are among the most opulent in the world. Traversed by the Skytrain, this area is especially good for eating and for gay and straight nightlife, mostly near the east end of Thanon Silom (around which several gay-friendly hotels are scattered). Staying by the river itself in the atmospheric area around Thanon Charoen Krung, also known as New Road, has the added advantage of easy access to express boats.

★ **Anantara Riverside** 257 Thanon Charoennakorn ☎02 476 0022, ⓦanantara.com; map p.78. A luxury retreat from the frenetic city centre, well to the south on the Thonburi bank, but connected to Taksin Bridge (for the Skytrain and Chao Phraya express boats), 15min away, by hotel ferries every 20min. Arrayed around a highly appealing, landscaped swimming pool, the tranquil, riverside gardens are filled with birdsong, while the stylish and spacious bedrooms come with varnished hardwood floors, balconies and complimentary smartphones. There's a fitness centre, tennis courts, kids' club, a spa, and among a wide choice of places to eat, a good Japanese teppanyaki house. B5085

Avani Riverside 257 Thanon Charoennakorn ☎02 365 9110, ⓦminorhotels.com; map p.78. Thoroughly modern luxury hotel with creative touches such as stylish work stations in the Long Bar and a deli-coffee bar. Though the hotel is set back a little from the Chao Phraya, towering views of the city and its riverscape are enjoyed by all of the rooms, the rooftop, infinity-edge pool and the excellent bar-restaurant on the same floor, Attitude, which is staffed by fine chefs, mixologists and late-night DJs. Guests can use most of the facilities of the adjacent Anantara Riverside (see above), including its shuttle boats. B5600

Baan Saladaeng 69/2 Soi 3, Thanon Saladaeng ☎02 636 3038, ⓦbaansaladaeng.com; map p.124. On a tiny, central alley, this chic, gay-friendly designer guesthouse offers sixteen individually styled and priced rooms, such as the Pop Art Mania Room and the Mediterranean Suite, some with bathtubs and balconies and one with its bath on the balcony. Rain showers, mini-bars, cable TV and comfy beds throughout. Breakfast included. B1250

Como Metropolitan 27 Thanon Sathorn Tai ☎02 625 3333, ⓦcomohotels.com; map p.124. The height of chic, minimalist urban living, where the spacious, Zen-like rooms are decorated in dark wood and creamy Portuguese limestone. There's a very seductive pool, a fine spa, a well-equipped fitness centre with bubbling hydro-pools, a yoga studio with free daily classes, and an excellent restaurant, Nahm (see page 158). B5000

ETZ Hostel 5/3 Soi Ngam Duphli ☎02 286 9424, ⓦetzhostel.com; map p.80. Helpful and very clean, ETZ sports playful contemporary decor in primary colours, a popular roof terrace and a large, attractive lounge. It's very handy for Lumphini subway and Thanon Rama IV, though consequently a little noisy. The a/c dorms share hot showers and fit four to twelve people (one is women-only), or you could upgrade to a bright white double with large, en-suite, hot-water bathroom. Breakfast and luggage storage are available. Dorms B200, doubles B800

Le Siam 3 Thanon Convent ☎02 233 5345, ⓦlesiam hotel.com; map p.124. Friendly – and genuinely eco-friendly – boutique hotel, with high standards of service, just off Thanon Silom and ideally placed for business and nightlife. The swish, well-designed rooms offer very good value, and there's a tiny terrace swimming pool. Staying true to the origins of the hotel, which was founded as Bangkok's first guesthouse, The Swiss Guesthouse, in 1953, the restaurant offers a range of savoury and sweet fondues. Buffet breakfast included. B2040

★ **Lub d** 4 Thanon Decho ☎02 634 7999, ⓦlubd.com; map p.124. Meaning "sleep well" (*lap dii*), this buzzing, upmarket hostel has a/c and hot water throughout and an industrial feel to its stylishly lit decor. This crisp modernity extends to the bedrooms, among which the dorms (some women-only) and the bunk-bedded "Railway" private rooms ("Railway" twin B800) share large bathroom areas, while the top-of-the-range en-suite doubles boast TVs and iPod docks. The hostel lays on some interesting activities and tours, and there's a popular bar and café, a movie lounge, washing machines and free storage facilities, but no kitchen. Dorms B300, doubles B1300

Luxx 6/11 Thanon Decho ☎02 635 8800, ⓦstaywith luxx.com; map p.124. Welcoming boutique hotel offering a good dose of contemporary style at reasonable prices. Decorated in white, grey and natural teak, the rooms feature DVD players and cute wooden baths surmounted by rain showers. B2500

★ **New Road Guest House** 1216/1 Thanon Charoen Krung, between sois 34 and 36 ☎02 630 9371, ⓦnewroadguesthouse.com; map p.124. Thai headquarters of Danish backpacker tour operator, Go Beyond, offering a wide choice of accommodation around a courtyard off New Road, as well as a helpful service centre and travel agent, and interesting Thailand tours. There are mixed and women-only a/c dorms, as well as small "Backpackit" fan rooms with mini-bars and well-equipped, hot-water bathrooms; a/c rooms sport attractive wooden floors and Thai decorative touches. Guests can hang out in the restaurant, the sociable bar or the rooftop hammocks; free baggage storage available and free showers after checkout. Dorms B350, fan doubles B700, a/c doubles B1000

Oldtown Hostel 1048 Thanon Charoen Krung, between sois 26 and 28 ☎02 639 4879, ⓦoldtownhostelbkk.com; map p.124. Handy for Hualamphong Station, this hundred-bed hostel features spruce a/c bunk beds and double beds, shared hot showers and extensive common areas, including a ground-floor café and pool table. Dorms B230, doubles B800

Peninsula Bangkok 333 Thanon Charoennakorn ☎02 020 2888, ⓦpeninsula.com; map p.124. Located on the Thonburi bank, with shuttle boats down to Taksin Bridge and its BTS station, this is an excellent top-class hotel, where the ultra-luxurious decor stylishly blends traditional Western and Asian design, and every room has a panoramic view of the Chao Phraya. The lovely riverside gardens shelter a three-tiered pool, a beautiful spa, a fitness centre and a tennis court, while restaurants include the classy Mei Jiang Cantonese restaurant (see page 158). B9480

Rose 118 Thanon Suriwong ☎02 266 8268–72, ⓦrosehotelbkk.com; map p.124. Set back from the main road but very handy for the city's nightlife, the compact rooms here (all with bathtubs) boast a simple but stylish, modernist look, enhanced by paintings and silk cushions. The ground-floor public rooms are more elegant again, and there's a beautiful swimming pool, a small gym, saunas and a good Thai restaurant, Ruen Urai (see page 158), at the back. B1800

★ **Sala Thai Daily Mansion** 15 Soi Saphan Khu ☎02 287 1436, ⓔsalathai.guesthouse@hotmail.com; map p.80. The last and best of several budget guesthouses on this quiet, narrow alleyway, the first right off Soi Saphan Khu, coming from Soi Sri Bamphen. A clean and efficiently run place, with bright, cheerful rooms with wall

fans, sharing hot-water bathrooms, and a large, leafy roof garden. Decent rates for single rooms. Fan B400, a/c B600

★ **Sukhothai** 13/3 Thanon Sathorn Tai ☎02 344 8888, ⓦsukhothai.com; map p.124. The most elegant of Bangkok's top hotels, its decor inspired by the walled city of Sukhothai, offers low-rise accommodation, as well as a beautiful garden spa, all coolly furnished in silks, teak and granite. Service is of the highest standard and the architecture makes the most of the views of the surrounding six acres of gardens, lotus ponds and pools dotted with statuary. There's also a health club, a 25m infinity pool and excellent restaurants including Celadon (see page 156). B7650

Swan 31 Soi 36, Thanon Charoen Krung ☎02 235 9271–3, ⓦswanhotelbkk.com; map p.124. Next to the stately residence of the French ambassador, this good-value Chinese hotel is well run and welcoming. Arrayed around a 15m pool, the rooms are bright, clean and of a decent size (though bathrooms in the cheaper rooms are small), with hot water, cable TV, mini-bars and safes; some have balconies with armchairs. Good rates for singles. B1000

Tarntawan Hotel 119/5–10 Thanon Suriwong ☎02 238 2620, ⓦtarntawansurawong.com; map p.124. Set back from the main road, a pretty, flower-strewn lobby announces this welcoming and well-run, gay-friendly hotel. The decent-sized, well-equipped rooms are gracefully furnished in natural colours with traditional Thai design elements, and all have bathtubs. B2200

SUVARNABHUMI AIRPORT

Mariya Boutique Residence 1627/2 Thanon Latkrabang ☎02 326 7854, ⓦmariyahotel.com; map p.78. A 5min drive from the airport to the northeast (with pick-ups available 24hr), this well-organized hotel offers hot showers, double-glazed windows, minibars, cable TV, microwaves, kettles and DVD players (on request) in all of the bedrooms, which feature some traditional Thai touches in the appealing decor. B1150

Novotel Suvarnabhumi ☎02 131 1111, ⓦnovotel.com; map p.78. The official airport hotel, set within the complex and a 10min walk from arrivals via a walkway in the basement (or catch the shuttle bus from outside arrivals Gate 4). Offering smart, contemporary rooms with marble bathrooms, Thai, Japanese, Cantonese and international restaurants, a swimming pool and fitness centre, the eco-friendly Novotel operates on a 24hr basis – you can check in at any time, and check out 24hr later. Breakfast included. B5865

EATING

As you'd expect, nowhere in Thailand can compete with Bangkok's diversity when it comes to food: it boasts an astonishing fifty thousand places to eat, almost one for every hundred citizens. Although prices are generally higher here than in the provinces, it's still easy to dine well on a budget.

For **Thai** food, the best gourmet restaurants in the country operate from the downtown districts, proffering wonderful royal, traditional and regional cuisines that definitely merit a visit. At the lower end of the price scale, one-dish meals from around the country are rustled up at the **food courts**

1

of shopping centres and department stores, as well as at **night markets** and **street stalls**. However in 2017 – just after CNN declared Bangkok the best city in the world for street food – the city authorities announced that they were going to rid the pavements of all vendors. They later backtracked, saying that the street stalls in Chinatown and Banglamphu could stay, and at the time of research it didn't seem that the ban was being rigorously enforced in the rest of the city. For the non-Thai cuisines, Chinatown naturally rates as the most authentic district for pure **Chinese** food; likewise neighbouring Pahurat, the capital's Indian enclave, is best for unadulterated **Indian** dishes, while there's a sprinkling of Indian and (mostly southern Thai) **Muslim** restaurants around Silom's Maha Uma Devi Temple and nearby Thanon Charoen Krung. Sukhumvit's Soi 3 is a hub for **Middle Eastern** cafés, complete with hookah pipes at the outdoor tables; good, comparatively cheap **Japanese** restaurants are concentrated, for example, on and around Soi Thaniya, at the east end of Thanon Silom; and there's a Korean enclave in Sukhumvit Plaza, at the corner of Soi 12. In the more expensive restaurants listed below you may have to pay VAT (currently seven percent) and a ten percent **service charge**.

RATANAKOSIN

The places reviewed below are especially handy for sightseers, but there are also plenty of street stalls around Tha Chang and a load of simple, studenty restaurants off the north end of Thanon Maharat near Thammasat University.

★ **Err** Soi Maharat, Thanon Maharat ☎ 02 622 2291–2, ⓦ errbkk.com; map p.83. A more basic offshoot of *Bolan*, one of Bangkok's finest restaurants (see page 155), Err rustles up "urban rustic" dishes such as delicious *moo hong*, braised pork belly with pepper (B230), in a chic, retro space; wash it down with rice whisky. Tues–Sun 11am–10pm.

Navy Club (Krua Khun Kung) Tha Chang ☎ 02 222 0081; map p.83. This place is immediately on the south side of the express-boat pier, but a little tricky to get to: ignore the prominent but overpriced *Navy Club 77 Café* on the corner of Na Phra Lan and Maharat roads, walk down Thanon Maharat a short way and go in through the car park of the navy compound. The decor's deeply institutionalized but the real draw is the shaded terrace built over the river, where you can enjoy excellent dried prawn and lemongrass salad (B130), *haw mok thalay* (seafood curry soufflé; B200) and other marine delights. Daily 11am–10pm; Mon–Fri kitchen closes 3–4pm & terrace closes 2–6pm (though you're welcome to finish your meal there after 2pm).

★ **Supanniga Eating Room** Riva Arun Hotel, 392/25–26 Thanon Maharat ☎ 02 714 7608; also at Soi 55 (Soi Thonglor), Thanon Sukhumvit ☎ 02 714 7508; and 28 Soi 10, Thanon Sathorn ☎ 02 635 0349; ⓦ supannigaeatingroom.com; map pages 83, 122 and 124. The upstairs terrace at this riverside restaurant-coffee bar, with head-on views of freshly renovated Wat Arun, is a great place to try the distinctive cuisine of Chanthaburi, famous for its herbs and spices – the delicious mixed appetiser platter is a great place to start, followed by *moo cha muang* (B240), a mild red curry of stewed pork. The restaurant's other speciality is food from Isaan, where the

---

DINNER AND COCKTAIL CRUISES

The **Chao Phraya River** looks fabulous at night, when most of the noisy longtails have stopped terrorizing the ferries, and the riverside temples, other fine monuments such as the Grand Palace and an increasing number of historic houses are elegantly illuminated. Joining one of the nightly **dinner cruises** along the river is a great way to appreciate it all, especially on one of the barges listed below, which are far preferable to the big, modern party boats. Call ahead to reserve a table and check departure details – some cruises may not run during the rainy season (May–Oct).

Loy Nava ☎ 02 437 4932, ⓦ loynava.com. The original, 40-year-old converted wooden rice-barge service still departs Si Phraya pier twice nightly, at 6pm (to catch the sunset) and 8.10pm, with pick-ups also at Tha Sathorn. During the cruise you can enjoy a Thai, seafood or vegetarian meal, accompanied by live traditional music and dancing. B1550, including hotel pick-up in central Bangkok.

Manohra ☎ 02 476 0022, ⓦ manohracruises.com. Beautiful converted rice-barge operated by the *Anantara Riverside Resort*, south of Taksin Bridge in Thonburi, serving Thai set dinners. Departs hotel at 7.30pm, returning 9.30pm, with pick-ups at Tha Sathorn possible. From B2300.

Supanniga ☎ 02 714 7608, ⓦ supannigacruise.com. An elegant setting of dark woods and silks for a six-course menu of delicious specialities from the Chanthaburi region, with a glass of champagne to tickle your taste buds (departing from River City at 6.15pm; B3250). Also offers cocktail cruises on weekdays (from B1250 including canapés) and champagne cruises on weekends (from B1550 including canapés), departing from *Supanniga Eating Room* on the river (see page 150) at 4.15pm, with a pick-up at River City at 4.45pm available.

family have a boutique hotel in Khon Kaen (see page 471). Daily 11.30am–10pm.

BANGLAMPHU AND THE DEMOCRACY MONUMENT AREA

Copycat entrepreneurship means that Khao San is stacked full of backpacker restaurants serving near-identical Western and (mostly) watered-down Thai food; there's even a lane, one block east, parallel to Thanon Tanao (behind *Burger King*), that's dominated by vegetarian cafés, following a trend started by *May Kaidee*. Hot-food stalls selling very cheap night-market snacks operate until the early hours. Things are more varied down on Thanon Phra Arthit, with its arty little café-restaurants favoured by Thammasat University students, while the riverside places, on Phra Arthit and further north off Thanon Samsen and in Thewet, tend to be best for seafood with a view. For the real old-fashioned Thai taste though, browse southern Thanon Tanao, where traditional shophouses have been selling specialist sweets and savouries for generations.

AROUND THANON KHAO SAN

Chabad House 96 Thanon Ram Bhuttri @kosher thailand.com; map p.100. A little piece of Israel, run by the Bangkok branch of the Jewish outreach Chabad-Lubavitch movement. Serves a well-priced, tasty kosher menu of schnitzels (B220), kebabs, baba ganoush, falafels, hummus, salads and Jewish breads in a/c calm, on the ground floor of a long-established community centre and guesthouse. Mon–Thurs & Sun 10am–11pm, Fri 10am–3pm, Sat 8–11pm.

Madame Musur Soi Ram Bhuttri; map p.100. Mellow bar-restaurant festooned with vines and paper lanterns with good people-watching tables on the alley, serving a wide range of drinks, including good espressos, and authentic northern Thai food – try the khantoke, two kinds of chilli dip with pork scratchings and organic vegetables (B150). Daily 9am–midnight.

★ **May Kaidee** East off Thanon Tanao @maykaidee. com; map p.100. Simple, neighbourhood Thai vegetarian restaurant that still serves some of the best veggie food in Banglamphu despite having spawned several competitors on the same alley. Come for Western breakfasts or try the tasty green curry, the Vietnamese-style veggie spring rolls or the sticky black-rice pudding with mango or banana. Most dishes around B100. Also runs a variety of cookery courses (see page 153). Daily 9am–10pm.

Nittaya 136 Thanon Chakrabongse; map p.100. This shop is nationally famous for its *nam phrik* (chilli dips) and curry pastes (which are available vacuum-packed), but it serves all kinds of food to take away – perhaps to eat in nearby Santichaiprakarn Park (see page 99) – including snacks and desserts. Mon–Sat 9am–6.30pm.

THANON PHRA ARTHIT

Aquatini *Navalai River Resort*, 45/1 Thanon Phra Arthit ☎02 280 9955; map p.100. Occupying a nice wooden deck in a perfect breezy riverfront spot beside the express-boat pier (even better after sunset when the boats stop running), this hotel restaurant does good mid-priced Thai food. Seafood's a speciality: the deep-fried ruby fish served with cashew nuts and bell peppers is very good, and their tangy coconut-milk *tom kha kai* soup is especially delicious. Most seafood mains B300–400. Daily 6.30am–midnight.

Gingerbread House Thanon Phra Sumen, opposite the fortress; map p.100. Sweet little retro café with clapboard walls and marble-topped tables, serving good espresso coffees, teas, sodas and scrummy cakes. Mon–Sat 10.30am–6pm.

★ **Hemlock** 56 Thanon Phra Arthit ☎02 282 7507; map p.100. Small, stylish, a/c restaurant that's very popular with students and young Thai couples. Offers a long, mid-priced menu, including delicious tom yam and green and phanaeng curries (around B150), as well as more unusual dishes such as several kinds of *laap* (spicy ground meat salad). The traditional *miang* starters (shiny green wild tea leaves filled with chopped vegetables, fish, prawn or meat) are also very tasty, and there's a good vegetarian selection. Worth reserving a table on Fri and Sat nights. Mon–Sat 5–11pm.

Kway Jap Yuan Khun Daeng Thanon Phra Arthit ☎085 246 0111; map p.100. This basic, bustling canteen does a roaring trade with Thammasat University students, who come for the delicious *kway jap yuan*, noodle soup similar to Vietnamese *pho* but a little starchier – go for the "extra" version with egg (B65) and you're set up for the day. Find it in an historic shophouse, unmistakably painted white and green – colours which the flamboyant owner often sports himself. Mon–Sat 11am–9.30pm.

Roti Mataba Karim 136 Thanon Phra Arthit ☎02 282 2119; map p.100. Famous 70-year-old outlet for the ever-popular fried Indian breads, or *rotis*, served here in lots of sweet and savoury varieties, including stuffed with meat and veg (*mataba*; from B44), served with vegetable and meat curries, or with bananas and condensed milk; biryanis (*khao mok*) are also on offer. Choose between pavement tables and a basic upstairs a/c room. Tues–Sun 10am–9pm.

THANON SAMSEN AND THEWET

Jok Phochana On a side soi running between Soi 2 and Soi 4, Thanon Samsen; map p.100. This bare-basics, forty-year-old restaurant, which has featured on national TV, is about as real as you're going to get near Thanon Khao San; a green curry costs B80. The day's ingredients are colourfully displayed at the front of the shop, and the quiet pavement tables get more crowded as the night wears on. Daily 4pm–midnight.

1

Kaloang Home Kitchen Beside the river (follow the bend round) at the far western end of Thanon Sri Ayutthaya ⓣ02 281 9228; map p.100. Flamboyant service and excellent seafood attracts a largely Thai clientele to this open-air, no-frills, bare-wood restaurant that perches on a stilted deck over the river. Dishes well worth sampling include the fried rolled shrimps served with a sweet dip and any of the host of Thai salads. Most mains are B100–150; expect to pay more for crab, shrimp and some fish dishes. Daily 11am–10pm.

Kinlom Chom Saphan Riverside end of Soi 3, Thanon Samsen ⓣ02 628 8382, ⓦkhinlomchomsaphan.com; map p.100. This sprawling, waterside restaurant merits its poetic name, "breathe the wind and savour the bridge", enjoying river breezes and close-up views of the lyre-like Rama VIII Bridge. It's always busy with a youngish Thai crowd who are entertained by live music. The predominantly seafood menu (mostly B150–300) features everything from crab to grouper cooked in multiple ways, including with curry, garlic or sweet basil sauces, but never with MSG. Daily 11am–midnight.

★ **Krua Apsorn** Thanon Samsen, opposite Thanon Uthong Nok on the southwestern edge of Dusit ⓣ02 668 8788; Thanon Dinso ⓣ02 685 4531; map page 100. Very good, spicy and authentic food and a genteel welcome make this unpretentious, a/c restaurant popular with the area's civil servants – as well as the royalty whom they serve. Try the green fish-ball curry (B120) or the yellow curry with river prawns and lotus shoots, both recommended by the leading Thai restaurant guide, MacDang, and then put out the fire in your mouth with home-made coconut sorbet. Thanon Samsen Mon–Sat 10.30am–8pm (generally closes early on Sat); Thanon Dinso Mon–Sat 10.30am–8pm.

Somsong Pochana 173 Thanon Samsen ⓣ061 971 1883; map p.100. Excellent simple lunch place serving unusual dishes such as traditional Sukhothai-style noodles (B40) and khanom jiin sao nam, rice noodles with pineapple, dried shrimp and coconut cream. Daily 9am–roughly 5pm.

Steve Café and Cuisine Wat Thawarad ⓣ02 281 0915, ⓦstevecafeandcuisine.com; map p.100. In a lovely riverside setting with views of Rama VIII Bridge, come here for great service and a huge menu that encompasses southern, northern and northeastern Thai specialities and fusion dishes, including a very tasty and spicy salmon *laap* (B210). It's easy to see, right across the mouth of Khlong Krung Kasem from Tha Thewet express-boat pier, though harder to get there, walking round and right through the grounds of the temple. Daily 11am–10.30pm.

SOUTH OF DEMOCRACY

In this area, there's also a branch of *Krua Apsorn* (see page 152).

Kai Yang Boran 474–476 Thanon Tanao, immediately to the south of the Chao Poh Seua Chinese shrine ⓣ02 622 2349; map p.100. Locally famous grilled chicken (B130 for half a bird) and *som tam* (green papaya salad; B80) restaurant (with a/c), wallpapered with photos of celebrities who have eaten here. *Nam tok* salad with roast pork and several kinds of *laap* round out the northeastern menu. Daily 8.30/9am–9pm.

Kor Panit 431–433 Thanon Tanao, on the east side, directly opposite Thanon Phraeng Phuton; map p.100. Outstanding coconut-laced sticky rice has been sold here since 1932; no English sign, but look for the mango vendors outside. You can choose your own variety to accompany the delicious *khao niaw* (sticky rice with coconut milk) to take away, or the shop will do you a plate of *khao niaw mamuang* (B100) to eat in, sitting on their one large wooden bench. Mon–Sat 7am–6pm.

Nattaporn 94 Thanon Phraeng Phuton, just off Thanon Kanlayana Maitri ⓣ02 221 3954; map p.100. This family has been specializing in its famous ice cream homemade from the milk of fresh coconuts for over sixty years, topping it with classic Thai condiments like sweetcorn, red beans and taro balls. They also do coconut-milk ice cream in mango, chocolate, coffee and tea flavours, as well as durian when in season. No English sign, but it's a basic shophouse, right next door to *The Bhuthorn* guesthouse. Mon–Sat 8am–4pm.

Padthai Thipsamai 313 Thanon Mahachai, near Wat Rajnadda ⓣ02 221 6280; map p.100. The most famous *phat thai* in Bangkok, flash-fried by the same family since 1966. The "special" option is huge, comes with especially juicy prawns, and is wrapped in a translucent, paper-thin omelette. Best washed down with fresh coconut juice. Daily, except alternate Mon, 5pm–2am.

HUALAMPHONG, CHINATOWN AND PAHURAT

Much of the fun of Chinatown dining is in the browsing of the night-time hot-food stalls that open up all along Thanon Yaowarat, around the mouth of Soi Issaranuphap (Yaowarat Soi 11) and along Soi Phadungdao (Soi Texas); wherever there's a crowd you'll be sure of good food. Pan Siam's *Good Eats: Chinatown* map, available from major bookshops, is a great resource for the weirder local specialities.

Hua Seng Hong 371 Thanon Yaowarat ⓣ02 222 7053, ⓦhuasenghong.co.th; map p.107. Vibrant, ever-popular, few-frills restaurant with an open kitchen out front, the original branch of what's now a citywide chain. Dishes from around B100, less for noodle soup, dim sum or roast duck on rice, more for delicacies such as braised geese's feet. Daily 9am–1am.

Raan Khun Yah Wat Traimit; map p.107. Just to the right inside the temple's Thanon Mittaphap entrance, this basic, very cheap central Thai restaurant (dishes from

THAI COOKERY CLASSES IN BANGKOK

Baipai 8/91 Soi 54, Thanon Ngam Wongwan ☎02 561 1404, ⓦbaipai.com. Thorough, four-hour classes in an attractive garden house in northern Bangkok. The classes cost B2200, including transfers from central hotels. Closed Sun.

Bangkok Bold Cooking Studio 503 Thanon Phra Sumen ☎098 829 4310, ⓦbangkokbold.com. Three-hour classes (from B2500) in an old converted shophouse in Banglamphu, which also hosts chef's table dinners (B1500/person). Different dishes are taught at each class, according to a monthly schedule that's posted on their website.

Cooking with Poo and Friends Klong Toey ☎080 434 8686, ⓦcookingwithpoo.com. Set up by the ebullient Khun Poo with the help of a Christian charity, a chance to experience the slums of Klong Toey and spend a morning learning to cook. The price of B1500 includes a market tour and free transfers from next to

Phrom Pong BTS station. Also offers classes on Phra Pradaeng, an undeveloped river island on the south side of Bangkok, including a short longtail trip and a bicycle ride.

May Kaidee East of Thanon Khao San, off Thanon Tanao ☎089 137 3173, ⓦmaykaidee.com. Banglamphu's famous vegetarian restaurant (see page 151) offers a huge variety of courses lasting anything from 2hr (B1000) to 10 days (B15,000), including raw food, desserts and fruit-carving classes.

Thai House 22km from central Bangkok in Bangmuang ☎02 997 5161, ⓦthaihouse.co.th. Set in a rural part of Nonthaburi province, here you can do one- (B3800) to three-day (B16,650) cooking courses, all including transfers from downtown. The three-day course includes a market visit, all meals and homestay accommodation in a lovely traditional teak house with a kitchen garden.

B40), now in its third generation of operation, is especially famous for its delicious *kaeng khiaw wan neua* (green beef curry), on a menu that otherwise changes daily – look out for *lon*, a chilli dip with coconut milk, and *khanom jiin nam yaa*, rice noodles topped with spicy fish sauce. Mon–Fri 6.30am–1pm (some things will sell out earlier than that).

Royal India Just off Thanon Chakraphet at 392/1 ☎02 221 6565; map p.107; basement, Siam Paragon ☎02 610 7667; map p.117; Floor 5, Emporium shopping centre ☎086 973 8266; map p.122; ⓦroyalindiathailand.com. Great dhal, perfect parathas and famously good North Indian curries (from B125), with plenty of vegetarian options, served in a dark, basic little a/c restaurant in the heart of Bangkok's most Punjabi of neighbourhoods to an almost exclusively South Asian clientele. Daily 10am–10pm.

T&K (Toi & Kid's Seafood) 49 Soi Phadungdao, corner of Thanon Yaowarat ☎02 223 4519, ⓦfacebook. com/tkseafood; map p.107. Hectic, rough-hewn street restaurant famous for its barbecued seafood, with everything from prawns and cockles (from B60 a serving) to whole fish and crabs (from B300) on offer, as well as more complex dishes such as seafood som tam. Eat at crowded pavement tables by the busy road or inside in the basic a/c rooms. Daily 4.30pm–2am.

DOWNTOWN: AROUND SIAM SQUARE AND THANON PLOENCHIT

In this neighbourhood, there are also branches of *Royal India* (see page 153), *Aoi* (see page 156) and *Somboon Seafood* (see page 158). Notable street food in this area

includes delicious *khao man kai*, boiled chicken breast with broth, dipping sauces and rice that's been cooked in chicken stock, which is served at a strip of late-night canteens on the south side of Thanon Phetchaburi, running east from the corner of Thanon Rajdamri.

Coffeeology Open House, Floor 6, Central Embassy; map p.117. Possibly the best espresso in Bangkok, made with beans from Chiang Dao in northern Thailand. Also offers drip, cold-brew and nitro-cold-brew coffees. Daily 10am–10pm.

Din Tai Fung Floor 5, Central Embassy ☎02 160 5918, ⓦdintaifung.com.sg; map p.117. At this attractive and efficient all-day dim sum place, the superb speciality is steamed pork dumplings with clear broth inside each one (B160), but other dishes such as spring rolls with duck and spring onion (B170) are also very tasty. Mon–Fri 11am–9.30pm, Sat & Sun 10.30am–9.30pm.

Eathai Basement, Central Embassy ⓦcentralembassy. com/eathai; map p.117. This upmarket food court – including a branch of *Krua Apsorn* (see page 152) – is a great place to learn about the huge variety of Thai food, with kitchens from the various regions rustling up their local dishes, plus seafood and vegetarian specialities, traditional drinks and dessert stalls and a section devoted to street food. Daily 10am–10pm.

Food Loft Floor 7, Central Chidlom, Thanon Ploenchit; map p.117. Bangkok's top department store lays on a suitably upscale food court of all hues – Thai, Vietnamese, Chinese, Japanese, Korean and Indian, as well as Italian by *Gianni* (see below) and Lebanese by *Beirut* (see page 155). Choose your own ingredients and watch them cooked in front of you, eat by the huge windows in the stylish,

1

YELLOW-FLAG HEAVEN FOR VEGGIES

Every year, for nine days during the ninth lunar month (between late Sept and Nov), Thailand's Chinese community goes on a **meat-free** diet to mark the onset of the Vegetarian Festival (Ngan Kin Jeh), a sort of Taoist version of Lent. Though the Chinese citizens of Bangkok don't go in for skewering themselves like their compatriots in Phuket (see page 620), they do celebrate the Vegetarian Festival with gusto: some people choose to wear only white for the duration, all the temples throng with activity, and nearly every restaurant and food stall in Chinatown turns vegetarian for the period, flying small yellow flags to show that they are upholding the tradition and participating in what's essentially a nightly veggie food jamboree. For vegetarian tourists this is a great time to be in town – just look for the yellow flag and you can be sure all dishes will be one hundred percent vegetarian. Soya substitutes are a popular feature on the vegetarian Chinese menu, so don't be surprised to find pink prawn-shaped objects floating in your noodle soup or unappetizingly realistic slices of fake duck. Many hotel restaurants also get in on the act during the Vegetarian Festival, running special veggie promotions for a week or two.

minimalist seating areas and then ponder whether you have room for a Thai or Western dessert. Daily 10am–10pm.

Gianni 34/1 Soi Tonson, Thanon Ploenchit ☎02 652 2922, ⊕giannibkk.com; map p.117. Probably Bangkok's best independent Italian restaurant, offering a sophisticated blend of traditional and modern in both its decor and food. Twice-weekly shipments of artisan ingredients from the old country are used in dishes such as risotto with porcini mushrooms and parmesan and squid-ink spaghetti with clams, prawns and asparagus. Best to come for lunch Mon–Fri when there's a good-value set menu (two courses for B490). Daily 11.30am–2pm & 6–10pm.

★**Hinata** Central Embassy, Thanon Ploenchit ☎02 160 5935, ⊕shin-hinata.com; map p.117. This branch of a famous Nagoya restaurant offers exquisite sushi (starting at B1000 for six pieces of nigiri sushi), good wines by the glass and great views over the leafy British Embassy grounds. Simpler rice dishes are available as part of lunchtime sets before 2pm (B500), or you could blow up to B6000 on a multi-course kaiseki meal, featuring appetizers, sushi, sashimi, seasonal dishes, soup and dessert. Daily 11am–11pm (last orders 9.30pm).

Home Kitchen (Khrua Nai Baan) 94 Soi Lang Suan ☎02 255 8947, ⊕khruanaibaan.com; map p.117. This congenial, unpretentious spot in an attractive a/c villa is like an upcountry restaurant in the heart of the city. On the reasonably priced Thai and Chinese picture menu, you're bound to find something delicious, including dozens of soups – try the kaeng som, with shrimp and acacia shoot omelette, for B200 – six kinds of laap and a huge array of seafood. Daily 8am–midnight.

Honmono Sushi Floor 4, Siam Paragon, Thanon Rama I ☎02 610 9240; map p.117. Owned by the Japanese expert on Thailand's version of Iron Chef, this place imports its seafood from Tokyo's Tsukiji Market five times a week and offers delights such as lobster sushi (B550) and scallop sashimi (B290). Daily 11am–10pm.

Inter 432/1–2 Soi 9, Siam Square ☎02 251 4689; map p.117. Honest, efficient Thai restaurant that's popular with students and shoppers, serving good one-dish meals from B68, as well as curries, soups, salads and fish, in a no-frills, fluorescent-lit canteen atmosphere. Daily 11am–9.30pm.

Jim Thompson's Restaurant and Wine Bar Jim Thompson's House, 6 Soi Kasemsan 2, Thanon Rama I ☎02 612 3601, ⊕jimthompsonrestaurant.com; map p.117. A civilized, reasonably priced haven in the must-see house museum (see page 118), serving delicious dishes such as pomelo salad with prawns (B260) and matsaman curry with chicken (B200), as well as cakes and Thai desserts. Daily 11am–5pm & 6–10pm.

Mah Boon Krong Food Courts Corner of Rama I and Phrayathai rds ⊕mbk-center.co.th; map p.117. Two decent food-courts at the north end of MBK: the long-running area on Floor 6 is a good introduction to Thai food, with English names and pictures of a huge variety of tasty, cheap one-dish meals from all over the country displayed at the various stalls (including vegetarian options), as well as fresh juices and a wide range of desserts; the slightly more upmarket version on Floor 5 is an international affair, spanning India, Italy, Vietnam, Lebanon, Indonesia, Mexico and Japan. Floor 6 daily 10am–roughly 9pm; Floor 5 daily 10am–9.30pm.

★**Polo Fried Chicken (Kai Thawt Jay Kee Soi Polo)** 137/13 Soi Polo, Thanon Witthayu ☎02 655 8489; map p.117. On the access road to the snobby polo club, this simple restaurant is Bangkok's most famous purveyor of the ultimate Thai peasant dish, fried chicken. All manner of northeastern dishes, including fish, sausages and loads of salads, fill out the menu, but it would be a bit perverse to come here and not have the classic combo of finger-licking chicken (B130 for a half), som tam and sticky rice. Daily 7am–9pm.

Red Sky Centara Grand at Central World Hotel, 999/99 Thanon Rama I ☎02 100 1234, ⊕centarahotelsresorts. com; map p.117. Opulent, blow-out restaurant, named

1

for the great sunset views from its indoor-outdoor, rooftop perch on the fifty-fifth floor. It purveys "the best of the land, sky and water" – be that Maine lobster, Hokkaido scallops or wagyu beef – beautifully presented in complex, meticulous preparations (mains from B850). Daily 6pm–1am (last food orders 11pm).

★ **Sanguansri** 59/1 Thanon Witthayu ☎ 02 251 9378; map p.117. The rest of the street may be a multi-storey building site but this low-rise, canteen-like old-timer, run by a friendly bunch of middle-aged women, clings on. And where else around here can you lunch on a sweet, thick and toothsome *kaeng matsaman* for B70? It goes well with *kung pla*, a tasty, fresh prawn and lemon-grass salad that can be spiced to order. The menu changes daily, and in the hot season they serve delicious khao chae, rice in chilled, flower-scented water served with delicate, fried side dishes. If possible, avoid the lunchtime rush between noon and 1pm. Mon–Sat 10am–3pm.

Som Tam (Nua) Floor 5, Central Embassy; map p.117. This lively modern restaurant is a great place to get to know the full range of Thai spicy salads. The *som tam* with pork crackling and sausage goes well with the very tasty deep-fried chicken (B180), or there's northeastern *laap* and *nam tok*, and central Thai salads (*yam*) by the dozen. Daily 10am–9.15pm.

Sra Bua Siam Kempinski Hotel (see page 147); map p.117. Molecular gastronomy comes to Bangkok, with great success. Operated by Copenhagen's Thai Michelin one-star, *Kiin Kiin*, this place applies some serious creativity and theatricality to Thai cuisine. Dishes such as frozen red curry with lobster salad (B650), which perfectly distils the taste of the *kaeng daeng*, match the dramatic decor, which encompasses two lotus ponds (*sra bua*). Daily noon–2.30pm & 6–10.30pm.

THANON SUKHUMVIT

In this area, there are also branches of *Aoi* (see page 156), *Royal India* (see page 153), *Supanniga* (see page 150) and *Ramentei* (see page 158).

Baan Khanitha 36/1 Soi 23 ☎ 02 258 4181; map p.122; 69 Thanon Sathorn Tai, at the corner of Soi Suan Phlu ☎ 02 675 4200–1; ⓦ baan-khanitha.com. The big attraction at this long-running favourite haunt of Sukhumvit expats is the setting in a traditional Thai house and leafy garden. The food is upmarket Thai and fairly pricey, and includes lots of fiery salads (*yam*) and a good range of *tom yam* soups, as well as green, matsaman and seafood curries. Most mains cost B200–500. Daily 11am–11pm.

Barcelona Gaudí Ground floor, Le Premier 1 Condo, Soi 23 ☎ 02 661 7410, ⓦ facebook.com/barcelona gaudithailand; map p.122. This appealing Catalan café offers lovely outdoor tables under a broad, shady tree and a short menu of very good Spanish dishes, including salads, paellas and tapas, as well as tasty *crema catalana* (a bit like

a crème brûlée) and on-the-money espressos. It's especially good value at lunchtime (Mon–Fri), when you can get four tapas and a soft drink for B290, and is also popular at weekends for watching Barcelona's football games, when the house wine at B95/glass goes down a storm. Mon–Fri 11am–11pm, Sat & Sun noon–11pm.

★ **Beirut** Basement, Ploenchit Centre, at the mouth of Soi 2 ☎ 02 656 7377; also at 64 Silom Building, set back off Thanon Silom between Soi 4 and Soi Thaniya ☎ 02 632 7448; ⓦ beirut-restaurant.com; map p.122. It's worth crossing the road from Bangkok's main Middle Eastern ghetto (Soi 3 and Soi 3/1) for the top-notch Lebanese food in this comfortable, a/c restaurant. Among dozens of salads and stuffed breads, the superb *motabel* (baba ganoush; B140) is fluffy and smoky, while the falafels are suitably moist inside and crunchy out. Good baklava, too. Ploenchit Centre daily 10am–10pm; 64 Silom Building daily 11.30am–midnight.

★ **Bolan** 24 Soi 53 (5min walk from BTS Thong Lo) ☎ 02 260 2961–2, ⓦ bolan.co.th; map p.122. Meticulous and hugely successful attempt to produce authentic traditional food in all its complexity, while upholding the "Slow Food" philosophy. It'll give you a lipsmacking education in Thai cuisine, best enjoyed on the "Bolan Balance" set dinner menu (B2680). Single-plate lunch sets start at B420. Tues–Fri 6–10.30pm (last orders), Sat & Sun noon–2.30pm & 6–10.30pm.

Cabbages and Condoms 10 Soi 12 ☎ 02 229 4610–28, ⓦ pda.or.th/restaurant; map p.122. The Population and Community Development Association of Thailand (PDA) runs this relaxing restaurant, decorated with condoms from around the world and the slogan "our food is guaranteed not to cause pregnancy". Try the chicken in pandanus leaves (B250) or the seafood green curry (B270); there's also a varied vegetarian menu. Daily 11am–10pm.

Dosa King Soi 11/1, with a back entrance on Soi 11 ☎ 02 651 1700, ⓦ dosaking.net; map p.122. Usually busy with expat Indian diners, this vegetarian Indian restaurant serves good food from both north and south, including over a dozen different dosas (southern pancake dishes), tandooris and the like. It's an alcohol-free zone so you'll have to make do with sweet lassi instead. Most dishes B100–200. Daily 11am–11pm.

Le Dalat 57 Soi 23 (Soi Prasanmit) ☎ 02 664 0670, ⓦ facebook.com/ledalatrestaurant; map p.122. There's Indochinese romance aplenty at this delightful, re-created Vietnamese brick mansion decked out with pot plants, plenty of photos and eclectic curiosities. The extensive, high-class Vietnamese menu features favourites such as a *goi ca* salad of aromatic herbs and raw fish (B360) and *chao tom* shrimp sticks on sugar cane (B250 per piece). Daily 11.30am–2.30pm & 5.30–10.30pm.

MahaNaga 2 Soi 29 ☎ 02 662 3060, ⓦ mahanaga. com; map p.122. The dining experience at this tranquil,

1

plush enclave is best appreciated after dark, when the courtyard tables are romantically lit. Cuisine is Thai fine dining, updated with contemporary techniques and some Western ingredients, featuring such tasty delights as *kaeng matsaman* with chicken and avocado (B350). Daily 5.30pm–midnight.

Prai Raya 59 Soi 8 ☎02 253 5556; map p.122. Set in a grand, modern villa done out in Sino-Portuguese style, this branch of a famous Phuket Town restaurant brings that city's distinctive cuisine to the capital – with a welcome offer to spice things down if requested. Most dishes are B200–250, including muu hong (stewed pork belly with cinnamon), but it's worth forking out a bit extra for the yellow curry with coconut milk and big chunks of fresh crabmeat. Also offers a good selection of vegetarian southern Thai dishes. Daily 11pm–10.30pm, last orders roughly 9.30pm.

Soul Food Mahanakorn 56/10 Soi 55 (Soi Thonglor; Exit 3 from BTS Thong Lo, then it's 100m up the soi on the right) ☎02 714 7708, ⓦsoulfoodmahanakorn. com; map p.122. If you already have your favourite stall for *som tam* or *laap*, this is not for you, but if not, this trim, welcoming, American-Thai bistro makes a great introduction to street food from around Thailand, using top-quality ingredients. The beef *khao soi* (curried noodle soup; B300) is thick and creamy, and the *som tam* (B150) is served with crispy chicken skin. Daily blackboard specials, and a wide selection of creative cocktails, craft beers and wines, including several by the glass. Daily 5.30pm–midnight (last food orders 11pm).

Vientiane Kitchen (Khrua Vientiane) 8 Soi 36, about 50m south off Thanon Sukhumvit ☎02 258 6171, ⓦvientiane-kitchenbkk.com; map p.122. Just a 3min walk west then south from BTS Thong Lo (Exit 2) and you're transported into a little piece of Isaan, where the menu's stocked full of northeastern delicacies, a live band sets the mood with heart-felt, sometimes over-amplified *pong lang* folk songs (see page 762), and there are even performances by a troupe of traditional dancers (daily from 7.30pm). The Isaan-accented menu (mostly B100–300) includes red ants' eggs salad, spicy-fried frog, jackfruit curry and grilled minced fish salad, plus there's a decent range of veggie options such as *som tam* and Thai desserts. With its airy, barn-like interior and mixed clientele of Thais and expats, it's a very enjoyable dining experience. Daily noon–11.30pm (last food orders 10.30pm).

DOWNTOWN: SOUTH OF THANON RAMA IV

In this area, there are also branches of *Baan Khanitha* (see page 155), *Supanniga* (see page 150) and *Beirut* (see page 155).

★**Aoi** 132/10–11 Soi 6, Thanon Silom ☎02 235 2321–2; map p.124; ground floor, Siam Paragon ☎02 129 4348–50; map p117.; 3rd Floor, Emporium

shopping centre; ☎02 664 8590–2; map p.122; ⓦaoi-bkk.com. One of the best places in town for a Japanese blowout, justifiably popular with the expat community, with excellent authentic food and elegant décor. Prices are higher in the evening, when a superb sushi set will set you back B1200, but at lunchtime you can get a bento box for B500. Thanon Silom daily 11.30am–1.45pm (last orders) & 5.30pm–9.45pm; Siam Paragon Mon–Fri 11.30am–2.15pm & 5.30–9.30pm, Sat & Sun 11am–9.30pm; Emporium shopping centre daily 11/11.30am–1.45/2.30pm & 5/5.30–9.45pm.

Bangkok Bold Kitchen Floor 2, Riverside Plaza, Thanon Charoennakorn ☎096 626 4519, ⓦbangkokbold.com; map p.78. This restaurant's retro look is in keeping with its menu of traditional, home-style recipes with bold flavours, mostly from central Thailand. Don't miss the excellent signature dish, stir-fried mackerel with acacia and pork crackling (B170), which goes well with the crabmeat "relish" (lon). Also offers a chef's table and cooking classes, both here and at its cooking studio on Thanon Phra Sumen in Banglamphu (see page 153). A bit out of the centre, but you can use the Anantara Riverside Hotel's shuttle boats (see page 148) from Saphan Taksin to get here (Riverside Plaza is right behind the hotel). Daily 11am–10pm.

★**Celadon** Sukhothai Hotel, 13/3 Thanon Sathorn Tai ☎02 344 8888; map p.124. Consistently rated as one of the best hotel restaurants in Bangkok and a favourite with locals, serving outstanding traditional and contemporary Thai food from all over the country – try the delicious pomelo salad with chicken and prawns (B450) and the northern-style egg noodles in curry soup (khao soi) – in an elegant setting surrounded by lotus ponds. Nightly performances of classical Thai dancing (7.30 & 8.30pm). Daily noon–2.30pm (last orders) & 6.30–10.30pm.

★**Eat Me** 1/6 Soi Phiphat 2, Thanon Convent ☎02 238 0931, ⓦeatmerestaurant.com; map p.124. Justly fashionable art gallery and restaurant in a striking, white modernist building, with changing exhibitions on the walls and a temptingly relaxing balcony. The eclectic, far-reaching menu features such mains as grilled squid with fennel, pomegranate and white bean purée (B790), there's an extensive wine list with many available by the glass, and the lemon-grass crème brûlée is not to be missed. Daily 3pm–1am.

Harmonique 22 Soi 34, Thanon Charoen Krung, on the lane leading to Wat Muang Kae express-boat pier ☎02 237 8175; map p.124. A relaxing, welcoming, moderately priced restaurant that's well worth a trip: tables are scattered throughout several converted shophouses, decorated with antiques and bric-a-brac, and a quiet, leafy courtyard, and the Thai food is varied and excellent, notably the house speciality crab curry (B240). Mon–Sat 11am–10pm.

JIM THOMPSON'S HOUSE

1

Home Cuisine Islamic Restaurant 186 Soi 36, Thanon Charoen Krung ☎02 234 7911, ⓦfacebook.com/homecuisineislamic; map p.124. The short, cheap menu of Indian and Thai Muslim dishes here has proved popular enough to warrant a refurbishment in green and white, with comfy booths, pot plants, a/c inside and a few outdoor tables overlooking the colonial-style French embassy. The *khao mok kai* signature dish (B85), a typical hybrid version of a chicken biryani, served with pickled aubergine and raita, is delicious. Mon–Sat 11am–9.30pm, Sun 6–9.30pm.

Indian Hut 418 Thanon Suriwong ☎02 236 5672–3, ⓦindianhutbangkok.com; map p.124. Bright, white-tablecloth, North Indian restaurant – look out for the Pizza Hut-style sign – that's justly popular with local Indians. For carnivores, tandoori's the thing (B375 for half a chicken), but there's also a wide selection of mostly vegetarian pakoras and other appetizers, as well as plenty of veggie main courses and breads, and a hard-to-resist house dhal (B250). Daily 11am–11pm.

Jim Thompson's Restaurant 149/4–6 Thanon Suriwong ☎02 235 8932, ⓦjimthompsonrestaurant.com; map p.124. Airy, elegant restaurant and lounge bar festooned with plants and signature fabrics (see page 119), which serves up tasty Thai dishes such as stir-fried soft-shell crab in yellow curry (B280), as well as burgers, salads, cakes, Thai desserts and a good selection of drinks. Also has a branch (closes 6pm) in the main Jim Thompson shop on the same street (see page 166). Daily 11am–10pm.

★**Krua Aroy Aroy** 3/1 Thanon Pan (opposite the Maha Uma Devi Temple) ☎02 635 2365, ⓦfacebook.com/kruaaroyaroy; map p.124. Aptly named "Delicious, Delicious Kitchen", this simple shophouse restaurant stands out for its choice of cheap, tasty, well-prepared dishes from all around the kingdom, notably chicken *matsaman* curry (B90), *khao soi* (a curried soup with egg noodles from northern Thailand) and *khanom jiin* (rice noodles topped with curry). Daily roughly 10am–6pm, or earlier if the food runs out.

Le Bouchon 37/17 Patpong 2, near Thanon Suriwong ☎02 234 9109; map p.124. Cosy Lyonnais bar-bistro in the heart of the red-light district that's much frequented by the city's French expats, offering home cooking such as duck confit (B490) and a good-value lunch set menu (B450 for two courses); booking is strongly recommended. Mon–Sat noon–3pm & 6.30–10.45pm.

★**Le Du** 399/3 Soi 7, Thanon Silom ☎092 919 9969, ⓦledubkk.com; map p.124. Excellent new restaurant that takes authentic Thai flavours and ingredients and develops them creatively and very successfully with modern cooking techniques. The regularly changing menu is strong on fish and seafood, in dishes such as superb soft-shell crab with bitter gourd and pineapple in a southern-style curry, accompanied by excellent wines, many available by

the glass. Leave room for a delicious dessert – or push the boat out for one of the tasting menus (with wine pairings available). Mon–Sat 6–11pm.

Mei Jiang Peninsula Hotel, 333 Thanon Charoennakorn ☎02 020 2888, ⓦpeninsula.com; map p.124. Probably Bangkok's best Chinese restaurant, with beautiful views of the hotel's riverside gardens, and very attentive and graceful staff. Cantonese specialities include excellent lunchtime dim sum, lobster rolls, lobster dumplings and brassica in clear broth (B480) and delicious teas. Free shuttle boats from Taksin Bridge. Daily 11.30am–2.30pm & 6–10.30pm.

★**Nahm** Como Metropolitan Hotel, 27 Thanon Sathorn Tai ☎02 625 3333, ⓦcomohotels.com/metropolitanbangkok; map p.124. Flagship restaurant of Australian David Thompson, the doyen of foreign chefs of Thai cuisine, with a seductive Japanese-designed interior and poolside tables. Expect esoteric authentic dishes such as oyster and Thai samphire salad, which are complex, intensely flavoured but well balanced, using the best of local ingredients. Go in the evening for the full effect, and book early; lunchtime sees a lighter, shorter menu that's more affordable and accessible (main dishes from B560). Mon–Fri noon–2pm & 6.30–10.15pm, Sat & Sun 6.30–10.15pm.

★**Ramentei** 23/8–9 Soi Thaniya ☎02 234 8082; map p.124; Sukhumvit Soi 33/1 ☎02 662 0050; map p.122. Excellent Japanese noodle café, bright, clean and welcoming, under the same ownership as *Aoi* (see page 156). The open kitchen turns out especially good, huge bowls of miso ramen (B230), which goes very well with the gyoza dumplings. Soi Thaniya daily 11am–2am; Soi 33/1 daily 11am–midnight.

Ruen Urai Rose Hotel, 118 Thanon Suriwong ☎02 266 8268–72, ⓦruen-urai.com; map p.124. Set back behind the hotel, this peaceful, hundred-year-old, traditional house, with fine balcony tables overlooking the beautiful hotel pool, comes as a welcome surprise in this full-on downtown area. The varied Thai food, which includes a good matsaman curry (B350), is of a high quality. Daily noon–11pm.

Sara Jane's 55/21 Thanon Narathiwat Ratchanakharin, between sois 4 & 6 ☎02 676 3338; map p.124. Long-standing, basic, a/c restaurant, popular with Bangkok's Isaan population, serving good, simple northeastern dishes, including a huge array of *nam tok*, *laap* and *som tam*, as well as Italian food – and a very tasty fusion of the two, spaghetti with *sai krok*, spicy Isaan sausage (B260). Daily 11am–3.30pm & 5.30–10pm.

Somboon Seafood Thanon Suriwong, corner of Thanon Narathiwat Ratchanakharin ☎02 233 3104; map p.124; Floor 5, Central Embassy ☎02 160 5965–6; map p.117; ⓦsomboonseafood.com. Highly favoured, bustling seafood restaurant, known especially for its crab curry (from about B300, depending on weight), with functional, modern decor and an array of marine life lined up in tanks awaiting its gastronomic fate. Thanon Suriwong daily 4–11.30pm; Central Embassy daily 11am–10pm.

★**Taling Pling** 653 Building 7, Ban Silom Arcade, Thanon Silom ☎02 236 4829; map p.124. One of the best Thai restaurants in the city outside of the big hotels, specializing in classic dishes from the four corners of the kingdom. The toothsome green beef curry (B145) with roti, which is recommended by the leading Thai restaurant guides, goes well with the delicious and refreshing house deep-fried fish salad. The atmosphere's convivial and relaxing, too. Daily 11am–10pm.

Tsukiji 62/19–20 Soi Thaniya ☎02 233 9698; map p.124. Named after Tokyo's famous fresh market, this coolly elegant restaurant serves high-quality sushi at a long counter and a few booth tables. Lunch on a weekday is the best time to come, when a nigiri sushi set with lots of side dishes costs just B300. Daily 11.30am–2pm & 5.30–10.30pm.

DRINKING AND NIGHTLIFE

Bangkok's **nightlife** has thoroughly grown up in the past decade and although for some male visitors, nightfall is the signal to hit the city's sex bars (most notoriously in the area off the east end of Thanon Silom known as Patpong), fortunately, Bangkok now also offers everything from craft-beer pubs and vertiginous, rooftop cocktail bars to fiercely chic clubs and dance bars, hosting top-class DJs. The high-concept bars of Sukhumvit and the lively, teeming venues of Banglamphu, in particular, pull in the style-conscious cream of Thai youth and are tempting an increasing number of travellers to stuff their party gear into their rucksacks. During the cool season, an evening out at one of the pop-up **beer gardens (usually Dec)** is a pleasant way of soaking up the urban atmosphere (and the traffic fumes); you'll find them in hotel forecourts or sprawled in front of dozens of shopping centres all over the city. Among the city's **club nights**, look out for the interesting regular events organized by Zudrangma Record Store (ⓦ zudrangmarecords.com), especially at their own bar *Studio Lam*, which mix up dance music from all around Thailand and from all over the world; Dudesweet's parties all over town, featuring Thai and international DJs and indie bands; and weekend DJ and band nights and creative events at Whiteline on Soi 8, Thanon Silom (ⓦ facebook.com/whitelinebangkok). Getting back to your lodgings should be no problem in the small hours: many bus routes run a (reduced) service throughout the night, and tuk-tuks and taxis are always at hand – though it's probably best for women travelling alone to avoid using tuk-tuks late at night.

BANGLAMPHU AND THE DEMOCRACY MONUMENT AREA

The travellers' enclave of Banglamphu takes on a new personality after dark, when its hub, Thanon Khao San, becomes a "walking street", closed to all traffic but open to almost any kind of makeshift stall, selling everything from fried bananas and buckets of "very strong" cocktails to share, to bargain fashions and one-off artworks. Young Thais come to the area to browse and snack before piling in to Banglamphu's more stylish bars and live-music clubs, most of which are free to enter (though some ask you to show ID first).

Ad Here the 13th (Blues Bar) 13 Thanon Samsen, opposite Soi 2, right by the start of the bridge over Khlong Banglamphu ☎089 769 4613; map p.100. Relaxed little neighbourhood live-music joint with sociable seats out on the pavement, where musos congregate nightly to listen to Thai and expat blues and jazz bands (from about 9.30pm onwards). Well-priced beer and plenty of cocktails. Daily 6pm–midnight.

Bottle Rocket 76/1 Thanon Phra Arthit ⓦ facebook.com/bottlerocketcraftbeerbar; map p.100. Gunning for the title of Thailand's smallest bar, with a petite streetside snug

---

NIGHTLIFE HOURS, ID CHECKS AND ADMISSION CHARGES

Most bars and clubs in Bangkok are meant to **close** at 1am, while those at the east end of Silom and on Royal City Avenue can stay open until 2am. In previous years, there have been regular "social order" clampdowns by the police, strictly enforcing these closing times, conducting occasional urine tests for drugs on bar customers, and setting up widespread ID checks to curb under-age drinking (you have to be 20 or over to drink in bars and clubs). However, at the time of writing, things were more chilled, with some bars and clubs staying open into the wee hours on busy nights and ID checks in only a few places. It's hard to predict how the situation might develop, but you'll soon get an idea of how the wind is blowing when you arrive in Bangkok – and there's little harm in taking a copy of your passport out with you, just in case. Nearly all bars and clubs in Bangkok are free, but the most popular of them will sometimes levy an admission charge of a couple of hundred baht on their busiest nights (which will usually include a drink or two), though this can vary from week to week.

that will appeal to smokers, Bottle Rocket pours half a dozen Thai and international craft beers on tap and plenty more in bottles. Happy hour till 8pm. Tues–Sun 5pm–midnight.

Brick Bar Buddy Village complex, 265 Thanon Khao San ⓦ brickbarkhaosan.com; map p.100. Massive red-brick vault of a live-music bar whose regular roster of reggae, ska, rock'n'roll and Thai pop bands, and occasional one-off appearances, is hugely popular with Thai twenty-somethings and teens. Big, sociable tables are set right under the stage and there's food too. The biggest nights are Fri and Sat when there's sometimes an entry charge, depending on who's on. Daily 7pm–1.30am.

Brown Sugar 469 Thanon Phra Sumen ⓞ 081 805 7759, ⓦ brownsugarbangkok.com; map p.100. Bangkok's best and longest-running jazz club moved in 2012 into smart, atmospherically lit premises in Banglamphu, which are hung with colourful modernist gig posters and include a leafy canalside terrace. It still has its famous Sun jam session, but is now allowing in a few early-evening acoustic sessions each week; music usually starts around 8.30pm. The prices of drinks are pumped up to pay for the talent, though they include imported beers on draught and in bottles. Tues–Thurs & Sun 5pm–1am, Fri & Sat 5pm–2am.

The Club 123 Thanon Khao San ⓞ 02 629 1010, ⓦ theclubkhaosan.com; map p.100. Thumping electronic dance music from an elevated, central DJ station with state-of-the-art lighting draw a young Thai and international crowd; check the website for upcoming events with imported DJs. Daily 10pm–late.

★ **Hippie de Bar** 46 Thanon Khao San ⓞ 081 820 2762; map p.100. Inviting courtyard bar set away from the main fray, with an indie-pop soundtrack and its own-brand fashion boutique. Attracts a mixed studenty/arty/high-society, mostly Thai crowd, to drink cheapish beer at its wrought-iron tables and park benches. Indoors is totally given over to retro kitsch, with plastic armchairs, Donny Osmond posters and floral prints. Daily 4pm–2am.

Jazz Happens 62 Thanon Phra Arthit ⓞ 084 450 0505, ⓦ facebook.com/jazzhappens; map p.100. Typical Phra Arthit bar, full of students, with just one small room and a few sociable pavement tables, but what sets this place apart is that some of the students are from Silpakorn University's Faculty of Jazz, playing jazz here most nights. Tuck into a decent selection of well-priced cocktails and a narrower choice of food while you're listening. Daily except Thurs 5pm–1am.

Phra Nakorn 58/2 Soi Damnoen Klang Tai ⓞ 02 622 0282, ⓦ facebook.com/phranakornbarandgallery; map p.100. Styles itself as "a hangout place for art lovers", and it successfully pulls in the capital's artists and art students, who can admire the floodlit view of the Golden Mount from the candlelit rooftop terrace, tuck into good food and reasonably priced drinks and browse one of the regular exhibitions on the first floor. Daily 6pm–1am.

Residence de Canal 463/72 Thanon Luk Luang ⓞ 02 061 8289, ⓦ facebook.com/residencebkk; map p.80. On the eastern edge of Banglamphu by Khlong Krung Kasem, this is about as underground as Bangkok's clubs get, set in a gritty, minimally converted warehouse, with just a few chairs and tables scattered around the white walls to distract from the music. Trance, house, techno, everything's on offer – "Fuck Genres Just Dance" is the motto – check out their Facebook page for line-ups, which currently include an open decks night on Mon. Daily 9pm–1am.

Sheepshank Tha Phra Arthit express-boat pier ⓞ 02 629 5165, ⓦ sheepshankpublichouse.com; map p.100. Set in a former boat-repair yard overlooking the Chao Phraya and the riverside walkway, this cool bar-restaurant sports an industrial look that features black leather, silver studs, pulleys and girders. There's a wide selection of bottled craft beers from the US and Japan, as well as imaginative bar snacks and a long menu of more substantial gastropub dishes. Mon 5pm–1am, Tues–Sun 11am–1am.

CHINATOWN

Chinatown has never had a reputation for its bars, but a handful of chic places, all affecting a rough-edged air of oriental mystique, have made Soi Nana a small hub of nightlife, just 5min walk from Hualampong subway station.

★ **Ba Hao** 8 Soi Nana, Thanon Maitri Chit ⓦ facebook. com/8bahao; map p.107. Announced by paper lanterns, friendly Ba Hao conjures up the spirit of old Chinatown with low red lighting and traditional, marble-topped tables and seats. As well as teas, ginseng shots and a short menu of Chinese food, it serves creative, Chinese-inspired cocktails – which Jamie Oliver likes, apparently – such as Opium, a Negroni using a ginseng and herbs liquor. Tues–Sun 6pm–midnight.

Let the Boy Die 542 Thanon Luang ⓦ facebook.com/ltbdbar; map p.107. At the time of research, Bangkok's pioneering craft-beer bar, under the same ownership as Golden Coins Taproom (see page 161), was about to reopen, offering a huge selection of Bangkok's finest brews. Tues–Sun 5–11pm.

Let the Girl Kill 747 Thanon Charoen Krung ⓦ facebook. com/let.the.girl.kill; map p.107. Offshoot of the above, with weathered wooden tables and stark grey walls, serving ten Thai craft beers on tap in the full rainbow of styles, from white and red beers to amber ales and stout. B300 for a flight of three beers to taste. Tues–Sun 6pm–midnight.

Teens of Thailand (TOT) 76 Soi Nana, Thanon Maitri Chit ⓦ facebook.com/teensofthailand; map p.107. The creaking of an ancient wooden door announces your arrival at this misleadingly named bar. Inside, old movie posters and a piano provide the setting for a cocktail menu that uses dozens of gins from around the world. Tues–Thurs & Sun 7pm–midnight, Fri & Sat 7pm–1am.

Tep Bar 69–71 Soi Nana, Thanon Maitri Chit ⓦfacebook.com/tepbarth; map p.107. Down a side alley off the main Soi Nana, Tep evokes the atmosphere of Bangkok of yore, with a bar that looks like the base of a chedi, candles and distressed walls, while a live group plays Thai classical music every evening. There's a long menu of Thai snacks, grilled meats and rice dishes, to be washed down with Thai rice whisky and herb liquor cocktails. Mon–Thurs & Sun 5pm–midnight, Fri & Sat 5pm–1am.

DOWNTOWN: AROUND SIAM SQUARE AND THANON PLOENCHIT

Downtown, Siam Square has much less to offer after dark than Thanon Sukhumvit, further east. Out to the northeast, running south off Thanon Rama IX, lies RCA (Royal City Avenue). An officially sanctioned "nightlife zone" that's allowed to stay open until 2am, it's lined mostly with warehouse-like clubs that have a reputation as meat markets.
Coco Walk Thanon Phrayathai; map p.117. It would be hard not to enjoy yourself at this covered parade of loosely interchangeable but buzzing good-time bars, right beside Ratchathevi BTS. Popular with local students, they variously offer pool tables, live musicians, DJs and a small skateboarding ramp, but all have reasonably priced beer and food. Daily roughly 6pm–1am.
Hyde and Seek Ground floor, Athenée Residence, 65/1 Soi Ruam Rudee ☎02 168 5152, ⓦhydeandseek.com; map p.117. Classy but buzzy gastrobar, with nightly DJs and lots of attractive garden seating. Amid a huge range of drinks, there's a good selection of wines by the glass and imported beers on draught; the food menu features bar bites, pastas, salads and familiar dishes such as bangers and mash. Daily 4.30pm–1am (last food orders 11.45pm).
Raintree 116/63–4 Soi Ruamjit, Thanon Rangnam ☎02 245 7230, ⓦraintreepub.com; map p.80. Near Victory Monument, two ordinary shophouses have been converted into this friendly, typical "good ol' boys" bar, with good food, lots of rough timber furniture and the biggest water-buffalo skulls you've ever seen. Live, nightly music (from about 9pm) is mostly Songs for Life (see page 763), mixed in with some *luk thung*, starting out low-key and soothing, and getting more raucous and danceworthy as the night hots up. Daily 6pm–1am.
Saxophone 3/8 Victory Monument (southeast corner), just off Thanon Phrayathai ☎02 246 5472, ⓦsaxophonepub.com; map p.80. Lively, easy-going, spacious venue with decent Thai and Western food and a diverse roster of bands – acoustic from 7.30pm, then mostly jazz and blues, plus funk, rock and reggae from 9pm (details on their website) – which attracts a good mix of locals and foreigners. Daily 6pm–2am.

THANON SUKHUMVIT

A night out on Thanon Sukhumvit could be subsumed by the girlie bars and hostess-run bar-beers on sois Nana and Cowboy, but there's plenty of style on Sukhumvit too, especially in the rooftop bars and craft-beer pubs. The scene has been gravitating eastwards over the last few years: the fashionable bars and clubs on and around Soi Thonglor (Soi 55) attract a "hi-so" (high-society) crowd, while those over on Soi Ekamai (Soi 63) are perhaps a little more studenty.
Brewski Radisson Blu Plaza Hotel, Thanon Sukhumvit between sois 25 and 27 ⓦvenuesbkk.com; map p.122. Winning (though pricey) combination of views and brews: a thirtieth-floor rooftop bar (smoking allowed) with a 270-degree vista of all the other downtown skyscrapers; plus a dozen craft beers on tap (a hundred more in bottles), with regular takeovers by the likes of Scotland's Brewdog. Daily 5pm–1am.
★ **Changwon Express** 37 Thanon Asok–Din Daeng ⓦfacebook.com/changwonexpress; map p.122. Off-strip but right next to Phetchaburi subway station, this small, friendly, Korean-owned bar brews its own excellent light stout and pale ale. Staff know what they're talking about and there are plenty of other Thai craft beers on tap, as well as British and US imports – plus Korean fusion food. Mon–Sat 5pm–midnight.
Glow 96/4–5 Soi 23 ⓦfacebook.com/glowbkk; map p.122. This intimate, unpretentious, two-floor venue with a great sound system is one of Bangkok's best underground clubs, attracting an interesting roster of Thai and international DJs, such as Dubfire and Nakadia, to play mostly house and techno. Wed–Sun 9.30pm–roughly 3am.
Golden Coins Taproom Ekamai Mall, at the entrance to Soi 10, Soi Ekamai (Soi 63) ⓦfacebook.com/goldencoinsinstaproom; map p.122. Small, brick-lined bar with rough-hewn wooden tables, serving its own great craft beers on tap and pub grub from around the world. Daily 5pm–midnight.
Iron Balls Park Lane shopping mall, 5min walk up Soi Ekamai (Soi 63) from the Skytrain ⓦfacebook.com/ironballsdistillery; map p.122. An unlikely spot for a gin distillery, but the product – using German juniper, ginger and lemongrass – is great; try their excellent Negroni, with Campari and charred sandalwood bitters. The small, attached bar mixes clubbiness – leather armchairs, library lamps – with a low-tech, early industrial feel – bell jars, coils and lots of wrought iron. Daily 6pm–1am.
The Iron Fairies Just over 1km up Soi Thonglor (Soi 55) from BTS Thong Lo ☎099 918 1600, ⓦtheironfairies.com; map p.122. High-concept bar that's designed to evoke a magical fairytale factory, with low lighting, jars of glitter (fairy dust) lining the walls and windows, gargoyles and lots of wooden structures including higgledy-piggledy staircases. Nightly live music including an open-mike night on Monday. Daily 6pm–2am.
Mikkeller 26 Yaek 2, Soi 10, Soi Ekamai (Soi 63) ☎02 381 9891, ⓦmikkellerbangkok.com; map p.122. This

1

branch of the famous Danish microbrewery offers thirty craft beers on tap in a handsome 1950s villa furnished in blonde wood, with bean bags out on the lawn. Located (and signposted) down a sub-soi of a sub-soi of Ekamai and with the beer working out at about B500/pint, it's one for the beer geeks. Daily 5pm–midnight.

★ **Studio Lam** About 100m up Soi 51 on the left, on the corner of the first sub-soi, about 5min walk west of BTS Thong Lo ☎02 261 6661, ⊛facebook.com/studiolambangkok; map p.122. This friendly, cosy neighbourhood bar is the latest project of Zudrangma Records (see page 767), whose record shop is just up the sub-soi to the left. The soundproofing and massive, purpose-built sound system give the game away: the music's the thing here, with DJs and live musicians playing driving *mor lam* and an eclectic choice of world sounds nightly. Tues–Sun 6pm–late.

★ **WTF** 7 Soi 51 ☎02 662 6246, ⊛wtfbangkok.com; map p.122. Small, Spanish-influenced bar-café and art gallery, which hosts occasional performance art, poetry and movie nights. Adorned with luridly coloured Thai film posters and a great soundtrack, it offers global tapas and a tempting variety of cocktails and drinks. It's 5min walk west of BTS Thong Lo, 100m up Soi 51, near the mouth of a small sub-soi on the left. Tues–Sun 6pm–1am.

DOWNTOWN: SOUTH OF THANON RAMA IV

There are one or two mixed bars on the mostly gay Soi 4 at the east end of Thanon Silom – and, of course, a slew of go-go bars on Patpong – but otherwise the action in this area is widely scattered. If, among all the choice of nightlife in Bangkok, you do end up at one of Patpong's sex shows, watch out for hyper-inflated bar bills and other cons – plenty of customers get ripped off in some way, and stories of menacing bouncers are legion.

Namsaah Bottling Trust Soi 7, Thanon Silom ☎02 636 6622; map p.124. Playful gastropub in a century-old villa – now shocking pink – with dwarfing views of the new 300-metre Mahanakhon skyscraper from its leafy patio. Down creative cocktails with a Thai twist and good fusion food (last orders midnight), amidst the plush of velvet drapes, pink hogs' heads and suits of Samurai armour. Daily 5pm–2am.

★ **The Sky Bar & Distil** Floors 63 & 64, State Tower, 1055 Thanon Silom, corner of Thanon Charoen Krung ☎02 624 9555, ⊛lebua.com; map p.124. Thrill-seekers and view addicts shouldn't miss forking out for an alfresco drink here, 275m above the city's pavements – come around 6pm to enjoy the stunning panoramas in both the light and the dark. It's standing-only at *The Sky Bar*, a circular restaurant-bar built over the edge of the building with almost 360-degree views, but for the sunset itself, you're better off on the outside terrace of *Distil* one floor up on the other side of the building (where bookings are accepted), which has a wider choice of drinks, charming service and huge couches to recline on. The bars have become very popular since featuring in *The Hangover II* movie and have introduced a strict, smart-casual dress code. Sky Bar daily 6pm–1am; Distil daily 5pm–1am.

★ **Tawandang German Brewery** 462/61 Thanon Rama III ☎02 678 1114–6, ⊛tawandang.com; map p.124. A taxi-ride south of Chong Nonsi BTS down Thanon Narathiwat Ratchanakharin – and best to book a table in advance – this vast all-rounder is well worth the effort. Under a huge dome, up to 1600 revellers enjoy good Thai and German food, great micro-brewed German beer and a mercurial, hugely entertaining cabaret, featuring live pop and luk thung, magic shows and dance numbers. Daily 5pm–1am.

Viva Aviv: The River Ground floor, River City shopping centre (free shuttle boat from Taksin Bridge) ☎02 639 6305, ⊛vivaaviv.com; map p.124. With a lovely open deck right on the river and a gnarly interior decor of hidebound chairs and ships' winches, this bar offers cool sounds, some serious cocktails, good coffees and smoothies, as well as comfort food such as gourmet hot dogs, pizzas and salads. Daily 11am–midnight.

CHATUCHAK WEEKEND MARKET

Viva 8 Section 8 ☎02 618 7425; map p.78. Classy, relaxing bar that serves great cocktails, juices and coffees, where you can rest your feet while listening to DJs (from about 4pm) or tuck into paella that's theatrically prepared in a huge pan by a Spanish chef. Sat & Sun 7am–10pm.

KO KRED

Chit's 5min walk south of the pier on the river ⊛facebook.com/chitbeer; map p.78. Huge selection of craft beers on tap and in bottle by Thailand's most famous home brewer, Chit (motto: "It's Good Chit"), plus Thai guest beers, pub grub and lovely riverside tables. Sat & Sun noon–9pm.

LGBTQ+ BANGKOK

Bangkok's gay bars, clubs and café-restaurants are concentrated around the east end of Thanon Silom, especially in the narrow alleys of Soi 2 and Soi 4. After a break of more than ten years, Bangkok Pride is scheduled to return to the city in 2018, with a parade, parties and social events across the city, workshops and film festivals, hosted by Out Bkk (⊛facebook. com/outinbkk). More general background on LGBTQ+ life in Thailand, plus contacts and sources of information, most of them concentrated in Bangkok, can be found in Basics (see page 69). Advice on opening hours, admission charges and ID is given in Drinking and Nightlife (see page 159) – Soi 2, for example, operates a strict ID policy.

The Balcony Soi 4, Thanon Silom ☎02 235 5891, ⓦbalconypub.com; map p.124. Unpretentious, fun place with plenty of outdoor seats for people-watching, welcoming staff, reasonably priced drinks, upstairs karaoke and decent Thai and Western food. Happy hour till 8pm. Daily 5.30pm–2am.

Dick's Café Duangthawee Plaza, 894/7–8 Soi Pratuchai (aka Soi Twilight), Thanon Suriwong ☎02 637 0078, ⓦdickscafe.com; map p.124. Elegant day-and-night café-bar-restaurant, with a *Casablanca* theme to the decor (styling itself on *Rick's Café Americain*) and occasional art exhibitions. On a traffic-free soi of go-go bars off the north side of Suriwong, it's ideal for drinking, eating decent Thai and Western food or just chilling out. Daily 10.30am–2am.

DJ Station Soi 2, Thanon Silom ☎02 266 4029, ⓦdj-station.com; map p.124. Bangkok's most famous club, a highly fashionable but unpretentious three-storey venue, packed at weekends, attracting a mix of Thais and farangs, with a cabaret show nightly at around 11pm. Daily 9.30pm–2am.

G Bangkok 60/18–21 Soi 2/1, Thanon Silom, in a small pedestrianized alley between Soi Thaniya and Soi 2 ☎02 632 8033; map p.124. Large, full-on, three-level club, somewhat more Thai-oriented than *DJ Station*, that's still often referred to by its former name, GOD (for Guys on Display). It tends not to fill up until *DJ Station* has closed. Hosts a big festival of parties over Songkran. Daily 11pm–3am, sometimes later on Sat.

JJ Park 8/3 Soi 2, Thanon Silom ☎02 235 1227; map p.124. Classy, Thai-oriented bar, for relaxed socializing among an older set rather than raving, with karaoke and live music. Daily 10pm–2am.

The Stranger Bar Soi 4, Thanon Silom ☎02 632 9425, ⓦfacebook.com/thestrangerbar; map p.124. Recently opened, stylish "pub theatre" with drag shows most nights at 10.30pm and good cocktails. Happy hour till 9pm. Daily 5.45pm–2am.

Telephone Pub 114/11–13 Soi 4, Thanon Silom ☎02 234 3279, ⓦfacebook.com/telephonebkk; map p.124. Bangkok's first Western-style gay bar when it opened in 1987, this cruisy, dimly lit eating and drinking venue has a terrace on the alley and a restaurant and karaoke upstairs. Daily 6pm–2am.

ENTERTAINMENT

On the cultural front, the most accessible of the capital's performing arts is **Thai dancing**, particularly when served up in bite-size portions in tourist shows. **Thai boxing** is also well worth watching: the raucous live experience at either of Bangkok's two main national stadiums far outshines the TV coverage.

CINEMAS

Central Bangkok has more than forty cinemas, many of them on the top floors of shopping centres. Most show recent American and European releases with their original dialogue and Thai subtitles, screening shows around four times a day. Several websites give showtimes of movies in Bangkok, including ⓦmoveedoo.com/th. Whatever cinema you're in, you're expected to stand for the king's anthem, which is played before every performance.

Alliance Française Off Thanon Witthayu, opposite the east side of Lumpini Park behind the Japanese Embassy ☎02 670 4200, ⓦafthailande.org. The frequent movie screenings at the French cultural centre are usually subtitled in English.

Apex Scala Thanon Rama I, Siam Square ☎02 251 2861, ⓦapexsiam-square.com. Among half a dozen cinemas in and around Siam Square, this is your best bet for independent foreign films.

Bangkok Screening Room Woof Pack Building, Soi Saladaeng 1, corner of Thanon Rama IV ☎090 906 3888, ⓦbkksr.com. New fifty-seat venue for independent movies, shorts and documentaries by international and Thai directors, as well as retrospective classics.

House Royal City Avenue (RCA) ☎02 641 5177, ⓦhouserama.com. Bangkok's main art-house cinema, well to the northeast of the centre. The nearest subway station, Phetchaburi, is a long walk away, so it's best to come by taxi.

CULTURE SHOWS AND PERFORMING ARTS

Because of the language barrier, most Thai theatre is inaccessible to foreigners and so, with a few exceptions, the best way to experience the traditional performing arts is at shows designed for tourists, most notably at Siam Niramit. You can, however, witness Thai dancing being performed for its original ritual purpose, usually several times a day, at the Lak Muang Shrine behind the Grand Palace (see page 93) and the Erawan Shrine on the corner of Thanon Ploenchit (see page 121). Background information on Thai classical dance and traditional theatre can be found in Basics (see page 49). Meanwhile, more glitzy and occasionally ribald entertainment is the order of the day at the capital's ladyboy cabaret shows.

Calypso Cabaret Asiatique (see page 165), Thanon Charoen Krung, 2km south of Saphan Taksin BTS ☎02 688 1415–7, ⓦcalypsocabaret.com. Expect glamorous outfits and over-the-top song-and-dance routines twice a night. B1200, or B900 if booked online, including one drink.

Chalermkrung Theatre (Sala Chalermkrung) 66 Thanon Charoen Krung, on the intersection with Thanon Triphet in Pahurat, next to Old Siam Plaza ☎02 224 4499, ⓦsalachalermkrung.com or ⓦthaiticketmajor.com. This Art Deco former cinema, dating from 1933, hosts *khon* performances with English subtitles every Thurs and Fri at 7.30pm. Tickets from B800.

National Theatre Sanam Luang, Ratanakosin ☎02 224 1342. Hosts traditional performing arts such as *khon*, *lakhon* and medley shows of music and dancing roughly twice a month (not in the hot season), usually on Sun. However, it's difficult to get information about what's on in English – the nearby Bangkok Tourism Division (see page 141) often has a schedule.

Siam Niramit 19 Thanon Tiam Ruammit, 5min walk (or a free shuttle ride from Exit 1) from Thailand Cultural Centre subway, following signs for the South Korean embassy ☎02 649 9222, ⊕ siamniramit.com. Unashamedly tourist-oriented but the easiest place to get a glimpse of the variety and spectacle intrinsic to traditional Thai theatre. The show presents a history of regional Thailand's culture and beliefs in a high-tech spectacular of fantastic costumes and huge chorus numbers, enlivened by acrobatics and flashy special effects. The complex also includes a kitschy handicrafts village, souvenir shops and a buffet restaurant (dinner plus show from B1850). Tickets (from B1500) can be bought on the spot, online or through most travel agents. Daily 8pm.

Thailand Cultural Centre Thanon Ratchadapisek ☎02 247 0028, ⊕ thaiticketmajor.com; Thailand Cultural Centre subway. All-purpose venue, under the control of the Ministry of Culture, that hosts mainstream classical concerts, traditional and contemporary theatre, and visiting international dance and theatre shows.

THAI BOXING

The violence of the average Thai boxing match (see page 50) may be off-putting to some, but spending a couple of hours at one of Bangkok's two main stadiums, Rajdamnoen and Lumphini, can be immensely entertaining, not least for the enthusiasm of the spectators and the ritualistic aspects of the fights. Seats for foreigners cost B1000–2000 (cheaper, standing tickets are reserved for Thais). Sessions usually feature at least ten bouts, each consisting of five 3min rounds with 2min rests in between each round, so if you're not a big fan it may be worth turning up late, as the better fights tend to happen later in the billing. To engage in a little *muay thai* yourself, visit one of several gyms around Bangkok that offer classes to foreigners.

Chacrit Muay Thai School 15/2 Soi 39, Thanon Sukhumvit ☎089 499 2052, ⊕ chacritmuaythaischool. com. Drop-in one-on-one sessions cost B800/hr; longer courses are available.

Lumphini Stadium Thanon Ram Intra ⊕ muaythai lumpinee.net. This sixty-year-old stadium recently moved way out into the northern suburbs near Don Muang Airport, but will become more accessible once the northern extension of the Skytrain opens. The schedule of upcoming fights is posted on its website. Usually Tues 6.30pm, Fri 7pm, Sat 4pm.

Rajdamnoen Stadium Thanon Rajdamnoen Nok ⊕ rajadamnern.com. Thailand's oldest stadium (established in 1945) is handily located next to the TAT office near Banglamphu (and handily surrounded by restaurants selling northeastern food). Usually Mon, Wed, Thurs & Sun 6.30pm.

Sor Vorapin's Gym 13 Trok Kasap, off Thanon Chakrabongse in Banglamphu ☎02 282 3551, ⊕ thaiboxings.com. Holds one-hour-thirty-minute *muay thai* classes twice daily (B500 per session), as well as one-on-one sessions (B1000 for 1hr 30min). Also offers extended training and a homestay at a second gym in Thonburi – see the website for details.

SHOPPING

Bangkok has a good reputation for shopping, particularly for antiques, gems, contemporary interior design and fashion, where the range and quality are streets ahead of other Thai cities. Fabrics and handicrafts are good buys too, though shopping for these in Chiang Mai has many advantages. As always, watch out for **fakes**: cut glass masquerading as precious stones, old, damaged goods being passed off as antiques, counterfeit designer clothes and accessories, even mocked-up international driver's licences (though Thai travel agents and other organizations aren't that easily fooled). Bangkok also has the best English-language bookshops in the country. Downtown is full of smart, multi-storey **shopping plazas** like Siam Centre, Siam Paragon and Central World on Thanon Rama I, Central Embassy on Thanon Ploenchit and Emporium and EmQuartier on Thanon Sukhumvit, which is where you'll find the majority of the city's fashion stores, as well as designer lifestyle goods and bookshops. The plazas tend to be pleasantly air-conditioned and thronging with trendy young Thais, but don't hold much interest for tourists unless you happen to be looking for a new outfit. Shopping centres, department stores and tourist-oriented shops in the city keep late **hours**, opening daily at 10 or 11am and closing at about 9pm; many small, upmarket boutiques, for example along Thanon Charoen Krung and Thanon Silom, close on Sundays, one or two even on Saturdays. Monday is meant to be no-street-vendor day throughout Bangkok, a chance for the pavements to get cleaned and for pedestrians to finally see where they're going, but plenty of stalls manage to flout the rule.

MARKETS

For travellers, spectating, not shopping, is apt to be the main draw of Bangkok's neighbourhood markets and the bazaars of Chinatown. The massive Chatuchak Weekend Market is an exception, being both a tourist attraction and a marvellous shopping experience (see page 128). With the notable exception of Chatuchak, most markets operate daily from dawn till early afternoon; early morning is often the best time to go to beat the heat and crowds.

Asiatique About 2km south of Taksin Bridge, between the river and Thanon Charoen Krung ⓦwww.asiatiquethailand.com. Night-time market for tourists in ten rebuilt 1930s warehouses and sawmills that belonged to the Danish East Asiatic Company. Several of them are given over to souvenirs and to clothes stalls, which tend to morph into bigger, more chic and expensive fashion outlets the closer to the river you get. Warehouse 1, devoted to furniture and home decor is probably the most interesting section, featuring some creative contemporary designs. There's plenty to eat, of course, with the poshest restaurants, including a branch of *Baan Khanitha* (see page 155), occupying the pleasant riverside boardwalk, while attractions include a sixty-metre ferris wheel and Calypso Cabaret (see page 163). Free ferries shuttle back and forth from Tha Sathorn pier, though the queues are often very long. Currently, the Chao Phraya Express tourist boats leaving Phra Arthit between 4pm and 6pm are extending their route from Tha Sathorn to Asiatique. You could also catch an orange-flag express boat to Wat Rajsingkorn, leaving a 10min walk through the wat and down Thanon Charoen Krung to the shopping complex. Asiatique is planning to expand, including floating restaurants, five-star hotels and improved access by boat. Daily 4pm–midnight.

Talat Rot Fai 2 Behind Esplanade Mall, Thanon Ratchadaphisek; map p.78. Fun outdoor market that's the most accessible of several similar night-time operations in Bangkok, as it's 5min walk from Thailand Cultural Centre subway station. Among the nail bars, tattoo parlours and pop-up barbers, hundreds of stalls purvey all the cool stuff a twenty-something urbanite might want, including new and pre-loved clothes, caps, bags and general kitsch. Dozens of food stalls and vibrant outdoor bars, some with live music, round out the picture. Daily 5pm–midnight.

HANDICRAFTS, TEXTILES AND CONTEMPORARY DESIGN

Samples of nearly all regionally produced handicrafts end up in Bangkok, so the selection is phenomenal. Many of the shopping plazas have at least one classy handicraft outlet, and competition keeps prices in the city at upcountry levels, with the main exception of household objects – particularly wickerware and tin bowls and basins – which get palmed off relatively expensively in Bangkok. Several places on and around Thanon Khao San sell reasonably priced triangular "axe" pillows (*mawn khwaan*) in traditional fabrics, which make fantastic souvenirs but are heavy to post home; some places sell unstuffed versions which are simple to mail home, but a pain to fill when you return. The cheapest outlet for traditional northern and northeastern textiles is Chatuchak Weekend Market (see page 128), where you'll also be able to nose out some interesting handicrafts. Most Thai silk, which is noted for its thickness and sheen, comes from the northeast and the north, where shopping for it is probably more fun. However, there is a decent range of outlets in the capital, including many branches of Jim Thompson. Bangkok also has a good reputation for its contemporary interior design, fusing minimalist Western ideals with traditional Thai and other Asian craft elements.

RATANAKOSIN

Doi Tung Lifestyle Thanon Na Phra Lan (plus several other branches around town) ⓦdoitung.org; map p.83. Part of the late Princess Mother's development project based at Doi Tung near Chiang Rai, selling very striking and attractive cotton and linen in warm colours, made up into clothes, cushion covers, rugs and so on, as well as coffee and macadamia nuts from the Chiang Rai mountains. Daily 8am–8pm.

SHOPPING FOR EVERYDAY STUFF

You're most likely to find useful everyday items in one of the city's numerous **department stores**: seven-storey Central Chidlom on Thanon Ploenchit (daily 10am–10pm; ⓦcentralchidlom.com), which boasts handy services like watch-repair booths as well as a huge product selection (including large sizes), is probably the city's best. For **children's stuff**, Central Chidlom also has a branch of Mothercare (ⓦmothercarethailand.com), as do the Emporium, Central World and Siam Paragon shopping centres. Meanwhile, the British chain of **pharmacies**, Boots (ⓦth.boots.com), has scores of branches across the city, including on Thanon Khao San in Banglamphu, in Siam Paragon, in Central World, in EmQuartier and at the Thanon Suriwong end of Patpong 1.

The best place to buy anything to do with **mobile phones** (see page 72) is the scores of small booths on Floor 4 of Mah Boon Krong (MBK) Shopping Centre at the Rama I/Phrayathai intersection. For **computer** hardware and genuine and pirated software, as well as cameras, Panthip Plaza, at 604/3 Thanon Phetchaburi, is the best place; it's slightly off the main shopping routes, but handy for Khlong Saen Saeb boat stop Tha Pratunam, or a longer walk from BTS Ratchathewi. Mac-heads are catered for here, including authorized resellers, and there are dozens of repair and secondhand booths, especially towards the back of the shopping centre and on the upper floors.

1

Queen Sirikit Museum of Textiles Shop Grand Palace (on the right just inside the Gate of Glorious Victory) ⓦqsmtthailand.org/shop; map p.83. Not-for-profit shop under the auspices of the Queen Mother's Support Foundation, which is especially good for beautiful, top-quality *yan lipao*, traditional basketware made from delicately woven fern stems. Daily 9am–4.30pm (except when the Grand Palace is closed for royal events).

BANGLAMPHU AND THE DEMOCRACY MONUMENT AREA

Heritage Craft 35 Thanon Bamrung Muang ⓦheritage craft.org; map p.100. In an atmospheric old shophouse with a small café, a permanent outlet for the fair-trade products of ThaiCraft (see page 166), including jewellery, silk and indigo batiks made by the Hmong of northern Thailand. Mon–Fri 11am–6pm.

Lofty Bamboo Buddy Hotel shopping complex, 265 Thanon Khao San; map p.100; ⓦloftybamboo.com. Also at Floor 2, Mah Boon Krong (MBK) Centre, corner of Thanon Phrayathai and Thanon Rama I. Fair-trade outlet for crafts, accessories, clothes, bags and jewellery, including textiles and accessories made by Lisu people from northern Thailand. Buddy Hotel shopping complex daily 10.30am–7.30pm; Mah Boon Krong (MBK) Centre daily 10.30am–8pm.

Taekee Taekon 118 Thanon Phra Athit ☎02 629 1473; map p.100. Tasteful assortment of handicraft gifts, souvenirs and textiles, plus a selection of Thai art cards and black-and-white photocards. Mon–Sat 9am–5pm.

DOWNTOWN: AROUND SIAM SQUARE AND THANON PLOENCHIT

Alexander Lamont Floor 3, Gaysorn Village; Floor 2, Central Embassy; ⓦalexanderlamont.com; map p.117. Beautiful lacquerware bowls, vases and boxes, as well as objects using bronze, glass, crystal, ceramic, parchment, gold leaf and petrified wood, all in imaginative contemporary, Asian-inspired styles. Daily 10am–8pm.

Chabatik Floor 2, River City ⓦchabatik.com; map p.117. Gorgeous scarves, wraps, bags, accessories and hangings in a rainbow of colours, made from soft Khon Kaen silk, combining traditional weaving methods with contemporary designs. Daily 10am–8pm.

Exotique Thai Floor 4, Siam Paragon ⓦsiamparagon. co.th; map p.117. A collection of small outlets from around the city and the country – including silk-makers and designers from Chiang Mai – makes a good, upmarket one-stop shop, that is much more interesting than Narai Phand (see below). There's everything from jewellery and beauty products to celadons and axe pillows (see page 468). Daily 10am–10pm.

Narai Phand Ground floor, President Tower Arcade, just east of Gaysorn Village, Thanon Ploenchit ⓦnaraiphand.com; map p.117. This souvenir centre was set up to ensure the preservation of traditional crafts and to maintain standards of quality, as a joint venture with the Ministry of Industry in the 1930s, and has a duly institutional feel, though it makes a reasonable one-stop shop for last-minute presents. It offers a huge assortment of reasonably priced, good-quality goods from all over the country, including silk and cotton, *khon* masks, *bencharong*, celadon, woodcarving, lacquerware, silver, brass, bronze, *yan lipao* basketware and axe cushions. Daily 10am–8pm.

OTOP Floor 4, Central Embassy ⓦcentralembassy. com/brands/otop-heritage; map p.117. An attractive selection of the more high-end handicrafts made under the national OTOP (One Tambon, One Product) scheme, including ceramics, bags and clothes, including silk. Daily 10am–8pm.

Creative Lab Siam Discovery, Thanon Rama I ⓦsiamdiscovery.co.th; map p.117. Recently renovated, Floor 3 of this mall is now an open-plan bazaar for all manner of contemporary Thai design, including lamps, vases, rugs, accessories, spa products and stationery. Daily 10am–10pm.

THANON SUKHUMVIT

Another Story Floor 4, EmQuartier ⓦfacebook.com/ anotherstoryofficial; map p.122. Another Story shelters a bewildering anthology of cool stuff: lamps and interior décor; lovely leather bags and accessories by Labrador; stationery and art books; sunglasses; and excellent breads, patisserie, cheese and wine at its deli-café. Daily 10am–10pm.

Sop Moei Arts 8 Soi 49 ⓦsopmoeiarts.com; map p.122. If you're not going up to Chiang Mai, it's well worth checking out the lovely fabrics and basketware at this small branch shop. Tues–Sat 9.30am–5pm.

ThaiCraft Fairs Floor L, Jasmine City Building, corner of Thanon Sukhumvit and Soi 23 ⓦthaicraft.org; map p.122. One-off craft sales and demonstrations, involving about fifty groups of artisans from all over the country, run on fair-trade principles by ThaiCraft, an independent development organization – check the website for dates.

DOWNTOWN: SOUTH OF THANON RAMA IV

Jim Thompson 9 Thanon Suriwong, corner of Thanon Rama IV; map p.117; branches at the Jim Thompson House Museum (see page 124), the airports and many department stores, malls and hotels around the city; ⓦjimthompson.com. A good place to start looking for traditional Thai fabric, or at least to get an idea of what's out there. Stocks silk, linen and cotton by the metre and ready-made items from shirts to cushion covers, which are well designed and of good quality, but pricey. They also have a home-furnishings section (daily 9am–7pm). Daily 9am–9pm.

Khomapastr 56–58 Thanon Naret, between Suriwong and Si Phraya roads ⓦkhomapastrfabrics.com; map p.124. Branch of the famous Hua Hin shop (see page 518), selling brightly coloured, hand-printed cotton in traditional Thai patterns. Mon–Sat 9am–5.30pm.

The Legend Floor 3, Thaniya Plaza, corner of Soi Thaniya and Thanon Silom ☎02 231 2170; map p.124. Stocks a small selection of well-made Thai handicrafts, notably wood, wickerware, celadon and other ceramics, at reasonable prices. Daily 10am–7pm.

The Shop @ TCDC Thailand Creative and Design Centre, Grand Postal Building, Thanon Charoen Krung ⓦtcdc. or.th; map p.124. The retail outlet at Bangkok's design centre sells innovative products dreamt up by local creatives, mostly stocking-fillers, bags, T-shirts and art books, with more than a whiff of kitsch. Tues–Sun 10.30am–9pm.

Tamnan Mingmuang Floor 3, Thaniya Plaza, corner of Soi Thaniya and Thanon Silom ☎02 231 2120; map p.124. Subsidiary of *The Legend* (see above), which sells lovely, aromatic basketry from all over the country: among the unusual items on offer are trays and boxes for tobacco and betel nut made from *yan lipao* (intricately woven fern vines), and bambooware sticky-rice containers, baskets and lampshades. Daily 10am–7pm.

TAILORED CLOTHES

Inexpensive tailoring shops crowd Silom, Sukhumvit and Khao San roads, but the best single area to head for is the short stretch of Thanon Charoen Krung between Thanon Suriwong and Thanon Silom (near the Chao Phraya express-boat stops at Tha Oriental and Tha Wat Muang Kae, or a 10min walk from Saphan Taksin Skytrain station). It's generally advisable to avoid tailors in tourist areas such as Thanon Khao San, shopping malls and Thanon Sukhumvit, although if you're lucky it's still possible to come up trumps here. For cheap and reasonable shirt and dress material other than silk go for a browse around Pahurat market (see page 109), though the suit materials are mostly poor and best avoided.

A Song Tailor 8 Trok Chartered Bank, just round the corner from OP Place shopping centre off Thanon Charoen Krung, near the Oriental Hotel ☎02 630 9708, ⓦasongtailor.com; map p.124. Friendly, helpful small shop that's a good first port of call if you're on a budget. Men's and women's suits and shirts; preferably at least three to five days with two fittings, but can turn work around in a day or two. Tues–Sat noon–7pm.

Golden Wool 1340–2 Thanon Charoen Krung ☎02 233 0149, ⓦgolden-wool.com; map p.124. A larger operation than nearby A Song, which can turn around decent work for men and women in two days, though prices are slightly on the high side. Mon–Sat 10am–8pm.

Marco Tailor Soi 7, Siam Square ☎02 252 0689; map p.117. Long-established tailor with a good reputation, making men's suits in two or three weeks. Mon–Sat 10am–7pm.

FASHION

Thanon Khao San is lined with stalls selling low-priced fashion clothing: the baggy cotton fisherman's trousers, elephant pants and embroidered blouses are all aimed at backpackers, but they're supplemented by cheap contemporary fashions that appeal to urban Thais as well. Downtown, the most famous area for low-cost, low-quality casual clothes is the warren-like Pratunam Market and surrounding malls such as Platinum Fashion Mall around the junction of Phetchaburi and Ratchaprarop roads (see page 117), but for the best and latest trends from Thai designers, you should check out the shops in Siam Square and across the road in the more upmarket Siam Centre. Prices vary considerably: street gear in Siam Square is undoubtedly inexpensive, while genuine Western brand names are generally competitive but not breathtakingly cheaper than at home; larger sizes can be hard to find. Shoes and leather goods are good buys in Bangkok, being generally handmade from high-quality leather and quite a bargain.

Central Embassy Thanon Ploenchit ⓦcentralembassy. com; map p.117. This recently built mall, constructed on land sold off by the British Embassy, is bidding to become the most chic of the city's shopping plazas: here you'll find Gucci and McQ – and gentlemen can get a very civilized haircut or shave at a branch of the London barber, Truefitt and Hill – while a few upmarket Thai names have made it to the party, notably Sretsis and Scotch and Soda. Daily 10am–10pm.

Central World Ratchaprasong Intersection, corner of Rama I and Rajdamri roads ⓦcentralworld.co.th; map p.117. This shopping centre is so huge that it defies easy classification, but you'll find plenty of Thai and international fashions on its lower floors and in the attached Zen department store at its southern end. Daily 10am–9/10pm.

Emporium Thanon Sukhumvit, between sois 22 and 24 ⓦemporiumthailand.com; map p.122. Large and rather glamorous shopping plaza, with its own department store and a good range of fashion outlets, from exclusive designer wear to trendy high-street gear. Genuine brand-name shops include Prada, Chanel and Burberry, as well as established local labels such as Soda. Daily 10am–8/10pm.

EmQuartier Thanon Sukhumvit, opposite Emporium ⓦemquartier.co.th; map p.122. Sprawling across three buildings, this mall runs the gamut from Miu Miu, Chanel and Jimmy Choo to Boots the Chemist. Less exclusive brands such as Hilfiger also find space alongside Soda, Jaspal and other local names (and lots of good eating options). Daily 10am–10pm.

Mah Boon Krong (MBK) At the Rama I/Phrayathai intersection ⓦmbk-center.co.th; map p.117. Vivacious, labyrinthine shopping centre which most closely resembles a traditional Thai market that's been rammed into a huge mall. It houses hundreds of small, mostly fairly inexpensive outlets, including plenty of high-street fashion shops. Daily 10am–9/10pm.

1

HAVING CLOTHES TAILOR-MADE

Bangkok can be an excellent place to get tailor-made suits, dresses, shirts and trousers at a fraction of the price you'd pay in the West. Tailors here can copy a sample brought from home and will also work from any photographs you can provide; most also carry a good selection of catalogues. The bad news is that many tourist-oriented tailors aren't terribly good, often attempting to get away with poor work and shoddy materials (and sometimes trying to delay delivery until just before you leave the city, so that you don't have time to complain). However, with a little effort and thought, both men and women can get some fantastic clothes made to measure.

Choosing a tailor can be tricky, and unless you're particularly knowledgeable about material, shopping around won't necessarily tell you much. However, don't make a decision wholly on prices quoted – picking a tailor simply because they're the cheapest usually leads to poor work, and cheap suits don't last. Special deals offering two suits, two shirts, two ties and a kimono for US$99 should be left well alone. Above all, ignore recommendations by anyone with a vested interest in bringing your custom to a particular shop.

Prices vary widely depending on material and the tailor's skill. As a very rough guide, for labour alone expect to pay B5000–6000 for a two-piece suit, though some tailors will charge rather more (check whether or not the price you're quoted includes the lining). For middling **material**, expect to pay about B3000–5000, or anything up to B20,000 for top-class cloth. With the exception of silk, local materials are frequently of poor quality and for suits in particular you're far better off using English or Italian cloth. Most tailors stock both imported and local fabrics, but bringing your own from home can work out significantly cheaper.

Give yourself as much **time** as possible. For suits, insist on two fittings. Most good tailors require around three days for a suit (some require ten days or more), although a few have enough staff to produce good work in a day or two. The more **detail** you can give the tailor the better. As well as deciding on the obvious features such as single- or double-breasted and number of buttons, think about the width of lapels, style of trousers, whether you want the jacket with vents or not, and so forth. Specifying factors like this will make all the difference as to whether you're happy with your suit, so it's worth discussing them with the tailor; a good tailor should be able to give good advice. Finally, don't be afraid to be an awkward customer until you're completely happy with the finished product – after all, the whole point of getting clothes tailor-made is to get exactly what you want.

Siam Centre Thanon Rama I ⓦsiamcenter.co.th; map p.117. Particularly good for local labels – look out for Greyhound, Senada and Fly Now, which mounts dramatic displays of women's party and formal gear – many of which have made the step up from the booths of Siam Square across the road, as well as international names like Superdry and Cath Kidston. Daily 10am–10pm.

Siam Square map p.117. It's worth poking around the alleys here and the "mini-malls" inside the blocks. All manner of inexpensive boutiques, some little more than booths, sell colourful street-gear to the capital's fashionable students and teenagers.

Viera by Ragazze Floor 2, Central World and in the attached Isetan and Zen department stores ⓦviera byragazze.com; map p.117. Stylish, Italian-influenced leather goods. Daily 10am–9/9.30pm.

BOOKS

English-language bookshops in Bangkok are always well stocked with everything to do with Thailand, and most carry fiction classics and popular paperbacks as well. The capital's secondhand bookshops are not cheap, but you can usually part-exchange your unwanted titles.

Asia Books Flagship store in Central World on Thanon Rama I, plus dozens of other branches around town ⓦasiabooks.com; map p.117. English-language bookshop (and publishing house) that's especially recommended for its books on Asia – everything from guidebooks to cookery books, novels to art. Also stocks bestselling novels and coffee-table books. Daily 10am–9.30pm.

B2S Floor 7, Central Chidlom, Thanon Ploenchit ⓦb2s. co.th; map p.117. This shop sells a decent selection of English-language books, but is most notable for its huge selection of magazines, newspapers and stationery. There are dozens of branches around town. Daily 10am–10pm.

Books Kinokuniya Floor 3, EmQuartier Shopping Centre, Thanon Sukhumvit; map p.122; Floor 6, Isetan, in Central World, Thanon Rama I; Floor 3, Siam Paragon, Thanon Rama I; map p.117; ⓦthailand.kinokuniya.com. Huge, efficient, Japanese-owned, English-language bookshop with a wide selection of books ranging from bestsellers to travel literature and from classics to sci-fi; not so hot on books about Asia, though. All daily 10/10.30am–10pm.

Dasa Book Cafe Between sois 26 and 28, Thanon Sukhumvit ⓦ dasabookcafe.com; map p.122. Bangkok's best secondhand bookshop, Dasa is appealingly calm and intelligently, and alphabetically, categorized, with sections on everything from Asia to biography and a large children's area. Browse its thrice-weekly updated spreadsheet of stock online, or enjoy coffee and cakes *in situ*. Daily 10am–8pm.

Open House Floor 6, Central Embassy, Thanon Ploenchit ⓦ centralembassy.com. As well as posh restaurants and a great coffee bar (see page 153), this novel take on a food court shelters lots of sofas and books to browse and to buy in a bright and welcoming space. Daily 10am–10pm.

JEWELLERY AND GEMS

Bangkok boasts the country's best gem and jewellery shops, and some of the finest lapidaries in the world, making this *the* place to buy cut and uncut stones such as rubies, blue sapphires and diamonds. However, countless gem-buying tourists get badly ripped off, so remember to be extremely wary.

Asian Institute of Gemological Sciences Jewelry Trade Center, 919 Thanon Silom ⓣ 02 267 4325 (laboratory) or ⓣ 02 267 4315 (school), ⓦ aigsthailand. com; map p.124. Independent professional advice and precious stones certification from its laboratory. Also runs reputable courses, such as a five-day introduction to gems and gemology (US$700). Mon–Fri 9am–6pm.

Jewelry Trade Center West end of Thanon Silom ⓦ jewelrytradecenter.com; map p.124. Dozens of members of the Thai Gem and Jewelry Traders Association

have outlets in this shopping mall (and on the surrounding streets). Mon–Sat roughly 11am–8pm.

Lambert Floor 4, Shanghai Building, Soi 17, 807–9 Thanon Silom ⓣ 02 236 4343, ⓦ lambertgems.com; map p.124. Thoroughly reputable, forty-year-old, American-owned outlet, offering a full service: loose stones and pearls, including collectors' stones, ready-made pieces, cutting, design, redesign and repairs. Mon–Fri 9am–5pm, Sat 9am–4pm.

ANTIQUES

Bangkok is the entrepôt for the finest Thai, Burmese and Cambodian antiques, but the market has long been sewn up, so don't expect to happen upon any undiscovered treasure. Even experts admit that they sometimes find it hard to tell real antiques from fakes, so the best policy is just to buy on the grounds of attractiveness. The River City shopping complex (ⓦ rivercitybangkok.com) off Thanon Charoen Krung, which is near Si Phraya express-boat pier, devotes its third, fourth and some of its second floors to a bewildering array of pricey treasures, ranging from Buddha images to tribal masks, as well as holding a bi-monthly auction (viewing during the preceding week; ⓦ rcbauctions. com). The other main area for antiques is the nearby section of Charoen Krung that runs down to the bottom of Thanon Silom, and the stretch of Silom running east from here up to and including the multistorey Jewelry Trade Center. Here you'll find a good selection of largely reputable individual businesses specializing in woodcarvings, ceramics, bronze statues and stone sculptures culled from all parts of Thailand and neighbouring countries as well. Remember that most antiques require an export permit (see page 64).

GEM SCAMS

Gem scams are so common in Bangkok that TAT has published a brochure about it and there are lots of web pages on the subject, including ⓦ en.wikipedia.org/wiki/Gem_scam and the very informative ⓦ 2bangkok.com/2bangkok-scams-sapphire.html, which describes typical scams in detail. Never buy anything through a tout or from any shop recommended by a "government official"/"student"/"businessperson"/tuk-tuk driver who just happens to engage you in conversation on the street, and note that there are no government jewellery shops, despite any information you may be given to the contrary, and no special government promotions or sales on gems.

The basic **scam** is to charge a lot more than what the gem is worth based on its carat weight – at the very least, get it **tested** on the spot, ask for a written guarantee and receipt. Don't even consider **buying gems in bulk** to sell at a supposedly vast profit elsewhere: many a gullible traveller has invested thousands of dollars on a handful of worthless multicoloured stones, believing the vendor's reassurance that the goods will fetch at least a hundred percent more when resold at home.

If you're determined to buy precious stones, check that the shop is a member of the **Thai Gem and Jewelry Traders Association** by visiting their website, which has a directory of members (ⓦ thaigemjewelry.or.th). To be doubly sure, you may want to seek out shops that also belong to the TGJTA's **Jewel Fest Club** (look for the window stickers; ⓦ jewelfestclub. com), which guarantees quality.

1

DIRECTORY

Banks and exchange The Suvarnabhumi Airport exchange desks are open 24hr, while many other exchange booths stay open till 8pm or later, especially along Khao San, Sukhumvit and Silom roads and in the major shopping malls. You can also withdraw cash from hundreds of ATMs around the city and at the airports.

Couriers DHL Worldwide (📞02 345 5000, 🌐dhl.co.th) has several Bangkok depots.

Embassies and consulates Australia, 181 Thanon Witthayu 📞02 344 6300, 🌐thailand.embassy.gov.au; Cambodia, 518/4 Thanon Pracha Uthit (Soi Ramkamhaeng 39) 📞02 957 5851–2 or 063 320 6370; Canada, 15th floor, Abdulrahim Place, 990 Thanon Rama IV 📞02 646 4300, 🌐thailand.gc.ca; Ireland, Floor 12, 208 Thanon Witthayu 📞02 016 1360; Laos, 502/1–3 Soi Sahakarnpramoon, Thanon Pracha Uthit 📞02 539 6667–8 ext 106; Malaysia, 35 Thanon Sathorn Tai 📞02 629 6800; Myanmar (Burma), 132 Thanon Sathorn Nua 📞02 234 4789; New Zealand, 14th Floor, M Thai Tower, All Seasons Place, 87 Thanon Witthayu 📞02 254 2530, 🌐nzembassy.com/thailand; South Africa, Floor 12A, M Thai Tower, All Seasons Place, 87 Thanon Witthayu 📞02 092 2900, 🌐www.dirco.gov.za/bangkok; UK, 14 Thanon Witthayu 📞02 305 8333; US, 120 Thanon Witthayu 📞02 205 4000; Vietnam, 83/1 Thanon Witthayu 📞02 650 8979. For further details about Bangkok's diplomatic corps, go to 🌐mfa.go.th/main/en/information on the Thai Ministry of Foreign Affairs' website.

Emergencies For English-speaking help in any emergency, call the tourist police on their free 24hr phoneline 📞1155. The tourist police are based on the grounds of Suvarnabhumi Airport (🌐touristpolice.go.th), or drop in at the more convenient Chana Songkhram Police Station at the west end of Thanon Khao San in Banglamphu (📞02 282 2323).

Hospitals, clinics and dentists Most expats rate the private Bumrungrad International Hospital, 33 Sukhumvit Soi 3 (📞02 066 8888, emergency 📞02 011 5222, 🌐bumrungrad.com), as the best and most comfortable in the city, followed by the BNH (Bangkok Nursing Home) Hospital, 9 Thanon Convent (📞02 022 0700, emergency 📞02 632 1000, 🌐bnhhospital.com); and the Bangkok Hospital Medical Centre, 2 Soi Soonvijai 7, Thanon Phetchaburi Mai (📞02 310 3000 or 📞1719, 🌐bangkokhospital.com). You can get travel vaccinations and malaria advice, as well as rabies advice and treatment, at the Thai Red Cross Society's Queen Saovabha Memorial Institute (QSMI) and Snake Farm on the corner of Thanon Rama IV and Thanon Henri Dunant (Mon–Fri 8.30am–4.30pm, Sat 8.30am–noon; 📞02 252 0161–4 ext 125 or 132, 🌐saovabha.com). Among general clinics, Global Doctor, Ground Floor, *Holiday Inn Hotel*, 981 Thanon Silom (corner of Thanon Surasak; 📞02 236 8444, 🌐globaldoctorclinic.com), is recommended. For dental problems, try the Bumrungrad Hospital's dental department on 📞02 011 4100; the Dental Hospital, 88/88 Sukhumvit Soi 49 (📞02 260 5000–15, 🌐dentalhospitalbangkok.com); or Siam Family Dental Clinic, Soi 3, Siam Square (📞081 987 7700, 🌐siamfamilydental.com).

Immigration office North of the centre off Thanon Wiphawadi Rangsit at Floor 2, B Building, Government Complex, Soi 7, Thanon Chaengwattana (Mon–Fri 8.30am–noon & 1–4.30pm; 📞02 141 9889, 🌐bangkok.immigration.go.th, which includes a map). When trying to extend your visa (see page 65), be very wary of any Khao San tour agents who offer to organize a visa extension for you: some are reportedly faking the relevant stamps and this has caused problems at immigration.

Internet access As well as 4G (see page 72), there's free wi-fi in nearly all hotels and guesthouses and most restaurants, bars and shopping centres in Bangkok. Internet cafés are now generally only found in the suburbs, full of schoolkids playing games, but most hotels and guesthouses will have computers and printers for printing out boarding passes and the like.

Laundry Nearly all guesthouses and hotels offer same-day laundry services (about B40–50/kg at a guesthouse, much more at a hotel), or there are several self-service laundries on and around Thanon Khao San.

Left luggage Luggage can be left at Suvarnabhumi Airport (B100/day); Don Muang Airport (B75/day); Hualamphong train station (B20–80/day); the bus terminals and most hotels and guesthouses.

Post offices If you're staying in Banglamphu, it's probably most convenient to use the local postal, packing and poste restante services at Banglamphubon PO, Soi Sibsam Hang, Bangkok 10203 (daily 8am–5pm). Downtown, Nana PO, between sois 4 and 6, Thanon Sukhumvit, Bangkok 10112 (Mon–Fri 8am–6pm, Sat & Sun 9am–5pm), is handy for the BTS.

Telephones It's best to buy a Thai SIM card for both international and domestic calls (see page 72). Otherwise, you can easily access Skype or the like with your own device through Bangkok's plentiful wi-fi networks.

Travel agents If you are buying onward international air tickets, be warned that there are many dodgy, transient travel agents in Bangkok, particularly on and around Thanon Khao San, which is known for its shady operators who display fake TAT licences, issue false tickets and flee with travellers' money overnight. The best advice is to use one of the tried and tested agents listed here. Never hand over any money until you've been given the ticket and checked it carefully. Asian Trails, 9th Floor, SG Tower, 161/1 Soi Mahadlek Luang 3, Thanon Rajdamri (📞02 626 2000, 🌐asiantrails.travel), does interesting Thailand tours and day-trips and runs airport transfers; *New Road Guest House* (see page 149) is a reliable agent for train and bus tickets, as well as their own unusual tours; Olavi Travel sells air, train and bus tickets and is opposite the west end of Thanon Khao San at 53 Thanon Chakrabongse, Banglamphu (☎02 629 4710, ⓦolavi.com); and the Bangkok branches of the worldwide STA Travel (☎02 160 5200, ⓦstatravel.co.th) are reliable outlets for cheap international flights and local tours: Baan Chart Hotel, Thanon Chakrabongse, opposite Wat Chana Songkhram, Banglamphu, and Floor 3, Chamchuri Square Building, corner of Phrayathai and Rama IV roads, as well as at both Lub D hostels (see pages 146 and 148).

The central plains

AUTTAMANUSORN WOODEN BRIDGE, MON VILLAGE

The central plains

North and west of the capital, the unwieldy urban mass of Greater Bangkok peters out into the vast, well-watered central plains, a region that for centuries has grown the bulk of the nation's food and been a tantalizing temptation for neighbouring power-mongers. The most densely populated region of Thailand, with sizeable towns sprinkled among patchworks of paddy, orchards and sugar-cane fields, the plains are fundamental to Thailand's agricultural economy.

Its rivers are the key to this area's fecundity, especially the Nan and the Ping, whose waters irrigate the northern plains before merging to form the Chao Phraya, which meanders slowly south through Bangkok and out into the Gulf of Thailand. Further west, the Mae Klong River sustains the many market gardens and fills the canals that dominate the hinterlands of the estuary at Samut Songkhram, a centre for the few remaining floating markets in the country.

Sited at the confluence of the Kwai Yai and Kwai Noi rivers, the town of **Kanchanaburi** has long attracted visitors to the notorious **Bridge over the River Kwai** and is now well established as a tourist hub, with everything from floating raft-house accommodation to waterside boutique hotels. Few tourists venture much further upriver, except as passengers on the remaining stretch of the **Death Railway** – the most tangible wartime reminder of all – but the remote little hilltop town of **Sangkhlaburi** holds enough understated allure to make the extra kilometres worthwhile.

On the plains north of Bangkok, the historic heartland of the country, the major sites are the **ruined ancient cities**, most of which are conserved as historical parks, covering the spectrum of Thailand's art and architecture. Closest to Bangkok, **Ayutthaya** served as the country's capital for the four hundred years prior to the 1782 foundation of Bangkok, and its ruins evoke an era of courtly sophistication. A short hop to the north, the remnants of **Lopburi** hark back to an earlier time, when the predominantly Hindu Khmers held sway over this region.

A separate nucleus of sites in the northern neck of the plains centres on **Sukhothai**, birthplace of the Thai kingdom in the thirteenth century. The buildings and sculpture produced during the Sukhothai era are the acme of Thai art, and the restored ruins of the country's first official capital are the best place to appreciate them, though two satellite cities – **Si Satchanalai** and **Kamphaeng Phet** – make good alternatives if you don't like crowds, and the city of **Phitsanulok** also serves as a good base for exploring the area. West of Sukhothai, on the Burmese border, the town of **Mae Sot** makes a refreshing change from ancient history and is the departure point for the rivers and waterfalls of **Umphang**, a remote border region that's becoming increasingly popular for trekking and rafting.

Chiang Mai makes an obvious next stop after exploring the sights north of Bangkok, chiefly because the **Northern Rail Line** makes connections painless. Or you could branch east into Isaan, by train or bus. It's also possible to **fly** out of Sukhothai, Phitsanulok and Mae Sot.

Nakhon Pathom

Even if you're just passing through, you can't miss the star attraction of **NAKHON PATHOM**: the enormous stupa **Phra Pathom Chedi** dominates the skyline of this otherwise unexceptional provincial capital, 56km west of Bangkok. Probably Thailand's

DEATH RAILWAY, KANCHANABURI

Highlights

❶ Kanchanaburi and the River Kwai Stay in a raft house, take a scenic train ride along the Death Railway and visit some moving World War II memorials. See page 187

❷ Erawan Waterfall Seven breathtakingly beautiful crystal pools in a jungle setting. See page 198

❸ Sangkhlaburi Search for sunken temples at this peaceful lakeside town near the Burmese border. See page 207

❹ Ayutthaya Atmospheric ruined temples, three fine museums and laidback guesthouses in the broad, grassy spaces of the former capital. See page 213

❺ Wat Phra Phutthabat A vibrant introduction to Thai religion at the Temple of the Buddha's Footprint. See page 229

❻ Sergeant Major Thawee Folklore Museum, Phitsanulok Housed in a series of wooden pavilions, this is one of the country's best ethnology museums, offering a fascinating insight into rural life. See page 234

❼ Sukhothai The nation's first capital is packed with elegant thirteenth-century ruins and inviting guesthouses. See page 237

❽ Umphang Wildlife Sanctuary A remote border region with spectacular waterfalls, river-rafting and Karen villages. See page 264

HIGHLIGHTS ARE MARKED ON THE MAP ON PAGE 176

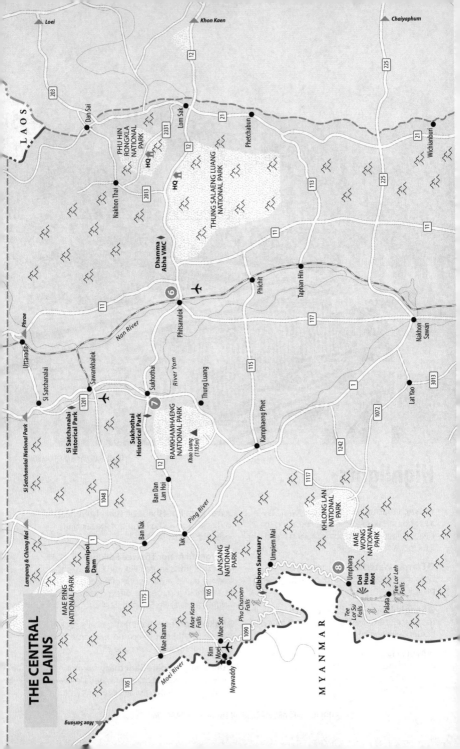

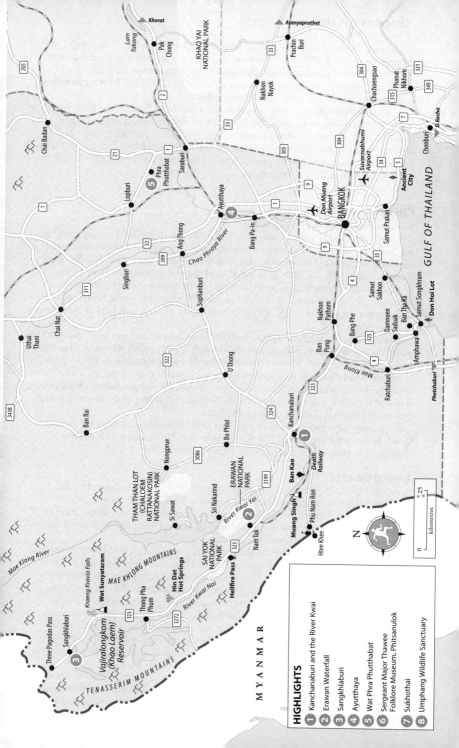

KHORAT
Khorat

Lam Takong

Pak Chong

KHAO YAI NATIONAL PARK

Aranyaprathet

Prachin Buri

205

33

Chai Badan

21

2

Nakhon Nayok

33

Chachoengsao

304

331

331

Phanat Nikhon

349

315

Pra Phutthabat

5

Saraburi

1

305

1

9

Suvarnabhumi Airport

34

7

Si Racha

Chonburi

Lopburi

1

Ayutthaya

4

305

Don Muang Airport

BANGKOK

3

Ancient City

32

Ang Thong

Bang Pa-In

1

9

Samut Prakan

GULF OF THAILAND

309

Chao Phraya River

311

Singburi

35

Chai Nat

Suphanburi

Samut Sakhon

Samut Songkhram

4

Don Hoi Lot

Uthai Thani

U Thong

Nakhon Pathom

Bang Phe

Damnoen Saduak

325

Ban Tha Ka

Amphawa

322

Ban Pong

4

Mae Klong

Ratchaburi

323

3438

Ban Rai

Bo Phloi

324

Kanchanaburi

Phetchaburi

Nongrue

3066

1

Death Railway

Si Sawat

Sri Nakarind

ERAWAN NATIONAL PARK

3199

Ban Kao

Muang Singh

Phu Nam Ron

THAM THAN LOT (CHALOEM RATTANAKOSIN) NATIONAL PARK

River Kwai Yai

2

Nam Tok

Htee Khee

MAE KHLONG MOUNTAINS

Kraeng Kravia Falls

Wat Sunyataram

Hin Dat Hot Springs

SAI YOK NATIONAL PARK

323

Hellfire Pass

River Kwai Noi

Mae Klong River

Thong Pha Phum

323

3272

Sangkhlaburi

Three Pagodas Pass

3

Vajiralongkorn (Khao Laem) Reservoir

TENASSERIM MOUNTAINS

MYANMAR

N

0   25
kilometres

HIGHLIGHTS

1 Kanchanaburi and the River Kwai
2 Erawan Waterfall
3 Sangkhlaburi
4 Ayutthaya
5 Wat Phra Phutthabat
6 Sergeant Major Thawee Folkiore Museum, Phitsanulok
7 Sukhothai
8 Umphang Wildlife Sanctuary

oldest town, Nakhon Pathom (derived from the Pali for "First City") is thought to be the point at which **Buddhism** first entered the region now known as Thailand, more than two thousand years ago. Then the capital of a sizeable Mon kingdom, it was important enough to rate a visit from two missionaries dispatched by King Ashoka of India, one of Buddhism's great early evangelists.

The **Phra Pathom Chedi** is easily visited as a day-trip from Bangkok or while travelling from the capital west to Kanchanaburi or south to Phetchaburi, Surat Thani and Malaysia, with plenty of overnight trains on the latter route passing through in the evening. As such, there's no earthly reason to overnight in Nakhon Pathom – which is reflected in the town's poor choice of hotels. Everything described below is within walking distance of the railway station.

Phra Pathom Chedi

400m south of the train station • Daily 5am–8pm • B60

Although the Buddha never actually came to Thailand, legend held that he rested in Nakhon Pathom after wandering the country, and the original **Phra Pathom Chedi** may have been erected to represent this. The first structure resembled Ashoka's great stupa at Sanchi in India, with its inverted bowl shape and spire that topped 39m. Local chronicles, however, tell how the chedi was built in the sixth century as an act of atonement by the foundling Phraya Pan who murdered the tyrant Mon king before realizing that he was his father. Statues of both father and son stand inside the viharns of the present chedi.

Whatever its true origins, the first chedi fell into disrepair and was later rebuilt with a prang during the Khmer period, between the eighth and twelfth centuries. Abandoned to the jungle once more, it was rediscovered by the future Rama IV in 1853 who, mindful that all Buddhist monuments are sacred however dilapidated, set about encasing the old prang in the enormous new 120m-high plunger-shaped chedi, making it one of the tallest stupas in the world. Its distinctive cladding of shimmering golden-brown tiles was completed several decades later.

The present-day chedi is much revered and holds its own week-long Phra Pathom Chedi **fair**, around the time of Loy Krathong in mid-November, which attracts musicians, fortune-tellers and of course plenty of food stalls.

Around the chedi

Approaching the chedi from the main (northern) staircase, you're greeted by the 8m-high Sukhothai-style Buddha image known as **Phra Ruang Rojanarit**, which contains some of Rama VI's ashes and stands in front of the north viharn. There's a viharn at each of the cardinal points and they all have an inner and an outer chamber containing tableaux of the life of the Buddha.

Proceeding clockwise around the chedi, as is the custom at all Buddhist monuments, you can weave between the outer promenade and the inner cloister via ornate doors that punctuate the dividing wall. The outer promenade is ringed by Buddha images employing a wide variety of mudras, or hand gestures, each of which has a specific meaning for Buddhists, and most of them are explained on plaques beside them. Throughout the rest of the country, most Buddha images portray one of just five or six common mudras, making this collection rather unique. The promenade is also dotted with **trees**, many of which have religious significance, such as the bodhi tree (*ficus religiosa*), under one of which the Buddha was meditating when he achieved enlightenment.

In the **east viharn**, look out for a mural showing a diagrammatic cross-section of the chedi with the encased original at its core. Further round, the **south viharn** staircase, about halfway up, is flanked by a three-dimensional replica of the original chedi topped by a Khmer prang (east side) and a model of the venerated chedi at Nakhon

Si Thammarat (west side). The **west viharn** houses two reclining Buddhas: a sturdy, 9m-long figure in the outer chamber and a more delicate portrayal in the inner one.

Phra Pathom Chedi National Museum

Just east from the bottom of the chedi's south staircase • Wed–Sun 9am–4pm • B100

Within the chedi compound are a couple of similarly named museums. The newer, more formal setup, the **Phra Pathom Chedi National Museum**, displays a good collection of Dvaravati-era (sixth to eleventh centuries) artefacts excavated nearby, including Wheels of Law (*dharmachakra*) – an emblem introduced by Theravada Buddhists before naturalistic images were permitted – and Buddha statuary with the U-shaped robe and thick facial features characteristic of Dvaravati sculpture. Together, the exhibits tell the story of how external influences, particularly those from India, shaped local beliefs.

2

Phra Pathom Chedi Museum

Halfway up the steps near the east viharn • Wed–Sun 9am–noon & 1–4pm • Free

The **Phra Pathom Chedi Museum** is a magpie's nest of a collection, offering a broader, more domestic introduction to Nakhon Pathom's history than the National Museum. More a curiosity shop than a museum, the small room and entranceway are filled with Buddhist amulets, seashells, gold and silver needles, Chinese ceramics, Thai musical instruments and ancient statues – enough for a short but satisfying browse.

Sanam Chandra Palace

A 10min walk west of the chedi along Thanon Rajdamnoen (or a B30 ride on a motorbike taxi) • Daily 9am–4pm (ticket office closes at 3.30pm) • B50 • ⓦ palaces.thai.net

Before ascending to the throne in 1910, Rama VI made several pilgrimages to the Phra Pathom Chedi, eventually choosing this 335-acre plot west of the pagoda as the location for a convenient new country retreat. The resulting complex of elegant wooden buildings, known as **Sanam Chandra Palace**, was designed to blend Western and Eastern styles, and a handful of its main buildings are now open to the public. Its principal structure, the **Jalimangalasana Residence**, evokes a miniature Bavarian castle, complete with turrets and red-tiled roof; the **Marirajrattabalang Residence** is a more oriental-style pavilion, built of teak and painted a deep rose colour inside and out; and the **Thub Kwan Residence** is an unadorned traditional Thai-style house of polished, unpainted golden teak. They each contain royal artefacts and memorabilia and, as such, visitors should take care to dress appropriately.

Sanamchandra Art Gallery

Just outside Sanam Chandra Palace's southern perimeter, behind the Thub Kwan Residence on Thanon Rajamanka Nai • Mon–Fri 9am–4pm • Free • ⓦ art-centre.su.ac.th • If coming from the chedi, expect to pay around B30 for a motorbike taxi

If you're interested in modern Thai art, it's well worth seeing what's on at the **Sanamchandra Art Gallery**. A purpose-built art centre set among outlying Sanam Chandra villas, it's one of the exhibition spaces for Bangkok's premier art school, Silpakorn University, whose satellite campus is just across the road. Their annual student show, held here every September and October, is usually very interesting.

ARRIVAL AND DEPARTURE	**NAKHON PATHOM**
By train To get to the chedi compound's northern gate from the train station, walk south for 200m down Thanon Rotfai, across the khlong and past the covered market. Destinations Bangkok Hualamphong (12 daily; 1hr 35min);	Bangkok Thonburi (5 daily; 1hr 10min); Chumphon (11 daily; 5hr 40min–8hr 30min); Hua Hin (13 daily; 2hr–3hr 40min); Kanchanaburi (2 daily; 1hr 30min); Nakhon Si Thammarat (2 daily; 13–15hr); Nam Tok (2 daily; 3hr

2

30min); Padang Besar (for trains to Malaysia; 1 daily; 16hr 15min); Phetchaburi (13 daily; 1hr 20min–2hr 30min); Surat Thani (10 daily; 8hr–11hr 30min); Trang (2 daily; 12hr 30min–13hr 30min).

By bus There are buses and a/c minibuses to Nakhon Pathom from Bangkok's Southern Bus Terminal, and buses from Damnoen Saduak and Kanchanaburi. On arrival, buses drop passengers either in front of the police station across Thanon Kwaa Phra from the chedi's southern entrance, or

beside the khlong, 100m from the northern gate towards the train station. Buses heading for Kanchanaburi and Damnoen Saduak collect passengers outside the police station across from the chedi's southern gate. Buses bound for Bangkok pick up from Thanon Phaya Pan on the north bank of the khlong near the train station.

Destinations Bangkok (every 30min; 40min–1hr 20min); Damnoen Saduak (roughly hourly; 1hr); Kanchanaburi (every 20min; 1hr 45min–2hr).

EATING

Hot-food stalls can be found just outside the chedi compound's southern wall, near the museum and are the obvious place to eat during the day (roughly 8am–5pm). There are lots of options, from noodle soup to grilled chicken and rice dishes (mostly B30–60).

Fairy Tale West side of Thanon Rotfai at no. 307, just south of the train station ☎ 081 913 8033. Almost hidden behind the food stalls that line the street, this cosy a/c café-bakery serves yummy crêpes, waffles and even French fries. It's an ideal spot to while away time waiting for a train. Mon–Sat 10.30am–7pm.

Lung Loy Pa Lan North side of Highway 4: to get there from the southwest corner of the chedi compound, head west on Thanon Rajvithee, then immediately south on winding Thanon Bhudtharucksa for just over 1km ☎ 034 255767. Nakhon Pathom's best local restaurant is very popular with pilgrims visiting the chedi. Top choices are whole snakehead fish, salted and grilled on bamboo sticks (B300), as well as very good grilled river prawns, but there are also more affordable regional specialities such as very spicy kaeng pa (jungle curry) with catfish (B80). Daily 10am–10pm.

Damnoen Saduak

To get an idea of what shopping in Bangkok used to be like before all the canals were tarmacked over, many people take an early-morning trip to the century-old **floating market** at **DAMNOEN SADUAK**. Sixty kilometres south of Nakhon Pathom and just over a hundred kilometres from Bangkok, it's just about accessible on a day-trip from the capital with a very early start. Vineyards and orchards here back onto a labyrinth of narrow canals, and every morning local market gardeners ply these waterways in paddleboats full of fresh fruit, vegetables and tourist-tempting soft drinks and souvenirs. Most dress in the blue denim jacket and high-topped straw hat traditionally favoured by Thai farmers, so it all looks very picturesque; however, the setup is clearly geared to tourists rather than locals, so the place lacks an authentic aura. For a more engaging experience, consider going instead to the floating markets at Amphawa, 10km south of Damnoen Saduak (see page 184), or at Tha Kha, 10km to the east of Damnoen Saduak (see page 187).

The market

Daily roughly 6–11am

The target for most tour groups is **Talat Khlong Ton Kem**, 2km west of Damnoen Saduak's tiny town centre at the intersection of Khlong Damnoen Saduak and Khlong Thong Lang. Many of the wooden houses here have been converted into warehouse-style souvenir shops and tourist restaurants, diverting trade away from the khlong vendors and into the hands of large commercial enterprises. Nonetheless, a semblance of traditional water trade continues, and the two bridges between Ton Kem and **Talat Khlong Hia Kui** (a little further south down Khlong Thong Lang) make decent vantage points.

Touts invariably congregate at the Ton Kem pier to hassle you into taking a **rowing boat trip** around the khlong network; this is worth considering and far preferable to being propelled between markets at top speed in one of the noisy longtail boats,

2

VISITING THE FLOATING MARKETS

For many visitors to Thailand, an essential item on their itinerary is a trip to a **floating market** (*talat nam*), to witness scenes of vendors selling fruit, flowers, vegetables and noodle dishes from **sampans** on the canals that were once the principal means of travelling around the country. Unfortunately, such bucolic scenes are from a bygone era, and while it's still possible to visit a floating market, many visitors regret the experience, feeling they've been led into a tourist trap, which is often exactly the case.

Most day tours from Bangkok head for **Damnoen Saduak**, where visitors are whisked around in noisy longtail boats, which pause for souvenir hawkers to make their pitch in between staged photos of smiling vendors dressed in traditional outfits with neatly arranged boatloads of produce. Such day-trips also include visits to dubious animal shows or handicraft workshops in an attempt to extract more tourist dollars.

In recent years, Thais have started heading for **Amphawa** (see page 184) at weekends, which has a more authentic atmosphere than Damnoen Saduak, though the least commercialized floating market is at **Tha Kha** (see page 187) on weekends. While most boat trips in these places focus on the markets, it's also possible to venture out onto the canals after dark to **watch the fireflies** twinkling romantically in their favourite lamphu trees like delicate strings of fairylights (best in the rainy season).

One problem of visits to this area is that most markets, with the exception of Amphawa, are at their best at the crack of dawn, but since they are around 100km from Bangkok, it takes at least a couple of hours for tour groups to get there. If you're keen to see them in the early hours, it's worth staying overnight in Damnoen Saduak, Amphawa or even Samut Songkhram (see page 182) and making arrangements for an early morning start; Tha Kha market is about 10km from each of these places.

While they cover less distance than the longtail boats, rowing boats make for a much more relaxing experience, and generally offer a one-hour-thirty-minute ride for around B300–400; they are available for hire from Ton Kem pier in Damnoen Saduak and at Tha Kha. Don't forget to take a hat or umbrella and plenty of sunscreen. There are no longer any rowing boats at Amphawa, where longtail boats charge B500/hr, or B600 for a roughly hour-long trip to see the fireflies.

which cost far more to charter. For a less hectic and more sensitive look at the markets, explore via the walkways beside the canals.

ARRIVAL AND DEPARTURE DAMNOEN SADUAK

BY BUS

From/to Bangkok Damnoen Saduak is 109km from Bangkok, so to reach the market in good time you have to catch one of the earliest buses or a/c minibuses from the capital's Southern Bus Terminal (roughly every 30min from 5.30am; 1hr 30min–2hr). Alternatively, you can join one of the day-trips from Bangkok, which generally give you two hours at the market, then stop at a handicraft village and/or animal show before dropping you back in the capital.

From Kanchanaburi Take a Ratchaburi-bound bus as far

as Bang Phe (every 20min from 5.10am; 1hr 30min), then change for the 30min journey to Damnoen Saduak.

From Phetchaburi and beyond To get to Damnoen Saduak from Phetchaburi or points further south, catch any Bangkok-bound bus and change at Samut Songkhram.

Getting into town Damnoen Saduak's bus terminal is just north of Thanarat Bridge and Khlong Damnoen Saduak, on the main Nakhon Pathom–Samut Songkhram road, Highway 325. Frequent yellow songthaews cover the 2km to Ton Kem.

ACCOMMODATION

Maikaew Damnoen Resort 333 Moo 9 ☎032 245120–1, ⓦmaikaew.com. Just a few steps east of the floating market, this relaxing resort has a variety of smart, comfortable rooms, bungalows and traditional-style teak houses, a canalside restaurant that uses vegetables from their hydroponic farm, two saltwater swimming pools,

a kids' pool and a Jacuzzi. They also have complimentary bicycles and offer a range of boat trips in the area (see website for details), so it makes a good springboard for exploration of the nearby canals. Breakfast included. Prices rise a little at weekends. B1650

Samut Songkhram

Rarely visited by foreign tourists and yet within easy reach of Bangkok, the tiny estuarine province of **Samut Songkhram** is nourished by the Mae Klong River as it meanders through on the last leg of its route to the Gulf. Fishing is an important industry round here, and big wooden boats are still built in riverside yards near the estuary; further inland, fruit is the main source of income, particularly pomelos, lychees, guavas and coconuts. But for visitors it is the network of three hundred **canals** woven around the river, and the traditional way of life the waterways still support, that makes a stay of a few days appealing. As well as some of the most interesting **floating markets** in Thailand – notably at **Amphawa** and **Tha Kha** – there are chances to witness traditional cottage industries such as palm-sugar production and *bencharong* ceramic-painting, plus more than a hundred historic temples to admire, a number of them dating back to the reign of Rama II, who was born in the province. The other famous sons of the region are Eng and Chang, the "original" Siamese twins, who grew up in the province (see page 183).

Samut Songkhram town

The provincial capital – officially called **SAMUT SONGKHRAM** but usually referred to by locals as **Mae Klong**, after the river that cuts through it – is a useful base for trips to the floating markets at Amphawa and Tha Kha. It's a pleasant enough market town, which, despite its proximity to Bangkok, remains relatively unaffected by Western influences. However, there's little reason to linger here during the day as all the local sights are out of town, mainly in **Amphawa** district a few kilometres upriver (see page 184).

To savour a real Thai seaside atmosphere, make the 10km trip to **Don Hoi Lot** at the mouth of the Mae Klong estuary (regular songthaews run there from the bus station), from where you can gaze out across the murky waters of the Gulf of Thailand from the shade of casuarina trees. Thais flock here in droves to gobble up *hoi lot*, or razor clams, which are harvested in their sackloads at low tide and typically served sun-dried and grilled on a stick or in a spicy stir-fry, hoi lot pat cha. You can order them – and lots of other cheap seafood – in any restaurant here, or buy them from street stalls, rent a mat and enjoy a picnic Thai-style.

THE SLOW TRAIN TO SAMUT SONGKHRAM

The most enjoyable way of travelling to Samut Songkhram is by **train** from Bangkok – a scenic, albeit convoluted journey that involves changing lines and catching a boat across the river in Samut Sakhon and could take up to three hours. It's a very unusual route, being single track and for much of the way squeezed in between homes, palms and mangroves, and, most memorably, between market stalls, so that at both the Samut Sakhon and Samut Songkhram termini the train really does chug to a standstill amid the trays of seafood.

Trains to Samut Sakhon (1hr) leave approximately hourly from Bangkok's **Wongwian Yai Station** in southern Thonburi (which is within walking distance of Wongwian Yai Skytrain station). The train pulls up right inside the wet market at **Samut Sakhon** (also known as **Mahachai** after the main local canal), a busy fishing port near the mouth of the Maenam Tha Chin. From the station, work your way through the market and take a ferry across the river to get the connecting train from **Ban Laem** on the opposite, west bank.

There are only four trains a day in each direction between Ban Laem and Samut Songkhram at the end of the line (called "Mae Klong" on railway timetables; 1hr), a journey through marshes, lagoons, prawn farms, salt flats and mangrove and palm growth. Once again, at Samut Songkhram, the station is literally enveloped by the town-centre market, with traders gathering up their goods and awnings from the trackside for the arrival and departure of the service.

2

ENG AND CHANG, THE SIAMESE TWINS

Eng (In) and Chang (Chan), the "original" **Siamese twins**, were born in Samut Songkhram in 1811, when Thailand was known as Siam. The boys' bodies were joined from breastbone to navel by a short fleshy ligament, but they shared no vital organs and eventually managed to stretch their connecting tissue so that they could stand almost side by side instead of permanently facing each other.

In 1824 the boys were spotted by entrepreneurial Scottish trader Robert Hunter, who returned five years later with an American sea merchant, Captain Abel Coffin, to convince the twins' mother to let them take her sons on a world tour. Hunter and Coffin anticipated a lucrative career as producer-managers of an exotic **freak show**, and were not disappointed. They launched the twins in Boston, advertising them as "the Monster" and charging the public 50 cents to watch the boys demonstrate how they walked and ran. Though shabbily treated and poorly paid, the twins soon developed a more theatrical show, enthralling their audiences with acrobatics and feats of strength, and earning the soubriquet "the eighth wonder of the world". At the age of 21, having split from their exploitative managers, the twins became self-employed, but continued to tour with other companies across the world. Wherever they went, they would always be given a thorough examination by local **medics**, partly to counter accusations of fakery, but also because this was the first time the world and its doctors had been introduced to conjoined twins. Such was the twins' international celebrity that the term "Siamese twins" has been used ever since. Chang and Eng also sought advice from these doctors on surgical separation – an issue they returned to repeatedly right until their deaths but never acted upon, despite plenty of gruesome suggestions.

By 1840 the twins had become quite wealthy and decided to settle down. They were granted American citizenship, assumed the family name Bunker, and became slave-owning **plantation farmers** in North Carolina. Three years later they married two local sisters, Addie and Sally Yates, and between them went on to father 21 children. The families lived in separate houses and the twins shuttled between the two, keeping to a strict timetable of three days in each household; for an intriguing imagined account of this bizarre state of affairs, read Darin Strauss's novel *Chang and Eng* (see page 782). Chang and Eng had quite different personalities, and relations between the two couples soured, leading to the division of their assets, with Chang's family getting most of the land, and Eng's most of the slaves. To support their dependants, the twins were obliged to take their show back on the road several times, on occasion working with the infamous showman P. T. Barnum. Their final tour was born out of financial desperation following the 1861–65 Civil War, which had wiped out most of the twins' riches and led to the liberation of all their slaves.

In 1874, Chang succumbed to bronchitis and died; Eng, who might have survived on his own if an operation had been performed immediately, died a few hours later, possibly of shock. They were 62. The twins are buried in White Plains in North Carolina, but there's a **statue** of them near their birthplace in Samut Songkhram, on an untended plot of land surrounded by local government buildings just south of Route 3092, aka Thanon Ekachai, about 4km northeast of town.

ARRIVAL AND INFORMATION

SAMUT SONGKHRAM TOWN

BY TRAIN
Samut Songkhram's train station is in the middle of town, on the eastern side of the Mae Klong River, with four trains a day making the 1hr trip from and to Ban Laem, where you can connect with trains from/to Bangkok (see page 182).

BY BUS FROM BANGKOK
The journey to Samut Songkhram by bus or a/c minibus from Bangkok's Southern Bus Terminal (every 20min in both directions; 1hr 30min) is fast, but the views are mostly dominated by urban sprawl. Samut Songkhram's bus station is south of the market, across from the Siam Commercial Bank off Thanon Ratchayadruksa.

CONNECTIONS TO AMPHAWA AND DAMNOEN SADUAK
By songthaew or a/c minibus Songthaews to Amphawa (approximately every 30min; 15min) and a/c minibuses to Amphawa and Damnoen Saduak, via Highway 325, leave from the bus station.

By taxi-boat Taxi-boats operate from the Mae Klong River pier, 50m west of the train station and market in the town centre. The journey upstream to Amphawa should take 20–30min.

ACCOMMODATION AND EATING

For accommodation, choose between staying in the town itself and a growing number of well-equipped resorts tucked away in the countryside. The **food stalls** near the pier, in the centre of town, make a pleasant spot for a cheap seafood lunch – for dessert, head to the **market**, near the train station, where you can buy fresh bananas, rambutans and watermelon slices. In the evening, food stalls along Thanon Si Jumpa just north of the railway station offer a wide variety of options.

Asita Eco Resort Beside a small canal about 4km southwest of the train station and just north of Highway 35 (Thanon Rama II) ☎034 767333, ⊛asitaresort.com. Choose between a Thai house and thatched villa at this small, luxurious resort, which is crafted from eco-friendly materials. There's a good-sized pool, a spa and bicycles for rent, plus a variety of tours on offer. Considerable discounts for weekday stays. Breakfast included. B5000

SERVICES

Banks and ATMs Currency exchange and ATMs are available at the branches of the main banks around the edge of Samut Songkhram market.

Baan Tai Had Resort On the west bank of the Mae Klong River, a couple of kilometres northwest of town ☎034 767220–4, ⊛baantaihad.com. Good-value resort, 15min by taxi-boat from Samut Songkhram's pier (alternatively, take the ferry across the river, then a 10min ride on a motorbike taxi). With its stylish, comfortable rooms and bungalows set around an attractive garden, swimming pool and restaurant, Baan Tai Had makes a good base, not least because of its local tour programmes. Also offers kayak rental. B1600

The Legend Maeklong 1285 Thanon Pathummalai ☎034 701121 ⊛thelegendmaeklong.com. Located 100m north of the ferry landing on the western edge of the river, this classy place in a pretty garden offers rooms in two Thai-style wooden houses and a shuttered colonial building that dates back to the early 1900s. There's also a waterside restaurant with excellent river views. Breakfast included. B1270

Amphawa

The district town of **AMPHAWA** is smaller and more atmospheric than Samut Songkhram, retaining original charm alongside modern development. Its old neighbourhoods hug the banks of the Mae Klong River and the Khlong Amphawa tributary, the wooden homes and shops facing the water and accessed either by boat or on foot along one of the waterfront walkways. The tradition of holding a **floating market** on the canal near Wat Amphawan has been revived for weekending Bangkokians and tourists, with traders setting up at around 9am (11am on Fri) and staying out until around 9pm every Friday, Saturday and Sunday. Amphawa's main street, Thanon Prachaset, runs west for about a kilometre from a T-junction with Highway 325 (the road from Damnoen Saduak to Samut Songkhram), before hitting the floating market at Khlong Amphawa (about 200m north of its confluence with the Mae Klong River), then Wat Amphawan and the Rama II Memorial Park.

Rama II Memorial Park

5min walk west of Amphawa market and khlong · **Park and Museum** daily 8.30am–5pm · B30

Rama II was born in Amphawa (his mother's home town) in 1767 and is honoured with a memorial park and temple erected on the site of his probable birthplace, beside the Mae Klong River on the western edge of Amphawa town.

Rama II, or Phra Buddhalertla Naphalai as he is known in Thai, is remembered as a cultured king who wrote poems and plays, and the **museum** at the heart of the **Rama II Memorial Park** displays lots of rather esoteric kingly memorabilia in traditional Thai-style houses, including a big collection of nineteenth-century musical instruments and a gallery of *khon* masks used in traditional theatre.

On the eastern edge of the park, **Wat Amphawan** is graced with a statue of the king and decorated with murals that depict scenes from his life, including a behind-the-altar panorama of nineteenth-century Bangkok, with Ratanakosin Island's Grand Palace, Wat Pho and Sanam Luang still recognizable to modern eyes.

2

Amphawa Chaipattananurak

On the west bank of Khlong Amphawa, a 5min walk north of Amphawa market • W amphawanurak.com • Mon–Thurs 8.30am–4pm;
Fri–Sun 8.30am–9pm • Free

The **Amphawa Chaipattananurak** centre was established to conserve the cultural heritage of the town, and is divided into five areas, each of which provides interesting information about the traditional lifestyle of the region. The Community Exhibition Room reflects the way of life of local communities, the Agricultural Demonstration Farm features many of the local fruit trees, and the Nakhawarang Cultural Ground is used for performances of traditional music, puppet shows and cooking demonstrations. There are also community shops selling local products and souvenirs, and an atmospheric coffee shop and tea house beside the canal with a retro interior.

Pinsuwan bencharong showroom and workshop

About 1km (15min walk) east of Amphawa Chaipattananurak, just west of H325 (look for the P Ben sign in front of a compound of traditional houses) • ☎ 034 751322 • Showroom daily 8am–noon & 1–5pm, workshop Mon–Sat 8am–noon & 1–5pm • Free

The Pinsuwan **bencharong workshop** specializes in reproductions of famous antique *bencharong* ceramics, the exquisite five-coloured pottery that used to be the tableware of choice for the Thai aristocracy and is now a prized collectors' item. Here you can watch the manufacturing process in action (though the workshop is closed on Sundays), and then buy items off the shelf or even order your own glittering, custom-made bowls, which can be delivered to your hotel or shipped back home.

Wat Chulamani

A few hundred metres east of Pinsuwan, across H325, or a 5min boat ride from Amphawa market along Khlong Amphawa

The canalside **Wat Chulamani** was until the late 1980s the domain of the locally famous abbot Luang Pho Nuang, a man believed by many to possess special powers, and followers still come to the temple to pay respects to his body, which is preserved in a glass-sided coffin in the main viharn. The breathtakingly detailed decor inside the viharn is testament to the devotion he inspired: the intricate black-and-gold lacquered artwork that covers every surface took years and cost millions of baht to complete. Across the temple compound, the bot's modern, pastel-toned murals tell the story of the Buddha's life, beginning inside the door on the right with a scene showing the young Buddha emerging from a tent (his birth) and being able to walk on lilypads straight away. The death of the Buddha and his entry into Nirvana are depicted on the wall behind the altar.

ARRIVAL AND DEPARTURE   AMPHAWA

From/to Bangkok A/c minibuses (at least hourly; 2hr; ☎ 085 385 9393) run to Amphawa, via Samut Songkhram, from Bangkok's Old Southern Bus Terminal (Sathaanii Sai Tai Kao, aka Pinklao), before continuing to Damnoen Saduak. On Friday, Saturday and Sunday, you can pick up some of these services at Bang Wa Skytrain station (Exit 4). There's no bus station in tiny Amphawa, but you'll find the a/c minibus offices on the high street just east of Khlong Amphawa in the town centre.

From/to Samut Songkhram Frequent songthaews from the market in Samut Songkhram (approximately every 30min; 15min) arrive at Amphawa's high street just east of Khlong Amphawa.

GETTING AROUND AND INFORMATION

By boat The most appealing way to explore the area is by boat (see page 181).
By bicycle Some resorts, such as *Baan Amphawa Resort & Spa* and *Amphawa Na Non* (see below), rent out bicycles.

Tourist office TAT have a new office on the east side of H325, just south of the T-junction with Thanon Prachaset (daily 8.30am–4.30pm; ☎ 034 752847–8)

ACCOMMODATION AND EATING

Amphawa Na Non 96 Thanon Prachaset ☎ 034 752111, W amphawananon.com. This stylish place sits on Amphawa's main street just a minute's walk east of the floating market. It caters mostly to Thais but staff speak good English and the big, bright, balconied rooms offer every comfort. Breakfast included. Higher rates on Fri & Sat nights. B2550

Baan Amphawa Resort & Spa 22 Thanon Bangkapom Kaewfah, off Highway 325 about 2km south of the T-junction with Thanon Prachaset ☎ 081 705 1317, ⓦ baanamphawa.com. A large, business-friendly hotel on the Mae Klong River, with attractive rooms in a series of traditional-style wooden buildings as well as more contemporary villas. There are two swimming pools, a spa, and a good riverfront restaurant. Breakfast included. B3800

Chaba Baan Cham Resort Just across Khlong Amphawa from Amphawa Chaipattananurak ☎ 081

984 1000, ⓦ chababaancham.com. Twelve appealing contemporary rooms with French windows and lots of varnished wood, equipped with a/c, hot showers, TVs and fridges. Breakfast included. Slightly higher rates on Fri & Sat nights. B1500

Jao Sam Ran On the bank of the Mae Klong River, about 100m east of Khlong Amphawa, near the police station (the English sign says "Chal Sam Rhand") ☎ 034 751811. On a shady terrace overlooking the broad river, this restaurant specializes in fresh seafood, including lots of mackerel dishes and very good grey mullet in a three-flavoured sauce (B160), and hosts live music in the evening. Mon–Thurs 3–11pm, Fri–Sun 3pm–midnight.

Tha Kha floating market

Ban Tha Kha, 10km northeast of Amphawa and 10km north of Samut Songkhram • Sat, Sun & public holidays roughly 7am–noon • By boat, it can be reached in about 30min from Amphawa; by car, it's signposted to the east of H325 between Damnoen Saduak and Amphawa

Unlike at the over-touristed market at nearby Damnoen Saduak, the **floating market** in the village of **Tha Kha** is still largely the province of local residents. It's possible to get here by boat from Amphawa, though most visitors come by road and begin their boat tour here. Market gardeners paddle up here in their small wooden sampans, or motor along in their noisy longtails, the boats piled high either with whatever's in season, be it pomelos or betel nuts, rambutans or okra, or with perennially popular snacks like hot noodle soup and freshly cooked satay. Their main customers are canalside residents and other traders, so the atmosphere is still pleasingly, but not artificially, traditional. As with the other markets in the area, boatmen also offer evening rides to watch the fireflies. The Tha Kha market attracts Thai tourist groups and occasional adventurous foreigners. It's best to pre-arrange a trip the day before through your accommodation in the area; expect to pay around B1000 for a half-day tour.

Kanchanaburi

Set at the confluence of two rivers, the Kwai Noi and the Kwai Yai, the provincial capital of **KANCHANABURI** makes the perfect getaway from Bangkok, 140km away. With its rich wartime history, plentiful supply of traveller-oriented accommodation and countless possibilities for easy forays into the surrounding countryside, there are plenty of reasons to linger here, and many visitors end up staying longer than planned. The big appeal is the river: that it's the famous River Kwai (pronounced "khwae" as in "quell" rather than "kwai" as in "quite") is a bonus, but the more immediate attractions are the guesthouses and restaurants that overlook the waterway, many of them offering fine views of the jagged limestone peaks beyond.

The heart of Kanchanaburi's ever-expanding travellers' scene dominates the southern end of **Thanon Maenam Kwai** (also spelt Kwae) and is within easy reach of the train station, but the real town centre is some distance away, running north from the bus station up the town's main drag, **Thanon Saeng Chuto**. Between this road and the river you'll find most of the town's war sights, with the infamous **Bridge over the River Kwai** marking the northern limit. Every day, tour groups and day-trippers descend on the Bridge, a symbol of Japanese atrocities in the region that's now insensitively commercialized – the town's main **war museums** and **cemeteries** are actually much more moving. Overlooking the huge **Don Rak Kanchanaburi war cemetery**, the **Thailand–Burma Railway Centre** provides shockingly instructive accounts of a period not publicly documented outside this region. The **JEATH War Museum** at the southeast end of town is also worth a visit, though you're strongly advised to avoid the crass World War II Museum by the Bridge (which also misleadingly labels itself as the "JEATH War Museum").

The **Chungkai war cemetery** and a handful of moderately interesting temples – including cave temples at **Wat Tham Khao Poon** and **Wat Ban Tham**, the hilltop twins of **Wat Tham Sua** and **Wat Tham Khao Noi** – provide the focus for pleasurable trips west of the town centre.

It's worth noting that Kanchanaburi gets packed during its annual *son et lumière* **River Kwai Bridge Festival**, held over ten nights from the end of November to commemorate the first Allied bombing of the Bridge on November 28, 1944, so book accommodation well ahead if you're planning a visit then.

Thailand–Burma Railway Centre

Opposite the train station, next to the Don Rak Kanchanaburi War Cemetery on Thanon Jaokannun • Daily 9am–5pm • B140 • ⓦ tbrconline.com

The modern **Thailand–Burma Railway Centre** is by far the best place to start any tour of Kanchanaburi's World War II memorials. It was founded to provide an informed context and research centre for the thousands who visit the POW graves every week. The result is a comprehensive and sophisticated history of the entire Thailand–Burma Railway line, with plenty of original artefacts, illustrations and scale models, and particularly strong sections on the planning and construction of the railway, and on the subsequent operation, destruction and decommissioning of the line. There is more of a focus on the line itself here than at the more emotive Hellfire Pass Memorial Museum (see page 205), but the human stories are well documented too, notably via some extraordinary original photographs and video footage shot by Japanese engineers, as well as through unique interviews with surviving Asian labourers on the railway.

Admission includes a free tea or coffee in the upstairs café, and the shop inside the entrance stocks some interesting books on the railway. If you want to learn more about the area's World War II history, guides can be hired for half- and full-day tours.

Kanchanaburi War Cemetery (Don Rak)

Opposite the train station on Thanon Saeng Chuto • Free

One Allied POW died for each railway sleeper laid on the Thailand–Burma Railway (see page 190), or so the story goes, and many of them are buried in Kanchanaburi's two war cemeteries, **Don Rak Kanchanaburi War Cemetery** and Chungkai Cemetery (see page 191). Of all the region's war sights, the cemeteries are the only places to have remained untouched by commercial enterprise. Don Rak is the bigger of the two, with 6982 POW graves laid out in straight lines amid immaculate lawns and flowering shrubs, maintained by the Commonwealth War Graves Commission. It was established after the war, on a plot adjacent to the town's Chinese cemetery, as the final resting place for the remains that had been hurriedly interred at dozens of makeshift POW-camp gravesites all the way up the line. Many of the identical stone memorial slabs in Don Rak state simply, "A man who died for his country"; others, inscribed with names, dates and regiments, indicate that the overwhelming majority of the dead were under 25 years old. A commemorative service is held here, and at Hellfire Pass (see page 205), every year on April 25, Anzac Day.

The Bridge over the River Kwai

Just west of the River Kwai Bridge Train Station • The public songthaews along Thanon Saeng Chuto pass close by or it's a 15–20min walk north of the main Thanon Maenam Kwai guesthouse area

For most people, the plain steel arches of the **Bridge over the River Kwai** come as a disappointment: as a war memorial it lacks both the emotive punch of the museums

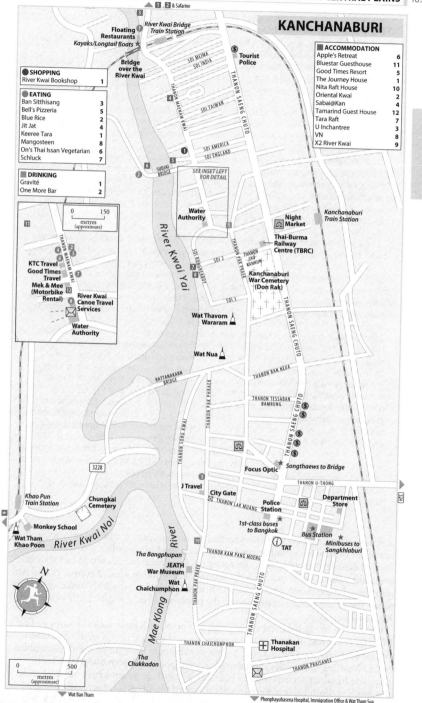

KANCHANABURI

1, **2** & Safarine

River Kwai Bridge
Train Station

Floating
Restaurants
Kayaks/Longtail Boats

Bridge
over the
River Kwai

Tourist
Police

SOI MEIMA
SOI INDIA

SOI TAIWAN

SOI AMERICA
SOI ENGLAND

SUDJAI
BRIDGE

SEE INSET LEFT
FOR DETAIL

Water
Authority

Night
Market

Thai-Burma
Railway
Centre (TBRC)

Kanchanaburi
War Cemetery
(Don Rak)

Kanchanaburi
Train Station

Wat Thavorn
Wararam

Wat Nua

RATTANAKARN
BRIDGE

River Kwai Yai

Khao Pun
Train Station

Chungkai
Cemetery

Monkey School

Wat Tham
Khao Poon

River Kwai Noi

River Mae Klong

3228

J Travel

City Gate

Police
Station

Focus Optic

Songthaews to Bridge

Department
Store

1st-class buses
to Bangkok

Bus Station

Minibuses to
Sangkhlaburi

TAT

Tha Bangphupan

JEATH
War Museum

Wat
Chaichumphon

Thanakan
Hospital

Tha
Chukkadon

Wat Ban Tham

Phonphayuhasena Hospital, Immigration Office & Wat Tham Sua

THANON MAEKHAM KWAI
THANON SAENG CHUTO
THANON PAK PRAEK
THANON JAO KANNUN
SOI RONGLABONG
SOI 2
SOI 1
THANON SAENG CHUTO
THANON BAN NEUA
THANON TESSABAN BAMRUNG
THANON SAENG CHUTO
THANON U-THONG
THANON LAK MUANG
THANON SONG KWAI
THANON PAK PRAEK
THANON KAM PANG MOENG
THANON PAK PRAEK
THANON CHAICHUMPHON
THANON SAENG CHUTO
THANON PRAISANEE
RATTANAKARN
N

SHOPPING
River Kwai Bookshop · · · · · · · · · · · · · · 1

EATING
Ban Sitthisang · 3
Bell's Pizzeria · 5
Blue Rice · 2
Jit Jat · 4
Keeree Tara · 1
Mangosteen · 8
On's Thai Issan Vegetarian · · · · · · · · · 6
Schluck · 7

DRINKING
Gravité · 1
One More Bar · 2

ACCOMMODATION
Apple's Retreat · 6
Bluestar Guesthouse · · · · · · · · · · · · · · 11
Good Times Resort · · · · · · · · · · · · · · · · · · 5
The Journey House · · · · · · · · · · · · · · · · · · 1
Nita Raft House · 10
Oriental Kwai · 2
Sabai@Kan · 4
Tamarind Guest House · · · · · · · · · · · · · 12
Tara Raft · 7
U Inchantree · 3
VN · 8
X2 River Kwai · 9

KTC Travel
Good Times
Travel
Mek & Mee
(Motorbike
Rental)
River Kwai
Canoe Travel
Services
Water
Authority

THANON MAEKHAM KWAI

0   150
metres
(approximate)

0   500
metres
(approximate)

2

2

THE DEATH RAILWAY

Shortly after entering World War II in December 1941, with the Straits of Malacca still mined and patrolled by the Allies, Japan began looking for an alternative supply route to connect its newly acquired territories that stretched from Singapore to the Myanmar-India border, with the eventual aim of being able to invade India from the northeast. In spite of the almost impenetrable terrain, the River Kwai basin was chosen as the route for a new **Thailand–Burma Railway**, the aim being to join the existing terminals of Nong Pladuk in Thailand (51km southeast of Kanchanaburi near Ban Pong, on Thailand's Southern Railway Line) and Thanbyuzayat in Myanmar – a total distance of 415km. British engineers had investigated the possibility of constructing such a railway before the war and had estimated it would take six years to build.

Over 60,000 British, Australian, Dutch and American POWs were shipped up from captured Southeast Asian territories to work on the link, their numbers augmented by as many as 250,000 conscripted Asian labourers. Work began at both ends in October 1942. Three million cubic metres of rock were shifted and 14km of bridges built with little else but picks and shovels, dynamite and pulleys. By the time the line was completed, just a year later, it had more than earned its nickname, the **Death Railway**: 12,400 POWs and an estimated 90,000 Asian labourers died while working on it.

The appalling conditions and Japanese brutality were the consequences of the **samurai code**: Japanese soldiers abhorred the disgrace of imprisonment – to them, ritual suicide was the only honourable option open to a prisoner – and therefore considered that Allied POWs had forfeited any rights as human beings. Food rations were meagre for men forced into backbreaking eighteen-hour shifts, often followed by night-long marches to the next camp. Many suffered from beriberi, many more died of dysentery-induced starvation, but the biggest killers were cholera and malaria, particularly during the monsoon. It is said that one man died for every sleeper laid on the track.

The two lines finally met at Konkoita, just south of present-day Sangkhlaburi, in October 1943. But as if to underscore its tragic futility, the Thailand–Myanmar link saw less than two years of active service: after the Japanese surrender on August 15, 1945, the railway came under the jurisdiction of the British who, thinking it would be used to supply Karen separatists in Myanmar, tore up 4km of track at Three Pagodas Pass, thereby cutting the Thailand–Myanmar link forever. When the Thais finally gained control of the rest of the railway, they destroyed the track all the way down to Nam Tok, apparently because it was uneconomic. Recently, however, an Australian–Thai group of volunteers and former POWs has salvaged sections of track near the fearsome stretch of line known as **Hellfire Pass**, creating a memorial walk at the pass and founding an excellent museum at the site (see page 205). There have been a number of **books** written about the Death Railway, including The Bridge over the River Kwai by Pierre Boulle and *The Railway Man* by Eric Lomax, both of which were made into successful films, and the 2014 Booker Prize-winning Narrow Road to the Deep North by Richard Flanagan. The Thailand–Burma Railway Centre stocks a selection of such books, as do the town's bookshops.

and the perceptible drama of spots further up the line, and as a bridge it looks nothing out of the ordinary – certainly not as awesomely hard to construct as it appears in David Lean's famous 1957 film, *Bridge on the River Kwai* (which was in fact shot in Sri Lanka). But it is the link with the multi-Oscar-winning film, of course, that draws tour buses by the dozen, and makes the Bridge approach seethe with trinket-sellers and touts. For all the commercialization of the place, however, you can't really come to the Kwai and not see it.

The fording of the Kwai Yai at the point just north of Kanchanaburi known as Tha Makkham was one of the first major obstacles in the construction of the Thailand–Burma Railway. Sections of a steel bridge were brought up from Java and reassembled by POWs using only pulleys and derricks. A temporary **wooden bridge** was built alongside it, taking its first train in February 1943; three months later the steel bridge was finished. Both bridges were severely damaged by Allied bombers (rather than commando-saboteurs as in the film) in 1944 and 1945, but the steel bridge was repaired after the war and is still in use today. The best way to see the bridge is by walking gingerly across it, or taking the **train** right over it: the Kanchanaburi–Nam Tok service crosses it three times a day in each direction, stopping briefly at the River Kwai Bridge station on the east bank of the river.

Thanon Pak Phraek

Between Rattanakarn Bridge and the City Gate

The historical significance of the stretch of **Thanon Pak Phraek** that runs north from Kanchanaburi's only remaining city gate has led the TAT to place information boards outside many of the old buildings, explaining their origin and use over the years. Most of these houses were built just outside the city walls in the late nineteenth or early twentieth century by Chinese and Vietnamese immigrants and reflect a variety of architectural styles. While some of the properties along the street are nothing more than run-down shophouses, others have been carefully restored and boast elaborate balconies with balustrades. Sadly, the tangle of electric cables along the street makes them less photogenic than they would otherwise be.

The more interesting buildings include the former Sumitrakarn Hotel, the first hotel in Kanchanaburi, which was built in 1937 and finally closed its doors to the public in 1979; it now functions as a shop selling household goods. Others worth a close look are Sitthisang house, built in 1920, renovated in 2009 and recently opened as a charming coffee shop (see page 195); and Boonyiam Jiaranai house, which has some elaborate stucco arches on the upstairs balcony.

JEATH War Museum

Beside the Mae Klong River on Thanon Pak Phraek, at the southern end of town • Daily 8am–5pm • B50

Founded by the abbot of adjacent Wat Chaichumphon in 1977 and housed partly in reconstructed Allied POW huts of attap (thatched palm), the unashamedly low-tech **JEATH War Museum** was the town's first public repository for the photographs and memories of the POWs who worked on the Death Railway. The name JEATH is an acronym of six of the countries involved in the railway: Japan, England, Australia, America, Thailand and Holland. The museum has since been surpassed by the slicker and more informative exhibitions at the Thailand–Burma Railway Centre and the Hellfire Pass Memorial Museum and is now of most interest for its small collection of wartime photographs and for its archive of newspaper articles about and letters from former POWs who have revisited the River Kwai.

Chungkai Cemetery

On the west bank of the Kwai Noi, 2km from Rattanakarn Bridge, along Route 3228 • Usually included in boat trips from the bridge (see page 194)

Scrupulously well-trimmed **Chungkai Cemetery** occupies a fairly tranquil roadside spot on the west bank of the Kwai Noi, at the site of a former POW camp. Some 1750 POWs are buried here; most of the gravestone inscriptions include a name and regimental insignia, and some with epitaphs such as "One corner of the world which is forever England". However, a number of the graves remain unnamed – at the upcountry camps, bodies were thrown onto mass funeral pyres, making identification impossible. The cemetery makes a pleasant cycle ride from Rattanakarn Bridge – much of the land in this area is sugar-cane country, for which Kanchanaburi has earned the title "sugar capital of Thailand".

Wat Tham Khao Poon

On the west bank of the Kwai Noi, 2km west along Route 3228 from Chungkai Cemetery and then Route 3305 (turn left at the railway line) • Daily dawn–dusk • B30 • Usually included in boat trips from the bridge (see page 194)

At the top of Route 3305's only hill, the cave temple **Wat Tham Khao Poon** stands on the former site of a POW camp. The attraction here is a nine-chambered cave connected by a labyrinth of dank stalactite-filled passages, where almost every ledge and knob of rock is filled with religious icons, the most important being the Reclining Buddha in the main chamber. Once out of the cave system, you can walk through a bamboo "museum" with some blurry pictures from World War II. If you arrived by road, follow the sealed road through the temple compound for 150m to reach a good vantage point over the Kwai Noi, just above the train tracks, presided over by an outsized, pot-bellied golden Buddha statue; if arriving by boat, you enter the wat compound via the cliff-side steps here.

Wat Ban Tham

12km south of town on the south bank of the Mae Klong River • Head south down Thanon Saeng Chuto for about 5km, turn right onto Thanon Mae Klong (Route 3429) to cross the Mae Klong River, then turn left along the south bank of the river; alternatively, it can be reached by boat in around 30min from the centre

Because of the limestone landscape, caves are found right around Kanchanaburi and many of them have been sanctified as shrines. **Wat Ban Tham** is one such place, and is intriguing enough to make the 12km trip from the town centre worthwhile. Travelling south down the Mae Klong to get to the temple is especially pleasant by longtail or kayak, but can also be done by road.

Wat Ban Tham was founded around six hundred years ago but its fame rests on the seventeenth-century love story that was supposedly played out in a cave on this site. A young woman called Nang Bua Klee was forced to choose between duty to her criminal father and love for the local hero by whom she had fallen pregnant; her father eventually persuaded Bua Klee to poison her sweetheart's food, but the soldier learned of the plot and killed both Bua Klee and their unborn son, whose souls are now said to be trapped in the cave at Wat Ban Tham. The cave is approached via an ostentatious Chinese-style dragon's mouth staircase, whose upper levels relate the legend in a gallery of brightly painted modern murals on the right-hand walls. Inside the cave, a woman-shaped stone has been painted in the image of the dead mother and is a popular object of worship for women trying to conceive: hopeful devotees bring pretty dresses and shoes for the image, which are hung in wardrobes to the side of the shrine, as well as toys for her son.

Wat Tham Sua and Wat Tham Khao Noi

17km south of the town centre • From Wat Ban Tham, follow the river road east for 5km and you'll see the hilltop complex on the south side of the road. If coming direct from town, the quickest route is to head south along Thanon Saeng Chuto, which becomes Highway 323, and cross the river via the signed Mae Klong Dam, then follow signs to the right; otherwise, take any local bus as far as Tha Muang, 12km south along Highway 323, then change to a motorbike taxi to the temples (about B50) • **Cable car** at Wat Tham Sua Mon–Fri 7.30am–4.30pm, Sat & Sun 7am–5.30pm • B20

If you're in the mood for more temples, the modern hilltop wats of Tham Sua and Tham Khao Noi both afford expansive views over the Mae Klong River valley and out to the mountains beyond. Designed by a Thai architect at the end of the twentieth century, **Wat Tham Sua** was conceived in typical grandiose style and boasts a very short funicular railway. It centres on a massive seated Buddha, sheltering under a strange half-chedi, his huge palm facing forward to show the Wheel of Law inscribed across it like one of Christ's stigmata. The neighbouring Chinese-designed **Wat Tham Khao Noi** was built at the same time and is a fabulously gaudy, seven-tiered Chinese pagoda, within which a laughing Buddha competes for attention with a host of gesturing and grimacing statues and painted characters. Neighbourly relations are now obviously a little frosty: Wat Tham Seua has built an eight-storey tower that partly obstructs the pagoda's view; and, though they share the same hilltop, a wall and barbed wire now separates the two temples, so that you're obliged to descend the slope and ascend again to get from one to the other.

ARRIVAL AND DEPARTURE   KANCHANABURI

BY TRAIN

The main Kanchanaburi train station (not to be confused with the River Kwai Bridge station) is just off Thanon Saeng Chuto, about 2km north of the town centre. It's within walking distance of some of the Thanon Maenam Kwai accommodation, or a tuk-tuk ride will cost around B50.

Services to Kanchanaburi Trains are the most scenic way to get to Kanchanaburi, but there are only two daily from Bangkok's Thonburi station via Nakhon Pathom (7.50am and 1.55pm), both of which are slow, all-third class (no a/c), ordinary trains and continue along the "Death Railway" to Nam Tok (see page 203). If coming from Phetchaburi, Hua Hin, Chumphon and points further south, take the train to Nong Pla Duk Junction, just east of Ban Pong (or Nakhon Pathom) and then change to a Kanchanaburi-bound train.

Moving on To get to northern Thailand, it's possible to take a minibus to Ayutthaya (see page 213), where you can pick up the Northern Rail Line. For southern Thailand, take a train to Nong Pla Duk Junction east of Ban Pong (or Nakhon Pathom) and change to a night train headed for Chumphon, Surat Thani or beyond.

Reservations and tickets Reservations for any rail journey in Thailand can be made at Kanchanaburi train station, though seats for the train ride to Bangkok are not reservable.

Destinations Bangkok Thonburi (2 daily; 2hr 35min); Nakhon Pathom (2 daily; 1hr 25min); Nam Tok (3 daily; 2hr); Nong Pla Duk Junction (2 daily; 1hr).

BY BUS

Kanchanaburi's bus station is at the southern edge of the town centre, a good 2km from most accommodation. Tuk-tuks wait here and will run you into the main Thanon Maenam Kwai accommodation area for around B80, or you

could catch a public songthaew (see page 194) up Thanon Saeng Chuto and walk.

Services to Kanchanaburi The buses and a/c minibuses from Bangkok's Southern Bus Terminal and Northern Mo Chit terminal are generally faster than the train. From Ayutthaya (connecting with trains from Chiang Mai), or points further north, you'll have to return to Bangkok, use a tourist a/c minibus service or change buses at Suphanburi, about 90km north of Kanchanaburi. Coming from Phetchaburi and Hua Hin, there's now a government-licensed a/c minibus service.

Moving on Government buses and a/c minibuses run from the bus station to Bangkok's Northern Mo Chit bus terminal, the Southern Bus Terminal, and to all destinations listed below. The first-class ticket office and departure point is beside the main road on the edge of the bus station, while the office for all other services is in the middle of the depot.

Destinations Bangkok (Northern Mo Chit terminal; roughly hourly; 3hr); Bangkok (Southern Bus Terminal; every 20min; 2hr 30min); Chiang Mai (3 daily; 11hr); Erawan National Park (every 50min; 1hr 30min); Hua Hin (every 60–90min; 3hr 30min); Kamphaeng Phet (3 daily; 6hr); Lampang (3 daily; 9hr); Nam Tok (every 30min; 1hr 30min); Nong Khai (1 daily; 11hr); Pattaya (3 daily; 6hr); Phetchaburi (every 60–90min; 2hr 30min); Phu Nam Ron (4 daily; 1hr 30min); Rayong (3 daily; 7hr 30min); Sai Yok (every 30min; 2hr 30min); Sangkhlaburi (every 30min; 3–5hr); Suphanburi (every 20min; 2hr 30min); Thong Pha Phum (every 30min; 3hr 30min); Three Pagodas Pass (2 daily; 7hr 30min).

BY TOURIST A/C MINIBUS

Guesthouses and travel agents can book you on a/c minibuses for Ayutthaya, Suvarnabhumi Airport and Thanon Khao San in Bangkok, which will usually pick you up at your guesthouse at a designated time.

CROSSING THE MYANMAR BORDER AT PHU NAM RON

If you have a visa for Myanmar, you can enter the country via the international border crossing at **Phu Nam Ron** (daily 6am–8pm), 70km west of Kanchanaburi and 200km from Bangkok. Four a/c minibuses run here daily from Kanchanaburi's bus station, taking about 1hr 30min. Until recently, the crossing was mostly used for renewing Thai visas; however, it is possible to get from Htee Khee on the Myanmar side of the border to Dawei on the coast. The Thai government are planning to pave the 160km road to the coast (where they're building a deep-water port for access to the Bay of Bengal) – contact Kanchanaburi's tourist office or J Travel, on the corner of Thanon Pak Phraek and Thanon Lak Muang (☎034 513455), for the latest information on transport.

2

GETTING AROUND

With songthaews plying the main route between the bus station and the Bridge, and boatmen waiting to ferry you along the waterways, it's easy to get to and from Kanchanaburi's main sights.

By tuk-tuk A tuk-tuk for a medium-length journey, for example from the railway station to the Bridge, will cost B80.

By songthaew Orange public songthaews run along Thanon Saeng Chuto, originating from outside the Focus Optic optician's, three blocks north of the bus station, and travelling north via the Kanchanaburi War Cemetery (Don Rak), Thai–Burma Railway Centre, train station and access road to the Bridge (#2; roughly every 20min until 7pm; 15min to the Bridge turn-off; B10).

By motorbike Many outlets, such as Mek and Mee (☎081 757 1194) on Thanon Maenam Kwai, rent out motorbikes for

around B200 per day.

By longtail boat Boats wait beside the Bridge for trips to riverside sights. A typical tour of the JEATH War Museum, Chungkai Cemetery and Wat Tham Khao Poon will cost B1000 and last 1hr 30min–2hr, though shorter, 30min jaunts on the water are also possible for B600.

By bicycle Guesthouses and tour agencies rent out bicycles for B50 a day – ideal for exploring the main town sights and the quiet rural backroads.

By kayak A green and sedate way of exploring the area is on a kayak tour. Try River Kwai Canoe Travel Services, 11 Thanon Maenam Kwai (☎086 168 5995, ⌨facebook.com/riverkwaicanoetravel), who charge from B400/person for 2hr, or Safarine (see page 198), who charge from B350 for 1hr 30min.

INFORMATION

Tourist information The TAT office (daily 8.30am–4.30pm; ☎034 511200 or 034 512500, ✉tatkan@tat.or.th) is just south of the bus station on Thanon Saeng Chuto and keeps up-to-date bus and train timetables. They can also

provide a decent map of the town and province, and let you look at a booklet on Pak Phraek Cultural Road in their office (no copies are available).

ACCOMMODATION

Many people choose to make the most of the inspiring scenery by staying on or near the river, in a **raft house**, a **guesthouse or a hotel**, and the options are constantly increasing as the town's building boom continues. The most popular area is the southern end of **Thanon Maenam Kwai**, which is *the* backpackers' hub, crammed with sometimes-noisy bars, restaurants and tour agents; most guesthouses are at the riverside end of the small sois running off this thoroughfare, though few rooms actually have river views. For those that have views (which naturally have higher rates), the idyll can be disturbed by roaring longtail engines and jet-skis during the day, so you might want to book in for just one night until you've experienced the decibel levels for yourself. Bring mosquito repellent too, as many huts float among lotus swamps. There is also raft-house accommodation further **upstream** at Nam Tok (see page 202) and near Tham Lawa (see page 204).

KANCHANABURI

Apple's Retreat On the west side of the river, 600m from Thanon Maenam Kwai (☎034 512017, ⌨applenoikanchanaburi.com; map p.189. *Apple's Retreat* sits in a green and tranquil spot, with a lovely Kwai-side restaurant, Blue Rice (see page 195), and terrace on the opposite side of the road by the river. The rather plain a/c rooms with platform beds and en-suite hot showers are in a two-storey building, enjoying views across farmland to the hills beyond, and there's a peaceful garden. Breakfast included. B990

Bluestar Guesthouse 241 Thanon Maenam Kwai (☎034 512161, ⌨bluestar-guesthouse.com; map

p.189. Popular, clued-up guesthouse in a quiet, leafy garden that runs down to the riverside, with a wide range of good-value accommodation including very cheap, basic fan bungalows with en-suite cold showers, smarter fan rooms with hot water and a choice of a/c bungalows and rooms, some with good views of the river. Fan B300, a/c B450

Good Times Resort 265/5–7 Thanon Maenam Kwai (☎090 143 4925, ⌨good-times-resort.com; map p.189. This is one of the most attractive resorts in town, with a prime location by the river just north of the Sudjai Bridge. Just about all of the 36 spacious rooms have a balcony, some with a view of the small swimming pool, but only one with river view. It's a good base for families as some rooms are connecting. Rates include a filling breakfast. B1250

The Journey House Just off Thanon Maenam Kwai, about 3km northwest of the Bridge (☎092 260 9903, ⌨thejourneyhousethailand.com; map p.189. Set in a large white villa with a pretty lily pond and swimming pool in the tranquil garden, this welcoming boutique hotel provides spacious rooms that are stylishly decorated with dark teak furniture. B2610

Nita Raft House Thanon Pak Phraek (☎034 514521, ✉nita_rafthouse@yahoo.com; map p.189. Away from the Thanon Maenam Kwai fray, a friendly, laidback, old-school guesthouse, whose simple floating rooms, some en-suite with river views, are among the cheapest in town; the very cheapest share bathrooms and face inland. Also does great food. B200

★**Sabai@Kan** 317/4 Thanon Maenam Kwai (☎092 997 4000, ⌨www.sabaiatkan.com; map p.189. This relaxing boutique hotel is located towards the northern end of Thanon Maenam Kwai, handy for the River Kwai Bridge railway station, and while there are no river views, all rooms have wall-to-wall windows that overlook a pleasant prospect of a swimming pool and shady garden. Rooms are spacious and well-equipped, with thick king-size mattresses on the beds. A decent buffet breakfast is included in the rate and staff are very efficient and helpful. B1400

Tamarind Guest House 29/1 Thanon Maenam Kwai ☎034 518790, ✉tamarind_guesthouse@yahoo. co.th; map p.189. Smaller rooms than in some of the other riverside guesthouses, but the place is very clean throughout and managed by considerate, friendly staff. Sleep in the two-storey house, or down by the waterfront in one of the rafthouse rooms (all en-suite with hot showers), which have river views and share a breezy, orchid-strewn terrace. No restaurant. Fan B350, a/c B550

★ **Tara Raft** 15/1 Soi Rongheaboy ☎092 829 9419, �W tararoom.com; map p.189. In a pretty location on a quiet stretch of the river just south of the Maenam Kwai hub, this place has probably the nicest raft-house rooms in town (B900): colourfully decorated, they come with king-size beds, a/c, hot showers, safes, fridges, big TVs and lovely outlooks from tiny terraces. The cheapest rooms are back on land with no view, but have the same facilities. They also run *Tara Bed and Breakfast* (fan from B250, a/c from B350) at 99–101 Thanon Maenam Kwai. B600

U Inchantree 443 Thanon Maenam Kwai ☎034 521584, Wukanchanaburi.com; map p.189. Spectacularly located on a bend in the Kwai Yai River, a 5min walk north of the Bridge (get off at the River Kwai Bridge station if arriving by train), this luxurious, 50-room retreat has charming staff and what must be Kanchanaburi's most style-conscious rooms. Standard rooms aren't huge, but the powerful rain showers and snuggly white duvets more than compensate. Outside, facilities include a waterfront pool, a peaceful glass-fronted library and an attractive restaurant by the river. All-day breakfast included; discounts available for early booking and for midweek stays. B3180

VN 44 Soi Rongheaboy ☎034 514082, W vnguesthouse. net; map p.189. A quiet, pretty place just south of the Maenam Kwai hub, with good food and decent raft-house rooms: they're large and come with terraces, en-suite hot showers and either fan or a/c. The cheapest rooms are in a concrete building but all have hot-water bathrooms. Fan B375, a/c B500

OUT OF TOWN

★ **Oriental Kwai** 194/5 Moo 1, Ladya (off Route 3199) ☎061 673 0670, W orientalkwai.com; map p.189. In a lovely, quiet spot beside the Kwai Yai, 15km north of town, this Dutch–Thai-run little hotel offers thoughtfully designed cottages in a lush tropical garden with a pool and gym, and gracious service. Cottages are a/c, have DVD players (with a big library of films to choose from) and are tastefully decorated in modern Asian accents; some are wheelchair accessible. The owners will give you plenty of ideas for exploring the area, including boat rides to the Bridge and route maps for tours by bicycle or motorbike (both available for rent). Free pick-ups from town on arrival. Breakfast included. B2800

X2 River Kwai Southwest of town off Route 3228, about 10km beyond Chungkai Cemetery ☎034 552124, W x2resorts.com/resorts/river-kwai; map p.189. The idea – a resort built mostly of shipping containers on the banks of the River Kwai Noi – may not sound promising, but the execution is stunningly and ingeniously modern, with bold architectural features and elements of industrial chic and Japanese style. Most of the rooms float on the placid waters, with riverside balconies and chill-out rooftops, while some give directly onto the infinity-edged pool. There are bicycles to explore the neighbourhood, kayaks and jet-skis for the river. B4560

EATING

Most of Kanchanaburi's guesthouses and raft houses have **restaurants**, and there's a cluster of floating restaurants beside the Bridge, serving good if rather pricey seafood to accompany the river views. A cheaper place to enjoy genuine local food is at the ever-reliable **night market**, which sets up alongside Thanon Saeng Chuto on the edge of the bus station. There are also a few food stalls at the **night bazaar**, which operates in front of the train station (Mon, Tues & Thurs–Sun 6–10pm), and at Thanon Lak Muang's "walking street" market on Saturday evenings from about 6pm.

Ban Sitthisang Thanon Pak Phraek; map p.189. This attractively renovated, hundred-year-old mansion, with ornate wooden lintels and sepia-toned décor, serves good espresso coffees, speciality teas, cakes and ice cream. Daily 8am–6pm.

Bell's Pizzeria 24/5 Thanon Maenam Kwai ☎081 010 6614; map p.189. Lively, Swiss-run place with pavement tables that's justly popular for its great pizzas (from B170). Also offers pastas, salads and a handful of Thai dishes. Daily 4–11pm or later.

★ **Blue Rice** Apple's Retreat Guesthouse, 153/4 Moo 4, Tamakam (cross the Sudjai Bridge then turn north) ☎034 512017, W applenoikanchanaburi.com; map p.189. In a lovely riverside guesthouse, reliably tasty food prepared to traditional Thai recipes. The short menu (B100–250) includes coconut- and cashew-laced *matsaman* curries – both meat and vegetarian varieties – as well as outstanding yellow curries. Every dish is prepared to order, so service can be slow. Also offers cookery classes (see page 196). Daily noon–2pm & 6–9.30pm.

Jit Jat 89 Thanon Maenam Kwai; map p.189. This

simple thatched hut turns out classic Thai dishes such as chicken with cashew nuts (B70) and northeastern salads at very reasonable prices, and cheap beers too. Daily 10am–11pm.

★ **Keeree Tara** 431/1 Thanon Maenam Kwai, about 100m north of the Bridge ☎ 034 513855, ⓦ keereetara.com; map p.189. Beyond the grandiose fountain at the entrance, scenic terraces slope down to a floating platform, all with fine views of the Bridge. Fortunately, the style is matched by the substance, on a diverse, creative menu: the laap muu thawt (deep-fried spicy pork salad; B150) and the kaeng khua muu yang khamin khao (roast pork and white turmeric curry) are both very good, and there's plenty of river fish and prawns. Daily 10.30am–9.45pm.

Mangosteen 13 Thanon Maenam Kwai ☎ 081 793 5814, ⓦ mangosteencafe.net; map p.189. This cheery and congenial shophouse café has books to browse or buy, as well as a few games and books for kids. Its imaginative, wide-ranging menu includes good Thai stir-fries, salads, set meals and Burmese chicken curry (B120), as well as desserts and all manner of Western offerings, from budget breakfasts to jacket potatoes. Wash it down with one of their shakes, smoothies or imported beers. Daily 10.30am–10pm.

On's Thai Issan Vegetarian 268/1 Thanon Maenam Kwai ☎ 087 364 2264, ⓦ onsthaiissan.com; map p.189. There's a lively buzz around this simple streetside place, which only serves vegetarian dishes such as seaweed soup and *phat thai* (B70 a dish). The buzz comes from On's students who learn how to make their favourite dishes during the day (see page 196). Daily 10am–9pm.

Schluck 20/1 Thanon Maenam Kwai ☎ 081 355 9477; map p.189. Cosy a/c restaurant serving salads, pizzas and steaks (from B160) as well as Thai food, but what really makes it stand out are the mouthwatering, home-made cakes such as vanilla choux buns and lemon meringue tart. Tues–Sun 4–10pm.

DRINKING

Nightlife in Kanchanaburi is relatively low-key, though there's a string of hostess bars at the southern end of Thanon Maenam Kwai, offering loud music and cheapish beer, with sports on TV as an added attraction. Further north up the strip are several simple bars without hostesses, and some classy venues that attract a mostly Thai crowd.

Gravité The Nine Guesthouse, Thanon Maenam Kwai; map p.189. Cool, friendly little café-bar serving drip coffee – their own blend is very good, but you can also try Ethiopian and Guatemalan beans – as well as homemade cakes and Thai craft beers. Daily 9am–9pm.

One More Bar 44/3 Thanon Maenam Kwai ☎ 084 801 3933; map p.189. A lively, sociable place to head to after dark, not least because it has a refreshing no-bar-girls policy. Staff are friendly, and there's a range of Thai and Western food complemented by a wide selection of beers, spirits and cocktails and live sports on TV. Daily 8am–12.30/1am.

SHOPPING

River Kwai Bookshop 293 Thanon Maenam ☎ 034 511676; map p.189. There are several secondhand bookshops on Thanon Maenam Kwai, but this is the best stocked, and staff are friendly and helpful. Mon, Tues & Thurs–Sun 12.30am–9pm.

DIRECTORY

Airline tickets Domestic and international tickets can be bought from Good Times Travel, 63/1 Thanon Maenam Kwai (☎ 034 915484, ⓦ good-times-travel.com).

Banks and ATMs There are several banks with money-changing facilities and ATMs on Thanon Saeng Chuto, immediately to the north of the Thanon U Thong junction, and around the Bridge.

Cookery classes Most famously at *Blue Rice* (see page 195): shop at the morning market, pick herbs and vegetables from their organic garden and learn how to cook the basic Thai dishes at professional cooking stations (daily 9.30am–2.30pm; B1990). Vegetarians should sign up for classes with Khun On at On's Thai Issan Vegetarian (see page 196); she'll teach you how to make three dishes in two hours for B600, any time between 10am and 6pm.

Hospitals The private Thanakan Hospital (☎ 034 622358) is at 20/20 Thanon Saeng Chuto, at the southern end of town, near the junction with Thanon Chukkadon; the government-run Phahon Phonphayulasena Hospital (☎ 034 511233 or ☎ 034 622999) is further south at 572/1 Thanon Saeng Chuto, near the junction with Thanon Mae Klong.

Immigration office At 100/22 Thanon Mae Klong ☎ 034 564279.

Post office The GPO is 1km south of the TAT office on Thanon Saeng Chuto.

Tourist police For all emergencies, call the tourist police on the free, 24hr phone line (☎ 1155), or contact them at their office on Thanon Saeng Chuto (☎ 034 512795) or one of their booths at the Bridge, the train station or the bus station.

Around Kanchanaburi

The parallel valleys of the Kwai Noi and the Kwai Yai, northwest of Kanchanaburi, are stacked full of great day-tripping opportunities, from **elephant camps**, through the exceptionally beautiful **Erawan Falls** and **Huay Mae Khamin Falls**, to the drama of a ride on the **Death Railway** and the pathos of the **Hellfire Pass Memorial Museum and Walk**. There are Stone Age artefacts at the **Ban Kao National Museum**, twelfth-century Khmer temple ruins at **Prasat Muang Singh**, and several good caves, including at **Tham Than Lot National Park** and **Sai Yok National Park**.

Many of these attractions are served by public **transport**, the train being an obvious option along the Kwai Noi valley as far as its **Nam Tok** terminus, with buses useful along both valleys. However, many people find it more convenient to combine several attractions and activities by signing up for one of the many mix-and-match **tours** offered by Kanchanaburi agents (see page 198), or rent a motorbike for a day. Distances are not large, and there's a handy connecting road between the two valleys just south of Nam Tok.

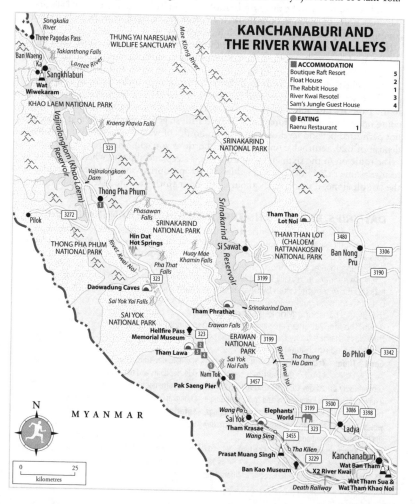

KANCHANABURI AND THE RIVER KWAI VALLEYS

■ ACCOMMODATION

Boutique Raft Resort	5
Float House	2
The Rabbit House	1
River Kwai Resotel	3
Sam's Jungle Guest House	4

● EATING

Raenu Restaurant	1

2

Elephants' World

99/4 Moo 4, Ban Nong Hoi, Tambon Wang Dong (32km northwest of Kanchanaburi) • ☏ 086 335 5332, ⓦ elephantsworld.org

Elephants' World is the most popular of several elephant camps in the vicinity of Kanchanaburi, probably because of their sensitive and non-exploitative way of dealing with these gentle giants. You can sign up on their website for programmes lasting from a day to four weeks, with prices starting from B2500, for which they will pick you up and drop you off and provide all meals and accommodation. Their motto is "We work for the elephants, and not the elephants for us", and activities include preparing food for them, feeding them and bathing them. Don't forget to take along a change of clothes, as caring for these huge beasts can be a messy business.

Erawan Falls

Daily 8am–4.30pm, though rangers start clearing the upper levels of the falls earlier • National park fee B300 • ☏ 034 574222, ⓦ nps. dnp.go.th

Considered by many to be the most beautiful falls in Thailand, the **Erawan Falls** are the star attraction of **Erawan National Park**. It's a great day out and, if you're on a tour, it combines well with a ride on the Death Railway.

The falls really are astonishingly lovely: the clear glacial-blue waters gush through the forest, dropping in a series of seven tiers along a route of around 2km. At each tier, cascades feed a pool shaded by bamboo, rattan and liana, and the whole course can be walked, along a riverside trail that gets increasingly tricky the further up you go. The distance between tiers, and the ascent to each, is clearly spelled out on signs in the park. It's just 500m from the visitor centre to level one, and then fairly easy going on and up to the dramatically stepped fifth stage (1800m). Food and drink are not permitted beyond level two, apart from bottles of water for which you must pay a deposit of B20, returnable on showing the bottle as you come down.

The route on to the sixth and seventh levels is steep and slippery when wet, and features some rickety bridges and ladders: wear appropriate shoes and avoid doing the last bit alone, if you can; it's about a one-hour-thirty-minute hike from bottom

---

DAY-TRIPS, RAFTING AND TREKKING AROUND KANCHANABURI

All the places listed below advertise **day-trips** around the Kanchanaburi and Sangkhlaburi areas, including infinite permutations of bamboo rafting, elephant-riding, Erawan Falls, Hellfire Pass and the Death Railway, sometimes with a short trek thrown in; most companies include the floating market at Damnoen Saduak in their programmes and offer multi-day trips. Prices listed are per person, usually for a minimum of four. They usually also do tailor-made guided tours to the war sights (often by boat or raft) and will provide a cheap transport service – car plus driver but no guide – for the more accessible attractions. If you're given the opportunity to visit Kanchanaburi's "**Monkey School**" as part of your tour, you're strongly advised to turn it down. The monkeys here are said to have been rescued from abusive owners, but they spend their days chained up by the neck or being coerced into performing circus tricks like shooting hoops and riding children's bicycles.

Good Times Travel 63/1 Thanon Maenam Kwai ☏ 034 915484, ⓦ good-times-travel.com. Competitively priced day-trips (from B1900/person for a group of four) and longer tours and treks, including a two-day trip to a Karen area near Hin Dat hot springs, which includes three–four hours' trekking each day (B4700/person, based on four sharing).

KTC (Kanchanaburi Travel Centre) 99–101 Thanon Maenam Kwai ☏ 086 396 7349 or ☏ 087 153 4147, ⓦ tourkanchanaburi.com. Offers the standard day-trips, as well as a twice-daily trip out to ride elephants and bathe them in the river (from B690) and an afternoon longtail trip to Wat Tham Khao Poon, Chungkai Cemetery and the Bridge (B400).

Safarine 117 Soi Tha Makham, Moo 2 (to the northwest of town) ☏ 086 049 1662, ⓦ safarine. com. French-run private-tour company, whose offerings include short and half-day canoeing trips in the Kanchanaburi area for B350–550.

to top. The best pools for swimming are level two (which gets the most crowded) and level seven, which is a hard slog but rarely busy, and also boasts stunning views over the jungle, while level four boasts a natural rock slide; at many of the pools small fish nibble at swimmers, giving you a free, natural fish spa. The seventh tier is topped by a triple cascade and is the one that gave the falls their name: Erawan is the three-headed elephant of Hindu mythology, vehicle of the god Indra.

Tham Phrathat

12km from Erawan Waterfall · Daily 8am–4.30pm (last entry 3pm)

With your own transport you might also want to visit the park's other significant feature, the 200m-long stalactite-filled cave, **Tham Phrathat**, 12km by road from the falls, then a 500m walk. It's of particular interest to geologists for its clearly visible disjointed strata, evidence of the Sri Sawat fault line that runs under the Kwai Yai.

ARRIVAL AND DEPARTURE

ERAWAN FALLS

Erawan Waterfall is 70km northwest of Kanchanaburi, via Route 3199 along the Kwai Yai valley, or 40km from Nam Tok. Most foreign tourists **charter return transport** to Erawan Falls from Kanchanaburi but you can also get a public **bus**. On day tours, the falls are commonly combined with a ride on the Death Railway.

By bus From Kanchanaburi, buses run to the national park visitor centre (every 50min; 1hr 30min); the last bus back to Kanchanaburi (very crowded on weekends and public holidays) departs at 4pm.

By chartered transport Guesthouses in Kanchanaburi can arrange private transport to the falls (around B1500/car, depending on fuel prices).

ACCOMMODATION AND EATING

You'll find several food stalls, restaurants, showers and shops near the trailhead that are open daily from around 8am–8pm.

National park accommodation ☏ 034 574222, ⓦ nps. dnp.go.th. The park has a series of basic bungalows, terraced "houses" and tents, which can be reserved online or at the visitor centre. You can also pitch your own tent in the park. Camping per person B̲3̲0̲, bungalows B̲8̲0̲0̲, tents B̲2̲2̲5̲

Huay Mae Khamin Falls

30km northwest of Tham Phrathat and 110km from Kanchanaburi · National park fee (Srinakarind National Park, aka Khuean Srinagarindra National Park) B300 · ☏ 081 010 6966, ⓦ nps.dnp.go.th

Though the Erawan Falls are certainly beautiful, they're often crowded, which can make it difficult to relax there. Arguably just as attractive but much less crowded (though it can get busy at weekends), the **Huay Mae Khamin Falls** also consist of seven levels, which are spread over 2km, with the most spectacular cataract at level four right beside the national park headquarters. The peculiar beauty of these falls is that mineral deposits create symmetrical ledges, over which the clear waters flow like a curtain. Informative signboards beside the wooden walkway and stairway (levels one to four) point out intriguing features of the landscape. Above level four, there's a trail through groves of bamboo and plenty of pools where you can plunge in and cool off in the therapeutic waters.

Getting to the falls once necessitated a long and expensive boat ride across the **Srinakarind Reservoir**, which is fed by the dammed waters of the Mae Klong and the Kha Khaeng and gives rise to the Kwai Yai, but there's now a sealed road (Route 6073) leading up the west side of the reservoir from Tham Phrathat in Erawan National Park. It's not on many tour itineraries yet, but that may change given the relatively easy access.

ARRIVAL AND ACCOMMODATION

HUAY MAE KHAMIN FALLS

There's no public transport to the falls, so you'll need a rented vehicle or to join a tour. Follow directions to Erawan Falls and on to Tham Phrathat, then keep going for another 30km along a rollercoaster of a road (R6073) to the national park headquarters. There are several food stalls, for which you'll need to buy coupons, beside the visitor centre. They serve simple rice and noodle dishes as well as drinks and are open daily from dawn to dusk.

National park accommodation ☎034 532027, ⓦ dnp.go.th. There are several concrete, stilted bungalows with balconies and hot showers, sleeping three people, and a large campsite that is very popular among Thais at weekends. Reserve online or at the visitor centre. You can also pitch your own tent in the park. Camping per person B30, bungalows B900, tents B225

Tham Than Lot (Chaloem Rattanakosin) National Park

97km north of Kanchanaburi • B200 • ☎034 547020, ⓦ nps.dnp.go.th

Tiny **Tham Than Lot National Park** (also known as **Chaloem Rattanakosin National Park**) covers just 59 square kilometres, but is home to leopards, oriental pied hornbills and barking tree frogs, and boasts two stalactite-strewn **caves** (bring a torch), a decent **waterfall** and an enjoyable hiking trail that links them.

From the visitor centre, follow the signed trail for about ten minutes to reach the first cave, **Tham Than Lot Noi**, which is 400m deep and illuminated if there are enough people (for example at weekends). A very picturesque 2.5km, two-hour **trail** runs on from the other side of Tham Than Lot Noi, along a stream and through a ravine to the first of three **waterfalls**, about an hour and a half's easy walk away and passing towering dipterocarps, fine jungle views and plenty of butterflies en route. The path gets more difficult after the first waterfall, and dangerously slippery in the wet season, running via another couple of waterfalls before coming to the larger of the park's two caves, the impressively deep sink-hole **Tham Than Lot Yai**, site of a small Buddhist shrine. Another ten minutes along the trail brings you to a small forest temple, from where you'll need to retrace your steps to return to the visitor centre.

ARRIVAL AND ACCOMMODATION	**THAM THAN LOT NATIONAL PARK**

If you'd rather not drive, your best bet is to organize a private tour from Kanchanaburi. If you're hungry, there's a very basic restaurant at the park's headquarters.

By car From the city, follow Route 3199 until you reach Ladya, and then join Route 3086. Turn left at Amphoe Nong

Pru and then follow the road for 18km until you reach the park.

National Park accommodation A handful of simple, government-owned bungalows sit within the park – bedding, hot showers and fan are provided. 4 people from B1200

Ban Kao National Museum

35km west of Kanchanaburi and 8km from Prasat Muang Singh • Wed–Sun 8.30am–4.30pm • B50 • ☎081 994 9873 • No public transport; follow Highway 323 north out of Kanchanaburi until you get to the junction with minor road 3229, then follow this road southwest for about 16km before joining minor road 3445 for the last 2km

The **Ban Kao National Museum** is devoted to relics from an advanced prehistoric civilization on the banks of the Kwai Noi (8000 to 1000 BC), which was first discovered by a Dutch POW working on the Death Railway who unearthed a burial site. Items on display include unique, curiously designed pots dated to around 1770 BC that were found buried at the head and feet of fifty skeletons; polished stone tools from around 8000 BC; and inscribed bronze pots and bangles transferred from a nearby bronze-culture site, which have been placed at around 1000 BC – somewhat later than the bronze artefacts from Ban Chiang in the northeast (see page 477). The hollowed-out tree trunks in the museum once functioned as coffins.

Prasat Muang Singh

8km northwest of Ban Kao National Museum, on minor road 3445 • Daily 8am–4.30pm • B100, plus B50/car, B20/motorbike or B10/bicycle • ☎034 591122 or ☎034 670264–5

Eight hundred years ago, the Khmer empire extended west as far as Muang Singh (City of Lions), an outpost strategically sited on the banks of the River Kwai Noi, 43km west

2

of present-day Kanchanaburi. Thought to have been built at the end of the twelfth century, the temple complex of **Prasat Muang Singh** follows Khmer religious and architectural precepts, but its origins are obscure – the City of Lions gets no mention in any of the recognized chronicles until the nineteenth century.

Prasat Muang Singh covers one-third of a square kilometre, bordered by moats and ramparts that had cosmological as well as defensive significance, and with an enclosed **shrine complex** at its heart. Restorations now give an idea of the crude grandeur of the original structure, which was constructed entirely from blocks of rough, russet laterite.

As with all Khmer prasats, the pivotal feature of Muang Singh is the main prang, surrounded by a series of walls and a covered gallery, with gateways marking the cardinal points. The prang faces east, towards Angkor, and is guarded by a fine sandstone statue of **Avalokitesvara**, one of the five great *bodhisattvas* of Mahayana Buddhism, would-be Buddhas who have postponed their entrance into Nirvana to help others attain enlightenment. He's depicted here in characteristic style, his eight arms and torso covered with tiny Buddha reliefs and his hair tied in a topknot. In Mahayanist mythology, Avalokitesvara represents mercy, while the other statue found in the prasat, the female figure of **Prajnaparamita**, symbolizes wisdom – when wisdom and mercy join forces, enlightenment ensues. Just visible on the inside of the north wall surrounding the prang is the only intact example of the stucco carving that once ornamented every facade. Other fragments and sculptures found at this and nearby sites are displayed in a small museum; especially tantalizing is the single segment of what must have been a gigantic face hewn from several massive blocks of stone.

ARRIVAL AND DEPARTURE — PRASAT MUANG SINGH

By car From Kanchanaburi either follow directions given for Ban Kao National Museum to start with (see page 200), or continue along Highway 323, turn left onto Route 3445 and head southwest to Muang Singh.

By train You can get to Muang Singh by taking the Death Railway train: get off at Tha Kilen (1hr 15min from Kanchanaburi; see page 203), walk straight out of the station for 500m, turn right at the crossroads and continue for another 1km to reach the ruins.

Nam Tok

There's not much more to the tiny town of **NAM TOK** than the terminus of the Death Railway line. Tour groups of Thais and foreigners flock to the pretty, roadside **Sai Yok Noi Falls**, 2km north, and if you're filling time between trains, you could walk along the continuation of the railway tracks to join them. It's also straightforward to get a bus on to Hellfire Pass.

ARRIVAL AND DEPARTURE — NAM TOK

By train The train station is at the top of the town, 900m north of Highway 323, and a further 2km from the Kwai Noi River. To reach the highway from the station, walk up the station approach road, cross the tracks, turn left at the spirit-house roundabout, then first right through the small town, passing a water tower and market on your left.

By bus All Kanchanaburi–Hellfire Pass–Thong Pha Phum/ Sangkhlaburi buses pass through Nam Tok, generally making a stop near the T-junction of the highway and the station road (every 30min; last bus back to Kanchanaburi at about 5.30pm); it's about 1hr 30min from Kanchanaburi to Nam Tok and 30min from Nam Tok to Hellfire Pass.

ACCOMMODATION

Boutique Raft Resort Just west of Pak Saeng pier (see page 204) on the river bank ☎ 081 353 1065, ⓦ boutiqueraft-riverkwai.com; map p.197. In a tranquil spot, accommodation either on land or in large, thatched bamboo and wood floating rafthouses with a/c, hot showers, fridges and their own waterside balconies, from which you could dive into the river. There's also a large raft enclosing a river-water swimming pool and plenty of simple bamboo rafts for pootling about on. Breakfast included. B2200

RIDING THE DEATH RAILWAY

The two-hour journey along the notorious Thailand–Burma **Death Railway** from Kanchanaburi to Nam Tok is one of Thailand's most scenic and most popular train rides. Though the views are lovely, it's the history that makes the ride so special, so it's worth visiting the Thailand–Burma Railway Centre in Kanchanaburi before making the trip, as this provides a context for the enormous loss of human life and the extraordinary feat of engineering behind the line's construction (see page 190). Alternatively, take a bus from Kanchanaburi to the **Hellfire Pass Memorial Museum and Walk** (see page 205), 18km from the line's current Nam Tok terminus, which provides an equally illuminating introduction to the railway's history, then take a bus back to Nam Tok and return to Kanchanaburi by train. A good tip, to get the best views, is to make sure you sit (or stand) on the right-hand side of the train on the journey back to Kanchanaburi, and on the left-hand side when travelling towards Nam Tok.

Leaving Kanchanaburi via the Bridge over the River Kwai, the train chugs through the fertile, red-soiled Kwai Noi valley, passing plantations of teak, tapioca, sugar cane, papaya and watermelon, and stopping frequently at country stations decked with frangipani and jasmine. The first stop of note is Tha Kilen (1hr 15min), where you can alight for Prasat Muang Singh (see page 200). About twenty minutes later the most hair-raising section of track begins: at **Wang Sing**, also known as Arrow Hill, the train squeezes through 30m-deep solid rock cuttings, dug at the cost of numerous POW lives; 6km further, it slows to a crawl at the approach to the **Wang Po viaduct**, where a 300m-long trestle bridge clings to the cliff face as it curves with the Kwai Noi – almost every man who worked on this part of the railway died. The station at the northern end of the trestle bridge is called **Tham Krasae**, after the cave that's hollowed out of the rock face beside the bridge; you can see the cave's resident Buddha image from the train. North of Tham Krasae, the train pulls in at **Wang Po Station** before continuing alongside a particularly lovely stretch of the Kwai Noi, its banks thick with jungle and not a raft house in sight, the whole vista framed by distant tree-clad peaks. Thirty minutes later, the train reaches **Nam Tok**, a small town that thrives chiefly on its position at the end of the line.

Three trains operate daily along the Death Railway in both directions, but they don't always run on time. Currently they're scheduled to leave Kanchanaburi at 6.07am (originating at Nong Pladuk Junction), 10.35am and 4.26pm (the latter two originating at Bangkok's Thonburi Station) and to return from Nam Tok at 5.20am, 12.55pm (both continuing to Thonburi Station) and 3.30pm (terminating at Nong Pla Duk Junction). If you're up at the Bridge, you can join the train five minutes later, though you're more likely to get a seat if you board at the main station. The Death Railway is classified as a historic line, so foreigners are charged an over-the-odds B100 to go to Nam Tok, even though the carriages are third class without a/c. If you're really worried about getting a seat, you can buy a "special ticket" at the station for B300 (one way), which includes a cushion, a snack, a drink and a reservation in a "historic" third-class carriage, ie one that's even older than the regular rolling stock.

EATING

There are several tourist-oriented **restaurants** at the station (open all day), and cheap **hot-food stalls** in the market (evening only), halfway along the station road, but your best bet for something to eat is Raenu Restaurant on Highway 323, about 2km north of town.

Raenu Restaurant Opposite Sai Yok Noi Falls on the main road ☎ 034 634360 or ☎ 081 880 1987; map p.197. Big, open-sided wooden restaurant overlooking the valley, that's hugely popular with Thai tourists, and for good reason: dished up in generous portions, the pla khao thawt man pla, a locally caught river fish deep-fried with fish sauce (B220), is delicious, and goes well with stir-fried local vegetables served with spicy shrimp-paste relish (B100). Daily 7/8am–8pm, until 9pm Sat & Sun.

Upriver on the Kwai Noi from Nam Tok

About 10km north of Nam Tok, a side road turns off Highway 323 at kilometre-stone 129 and winds down to the east bank of the river for about 2km, giving access to a beautiful stretch of the Kwai Noi and the **Resotel pier**. There's no development along the banks apart from a few raft houses and shore-bound little hotels. The west bank of the river here, where you'll find Tham Lawa, the Mon village and a couple of pleasant

2

> ## BOAT TRIPS FROM NAM TOK
>
> You can rent a longtail **boat** (plus driver) from the Nam Tok's **Pak Saeng pier** ("Tha Pak Saeng") for the ride upstream to **Tham Lawa** or **Sai Yok Yai Falls**. To reach the pier from the Highway 323 T-junction, cross the road, turn southeast towards Kanchanaburi, then take the first road on your right; it's 2km from here to the river. The return journey to the cave takes roughly two hours, including 30–45min there, and costs B1200 for the eight-seater boat; for an extra B3000–4000 you could continue to Sai Yok Yai Falls, a five- or six-hour return trip, though this trip is not possible when water levels are low (Feb–May). You can also rent a boat for an hour's sightseeing (around B1200) along this pretty stretch of river.

places to stay, can be reached either by boat from the Resotel pier or by car, crossing the bridge over the Kwai Noi by the Pak Saeng pier in Nam Tok and working your way up the minor roads.

Tham Lawa

60km northwest of Kanchanaburi and 15km northwest of Nam Tok, on the west bank of the Kwai Noi • Daily roughly 8.30am–4.30pm • Sai Yok National Park fee B300 • Can be reached via a longtail ride upriver from the Pak Saeng pier in Nam Tok (see page 204), by road on the west side of the river from Nam Tok, or by walking from nearby accommodation

The most famous attraction around here is **Tham Lawa**, the largest stalactite cave in the area and home to three species of bat. A steep set of stairs leads to the entrance, beyond which are five large chambers, connected by an illuminated concrete path. There are also light switches that should illuminate the more striking formations, but often don't work; it's best to take your own torch. The walk through the cave and back takes around thirty minutes, but the stalactites and stalagmites are not especially impressive and you'd need to be very keen on caves to find it worthwhile.

The Mon village

You can visit the **Mon village** just below Tham Lawa, where you're encouraged to browse the sarongs and other artefacts made and sold by the villagers, take an elephant ride and visit the local school. The Mon villagers fled here from Myanmar in the late 1950s (see page 210) but have still not been granted Thai ID papers, which means the children can't study at Thai secondary schools and adults have difficulty finding work. This village has close links with resorts operated by Serenata (including the *Resotel* and *Float House*), and many of its residents work at the hotels.

ARRIVAL AND DEPARTURE   UPRIVER ON THE KWAI NOI FROM NAM TOK

By bus Any Kanchanaburi–Hellfire Pass–Thong Pha Phum/ Sangkhlaburi bus will drop you at the turn-off to the Resotel pier. Heading back to Kanchanaburi, you should be able to flag down buses at the same spot.

ACCOMMODATION

Float House Just upstream from the Resotel (see below) and Tham Lawa (take a boat from the Resotel pier) ☎02 642 5497, ⓦ thefloathouseriverkwai.com; map p.197. This is the newest resort operated by Serenata, a company with something of a monopoly on luxury accommodation in the region. In a gorgeous setting, with lush jungle all round and the river flowing beneath, this floating resort features beautiful thatched but a/c rooms with every comfort, including private terraces looking out over the river. Breakfast included. B5230

River Kwai Resotel On the west bank of the river (take a boat from the Resotel pier) ☎02 642 5497, ⓦ riverkwairesotel.net; map p.197. Serenata's flagship resort is a classy, upmarket spot, comprising an open-air restaurant, some charming and spacious thatched riverside chalets with their own balconies and a turquoise swimming pool. Breakfast included. B2850

Sam's Jungle Guest House About 1km off the highway at kilometre-stone 129 ☎081 948 3448, ⓦ samsguesthouse. com; map p.197. Occupying a large swathe of steep and densely grown riverbank, this place offers a range of well-priced fan and a/c accommodation with hot showers and terraces, in a strange and rather unstylish assortment of buildings that nonetheless enjoy an exceptionally tranquil setting; there's kayak rental too. Staff keep the front gate closed while working down by the river, so call ahead if you can. Fan B400, a/c B500

Hellfire Pass

Although the rail line north of Nam Tok was ripped up soon after the end of World War II, it casts its dreadful shadow all the way up the Kwai Noi valley into Myanmar. The remnants of track are most visible at **Hellfire Pass**, and many of the villages in the **area** are former POW sites – locals frequently stumble across burial sites, now reclaimed by the encroaching jungle. To keep the Death Railway level through the uneven course of the Kwai valley, the POWs had to build a series of embankments and trestle bridges and, at dishearteningly frequent intervals, gouge deep cuttings through solid rock. The most concentrated digging was at **Konyu**, 18km beyond Nam Tok, where seven separate cuttings were made over a 3.5km stretch. The longest and most brutal of these was Hellfire Pass, which got its name from the hellish-looking lights and shadows of the fires the POWs used when working at night. The job took three months of round-the-clock labour with the most primitive tools.

2

Hellfire Pass Memorial Museum
Daily 9am–4pm • Donation requested • ☎ 034 919605, ⊕ dva.gov.au

The story of the POWs who died on the Hellfire Pass is documented at the beautifully designed **Hellfire Pass Memorial Museum**, the best and most informative of all the World War II museums in the Kanchanaburi region. Inside, wartime relics, POW memorabilia, photos and informative display boards tell the sobering history of the construction of this stretch of the Thailand–Burma Railway, along with slide shows and videos. Founded by an Australian–Thai volunteer group, the museum now serves as a sort of pilgrimage site for the families and friends of Australian POWs.

Hellfire Pass Memorial Walk
No set hours for the walk, but the audio tour must be returned to the museum by 4pm

The same Australian–Thai group responsible for the Hellfire Pass Memorial Museum has also cleared a one-hour circular **memorial walk**, which begins at the museum and descends to follow the old rail route through the 20m-deep, 70m-long cutting and back. Only adding to the poignancy, it's a beautiful trail through woods and bamboo stands, with bucolic views of the mountain ridges across the valley. It's also possible to extend the walk by continuing northwards along the line of the railway to the Hin Tok Road, just beyond Hin Tok Cutting, along a course relaid with some of the original narrow-gauge track (about 2hr 30min out and back; if you have a car with driver, you could arrange to be picked up at the Hin Tok Road). It's well worth getting the excellent, free **audio tour** available at the museum (leave your passport or driving licence as deposit), which gives a detailed commentary, including vivid first-person testimonies by Australian former POWs, all along both sections of walk. Bring water and sturdy shoes as the walk along the old railway line goes over large chippings.

ARRIVAL AND DEPARTURE   HELLFIRE PASS

Hellfire Pass is 18km north of Nam Tok, on a military base on the west side of Highway 323 just after kilometre-stone 139. Most Kanchanaburi tour-operators offer **day-trips** featuring Hellfire Pass. It's also easy to get here on your own by bus, or by a combination of train and bus, taking the Death Railway (see page 203) to Nam Tok, then a bus to Hellfire Pass.

By bus From Kanchanaburi or Nam Tok, take any bus bound for Thong Pha Phum or Sangkhlaburi and ask to be dropped off at Hellfire Pass; it's about a 2hr journey from Kanchanaburi or 30min from Nam Tok. The last return bus to Kanchanaburi passes Hellfire Pass at about 5pm; if you're continuing to Sangkhlaburi, the last onward bus comes past at about 2pm, the last a/c minibus at about 6.30–7pm.

Sai Yok National Park
B300 • ☎ 034 686024, ⊕ nps.dnp.go.th

Expanses of impenetrable mountain wilderness characterize the Kwai Noi valley to the north of Hellfire Pass, a landscape typified by the dense monsoon forests

2

of **Sai Yok National Park**, which stretches all the way to the Burmese border. The park makes a refreshing enough stopover between Nam Tok and Sangkhlaburi, particularly if you have your own transport. Its teak forests are best known for the much-photographed though unexceptional **Sai Yok Yai Falls** flowing into the Kwai Noi River, the eight stalactite-filled chambers of **Daowadung Caves**, and **Kang Kao Cave**, which is home to one of the smallest-known mammals in the world, the elusive Kitti's hog-nosed or bumblebee bat, which weighs as little as 1.75g when fully grown. Short trails to Sai Yok Yai Falls and Kang Kao Cave start from near the park's visitor centre, while Daowadung Cave is 6km away by road or longtail boat.

ARRIVAL AND DEPARTURE   SAI YOK NATIONAL PARK

The park is 19km from Hellfire Pass, 97km north of Kanchanaburi, signed off Highway 323 between kilometre-stones 155 and 156.

By bus Any of the Kanchanaburi–Thong Pha Phum/Sangkhlaburi buses will stop at the road entrance to Sai Yok, from where it's a 3km walk to the visitor centre, trailheads

and river (motorbike taxis sometimes hang around the road entrance). The last bus to Sangkhlaburi passes at around 2.30pm and the last bus to Kanchanaburi at about 4.30pm.

By boat The most scenic approach to Sai Yok is by longtail from Nam Tok, a 5–6hr return trip (see page 204), though it's not always possible in the dry season (Feb–May).

ACCOMMODATION AND EATING

There are plenty of **hot-food stalls**, restaurants and floating restaurants near the visitor centre.

National park accommodation ☎034 686024, ⓦdnp.go.th. You can stay in the national park's simple,

fan-cooled bungalows, sleeping between four and seven people, some with hot showers, but it's worth booking ahead online. B800

Pha Tad Falls and Hin Dat hot springs

Pha Tad Falls (Srinakarind National Park fee) B300 • Hin Dat hot springs B60

North of Sai Yok National Park, signs off Highway 323 direct you to the two long, gently sloping cascades of **Pha Tad Falls**, which are very attractive in the wet season (June–Nov), though there's almost no water in the late dry season (Feb–May). Nearer the main road is **Hin Dat** (Hindad) **hot springs**, where, after paying the entry fee, you can immerse yourself in pools of soothingly warm water. Close by is a much cooler stream – perfect for leaping into after a good soak in the springs – and you can make use of the nearby showers and food stalls.

ARRIVAL AND DEPARTURE   PHA TAD FALLS AND HIN DAT HOT SPRINGS

Both Pha Tad Falls and Hin Dat hot springs are east off Highway 323.

To/from Pha Tad Falls The falls are 10km east from kilometre-stone 178 and can only be reached with your own transport or on a tour.

To/from Hin Dat The hot springs are 1km east from

kilometre-stone 180; any Thong Pha Phum/Sangkhlaburi bus from Kanchanaburi will drop you at the Hin Dat access track, from where it's an easy walk across to the springs. Returning in the afternoon, flag down a bus from Thong Pha Phum or Sangkhlaburi for the trip back to Kanchanaburi (last bus around 4pm).

Thong Pha Phum and around

The first significant settlement northwest of Sai Yok is **Thong Pha Phum** (147km from Kanchanaburi), a mid-sized market town with bus connections to Sangkhlaburi and Kanchanaburi and plenty of small food shops. With your own transport, you could drive northwest of town to explore the southeastern fringes of nearby **Vajiralongkorn Reservoir** (formerly Khao Laem Reservoir, but renamed after the current king), set in a refreshing, almost Scandinavian, landscape of forested hills and clear, still water. This vast body of water stretches all the way from the dam, 12km northwest of Thong Pha Phum market, to Sangkhlaburi 73km to the north and, when created in the early 1980s, flooded every village in the vicinity.

ARRIVAL AND DEPARTURE   THONG PHA PHUM

By bus Take a bus or a/c minibus from Kanchanaburi (2hr 30min–3hr 30min) or from Sangkhlaburi (1hr–1hr 30min). Occasional yellow songthaews travel to the reservoir from Thong Pha Phum market.

ACCOMMODATION

The Rabbit House Down a lane that runs behind the hospital, opposite Wat Thong Pha Phum ☎ 034 910190, ⓦ therabbithouse1.tht.in.th; map p.197. Thong Pha Phum's best hotel is a surprisingly modern-looking affair, offering bright, tiled rooms with a/c, hot showers, fridges and cable TV. B790

Thong Pha Phum National Park

About 60km west of Thong Pha Phum along Route 3272 • B200 • ☎ 034 510979, ⓦ nps.dnp.go.th

After skirting round the southern branch of Vajiralongkorn Reservoir, the final 30km of the road to **Thong Pha Phum National Park** twists like a roller coaster and is slow but surfaced. If you have your own wheels the effort is worth it; this is a remote and lovely place to escape to, barely visited by foreign tourists and home to a population of wild elephants, mountain goats and barking deer. If you stay overnight, the big pleasure here is waking to see the foggy jungle below. During the day you can follow several **trails** that lead to the park's waterfalls.

ARRIVAL   THONG PHA PHUM NATIONAL PARK

By songthaew Occasional songthaews head to Pilok on the Myanmar border from the market in Thong Pha Phum, taking around 1hr 30min.

ACCOMMODATION AND EATING

In high season, there's a restaurant on site but options are limited, so it's worth bringing some of your own supplies. **National park accommodation** ☎ 034 510979. There are a number of rather basic bungalows near park headquarters. Call in advance to reserve. It's also possible to camp here – you can bring your own tent, or rent one. Camping B30, tents B225, bungalows B800

Sangkhlaburi and around

Beyond Thong Pha Phum the views get increasingly spectacular as Highway 323 climbs through the remaining swathes of montane rainforest, occasionally hugging the eastern shore of the Vajiralongkorn Reservoir until 73km later it comes to an end at **Sangkhlaburi** (often called **Sangkhla** for short). In the early 1980s, the old town was lost under the rising waters of the newly created Khao Laem (now Vajiralongkorn) Reservoir, when the Kwai Noi River was dammed. Its residents were mostly relocated to the northern tip of the lake, beside the Songkalia River, where modern-day Sangkhla now enjoys an eerily beautiful view of the water. It's a tiny town with no unmissable attractions, but the atmosphere is pleasantly low-key and the best of the accommodation occupies scenic lakeside spots so it's a great place to slow down for a while.

Cultural interest is to be found in the villages, markets and temples of the area's Mon, Karen and Thai populations, including at **Ban Waeng Ka** across the water. It sees relatively few farang tourists, but it's a popular destination for weekending Thais (come during the week for better deals on accommodation) and resident NGO volunteers add a positive vibe. Though the Burmese border is just 22km away at **Three Pagodas Pass**, at the time of writing it was closed to foreigners.

Boating on the lake

Aside from crossing the famous wooden bridge over the lake to the Mon village of Ban Waeng Ka, the main pastime in Sangkhlaburi is **boating** across the reservoir in search of the old village that was submerged when the valley was flooded. Water levels in the reservoir have dropped over the last few years, and vary between the dry and rainy seasons, but you should be able to see the "old" Wat Wang Wiwekaram and the "old" Wat Si Suwan; early morning and late afternoon are the best times to go. *P Guest House* rents out two-person **canoes** for independent exploring (B60/hr, B250/day or B150 for half a day) and offers longtail boat trips (B600 for up to six people; about 1hr 30min).

Ban Waeng Ka

The Mon village of **BAN WAENG KA**, across the reservoir from Sangkhlaburi, was founded in the late 1940s after the outbreak of civil war in Myanmar forced many to flee across the Thai border (see page 210). The **Mon** people's homeland, Mon State, lies just west of the Tenasserim Mountains, so thousands of Mon ended up in Sangkhlaburi, illegal immigrants whose presence was permitted but not officially recognized. Most now have official Sangkhlaburi residency, but still endure limited

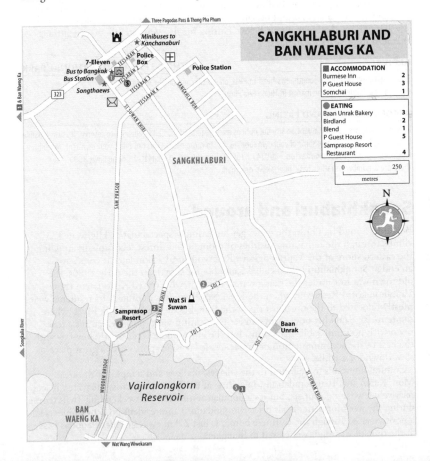

BAAN UNRAK FOUNDATION

Sangkhla's location so close to the Burmese border, along with the upheavals caused by the creation of the reservoir, mean that the town is full of displaced people, many of whom are in dire straits. Several organizations work with refugees in the area, including **Baan Unrak Foundation** (☎ 034 510778, ⊛ baanunrak.org), a farang-managed programme founded by the Neo Humanist Foundation that has run a children's home here since 1991 and has also established a primary school and a weaving project for destitute women. To help support the project you can buy handicrafts at the *Baan Unrak Bakery* (see page 211) or make a donation. Volunteer placements are also possible, including teaching English.

rights and must apply for expensive seven-day permits if they wish to travel out of the district, a system that lends itself to corruption.

Getting to Ban Waeng Ka entails crossing the narrow northern neck of the lake, near the influx of the Songkalia River. Drivers have to use a concrete bridge and a winding road of several kilometres to get there, but pedestrians can walk over the spider's web of a **wooden bridge** that is Sangkhla's unofficial town symbol. At almost 400m it is said to be the longest hand-built wooden bridge in the world and it can be reached either by following signs from near the post office to *Samprasop Resort*, which overlooks the structure, or by using the connecting footbridge near the *Burmese Inn*. Once across the wooden bridge, turn left to get into the village – a sprawling collection of traditional wooden houses lining a network of steep tracks, with a small but lively dry-goods market at its heart.

Wat Wang Wiwekaram

About 2km south from the bridgehead

Wat Wang Wiwekaram (also known as **Wat Luang Pho Uttama**) is Ban Waeng Ka's most dramatic sight, its massive, golden **chedi** clearly visible from Sangkhlaburi. Built in a fusion of Thai, Indian and Burmese styles, the imposing square-sided stupa is modelled on the centrepiece of India's Bodh Gaya, the sacred site of the Buddha's enlightenment, and contains a much-prized Buddha relic (said to be a piece of his skeleton) brought to Ban Waeng Ka from Sri Lanka. It's a focal point for the Mon community on both sides of the Thai–Myanmar border, particularly at Mon New Year in April. There's a **tourist market** in the covered cloisters at the chedi compound, with plenty of reasonably priced Burmese woodcarvings, checked *longyis* and jewellery.

The wat is spread over two compounds (you might want to hail a motorbike taxi to get here from the bridgehead), with the bot, **viharn** and monks' quarters about 1km away from the chedi, at the end of the left-hand fork in the road. The interior of the viharn is decorated with murals showing tableaux from the five hundred lives of the Buddha, designed to be viewed in anticlockwise order.

Three Pagodas Pass and the border

24km north of Sangkhlaburi • Songthaews leave Sangkhla bus station roughly every 40min from 6.40am until about 6.30pm and take 40min; the last songthaew back to Sangkhla leaves at about 5pm

All border trade for hundreds of kilometres north and south has to come through **Three Pagodas Pass** (signed as **Jadee Sam Ong**), but at the time of writing the crossing was **closed** to foreigners. Unless you're looking for heavy teak furniture or orchids, that means it's currently not worth making the trip as there's nothing more than a small market on the Thai side, in the village of **Ban Chedi Sam Ong**, plus the three eponymous little **chedis** said to have been erected in the eighteenth century by the kings of Myanmar and Thailand as a symbolic peace gesture. If and when full border operations resume, foreigners will probably once again be allowed access to the Burmese border village of **Payathonzu**, whose main attraction is the Mon temple **Wat**

THE MON IN THAILAND

Dubbed by some "the Palestinians of Asia", the **Mon** people – numbering between roughly two and four million in Myanmar and an estimated one hundred thousand in Thailand (chiefly in the western provinces of Kanchanaburi and Ratchaburi, in the Gulf province of Samut Sakhon and in Nonthaburi and Pathum Thani, just north of Bangkok) – have endured centuries of persecution, displacement and forced assimilation.

Ethnologists speculate that the Mon originated either in India or Mongolia, travelling south to settle on the western banks of the Chao Phraya valley in the first century BC. Here they founded the **Dvaravati kingdom** (sixth to eleventh centuries AD), building centres at U Thong, Lopburi and Nakhon Pathom and later consolidating a northern kingdom in Haripunchai (modern-day Lamphun). They probably introduced Theravada Buddhism to the region, and produced some of the earliest Buddhist monuments, particularly Wheels of Law and Buddha footprints.

Over on the Burmese side of the border, the Mon kingdom had established itself around the southern city of Pegu well before **the Burmese** filtered into the area in the ninth century, but by the mid-eighteenth century they'd been stripped of their homeland and were once again relocating to Thailand. The Thais welcomed them as a useful source of labour, and in 1814 the future Rama IV arrived at the Kanchanaburi border with three royal warboats and a guard of honour to chaperone the exiles. Swathes of undeveloped jungle were given over to them, many of which are still Mon-dominated today.

The **persecution** of the Burmese Mon continued after independence in 1948 and, even though the New Mon State Party (NMSP) entered into a ceasefire agreement with the military junta in June 1995, international human-rights organizations continued to report violations against civilian Mon living in Myanmar. Thousands of Mon men, women and children were press-ganged into unpaid labour, and soldiers occupied some Mon villages and confiscated farmland and livestock. In an attempt to wipe out Mon culture, the military leaders also banned the teaching of Mon language, literature and history in government schools. Not surprisingly, Mon fled these atrocities in their thousands, the majority ending up in five **resettlement camps** collectively known as Halockhani, in a Mon-controlled area near the Thai border opposite Sangkhlaburi; from there, many have been resettled in the USA, Canada, Australia, Scandinavia and the Netherlands.

The oppression has abated since the 2011 and 2015 elections which eventually brought Aung San Suu Kyi's National League for Democracy to power, and the population of Halockhani was down to three thousand in August 2015. However, there are still reports of human rights abuses, and the Mon continue to struggle for the right to administer their own independent Mon State in their historical homelands in lower Myanmar. As one commentator has described it, while some of Myanmar's ethnic minority groups seek to *establish* autonomy, the Mon are attempting to *reclaim* it, and they still celebrate their national day in the town of Ye each year, usually in February. For more information, see the website of the Human Rights Foundation of Monland (HURFOM; ⓦ rehmonnya.org).

Like Thais, the Mon are a predominantly Buddhist, rice-growing people with strong animist beliefs. All Mon families have totemic **house spirits**, such as the turtle, snake, chicken or pig, which carry certain taboos; if you're of the chicken-spirit family, for example, the lungs and head of every chicken you cook have to be offered to the spirits, and although you're allowed to raise and kill chickens, you must never give one away. Guests belonging to a different spirit group from their host are not allowed to stay overnight. Mon **festivals** also differ slightly from Thai ones – at Songkhran (Thai New Year), the Mon spice up the usual water-throwing and parades with a special courtship ritual in which teams of men and women play each other at bowling, throwing flirtatious banter along with their wooden discs.

Sao Roi Ton, known in Burmese as **Tai Ta Ya temple**, or the Temple of One Hundred Teakwood Posts.

ARRIVAL AND DEPARTURE   SANGKHLABURI

By bus A/c buses currently run from Bangkok's Northern Mo Chit bus terminal via Kanchanaburi to Thanon Tessaban 1, near Sangkhla's bus station, before heading on to Three Pagodas Pass (2 daily; 7hr 30min); however, this service is losing popularity and may disappear. In addition, there are four daily, non-a/c Kanchanaburi–Sangkhla buses that take about 5 hours.

By minibus The fastest way to get to Sangkhlaburi from Kanchanaburi is by a/c minibus (every 30min; 3–4hr; reserve a few hours ahead if possible and be prepared to buy an extra seat if you have luggage); they also pick up from Thong Pha Phum. Minibuses terminate on Thanon Tessaban 1, with services in the opposite direction departing from the same spot.

By car or motorbike Driving from Kanchanaburi to Sangkhlaburi can be tiring as the road is full of twists after Thong Pha Phum; the last 25km are particularly nerve-wracking due to the switchback bends. Nonetheless, the scenery is fabulous, particularly at the lakeside viewpoint just north of kilometre-stone 35 (about 40km south of Sangkhlaburi). As this is a border area, there may be police checkpoints en route – after a quick look at your passport, the officers should wave you through.

GETTING AROUND AND INFORMATION

Sangkhlaburi itself is small enough to walk round in an hour, but if the sun is beating down hard, you might want to look for an alternative.

By motorbike taxi Motorbikes from the bus station usually charge B20 to the guesthouses and B50 for a ride to Wat Wang Wiwekaram across the water.

By bicycle or motorbike *P Guest House* rents out bicycles

(B100/day) and motorbikes (B200/day).

By pick-up truck *Burmese Inn* or *P Guest House* should be able to arrange a pick-up truck and driver; prices depend on the length of hire and distances travelled.

Services Siam Commercial Bank, on the edge of the market in the town centre, changes money and has an ATM.

ACCOMMODATION

Reservations are essential at all accommodation for weekends and national holidays.

Burmese Inn Soi 1 ☏ 086 168 1801, ⊚ burmese-inn. com; map p.208. This rambling, traveller-oriented guesthouse overlooks the northeastern spur of the lake just behind the newer bridge, offering easy access to the Mon village, but hardly any rooms have lake views. Most of the rooms and bungalows feel run-down, but all have hot showers and there's a decent restaurant serving Burmese food. Fan B500, a/c B1000

P Guest House Thanon Si Suwan Khiri ☏ 034 595061, ⊚ p-guesthouse.com; map p.208. Large, popular, Mon-owned place that's efficiently run, clued-up and friendly. It's arrayed on terraces that now slope a long way down to the lakeshore, affording great views across to Ban Waeng Ka and Wat Wang Wiwekaram. There are basic, stone-studded rooms with shared bathrooms that have partial lake views, or much more luxurious en-suite rooms with a/c and hot showers that are bigger and brighter and have sweeping views. Reservations strongly advised. Fan B400, a/c B950

Somchai About 1km west of Ban Waeng Ka on Route 3024 (the road that winds round the lake to the Mon village) ☏ 034 595180, ⊚ facebook.com/somchaicoffeeofficial; map p.208. Basic, compact rooms with hot showers and balconies on stilts, at the top of a steep slope overlooking the tree-lined hillside opposite. Fan B700, a/c B1000

EATING

Day and night, the cheapest places to eat are at and around the **market** in the town centre. On Saturday evenings in high season and bank-holiday weekends, there's a much wider choice of food stalls here when this area turns into a "walking street" market, accompanied by live bands, local dances and, of course, souvenirs. If you're hankering after a decent latte, drop into one of the new a/c coffee shops that have popped up across town. Note that most places close quite early.

Baan Unrak Bakery Thanon Si Suwan Khiri, opposite Soi 3; map p.208. Part of the Baan Unrak foundation (see page 209), this sociable café and bookstore serves hot vegetarian meals (B60–100) and great cakes, as well as selling their woven products. Mon–Sat 8am–8pm.

Birdland 13/1 Thanon Si Suwan Khiri ☏ 086 801 6738; map p.208. Open-sided place in front of a secondhand bookstore, serving everything from pancakes, pizzas and yummy potato balls (B90) to Burmese curry, in generous

portions. Daily 7am–8pm.

Blend Tessaban 1, just across from the bus station ☏ 034 595204; map p.208. A handy place to wait before catching a bus, this diddy a/c café serves scrummy home-baked cakes and good espresso coffees (from B30). Daily 8am–6pm.

P Guest House Thanon Si Suwan Khiri ☏ 034 595061; map p.208. The large, Wild-West style restaurant at *P Guest House* offers fine lake views from its terrace and serves a short menu of Thai and Burmese food (most dishes around B120), as well as a few Western dishes, such as an American breakfast (B150 including coffee). Daily 7am–8.30pm.

Samprasop Resort Restaurant By the north end of the wooden bridge; map p.208. Very popular with visiting Thais, this open-air restaurant offers lofty views of the bridges, the lake and Wat Wang Wiwekaram, and very good dishes such as thawt man pla grai, fishcakes with a cucumber dip (B130). Daily 5pm–8.30pm (last orders).

Bang Pa-In

Little more than a roadside market, the village of **BANG PA-IN**, 60km north of Bangkok, has been put on the tourist map by its extravagant and rather surreal **Royal Palace**, even though most of the buildings can be seen only from the outside. King Prasat Thong of Ayutthaya first built a temple and palace on this site, 20km downstream from his capital, in the middle of the seventeenth century, and it remained a popular country residence for the kings of Ayutthaya. The palace was abandoned a century later when the capital was moved to Bangkok, only to be revived in the middle of the nineteenth century when the advent of steamboats shortened the journey time upriver. Rama IV (1851–68) built a modest residence here, which his son Chulalongkorn (Rama V), in his passion for westernization, knocked down in the 1870s to make room for the eccentric melange of European, Thai and Chinese architectural styles visible today.

The palace

Daily 8am–4pm, ticket office closes around 3.30pm • B100 • ⓦ palaces.thai.net/index_bp.htm • Visitors are asked to dress respectfully, so no vests, shorts, short skirts, see-through shirts or backless sandals

Set in manicured grounds on an island in the Chao Phraya River, and based around an ornamental lake, the **palace** complex is flat and compact, and easy to see on foot. The best approach is to explore slowly, following walkways that crisscross the lake.

The lakeside and covered bridge

On the north side of the lake stand a two-storey, colonial-style residence for the royal relatives and the Italianate **Varobhas Bimarn** (**Warophat Phiman**, "Excellent and Shining Heavenly Abode"), which housed Chulalongkorn's throne hall and still contains private apartments where the present royal family sometimes stays, though the lavishly furnished rooms by the entrance are usually open to the public. A covered bridge links this outer part of the palace to the **Pratu Thewarat Khanlai** ("The King of the Gods Goes Forth Gate"), the main entrance to the inner palace, which was reserved for the king and his immediate family. The high fence that encloses half of the bridge allowed the women of the harem to cross without being seen by male courtiers.

Aisawan Thiphya-art

You can't miss the glittering **Aisawan Thiphya-art** ("Divine Seat of Personal Freedom") in the middle of the lake: named after King Prasat Thong's original palace, it's the only example of pure Thai architecture at Bang Pa-In. The elegant tiers of the pavilion's roof shelter a bronze statue of Chulalongkorn.

The inner palace

In the inner palace, the **Uthayan Phumisathian** ("Garden of the Secured Land"), recently rebuilt in grand, neocolonial style, was Chulalongkorn's favourite house. After passing the candy-striped **Ho Withun Thasana** ("Sage's Lookout Tower"), built so that the king could survey the surrounding countryside, you'll come to the main attraction of Bang Pa-In, the **Phra Thinang Wehart Chamrun** ("Palace of Heavenly Light"), which was the favourite residence of Vajiravudh (Rama VI). A masterpiece of Chinese design, the mansion and its contents were shipped from China and presented as a gift to Chulalongkorn in 1889 by the Chinese Chamber of Commerce in Bangkok. The sumptuous interior gleams with fantastically intricate lacquered and gilded wooden screens, hand-painted porcelain floor tiles and ebony furniture inlaid with mother-of-pearl.

The obelisk

The simple marble **obelisk** behind the Uthayan Phumisathian was erected by Chulalongkorn to hold the ashes of Queen Sunandakumariratana, his favourite wife.

In 1881, Sunanda, who was then 21 and expecting a child, was taking a trip on the river here when her boat capsized. She could have been rescued quite easily, but the laws concerning the sanctity of the royal family left those around her no option: "If a boat founders, the boatmen must swim away; if they remain near the boat [or] if they lay hold of him [the royal person] to rescue him, they are to be executed." Following the tragedy, King Chulalongkorn set about reforming Thai customs and strove to make the monarchy more accessible.

Wat Niwet Thammaprawat

2

Perhaps the oddest building of all in Bang Pa-In's architectural melange is **Wat Niwet Thammaprawat**, reached by a cable car across the canal on the north side of the grounds. Chulalongkorn wanted a royal temple for his palace but, in his thirst for Westernization, employed an Italian architect to build it in the style of a Gothic Revival church. Surmounted by a spire with a weather vane and lit by stained-glass windows, the main Buddha image sits under the pointed arches of a typically Gothic three-part altar.

ARRIVAL AND DEPARTURE
BANG PA-IN

Bang Pa-In can easily be visited on a day-trip from Bangkok, and tours to Ayutthaya from the capital usually feature a stop here (see page 217). From Ayutthaya, about 20km to the north, you could cycle or motorbike down the riverside Route 3477 beginning at Wat Phanan Choeng, or catch the train.

By train The best route from Bangkok is by train from Hualamphong station, which takes about one-hour-thirty-minutes to reach Bang Pa-In (on arrival, note the separate station hall built by Chulalongkorn for the royal family). All trains continue to Ayutthaya, with half going on to Lopburi. From Bang Pa-In's train station it's a 20min walk to the palace, or you can take a motorbike taxi for about B40.

Returning to the station, catch a motorized samlor from the market, about 300m southwest of the palace entrance.

Destinations Ayutthaya (15 daily; 15min); Bangkok Hualamphong (15 daily; 1hr 30min).

By bus Buses leave Bangkok's Northern Mo Chit terminal (roughly every 30min; 1hr 30min–2hr) and stop at Bang Pa-In market, about 300m southwest of the palace entrance. This is also the easiest place to catch a bus back to Bangkok.

By songthaew From Ayutthaya, irregular and interminably slow songthaews leave Chao Phrom market for the journey to Bang Pa-In market (very roughly hourly; about 1hr 30min), returning from the same spot.

EATING

There are food stalls just outside the palace gates, and at Bang Pa-In market, plus a couple of well-appointed riverside restaurants (no English signs) between the railway station and the palace, opposite Wat Chumpol Nikarayam.

Ayutthaya

In its heyday as the booming capital of the Thai kingdom, **AYUTTHAYA**, 80km north of Bangkok, was so well-endowed with temples that sunlight reflecting off their gilt decoration was said to dazzle from 5km away. Wide, grassy spaces today occupy much of the atmospheric site, which now resembles a graveyard for temples: grand, brooding red-brick ruins rise out of the fields, satisfyingly evoking the city's bygone grandeur while providing a soothing contrast to more glitzy modern temple architecture. A few intact buildings help form an image of what the capital must have looked like, while several fine museums flesh out the picture.

The core of the ancient capital was a 4km-wide **island** at the confluence of the Lopburi, Pasak and Chao Phraya rivers, which was once encircled by a 12km-long wall, crumbling parts of which can be seen at the Phom Petch fortress in the southeast corner. A grid of broad roads now crosses the island, known as **Ko Muang**: the hub of the small modern town occupies its northeast corner, around the Thanon U Thong and Thanon Naresuan junction, but the rest is mostly uncongested and ideal for exploring by bicycle.

There is much pleasure to be had, also, from soaking up life on and along the encircling **rivers**, either by taking a boat tour or by dining at one of the waterside restaurants. It's very much a working waterway, busy with barges carrying cement, rice and other heavy loads to and from Bangkok and the Gulf and with cross-river ferry services that compensate for the lack of bridges. In addition, kids – and children at heart – will enjoy the Million Toy Museum, which provides light relief from the sombre mood of Thailand's ancient heritage.

Ayutthaya comes alive each year for a week in mid-December, with a **festival** that commemorates the town's listing as a **World Heritage Site** by UNESCO on December

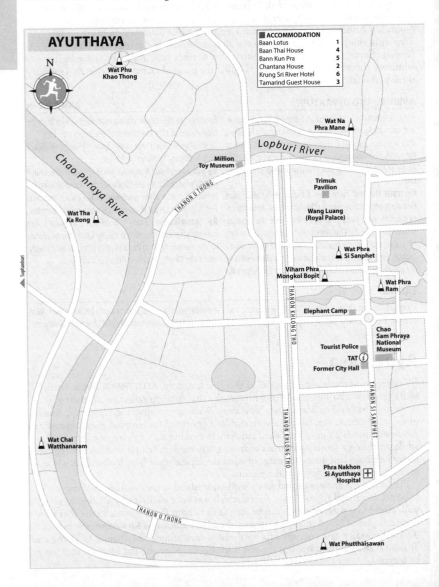

AYUTTHAYA

N

ACCOMMODATION	
Baan Lotus	1
Baan Thai House	4
Bann Kun Pra	5
Chantana House	2
Krung Sri River Hotel	6
Tamarind Guest House	3

Wat Phu Khao Thong

Wat Na Phra Mane

Lopburi River

Million Toy Museum

Chao Phraya River

THANON U THONG

Trimuk Pavilion

Wang Luang (Royal Palace)

Wat Tha Ka Rong

Suphanburi

Wat Phra Si Sanphet

Viharn Phra Mongkol Bopit

Wat Phra Ram

THANON KHLONG THO

Elephant Camp

Chao Sam Phraya National Museum

Tourist Police

TAT (i)

Former City Hall

THANON SI SANPHET

Wat Chai Watthanaram

THANON KHLONG THO

Phra Nakhon Si Ayutthaya Hospital

THANON U THONG

Wat Phutthaisawan

13, 1991. The highlight is the nightly *son et lumière* show, featuring fireworks and elephant-back fights, staged around the ruins.

Brief history

Ayutthaya takes its name from the Indian city of Ayodhya (Sanskrit for "invincible"), the legendary birthplace of Rama, hero of the *Ramayana* epic. It was founded in 1351 by U Thong – later **Ramathibodi I** – after Lopburi was ravaged by smallpox, and it rose rapidly through exploiting the expanding trade routes between India and China. Stepping into the political vacuum left by the decline of the Khmer empire at Angkor

2

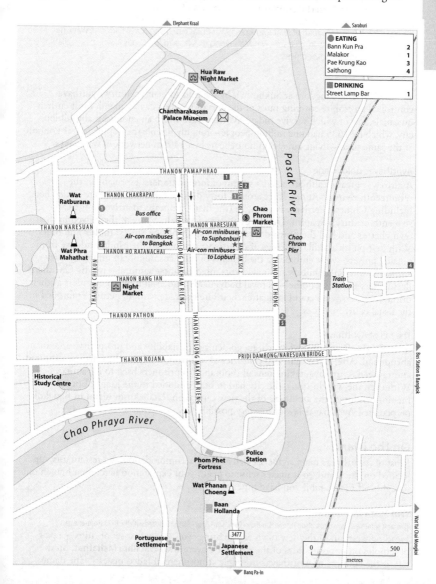

2

VISITING AYUTTHAYA – ORIENTATION AND TEMPLE PASS

The majority of Ayutthaya's ancient remains are spread out across the western half of the island in a patchwork of parkland: **Wat Phra Mahathat** and **Wat Ratburana** stand near the modern centre, while a broad band runs down the middle of the parkland, containing the **Royal Palace** (Wang Luang) and temple, the most revered Buddha image, at **Viharn Phra Mongkol Bopit**, and the two main **museums**. To the north of the island you'll find the best-preserved temple, **Wat Na Phra Mane**, and **Wat Phu Khao Thong**, the "Golden Mount"; to the west stands the Khmer-style **Wat Chai Watthanaram**; while to the southeast lie the giant chedi of **Wat Yai Chai Mongkol**, **Wat Phanan Choeng**, still a vibrant place of worship, and **Baan Hollanda**, which tells the story of the Dutch settlement in Ayutthaya. The city's main temples can be visited for a reduced rate when you buy the special six-in-one **pass** for Wat Phra Mahathat, Wat Ratburana, Wat Phra Ram, Wat Phra Si Sanphet, Wat Chai Watthanaram and easily missable Wat Maheyong (B220; valid for 30 days), which is available from the temples' ticket offices.

---

and the first Thai kingdom at Sukhothai, by the mid-fifteenth century Ayutthaya controlled an empire covering most of the area of modern-day Thailand. Built entirely on canals, few of which survive today, Ayutthaya grew into an enormous amphibious city, which by 1685 had one million people – roughly double the population of London at the same time – living largely on houseboats in a 140km network of waterways.

Ayutthaya's golden age

Ayutthaya's great wealth attracted a swarm of **foreign traders**, especially in the seventeenth century. At one stage around forty different nationalities were settled here, including Chinese, Persians, Portuguese (the first Europeans to arrive, in the early sixteenth century), Spanish, Dutch, English and French. Many of them lived in their own ghettos and had their own docks for the export of rice, spices, timber and hides. With deft political skill, the kings of Ayutthaya maintained their independence from outside powers, while embracing the benefits of their cosmopolitan influence: they employed foreign architects and navigators, used Japanese samurai – mostly Christians fleeing persecution at home – as royal bodyguards, and even took on outsiders as their prime ministers, who could look after their foreign trade without getting embroiled in the usual court intrigues.

The fall of Ayutthaya

In 1767, this four-hundred-year-long golden age of stability and prosperity came to an abrupt end. After more than two centuries of recurring tensions, the Burmese captured and ravaged Ayutthaya, taking tens of thousands of prisoners back to Myanmar. With even the wats in ruins, the city had to be abandoned to the jungle, but its memory endured: the architects of the new capital on Ratanakosin island in Bangkok perpetuated Ayutthaya's layout in every possible way.

On the island

Most of Ayutthaya's main sights, as well as most accommodation and restaurants, are located on the island, so it makes sense to begin your exploration here, then branch out to sights off the island if you have time.

Wat Phra Mahathat

1km west of the new town centre along Thanon Naresuan • Daily 8am–6pm • B50, or included with the B220 six-in-one pass

Heading west out of the new town centre brings you to the first set of ruins – a pair of temples on opposite sides of the road. The overgrown **Wat Phra Mahathat**, on the left, is the epitome of Ayutthaya's nostalgic atmosphere of faded majesty. The name

"Mahathat" (Great Relic Chedi) indicates that the temple was built to house remains of the Buddha himself: according to the royal chronicles – never renowned for historical accuracy – King Ramesuan (1388–95) was looking out of his palace one morning when ashes of the Buddha materialized out of thin air here. A gold casket containing the ashes was duly enshrined in a grand 38m-high prang, and the temple became home to Ayutthaya's supreme patriarch. The prang later collapsed, but the reliquary was unearthed in the 1950s, along with a hoard of other treasures, including a gorgeous marble fish, which opened to reveal gold, amber, crystal and porcelain ornaments – all now on show in the Chao Sam Phraya National Museum (see page 219).

You can climb what remains of the prang to get a good view of the broad, grassy complex, with dozens of brick spires tilting at impossible angles and headless Buddhas scattered around like spare parts in a scrapyard; look out for the serene (and much photographed) head of a stone Buddha that has become nestled in the embrace of a bodhi tree's roots.

2

AYUTTHAYA TOURS AND CRUISES

Ayutthaya is relatively spread out, so if you're really pushed for time, you might consider joining one of the **day-trips from Bangkok**. With a little more time, you can tour by tuk-tuk, bicycle or boat. The widest choice of **tours** is offered by Ayutthaya Boat & Travel (☎081 733 5687, ⓦayutthaya-boat.com), whose itineraries include **cycling** around the ruins and to Bang Pa-In (see page 212), homestays, boat tours, lunch and dinner cruises on a teak rice barge, cooking classes and packages by train and boat from Bangkok. For a serious **guided historical tour** of the ruins, local expert Professor Monton at Classic Tour (☎081 832 4849; about B2000/person/day, depending on group size) comes highly recommended.

FROM BANGKOK

The most popular **day-trips** by bus to Ayutthaya from Bangkok feature only the briefest whizz around the old city's two or three main temples, making a stop at the Bang Pa-In summer palace en route (see page 212) and rounding the day off with a short river cruise down the Chao Phraya from just north of Bangkok; Grand Pearl Cruise is one of the main operators (ⓦgrandpearlcruise.com; B1900). You can also cruise the river in more style, spending one or more nights on plushly converted teak rice-barges such as the *Mekhala* (ⓦasian-oasis. com), the two owned by the *Anantara Riverside Hotel* (ⓦbangkok-cruises.anantara.com) or the Thanatharee (ⓦthanatharee.com; also offers day-trips).

BY TUK-TUK, BOAT OR ELEPHANT

If you're pushed for time you could hire a **tuk-tuk** for a whistle-stop tour of the old city. This will cost B300 an hour from the station, where on busy days a queue forms, which is then divided into groups of four or five for the tours; or around B200 an hour if you walk away from the tourist hotspots and flag a tuk-tuk down on the street. (Sunset tuk-tuk tours to see the ruins illuminated may be organized by guesthouses again if the temples' floodlights ever get fixed.)

Circumnavigating Ayutthaya by boat is a very enjoyable way to take in some of the outlying temples, and possibly a few lesser-visited ones too; many of the temples were designed to be approached and admired from the river, and you also get a leisurely look at twenty-first-century riverine residences. All guesthouses and agencies offer **boat tours**, typically charging B180 per person for a two-hour trip in the early evening; tours can also be arranged – and boats chartered (B700 for 2hr) – from Chao Phrom pier.

It's also possible to take a brief **elephant ride** past a couple of the central ruins from the roadside elephant "camp" on Thanon Pathon (B400/person for 15min, B500 for 25min; ☎035 242417). The elephants and their mahouts are photogenically clad in period costume and you can buy the elephants bananas while they wait for custom, or simply watch them return home after 6pm when they rumble across to the northeast side of town to bathe and bed down in the restored sixteenth-century kraal. Wild elephants were formerly driven to the kraal for capture and taming, but these days it's the headquarters of Elephantstay (ⓦelephantstay. com), an organization that runs one- to fourteen-day packages for visitors who want to ride, feed, water and bathe the sixty resident elephants.

Wat Ratburana
Across the road from Wat Phra Mahathat • Daily 8am–6pm • B50, or included with the B220 six-in-one pass

The towering **Wat Ratburana** was built in 1424 by King Boromraja II to commemorate his elder brothers, Ay and Yi, who managed to kill each other in an elephant-back duel over the succession to the throne, thus leaving it vacant for Boromraja. Here, four elegant Sri Lankan-style chedis lean outwards as if in deference to the main prang, on which some of the original stuccowork can still be seen, some of which has been restored, including fine statues of garudas swooping down on nagas. It's possible to descend steep steps inside the prang to the crypt, where on two levels you can make out fragmentary murals of the early Ayutthaya period.

Wat Phra Ram
West of Wat Phra Mahathat • Daily 8am–6pm • B50, or included with the B220 six-in-one pass

West of Wat Phra Mahathat you'll see a lake, now surrounded by a popular park, and the slender prang of **Wat Phra Ram**, built in the late fourteenth century on the site of Ramathibodi's cremation by his son and successor as king, Ramesuan. Sadly, not much of the prang's original stuccowork remains, but you can still get an idea of how spectacular it would have looked when the city was at its zenith.

Wat Phra Si Sanphet and the Wang Luang (Royal Palace)
To the west of Thanon Si Sanphet • Daily 8am–6pm • B50, or included with the B220 six-in-one pass

Wat Phra Si Sanphet was built in 1448 by King Boromatrailokanat as a private royal chapel, and was formerly the grandest of Ayutthaya's temples. Even now, it's one of the best preserved.

The wat took its name from one of the largest standing metal images of the Buddha ever known, the **Phra Si Sanphet**, erected here in 1503. Towering 16m high and covered in 173kg of gold, it did not survive the ravages of the Burmese, though Rama I rescued the pieces and placed them inside a chedi at Wat Pho in Bangkok. The three remaining grey chedis in the characteristic style of the old capital were built to house the ashes of three kings, and have now become the most familiar image of Ayutthaya.

The site of this royal wat was originally occupied by Ramathibodi I's wooden palace, which Boromatrailokanat replaced with the bigger **Wang Luang** (Royal Palace; same hours and ticket as Wat Phra Si Sanphet, though it was under renovation at the time of writing), stretching to the Lopburi River on the north side. Successive kings turned the Wang Luang into a vast complex of pavilions and halls, with an elaborate system of walls designed to isolate the inner sanctum for the king and his consorts. The palace was destroyed by the Burmese in 1767 and plundered by Rama I for its bricks, which he needed to build the new capital at Bangkok. Now you can only trace the outlines of a few walls in the grass and inspect an unimpressive wooden replica of an open pavilion – better to consult the model of the whole complex in the Historical Study Centre (see page 219).

The Million Toy Museum
In the northwest corner of the island, just west of the Royal Palace and the westernmost bridge over the Lopburi River • Tues–Sun 9am–4pm • B50 • ⓦ milliontoymuseum.com

After a few hours gazing at the ruins of ancient temples, it comes as a welcome relief to enter the quirky, private **Million Toy Museum**, where cabinets on two floors are packed not only with toys, but also with odd items like Queen Elizabeth II coronation mugs from 1953. Kids love it, and even adults will recognize a few favourites from childhood, such as Superman, Minnie Mouse, Donald Duck and Goofy. There's a café out front that is also full of toy characters, and seats in a shady garden where you can rest your legs.

Viharn Phra Mongkol Bopit
On the south side of Wat Phra Si Sanphet • Closed for repair at the time of writing, but usually daily 8am–4.30pm • Free

Viharn Phra Mongkol Bopit attracts tourists and Thai pilgrims in about equal measure. The pristine hall – a replica of a typical Ayutthayan viharn, with its characteristic chunky lotus-capped columns around the outside – was built in 1956, with help from the Burmese to atone for their flattening of the city two centuries earlier, in order to shelter the revered **Phra Mongkol Bopit**, which, at 12.45m high (excluding the base), is one of the largest bronze Buddhas in Thailand. The powerfully austere image, with its flashing mother-of-pearl eyes, was cast in the fifteenth century, then sat exposed to the elements from the time of the Burmese invasion until its new home was built. During restoration, the hollow image was found to contain hundreds of Buddha statuettes, some of which were later buried around the shrine to protect it.

2

Chao Sam Phraya National Museum
10min walk south of Viharn Phra Mongkol Bopit • Daily 8.30am–4pm • B150

The largest of the town's three museums is the **Chao Sam Phraya National Museum**, where most of the moveable remains of Ayutthaya's glory – those that weren't plundered by treasure-hunters or taken to the National Museum in Bangkok – are exhibited. Apart from numerous Buddhas and some fine woodcarving, the museum is bursting with **gold treasures**, including the original relic casket from Wat Mahathat, betel-nut sets and model chedis, and a gem-encrusted fifteenth-century crouching elephant found in the crypt at Wat Ratburana.

Historical Study Centre
Thanon Rotchana, a 5min walk from Chao Sam Phraya National Museum • Scheduled to reopen after renovation in 2018, but usually Tues–Sun 9am–4pm • B100

It's worth paying a visit to the **Historical Study Centre**, if only to check out its scale model of the Royal Palace before you set off to wander around the real thing. The visitors' exhibition upstairs puts Ayutthaya's ruins in context, dramatically presenting a broad social history of the city through videos, sound effects and reconstructions of temple murals. Other exhibits include model ships and a peasant's wooden house.

Chantharakasem Palace Museum
In the northeast corner of the island • Wed–Sun 8.30am–4pm • B100

The **Chantharakasem Palace** was traditionally the home of the heir to the Ayutthayan throne. The Black Prince, Naresuan, built the first *wang na* (palace of the front) here in about 1577 so that he could guard the area of the city wall that was most vulnerable to enemy attack. Rama IV (1851–68) had the palace restored and it now houses a **museum** displaying many of his possessions, including a throne platform overhung by a white *chat*, a ceremonial nine-tiered parasol that is a vital part of a king's insignia. The rest of the museum features beautiful ceramics and Buddha images, and a small arsenal of cannon and musketry.

Off the island

It's easy enough to visit places off the island via various bridges across the river, especially if you're travelling around on a bike. If you're pushed for time, the two main sights are Wat Chai Watthanaram to the west, and Wat Yai Chai Mongkol to the southeast of the island.

Wat Na Phra Mane
On the north bank of the Lopburi River, opposite the Wang Luang • Daily 8am–5pm • B20

Wat Na Phra Meru is in some respects Ayutthaya's most rewarding temple, being the only one from the town's golden age that survived the ravages of 1767 (because the Burmese used it as their main base during the siege), though frequent refurbishments make it appear quite new.

The main **bot**, built in 1503, shows the distinctive features of Ayutthayan architecture – outside columns topped with lotus cups, and slits in the walls instead of windows to let the air circulate. Inside, underneath a rich red-and-gold coffered ceiling that represents the stars around the moon, sits a powerful 6m-high Buddha in the disdainful, over-decorated royal style characteristic of the later Ayutthaya period.

In sharp contrast is the dark-green **Phra Khan Thavaraj** Buddha, which dominates the tiny viharn behind to the right. Seated in the "European position", with its robe delicately pleated and its feet up on a large lotus leaf, the gentle figure conveys a reassuring serenity. It's advertised as being from Sri Lanka, the source of Thai Buddhism, but more likely is a seventh- to ninth-century Mon image from Wat Phra Mane at Nakhon Pathom.

Wat Phu Khao Thong
2km northwest of Wat Na Phra Mane • Daily dawn–dusk • Free

Head northwest of Wat Na Phra Mane and you're in open country, where the 50m-high chedi of **Wat Phu Khao Thong** rises steeply out of the fields. In 1569, after a temporary occupation of Ayutthaya, the Burmese erected a Mon-style chedi here to commemorate their victory. Forbidden by Buddhist law from pulling down a sacred monument, the Thais had to put up with this galling reminder of the enemy's success until it collapsed nearly two hundred years later, when King Borommakot promptly built a truly Ayutthayan chedi on the old Burmese base – just in time for the Burmese to return in 1767 and flatten the town. This "Golden Mount" has recently been restored, with a colossal equestrian statue of King Naresuan, conqueror of the Burmese, to keep it company. You can climb 25m of steps up the side of the chedi to look out over the countryside and the town, with glimpses of Wat Phra Si Sanphet and Viharn Phra Mongkok Bopit in the distance.

Wat Tha Ka Rong
Opposite the northwest corner of the island, near the confluence of the Chao Phraya and Lopburi rivers • Daily dawn–dusk • Free

This modern temple is wild – think Buddha goes to Disneyland. Highlights include a room full of enormous statues of famous monks, motion-activated skeletons, robots and other mannequins that *wai* as you pass and ask for a donation, and the plushest bathrooms you'll see in town. There's also a floating market on the riverside selling souvenirs, and an interesting display of Buddha images from neighbouring countries.

Wat Chai Watthanaram
Across the river, west of the island • Daily 8am–6pm • B50, or included with the B220 six-in-one pass

It's worth the bike or boat ride to reach the elegant brick-and-stucco latticework of Khmer-style stupas at **Wat Chai Watthanaram**. Late afternoon is a popular time to visit, as the sun sinks photogenically behind the main tower.

King Prasat Thong commissioned the building of Wat Chai Watthanaram in 1630, possibly to commemorate a victory over Cambodia, designing it as a sort of Angkorian homage, around a 35m-high central Khmer corncob **prang** encircled by a constellation of four minor prangs and eight tiered and tapered chedis. Most of the stucco facing has weathered away to reveal the red-brick innards in pretty contrast, but a few tantalizing fragments of stucco relief remain on the outside of the chedis, depicting episodes from the Buddha's life. Around the gallery that connects them sits a solemn phalanx of 120 headless seated Buddhas, each on its own red-brick dais but showing no trace of their original skins, which may have been done in black lacquer and gold-leaf. To the east a couple of larger seated Buddhas look out across the river from the foundations of the old bot.

Wat Yai Chai Mongkol

Southeast of the island, about 2km from the station • Daily 8am–5pm • B20 • If cycling here, avoid the multi-laned Pridi Damrong/
Naresuan Bridge and Bangkok road by taking the river ferry across to the train station and then heading south 1.5km before turning east
to the temple

Across the Pasak River southeast of the island, you pass through Ayutthaya's
new business zone and some rustic suburbia before reaching the ancient but still
functioning **Wat Yai Chai Mongkol**. Surrounded by formal lawns, flowerbeds and much-
photographed saffron-draped Buddhas, the wat was established by Ramathibodi I in
1357 as a meditation site for monks returning from study in Sri Lanka. King Naresuan
put up the beautifully curvaceous **chedi** to mark the decisive victory over the Burmese
at Suphanburi in 1593, when he himself is said to have sent the enemy packing by
slaying the Burmese crown prince in an elephant-back duel. Built on a colossal scale
to outshine the Burmese Golden Mount on the opposite side of Ayutthaya, the chedi
has come to symbolize the prowess and devotion of Naresuan and, by implication, his
descendants right down to the present king. By the entrance, the **reclining Buddha** was
also constructed by Naresuan. A huge modern glass-walled shrine to the revered king
dominates the back of the temple compound.

Wat Phanan Choeng

Near the confluence of the Chao Phraya and Pasak rivers, to the west of Wat Yai Chai Mongkol • Daily 8am–5pm • B20

In Ayutthaya's most prosperous period, the docks and main trading area were located
near the confluence of the Chao Phraya and Pasak rivers, and this is where you'll find
the oldest and liveliest working temple in town, **Wat Phanan Choeng**. The main viharn
is often filled with the sights, sounds and smells of an incredible variety of merit-
making activities, as devotees burn huge pink Chinese incense candles, offer food and
rattle fortune sticks. If you can get here during a festival, especially Chinese New Year,
you're in for an overpowering experience.

The 19m-high Buddha, which almost fills the hall, has survived since 1324, shortly
before the founding of the capital, and tears are said to have flowed from its eyes when
Ayutthaya was sacked by the Burmese. However, the reason for the temple's popularity
with the Chinese is to be found in the early eighteenth-century shrine by the pier, with
its image of a beautiful Chinese princess who drowned herself here because of a king's
infidelity: his remorse led him to build the shrine at the place where she had walked
into the river.

Baan Hollanda

Just south of Wat Phanan Choeng • Wed–Sun 9am–5pm • B50 • ⓦ baanhollanda.org

During Ayutthaya's heyday in the sixteenth and seventeeth centuries, foreign merchants
were attracted here to trade with the Siamese, and were permitted to set up trading
posts on either side of the Chao Phraya River to the southeast of the island. Three
settlements have now been turned into museums recounting foreign relations with
Siam, and of these, **Baan Hollanda** (the Dutch settlement) is the most interesting (the
others are those of the Japanese and Portuguese). Established in 2013 in order to
inform visitors about the history of the Dutch in Siam, the exhibition covers Siamese–

ART AND HISTORY AT THE AYUTTHAYA TOURIST OFFICE

While visiting the Tourist Information Centre, it's well worth heading upstairs to the smartly
presented multi-media **exhibition** on Ayutthaya (daily 8.30am–4.30pm; free), which provides
an engaging introduction to the city's history, an overview of all the sights, including a
scale-model reconstruction of Wat Phra Si Sanphet, and insights into local traditional ways of
life. Also on this floor, there's the **Ayutthaya National Art Museum** (daily 8.30am–roughly
4.30pm; free), which houses depictions of animals, people and landscapes by Thai artists as
well as temporary exhibitions.

Dutch relations from the first arrival of the Dutch East India Company in 1604. It's housed in a reconstruction of the original Dutch colonial-style lodge, following a description in the diary of a seventeenth-century Dutch merchant. The Dutch bought rice, tin, deerskins and wood from Siam and in return sold Japanese silver and Indian printed textiles to the Siamese. The centre also demonstrates how the Dutch have mastered the art of flood protection in their own country so that a large percentage of its population lives below sea level without fear, and there's a café and an opportunity for visitors to pick up a pair of ceramic clogs or a windmill at the museum shop.

2

ARRIVAL AND DEPARTURE

AYUTTHAYA

BY TRAIN

The best way of getting to Ayutthaya from Bangkok is by train (with departures mostly in the early morning and evening); trains continue on to Nong Khai and Ubon Ratchathani in the northeast, and to the north and Chiang Mai. The station is on the east bank of the Pasak; to get to the centre of town, take a ferry from the jetty 100m west of the station (last ferry around 8pm; B5) across and upriver to Chao Phrom pier; it's then a 5min walk to the junction of Thanon U Thong and Thanon Naresuan, near most guesthouses. The station has a useful left-luggage service (24hr; B10 per piece per day).

Destinations Bangkok Hualamphong (23–32 daily; 1hr 30min–2hr); Chiang Mai (5 daily; 10hr 45min–13hr 10min); Lopburi (14–16 daily; 45min–1hr 30min); Nong Khai (3 daily; 9hr 30min); Phitsanulok (11 daily; 3hr 30min–6hr 20min); Ubon Ratchathani (6 daily; 7hr 20min–10hr 30min).

BY BUS OR MINIBUS

From/to Bangkok Frequent a/c minibuses to Ayutthaya depart Bangkok's Northern (Mo Chit) and Southern bus terminals, pulling in at the stop on Thanon Naresuan, near the main accommodation area.
From/to Lopburi Frequent a/c minibuses to Lopburi depart from Soi 2, Thanon Bang Ian, near Chao Phrom Market.

From/to northern Thailand Long-distance buses to/ from the north only stop at Ayutthaya's Northern Bus Terminal, 5km to the east of the centre on the main north–south highway, from where you'll need a tuk-tuk to get into town (B150–200). On departure, there's an office for these services on Thanon Naresuan, where you can buy tickets.
From/to Kanchanaburi Travelling from Kanchanaburi, it's possible to bypass the Bangkok gridlock, either by hooking up with an a/c tourist minibus direct to Ayutthaya (daily; 3hr) arranged through guesthouses in Kanchanaburi or, under your own steam, by taking a public bus to Suphanburi (every 20min; 2hr 30min), then changing to an Ayutthaya a/c minibus, which will drop you off on Soi 2, Thanon Bang Ian, near Chao Phrom Market. To travel from Ayutthaya to Kanchanaburi, the easiest option is to book a seat on a minibus through one of the guesthouses.

Destinations Bangkok (every 20min; 1hr 30min–2hr); Chiang Mai (11 daily; 9hr); Chiang Rai (7 daily; 12hr); Kamphaeng Phet (8 daily; 5hr); Lopburi (every 30min; 1hr 30min); Mae Sot (8 daily; 6hr); Phitsanulok (roughly hourly; 5hr); Sukhothai (over 30 daily; 5–6hr); Suphanburi (every 10min; 1hr 30min); Tak (6 daily; 6hr).

GETTING AROUND

Busloads of tourists descend on Ayutthaya's sights during the day, but the area covered by the old capital is large enough not to feel swamped. Distances are deceptive, so it's not a good idea to walk everywhere. There are plenty of bicycle and other tours around Ayutthaya, and tuk-tuks can be hired by the hour.
By bicycle or motorbike As well as at guesthouses, bicycles (from B50/day) can be rented around the train station and, more conveniently, from Chao Phrom pier across the river and at Wat Phra Mahathat; if you do rent from the station, put the bike on the ferry to Chao Phrom pier rather than take on the busy, steep Pridi Damrong Bridge. Some guesthouses and a few outlets in front of the station and at Chao Phrom pier rent small motorbikes (from B200/day).
By tuk-tuk Tuk-tuks are easy enough to flag down on the street, charging around B40 for a typical medium-range journey in town on your own.
By motorbike taxi Motorbikes charge around B30 for short journeys.

INFORMATION

Tourist information TAT's helpful Ayutthaya Tourist Information Centre (daily 8.30am–4.30pm; ☎ 035 246076–7, ✉ tatyutya@tat.or.th) is in a room on the ground floor of the former city hall (on the west side of Thanon Si Sanphet, opposite the Chao Sam Phraya National Museum).

Useful website If you want to delve further into the city's history, have a look at Ayutthaya Historical Research (🌐 ayutthaya-history.com), a labour of love by three expat enthusiasts.

ACCOMMODATION

Ayutthaya offers a good choice of accommodation, including a small ghetto of **budget guesthouses** on and around the soi that runs north from Chao Phrom market to Thanon Pamaphrao; it's sometimes known as Soi Farang but is actually signed as Naresuan Soi 2 at the southern end and Pamaphrao Soi 5 at the northern.

Baan Lotus 20 Thanon Pamaphrao ☎ 035 251988; map p.214. Two old wooden houses with polished wooden floors and large, plain, but clean rooms (with either shared or en-suite hot showers), at the end of a long-overgrown garden with a lotus pond and pavilion for relaxing at the back. It's a wonderfully restful location just a few steps from the restaurants and bars on Soi Farang. Fan B350, a/c B600

Baan Thai House 199/19 Moo 4, Sri Krung Villa, 600m east of the train station ☎ 035 259760, ⓦ baanthaihouse.com; map p.214. Twelve immaculate a/c villas with traditional sloping roofs, set around manicured tropical gardens and a huge artificial pond with its own wooden water wheel. Rooms have flatscreen TVs, wooden floors and delicately carved furnishings, plus classy outdoor showers. Perks include free bicycles, a spa and an outdoor pool. Breakfast included. B2400

Bann Kun Pra 48/2 Thanon U Thong, just north of Pridi Damrong Bridge ☎ 035 241978, ⓦ bannkunpra.com; map p.214. The best rooms in the rambling, hundred-year-old teak house here have shared bathrooms and gorgeous river-view balconies. There are also two newer and slightly noisier blocks near the road, where you can choose between basic, single-sex dorm rooms with individual lockable tin trunks, or stylish en-suite doubles with a/c, attractive wooden floors and private terraces overlooking

the waterway. They also offer river tours, a warm welcome and a good restaurant (see page 224). Dorms B250, fan doubles B500, a/c doubles B1100

Chantana House 12/22 Naresuan Soi 2 ☎ 035 323200, ⓔ chantanahouse@yahoo.com; map p.214. Towards the quieter end of the travellers' soi, this low-key guesthouse has simple, boxy but spotlessly clean rooms with en-suite hot showers, though not all have outward-facing windows; it's set in a two-storey house with lots of common areas behind a well-kept garden. Kind, friendly staff, but not much English spoken. Fan B500, a/c B600

Krung Sri River Hotel 27/2 Moo 11, Thanon Rojana ☎ 035 244333, ⓦ krungsririver.com; map p.214. Ayutthaya's most prominent central hotel occupies nine storeys in a prime if noisy position beside the Pridi Damrong Bridge, with some standard rooms and all suites enjoying river views. Furnishings aren't exactly chic, but there are minibars, safes and TVs in all two hundred large bedrooms, as well as an attractive third-floor pool and a fitness centre. Breakfast included. B2650

★ **Tamarind Guest House** On a lane off Thanon Chikun in front of the entrance to Wat Mahathat ☎ 081 655 7937; map p.214. Tucked away from the main road, this quirky guesthouse has bags of character and its stylish a/c rooms are all different in design, though all have attractive wooden floors, bright colour schemes and en-suite hot showers. There's a great, multi-level family room and the owner can help with sightseeing plans. Free coffee, tea, fruit and biscuits. If this place is full, ask about nearby Good Morning, a similar, slightly cheaper guesthouse under the same ownership. B650

EATING

Other than the restaurants listed below, the *roti* (Muslim pancake) stalls near the hospital at the southern end of Thanon Si Sanphet are good for daytime snacks and after dark there are a couple of **night markets**. There's an excellent one with a wide range of food beside the river at Hua Raw, about ten minutes' walk north of Naresuan Soi 2, and another at the west end of Thanon Bang Ian, 150m south of Wat Phra Mahathat.

Bann Kun Pra Thanon U Thong, just north of Pridi Damrong Bridge ☎ 035 241978, ⓦ bannkunpra.com; map p.214. The riverside dining terrace here is just as atmospheric as the lovely guesthouse upstairs, and enjoys fine views. It specializes in creative and reasonably priced fish, seafood and river prawns, in dishes such as an intensely flavoured seafood tom yam, with a thicker soup than usual. Most mains around B150. Daily 7am–10.30pm.

★ **Malakor** Thanon Chikun, opposite Wat Ratburana; map p.214. Handy for the sights, this all-round café-restaurant is set on appealing wooden decks among shady trees. As well as a wide choice of breakfasts, espresso coffees and icy-cold beers, it offers some tasty and unusual

Thai dishes that can be spiced to order, such as tom klong pla yang (sour and spicy smoked fish soup; B150), and one-plate meals and salads for under B100. Daily 8am–9.30pm (kitchen closes 3–4.30pm).

★ **Pae Krung Kao** Thanon U Thong, just south of Pridi Damrong Bridge; map p.214. Festooned with plants, mai dut (Thai bonsai trees), waterfalls and curios, this rustic restaurant with breezy wooden decks built over the river specializes in river prawns. They're pricy (B700 each) but huge, sweet and juicy and come with a delicious nam jim, spicy, sour dipping sauce. Other noteworthy dishes include green curry with fish balls (B150). Daily 10am–8.30pm.

Saithong 45 Moo 1, Thanon U Thong ☎ 035 241449; map p.214. On the south side of the island, this place has an attractive riverside terrace and a cosy a/c room, and its reasonably priced seafood (most dishes B150–200) is popular with locals, so it's often full on weekend evenings. Try the seabass with spicy lemon sauce or the yum Saithong – a spicy salad with shrimp, chicken, squid and ham. Live music from 6pm each evening. Daily 10am–9.30pm.

DRINKING

Competing singers at the clutch of **bar-restaurants** along Soi Farang (Naresuan Soi 2) can mean this stretch turns into a battle of the bands after 9pm, but it's fun and lively, and free with your beer.

Street Lamp Bar Naresuan Soi 2; map p.214. One of the most popular bars on the street, with regular live music, ranging from country to rock and blues, and cheap, ice-cold beer. Simple dishes like fried rice from B65. Daily roughly 8.30am–midnight.

DIRECTORY

Banks and ATMs There are plenty of banks with exchange services and ATMs around the junction of Thanon Naresuan and Naresuan Soi 2.

Hospital The government Phra Nakhon Si Ayutthaya

hospital is at the southern end of Thanon Si Sanphet (☎035 211888).

Tourist police Based just to the north of the TAT office on Thanon Si Sanphet (☎035 241446 or ☎1155).

Lopburi and around

Mention the name **LOPBURI** to Thais and the chances are that they'll start telling you about monkeys – the central junction in the old town of this unexceptional provincial capital, 150km due north of Bangkok, swarms with around two thousand **macaques**. So beneficial are the beasts to the town's tourist trade that a local hotelier treats them to a mostly fruitarian meal laid out on a hundred tables at Phra Prang Sam Yod temple every year on the last Sunday of November, as a thank you for their help. In fact, the monkeys can be a real nuisance, so make sure to close your windows at night and take care with bags while out and about.

The town's central **Khmer buildings**, though historically important, are rather unimpressive. More illuminating are the **Somdet Phra Narai National Museum**, housed in a partly reconstructed seventeenth-century palace complex, **Ban Vichayen**, once home to the Greek adventurer Constantine Phaulkon, and distant **Wat Phra Phutthabat**, a colourful eye-opener for non-Buddhists. Lopburi's main festival is the nine-day **King Narai Reign Fair** in February, which commemorates the seventeenth-century king's birthday with costumed processions, cultural performances, traditional markets and a *son et lumière* show at Phra Narai Ratchanivet.

The old centre of Lopburi sits on an egg-shaped island between canals and the Lopburi River, with the railway line running across it from north to south. **Thanon Vichayen**, the main street, crosses the rail tracks at the town's busiest junction before heading east – now called Thanon Narai Maharat – through the newest areas of development, via Sakeo roundabout (aka Sri Suriyothai roundabout) and the bus station, to meet Highway 1 at the Narai roundabout. Most of the town's accommodation and restaurants are set within the quiet, partly residential core between Phra Narai Ratchanivet to the west and Thanon Na Phra Karn to the east.

Brief history

Originally called Lavo, Lopburi is one of the longest-inhabited towns in Thailand, and was a major centre of the Mon (Dvaravati) civilization from around the sixth century. It maintained a tenuous independence in the face of the advancing Khmers until as late as the early eleventh century, when it was incorporated into the empire as the provincial capital for much of central Thailand. Increasing Thai migration from the north soon tilted the balance against the Khmers, and Lopburi was again independent from some time early in the thirteenth century until the rise of Ayutthaya in the middle of the fourteenth. Thereafter, Lopburi was twice used as a second capital, first by King Narai of Ayutthaya in the seventeenth century, then by Rama IV of Bangkok in the nineteenth, because its remoteness from the sea made it less vulnerable to European expansionists. Rama V downgraded the town, turning the royal palace into a provincial government office and museum; Lopburi's modern role is as the site of several huge military barracks.

Wat Phra Si Ratana Mahathat

Just south of Thanon Na Phra That • Wed–Sun 7am–5pm • B50

The impressive centrepiece of the sprawled grassy ruins of **Wat Phra Si Ratana Mahathat** is a laterite prang in the Khmer style of the twelfth century, decorated with finely detailed stuccowork and surrounded by a ruined cloister. Arrayed in loose formation around this central feature are several more rocket-like Khmer prangs and a number of graceful chedis in the Ayutthayan style, among them one with a bulbous peak and faded bas-reliefs of Buddhist saints. King Narai added to the mishmash of styles by building a "Gothic" viharn on the eastern side of the main prang, now roofless, which is home to a lonely, headless stone Buddha, often draped in photogenic saffron.

Phra Narai Ratchanivet (King Narai's palace)

Sandwiched between Thanon Ratchadamnern and Thanon Phetracha; main entrance on Thanon Sorasak • Wed–Sun 8am–4pm • B150

The imposing gates and high crenellated walls of the **Phra Narai Ratchanivet** make it easy to imagine how visitors from afar would have been in awe of the palace in its seventeenth-century heyday. The extensive grounds are a pleasant place to stroll, and

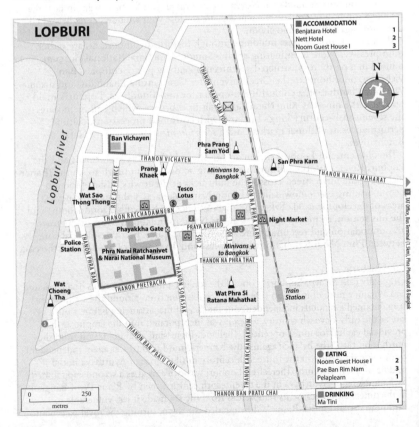

LOPBURI

◼ ACCOMMODATION	
Benjatara Hotel	1
Nett Hotel	2
Noom Guest House I	3

THANON PRANG SAM YOD

Lopburi River

Ban Vichayen

THANON VICHAYEN

Phra Prang Sam Yod

San Phra Karn

THANON NARAI MAHARAT

Prang Khaek

Minivans to Bangkok

RUE DE FRANCE

Wat Sao Thong Thong

Tesco Lotus

THANON NA PHRA KARN

THANON RATCHADAMNERN

Phayakkha Gate

PRAYA KUMJUD

Night Market

SOI 2

SOI 1

Police Station

Phra Narai Ratchanivet & Narai National Museum

THANON PHRA RAM

Minivans to Bangkok

THANON NA PHRA THAT

Wat Choeng Tha

THANON PHETRACHA

THANON SORASAK

Wat Phra Si Ratana Mahathat

Train Station

THANON BAN PRATU CHAI

THANON KANCHANAKHOM

THANON BAN PRATU CHAI

TAT Office, Bus Terminal (1.5km); Phra Phutthabat & Bangkok

● EATING	
Noom Guest House I	2
Pae Ban Rim Nam	3
Pelaplearn	1

◼ DRINKING	
Ma Tini	1

0 ————— 250
metres

LOPBURI ROCK-CLIMBING

Khao Chin Lae, a 240m-high limestone pinnacle on Lopburi's northeastern edge, features over forty climbing routes of all difficulty levels. Surrounded by fields of rice and sunflowers that bloom roughly from November to February, the craggy peak looms behind Wat Pa Suwannahong at the eastern end of the mountain. The monks themselves maintain the climbing area (donations welcome), asking visitors to register before and after their climb and to dress respectfully while passing through the temple. Noom Guesthouse (see page 230) rents out gear and runs climbing trips.

2

the informative museum in the centre of the complex is a good place to begin a tour of Lopburi. King Narai, with the help of French architects, built the heavily fortified palace in 1666 as a precaution against any possible confrontation with the Western powers, and for the rest of his reign he was to spend eight months of every year here, entertaining foreign envoys and indulging his love of hunting. After Narai's death, Lopburi was left forgotten until 1856, when Rama IV – worried about British and French colonialism – decided to make this his second capital and lavishly restored the central buildings of Narai's palace.

Phayakkha Gate

The main entrance to the palace complex is through the **Phayakkha Gate** on Thanon Sorasak. You'll see the unusual lancet shape of this arch again and again in the seventeenth-century doors and windows of Lopburi – just one aspect of the Western influences embraced by Narai. Around the **outer courtyard**, which occupies the eastern half of the complex, stand the walls of various gutted buildings – twelve warehouses for Narai's treasures, stables for the royal hunting elephants and a moated reception hall for foreign envoys. With their lily ponds and manicured lawns, these well-shaded grounds are ideal for a picnic or a siesta.

Somdet Phra Narai National Museum

Straight ahead from the Phayakkha Gate another arch leads into the **central courtyard**, where the three buildings of the museum are located. The typically Ayutthayan **Chanthara Phisan Throne Hall** contains a fascinating exhibition on Narai's reign – check out the pointed white cap typical of those worn by noblemen of the time, which increased their height by no less than 50cm. The colonial-style **Phiman Mongkut Pavilion** houses exhibits that show the development of Lopburi from prehistory to the present, spread across three floors. On the first floor are artefacts unearthed in excavations around town, mostly dating to the Dvaravati era. On the second floor are objects of Khmer art, as well as objects from the Ayutthaya and Rattanakosin eras, while the top floor is dedicated to **King Mongkut**, filled with his furniture and assorted memorabilia of his reign, including his very short and uncomfortable-looking bed and eerie painted statues of his equally vertically challenged near-contemporaries, Napoleon and Queen Victoria. Finally, the **Phra Pratiep Building**, which used to be Rama IV's harem, contains examples of Lopburi's arts and crafts and gives a taste of local culture.

Dusit Sawan Hall

On the south side of the museum lies the shell of the **Dusit Sawan Hall**, where foreign dignitaries came to present their credentials to King Narai. Inside you can still see the niche, raised 3.5m above the main floor, where the throne was set; beneath the niche, a modern plaque showing Narai receiving the French envoy, the Chevalier de Chaumont, in 1685 is revered as an icon of the king, with offerings of gold leaf, joss sticks and garlands. The whole building is divided in two around the throne: the front half has "foreign" doors and windows with pointed arches; the rear part, from where the king would have made his grand entrance, has traditional Thai openings. The hall used to be lined with French mirrors in imitation of Versailles, with Persian carpets and a pyramidal roof of golden glazed tiles rounding off the most majestic building in the palace.

Wat Sao Thong Thong

Rue de France

The street that runs from the north wall of Phra Narai Ratchanivet to Ban Vichayen is named rue de France, to commemorate the establishment of diplomatic ties between Siam and France in the 1680s (following the usual diplomatic niceties, the main street in the French city of Brest, where the Siamese envoys first landed, is "rue de Siam"). Halfway along the street is a building whose plain terracotta roof tiles and whitewashed exterior give it a strangely Mediterranean look. This is in fact the viharn of **Wat Sao Thong Thong**, and is typical of Narai's time in its combination of Thai-style tiered roof with "Gothic" pointed windows. Erected as either a Christian chapel or a mosque for the Persian ambassador's residence, it was later used as a Buddhist viharn and has now been tastefully restored, complete with brass door-knockers and plush red carpet. Inside there's an austere Buddha image of the Ayutthaya period and, in the lamp niches, some fine Lopburi-style Buddhas.

Ban Vichayen

Thanon Vichayen • Wed–Sun 7am–5pm • B50

The complex of **Ban Vichayen** was originally built by Narai as a residence for foreign ambassadors, with a Christian chapel incongruously stuccoed with Buddhist flame and lotus-leaf motifs. Though now just a nest of empty shells, it still conjures up the atmosphere of court intrigue and dark deeds which, towards the end of Narai's reign, centred on the colourful figure of its most famous resident, **Constantine Phaulkon**, a Greek adventurer who came to Ayutthaya with the English East India Company in 1678. He entered the royal service as interpreter and accountant, rapidly rising to the position of prime minister. It was chiefly due to his influence that Narai established close ties with Louis XIV of France, a move that made commercial sense but also formed part of Phaulkon's secret plan to turn Narai and his people to Christianity, with the aid of the French. (It was around this time that the word for Westerner, *farang*, entered the Thai language, from the same derivation as *français*, which the Thais render *farangset*.) In 1688, a struggle for succession broke out, and leading officials persuaded the dying Narai to appoint as regent his foster brother, Phetracha, a great rival of Phaulkon's. Phetracha promptly executed Phaulkon on charges of treason, and took the throne himself when Narai died. Under Phetracha, Narai's open-door policy towards foreigners was brought to a screeching halt and the Thai kingdom returned to traditional, smaller-scale dealings with the outside world.

Prang Khaek

The junction of Thanon Vichayen and Thanon Sorasak is marked by an unusual traffic island on which perch the three stubby red-brick towers of **Prang Khaek**, a well-preserved Hindu shrine, possibly to the god Shiva, dating from as early as the eighth century. The three towers, which face east and are aligned in a row, have been restored on several occasions – most notably in the seventeenth century under the auspices of King Narai.

Phra Prang Sam Yod

On the corner of Thanon Prang Sam Yod and Thanon Vichayen • Wed–Sun 6am–8pm • B50

Like nearby Prang Khaek, **Phra Prang Sam Yod**, at the top of Thanon Na Phra Karn, seems to have originally been a Hindu temple, later converted to Buddhism under the Khmers. The three chunky prangs, made of dark laterite with some restored stuccowork, and symbolizing the Hindu triumvirate of Brahma, Vishnu and Shiva, are Lopburi's most photographed sight, though they'll only detain you for a minute or two – while you're here, check out some carved figures of seated hermits at the base of the door columns.

The shrine's grassy knoll is a good spot for **monkey-watching** – monkeys run amok all over this area, so keep an eye on your bags and pockets. Across the railway line at the modern red-and-gold shrine of **San Phra Karn**, there's even a monkey's adventure playground, beside the base of what must have been a huge Khmer prang.

Wat Phra Phutthabat (Temple of the Buddha's Footprint)

17km southeast of Lopburi, off Highway 1 • Any of the frequent buses to Saraburi or Bangkok from Lopburi's Sakeo roundabout will get you there (30min)

The most important pilgrimage site in central Thailand, **Wat Phra Phutthabat** is believed to house a footprint made by the Buddha.

The **legend** of Phra Phutthabat dates back to the beginning of the seventeenth century, when King Song Tham of Ayutthaya sent some monks to Sri Lanka to worship the famous Buddha's footprint of Sumankut. To the monks' surprise, the Sri Lankans asked them why they had bothered to travel all that way when, according to the ancient Pali scriptures, the Buddha had passed through Thailand and had left his footprint in their own backyard. As soon as Song Tham heard this he instigated a search for the footprint, which was finally discovered in 1623 by a hunter named Pram Bun, when a wounded deer disappeared into a hollow and then emerged miraculously healed. The hunter pushed aside the bushes to discover a foot-shaped trench filled with water, which immediately cured him of his terrible skin disease. A temple was built on the spot, but was destroyed by the Burmese in 1765 – the present buildings date from the Bangkok era.

A staircase flanked by nagas leads up to a marble platform, where an ornate mondop with mighty doors inlaid with mother-of-pearl houses the **footprint**, which in itself is not much to look at. Sheltered by a mirrored canopy, the stone print is nearly 2m long and obscured by layers of gold leaf presented by pilgrims; people also throw money into the footprint, some of which they take out again as a charm or merit object. The hill behind the shrine, which you can climb for a fine view over the gilded roofs of the complex to the mountains beyond, is covered in shrines. The souvenir village around the temple includes plenty of **food stalls**.

THE FESTIVAL OF THE HOLY FOOTPRINT

During the dry season in January, February and March, hundreds of thousands of pilgrims from all over the country flock to Wat Phra Phutthabat for the **Ngan Phrabat (Festival of the Holy Footprint)**. During the fair, which reaches its peak in two week-long lunar periods, one usually at the beginning of February and the other at the beginning of March, stalls selling souvenirs and traditional medicines around the entrance swell to form a small town, and traditional entertainments, magic shows and a Ferris wheel are laid on. The fair is still a major religious event, but before the onset of industrialization it was the highlight of social and cultural life for all ages and classes; it was an important place of courtship, for example, especially for women at a time when their freedom was limited. Another incentive for women to attend the fair was the belief that visiting the footprint three times would ensure a place in heaven – for many women, the Phrabat Fair became the focal point of their lives, as Buddhist doctrine allowed them no other path to salvation. Up to the reign of Rama V (1868–1910) even the king used to come, performing a ritual lance dance on elephant-back to ensure a long reign.

BY TRAIN

Lopburi is on the main line north to Chiang Mai and is best reached by train from Bangkok's Hualamphong Station, via Ayutthaya. A popular option is to arrive in Lopburi in the morning, leave your bags at the conveniently located station while you look around the old town, then catch one of the night trains to the north.

Destinations Ayutthaya (16 daily; 45min–1hr 30min); Bangkok Hualamphong Station (16 daily; 2hr 30min–3hr); Chiang Mai (5 daily; 10–12hr); Phitsanulok (11 daily; 3hr–5hr 15min).

BY BUS OR MINIBUS

The long-distance bus terminal is on the southwest side of the huge Sakeo roundabout (aka Sri Suriyothai roundabout), 2km east of the old town. From there, shared songthaews head west on Thanon Narai Maharat to Narai's palace (B10).

From/to Bangkok Besides regular buses from the Northern Bus Terminal (Mo Chit), a couple of companies operate fast a/c minibuses between the same bus terminal and Lopburi, which leave when full (roughly 5am–8pm) and terminate outside their offices on Thanon Na Phra Karn, between the train station and Phra Prang Sam Yod. They depart from the same locations.

Destinations Ayutthaya (every 30min; 1hr 30min); Bangkok (every 20min; 2–3hr); Chiang Mai (4 daily; 9–11hr); Khorat (hourly; 3hr–3hr 30min).

GETTING AROUND AND INFORMATION

By motorbike Lopburi is easily explored on foot, but if you want to get further afield, *Noom Guesthouse I* rents out automatic motorbikes for B250–300/day.

Tourist information The TAT office is in Lopburi Provincial Hall at the Narai roundabout, about 4km east of the old town on Thanon Narai Maharat (daily 8.30am–4.30pm; ☎036 770096–7, ✉tatlobri@tat.or.th); it's too far from the city's main sights to be of much use, though they can provide a good map of the town and a booklet of nearby attractions.

ACCOMMODATION

Benjatara Hotel 123/33 Moo 1, Tambon Khao Sam Yod (just east of the Narai roundabout, on a lane to the north off Highway 1 immediately after the Ford dealership) ☎036 422 608–9, ⓦfacebook.com/benjatara; map p.226. This smart, modern place offers the town's most comfortable mid-range lodging, but it's about 5km from the centre. The large, tiled rooms all have a/c, hot showers, fridges and TVs, and some have balconies. B550

Nett Hotel 17/1–2 Soi 2, Thanon Ratchadamnern ☎036 411738; map p.226. The best alternative to *Noom* (see below) is this clean and friendly place, announced by a multicoloured, three-storey mosaic of a dragon and a cockerel. It offers unadorned en-suite fan or a/c rooms, the latter with hot water, TVs and fridges, though don't expect a view. Fan B250, a/c B400

★ **Noom Guesthouse I** 15–17 Thanon Praya Kumjud ☎036 427693, ⓦnoomguesthouse.com; map p.226. Most travellers make a beeline for the rooms at friendly *Noom Guesthouse I*, whose centrally located old wooden house is fronted by a streetside restaurant and bar. There's a good mix of teak-floored rooms upstairs in the main house sharing hot-water bathrooms, including single and family rooms at decent rates, or you can stay in one of the a/c bungalows with en-suite hot showers and TVs in the back garden. As well as rock-climbing (see page 227), Noom offers half-day tours to a cave packed with bats, and one-day (combined with a visit to Wat Phra Phutthabat) and overnight trekking trips. Fan B350, a/c B550

EATING

Lopburi's dining scene is pretty limited, but the **night market**, which sets up all along the west side of the railway tracks, is a reliable choice for cheap eats.

★ **Noom Guesthouse I** 15–17 Thanon Praya Kumjud ☎036 427693, ⓦnoomguesthouse.com; map p.226. This classic travellers' café serves a great range of Thai and Western dishes (mostly B100–150) in its cosy, ground-floor restaurant, with tables spilling on to the street in the evening. They serve a wide range of breakfasts and draught beer and cocktails in the evening. Owner Noom is the man to ask if you have any queries about attractions near Lopburi or onward travel. Restaurant daily 8am–9pm (bar often stays open later).

Pae Ban Rim Nam 57/68 Soi Wat Choeng Tha, off Thanon Phetracha ☎036 618005; map p.226. This floating restaurant, located just southwest of King Narai's Palace, makes a good spot for lunch after exploring the palace grounds and the museum. Dishes are a bit expensive but portions are huge (they cater mostly to Thai groups), with lots of seafood and classics like green curry (B120) on the menu. They sometimes host karaoke parties in the evening, when it's not such a pleasant experience. Daily 10am–10pm.

Pelaplearn Thanon Ratchadamnern; map p.226. Stylish little a/c café – think polished concrete walls and retro armchairs – serving tasty cakes, snacks and a good range of espresso coffees (latte B35). Tues–Sun 10.30am–5.30pm.

DRINKING

The most popular places for a **beer**, day or night, are *Ma Tini* and the sociable pavement tables at *Noom Guesthouse I*.

Ma Tini 18 Thanon Praya Kumjud ☎088 680 7335; map p.226. *Ma Tini*, meaning "come here", is run by Tee, a musician who sometimes plays with his band and other times puts on classic rock songs. Seating is on a shady outdoor terrace, and though the menu covers a wide range of Thai, Western and vegetarian dishes (mostly around B100), it's more bar than restaurant, and a cool place to hang out in the evening, enjoying the music or playing pool over a beer or a cocktail. Daily 9am–midnight.

Phitsanulok

Handily located midway up the railway line between Bangkok and Chiang Mai, the provincial capital of **PHITSANULOK** ("Abode of Vishnu") makes a useful stopover with reasonable hotels and good transport connections, especially to the historical centres of Sukhothai and Kamphaeng Phet. The main sight in town is the country's second-most important Buddha image, enshrined in historic **Wat Mahathat** and the focus of pilgrimages from all over Thailand; it is complemented by one of the best ethnology collections in Thailand, at the **Sergeant Major Thawee Folklore Museum**. There are also several potentially rewarding national parks within an hour or two's drive along Highway 12, the so-called "**Green Route**".

Typically for a riverside town, "Phit'lok" as it's often nicknamed, is long and narrow. The heart of the city, which occupies the east bank of the Nan River, is easily walkable and exudes plenty of urban grit, with its Thai-Chinese shophouses and traditional restaurants, particularly along Thanon Boromtrailoknat between the police station and the *Pailyn Hotel*. The two main sights, however, lie at opposite extremities: Wat Mahathat to the north, and the folklore museum 2.5km south.

Brief history

Huge swathes of Phitsanulok were destroyed by fire in 1957, but the town's history harks back to a heyday in the late fourteenth and early fifteenth centuries when, with Sukhothai waning in power, it rose to prominence as the favoured home of the crumbling capital's last rulers. After supremacy was finally wrested by the emerging state of Ayutthaya in 1438, Phitsanulok was made a provincial capital, subsequently becoming a strategic army base during Ayutthaya's wars with Lanna and the Burmese, and adoptive home to Ayutthayan princes. The most famous of these was **Naresuan**, who was governor of Phitsanulok before he assumed the Ayutthayan crown in 1590. The foundations of fifteenth-century Chandra Palace, where both Naresuan and his younger brother Akkathasaroth were born, have been excavated in the grounds of a former school northwest of Naresuan Bridge; the tramway tour makes a stop there.

Wat Phra Si Ratana Mahathat (Wat Yai)

Entrances on Thanon Bhudhabucha on the east bank of the Nan River, and on Thanon Jakarnboon • Daily 6am–9pm • Free • No shorts or skimpy clothing

Officially called **Wat Phra Si Ratana Mahathat** (and known locally as **Wat Yai**, meaning "big temple"), this fourteenth-century temple was one of the few buildings miraculously to escape Phitsanulok's great 1957 fire. It receives a constant stream of worshippers eager to pay homage to the highly revered Buddha image inside the viharn. Because the image is so sacred, a **dress code** is strictly enforced here, forbidding shorts and skimpy clothing.

Phra Phuttha Chinnarat

Delicately inlaid mother-of-pearl doors made in the eighteenth century mark the entrance to the main viharn, opening onto the low-ceilinged interior, painted mostly in dark red and black, with gold leaf motifs, and dimly lit by narrow slits along the upper walls. In the centre of the far wall sits the much-cherished **Phra Phuttha Chinnarat**: late Sukhothai in style and probably cast in the mid-fourteenth century for King Lithai, this gleaming, polished-bronze Buddha is one of the finest of the period and, for Thais, second in importance only to the Emerald Buddha in Bangkok. Tales of the statue's miraculous powers have fuelled the devotion of generations of pilgrims

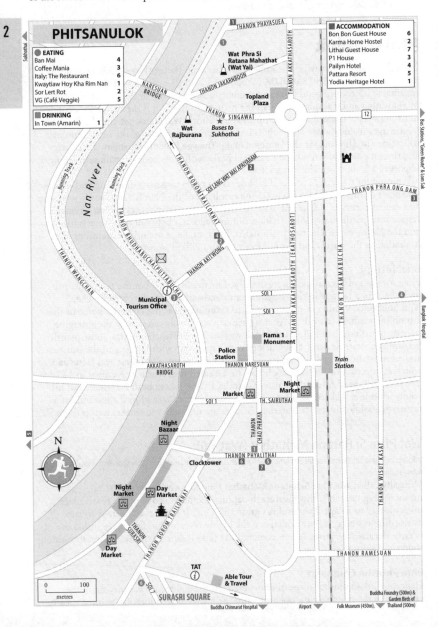

PHITSANULOK

EATING
Ban Mai	4
Coffee Mania	3
Italy: The Restaurant	6
Kwaytiaw Hoy Kha Rim Nan	1
Sor Lert Rot	2
VG (Café Veggie)	5

DRINKING
In Town (Amarin)	1

ACCOMMODATION
Bon Bon Guest House	6
Karma Home Hostel	2
Lithai Guest House	7
P1 House	3
Pailyn Hotel	4
Pattara Resort	5
Yodia Heritage Hotel	1

FESTIVALS AND EVENTS IN PHIT'LOK

In late January or February, Phitsanulok honours the **Phra Buddha Chinnarat** with a **week-long festival**, which features *likay* folk-theatre performances (see page 50) and dancing. Then, later in the year, on the third weekend of September, traditional **longboat races** are staged on the Nan River, in front of Wat Mahathat. Phitsanulok also hosts three lively **food festivals** every year, during Songkhran, the Thai New Year, in April, over the Loy Krathong period in November, and over the Christmas and Western New Year period. Almost every restaurant in town participates, selling their trademark dishes from special stalls set up along the east bank of the river, and there's traditional Thai dance and other entertainments.

2

– one legend tells how the Buddha wept tears of blood when Ayutthayan princes arrived in Phitsanulok to oust the last Sukhothai regent. The Phra Phuttha Chinnarat stands out among Thai Buddha images because of its *mandorla*, the flame-like halo that symbolizes extreme radiance and frames the upper body and head like a chairback, tapering off into nagas at the arm rests. There's an almost perfect replica of the Phitsanulok original in Bangkok's Marble Temple (see page 114), commissioned by Rama V in 1901. Visitors are asked not to photograph this image in a standing position, but to kneel respectfully in front of it as locals do.

The prang

Behind the main viharn, the gilded mosaic **prang** houses the holy relic that gives the wat its name (Mahathat means "Great Relic Stupa") – though which particular remnant of the Buddha lies entombed here is unclear – and the cloister surrounding both structures contains a gallery of Buddha images of different styles.

Phra Phuttha Chinnarat National Museum

Daily 8am–4pm • Free

The viharn on the north side of the prang is the unlikely setting for what must be Thailand's smallest national museum, sheltering a desultory display of bencharong, Sangkhalok (see page 244) and blue and white ceramics. The highlights are two alms bowl lids made for Rama V and beautifully inlaid with mother-of-pearl, one showing a mythical lion, the other the king's insignia, the three-headed elephant Erawan surmounted by a coronet.

The river bank

South of Wat Mahathat and Naresuan Bridge, **the east and west banks** of the Nan River have been landscaped into a pleasant riverside park and jogging track that runs all the way down to Akkathasaroth (Ekathosarot) Bridge. There are no exceptional attractions along its course, but you may want to make a stop at Wat Rajburana, or join the locals who come out in their thousands each evening to exercise in this area. South of Akkathasaroth Bridge, the east bank of the river is dominated by the permanent stalls of the **night bazaar**, the place for locals and tourists to shop for bargain-priced fashions and a cheap meal.

Wat Rajburana

Just south of Naresuan Bridge • Daily 6am–8.30pm

Like Wat Mahathat, **Wat Rajburana** survived the 1957 fire. Recognizable by the huge brick-based chedi that stands in the compound, the Sukhothai-era wat is chiefly of interest for the *Ramakien* **murals** (see page 88) that cover the interior walls of the bot. Now fading, they were probably painted in the mid-nineteenth century. Other interesting features are a wooden scripture library raised on concrete piles, and a boat once used by King Rama V that is protected by a shelter and bedecked with floral garlands.

The Sergeant Major Thawee Folk Museum

26/138 Thanon Wisut Kasat, just over 1km southeast of the train station • Daily 8.30am–4/4.30pm • B50

The **Sergeant Major Thawee Folk Museum** (Phiphitaphan Ja Tawee) displays a variety of exhibits on the region's culture and its fascinating look at traditional rural life makes this one of the best ethnology museums in the country. The collection, which is housed in a series of wooden pavilions, belongs to Sergeant Major Dr Thawee, a former military cartographer who has pursued a lifelong personal campaign to preserve and document a way of life that's gradually disappearing. Highlights include the reconstructed kitchen, veranda and birthing room of a typical village house, known as a "tied house" because its split-bamboo walls are literally tied together with rattan cane; and an exceptionally comprehensive gallery of traps: dozens of specialized contraptions designed to ensnare everything from cockroaches to birds perched on water buffaloes' backs. There's also a display on weaving and natural dyes, a collection of traditional toys and some fearsome-looking wooden implements for giving yourself a massage. A recent addition to the museum is an aquarium of fish found in local rivers, including the snakehead fish and the Mekhong giant catfish (see page 373).

Buddha Foundry

26/43 Thanon Wisut Kasat, about 50m south of the Folk Museum ☎ 055 301668 • Daily roughly 8am–5pm • Free

For a rare chance to see Buddha images being forged, head to Sergeant Major Thawee's **Buranathai Buddha Bronze-Casting Foundry**. Anyone can drop in to see the fairly lengthy procedure, which is best assimilated from the illustrated explanations along the entrance lane. Images of all sizes are made here, from 30cm-high household icons to mega models destined for wealthy temples. The Buddha business is quite a profitable one: worshippers can earn a great deal of merit by donating a Buddha statue, particularly a precious one, to their local wat, so demand rarely slackens. There's a gift shop on site.

Garden Birds of Thailand

Behind the Buddha Foundry on Thanon Wisut Kasat • Daily 8.30am–5pm • B50 • Accessible from the foundry or via Soi 17

Garden Birds of Thailand (Suan Nok) is another of Sergeant-Major Thawee's enthusiasms: a zoo containing hundreds of breathtakingly beautiful Thai birds, each one segregated and informatively described. It's an astonishing collection that offers a unique chance to admire at close range such beauties as the blue magpie, the Eurasian jay and the common hoopoe.

ARRIVAL AND DEPARTURE   PHITSANULOK

Phitsanulok stands at the hub of an efficient transport network that works well as a transit point between Bangkok, the far north and Isaan. Every Bangkok–Chiang Mai **train** stops here, and assorted **buses** head east towards the Isaan towns of Loei and Khon Kaen.

Destinations Ayutthaya (11 daily; 4hr 30min–5hr 30min); Bangkok Hualamphong (11 daily; 5hr 30min–8hr); Chiang Mai (6 daily; 5hr 50min–8hr 15min); Den Chai (for Phrae; 8 daily 2–3hr); Lampang (6 daily; 4hr–5hr 30min); Lamphun (6 daily; 5hr 40min–7hr 20min); Lopburi (11 daily; 3hr–5hr 15min).

BY PLANE

Phitsanulok airport is 7km south of town and B120 by tuk-tuk from the train station or about B200 in a taxi. The airport is served by Air Asia, Nok Air and Thai Lion Air flights to and from Bangkok's Don Muang Airport (5–10 daily; 1hr).

BY TRAIN

Phitsanulok train station is in the town centre; tuk-tuk rates from here to various attractions are posted outside (from B60).

BY BUS

Buses for Sukhothai, Lom Sak and other adjacent provinces use the old bus station, about 4km east of Naresuan Bridge on the south side of Highway 12; Sukhothai buses also make useful stops in the centre near the bridge, as marked on our map (B60 by tuk-tuk from the train station). Long-distance buses are meant to use the new bus station (Bus Terminal 2), but it's about 10km east of Naresuan Bridge near Indochina Junction, where highways 11 and 12 meet, and understandably unpopular with locals. Accordingly, some

THE GREEN ROUTE

East of Phitsanulok and served by frequent buses, Highway 12 towards Lom Sak has been tagged **"the Green Route"** by TAT because it gives access to several national parks and rapids, and provides an excuse for a pleasant day or two's excursion from the city. Their Phitsanulok office can provide a simple map outlining routes. Beyond Lom Sak on the same road lies Nam Nao National Park (see page 482).

The first highlight is the chance to go **whitewater rafting** on the Class 1–5 rapids of the Khek River; the *Sappraiwan Resort* (☎055 293293, ⓦsappraiwan.com; doubles B2800 including breakfast) at kilometre-marker 53 on Highway 12 arranges an overnight trip (roughly June–Nov; B1950/person including three meals and one night's accommodation). The resort also has a swimming pool and an elephant sanctuary where you can watch the pachyderms playing together.

Next up is **Phu Hin Rongkla National Park** (B500; ☎055 233527, ⓦnps.dnp.go.th), about 100km northeast of Phitsanulok: turn north off Highway 12 at kilometre-stone 68 onto Route 2013, then east onto Route 2331 to reach the visitor centre. Formerly the notorious stronghold of the insurgent Communist Party of Thailand from 1967 to 1982, the park still contains some relics from that period, though its short trails through montane forests and natural rock gardens are now the main point of interest. Should you want to stay, the park offers bungalows (from B800).

Also on the Green Route is **Thung Salaeng Luang National Park** (B200–500 depending on which areas you want to visit; ☎055 268019, ⓦnps.dnp.go.th), 82km east of Phitsanulok (turn south off Highway 12 at kilometre-stone 79). Thung Salaeng is famous for Kaeng Sopha waterfall, which is spectacular towards the end of the rainy season, and for the flowers that carpet its grasslands at Thung Nonson for a brief period after the end of the rainy season (November is the best time to go). Bungalows are available in the park from B1000.

The Dhamma Abha Vipassana meditation centre (☎081 827 7331, ⓦabha.dhamma.org), which follows the teachings of S.N. Goenka, holds frequent ten-day **meditation** courses throughout the year (sign up on the website), and is also in this area, in Ban Huayplu; turn north off Highway 12 at kilometre-stone 49.

long-distance buses, including some services to Bangkok, Chiang Mai, Chiang Rai and Mae Sot, use the old bus station; however, if you make the trek out to the new terminal, you'll have a wider choice of long-distance services with more frequent departures. Shared purple songthaews (B15–30) shuttle between the new bus station and the train station in the centre of town, via the old bus station, while a taxi or a tuk-tuk to the centre will cost about B150 from the new terminal, B60 or more from the old terminal.

Destinations Bangkok (over 40 daily; 5–6hr); Chiang Mai (over 30 daily; 5–7hr); Chiang Rai (over 20 daily; 6–8hr); Kamphaeng Phet (roughly hourly; 2–3hr); Khon Kaen (roughly hourly; 5–6hr); Loei (3 daily; 4–5hr); Lom Sak (roughly hourly; 2hr); Mae Sot (roughly hourly; 3hr 30min–5hr); Nan (5 daily; 5–6hr); Phrae (17 daily; 2–3hr); Sukhothai (hourly; 1hr); Udon Thani (3 daily; 6–7hr).

GETTING AROUND

Phitsanulok has a handful of city buses but their schedules are so infrequent that they're to all intents and purposes useless.

By tuk-tuk Tuk-tuks buzz around town and hang out at the train station, where rates are posted on a board outside, including B60 to Wat Phra Si Ratana Mahathat and the Sergeant Major Thawee Folk Museum; you might have to walk to the station to get these rates, as a tuk-tuk flagged down on the street is likely to quote a higher fare.

By taxi For an a/c taxi, call ☎055 338888; a few will turn the meter on, but most will want to agree a fare in advance.

By car or motorbike Avis (ⓦavisthailand.com), who will deliver and collect anywhere in town, and Budget (ⓦbudget.co.th) have desks at the airport. Motorbike rental is available for B200–300 per day at Lady Motor (☎086 209 9988) on the northwest side of the old bus station.

INFORMATION

Tourist information The helpful municipal tourist office occupies a traditional-style wooden building next to Coffee Mania on Thanon Bhudhabucha (Mon–Fri 8.30am–4.30pm; ☎055 252148). There's also a TAT office (daily 8.30am–4.30pm; ☎055 252742, ⓔtatphlok@tat.or.th) in Surasri Square (aka Surasi Trade Centre), a small grid of businesses off the eastern side of Thanon Boromtrailoknat.

2

PHITSANULOK BY TRAM

For a cheap whizz around some of the town's sights, you could take a 45-minute **"tramway tour"** in a kind of open-sided bus (in Thai *rot rang*), which starts in front of the tourist police booth inside Wat Phra Si Ratana Mahathat (daily roughly 8/9am–4pm, though the driver will knock off early if there are no tourists around; departs when it has at least ten passengers; B40). Commentary is in Thai but one of the students who works at the tourist police booth might offer to accompany you to translate; there are printed English-language summaries, but they're only available at the TAT office. The route takes in some remains of the town's Ayutthaya-era walls and moat, as well as a couple of excavated ruins across the river – King Naresuan's place of birth, Chandra Palace, plus the Sukhothai-era Wat Wihanthong – neither of which is really worth making the effort to walk to.

ACCOMMODATION

Bon Bon Guest House 77 Thanon Phayalithai ☎ 055 219058 or ☎ 081 707 7649; map p.232. The only thing approaching a genuine guesthouse in the town centre, this three-storey place is set back from the road around a small yard. The twenty rooms all have small balconies, en-suite hot showers and TVs and are kept nice and clean. Fan B350, a/c B400

Karma Home Hostel 26/54 Soi Lang Wat Mai Apaiyaram ☎ 088 814 1268, ☒ facebook.com/karmahomehostel; map p.232. Welcoming and informative hostel-cum-homestay in the centre of town, offering fan-cooled bunk beds and hammocks for chilling on the roof terrace, as well as informal cooking classes and temple tours. Dorms B200

Lithai Guest House 73/1–5 Thanon Phayalithai ☎ 055 219626–9, ☒ lithaiphs@yahoo.com; map p.232. Good but bland option, used mainly by salespeople so not especially cosy and much more of a hotel than a guesthouse. The clean, bright rooms come with hot shower, TV and either fan or a/c. Decent rates for singles. Fan B300, a/c B580

P1 House Northeast of the centre at 9/15–19 Thanon Phra Ong Dam ☎ 055 211007; map p.232. Above a retro-styled café that gives onto a garden at the back, stylish, well-maintained, good-sized rooms with a/c, hot showers, TVs and fridges. Simple breakfast included. B650

Pailyn Hotel 38 Thanon Boromtrailoknat ☎ 055 252411–5; map p.232. Central, long-running three-star tourist and business hotel that's old-fashioned and unstylish but offers good-sized a/c rooms with comfortable beds. Upper-floor rooms in the twelve-storey tower enjoy long-range river views from their balconies. Breakfast included. B850

Pattara Resort 349/40 Thanon Chaiyanupap, 2km west of the town centre ☎ 055 282966, ☒ pattararesort.com; map p.232. Situated out of town in a residential area, this rambling resort is the best place in Phitsanulok to really relax. All rooms, from the large superior rooms up to the huge villas with their own pools, are surrounded by greenery and furnished with thick-mattress beds, rain showers, DVD players and subtle lighting. There's also a large swimming pool, a spa and a good restaurant. Breakfast included. B3800

Yodia Heritage Hotel 89/1 Thanon Buddhabucha (Puttabucha), 250m north of Wat Phra Si Ratana Mahathat ☎ 055 214677, ☒ yodiaheritage.com; map p.232. This classy boutique hotel beside the river provides spacious, contemporary-styled rooms, all with a/c, wooden floors, elegantly restrained decor, bathtubs and a balcony overlooking the small garden. The on-site *Amore* restaurant enjoys river views, and there's also a swimming pool and a library. Free pick-up from the airport. Breakfast included. B2800

EATING

In the evening, **night market** stalls set up south of the night bazaar along the east bank of the river, south of Akkathasaroth Bridge. *Phat thai* and *hawy thawt* (omelette stuffed with mussels) are popular choices, but the most famous dish is "flying vegetables", in which strong-tasting morning-glory (*phak bung*) is stir-fried before being tossed flamboyantly in the air towards the plate-wielding waiter or customer. Also famous in Phit'lok are *kwaytiaw hoy kha*, or dangling leg noodles, so named for the style of eating noodles while sitting with legs dangling over the side of a raised pavilion.

Ban Mai 93/30 Thanon Wisut Kasat ☎ 055 303122; map p.232. It's worth heading east across the railway tracks to this smart restaurant in a residential lane off Thanon Wisut Kasat (opposite the *Ayara Grand Palace*). Expect white tablecloths, sturdy furnishings and attentive service, complementing classic Thai dishes, such as chicken green curry (B150). Daily 11am–10pm, last orders 8.30pm.

Coffee Mania Thanon Bhudhabucha, next to the municipal tourist office ☎ 055 251133; map p.232. This laidback café enjoys an excellent riverside location, with seating in and around an attractive traditional-style wooden building overlooking a pond. They serve delicious milky cappuccinos (B40), as well as a few snacks such as cakes and biscuits. Daily 8am–7pm.

Italy: The Restaurant Soi 7, Thanon Boromtrailoknat ☎055 219177; map p.232. Offers a huge choice of pizzas (B120–270), pastas, meat and fish dishes, plus wines, in a slightly quieter part of town, away from the worst of the traffic noise. Daily 10am–10pm.

Kwaytiaw Hoy Kha Rim Nan 100m north of Wat Mahathat ☎081 379 3172; map p.232. The noodles here are so famously tasty they've been featured on several TV channels. Choose from *phat thai*, Sukhothai noodles with red pork in a sweet and spicy broth, *tom yam* soup with noodles, or yellow noodles with pork; tofu versions are also available (B30–50). You sit on the raised floor with legs dangling (*hoy kha*) under the table. There's no English sign, but it's an open-sided pavilion with a brown awning and is always packed. Daily 9am–4pm.

Sor Lert Rot Thanon Boromtrailoknat, immediately south of the Pailyn Hotel; map p.232. It doesn't look much, but this basic, rather untidy, Thai-Chinese restaurant cooks up some of the best food in town. Try the fried chicken (B120) and the salted fish with Chinese kale (*khana pla khem*; B50). Mon–Sat 8am–9/10pm.

VG (Café Veggie) 93/2 Thanon Phayalithai ☎080 786 3405; map p.232. This chic, industrial-look café, with bare concrete walls, marble-topped tables and stylish lighting, features an appetizing menu of salads, soups and sandwiches, but, despite the name, it's far from exclusively vegetarian, and you can indulge in delicious burgers and fish and chips too (most dishes B150–200), along with delicious juices to wash it down and spectacular desserts such as french toast with ice cream and strawberries. Daily 11.30am–9pm (kitchen closes 8pm).

DRINKING

In Town (Amarin) 50–52 Thanon Phayalithai ☎096 665 5186; map p.232. Small, buzzy, open-sided bar, with bare brick walls and sports on the TV, that's something of a beer drinker's paradise – though one with deep pockets (around B200/bottle). There's a huge range of brews on offer, including Czech, German, Belgian, British, American and Japanese, with several draught beers at any one time. Daily 6pm–midnight.

DIRECTORY

Banks and ATMs There are several banks on Thanon Boromtrailoknat, and ATMs can be found here and outside most convenience stores.

Hospitals Bangkok Hospital on Thanon Phra Ong Dam (☎055 212222) is private, and Buddha Chinnarat Hospital, Thanon Sithamtraipidok (☎055 270300), is government-run.

Left luggage At the train station (daily 7am–11pm; B20–30/item).

Tourist police For all emergencies, call the tourist police

on the free 24hr phoneline ☎1155, or contact them at their booth in the southwest corner of the compound of Wat Phra Si Ratana Mahathat (their main office is in the far northern suburbs near the stadium).

Travel agent Able Tour and Travel (Mon–Fri 8.30am–5pm, Sat 8.30am–4pm; ☎055 242206, ✉ablegroup@hotmail. com), near the TAT office in Surasri Square, sells air tickets and can arrange minibuses to Sukhothai or Kamphaeng Phet (B1800 excluding petrol).

Sukhothai

For a brief but brilliant period (1238–1376), the walled city of **SUKHOTHAI** presided as the capital of Thailand, creating the legacy of a unified nation of Thai peoples and a phenomenal artistic heritage. Some of Thailand's finest buildings and sculpture were produced here, but by the sixteenth century the city had been all but abandoned to the jungle. Now an impressive assembly of elegant ruins, the Old City, 58km northwest of Phitsanulok, has been preserved as **Sukhothai Historical Park** and is one of Thailand's most visited ancient sites.

There are several accommodation options near the historical park, but travellers looking for urban comforts tend to stay in so-called **NEW SUKHOTHAI**, a modern market town 12km to the east, which has good travel links with the Old City and is also better for restaurants and long-distance bus connections. It's a small, friendly town, used to seeing tourists but by no means overrun with them. The town straddles the Yom River, which burst its banks and caused serious flooding in 2011, since when an ugly flood wall has been erected along its course through town.

Sukhothai makes a peaceful and convenient base for visiting Ramkhamhaeng National Park, as well as the ruins of Si Satchanalai and Kamphaeng Phet, which, while not as extensively renovated, are still worth visiting – if only for their relative wildness

2

and lack of visitors. Most of these outlying places can be reached fairly easily by public transport, but for trips to Wat Thawet and Ramkhamhaeng National Park you'll need to rent your own vehicle or arrange a driver through your accommodation.

The Historical Park (Muang Kao Sukhothai)

12km west of New Sukhothai ⏱ 055 697527 • Daily: central zone 6.30am–7.30pm, floodlit Sat 6.30–9pm; northern zone 7.30am–5.30pm; western zone 8am–4.30pm • B100 per zone (central, north and west), plus B10 per bicycle per zone • iPad guide rental B690/day, including admission fees and either bike hire (and bike admission fees) or tram ticket (🌐 sukhothaikingdom.com)

In its prime, the Old City boasted around forty separate temple complexes and covered an area of about seventy square kilometres between the Yom River and the low range of hills to the west. At its heart stood the walled royal city, protected by a series of moats and ramparts. **SUKHOTHAI HISTORICAL PARK**, or **Muang Kao Sukhothai**, covers all this area and is divided into five **zones**: all the most important temples lie within the central zone, with the Ramkhamhaeng Museum just outside it; the ruins outside the city walls are spread out over a sizeable area and divided into north, south, east and west zones.

With the help of UNESCO, the Thai government's Fine Arts Department has restored the most significant ruins and the result reveals the original town planners' keen aesthetic sense, especially their astute use of water to offset and reflect the solid monochrome contours of the stone temples. Although there is a touch of the too

NEW SUKHOTHAI

ACCOMMODATION	
At Home	3
Blue House & Green House	5
J&J Guest House	4
Ruean Thai Hotel	2
Sawasdipong Hotel	6
Sukhothai Heritage Resort	1
TR Guest House	7

EATING	
Baan Kru Iw	2
Dream Café	5
Hong Rama Tearoom	3
Mai Klang Kroong	1
Poo Restaurant	6
Tai Ton Krajee	4

DRINKING	
Chopper Bar	1

THE SUKHOTHAI BUDDHA

The classic Buddha images of Thailand were produced towards the end of the Sukhothai era. Ethereal, androgynous figures with ovoid faces and feline expressions, they depict not a Buddha meditating to achieve enlightenment – the more usual representation – but an already **enlightened Buddha**: the physical realization of an abstract, "unworldly" state. Though they produced mainly seated Buddhas, Sukhothai artists are renowned for having pioneered the **walking Buddha**, one of four postures described in ancient Pali texts but without precedent in Thailand.

perfectly packaged theme park about the central zone (and, in some critics' opinions, too liberal an interpretation of thirteenth-century design), it's a serene and rewarding site, with plenty to investigate should you want to look more closely. It does, however, take a determined imagination to visualize the ancient capital as it must once have looked, not least because houses and palaces would have filled the spaces between the wats – like their Khmer predecessors, the people of Sukhothai constructed their secular buildings from perishable materials such as wood, only using expensive, durable stone for their sacred structures. Private vehicles have recently been banned from the **central zone**, which covers three square kilometres: a bike is the best way to get around, or you could hire an electric tuk-tuk with driver (from B200/hour) or join one of the regular, hour-long tram tours (B60). Of the eleven ruins here, Wat Mahathat is the one that should definitely not be missed.

There's a much less formal feel to the ruins in the **outer zones**, where you're as likely to find cows trampling through the remains as tourists; with some clever planning, you could visit several lesser-known ruins without paying the zone fee. You'll need a bicycle or car to get around, but all sites are clearly signposted from the gates encircling the central zone. The **north** zone is the closest and most rewarding, followed by the **east** zone (no fee) just off the road to New Sukhothai. If you're feeling energetic, head for the **west** zone, which requires a much longer bike ride and some hill climbing. The ruins to the **south** (no fee) are rarely visited, but Wat Chetuphon and Wat Chedi Si Hong are definitely worth a look.

Brief history

Prior to the thirteenth century, the land now known as Thailand was divided into a collection of petty principalities, most of which owed their allegiance to the Khmer empire and its administrative centre Angkor (in present-day Cambodia). With the Khmers' power on the wane, two Thai generals joined forces in 1238 to oust the Khmers from the northern plains, founding the kingdom of **Sukhothai** ("Dawn of Happiness" in Pali) under the regency of one of the generals, Intradit. In short order they had extended their control over much of present-day Thailand, as well as parts of Myanmar and Laos.

King Ramkhamhaeng

The third and most important of Sukhothai's eight kings, Intradit's youngest son **Ramkhamhaeng** (r.1279–98) laid the foundations of a unique Thai identity by establishing Theravada (Hinayana) Buddhism as the common faith and introducing the forerunner of the modern Thai alphabet; of several inscriptions attributed to him, the most famous, found on what's known as Ramkhamhaeng's Stele and housed in Bangkok's National Museum (with a copy kept in Sukhothai's Ramkhamhaeng Museum), tells of a utopian land of plenty ruled by a benevolent monarch.

Ramkhamhaeng turned Sukhothai into a vibrant spiritual and commercial centre, inviting Theravada monks from Nakhon Si Thammarat and Sri Lanka to instruct his people in the religion that was to supplant Khmer Hinduism and Mahayana Buddhism, and encouraging the growth of a ceramics industry with the help of

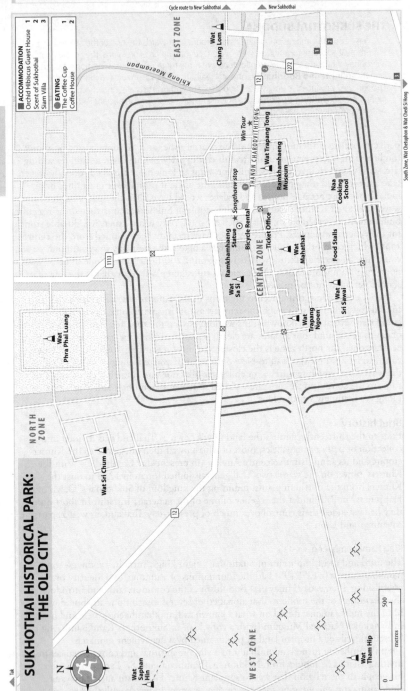

SUKHOTHAI HISTORICAL PARK:
THE OLD CITY

ACCOMMODATION
Orchid Hibiscus Guest House   1
Scent of Sukhothai   2
Siam Villa   3

EATING
The Coffee Cup   1
Coffee House   2

Cycle route to New Sukhothai   New Sukhothai

EAST ZONE

Wat Chang Lom

Khlong Maerampan

Win Tour

Wat Trapang Tong

Songthaew stop

THANON CHAROD VITHITONG

Ramkhamhaeng Museum

Ramkhamhaeng Statue

Bicycle Rental

Ticket Office

Naa Cooking School

Wat Sa Si

CENTRAL ZONE

Wat Mahathat

Food Stalls

Wat Trapang Ngoen

Wat Sri Sawai

NORTH ZONE

Wat Phra Phai Luang

Wat Sri Chum

WEST ZONE

Wat Saphan Hin

Wat Tham Hip

South Zone, Wat Chetuphon & Wat Chedi Si Hong

N

0   500
metres

Chinese potters. By all accounts, Ramkhamhaeng's successors lacked his kingly qualities, and so, by the second half of the fourteenth century, Sukhothai had become a vassal state of the newly emerged kingdom of Ayutthaya; finally, in 1438, it was forced to relinquish all vestiges of its independent identity.

Ramkhamhaeng National Museum
Just outside the main entrance to the central zone • Daily 9am–4pm • B150

The well-presented **Ramkhamhaeng National Museum** features several illuminating exhibitions and contains some of the finest **sculptures** and reliefs found at the temples of Sukhothai's Old City and nearby Si Satchanalai. Outstanding artefacts in the downstairs gallery of the main building include the fourteenth-century bronze statue of a walking Buddha, and the large Buddha head that was found at Wat Phra Phai Luang in the north zone of Sukhothai Historical Park. Also here is a useful guide to the many different **stucco motifs** that once decorated every Sukhothai-era temple, along with a copy of one of the finest local examples of stucco relief, depicting the Buddha being sheltered by a naga, whose original is still *in situ* at Si Satchanalai's Wat Chedi Jet Taew. The wide-ranging section on Ramkhamhaeng's famous **stele** features a complete translation of the inscription, plus a detailed look at the origins and evolution of the original "Tai" script. The upstairs gallery provides an informative introduction to **Sangkhalok ceramics** (see page 244).

Statue of King Ramkhamhaeng
A modern **statue** of King Ramkhamhaeng sits to the right inside the main entrance to the central zone, just beyond the ticket office. Cast in bronze, he holds a palm-leaf book in his right hand – a reference to his role as founder of the modern Thai alphabet. Close by stands a large bronze **bell**, a replica of the one referred to on the famous stele (also reproduced here), which told how the king had the bell erected in front of his palace so that any citizen with a grievance could come by and strike it, whereupon the king himself would emerge to investigate the problem.

Wat Mahathat
Central zone

Your first stop in the central zone should be Sukhothai's most important site, the enormous **Wat Mahathat** compound. It's packed with the remains of scores of monuments and surrounded, like a city within a city, by a moat. This was the spiritual focus of the city, the king's temple and symbol of his power; successive regents, eager to add their own stamp, restored and expanded it so that by the time it was abandoned in the sixteenth century it numbered ten viharns, one bot, eight mondops and nearly two hundred small chedis. Looking at the wat from ground level, it's hard to distinguish the main structures from the minor ruins. Remnants of the viharns and the bot dominate the present scene, their soldierly ranks of pillars, which formerly supported wooden roofs, directing the eye to the Buddha images seated at the far western ends.

The principal chedi complex, which houses the Buddha relic, stands grandly, if a little cramped, at the heart of the compound, built on an east–west axis in an almost continuous line with two viharns. Its elegant centrepiece follows a design termed **lotus-bud chedi** (after the bulbous finial ornamenting the top of a tower), and is classic late Sukhothai in style. This lotus-bud reference is an established religious symbol: though Sukhothai architects were the first to incorporate it into building design – since when it's come to be regarded as a hallmark of the era – the lotus bud had for centuries represented the purity of the Buddha's thoughts nudging through the muddy swamp and finally bursting into flower. The chedi stands surrounded by eight smaller towers – some with their stucco decoration partially reapplied, and some with a Buddha image in one of their four alcoves – on a square platform decorated with a procession of walking Buddha-like monks, another artistic innovation of the Sukhothai school, here

2

LOY KRATHONG

Every year on the evening of the full moon of the twelfth lunar month (usually in November), Thais all over the country celebrate the end of the rainy season with **Loy Krathong**, also known as the Festival of Light. One of Thailand's most beautiful festivals, it's held to honour and appease the spirits of the water at a time when all the fields are flooded and the canals and rivers are overflowing their banks. The festival is said to have originated seven hundred years ago, when **Nang Noppamas**, the consort of a Sukhothai king, adapted an ancient Brahmin tradition of paying homage to the water goddess.

At this time, nearly everyone makes or buys a **krathong** and sets it afloat (*loy*) on the nearest body of water, to cast adrift any bad luck that may have accrued over the past year. *Krathongs* are miniature basket-boats made of banana leaves that have been elegantly folded and pinned, origami style, and then filled with flowers, three sticks of incense and a lighted candle; the traditional base is a slice of banana tree trunk, but it's increasingly popular to buy your *krathong* ready-made from the market, sometimes with an eco-unfriendly polystyrene bottom. Some people slip locks of hair and fingernail clippings between the flowers, to represent sinful deeds that will then be symbolically released along with the *krathong*; others add a coin or two to persuade the spirits to take away their bad luck (swiftly raided by opportunist young boys looking for small change). It's traditional to make a wish or prayer as you launch your *krathong* and to watch until it disappears from view: if your candle burns strong, your wishes will be granted and you will live long.

Chiang Mai goes to town over Loy Krathong (see page Loy Krathong), but **Sukhothai Historical Park** is the most famous place in Thailand to celebrate the festival, and the ruins are the focus of a spectacular festival held over several nights around the full moon. The centrepiece is a charming *son et lumière* performance at Wat Mahathat, complemented by firework displays, the illumination of many Old City ruins, thousands of candles floating on the shimmering lotus ponds, a parade of charming Nang Noppamas (Miss Loy Krathong) lookalikes and all sorts of concerts and street-theatre shows. All accommodation gets packed out during the festival, so book ahead if possible.

depicted in stucco relief. Flanking the chedi platform are two square mondops, built for the colossal standing Buddhas still inside them today.

The grassy patch across the road to the east of Wat Mahathat was until recently thought to be the site of the royal palace, but archeologists now think it is more likely to have been located north of Wat Sa Si towards the northern gate.

Wat Sri Sawai
300m southwest of Wat Mahathat, central zone

The triple corn-cob-shaped prangs of **Wat Sri Sawai** make for an interesting architectural comparison with Wat Mahathat. Just as the lotus-bud chedi epitomizes Sukhothai aspirations, the prang represents Khmer ideals: Wat Sri Sawai was probably conceived as a Hindu shrine several centuries before the Sukhothai kingdom established itself here. The stucco reliefs decorating the prangs feature a few weatherworn figures from both Hindu and Buddhist mythology, which suggests that the shrine was later pressed into Buddhist service; the square base inside the central prang supported the Khmer Shiva lingam (phallus), while the viharn out front is a later, Buddhist, addition.

Wat Trapang Ngoen
Just west of Wat Mahathat, central zone

Wat Trapang Ngoen is distinguished by a particularly fine lotus-bud chedi. Aligned with the chedi on the symbolic east–west axis are the dilapidated viharn and, east of that, on an island in the middle of the "silver pond" after which the wat is named, the remains of the bot. Walk across the bridge to the bot to appreciate the setting from the water. North of the chedi, notice the fluid lines of the walking Buddha mounted onto a brick wall – a classic example of Sukhothai sculpture.

Wat Sa Si
North of Wat Trapang Ngoen, central zone

Entirely surrounded by water, **Wat Sa Si** commands a fine position on two connecting islands north of Wat Trapang Ngoen. The bell-shaped chedi with a tapering spire and square base shows a strong Sri Lankan influence, and the metallic replica of a freestanding walking Buddha is typical Sukhothai.

Wat Phra Phai Luang
North zone, about 500m north of the old city walls: exit the central zone north of Wat Sa Si

About 500m north of the earthen ramparts of the old city walls, a footbridge (also accessible to bicycles and motorbikes) leads you across to **Wat Phra Phai Luang**, one of the ancient city's oldest structures, surrounded by around fifty Sangkhalok pottery kilns. The three prangs, only one of which remains intact, were built by the Khmers before the Thais founded their own kingdom here, and, as at the similar Wat Sri Sawai, you can still see some of the stucco reliefs showing both Hindu and Buddhist figures. Others are displayed in Ramkhamhaeng National Museum (see page 241). It's thought that Wat Phra Phai Luang was at the centre of the old Khmer town and that it was as important then as Wat Mahathat later became to the Thais. When the shrine was converted into a Buddhist temple, the viharn and chedi were built to the east of the prangs: the reliefs of the (now headless and armless) seated Buddhas are still visible around the base of the chedi. Also discernible among the ruins are parts of a large reclining Buddha and a mondop containing four huge standing Buddhas in different postures.

Wat Sri Chum
About 750m southwest from the Wat Phra Phai Luang compound, north zone

Wat Sri Chum boasts Sukhothai's largest surviving Buddha image, the Phra Achana, which is mentioned on Ramkhamhaeng's Stele as the "statue of the Teacher". This enormous, heavily restored brick-and-stucco seated Buddha, measuring more than 11m from knee to knee and almost 15m high, peers through the slit in its custom-built mondop. Check out the elegantly tapered fingers, complete with gold-leaf nail varnish. A passageway – rarely opened up, unfortunately – runs inside the mondop wall, taking you from ground level on the left-hand side to the Buddha's eye level and then up again to the roof, affording a bird's-eye view of the image. Legend has it that this Buddha would sometimes speak to favoured worshippers, and this staircase would have enabled tricksters to climb up and hold forth, unseen; one of the kings of Sukhothai is said to have brought his troops here to spur them on to victory with encouraging words from the Buddha.

Wat Chang Lom
East zone, about 1.5km east of the main entrance

The only temple of interest in the **east zone** is canalside **Wat Chang Lom**, beside the bicycle track to New Sukhothai and just off the road to the new city. Chang Lom means "surrounded by elephants" and the main feature here is a large Sri Lankan-style, bell-shaped chedi encircled by a sculpted frieze of more than thirty elephants.

Wat Saphan Hin
West zone, almost 5km west of the Ramkhamhaeng National Museum

Be prepared for a long haul out to the **west zone**, in the forested hills off the main road to Tak. Marking the western edge of the Old City, the hilltop temple of **Wat Saphan Hin** should – with sufficiently powerful telescopic lenses – give a fantastic panorama of the Old City's layout, but with the naked eye conjures up only an indistinct vista of trees and stones. The wat's ruinous viharn is reached via a steep 300m-long pathway of stone slabs (hence the name, meaning "Stone Bridge"), which starts from a side road running south from the main Tak road. This is the easiest approach if you're on a bike, as it's completely flat; the other route, which follows a lesser, more southerly road out of the Old City's west side via Wat Tham Hip, takes you over several hills (it's not known which route was taken by King Ramkhamhaeng, who is said to have visited this temple on a white elephant on every Buddhist holy day). Inside the viharn you'll find a well-preserved, 12m standing Buddha image called Phra Attharot, which is mentioned on Ramkhamhaeng's Stele.

Wat Chetuphon and Wat Chedi Si Hong
South zone; follow Route 1272 south from just southwest of Wat Chang Lom

Surrounded by a narrow moat that is smothered with pink water lilies which open for a few hours every morning, **Wat Chetuphon**'s main feature is a headless walking Buddha framed by laterite columns of what was once the viharn. Behind it is a headless standing Buddha, and the mondop that once protected them also housed a sitting and reclining Buddha. Just opposite, **Wat Chedi Si Hong** is largely overgrown, though it's possible to make out a few stucco elephants round the base of the chedi and the crossed legs of a large Buddha image that is also framed by laterite columns.

Sangkhalok Museum
2km east of New Sukhothai on the northern bypass (Highway 101), close to the junction with Highway 12, the road to Phitsanulok • Daily 8am–5pm • B100 • Tuk-tuk ride from central New Sukhothai should cost around B100

If you have a serious interest in ceramics you'll probably enjoy the Sukhothai-era exhibits at the privately owned **Sangkhalok Museum** – ask for one of the informative museum booklets at the ticket desk to get the most out of a visit. The ground floor of the museum displays ceramic artefacts from thirteenth- to seventeenth-century Sukhothai, including **water pipes** used in the city's widely admired irrigation system, and the lotus-bud **lamps** whose gracefully shaped perforations both shield the flame and diffuse its light and are still popular in Thailand today. Some of the finest pieces are the characteristically expressive **figurines**, many of which are signed by the potter, and the **bowls**, which fall into two main types: light green celadon with incised patterns, sometimes with scalloped rims; and cream with underglazed black painting, often with floral or fish designs. This style of pottery has become known as Sangkhalok, after the prosperous city of Sawankhalok, near Si Satchanalai (see page 248), which was part of the kingdom of Sukhothai at that time. Also on show are some of the most exquisite ceramics produced in northern Thailand during the Lanna era (fourteenth to sixteenth centuries). Upstairs, the focus is on the cultural significance of certain artefacts and how they represent traditional Thai philosophy.

Wat Thawet
10km north of New Sukhothai on the west bank of the River Yom • Donation requested

Famous for its one hundred different, brightly painted, concrete statues depicting morality tales and Buddhist fables, **Wat Thawet** makes a stark contrast to the temples in the historical park. The main attraction is a **sculpture park** that was conceived by a local monk in the 1970s, with the aim of creating a "learning garden" where visitors could learn about the Buddhist ideas of hell and karmic retribution. For example, people who have spent their lives killing animals are depicted here with the head of a buffalo, pig, cock or elephant, while those who have been greedy and materialistic stand naked and undernourished, their ribs and backbones sticking out. Then there's the alcoholic who is forced to drink boiling liquids that make his concrete guts literally explode on to the ground.

Part of the appeal of Wat Thawet is that it makes a good focus for a very pleasant **bicycle trip** from Sukhothai. Peaceful minor roads follow the west bank of the winding

River Yom pretty much all the way from the main bridge in New Sukhothai to the temple, crossing two bypasses on the way and passing typical wooden houses and several banana plantations.

Ramkhamhaeng National Park

Around 30km southwest of Sukhothai • B200 • ☏ 055 910000, ⓦ nps.dnp.go.th • To get to the main park entrance from New Sukhothai, follow Highway 101 towards Kamphaeng Phet for 19km, then take side road 1319 (signed to Khao Luang) for the final 16km to park headquarters; Kamphaeng Phet-bound buses will take you to the junction, but you'll have trouble hitching to the park from here, so renting private transport is advised

The forested area immediately to the southwest of Sukhothai is protected as **Ramkhamhaeng National Park** and makes a pleasant day-trip on a motorbike. The park is home to waterfalls and herbal gardens and, if you're feeling sufficiently energetic, there's the possibility of a challenging mountain climb.

The headquarters stands at the foot of the eastern flank of the highest peak, **Khao Luang** (1185m), which can be climbed in around four hours, but only safely from November to February. Several very steep trails run up to the summit from here, but they are not very clearly marked; the first couple of kilometres are the worst, after which the incline eases up a little. From the top you should get a fine view over the Sukhothai plains. If you want to camp on the summit, simply alert the rangers at the park headquarters, and they will arrange for their colleague at the summit to rent you a tent; you need to take your own food and water. Fan-cooled **bungalows** in the area around the park headquarters can be rented for B1200–1800.

Thung Luang Pottery Village

16km south of New Sukhothai on Highway 101

En route to or from Ramkhamhaeng National Park you could make a detour to **Thung Luang Pottery Village** (signposted), where nearly every household is involved in the production of earthenware pots, vases and statuary. Their lamps and table decorations are often purchased by Thai resort hotels and used to add colour to outdoor restaurants. Once you've turned off the main road, you'll pass a line of roadside stalls, but to enter the heart of the pottery neighbourhoods continue for another kilometre or so, past a school and two temples.

ARRIVAL AND DEPARTURE SUKHOTHAI

By plane The tiny airport is about 25km north of town (halfway to Si Satchanalai) and is served by three daily Bangkok Airways' flights to and from Bangkok's Suvarnabhumi Airport (1hr 20min). Shuttle buses transfer passengers to or from New Sukhothai hotels for B180 per person, while Eddy Rent-a-car offers car rental, with or without a driver (☏ 093 131 5597, ⓦ eddy-rentacar.com). Air Asia and Nok Air offer minivan transfers to Old Sukhothai from Phitsanulok Airport (see page 234).

By bus Sukhothai has direct bus connections with many major provincial capitals and makes a good staging point between Chiang Mai and Bangkok, as well as an easy day-trip from Phitsanulok. All buses use the Sukhothai bus terminal, located about 3km west of New Sukhothai's town centre, just off the bypass (note that many buses from Chiang Mai and Tak pass the Old City en route). To get from the bus station to the New Sukhothai guesthouses, songthaews are currently charging as much as B60/person,

which is way over the odds. However, many guesthouses will pick you up for free – just ring ahead. In Old Sukhothai, Win Tour has an office on Thanon Charodvithitong (☏ 099 135 5645, ⓦ sukhothaiwintour.com) where you can catch a bus to Bangkok via Ayutthaya three times a day, or to Chiang Mai via Lampang five times a day.

Destinations Ayutthaya (over 30 daily; 5–6hr); Bangkok (over 30 daily; 6–7hr); Chiang Mai (over 20 daily; 5–6hr); Chiang Rai (3 daily; 8–9hr); Kamphaeng Phet (roughly hourly, best in the morning; 1hr–1hr 30min); Khon Kaen (9 daily; 6–7hr); Lampang (over 20 daily; 4hr); Mae Sot (roughly hourly; 2hr 30min–4hr); Nan (2 daily; 4–5hr); Phitsanulok (hourly; 1hr); Phrae (6 daily; 3–4hr); Si Satchanalai (every 30min; 1–2hr); Tak (roughly hourly; 1hr 30min).

By train and bus If you're coming from Bangkok, Chiang Mai or anywhere in between, one option is to take the train to Phitsanulok and then change onto a bus to Sukhothai.

2

CYCLING AROUND SUKHOTHAI

You can **cycle** from New Sukhothai to the historical park along a peaceful canalside track. To pick up the track, start from the bridge in New Sukhothai, cycle west along the main road towards the historical park for about 3km (beyond Sukhothai Hospital, just before the Big C hypermarket) until you reach a temple with an impressive gold-and-white-decorated gateway on the right-hand side. A narrow track between this temple and the adjacent petrol station takes you via a small bridge to a track that runs along the north bank of Khlong Maerampan, nearly all the way to the Old City. It's an easy 14km ride. Near the end you cross a major road to pick up the final stretch of track; then, after reaching the elephant statues at the ruins of Wat Chang Lom (see page 243), cross the bridge on your left to regain the main road into the historical park, about 1.5km away. **Bicycle rental** is available from a few guesthouses in New Sukhothai and in great numbers at the historical park where outlets near the songthaew stop rent them out for B30.

Alternatively, join a full-day **guided cycle tour** around the historical park (B990 including lunch) with Belgian–Thai-run Cycling Sukhothai (☎ 085 083 1864, ⍟ cycling-sukhothai.com). They also offer morning, sunset and full-day cycle tours around local villages and countryside. All trips include mountain bike and transfers, and are bookable through most guesthouses.

From Phitsanulok station, take a tuk-tuk (about B60) to the bus stop opposite Topland Plaza near Naresuan Bridge, then catch one of the hourly buses to New Sukhothai bus terminal (1hr, coming from Phitsanulok old bus station).

GETTING AROUND

By bus Many buses from the bus terminal in New Sukhothai that are heading for Chiang Mai or Tak will drop you off in the Old City.

By songthaew Large songthaews from New Sukhothai (roughly every 30min; 20min; B30; see map for location) terminate at the central zone entrance point in the Old City, beside a couple of cycle-rental outlets.

By tuk-tuk New Sukhothai guesthouses can organize a tuk-tuk to drop you in Old Sukhothai for B200.

By bicycle Cycling makes a peaceful and pleasant way to see Sukhothai and its surroundings (see page 246).

By motorbike For getting around the wider area, motorbike rental (around B250/day) is available at guesthouses or the shop underneath *Chopper Bar* on New Sukhothai's Thanon Pravetnakorn.

INFORMATION

Tourist information The TAT office is at 200 Thanon Charodvithitong in the new city (daily 8.30am–4.30pm; ☎ 055 616228, Etatsukho@tat.or.th), but you'd be better off asking for information at your guesthouse or hotel. Alternatively, friendly tour guide Naa offers free information and advice by phone or in person at her cookery school in the old city (see page 248).

Guidebook Dawn F. Rooney's lively and beautifully photographed *Ancient Sukhothai* is a great guidebook, not only to Sukhothai's Old City but also to those of Si Satchanalai and Kamphaeng Phet; you'll need to buy it before you arrive, though.

ACCOMMODATION

There's plenty of attractive accommodation in Sukhothai; just be wary of commission-hungry tuk-tuk drivers falsely claiming places are full, no good or no longer in business.

NEW SUKHOTHAI

At Home 184/1 Thanon Wichien Chamnong ☎ 055 610172; map p.238. Delightful, genuinely welcoming guesthouse that's been converted from a fifty-year-old family home to accommodate eleven large, attractive rooms. The most atmospheric are upstairs in the teak-walled, teak-floored part of the house, which is set back from the road in a garden with a large pond, where there are a few smart new a/c bungalows with DVD players too (B1100). Free bicycles. Breakfast included. Fan B700, a/c B900

Blue House & Green House 295/34 & 295/31 Soi Sri Samarang ☎ 080 506 8402, ⍟ sukhothaibluehouse. wordpress.com; map p.238. Two houses at the end of a quiet, central lane, operated by the same welcoming family. Green is a more basic wooden house, sheltering tightly packed fan dorms and private rooms with shared, cold or en-suite, hot showers. A gleaming modern villa, Blue provides tiled a/c rooms with comfortable wooden beds, TVs, fridges and en-suite hot water. Dorm B140, fan B250, a/c B600

J&J Guest House 12 Soi Wat Kuhasuwan, around 100m north of the bridge ☎ 055 620095; map p.238. Located on the west side of the River Yom, J&J offers well-designed wooden bungalows with a/c, en-suite hot-water bathrooms, TVs, balconies and pretty ceramic handbasins in the shape of blooming flowers. The rooms are set around a shady garden. B750

Ruean Thai Hotel 181/20 Soi Pracha Ruam Mit, off Thanon Charodvithitong ☎055 612444, Ⓦrueanthaihotel.com; map p.238. This idiosyncratic thirty-room hotel has been painstakingly assembled from ten century-old teak houses from the Sukhothai area. The main two-storey complex is built around a central swimming pool, its attractive facades fashioned from salvaged teak walls, windows and doors, and steeply gabled roofs; room interiors are modern, individually furnished and with good-quality contemporary bathrooms. Those with most character are the deluxe and family rooms; all rooms have a/c and fridges. There is a restaurant, free bicycle use and free transfers from the bus station. Rates include a good buffet breakfast. B1480

Sawasdipong Hotel 56/2–5 Thanon Singhawat ☎055 611567, Ⓦsawasdipong.com; map p.238. A good-value option in a central location, with fifty rooms that all have a/c, TVs, fridges and en-suite hot-water bathrooms, set back from the busy main road so it's reasonably quiet. B600

TR Guest House 27/5 Thanon Pravetnakorn ☎055 611663, Ⓦsukhothaibudgetguesthouse.com; map p.238. Large a/c doubles in a spotlessly clean concrete block, plus slightly less stylish but otherwise identical fan rooms, and a handful of spacious, wooden, fan or a/c bungalows with verandas in the back garden; all accommodation types have en-suite hot-water bathrooms. Toh and Long, the helpful and knowledgable couple who run the place, can provide you with an excellent map of the area, and can help out with travel plans. Fan B300, a/c B450

THE OLD CITY AREA

Orchid Hibiscus Guest House Just off Route 1272, about 1km southeast of the main entrance to the historical park ☎084 714 2256, Ⓦorchidhibiscus-

guesthouse.com; map p.240. Tranquil Italian–Thai-managed garden haven within easy cycling reach of the Old City. The smart rooms and bungalows are furnished with a/c, hot showers and fridges and are ranged around a pretty tropical flower garden and swimming pool. Their second branch up on the main road, Pin Pao Guest House, has a pool and a Jacuzzi and is slightly cheaper. Breakfast included. B900

Scent of Sukhothai 95/14 Moo 3, off Route 1272 ☎083 211 8898; map p.240. This new resort about 1km southeast of the Ramkhamhaeng National Museum constitutes very good value. Smart, bright, tasteful rooms with a/c, hot showers, TVs, fridges and balconies overlook a well-tended garden, a saltwater swimming pool and a Jacuzzi, and a good breakfast is included. B1250

★ **Siam Villa** Route 1272, about 1km southeast of the Ramkhamhaeng National Museum T055 019956, Ⓦsiamvillasukhothai.com; map p.240. Excellent-value choice with oodles of charm: a/c rooms with hot showers, fridges and TVs in traditional Thai-style villas with steep roofs and wood-panelled walls, set around a lotus pond in a leafy garden. Double B720

SUKHOTHAI AIRPORT

Sukhothai Heritage Resort Just outside the airport compound ☎055 647567, Ⓦsukhothaiheritage.com; map p.238. Tastefully designed four-star hotel owned by Bangkok Airways, set in lovely rural surrounds of organic rice fields (where guests can learn about rice farming), an orchid farm and lotus ponds. The hotel garden is artfully planted with shrubs and hedges and there are two pools, two restaurants and a library. Rooms are modern with verandas overlooking the pools, flatscreen TVs and DVD players. Bicycles are free for guests' use. It's about halfway between Sukhothai and Si Satchanalai, so well placed for a visit to both. Breakfast included. B2970

EATING

The local speciality is a pungent bowl of **Sukhothai noodles**: thin rice noodles served in a dark, slightly sweet broth flavoured with soy sauce, coriander and chilli and spiked with chunks of pork crackling, green beans and peanuts. In New Sukhothai, as well as at the places noted below, you can find them at the **hot-food stalls** and streetside tables that set up every evening in front of Wat Ratchathani on Thanon Charodvithitong. There's also a permanent covered area for night-market-style **restaurants** on the soi between Thanon Ramkhamhaeng and Thanon Nikhon Kasem. In the Old City, there is a string of restaurants serving hot food and fresh coffee on the main street just east of the central zone entrance. On Saturday evenings, there are "**walking street**" markets selling food and crafts on the main street to the east of the central zone in the Old City (Dec–Feb weekly, March–Nov fortnightly),

and on Thanon Nikhon Kasem just south of the bridge in New Sukhothai.

NEW SUKHOTHAI

Baan Kru Iw 203/25 Thanon Wichien Chamnong, corner of Soi Mahasaranon 1, about 75m north of At Home guesthouse; map p.238. This award-winning, folksy lunch spot is famous locally for its duck noodles (B45), its aromatic parcels of *phat thai* wrapped in thin omelette, *khanom jiin nam yaa* (rice noodles with fish curry) – and Sukhothai noodles. Watch the white-capped cooks in their open-plan kitchens. Daily 9am–3.30pm.

★ **Dream Café** 86/1 Thanon Singhawat ☎094 626 1065; map p.238. Dark and cosy, with wood-panelled walls and windowsills full of curios and Thai antiques, this long-running Sukhothai institution serves great food (main

2

dishes around B150–200) and is very popular. Highlights include delicious green curry, tom yam with pork spare ribs and young tamarind leaves, fiery wing-bean salad, and deep-fried banana-flower fritters. Daily 5–11pm.

Hong Rama Tearoom Nakorn de Sukhothai, 35/1 Thanon Prasertpong ☎ 055 611833; map p.238. On the ground floor of a boutique hotel, this welcoming restaurant is right opposite the covered night market, yet still tempts plenty of diners in with its smart design and eager-to-please staff. Mostly Thai cuisine (mostly B80–150), but several Western dishes too such as pizza and spaghetti carbonara (B100), plus beer served in chilled glasses, espresso coffees, teas and smoothies. Daily 7.30am–9pm.

Mai Klang Kroong 139 Thanon Charodvithitong ☎ 055 621882; map p.238. No Roman-script sign but look out for the shopfront festooned with ferns. This is a great place to sample Sukhothai noodles (B35) and other local specialities from the short menu (in English), and soak up the mood of a bygone era. Staff wear traditional dress and there's also a small gift shop selling traditional clothing. Daily roughly 8am–3pm.

Poo Restaurant 24/3 Thanon Charodvithitong; map p.238. Friendly streetside travellers' bar-restaurant that serves all the standard Thai dishes (around B100) and a few simple Western dishes, plus cheap draught Chang beer and lots of bottled Belgian beer. Daily 9am–10pm.

Tai Ton Krajee Thanon Charodvithitong, about 500m west of the bridge on the south side of the road; map p.238. This basic restaurant in an ancient one-storey wooden building is one of the best places to try the very more-ish Sukhothai noodle soup (B30). English menu but no English sign. Daily 8/9am–4pm.

THE OLD CITY AREA

The Coffee Cup Thanon Charodvithitong, opposite the museum ☎ 098 347 5496; map p.240. At this clean and airy café, the menu of Thai, Western and fusion dishes is huge (with photos to help), including bagels, baguettes, massaman chicken curry (B100), espresso coffees and delicious fruit shakes. Daily 7am–10pm.

Coffee House Sinvana Resort, Thanon Charodvithitong, corner of Route 1272; map p.240. Congenial restaurant with a/c or veranda tables, serving tasty basics like phat thai (from B50) and more interesting dishes such as kaeng som with acacia-shoot omelette and shrimp (B100), as well as espresso coffees, ice cream and other desserts. Daily 8am–9pm.

DRINKING

NEW SUKHOTHAI

Chopper Bar 95/1–2 Thanon Pravetnakorn ☎ 055 611190; map p.238. This popular balcony bar with cheap beer and an extensive menu of Thai dishes (mostly B90–120) is a great place to meet other travellers or just watch the world go by. Daily 3pm–midnight.

DIRECTORY

Banks, exchange and ATMs In the Old City, there are several ATMs on the approach road to the historical park, and the Government Savings Bank dispatches an a/c minibus to a spot opposite the museum entrance to act as a currency exchange booth (Mon–Wed, Sat & Sun 10am–3pm; ☎ 055 610081). New Sukhothai has many banks and ATMs.

Cookery courses One- and two-day courses led by excellent tour guide Naa at her cooking school in the Old City (423/6 Moo 3, 300m south of the museum; ☎ 089 858 9864, ✉ ninetynine_gh@yahoo.com; B800/person for 1 day, B1500 for 2 days). Accommodation is available for those on two-day courses (B400/night with a/c and hot shower).

Guides Khun Tan, the former owner of Lotus Village Guesthouse who speaks excellent English and French

(☎ 081 533 6288, ✉ lotus.village@ymail.com), offers guiding services to Sukhothai and Si Satchanalai by appointment, as does Khun Naa when she's not busy at her cooking school.

Hospital The government-run Sukhothai Hospital (☎ 055 610903) is about 2km west of New Sukhothai on the road to Sukhothai Historical Park.

Post office Thanon Nikhon Kasem, about 1km south of the bridge in New Sukhothai (Mon–Fri 8.30am–4.30pm).

Tourist police For all emergencies, call the tourist police on ☎ 1155, or go to the local police station on Thanon Si Intharadit (the continuation southwards of Thanon Singhawat) or the more central police box on Thanon Wichien Chamnong in New Sukhothai.

Si Satchanalai

In the mid-thirteenth century, Sukhothai cemented its power by establishing several satellite towns, of which the most important was **SI SATCHANALAI**, 57km upriver from Sukhothai on the banks of the Yom. Now a UNESCO-listed **historical park**, the partially restored ruins of **Muang Kao Si Satchanalai** have a quieter ambience than the grander models at Sukhothai Historical Park, and the additional attractions of the

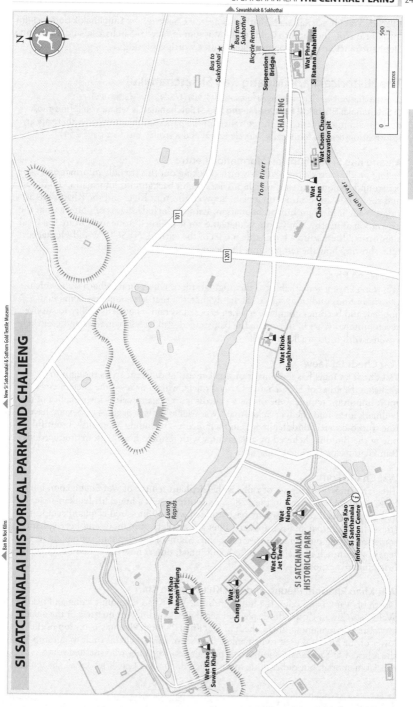

SI SATCHANALAI HISTORICAL PARK AND CHALIENG

N

Sawankhalok & Sukhothai

Ban Ko Noi Kilns

New Si Satchanalai & Sathorn Gold Textile Museum

Bus to Sukhothai

Bus from Sukhothai

Bicycle Rental

Suspension Bridge

CHALIENG

Wat Phra Si Ratana Mahathat

Wat Chom Chuen excavation pit

Wat Chao Chan

Yom River

Yom River

101

1201

Wat Khok Singkharam

Luang Rapids

Wat Khao Phanom Pleung

Wat Chang Lom

Wat Chedi Jet Taew

Wat Nang Phya

Wat Khao Suwan Khiri

SI SATCHANALAI HISTORICAL PARK

Muang Kao Si Satchanalai Information Centre

0   500
metres

2

riverside **Wat Phra Si Ratana Mahathat** in nearby Chalieng, the **Sangkhalok pottery kilns** in Ban Ko Noi, the **Sathorn Gold Textile Museum** in New Si Satchanalai and **Boon Lott's Elephant Sanctuary** combine to make the area worth exploring.

The Historical Park (Muang Kao Si Satchanalai)

South bank of the Yom River, 11km south of New Si Satchanalai ☎ 055 950714 · Daily 8.30am–4.30pm · B100

Si Satchanalai Historical Park, or **Muang Kao Si Satchanalai**, is where you'll find most of the main monuments. At the entrance on the park's southeastern side, there are an information centre, food stalls, bicycle rental and a trolley bus (see page 254).

Muang Kao Si Satchanalai Information Centre

Before heading inside the park it's worth checking out this friendly information centre, set around tranquil gardens, which provides useful background information on the area and shows how its location, on a plain between the Yom River and the Khao Phra Sri ridge, made it ideal for human habitation. Exhibits include shards of pottery from the excavation at nearby Wat Chom Chuen and some polished stone tools from Tha Chai subdistrict. There's also a large-scale model of the entire UNESCO World Heritage Site, showing how the temples hug the bend in the river.

Wat Nang Phya

Wat Nang Phya is remarkable for the original stucco reliefs on its viharn wall, which remain in fine condition; stucco is a hardy material that sets soon after being first applied, and becomes even harder when exposed to rain – hence its ability to survive seven hundred years in the open. The balustraded wall has slit windows and is entirely covered with intricate floral motifs.

Wat Chedi Jet Taew

Wat Chedi Jet Taew has seven rows of small chedis of different styles thought to enshrine the ashes of Si Satchanalai's royal rulers, which makes it the ancient city's most important temple. One of the 34 chedis is an elegant scaled-down replica of the hallmark lotus-bud chedi at Sukhothai's Wat Mahathat (see page 241). Several have fine stucco-covered Buddha images in their alcoves, including a famously beautiful one of the Buddha sheltered by a naga (now with restored head), also reproduced in Ramkhamhaeng National Museum.

Wat Chang Lom

The park's most striking set of ruins is the elephant temple of **Wat Chang Lom**, built by King Ramkhamhaeng in the 1280s. Its centrepiece is a huge, Sri Lankan-style, bell-shaped chedi set on a square base studded with 39 life-sized elephant sculptures (those in Sukhothai and Kamphaeng Phet are smaller). A mahout and his elephant sometimes hang out here to prove the point. Many of the elephant statues are in good repair, with much of their stucco flesh still intact; others now have their bulky laterite-brick innards exposed.

Wat Khao Phanom Pleung and Wat Khao Suwan Khiri

North of Wat Chang Lom, the hilltop ruins of Wat Khao Phanom Pleung and nearby Wat Khao Suwan Khiri afford splendid aerial views of different quarters of the ancient city. The sole remaining intact chedi of **Wat Khao Phanom Pleung** sits on top of the lower of the hills and used to be flanked by a set of smaller chedis built to entomb the ashes of Si Satchanalai's important personages – the ones who merited some special memorial, but didn't quite make the grade for Wat Chedi Jet Taew. The temple

presumably got its name, which means "mountain of sacred fire", from the cremation rituals held on the summit.

Wat Khao Suwan Khiri's huge chedi, which graces the summit 200m northwest, has definitely seen better days, but the views from its platform – south over the main temple ruins and north towards the city walls and entrance gates – are worth the climb.

Wat Phra Si Ratana Mahathat

Just over 2km east of the Historical Park • B20

Before Sukhothai asserted control of the region and founded Si Satchanalai, the Khmers governed the area known as **Chalieng**, which is cradled in a tight bend in the Yom River. Just about all that now remains of Chalieng is **Wat Phra Si Ratana Mahathat** (known locally as Wat Phra Prang), whose compound, aligned east–west and encircled by a now sunken wall of pock-marked laterite blocks, contains structures thought to date back to the early thirteenth century, in the Khmer era, but with later additions by Sukhothai and Ayutthayan builders.

If you approach from the wooden suspension bridge, you'll pass some simple food and coffee stalls and enter the ancient temple via its semi-submerged eastern gateway, passing beneath a hefty Khmer-style lintel carved with both Buddhist and Hindu images. Inside, the compound is dominated by a towering corncob prang, the main shrine, which was likely remodelled during the Ayutthayan era and whose exterior has been renovated with all-over stucco decorations. The ruined viharn in front of the prang enshrines a large seated Buddha sculpted in typical Sukhothai style, with hand gestures symbolizing his triumph over temptation. The gracefully curving stucco of a walking Buddha in high relief to the left is also classic Sukhothai and is regarded as one of the finest of its genre. Immediately to the west of the prang, the remains of the octagonal laterite platform and its bell-shaped chedi are believed to date from a different era, possibly considerably earlier. A mondop built around a large standing Buddha guards one side and looks north; beyond lies another viharn, containing two seated Buddha images.

Ban Ko Noi kilns

Endowed with high-quality clay, the area around Si Satchanalai – known as Sawankhalok or Sangkhalok during the Ayutthaya period – commanded an international reputation as a ceramics centre from the mid-fourteenth to the end of the fifteenth century, producing pieces still rated among the finest in the world. Several of Thailand's major museums feature collections of ceramics from both Si Satchanalai and Sukhothai under the umbrella label of Sangkhalok, and there's a dedicated collection of Sangkhalok wares just outside New Sukhothai (see below). More than two hundred **kilns** have been unearthed in and around Si Satchanalai to date, and it's estimated that there could once have been a thousand in all. One of the main groups of kilns is in the village of **BAN KO NOI**, which is about 5km upstream from Si Satchanalai Historical Park and can be reached by bicycle by following the very pleasant, almost traffic-free road up the west bank of the Yom River through hamlets fringed with flowering shrubs and fruit trees.

Centre for the Study and Preservation of Sangkhalok Kiln

Daily 8.30am–4.30pm • B100 • ☏ 055 259414

Two groups of excavated kilns, about 800m apart along the river road at Ban Ko Noi, have been roofed and jointly turned into the **Centre for the Study and Preservation of Sangkhalok Kiln**. The first site you'll reach shelters four kilns and is often referred to as **Kiln 61** after the most important of the four, which still contains broken vases of all sizes in situ. Two of the kilns here are up-draught kilns and two, including #61, are cross-draught kilns, the latter generating a greater and more consistent heat, which enabled the production of glazed ware. Most Sangkhalok ceramics were glazed – the grey-green celadon, probably introduced by immigrant Chinese potters, was especially popular – and typically decorated with fish or chrysanthemum motifs. A small display of **Sangkhalok ceramics** gives a hint of the pieces that were fired here: domestic items such as pots, decorated plates and lidded boxes; decorative items like figurines, temple sculptures and temple roof tiles; and items for export, particularly to Indonesia and the Philippines, where huge Sangkhalok storage jars were used as burial urns. Across the road from Kiln 61, shops sell reproduction ceramics and "antiques".

Sitting pretty among trees on the west bank of the River Yom, the centre's other site contains two much bigger kilns. Of these, the more important is **Kiln 42**, which actually consists of nine layers of kilns built on top of one another to a depth of seven metres. There are only a smattering of exhibits at this second site, but it does have very informative display boards about all aspects of Sangkhalok ware. Kiln 42 sits at the junction of the river road with Route 1201, which after 5km will bring you across the Yom into New Si Satchanalai.

Sathorn Gold Textile Museum

11km north of the Historical Park, at the northern end of the modern town of Si Satchanalai, on the east side of Highway 101 ☎ 055 671143, ⓦ sathorngoldtextilemuseum.com • Daily 8.30am–5.30pm • Free • Any Sukhothai guesthouse can include a visit to the museum in a Si Satchanalai day-trip, or you can come here on the bus from New Sukhothai, getting off in modern Si Satchanalai rather than at the ruins

The **Sathorn Gold Textile Museum** houses the private collection of Khun Sathorn, who also runs the adjacent textile shop, which now sits in a small complex of cafés, jewellery and souvenir shops; he or his staff open up the one-room exhibition for anyone who shows an interest.

Most of the **textiles** on show come from the nearby village of Hat Siew, whose weavers, descendants of Thai Puan migrants from Laos, specialize in the art of *teen jok*, or hem embroidery, whereby the bottom panel of the sarong or *phasin* (woman's sarong) is decorated with a band of supplementary weft, usually done in exquisitely intricate patterns. Some of the textiles here are almost a hundred years old and many of the *teen jok* **motifs** have symbolic meaning showing what the cloths would have been used for – a sarong or *phasin* used for a marriage ceremony, for example, tends to have a double image, such as two birds facing each other. Elephants also feature quite a lot in Hat Siew weaving, probably a reference to the village custom in which young men who are about to become monks parade on elephants to their ordination ceremony. The tradition continues to this day and elephant parades are held at the mass ordination ceremony every year on April 7 and 8. Modern Hat Siew textiles are sold at the adjacent Sathorn **shop** and at other outlets further south along the main road.

Boon Lott's Elephant Sanctuary (BLES)

304 Moo 5, Ban Na Ton Jan, Tambon Ban Tuek (about 30km northeast of Si Satchanalai, on the way to Uttaradit; arrange pick-up at Sukhothai Airport or Uttaradit) • B6000/person/night (advance booking necessary) • ⓦ blesele.org

Named after a baby elephant that succumbed to various injuries, **Boon Lott's Elephant Sanctuary (BLES)** was started by Katherine Connor in 2004 and is now one of the most popular sanctuaries in the country, home to around twenty elephants that have been saved from abuse and sickness. The sanctuary is only open to guests staying overnight; accommodation consists of three teak cottages and prices are inclusive of all meals. Guests are involved in every aspect of caring for the elephants, from collecting food for them to repairing elephant pens and bathing the pachyderms. Typically people stay around three to five days, but at the time of writing it was fully booked six months ahead, so this is one experience that needs some advance planning.

2

ARRIVAL AND DEPARTURE

SI SATCHANALAI

A visit to Si Satchanalai Historical Park works best as a day-trip from Sukhothai (60km away). The easiest option is to travel with a **car** or **motorbike** from New Sukhothai, or join a **tour** from there, which can be organized through many of the guesthouses.

By bus The fastest way to get here by public transport from Sukhothai is on one of the a/c buses bound for Chiang Rai from the New Sukhothai bus station (3 daily); there's a convenient departure at 9am, which will get you to Si Satchanalai in just over an hour. Local buses towards

Uttaradit depart about every half-hour (also from the bus station), but take around two hours to reach Si Satchanalai and sometimes require a change of bus in Sawankhalok. All buses drop passengers on Highway 101 at the signpost for Wat Phra Si Ratana Mahathat, beside a pink archway gate. Pass through it, follow the narrow road and cross the suspension bridge to the temple, from where it's a further 2km west to Si Satchanalai Historical Park. Heading back, the last bus to New Sukhothai passes Old Si Satchanalai at about 4pm.

GETTING AROUND

By bicycle If arriving by bus, the best place to rent a bike (B30) is the shop at the end of the suspension bridge, close to Wat Phra Si Ratana Mahathat. Bikes are also available for rent for the same price at the entrance to the historical park by the information centre.

By trolley bus Cars are no longer admitted to the historical park, so if you don't fancy walking or cycling, you'll need to hire an open-sided trolley bus to take you around (B300; duration flexible).

Kamphaeng Phet

KAMPHAENG PHET, 77km south of Sukhothai, was probably founded in the fourteenth century by the kings of Sukhothai as a buffer city between their capital and the increasingly powerful city-state of Ayutthaya. Strategically sited 100m from the east bank of the Ping, the ruined old city has, like Sukhothai and Si Satchanalai before it, been partly restored and opened to the public as a **historical park** and is similarly listed as a UNESCO World Heritage Site. The least visited of the three, it rivals both Sukhothai and Si Satchanalai for your attention mainly because of the untamed tree-shaded setting and the gracefully weathered statues of its main temple.

A new city has grown up over and around the old. Municipal and provincial edifices dot the area within the old city walls, while the commercial centre now lies to the southeast, the usual commercial blandness offset by a riverside park, plentiful flowers and an unusual number of historic wooden houses dotted along the main thoroughfares. You can even swim off an island in the middle of the river, accessible via a footbridge near Soi 21, a few hundred metres south of the night market.

Kamphaeng Phet National Museum

Thanon Pin Damri • Wed–Sun 9am–4pm • B100

Kamphaeng Phet National Museum takes a look at the fascinating development of the ancient city. The prize exhibit in its upstairs sculpture gallery is the bronze standing **Shiva**: cast in the sixteenth century in Khmer-Ayutthayan style, the statue has had a chequered history – including decapitation by a nineteenth-century German admirer. Also on this floor is an unusual wooden, seventeenth- or eighteenth-century Ayutthayan-style standing Buddha, whose diadem, necklace and even hems are finely carved.

Kamphaeng Phet Ruan Thai Provincial Museum

Thanon Pin Damri ☎ 055 722342 • Daily 9am–4.30pm • B100

While you're at the National Museum, you can't miss the alluring group of traditional-style, stilted teak buildings in the adjacent landscaped compound – nor the barking of its resident dogs. This is the **Kamphaeng Phet Ruan Thai Provincial Museum**, whose exhibits and scale models introduce the history, traditions and contemporary culture of Kamphaeng Phet province.

Historical Park (Muang Kao Kamphaeng Phet)

Daily 6am–6pm • B150 for both main zones or B100 for one zone; vehicle entry for the arunyik zone B10–50 • Bicycle rental B30

Ruins surround modern Kamphaeng Phet on all sides, but the **Historical Park** – or **Muang Kao Kamphaeng Phet** – takes in the two most interesting areas: the zone around the two main temples, Wat Phra Kaeo and Wat Phra That, inside the old city walls,

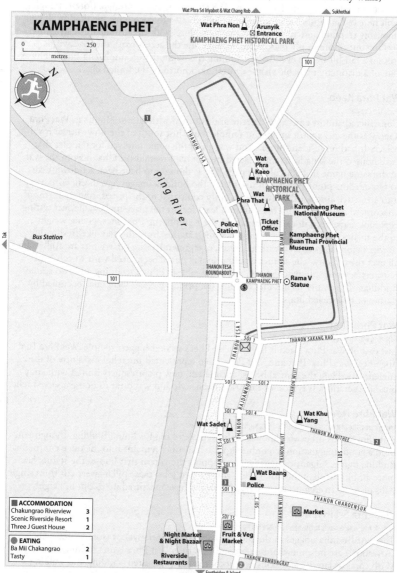

KAMPHAENG PHET

0   250
metres

Wat Phra Sri Iriyabot & Wat Chang Rob   Sukhothai

Wat Phra Non
Arunyik
Entrance
KAMPHAENG PHET HISTORICAL PARK

101

Ping River

Tak

Bus Station

THANON TESA 2

1

Wat Phra Kaeo
KAMPHAENG PHET HISTORICAL PARK
Wat Phra That
Kamphaeng Phet National Museum

Police Station
Ticket Office
Kamphaeng Phet Ruan Thai Provincial Museum

THANON PIN DAMRI

THANON TESA ROUNDABOUT
101
THANON KAMPHAENG PHET
Rama V Statue

THANON TESA 1
SOI 1
THANON SAKANG RAO

SOI 5   SOI 2
RADAMDOEN
THANON WIJIT

SOI 4
SOI 5
Wat Khu Yang
THANON RAJWITHEE
2

Wat Sadet
THANON TESA
SOI 9
THANON WIN MUANG
THANON WIJIT
SOI 1

SOI 11
1
SOI 5

3
SOI 13
Wat Baang
Police
SOI 2
THANON WIJIT
Market
THANON CHAROENSUK

ACCOMMODATION
Chakungrao Riverview   3
Scenic Riverside Resort   1
Three J Guest House   2

EATING
Ba Mii Chakangrao   2
Tasty   1

SOI 15
Night Market & Night Bazaar
Fruit & Veg Market
Riverside Restaurants
THANON BUMRUNGRAT

Footbridge & Island

2

and the forested ("*arunyik*") area just north of that. A tour of both areas involves a 5km round-trip, so you'll need transport; a bicycle is the best option. Parts of the **city walls** that gave Kamphaeng Phet its name ("Diamond Walls") are still in good condition, though Highway 101 to Sukhothai now cuts through the enclosed area and a few shops have sprung up along the roadside, making it hard to visualize the fortifications as a whole. The ruins that dot the landscape across the Ping River, west of the Thanon Tesa roundabout, belong to the even older city of Nakhon Chum, but are very dilapidated.

The two dozen or so ruins in the forested area north of the city walls – head north for 100m along Highway 101 from behind Wat Phra Kaeo, cross the moat and turn up a road to the left – are all that remains of Kamphaeng Phet's **arunyik** (forest) temples, built here by Sukhothai-era monks in a wooded area to encourage meditation. It's an enjoyably tranquil and atmospheric area to explore, with the tumbledown structures peeking out of the thinly planted groves that line the access road; the road winds around a fair bit before eventually rejoining the Sukhothai–Kamphaeng Phet highway (site of a distinctly missable visitor centre) 3km north of the walled city.

Wat Phra Kaeo
Inside the city walls

Constructed almost entirely of laterite and adorned with laterite Buddhas, **Wat Phra Kaeo** was the city's most important temple, built just south of the now-ruined royal palace. It had no resident monks and was given the name reserved for temples that have housed the kingdom's most sacred image: the Emerald Buddha, now in the wat of the same name in Bangkok (see page 85), is thought to have been set down here to rest at some point. Seven centuries later, the Buddha images have been worn away into attractive abstract shadows, often aptly compared to the pitted, spidery forms of Giacometti sculptures, and the tranquil, leafy feel to the place makes a perfect setting. Few tools have been unearthed at any of the Kamphaeng Phet sites, giving weight to the theory that the sculptors moulded their statues from the clay-like freshly dug laterite before leaving it to harden. Small, overgrown laterite quarry pits are still visible all over the old city. The statues would originally have been faced with stucco, and restorers have already patched up the central tableau of one reclining and two seated Buddhas. The empty niches that encircle the principal chedi were once occupied by statues of bejewelled lions.

Wat Phra That
Adjoining Wat Phra Kaeo, inside the city walls

Just east of Wat Phra Kaeo is Kamphaeng Phet's second-biggest temple, **Wat Phra That**. Together, Wat Phra That and Wat Phra Kaeo represented the religious centre of the ancient city. Here the central bell-shaped chedi, now picturesquely dotted with stray bits of vegetation, is typical of the Sri Lankan style and was built to house a sacred relic.

Wat Phra Non
Arunyik area: the first temple on the left once through the entrance

Wat Phra Non is otherwise known as the Temple of the Reclining Buddha, though you need a good imagination to conjure up the indistinct remains into the once enormous Buddha figure. Gigantic laterite pillars support the viharn that houses the statue; far more ambitious than the usual brick-constructed jobs, these pillars were cut from single slabs of stone from a nearby quarry and would have measured up to 8m in height.

Wat Phra Sri Iriyabot
Arunyik area: immediately to the north of Wat Phra Non

The four Buddha images in the mondop of **Wat Phra Sri Iriyabot** (sometimes spelt "Ariyabot") are in somewhat better condition than Wat Phra Non's reclining Buddha. With cores of laterite and skins of stucco, the partly restored standing and walking images tower over the viharn, while the seated (south-facing) and reclining (north-facing) Buddhas have been eroded into indistinct blobs. The full-grown trees rooted firmly in the raised floor are evidence of just how old the place is.

Wat Chang Rob

Arunyik area: 1km northwest of the entrance gate • Follow the road around the bend from Wat Phra Sri Iriyabot

Wat Chang Rob is crouched on top of a laterite hill. Built to the same Sri Lankan model as its sister temples with a similar name in Sukhothai and Si Satchanalai (Wat Chang Lom; see pages 243 and 250 respectively), this "temple surrounded by elephants" retains only the square base of its central bell-shaped chedi. Climb one of its four steep staircases for a view out over the mountains in the west, or just for a different perspective of the 68 elephant buttresses that encircle the base. Sculpted from laterite and stucco, they're dressed in the ceremonial garb fit for such revered animals; floral reliefs can just be made out along the surfaces between neighbouring elephants – the lower level was once decorated with a stucco frieze of flying birds.

ARRIVAL AND DEPARTURE

KAMPHAENG PHET

Most people visit Kampheng Phet as a **day-trip** from Sukhothai, either on one of the direct buses or by arranging a car and driver through their guesthouse – though there are buses here from other towns, too.

By bus Arriving by bus from Sukhothai or Phitsanulok, you'll enter Kamphaeng Phet from the east and should get off either inside the old city walls or at the Thanon Tesa roundabout rather than wait to be deposited across the river

at the terminal, 1km west of the river on Highway 101. From the bus station, you'll need to hop on a motorbike taxi (B50) to get to the town centre.

Destinations Bangkok (hourly; 6–7hr); Chiang Mai (hourly; 6hr); Kanchanaburi (3 daily; 6hr); Mae Sot (8 daily; 2hr 30min); Phitsanulok (roughly hourly; 2–3hr); Sukhothai (roughly hourly; 1hr–1hr 30min); Tak (hourly; 1hr).

GETTING AROUND

By bicycle or motorbike Bicycles are available for rent (B30–50/day) at the entrance to both sections of the historical park, and at all the hotels we list below. *Three J* is

the only place that rents out motorbikes (B200/day) – not very convenient for day-trippers, however.

ACCOMMODATION

Chakungrao Riverview 149 Thanon Tesa 1 ☏055 714900–4, ⓦchakungraoriverview.com; map p.255. The best hotel in central Kamphaeng Phet, recently tastefully renovated, where large rooms all have polished wooden floors, balconies, a/c, TVs and en-suite hot showers. Those out front have river views, and those out back look over a temple. Staff are very helpful and breakfast is included. B1000

Scenic Riverside Resort 325/16 Thanon Tesa 2 ☏055 722009, ⓦscenicriversideresort.com; map p.255. At this quirky, kitsch resort on the banks of the Ping, nearly all of the accommodation is in large, gleaming-white, a/c cottages that wouldn't look out of place on a Greek island. All have spacious bathrooms with hot showers

and bathtubs, TVs with karaoke players and rooftop decks with barbecues, and there's a swimming pool. Breakfast included. B1500

Three J Guest House 79 Thanon Rajwithee, 600m east of the main drag ☏081 887 4189, ⓦthreejguesthouse. com; map p.255. The most traveller-oriented place in Kamphaeng Phet, this pleasant, secluded homestay with a dozen comfortable bungalows is built from rough-cut logs and set in a Chinese-style rock garden at the back of a family home. All rooms have cosy verandas; the cheapest options share bathrooms and the priciest have a/c, and there are family rooms sleeping four people (B800). There's bicycle and motorbike rental (B50/B200 per day), and the owners offer tours to nearby waterfalls and lakes. Fan B300, a/c B400

EATING

From late afternoon the **night market** is the most enjoyable place to eat. Occupying a covered area in the southern part of the new town between the river and Thanon Tesa 1, it offers a mouthwateringly wide selection of specialist sweet and savoury stalls, including *ba mii cha kang rao* (see below).

Ba Mii Chakangrao Thanon Rajdamnoen, at the corner of Soi 9; map p.255. This basic streetside restaurant (look for the green signs) is one of the best places to try Kamphaeng Phet's signature dish, *ba mii cha kang rao*, freshly made egg noodles with cowpeas and pork (B30), which can be eaten here with pork satay. Daily 9am–3pm, sometimes earlier if the food runs out.

Tasty 115–119 Thanon Tesa 1 ☎055 712594; map p.255. If you'd rather eat in smart a/c comfort than in the night market, head for this cosy spot, where prices are only marginally higher, with one-dish noodles and rice meals such as khao phat kunchiang (fried rice with sweet Chinese sausage) starting at B45. The Thai and a few Western dishes are well prepared and presented, and they also serve espresso coffees, cakes and a few imported beers. Daily 10.30am–10.30pm.

Mae Sot and the border

Located just 6km from Myanmar, and 100km west of Tak, **MAE SOT** is very much a border town, populated by a rich ethnic mix of Burmese, Karen, Hmong and Thai. It is dependent on its thriving trade in Burmese gems and teak as well as, reportedly, on an even more lucrative cross-border black market in drugs, labourers and sex workers. For the casual visitor, however, it's a relaxed place to hang out, with several good restaurants to enjoy, although there are no unmissable sights. The short ride to the border market provides additional, if low-key, interest, and there are several caves and waterfalls within day-tripping distance.

For many people, Mae Sot is just an overnight stop on the way to **Umphang** (see page 263), a remote village 164km further south. Since the road to Umphang is full of twists and bends and the journey takes at least four hours, it is advisable to set out in the morning, either in a bumpy songthaew or with your own wheels.

In Mae Sot the Burmese influence is palpable in everything from food to fashions; many of the guesthouses are run by Burmese staff, who often speak good English, and the only real sights in the town are its handful of glittering Burmese-style temples.

Rim Moei market

Frequent songthaews (B25) ferry Thai traders and a meagre trickle of tourists the 6km from the market in Mae Sot (Thanon Banthung), via the bus station, to the border at **RIM MOEI**, where a market has grown up beside the banks of the Moei River. It's a

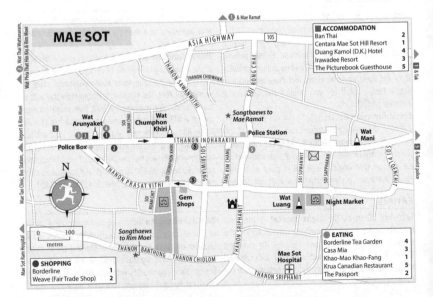

MAE SOT

ASIA HIGHWAY

ACCOMMODATION
Ban Thai	2
Centara Mae Sot Hill Resort	1
Duang Kamol (D.K.) Hotel	4
Irawadee Resort	3
The Picturebook Guesthouse	5

SHOPPING
Borderline	1
Weave (Fair Trade Shop)	2

EATING
Borderline Tea Garden	4
Casa Mia	3
Khao-Mao Khao-Fang	1
Krua Canadian Restaurant	5
The Passport	2

HELPING MAE SOT'S BURMESE REFUGEES

There are currently five camps for **refugees** from Myanmar along the border to the north and south of Mae Sot, and Mae Sot itself was the headquarters for dozens of related international **aid projects**, though many have now relocated to Yangon. Most of these organizations welcome donations and some are happy to receive visitors and even short-term volunteers; ask at *Ban Thai* guesthouse, Borderline shop and *Krua Canadian* restaurant. One of the most famous organizations in Mae Sot is the **Mae Tao Clinic** (maetaoclinic.org), which provides free medical care for around 110,000 Burmese migrants and refugees a year, focusing on those who fall outside the remit of the camps and cannot use the Thai health system. It also trains Burmese medical workers and runs a child protection programme, encompassing a primary and secondary school, a boarding house and a children's home. The clinic was founded in 1989 by a Karen refugee, Dr Cynthia, who has won several prestigious international awards for her work. The clinic is in urgent need of donations and welcomes volunteer health-workers who can commit for several months – see their website on how to donate and how to apply for a placement.

bit tacky, and not as fun to browse as Mae Sot's markets, but in amongst the electrical goods, clothes and teak furniture, it's not a bad place to pick up Burmese **handicrafts**, particularly wooden artefacts such as boxes and picture frames, woven Karen shoulder-bags and checked *longyi*.

Wat Thai Wattanaram and Wat Phra That Doi Hin Kiu

Both temples are located on a turn to the north off the Asian Highway, about 500m east of the Friendship Bridge in Rim Moei: Wat Thai Wattanaram is just 100m up this road, so walkable; Wat Phra That Doi Hin Kiu, for which you'll need your own transport, is 7km further north on the same road – take the right fork at a police checkpoint along this road and look for the temple on the hill to the right (no English sign)

If you're heading out to the Rim Moei market, it's worth taking a look at nearby **Wat Thai Wattanaram**, a Shan temple built in 1857. The main attractions here are a 45m reclining Buddha with bright red lips that's protected by an open-sided shelter, and a cloister of 28 sitting Buddha images just beyond this. There's also a large replica of the Shwedagon Pagoda in Yangon, while the viharn has a display of Shan musical instruments on the second floor. If you're not heading into Myanmar where you can visit the Kyaiktiyo Pagoda (Golden Rock), you can see Thailand's smaller equivalent at **Wat Phra That Doi Hin Kiu** on a hill that looks out over the Moei River – an idyllic pastoral scene. A 5m-tall standing Buddha marks the beginning of the steep stairway that leads up to the gold-painted rock, which is surmounted by a small chedi surrounded by Burmese figurines. The rock is precariously balanced and seems about to tumble down the mountain, and its gleaming gold colour makes a stark contrast with the lush green background.

Waterfalls, springs and caves near Mae Sot

There are several minor caves and waterfalls around Mae Sot, which are easy enough to explore if you have your own transport, though none can compare with Umphang's far mightier Thi Law Su Falls. Borderline shop or Krua Canadian (see page 262) should be able to provide you with further information.

To reach the three-tier **Mae Kasa Falls** (rainy season only) and hot springs (around 14km from town) head north out of Mae Sot, along Highway 105 towards Mae Ramat, then take a side road at around kilometre-stone 13 for 7km. Much further north, just after kilometre-stone 95 on Highway 105, a sign directs you the 2km off the highway to the enormous 800m-deep bat-cave, **Tham Mae Usu** (inaccessible July–Oct because of flooding).

South out of town, off Route 1090 to Umphang, the 97 tiers of **Pha Charoen Falls** are 41km from Mae Sot; take any songthaew bound for Umphang. The falls drop down through the jungle like a wonky staircase, and are a popular photo spot for day-tripping Thais.

Highland Farm Gibbon Sanctuary

A couple of kilometres on from Pha Charoen Falls, 43km south of Mae Sot on Route 1090 to Umphang • ☏ 081 727 1364, ⓦ gibbonathighlandfarm.org/index • Take any songthaew bound for Umphang • Free for brief visits

Highland Farm Gibbon Sanctuary cares for over sixty injured and abandoned gibbons, most of which have been rescued from abusive owners and are unable to live in the wild. They also take care of around twenty monkeys, a jackal and an Asiatic bear. The sanctuary welcomes day-trippers, and also offers long-term placements for serious, self-motivated volunteers.

ARRIVAL AND DEPARTURE   MAE SOT

By plane Nok Air operates flights from Bangkok (Don Muang; 4 daily; 1hr 15min) and Yangon (Myanmar; 5 weekly; 1hr) to Mae Sot's airport, 3km west of town. Motorbike taxis and metered taxis are on hand for the run into the centre.

By bus, minibus or songthaew Nearly all buses, a/c minibuses and songthaews (including those to Umphang and Mae Sariang) now use the government bus station west of town at the Thanon Indharakiri/Highway 105 intersection; a motorbike taxi into town costs around B50. Songthaews to Mae Ramat leave from Soi Rongchai, while

songthaews to Rim Moei leave from Thanon Banthung. It's sometimes quicker to change at Tak bus station, which has a wider choice of long-distance services than Mae Sot.
Destinations Bangkok (13 daily; 8–9hr); Chiang Mai (2 daily; 6hr); Chiang Rai (1 daily; 9–10hr); Mae Ramat (songthaews every 30min; 1hr); Mae Sai (1 daily; 10–11hr); Mae Sariang (songthaews roughly hourly until around noon; 5–6hr); Phitsanulok (roughly hourly; 3hr 30min–5hr); Sukhothai (roughly hourly; 2hr 30min–4hr); Tak (every 30min; 2hr); Umphang (songthaews hourly until roughly 2pm; 4–5hr).

GETTING AROUND AND INFORMATION

By bicycle or motorbike Several guesthouses rent motorbikes (around B200–250/day) and bicycles (around B50/day).

By car Avis (ⓦ avisthailand.com) has an office at the airport and will deliver and collect anywhere in Mae Sot.

By taxi Mae Sot has a small fleet of metered taxis (ⓦ facebook.com/taximaesot), charging around B60

between the airport and town; call ☏ 055 030357 or 098 101 9345 to book one. There are only a few in town and you can't pick them up on the street.

Tourist information There is no TAT office here, but both Borderlines shop and *Krua Canadian* restaurant are good sources of local information (see page 262), as are the guesthouses.

ACCOMMODATION

Because of all the volunteers in town, many guesthouses offer monthly or weekly discounts.

★ **Ban Thai** 740/1 Thanon Indharakiri ☏ 055 531590, ⓔ banthai_mth@hotmail.com; map p.258. The most appealing guesthouse in Mae Sot occupies several traditional-style, wooden-floored houses in a peaceful garden compound at the west end of town. All rooms are tastefully and comfortably furnished; those in the main house share hot-water bathrooms, while those in the more expensive and spacious compound houses have en-suite hot showers and cable TV. It's often full so advance bookings are recommended. Fan B280, a/c B850

Centara Mae Sot Hill Resort 100 Asia Highway/Highway 105 ☏ 055 532601–8, ⓦ centarahotelsresorts.com; map p.258. The top hotel in the area has a large swimming pool with a children's pool, floodlit tennis courts,

a gym and luxurious, recently renovated rooms; it's a 10min drive northeast of the town centre. B1400

Duang Kamol (D.K.) Hotel 298/2 Thanon Indharakiri ☏ 055 531699; map p.258. The nicest and best value of the town-centre budget hotels has huge, clean rooms with hot showers, many of them with little balconies and some with a/c and TVs. The entrance is on the first floor, above a series of shops. Fan B250, a/c B380

Irawadee Resort 758/1–2 Thanon Indharakiri ☏ 055 535430, ⓦ irawadee.com; map p.258. The rooms here definitely have character, though you might find the gold-painted furnishings, red walls and canopied beds a bit over the top. The "resort" tag is a bit of a misnomer – it's more like a boutique hotel – but it has a good central location and helpful staff. B1200

★ **The Picturebook Guesthouse** 125/4–6 Soi

REFUGEES FROM MYANMAR: THE KAREN

With a population of five to seven million, the **Karen** are Myanmar's largest ethnic minority, but their numbers have offered no protection against persecution by the Burmese. This mistreatment has been going on for centuries, and entered a new phase after the country won its independence from Britain in 1948. Unlike many other groups in Myanmar, the Karen had remained loyal to the British during World War II and were supposed to have been rewarded with autonomy when Britain pulled out; instead they were left to battle for that themselves. Fourteen years after the British withdrawal, the **Burmese army** took control, setting up an isolationist state run under a bizarre ideology compounded of militarist, socialist and Buddhist principles. From that time, the military were engaged in armed conflict with all ethnic minority groups in the country until 2011, when a new government, consisting of military and civilians, brought about a fragile stability.

However, despite positive steps in a nationwide peace process, which has seen numerous ceasefires signed since 2011, and despite a landslide victory for the National League for Democracy, led by Aung San Suu Kyi, in the 2015 general election, clashes continue to erupt between government forces and armed factions of some minority groups. The Karen people, whose homeland state of Kawthulay borders northwest Thailand from Mae Sariang down to Three Pagodas Pass, are among those affected. The Karen National Union (KNU) signed a ceasefire in 2012, but armed Karen factions were still involved in skirmishes with Burmese government troops at the time of this update. (The Karen are distinct from the Karenni, or Red Karen, whose homeland is north of Kawthulay and borders Thailand's Mae Hong Son province.)

As a result of these conflicts, many Karen continue to flee across the Thai border. For many years **Thai government policy** has been to admit only those who are fleeing active fighting, not human rights violations. Thailand is not a signatory to the 1951 Convention Relating to the Status of Refugees and has no legal framework for processing asylum seekers. The hundreds of thousands who have left their homeland because of politically induced economic hardship – forced labour, theft of their land and livestock, among other factors – must therefore either try to enter the refugee camps illegally, or attempt to make a living as **migrant workers**. There are between two and three million migrants from Myanmar currently in Thailand. Without refugee status, these exiles are extremely vulnerable to abuse, both from corrupt officials and from exploitative employers. In Mae Sot, for example, where Burmese migrants are a mainstay of the local economy, many of them are reportedly paid as little as B100 a day (a third of the national minimum wage) to work in the worst jobs available, in gem and garment factories, and as prostitutes. Demands for better wages and improved conditions, however, nearly always result in deportation.

Reactions in the **Thai press** to Burmese refugees are mixed, with humanitarian concerns tempered by economic hardships in Thailand and by high-profile cases of illegal Burmese workers involved in violent crimes and drug-smuggling (Myanmar is now one of the world's leading producers and smugglers of methamphetamines, also known as *ya baa*, or Ice, much of which finds its way into Thailand).

For recent **news** and archive reports on the situation in Myanmar and on its borders, see Burma News International's website, Ⓦ bnionline.net. For information on how to offer **support** to refugees from Myanmar in this area, see the website of The Border Consortium, Ⓦ theborderconsortium.org. A good book about the Karen struggle and the refugee situation in Mae Sot is *Restless Souls: Rebels, Refugees, Medics and Misfits* by Phil Thornton, a Mae Sot-based journalist.

19, Thanon Indharakiri, about 1km east of the centre, behind the J2 Hotel ☎090 459 6990, Ⓦ picturebookthailand.org; map p.258. A welcoming boutique hotel and social enterprise that acts as a training centre for mostly Burmese young people. Ten polished concrete a/c rooms with wooden furniture, charming artworks, large hot-water bathrooms and terraces overlook a pretty little garden. Bike rental. Breakfast included. <u>B600</u>

2

CROSSING THE MYANMAR BORDER AT MAE SOT

If you have a visa arranged in advance, you can enter Myanmar via the international border crossing (daily 6am–8pm) at the Thai-Myanmar Friendship Bridge, just 7km west of Mae Sot. Regular songthaews go there from Thanon Banthung in Mae Sot via the bus station, and from the bridge it's just 1km to the town of Myawaddy in Myanmar. There's a separate window for foreigners, so the process of crossing the border is fairly rapid. From Myawaddy, it's possible to travel on to popular tourist destinations like the Kyaiktyo Pagoda (the Golden Rock) and Mawlamyine. Before the opening of the border to foreigners, this border post was used mostly by long-stay visitors to Thailand on visa runs, but now that the Thai government has clamped down on visa extensions it's becoming more popular as the starting point for an exploration of Myanmar.

EATING

Thanon Prasat Vithi is well stocked with noodle shops and **night-market stalls**, there's lots of Muslim and Burmese food for sale in the market, and there are several bars and restaurants on the new ring road east of town between Thanon Indharakiri and the Asian Highway; this is the best area to go looking for nightlife.

Borderline Tea Garden 674/14 Thanon Indharakiri ☎ 055 546584, ⓦ borderlinecollective.org; map p.258. In the garden behind their fair-trade handicrafts shop, this very relaxed, social enterprise café serves cheap Burmese snacks – including vegetable pakoras (B60), tea leaf salad (B40) and potato curry with flat bread (B55) – washed down with Burmese tea, lemon grass and other freshly made juices. Everything on the menu is vegetarian and no alcohol is served. They also have an art gallery, and run cookery classes (see page 263). Tues–Sun 7.30am–9pm.

Casa Mia Thanon Don Kaew, 5min walk west of Ban Thai guesthouse ☎ 087 204 4701; map p.258. Popular especially for its home-made pastas, including a delicious spicy tortellini pomodoro, at rock-bottom prices (under B100). Also does pizzas, a big range of Thai dishes, salads, veggie options and a daily roster of cakes and desserts – cheesecake, banoffee pie and the like. Daily except Sat 8am–9.30pm.

★ **Khao-Mao Khao-Fang** 382 Moo 9, Thanon Mae Sot-Mae Ramat (about 2km north of town on the west side of Highway 15) ☎ 055 532483, ⓦ khaomaokhaofang. com; map p.258. A garden restaurant extraordinaire, styling itself an "imaginary jungle", where the artfully landscaped cascades, rivulets, rock features and mature

trees make you feel as if you're sitting in a primeval forest film set, especially at night when sea-green lighting adds to the effect. Even the chairs and tables are carved from tree trunks and branches. A popular spot for dates and VIP lunches, it serves a fantastic range of food, including some unusual Thai dishes, such as banana blossom and coconut milk spicy salad (B130). Everything is beautifully prepared and presented, and there are some yummy desserts too, like banana fritters with sesame glaze. Don't miss the bathrooms, which are something special. During the day you could use the Mae Ramat/Mae Sariang songthaew service, but after dark you'll need to call a taxi or use your own transport. Daily 11am–3pm & 5–10pm.

Krua Canadian Restaurant 3 Thanon Sri Phanit ☎ 055 534659; map p.258. There's a great menu of delicious dishes (mostly B100–150) at this simple restaurant, including the best Western breakfasts in town, plus bangers and mash, burgers, steaks, pizzas and a good range of Thai, Mexican and vegetarian dishes. Also serves several blends of local hill-tribe coffee, and owner Dave is a mine of local information. Daily 8am–2pm & 5–9.30pm.

The Passport at HCTC 507 Moo 10, Maepa, about 2km northwest of the town centre ☎ 063 668 4494, ⓦ hctcmaesot.org; map p.258. This excellent restaurant is a training school (the Hospitality & Catering Training Centre) for underprivileged Karen, and the students are enthusiastic and charming. Choose one of the three-course menus (Thai or Western), which change weekly, for around B200–250, and enjoy the attractive, minimalist decor. Fri & Sat 6.30–9pm.

SHOPPING

For fashions, Burmese sarongs and daily necessities, you can't beat the well-stocked **day market** that runs south off Thanon Prasat Vithi. Mae Sot is most famous, however, as a good place to buy jewellery: the **gem and jade shops** on central Thanon Prasat Vithi offer a larger and less expensive selection than the stalls at the Rim Moei border market, and even if you don't intend to buy, just watching the theatrical haggling is half the fun. On

Saturday evenings, Soi Rongchai next to the police station is pedestrianized as a **walking street market**, selling food, T-shirts and handicrafts.

Borderline 674/14 Thanon Indharakiri (next to Wat Arunyaket) ☎ 055 546584, ⓦ borderlinecollective.org; map p.258. This place stocks an eye-catching range of crafts, such as sarongs, scarves, slippers, cushion covers, yoga mats and laptop bags. They also sell an excellent hand-painted map of the town for B90, and their most popular item is the bags of tea from Myanmar (B150 for 250g). The items are made by Karen women living in refugee camps along the border and other Burmese women's groups. Tues–Sun 7.30am–9pm.

Weave (Fair Trade Shop) 541 Thanon Indharakiri (opposite Bai Fern restaurant) ☎ 055 544863,

ⓦ weave-women.org; map p.258. A similar operation to Borderline, with a name that's short for "Women's Education for Advancement and Empowerment". Traditional patterns, dyes and colour combinations are used to create a variety of woven products, such as traditional Karen shifts, thus helping to preserve traditional culture and give local refugee women an income. Mon–Sat 9am–6pm.

DIRECTORY

2

Cookery lessons Learn how to rustle up Shan, Karen and Burmese dishes at *Borderline Tea Garden*. Classes cost B1000 for one person, B600 for two, and B500 for three to six people, including a trip to the market and a cookbook. Book at least a day in advance.

Hospitals The public Mae Sot Hospital is on the southeastern edge of town (☎ 055 531229) and the private Mae Sot Ram (Phawo) Hospital is on the southwestern edge (☎ 055 533912–4).

Immigration office At Rim Moei border crossing (see page 262).

Language lessons Informal Burmese lessons are available through most guesthouses and several restaurants.

Tourist police For all emergencies, call the tourist police on their free, 24hr phoneline ☎ 1155, or contact them at their office about 1km east of the centre on Thanon Indharakiri.

Umphang

Surrounded by mountains and situated at the confluence of the Mae Klong and Umphang rivers, the small and very quiet village of **UMPHANG** is made up of little more than a thousand or so wooden houses and a wat. It won't take long to explore the minute grid of narrow roads that bisects the village, and although it's popular among Thai visitors, foreign tourists are still relatively rare here, so communication could be a challenge. Coming here is all about trips to **Thi Law Su Waterfall**, which many believe to be the most beautiful in the country, with a drop of around 200m and a width of around 400m during the rainy season. Even if you don't fancy trekking or rafting to the falls, it's worth making the spectacular trip 164km south from Mae Sot to Umphang, both for the stunning mountain scenery you'll encounter along the way, and for the buzz of being in such an isolated part of Thailand. Bring some warm clothes as it can get pretty cool at night and in the early mornings – and the songthaew ride along the Sky Highway from Mae Sot is often windy.

Riding the Sky Highway

The 150-kilometre drive from Mae Sot to Umphang generally takes about four hours and for the first hour proceeds in a fairly gentle fashion through the maize, cabbage and banana plantations of the Moei valley, before passing Pha Charoen Falls (see page 260). The fun really begins when you start climbing into the mountains and the road – accurately dubbed the "**Sky Highway**" – careers round the edges of steep-sided valleys, undulating like a fairground rollercoaster (there are 1219 bends in all). The scenery is glorious, but if you're prone to car sickness, dose up on preventative tablets as the ride can be very unpleasant: the songthaews get so crammed with people and produce that there's often no possibility of distracting yourself by staring out of the window.

Karen, Akha, Lisu and Hmong people live in the few hamlets along the route, many growing cabbages along the cleared lower slopes with the help of government incentives (part of a national campaign to steer upland farmers away from the opium trade). The **Hmong** in particular are easily recognized by their distinctive embroidered jackets and skirts edged in bright pink, red and blue bands (see page 771). In 2000, the local

Karen population mushroomed when three refugee camps from the Rim Moei area were relocated to the purpose-built village of Umpiem Mai alongside the Sky Highway midway between Mae Sot and Umphang. Umpiem Mai is currently home to around twelve thousand Karen refugees.

EXPLORING THE UMPHANG WILDLIFE SANCTUARY

Most people who visit Umphang sign up for a trip of two to three days (see tour operators) to the three-tiered **Thi Law Su Waterfall** (Nam Tok Thilawsu), star feature of the Umphang Wildlife Sanctuary (entry B200, normally included in a tour package), which, unusually for Thailand, flows all year round. These trips usually involve rafting along spectacular rivers, often passing through narrow gorges (which many find the highlight of the trip), as well as trekking and camping near the base of the falls. The waterfall is at its most impressive just after the rainy season in November, when it extends to a dramatic 400m across. During this period you can swim in the beautifully blue lower pool, but trails can still be muddy, which makes for tough going; trek leaders often recommend wearing rubber boots (best bought in Mae Sot as they're hard to find in Umphang). Nonetheless, November to February is the best **season** for trekking, even if the nights get pretty chilly. From December to April (the dry season), it's usually possible to climb to one of the waterfall's upper tiers, mud permitting. By contrast, at the height of the rainy season (July–Sept), it's often impossible to trek anywhere, the rugged access road from the wildlife sanctuary entrance to the ranger station (mostly unsealed) is frequently impassable and the falls are hidden behind a sea of mist. Around the falls, the vegetation is mainly montane forest, home to numerous varieties of orchid and over a thousand types of palm, and plenty of commonly encountered monkeys and hornbills, plus elusive wild elephants, tapirs and clouded leopards.

Access to the falls is strictly controlled by national park rangers, who forbid people from taking food or plastic water bottles beyond the ranger station and campsite, from where it is a comfortable 1.5km walk along a raised wooden walkway to the falls. As yet, the number of visitors is reasonably small – except on public holidays, during school holidays and on some weekends, when Thai trippers flood the area.

A **typical tour** to Thi Law Su lasts three days and follows something like this increasingly standard itinerary. Day one: rafting down the Mae Klong River via Thi Law Jor Falls, a hot spring and some striking honeycombed cliffs; then a 9km trek (3–4hr) to the official campsite near Thi Law Su Falls. Day two: morning at the falls, then a two-hour trek to a homestay at the Karen village of Khotha. Day three: a three-hour elephant ride (or trek) to Mae Lamoong junction; return to Umphang by car. Some trekkers find the three-day itinerary too baggy, with quite a lot of empty time at day's end (bring a book), so if you want a more challenging experience try to persuade your trekking agency to cover the same itinerary in two days. **Prices** start at about B3000 per person for the standard three-day Thi Law Su trek without elephant riding, in a group of around six people (more expensive in a smaller group), B4000 with elephant riding. Some tour operators offer a one-day trip from Umphang (around B2000/person), rafting down the Mae Klong River via Thi Law Jor Falls and a hot spring, then driving the rest of the way to the Umphang Wildlife Sanctuary campsite, before walking to Thi Law Su falls and back, then driving all the way back to Umphang in the afternoon. Prices do vary between operators: smaller outfits can't afford to undercut the big operators and cost savings can mean lower wages – and morale – for guides. If you haven't pre-arranged a tour, the best time to contact **trek leaders** at the smaller outfits in Umphang is often after about 4pm, when they've returned from their last trip. Guides should provide tents, bedrolls, mosquito nets and sleeping bags, plus all meals and drinking water; trekkers may be asked to help carry some of the gear.

Although Thi Law Su is the most famous destination in the Umphang area, other programmes are available on request. From roughly June or July to November or December there's **whitewater rafting** from the Karen village of **Umphang Khi** via the forty-plus rapids of the Umphang River, which can also include a fairly long trek and a night in the village. Alternatively, there are one- and two-day rafting trips to **Thi Law Leh Falls**, which involve four to eight hours' rafting (depending on water levels) via a series of cataracts along the Mae Klong River, and the possibility of a seven-hour trek on the second day. For bird-spotting, ask about trips to Thung Yai Naresuan Wildlife Sanctuary.

In fact the Umphang region was inhabited by Karen hill tribes before the Thais came to settle in the area in the early twentieth century; later, when the Thais began trading in earnest with their neighbours across the Burmese border, the Karen traders from Myanmar used to carry their identification documents into Thailand in a bamboo container which they called an "umpha" – this is believed to be the origin of the name Umphang.

ARRIVAL AND DEPARTURE

UMPHANG

When it comes to public transport, Umphang is effectively a dead end, so the only way to travel on from here is to go back to **Mae Sot** first.

By songthaew The only public transport access to Umphang is along the Sky Highway from Mae Sot's bus station by songthaew, which should drop you off at your accommodation (hourly until roughly 2pm; 4–5hr; B130; if you're prone to motion sickness, ask the driver about sitting in the front seat, for which you'll probably have to pay a bit extra). Heading back to Mae Sot, songthaews leave at least hourly until about 12.30pm from the top of the town, though it's usual for guesthouses to phone ahead and get the songthaew to pick you up.

GETTING AROUND AND TOUR OPERATORS

Just about every guesthouse and resort in Umphang can help arrange a trip to Thi Law Su, but many cater exclusively to Thais. Those listed below have English-speaking guides and a reputation for reliability. Most tour operators offer a pick-up in Mae Sot; contact individual companies for details. Nearly all guesthouses can arrange a 4WD with driver for exploring the area (price dependent on destination – about B2500 to Thi Law Su Falls and back). There's no official motorbike rental in Umphang, but it's worth asking around as guesthouse owners may be able to help you.

Mr Boonchuay 360 Moo 1, Thanon Pravitpaiwan ☎ 055 561020 or 081 379 2591, ⓦ boonchuaytour.net.

Umphang-born and bred, Mr Boonchuay knows the area well and has a good reputation; his English is not perfect, but he has English-speaking guides. Offers standard Thi Law Su programme, with optional elephant riding, as well as other trekking and rafting tours; pick-ups from Mae Sot offered.

Phu Doi Campsite and Resort Soi 4, Thanon Pravitpaiwan ☎ 055 561049, ⓦ phudoi.com. As well as whitewater rafting in season, Phu Doi runs the standard Thi Law Su programme or an option with less trekking (both with optional elephant riding); pick-ups from Mae Sot offered.

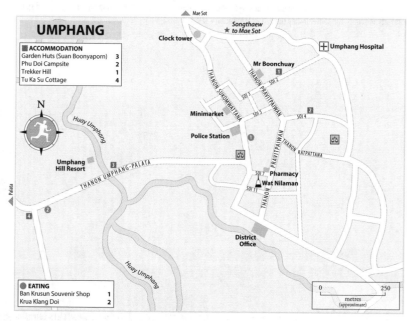

UMPHANG

ACCOMMODATION	
Garden Huts (Suan Boonyaporn)	3
Phu Doi Campsite	2
Trekker Hill	1
Tu Ka Su Cottage	4

EATING	
Ban Krusun Souvenir Shop	1
Krua Klang Doi	2

Mae Sot

Songthaew to Mae Sot

Clock tower

Umphang Hospital

Mr Boonchuay

THANON SUKHWATTANA

THANON PRAVITPAIWAN

Minimarket

Police Station

THANON PRAVITPAIWAN

THANON RATPATTANA

Pharmacy

Wat Nilaman

Huay Umphang

Umphang Hill Resort

THANON UMPHANG-PALATA

Palata

District Office

Huay Umphang

0   250
metres (approximate)

2

Tu Ka Su At Tu Ka Su Cottage, 40 Moo 6 ☎ 055 561295, ⓦ tukasu.com. One of the best organized tour operators in Umphang, Tu Ka Su offers a wide variety of well-priced three- and four-day trekking and rafting trips to Thi Law Su, Thi Law Leh, Umphang Khi and Palata Falls. Unfortunately most of their website is in Thai, but you can email them for details.
Umphang Hill At Umphang Hill Resort, 59 Moo 6 ☎ 055 561063–4; and in Mae Sot at 296/2 Thanon Indharakhiri, next to the Duang Kamol Hotel ☎ 055 542942; ⓦ umphanghill.com. This large, slightly upmarket outfit offers eleven itineraries and tailor-made permutations, ranging from three-day trips to Thi Law Su (B6650/person for 2–4 people, including Mae Sot transfers) to seven-day trips to Umphang Khi and Thi Law Su, including elephant riding and whitewater rafting (B17,000/person for 2–4 people, including Mae Sot transfers).

ACCOMMODATION

A night's accommodation in Umphang is often included in the price of a tour.
Garden Huts (Suan Boonyaporn) 8/1 Thanon Umphang-Palata ☎ 055 561093; map p.265. A spread of spacious rooms, all with fans, TVs and hot showers, set in wood, brick and concrete builings around a pretty riverside flower garden. B300
Phu Doi Campsite and Resort Soi 4, Thanon Pravitpaiwan ☎ 055 561049, ⓦ phudoi.com; map p.265. In a central location overlooking a pond, a decent set of en-suite rooms in several wooden houses with verandas, hot water, TV and air-con (you can score a discounted rate by asking for the a/c to be switched off). B600

Trekker Hill Soi 2, Thanon Pravitpaiwan ☎ 055 561090; map p.265. Easy-going place with pleasant views from its hillside on the east side of town, where the basic wooden bungalows stretch to fans, mosquito nets and hot showers. B300
Tu Ka Su Cottage Thanon Umphang-Palata ☎ 055 561295, ⓦ tukasu.com; map p.265. In a pretty garden up the hill from the river, this quite stylish place is the most attractive in Umphang and offers nicely designed en-suite wooden cabins and rooms, all with TV, hot water, air-con and good-sized verandas; the smallest bungalows sleep three, and some have cute, semi-garden-style bathrooms. B600

EATING

Unsurprisingly, Umphang is no gourmet mecca and most visitors just eat at their guesthouse, though there are cheap **food stalls** that set up close to the temple at dusk.
Ban Krusun Souvenir Shop Thanon Sukomwattana ☎ 089 824 0890; map p.265. Along with postcards and local arts and crafts, this souvenir shop run by a local musician sells good espresso coffees (from B40). Daily 7am–8pm.
Krua Klang Doi 19/1 Moo 6, Umphang (just east of Tu Ka Su) ☎ 081 284 7926; map p.265. Popular with locals and visitors, this simple restaurant serves good cheap Thai standards (from B50), including some fresh and spicy salads. Daily 8/9am–9/10pm.

The north

RICE TERRACES IN WWW, CHIANG MAI

1

The north

Travelling up by rail through the central plains, there's no mistaking when you've reached the north of Thailand: somewhere between Uttaradit and Den Chai, the train slows almost to a halt, as if approaching a frontier post, to meet the abruptly rising mountains that continue largely unbroken to the borders of Myanmar (Burma) and Laos. Beyond this point the climate becomes more temperate (downright cold at night between December and February), nurturing the fertile land that gave the old kingdom of the north the name of Lanna, "the land of a million rice fields". Although only one-tenth of the land can be used for rice cultivation, the valley rice fields here are three times more productive than those in the dusty northeast, and the higher land yields a great variety of fruits, as well as beans, groundnuts and tobacco.

Until the beginning of the last century, Lanna was a largely independent region. On the back of its agricultural prosperity, it developed its own styles of art and architecture, which can still be seen in its flourishing temples and distinctive handicraft traditions. The north is also set apart from the rest of the country by its exuberant festivals, a cuisine that has been heavily influenced by Myanmar and a dialect quite distinct from central Thai. Northerners proudly call themselves *khon muang*, "people of the principalities", and their gentle sophistication is admired by the people of Bangkok, whose wealthier citizens build their holiday homes in the clean air of the north's forested mountains.

Chiang Mai, the capital and transport centre of the north, is a great place just to hang out or prepare for a journey into the hills. For many tourists, this means joining a trek (see page 57) to visit one or more of the **hill tribes**, who comprise one-tenth of the north's population and are just about clinging onto the ways of life that distinguish them from one another and the Thais around them (see page 769). For those with qualms about the exploitative element of this ethnological tourism, there are plenty of other ways of enjoying the great outdoors in northern Thailand.

A trip eastwards from Chiang Mai to the ancient city-states of Lampang, Phrae and Nan can be highly rewarding, not only for the dividends of going against the usual flow of tourist traffic, but also for the natural beauty of the region's upland ranges – seen to best effect from the well-marked trails of **Doi Khun Tan National Park** – and for its eccentric variety of Thai, Burmese and Lao art and architecture. Congenial **Lampang** contains wats to rival those of Chiang Mai for beauty – in Wat Phra That Lampang Luang the town has the finest surviving example of traditional northern architecture anywhere – while little-visited **Phrae**, to the southeast, is a step back in time to a simpler Thailand. Further away but a more intriguing target is **Nan**, with its heady artistic mix of Thai and Lao styles and steep ring of scenic mountains.

To the west of Chiang Mai, the trip to **Mae Hong Son** takes you through the most stunning mountain scenery in the region into a land with its roots across the border in Myanmar, with the option of looping back through **Pai**, a laidback, sophisticated hill station that's become a popular hub for treks and activities. Bidding to rival Chiang Mai as a base for exploring the countryside is **Chiang Rai** to the north, which is also home to an intriguing diversity of museums and temples; above Chiang Rai, the northernmost tip of Thailand is marked by the Burmese border crossing at **Mae Sai** and the junction of Thailand, Laos and Myanmar at **Sop Ruak**. Fancifully dubbed the "Golden Triangle", Sop Ruak is a must on every bus party's itinerary – but you're more likely to find peace and quiet among the ruins of nearby **Chiang Saen**, set on the leafy banks of the Mekong River.

KHAO SOI

Highlights

❶ Hill-tribe trekking A chance to visit the diverse hill tribes of northern Thailand and explore dramatic countryside along the way. See page 57.

❷ Chiang Mai Old-town temples, the best of Thai crafts, cookery courses and fine restaurants – the north's sophisticated capital is a great place to hang out. See page 275.

❸ Festivals Exuberant Songkhran, glittering Loy Krathong and colourful Poy Sang Long are the pick of many. See pages 284 and 339.

❹ Khao soi Delicious, spicy, creamy noodle soup, the northern Thai signature dish. See page 292.

❺ Wat Phra That Doi Suthep Admire the towering views from this stunning example of temple architecture, just outside Chiang Mai. See page 301.

❻ Nan A welcoming riverside town offering fascinating temple murals, attractive handicrafts and dramatic mountainscapes. See page 320.

❼ The Mae Hong Son loop A rollercoaster journey – with a chill-out break in laidback Pai – through the country's wildest mountain scenery. See page 328.

❽ Whitewater rafting on the Pai River Well-organized excitement taking in rapids, gorges and beautiful waterfalls. See page 346.

HIGHLIGHTS ARE MARKED ON THE MAP ON PAGE 272

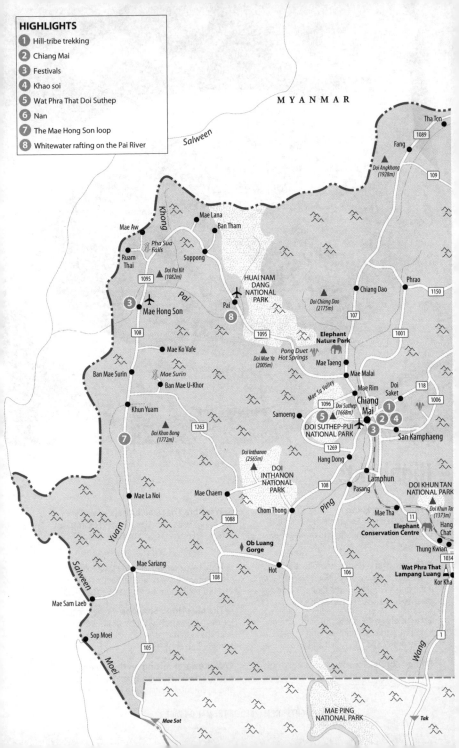

HIGHLIGHTS

1. Hill-tribe trekking
2. Chiang Mai
3. Festivals
4. Khao soi
5. Wat Phra That Doi Suthep
6. Nan
7. The Mae Hong Son loop
8. Whitewater rafting on the Pai River

MYANMAR

Salween

Tha Ton

1089

Fang

109

Doi Angkhang
(1928m)

Khong

Mae Lana

Ban Tham

Mae Aw

Pha Sua
Falls

Soppong

Ruam
Thai

Doi Pai Kit
(1082m)

1095

HUAI NAM
DANG
NATIONAL
PARK

Chiang Dao

Phrao

1150

Doi Chiang Dao
(2175m)

107

3

Mae Hong Son

Pai

1095

8

Pai

Elephant
Nature Park

1001

108

Mae Ko Vafe

Doi Mae Ya
(2005m)

Pong Duet
Hot Springs

Mae Taeng

Mae Malai

Doi
Saket

118

Ban Mae Surin

Mae Surin

Ban Mae U-Khor

Mae Sa Valley

Mae Rim

1006

Khun Yuam

1263

Doi Khun Bong
(1772m)

Samoeng

1096

Doi Suthep
(1668m)

5

CHIANG
MAI

1

2

4

7

DOI SUTHEP-PUI
NATIONAL PARK

3

San Kamphaeng

Doi Inthanon
(2565m)

DOI
INTHANON
NATIONAL
PARK

1269

Hang Dong

Lamphun

DOI KHUN TAN
NATIONAL PARK

Mae La Noi

Mae Chaem

108

Pasang

Doi Khun Tan
(1373m)

11

Hang
Chat

1088

Chom Thong

Ping

Mae Tha

Elephant
Conservation Centre

Thung Kwian

Yuam

Ob Luang
Gorge

Hot

106

1034

Wat Phra That
Lampang Luang

Kor Kha

Mae Sariang

108

Salween

Wang

1

Mae Sam Laeb

Sop Moei

105

Moei

Mae Sot

MAE PING
NATIONAL PARK

Tak

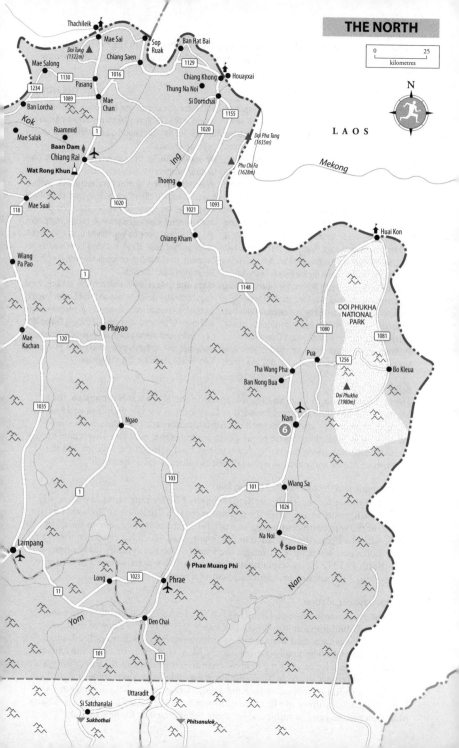

THE NORTH

0   25
kilometres

N

LAOS

Thachileik

Mae Sai
Doi Tung
(1322m)
Sop
Ruak
Ban Hat Bai

Mae Salong
Chiang Saen
1129

1130
Pasang
1016
Chiang Khong
Houayxai

1234
Thung Na Noi
Ban Lorcha
1089
Mae Chan
Si Dornchai

Kok
Ruammid
1
1155

Mae Salak
1020
Doi Pha Tang
(1635m)

Baan Dam
Chiang Rai
Phu Chi Fa
(1628m)

Wat Rong Khun
Mekong

Thoeng

Mae Suai
1020
1021
1093

118
Huai Kon

Wiang
Pa Pao
Chiang Kham

1
1148

DOI PHUKHA
NATIONAL
PARK

Phayao
1080
1081

Mae
Kachan
120
Pua
1256
Bo Kleua

Tha Wang Pha
Ban Nong Bua
Doi Phukha
(1980m)

1035
Ngao
Nan
6

103
101
Wiang Sa

1
1026

Na Noi
Sao Din

Lampang

Phae Muang Phi

Long
1023
Phrae
Nan

11
Yom
Den Chai

101
11

Si Satchanalai
Uttaradit

Sukhothai
Phitsanulok

Ing

East of Chiang Saen on the Mekong River, **Chiang Khong** is an important crossing point to Houayxai in Laos, from where boats make the scenic two-day trip down the Mekong to Luang Prabang.

GETTING THERE AND AROUND THE NORTH

As elsewhere in Thailand, buses are by far the most important form of transport for getting to and around the north. However, the mountainous topography makes **getting around** the region necessarily roundabout, with bus routes divided into three main areas: east from Chiang Mai, through Lampang and Phrae to Nan (though one very slow bus a day winds its way over some spectacular hills to Chiang Rai); west from Chiang Mai around the Mae Hong Son loop through Mae Sariang and Pai; and north of Chiang Rai, an area that is well served by buses along the main routes, fed by songthaews on the minor roads. To get between Chiang Mai and Chiang Rai, you can either take a fast, direct service along Highway 118 or catch a bus to Tha Ton, followed by a boat down the Kok River to Chiang Rai.

By plane There are domestic flights to the airports at Chiang Mai, Lampang, Phrae, Nan, Mae Hong Son and Chiang Rai. In addition, Chiang Mai is served by international flights from and to dozens of cities in China, East Asia and Southeast Asia. There are also flights between China and Chiang Rai.

By train The Northern Rail Line offers several daily services, mostly overnight, between Bangkok and Chiang Mai. Although trains are generally slower than buses, the stations at Den Chai (from where buses and songthaews run to Phrae and Nan) and Lampang are useful if you're coming up from Bangkok.

By motorbike To fully appreciate the mountainous landscape of the north, many people take to the open roads on rented motorbikes, which are available in most northern towns (Chiang Mai offers the best choice) and are relatively inexpensive. You should be cautious about biking in the north, however, especially if you're an inexperienced rider, and avoid riding alone on any remote trails – for expert advice on motorbike travel, including tips on safety for beginners, check out ⓦ gt-rider.com, the website of Chiang Mai resident David Unkovich.

Maps and guides David Unkovich also produces good maps of the Mae Hong Son loop and "The Golden Triangle" (available locally and online through ⓦ gt-rider.com, which also covers GPS routes). Meanwhile, Exploring Chiang Mai: City, Valley and Mountains is a fascinating, thoroughly researched and in-depth guide to northern Thailand by long-time local resident, Oliver Hargreave.

Brief history

The first civilization to leave an indelible mark on the north was **Haripunjaya**, the Mon (Dvaravati) state that was founded at Lamphun in the late eighth or early ninth century. Maintaining strong ties with the Mon kingdoms to the south, it remained the cultural and religious centre of the north for four centuries. The Thais came onto the scene after the Mon, migrating down from China between the seventh and the eleventh centuries and establishing small principalities around the north.

King Mengrai and the founding of Chiang Mai

The prime mover for the Thais was **King Mengrai** of Ngon Yang (around present-day Chiang Saen), who, shortly after the establishment of a Thai state at Sukhothai in the middle of the thirteenth century, set to work on a parallel unified state in the north. By 1296, when he began the construction of Chiang Mai, which has remained the capital of the north ever since, he had brought the whole of the north under his control, and at his death in 1317 he had established a dynasty which was to oversee a two-hundred-year period of unmatched prosperity and cultural activity.

The Burmese occupation

After the expansionist reign of Tilok (1441–87), who hosted the eighth world council of Theravada Buddhism at Wat Jet Yot in Chiang Mai in 1477, a series of weak, squabbling kings came and went, while Ayutthaya increased its unfriendly advances. But it was the **Burmese** who finally snuffed out the Mengrai dynasty by capturing Chiang Mai in 1558, and for most of the next two centuries they controlled Lanna through a succession of puppet rulers. In 1767, the Burmese sacked the Thai capital at Ayutthaya, but the Thais soon regrouped under King Taksin, who with the help of **King Kawila** of Lampang gradually drove the Burmese northwards. In 1774 Kawila recaptured Chiang Mai, then deserted and in ruins, and set about rebuilding it as his new capital.

The colonial period

Kawila was succeeded as ruler of the north by a series of incompetent princes for much of the nineteenth century, until colonialism reared its head. After Britain took control of Upper Burma, **Rama V** of Bangkok began to take an interest in the north – where, since the Bowring Treaty of 1855, the British had established lucrative logging businesses – to prevent its annexation. He forcibly moved large numbers of ethnic Thais northwards, in order to counter the British claim of sovereignty over territory occupied by Thai Yai (Shan), who also make up a large part of the population of Upper Burma. In 1877 Rama V appointed a commissioner over Chiang Mai, Lamphun and Lampang to better integrate the region with the centre, and links were further strengthened in 1921 with the arrival of the railway from Bangkok.

The north today

Since the early twentieth century, the north has built on its agricultural richness to become relatively prosperous, though the economic booms of the last thirty years have been concentrated, as elsewhere in Thailand, in the towns, due in no small part to the increase in tourism. The eighty percent of Lanna's population who live in rural areas – of which the vast majority are subsistence farmers – are finding it increasingly difficult to earn a living off the soil, due to rapid population growth and land speculation for tourism and agro-industry.

3

Chiang Mai

Although rapid economic progress in recent years has brought problems such as pollution and traffic jams, **CHIANG MAI** still manages to preserve some of the atmosphere of an ancient village alongside its modern urban sophistication. It's the kingdom's second city, with a youthful population of about 400,000 (more than 60,000 of them are students), and the contrast with the maelstrom of Bangkok is pronounced: the people here are famously easy-going and even speak more slowly than their cousins in the capital, a lilting dialect known as *kham muang*. Chiang Mai's moated old quarter, where new buildings are limited to a height of four storeys, has retained many of its traditional wooden houses and quiet, leafy gardens, as well as the most famous and interesting **temples** in the city – Wat Phra Singh, Wat Chedi Luang and Wat Chiang Man – clustered conveniently close to each other. These elegant wats may be Chiang Mai's primary tourist sights, but they're no pre-packaged museum pieces – they're living community centres, where you're quite likely to be approached by monks keen to chat and practise their English. Inviting handicraft **shops**, some interesting **museums**, good-value accommodation, rich cuisine and riverside bars further enhance the city's allure, making Chiang Mai a place that detains many travellers longer than they expected. These days, increasing numbers of travellers are also taking advantage of the city's relaxed feel to indulge in a burst of self-improvement, enrolling for **courses** in **cookery**, **massage** and the like (see page 281).

Many colourful **festivals** (see page 284) attract throngs of visitors here too: Chiang Mai is one of the most popular places in Thailand to see in the Thai New Year – Songkhran – in mid-April, and to celebrate Loy Krathong at the full moon in November, when thousands of candles are floated down the Ping River in lotus-leaf boats. And a pilgrimage to **Doi Suthep**, the mountain to the west of town, should not be missed, to see the sacred, glittering temple and the towering views over the valley of the Ping River, when weather permits. Beyond the city limits (see page 300), a number of other day-trips can be made, such as to the ancient temples of Lamphun – and, of course, Chiang Mai is the main centre for hill-tribe **trekking**, as well as all sorts of other outdoor activities (see page 278).

Orientation is simple in central Chiang Mai, which divides roughly into two main parts: the **old town**, surrounded by the well-maintained moat and occasional remains of the city wall, where you'll find most of the temples, and the **new town centre**, between the moat and the Ping River to the east, the main market and shopping area. The biggest concentration of guesthouses and restaurants hangs between the two, centred on the landmark of **Tha Pae Gate** (*Pratu Tha Pae*) in the middle of the east moat. Also noteworthy is the area around **Thanon Nimmanhaemin**, near the university to the west of the old town, which is home to an ever-expanding choice of bars and restaurants, especially in the sois on its east side. On the outskirts, the town is bounded to the

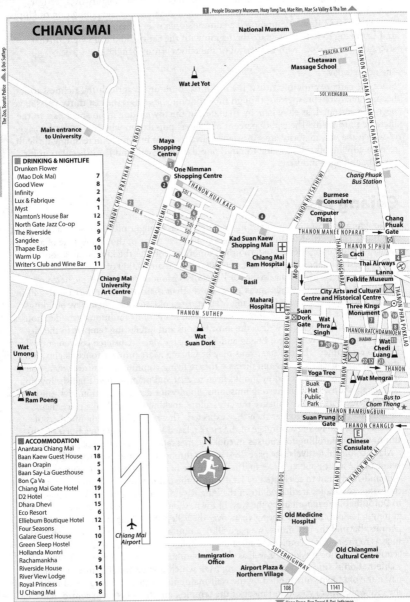

CHIANG MAI

People Discovery Museum, Huay Tung Tao, Mae Rim, Mae Sa Valley & Tha Ton

National Museum

PRACHA UTHIT
Chetawan
Massage School

Wat Jet Yot

SOI VIENGBUA

Main entrance
to University

Maya
Shopping
Centre

One Nimman
Shopping Centre

THANON HUAI KAEO

SOI 1
SOI 3
SOI 5
SOI 7
SOI 9
SOI 11
SOI 17

Chang Phuak
Bus Station

Burmese
Consulate

Computer
Plaza

THANON MANEE NOPARAT

Chang
Phuak
Gate

THANON SI PHUM

Cacti

Thai Airways

Lanna
Folklife Museum

City Arts and Cultural
Centre and Historical Centre

Three Kings
Monument

THANON RATCHADAMNOEN

Wat
Chedi
Luang

THANON

Wat Mengrai

Bus to
Chom Thong

THANON BAMRUNGBURI

Suan Prung
Gate

THANON CHANGLO

Chinese
Consulate

Kad Suan Kaew
Shopping Mall

Chiang Mai
Ram Hospital

Basil

Maharaj
Hospital

THANON SUTHEP

Suan
Dork
Gate

Wat
Phra
Singh

JHABAN

Yoga Tree

Buak
Hat
Public
Park

Chiang Mai
University
Art Centre

Wat
Suan Dork

Wat
Umong

Wat
Ram Poeng

Old Medicine
Hospital

Chiang Mai
Airport

Immigration
Office

Airport Plaza &
Northern Village

SUPERHIGHWAY

Old Chiangmai
Cultural Centre

108   1141

Hang Dong, Ban Tawai & Doi Inthanon

The Zoo, Tourist Police ◄ & Doi Suthep

3

THANON CHON PRATHAN (CANAL ROAD)

THANON NIMMANHEMIN

SOI 6

SIRIMANGKARAJAN

THANON HATSAT/HEWI

Moat

THANON SINGHARAT

THANON BOON RUANGRIT

THANON ARAK

THANON SAMLARN

THANON PHRA POKKLAO

THANON THIPHANET

THANON WUALAI

THANON MAHIDOL

N

DRINKING & NIGHTLIFE

Drunken Flower (Mao Dok Mai)	7
Good View	8
Infinity	2
Lux & Fabrique	4
Myst	1
Namton's House Bar	12
North Gate Jazz Co-op	5
The Riverside	9
Sangdee	6
Thapae East	10
Warm Up	3
Writer's Club and Wine Bar	11

ACCOMMODATION

Anantara Chiang Mai	17
Baan Kaew Guest House	18
Baan Orapin	5
Baan Say-La Guesthouse	3
Bon Ça Va	4
Chiang Mai Gate Hotel	19
D2 Hotel	11
Dhara Dhevi	15
Eco Resort	6
Elliebum Boutique Hotel	12
Four Seasons	1
Galare Guest House	10
Green Sleep Hostel	7
Hollanda Montri	2
Rachamankha	9
Riverside House	14
River View Lodge	13
Royal Princess	16
U Chiang Mai	8

north, east and south by the Superhighway and two further huge but incomplete ring roads, with Thanon Chon Prathan (Canal Road) providing a western bypass.

Brief history

Founded as the capital of Lanna in 1296, on a site indicated by the miraculous presence of deer and white mice, Chiang Mai – "New City" – has remained the north's

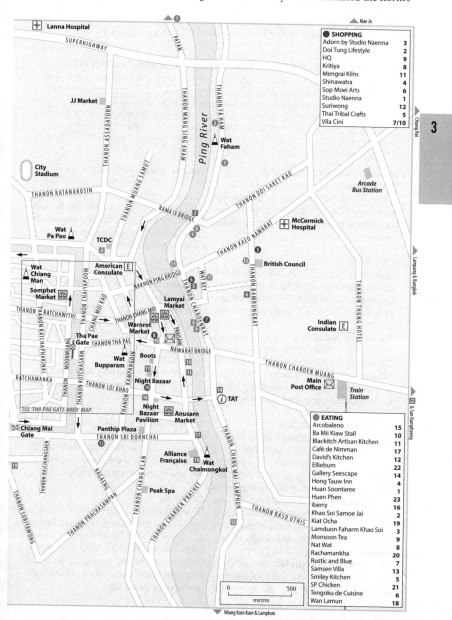

SHOPPING

Adorn by Studio Naenna	3
Doi Tung Lifestyle	2
HQ	9
Kritiya	8
Mengrai Kilns	11
Shinawatra	4
Sop Moei Arts	6
Studio Naenna	1
Suriwong	12
Thai Tribal Crafts	5
Vila Cini	7/10

EATING

Arcobaleno	15
Ba Mii Kiaw Stall	10
Blackitch Artisan Kitchen	11
Café de Nimman	17
David's Kitchen	12
Elliebum	22
Gallery Seescape	14
Hong Tauw Inn	4
Huan Soontaree	1
Huen Phen	23
iberry	16
Khao Soi Samoe Jai	2
Kiat Ocha	19
Lamduon Faharm Khao Soi	3
Monsoon Tea	9
Nat Wat	8
Rachamankha	20
Rustic and Blue	7
Samsen Villa	13
Smiley Kitchen	5
SP Chicken	21
Tengoku de Cuisine	6
Wan Lamun	18

most important settlement ever since. Lanna's golden age under the Mengrai dynasty, when most of the city's notable temples were founded, lasted until the Burmese captured the city in 1558. Two hundred years passed before the Thais pushed the Burmese back beyond Chiang Mai to roughly where they are now, and the **Burmese influence** is still strong – not just in art and architecture, but also in the rich curries and soups served here. After the recapture of the city, the *chao* (princes) of Chiang Mai remained nominal rulers of the north until 1939, but, with communications rapidly improving from the beginning of the last century, Chiang Mai was brought firmly into Thailand's mainstream as the region's administrative and service centre.

TREKKING AND OTHER OUTDOOR ACTIVITIES IN CHIANG MAI

The **trekking** industry in Chiang Mai offers an impressive variety of itineraries, with dozens of agencies covering nearly all trekkable areas of the north – choose a tour operator carefully. Many treks include a ride on an elephant (see page 314) and a bamboo-raft excursion, though the amount of actual walking included can vary greatly. Below we have listed a couple of operators who offer something a little different. Most of the companies detailed below include free pick-ups and drop-offs in the price of their tours, which can easily be arranged through your accommodation.

GENERAL ADVENTURE TOURS

Contact Travel Tasala, to the east of town ☎ 053 850160, ⊚ activethailand.com. Long-standing, general agency that offers a wide range of adventure tours, including whitewater rafting, trekking, cycling and kayaking.

TREKKING

Eagle House See page 289. This well-run guesthouse runs the standard type of trek, but to carefully chosen quiet areas and with an educational bent, and passes on a proportion of costs towards funding projects in hill-tribe villages.
The Trekking Collective 3/5 Soi 1, Thanon Loi Khro ☎ 053 208340, ⊚ trekkingcollective.com. This upmarket outfit arranges pricey but high-quality customized treks from one to six days and can cater for specific interests such as animal-watching; it too is involved in community programmes to help tribal people.

CYCLING AND KAYAKING

Chiang Mai Mountain Biking 1 Thanon Samlarn, opposite Wat Phra Singh ☎ 081 024 7046, ⊚ mountainbikingchiangmai.com. Mountain-biking tours, ranging from single-track downhill rides, mostly on Doi Suthep, that are tough for beginners, to cross-country leisure or hike-and-bike trips. The same company offers one- and multi-day kayaking trips on the north's lakes and rivers, including whitewater trips, paddles on the Ping River through Chiang Mai and bike-and-kayak trips (⊚ chiangmaikayaking.com).
Chiang Mai Sunday Bicycle Club ⊚ cmcycling.org. Interesting rides (part of a local cycling campaign) every Sunday morning from Tha Phae Gate that are open to all.

Click and Travel 158/40 Thanon Chiang Mai–Hod ☎ 053 281553, ⊚ clickandtravelonline.com. Belgian–Thai company that offers guided and self-guided cycling tours of Chiang Mai and the north, lasting from a few hours to four days, and maintains a useful website, ⊚ chiangmaicycling.org, full of all manner of information for cyclists.

WHITEWATER RAFTING

Siam Rivers 17 Thanon Ratchawithi ☎ 089 515 1917, ⊚ siamrivers.com. Chiang Mai's longest-standing whitewater rafting outfit, with high standards of safety (trips run roughly late May to Feb/March), which also offers full-moon trips and whitewater kayaking.

ROCK-CLIMBING

Chiang Mai Rock Climbing Adventures 55/3 Thanon Ratchaphakinai ☎ 053 207102 or ☎ 086 911 1470, ⊚ thailandclimbing.com. Climbing trips and courses to Crazy Horse Buttress, a limestone outcrop in the San Kamphaeng area, 50km east of town, which offers highly varied climbing with more than a hundred routes. Also caving courses and trips, bouldering trips and a bouldering wall, as well as equipment rental and sales, private guides and a partner-finding service.

ZIPLINING

Flight of the Gibbon ☎ 053 010660, ⊚ treetopasia.com. Full-day rainforest canopy tours on zip lines and sky bridges in the hills to the east of town.
Jungle Flight ☎ 053 208666, ⊚ jungleflightchiangmai.com. The first, and probably the best, of Flight of the Gibbon's several imitators, offering similar ziplining trips at cheaper prices.

CHIANG MAI BOAT TRIPS

A pleasant way to get a feel for the city and its layout is to take a **boat trip** on the Ping River. Hourly two-hour cruises operated by Mae Ping River Cruises (☎053 274822 or ☎081 884 4621, ⓦmaepingrivercruise.com) depart from Wat Chaimongkol on Thanon Charoen Prathet, sailing 8km upstream through lush countryside to a riverside farmhouse for a look around the fruit, herb and flower gardens, plus refreshments and fruit-tasting (B550/person; minimum two people, includes pick-up from your accommodation). Mae Ping River Cruises also offer trips to Wiang Kum Kam (see page 302).

Wat Phra Singh

At the far western end of Thanon Ratchdamnoen in the old town

If you see only one temple in Chiang Mai it should be **Wat Phra Singh**, perhaps the single most impressive array of buildings in the city. Just inside the gate to the right, the wooden scripture repository is the best example of its kind in the north, inlaid with glass mosaic and set high on a base decorated with stucco angels. The largest building in the compound, a colourful modern viharn fronted by naga balustrades, hides from view a rustic wooden bot, a chedi with a typical northern octagonal base constructed in 1345 to house the ashes of King Kam Fu, and – the highlight of the whole complex – the beautiful **Viharn Lai Kam**. This wooden gem is a textbook example of Lanna architecture, with its squat, multi-tiered roof and exquisitely carved and gilded pediment: if you feel you're being watched as you approach, it's the sinuous double arch between the porch's central columns, which represents the Buddha's eyebrows.

Inside sits one of Thailand's three **Phra Singh** (or Sihing) Buddha images (see page 283), a portly, radiant and much-revered bronze in a fifteenth-century Lanna style. Its setting is enhanced by the partly damaged but colourful **murals** of action-packed tableaux, which give a window on life in the north a hundred years ago. The murals illustrate two different stories: on the right-hand wall is an old folk tale, the *Sang Thong*, about a childless king and queen who are miraculously given a beautiful son, the "Golden Prince", in a conch shell. The murals on the left show the story of the mythical swan Suwannahong, who forms the magnificent prow of the principal royal barge in Bangkok. Incidentally, what look like Bermuda shorts on the men are in fact **tattoos**: in the nineteenth century, all boys in the north were tattooed from navel to kneecap, an agonizing ordeal undertaken to show their courage and to enhance their appeal to women. On one side of the wat is a high school for young yellow-sashed novices and schoolboys in blue shorts, who all noisily throng the temple compound during the day. Dally long enough and you'll be sure to have to help them with their English homework.

Wat Chedi Luang

Main entrance on Thanon Phra Pokklao, 10min walk east along Thanon Ratchdamnoen from Wat Phra Singh, with a back entrance on Thanon Jhaban • Daily 5am–10.30pm; B40 • Museum daily except Tues 8.30am–5pm • Monk Chat daily 9am–6pm

At **Wat Chedi Luang**, an enormous chedi, built in 1421 to house the ashes of King Ku Na but toppled from 90m to its present 60m by an earthquake in 1545, is the temple's most striking feature. You'll need a titanic leap of the imagination, however, to picture the beautifully faded pink-brick chedi, in all its crumbling grandeur, as it was in the fifteenth century, when it was covered in bronze plates and gold leaf, and housed the Emerald Buddha (see page 85) for eighty years. Recent attempts to rebuild the entire chedi to its former glory, now abandoned, have nevertheless led to modern replacements of the elephants at the base, the nagas that line the lengthy staircases and the Buddha images in its four niches, including an oversized replica of the Emerald Buddha, funded by the present king for Chiang Mai's seven-hundredth anniversary in 1996, in its old spot on the eastern side. A cup on a wire stretching to the pinnacle

MENGRAI MANIA

The spirit of **King Mengrai**, the heroic founder of the Lanna kingdom (see page 723), is still worshipped at dozens of shrines in Chiang Mai and the north seven hundred years after his death, but three in the old city stand out. About halfway between Wat Phra Singh and Wat Chedi Luang on Soi 6, Thanon Ratchamanka, Wat Kawt Kala was the second temple founded by the king in Chiang Mai (after Wat Chiang Man) and had its name changed to **Wat Phra Chao Mengrai** (or just **Wat Mengrai**) in the 1950s. The standing Buddha in its own *sala* just to the right of the main viharn here is said to replicate exactly King Mengrai's dimensions – and no wonder he was capable of such heroic deeds, as the image is 4m tall. By the beautiful, stately *bo* tree at the back of the compound stands a more plausible life-size modern statue of the king himself holding an elephant hook, where people leave all kinds of offerings, including swords.

Between Wat Chedi Luang and Chiang Mai City Arts and Cultural Centre stand two further monument-shrines to the great king. The site where he was killed by lightning in 1317, aged 79, is marked by a glittering, much-venerated **shrine** in its own small piazza on the corner of Thanon Ratchdamnoen and Thanon Phra Pokklao. A few minutes on up Thanon Phra Pokklao, Mengrai features again in the bronze **Three Kings Monument** in front of the arts and cultural centre, showing him discussing the auspicious layout of his "new city", Chiang Mai, with his allies, Ramkhamhaeng of Sukhothai and Ngam Muang of Phayao. The three kings had studied together under a religious teacher in Lopburi, but when they met up again, things were actually rather different from the harmonious picture portrayed by the monument: on a visit to Phayao, Ramkhamhaeng had an affair with Ngam Muang's wife, and Mengrai had to step in and mediate.

is used to bless the chedi during major Buddhist festivals: it's filled with water, and a pulley draws it to the spire where the water is tipped out over the sides of the chedi.

In a modern building (which women are not allowed to enter) by the main entrance stands the city's *lak muang* or foundation pillar, here called the **Sao Inthakin** (Pillar of Indra), a brick structure covered in coloured glass and topped by a Buddha. Built by King Mengrai at Wat Sadeu Muang (on Thanon Inthrawarorot) when he established Chiang Mai, the pillar was moved here to the city's geographical centre by King Kawila in 1800, while he was re-founding the city after the ravages of the wars with the Burmese. The building has recently been renovated, with colourful murals depicting the foundation legends of Wat Chedi Luang and the *Sao Inthakin*. Above, the *Sao Inthakin* building is sheltered by a stately gum tree which, the story has it, will stand for as long as the city's fortunes prosper.

On the northeast side of the chedi, **Monk Chat** is advertised, giving you a chance to meet and talk to the monks in English. There's a mildly diverting museum on the chedi's north side, while on the southwest side, a couple of small viharns shelter astonishingly lifelike waxworks of two much-revered but recently deceased monks.

Wat Pan Tao

Thanon Phra Pokklao, next door to Wat Chedi Luang on the north side

While you're in the vicinity, pop in on **Wat Pan Tao** to see the recently renovated, fourteenth-century, all-teak viharn. Constructed of unpolished panels, it's supported on enormous pillars and protected by carved wooden bars on the windows, a classic of graceful Lanna architecture. The teak panels apparently came from a royal palace and still sport a beautiful carved peacock over the main door, the emblem of the Chiang Mai kings. With a very active abbot, this temple is a good place to catch festivals, especially Songkhran, when it's filled with enormous sandcastles planted with coloured flags.

Chiang Mai central museums

Thanon Phra Pokklao • Tues–Sun 8.30am–5pm • B90 for each or B180 combined ticket • ☎ 053 217793, ⓦ cmocity.com

Around the landmark Three Kings Monument (see page 280) and its tree-lined piazza, the municipality runs three museums of varying levels of interest.

Chiang Mai City Arts and Cultural Centre

Immediately behind the monument, the elegant 1920s former provincial office houses the recently renovated, main **Chiang Mai City Arts and Cultural Centre** – essentially a museum with the aim of conveying the identity of the city and the region through its history, customs and culture. To this end, scale models and plenty of high-quality English-language audiovisuals are thoughtfully deployed. Displays include a recreated streetscape and traditional house, and a whole room devoted to the packed calendar of

---

COURSES IN CHIANG MAI

The most popular course on offer is how to **cook** Thai food (especially at the cluster of small schools on and around Soi 5, Thanon Ratchdamnoen), followed by **Thai massage**. Chiang Mai is also a popular place for meditation retreats (see page 285), while other skills to be tackled, besides rock-climbing (see page 278), include: **t'ai chi**, on ten-day programmes at Naisuan House, off Thanon Doi Saket Kao (☎085 714 5537, ⌨taichithailand.com); **yoga**, and many other wellness classes, at the Yoga Tree, 65/1 Thanon Arak (☎062 283 9915, ⌨theyogatree.org); one-to five-day workshops in silver **jewellery-making** through Nova, 179 Thanon Tha Pae (☎053 273058, ⌨nova-collection.com); indigo and weaving workshops at Studio Naenna (see page 298); and **Lanna arts and culture** with Origin Asia (see page 28).

COOKERY COURSES

Asia Scenic 31 Soi 5, Thanon Ratchdamnoen ☎053 418147–8. This much-recommended school covers all the bases, with an organic farm outside of town (B1200 full day or B1000 morning class) and an organic garden at its in-town school (B1000 full day or B800 morning or evening class). Market visit, recipe book and transfers included.

Basil 22/4 Soi 5, Thanon Sirimuangkarajan ☎083 320 7693, ⌨basilcookery.com. Highly regarded school with small class sizes, offering long morning or evening classes (B1000) on which you'll learn to cook six dishes (plus a curry paste). Market visit, recipe book and transfers included. Closed Sun.

Chiang Mai Thai Cookery School Office at 47/2 Thanon Moonmuang ☎053 206388, ⌨thaicookeryschool.com. The original – and still one of the best – offering courses of one (B1450) to five (B6700) days, as well as more advanced masterclasses. Courses are held about 30min drive out of town (transport provided). Market visit and recipe book included.

THAI MASSAGE COURSES

We give details on having a massage in Chiang Mai later in the chapter (see page 290).

Baan Hom Samunprai 9km south of town beyond Wiang Kum Kam ☎053 817362, ⌨homprang.com. Live-in massage courses out in the countryside costing B2200/day, including accommodation in a traditional village-style house with full board and the use of steam baths and bicycles; live-out courses from B1600/day.

Chetawan Massage School 7/1–2 Soi Samud Lanna, Thanon Pracha Uthit, off Thanon Chotana ☎053 410360–1, ⌨watpomassage.com. A branch of the massage school at Bangkok's Wat Pho (see page 90), which is considered to be the best place to study Thai massage in Thailand. Thirty-hour courses (6hr/day for 5 days) in traditional Thai (B9500) or foot (B7500) massage.

Old Medicine Hospital Off Thanon Wualai, opposite the Old Chiangmai Cultural Centre ☎053 201663 or ☎090 320 2712, ⌨thaimassageschool.ac.th. The longest-established centre in Chiang Mai, aka Shivagakomarpaj after the Indian hermit who is said to have founded the discipline over two thousand years ago. Highly respected five-day courses (B5000) with basic accommodation available; foot, oil and herbal compress courses are also offered.

Sunshine Network ⌨asokananda.com. An international group of practitioners and teachers founded by the highly respected German teacher, Harald Brust, aka Asokananda, who died in June 2005. Asokananda emphasized the spiritual aspect of what he called Thai yoga massage or Ayurvedic bodywork. Led by one of Asokananda's followers, twelve-day beginners' courses (B19,500, including basic accommodation, simple vegetarian rice meals and transport) are held at a rural retreat in a Lahu village between Chiang Mai and Chiang Rai, often with optional yoga, t'ai chi and Vipassana meditation classes.

Thai Massage School of Chiangmai Northeast of town on the Mae Jo road, 2km beyond the Superhighway ☎053 854330, ⌨tmcschool.com. Accredited by the Ministry of Education and highly recommended by past pupils. Five-day courses (B8500), as well as longer professional courses and foot massage courses. All courses include transport.

3

annual festivals in Lanna, and there's an engaging exhibit on the hill tribes upstairs. The courtyard in the back half of the building shelters temporary exhibitions, a souvenir shop and a small coffee shop with nice outdoor tables.

Lanna Folklife Museum

Across Thanon Phra Pokklao, the former courthouse, built in colonial style in 1935, is now the smartly designed **Lanna Folklife Museum**, with an attractive coffee shop in the grounds. An anthropological survey of Lanna culture and traditions, it's a bit listy and would benefit from more contextual information, but the curators have persuaded some notable local collectors to lend some beautiful artefacts: ceramics, lacquerware, ceremonial wooden betel sets (see page 322) and textiles. You'll also learn about local styles of mural painting and Buddhist ritual, as well as the *fon lep* (nail dance), a Lanna women's dance that's enhanced by the wearing of 20cm brass fingernail extensions.

Chiang Mai Historical Centre

Behind the City Arts and Cultural Centre, with its entrance on Thanon Ratchawithi, the **Chiang Mai Historical Centre** is the most disappointing of the three museums – you'll get little more out of it than you would from reading a half-decent history of the region.

Wat Chiang Man

Thanon Ratchaphakinai

Erected by Mengrai on the site where he first pitched camp, **Wat Chiang Man** is the oldest temple in Chiang Mai and most notable for two dainty and very holy Buddha images housed in the viharn to the right of the entrance. The **Phra Sila**, a graceful marble bas-relief carved in northern India, supposedly in the sixth century BC, stands in the typical *tribunga*, or hip-shot stance. Its partner, the **Phra Setangamani** (or Crystal Buddha), supposedly made in the second century BC, was taken from Lopburi to Haripunjaya (Lamphun) as a talisman by Chama Thevi when she became queen there, and was later captured by King Mengrai; it's much revered by the inhabitants of Chiang Mai for its rainmaking powers and is carried through the streets during the Songkhran festival to help the rainy season on its way.

Thailand Creative and Design Centre (TCDC)

1/1 Thanon Muang Samut, behind Muang Mai market • Tues–Sun 10.30am–6pm • Free • ☎ 052 080500, ⓦ tcdc.or.th/chiangmai

The Chiang Mai branch of this resource centre for designers occasionally hosts interesting temporary shows that are worth looking out for. It's the main hub for Chiang Mai Design Week (ⓦ chiangmaidesignweek.com), an ambitious and diverse festival of creativity that takes place all over town every year in early December.

Highland People Discovery Museum

About 4km northwest of Chang Puak Gate, signposted off the north side of Route 1266, which runs between Thanon Chotana and Thanon Chon Prathan • Mon–Fri 8.30am–noon & 1–4pm • donation requested

Also known as the Tribal Museum (in Thai, Phiphithaphan Chao Khao), this museum provides a valuable introduction to the hill tribes before setting off on a trek. Set in an artificial lake, Norng Hor, that's surrounded by restaurants on stilts, the pagoda-like edifice covers the six main highland peoples, with smaller sections on another four ethnic minorities who live in northern Thailand, the Lawa, the Htin, the Khamu and the Mrabri. The collection is especially strong on the tribes' beautiful traditional fabrics, with labels, display boards and a video in English to flesh out the picture. Behind the restaurants on the south side of the lake, you'll find reconstructions of the typical houses of each of the ten minorities.

Chiang Mai National Museum

On the northwestern outskirts on the Superhighway • Wed–Sun 9am–4pm • B100

In telling the history of Lanna art and culture, the **National Museum** – despite a very lengthy recent renovation – is not as informative and user-friendly as its rival, the Chiang Mai Arts and Cultural Centre, though in terms of the quality of artefacts on display, it has the edge. Upstairs, it illustrates Lanna's history with votive tablets and Buddha heads from Wiang Kum Kam (see page 302) and a two-metre-long footprint of the Buddha from around 1600, made of teak inlaid with mother-of-pearl. Downstairs, the highlight of the museum's run through the region's artistic development is the huge, smiling head of the Phra Saen Swe, a lion-type Buddha image (see page 283); cast in bronze in Chiang Mai, it would originally have stood 6m tall. Look out also for some lovely ceramics from San Kamphaeng and a gilded teak candelabra, elaborately carved with nagas and floral patterns – such sattaphan are found in front of the main Buddha images of temples all over northern Thailand, their seven candles representing the seven mountains that surround Mount Meru at the centre of the Buddhist universe. There's a good spot for lunch, a branch of *Lamduon Faharm Khao Soi* (see page 294), just east of the museum on the north side of the Superhighway.

Wat Jet Yot

Set back from the Superhighway, a 10min walk west of the National Museum

The peaceful garden temple of **Wat Jet Yot** is named after the "seven spires" of its unusual chedi. It was built in 1455 by King Tilok, after a model of the great temple at Bodh Gaya in India, and represents the seven places around Bodh Gaya which the Buddha visited in the seven weeks following his enlightenment; it also houses the king's ashes. Around the base of the chedi, delicate stuccos portray flowers and cross-legged deities serenely floating in the sky, whose faces are said to be those of Tilok's relatives. They represent the angels who gathered to rejoice at the Buddha's enlightenment, showering him with heavenly flowers.

Chiang Mai Zoo and Aquarium

Thanon Huai Kaeo

About 1km beyond Wat Jet Yot at the busy Rin Kham crossroads, the Superhighway meets Thanon Huai Kaeo, a broad avenue that runs from the northwest corner of the moat to the foot of Doi Suthep, where it becomes the winding road up to the summit. Heading out up Thanon Huai Kaeo, past the sprawling campus of Chiang Mai University (CMU or "*Mor Chor*"), brings you to **Chiang Mai Zoo and Aquarium**, in an attractive park at the base of the mountain.

LANNA BUDDHA IMAGES

In the golden age of the Lanna kingdom, from the fourteenth to the sixteenth centuries, Buddha images were produced in the north in two main contrasting styles (Ayutthaya-style images also became popular from the fifteenth century onwards). One group, which resembles images from northern India, has been called the **lion-type**, after the Shakyamuni (Lion of the Shakyas) archetype at the great Buddhist temple at Bodh Gaya, the site of the Buddha's enlightenment. It's been conjectured that a delegation sent by King Tilok to Bodh Gaya in the 1450s brought back a copy of the statue, which became the model for hundreds of Lanna images. These broad-shouldered, plump-bellied Buddhas are always seated with the right hand in the touching-the-earth gesture, while the face is well rounded with pursed lips and a serious, majestic demeanour. The second type is the **Thera Sumana** style named after the monk Mahathera Sumana, who came from Sukhothai in 1369 to establish his Sri Lankan sect in Lanna. The Chiang Mai National Museum is well stocked with this type of image, which shows strong Sukhothai influence, with an oval face and a flame-like *ushnisha* on top of the head.

CHIANG MAI FESTIVALS

Chiang Mai is the best and busiest place in the country to see in the Thai New Year, **Songkhran**, which takes over the city between April 13 and 15 and during the preceding days. The most obvious role of the festival is as an extended "rain dance" in the driest part of the year, when huge volumes of canal water are thrown about in a communal water-fight that spares no one a drenching. The other elements of this complex festival are not as well known but no less important. In the temple compounds, communities get together to build sandcastles in the shape of chedis, which they cover with coloured flags – this bestows merit on any ancestors who happen to find themselves in hell and may eventually release them from their torments, and also shows an intent to help renovate the wat in the year to come. Houses are given a thorough spring-clean to see out the old year, while Buddha images from the city's main temples are cleaned, polished and sprinkled with lustral water, before being ceremonially carried through the middle of the water-fight to give everyone the chance to throw water on them and receive the blessing of renewal. Finally, younger family members formally visit their elders during the festival to ask for their blessings, while pouring scented water over their hands.

Loy Krathong, on and around the night of the full moon in November, has its most showy celebration at Sukhothai (see page 242), but Chiang Mai – where it is also known as **Yipeng** – is not far behind. Thousands of candles are gently floated down the Ping River in beautiful lotus-leaf boats, and people release **khom loy**, paper hot-air balloons that create a magical spectacle as they float heavenward, sometimes with firecrackers trailing behind. As with krathongs, they are released to carry away sins and bad luck, as well as to honour the Buddha's topknot, which he cut off when he became an ascetic (according to legend, the topknot is looked after by the Buddha's mother in heaven).

Chiang Mai's brilliantly colourful **flower festival**, centred on Buak Hat Park at the southwest corner of the old town usually on the first weekend of February, also attracts huge crowds. The highlight is a procession of floats, modelled into animals, chedis and even scenes from the *Ramayana*, and covered in flowers. In early April, the **Poy Sang Long** festival, centred around Wat Pa Pao near the northeast corner of the old city, is an ordination ritual for young Thai Yai (Shan) men, who are paraded round town on the shoulders of relatives. The boys are dressed in extravagant, colourful clothing with huge floral headdresses, which they symbolically cast off at the end of the festival to don a saffron robe – its most elaborate manifestation in Thailand is in Mae Hong Son (see page 328). In late May or early June, the week-long **Inthakin Festival**, a life-prolonging ceremony for the city of Chiang Mai, using holy water from Doi Luang Chiang Dao, is focused around the city foundation pillar at Wat Chedi Luang, which is thronged with market stalls and local people making offerings.

The zoo

Daily 8am–6pm • B150, children B70 • ⓦ chiangmai.zoothailand.org

Originally a menagerie of a missionary family's pets, the **zoo** now houses an impressive collection of about eight thousand animals, including rare Thai species, in modern, relatively comfortable conditions. There's a children's zoo and a colourful aviary, while larger mammals include elephants, giraffes, penguins, koalas, a rhino and the current favourites, two **giant pandas** on an extended loan from China (B100 extra, children B50). Despite a disorientating layout, it makes a diverting visit, especially for kids, though visitors from temperate countries can probably do without entering the Snow Dome. Feeding and activity times for animals are posted clearly (including on the website), and refreshment stalls for humans are never far away.

The zoo is better visited in the morning to avoid the afternoon heat. The grounds are too big to walk round, but shuttle buses (B30, children B20) are available to take you around, or you can hire your own golf cart (B300–350/hour).

The aquarium

Mon–Fri 10am–4pm, Sat & Sun 9am–4.30pm • B520, B390 children (includes admission to zoo) • ⓦ chiangmaiaquarium.com

Towards the western side of the zoo (linked to the entrance by shuttle bus), the **aquarium** is the biggest in Southeast Asia, with what's said – at 130m – to be the longest underwater viewing tunnel in the world. With the aim of showing landlocked Chiang Mai some rarely seen species, the huge edifice is strictly divided in half: in the freshwater section, you can see not only the Mekong giant catfish (see page 373), but also *thae pha*, the Chao Phraya giant catfish; while the salty half displays rare white-tip reef sharks, rays and moray eels. There's a saltwater touch pool, and a long menu of feeding times, detailed on the website; it's also possible to snorkel (B1000) and scuba-dive (B4290) with the fishes.

Wat Suan Dork

Thanon Suthep • Monk Chat Mon–Fri 5–7pm • Ⓦ monkchat.net

Wat Suan Dork, the "Flower Garden Temple", is surrounded by walls as part of Chiang Mai's fortifications. Legend says that Mahathera Sumana, when he was invited to establish his Sri Lankan Buddhist sect here in 1369, brought with him a miraculous glowing relic. Ku Na, the king of Chiang Mai, ordered a huge chedi – the one you see today – to be built in his flower garden, but as the pea-sized relic was being placed inside the chedi, it split into two parts: one half was buried here, the other found its way to Doi Suthep, after further adventures (see page 300).

The brilliantly whitewashed chedi now sits next to a garden of smaller, equally dazzling chedis containing the ashes of the Chiang Mai royal family; framed by Doi Suthep to the west, this makes an impressive and photogenic sight, especially at sunset. At the back of the dusty compound, the bot is decorated with lively *Jataka* murals and enshrines a beautifully illuminated, 500-year-old bronze Buddha image. Nearby signs point the way to **Monk Chat**, organized by the Mahachulalongkorn Buddhist University based at the temple, which gives the monk-students the opportunity to meet foreigners and practise their English, and you the chance to talk to monks about anything from Buddhism to the weather – or about the university's overnight Buddhist culture and meditation courses (see page 285).

Chiang Mai University Art Centre

Thanon Nimmanhemin, near the corner of Thanon Suthep • Tues–Sun 9am–5pm • Free • ☎ 053 218279, Ⓦ facebook.com/cmuartcenter

The modern **Chiang Mai University Art Centre** is not only confirmation of the city's growing importance, but also a boon to the large local artistic community. The large,

---

MEDITATION IN CHIANG MAI

The peace and quiet of the northern capital make it ideally suited to **meditation** sessions, short courses and longer retreats, many of which are conducted in English. General information and advice about meditation is given in Basics (see page 52), where you'll also find details of the retreats at Wat Phra That Chom Thong, 60km south of Chiang Mai.

Green Papaya Sangha Ⓦ greenpapayasangha.org. Offers meditation in the tradition of Vietnamese Zen Master Thich Nhat Hanh on Thursday evenings at 7.30pm at the Yoga Tree (see page 281). It also hosts dhamma talks from teachers of other Buddhist traditions. By donation.

International Buddhist Meditation Centre Wat Phra That Doi Suthep ☎ 053 295012, Ⓦ fivethousandyears.org. A variety of Vipassana meditation courses for beginners and experienced students, from five to 21 days. Registration must be made in advance (courses are often full). By donation.

Mahachulalongkornrajavidiyalaya Buddhist University Wat Suan Dork Ⓦ monkchat.net. Introductory retreat courses on meditation and Thai Buddhist culture, for which you need to wear white clothes, available for B300. Including yoga, chanting and almsgiving, they begin at about 1pm on a Tuesday, before departure to the training centre, returning to Wat Suan Dork at about 3pm the next day (B500). Courses are sometimes cancelled so check the schedule on the website.

Northern Insight Meditation Centre Wat Ram Poeng (aka Wat Tapotaram), off Thanon Chon Prathan near Wat Umong ☎ 053 278620, Ⓦ palikanon.com/vipassana/tapotaram/tapotaram.htm. Disciplined Vipassana courses (with a rule of silence, no food after noon and so on), taught by Thai monks with translators. The minimum stay is ten days, with a basic course lasting 26 days, and payment is by donation.

purpose-built exhibition areas are well designed and lit, and the exhibitions generally change each month, giving visitors an insight into modern Thai art, as well as anything from Japanese lacquerware sculpture to Iranian carpetry art. There's a shop and a good café, and films and concerts are regularly put on here.

Wat Umong

Off Thanon Suthep: turn left (south) after Wang Nam Gan (a royal agricultural produce project), then follow the signs to the wat for about 1km along a winding lane

More of a park than a temple, **Wat Umong** makes an unusual, charming place for a quiet stroll, at the centre of an up-and-coming creative neighbourhood dotted with coffee shops and boutiques. According to legend, the wat was built by King Mengrai, but renovated in the 1380s by King Ku Na for a brilliant but deranged monk called Jan, who was prone to wandering off into the forest to meditate. Because Ku Na wanted to be able to get Jan's advice at any time, he founded this wat and decorated the **tunnels** (*umong*) beneath the chedi with paintings of trees, flowers and birds to simulate the monk's favoured habitat. Some of the old tunnels can still be explored, where obscure fragments of paintings and one or two small modern shrines can be seen. Above the tunnels, frighteningly lavish nagas guard the staircase up to the bell-shaped, Sri Lankan-style **chedi** and a grassy platform that supports a grotesque black statue of the fasting Buddha, all ribs and veins: he is depicted as he was during his six years of self-mortification, before he realized that he should avoid extremes along the Middle Path to enlightenment. Behind the chedi, the ground slopes away to a tree-lined **lake** inhabited by hungry carp, where locals come to relax and feed the fish. On a tiny island here, reached by a concrete bridge, stands a statue of the late Buddhadasa Bhikkhu (see page 530), a famous southern Thai monk who re-established the monastic community here in the 1960s.

ARRIVAL AND DEPARTURE   CHIANG MAI

On arrival at the train station or one of the bus stations, you can either flag down a red songthaew out on the road or charter a tuk-tuk or songthaew (see page 287) to get to the centre. To **book tickets** for departure, there are several ways to dodge a long, extra trip out to Arcade (see pages 30 and 287), including just asking your guesthouse or hotel. Queen Bee, 5 Thanon Moonmuang (☎053 275525, ⓦqueenbeetours.com), is a reliable **travel agent** for train tickets and all manner of minibus, bus and domestic plane tickets, as well as for a wide range of tours. STA Travel on Floor 3 of Maya shopping centre, at the corner of Thanon Nimmanhemin and Thanon Huai Kaeo (☎052 081140, ⓦstatravel.co.th), is a good agent for cheap international plane tickets.

BY PLANE

Chiang Mai Airport is 3km southwest of the centre. Its busiest route is Bangkok, which is served by all seven of the main Thai carriers (only Thai, Thai Smile, Vietjet and Bangkok Airways fly to Suvarnabhumi from here). Meanwhile Bangkok Airways does Ko Samui, Mae Hong Son and Phuket, Thai Smile Phuket, Air Asia Hat Yai, Khon Kaen, Krabi, Phuket, Surat Thani, U-Tapao (near Pattaya) and Ubon Ratchathani, and Nok Air Udon Thani. There are also dozens of international routes from China, East and Southeast Asia. **Airport facilities** You'll find currency exchange booths and ATMs, cafés, a tourist police booth, a post office, left

luggage and car rental offices such as Avis (☎02 251 1131, ⓦavisthailand.com).

Getting to/from the centre Two licensed a/c taxi companies have booths in the domestic baggage hall and in the arrivals hall, charging from B160 to Tha Pae Gate, for example (they don't use their meters). From the exit by the international arrivals hall, at the south end of the terminal, a/c minibuses run to hotels in town every half-hour (B40/ person). Tuk-tuks and red songthaews can bring departing passengers to the airport (around B120 from the city centre), but are not allowed to pick up fares there. A new R3 blue bus service started in 2018, linking the airport with Thanon Nimmanhemin, the Old Town and the night bazaar (every 20–30min; B20 flat fare).

Destinations Bangkok (25 daily; 1hr); Hat Yai (2 daily; 2hr); Khon Kaen (1 daily; 1hr 10min); Ko Samui (1 daily; 1hr 50min); Krabi (2 daily; 2hr); Mae Hong Son (2 daily; 45min); Phuket (5 daily; 2hr); Surat Thani (2 daily; 2hr); Ubon Ratchathani (1 daily; 1hr 45min); Udon Thani (3 daily; 1hr); U-Tapao (3 daily; 1hr 15min–2hr).

BY TRAIN

Many people arrive – sometimes an hour or two later than scheduled – at the train station (which has a left-luggage office) on Thanon Charoen Muang, just over 2km from Tha Pae Gate on the eastern side of town. There's usually a welcoming committee of guesthouse staff, plugging their accommodation and offering free lifts.

Destinations Bangkok (5 daily; 12hr–14hr 30min); Den Chai (for Phrae and Nan; 6 daily; 4–5hr); Doi Khun Tan (6 daily; 1hr–1hr 30min); Lampang (6 daily; 2hr–2hr 30min).

BY BUS

Arcade bus station Chiang Mai's main bus station **(which has left-luggage facilities)** is off the south side of Thanon Kaeo Nawarat, about 3km from Tha Pae Gate to the northeast.

Chang Phuak bus station This small station off the east side of Thanon Chotana handles services from the rest of Chiang Mai province (including Chom Thong and Tha Ton); buses from Lamphun also end up here.

Bus companies The main Chiang Mai-based long-distance bus company, Green Bus (☎ 053 266480, ⓦ greenbusthailand.com), maintains a ticket office in the centre of town, on the corner of Thanon Singharat and Thanon Ratchdamnoen, opposite Wat Phra Singh. If you insist on travelling here with one of the low-cost tourist bus companies on Bangkok's Thanon Khao San despite our warnings (see page 137), try to find out exactly where you'll be dropped in Chiang Mai before making a booking: these companies' buses have been known to stop on a remote part of the Superhighway, where they "sell" their passengers to various guesthouse touts.

Destinations Bangkok (30 daily; 9hr 30min–11hr); Chiang Khong (2 daily; 5–6hr); Chiang Rai (roughly every 30min; 3hr); Chiang Saen (2 daily; 5–7hr); Chom Thong (every 20min; 1hr–1hr 30min); Fang (every 30min; 2hr 30min–3hr 30min); Kanchanaburi (3 daily; 11hr); Khon Kaen (9 daily; 12hr); Khorat (10 daily; 12hr); Lampang (roughly every 30min; 1hr 30min–2hr); Lamphun (every 20min; 30min–1hr); Luang Prabang, Laos (4 weekly; 20hr); Mae Hong Son (3 daily via Mae Sariang, 8hr; 10 daily via Pai, 6–8hr 30min); Mae Sai (6–8 daily; 4hr 40min–5hr 15min); Mae Sot (2 daily; 6hr); Nan (13 daily; 5–6hr); Pai (hourly; 3hr–4hr 30min); Phitsanulok (over 30 daily; 5–7hr); Phrae (11 daily; 4hr); Sukhothai (over 20 daily; 5–6hr); Tha Ton (6 daily; 4hr); Udon Thani (2 daily; 12hr).

3

GETTING AROUND

BY BICYCLE

Although you can comfortably walk between the most central temples, bicycles are the best way of getting around the old town and, with a bit of legwork, out to the attractions beyond the moat too. Rickety sit-up-and-beg models and basic mountain bikes are available at many outlets around the old town, especially on the roads along the eastern moat, for about B50/day, while knowledgeable and helpful Cacti, 94/1 Thanon Singharat, near the corner of Si Phum (☎ 053 212979 or ☎ 089 757 9150), rents good-quality, well-maintained road and mountain bikes (B150–450/day), as well as selling new and used bikes and doing repairs.

BY SONGTHAEW

Chiang Mai has a handful of city buses that mostly operate out of Arcade Bus Station, but their schedules are so infrequent that they're next-to-useless. Instead, people use red songthaews (rot daeng) within the city (songthaews of other colours serve outlying villages and suburbs). A small number of these vehicles run along fixed routes that are popular with locals (B15/person), but the vast majority act as shared taxis, picking up a number of passengers headed in roughly the same direction and taking each to their specific destination. A journey in the centre of town, for example from Tha Pae Gate to Wat Phra Singh, will set you back B30/person, but it'll naturally cost more to go somewhere off the beaten track or if the driver thinks you want to charter (mao) the whole vehicle.

BY TAXI, TUK-TUK OR SAMLOR

Chiang Mai's so-called "meter taxis" never switch on their meters, they only quote flat fares, typically B150 for a 2km journey. You can't flag them down on the street – ask at your accommodation or try calling ☎ 053 262878 or ☎ 053 241955 for a pick-up. More prevalent are tuk-tuks, for which heavy bargaining is expected – allow around B60 for a short journey, say from the Night Bazaar to Tha Pae Gate. The town still has a few samlors, which are cheap when used by locals to haul produce home from the market, but not so cheap when chartered by groups of upmarket tourists on sightseeing tours from their hotel. App-based taxi services have recently come to Chiang Mai, of which the most popular is Uber's Southeast Asian equivalent, Grab.

BY MOTORBIKE

Motorbikes – most useful for exploring places outside of Chiang Mai – are available to rent in all shapes and sizes around Tha Pae Gate, costing around B200–250/day for a 125cc automatic. Among reliable rental outlets, Queen Bee, 5 Thanon Moonmuang (☎ 053 275525, ⓦ queen-bee.com), and Mr Mechanic, Thanon Moonmuang, near the corner of Thanon Ratchawithi (☎ 053 214708, ⓦ mr-mechanic1994.com), who has bikes of all sizes, can also offer insurance.

BY CAR

Many outlets in the Tha Pae Gate area rent out cars and 4WDs, from as little as B800/day: reliable companies offering insurance and breakdown recovery include Avis, at Chiang Mai airport (☎ 02 251 1131, ⓦ avisthailand.com;

delivery and collection anywhere in Chiang Mai); Journey Smile, 283 Thanon Tha Pae (☎053 208787, ⓦjourneysmile.

com); North Wheels, 70/4–8 Thanon Chaiyapoom (☎053 874478, ⓦnorthwheels.com); and Queen Bee (see above).

INFORMATION

Tourist information The TAT office (daily 8.30am–4.30pm; ☎053 248604–5) is on Thanon Chiang Mai–Lamphun, on the east bank of the river south of Nawarat Bridge. It's not to be confused with TAD Travel and Tours on Thanon Ratchaphakinai and other similarly named outlets prominently displaying "INFORMATION" signs, which pretend to be government information offices but are in fact private travel agents.

Maps *Nancy Chandler's Map of Chiang Mai*, sold in many outlets in the city (B320) and online in either paper or pdf form (ⓦnancychandler.net), is very handy for a detailed exploration: like their brightly coloured Bangkok map, it gives a personal choice of sights, shops, restaurants and various oddities.

Listings Several free, monthly, locally published magazines such as *Citylife* contain information about upcoming events in town and articles about local culture; they're distributed in spots where tourists tend to congregate, including hotel lobbies. *Citylife* also has a website at ⓦchiangmaicitylife.com and produces a fortnightly map with events listings, *City Now*.

ACCOMMODATION

Chiang Mai is well stocked with every kind of accommodation to suit all budgets, though places may fill up from December to February and are very busy at festival time, particularly during Songkhran (April), Loy Krathong (Nov) and around New Year's Eve. **Basic guesthouses**, often friendly, quiet affairs with their own outdoor cafés, are gathered on the narrow sois inside the old city. Situated close to the eastern side of the moat and Tha Pae Gate, **Thanon Moonmuang's Soi 9** and the **south end of Thanon Ratchaphakinai** almost warrant being called travellers' ghettoes (though nothing like on the scale of Bangkok's Thanon Khao San), but there are plenty of other, quieter options within the moat where you can better soak up the old town's charm. In the moderate price range, by far the best options are the **upmarket guesthouses and boutique hotels**, which, as well as good facilities, generally offer much more appealing decor and atmosphere than similarly priced chain hotels. At the top end, there has been a recent explosion of **luxury accommodation** in Chiang Mai, most of them enhanced by traditional Lanna architectural touches.

ESSENTIALS

Scams Beware of tuk-tuk and songthaew drivers at the bus and train stations offering a free ride if you stay at a particular guesthouse – perhaps adding, falsely, that the place you had planned to stay is full or closed – as you'll probably find that the price of a room is bumped up to pay for your ride. To get around this, some guesthouses send their own staff to the stations, who will genuinely give you a free ride; and many places will offer a free pick-up when you book.

Trekking hassles Many of the least expensive places in Chiang Mai make their money from trekking and tours, which can be convenient as a trek often needs a lot of organizing beforehand, but can equally be annoying if you're in Chiang Mai for other reasons and are put under pressure to trek; most of the guesthouses we've listed can

arrange trekking, but at none of them should you get this kind of undue hassle.

THA PAE GATE AREA

GUESTHOUSES

60 Blue House 32–34 Thanon Ratchaphakinai ☎053 206126, ⓦ60bluehouse.com; map p.289. Helpful, eco-friendly guesthouse with lots of local information and a small, leafy garden. Most of the turquoise-themed accommodation shares bathrooms: an eight-bed dorm (not bunks), good-value fan or a/c single rooms and a/c doubles or twins. Larger rooms sleeping three or four are en suite and have mini-kitchens. Dorms B250, doubles B800

★ **Awana House** 7 Soi 1, Thanon Ratchdamnoen ☎053 419005, ⓦawanahouse.com; map p.289. This welcoming, Thai-Dutch guesthouse has a tiny, covered pool and large, nicely furnished rooms (most with balconies), complete with colourful trompe l'oeil paintings, a/c, hot water, cable TV and fridge. There's also a pleasant, mostly covered rooftop terrace, which shelters two fan rooms with double beds, sharing a hot-water bathroom. Fan B495, a/c B690

Chiang Mai Thai House 5/1 Soi 5, Thanon Tha Pae ☎053 904110, ⓦchiangmaithaihouse.com; map p.289. There's a choice of smallish but well-furnished rooms with fan and cable TV, or bigger ones with a/c and mini-bar (some with cute mini-gardens on the ground floor), in this centrally located but fairly quiet place, which also has a tiny pool. Fan B600, a/c B1200

Diva Guesthouse 84/13 Thanon Ratchaphakinai ☎053 273851, ⓦdivaguesthouse.com; map p.289. Helpful spot with richly coloured murals on the walls, a sociable ground-floor café and a wide choice of clean rooms with en-suite hot showers: mixed, six-bed, fan-cooled or a/c dorms and fan and a/c private rooms of all sizes. Success has spawned two overspill branches nearby. Dorms B120, fan doubles B300, a/c doubles B500

★ **Eagle House** 16 Soi 3, Thanon Chang Moi Kao ☎053 235387, ⓦeaglehouse.com; map p.289. Run by an Irishwoman who is keen to promote ethical ecotourism, this friendly, quiet, well-maintained guesthouse offers a spacious garden terrace area with a good café and well-organized treks, as well as Thai cookery courses. Choose from a wide variety of en-suite rooms of different sizes, most with hot water, some with a/c. Fan B300, a/c B500

Gap's House 3 Soi 4, Thanon Ratchdamnoen ☎053 278140, ⓦgaps-house.com; map p.289. Set around a relaxing, leafy compound strewn with objets d'art is a wide range of a/c rooms with antique furniture and hot showers.

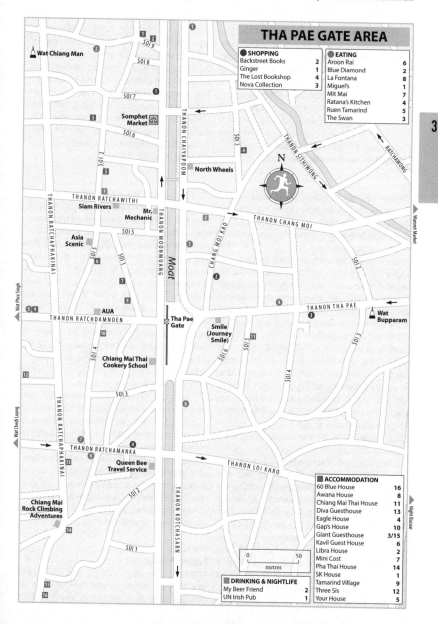

THA PAE GATE AREA

3

● SHOPPING
Backstreet Books	2
Ginger	1
The Lost Bookshop	4
Nova Collection	3

● EATING
Aroon Rai	6
Blue Diamond	2
La Fontana	8
Miguel's	1
Mit Mai	7
Ratana's Kitchen	4
Ruen Tamarind	5
The Swan	3

■ ACCOMMODATION
60 Blue House	16
Awana House	8
Chiang Mai Thai House	11
Diva Guesthouse	13
Eagle House	4
Gap's House	10
Giant Guesthouse	3/15
Kavil Guest House	6
Libra House	2
Mini Cost	7
Pha Thai House	14
SK House	1
Tamarind Village	9
Three Sis	12
Your House	5

■ DRINKING & NIGHTLIFE
My Beer Friend	2
UN Irish Pub	1

Wat Chiang Man
Somphet Market
North Wheels
Siam Rivers
Mr. Mechanic
Asia Scenic
AUA
Tha Pae Gate
Smile (Journey Smile)
Chiang Mai Thai Cookery School
Queen Bee Travel Service
Chiang Mai Rock Climbing Adventures
Wat Bupparam
Moat
Wat Phra Singh
Wat Chedi Luang
Warorot Market
Night Bazaar

THANON CHAIYAPOOM
THANON RATCHAWITHI
THANON RATCHAPHAKINAI
THANON MOONMUANG
THANON RATCHDAMNOEN
THANON RATCHAMANKA
THANON KOTCHASARN
THANON LOI KHRO
THANON CHANG MOI
THANON THA PAE
THANON SITHIWONG
CHANG MOI KAO
RATCHAWONG

0 50
metres

3

MASSAGES AND SPAS IN CHIANG MAI

Many of Chiang Mai's top hotels have full-service **spas**, and there are several upmarket stand-alones. However, some of the best traditional **massages** in town – no frills but highly skilled and good value – are likely to be had at schools such as the Old Medicine Hospital, which offers consistently good Thai (B250/hour), herbal and foot massages; and out in the countryside Baan Hom Samunprai offers great two-hour massages for B800, as well as foot massages, herbal compress massages and steam baths (for both, see page 281).

Let's Relax Night Bazaar Pavilion, Thanon Chang Klan ☎ 053 818498, ⊌ letsrelaxspa.com. Part of a nationwide chain, with several other branches around town, this reasonably priced spa lays on a few more frills, longer opening hours and a wider range of treatments than the basic massage centres (B600 for a 1hr Thai massage).

Oasis Spa 4 Thanon Samlan, just south of Wat Phra Singh, & 102 Thanon Sirimuangkarajan ☎ 053 920111, ⊌ oasisspa.net. Upmarket spa with a good reputation (B1990 for a 2hr traditional massage).

The Peak Spa & Beauty Salon Twin Peaks Condo, 187/13 Thanon Chang Klan ☎ 053 818869, ⊌ peak-spa.com. Excellent choice, offering a wide range of treatments at moderate prices, but with service and facilities comparable to an upmarket hotel spa (from B800 for 90min Thai massage). Free transfers included.

Thai Massage Conservation Club 99 Thanon Ratchamankha, near Wat Chedi Luang ☎ 083 864 1184, ⊌ thaiblindmassage.com. Basic setup with traditional massages by extremely competent, blind masseurs (B200/hr), who focus on vigorous acupressure rather than stretching.

The room price includes a simple cooked breakfast, and a vegetarian buffet is served in the evening (not Sun); one-day cookery courses available. Decent rates for singles. B550

Giant Guesthouse Soi 6, Thanon Moonmuang ☎ 053 227338, ⊌ giantguesthouse.com; map p.289. This popular option is right next to the market and has its own kitchen – ideal if you fancy practising your Thai cooking. The helpful staff put on films in the comfortable lounge, and there's a small leafy patio. Rooms come with fan (shared or en-suite bathrooms) or a/c. There's another, fan-only branch at the bottom of Thanon Ratchaphakinai with dorm beds (B120). Fan B240, a/c B450

Kavil Guest House 10/1 Soi 5, Thanon Ratchdamnoen ☎ 053 224740 or ☎ 089 852 1875; map p.289. Friendly, recently renovated place in a modern four-storey building on a central but quiet soi, offering smart, bright, a/c rooms with small en-suite hot-water bathrooms. The downstairs café is at the front, which means there's no noisy courtyard effect. Breakfast included. B1200

Libra House 28 Soi 9, Thanon Moonmuang ☎ 053 210687, ⊌ librahousechiangmai.com; map p.289. Excellent, family-run, trekking-oriented guesthouse with keen, helpful service and 24hr check-in. Forty large, plain but well-maintained rooms, spread across five buildings with some quiet sitting areas, are en suite with hot showers. Free daytime pick-ups for advance bookings. Fan B400, a/c B600

Mini Cost 19–19/4 Soi 1, Thanon Ratchdamnoen ☎ 053 418787–8, ⊌ minicostcm.com; map p.289. Smart ochre-painted guesthouse and apartment block with helpful staff, offering comfortable rooms with some colourful modern Thai decorative touches, as well as a/c, hot water, fridges, safes, balconies and cable TV. B1150

Pha Thai House 48/1 Thanon Ratchaphakinai ☎ 053 278013 or ☎ 081 998 6933, ⊌ phathaihouse.com; map p.289. Wide variety of rooms, all with en-suite hot showers, in a leafy garden setting with a small swimming pool: most boast balconies, colourful decor, fridges, TVs, a/c and antique-style furniture, while plainer fan rooms at the front of the compound by the road are much cheaper. Family rooms also available. Fan B800, a/c B1000

SK House 30 Soi 9, Thanon Moonmuang ☎ 053 210690, ⊌ theskhouse.com; map p.289. Efficient, brick-built high-rise with a ground-floor café, a small, shaded swimming pool and a slightly institutional feel. Fan rooms come with hot-water bathrooms, while the a/c rooms are much more colourful and attractive, with cable TV. Free pick-ups from the train station. Fan B250, a/c B600

★ **Your House** 8 Soi 2, Thanon Ratchawithi ☎ 053 217492, ⊌ yourhouseguesthouse.com; map p.289. Very welcoming, old-town atmosphere (though some rooms get a bit of noise from nearby bars) and a wide choice of accommodation: in the attractive, original teak house, six airy rooms share three bathrooms with hot showers; the two modern annexes across the lane, both with hot water en suite, include lovely, big rooms with polished teak floors, small balconies and well-equipped bathrooms. Optional a/c in most rooms. The attractive garden restaurant serves good Thai and French food, with buffalo steak and chips a speciality. Good for treks, day-trips and train, plane and bus tickets. Discounts for singles. Fan B250, a/c B450

HOTELS

Tamarind Village 50/1 Thanon Ratchdamnoen ☎ 053 418896–9, ⊌ tamarindvillage.com; map p.289. Named for a huge, 200-year-old tamarind tree that shades the compound, this small, tranquil boutique resort in the heart of Chiang Mai's old city is designed in Lanna style around a series of courtyards, though the extremely comfortable rooms, which all enjoy lovely garden views, have modern touches. Good-sized pool, attractive spa, an interesting programme of art and cultural exhibitions and excellent restaurant (see page 293) too. Breakfast included. B7000

Three Sis 1 Soi 8, Thanon Phra Pokklao ☎053 273243, ⊕the3sis.com; map p.289. Genteel B&B opposite Wat Chedi Luang with lots of attractive open-plan public areas to loll about in. Rooms in the new building have wooden floors and tasteful furnishings that also feature a lot of dark wood, while those in the original building are almost as spacious but less stylish; all have a/c, hot water, cable TV and fridge. Breakfast included. B1890

REST OF CHIANG MAI

GUESTHOUSES

★ **Baan Kaew Guest House** 142 Thanon Charoen Prathet ☎053 271606, ⊕baankaew-guesthouse.com; map p.276. Set back from the road in a quiet, pretty garden, this attractive modern building has twenty large, simple but well-equipped and well-maintained rooms with hot water, mini-bars and a/c. B800

Baan Orapin 150 Thanon Charoenrat ☎053 243677, ⊕baanorapin.com; map p.276. Pretty compound overshadowed by tall longan trees, offering big, comfy and characterful rooms with teak and rattan furnishings and wooden floors. Some rooms come with four-poster beds and balconies. Breakfast included; minimum stay two nights. B2500

Baan Say-La Guesthouse 4–4/1 Soi 5, Thanon Nimmanhemin ☎053 894229, ⊕baansaylaguesthouse.com; map p.276. Handy for Nimman nightlife, this good-value, well-maintained, all-a/c guesthouse has a subtle Thai retro feel, with lots of dark wood everywhere and four-poster beds in some rooms. Some bedrooms have balconies, while the cheapest share bathrooms. Breakfast isn't offered, but bread and coffee are free. B790

Bon Ça Va 252/13–14 Thanon Phra Pokklao ☎053 418266, ⊕facebook.com/boncavahotel; map p.276. Small, friendly guesthouse with a tasteful antique look, just south of Chang Puak Gate, offering large, clean rooms with a/c, hot showers, fridges, safes and cable TV, some with balconies. B940

Eco Resort 109 Thanon Bamrungrat ☎053 247111, ⊕ecoresortchiangmai.com; map p.276. This former school in huge, lush, quiet gardens has been tastefully transformed into a modern, eco-friendly hostel-cum-hotel, with a/c and hot water throughout. Choose between well-equipped dorms with smart, white bedding, basic private rooms with shared bathrooms and attractive "superior" options with large bathrooms in a subtle contemporary style. There's a lovely, 25m pool surrounded by hanging plants, an outdoor gym, table tennis and table football. Dorms B450, doubles B1180

Galare Guest House 7 Soi 2, Thanon Charoen Prathet ☎053 818887 or ☎053 821011, ⊕galare.com; map p.276. Near Nawarat Bridge, this long-standing, well-run upmarket guesthouse is justly popular. Plain a/c rooms, each with hot-water bathroom, TV and fridge, overlook a shady lawn that gives way to a riverside terrace restaurant. B1200

Green Sleep Hostel 5/10 Soi 7, Thanon Ratchdamnoen ☎061 464 0919, ⊕greensleephostel.com; map p.276. Sociable, architect-designed hostel with appealing common areas strewn with pot plants, a kitchen and a washing machine. Hot-water bathrooms are shared by smart, a/c dorms with 4–10 bunk beds (some women only) and by small, windowless doubles. Free bicycles. Light breakfast included. Dorms B350, doubles B540

★ **Hollanda Montri** 365 Thanon Charoenrat ☎053 242450, ⊕hollandamontri.com; map p.276. North of the centre by the busy Rama IX Bridge, in a modern building by the river, this Dutch–Thai guesthouse has large, comfortable and attractive fan or a/c rooms with TVs and hot-water bathrooms, and cheerful staff. A very pleasant, terraced riverside bar-restaurant offers a long menu of Thai and European dishes. Free daytime bicycles. Fan B550, a/c B750

Riverside House 101 Thanon Chiang Mai–Lamphun ☎053 241860, ⊕riverside house-chiangmai.com; map p.276. Welcoming place with a lush garden on the east bank of the river, though just a short walk from the night bazaar, with plain but clean and good-sized a/c rooms with cable TV, fridges and hot showers, many with balconies, plus a small swimming pool. B1000

River View Lodge 25 Soi 4, Thanon Charoen Prathet ☎053 271109, ⊕riverviewlodgch.com; map p.276. Tasteful, well-run and good-value alternative to international-class hotels, with a small swimming pool and neat decorative touches in the rooms; the most expensive have balconies overlooking the river. Breakfast included. B1800

HOTELS

Anantara Chiang Mai 123 Thanon Charoen Prathet ☎053 253333, ⊕anantara.com; map p.276. Occupying a prime riverside site (with an annexe of serviced suites across Thanon Charoen Prathet), this luxury place offers sleek high-concept design in its spacious rooms, along with balconies and river views. There's a good-looking spa, a cooking school and a 34m riverside swimming pool, while a century-old teak house – formerly the British Consulate – serves afternoon teas, cocktails and Asian food, and the waterfront restaurant dishes up excellent Indian and Peruvian food. B10,640

Chiang Mai Gate Hotel 11/10 Thanon Suriyawong ☎053 203895–9, ⊕chiangmaigatehotel.com; map p.276. Located just to the south of the old city, this place has 120 well-equipped rooms with Lanna touches in the design, a/c, TVs, fridges and hot water, plus a small swimming pool and helpful staff. B830

D2 Hotel 100 Chang Klan ☎053 999999, ⓦdusit.com; map p.276. With its muted orange theme and helpful staff in street fashions, plus stylish lighting and minimalist furnishings, this place in the heart of the night bazaar, run by the Dusit Group, is probably the coolest luxury hotel in Chiang Mai. A spa, fitness centre and rooftop pool are among the amenities. B5420

Dhara Dhevi 51/4 Thanon Chiang Mai–Sankamphaeng ☎053 888888, ⓦdharadhevi.com; map p.276. Occupying huge grounds a few kilometres east of the city centre, the *Dhara Dhevi* transports its guests into another era, the heyday of the Lanna Kingdom. Traditional Lanna architecture is complemented by modern touches in the villas and residences, which are equipped with every conceivable comfort and look out over rice fields and vegetable gardens. With a breathtaking spa (modelled on the royal palace of Mandalay), cooking school, a daily programme of crafts demonstrations, shopping centre, library of books and DVDs, a kids' club, two swimming pools, tennis courts, a patisserie and five restaurants, guests need never leave the premises. Breakfast included. B20,480

★ **Elliebum Boutique Hotel** 114/3–5 Thanon Ratchamanka ☎090 318 6429, ⓦelliebum.com; map p.276. Stylish small hotel right in the centre of the old town, offering warm hospitality and plenty of clued-up advice about the city. The elegant bedrooms blend carved wooden lintels and other traditional Thai features into an appealing modern look; the cheapest have small hot-water bathrooms but represent good value, while the largest sport bathtubs; all have bay window seats, a/c, fridges and Bluetooth-enabled smart TVs. Also on offer are culinary walking tours

(see page 293). Tasty breakfasts included. B2000

★ **Four Seasons** About 15km north of Chiang Mai on Mae Rim–Samoeng Old Road, at the start of the Mae Sa valley ☎053 298181, ⓦfourseasons.com; map p.276. The last word in Lanna luxury, with superbly appointed rooms and apartments, a swimming pool and a gorgeous spa, all set around a picturesque lake and rice paddies (where you can learn to plant rice) with fine views of Doi Suthep behind. On a long menu of activities, the highlight is a top-quality cooking school. B23,700

★ **Rachamankha** 6 Soi 9, Thanon Ratchamanka ☎053 904111, ⓦrachamankha.com; map p.276. Looking more like a temple than a hotel, this spacious, architect-owned property with just 25 elegant rooms arrayed around quiet courtyards is hidden in the backstreets of the old city. There's a lovely, large pool, a spa, an excellent restaurant (see page 294) and a well-stocked library with sherry laid out for browsers. B11,800

Royal Princess 111 Thanon Chang Klan ☎053 253900, ⓦdusit.com; map p.276. Tidy, centrally located, long-running hotel close to the night bazaar, with two hundred comfortable rooms, a small swimming pool, a fitness centre and a good Chinese restaurant. B2350

U Chiang Mai 70 Thanon Ratchdamnoen ☎053 327000, ⓦuhotelsresorts.com; map p.276. Innovative hotel that offers 24hr use of room (no matter what time you check in), breakfast (included) available in your bedroom all day, and free bikes. The reading room and spa occupy the hundred-year-old former governor's residence, while some of the rooms – decorated in contemporary Thai style, with daybeds on the balconies, rain showers, DVD players and iPods – give straight onto the small, black swimming pool in the central courtyard. Discounts if you book over a month in advance. B8330

EATING

The main difficulty with **eating** in Chiang Mai is knowing when to stop. All over town there are inexpensive and enticing restaurants serving typically northern food, which has been strongly influenced by Burmese cuisine, especially in curries such as *kaeng hang lay* (usually translated on menus as "Northern Thai curry"), made with pork belly, ginger, garlic and tamarind. At **lunchtime** the thing to do is to join the local workers in one of the simple, inexpensive cafés that put all their efforts into producing just one or two special dishes – the traditional meal at this time of day is *khao soi*, a thick broth of curry and coconut cream, with egg noodles and a choice of meat. The main **night markets** are at the back and front entrances to Chiang Mai University on Thanon Suthep and Thanon Huai Kaeo; along Thanon Bamrungburi by Chiang Mai Gate; along Thanon Manee Noparat by Chang Puak Gate; plus a few stalls in front of Somphet market on Thanon Moonmuang. Also in the evening you'll find restaurants which lay on touristy **cultural shows** with *khan toke* dinners, a selection of

northern dishes traditionally eaten on the floor off short-legged lacquer trays. Of these, the Old Chiangmai Cultural Centre, 185/3 Thanon Wualai (B570; ☎053 202993–5, ⓦoldchiangmai.com), with its show of northern Thai and hill-tribe dancing, has the best reputation. Many of the **bars** listed in "Drinking and nightlife" (see page 295) have good reputations for their food, especially *The Riverside*.

THA PAE GATE AREA

THAI

Aroon Rai Thanon Kotchasarn ☎053 276947; map p.289. This basic, long-standing restaurant by Tha Pae Gate serves great northern Thai dishes, such as tasty *kaeng hang lay muu* (B60), *khao soi* and a very good *kaeng khae*, a typical local curry without coconut milk, with lots of herbs and vegetables. They also sell their curry pastes for you to take home. Daily roughly 11.30am–9.30pm.

★ **Ratana's Kitchen** 320–322 Thanon Tha Pae ☎053

233739; map p.289. A good-value favourite among locals and visitors both for northern specialities (B70–130) such as *kaeng hang lay*, *khao soi* and mixed hors d'oeuvres, and for tasty Western breakfasts, sandwiches, cottage pie and steaks. Extensive vegetarian menu, wine and cocktails too. Daily 7.30am–11.30pm.

Ruen Tamarind 50/1 Thanon Ratchdamnoen ☎053 418896–9; map p.289. Overlooking the pool at the *Tamarind Village* hotel (see page 290), this elegant restaurant serves up excellent Thai cuisine, including mainstream fare such as *tom kha thaleh* (coconut soup with seafood) and more creative offerings such as duck-breast laap (B350), as well as a long and interesting selection of northern Thai favourites. Also does afternoon tea. Daily 7am–11pm.

INTERNATIONAL

Blue Diamond Soi 9, Thanon Moonmuang; map p.289. Popular, mostly vegetarian restaurant with a pleasant garden in a quiet neighbourhood of guesthouses, serving very good Thai dishes, Western breakfasts (sets from B140), home-made bread, shakes, herbal teas and espresso coffee. Mon–Sat 7am–8.30pm.

★ **La Fontana** 39/7–8 Thanon Ratchamanka ☎053 207091, ⓦlafontanachiangmai.com; map p.289. Chiang Mai's best Italian, dishing up great home-made pastas (B150–200), risottos, pizzas, meat and fish dishes, as well as tempting antipasti and panna cotta, ice cream and other desserts, all washed down with imported Italian wine. Daily 11.30am–10.30pm; in low season, sometimes closes Tues and at lunchtimes.

Miguel's Thanon Chaiyapoom ☎053 874148, ⓦfacebook.com/miguelscafechiangmai; map p.289. A warm welcome, a relaxing terrace and good Mexican food: feast on the *nachos grande* with chicken for B205, perhaps with a side order of guacamole (in season). Daily 9am–11pm.

Mit Mai 42/2 Thanon Ratchamanka ☎053 275033; map p.289. It looks like a simple Thai restaurant from the street, but in fact *Mit Mai* serves up excellent food in large portions from Yunnan province in southwest China, including a zesty chicken salad and delicious snow peas stir-fried with Yunnanese ham (B90), as well as more exotic dishes such as *fong nom thawt* (fried cheese) and white bamboo grubs. Daily 10am–10pm.

The Swan 48 Thanon Chaiyapoom ☎082 893 6670; map p.289. Don't let this Burmese restaurant's narrow frontage on the busy road around the moat put you off: walk through to the lovely courtyard garden and enjoy delicious dishes from across the border, such as tea-leaf salad, aubergine salad and pork curry (main dishes around B100). Daily 11am–11pm.

REST OF CHIANG MAI

THAI

Ba Mii Kiaw Stall Thanon Manee Noparat, just west of Wat Lok Malee; map p.276. When the DTAC phone shop closes for the night, this pushcart kitchen with plenty of tables turns up on the forecourt and starts serving the best noodle soup in town, stuffed with roast red pork and wonton (*ba mii kiaw*; B35). Mon–Sat 6pm–midnight.

★ **Blackitch Artisan Kitchen** 27/1 Soi 7, Thanon Nimmanhemin ☎081 881 9144, ⓦblackitch.com; map p.276. Chiang Mai's most innovative culinary experience, in a simple, tiled restaurant above an ice cream shop. Chef Black conjures up set menus of around ten courses (B1800) that vary according to what is fresh and seasonal, sourcing the best of Thai ingredients and making creative use of regional Thai preparation styles (with Japanese influences). Expect a lot of seafood (as well as home-cured fish) in dishes such as sun-dried squid stuffed with fermented pork, salted egg and rice, served with pomelo. Wash it down with home-made umeshu (plum wine) and Thai craft beer. Reserve at least 24hr in advance. Daily 11am–2pm & 6–10pm.

Café de Nimman Soi 13, Thanon Sirimuangkarajan ☎053 218405; map p.276. Excellent, creative Thai food such as som tam salad with salted egg (B110), at this stylish, reasonably priced restaurant with lots of attractive outdoor tables. Daily 11am–11pm.

Hong Tauw Inn 95/17–18 Nantawan Arcade, Thanon Nimmanhemin ☎053 218333; map p.276. Comfortable a/c restaurant done out in "country inn" style, with antiques, plants and old clocks, making for a relaxing environment. The varied menu of home-style cuisine ranges from rice and noodle dishes such as *khanom jiin*, to delicious central and northern Thai main dishes (around B100), and includes a wide range of *nam phrik*, spicy relishes, as well as *lon*, chilli dips with coconut milk. Daily 11am–10pm.

★ **Huan Soontaree** 208 Thanon Patan, 3km north of the

FOOD WALKS AND DINNER CRUISES

In the mornings, *Elliebum Boutique Hotel* (see page 292) offers fascinating guided **food walks** around the old town (4hr; from B850/person), taking in Chiang Mai Gate Market and the locals' favourite street restaurants and dessert stalls. With plenty of insights about Thai cuisine and culture along the way, they're a great way to get to know the city.

Every evening, *The Riverside* (see page 296) runs a **dinner cruise**, charging B180/person on top of whatever you order from its very good menu. Booking is recommended, but you'll certainly need to get there by 7.15pm to put your orders in (boat departs at 8pm).

Superhighway ☎083 860 8196, ⓦhuansoontaree.com; map p.276. A convivial riverfront restaurant owned by the famous northern Thai folk-singer Soontaree Vechanont, who along with her singer daughter Lanna Commins entertains diners nightly from the balcony-level stage. Delicious, reasonably priced northern specialities such as kaeng hang lay (B140). Split levels allow a choice of seating, including on a leafy riverside terrace hung with paper lanterns, or on a balcony near the stage. Daily 4–11pm.

★ **Huen Phen** 112 Thanon Ratchamanka; map p.276. One of Chiang Mai's best northern Thai restaurants – and certainly the most famous. Try local specialities such as sai oua (sausage), kaeng hang lay (pork curry) and khao soi (noodle curry; B40). In the evening, the restaurant opens in an old wooden house decorated with antiques around the back (with a pricier menu). Daily roughly 8am–4pm & 5–10pm.

Khao Soi Samoe Jai Thanon Faham, just north of Wat Faham; map p.276. Thick, tasty and very cheap khao soi (spiced to order) and other northern specialities, plus delicious satay, som tam. No English sign – it's a wooden house with a red, white and blue awning. Daily 7/8am–5pm.

Kiat Ocha 41–43 Thanon Inthrawarorot, off Thanon Phra Pokklao (the English sign says "Hainanese chicken"); map p.276. Delicious and very popular satay and khao man kai – boiled chicken breast served with dipping sauces, broth and rice – from around B40 a dish. This and the surrounding cafés are especially handy if you're looking round the old town. Daily 6am–3pm, or until the food runs out.

Lamduon Faharm Khao Soi 352/22 Thanon Charoenrat; map p.276. Excellent, very cheap khao soi prepared to a secret recipe, which can be spiced according to your taste; delicious crackling with the pork version. Also satay, som tam, waffles and an assortment of juices. Daily 8.30am–4/4.30pm.

★ **Monsoon Tea** 328/3 Thanon Charoenrat ☎052 007758; ⓦmonsoon-tea-company.com; map p.276. At the charming teahouse on Thanon Charoenrat, you can not only taste and buy their aromatic, deeply flavoured, organic teas, which are grown wild in the traditional way among the forests of northern Thailand, but also tuck into some excellent Thai and fusion dishes, including nam phrik noom (northern Thai chilli dip with young aubergines; B89), laap burgers, tea-leaf salad and delicious deep-fried chicken with fermented tea paste (B150). They also have a new branch selling teas at One Nimman (north end of Thanon Nimmanhemin t097 918 9892). Mon–Sat 10am–8pm.

Rachamankha 6 Soi 9, Thanon Ratchamanka ☎053 904111; map p.276. In the courtyard of the boutique hotel of the same name (see page 292), this is one of Chiang Mai's classiest places to eat, with starched linen tablecloths and elegant cutlery and often with live traditional or classical music in the evening. From an unusual menu of northern Thai, Shan and Burmese food (main courses around B250) and Western dishes (from

around B450), try the delicious Burmese-style beef curry. Daily 7am–11pm.

★ **Samsen Villa** Rimping Condominium, 201 Thanon Charoenrat ☎081 951 4415, ⓦsamsenvilla.com; map p.276. The best of several restaurants on the east bank of the Ping River, serving excellent, creative Thai food (most dishes B100–200) in the charming waterfront garden of this prominent condo by Nakhon Ping Bridge. Don't miss the grilled beef with elephant garlic and the lon (chilli dip with coconut milk), but avoid the signature "jelly beer" – unless you like your beer flat and frozen like a Slurpie. Daily 11am–10.30pm.

SP Chicken 9/1 Soi 1, Thanon Samlarn ☎080 500 5035; map p.276. Justly famous basic northeastern restaurant that's featured in the New York Times. The signature chickens (B90 for a half) are slowly cooked whole on a rotisserie and eaten with som tam and sticky rice, but the laap is also very good. Daily 10am–5pm.

Wan Lamun Thanon Inthrawarorot (no English sign, but look for the pink flower on its Thai sign); map p.276. Delightful spot purveying excellent lunches such as khanom jiin and phat thai and delicious Thai and Western desserts, to take away – perhaps to the square in front of the City Arts and Cultural Centre. Daily 7am–3/4pm, though some things will sell out earlier.

INTERNATIONAL

Arcobaleno 60 Thanon Na Wat Ket ☎053 306254, ⓦarcobaleno-cm.com; map p.276. Tasty Italian food (main dishes from around B200) served in and around an attractive wooden house on a quiet lane near Nakhon Ping Bridge. Try the spaghetti arcobaleno (with smoked bacon, mushrooms and tomato sauce) and the delicious panna cotta for dessert. Daily except Wed 11am–2pm & 5.30–10pm.

★ **David's Kitchen** 113 Thanon Bamrungrat ☎091 068 1744, ⓦdavidskitchen.co.th; map p.276. Chiang Mai's best restaurant for fine dining, in a lovely setting with warm hospitality. The food is mostly classic French, with beef and veal a speciality in dishes such as deliciously tender braised beef cheek in red wine sauce (B1050), while desserts like sticky toffee pudding show some British influence. Main courses start at around B500, while a four-course set menu goes for B1450, and there's a great wine list, with lots of choice by the glass. Mon–Sat 5–10pm.

Elliebum 114/3–5 Thanon Ratchamanka ☎090 318 6429, ⓦelliebum.com; map p.276. This stylish and welcoming café with a shady garden patio serves excellent espresso coffees, made with arabica beans sustainably grown in the nearby mountains, delicious fruit smoothies, all-day breakfasts such as blueberry pancakes with maple syrup and fresh fruit, and great Thai and Western lunches, using local, seasonal and organic ingredients wherever possible. Daily 7am–5pm.

Gallery Seescape Soi 17, Thanon Nimmanhemin wfacebook.com/galleryseescape; map p.276. Gallery, design shop and café run by a famous local artist, offering shady garden tables, very good espressos and creative, attractively presented Western breakfasts and lunches (around B150). Tues–Sat 8am–6pm.

iberry Off the south side of Soi 17, Thanon Nimmanhemin ☎053 895181; map p.276. Chiang Mai's best and most famous ice-cream shop, owned by comedian "Nose" Udom – who is portrayed as a pink dog in a huge statue in the quirky garden. Also does home-made sorbets and cakes and good coffee. Daily 10am–10pm.

Nat Wat 330/2 Thanon Charoenrat ☎081 716 1608; map p.276. Relax amidst the polished grainy wood of the interior or out in the pretty little waterfall garden and chow down on some seriously good Western food: specials such as duck confit with spiced lentils and tomato jam (B280), eggs benedict (B165), pastas, salads and sandwiches, as well as cakes, freshly squeezed juices and drip or espresso coffee. Tues–Sun 8.30am–5pm.

Rustic and Blue Soi 7, Thanon Nimmanhemin ☎053 216420; map p.276. American-style deli-café that's hugely popular during the day, quieter (especially the patio tables at the rear) for dinner. Huge selection of brunches, as well as comfort dishes such as fish'n'chips (B345), which you can wash down with Japanese, US and European beers. Daily 8.30am–8.30/9pm (last orders).

Smiley Kitchen Soi 3, Thanon Nimmanhemin ☎087 176 7566; map p.276. Excellent small restaurant serving authentic Japanese home-style cooking, such as a tonkatsu (pork cutlet) set for B190. Mon–Sat 11.30am–2.30pm & 5.30–9pm.

Tengoku de Cuisine Soi 5, Thanon Nimmanhemin ☎087 725 9888; map p.276. At this popular, stylish Japanese restaurant, the sushi and the tartare (tataki) are both very good, while the aubergine with miso sauce is not to be missed – best sampled on an all-you-can-eat "buffet" menu (though all dishes are prepared to order) for B800. Daily 11am–2pm & 5.30–10pm.

DRINKING AND NIGHTLIFE

Although there's a clutch of hostess bars bordering the east moat and along Loi Khro, and several gay bars offering sex shows, Chiang Mai's **nightlife** generally avoids Bangkok's sexual excesses, but offers plenty of opportunities for a good night out. The main concentrations of **bars** are on the east bank of the Ping River, around Tha Pae Gate and to the west of town around Thanon Nimmanhemin. It's also well worth checking out the strip of good-time bars at **JJ Market** on Thanon Assadatorn on the north side of town, which sport aspirational Bangkok names like *Tha Chang* and *Hualamphong* and which heave at weekends with the youth of Chiang Mai, drinking and watching the live bands.

THA PAE GATE AREA

★ **My Beer Friend** Thanon Chang Moi ⓦfacebook.com/mybeerfriend; map p.289. No expense has been spent on décor at this small, friendly bar, allowing you to concentrate on the great Thai craft beers. Ranging from porters to IPAs and English-style bitters, most are brewed by the owners themselves (in Japan, because of Thai brewing laws), some by their beer friends. At B100 for a 200ml glass, you might be able to work your way across all the taps. Daily except Tues 5pm–midnight.

UN Irish Pub 24/1 Thanon Ratchawithi ⓦunirishpub.com; map p.289. Though it hasn't had an Irish owner for a few years now, this is a cordial, well-run pub that serves Guinness on tap, as well as good food, including home-made bread for satisfying breakfasts and sandwiches, pies and pizzas. Appealing beer garden, quiz night on Thursday, and all manner of sports on TV (the schedule is posted weekly on its website). Daily roughly 9am–midnight.

REST OF CHIANG MAI

Drunken Flower (Mao Dok Mai) Soi 17, Thanon Nimmanhemin ☎097 523 5666, ⓦfacebook.com/thedrunkenflower; map p.276. Laidback and very congenial, this quirky venue is a favourite among university students and 20-somethings, both Thai and farang. Reasonable prices for drinks, Thai and Mexican food and an eclectic range of background music, often with live acoustic music. Wed–Sun 5pm–midnight.

Good View 13 Thanon Charoenrat ☎053 241866, ⓦgoodview.co.th; map p.276. A near-clone of the neighbouring *Riverside*, this large venue on the banks of the Ping River appeals to fashionable Thais with its smart staff, extensive menu of Thai, Chinese, Japanese and Western food, and slick, competent musicians, who play anything middle of the road from country to jazz. Daily 10am–1am.

GAY NIGHTLIFE IN CHIANG MAI

For an introduction to the city's **gay scene**, check out the roads off the west side of Thanon Chotana, where there's a clutch of bars around the gay-owned *Lotus Hotel*, which itself has a popular garden bar. At 1/21–22 Soi Viengbua here, the long-running *Adam's Apple* (daily 9pm–1am; ⓦadamsappleclub.com) hosts go-go dancers and cabaret shows. Meanwhile, out on Thanon Chon Prathan (Canal Road) just south of Thanon Huai Kaeo, *See Man Pub* is Chiang Mai's biggest gay dance club, with live bands and Coyote dancers (daily roughly 9pm–midnight).

Infinity Soi 6, Thanon Nimmanhemin ☏053 400085, ⓦfacebook.com/infinityclub.chiangmai; map p.276. At the end of Soi 6 in what's known as Prasertland or Kad Cherng Doi (a huge car park and loosely designated entertainment zone), this stylish and spacious venue, with live bands, Thai and international DJs and lots of outdoor tables, is one of the clubs of the moment in Chiang Mai. Daily 6pm–12.30am.

Lux & Fabrique 226 Thanon Wichayanon ⓦfacebook. com/lux.fabrique; map p.276. The ground floor of the *President Hotel* has been taken over by this highly fashionable club, which features a huge dance hall, industrial-look bars and attractive garden areas for chilling, and occasionally attracts big-name international DJs. Daily 5pm–1am.

Myst Floor 6, Maya Shopping Centre, Thanon Huai Kaeo ⓦfacebook.com/mystmaya; map p.276. Chiang Mai branch of a venue on Bangkok's Soi Thong Lo, this sophisticated rooftop bar offers creative cocktails – what they call "molecular mixology" – imported beers such as Hoegaarden on draught and cool views of Doi Suthep at sunset and the city at night. Daily 6pm–1am.

Namton's House Bar 196/2 Thanon Chiang Mai–Lamphun ⓦfacebook.com/namtonshousebar; map p.276. Cosy bar with wooden terraces overlooking a canal, serving well-kept, pricy craft beers from around the world, including the likes of Brew Dog, Mikkeller and Coedo. It's a bit far from the action, but at the time of writing, *Namton's* and *My Beer Friend* (see page 295) were about to jointly open a Thai craft beer bar, PUOL2OHM, on the rooftop of One Nimman, a shopping mall at the north end of Thanon Nimmanhemin. Daily except Wed 3–11/11.30pm.

North Gate Jazz Co-op Thanon Si Phum ⓦfacebook. com/northgate.jazzcoop; map p.276. Chilled, open-fronted bar with pavement tables overlooking Chang Phuak Gate and upstairs seats for more serious listeners, featuring high-quality live jazz nightly; Tuesday's open-mike night is the big event of the week. Open most nights roughly 8pm–midnight.

★ **The Riverside** Thanon Charoenrat ☏053 243239, ⓦtheriversidechiangmai.com; map p.276. On one side of the road candlelit terraces by the water (best to book if you want a table here) and an often heaving, lively bar for gigs, on the other a spacious complex of rooms, terraces, a stage and a bar area for imported craft beers. Various soloists and bands perform nightly on the two stages, with the tempo increasing as the night wears on. Long, high-quality menu of Western and Thai food (including northern specialities) also on offer, as well as dinner cruises (see page 293). Daily 10am–1am.

Sangdee 5 Soi 5, Thanon Sirimuangkarajan ☏053 894955, ⓦfacebook.com/sangdeeart; map p.276. An all-rounder that's worth checking out, this non-profit art gallery-café-bar hosts regular DJ parties. Tues–Sat roughly 3pm–midnight.

★ **Thapae East** 88 Thanon Tha Pae ⓦfacebook.com/ thapaeeast; map p.276. Set in atmospheric red-brick houses and a garden of half-constructed buildings, this "venue for the creative arts" serves craft beers and usually has something interesting on, notably live music. Mon–Sat 6–11pm.

Warm Up 40 Thanon Nimmanhemin ☏053 400677, ⓦfacebook.com/warmupcafe1999; map p.276. Hugely popular venue with students and young locals, offering both live bands and local and international DJs spinning the latest sounds in different indoor and outdoor zones. Daily 6pm–1am.

Writer's Club and Wine Bar 141/3 Thanon Ratchdamnoen ☏053 814187; map p.276. An unofficial foreign correspondents' club for Chiang Mai, this welcoming bar near the centre of the old city is popular among farang residents and visitors, serving a range of beers and wines, plus good Thai and Western food. Daily except Sat noon–midnight.

ENTERTAINMENT

Cinemas All of the city's big shopping centres have top-floor cineplexes. Your best bet for English-soundtrack or English-subtitled films near the centre is the Major Cineplex (ⓦmajorcineplex.com/en/cinema/major-chiangmai) on top of Airport Plaza, southwest of the old town, or SF Cinema City at Maya, at the corner of Thanon Nimmanhemin and Thanon Huai Kaeo (ⓦsfcinemacity.com). French-language films with English subtitles are screened at the Alliance Française, 138 Thanon Charoen Prathet, on Fridays at 8pm (☏053 275277).

SHOPPING

Shopping is an almost irresistible pastime in Chiang Mai, whether it be for traditional silver bracelets, chic contemporary lacquerware or even secondhand books. Serious shoppers should get hold of a copy of *Nancy Chandler's Map of Chiang Mai* (see page 288).

MARKETS AND THE SAN KAMPHAENG ROAD

Two main tourist shopping areas, the San Kamphaeng road and the night bazaar, conveniently operating at different times of the day, sell the full range of local handicrafts, backed up by markets, shopping malls and the weekend walking streets.

THE SAN KAMPHAENG ROAD

The road to San Kamphaeng, which extends due east from the end of Thanon Charoen Muang for 13km, is the main daytime strip, lined with every sort of handicrafts shop and factory, where you can usually watch the craftsmen at work. The biggest concentrations are at Bo Sang, the "umbrella village", 9km from town (see page 299), and at San Kamphaeng itself, once important for its kilns but now famous for its silk weaving.

Getting there Frequent white songthaews to San Kamphaeng leave Chiang Mai from the central Lamyai market, but it's difficult to decide when to get off if you don't know the area. You could sign up for a tour or hire a tuk-tuk for a few hundred baht, but the catch here is that the drivers will want to take you to the shops where they'll pick up a commission. The best way to go is by bicycle or motorbike, which allows you to stop where and when you please, but take care with the fast-moving traffic on the narrow road.

THE NIGHT BAZAAR

The other main shopper's playground is the night bazaar, sprawling around the junction of Thanon Loi Khro and Thanon Chang Klan (and into the adjacent, quieter Anusarn market). Here bumper-to-bumper street stalls and several indoor areas (including the original Chiang Mai Night Bazaar shopping centre on the west side of Thanon Chang Klan) sell just about anything produced in Chiang Mai, plus crafts from other parts of Thailand and Southeast Asia, as well as counterfeit designer goods; the action starts up at around 5pm, and there are plenty of real bargains.

WARO ROT MARKET

During the day, bustling Warorot market (known locally as "Kad Luang") on Thanon Chang Moi has lots of cheap and cheerful cotton, linen and ceramics for sale on the upper floors. In the heart of the market, you can watch locals buying chilli paste, sausage and sticky rice from their favourite stalls, and maybe even join the queue. There's also a pungent and colourful flower market just east of here, on Thanon Praisani by the river, while the atmospheric warren of narrow lanes to the south and west of the market is well worth a browse, for everything from silk, cotton and hill-tribe crafts to stationery and plastic.

THE NORTHERN VILLAGE

The Northern Village in the Airport Plaza shopping centre (Mon–Fri 11am–9pm, Sat & Sun 10am–9pm), at the corner of the Superhighway and Highway 108, is like a market of stalls moved into an a/c mall. It has all manner of

slightly upmarket handicrafts and contemporary decorative products, ranging from silver and wood to textiles and herbal products, and includes a branch of Doi Tung Lifestyle.

FABRICS, CLOTHES AND CONTEMPORARY INTERIOR DESIGN

Few visitors leave Chiang Mai without some new item of clothing and, to tempt you to dig deeper into your purse, upmarket silks and cottons often share shelf-space with bold examples of modern interior design.

Silk The silk produced out towards San Kamphaeng, to the east of Chiang Mai, is richly coloured and hard-wearing, with various attractive textures. Bought off a roll, the material is generally cheaper than in Bangkok, and can cost as little as B400/metre for top-quality four-ply (suitable for shirts and suits). Ready-made silk clothes, though inexpensive, are generally staid and more suited to formal wear.

Cotton In Chiang Mai you'll also see plenty of traditional, pastel-coloured cotton, which is nice for furnishings, most of it from the village of Pa Sang southwest of Lamphun. Outlets in the basement of the main Chiang Mai night bazaar shopping centre on Thanon Chang Klan have good, cheap selections of this sort of cloth at around B300/metre, plus hand-painted and batik-printed lengths, and ready-made tablecloths and the like.

Fashion and interior design You'll find some stunning contemporary design in Chiang Mai, often fusing local crafts with modern, minimalist elements. A fruitful place for this kind of shopping is Thanon Nimmanhemin, on the west side of the city, which savvy locals sometimes tag Chiang Mai's Sukhumvit for its services to well-to-do expats. Its northern end towards Thanon Huai Kaeo, particularly on and around Soi 1, has a concentration of interesting fashion and decor boutiques. Thanon Charoenrat, on the east side of the river, also hosts several stylish outlets for clothes and interior design between Nawarat and Nakhon Ping bridges, while Ban Tawai (see page 298) boasts some creative decor shops.

Doi Tung Lifestyle Thanon Nimmanhemin, opposite Soi 1 ☎053 217981, ✆doitung.org; map p.276. Part of the late Princess Mother's development project based at Doi Tung, selling very striking and attractive cotton and linen in warm colours, made up into clothes, cushion covers, rugs and so on. Daily 10am–8pm.

3

CHIANG MAI'S WALKING STREETS

If you're in Chiang Mai at the weekend it's worth heading down to **Thanon Wualai**, just south of the old city, on a Saturday between about 5pm and 11pm, or to the larger affair on **Thanon Ratchdamnoen** and part of **Thanon Phra Pokklao** in the old city on a Sunday at the same time. Closed to traffic for the duration, these "**walking streets**" become crowded with vendors selling typical northern Thai items such as clothes, musical instruments and snacks, as musicians busk to the throngs of people. The walking streets have become even more popular than the night bazaar, as they are ideal places to pick up a souvenir and mingle with a very mixed crowd of Thais and farangs.

3

Ginger 199 Thanon Moonmuang ☎053 287681–2, ⓦthehousethailand.com; map p.289. Chichi boutique selling striking and original women's and men's wear, accessories and contemporary home décor and kitchenware. Daily 10am–11pm.

Kritiya 46 Thanon Khwang Men, the lane that runs south from the west side of Warorot Market ☎053 234478; map p.276. This small, atmospheric shop is probably the best place in town to buy bolts of high-quality local silk at competitive prices. Mon–Sat 9/10am–4.30/5pm.

Shinawatra 7km out on the San Kamphaeng road ☎053 338053–5, ⓦshinawatrathaisilk.co.th (with a shop at 18/1 Thanon Huai Kaeo ☎053 223264); map p.276. Century-old silk factory and showroom, which has entertained luminaries such as Princess Diana and is a good place to follow the silk-making process right from the cocoon. Daily 9am–5.30pm.

Sop Moei Arts 150/10 Thanon Charoenrat ☎053 306123, ⓦsopmoeiarts.com; map p.276. Gorgeous fabrics – scarves, wall-hangings, bags and cushion covers – and stylish basketware, with part of the profits going back to the eponymous Karen village and nearby refugee camp near Mae Sariang, where they're made. Mon–Fri & Sun 10am–6pm, Sat 10am–5pm.

Studio Naenna 138/8 Soi Changkhian, Thanon Huai Kaeo ☎053 226042; & Adorn by Studio Naenna, 22 Soi 1, Thanon Nimmanhemin ☎053 895136; ⓦstudio-naenna. com; map p.276. If you're interested in the whole process of traditional fabric production, particularly the use of natural dyes, you can contact Studio Naenna about their 3-day indigo workshops (roughly Sept–Nov) and 5-day one-on-one weaving workshops. It's part of an eco-friendly, sustainable project set up by Patricia Cheesman, an expert on Thai textiles (her collection of textiles is on display in a gallery at Studio Naenna on Wed or by appointment). Their products, which consist of top-quality, ready-made silk and cotton garments, accessories, home furnishings and art pieces, are on sale at Studio Naenna and their more central outlet, Adorn. Studio Naenna Mon–Fri 9am–5pm; Adorn daily 10am–6pm.

Vila Cini 30 Thanon Charoenrat ☎053 246246, ⓦvilacini.com; map p.276. Sumptuously coloured silk scarves, bags, shirts, ties and cushion covers, as well as bolts

CHIANG MAI'S TRADITIONAL CRAFTS

Chiang Mai is the best place in Thailand to buy handicrafts, and it's a hotbed of traditional cottage industries offering generally high standards of workmanship at low prices.

WOODCARVING

The city has a long tradition of **woodcarving**, which expresses itself in everything from salad bowls to half-size elephants. In the past the industry relied on the cutting of Thailand's precious teak, but manufacturers are now beginning to use other imported hardwoods, while bemoaning their inferior quality.

Wooden objects are sold all over the city, but the most famous place for carving is **Ban Tawai**, a large village of shops and factories where prices are low and where you can watch the woodworkers in action. One of Thailand's most important woodcarving centres, Ban Tawai relied on rice farming until forty years ago, but today virtually every home here has carvings for sale outside and each back yard hosts its own cottage industry. There's an a/c minibus service from Chang Puak bus station, via the Three Kings Monument and Chiang Mai Gate in the old city, to Ban Tawai six times a day (see ⓦfacebook.com/taxitawai for times; 1hr; B20–30), but it'll be easier if you have your own transport: follow Highway 108 south from Chiang Mai 13km to Hang Dong, then head east for 2km. A regularly updated, free **map** of Ban Tawai's outlets, which now include all manner of antiques and interior decor shops, is available around town (or go to ⓦban-tawai.com).

LACQUERWARE

Lacquerware can be seen in nearly every museum in Thailand, most commonly in the form of **betet sets**, which used to be carried ceremonially by the slaves of grandees as an insignia of rank and wealth (see page 322). Betel sets are still produced in Chiang Mai according to the traditional technique, whereby a woven bamboo frame is covered with layers of rich red lacquer and decorated with black details. A variety of other objects, such as trays and jewellery boxes, is also produced, some decorated with gold leaf on black gloss. Lacquerware makes an ideal choice for gifts, as it is both light to carry, and at the same time typically Thai, and is available in just about every other shop in town.

CELADON

Celadon, sometimes known as greenware, is a delicate variety of stoneware which was first of silk by the metre. The 150-year-old teak Sino-Portuguese shophouse in the Wat Ket neighbourhood – site of the first expat community in Chiang Mai in the late nineteenth century – is an attraction in itself. Daily 8.30am–10.30pm.

HILL-TRIBE CRAFTS
Thai Tribal Crafts 208 Thanon Bamrungrat ⊕ 053 241043, ⓦ ttcrafts.co.th; map p.276. Long-running, non-profit, fair-trade shop, sponsored by a Christian charity, with a huge range of products made by seven of the region's hill tribes, from bags, scarves, home furnishings and silverware to musical instruments and bamboo basketry. Mon–Sat 9am–5pm.

BOOKS
Backstreet Books 2/8 Thanon Chang Moi Kao ⊕ 053 874143, ⓦ backstreetbooksiam.com; map p.289. Large, well-organized, Irish-run secondhand bookshop (plus a few new books) near Tha Pae Gate, where you can buy or exchange books. Daily 10am–8pm.

Suriwong 54/1 Thanon Sri Dornchai ⊕ 053 281052–6; map p.276. The best place for new English-language publications, stocking a wide selection of novels, books about Thailand and maps in an organized display; it also features newspaper and stationery sections. Mon–Fri 10am–8pm, Sat & Sun 9am–8pm.

The Lost Bookshop 34/3 Thanon Ratchamanka ⊕ 053 206656; map p.289. A smaller branch of Backstreet Books, but with plenty of titles (mostly secondhand) available in English. Daily 10am–8pm.

COMPUTERS AND PHONES
For sales and repairs, either Panthip Plaza, corner of Chang Klan and Sri Dornchai roads, or Computer Plaza, Thanon Manee Nopparat on the north side of the moat.

DIRECTORY
Banks, ATMs and exchange Dozens of banks with ATMs are dotted around Thanon Tha Pae and Thanon Chang Klan, and many exchange booths here stay open for evening shoppers.
Consulates Canada, 151 Superhighway ⊕ 053 850147;

3

made in China over two thousand years ago, and later produced in Thailand, most famously at Sukhothai and Sawankhalok (Si Satchanalai).

Mengrai Kilns 79/2 Soi 6, Thanon Samlarn ⊕ 053 272063, ⓦ mengraikilns.com; map p.276. The best of several kilns in Chiang Mai that have revived the art of celadon. Sticking to the traditional methods, Mengrai produces beautiful and reasonably priced vases, crockery and larger items, thrown in elegant shapes and covered with transparent green, blue and purple glazes. Daily 8am–5pm.

UMBRELLAS AND PAPER
The village of **Bo Sang**, 9km east of Chiang Mai, bases its fame on souvenir **umbrellas** – made of silk, cotton or mulberry (sa) paper and decorated with bold, painted colours – and celebrates its craft with a colourful **umbrella fair** every January. The artists who work here can paint a small motif on your bag or camera in two minutes flat. The grainy **mulberry paper**, which makes beautiful writing or sketching pads, is sold almost as an afterthought in many of Bo Sang's shops.

HQ 3/31 Thanon Samlarn ⊕ 053 814717–8, ⓦ hq papermaker.com; map p.276. Down a small soi opposite Wat Phra Singh, HQ is the best place to buy sheets of beautifully coloured mulberry paper, along with a range of other specialist papers. Mon–Sat 9am–6pm.

SILVER AND JEWELLERY
Chiang Mai's traditional **silversmiths**' area is on **Thanon Wualai**, on the south side of the old town, though the actual smithing is now done elsewhere. If you're serious about buying silver, however, this is still the place to come, with dozens of small shops on Wualai itself and on Soi 3 selling repoussé plates, bowls and cups, and attractive, chunky jewellery. For sterling silver, check the stamp that shows the item is 92.5 percent pure; some items on sale in Chiang Mai are only eighty percent pure and sell much more cheaply.

Nova Collection 179 Thanon Tha Pae ⊕ 053 273058, ⓦ nova-collection.com; map p.289. A good general **jewellery** store which has some lovely rings and necklaces blending gold, silver, platinum, steel and precious stones in striking and original designs. Mon–Sat 9am–7.30pm & Sun 10am–6pm.

China, 111 Thanon Chang Lo ☎053 280380; India, 33/1 Thanon Thung Hotel ☎053 243066; Myanmar, 9/4 Soi 3, Thanon Manee Noparat ☎052 004211; US, 387 Thanon Witchayanon ☎053 107700.

Hospitals Lanna, at 103 Superhighway (☎053 999777, ⊛lanna-hospital.com), east of Thanon Chotana, has a 24hr emergency and ambulance service and dentistry department; McCormick (☎053 921777, ⊛mccormick.in.th) is cheaper, used to farangs and is nearer, on Thanon Kaeo Nawarat; Chiang Mai Ram, at 8 Thanon Boonruangrit (☎053 920300, ⊛chiangmairam.com), also has a good reputation.

Immigration office In Promenada Mall, 5km southeast of the old city on H1141 (Mon–Fri 8.30am–4.30pm; ⊛chiangmaiimm.com), but may move back to its old location by the airport – check ⊛thaivisa.com.

Pharmacies Boots branches include Thanon Tha Pae, opposite Tha Pae Gate, and on Thanon Chang Klan near the Night Bazaar.

Post offices The GPO is way out of the centre on Thanon Charoen Muang near the train station, but there's a far more convenient post office at 43 Thanon Samlarn (Phra Singh PO), near Wat Phra Singh (Mon–Fri 8.30am–4pm, Sat 9am–noon), which offers a packing service. There are also post offices on Thanon Phra Pokklao at the junction with Thanon Ratchawithi in the old town (Sri Phum PO), on Thanon Wichayanon near Nawarat Bridge (Mae Ping PO), and at the airport.

Swimming pool At the Eco Resort (see page 291), B150/day for non-guests.

Thai language courses AUA (American University Alumni), 24 Thanon Ratchdamnoen (☎053 214120, ⊛learnthaiinchiangmai.com), is the longest-established and best place to learn Thai, certified by the Ministry of Education. Several levels of classes are offered, starting with spoken Thai for beginners (60hr over about six weeks; B5300), with class sizes limited to five to twelve students. Individual and small-group instruction can also be arranged.

Tourist police At the far end of Thanon Huai Kaeo, at the start of the road up Doi Suthep, opposite the zoo, and at the airport ☎1155.

Around Chiang Mai

You'll never feel cooped up in Chiang Mai, as the surrounding countryside is dotted with day-trip options in all directions. Dominating the skyline to the west, **Doi Suthep** and its eagle's-nest temple are hard to ignore, and a wander around the pastoral ruins of **Wiang Kum Kam** on the southern periphery has the feel of fresh exploration. Much further south, the quiet town of **Lamphun** offers classic sightseeing in the form of historically and religiously significant temples and a museum. To the north, the **Mae Sa valley** may be full of tour buses, but its highlights, the **Queen Sirikit Botanic Gardens**, the intriguing **Elephant Poopoopaper Park** and the **Siam Insect Zoo**, as well as the nearby lake of **Huay Tung Tao** and **Darapirom Palace**, merit an independent jaunt. Distinctly missable, however, is the Chiang Mai **Night Safari** to the southwest of the city, which has encroached on land belonging to Doi Suthep National Park, and even announced as an opening promotion when it was launched in 2006 that the meat of all the animals on display would also be available in its restaurant (though the offer has now been withdrawn) – much better to spend your money at Chiang Mai Zoo (see page 283).

All the excursions described here can be done in half a day; not all of them are covered by public **transport**, but a car with driver arranged through a Chiang Mai guesthouse should cost you around B1000 for a half-day local trip. There are also some good options for longer jaunts that could be done in a day out of Chiang Mai, notably to Doi Inthanon National Park (see page 329), to Lampang and the Thai Elephant Conservation Centre (see page 313) and to the Elephant Nature Park (see page 350).

Doi Suthep

A jaunt up **DOI SUTHEP**, the mountain which rises steeply at the city's western edge, is the most satisfying brief trip you can make from Chiang Mai, chiefly on account of beautiful **Wat Phra That Doi Suthep**, which dominates the hillside and gives a towering view over the goings-on in town. This is the north's holiest shrine, its pre-eminence deriving from a magic relic enshrined in its chedi and the miraculous legend of its founding. The original chedi was built by King Ku Na at the end of the fourteenth century, after the glowing relic of Wat Suan Dork had self-multiplied just before being enshrined. A place had to be found for the clone, so Ku Na put it in a travelling shrine on the back of a white elephant and waited to see where the sacred animal would lead: it eventually climbed Doi Suthep, trumpeted three times, turned round three times, knelt down and died, thereby indicating that this was the spot. Ever since, it's been northern Thailand's most important place of pilgrimage, especially for the candlelit processions on **Makha Puja**, the anniversary of the sermon to the disciples, and **Visakha Puja**, the anniversary of the Buddha's birth, enlightenment and death, when thousands of people walk up to the temple through the night from Chiang Mai.

Doi Suthep-Pui National Park

Park headquarters are about 1km beyond the wat • B200 • ☎ 053 210244, ⓦ nps.dnp.go.th

A signpost halfway up the road to the temple is about the only indication that you're in **Doi Suthep-Pui National Park**, which also encompasses the 1685m peak of Doi Pui to the northwest of Doi Suthep; however, an entry fee is not levied if you are only visiting the wat, Phuping Palace and Ban Doi Pui, a highly commercialized Hmong village near the palace that's worth avoiding. Despite the nearness of the city, the park's rich mixed forests support 330 species of bird and are a favoured site for nature study, second in the north only to the larger and less-disturbed Doi Inthanon National Park.

About 5km from the base of the mountain road, a road on the right leads 3km to **Mon Tha Than Falls**, a beautiful spot, believed by some to be home to evil spirits. The higher fall is an idyllic 5m drop into a small bathing pool, completely overhung by thick, humming jungle.

Wat Phra That Doi Suthep

B30, or B50 including the cable car • ⓦ doisuthep.com • Monk Chat (a chance to talk to the monks in English), southwest corner of the lower terrace Mon–Sat 9am–5pm • Meditation courses are held here (see page 285)

KHRUBA SRIVIJAYA

Khruba Srivijaya, widely regarded as the "patron saint" of northern Thailand, was born in 1878 in a small village 100km south of Chiang Mai. His birth coincided with a supernatural thunderstorm and earthquake, after which he was given the auspicious nickname Faa Rawng (Thunder) until he joined the monkhood. Appointed abbot of his local temple by the age of 24, he came to be regarded as something of a rebel – though a hugely popular one among the people of Lanna. Despite the suspicions of the Sangha, both locally and in Bangkok, he became abbot of Lamphun's Wat Chama Thevi, which he set about restoring with gusto. This was the beginning of a tireless campaign to breathe life into Buddhist worship in the north by renovating its religious sites: over a hundred temples got the Khruba treatment, including Chiang Mai's Wat Phra Singh, Wat Phra That Haripunjaya in Lamphun and Wat Phra That Doi Tung near Mae Sai, as well as bridges, schools and government buildings. His greatest work, however, was the construction in 1935 of the paved road up to Wat Phra That Doi Suthep, which beforehand could only be reached after a climb of at least five hours. The road was constructed entirely by the voluntary labour of people from all over the north, using the most primitive tools. The project gained such fame that it attracted donations of B20 million, and on any one day as many as four thousand people were working on it. So that people didn't get in each other's way, Khruba Srivijaya declared that each village should contribute 15m of road, but as more volunteers flocked to Chiang Mai, this figure had to be reduced to 3m. The road was completed after just six months, and Khruba Srivijaya took the first ride to the temple in a donated car.

When Khruba Srivijaya died back in his native village in 1938, Rama VIII was so moved that he sponsored a royal cremation ceremony. The monk's relics were divided up and are now enshrined at Wat Suan Dork in Chiang Mai, Wat Phra Kaeo Don Tao in Lampang and at many other holy places throughout the north. There's a statue of him at the end of Thanon Huai Kaeo, where the road to Wat Phra That Doi Suthep starts, and you'll see photos of him in temples, shops and restaurants all over the north, where Khruba amulets are still hugely popular, eighty years after his death.

Opposite a car park and souvenir village, 11km from the base of the mountain road, a flight of three hundred naga-flanked steps – or the adjacent cable car – is the last leg on the way to **Wat Phra That Doi Suthep**. From the temple's **lower terrace**, the magnificent views of Chiang Mai and the surrounding plain, 300m below, are best in the early morning or late afternoon in the cool season, though peaceful contemplation of the view is frequently shattered by people sounding the heavy, dissonant bells around the terrace – they're supposed to bring good luck. At the northwestern corner is a 2m-high statue of the elephant, which, so the story goes, expired on this spot.

Before going to the **upper terrace** you have to remove your shoes – and if you're showing a bit of knee or shoulder, the temple provides wraps to cover your impoliteness. This terrace is possibly the most harmonious piece of temple architecture in Thailand, a dazzling combination of red, green and gold in the textures of carved wood, filigree and gleaming metal – even the tinkling of the miniature bells and the rattling of fortune sticks seem to keep the rhythm. A cloister, decorated with gaudy murals, tightly encloses the terrace, leaving room only for a couple of small minor viharns and the altars and ceremonial gold umbrellas which surround the central focus of attention, the **chedi**. This dazzling gold-plated beacon, a sixteenth-century extension of Ku Na's original, was modelled on the chedi at Wat Phra That Haripunjaya in Lamphun – which previously had been the region's most significant shrine – and has now become a venerated emblem of northern Thailand. Look out for an old black-and-white photograph opposite the northeastern corner of the chedi, showing a cockerel that used to peck the feet of visitors who entered with their shoes on.

Phuping Palace

4km up the paved road from the wat • Daily 8.30am–4.30pm, last ticket sales 3.30pm; usually closed between Jan and March when the royals are in residence • B50 • ⓦ bhubingpalace.org • Dress politely – no shorts or bare shoulders

Phuping Palace is the residence for the royals when they come to visit their village development projects in the north. There's a viewpoint over the hills to the south, rose and fern gardens and some pleasant trails through the grounds, but the buildings themselves are off-limits.

ARRIVAL AND DEPARTURE   DOI SUTHEP

The best way to get up the mountain is in a rented vehicle, allowing you to stop along the way to admire the views. The road, although steep and winding, is paved and well suited for motorbikes.

By shared songthaew Red shared songthaews to Doi Suthep leave from Thanon Huai Kaeo in front of the zoo or Chiang Mai University, but will only set off once they have a complement of at least six passengers (B40 one-way to the wat; at least B70 one-way to Phuping Palace, for which you're likely to have to wait a bit longer for a full complement of passengers). Some Doi Suthep shared songthaews also hang out on Thanon Manee Noparat near Chang Puak Gate and at Wat Phra Singh, but you're probably going to have to wait longer for enough passengers to show up here and/or have to pay the driver a bit more money to get him to go.

By chartered vehicle It costs around B600 to charter a whole songthaew, about B800 to arrange a car and driver through your guesthouse.

On foot It's possible to walk up the mountainside along the scenic Pilgrims' Trail from the outskirts of Chiang Mai to the temple in about 1hr 30min (without stops). To get to the trailhead, go to the end of Thanon Suthep and turn right, following signs for the zoo (the back entrance), which will bring you to the signboards at the start of the path by a red and white, Channel 7 TV mast (for further details, go to ⓦ globotreks.com/destinations/thailand-destinations/hiking-monks-trail-wat-pha-lat-chiang-mai/). About halfway up, you'll reach Wat Palad, a pretty, tranquil and rustic temple by a waterfall, after which you'll need to cross the main road up the mountain to regain the trail.

Wiang Kum Kam

5km south of Chiang Mai city centre, beyond the Superhighway, on the east bank of the Ping River

The well-preserved and little-visited ruins of the ancient city of **WIANG KUM KAM** – traditionally regarded as the prototype for Chiang Mai – are hidden away in the

SKY LANTERNS AT LOY KRATHONG

picturesque, rural fringe of town. According to folklore, Wiang Kum Kam was built by King Mengrai as his new capital of the north, but was soon abandoned because of inundation when the Ping River changed course. Recent excavations, however, have put paid to that theory: Wiang Kum Kam was in fact established much earlier, as one of a cluster of fortified satellite towns that surrounded the Mon capital at Lamphun. After Mengrai had conquered Lamphun in 1281, he resided at Kum Kam for a while, raising a chedi, a viharn and several Buddha statues before moving on to build Chiang Mai. Wiang Kum Kam was abandoned some time before 1750, probably as a result of a Burmese invasion. About half of Wiang Kum Kam's 22 known temple sites have now been excavated, along with a stone slab (now housed in the Chiang Mai National Museum) inscribed in a unique forerunner of the Thai script.

Chedi Si Liam
1km south of the Superhighway on the east bank of the river

Head first for **Chedi Si Liam**, which provides a useful landmark: this Mon chedi, in the shape of a tall, squared-off pyramid with niched Buddha images, was built by Mengrai in memory of his dead wife. Modelled on Wat Kukut in Lamphun, it was restored in 1908 by a wealthy Mon resident of Chiang Mai using Burmese artisans and is still part of a working temple.

Wat Kan Thom
About 2km from Chedi Si Liam: backtrack along the river road you've travelled down from Chiang Mai, take the first right turn, turn right again and keep left through a scattered farming settlement

Wat Kan Thom (aka Wat Chang Kham) lay at the centre of the old city and is still an important place of worship. Archeologists were only able to get at the site after much of it had been levelled by bulldozers building a playground for the adjacent school, but they have managed to uncover the brick foundations of Mengrai's viharn. The modern shrine next to it is where Mengrai's soul is said to reside. Also in the grounds are a white chedi and a small viharn, both much restored, and a large new viharn displaying fine craftsmanship.

If you have your own transport, from here you can head off along the trails through the thick foliage of the longan plantations to the northwest of Wat Kan Thom, back towards Chedi Si Liam. On this route, you come across surprisingly well-preserved chedis and the red-brick walls of Wiang Kum Kam's temples in a handful of shady clearings set between rural dwellings.

ARRIVAL AND DEPARTURE   **WIANG KUM KAM**

By boat and horse carriage A nice way of seeing Wiang Kum Kam is on a trip with Mae Ping River Cruises (2–4 daily, minimum 2 people; 2hr altogether; B800/person including pick-up from your accommodation), which involves a 15min cruise down the river followed by a horse-and-carriage ride around six of the temples (see page 279).

By motorbike or bicycle About 3km square, the ancient city can be explored on a bicycle or a motorbike, though it's easy to get lost in the maze of lanes connecting the ruins. If you're happy to look around under your own steam, the best way to approach Wiang Kum Kam is by heading down Thanon Chiang Mai–Lamphun, then forking right at Nong Hoi market (a short way after the *Holiday Inn*) onto Thanon Koh Klang, which will bring you under the Superhighway to Chedi Si Liam.

Lamphun

Though capital of its own province, **LAMPHUN** lives in the shadow of the tourist attention (and baht) showered on Chiang Mai, 26km to the north. Yet for anyone interested in history, a visit to this former royal city is a must and, if you have your own transport, combines very well with a trip to Wiang Kum Kam. The town's largely plain architecture is given some character by the surrounding waterways, beyond which stretch lush rice-fields and plantations of *lamyai* (longan); the sweetness of the local variety is celebrated every year at the peak of the harvest season in early August at the **Ngan Lamyai** (Longan Festival), when the town comes alive with processions of fruity floats, a drum-beating competition and a Miss Lamyai beauty contest. Lamphun also offers a less frantic alternative to Chiang Mai during the Songkhran and Loy Krathong festivals, the Khuang River being a far less congested place to float your *krathong* than Chiang Mai's Ping River. Though the streets of the town are usually sleepy, the ancient working **temples** of Wat Phra That Haripunjaya and Wat Kukut are lively and worth aiming for on a half-day trip from Chiang Mai.

Lamphun claims to be the oldest continuously inhabited town in Thailand, and has a history dating back to the late eighth or early ninth century when the ruler of the major Dvaravati centre at Lopburi sent his daughter, Chama Thevi, to found the Theravada Buddhist city-state of **Haripunjaya** here. Under the dynasty she established, Haripunjaya flourished as a link in the trade route to Yunnan in southwest China and managed to resist coming under the suzerainty of the Khmers at Angkor, who absorbed Lopburi and the other Dvaravati cities in central Thailand in the eleventh century. In 1281, after a decade of scheming, the great Lanna king Mengrai conquered Lamphun and brought it under his control.

Chama Thevi's planners are said to have based the **layout** of the town on the shape of an auspicious conch shell. The rough outcome is a rectangle, narrower at the north end than the south, with the Khuang River running down its kilometre-long east side, and moats around the north, west and south sides. The main street, Thanon Inthayongyot, bisects the conch from north to south, while the road to Wat Chama Thevi (Thanon Chama Thevi) heads out from the middle of the west moat.

Wat Phra That Haripunjaya

Easiest access through the rear entrance on Thanon Inthayongyot • Daily 6am–9pm • B20

One of the north's grandest and most important temples, **Wat Phra That Haripunjaya** has its bot and ornamental front entrance facing the Khuang River. Its main festival is Visakha Puja, the anniversary of the Buddha's birth, enlightenment and death, which is said to coincide with the anniversary of the temple's establishment, when the main chedi is bathed in holy water donated by the king. However, the date of its founding is actually hard to fathom: the earliest guess is 897, when the king of Haripunjaya is said to have built a chedi to enshrine a hair of the Buddha on the site of Queen Chama Thevi's original palace. More certain is the date of the main rebuilding of the temple, under King Tilok of Chiang Mai in 1443, when the present ringed chedi was erected in the then-fashionable Sri Lankan style (later copied at Doi Suthep and Lampang). Clad in brilliant copper plates, it has since been raised to a height of about 50m, crowned by a gold umbrella.

The plain open courtyards around the chedi contain a compendium of religious structures in a wild mix of styles and colours. On the north side, the tiered, twenty-metre-high, Haripunjaya-style pyramid of **Chedi Suwanna** was built in 1418 as a replica of the chedi at nearby Wat Chama Thevi. You get a whiff of southern Thailand in the open space beyond the Suwanna chedi, where the **Chedi Chiang Yan** owes its resemblance to a pile of flattened pumpkins to the Srivijayan style. On either side of the viharn (to the east of the main chedi) stand a dark red **bell tower**, containing what's claimed to be the world's largest bronze gong, and a weather-beaten **library** on a raised base. Just to add to the temple's mystique, an open pavilion at the southwest corner of the chedi shelters a stone indented with four overlapping **footprints**, believed by fervent worshippers to confirm an ancient legend that the Buddha once passed this way. Next to the pavilion is a small **museum** which houses bequests to the temple, including some beautiful Buddha images in the Lanna style. Finally, beside the back entrance, is the **Phra Chao Tan Jai**, a graceful standing Buddha, surrounded by graphic murals that depict a horrific version of Buddhist hell.

Hariphunchai National Museum

Thanon Inthayongyot, across the road from Wat Phra That Haripunjaya's back entrance • Wed–Sun 9am–4pm • B100

The **Hariphunchai National Museum** contains a well-organized but not quite compelling collection of religious finds and stone inscriptions, and occasionally stages some interesting temporary exhibitions. The terracotta and bronze Buddha images here give the best overview of the distinctive features of the Haripunjaya style: large curls above a wide, flat forehead, bulging eyes, incised moustache and enigmatic smile.

Wat Chama Thevi

Thanon Chama Thevi

Art-history buffs will get a thrill out of **Wat Chama Thevi** (also known as Wat Kukut), where the main brick chedi, Suwan Chang Kot, which was built around 1150 and repaired in 1218, is the only complete example of Haripunjaya architecture.

Queen Chama Thevi is supposed to have chosen the site by ordering an archer to fire an arrow from the city's western gate – to retrace his epic shot, follow the road along the National Museum's southern wall to the west gate at the city moat, and keep going for nearly 1km along Thanon Chama Thevi. Chedi Suwan Chang Kot is five-tiered and rectangular, inset with niches sheltering beautiful, wide-browed Buddha images in stucco, typical of the Haripunjaya style. Believed to enshrine Chama Thevi's ashes, it lost its pinnacle at some stage, giving rise to the name Wat Kukut, the temple with the "topless" chedi. On your way back to the town centre from Wat Chama Thevi, you might like to pop in at **Wat Mahawan**, famous for the Buddha image amulets on sale there.

ARRIVAL AND DEPARTURE   LAMPHUN

It's not worth considering catching the train from Chiang Mai to Lamphun as schedules are unreliable and the station there is way out to the northeast of the town centre.

By bus Small, a/c buses from Chiang Mai's Chang Puak bus station, via Lamyai market on Thanon Praisani, will put you off outside the back entrance of Wat Haripunjaya.

By motorbike or car The direct (and scenic) route from Chiang Mai to Lamphun is Thanon Chiang Mai–Lamphun, which becomes Highway 106, for much of the way a stately avenue lined by 30m-tall *yang* trees that makes for a pleasant motorbike or car ride.

ACCOMMODATION AND EATING

Lamphun Ice 6 Thanon Chaimongkol ☎ 090 891 8708. This neat little a/c place with nice booth tables serves tasty Thai food at reasonable prices, with simple dishes such as chicken on rice starting at B35, as well as delicious homemade longan ice cream and espresso coffees; it's conveniently situated on the road that runs along the south wall of Wat Haripunjaya. Daily except Fri 11am–10pm.

Lamphun Will Hotel Thanon Chama Thevi opposite Wat Kukut ☎ 053 534865–6, ⓦ lamphunwillhotel.com. It's unlikely you'll want to stay overnight in Lamphun, but this reasonably stylish, 80-room hotel is a decent choice. There's a swimming pool, a restaurant, and en-suite hot-water bathrooms, a/c, fridges and cable TV in all the bedrooms. B1500

Huay Tung Tao

Signed off Thanon Chon Prathan (Canal Rd) about 10km north of Chiang Mai, just before it joins Highway 107 (the continuation of Thanon Chotana); it's then 2km northwest from the turn-off to the paved road around the lake

With your own transport, **Huay Tung Tao**, a large man-made lake at the base of Doi Suthep, is a great place to cool off during the hot season; it's safe to swim in, with canoes and inner tubes to rent, and is also used by anglers and windsurfers. Wooden shelters along the water's edge provide shade from the sun, and you can order simple food such as sticky rice, grilled chicken and *som tam*.

Darapirom Palace

16km north of Chiang Mai in Mae Rim: look out for a sign on the left of Highway 107 just before Mae Rim police station, then it's about 400m from the turn-off • Tues–Sun 9am–5pm • B20 • ☎ 053 299175, ⓦ chula.ac.th

In **Mae Rim**, a small market town that's now almost a suburb of Chiang Mai, the **Darapirom Palace** is a gorgeous colonial-style building from the early twentieth century. The palace was once the home of Princess Dara Rasamee (1873–1933), daughter of Chao Inthanon, the lord of Chiang Mai, who became the favourite concubine of King Chulalongkorn (Rama

V) in the days before Chiang Mai was fully integrated into the Siamese state. Extremely proud of her northern heritage – and now something of a heroine to lovers of Lanna culture – the princess had this residence built in 1914, a few years after Chulalongkorn's death, when she returned from Bangkok to live out her later years in her homeland. Bangkok's Chulalongkorn University has opened the palace as a museum, featuring period furnishings and many items that once belonged to the princess. Photographs of her show her knee-length hair – which contrasted strongly with the fashion among Siamese women of the time to sport short-cropped hair – and the various rooms of the museum display her wardrobe and personal effects including musical instruments.

The Mae Sa valley

About 1km north of central Mae Rim on Highway 107, Route 1096, a good sealed road, heads west up the valley

Running west from Mae Rim, the **Mae Sa valley** has the atmosphere of a theme park, sheltering a menagerie of snake farms, monkey shows, elephant camps, tiger sanctuaries, "adventure sports" venues, and orchid and butterfly farms, but its highlight, the lovely botanic gardens, is well worth the trip. The main Route 1096 through the valley also passes the unspectacular **Mae Sa Waterfall** (part of Doi Suthep-Pui National Park; B200), where you can walk up a peaceful trail passing lots of little cascades along the way. Once you've seen all you want to in the valley, you have the option of continuing west for a scenic drive in the country: turn left on to Route 1269 before Samoeng, and follow this road as it swoops up and down over hills, skirting all the way round Doi Suthep to join Highway 108 8km south of Chiang Mai, a two-hour drive in all.

3

Elephant Poopoopaper Park

200m up Route 1096 from the Mae Rim turn-off, turn right for about 1km (signposted) • Daily 9am–5.30pm • B100 • Ⓦ poopoopaperpark.com

Elephants eat between 200 and 500kg of food every day, and download the results 15–20 times a day, so what's to be done with this mountain of dung? **Elephant Poopoopaper Park** provides an unlikely but eco-friendly, sustainable and fair-trade answer, that's also a lot of fun for all the family and surprisingly odour-free (given the creatures' speedy digestive systems). Entertaining tours guide you through the stages of turning poo into paper in a pretty garden setting, and there are plenty of hands-on activities including the chance to screen the pulp mixture to make sheets. Everything from greeting cards to sun visors made out of the coarse, colourful paper is on sale, and kids of all ages will love customizing their souvenirs with their own designs.

Siam Insect Zoo

4km up Route 1096 from the Mae Rim turn-off, turn right (signposted) and it's 100m on your right • Daily 9am–5pm • B200 • Ⓦ siaminsectzoo.com

Founded by a professor of entomology, **Siam Insect Zoo** shelters just about anything that creeps or crawls in Thailand – whether alive in cages or pinned in glass cases – plus hundreds of specimens from around the world. Detailed labels and display boards in English explain how insects see and how cockroaches can survive decapitation for weeks, and you'll get the chance to handle caterpillars and stick insects with staff supervision. Outside is a delightful butterfly garden, covered with netting and landscaped with streams and bridges. There's also an insect-themed souvenir shop and a nice little café.

Queen Sirikit Botanic Gardens

12km up Route 1096 from the Mae Rim turn-off • Daily 8.30am–5pm, Natural Science Museum daily 9am–4pm • B100, plus B100 per car • Shuttle buses B30 (unlimited rides) • Ⓦ qsbg.org

The magnificent **Queen Sirikit Botanic Gardens**, which offer fine views across the mountain valley, are the main reason for coming to Mae Sa. If you are at all botanically inclined, you could easily spend half a day here, exploring the four nature trails that link its arboretum, ornamental beds, fern garden, orchid nursery, areas of climbers and medicinal plants and a complex of a dozen glasshouses. There's also a vertiginous canopy walkway with great views near the top of the park and an interesting and attractive Natural Science Museum, with English labels, to put things in context. Hop-on, hop-off shuttle buses run around the steep, extensive grounds, if the heat gets too much; cars are also allowed to drive round, but motorbikes must park at the entrance.

EATING

MAE SA VALLEY

★ **Pongyang Angdoi Restaurant** About 500m beyond the botanic gardens on the south side of the road ☎ 053 879151, ⓦ facebook.com/pongyangangdoirestaurant. By far the best place to eat hereabouts (most dishes B150–200), set on terraced platforms overlooking landscaped gardens and the Mae Sa river. Specialities include muu det diaw, sun-dried then deep-fried pork, and kaeng khua het thawp, a delicious curry made with a highly prized local fungus. Daily 10.30am–8.30pm, closes 5pm on Wed.

Doi Khun Tan National Park

Around 50km southeast of Chiang Mai • B100 • ☎ 053 546335, ⓦ nps.dnp.go.th

One of three major national parks close to Chiang Mai, along with Suthep and Inthanon, **DOI KHUN TAN NATIONAL PARK** is accessible by train from Chiang Mai and Bangkok: a 1352m-long rail tunnel, the longest in Thailand, built between 1907 and 1918 by German engineers and Thai workers (of whom over a thousand died due to accidents, malaria and tigers), cuts through the mountain that gives the park its name. Despite this, and the fact that the king has famously holidayed here, the park remains unspoiled, but has enough infrastructure to encourage overnighting. The park is most popular on weekends, when groups of Thai schoolchildren visit, and during the cool season.

Covering 255 square kilometres, the park's vegetation varies from bamboo forest at an altitude of 350m to tropical evergreen forest between 600m and 1000m; the 1373m summit of Doi Khun Tan is known for its wild flowers, including orchids, gingers and lilies. Most of the small mammal species in the park are squirrels, but you're more likely to see some birds, with over 182 species found here.

Trails through the park

The park's **trails** are clearly marked, ranging from short nature trails around the park headquarters (where maps are available) to the major trail that leads to the summit of **Doi Khun Tan** – with impressive views of the surrounding countryside, it's clear how it fulfilled its role as a World War II military lookout. This main 8.3km trail from the train station to the summit, though steep, is very easy, divided into four quarters of approximately 2km each, with each quarter ending at a resting place. While you shouldn't have a problem getting to the summit and back in a day, a more rewarding option is to do the walk in two days, staying overnight in the bungalows or at one of the campsites along the trail. Alternatively, you can take a circular route to the summit and back, forsaking a large chunk of the main trail for a subsidiary trail that curves around the north side, taking in a **waterfall**.

ARRIVAL AND DEPARTURE

DOI KHUN TAN NATIONAL PARK

By train There are three morning trains daily from Chiang Mai to Khun Tan station on their way to Lampang and beyond, and there's one evening train back (scheduled for 6.23pm), making a day-trip by rail from Chiang Mai possible. The park headquarters is a 1300m walk up the summit trail from the train station.

Destinations Bangkok (5 daily; 11–13hr); Chiang Mai (6 daily; 1hr 30min); Lampang (6 daily; 50min).
By car or motorbike A car or motorbike can take you to the park headquarters, though no further: from Chiang Mai follow Highway 11 to the turn-off to Mae Tha and head northeast for 18km, following signs for the park.

ACCOMMODATION AND EATING

If you want to stay in the park, consider booking in advance through the Department of National Parks website (🌐 nps. dnp.go.th). There's a basic **restaurant** at the headquarters and beside the bungalows.

Bungalows The park's bungalows, scattered for over 1km up the main trail from the headquarters, are mostly spacious and well-appointed log cabins with hot-water bathrooms, sleeping up to six people. Some have outside seating areas with great views over the rolling hills. B500

Camping There's a well-equipped (and often very busy) campsite near the park headquarters; if you don't have your own tent you can rent one here. B150

Lampang and around

A high road pass and a train tunnel breach the narrow, steep belt of mountains between Chiang Mai and **LAMPANG**, the north's second-largest town, 100km to the southeast. Lampang is an important transport hub – Highway 11, Highway 1 and the Northern

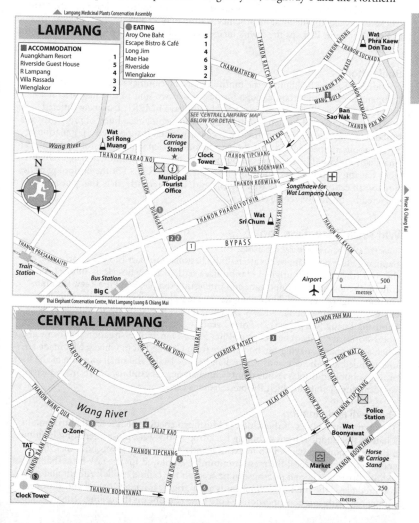

3

Lampang Medicinal Plants Conservation Assembly

LAMPANG

■ ACCOMMODATION
Auangkham Resort	1
Riverside Guest House	5
R Lampang	4
Villa Rassada	3
Wienglakor	2

● EATING
Aroy One Baht	5
Escape Bistro & Café	1
Long Jim	4
Mae Hae	6
Riverside	3
Wienglakor	2

Thai Elephant Conservation Centre, Wat Lampang Luang & Chiang Mai

CENTRAL LAMPANG

Rail Line all converge here – and given its undeniably low-key attractions, nearly all travellers sail through it on their way to the more trumpeted sights further north. But unlike most other provincial capitals, Lampang has the look of a place where history has not been completely wiped out: houses, shops and temples survive in the traditional style, and the town makes few concessions to tourism. Out of town, the beautiful complex of **Wat Phra That Lampang Luang** is the main attraction in these parts, but while you're in the neighbourhood you could also stop by to watch a show at the **Elephant Conservation Centre**, on the road from Chiang Mai.

The modern centre of Lampang sprawls along the south side of the Wang River, with its most frenetic commercial activity taking place along Thanon Boonyawat and Thanon Robwiang near Ratchada Bridge. Here, you'll find stalls and shops selling the famous local **pottery**, a kitsch combination of whites, blues and browns, made from the area's rich and durable kaolin clay. On all street signs around town, and in larger-than-life statues at key intersections, is a **white chicken**. This symbol of Lampang relates to a legend concerning the Buddha, who sent down angels from Heaven in the form of chickens to wake up the local inhabitants in time to offer alms to the monks at the end of Buddhist Lent. Perhaps the town's image as a laidback, sleepy place is justified in the light of this tale.

Brief history

Founded as Kelang Nakhon by the ninth-century Haripunjaya queen Chama Thevi, Lampang became important enough for one of her two sons to rule here after her death. After King Mengrai's conquest of Haripunjaya in 1281, Lampang suffered much the same ups and downs as the rest of Lanna, enjoying a burst of prosperity as a **timber** town at the end of the nineteenth century, when it supported a population of twenty thousand people and four thousand working elephants. Many of its temples are financially endowed by the waves of outsiders who have settled in Lampang: refugees from Chiang Saen (who were forcibly resettled here by Rama I at the beginning of the nineteenth century), Burmese teak-loggers and, more recently, rich Thai pensioners attracted by the town's sedate charm.

Wat Phra Kaew Don Tao

Thanon Phra Kaeo, 1km northeast of the Ratchada Bridge

Lampang's few sights are well scattered; the best place to start is on the north side of the river (the site of the original Haripunjaya settlement), whose leafy suburbs today contain the town's most important and interesting temple, **Wat Phra Kaew Don Tao**. An imposing, rather forbidding complex, the temple was founded in the fifteenth century to enshrine the Phra Kaew Don Tao image, now residing at Wat Phra That Lampang Luang (see page 312). For 32 years it also housed the Emerald Buddha (local stories aver this to be a copy of Phra Kaew Don Tao), a situation that came about when an elephant carrying the holy image from Chiang Rai to Chiang Mai made an unscheduled and therefore auspicious halt here in 1436. The small **museum** at the back of the compound displays some dainty china among its exhibits, but its main focus is woodcarving, a craft at which Burmese artisans excel.

The chedi and mondop

The clean, simple lines of the white, gold-capped **chedi**, which is reputed to contain a hair of the Buddha, form a shining backdrop to the wat's most interesting building, a Burmese **mondop** stacked up in extravagantly carved tiers; it was built in 1909 by craftsmen from the local Burmese community, employed for the task by a Thai prince (whose British-style coat of arms can be seen on the ceiling inside). All gilt and gaudy coloured glass, the interior decoration is a real fright, mixing Oriental and European influences, with some incongruously cute little cherubs on the ceiling. The mondop's boyish bronze centrepiece has the typical features of a Mandalay Buddha, with its jewelled headband, inset black and white eyes, and exaggerated, dangling ears, which denote the Buddha's supernatural ability to hear everything in the universe. In front of the Buddha is an image of Khruba Srivijaya, the north's most venerated monk (see page 301).

Ban Sao Nak

6 Thanon Ratwattana • Daily 10am–5pm • B50

Not far from Wat Phra Kaew Don Tao can be found **Ban Sao Nak** ("house of many pillars"), a private museum containing a fine display of ceramics, lacquerware and teak furnishings. Built in 1895 in a mixture of Burmese and Lanna styles, this sprawling wooden mansion is supported by a maze of 116 teak pillars and contains some interesting fading photographs of its former occupants, who were local notables. Here and outside, in the carefully landscaped grounds, you'll get a sense of how life would have been for the north's wealthier residents at the turn of the twentieth century.

3

Wat Sri Chum

Thanon Sri Chum, a 5min walk south of Thanon Robwiang

The Burmese who worked on Wat Phra Kaew Don Tao were brought to Lampang in the late nineteenth century when, after the British conquest of Upper Burma, timber companies expanded their operations as far as northern Thailand. Fearing that the homeless spirits of fallen trees would seek vengeance, the Burmese loggers often sponsored the building of temples, most of which still stand, to try to appease the tree spirits and gain merit. Though the spirits had to wait nearly a century, they seem to have got their revenge: due to a short circuit in some dodgy wiring, the viharn of **Wat Sri Chum**, which is the biggest Burmese temple in Thailand as well as the most important and beautiful Burmese temple in town, was damaged by fire in 1992. Now restored to its former glory, with fresh carvings and murals by Burmese craftsmen, it's sited in a small grove of bodhi trees.

Wat Sri Rong Muang

Towards the west end of Thanon Takrao Noi

To get more of a flavour of Myanmar, head for 100-year-old **Wat Sri Rong Muang**, which presents a dazzling ensemble: the crazy angles of its red-and-yellow roof shelter Mandalay Buddhas and several extravagantly carved gilt sermon-thrones, swimming in a glittering sea of coloured-glass wall tiles.

Thanon Talat Kao

South bank of the river • Walking street Sat & Sun roughly 5–10pm

When you've had your fill of temples, **Thanon Talat Kao**, the "Old Market Street", is good for a quiet stroll in the early morning. It has some very old shophouses and mansions, with intricate balconies and gables and unusual sunburst designs carved over some of the doors, showing a mixture of European, Burmese and Chinese influences – it used to house the offices of English and Burmese logging companies and was known as Talat Jiin, "Chinese market" (or in northern dialect, Kad Kong Ta, which means "Pier Street Market"), but went into decline with the advent of the railway in 1916. On Saturday and Sunday evenings, Talat Kao comes to life as a "**walking street**", similar to those in Chiang Mai, with food, clothes, silk and other crafts for sale and musicians playing. (There's a smaller walking street market on Friday early evening just across the river on Thanon Wang Nuea.)

Wat Phra That Lampang Luang

18km southwest of Lampang • Blue songthaews from Lampang's Thanon Robwiang run to Kor Kha, about 3km south of Wat Phra That Lampang Luang, every 30min (B40), but then you'll have to hire a motorbike taxi to take you to the temple and pay the driver to wait for you; alternatively, one of the Kor Kha songthaew drivers, Khun Awt, is now offering to continue to the temple once a day (departing Lampang at 11.30am), with a pick up at 6pm, charging B100/person return (ask at the municipal tourist office if you want more information)

A grand and well-preserved capsule of Lanna art and design, **Wat Phra That Lampang Luang** is one of the architectural highlights of northern Thailand. The wat was built early in the Haripunjaya era as a *wiang* (fortress), one of a satellite group around Lampang – you can still see remains of the threefold ramparts in the farming village around the temple. Outside the wat, simple snacks, handicrafts and antiques can be bought from market stalls. If you're driving yourself to the temple, head south from Lampang on Highway 1, then cross the bridge over the Wang River at Kor Kha and turn right, heading north for about 3km on Route 1034; if you're coming from Chiang Mai or the elephant centre, just after Hang Chat (before you reach Lampang) turn right off Highway 11 onto Route 1034.

The main viharn

At the main entrance, a naga staircase leads you up to a wedding cake of a gatehouse, richly decorated with stucco, which is set in the original brick boundary walls. Just inside, the oversized fifteenth-century **viharn** is open on all sides in classic Lanna fashion, and shelters a spectacular centrepiece: known as a *ku*, a feature found only in the viharns of northern Thailand, this gilded brick tower looks like a bonfire for the main Buddha image sitting inside, the Phra Chao Lan Thong. Tall visitors need to mind their heads on the panels hanging from the low eaves, which are decorated with attractive, though fading, early nineteenth-century paintings of the Jataka (the Buddha's previous lives), showing battles, palaces and nobles in traditional Burmese gear.

The rest of the main compound

The temple's main walled compound is home to no fewer than four other viharns. In front of the murky, beautifully decorated viharn to the left, look out for a wooden *tung chai* carved with flaming, coiled nagas, used as a heraldic banner for northern princes. The battered, cosy **Viharn Nam Tame**, second back on the right, dates to the early sixteenth century. Its drooping roof configuration is archetypal: divided into three tiers, each of which is divided again into two layers, it ends up almost scraping the ground. Under the eaves you can just make out fragments of panel paintings, as old as the viharn, illustrating a story of one of the exploits of the Hindu god Indra.

Dating from the fifteenth century, the wat's huge central **chedi** enshrines a hair of the Buddha and ashes from the right side of his forehead and neck. By its northwest corner, a sign points to a drainage hole in the wat's boundary wall, once the scene of an unlikely act of derring-do: in 1736, local hero Thip Chang managed to wriggle through the tiny hole and free the *wiang* from the occupying Burmese, before going on to liberate the whole of Lampang.

At the chedi's southwest corner, the **Haw Phra Phuttabhat** (no entry for women) is a small chamber that acts as a camera obscura. If you close the door behind you, an image of the chedi is projected through a small hole in the door onto a sheet hung from the ceiling.

Phra Kaew Don Tao

A gate in the south side of the main compound's boundary wall leads first to a spreading **bodhi tree** on crutches: merit-makers have donated hundreds of supports to prop up its drooping branches. The tree, with its own small shrine standing underneath, is believed to be inhabited by spirits, and the sick are sometimes brought here in search of a cure.

The path beyond the bodhi tree will bring you to a small, unimpressive viharn to the west of the main compound, which is the home of **Phra Kaew Don Tao**, the much-revered companion image to Bangkok's Emerald Buddha, and the wat's main focus of pilgrimage. Legend has it that the statuette first appeared in the form of an emerald found in a watermelon presented by a local woman to a venerated monk. The two of them tried to carve a Buddha out of the emerald, without much success, until the god Indra appeared and fashioned the marvellous image, at which point the ungrateful townsfolk accused the monk of having an affair with the woman and put her to death, thus bringing down upon the town a series of disasters which confirmed the image's awesome power. In all probability, the image was carved at the beginning of the fifteenth century, when its namesake wat in Lampang was founded. Peering through the rows of protective bars inside the viharn, you can just make out the tiny meditating Buddha, which is actually made of jasper, not emerald. Like the Emerald Buddha in Bangkok, Phra Kaew Don Tao has three costumes, one for each season of the year (see page 85).

Thung Kwian market

21km from Lampang on Highway 11, en route to the Thai Elephant Conservation Centre

If you have your own vehicle, the **Thung Kwian market** (open daily) offers not only a useful stop for refreshments near the elephant centre, but also a chance to view the panoply of products on sale – rabbits and birds, honeycombs, bugs and creepy-crawlies of every description. This is a favourite spot for city Thais to pick up some exotic taste to take back home with them.

The Thai Elephant Conservation Centre

30km west of Lampang on Highway 11 • Shows daily at 10am, 11am & 1.30pm, with the chance to see the elephants bathing at 9.40am & 1.10pm • B200 • ☎ 054 829333, ⓦ thailandelephant.org • The centre is on the bus route between Chiang Mai and Lampang; from the gates, there are regular shuttle buses into the elephant showground 2km away

The **Thai Elephant Conservation Centre** (aka the National Elephant Institute) is the most authentic and worthwhile place in Thailand to see elephants displaying their skills. Entertaining **shows** put the elephants through their paces, with plenty of loud trumpeting for their audience. After some photogenic bathing, they walk together in formation and go through a routine of pushing and dragging logs, then proceed to paint pictures and play custom-made instruments. You can feed them bananas and sugar cane after the show, and even take a **ride** on one (available daily 8am–3.30pm) – B500 gets you thirty minutes (maximum two people), while B1000 gives you an hour's ride, with a chance to get out into the nearby forest (longer day-trips, overnight treks and mahout training programmes are also on offer – see the website). Visitors are also free to look around the hospital (best in the early morning), but not the royal stables, where six of Rama IX's ten white elephants are kept.

Run by the Thai government, the conservation centre was originally set up in 1969 in another nearby location as a young elephant-training centre, the earliest of its kind in Thailand. However, since the ban on logging, the new centre, opened in 1992, emphasizes the preservation of the elephant in Thailand (see page 314). By promoting ecotourism the centre is providing employment for the elephants and enabling Thai people to continue their historically fond relationship with these animals. Money raised from entrance fees and donations helps to finance the **elephant hospital** here, which cares for sick, abused, ageing and abandoned elephants. The centre has three simple **restaurants** on site, and offers the possibility of **homestays** and bungalow **accommodation** (from B1000; see the website for more details).

ARRIVAL AND DEPARTURE | LAMPANG

By plane Bangkok Airways (Suvarnabhumi Airport; 3 daily; 1hr 30min) and Nok Air (Don Muang Airport; 4 daily; 1hr 20min) run flights from Bangkok. The airport is just south of town, and songthaews and a/c taxis are on hand for the short ride to the centre.

By train The train station lies less than 1km southwest

THE ELEPHANT IN THAILAND

To Thais the **elephant** has profound **spiritual significance**, derived from both Hindu and Buddhist mythologies. Carvings and statues of **Ganesh**, the Hindu god with an elephant's head, feature on ancient temples and modern shrines all over the country and, as the god of knowledge and remover of obstacles, Ganesh has been adopted as the symbol of the Fine Arts Department – and is thus depicted on all entrance tickets to historical sites. The Hindu deity Indra rarely appears without his three-headed elephant mount **Erawan**, and miniature devotional elephant effigies are sold at major Brahmin shrines, such as Bangkok's Erawan Shrine. In Buddhist legend, the future **Buddha's mother** was able to conceive only after she dreamt that a white elephant had entered her womb: that is why elephant balustrades encircle many of the Buddhist temples of Sukhothai, and why the rare white elephant is accorded royal status (see page 114) and featured on the national flag until 1917.

The **practical** role of the elephant in Thailand was once almost as great as its symbolic importance, and it's thought that elephants were first captured and tamed over four thousand years ago. The kings of Ayutthaya relied on elephants to take them into battle against the Burmese – one king assembled a trained elephant army of three hundred – and during the nineteenth century King Rama IV offered Abraham Lincoln a male and a female to "multiply in the forests of America" and to use in the Civil War. In times of peace, the phenomenal strength of the elephant has made it invaluable as a beast of burden and transport: elephants hauled the stone from which the gargantuan Khmer temple complexes of the northeast were built, and for centuries they have been used to clear forests and carry timber and people.

The traditional cycle for domestic elephants born in captivity was to spend the first three years of their lives with their mothers (who are pregnant for 18–22 months and would get five years' maternity leave), before being separated and raised with other calves in training schools. Each elephant was then looked after by a **mahout** (*kwan chang*), a trainer, keeper and driver rolled into one. Traditionally the mahout would have stayed with the elephant for the rest of its life, but nowadays this rarely happens, as being a mahout is seen as a low-status job.

Training began with mahouts taking months to systematically break down the elephants' natural instincts – training methods often included being confined to tiny pens, and starved or beaten. Over the next thirteen years the elephant was taught about forty different commands, from simple "stop" and "go" orders to complex instructions for hooking and passing manoeuvres with the trunk. By the age of 16, elephants were ready to be put to work and were expected to carry on working until they reached 50 or 60, when they were retired.

Today there are around 2500 domesticated elephants in Thailand and the population of wild elephants is thought to be under two thousand – down from a roughly estimated total population of one hundred thousand in 1900 (the Asian elephant is now officially classified as an endangered species). Mechanized logging destroyed the wild elephant's preferred river-valley grassland and forest habitats, forcing them into isolated upland pockets that have shrunk even further due to agricultural expansion. The 1989 **ban on commercial logging** within Thai borders – after the 1988 catastrophe when the effects of deforestation caused mudslides that killed a hundred people and wiped out villages in Surat Thani province – came too late.

A small number of elephants still work in the illegal teak-logging trade along the border with Myanmar, and some are used as cute begging props, but most mahouts struggle to find the vast amount of food needed to sustain their charges – about 125kg per beast per day. Tourism was touted as an alternative to unemployment for elephants and their mahouts, though it's been a mixed blessing to say the least, as the elephants are often poorly treated, overworked or downright abused. Along with most major tourist companies we don't recommend riding elephants – if you want to interact with these magnificent beasts, then it's far better for the elephant (and many would say more rewarding for the tourist) to "walk" with them in their natural environment, tracking them and keeping at a respectful distance. Thailand has emerged at the forefront of **ethical elephant tourism** and places near Chiang Mai like the Elephant Nature Park (see page 350) and Burm and Emily's Elephant Sanctuary (❀ bees-elesanctuary.org) are open to visitors or volunteers.

If you really must ride an elephant, do your research and consider somewhere like the Thai Elephant Conservation Centre (see page 313), where the mahouts are well trained, the howdahs (saddles) are well designed, and where the animals get plenty of shade and carry a maximum of two people at a time for limited periods each day.

of the centre of Lampang (listed on some timetables as "Nakhon Lampang"). A shared yellow-and-green songthaew from here to the centre costs B20/person.
Destinations Bangkok (5 daily; 10–12hr); Chiang Mai (6 daily; 2hr–2hr 30min).
By bus The bus station is southwest of the town centre, just off the bypass, though some buses also make a stop on Thanon Phaholyothin in the centre. Yellow-and-green songthaews wait at the edge of the terminal, departing when full up (B20/person within the city).
Destinations Bangkok (at least hourly, with a concentration of overnight buses leaving around 8–9pm; 8hr); Chiang Mai (roughly every 30min; 1hr 30min–2hr); Chiang Rai (roughly every 30min; 4–5hr); Kanchanaburi (3 daily; 9hr); Mae Sai (1 daily; 5hr); Nan (7 daily; 4hr); Phitsanulok (roughly hourly; 4hr); Phrae (roughly hourly; 1hr 30min–2hr 30min); Sukhothai (over 20 daily; 4hr); Tak (roughly every 30min; 2hr 30min).

GETTING AROUND

The town centre can be covered on foot, but there are alternatives, including the town's horse-drawn carriages (see page 315).
By songthaew There are plenty of shared yellow-and-green songthaews that cruise the streets looking for custom (B20/person within the city).
By bicycle or motorbike Bicycles are available free at the municipal tourist office (bring your passport to photocopy). They can be rented (B50–60/day) at R-Lampang and *Riverside* guesthouses (see page 315) or at O-Zone on Thanon Tipchang (☎081 287 5527), who also have motorbikes (B250–500/day).
By rented car Avis (ⓦavisthailand.com) is based at the airport but will deliver and collect anywhere in Lampang.

INFORMATION

Tourist information The helpful, clued-up municipal tourist information centre (Mon–Fri 9am–4.30pm, plus Sat 9am–noon in high season; ☎054 237229), just west of the clocktower and next to the fire station on Thanon Takrao Noi, can provide a map of the town, which shows horse-drawn carriage routes. The TAT office is on Thanon Baan Chiangrai (daily 8.30am–4.30pm; ☎054 222214–5).

ACCOMMODATION

Auangkham Resort Thanon Wang Nuea ☎054 221305–6, ⓦauangkhamlampang.com; map p.309. At this friendly, leafy haven on the peaceful north bank of the river, the public areas have a colourful, retro feel while the large, bright bedrooms all have French windows and verandas overlooking the lovely garden, as well as a/c, hot showers, TVs and fridges. Free bicycles. B1100

★ **Riverside Guest House** 286 Thanon Talat Kao ☎054 227005, ⓦtheriverside-lampang.com; map p.309. This peaceful, traditional compound of century-old teak houses with a small, attractive garden offers tasteful en-suite rooms decorated with antiques and traditional textiles, all with access to hot showers (a few sharing) and many with a/c; some boast balconies or terraces overlooking the river. Varied breakfasts and all-day drinks are served on the relaxing terraces of the riverside café (not to be confused with the *Riverside* restaurant, further west). Fan B400, a/c B600

R Lampang Thanon Talat Kao, just east of Riverside Guest House ☎054 225278, ⓦr-lampang.com; map p.309. Part guesthouse, part doll's house, *R Lampang* occupies a prime spot on the riverfront, with shades of pastel green and soft pink providing the backdrop for a weird and wonderful collection of corridor curios – from white-painted samlors to clapped-out old TV sets. The fan rooms are too small, but the a/c rooms with TV and fridge are worth the investment. Fan B350, a/c B650

Villa Rassada 35 Thanon Charoen Pathet ☎085 365 9697, ⓦfacebook.com/villarassada; map p.309. Just across the river from Thanon Talat Kao, this good-value, welcoming small hotel offers stylish, contemporary rooms in muted tones, with a/c, hot showers, fridges, TVs and

---

LAMPANG'S HORSE-DRAWN CARRIAGES

If you want to get out to Wat Phra Kaew Don Tao you might want to employ the services of a **horse-drawn carriage**, which, along with white chickens, is a prevalent symbol of Lampang (in fact, Thais often refer to the city as *muang rot mah*, or "horse-cart city"). These colourfully decked-out carriages, complete with Stetson-wearing driver, can be hired at several stops around town, including towards the east end of Thanon Boonyawat and opposite the municipal tourist office. There are two "standard routes" around the town centre; the shorter one (3km) costs B200 (carrying two people), while the longer one (4–5km) costs B300. An alternative is the B400, one-hour city tour, which goes past Wat Sri Chum, Wat Phra Kaew Don Tao, Ban Sao Nak and Wat Sri Rong Muang (though you'll probably have to pay the driver a bit more for his time if you want to visit all of these sights properly).

balconies. Breakfast included. B790
Wienglakor 138/38 Thanon Phaholyothin ☎054
316430–5, ⊛lampangwienglakor.com; map p.309. Of
several big and expensive hotels in town, this one has the

cosiest rooms and the most tasteful decor, with coffered
ceilings, parquet floors and ornamental ponds in traditional
Thai style, as well as a good restaurant (see below).
Breakfast included. B1600

EATING

Artsy coffee houses line Thanon Talat Kao, while the
stretch of **Thanon Takrao Noi** between the clocktower
and Thanon Wienglakon is a lively part of town after dark,
featuring many simple restaurants and the Atsawin **night
market** running off its side streets to the south, as well as
pubs and **karaoke bars**.

★ **Aroy One Baht** Thanon Tipchang ☎054 219233;
map p.309. Cheap eats (most dishes around B50) in a nice
old wooden house with outdoor terraces, staffed by happy
young Thais. The tom kha kai and the prawn tempura are
recommended, and there's a decent choice for vegetarians.
Daily 4–11pm.

Escape Bistro & Café 357/37 Thanon Duangrat ☎054
322622; map p.309. The most refined snack-stop on
broad and busy Thanon Duangrat, this chilly a/c café is
adorned with stained glass and fountains and spreads
over two floors and a sunny outdoor terrace area. Try the
delicious raspberry panna cotta (B85) as you flick through
the huge selection of magazines. Daily 8.30am–8pm.

Long Jim 1583 Thanon Charoen Muang ☎082 892
5009, ⊛longjimpizza.com; map p.309. Uncomplicated
American-run bar-restaurant serving tasty New York-style
pizzas in two sizes (from B150) and calzone, as well as a few

simple pasta dishes and salads. Tues–Sun 5–9pm.
Mae Hae Thanon Uparaj; map p.309. This nondescript
sky-blue shophouse, 10m from Thanon Boonyawat, serves
some of the best sai oua (spicy pork sausage) you're likely to
encounter, bursting with flavour, as well as other excellent
northern Thai dishes such as tam khanun (jackfruit salad).
There's no English sign and no menu – just choose and point
at the tempting ready-made dishes, which cost around B50
each. Daily roughly 10am–7pm.

Riverside 328 Thanon Tipchang ☎054 221861;
map p.309. Behind its own good bakery-coffee house,
this cosy, relaxing restaurant on rustic wooden terraces
overlooking the water serves a wide variety of excellent
Thai dishes (from B70), including northern specialities, and
Western food, to the sounds of live music (quality variable)
in the evenings. Daily 10am–midnight.

Wienglakor 138/38 Thanon Phaholyothin ☎054
316430–5; map p.309. The best hotel restaurant in
town with a wide choice of well-prepared, good-value
northern dishes and an inviting ambience, overlooking the
landscaped gardens. Dinner on Friday and Saturday nights is
accompanied by live Thai traditional music (6–8pm). Daily
10am–midnight.

Phrae and around

Heading east out of Lampang on your way to the small city of **PHRAE**, you'll pass
through the tobacco-rich Yom valley, dotted with distinctive brick curing-houses. Phrae
province is famous for woodcarving and the quality of its seua maw hawm, the deep-
blue, collarless working shirt seen all over Thailand (produced and sold in abundance
in the village of Ban Thung Hong, 4km north of central Phrae on Highway 101). The
main reason to stop here, however, is to explore Phrae's old town, with its peaceful
lanes filled with temples and traditional teak houses – as in Lampang, the former
logging industry attracted Burmese workers and the influence is evident – and to enjoy
the old-fashioned and friendly nature of a place still virtually untouched by tourism.

Sited on the southeast bank of the Yom River, Phrae is clearly divided into old and new
towns; an earthen wall surrounds the roughly oval-shaped old town, with a dry moat on
its southeastern side and the new town centre beyond that. At the centre of the **old town**,
a large roundabout is the main orientation point; running northwest–southeast through
the roundabout, through Pratuchai (the main gate on the southeastern side of the old
town), and into the **new town** is Thanon Charoen Muang, where several shops sell the
trademark deep-indigo shirts. The main street in the new town, Thanon Yantarakitkoson,
intersects Thanon Charoen Muang about 300m southeast of the old town.

Vongburi House

Thanon Khamlue • Daily 9am–5pm • B30

The white-and-pink **Vongburi House** (Baan Wongburi) is a good place to begin an exploration of the old town. Built of teak between 1897 and 1907 in Thai–European style for the wife of the last lord of Phrae, it's smothered in elaborate, lace-like woodcarving on all the eaves, gables and balconies, and around doors and windows. Inside the house, exhibits include fine silverware, antique furniture, undershirts with magic spells written on them to ward off danger, and various documents such as elephant identity papers and artefacts that shed light on the history of the family, who still live in part of the complex.

Wat Luang

Just south of Thanon Rob Muang, around 100m from Vongburi House

Phrae's oldest temple complex, **Wat Luang**, dates from the town's foundation around the twelfth century; it contains the only intact original brick entrance gate to the city, though unfortunately it has been closed up and turned into an ugly shrine to Chao Pu, an early Lanna ruler. Apart from the gate, the oldest component of the wat is the crumbling early Lanna-style **chedi** called Chang Kham after the four elephants – now mostly trunkless – which sit at its octagonal base; these alternate with four niches containing Buddha images and some haphazardly leaning, gilded bronze parasols.

Over the years, Wat Luang has been added to and parts of it have been quite spoiled in a gaudy modernization process; until recently, a dishonest monk was even taking down parts of the temple to sell. Apart from the ruined entrance gate, this meddling is most evident in the **viharn**, opposite, where an ugly and very out-of-place laterite brick facade has been placed in front of the original Lanna-style sixteenth-century entrance. Opposite the chedi on the north side of the compound, a **museum** (irregular hours; free) on two floors houses some real treasures, the most important being a collection of

3

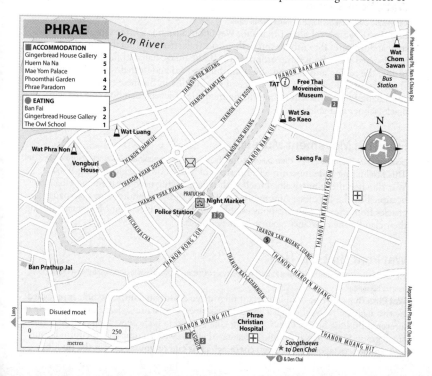

sixteenth-century bronze Buddhas and several glass cases containing old manuscripts with beautifully gilded covers, which are located upstairs.

Wat Phra Non

About a block west of Wat Luang along Thanon Rob Muang

In the far northwestern corner of the old city is **Wat Phra Non**, established three centuries ago, whose name comes from the 9m-long reclining Buddha housed in a small viharn; look out for the Lanna-style bot's finely carved and gilded wooden pediment showing scenes from the *Ramayana*.

Ban Prathup Jai

Beyond the old town's west gate • Daily 8am–5pm • B50

Signposted among the tranquil lanes out beyond the old town's west gate lies the massive two-storey teak house of **Ban Prathup Jai**, constructed out of nine old houses in the 1970s. A visit here allows you to appreciate the beauty and strength of the wood, even if the overall effect is a bit over the top. The lower floor has an impressive interior of 130 pillars of solid teak carved with jungle scenes; huge wooden elephants wander among the columns, and solid teak walls provide a backdrop for ornately carved furniture. There's also a souvenir shop where you can buy all things wooden. Upstairs has the feel of a traditional house, and the furniture and objects are those that you might find in a well-to-do Thai home: ornately carved cabinets crammed with bowls and other ordinary household objects, tables displaying framed family portraits, wall carvings and even a teak bar.

Wat Chom Sawan

Around 200m north of the bus station on Thanon Yantarakitkoson

Built in 1894 by local Shan (Thai Yai), **Wat Chom Sawan** is a fine example of Burmese-style architecture. Recently restored, the main teak structure (notable for its impressive multi-tiered roof) houses the ordination hall, the image hall and the monks' residence. Inside, the ceiling and columns are beautifully carved and dotted with glittering stained glass. Treasures include an ivory image of the Buddha in Burmese style, scripture slabs and Luang Pho San, a seated Buddha figure made of woven bamboo covered with black lacquer and gold leaf.

Free Thai Movement Museum

Tucked behind the Phrae Paradorn hotel • Daily 8am–5pm • Free • Enter via the hotel's reception area (ask at reception if doors are locked)

This fascinating little museum tells the story of Thailand's struggles during World War II, when the country allied itself with Japan, having been invaded and effectively occupied by the Japanese. Among the exhibits on show are photos and newspaper articles from the era, plus weapons used by **Seri Thai** (the Free Thai Movement) during their clandestine resistance against Japanese forces.

Wat Phra That Cho Hae

9km east of town (1km beyond the village of Padang) • Without your own transport, you'll need to charter a songthaew (about B500) from the bus station

Wat Phra That Cho Hae is an important pilgrimage centre sited on a low hill, approached by two naga stairways through a grove of teak trees. One staircase leads to a shrine where a revered Buddha image, Phra Chao Tan Chai, is said to increase women's fertility. The small grounds also house a brightly decorated viharn with an unusual cruciform layout and a gilded, octagonal, 33m-high **chedi**, which is said to house relics of the Buddha's hair and left elbow and is traditionally wrapped in the yellow satin-like cloth, *cho hae* (which gives the wat its name), in March or April. To the north of the main compound, a new viharn houses a shiny Buddha and some well-crafted murals and window carvings.

Phae Muang Phi

18km northeast of Phrae off Highway 101

Out of town are the so-called ghost pillars at **Phae Muang Phi**, a geological quirk of soil and wind erosion. Overzealous reports describe this as Thailand's Grand Canyon, but it's not a fair comparison, and it's probably only worth visiting if you're going on through to Nan with your own transport. It's recently been landscaped as a kind of park, but some locals still believe the place is haunted.

ARRIVAL AND DEPARTURE
PHRAE

By plane Nok Air runs two daily flights (1hr 30min) from Bangkok's Don Muang to Phrae's airport, 3km southeast of town. Some hotels offer free pick-ups from the airport, or you can take an airport taxi (B100).

By bus or minibus Buses and a/c minibuses stop at the main bus station off Thanon Yantarakitkoson, towards the northeast of town.

Destinations Bangkok (13 daily, mostly in the evening, some in the morning; 8hr); Chiang Mai (11 daily; 4hr); Chiang Rai (at least hourly; 4hr); Den Chai (at least hourly; 30min); Lampang (roughly hourly; 1hr 30min–2hr 30min);

Nan (every 40min; 1hr 30min–2hr); Phitsanulok (at least hourly; 2–3hr).

By train Den Chai train station, just 20km to the southwest, is on the main Bangkok–Chiang Mai line. Frequent songthaews and a/c minibuses run from Den Chai (20–40min), the former to a stand south of Phrae's old town, the latter to the bus station.

By car If you're driving here from Lampang, turn left from Highway 11 at Mae Khaem onto Route 1023 and approach the town via Long and some lovely scenery.

GETTING AROUND

By songthaew A shared songthaew from the TAT office to Wat Luang, for example, costs B20/person.

By bicycle or motorbike The *Mae Yom Palace Hotel* rents out bicycles (B100/day). Motorbikes can be rented for

B200/day at Saeng Fa (☎054 521598), next to the Bank of Ayudhaya on Thanon Yantarakitkoson.

By rented car Eddy Rent-a-car at Phrae Airport (☎093 139 8012 or ☎093 131 5597, ⒲eddy-rentacar.com).

INFORMATION

Tourist information The TAT office is at 2 Thanon Baan Mai

(daily 8.30am–4.30pm; ☎054 521127, ✉tatphrae@tat.or.th).

ACCOMMODATION

Gingerbread House Gallery Corner of Thanon Charoen Muang and Thanon Rong Sor ☎054 523671, ⒲facebook.com/gingerbreadhousegallery; map p.317. This landmark, two-storey former hotel is something of an artistic and cultural hub for Phrae and has returned to its original use: retaining many of its rich teak floors and walls, it now offers stylish rooms with a/c and hot showers. Breakfast and bicycles included. B1200

Huern Na Na 7/9 Thanon Sasibutr ☎054 524800, ⒲huernnana.com; map p.317. Phrae's best hotel boasts an impressive Lanna-style exterior, an attractive swimming pool, a spa and sauna. Bright, luxurious bedrooms have an appealing contemporary style that blends dark wood with occasional splashes of colour. Breakfast included. B2600

Mae Yom Palace Hotel 181/6 Thanon Yantarakitkoson ☎054 521028–34, ⒲maeyompalace.com; map p.317. Good-value traditional upmarket hotel, with a handy central location near the bus station. Facilities include

a large, attractive swimming pool, a restaurant with a pleasant outdoor terrace and bicycle rental. Decent-sized rooms are carpeted and air-conditioned, with hot showers, fridges and cable TV. Breakfast included in the price. B790

Phoomthai Garden Hotel 31 Thanon Sasibutr ☎054 627359, ⒲phoomthaigarden.com; map p.317. Attractive, low-rise fifty-room hotel to the south of the old town, featuring a lot of teak and earth tones in its decor and furniture. The bedrooms have balconies overlooking the leafy garden. Free pick-ups from airport and bus station and free bicycles for guests' use. Various rainy-season promotions offered on their website. Breakfast included. B1300

Phrae Paradorn 177 Thanon Yantarakitkoson ☎054 511177; map p.317. Not "absolutely clean" as the sign outside proclaims, but it comes pretty close and makes a good budget choice, with a simple breakfast thrown in. The a/c rooms include fridges, the fan rooms balconies, and all have hot water and TV. Fan B350, a/c B550

EATING

To get a cheap and varied dinner in the town centre, your best bet is to head for the lively **night market** that convenes each evening just outside Pratuchai, the main gate on the southeastern side of the old town, towards the western end of Thanon Charoen Muang. On Saturday evenings (roughly 4–7pm), a "walking street" market on Thanon Khamlue near Vongburi House sells lots of food, as well as handicrafts and souvenirs.

★ **Ban Fai** A couple of kilometres south out of town at the junction of the Den Chai road and the bypass towards Nan ☎054 523114; map p.317. This open-sided barn-like place is the best restaurant around, serving very good Thai food including northern specialities such as *nem* (spiced pork sausages), the typical Lanna pork curry, *kaeng hang lay*, and a tasty *kaeng ho*, a rich curry (originally from leftovers) mixing *kaeng hang lay*, glass noodles and aubergines. Daily 8am–10pm.

Gingerbread House Gallery Corner of Thanon Charoen Muang and Thanon Rong Sor ☎054 523671, ⓦfacebook.com/gingerbreadhousegallery; map p.317. With jazz on the soundtrack, this friendly, civilized café and boutique offers tasty all-day breakfasts (B120), one-dish Thai meals, salads and spaghetti, as well as gingerbread biscuits, waffles and good espresso coffees. Daily 8am–5pm.

The Owl School Thanon Khamlue, opposite Vongburi House ☎089 433 2595; map p.317. A likeable café set in an old shophouse overhung with ferns, dispensing home-roasted, single-origin drip coffees and homespun philosophy. Daily except Wed 9am–6pm.

Nan

After leaving the Yom River, Highway 101 gently climbs through rolling hills of cotton fields and teak plantations to its highest point, framed by limestone cliffs, before descending into the high, isolated valley of the **Nan River**, the longest in Thailand (740km) and one of the tributaries of the Chao Phraya. Ringed by high mountains, the small but prosperous provincial capital of **NAN**, 225km northeast of Lampang, rests on the grassy west bank of the river. Few Western visitors make it out this far, but it's a likeable place with a thriving handicrafts tradition, a good museum and some superb temple murals at **Wat Phumin**, as well as at Wat Nong Bua out in the countryside (see page 325). Nan's centre comprises a disorientating grid of crooked streets, around a small core of shops and businesses where Thanon Mahawong and Thanon Anantaworarichides meet Thanon Sumondhevaraj.

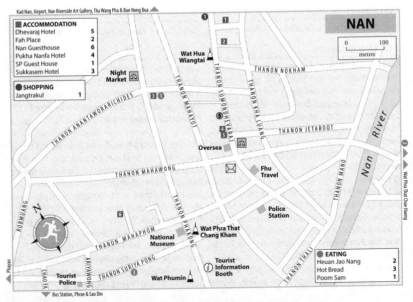

The town comes alive for the **Lanna boat races**, usually held in late October or early November, when villages from around the province send teams of up to fifty oarsmen to race in long, colourfully decorated canoes with dragon prows. The lush surrounding valley is noted for its cotton-weaving, sweet oranges and the attractive grainy paper made from the bark of local *sa* (mulberry) trees.

Brief history

Nan province has a history of being on the fringes, distanced by the encircling barrier of mountains. It flourished from the fourteenth to the sixteenth century as one of the city states that formed Lanna, but in 1558 the Burmese seized control, enslaved a large part of the population and allowed the principality to go into decline. Rama V brought Nan into his centralization programme at the start of the twentieth century, but left the traditional ruling house in place, making it the last province in Thailand to be administered by a local ruler (it remained so until 1931). During the troubled 1970s, Communist insurgents holed up in this twilight region and proclaimed Nan the future capital of the liberated zone, which only succeeded in bringing the full might of the Thai Army down on them; the insurgency faded after the government's 1982 offer of amnesty. Today, energies are focused on development, and the province has become less isolated with the building of several new roads.

Wat Phumin

Thanon Phakong

Wat Phumin will grab even the most over-templed traveller. Its late-sixteenth-century centrepiece is an unusual cruciform building, combining both the bot and the viharn, which balances some quirky features in a perfect symmetry. Two giant nagas pass through the base of the building, with their tails along the balustrades at the south entrance and their heads at the north, representing the sacred oceans at the base of the central mountain of the universe. The doors at the four entrances, which have been beautifully carved with a complex pattern of animals and flowers, lead straight to the four Buddha images arranged around a tall altar in the centre of the building – note the Buddhas' piercing onyx eyes and pointed ears, showing the influence of Laos, 50km away.

What really sets the bot apart are the **murals**, whose bright, simple colours seem to jump off the walls. Commissioned in the late nineteenth century by the last king of Nan and executed over two decades by a Thai Lue artist, Thit Buaphan, the paintings take you on a whirlwind tour of heaven, hell, the Buddha's previous incarnations, local legends and incidents from Nan's history. Packed with vivacious, sometimes bawdy, detail, including katoey (ladyboys), hill tribes and the moustachioed and tattooed artist himself whispering sweet nothings in a woman's ear (west wall), they provide a valuable pictorial record of that era.

The National Museum

Thanon Phakong • Wed–Sun 9am–4pm • Free

The **National Museum** is set in a tidy, century-old palace with superb teak floors, which used to be home to the rulers of Nan. It has been emptied of most of its displays in preparation for a planned refit (though with no signs of progress for some years), but its single prize exhibit is still on display upstairs: a talismanic elephant tusk with a bad case of brown tooth decay, which is claimed to be magic black ivory. The tusk was presented to the lord of Nan by the ruler of Keng Tung (now part of Myanmar) over three hundred years ago and sits on a colourful wooden *khut*, a mythological eagle. Around the tusk are a few kingly exhibits, including a lovely chased-silver betel-chewing set that belonged to the last ruler of Nan.

BETEL

Betel-chewing today is popular only among elderly Thais, particularly country women, but it used to be a much more widespread social custom, and a person's betel tray set was once a Thai's most prized possession and an indication of rank: royalty would have sets made in gold, the nobility's would be in silver or nielloware, and poorer folk wove theirs from rattan or carved them from wood. A set comprises at least three small covered receptacles, and sometimes a tray to hold these boxes and the knife or nutcracker used to split the fruit.

The three essential ingredients for a good chew are betel leaf, limestone ash and areca palm fruit. You chew the coarse red flesh of the narcotic fruit first (best picked when small and green-skinned), before adding a large heart-shaped betel leaf, spread with limestone-ash paste and folded into manageable size; for a stronger kick, you can include tobacco and/or marijuana at this point. An acquired and bitter taste, betel numbs the mouth and generates a warm feeling around the ears. Less pleasantly, constant spitting is necessary – which is why you'll often see spittoons in old-fashioned hotels in Thailand, re-used as waste baskets. It doesn't do much for your looks either: betel-chewers are easily spotted by their rotten teeth and lips stained scarlet from the habit.

Wat Phra That Chang Kham

Thanon Phakong

Wat Phra That Chang Kham was founded in 1406 as Wat Luang, a royal temple where oaths of allegiance ceremonies were held. The main feature here is a gorgeous, gold-capped, bell-shaped chedi, enshrining relics of the Buddha and supported by elephants (*chang kham*) on all sides; those on the corners are adorned with gold helmets and straps. In front of the chedi, the easterly of the two viharns used to be a ho trai (scripture library). It houses a beautiful, sinuous, Sukhothai-style, walking Buddha image in the gesture of dispelling fear, said to have been made of two-thirds solid gold in the fourteenth century. The western viharn used to be the third masterpiece of Thit Buaphan, the artist of Wat Phumin and Wat Nong Bua, but in the last century the abbot ordered the murals to be whitewashed over – faint traces of birds and rows of heads can just be made out. The temple is attached to a school, a reminder that temples were once the only source of education in the country.

Wat Phra That Chae Haeng

2km southeast of town, just off Highway 1168

Wat Phra That Chae Haeng is a must, as much for its setting on a hill overlooking the Nan valley as anything else. The wat was founded in the fourteenth century, at a spot determined by the Buddha himself when he passed through this way – or so local legend would have it. The nagas here outdo even Wat Phumin's: the first you see of the wat across the fields is a wide driveway flanked by monumental serpents gliding down the slope from the temple. A magnificent gnarled bodhi tree with hundreds of spreading branches and roots guards the main gate, set in high boundary walls. Inside the walls, the highlight is a slender, 55m-high, Lanna-style golden chedi, surrounded by four smaller chedis and four carved and gilded umbrellas, as well as small belfries and stucco lions. Close competition comes from the viharn roof, which has no fewer than fifteen Lao-style tiers, stacked up like a house of cards and supported on finely carved *kan tuei* (wood supports) under the eaves.

ARRIVAL AND DEPARTURE   NAN

BY PLANE

Nok Air (3 daily; 1hr 30min) and Air Asia (2 daily; 1hr 20min) run flights between Bangkok's Don Muang Airport and Nan. The airport is 2km northwest of town, and is served by a/c

taxis (about B100 to the centre; ☎ 054 773555).

BY BUS

The bus station is in the southwest corner of town, off the

main road to Phrae; motorbike taxis to the centre cost B20–50/person, depending on how far you're going.

From/to Chiang Mai The bus journey to Nan from Chiang Mai takes around 6hr, so it might be worth catching one of the more comfortable first-class or VIP vehicles that serve this route, shaving a little off the journey time.

From/to Chiang Rai One bus a day winds its tortuous way over the mountains from Chiang Rai, via Chiang Kham; if you're prone to motion sickness and want to avoid the worst of the twisting roads, change buses in Phrae instead.

From/to Luang Prabang, Laos In the far north of Nan province, the **border crossing** at **Huai Kon** is open to foreigners, with Lao visas available on arrival. This route is now served by one a/c bus a day that departs from Nan for Luang Prabang, via Sayaboury.

Destinations Bangkok (20 daily; 10–11hr); Chiang Mai (13 daily; 5–6hr); Chiang Rai (1 daily; 6–7hr); Den Chai (for the Bangkok–Chiang Mai railway line; every 40min; 2hr–2hr 30min); Luang Prabang (Laos; 1 daily; 10hr); Phitsanulok (5 daily; 5–6hr); Phrae (every 40min; 1hr 30min–2hr).

INFORMATION AND GETTING AROUND

Tourist information There's a helpful municipal tourist information booth (☎054 775769), which keeps bus timetables, and a national parks information booth (☎062 985 4709) opposite Wat Phumin (both daily 8.30am–4.30pm).
Tourist police Thanon Suriyapong (☎054 710216 or ☎1155).
Bicycle and motorbike rental If you want to explore the area on two wheels, Oversea, a bike and motorbike retailer on Thanon Sumondhevaraj, near the corner of Thanon Mahawong (☎054 710258 or ☎097 049 1982), rents out bicycles (B80/day) and motorbikes (B250/day).
Car rental Based at the airport, Avis (☎avisthailand.com) will deliver and collect anywhere in town.

ACCOMMODATION

Despite being a small town with few visitors, Nan has some attractive accommodation options, ranging from family-run guesthouses to clean, reasonably priced hotels. The only times of year when finding somewhere to stay might be a problem are during the Lanna boat races (late Oct or early Nov) and over Christmas and New Year.

Dhevaraj Hotel 466 Thanon Sumondhevaraj ☎054 710212, ☎dhevarajhotel.com; map p.320. Large, centrally positioned hotel, popular with tour groups, which has a slightly institutional feel but is a hub of Nan social life. There's an outdoor pool and a wide range of well-maintained though slightly old-fashioned a/c accommodation, all with hot water and nice cosy beds. Breakfast included. B1200

Fah Place Soi Kha Luang 1, 237/8 Thanon Sumondhevaraj ☎054 710222; map p.320. Just down a small soi off the main road, this striking, modern, cream block contains spacious, very good-value a/c rooms, done out with attractive tiles, tasteful wooden furniture and large hot-water bathrooms. Cheaper rooms are on the upper floors (no lift). B400

★ **Nan Guesthouse** 57/15 Soi 2, Thanon Mahaprom ☎054 771849, ☎nanguesthouse.net; map p.320. Proper guesthouse in a largely wooden house that's quiet and bucolic despite its central position, with lots of local information, a roof terrace and free drinking water. The very clean rooms either share bathrooms (fan) or have en-suite hot showers, fridges and TVs (fan or a/c). Bicycles and motorbikes for rent. You can get breakfast at their café

opposite, which serves espresso coffees and home-baked bread. Dorms B180, fan B350, a/c B600

Pukha Nanfa Hotel 369 Thanon Sumondhevaraj ☎054 771111, ☎pukhananfahotel.co.th; map p.320. An eye-catching wooden building on the city's main street, with an imposing chalet-like facade that sparkles with fairy lights. Inside, ornate carvings and wall hangings lead the way to a massive wooden staircase, which twists up towards the elegant, panelled bedrooms. There's a wonderful first-floor terrace with views over the street, and a small café downstairs. Breakfast included. B2600

SP Guest House 233 Thanon Sumondhevaraj ☎054 774897 or 088 529 5217; map p.320. Actually on Trok Hua Wiangtai, a narrow alley off the main road, this well-maintained, friendly guesthouse offers fourteen diverse, dimly lit but spacious a/c rooms, with hot-water bathrooms, fridges and TVs. The owners are extremely helpful, and there are big family rooms available. B500

Sukkasem Hotel 119–121 Thanon Anantaworarichides ☎054 772555, ☎sukkasemnan@gmail.com; map p.320. A small step up in price and style from its sister property, Fah Place, the Sukkasem provides smart a/c rooms with gleamingly polished timber floors, tasteful wooden furniture, en-suite hot showers, fridges and TVs. Rooms are above an attractive, airy lobby and priced according to size; at the back, there are also a few small dorms. Bike rental available. Dorms B450, doubles B600

EATING

Plenty of restaurants cluster around Thanon Anantaworarichides, while the **night market** is just around the corner on Thanon Phakong. The liveliest night-time scene in Nan is on **Kad Nan**, an alley of restaurants, bars, boutiques and gift shops, about 1km up Thanon Mahayot from Thanon Anantaworarichides on the right.

Heuan Jao Nang East bank of the Nan River, about 500m north of the bridge; map p.320. The most northerly and best of several restaurants above the bridge, with attractive tables on an embankment by the river

3

that are good for sunset-watching. The food's great, too (most dishes B150–250): lots of river fish – try the *pla khang patcha*, fish stir-fried with green peppercorns, ladyfinger roots and other herbs – and northern specialities, including delicious, tongue-tingling (literally) deep-fried chicken with Vietnamese mint (*kai thawt makhwen*). Daily noon–11pm.

Hot Bread Thanon Suriyapong; map p.320. This friendly café near Wat Phumin bakes its own white and wholewheat bread, scones and cakes, and serves good espresso coffees, lots of vegetarian dishes and Western breakfasts – you can't beat Cumberland sausages, eggs, toast and coffee for B150. Daily 8am–4pm; closes 2 midweek days around the midpoint of each month, and from mid-May to the end of June.

★ **Poom Sam (Poom 3)** Thanon Anantaworarichides ☎ 054 772100; map p.320. It may look like any other streetside restaurant, but nationally famous *Poom Sam* prepares excellent, creative Thai and Chinese food in generous portions at reasonable prices, and there's a comfy a/c room as well. Don't miss the chef's signature dish, delicious chicken *matsaman* curry with pineapple, served with roti and apple (B180). Daily 5/5.30pm–2am; closed last Mon of the month.

SHOPPING

Loyalty to local traditions ensures the survival of several good **handicrafts shops** in Nan, most of which are found on Thanon Sumondhevaraj around the junction with Anantaworarichides. On Friday, Saturday and Sunday evenings (roughly 6–9/10pm), the stretch of Thanon Phakong in front of Wat Phumin becomes a "**walking street**", similar to those in Chiang Mai, with crafts and food for sale.

Jangtrakul 304–6 Thanon Sumondhevaraj ☎ 054 710016; map p.320. The best all-rounder among the crafts shops on the street, selling local woodcarving, silks and cottons, including colourful Thai Lue weaving and hill-tribe textiles. Daily 8am–7pm.

Around Nan

The remote, mountainous countryside **around Nan** runs a close scenic second to the precipitous landscape of Mae Hong Son province, but its remoteness means that Nan has even worse transport and is even more poorly mapped. This does, of course, make it an exciting region to explore, where you may encounter the province's ethnic minorities: the Thai Lue (see page 325); the **Htin**, an upland Mon-Khmer people, most of whom have migrated since the Communist takeover of Laos in 1975; the **Khamu**, skilled metalworkers who have moved to Nan over the last 150 years from southwest China and Laos; and the little-known Mrabri (see page 325) – a good place to organize excursions is Fhu Travel (see page 324). More straightforward targets include the temple at **Nong Bua**, with its superb murals, and beautiful **Doi Phukha National Park**.

Nan Riverside Arts Space

20km north of Nan up Route 1080 • Daily except Wed 9am–5pm • B20 • ☎ 081 989 2912 • Served by buses (roughly hourly) from Nan bus station en route to Tha Wang Pha

The impressive **Nan Riverside Arts Space** was founded by local, nationally famous artist, Winai Prabripu, in a lovely setting by the banks of the Nan River. Various exhibition

---

TOURS AROUND NAN

Nan is a pleasant spot to spend a day or two, but if you fancy doing something a bit more energetic, it's worth heading out to the countryside. Your best option is to book with the long-standing **Fhu Travel** at 453/4 Thanon Sumondhevaraj (☎ 054 710636 or ☎ 081 287 7209, ✉ fhutravel@hotmail.com). As well as dispensing advice about the region, Fhu and Ung, his wife, organize enjoyable guided **tours** and **trekking** trips. One-day tours to Wat Nong Bua, include a visit to the local weavers, as well as to silversmiths, batik makers, rattan furniture makers and a waterfall, cost B1800/person in a group of two, including lunch. One-day treks (same price) head west, through tough terrain of thick jungle and high mountains, visiting Mrabri, Htin, Hmong and Mien villages. Fhu can also arrange one-day **kayaking** trips on the Nan River near town (B1500/person in a group of two).

SPIRITS OF THE YELLOW LEAVES

Inhabiting the remote hill country west of Nan, the population of about three hundred **Mrabri** represents the last remnants of nomadic hunter-gatherers in Thailand, though their way of life is rapidly passing. Believing that spirits would be angered if the tribe settled in one place, grew crops or kept animals, the Mrabri traditionally built only temporary shelters of branches and wild banana leaves, moving on to another spot in the jungle as soon as the leaves turned yellow; thus they earned their poetic Thai name, **Phi Tong Luang** – "Spirits of the Yellow Leaves". They eked out a hard livelihood from the forest, hunting with spears, trapping birds and small mammals, digging roots and collecting nuts, seeds and honey.

In recent decades, however, deforestation by logging and slash-and-burn farming has eaten into the tribe's territory, and the Mrabri were forced to sell their labour to Hmong and Mien farmers, often under slave-like conditions. But in the last few years, salvation for the Mrabri has come in the form of weaving **hammocks**: foreign visitors noticed their skill at making string bags out of jungle vines and helped them to set up a small-scale hammock industry. The hammocks are now exported to countries around the world, and the Mrabri weavers have the benefits of education, free healthcare and an unemployment fund. For more information, go to ⓦ jumbohammock.com.

3

spaces display his paintings – many of them local landscapes focusing on details of plants in season and paintings inspired by the Wat Phumin murals – as well as rotating exhibitions by other contemporary Thai artists, sculptures and photos. A visit to the gallery combines well with Ban Nong Bua.

Ban Nong Bua

About 40km north of Nan off the west side of Route 1080 • Roughly hourly services from Nan bus station to Tha Wang Pha, from whose southern outskirts signs in English point you left across the Nan River to Wat Nong Bua, 3km away (coming by bus, either hire a motorbike taxi in the centre of Tha Wang Pha, or walk the last 3km)

BAN NONG BUA, site of a famous muralled **temple** of the same name, makes a rewarding day-trip from Nan. The village and surrounding area are largely inhabited by **Thai Lue** people, distant cousins of the Thais, who've migrated from China in the past 150 years. They produce beautiful cotton garments in richly coloured geometric and floral patterns; just behind the wat, you can watch **weavers** at work and buy the opulent fabrics. The quality of design and workmanship is very high here, and prices, though not cheap, are reasonable for the quality.

Wat Nong Bua

Built in 1862 in typical Lanna style, **Wat Nong Bua**'s beautifully gnarled viharn has low, drooping roof tiers surmounted by stucco finials – here you'll find horned nagas and tusked makaras (elephantine monsters), instead of the garuda finial which invariably crops up in central Thai temples. The viharn enshrines a pointy-eared Lao Buddha, but its most outstanding features are the **murals** that cover all four walls. Executed between 1867 and 1888, probably by Thit Buaphan the painter of Wat Phumin, they depict with much humour and vivid detail scenes from the *Chanthakhat Jataka* (the story of one of the Buddha's previous incarnations, as a hero called Chanthakhat). This is a particularly long and complex *Jataka* (although a leaflet outlining the story in English is sometimes available, in return for a small donation to temple funds), wherein our hero gets into all kinds of scrapes, involving several wives, other sundry liaisons, some formidably nasty enemies and the god Indra transforming himself into a snake. The crux of the tale comes on the east wall (opposite the Buddha image): in the bottom left-hand corner, Chanthakhat and the love of his life, Thewathisangka, are shipwrecked and separated; distraught, Thewathisangka wanders through the jungle, diagonally up the wall, to the hermitage of an old woman, where she shaves her head and becomes a nun; Chanthakhat travels through the wilderness along the bottom of the wall, curing a wounded naga-king on the way, who out of gratitude gives him a magic crystal ball, which enables our hero to face another series of perils along the south wall, before finally rediscovering and embracing Thewathisangka in front of the old woman's hut, at the top right-hand corner of the east wall.

Doi Phukha National Park

Around 80km northeast of Nan off Route 1256 · B200 · ☎ 054 701000, ⊚ nps.dnp.go.th

East of Tha Wang Pha, Route 1080 curves towards the town of **Pua**, on whose southern outskirts Route 1256, the spectacular access road for **Doi Phukha National Park**, begins its journey eastwards and upwards. The paved road climbs up a sharp ridge, through occasional stands of elephant grass and bamboo, towards Doi Dong Ya Wai (1939m), providing one of the most jaw-droppingly scenic drives in Thailand. Across the valleys to the north and south stand rows of improbably steep mountains (including the 1980m Doi Phukha itself, far to the south), covered in lush vegetation with scarcely a sign of human habitation. The park is home to the rare and endangered chomphuu phukha (bretschneidera sinensis), a tree that grows up to twenty metres tall and produces spectacular bunches of pink and white flowers in February and March.

From the park headquarters, 24km up the road from Pua, there's a self-guided, 4km **trail**, but to hike up any of the park's many peaks, you'll need to hire a guide (by donation, about B200/day expected) from the headquarters.

ARRIVAL AND DEPARTURE | DOI PHUKHA NATIONAL PARK

It's difficult to get into the park on public transport, and you'll usually have to stay the night. The trip is most exciting if tackled on a motorbike (though watch out for loose chippings on the bends and, in the rainy season, landslides to the east of park headquarters on the way to Bo Kleua).

By bus and songthaew From Nan's bus station, buses and a/c minibuses (on their way from Den Chai to the border at Huai Kon) run to Pua roughly hourly (1–2hr), from where irregular songthaews from the market (best in the mornings, though you may find school songthaews in the late afternoon) serve the handful of villages along Route 1256 towards Bo Kleua.

ACCOMMODATION AND EATING

Food is available at the park's simple **restaurant**, and there are also several food stalls serving basic snacks.

Bo Klua View About 20km beyond the park headquarters towards Bo Kleua ☎ 054 778140 or ☎ 081 809 6392, ⊚ bokluaview.com. This mid-range resort has a dozen stylish a/c bungalows with large verandas and great views set around a terraced rice field, and a restaurant serving good Thai and Western food. B1850

National park bungalows Park headquarters, 24km up the road from Pua ☎ 054 701000, ⊚ nps.dnp.go.th. Accommodation ranges from large chalets sleeping six or seven through rooms for four (all the above with hot showers and fridges), to small, basic, A-frame bungalows for two with shared hot showers. B300

National park camping There's a large, open, grassy campsite near the park headquarters.

Sao Din

60km south of Nan; head south on Highway 101 to Wiang Sa, then turn left and follow Route 1026 to Na No, just after which a turning on the right leads into the site

One of several brief excursions from Nan possible with your own transport, **Sao Din** ("earth pillars") provides a more intriguing example of soil erosion than the better-known site at Phae Muang Phi near Phrae. Here the earth pillars cover a huge area and appear in fantastic shapes, the result of centuries of erosion by wind and rain. There's little in the surrounding area, which makes wandering among the formations a peaceful experience. If you come here, be sure to wear long trousers and boots, especially in the cool season, as a thorny plant that grows in the region can cause discomfort.

The Mae Hong Son loop

Two main roads head in opposite directions from Chiang Mai over the western mountains, meeting each other in Mae Hong Son, at the heart of Thailand's most remote province – and offering the irresistible prospect of tying the highways together into a 600km **loop**. The towns en route give a taste of Myanmar to the west, but the journey itself, winding over implausibly steep forested mountains and through tightly hemmed farming valleys, is what will stick in the mind.

The **southern** leg of the route, **Highway 108**, first passes **Doi Inthanon National Park**, with its twisting curves, lofty views over half of northern Thailand and enough waterfalls to last a lifetime; from here, with your own vehicle you could shortcut the southernmost part of the loop by taking the paved but very winding Routes 1088 and 1263 from Mae Chaem to Khun Yuam. Sticking to the main loop, however, you'll next reach **Mae Sariang**, an important town for trade across the border with Myanmar and a gentle, low-key base for trekking and trips on the Salween River. The provincial capital, **Mae Hong Son**, roughly at the midpoint of the loop, is a more developed hub

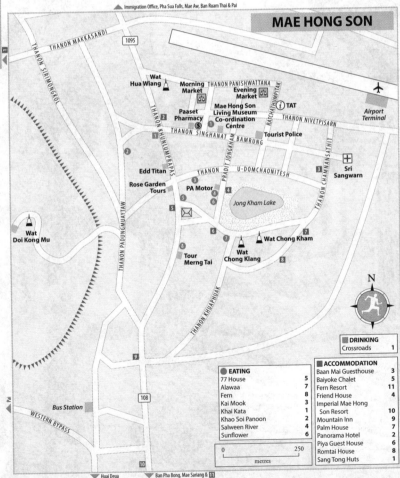

MAE HONG SON

Immigration Office, Pha Sua Falls, Mae Aw, Ban Ruam Thai & Pai

THANON MAKKASANDI
1095
THANON SIRIMONGKOL
Wat Hua Wiang
Morning Market
THANON PANISHWATTANA
Evening Market
Mae Hong Son Living Museum Co-ordination Centre
TAT
RAJCHATHUMPTIAK
THANON NIVETPISARN
Airport Terminal
Paaset Pharmacy
THANON KHUNLUMPRAPAS
THANON SINGHANAT
BAMRUNG
Tourist Police
PRADIT JONGKHM
THANON U-DOMCHAONITESH
THANON CHAMNANSATHIT
Sri Sangwarn
Edd Titan
THANON
Rose Garden Tours
PA MOTOR
Jong Kham Lake
Wat Doi Kong Mu
THANON PADUNGMUAYTAW
Wat Chong Kham
Tour Merng Tai
Wat Chong Klang
THANON KHUAPHUAK
N
Huai Deua
Ban Pha Bong, Mae Sariang &
Bus Station
WESTERN BYPASS
108
Pai

DRINKING
Crossroads   1

EATING
77 House   5
Alawaa   7
Fern   8
Kai Mook   3
Khai Kata   1
Khao Soi Panoon   2
Salween River   4
Sunflower   6

ACCOMMODATION
Baan Mai Guesthouse   3
Baiyoke Chalet   5
Fern Resort   11
Friend House   4
Imperial Mae Hong
  Son Resort   10
Mountain Inn   9
Palm House   7
Panorama Hotel   2
Piya Guest House   6
Romtai House   8
Sang Tong Huts   1

0   250
metres

for exploring the area's mountains, rivers and waterfalls, though it can become frantic with tour groups in the cool season, especially on November and December weekends when the sunflowers are out.

The **northern** leg follows **Route 1095**, much of which was established by the Japanese army to move troops and supplies into Myanmar after its alliance with Thailand during World War II. The road heads northeast out of Mae Hong Son towards the market town of **Soppong**, whose surroundings feature beautiful caves (notably **Tham Lot**), appealing accommodation and stunning scenery to trek or kayak through. Halfway back towards Chiang Mai from Mae Hong Son is **Pai**, a cosy, cosmopolitan and hugely popular tourist hangout with plenty of activities and some gentle walking trails in the lovely surrounding valley.

GETTING THERE AND AROUND   MAE HONG SON LOOP

We've covered the loop in a **clockwise** direction here, in part because Doi Inthanon is best reached direct from Chiang Mai, but you could just as easily go the other way round. Travelling the loop is straightforward, although the mountainous roads go through plenty of bends and jolts. The labour-intensive job of **paving** every hairpin bend was completed in the 1990s, but ongoing repair work can still give you a nasty surprise if you're riding a motorbike.

By plane From Chiang Mai, there are Bangkok Airways flights to Mae Hong Son.

By bus Mae Hong Son is 8hr 30min from Chiang Mai by a/c or ordinary bus, although services along the shorter but even more winding northern route are now augmented by faster, hourly a/c minibuses, which cover the ground via Pai in about six hours.

By motorbike or car Above all the loop is made for motorbikes and cars: the roads are generally quiet (but watch out for huge, speeding trucks) and you can satisfy the inevitable craving to stop every five minutes and admire the mountain scenery. A useful piece of equipment for this journey is the 1:375,000 map of the Mae Hong Son loop, with useful insets of Pai's and Mae Hong Son's environs, published by Golden Triangle Rider (W gt-rider.com) and available in local bookshops.

Doi Inthanon National Park

Traversed by Route 1009, which runs west off Highway 108 just north of Chom Thong • A checkpoint by Mae Klang Falls collects the B300 entrance fee • ☎ 053 286728, W nps.dnp.go.th

Covering a huge area to the southwest of Chiang Mai, **DOI INTHANON NATIONAL PARK**, with its Karen and Hmong hill-tribe villages, dramatic waterfalls and panoramas over rows of wild, green peaks to the west, gives a pleasant, if slightly sanitized, whiff of northern countryside, its attractions and concrete access roads kept in good order by the national parks department. The park, named after the highest mountain in the country and so dubbed the "Roof of Thailand", is geared mainly to wildlife conservation but also contains hill-tribe agricultural projects producing strawberries, apples and flowers for sale. Often shrouded in mist, Doi Inthanon's temperate forests shelter a huge variety of flora and fauna, which make this one of the major destinations for naturalists in Southeast Asia. The park supports about 380 **bird species**, the largest number of any site in Thailand – among them the ashy-throated warbler and a species of the green-tailed sunbird, both unique to Doi Inthanon – as well as, near the summit, the only red rhododendrons in Thailand and a wide variety of ground and epiphytic orchids. The waterfalls, birds and flowers are at their best in the cool season, but night-time temperatures sometimes drop below freezing, making warm clothing a must.

Wat Phra That Si Chom Thong

Chom Thong, 58km southwest of Chiang Mai on Highway 108

The gateway to the park is **CHOM THONG**, a market town with little to offer apart from the attractive **Wat Phra That Si Chom Thong**, whose impressive brass-plated chedi dates from the fifteenth century. The nearby bo tree has become an equally noteworthy architectural feature: dozens of Dalí-esque supports for its sagging branches have been sponsored by the devoted in the hope of earning merit. Inside the renovated sixteenth-century viharn, a towering, gilded *ku* housing a Buddha relic (supposedly from the right side of his skull) just squeezes in beneath the ceiling, from which hangs a huge, sumptuous red-and-green umbrella. Weaponry, gongs, umbrellas, thrones and an elephant-tusk arch carved with delicate Buddha images all add to the welcoming clutter. The temple is also famous for its meditation retreats (see page 285).

The main waterfalls
Four sets of waterfalls provide the main roadside attractions along Route 1009 from Chom Thong to the park headquarters: overrated **Mae Klang Falls**, 8km in, which with its picnic areas and food vendors gets overbearingly crowded at weekends; **Vachiratharn Falls**, the park's most dramatic, with a long, misty drop down a granite escarpment 11km beyond; **Sirithan Falls**, which looks like a smaller version of Vachiratharn and is just a couple of kilometres further up the hill; and finally the twin cascades of **Siriphum Falls**, backing the park headquarters a further 9km on. With your own wheels you could reach a fifth and much more beautiful cataract, **Mae Ya**, which is believed to be the highest in Thailand – the winding, 14km paved track to it heads west off Route 1009, 2km north of Highway 108.

The chedis
11km beyond the headquarters • Daily 8am–5pm • B40

For the most spectacular views in the park, continue 11km beyond the headquarters along the summit road to the sleek, twin chedis looming incongruously over the misty green hillside: on a clear day you can see the mountains of Myanmar to the west from here. Built by the Royal Thai Air Force, the granite chedis commemorate the sixtieth birthdays of Rama IX and Queen Sirikit; the late king's monument, **Napamaytanidol Chedi** (1987), is brown to the more feminine lilac of the queen mother's **Napapolphumsiri Chedi** (1992).

Kew Mae Pan Trail
Trailhead a short way up the summit road from the chedis • 2hr; open Nov–May • B200 for compulsory guide

Starting a short distance up the road from the chedis is the rewarding **Kew Mae Pan Trail**. This circular, three-kilometre walk wanders through sun-dappled forest and open savanna as it skirts the steep western edge of Doi Inthanon, where violent-red epiphytic rhododendrons (in bloom Dec–Feb) are framed against open views over the canyoned headwaters of the Pan River, when the weather allows. To do this walk, you have to hire a local Hmong guide at the trailhead.

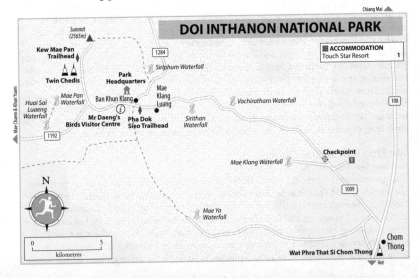

The summit and around

Doi Inthanon's **summit** (2565m), 6km beyond the chedis, is a big disappointment – from the car park you can see little beyond the radar installation. For many people, after a quick shiver and a snapshot in front of a board proclaiming this the highest point in Thailand, it's time to hop in the car and get back to warmer climes. A small, still-revered stupa behind this board contains the ashes of King Inthanon of Chiang Mai (after whom the mountain was renamed): at the end of the nineteenth century he was the first to recognize the importance of this watershed area in supplying the Ping River and ultimately the Chao Phraya, the queen of Thailand's rivers. A hundred metres back down the road, it's an easy stroll along a raised walkway to the bog known as **Ang Ka** (Crow's Pond), which is the highest source of these great waterways and one of the park's best bird-watching sites. The cream and brown sphagnum mosses that spread underfoot, the dense ferns that hang off the trees and the contorted branches of rhododendrons give the place a creepy, primeval atmosphere.

The Mae Chaem road

Around 7km after it turns off the main summit road, the paved **Mae Chaem road** skirts yet another set of waterfalls: look for a steep road to the right, leading down to a ranger station and, just to the east, the dramatic long drop of **Huai Sai Luaeng Falls**. A 500m trail from the car park will bring you to **Mae Pan Falls**, a series of short cascades in a peaceful, shady setting.

ARRIVAL AND DEPARTURE
DOI INTHANON NATIONAL PARK

The main road through the park, Route 1009, turns west off Highway 108, 1km north of the gateway town of Chom Thong, winding generally northwestwards for 48km to the top of Doi Inthanon, passing the park headquarters about 30km in. A second paved road forks left 10km before the summit, affording breathtaking views as it helter-skelters down for 20km to the sleepy, riverside weaving village of Mae Chaem, southwest of the park.

By bus Frequent non-a/c blue buses to Chom Thong (on their way to Hot) from Chiang Mai's Chang Puak bus station can be picked up at Chiang Mai Gate. At Chiang Mai Gate, it should also be possible to pick up a yellow songthaew (slower and only slightly cheaper) for the journey to Chom

Thong. Once there, you can charter a whole songthaew or a/c minibus to explore the park for around B1500 for the day.
By motorbike or jeep You could do the park justice in a day with an early start from Chiang Mai, or treat it as the first stage of a longer trip to Mae Hong Son: from Mae Chaem, either follow Route 1088 south to pick up Highway 108 again towards Mae Sariang, 25km west of Hot; or take Route 1088 north then Route 1263 west through remote countryside, joining Highway 108 just north of Khun Yuam.
With a tour Most tour operators in Chiang Mai offer day-trips to the national park (around B1500–3000/person, depending on group size) – if you don't have your own transport, this is the easiest way to visit.

INFORMATION

Park information For information on the park, stop at the park headquarters 23km beyond the Mae Klang checkpoint. Ask here about the new, 3km Pha Dok Sieo Trail, which begins about 500m east on the south side of Route 1009 – a Karen guide will lead you past a waterfall and scenic terraced paddyfields to Ban Mae Klang Luang, where you can have a cup of fresh coffee and perhaps watch weavers

at work.
Birding information 200m beyond the headquarters on the left-hand side of Route 1009, at Mr Daeng's Birds Visitor Centre & Restaurant (☎ 053 286731–2 or ☎ 081 884 8108), bird-watchers can consult a logbook of sightings, pick up a simple, photocopied map of birding sites, or hire a guide for B3000/day for up to five people.

ACCOMMODATION AND EATING

In the daytime, **food stalls and/or restaurants** operate at the twin chedis, the Kew Mae Pan trailhead, Mae Klang, Vachiratharn and Mae Ya falls (the last mentioned in high season only), while the restaurants beside the park headquarters and at the royal project near Siriphum Falls are open daytime and evening. Camping, an often chilly alternative to the accommodation below, is permitted on a

site about 500m from the park headquarters and another site at Huai Sai Luaeng Falls. Three-person tents can be rented at headquarters for B225/night (bedding extra).
National park bungalows ☎ 053 286730, ⊕ nps.dnp. go.th. Park accommodation comes in standard log-cabin or concrete varieties, with electricity, mattresses or beds and bedding. Three- to 23-berth bungalows, set among

dense stands of pine near the headquarters, have hot-water bathrooms, while simpler, fifteen-person bungalows at Huai Sai Luaeng Falls cost B1500/night. Accommodation is often fully booked at weekends and national holidays, but at other times you should be OK to turn up on the day. B1000–6500

Touch Star Resort 7km from Chom Thong just off the main park road ☎ 053 033594, ⚲ touchstarresort. com; map p.330. In extensive grassy grounds with a mineral-water pool and a restaurant, this cutesy place has spacious a/c rooms, cottages, thatched bungalows and even a log cabin that sleeps 12, all with hot-water bathrooms. Breakfast included. B1600

West towards Mae Sariang

Heading south from Chom Thong, the road flattens out a little, passing dusty and seldom-visited weaving villages as it follows the Ping River downstream. Just after Hot the road bends west, climbing up once again towards the **Ob Luang Gorge National Park**, where attractions include whitewater rafting down the Chaem River.

Pa-Da Cotton Textile Museum

On the east side of Highway 108 between kilometre-stones 68 and 69, in Ban Rai Pai Ngarm ☎ 098 656 6328 • Daily except Thurs 8am–noon & 1–4.30pm; closed the 1st and 16th days of the month • By donation • All buses between Chiang Mai and Hot or Mae Sariang pass Ban Rai Pai Ngarm

Among several weaving villages to the south of Chom Thong, the **Pa-Da Cotton Textile Museum** at Ban Rai Pai Ngarm is well worth a look; it's reached down a beautiful avenue of bamboo trees. The museum is dedicated to the work of Saeng-da Bansiddhi, a local woman who started a cooperative practising traditional dyeing and weaving techniques using only natural products and was made a National Artist in 1986. Saeng-da died in 1993, and the museum, which displays some of her personal effects as well as looms, fabrics and plants used in dyeing, was established to honour her efforts to revive these disappearing skills. It's situated on the upper floor of a large wooden building, while on the ground floor weavers can be seen busy at work. Lovely bolts of cloth and a small range of clothes and scarves in earthy and pastel colours are on sale at reasonable prices.

Ob Luang Gorge National Park

17km west of Hot on Highway 108 • B200 • ☎ 093 242 3458 or ☎ 089 263 5055, ⚲ nps.dnp.go.th

Weaving through pretty wooded hills up the valley of the Chaem River for 17km from Hot will bring you to **Ob Luang Gorge National Park**, which is billed with wild hyperbole as "Thailand's Grand Canyon". A wooden bridge over the short, narrow channel lets you look down on the Chaem River bubbling along between sheer walls 30m below. The park is also tagged "Land of Prehistoric Human" because of the discovery of Bronze Age graves here, containing seashell bracelets and other decorative items, as well as rock paintings of elephants and human figures. Upstream from the bridge near the park headquarters, you can relax at the roadside food stalls and swim in the river when it's not too fast. At the headquarters you can arrange hour-long 5km **whitewater-rafting** trips in the cool season on the river's class II–III rapids (from B1800 for four people up to B2500 for eight, including guides, transport, life jackets and helmets).

West of Ob Luang, the highway gradually climbs through pine forests, the road surface bad in patches and the countryside becoming steeper and wilder.

ARRIVAL AND DEPARTURE · OB LUANG GORGE NATIONAL PARK

By bus Buses travelling between Chiang Mai and Mae Sariang pass by the park headquarters, as do buses travelling between Bangkok and Mae Hong Son.

ACCOMMODATION

National park bungalows ☎ 053 315302, ⚲ nps. dnp.go.th. There are a few large bungalows with three bedrooms and two bathrooms with hot water, fridge and TV sleeping ten people; at quiet times, you might be able to persuade the rangers to rent you one of the bedrooms at a cheaper rate. B2100

Campsite The shady riverbank shelters a campsite; you can rent a two- to three-person tent for B225 (bedding extra).

Mae Sariang and around

After its descent into the broad, smoky valley of the Yuam River, Highway 108's westward progress ends at **MAE SARIANG**, 191km from Chiang Mai, a quietly industrious market town showing a marked Burmese influence in its temples and rows of low wooden shophouses. Halfway along the southern route between Chiang Mai and Mae Hong Son, this is an obvious place for a stopover. From here you can make an intriguing day-trip to the trading post of **Mae Sam Laeb** on the border with Myanmar and out onto the Salween River.

Soaking up the atmosphere is the main activity in this border outpost, which is regularly visited by local hill tribes and dodgy traders from Myanmar. If you want something more concrete to do, stroll around a couple of century-old temples off the north side of the main street, whose Burmese features provide a glaring contrast to most Thai temples. The first, **Wat Si Boonruang**, sports a fairytale castle of a bot with an intricate, tiered, corrugated roof in green and white piled high above. Topped with lotus buds, the unusual *sema* stones, which delineate the bot's consecrated area, look like old-fashioned street bollards. The open viharns here and next door at **Wat Utthayarom** (aka Wat Jong Sung) are mounted on stilts, with broad teak floors that are a pleasure to get your feet onto. Both wats enshrine Burmese-style Buddhas, white and hard-faced.

Mae Sam Laeb

46km southwest of Mae Sariang and accessible by hourly songthaews from the market in the morning (1hr 30min)

MAE SAM LAEB lies on the mighty, 3000km-long Salween (or Salawin) River, which, having descended from Tibet through Myanmar, forms the Thai-Myanmar border for 120km, before emptying into the Andaman Sea at Mawlamyine. The village is little more than a row of wooden stores and restaurants, but with its Thai, Chinese, Karen and Burmese inhabitants, it has a classic frontier feel about it. The only thing to do here is to take a **longtail trip** on the mighty river, lined with totally unspoilt jungle-clad hills. It'll cost you about B1500 for a roughly two-hour return trip if you arrange it yourself in Mae Sam Laeb, or you could book a tour through *Northwest Guest House* in Mae Sariang (B5000 for a group of two people, including transport from Mae Sariang, boat and lunch).

ARRIVAL AND DEPARTURE

MAE SARIANG

By bus The main company serving Mae Sariang is Prempracha (⦿premprachatransports.com), who run buses from Chiang Mai's Arcade bus station and Mae Hong Son and a/c minibuses from Chiang Mai, Mae Hong Son and Khun Yuam. Sombat Tour operates two buses a day from Bangkok's Northern Mo Chit Terminal to Mae Sariang (plus

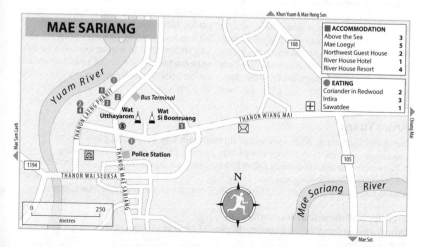

three more that continue to Mae Hong Son).

Destinations Bangkok (5 daily; 12hr); Chiang Mai (12 daily; 3hr 30min–4hr 30min); Khun Yuam (8 daily; 2–3hr); Mae Hong Son (4 daily; 4hr).

By songthaew Scenic Highway 105 up from Mae Sot (see page 258) is covered by songthaews (roughly hourly until around noon; 5–6hr), though the journey's really too long to make on a rattling bench seat.

GETTING AROUND

By bicycle or motorbike Bicycles (B50–100/day, free for guests) and motorbikes (B200), handy for exploring temples and Karen weaving villages in the surrounding Yuam valley, can be rented from *Northwest Guest House*.

Treks and tours Demand for trekking and tours from Mae Sariang is very low, so arrangements are ad hoc: try *Northwest Guest House* or send a message to Mae Sariang Tours, preferably a week in advance (no office; ⓦ facebook.com/maesariang.man).

ACCOMMODATION

Mae Sariang has a good range of accommodation for such a tiny town.

Above the Sea 75 Thanon Laeng Phanit ☎ 053 682264, ⓦ abovetheseaguesthouse.com; map p.333. Friendly guesthouse offering bright a/c rooms with exposed brickwork, quirky murals and hot showers, as well as a small swimming pool and bar-restaurant in the pretty garden. Breakfast included. B1200

Mae Loegyi Thanon Wiang Mai ☎ 086 920 2835 or ☎ 089 637 8899; map p.333. A little away from the riverside action, such as it is, this pleasant, welcoming, slightly quirky place offers creeper-clad, ochre rooms and bungalows with a/c, hot showers and TVs, some with separate sitting rooms. B600

Northwest Guest House 81 Thanon Laeng Phanit ☎ 098 360 3867 or ☎ 089 700 9928, ⓦ northwestgh.blogspot.com; map p.333. Clean, friendly spot with plenty of local information and tidy, polished-wood rooms; hot-water bathrooms are either shared (fan rooms) or en suite (a/c). Fan B250, a/c B500

River House Hotel Thanon Laeng Phanit ☎ 053 621201, ⓦ riverhousehotels.com; map p.333. Modern all-teak hotel in traditional open-plan style, where the rooms have simple, tasteful furnishings, fine river views, verandas, a/c and en-suite hot-water bathrooms. Guests can use the pool at River House Resort. Breakfast included. B1500

River House Resort Thanon Laeng Phanit ☎ 053 683066, ⓦ riverhousehotels.com; map p.333. Run by the owner of *River House Hotel*, this is Mae Sariang's fanciest place to stay, with a very attractive swimming pool set amidst lawns running down to the river. All rooms come with a/c, hot water, mini-bars and smart teak floors and furnishings; some have river-view balconies, while the more expensive ones boast bathtubs. Breakfast included. B1800

EATING

The small "walking street" market on Sunday evenings at the western end of Thanon Wiang Mai includes plenty of food stalls.

Coriander in Redwood River House Resort, Thanon Laeng Phanit; map p.333. The poshest restaurant in town, in a lovely, century-old redwood building that was once the residence of a British teak concessionary. As well as simple dishes such as phat thai (B50), it offers northern chilli dips (nam phrik) and other specialities such as pork-belly curry (kaeng hang lay) and fish from the Salween River. Daily 11am–9pm.

Intira Thanon Wiang Mai; map p.333. The locals' favourite, a slightly scruffy roadside restaurant with an a/c room, which does a good chicken with cashew nuts (B100) and some interesting local specialities such as boar in red curry. Daily 7/8am–9pm (last orders).

Sawatdee Thanon Laeng Phanit; map p.333. Popular with local NGO workers, *Sawatdee* bar-restaurant offers Thai and Isaan food (from B40), sandwiches, pastas and a few other Western dishes, on a terrace overlooking the river, with a pool table and some low tables, hammocks and axe cushions for chilling out – the view is superb. Daily roughly 5pm–midnight.

Khun Yuam

North of Mae Sariang, wide, lush valleys alternate with tiny, steep-sided glens – some too narrow for more than a single rice paddy – turning Highway 108 into a winding rollercoaster. The market town of **KHUN YUAM**, 95km north of Mae Sariang and served by all buses between Mae Sariang and Mae Hong Son, is a popular resting spot, especially for those who've taken the direct route here (Route 1263) over the mountains from Mae Chaem.

Thai-Japan Friendship Memorial Hall

On the left of the main thoroughfare, Thanon Rajaburana • Daily roughly 8.30am–noon & 1–4.30pm • B100

At the north end of town, the **Thai-Japan Friendship Memorial Hall** commemorates Khun Yuam's role as a supply base for the Japanese army's campaigns in Burma, including their largest hospital in Thailand. It hosts a curious collection of rusting relics from the period – old trucks, rifles, water canisters and uniforms – though there's no mention of the thousands of Thais who died building the Death Railway (see page 190), or indeed the road west from Chiang Mai to Mae Hong Son, for the Japanese. Lining the walls, hundreds of black-and-white photos document the later period of the war, when after their retreat from Myanmar in 1944, many of the Japanese rested or convalesced here for two years and longer; some stayed on and married locally, among whom the last survivor died in 2000.

ACCOMMODATION AND EATING
KHUN YUAM

Ban Farang Just off Thanon Rajaburana, north of the museum and well signposted ☎053 622086, ⓦ banfarang-guesthouse.com. In a leafy setting on the edge of town, each of the smart, very clean rooms and bungalows here has duvets and a hot-water bathroom; there are cheap dorm beds, too. The restaurant serves up good Thai and Western food, at reasonable prices. Dorms B150, doubles B500

The Buatong fields

Just north of Khun Yuam, Route 1263 branches off to the east over the hills towards Mae Chaem; after about 20km, a side road leads north towards Ban Mae U-Khor and the **Buatong fields** on the slopes of Doi Mae U-Khor, where Mexican sunflowers make the hillsides glow butter-yellow in November and early December. You'll often see the same flowers by the roadside at this time of year, but the sheer concentration of blooms at Mae U-Khor, combined with sweeping views over endless ridges to the west, draws dozens of tour groups in air-conditioned minibuses.

Mae Surin Waterfall

On the spur road that branches north from Route 1263 to the Buatong fields, around 15km beyond Ban Mae U-Khor • B200 • ☎053 061073, ⓦ nps.dnp.go.th

Mae Surin Waterfall in Nam Tok Mae Surin National Park is arguably the most spectacular waterfall in the whole country, the waters hurtling over a cliff and plunging almost 100m before crashing on huge boulders and foaming down a steep gorge. The kind topography of the region allows a great view of the falls from directly in front, but the best view, from below, requires a steep and at times precarious three-hour hike down and back from the park's well-appointed campsite.

Mae Ko Vafe and Ban Pha Bong

Back on Highway 108, 35km north of Khun Yuam, a right turn leads up to **Mae Ko Vafe** – a Thai rendition of "microwave", referring to the transmitters that grace the mountain's peak; the paved road climbs for 10km to a Hmong village, where the fantastic view west stretches far into Myanmar. Around 15km beyond this turn-off, Highway 108 climbs to a roadside **viewing area**, with fine vistas, this time to the east, of the sheer, wooded slopes and the Pha Bong Dam in the valley far below. Subsequently the road makes a dramatic, headlong descent towards Mae Hong Son, passing the **Ban Pha Bong** hot springs, 7km north of the viewing area (11km before Mae Hong Son). These have been turned into a small spa complex with hot spring-water baths, traditional masseurs, private treatment rooms and a restaurant.

Mae Hong Son and around

MAE HONG SON, capital of Thailand's northwestern-most province, sports more nicknames than a town of ten thousand people seems to deserve. In Thai, it's Muang

Sam Mok, the "City of Three Mists": set deep in a mountain valley, Mae Hong Son is often swathed in mist, the quality of which differs according to the three seasons (in the rainy season it's low cloud, while in the hot season it's mostly composed of unpleasant smoke from burning fields). In former times, the town, which wasn't connected to the outside world by a paved road until 1968, was known as "Siberia" to the troublesome politicians and government officials who were exiled here from Bangkok. Nowadays, thanks to its mountainous surroundings, it's increasingly billed as the "Switzerland of Thailand": eighty percent of Mae Hong Son province is on a slope of more than 45 degrees.

To match the hype, Mae Hong Son has become a popular tourist destination, sporting, alongside plenty of backpacker guesthouses, several upmarket hotels and resorts for Thai and farang tourists. Many visitors come here for **trekking** in the beautiful countryside, others just for the cool climate and lazy upcountry atmosphere. The town is still small enough and sleepy enough to hole up in for a quiet week, though in the high season (Nov–Feb) swarms of minibuses disgorge tour groups who hunt in packs through the souvenir stalls and fill up the restaurants. At this time of year, lakeside Thanon Pradit Jongkham and the small roads that run up to the post office become a pedestrianized "**walking street**" in the evening, allowing vendors to sell souvenirs, handicrafts and clothes and to serve food at low tables on the waterfront.

Running north to south, Mae Hong Son's main drag, **Thanon Khunlumprapas**, is intersected by Thanon Singhanat Bamrung at the traffic lights in the centre of town. Beyond the typical concrete boxes in the centre, Mae Hong Son sprawls lazily across

"LONG-NECK" WOMEN

The most famous – and notorious – of the Mae Hong Son area's spectacles is its contingent of **"long-neck" women**, members of the tiny **Kayan Lahwi** tribe of Myanmar (sometimes called Padaung) who have come across to Thailand to escape Burmese repression. Though the women's necks appear to be stretched to 30cm and more by a column of brass rings, the "long-neck" tag is a technical misnomer: a *National Geographic* team once X-rayed one of the women and found that instead of stretching out her neck, the pressure of eleven pounds of brass had simply squashed her collarbones and ribs. Girls of the tribe start wearing the rings from about the age of 6, adding one or two each year up to the age of 16 or so. Once fastened, the rings are generally for life, for to remove a full stack may eventually cause the collapse of the neck and suffocation – in the past, removal was a punishment for adultery.

The **origin** of the ring-wearing ritual remains unclear, despite an embarrassment of plausible explanations. Kayan Lahwi legend says that the mother of their tribe was a dragon with a long, beautiful neck, and that their unique custom is an imitation of her. Tour guides will tell you the practice is intended to enhance the women's beauty. In Myanmar, where the practice is now discouraged, it's variously claimed that ring-wearing arose out of a need to protect women from tiger attacks or to deform the wearers so that the Burmese court would not kidnap them for concubines.

In spite of their handicap (they have to use straws to drink, for example), the women are able to carry out some kind of an ordinary life: they can marry and have children, and they're able to weave and sew, although these days they spend most of their time posing for photographs like an exhibit in a carnival sideshow. Only half of the Kayan Lahwi women now lengthen their necks; left to follow its own course, the custom would probably die out, but the influence of **tourism** may well keep it alive for some time yet. The villages in Mae Hong Son, and now also in Chiang Mai and Chiang Rai provinces, where they live, are set up by Thai entrepreneurs as a money-making venture (visitors are charged B250–500 to enter these villages). At least, contrary to many reports, the "long necks" are not held as slaves: they are each paid a very basic wage of about B1500 per month, supplemented by whatever they can make selling handicrafts to tourists. However, their plight as refugees is certainly precarious and vulnerable; those in Mae Hong Son are in theory allowed to move around the province, but those in Chiang Mai and Chiang Rai are confined to their villages.

the valley floor and up the lower slopes of Doi Kong Mu to the west, trees and untidy vegetation poking through at every possible opportunity to remind you that open country is only a stone's throw away.

Brief history

Mae Hong Son was founded in 1831 as a training camp for elephants captured from the surrounding jungle for the princes of Chiang Mai (Jong Kham Lake, in the southeastern part of the modern town, served as the elephants' bathing spot). The hard work of hunting and rearing the royal elephants was done by the **Thai Yai** (aka Shan), who account for half the population of the province and bring a strong Burmese flavour to Mae Hong Son's temples and festivals. The other half of the province's population is made up of various hill tribes (a large number of Karen, as well as Lisu, Hmong and Lawa), with a tiny minority of Thais concentrated in the provincial capital. The latest immigrants to the province are **Burmese refugees** (see page 261), based in camps between Mae Hong Son and the border, who generally do not encourage visitors as they've got quite enough on their plates without having to entertain onlookers.

3

Wat Chong Kham
Towards the southeast of the town centre, just south of the lake

Mae Hong Son's classic picture-postcard view – either by day or when illuminated at night – is its twin nineteenth-century Burmese-style temples, Wat Chong Kham and Wat Chong Klang, from the opposite, north, shore of Jong Kham Lake (Nong Jong Kham), their gleaming white and gold chedis and the multi-tiered roofs and spires of their viharns reflected in the water. In the viharn of **Wat Chong Kham** is a huge, intricately carved sermon throne, decorated with the *dharmachakra* (Wheel of Law) in coloured glass on gold; the building on the left has been built around the temple's most revered Buddha image, the benign, inscrutable Luang Pho To.

Wat Chong Klang
Next to Wat Chong Kham, just south of the lake

Wat Chong Klang, the other of the two lakeside temples, is famous for its paintings on glass, which are said to have been painted by artists from Mandalay more than a hundred years ago; they're displayed over three walls on the left-hand side of the viharn. The first two walls behind the monks' dais (on which women are not allowed to stand) depict *Jataka* stories from the Buddha's previous incarnations in their lower sections, and the life of the Buddha himself in their upper, while the third wall is devoted entirely to the Buddha's life. A room to the left houses an unforgettable collection of **teak statues**, brought over from Myanmar in the middle of the nineteenth century. The dynamically expressive, often humorous figures are characters from the *Vessantara Jataka*, but the woodcarvers have taken as their models people from all levels of traditional Burmese society, including toothless emaciated peasants, butch tattooed warriors and elegant upper-class ladies.

Mae Hong Son Living Museum Co-ordination Centre
Thanon Singhanat Bamrung · Daily 8.30am–4.30pm

It's worth calling in on the **Mae Hong Son Living Museum Co-ordination Centre**, the welcoming information office for an interesting project to open up Mae Hong Son as a living cultural showcase. You'll be able to pick up a useful map showing good local restaurants and the remaining examples of Thai Yai teak architecture in town.

The morning market
Between Thanon Nivetpisarn and Thanon Panishwattana · Daily from dawn until around 9am

The town's vibrant, smelly **morning market** is worth dragging your bones up at dawn to see. People from the local hill tribes often come down to buy and sell, and the range of produce is particularly weird and wonderful, including, in season, porcupine meat, displayed with quills to prove its authenticity.

Wat Hua Wiang
Thanon Panishwattana

The many-gabled viharn of 150-year-old **Wat Hua Wiang** shelters, under a lace canopy, one of the most beautiful Buddha images in northern Thailand, the **Chao Palakeng**. Copied from the Mahamuni image in Mandalay and brought over to Mae Hong Son a hundred years ago, the strong, serene bronze has the regal clothing and dangling ears typical of Burmese Buddhas.

Wat Doi Kong Mu
On the hill to the west of town

For a godlike overview of the area, drive or climb up to **Wat Doi Kong Mu** on the steep hill to the west. From the temple's two chedis, which enshrine the ashes of respected nineteenth-century Thai Yai monks, you can look down on the town and out across the sleepy farming valley north and south. Behind the chedis, the viharn contains an unusual and highly venerated white marble image of the Buddha, surrounded in gold flames. If you've got the energy, trek up to the bot on the summit, where the view extends over the Burmese mountains to the west.

Pha Sua Falls, Mae Aw and Ban Ruam Thai
North of Mae Hong Son: if driving yourself, turn left off Route 1095 10km north of town, following signposts for Pha Sua

---

TOURS AND TREKKING AROUND MAE HONG SON

Once you've exhausted the few obvious sights in town, the first decision you'll have to grapple with is whether to visit one of the three villages of "long-neck" women around Mae Hong Son (see page 336). Our advice is don't: they're effectively human zoos for snap-happy tourists, offering no opportunity to discover anything about Kayan culture. Less controversially, the roaring **Pha Sua Falls** and the villages of **Mae Aw** and **Ruam Thai** to the north of town make a satisfying day out. Other feasible targets include the hot springs at **Ban Pha Bong** (see page 335) and, further out, **Mae Surin Waterfall** (see page 335) and **Tham Lot** (see page 342). If all that sounds too easy, Mae Hong Son is a popular centre for **trekking**.

There's no getting away from the fact that trekking up and down Mae Hong Son's steep inclines is tough, though the scenery is magnificent. Most of the hill-tribe villages here are Karen, interspersed with indigenous Thai Yai (Shan) settlements in the valleys. Heading east, where many villages are very unspoilt, having little contact with the outside world, is preferable to the more populous, less traditional west; to the southeast, you'll be able to visit Hmong and Karen, to the northeast, Lisu also. In the latter direction, if you're very hardy, you might want to consider the five- to six-day routes to Soppong or Pai, which have the best scenery of the lot. Several guesthouses and travel agencies in Mae Hong Son run multi-day treks, on which guides can often build a camp of natural materials while overnighting in the forest.

Chakraphan (Chan) Prawinchaikul ☎089 552 6899, ⓦnaturewalksthai-myanmar.com. Chan is a highly recommended, currently independent guide, who speaks good English, specializes in flowers and insects and offers everything up to a six-day trek to Pai (one-day treks from B1500/person).

Rose Garden Tours 86/4 Thanon Khunlumprapas ☎053 611681, ⓦrosegarden-tours.com. A reliable company for guided tours around the area, with day-long excursions starting from B1100.

Tour Merng Tai 89 Thanon Khunlumprapas ☎053 611979, ⓦtourmerngtai.com. Among a wide variety of trips, including cycling tours around town, Tour Merng Tai offers several community-based tourism programmes, employing village guides and cooks and contributing part of the profits to local communities. They include one-day treks, visiting Lahu, Thai Yai or Karen villages (from B1700/person, including 4WD transport where necessary, English-speaking guide and lunch), though longer homestays with trekking are possible.

POY SANG LONG

Mae Hong Son's most famous and colourful festival is **Poy Sang Long**, held over the first weekend of April, which celebrates the ordination into the monkhood, for the duration of the schools' long vacation, of Thai Yai boys between the ages of 7 and 14. Similar rituals take place in other northern Thai towns at this time, but the Mae Hong Son version is given a unique flavour by its Thai Yai elements. On the first day of the festival, the boys have their heads shaved and are anointed with turmeric and dressed up in the colours of a Thai Yai prince, with traditional accessories: long white socks, plenty of jewellery, a headcloth decorated with fresh flowers, a golden umbrella and heavy face make-up. They are then announced to the guardian spirit of the town and taken around the temples. The second day brings general merry-making and a spectacular **parade**, headed by a drummer and a richly decorated riderless horse, which is believed to carry the town's guardian spirit. The boys, still in their finery, are each carried on the shoulders of a chaperone, accompanied by musicians and bearers of traditional offerings. In the evening, the novices tuck into a sumptuous meal, waited on by their parents and relatives, before the ordination ceremony in the temple on the third day.

3

North of Mae Hong Son, a trip to **Pha Sua Falls** and the border villages of **Mae Aw** and **Ruam Thai** takes in some spectacular and varied countryside. Your best options are to rent a vehicle or join a tour (B1100–1400/person for a one-day excursion, including a visit to the highly overrated Fish Cave). With your own wheels, you can stop off en route at the Phu Klon Country Club (☎053 282579, ⊛phuklon.co.th), more commonly known as the **mud spa**, where you can get a face or body mask or a massage, or bathe in the hot spring water.

Pha Sua Falls

About 20km from the turn-off from Route 1095 you'll reach **Pha Sua Falls**, a wild, untidy affair, which crashes down in several cataracts through a dark overhang cut in the limestone. The waterfall flows all year round but is in full roar in October after the rainy season. Take care when swimming, as several people have been swept to their deaths here.

Mae Aw

Above the falls the paved road climbs precipitously, giving glorious, broad vistas of both Thai and Burmese mountains, before reaching the unspectacular half-Hmong, half-Thai Yai village of **Naphapak** after 11km. From here, a largely flat stretch of tarmac (built by the Thai military to help the fight against the opium trade) heads north for 7km to **MAE AW** (aka Ban Rak Thai), a settlement of Kuomintang anti-Communist Chinese refugees (see page 361), right on the border with Myanmar. The tight ring of hills around the village heightens the feeling of being in another country: delicate, bright-green tea bushes line the slopes, while Chinese ponies wander past long, unstilted bamboo houses. In the central marketplace on the north side of the village reservoir, shops sell great bags of Oolong and Chian Chian teas, as well as dried mushrooms.

Ban Ruam Thai

Heading 6km west from Naphapak along a fairly rough paved road, you'll come to **BAN RUAM THAI**, a Thai Yai settlement where a royal project has had a lot of success in substituting coffee for opium. At the western end of the village lies **Pang Oung**, a large reservoir surrounded by pine-clad slopes that's very popular with Thai tourists and has been dubbed "Switzerland in Mae Hong Son" – the locals have even put bells on their cows.

ARRIVAL AND DEPARTURE
MAE HONG SON

By plane Mae Hong Son airport is close to the centre (about B60 in a tuk-tuk), towards the northeast of town. Bangkok Airways runs direct flights from and to Chiang Mai twice a day (45min).

By bus The main company serving Mae Hong Son is Prempracha (ⓦpremprachatransports.com). From Chiang Mai's Arcade bus station, they run one daytime bus a day (plus two overnight) via Mae Sariang and one a day via Pai, as well as nine a/c minibuses a day via Pai. They also offer one a/c minibus a day from Mae Sariang. Minibuses coming into Mae Hong Son via Pai go past the *Crossroads* bar, so ask the driver to drop you there if you're staying in town. From the new bus station, tuk-tuks run north into the centre for about B80.

Destinations Bangkok (Sombat Tour; 3 daily; 15hr); Chiang Mai (13 daily; 6hr–8hr 30min); Mae Sariang (4 daily; 4hr); Pai (10 daily; 3hr–4hr 30min).

GETTING AROUND

Local transport, in the form of songthaews and tuk-tuks from the north side of the morning market, is thinly spread and unreliable, so for all excursions it's best to rent your own vehicle or join an organized tour through your guesthouse or one of the many travel agents in town.

By motorbike or four-wheel drive PA Motor on Thanon

Pradit Jongkham opposite *Friend House* (☎053 614220, ⓦpamotorcarrent.com) rents out motorbikes for B150–250/day, as well as cars and 4WDs from B1500.

By bicycle Edd Titan on Thanon Khunlumprapas (☎084 372 3515, ⓦfacebook.com/eddtitanbikerentals) rents out good-quality bikes for B100–150/day.

INFORMATION

Tourist information The TAT office is on Thanon Ratchathumpitak, towards the northeast of the city centre

(daily 8.30am–4.30pm; ☎053 612982–3).

ACCOMMODATION

Mae Hong Son has a healthy roster of **guesthouses**, many of them being good-value, rustic affairs set in their own quiet gardens; most huddle together around Jong Kham Lake while a few spread themselves out on the northern slopes of Doi Kong Mu on the northwestern edge of town, which greatly adds to their scenic appeal. If you've got a little more money to spend, you can get out into the countryside to one of several self-contained **resorts**, though staying at most of these is not exactly a wilderness experience – they're really designed for weekending Thais travelling by car. Finally, several **upmarket hotels** have latched onto the area's meteoric development, offering all the usual international-standard facilities.

Baan Mai Guesthouse Thanon Chamnansathit, northeast of the lake ☎080 499 1975, ⓦbaanmai guesthouse.com; map p.328. Welcoming homestay in a cosy, plant-strewn, traditional wooden house with shared hot-water bathrooms. Informal cooking classes offered. Light breakfast included. Fan B400, a/c B600

Baiyoke Chalet Thanon Khunlumprapas, just across from the post office ☎053 613132–9, ⓦbaiyokehotel. com; map p.328. Set around a a topiary-filled courtyard, this upmarket hotel offers standard rooms that are small, simple but more than serviceable, with varnished parquet floors, plain white walls, bedside lamps, a desk, a mini-bar, TV, a/c, hot shower and a balcony. Breakfast included (good-value half-board packages also offered). B1380

★**Fern Resort** 6km south of town on Highway 108, then signposted 2km east on a paved minor road ☎053 686110–1, ⓦfernresort.info; map p.328. By far the best resort around Mae Hong Son, this eco-friendly and sustainable place employs local villagers as much as possible. In a peaceful, shady valley, a brook runs through the beautiful, spacious grounds, past rice fields and stylish, large cottages with hot

water, a/c and verandas (no phones or TV, wi-fi only around the lobby and restaurant). There's an attractive swimming pool, nature trails in the surrounding Mae Surin National Park, mountain bikes for guests' use and campfires in the evening; free pick-ups from town and regular free shuttle buses to the *Fern Restaurant* in town. Breakfast included. B1700

Friend House 20 Thanon Pradit Jongkham ☎053 620119; map p.328. Basic but clean teak-and-concrete house with upstairs balcony giving views of the lake. Larger rooms have hot-water bathrooms, smaller ones share hot showers and have mattresses on the floor. B250

Imperial Mae Hong Son Resort 149 Moo 8, Tambon Pang Moo ☎053 684444–5, ⓦimperialhotels.com; map p.328. On the south side of the town by the turn-off for Huai Deua, this low-rise building is set in pretty, sloping landscaped gardens, overlooked by spacious, bright rooms featuring lovely polished-teak floors, satellite TV, balconies and mini-bars; there's a large swimming pool, too. B2680

Mountain Inn 112 Thanon Khunlumprapas ☎053 611802–3, ⓦmhsmountaininn.com; map p.328. Large, neat and tasteful rooms with a/c, hot-water bathrooms, mini-bars and TVs, set round a flower-strewn garden and swimming pool. Look out for the stencilled wall art and quirky smiling statues in the lobby. B1800

Palm House 22/1 Thanon Chamnansathit ☎053 614022; map p.328. The decor in this two-storey block near the lake is plain, to say the least, but the welcome's friendly and the clean, tiled a/c rooms have hot showers, TVs and fridges. B690

Panorama Hotel 51 Thanon Khunlumprapas ☎053 611757; map p.328. Welcoming, five-storey hotel near the town's main crossroads, where the no-frills but comfortable a/c rooms have hot showers, fridges and TVs. B800

★ **Piya Guest House** 1/1 Soi 3, Thanon Khunlumprapas ☎ 053 611260, ⓦ facebook.com/piyaguesthousemhs; map p.328. Friendly, well-run, hotel-like guesthouse, boasting large, brightly painted, clean bungalows with spacious, hot-water bathrooms and a/c, in a lush garden dotted with fruit trees and a small swimming pool beside the lake. B700

Romtai House 22 Thanon Chamnansathit ☎ 053 612437, ⓦ mhs-romtai.com; map p.328. There's a wide choice of spacious, well-kept rooms and bungalows with hot water at this tranquil place that's set around a rambling,

colourful garden and a big lotus pond. B400

Sang Tong Huts Down a small lane off Thanon Makkasandi ☎ 053 611680, ⓦ sangtonghuts.org; map p.328. Upmarket, German-run guesthouse with a cute swimming pool, offering rustic chic on a steep, jungly slope on the edge of town. Roofed with traditional, thatched *tong teung* leaves and equipped with mosquito nets on the beds, the posh cottages have verandas, rugs, tapestries and large, attractively tiled bathrooms with hot water. Home-baked bread, croissants, jam, yogurt and muesli for breakfast. B1200

EATING

In addition to *Khao Soi Panoon* listed below, you could head to the Mae Hong Son Living Museum Co-ordination Centre (see page 337) for information about other traditional restaurants favoured by locals. There's also a small, popular, takeaway-only **evening market** on Thanon Panishwattana, along from the day market, that closes around 8pm.

77 House 77 Thanon Khunlumprapas ☎ 053 611977, ⓦ facebook.com/housemaehongson; map p.328. Chic cafe-restaurant next door to its own boutique, with tables on the pavement for people-watching, sofas inside and French chansons on the soundtrack. It's popular for breakfast, with very good espresso coffees, and later in the day serves Thai and Western meals (from around B70), including Pon Yang Kham beef (Thailand's version of wagyu beef) and organic salads, washed down with imported beer and wine. Daily 7.30am–10.30pm.

Alawaa South side of Jong Kham Lake, across from Wat Chong Klang ☎ 053 611552; map p.328. Stylish, a/c, polished-concrete café with a small garden patio, serving good espresso coffees, teas, smoothies and cakes. Mon–Sat 8.30am–5.30pm.

Fern 87 Thanon Khunlumprapas ☎ 053 611374; map p.328. Large, justly popular eating place, set in a lovely teak building with a nice terrace, serving good Thai food (from B80), such as spicy coconut shoot salad and river fish with spicy mango salad. It also offers a few Thai Yai, northern Thai and Western dishes. Daily 10.30am–10pm.

Kai Mook Thanon U-Domchaonitesh; map p.328. Friendly and congenial old-timer with lots of interesting menu choices including northern Thai dishes: chilli dips (*nam phrik*), deep-fried mushrooms in soy sauce and a zingy

mixed nut salad (B90). Daily 10am–2pm & 5–10pm.

Khai Kata Just off Thanon Singhanat Bamrung, immediately inside the gate to the morning market opposite Krung Thai Bank; map p.328. Mae Hong Son's best breakfast – which may well leave you asking for seconds – is the Vietnamese-style *khai kata* here (fried eggs with minced pork), served with mini-baguettes and traditional coffee. Daily 5am–1pm.

★ **Khao Soi Panoon** Thanon Padungmuaytaw, next to Kadkam Plaza; map p.328. This simple housefront restaurant does a superb version of the northern breakfast and lunch soup with egg noodles, *khao soi*, creamy and toothsome, served with either chicken or pork (B40). Daily roughly 8am–4pm.

★ **Salween River** 23 Thanon Pradit Jongkham ☎ 084 687 8891; map p.328. Cosy, welcoming restaurant and bar with a book exchange. The kitchen serves up good breakfasts with home-made bread and a wide variety of Western favourites (main dishes B100 and up), as well as northern Thai, Thai Yai and Burmese food, including a delicious green tea salad (B50), and Arabica coffee produced by local hill tribes. Daily 8am–10pm.

Sunflower Thanon Pradit Jongkham ⓦ maehongsontravel.com/sunflower; map p.328. Despite the strange grotto-like architecture, this is a good, friendly place for breakfast, lunch, dinner or just a drink, with a large terrace overlooking the lake and the temples behind. Pizzas, espresso coffees, and some tasty Thai dishes, including Lanna specialities and Pai River fish. In high season you're likely to catch some live music here in the evenings. Daily 8am–midnight (kitchen closes 10pm).

DRINKING

Crossroads 16 Thanon Singhanat Bamrung ☎ 053 612500; map p.328. This welcoming, aptly named bar – located at the junction of the town's two main roads – is a great place to chill out in the evenings and watch the world

go by. Set in a lovely old Thai Yai teak house that's now filled with retro knick-knacks, it's best for a drink – including great shakes and cocktails – though it also serves Thai and Western food, including breakfasts. Daily 8am–midnight.

DIRECTORY

ATMs and exchange There are several ATMs, banks and exchange booths along Thanon Khunlumprapas and on Thanon Singhanat Bamrung.

Hospital Sri Sangwarn, Thanon Singhanat Bamrung ☎ 053 611378.

Immigration office Thanon Khunlumprapas, north of the

town centre (Mon–Fri 8.30am–4.30pm; ☎ 053 612106).   **Tourist police** Thanon Singhanat Bamrung ☎ 053 611812
Pharmacy Helpful, English-speaking Paaset, Thanon   or ☎ 1155.
Singhanat Bamrung (daily 7am–9pm).

Soppong and Tham Lot

The small market town of **SOPPONG**, 68km from Mae Hong Son on Route 1095 in
the district of Pang Ma Pha (which is sometimes used on signposts), gives access to the
most famous of over two hundred known caves in the area, **Tham Lot**, 9km north in
BAN THAM. Due to its proximity to Pai, Soppong has become popular for day-trippers,
and now even supports several ATMs. On Tuesday mornings, it hosts a weekly market
that draws many hill-tribe villagers down to sell their wares.

Tham Lot

Ban Tham, 9km north of Soppong; Thai Yai guide with lantern B150 per group (up to three people), bamboo raft B300–400 for up to three
people

Turn right in Ban Tham to find the entrance to the **Tham Lot Nature Education Station**,
set up to look after the cave. A short walk through the forest brings you to the entrance
of Tham Lot, where the Lang River begins a 600m journey through the cave. How you
access the various parts of the cave depends on the time of year and how much rain
there has been, and usually involves hiring a bamboo raft for some or all of your journey.
Normally two hours should allow you plenty of time for travelling through the broad,
airy tunnel, and for the main attraction, climbing up into the sweaty caverns in the roof.

The first of these, **Column Cavern**, 100m from the entrance on the right, is dominated
by a 20m-high cave stalagmite snaking up towards the ceiling – be sure not to touch
any of the cave formations. Another 50m on the left, bamboo ladders lead up into
Doll Cave, which has a glistening, pure white wall and a weird red and white formation
shaped like a Wurlitzer organ; deep inside, stalagmites look like dolls. Just before the
vast exit from the cave, wooden ladders on the left lead up into **Coffin Cave**, named
after the remains of a dozen crude log coffins discovered here, one of them preserved
to its full length of 5m. Hollowed out from teak trunks about 1700 years ago, they are
similar to those found in many of the region's caves: some are raised 2m off the ground
by wooden supporting poles, and some still contained bones, pottery and personal
effects when they were discovered. It's worth hanging round the cave's exit at sunset,
when hundreds of thousands of tiny black chirruping swifts pour into the cave in an
almost solid column, to find their beds for the night.

ARRIVAL AND DEPARTURE   SOPPONG AND BAN THAM

By bus All buses connecting Mae Hong Son with Pai and   (B70) or pick-up truck (B300) for the gentle run along the
Chiang Mai pass through Soppong. From the bus stop in the   paved forest road to Ban Tham, which branches off Highway
centre of Soppong, it's possible to pick up a motorbike taxi   1095 just east of *Little Eden Guesthouse*.

ACCOMMODATION AND EATING

SOPPONG   forest. Services here include motorbike rental and massage,
Little Eden Guest House A short walk east of Soppong's   and there are plenty of tours and treks on offer. B450
bus stop ☎ 053 617054, ⊚ littleeden-guesthouse.com.   ★ **Soppong River Inn** At the west end of town, about
This tranquil spot offers neat, attractive bungalows, plush   500m from the bus stop ☎ 053 617107, ⊚ soppong.
rooms and deluxe two-storey houses, each with a private   com. On this extensive, densely foliated, quiet riverside plot
hot-water bathroom. The pretty garden has a kidney-shaped   you'll find a variety of bungalows and cottage-style rooms,
swimming pool and slopes down towards the Lang River,   tastefully decorated and thoughtfully designed, all with hot
which is flanked by a relaxing pavilion and crossed by a   showers, many with outdoor bathrooms and some with
suspension bridge that leads to a short loop walk through the   luxuries such as a/c, DVD players and iPod docks. As well as

TOURS FROM CAVE LODGE

The owners of *Cave Lodge* (see below) can provide plenty of useful information about Tham Lot and other robust, active **caves** that can be explored in the region (many of which they themselves discovered), and organize **guided trips** (from B750/person, including equipment and lunch). They also offer a variety of **kayaking** tours year round, including trips through Tham Lot, plus 6km of fun rapids (roughly June–Jan; from B650). Maps (and packed lunches) for self-guided walking from the lodge to local Thai Yai, Karen, Lahu and Lisu villages are available, as well as local, English-speaking guides for one-day hikes and full-on **trekking** (typically B2500 for 3 days).

---

a good café serving Western, Thai and Thai Yai food, there's a lovely, partly thatched deck over the Pai River, which here runs swiftly through a craggy, jungly defile. Thai massage and treks available. B700

BAN THAM

★ **Cave Lodge** On the other side of Ban Tham from the cave ☎ 053 617203, ⓦ cavelodge.com. Set amongst trees above the Lang River, this long-established guesthouse makes an excellent, friendly base for exploring the area. The owners can arrange local sightseeing trips and activities (see page 344) and there's a good range of accommodation, from dorms to wooden rooms and bungalows, some with

shared hot showers and others with their own bathrooms. There's also a herbal steam sauna and a relaxing communal area around an open fire for hanging out and eating Thai, Thai Yai and Western food, including home-baked bread and muffins. Dorms B180, doubles B300

BAN NONG TONG

Lisu Homestay In the village of Ban Nong Tong, a 10min motorbike ride from Soppong ☎ 085 721 1575, ⓦ lisuhilltribe.com. A genuine Lisu homestay where you can go trekking, have a massage and herbal steam bath and learn the hill tribe's crafts, music, dance, massage and cooking (courses extra at B700/day). Full board per person B300

Pai

Set in a broad, gentle, mountain-ringed valley 43km beyond Soppong, **PAI** was once just a small-town stopover on the tiring journey to Mae Hong Son, but in recent years has

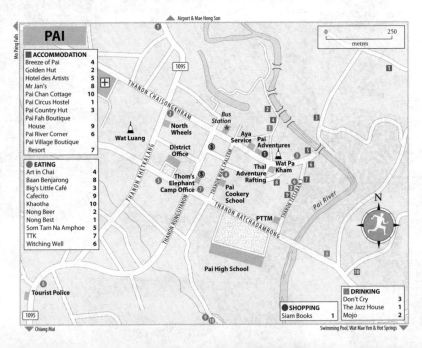

ACCOMMODATION	
Breeze of Pai	4
Golden Hut	2
Hotel des Artists	5
Mr Jan's	8
Pai Chan Cottage	10
Pai Circus Hostel	1
Pai Country Hut	3
Pai Fah Boutique House	9
Pai River Corner	6
Pai Village Boutique Resort	7

EATING	
Art in Chai	4
Baan Benjarong	8
Big's Little Café	3
Cafecito	9
Khaotha	10
Nong Beer	2
Nong Best	1
Som Tam Na Amphoe	5
TTK	7
Witching Well	6

SHOPPING	
Siam Books	1

DRINKING	
Don't Cry	3
The Jazz House	1
Mojo	2

PAI HOT SPRINGS, SPAS AND TRADITIONAL MASSAGE

Just because you're hundreds of kilometres from the nearest beach, that doesn't mean you can't enjoy a good soak. The Pai area is home to some natural hot springs and a clutch of decent spas, all of which offer massages.

Accessible from the minor road south from Wat Mae Yen, about 7km southeast of town (or by turning left off the main Chiang Mai road straight after the bridge over the Pai River), are some **hot springs** (B300), part of Huai Nam Dang National Park, which have one or two very hot, rough pools that aren't really up to much. Much better than the pools, however, are the nearby **spas**, which put the piped hot water from the springs to more productive use. *Pai Hotsprings Spa Resort* (☎ 053 065746, ⊛ paihotspringssparesort.com), down a side road about 1km north of the springs by the Pai River, has a large, shady mineral pool that's open to non-guests (B100), as well as offering various massages and accommodation with spa-water bathrooms.

Massages are available at several spots around town. Having trained at the Old Medicine Hospital in Chiang Mai, the staff at Pai Traditional Thai Massage (PTTM) on Thanon Tessaban 1 (☎ 083 577 0498) have a good reputation for traditional massages (B200/hr), and run government-approved, three-day **massage courses** (B3000).

3

established itself as a major tourist destination in its own right. There's nothing special to see here, but you can partake of all manner of outdoor activities, courses – there's even a circus school – and holistic therapies, not to mention retail therapy at the art studios, bookshops and jewellery shops. The guesthouses, out-of-town resorts and restaurants have tailored themselves to the flood of Westerners who make the journey out from Chiang Mai, some of whom settle into the town's full-on traveller culture and laidback, New-Agey feel for weeks or even months. Meanwhile, Pai is now firmly on the radar of Thai tourists, so in high season, especially on weekends when the sunflowers near Mae Hong Son are out (see page 335), the narrow through-streets get clogged with air-conditioned minibuses. It can be an odd mix, but an evening promenade along the "walking street" of Thanon Chaisongkhram, with its Thai-style galleries and gift shops in the traditional buildings at the western end and more traveller-oriented outlets to the east – plus a sprinkling of local hill-tribe people and shrouded Thai Muslims – is undoubtedly pleasant and *sanuk*.

Wat Mae Yen and the swimming pool

Fluid: daily 9am–6.30pm; closes for about 2 months during the rainy season • B60 • ⊛ facebook.com/fluidswimmingpool

Several undemanding walks can be made around Pai's broad, gently sloping valley. The easiest – a round-trip of about an hour – takes you across the river bridge on the east side of town and up the hill to Wat Mae Yen, which commands a great view over the whole district. On the way to the wat, you'll pass Fluid, the town's well-maintained open-air 25m swimming pool, with landscaped lawn areas for sunbathing and a popular bar-restaurant.

Towards Mo Pang Falls

To the west of town, beyond Pai Hospital, the continuation of Thanon Chaisongkhram will bring you, after 3km, to Wat Nam Hu, supposedly founded by sixteenth-century nationalist hero, King Naresuan, and housing a Buddha image with an unusual topknot containing miraculous holy water. A kilometre further on, you'll pass the Kuomintang village of Ban Santichon and its Chinese theme park of thatched adobe buildings, housing tea and souvenir shops and several popular Yunnanese restaurants – which appeal mostly to Pai's many Chinese visitors. As you continue, the road gradually climbs through comparatively developed Thai Yai, Lisu and Lahu villages to Mo Pang Falls, with a pool for swimming, about 10km west of Pai.

ARRIVAL AND DEPARTURE   PAI

Air Asia now offers combination tickets from Bangkok, including flight from Don Muang to Chiang Mai and a/c   minibus transfer to Pai. Aya Service, a travel agency on Thanon Chaisongkhram (☎ 053 699888, ⊛ ayaservice.

3

OUTDOOR ACTIVITIES AND COURSES IN PAI

Pai makes a good base for **trekking** which can be arranged through guesthouses or operators such as Thai Adventure Rafting (see below). The cost starts at around B800/day (in a large group), with bamboo rafting extra. Thai Adventure Rafting's two-day trek, for example, heads off to friendly, hassle-free Karen and Lahu villages to the north near the Myanmar border, taking in some beautiful scenery. Its one-day treks take in Lisu and Lahu villages and a three-tiered waterfall, and it also offers combination tours of one day trekking and one day rafting (from B2900/person), as well as afternoon **mountain-biking** tours (from B1100/person). Another reliable all-rounder is Pai Adventures on Thanon Chaisongkhram (☎053 699326, ⓦpaiadventures.com), which besides trekking and white-water rafting offers one-day **caving** trips (from B1800; Jan–May).

As well as trekking, agencies in town can arrange bamboo-rafting, kayaking and tubing on the Pai River. Pai also offers massage courses (see opposite).

COOKERY SCHOOL

Pai Cookery School Thanon Wan Chalerm ☎081 706 3799, ⓦpaicookeryschool.com. Thai cooking courses of 2hr in the morning (B600), 4hr in the afternoon, including a trip to the market to learn about ingredients (B750), or up to three days; vegetarians catered for.

ELEPHANT CAMP

Thom's Office in town on Thanon Rungsiyanon ☎053 065778, ⓦthomelephant.com. Among several elephant camps about 5km south of town on the minor road from Mae Yen towards the hot springs, Thom's offers a variety of experiences, starting from an hour-long trip, either riding bareback or bathing with an elephant (from B800, including transport from town and a free bathe in a hot spring pool), as well as mahout training courses (on-site accommodation is available).

WHITE-WATER RAFTING

Thai Adventure Rafting Thanon Chaisongkhram ☎053 699111, ⓦthairafting.com. The reliable and experienced, French-run Thai Adventure Rafting specializes in rubber-raft trips. Heading down the Pai River to Mae Hong Son, you'll pass through gorges and sixty rapids (up to class IV) and take in waterfalls and hot springs. The full journey lasts two days, including a night at a comfortable jungle camp by the river, and costs B3500/person, though one-day trips (B1800) are also available; the season normally runs from June or July to February, with the highest water in September, and participants must be able to swim.

YOGA RETREAT

Xhale Yoga In Pai Resort, 6km north of Pai ⓦxhaleyogapai.com. Certified tutor Bhud runs highly recommended, five-night yoga retreats (see the website for the schedule; from B12,500 including vegetarian meals, accommodation, transport from Pai bus station and guided meditation).

com), sells bus, air and train tickets. It also offers one-way motorbike rental between Chiang Mai and Pai for B300 plus the daily rental charge, with your luggage carried free on one of their a/c minibuses.

By bus Prempracha (☎053 492999, ⓦprempracha transports.com) runs one non-a/c bus a day from Chiang Mai Arcade bus station to Pai (4hr), which continues to Mae Hong Son (4hr 30min from Pai) via Soppong, as well as speedier, more expensive, hourly a/c minibuses on the same route. Aya Service (☎053 699888 in Pai, ☎053 231815 in Chiang Mai) runs hourly a/c minibuses from Chiang Mai only, but offers pick-ups from your accommodation.

Destinations Chiang Mai (hourly; 3–4hr); Mae Hong Son (hourly; 3–4hr 30min); Soppong (hourly; 1hr–1hr 30min).

GETTING AROUND

By car If you're driving yourself, note that the eastern part of Thanon Chaisongkhram, the north end of Rungsiyanon and Thanon Tessaban 1 are pedestrianized, at least in the tourist season. Wat Luang on Thanon Khetkalang is a handy place to park. North Wheels on Thanon Khetkalang rents out cars (☎053 698066, ⓦnorthwheels.com; from B1200/day).

By motorbike taxi Yellow-vested motorbike taxis and songthaew taxis wait on Thanon Chaisongkhram opposite the bus station, but if you're staying in one of the more central guesthouses it's easy enough to walk.

By rented motorbike Aya Service, on Thanon Chaisongkhram, rents motorbikes, charging from B100/day, not including insurance, which starts from B80/day. The reliable North Wheels (see page 288) charges B200/day including insurance.

INFORMATION

Events listings The free, monthly, English-language *Pai Events Planner*, available in bars such as The Jazz House, restaurants and guesthouses, has news about what's on.

ACCOMMODATION

The streets in the centre of town teem with places to stay, and there are dozens of hotels, resorts and "treehouse retreats" in the quiet countryside around Pai. However, you'll have to put up with guesthouse owners' penchant for Pai-based puns: think *Pai in the Sky*, *Pai Chart* and so on.

CENTRAL PAI

Breeze of Pai Just off Thanon Chaisongkhram near Wat Pa Kham ☎081 998 4597, ⓦfacebook.com/ breezeofpai; map p.344. Congenial, well-maintained place with large, simple but chic, ochre bungalows and single-storey rooms with nice parquet floors and hot showers. The compound's a little crowded but lent privacy by plenty of rich foliage, enhanced by seasonal flowers and fountains. Fan B500, a/c B800

Golden Hut North of The Jazz House, next to the river ☎053 699949, ⓦgoldenhut.wordpress.com; map p.344. Very cheap bamboo fan rooms with shared hot showers, in a quiet garden set back from the river, or riverside bungalows on stilts. B150

Hotel des Artists (Rose of Pai) Thanon Chaisongkhram, across from Pai River Corner ☎053 699539, ⓦhotelartists.com; map p.344. On a corner plot near the river and centred around an attractive glass-sided living room, this stylish hotel has just fourteen bedrooms, the best of which have fantastic terraces that face out across the water. In the spacious rooms, bell-shaped lanterns illuminate the beds (which are raised off the ground on platforms made from local wood) while facilities include a/c, TVs, DVD players, and artfully tiled en-suite bathrooms. Breakfast included. B4000

Mr Jan's Thanon Sukhaphibun 3 (Tessaban) ☎053 699554; map p.344. On one of a mess of small streets behind and to the east of Thanon Chaisongkhram, these quiet, comfy concrete rooms are set in a fragrant garden and offer good value for the facilities: a/c, hot shower, fridge and TV. B500

★ **Pai Chan Cottage** About 300m east of the bridge ☎081 180 3064, ⓦpaichan.com; map p.344. Overlooking paddyfields and the resort's attractive swimming pool and gardens, the thatched wooden bungalows here are colourful and tasteful, with en-suite hot showers and mosquito nets. Free pick-ups from town. Good rates for singles. B800

★ **Pai Circus Hostel** East side of the river ☎099 273 3678, ⓦpaicircushostel.com; map p.344. Free fire juggling lessons and a slack line give this spacious, popular resort its name, but there's also a swimming pool with great views of the valley, free yoga and a great party vibe. The cheapest dorms have bamboo bunks with mosquito nets, while the cheapest doubles are basic, thatched A-frames with shared bathrooms, but there's a wide range in both categories. Free pick-ups from town. Dorms B160, doubles B380

★ **Pai Country Hut** East side of the river ☎087 779 6541, ⓦpaicountryhut.com; map p.344. Friendly guesthouse in a lovely garden surrounded by very attractive bamboo bungalows thatched with leaves in the local style; all have hammocks on their balconies, while the cheapest share hot showers. Free pick-ups from town. B400

Pai Fah Boutique House Thanon Tessaban 1 ☎053 064448, ⓦpai-fah.com; map p.344. Terracotta-coloured walls separate this good-looking hotel from the road, creating a surprisingly quiet little enclave. Inside, the a/c rooms are small but tastefully pieced together, with spacious private bathrooms, and there are plenty of shady public areas to relax in on sunny afternoons. Fan B850, a/c B1000

Pai River Corner Eastern end of Thanon Chaisong-khram, by the river ☎053 699049, ⓦpairivercorner.

3

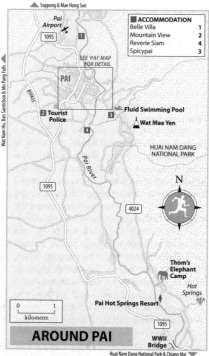

Soppong & Mae Hong Son

Pai Airport
1095

SEE 'PAI' MAP FOR DETAIL

PAI

BYPASS

Wat Nam Hu, Ban Santichon & Mo Pang Falls

Tourist Police

Fluid Swimming Pool
Wat Mae Yen

Pai River

1095

4024

N

HUAI NAM DANG NATIONAL PARK

Thom's Elephant Camp

Hot Springs

Pai Hot Springs Resort

0   1
kilometre

AROUND PAI

WWII Bridge

1095

ACCOMMODATION	
Belle Villa	1
Mountain View	2
Reverie Siam	4
Spicypai	3

Huai Nam Dang National Park & Chiang Mai

com; map p.344. Elegant, Mediterranean-style resort with beautifully furnished, balconied rooms, some of which have their own large jacuzzi in a private courtyard, set around an attractive garden and swimming pool. B5000

Pai Village Boutique Resort South off Thanon Chaisongkhram, by the river ☎053 698152, ⓦpaivillage.com; map p.344. In the heart of Pai, rural simplicity – bamboo and teak huts with roofs of *tong teung* leaves, traditional sunburst-design gables and golden-teak furniture – with plenty of home comforts, including verandas and large bathrooms with hot showers. About B500 more gets you a/c and more living space in a "Deluxe Village" bungalow. Clustered rather closely together in a lush garden, but with seductive corners for sitting out. Fan B3315, a/c B3835

OUT OF TOWN

Belle Villa About 1km north of town, signposted to the right off the Mae Hong Son road ☎053 698226–7, ⓦbellevillaresort.com; map p.347. Elegant luxury rooms and villas on stilts, all with balconies, mini-bars and safes. Traversed by a stream and decorated with rice fields, the grounds sport two stylish pools. Early-bird discounts and other promotions available on their website. Breakfast included. B2800

Mountain View 500m up a side road by the tourist police at the south end of town ☎086 180 5998, ⓦthemountainviewpai.com; map p.347. Laidback, old-style resort of wooden bungalows with private bathrooms and hammocks on the balconies, set in ten acres of hilltop land among a small arboretum of flowering trees, with a sociable campfire burning in the cool season. Call for free pick-up from the centre. Free access to Fluid swimming pool (see page 345). B270

★ **Reverie Siam** About 2km south of the centre on the west bank of the river ☎053 699870, ⓦreveriesiam. com; map p.347. Set in lush gardens by the river with two saltwater swimming pools, the large rooms and villas at this boutique hotel are decorated in a fetching colonial style, with repro antique furniture, curios, prints and a touch of Gallic flair; all have rain showers, DVD players and view-filled balconies or verandas. There's a good restaurant and a free shuttle service to town. Breakfast included. B2950

Spicypai Around 700m east of the Thanon Ratchadamrong bridge; keep right at the junctions you pass along the way and then follow the signs to the hostel ☎052 040177; map p.347. Ultra-cheap and ultra-sociable dorm beds with mosquito nets, in a series of lofty, stilted bamboo huts thatched with *tong teung* leaves, surrounded by vivid green paddy fields. Facilities include shared hot showers and lockers for your valuables. Simple breakfast included. Dorms B180

EATING

CENTRAL PAI

Art in Chai Thanon Wan Chalerm; map p.344. Old-school hippy café that's famous for its strong masala chai. It also serves tasty sandwiches (around B90), veggie and vegan salads, various porridges and homemade yoghurt, as well as cakes and cookies. Daily except Tues 9am–10pm.

Baan Benjarong South end of town on Thanon Rungsiyanon ☎053 698010; map p.344. In a town where you can get everything from sushi to falafel, this is one of the few places to offer a wide variety of authentic and tasty Thai dishes – the banana-flower salad (*yam hua plee*) is especially delicious. Small, often full on busy nights (no reservations) and service can be a little begrudging. Daily approximately 11am–1.30pm & 5–8pm, though hours are temperamental.

Big's Little Café Thanon Chaisongkhram ⓦfacebook. com/bigslittlecafepai; map p.344. Run by Big, who has worked as a chef in England, this tiny streetside café is renowned for its tasty and keenly priced burgers, sandwiches, jacket potatoes and Western breakfasts. Customers sit around on bar stools while their food is prepared right in front of them. A good spot for meeting other travellers. Daily except Sat 9am–4/5pm.

★ **Cafecito** Down a quiet soi off Thanon Rungsiyanon on the south side of town ☎086 587 2107, ⓦfacebook. com/cafecitopai; map p.344. It's well worth the trek out to this café for excellent home-roasted coffee, scrummy home-baked cakes and great Mexican food such as tacos (B110). Daily except Thurs 9am–5pm.

Khaotha Down a quiet soi off Thanon Rungsiyanon on the south side of town ⓦfacebook.com/khaothapai; map p.344. Coffee roaster and wholesaler that's also a cool café, decorated with graffiti and old fans, with jazz on the soundtrack and quiet seats on the front terrace. There are a few teas and sodas on the menu, but the main event here is the seriously good espresso coffee (B40). Daily 8.30/9am–5pm.

Nong Beer Corner of Chaisongkhram and Khetkalang ☎053 699103; map p.344. One of Pai's longest-standing and most popular places for cheap eats dishing up great *khao soi*, pork satay and a wide range of buffet stir-fries and curries, including northern pork belly curry (*kaeng hang lay*). Daily 8am–9pm.

Nong Best Thanon Khetkalang, just south of Pai Flora Resort; map p.344. This friendly bare-bones restaurant with an open streetside kitchen doesn't look like much from the outside but it's justifiably very popular with locals, and you can taste why – excellent pork with basil and chillies (B70) and crispy pork with snow peas (B70). Daily 9am–9pm.

Som Tam Na Amphoe Thanon Ratchadamrong, next to Payi Resort ☎053 698087; map p.344. The green papaya salad here (B40) is a must-eat for Thai visitors to Pai, served with grilled chicken (B70), or available in the Khorat version, *tam sua*, with rice noodles (B40). The sign's in Thai, but includes the phone number. Daily 10am–4.30/5pm.

TTK Thanon Ratchadamrong, next to TTK Guesthouse ☎053 698093; map p.344. Famous for its kebabs (B120), falafels and other Middle Eastern dishes, this large, welcoming indoor-outdoor restaurant also serves reasonably priced beer, espresso coffees and Western and Middle Eastern breakfasts. Daily 8am–9.30pm.

Witching Well Thanon Tessaban 1, opposite Pai River Corner ✪witchingwellrestaurant.com; map p.344. Choose between the cute garden with its waterfall fountain and the wine bar-like interior with its bare brick walls, and tuck into good Western food such as spaghetti with pesto (B185), burgers and breakfasts – or just sip a glass of wine, an imported beer or an espresso coffee. Daily 8am–9.30pm.

OUT OF TOWN

Silhouette Reverie Siam Resort (see page 348); map p.347. High-class bar-restaurant serving everything from tapas (around B100), through cheese and charcuterie boards, to sophisticated dishes such as salmon fillet with marinated cherry tomatoes and tarragon cream (B335), on a lovely terrace overlooking the hotel gardens and the valley. Live music nightly and free shuttle service from the centre. Daily 7.30am–10.30pm.

DRINKING AND NIGHTLIFE

Several **bars** around town offer live music and DJs: as well as those listed below, look out for posters around town, which sometimes announce one-off parties too. The free Pai Jazz and Blues **festival** rocked the town over a weekend in late July 2017 and hopefully will be staged again in future years.

Don't Cry Thanon Ratchadamrong; map p.344. Just across the river from the centre, this classic reggae bar (with a bit of EDM and hip-hop thrown in nowadays) features live bands, DJs and fire shows. It's the last place in town to close … Daily 7pm–late.

★ **The Jazz House** Just off Thanon Chaisongkhram near Wat Pa Kham ☎064 370 0182, ✪facebook.com/ jazzhousepai; map p.344. This mellow and sociable bar-restaurant on a quiet, leafy lane occupies a wooden house and a shady garden with hammocks, cats and low-slung tables. It offers Thai and creative Western food, live music from 7.30pm Mon–Sat and an open mike night on Sun from 6.30pm (as well as hostel rooms, if you really want to immerse yourself in Pai's music scene). Daily 9am–9.30pm.

Mojo Thanon Tessaban 1 ✪facebook.com/mojocafepai; map p.344. Cosy bar done out with dark wood and black-and-white photos of the blues greats, where a good blues band plays every night (about 8.45pm), with live acoustic as the overture (about 7.45pm). Wed is jam night (from about 10pm). Tues–Sun 5–11.30pm.

DIRECTORY

ATMs You'll find ATMs in the centre, on Thanon Chaisong-khram and Thanon Rungsiyanon.
Hospital Thanon Chaisongkhram ☎053 699211.
Bookshop Siam Books, Thanon Chaisongkhram (☎086 255 6944; daily 9am–8/10pm), has a good selection of used and new paperbacks.
Tourist police South end of town, on the road to Chiang Mai ☎1155.

From Pai to Chiang Mai

Once out of the Pai valley, Route 1095 climbs for 35km of hairpin bends, with beautiful views north to 2175m Doi Chiang Dao near the top. In the cool season, with your own transport, you can witness – if you get started from Pai an hour before dawn – one of the country's most famous views of the sun rising over a sea of mist at **Huai Nam Dang National Park** (B300). The viewpoint is signposted on the left 30km out of Pai; take this turning and go on 6km to the park headquarters. Back on Route 1095, once over the 1300m pass, the road steeply descends the south-facing slopes in the shadow of Doi Mae Ya (2005m), before working its way along the narrow, more populous lower valleys. After 55km (at kilometre-stone 42), a left turn leads 6.5km over some stomach-churning hills to **Pong Duet hot springs**, where scalding water leaps up to 4m into the air, generating copious quantities of steam in the cool season. A few hundred metres downstream of the springs, a series of pools allows you to soak in the temperature of your choice. The last appealing detour of the route is to **Mokfa Falls** (part of Doi Suthep-Pui National Park; B200), where a cascade tumbles about 30m into a sand-fringed pool that is ideal for swimming, making an attractive setting for a break – it's 2km south of the main road, 76km from Pai. Finally, at **Mae Malai**, turn right onto the busy Highway 107 and join the mad, speeding traffic for the last 34km across the wide plains to Chiang Mai.

To Chiang Rai via Tha Ton

If you're coming up from Chiang Mai, the quickest and most obvious **route to Chiang Rai** is Highway 118, a fast, 185km road that swoops through rolling hill country. A much more scenic approach, however, is to follow Highway 107 and Highway 1089; a two-day trip along this route will leave you enough time for an overnight stay in **Tha Ton** and a longtail boat trip along the **Kok River**. There are other diversions en route, including the famous **Elephant Nature Park** and several good guesthouses in the countryside near **Chiang Dao**.

The Elephant Nature Park

12km beyond Mae Taeng · Full-day trip costs B2500/person · Best to book your visit online as far in advance as possible, though they have an office in Chiang Mai at 1 Thanon Ratchamanka · ☎ 053 818932, ⓦ elephantnaturepark.org

From Chiang Mai the route towards Tha Ton heads north along Highway 107, retracing the Mae Hong Son Loop as far as Mae Malai. About 3km after Mae Taeng, a signposted left turn leads 9km to the **Elephant Nature Park**, which is essentially a rescue centre and hospital for sick, orphaned and neglected elephants, where hands-on educational visits by the public are encouraged. On a daytime visit, you'll get to feed, bathe and learn about the elephants close up, but it's also possible to stay for two days or sign up as a paying volunteer for a week. The park's owner, Sangduan ("Lek") Chailert, has become something of a celebrity in recent years, being featured on the BBC and in *Time* magazine for her conservation efforts. Visits must be booked in advance and include transport from and to your accommodation in Chiang Mai.

Chiang Dao

Around kilometre-stone 72, **CHIANG DAO**, which hosts an interesting hill-tribe fresh market on Tuesday mornings, stretches on and on along the old main road (now Route 1359) as the dramatic limestone crags and forests of Thailand's third-highest peak, Doi Luang Chiang Dao (or Doi Luang, "Great Mountain"; 2240m), loom up on the left. Highway 107 now follows a bypass that sweeps round to the west of town, carrying traffic heading straight for Fang and Tha Ton. From the high street just north of the market, Route 3024 heads west, crossing the bypass before passing the caves and the accommodation listed below.

Tham Chiang Dao

5km northwest of the town centre, across the bypass on Route 3024 · Daily roughly 8am–4pm · Admission to the caves is B40 and guides ask around B100 to take a group of up to four people on a roughly 30min tour · Access from Chiang Dao by yellow songthaews and motorbike taxis

An extensive complex of interconnected caverns, **Tham Chiang Dao** has an attached monastery (the caves were given religious significance by the local legend of a hermit sage who is said to have dwelt in them for a millennium). Several of the caverns can be visited; a couple have electric light but others need the services of a guide with a lantern; guides will point out unusual rock formations and keep you on the right track

---

TREKS UP DOI LUANG CHIANG DAO

Guided treks to the **summit of Doi Luang Chiang Dao**, famous for its many rare alpine plants and birds, can be arranged by both *Malee's* and *Chiang Dao Nest* (see page 351) during the cool season, roughly from November to early February. There's an altitude difference of 1100m from the trailhead to the summit: fit hikers can do it in one day (from B1100/person in a large group), though it's more pleasurable to spend two days (from B2200/person in a large group, including camping below the summit).

– it's said the deepest parts of the cave are 12km underground, and just a few of the caverns are considered safe to visit.

ARRIVAL AND DEPARTURE — CHIANG DAO

By bus Take one of the buses or a/c minibuses from Chiang Mai's Chang Phuak bus station bound for Fang or Tha Ton, which drive along the main street (Route 1359) through Chiang Dao town. Get off at the main bus stop (rather than the bus station further north), which is near Tesco Lotus Express opposite The Star, where you're most likely to find a motorbike taxi (B60) or yellow songthaew (B150) to take you to the cave or the guesthouses.

ACCOMMODATION AND EATING

Chiang Dao Nest About 1500m further north along Route 3024 from the caves ☎ 053 456612, ⓦ chiang daonest.com. There are two branches of this farang favourite, one on each side of *Malee's*, with around twenty bungalows in total – all with attached hot-water bathrooms and verandas. The one nearer to the caves has a/c and serves Thai food, while the further one – which has a small swimming pool – turns out gourmet Western dishes (mains at around B300–400). B1095

Chiang Dao Roundhouses Just off the east side of Route 3024 near the caves ☎ 087 496 1571, ⓦ chiangdao-roundhouses.com. Set on a landscaped grassy slope with attractive sitting areas and great views of Doi Luang, this laid-back resort offers three spacious and comfortable adobe roundhouses, one thatched, with indoor-outdoor hot-water bathrooms. Closed mid-March to June & Sept. Breakfast included. B1300

Malee's Nature Lovers Bungalows About 1500m further north along Route 3024 from the caves ☎ 081 961 8387, ⓦ maleenature.com. In a cosy orchid-filled garden, delightfully set in the shadow of the mountain, you'll find comfy bungalows of varying size, all with hot showers, as well as a camping area (B200/person), a saltwater plunge pool and good food. They can arrange treks and bird-watching trips, and have information for self-guided hiking and birding; mountain-bike and motorbike rental is available. B750

Doi Angkhang

Back on Highway 107, the road shimmies over a rocky ridge marking the watershed between the catchment areas of the Chao Phraya River to the south and the Mekong River ahead, before descending into the flat plain around Fang and the Kok River. Branching off to the left some 60km from Chiang Dao (at kilometre-stone 137), a steep and winding 25km road, Route 1249, for which you'll need your own transport, leads up to the mountain known as **Doi Angkhang** (1928m). Besides a royal agricultural project that produces peaches, raspberries and kiwis in the cool season, the mountain is home to a luxurious resort, where you can stop for food and spend a couple of hours soaking up the scenery.

ACCOMMODATION — DOI ANGKHANG

★ **Angkhang Nature Resort** 1/1 Moo 5 Baan Khum ☎ 053 450110, ⓦ mosaic-collection.com/angkhang. At this gorgeous hillside resort, the luxurious teak pavilions have balconies with great views (and electric blankets for the cool season), the restaurant uses organic produce from the royal project, and bird-watching, trekking, mule riding or mountain biking to nearby hill-tribe villages are the main activities. Breakfast included. B2600

Tha Ton and around

The tidy, leafy settlement of **THA TON**, nearly 180km north of Chiang Mai, huddles each side of a bridge over the Kok River, which flows out of Myanmar 4km to the north upstream. Life in Tha Ton revolves around the bridge – buses and boats pull up here, and most of the accommodation is clustered nearby. The main attraction here is the longtail-boat trip downstream to Chiang Rai.

Wat Tha Ton

On the west side of the bridge • ⓦ wat-thaton.org

The over-the-top ornamental gardens of **Wat Tha Ton**, endowed with colossal golden and white Buddha images and an equally huge statue of Kuan Im, the Chinese *bodhisattva* of mercy, are well worth the short climb. From any of the statues, the views up the narrow green valley towards Myanmar and downstream across the sun-glazed plain are heady stuff.

ARRIVAL AND DEPARTURE

By bus or songthaew Regular non-a/c buses run between Chiang Mai's Chang Phuak bus station and Tha Ton (every 90min–2hr; 4hr). Otherwise, you could take one of the half-hourly buses or a/c minibuses to the ugly frontier outpost of Fang, 153km from Chiang Mai, then change onto a roughly half-hourly songthaew to Tha Ton. From Tha Ton, it's also possible to move on to Mae Salong by songthaew

THA TON AND AROUND

(see page 362) or Mae Sai by a/c minibus (1 daily; 1hr 30min).

By car or motorbike If you're coming up Highway 107 with your own transport, you can give Fang a miss altogether by branching west on a bypass signposted to Mae Ai. In Tha Ton, you can rent a motorbike just south of the boat station for B400/day.

ACCOMMODATION AND EATING

There are several simple **restaurants** opposite the boat landing; in addition, the following resorts have restaurants that are open to non-guests.

Khun Mai Baan Suan Resort On the east bank of the river, about 500m north of the bridge ☎053 053551,

🌐 khunmaibaansuan.com. At a bend in the tree-lined river, this friendly resort has comfortable, tiled, log-cabin-style bungalows, some right on the water's edge, and brick-built rooms, all with a/c and hot showers and set around a lovely, big garden. Breakfast included. **B900**

BOAT TRIPS ALONG THE KOK RIVER

Travelling down the 100km stretch of the **Kok River** to Chiang Rai gives you a chance to soak up a rich diversity of typical northern landscapes, which you never get on a speeding bus. Heading out of Tha Ton, the river traverses a flat valley of rice fields and orchards, where it's flanked by high reeds inhabited by flitting swallows. After half an hour, you pass the 900-year-old **Wat Phra That Sop Fang**, with its small hilltop chedi and a slithering naga staircase leading up from the river bank. Beyond the large village of **Mae Salak**, 20km from Tha Ton, the river starts to meander between thickly forested slopes. From among the banana trees and giant wispy ferns, kids come out to play, adults to bathe and wash clothes, and water buffalo emerge simply to enjoy the river. About two hours out of Tha Ton the hills get steeper and the banks rockier, leading up to a half-hour stretch of small but feisty rapids, where you might well get a soaking. Beyond the rapids, crowds of boats suddenly appear, ferrying tour groups from Chiang Rai to the Karen village of **Ruammid**, 20km upstream, for elephant-riding. From here on, the landscape deteriorates as the bare valley around Chiang Rai opens up.

BOATS

The best time of year to make this trip is in the cool season (roughly Nov–Feb), when the river is high enough after the rainy season and the vegetation lush. Canopied **longtail boats** (B400/person) leave from the south side of the bridge in Tha Ton every day at around 12.30pm for the trip to Chiang Rai, which takes three to four rather noisy hours. The slower, less crowded journey upriver gives an even better chance of appreciating the scenery – the longtails leave Chiang Rai at 10.30am. However, if there are fewer than four passengers, these public boats won't depart – though there's always the option of buying up the extra seats. If you can get a group of up to six people together, it's better to charter a longtail from the boat landing in Tha Ton (B2500; ☎053 373224), which will allow you to stop at the hill-tribe villages and hot springs en route.

ACCOMMODATION

A peaceful **guesthouse** between Mae Salak and Ruammid, from which you can go trekking (guided or self-guided), might tempt you to break your river journey. *Akha Hill House* (☎064 229 9094, 🌐akhahill.com; dorm B80, fan double B250, a/c B1100), on the south bank of the Kok, 3km on foot from the riverside hot springs near Huai Kaeo waterfall, offers lofty views, comfortable rooms and bungalows, with shared or en-suite hot showers, and free transport daily to and from Chiang Rai, 1hr away.

Old Trees House About 400m east of the bridge on the north side of Route 1089 ☎081 168 9847, ⓦoldtrees house.net. This small, French-Thai resort is set in a lovely, lush, shady garden, with thatched salas for hanging out, an elevated terrace with a panorama over the valley and two landscaped swimming pools. The comfortable, roomy thatched bungalows sport sturdy bamboo furniture, verandas, hot showers, fridges, DVD players and fans. The owners can arrange one-day treks for B1000–1100/person, including lunch. Thai dinners served. Breakfast included. B1500

Ban Lorcha

Beyond Tha Ton, Route 1089 heads east towards Mae Chan and Highway 1; about 20km out of town, at Ban Kew Satai, a dramatic side road leads north for 16km to Mae Salong (see page 360). On the way, it's worth breaking your journey (about 1km west of Kew Satai on Route 1089, and accessible by songthaews from Tha Ton and Mae Salong) at **BAN LORCHA**. As part of a community-based tourism development project, owned and managed by the villagers, with technical assistance from the PDA in Chiang Rai (see page 355), this Akha settlement has been opened to visitors, who pay an entrance fee of B80 (income goes into a village development fund). A guide leads you on a 1km walk through the village, which is strategically dotted with interesting display boards in English, and you'll get a chance to have a go on an Akha swing (not the ceremonial one), see a welcome dance and watch people weaving and tool-making, for example.

Chiang Rai

Sprawled untidily over the south bank of the Kok River, **CHIANG RAI** continues to live in the shadow of the regional capital, Chiang Mai, but in the last few years has acquired several genuine sights of interest, notably the **Mae Fah Luang Art & Cultural Park**, a beautiful storehouse of Lanna art, and the contrasting inspirations of two local artists, **Baan Dam**, the "Black House Museum" and **Wat Rong Khun**, the "White Temple". There's now also a good choice of guesthouses and upmarket riverside hotels in which to lay your head, and from here you can set up a wide range of trekking, day-trips and other outdoor activities in the surrounding countryside. The town quietly gets on with its own business during the day, when most of its package tourists are out on manoeuvres, but at night the neon lights flash on and souvenir stalls and ersatz Western restaurants are thronged.

Brief history

Chiang Rai is most famous for the things it had and lost. It was founded in 1263 by King Mengrai of Ngon Yang who, having recaptured a prize elephant he'd been chasing around the foot of Doi Tong, took this as an auspicious omen for a new city. Tradition has it that Chiang Rai then prevailed as the capital of the north for thirty years, but historians now believe Mengrai moved his court directly from Ngon Yang to the Chiang Mai area in the 1290s. Thailand's two holiest images, the Emerald Buddha (now in Bangkok) and the Phra Singh Buddha (now either in Bangkok's National Museum, Chiang Mai or Nakhon Si Thammarat, depending on which story you believe), also once resided here before moving on – at least replicas of these can be seen at Wat Phra Kaeo and Wat Phra Singh.

Doi Tong

Northwest of the centre

A walk up to **Doi Tong**, the hummock to the northwest of the centre that was the site of Mengrai's original ring fort, is the best way to get your bearings in Chiang Rai and, especially at sunset, offers a fine view up the Kok River as it emerges from the mountains to the west. On the highest part of the hill stands a kind of phallic Stonehenge centred on the town's new **lak muang** (city pillar) representing the Buddhist layout of the universe. Historically, the erection of a *lak muang* marks the official founding of a Thai city, precisely dated to January 26, 1263 in the case of Chiang Rai; the new *lak muang* and the elaborate stone model around it were erected 725 years later to the day, as part of the celebrations of King Bhumibol's sixtieth birthday. The *lak muang* itself represents Mount Sineru (or Meru), the axis of the universe, while the series of concentric terraces, moats and pillars represent the heavens and the earth, the great oceans and rivers, and the major features of the universe. Sprinkling water onto the garlanded *lak muang* and then dabbing your head with the water after it has flowed into the basin below brings good luck. The old wooden *lak muang* can be seen in the viharn of **Wat Phra That Doi Tong** on the eastern side of the hill, which is said to be older than the city itself, dating back to the tenth century.

Wat Phra Kaeo

Thanon Trairat • Temple daily dawn–dusk • Sangkaew Hall daily 9am–5pm • Free • ⓦ watphrakaew-chiangrai.com

Thailand's most important image, the Emerald Buddha, which had supposedly been sculpted by the gods in Patna, India, in 234 BC, was placed in the chedi at **Wat Phra**

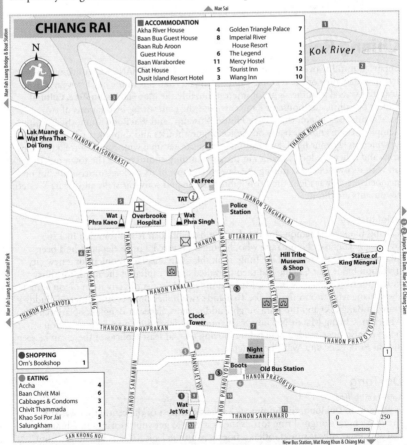

TOURS AND TREKKING FROM CHIANG RAI

Communities from all the hill tribes have settled around **Chiang Rai**, and the region offers the full range of terrain for **trekking**, from reasonably gentle walking trails near the Kok River to tough mountain slopes further north towards the border with Myanmar. However, this natural suitability has attracted too many tour and trekking agencies, and many of the hill-tribe villages, especially between Chiang Rai and Mae Salong, have become weary of the constant toing and froing; the south side of the river to the west of town is generally a better bet. Sizes of group treks from Chiang Rai tend to be smaller than those from Chiang Mai, often with just two or three people, with a maximum of about seven in a group. Most guesthouses in Chiang Rai can fit you up with a trek – *Chat House* is responsible and reliable, typically charging around B2500–3500 per person for three days and two nights in a group of between two and six people. It's worth avoiding the several camps of "long-neck" women (see page 336) around Chiang Rai, who live as virtual prisoners for the convenience of tourists. Different ways to see the countryside around Chiang Rai include Chiang Rai Bicycle Tour's half- to five-day **cycling tours**, which include hill-tribe villages, boat trips on the Kok, waterfalls and Wat Rong Khun (☎085 662 4347, ⓦchiangraibicycletour.com; from B1450/person including pick-up from your accommodation); and **horseback trail-riding** for beginners and experts with Appaloosa Stables (☎096 836 8701, ⓦappaloosa-stables.com; B900/hr).

More expensive treks are offered by several nonprofit foundations promoting **community-based tourism** that are based in and around Chiang Rai, as detailed below.

Natural Focus ☎053 758658 or ☎085 888 6869, ⓦnaturalfocus-cbt.com. Set up by the Hill Area and Community Development Foundation, this CBT initiative offers one- to five-day tours to learn about mountain life, as well as youth, community development and volunteer skills programmes.

PDA At the Hill Tribe Museum (see page 355) ☎053 740088, ⓦpdacr.org. This development agency offers one- to three-day jungle treks to non-touristy areas, usually including a longtail-boat trip. It also lays on a wide range of guided tours, to its Akha project at Ban Lorcha (see page 353), Mae Salong and other places of interest.

Thailand Ecotour ⓦthailandecotour.org. Part of the excellent Mirror Foundation (see page 60), with an interesting and well-received programme that includes one-day bicycle tours and one- to seven-day treks.

Kaeo by King Mahaprom of Chiang Rai in 1390. However, lightning destroyed the chedi 44 years later, allowing the image to continue its perambulations around Southeast Asia, finally settling down in Bangkok. A beautiful replica can now be seen here in a tiny, Lanna-style pavilion, the **Hor Phra Yok**. Carved in China from milky green Canadian jade, the replica was presented by a Chinese millionaire to mark the ninetieth birthday of the Princess Mother, Mae Fah Luang, in 1990, and consecrated by King Bhumibol himself. At 47.9cm wide and 65.9cm tall, it's millimetres smaller than the actual Emerald Buddha, as religious protocol dictated that it could not be an exact copy of the original. There's much else of interest in the temple complex, which has recently been renovated to a high standard, notably the **Sangkaew Hall**. Distinguished by its informative labels on Thai religious practice in English, this museum houses all sorts of Buddhist paraphernalia, including the belongings of famous monks from Chiang Rai.

The Hill Tribe Museum and Handicrafts Shop

620/25 Thanon Tanalai ☎053 719167, ⓦpdacr.org • Mon–Fri 8.30am–6pm, Sat & Sun 10am–6pm • Museum B50

The **Hill Tribe Museum and Handicrafts Shop** stocks an authentic selection of tasteful and well-made hill-tribe **handicrafts**. The shop, on the second floor, was started by the country's leading development campaigner, Meechai Viravaidya, under the auspices of the PDA (Population and Community Development Association), and all proceeds go to village projects. The museum is a good place to learn about the hill tribes before going on a trek, and includes a slick, informative slide show (20min). You can donate old clothes, toys or money for jumpers and blankets, and the PDA also organizes treks and tours themselves (see above).

Mae Fah Luang Art & Cultural Park (Rai Mae Fah Luang)

5km west of the city centre in Ban Pa Ngio • Tues–Sun 8.30am–5pm • B200 • ⓦ maefahluang.org • To get here, charter a songthaew for about B100 one-way, or B200 return; with your own transport, head west on Thanon Tanalai for 1.7km from Thanon Trairat, turn right at the traffic lights onto Thanon Hong Lee and follow the road for 2–3km until you see the entrance on the left-hand side

By far Chiang Rai's most compelling attraction is the **Mae Fah Luang Art and Cultural Park**, a beautiful showcase of Lanna art and architecture, and its influences from Myanmar, Laos and China. In particular, the museum displays the consummate skills of local woodcarvers, with a focus on teak, which in Thailand is associated with concepts of dignity. It's set in lovely parkland, including a young teak garden that holds 43 varieties from northern Thailand.

The main reason for coming here is to see the **Haw Kham**, an amazing, multi-tiered barn of a building on massive stilts. It took five years to construct in the 1980s, in honour of the auspicious 84th birthday of the Princess Mother, Mae Fah Luang, using materials from 32 old houses in Chiang Rai province. Look out especially for the *ben grit* (fish scales) roof tiles, which inevitably are also made of teak. The interior's dramatic centrepiece is a huge, slender, wooden prasat, representing the centre of the universe, Mount Meru, set in a sunken white sandpit – which not only symbolizes the Ocean of Milk, but also soaks up moisture to protect the teak. Dozens of very fine wooden artefacts surround the prasat, including a beautifully serene Burmese Buddha in a delicate, many-frilled robe that looks as if it's moving. Standouts among the displays in the nearby **Haw Kaew** – which is also made entirely of teak – are some ornate *oop*, or ceremonial alms bowls, and a bed headboard and footboard that sport scary carvings of Rahoo: the monster eating the moon connotes not only eclipses, but also a good night's sleep.

Wat Rong Khun (the White Temple)

13km south of Chiang Rai on the west side of Highway 1 • Mon–Fri 8am–5pm, Sat & Sun 8am–5.30pm; B50 • Catch one of the roughly half-hourly songthaews bound for Mae Khajan from the old bus station

Wat Rong Khun almost defies description. Begun in 1997, it's the life's work of local contemporary artist, **Chalermchai Kositpipat** (see page 751), who has rediscovered Buddhism in a big way since spending time as a monk in 1992; he is also training dozens of "disciples", as he calls them, to finish the temple long after his death, hopefully by 2070. Taking traditional Buddhist elements such as nagas and lotus flowers, and Lanna features such as long, slender *tung kradan* banners, Ajarn Chalermchai has enlarged and elaborated them, adding all sort of frills, layers and tiers. Surrounded by ponds, fountains and bridges (as well as a burgeoning village of souvenir shops and cafés for tourists), the temple is all white (to stand for the Buddha's purity), inlaid with clear glass tiles (to represent his wisdom); the end result is like a frosted wedding cake. Inside the bot, which houses an eerily lifelike waxwork of the wat's former abbot, you can often watch Chalermchai's disciples painting the golden-toned murals; an earthquake in 2014 damaged the plasterwork and toppled the temple's uppermost spire, but the work goes on. In the adjacent Hall of Masterwork, some of the artist's original paintings are on display, while reproductions are on sale (to raise money for the project) in the souvenir shop, along with a useful B100 booklet on the temple in English, which explains the meaning of the complex design.

If you're a fan of Chalermchai's work, you'll want to check out his new **clocktower**, back in Chiang Rai at the junction of Banphaprakan and Jet Yot roads, which hosts a mini *son et lumière* for five minutes every night at 7, 8 and 9pm. His designs can also be seen in the florid lampposts all over town.

Baan Dam (the Black House Museum)

About 1km west off Highway 1 (signposted), 10km north of Chiang Rai • Daily 9am–5pm; B80 • Catch any bus heading up Highway 1 (towards Mae Chan) from the old bus terminal and walk

If Wat Rong Khun almost defies description, **Baan Dam** thoroughly boggles the mind. The former residence and studio of the late, Chiang Rai-born National Artist, **Thawan Duchanee**, it houses a bizarre array of objects that were collected by Ajarn Thawan to inspire him in his work – blackened crocodile skins and conch shells, elephant skulls and stone circles, pinned insects in glass cases and bamboo fish traps. Set in a grassy, shady park, the collection is neatly displayed in and around forty or so buildings, many of which are exaggerated forms of traditional Thai structures: the ho trai (a library on stilts) is typical, painted black with a buffalo-horn staircase. Most of the buildings are locked, though you can look in through windows or doors, and none of the objects are labelled, so you're likely to be spending most time in the "main sanctuary hall", a lofty black "viharn" with an impossibly steep, multi-tiered roof. Here, as well as his inspirational objects, you'll find some typical examples of Thawan's paintings and woodcarvings, featuring gnarly, muscular and sharp-toothed mythical creatures – look out especially for the tung, traditional Lanna wooden banners, which in this artist's hands become more like totem poles.

ARRIVAL AND DEPARTURE — CHIANG RAI

By plane Bangkok Airways, Thai Smile, Vietjet (all use Bangkok's Suvarnabhumi Airport), Nok Air, Thai Lion Air and Air Asia (all Don Muang Airport) each fly between Bangkok and Chiang Rai 2–4 times daily (1hr 15min); Vietjet flies direct to Phuket once daily (2hr), Air Asia to Hat Yai once daily (2hr). The airport is 8km north of town on Highway 1 – about a B150 taxi ride.

By bus Chiang Rai's new bus station **(sometimes called Terminal 2)** is about 6km south of the centre on Highway 1. It handles inter-provincial routes (including a/c and some non-a/c services from/to Lampang), while the old bus station (Terminal 1) on Thanon Phaholyothin serves Chiang Rai province (Mae Sai, Chiang Saen, Chiang Khong and Sop Ruak), plus Nan and most non-a/c buses to Lampang; some services, to Chiang Mai and Mae Sot for instance, stop at both, however. Shared songthaews shuttle between the two bus stations for B20.

Destinations Bangkok (24 daily; 11–12hr); Chiang Khong (roughly every 30min; 2–3hr); Chiang Mai (roughly every 30min; 3hr); Chiang Saen (every 20min; 1hr–1hr 30min); Houayxai, Laos (1 daily; 4hr); Khon Kaen (6 daily; 12hr 30min); Khorat (6 daily; 12hr 30min); Lampang (roughly every 30min; 4hr–5hr 30min); Luang Prabang, Laos (4 weekly; 17hr); Mae Sai (every 20min; 1hr–1hr 30min); Mae Sot (2 daily; 9hr 30min); Nakhon Phanom (3 daily; 19hr); Nan (1 daily; 6hr); Phitsanulok (around 20 daily; 7hr); Phrae (around 20 daily; 3–5hr); Rayong (4 daily; 18–19hr); Sukhothai (4 daily; 7hr 30min); Udon Thani (3 daily; 13hr).

By boat Longtails from/to Tha Ton dock at the boat station, northwest of the centre on the north side of the Mae Fah Luang Bridge.

GETTING AROUND

By metered taxi or tuk-tuk The city's a/c metered taxis charge from B37 (plus a B20 call-out fee; ☎ 053 750773), while tuk-tuks start at around B50. App-based taxi service Grab has recently come to Chiang Rai.

By bicycle Fat Free, 448/2 Thanon Klang Wieng (☎ 086 430 5523, ⓦ fatfreebike.com), rents good sit-up-and-begs for B50/day and mountain bikes from B200/day.

By car or motorbike Car rental is available through North Wheels – who also have motorbikes with insurance – west of the centre at 88/14–15 Thanon Ratchayota (☎ 053 740585, ⓦ northwheels.com), or through Avis at the airport (☎ 02 251 1131, ⓦ avisthailand.com). Motorbikes, big and small, can also be rented at Chiang Rai Big Bikes on Thanon Jet Yot (☎ 090 891 0997, ⓦ crbigbikerentals.com), and several other places on the same street.

INFORMATION AND MAPS

Tourist information TAT has a helpful office at 448/16 Thanon Singhaklai (daily 8.30am–4.30pm; ☎ 053 717433 or ☎ 053 744674–5, ✉ tatchrai@tat.or.th) with some useful free maps and brochures. Ask here about the renovated old provincial office opposite, which may be turned into a museum, and, if the "White Temple" has given you a taste for big, gaudy, modern temples with catchy nicknames, you could also ask about Chiang Rai's "Blue Temple" (Wat Rong Seua Ten) and "Nine-tier Temple" (Wat Huai Pla Kang).

ACCOMMODATION

A wide choice of good **guesthouses** is within walking distance of central Chiang Rai, while several very appealing hotels hug the tranquil banks of the Kok River on the town's fringes.

3

Akha River House Just west of busy Thanon Ratannakhet, on the south bank of the Kok River ☎063 290 5662, ⓦakhahill.com; map p.354. Under the same Akha ownership as Akha Hill House (see page 352), with part of the profits going to an educational project. The cheapest rooms share bathrooms in an old building, but you might well be tempted to cough up for their smart, a/c offerings with terraces overlooking the lawn and the river channel, en-suite hot showers and chunky bamboo furniture. Fan B200 , a/c B800

Baan Bua Guest House 879/2 Thanon Jet Yot ☎053 718880; map p.354. Congenial and well-run establishment arrayed around a surprisingly large, quiet and shady garden, set back off the road. The very clean and attractive concrete, single-storey rooms and dorms all come with hot showers. Dorms B200, fan doubles B500, a/c doubles B600

★ **Baan Rub Aroon Guest House** 65 Thanon Ngam Muang ☎053 711827, ⓦbaanrubaroon.com; map p.354. In a pretty, quiet garden, this lovely early twentieth-century mansion has polished teak floors, lots of houseplants and immaculate hotel-style rooms with a/c and clean white sheets. The downside is that most rooms share hot-water bathrooms, but there's also a very well-equipped kitchen and a nice terrace for eating breakfast (included). Cooking classes available. B650

Baan Warabordee 59/1 Thanon Sanpanard ☎053 754488, ⓦfacebook.com/baanwarabordee; map p.354. Among a number of similar, slightly upmarket guesthouses on this surprisingly quiet, dead-end street in the town centre, a traditional wooden gate welcomes you into the pleasant, fountain-cooled garden here. The surrounding rooms are large and tastefully decked out in natural tones, with a/c, hot showers, TVs and fridges; some have their own balconies. B800

Chat House 3/2 Soi Sangkaew, Thanon Trairat ☎053 711481, ⓦchatguesthouse.com; map p.354. Located behind its own garden restaurant and bakery on a quiet soi, this is Chiang Rai's longest-running travellers' hangout, with a laidback, friendly atmosphere and backpacker-oriented facilities. The cheaper rooms (including a dorm for B150/bed and three singles for B250) are in an old, mostly wooden house with shared hot showers, while a concrete row of garden rooms have en-suite hot water, with either a/c or fan. Fan B350, a/c B600

Dusit Island Resort Hotel 1129 Thanon Kaisornrasit ☎053 607999, ⓦdusit.com; map p.354. Set on an expansive island in the Kok River offering unbeatable views

of the valley, this is one of the swankiest places to stay in town, with high standards of service. The huge rooms are lavishly furnished, with fancy bathrooms, mini-bars and big TVs. Hotel facilities include a rooftop steakhouse, fitness centre, tennis court, jogging track and an expansive swimming pool with a swim-up bar. B4000

Golden Triangle Palace 590 Thanon Phaholyothin ☎053 711339, ⓦgoldentrianglepalacecr.com; map p.354. Despite a gaudy recent makeover, this place still offers reasonable value, its main asset being its setting in a garden compound in the heart of town, where the large, comfortable rooms come with a/c, hot water, TVs and fridges. B1200

Imperial River House Resort 482 Moo 4, Thanon Mae Kok ☎053 750830, ⓦimperialriverhouse.com; map p.354. Opposite *The Legend* on the north bank of the Kok, this resort has elegantly designed and sumptuously furnished rooms and cottages with lovely wooden floors, all overlooking the large swimming pool and landscaped riverside gardens. Extremely relaxing location and excellent service. B3660

The Legend 124/15 Thanon Kohloy ☎053 910400, ⓦthelegend-chiangrai.com; map p.354. Describing itself as a "boutique river resort", this place offers large luxury rooms decorated in contemporary Lanna style with verandas, DVD players and indoor-outdoor bathrooms. Hugging the south bank of the Kok, the compound also features a huge infinity pool, a fitness centre and a top-class spa. Breakfast included. B4750

Mercy Hostel 1005/22 Thanon Jet Yot ☎053 711075, ⓦmercyhostelchiangrai.com; map p.354. At this friendly new hostel and coffee shop, arrayed around a small but attractive pool on a quiet soi, smart mixed and female-only dorms and private rooms come with a/c and hot showers (the rooms also have TVs and fridges). Dorms B250, doubles B800

Tourist Inn 1004/4–6 Thanon Jet Yot ☎053 752094, ⓦfacebook.com/touristinnhotel; map p.354. Clean guesthouse in a modern four-storey building run by a Japanese–Thai team. The reception area downstairs has books for guests' use and a European-style bakery, while bright, light rooms upstairs come with hot-water bathrooms. Breakfast included. Fan B400, a/c B500

Wiang Inn 893 Thanon Phaholyothin ☎053 711533, ⓦwianginn.com; map p.354. Set back off the main road, this 260-room hotel has a bright and spacious lobby, an attractive pool and comfortably furnished rooms equipped with all facilities and decorated with Thai murals. Breakfast included. B2800

EATING

Chiang Rai's **restaurants**, including a growing number of Western places, congregate mostly along Thanon Phaholyothin near the night bazaar, which itself shelters a huge but indifferent food centre. You need never go without

a good **coffee** fix in Chiang Rai: the stuff grown on nearby mountains such as Doi Wawee and Doi Chaang is served up at several cafés around the clocktower.

Accha Thanon Jet Yot ☎052 055223; map p.354. This

friendly restaurant with appealing courtyard tables under the trees does tasty versions of all the Indian classics (chicken tikka masala B170), with good breads and plenty of choice for vegetarians. The combo meals (dal, curry, rice and nan bread) are good value at B220. Daily 11am–3pm & 5–10pm.

Baan Chivit Mai 172 Thanon Prasobsuk, opposite the old bus station ☎ 053 712357, ⊛ bcmthai.com; map p.354. Bakery run by a Scandinavian charity that helps children in Chiang Rai and Bangkok slums. Very clean a/c café, serving excellent sandwiches, cakes (chocolate cake B45) and espresso coffees, plus Swedish meatballs and simple Thai dishes. Mon–Sat 8am–9pm.

Cabbages and Condoms At the Hill Tribe Museum (see p.358) ☎ 053 740657; map p.354. Proudly proclaiming "our food is guaranteed not to cause pregnancy", this restaurant covers its walls with paraphernalia devoted to family planning and HIV/AIDS prevention and hosts regular live music. The Thai food, including some traditional northern dishes and a few dishes suitable for vegetarians, is a bit hit and miss, but it's for a good cause. Daily 10am–midnight.

★ **Chivit Thammada** On the north bank of the Kok River, immediately west of the Highway 1 bridge – turn left at the first traffic lights over the bridge, then second left down a (signposted) soi ☎ 081 984 2925, ⊛ chivitthammada.com; map p.354. A destination café for visiting Thais, with leafy riverside terraces. Sustainably run, with high standards of service, it uses local, organic

and seasonal produce whenever possible, in Thai fusion and Western dishes such as decadent and tasty duck eggs Benedict with truffle hollandaise, bacon and smoked salmon (B220). The home-made cakes are also very tempting, as well as a huge range of very good coffees, smoothies, detox drinks and imported beers. Daily 8am–9pm.

Khao Soi Por Jai Thanon Jet Yot, opposite the Wangcome Hotel; map p.354. Run by the sisters of Chalermchai Kositpipat, the artist behind Wat Rong Khun, this simple, fluorescent-lit restaurant is hung with prints of his works. They offer tasty khao soi with chicken, prawn or fish (B40), good som tam and northern delicacies such as sai oua (spicy sausage), kep muu (pork scratchings) and nam prhik noom (chilli dip with young aubergine). Daily 7am–4pm.

★ **Salungkham** 834/3 Thanon Phaholyothin, on the east side of the road between King Mengrai's statue and the river ☎ 053 717192, ⊛ salungkham.com; map p.354. Justifiably rated by locals as serving the best Thai food in town (main dishes around B150), with a garden for evening dining. Try the superb *kaeng hang lay*, a northern Thai pork-belly curry, or the equally good banana-flower salad with fresh prawns; any dishes using their home-smoked ham or bacon (also on sale to take away) are well worth trying, too. There's no sign in English, but look out for Our Lady of the Nativity Church next door or the Cosmo petrol station opposite. Daily 10.30am–10pm.

SHOPPING

The night bazaar off Thanon Phaholyothin next to the old bus station is open daily roughly from 5–11pm. It sells all sorts of souvenirs and handicrafts, some of good quality and competitively priced – though it's usually crowded with tour groups. At weekends, Chiang Rai's **walking streets**, similar to those in Chiang Mai, come alive with musicians and all manner of stalls, including lots of food and local crafts and products such as coffee and macadamias.

There's one on Thanon Tanalai, around the junction with Wisetwiang, on Saturday evening; and another on Thanon San Khong Noi, to the southwest of the centre, on Sunday evening (aka "Happy Street"). There's also a good handicrafts shop at the Hill Tribe Museum (see page 355).

Orn's Bookshop 1051/61 Thanon Jet Yot, off Soi 1 ☎ 081 022 0818; map p.354. Secondhand fiction and travel books to buy or exchange. Daily 8am–8pm.

DIRECTORY

Cookery classes *Chat House* runs one-day cookery classes including transfers from your accommodation and a trip to the local market (B950/person).

Pharmacy Boots (Thanon Phaholyothin; daily 11am–

10pm) is a well-stocked chemist with English-speaking staff.

Tourist police The tourist police have moved their office out to Highway 1, 17km south of town, though they're still accessible to tourists by phone (☎ 1155 or ☎ 053 152547).

North of Chiang Rai

The northernmost tip of Thailand, stretching from the Kok River and Chiang Rai to the border, is split in two by Highway 1, Thailand's main north–south road. In the western half, rows of wild, shark's-tooth mountains jut into Myanmar, while to the east, low-lying rivers flow through Thailand's richest rice-farming land to the Mekong River, which forms the border with Laos here.

At a push, any one of the places described in this section could be visited in a day from Chiang Rai, while hardly anyone visits **Mae Sai** on the Burmese border except on a visa-run day-trip. If you can devote two or three days, however, you'd be better off moving camp to **Mae Salong**, a mountain-top Chinese enclave, or **Chiang Saen**, whose atmospheric ruins by the banks of the Mekong contrast sharply with the ugly commercialism of nearby **Sop Ruak**, the so-called Golden Triangle. Given more time and patience, you could also stop over at the palace, temple and arboretum of **Doi Tung** to look down over Thailand, Laos and Myanmar, and continue beyond Chiang Saen to **Chiang Khong** on the banks of the Mekong, which is now a popular crossing point to Laos.

For hopping around the main towns here by **public transport**, the setup is straightforward enough: frequent buses to Mae Sai run due north up Highway 1; to Chiang Saen and Sop Ruak, they start off on the same road before forking right onto Highway 1016; regular buses also run northeast from Chiang Rai to Chiang Khong; other routes are covered only by songthaews.

Hill Tribe Culture Centre and Ban Therd Thai

For driving to Mae Salong from Chiang Rai, locals recommend heading west from Mae Chan towards Tha Ton along Route 1089, then turning north at Ban Kew Satai along Route 1234, a longer journey but on slightly better roads. The old, more direct approach is on Route 1130, a dizzying, narrow rollercoaster of a road that ploughs its way westwards up to Mae Salong for 36km from **Ban Pasang**, 32km north of Chiang Rai on Highway 1. With your own transport, a few marginally interesting attractions might tempt you to stop along this route, notably the **Hill Tribe Culture Centre**, 12km from Ban Pasang, where there's a small hill-tribe handicrafts market, and a couple of Mien and Akha souvenir villages. At Sam Yaek, 24km from Ban Pasang, a paved side-road heads north for 13km to **Ban Therd Thai** ("Village to Honour Thailand"). In its former incarnation as Ban Hin Taek ("Village of Broken Stone"), this mixed village was the opium capital of the notorious Khun Sa (see page 361): the Thai army drove Khun Sa out after a pitched battle in 1983, and the village has now been renamed and "pacified" with the establishment of a market, school, hospital and even a Khun Sa museum in his former headquarters.

Mae Salong (Santikhiri)

Perched 1300m up on a ridge, commanding fine views of sawtoothed hills, stands the Chinese Nationalist outpost of **MAE SALONG** – the focal point for the area's fourteen thousand **Kuomintang**, who for three generations now have held fast to their cultural identity, if not their political cause. Though it has temples, churches and mosques, it's the details of Chinese life in the backstreets – the low-slung houses, the pictures of Chiang Kai-shek, ping-pong tables, the sounds of Yunnanese conversation – that make the village absorbing.

Mae Salong straggles for several kilometres along Highway 1130, which heads west to a central junction near the morning market, the 7–11 and the steps for the Princess Mother Pagoda, before turning southwards past the petrol station, a big souvenir market and the Thai Military Bank (the way out towards Tha Ton). It gets plenty of Thai visitors, especially at weekends in the cool season, when they come to admire the cherry blossoms and throng the main street's souvenir shops and stalls to buy such delicacies as sorghum whisky (pickled with ginseng, deer antler and centipedes) and locally grown Chinese tea, coffee, mushrooms and herbs. Free cups of tea are offered nearly everywhere, and it's possible to visit, for example, **Mae Salong Villa**'s own estate and factory – ask at the resort for directions and tea-processing times. It might also be worth braving the dawn chill to get to the **morning market**, held in the middle of town near *Shin Sane Guest House* between 6am and 8am, which pulls shoppers and vendors in from the surrounding Akha, Lisu and Mien villages.

Brief history

The ruling party of China for 21 years, the **Kuomintang** (Nationalists) were swept from power by the Communist revolution of 1949 and fled in two directions: one group, under party leader Chiang Kai-shek, made for Taiwan, where it founded the Republic of China; the other, led by General Li Zongren, settled in northern Thailand and Myanmar. The Nationalists' original plan to retake China from Mao Zedong in a two-pronged attack never came to fruition, and the remnants of the army in

DRUGS AND THE GOLDEN TRIANGLE

Opium will always be associated with the Far East in the popular imagination, but the opium poppy actually originated in the Mediterranean. It arrived in the East, however, over twelve centuries ago, and was later brought to Thailand from China with the hill tribes who migrated from Yunnan province. Opium growing was made illegal in Thailand in 1959, but during the 1960s and 1970s rampant production and refining of the crop in the lawless region on the borders of Thailand, Myanmar and Laos earned the area the nickname **the Golden Triangle**. Two main "armies" operated most of the trade within this area. The ten-thousand-strong **Shan United Army** (SUA), set up to fight the Burmese government for an independent state for the Shan (Thai Yai) people, funded itself from the production of heroin (a more refined form of opium). Led by the notorious warlord Khun Sa, the SUA attempted to extend their influence inside Thailand during the 1960s, where they came up against the troops of the **Kuomintang** (KMT). These refugees from China, who fled after the Communist takeover there, were at first befriended by the Thai and Western governments, who were pleased to have a fiercely anti-Communist force patrolling this border area. The Kuomintang were thus able to develop the heroin trade, while the authorities turned a blind eye.

By the 1980s, the danger of Communist incursion into Thailand had largely disappeared, and the government was able to concentrate on the elimination of the crop, putting the Kuomintang in the area around Mae Salong on a determined "**pacification**" programme. In 1983 the Shan United Army was pushed out of its stronghold at nearby Ban Hin Taek (now officially Ban Therd Thai), over the border into Myanmar, and in 1996, Khun Sa cut a deal with the corrupt Burmese military dictatorship. The man once dubbed the "Prince of Death", who had a US$2 million bounty on his head from the United States, was able to live under Burmese army protection in a comfortable villa in Yangon until his death in 2007.

The Thai government has succeeded in reducing the size of the opium crop within its borders to an insignificant amount, but Thailand still has a role to play as a conduit for heroin; most of the production and refinement of opium has simply moved over the borders into Myanmar and Laos. And in the last few years, opium growing within northern Thailand, although still at a very low level, has apparently started to increase again, based on small patches in remote mountains and using a high-yield, weather-resistant breed supplied by the Burmese drug barons.

The destruction of huge areas of poppy fields has had far-reaching repercussions on the **hill tribes**. In many cases, with the raw product not available, opium addicts have turned to injecting heroin from shared needles, leading to a devastating outbreak of AIDS. The Thai government has sought to give the hill tribes an alternative livelihood through the introduction of legitimate cash crops, yet these often demand the heavy use of pesticides, which later get washed down into the lowland valleys, incurring the wrath of Thai farmers.

The dangers of the heroin trade have in recent years been eclipsed by the flood of **methamphetamines** – either *yaa baa* (literally "crazy medicine") or the purer Ice (crystal meth) – that is infiltrating all areas of Thai society, but most worryingly the schools. Produced in vast quantities in factories just across the Burmese border, mostly by former insurgents, the United Wa State Army, *yaa baa* and Ice are the main objective of vehicle searches in border areas, with perhaps a billion tablets smuggled into Thailand each year. It's estimated that three million Thais are methamphetamine users, prompting the Thaksin government into a fierce crackdown in the first half of 2003 which, much to the consternation of human rights watchers, led to two thousand extra-judicial deaths and 51,000 arrests. Things have quietened down since then, but the frequent busts of methamphetamine dealers show that the problem has not gone away.

3

TREKS AND TOURS FROM MAE SALONG

Little Home Guest House produces a decent sketch map of Mae Salong's environs and staff can give out enough information to enable you to **walk** to some neighbouring hill-tribe and Chinese villages yourself. Alternatively, they can hook you up with an English-speaking Akha guide who leads **day-trips** on foot and/or by pick-up to Akha, Lahu and Lisu villages (from B1000/day); **homestays** in his village are also possible.

Thailand became major players in the **heroin trade** and, with the backing of the Thai government, minor protagonists in the war against Communism.

In the 1980s, the Thai government began to work hard to "pacify" the Kuomintang by a mixture of force and more peaceful methods, such as **crop programmes** to replace opium. Around Mae Salong at least, its work seems to have been successful, as evidenced by the slopes to the south of the settlement, which are covered with a carpet of rich green tea bushes. Since its rehabilitation, Mae Salong is now officially known as **Santikhiri** (Hill of Peace).

The Princess Mother Pagoda

Towering above the village on top of a hill, the **Princess Mother Pagoda**, a huge, gilt-topped chedi, is so distinctive that it has quickly become Mae Salong's proud symbol. It's a long and steep climb up 718 steps from near the morning market to get there, but with a rented vehicle you can follow the road to the southern end of the village and branch right beyond the bank on a road that carries you heavenward, revealing some breathtaking views on the way.

Chinese Martyrs Memorial Museum

At the southern edge of the village, on the way out towards Tha Ton • Daily 8am–5pm • B20

The **Chinese Martyrs Memorial Museum** recounts the origins of the Kuomintang in Thailand, giving details of battles such as the famous one fought against Thai and Lao Communists and Hmong at Phu Chi Fa near Chiang Khong, and depicting the Kuomintang as heroic protectors of the Kingdom of Thailand. The huge Chinese-style complex encompasses a shrine to the KMT martyrs who fell in the fighting.

ARRIVAL AND DEPARTURE   MAE SALONG

From Chiang Rai Buses (every 20min; 40min) leave Chiang Rai's old bus station for Mae Chan, 29km to the north on Highway 1. You'll then need to change to a green songthaew for the 1hr 30min–2hr chug up to Mae Salong from Mae Chan market, via Route 1089 and Ban Kew Satai (5 daily; last departure about 1pm). There are blue songthaews from Pasang, 3km north of Mae Chan on Highway 1, that head up the old Route 1130 to Mae Salong, but they only leave when full and are unreliable.

From Tha Ton There are four direct yellow songthaews a day between Tha Ton and Mae Salong (1hr 30min), via the interesting Akha village of Ban Lorcha (see page 353), with the last one leaving Tha Ton around noon.

Leaving Mae Salong When it's time to depart Mae Salong, you'll find the songthaews for Tha Ton and Mae Chan by *Little Home* and *Shin Shane* guesthouses, just west of the central junction.

By rented motorbike *Little Home Guest House* rents out motorbikes for B200/day.

ACCOMMODATION

You'll appreciate Mae Salong best if you spend the night here, after the day-trippers have left. Fortunately, there's a wide range of **accommodation**, including half a dozen budget guesthouses clustered around the central junction. Rates are significantly lower out of season, when the village feels wonderfully peaceful.

Baan Hom Muen Lee (Osmanthus House) Between the central junction and Mae Salong Villa, opposite

Sweet Mae Salong ☏ 053 765271, ⊕ baanhommuenlee. com. Boutique hotel done out in ochre and black paint and polished concrete adorned with Chinese calligraphy, where the spacious rooms provide fantastic views northwards from their large balconies and even from their bathrooms; they're equipped with platform beds, big-screen TVs, mini-bars and hot showers. B1200

★ **Little Home Guest House** Central junction ☏ 053

765389, ⓦmaesalonglittlehome.com. This friendly hillside spot offers smart bungalows in a tightly packed but pretty garden and new rooms with polished concrete floors and walls above their good Yunnanese restaurant, all with hot-water en-suite bathrooms and verandas/balconies. The staff bend over backwards to help guests in their explorations and make them feel at home. Fan B800, a/c B1000

Mae Salong Villa On the main road towards the eastern end of the village ☎053 765114–5, ⓦmaesalong-villa.com. Choose between large, comfortable rooms in a two-storey block and Chinese-style family bungalows with better views from their picture windows, all with hot showers and fridges. In a pretty, sloping garden facing the Princess Mother Pagoda and Burmese mountains. Breakfast included. B1200

Shin Sane Guest House Central junction ☎053 765026, ⓦshinsaneguesthouse.com. Prominent place with plenty of local information, offering small bedrooms with shared hot-water bathrooms in a funky wooden building and well-kept bungalows (with hot showers; B800) in the garden behind. B400

EATING

The choice of restaurants in Mae Salong is narrower than its hotel selection, but there are some excellent places to sample Yunnanese dishes.

Mae Salong Villa On the main road towards the eastern end of the village ☎053 765114–9. Has great views from its first-floor terrace and cooks up some of the best food in town, including delicious but expensive Chinese specialities like roast pork, *het hawm* (wild mushrooms) and *kai dam* (black chicken), which is usually served in soup with Chinese herbs (B300). Daily 7am–7.30pm.

Salima A short way west of the central junction before the bank. Welcoming Muslim-Chinese restaurant that rustles up delicious Yunnanese specialities such as deep-fried mushrooms in soy sauce (B120) and black chicken soup, as well as cheaper dishes on rice and noodle dishes (including beef and chicken khao soi; from B40) and fusion dishes such as spicy tuna and tea leaves salad. Daily 8am–8pm.

★ **Sweet Mae Salong** Between the central junction and Mae Salong Villa, on the south side of the road ☎089 874 9656. This place hits the spot with delicious, home-baked cakes and croissants, excellent espresso coffees, mellow sounds and awesome views from the rear terraces. Daily 8.30am–4.30pm.

Doi Tung

Steep, wooded hills rise abruptly from the plains west of Highway 1 as it approaches the Burmese border. Crowned both by a thousand-year-old wat and by the country retreat of the Princess Mother (the present king's late grandmother), the central peak here, 1322m **DOI TUNG**, makes a worthwhile outing just for the journey. A broad, new road, Route 1149, runs up the mountainside, beginning 43km north of Chiang Rai on Highway 1, just before the centre of **Ban Huai Khrai**.

Cottage Industries Centre and Outlet

Around 1km from Ban Huai Khrai • Daily 8.30am–4.30pm

The old road to the mountain from the centre of Ban Huai Khrai passes after 1km or so the **Cottage Industries Centre and Outlet**, set up by the Princess Mother, where you can watch crafts such as weaving, ceramics and paper-making from the bark of the *sa* (mulberry) tree in progress and buy the finished products in the on-site shop.

The Royal Villa complex

12km up the main summit road, then left up a side road • Royal Villa: daily 7am–6pm; closed if royals in residence • Villa B90; combined ticket to villa, Hall of Inspiration, Mae Fah Luang Garden & arboretum (see page 364) B220

The largely Swiss-style **Royal Villa** on Doi Tung was built for the Princess Mother (the grandmother of the present king, she was never queen herself, but was affectionately known as *Mae Fah Luang*, literally "royal sky mother"). She took up residence here on several occasions to work on development projects in the area, before her death in 1995.

In the Grand Reception Hall, which also features some beautiful floral wall panels made of embroidered silk, the positions of the planets and stars at the time of the Princess Mother's birth in 1900 have been carved into the ceiling. You can also visit her living room, bedroom and study, all left as when she lived here.

The Hall of Inspiration and the gardens

Hall of Inspiration Daily 8am–6pm · B90 **Mae Fah Luang Garden** Daily 6.30am–6pm · B90

On the access road to the Royal Villa, a few hundred metres back down the hill, the **Hall of Inspiration** contains hagiographical displays on the Princess Mother and her family and is strictly for royal-watchers. Next door, the immaculate ornamental **Mae Fah Luang Garden** throngs with snap-happy day-trippers at weekends. The Princess Mother's hill-tribe project has helped to develop local villages by introducing new agricultural methods: the slopes which were formerly blackened by the fires of slash-and-burn farming and sown with opium poppies are now used to grow teak and pine, and crops such as strawberries, macadamia nuts and coffee, which, along with pottery, *sa* paper, rugs and clothes, are sold in the shops and stalls near the entrance to the gardens. There's also an information booth that has simple maps of the mountain here.

Wat Phra That Doi Tung

Beyond the turn-off for the Royal Villa, a paved road heads northeast, climbing over a precarious saddle with some minor temple buildings and passing through a tuft of thick woods, before reaching **Wat Phra That Doi Tung** on top of the mountain. Pilgrims to the wat earn themselves good fortune by clanging the rows of dissonant bells around the temple compound and by throwing coins into a well, which are collected for temple funds. For non-Buddhist travellers, the reward for getting this far is the stunning view out over the cultivated slopes and half of northern Thailand. The wat's most important structures are its twin **chedis**, erected to enshrine relics of the Buddha's left collarbone in 911. When the building of the chedis was complete, King Achutaraj of Ngon Yang ordered a giant flag (*tung*), reputedly 2km long, to be flown from the peak, which gave the mountain its name.

Mae Fah Luang Arboretum

Daily 8am–6pm · B90

A very steep, sometimes rough, paved **back road** runs right along the border with Myanmar to Mae Sai (22km), via two army checkpoints and the Akha village of Ban Pha Mee, beginning near the saddle beneath the peak of Doi Tung. After about 4km of asphalt, you reach the delightful **arboretum** at the pinnacle of **Doi Chang Moob** (1509m), a landscaped garden planted with rhododendrons, azaleas, orchids and ferns and furnished with fantastic terrace viewpoints looking east to Chiang Saen, the Mekong and the hills of Laos beyond, and west to the mountains around Mae Salong. For the most awesome view, however, continue a short way up the Mae Sai road to the Thai military checkpoint, to gaze at the opposing Burmese camp and seemingly endless layers of Burmese mountain stacked up to the north.

ARRIVAL AND DEPARTURE   DOI TUNG

It's best to rent a vehicle from Chiang Rai or Mae Sai to explore Doi Tung. Otherwise, any bus between Chiang Rai and Mae Sai can put you off in Ban Huai Khrai, where you'll have to charter a songthaew (about B600) to take you up the mountain and back.

ACCOMMODATION AND EATING

There's a Doi Tung coffee shop, an excellent restaurant and a self-service café on the access road to the Royal Villa, in the complex of shops near Mae Fah Luang Garden.

Doi Tung Lodge In the woods below the Royal Villa ☏ 053 767015–7, ⓦ doitung.org. The spacious, bright, recently refurbished rooms at this upmarket, two-storey tourist lodge are set in tranquil, pretty gardens and all come with a/c, hot water, balcony, TV and fridge. Breakfast included. **B3000**

Mae Sai

With its bustling border crossing into Myanmar and kilometres of tacky souvenir stalls, **MAE SAI** can be an interesting place to watch the world go by, though most

foreigners only come here on a quick visa run. Thailand's most northerly town lies 61km from Chiang Rai at the dead end of Highway 1, which forms the town's single north–south street. Wide enough for an armoured battalion, this ugly boulevard still has the same name – **Thanon Phaholyothin**, after an early-twentieth-century general and revolutionary leader – as at the start of its thousand-kilometre journey north at Bangkok's Victory Monument. The road ends at the Mae Sai River, which here serves as the Thailand–Myanmar border.

For a lofty perspective on the comings and goings, climb up through the market stalls to the supposedly second-century BC chedi of **Wat Phra That Doi Wao**, which enshrines some of the Buddha's hair, five minutes' walk from the bridge on the west side of Phaholyothin, behind the *Top North Hotel*. As well as Doi Tung to the south and the hills of Laos in the east, you get a good view up the steep-sided valley and across the river to Thachileik.

ARRIVAL AND DEPARTURE   MAE SAI

By bus From Chiang Rai, frequent non-a/c buses and a/c minibuses to Mae Sai run due north up Highway 1. They stop 4km short of the frontier at the bus station, from where shared songthaews shuttle into town. Returning to the bus station, the songthaews head off from the corner of Soi 2 on the east side of Thanon Phaholyothin, about 50m south of the border bridge, or you should be able to flag one down further along its route.

Destinations Bangkok (12 daily; 12–13hr); Chiang Mai (6–8 daily; 4hr 40min–5hr 15min); Chiang Rai (every 20min; 1hr–1hr 30min); Mae Sot (1 daily; 10–11hr); Phitsanulok (6 daily; 8–9hr); Tha Ton (1 daily; 1hr 40min).

GETTING AROUND

By motorbike Motorbikes can be rented from Pornchai, about 500m south of the bridge on the west side of Thanon Phaholyothin, for B250/day.

ACCOMMODATION AND EATING

The huge night market that stretches far down Thanon Phaholyothin from the border is the best place to eat in the evening.

★ **Navy Home** About 1km south of the bridge on the east side of Thanon Phaholyothin ☎ 053 732929, ⓦ navyhome.com. Owned by a retired admiral, this hotel greets guests with a gangway over a pond, a display of his ceremonial uniforms and "Welcome aboard" signs, not to mention spent naval missile casings. It's even shaped like a ship and, although some of the rooms are cabin-like in size, they're all neat, clean and, well, shipshape, with a/c, hot showers, fridges and TVs. B500

Piyaporn Pavilion Just off the west side of Thanon Phaholyothin about 500m south of the bridge ☎ 053 731395, ⓦ piyapornpavilion.com. This imposing seven-storey block is one of Mae Sai's best hotels, with well-equipped rooms in a smart, contemporary style, plus a/c, hot-water bathtubs, TVs and fridges. B1120

Rim Nam (Riverside) Right under the western side of the bridge, down a slip road to the left of the border checkpoint. A popular, reasonably priced restaurant with a riverside terrace, which gets crowded during the day with tourists watching the border action and serves cheap one-dish meals as well as its speciality, crab with curry powder (B300). Daily 7/8am–8/9pm.

Sai Lom Joy 5min walk west of the bridge along the riverside Thanon Sailomjoy (Soi Tessaban 21) ☎ 081 952 1249, ⓦ sailomjoy.com. New boutique hotel with lots of Lanna design touches and a waterfall fountain in its relaxing garden. Spacious tiled rooms done out in earth tones come with a/c, hot showers and TVs. Breakfast included. B1200

Sop Ruak

The "**Golden Triangle**", a term originally coined to denote a huge opium-producing area spreading across Myanmar, Laos and Thailand, has, for the benefit of tourists, been artificially concentrated into the precise spot where the borders meet, 70km northeast of Chiang Rai. Don't come to the village of **SOP RUAK**, at the confluence of the Ruak (Mae Sai) and Mekong rivers, expecting to come across sinister drug-runners or poppy fields – instead you'll find souvenir stalls, pay-toilets, a huge, supremely tacky golden Buddha shrine, two opium museums and lots of signs saying "Golden Triangle" which pop up in a million photo albums around the world.

CROSSING THE MYANMAR BORDER TO THACHILEIK

Thanon Phaholyothin ends at a short pedestrianized **bridge** over the Mae Sai River, which forms the border with Myanmar. Armed with a visa, you can enter the country here, notably for trips to the historic Thai Yai (Shan) town of Keng Tung. Even without a visa, you can have the dubious pleasure, during daylight hours, of crossing over to **Thachileik**, the Burmese town opposite, for yet more tacky shopping. You'll first be stamped out by **Thai immigration** at the entrance to the bridge, then on the other side of the bridge, you pay US$10, or an exorbitant B500, to Burmese immigration for a one-day stay. Coming back across the bridge, unless you already have a multiple-entry Thai visa or re-entry permit, you'll be given a new fifteen-day entry stamp (the "tourist visa exemption") – thirty days for UK, US, Canadian and other G7 citizens – by Thai immigration. However, note that you're only allowed two tourist visa exemptions per year and that visa requirements change frequently – go to the forums on ⓦ thaivisa.com for the latest information.

Hall of Opium
At the Mae Sai end of the village • Tues–Sun 8.30am–5.30pm, last ticket sale 4pm • B200 • ⓦ doitung.org

Under the auspices of the Mae Fah Luang Foundation based at Doi Tung (see page 363), the ambitious **Hall of Opium** took B400 million and nine years to research and build, with technical assistance from the People's Republic of China. It provides a well-presented, largely balanced picture, in Thai and English, of the use and abuse of opium, and its history over five thousand years, including its spread from Europe to Asia and focusing on the nineteenth-century **Opium Wars** between Britain and China. Dioramas, games and audiovisuals are put to imaginative use, notably in a reconstruction of a nineteenth-century Siamese opium den, playing the interactive "Find the Hidden Drugs", and, most movingly, watching the personal testimonies of former addicts and their families.

House of Opium
On the main through-road near Wat Phra That Phu Khao • Daily 7am–7pm • B50

The **House of Opium** is smaller and cheaper than the similarly named Hall of Opium, which it imitates, and it tends more to glorify opium use. All the paraphernalia of opium growing and smoking is housed in several display cases, including beautifully carved teak storage boxes, weights cast from bronze and brass in animal shapes, and opium pipes.

The meeting of the waters
The confluence of the Ruak (Mae Sai) and Mekong rivers is undoubtedly monumental, but to get an unobstructed view of it you'll need to climb up to **Wat Phra That Phu Khao**, a 1250-year-old temple perched on a small hill above the village. To the north, beyond the puny Ruak River, you'll see the mountains of Myanmar marching off into infinity, while eastwards across the mighty Mekong are the hills and villages of Laos. This pastoral scene has now been marred, however, by the appearance of a Thai luxury hotel, which is actually over on an uninhabited strip of Burmese land immediately upstream of the confluence. The attached casino bypasses Thai laws against gambling, and the usually strict border formalities are waived for visitors coming from Thailand.

ARRIVAL AND DEPARTURE   **SOP RUAK**

By songthaew from Mae Sai Blue songthaews make the 45min trip in the morning to Sop Ruak's main river road from the corner of Soi 8 on the east side of Thanon Phaholyothin, about 300m south of the bridge in Mae Sai (they leave when they're full, sometimes only twice a day). **By songthaew or bicycle from Chiang Saen** You can take a blue songthaew from (and back to) Thanon Phaholyothin in Chiang Saen (best in the morning; 15min) or rent a bike and cycle there – it's an easy 10km ride on a quiet dual carriageway, which will give you the chance to gawp at the domes and half-built tower blocks of Kapok City, a Chinese-owned casino town across on the Lao bank of the Mekong.

A QUICK TRIP TO LAOS

Sop Ruak puts you tantalizingly close to Laos and, even if you don't have time to spend exploring the country properly, you can still have the thrill of stepping on Lao soil. A **longtail boat** from next to *Siwan Restaurant*, for example, will give you a kiss-me-quick tour of the "Golden Triangle" (B500), including a stop at a souvenir market on the Lao island of Done Xao (B30 admission).

ACCOMMODATION

There's nowhere decent to stay in Sop Ruak for budget travellers, but for those willing to splurge, there are some excellent options on the outskirts of the village, including a couple of places that offer great views of the Mekong River.

★**Anantara Golden Triangle Elephant Camp & Resort** Opposite the Hall of Opium, at the Mae Sai end of the village ☎ 053 784084, ⓦ goldentriangle. anantara.com. Tastefully designed in a blend of traditional and contemporary styles and set in huge, peaceful grounds, this palatial luxury hotel is one of the finest in northern Thailand. The balconies of all its rooms and its swimming pool offer breathtaking views over the countryside to the Mekong, Myanmar and the hills of Laos. Rates include round-trip limousine transfers from Chiang Rai airport, full-board meals, drinks and a range of daily activities, notably programmes at their excellent elephant camp (ⓦ helpingelephants.org), treatments at the spectacular spa, and Thai cooking classes. B44,800

Greater Mekong Lodge In the Golden Triangle Park, next to the Hall of Opium ☎ 053 784450–2, ⓦ doitung. org. Good-value if slightly institutional rooms, all with a balcony, fridge, hot water and a/c. You can choose between rooms in the main hotel building or stilted chalets (where the views are better). Includes breakfast. B1200

Serene at Chiang Rai About 500m south of the House of Opium, on the riverside ☎ 053 784500, ⓦ sereneatchiangrai.com. As well as good service, a handy location and an elegant pool right by the Mekong, this place offers big, contemporary a/c rooms with balconies and an all-day café on a riverside terrace. "River-view" rooms cost about B600 more than the cheapest "city-view" rooms. Breakfast included. B1800

EATING

As well as the places listed below, there's a row of ramshackle **restaurants** by the waterfront, serving up basic Thai food and some decent fruit shakes.

Baan Dhalia At the Anantara ☎ 053 784084, ⓦ golden triangle.anantara.com. This opulent Italian restaurant serves a wide range of antipasti, pizzas, Mediterranean main courses and an imaginative menu of pastas, such as pumpkin ravioli with saffron gazpacho and olive salsa (B560) and spaghetti prepared tableside in a parmesan wheel with black truffle cream (B1150). The resort's other restaurant, Sala Mae Nam, offers very good Thai and Western lunches and dinners on a panoramic terrace. Daily 6.30–11pm.

Siwan In front of the Imperial Golden Triangle Hotel, along the main river road. The best of the riverfront restaurants, welcoming *Siwan* specializes in *tom yam pla* (spicy and sour soup with river fish; B220), but also offers cheaper dishes such as fried rice (from B60), as well as great views of the Mekong. Daily 7am–8.30pm.

Chiang Saen

Combining dozens of tumbledown temple ruins with sweeping Mekong River scenery, **CHIANG SAEN**, 60km northeast of Chiang Rai, is a good base camp for the border region east of Mae Sai. The town's focal point, where the Chiang Rai road (Thanon Phaholyothin) meets Thanon Rim Khong (the main road along the banks of the Mekong), is a lively junction thronged by buses, songthaews and longtails and lined with market stalls selling goods from China. Turning left at this T-junction soon brings you to Sop Ruak, and you may well share the road with the tour buses that sporadically thunder through (though most of them miss out the town itself by taking its western bypass). Very few tourists turn right in Chiang Saen, passing the busy port for cargo boats from China, along the road to Chiang Khong, even though this is the best way to appreciate the slow charms of the Mekong valley.

The layout of the old, ruined city is defined by the Mekong River running along its east flank; a tall rectangle, 2.5km from north to south, is formed by the addition of the ancient ramparts, now fetchingly overgrown, on the other three sides. The grid of leafy streets inside the ramparts is now too big for the modern town, which is generously scattered along the river road and across the middle on Thanon Phaholyothin.

Brief history

Originally known as Yonok, the region around Chiang Saen seems to have been an important Thai trading crossroads from some time after the seventh century. The city of Chiang Saen itself was founded around 1328 by the successor to the renowned King Mengrai of Chiang Mai, Saen Phu, who gave up his throne to retire here. Coveted for its strategic location guarding the Mekong, Chiang Saen had multiple allegiances, paying tribute to Chiang Mai, Keng Tung in Myanmar and Luang Prabang in Laos, until Rama I razed the place in 1804. The present village was established only in 1881, when Rama V ordered a northern prince to resettle the site with descendants of the old townspeople mustered from Lamphun, Chiang Mai and Lampang, to reinforce the extent of Thai rule in the face of increasing colonial interest.

National Museum

Thanon Phaholyothin, just inside the old city walls • Wed–Sun 9am–4pm • B100

The **National Museum** makes an informative starting point for a visit, housing some impressive architectural features rescued from the surrounding ruins, with good labelling in English, as well as a plethora of Buddha images – the two typical northern Thai styles of Buddha are sometimes referred to jointly as the "Chiang Saen style", though most academics instead use the more helpful term "Lanna style" (see page 283). As in many of Thailand's museums, the back end is given over to exhibits on folk culture, one of many highlights being the beautiful wooden lintel carved with *hum yon* (floral swirls representing testicles), which would have been placed above the front door of a house to ward off evil and for ventilation.

Wat Phra That Chedi Luang

Thanon Phaholyothin, next door to the museum

Wat Phra That Chedi Luang, originally the city's main temple, is worth looking in on for its imposing octagonal chedi, said to house a relic of the Buddha's breastbone and now decorated with a huge yellow ribbon, while handicraft stalls in the grounds sell Thai Lue cloths among their wares. In March 2011, a 6.8-magnitude earthquake rocked Myanmar, and the aftershocks (felt strongly in Chiang Saen) caused the top of the spire to break off, though it's since been rather cack-handedly restored.

Wat Pa Sak

Just beyond the ramparts to the west • Open access, but there's a B50 admission fee if the custodian's around

Wat Pa Sak's brick buildings and laterite columns have been excavated and restored by the Fine Arts Department, making it the most accessible and impressive of Chiang Saen's many temples. The wat's name is an allusion to the hundreds of teak trees that Saen Phu planted in the grounds when he built the chedi in 1340 to house relics of the Buddha's right ankle from India. The chedi's square base is inset with niches housing alternating Buddhas and *deva* (angels) with flowing skirts, and above rises the tower for

the Buddha relic, topped by a circular spire. Beautiful carved stucco covers much of the structure, showing intricate floral scrolls and stylized lotus patterns as well as a whole zoo of mythical beasts.

Wat Phra That Chom Kitti
Outside the northwest corner of the ramparts

The open space around modern Chiang Saen, which is dotted with trees and another 140 overgrown ruins (both inside and outside the ramparts), is great for a carefree wander. A spot worth aiming for is the gold-topped, crooked chedi of tenth-century **Wat Phra That Chom Kitti** out on the western bypass, which houses yet another relic of the Buddha himself and gives a good view of the town and the river from a small hill.

Wat Phra That Pha Ngao
3km southeast along the river road – look out for the tall brick gate on the right

Wat Phra That Pha Ngao, well worth the short detour from the centre, is thought to have been the main temple of the Yonok principality, built originally in the sixth century. The temple contains a supposedly miraculous chedi perched on top of a large boulder, but the real attraction is the **new chedi** on the hillside above: take the 1km track which starts at the back of the temple and you can't miss the gleaming, white-tiled Phra Borom That Nimit, designed by an American, with attractive modern murals and built over and around a ruined brick chedi. From here, though you have to peer through the trees, the views take in Chiang Saen, the wide plain and the slow curve of the river. To the east, the Kok River, which looks so impressive at Chiang Rai, seems like a stream as it pours into the mighty Mekong. On the way down from the chedi, have a look at the new Lao-style viharn, which was inaugurated by Princess Sirindhorn in 1999 and is covered from tip to toe in beautiful woodcarving.

ARRIVAL AND DEPARTURE
CHIANG SAEN

By bus or songthaew Non-a/c buses and a/c minibuses from Chiang Rai (every 20min; 1hr–1hr 30min) and, in the morning, blue songthaews from Mae Sai (roughly 2 daily; 1hr) via Sop Ruak (15min) stop by the market on Thanon Phaholyothin. Songthaews from Chiang Khong (2hr; best done in the morning, usually involving a change at the Thai Lue weaving village of Ban Hat Bai) stop on the river road to the south of the T-junction. Motorized samlors wait to ferry people around town.

GETTING AROUND

By boat Speedboats congregate along the riverside near the central T-junction, offering local tours of the "Golden Triangle" lasting a couple of hours (B700), including the Lao souvenir market on Done Xao island (B30 admission).
By bicycle or motorbike To get around the ruins and the surrounding countryside, bicycles (B80/day) and motorbikes (B200/day) can be rented from the no-name barber shop opposite the Bangkok Bank on Thanon Phaholyothin. Motorbikes are also available for B200 at *Gin's Maekhong View Resort*. Fat Free, about 1km north of the T-junction on Thanon Rim Khong (☎086 430 5523, ⓦ fatfreebike.com), rents good sit-up-and-beg bicycles for B100/day and mountain bikes from B200/day.

INFORMATION

Tourist information The municipal tourist office (Mon–Fri 8am–4pm; ☎053 777084) on Thanon Phaholyothin, opposite the National Museum, houses some forlorn exhibits on the architecture and conservation of Chiang Saen and hands out a simple map of the city.

ACCOMMODATION

★ **Gin's Maekhong View Resort and Spa** Outside the ramparts, about 2km north of the T-junction ☎053 650847, ⓦ ginmaekhongview.com and ⓦ facebook. com/ginsmaekhongview (for bookings); map p.369. Set around a pretty lawn and an attractive, small swimming pool on the river side of Thanon Rim Khong, the a/c rooms and pricier bungalows at this friendly, clued-up resort are bright, tasteful and well equipped. All have verandas/balconies that offer vistas of the Mekong and a dry-season field of sunflowers, a view that's shared by the resort's café-restaurant. A few cheaper rooms (B680) in a thatched wooden "cowboy house" are also available. B1100

Pak Ping Rim Khong About 500m north of the T-junction ☎053 650151, ⓦfacebook.com/pakpingrimkhong; map p.369. Friendly boutique hotel with a pleasant garden area, where the bright, contemporary rooms are decked out with dark wooden furniture, crisp white linen and a few splashes of colour, and equipped with a/c, hot showers and fridges. Breakfast included. B1000

Tan Rak Home Just off Thanon Rim Khong, 250m north of the T-junction, down the soi by Chiang Saen Guesthouse ☎089 434 4345; map p.369. Friendly guesthouse in a modern, two-storey building providing clean, colourfully painted, tiled-floor rooms with a/c, TV, fridge and hot shower. B400

EATING

Food in Chiang Saen is nothing special; you could do worse than try the **street-food stalls** on the riverfront promenade just north of the T-junction, where you can sprawl on mats at low tables in the evening, followed by a drink at one of the small, lively bars opposite. On Saturday evenings, this stretch of Thanon Rim Khong becomes a "**walking street**" market, selling plenty of food and handicrafts.

Khong View Station Thanon Rim Khong, about 2km north of the T-junction, between Gin's Resort and the bypass ☎081 991 7301; map p.369. This appealing bar-restaurant gets its name from a railway carriage on the imaginary "Chiang Saen–Sipsongpanna" line that's now marooned on the property (Xishuangbanna, as the Chinese call it, is an ethnically Thai prefecture about 300km north up the Mekong in Yunnan). At the shady outdoor tables with views of the river, you can tuck into espresso coffees (during the day), cheap beer and good Thai food such as fried rice with naem (northern fermented sausage) and Mekong catfish fried with garlic (B150). Daily 7.30am–11pm.

Samying Thanon Phaholyothin, on the west side of the Krung Thai bank ☎053 777040; map p.369. Popular with locals, this is a cheap, clean, well-run restaurant serving river fish in various preparations (around B150), chicken khao soi (B40) and good Thai salads. Daily 7am–4pm.

Chiang Khong and around

As one of the jumping-off points into Laos from Thailand, **CHIANG KHONG** is constantly bustling with travellers waiting to go over the river to the Lao town of Houayxai and embark on the lovely Mekong boat journey down to Luang Prabang. On a high, steep bank above the water, Chiang Khong is strung out along a single, north–south street, Thanon Sai Klang, which runs down to the fishing port of Ban Hat Khrai. Once you've admired the elevated view of the traffic on the Mekong and glimpsed the ruined, red-brick turrets of the French-built Fort Carnot in Houayxai, there's little to do in the town itself. On Friday mornings, there's a bustling **market** at the District Office, while two "walking street" markets operate on weekend evenings: Fridays at Ban Hat Khrai, Saturdays on the main street in front of Wat Phra Kaew.

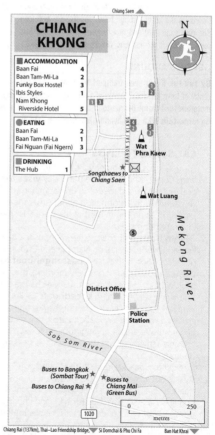

Chiang Saen ▲

CHIANG KHONG

N

3

■ ACCOMMODATION
Baan Fai	4
Baan Tam-Mi-La	2
Funky Box Hostel	3
Ibis Styles	1
Nam Khong Riverside Hotel	5

● EATING
Baan Fai	2
Baan Tam-Mi-La	1
Fai Nguan (Fai Ngern)	3

■ DRINKING
The Hub	1

Wat
Phra Kaew

Songthaews to
Chiang Saen

Wat Luang

Mekong River

District Office

Police
Station

Sob Som River

Buses to Bangkok
(Sombat Tour) ★
★ Buses to
Chiang Mai
(Green Bus)
Buses to Chiang Rai ★

1020

0   250
metres

Chiang Rai (137km), Thai–Lao Friendship Bridge, ▼ Si Dornchai & Phu Chi Fa   Ban Hat Khrai ▼

3

BOAT TRIPS ON THE MEKONG

If you're twiddling your thumbs in Chiang Khong while waiting to cross to Laos, or simply want to spend some time out on the water, ask at your guesthouse about one-hour **boat trips** on the Mekong (B700) from a pier near Wat Luang. As you leave Chiang Khong itself and chug past sandy outcrops, it's likely you'll catch glimpses of villagers fishing, playing or washing in the river (usually met with big smiles and lots of frantic waving).

ARRIVAL AND DEPARTURE
CHIANG KHONG

By bus or a/c minibus Direct buses between Chiang Khong and Chiang Rai follow three different routes taking roughly 2hr, 2hr 30min or 3hr (each route approximately hourly, from Chiang Rai's old bus station); be sure to ask for the quickest time, *sawng chuamohng*. All buses arriving in Chiang Khong stop on the main road at the south end of town, except services to Laos and some to Bangkok, which use the Baw Khaw Saw terminal on Route 1020, 4km south of town towards the new Mekong bridge. Because of the popularity of the border crossing here, there are now direct buses from and to Chiang Mai run by the Green Bus Company, as well as tourist a/c minibuses; you can arrange tickets for the latter through travel agents such as Queen Bee (see page 286) and guesthouses. Nok Air offer fast combination flight-and-bus tickets between Bangkok's

Don Muang Airport and Chiang Khong, via Chiang Rai Airport.

Destinations Bangkok (9 daily; 13hr); Chiang Mai (2 daily; 5–6hr); Chiang Rai (roughly every 20min; 2–3hr); Luang Prabang, Laos (4 weekly; 15hr).

By songthaew from/to Chiang Saen This 2hr journey is best done in the early morning and usually involves a change of vehicle at Ban Hat Bai. In Chiang Khong, songthaews drop off and leave from the roadside near the post office.

By car from/to Chiang Saen If you're driving yourself between Chiang Saen and Chiang Khong, it's more scenic to branch off the direct Route 1129 onto the winding, paved roads that hug the northward kink in the Mekong River.

GETTING AROUND

By tuk-tuk If you need transport from the bus to the centre of town, the local version of a tuk-tuk (a converted motorbike) will charge B40/person.

By mountain bike Good hybrid bikes (B100/day) can be

rented from *The Hub* (see page 373).

By motorbike or car *Baan Fai* rents motorbikes for around B300/day, cars for around B1500/day.

CROSSING TO LAOS

Tourists cross the border via the Fourth Thai-Lao Friendship Bridge, 8km downstream from Chiang Khong, where thirty-day **visas for Laos** are available on arrival (US$30 or B1500 and up, depending on nationality, plus $1 overtime fee after 4pm and at weekends) – for information about other means of getting a Lao visa, see Basics (see page 30). As paying in baht at the border is so unfavourable, banks and gold shops in Chiang Khong sell dollars.

From Houayxai, the Lao town opposite Chiang Khong, there are buses to Luang Prabang, Vientiane, Luang Namtha and Oudomxai, for example, but by far the most popular option is to catch a **passenger boat to Luang Prabang**. Generally departing between 10am and noon every morning, these glide down the scenic Mekong in two days, with an overnight and usually a change of boat at Pakbeng. An alternative is to take one of the early-morning **speedboats** (6–7hr), on which passengers should be provided with helmets and life jackets, but they're cramped, noisy and dangerous. More luxurious cruises down to Luang Prabang are also available, including an ultra-luxe two-night trip aboard the Anantara hotel group's Boheme, a thirteen-cabin barge with an on-board spa and activities along the way such as trekking, mountain-biking and cooking classes (W anantara.com).

To get to Houayxai from Chiang Khong, you'll need to catch a tuk-tuk to the bridge, then a shuttle bus across the bridge, then a songthaew on the Lao side to the pier for Luang Prabang boats in Houayxai – your best option is to book a passenger boat ticket through a travel agent or guesthouse such as *Baan Fai* in Chiang Khong for around B1350, which will include all transport from your guesthouse to the pier in Houayxai.

3

GIANT CATFISH

The **Mekong giant catfish** (*pla buk*) is the largest scaleless freshwater fish in the world, measuring up to 3m in length and weighing up to 300kg. Chiang Khong has traditionally been the catfish capital of the north, attracting fish merchants and restaurateurs from Chiang Rai, Chiang Mai and Bangkok – the mild, tasty meat of the *pla buk* is prized for its fine, soft texture, and one fish can fetch up to B100,000. The **catfish season** (when water levels in the river are low) is officially opened at the port of Ban Hat Khrai on April 18 with much pomp, including an elaborate ceremony by Thai and Lao fishermen to appease Chao Por Pla Buk, the giant catfish god. However, the fish is threatened by new (and proposed) dams on the Mekong in China and Laos, which affect water levels, and by the dynamiting of rapids to allow passage of large cargo boats to and from China – a plan to blast the stretch from Chiang Saen all the way down to Luang Prabang is currently being resisted by environmentalists. The season's haul used to be between thirty and sixty fish all told, but recent years have been so disappointing (some with no catches at all) that Thailand's Fishery Department has set up an artificial spawning programme.

ACCOMMODATION

Baan Fai 27 Thanon Sai Klang ☎053 791394, ✉baanfai-chiangkhong@hotmail.com; map p.371. This welcoming spot has a wide variety of rooms, from singles with shared hot showers (B200) to newly renovated doubles with fridges and attached hot-water bathrooms, in some nice old wooden houses tightly packed onto a small plot of land in front of *Nam Khong Riverside Hotel*. Fan B350, a/c B500

★ **Baan Tam-Mi-La** Soi 1, Thanon Sai Klang (signposted down a lane in the middle of town among a cluster of shops) ☎053 791234, ✉baantammila@gmail.com; map p.371. With helpful staff and a scenic, easy-going riverfront location, this place has tasteful, well-designed rooms and wooden bungalows on a leafy slope, with en-suite hot showers, and sells good hammocks. Basic bicycles free for guests to use. Fan B450, a/c B700

Funky Box Hostel Soi 2, Thanon Sai Klang ☎093 278 2928, ⓦfunkyboxhostel.com; map p.371. This hostel owned by *The Hub* (see page 373) does what it says on the tin: one large, fan-cooled, shed-like dormitory, decorated in bright, funky colours, is equipped with comfy beds, lockers and three hot-water bathrooms. They now also offer bright, fan-cooled private rooms with polished wood floors, shared hot showers and free use of bicycles (decent rates for singles). Good breakfasts can be had at the pub. Dorms B100, doubles B350

Ibis Styles Thanon Sai Klang ☎053 792008, ⓦibis.com; map p.371. This new outlet of the French Accor group offers tasteful, well-designed, upmarket rooms with all the usual amenities (half of them with river views) and a great, infinity-edge, riverfront swimming pool. Breakfast included. B1380

Nam Khong Riverside Hotel Thanon Sai Klang ☎053 791796, ⓦnamkhongriverside.com; map p.371. Low-rise, forty room hotel set around a pretty riverside garden with a river-view restaurant and smartly furnished rooms, all with a/c, hot water, fridges, balconies and Mekong views. Accordingly, ground-floor rooms tend to be cheapest. B1000

EATING

Baan Fai 27 Thanon Sai Klang ☎053 791394; map p.371. With some nice, shady streetside tables and a souvenir shop selling Thai Lue textiles, this welcoming guesthouse café serves decent espresso coffees, fruit shakes, all-day breakfasts and sandwiches (B70). Daily 6.30am–10pm.

Baan Tam-Mi-La 113 Thanon Sai Klang ☎053 791234; map p.371. Excellent guesthouse terrace restaurant with a sweeping view of the river, making it an ideal spot to while away the time. Very good Thai food, lots of vegetarian options and a few Western dishes, plus espressos, home-baked cakes and bread, and hearty breakfasts. Daily 7am–7pm.

Fai Nguan (Fai Ngern) Nam Khong Riverside Hotel, Thanon Sai Klang ☎053 791796; map p.371. Well-appointed hotel restaurant with great views of the river and a wide range of Thai dishes, notably salads (B150) and northern specialities. Daily 6.30am–9/10pm.

DRINKING

The Hub Soi 2, Thanon Sai Klang; map p.371. Fun, lively and sociable bar with a pool table, board games and Western comfort food such as fish'n'chips (plus veggie and vegan options), run by a Liverpudlian who used to hold the world record for going round the world on a bike (106 days). Daily 4–11pm.

The east coast

KO CHANG NATIONAL MARINE PARK, KO MAK

The east coast

Just a few hours' drive from the capital, the east-coast resorts attract a mixed crowd of weekending Bangkokians and sybaritic tourists. Transport connections are good and, for overlanders, there are several Cambodian border crossings within reach. Beautiful beaches aren't the whole picture, however, as the east coast is also crucial to Thailand's industrial economy, its natural gas fields and deep-sea ports having spawned massive development along the first 200km of coastline, an area dubbed the Eastern Seaboard. The initial landscape of refineries and depots shouldn't deter you though, as offshore it's an entirely different story, with beaches as glorious as more celebrated southern retreats and enough peaceful havens to make it worth packing your hammock.

The first worthwhile stop comes 100km east of Bangkok at the town of **Si Racha**, which is the point of access for tiny **Ko Si Chang**, whose dramatically rugged coastlines and low-key atmosphere make it a restful retreat. In complete contrast, nearby **Pattaya** is Thailand's number one package-tour destination, its customers predominantly middle-aged European men enticed by the resort's sex-market reputation, or snap-happy, package-tour groups, all undeterred by its lacklustre beach. Things soon look up, though, as the coast veers sharply eastwards towards Ban Phe, revealing the island of **Ko Samet**, the prettiest of the beach resorts within comfortable bus-ride range of Bangkok.

East of Ban Phe, the landscape becomes lusher and hillier around **Chanthaburi**, the dynamo of Thailand's gem trade and one of only two eastern provincial capitals worth visiting. The other is **Trat**, 68km further along the highway, and an important hub for transport, both into **Cambodia** via Hat Lek – one of this region's two main border points, the other being Aranyaprathet (see page 379) – and to the 52 islands of the Ko Chang Marine National Park. The most popular of this island group is large, forested **Ko Chang** itself, whose long, fine beaches have made it an appealing alternative to Phuket or Ko Samui on the southern peninsula. A host of smaller, less-developed islands fills the sea between Ko Chang and the Cambodian coast, most notably temptingly diverse **Ko Mak** and **Ko Kood**, which lie outside the national park boundaries.

GETTING AROUND   THE EAST COAST

By bus Highway 3 extends almost the entire length of the east coast, beginning in Bangkok as Thanon Sukhumvit, and known as such when it cuts through towns, and hundreds of buses ply the route, connecting all major mainland destinations. It's also possible to travel between the east coast and the northeast and north without doubling back through the capital: the most direct routes into Isaan start from Pattaya, Rayong and Chanthaburi.

By plane Bangkok's Suvarnabhumi Airport (see page 132) is less than 50km from Si Racha, and there are two domestic airports along the east coast itself: at U-Tapao naval base, southeast of Pattaya, and just west of Trat.

By train Though a rail line connects Bangkok with Si Racha and Pattaya, it is served by just one slow train a day in each direction; a branch line makes two journeys a day to Aranyaprathet near the Cambodian border.

Si Racha

The eastbound journey out of Bangkok is not at all scenic, dominated initially by traffic-choked suburban sprawl and then by the industrial landscape of the petrochemical and shipping industries that power Thailand's Eastern Seaboard. The first major population centre is the provincial capital of **Chonburi**, whose only notable

Highlights

❶ Ko Samet This pretty little island, fringed with a dozen or so beaches of fine, dazzlingly white sand, is easy to get to and offers a wide choice of accommodation, though it's suffering a little for its popularity these days. See page 392

❷ Chanthaburi The atmospheric Chantaboon Riverfront, the town's gem market and absence of tour buses make this small town worth a visit. See page 399

❸ Ko Chang Head for Lonely Beach if you're in the mood to party, or to Hat Khlong Phrao, Ao Bang Bao or Hat Khlong Kloi for progressively more tranquil scenes. See page 405

❹ Ko Mak Lovely, lazy, palm-filled island with peaceful white-sand beaches, a welcoming atmosphere and some stylish accommodation. See page 420

❺ Ko Kood The real beauty of the east, with some great beaches, Thailand's fourth-largest island is untamed and as yet largely undeveloped. See page 423

HIGHLIGHTS ARE MARKED ON THE MAP ON PAGE 378

attraction is its annual October bout of buffalo racing. Twenty kilometres on, you reach the fast-growing town of **SI RACHA**, a prosperous residential and administrative hub for the Eastern Seaboard's industries and home to a sizeable population of expat families. The town is best known though as the source of *nam phrik Si Racha* (commonly known as Sriracha sauce), the chilli-laced ketchup found on every kitchen table in Thailand, and as the departure point for the island of **Ko Si Chang** (see page 380). Si Racha's only sights are a seafront public park and **Wat Ko Loy**, a gaudy hexagon presided over by a statue of the Chinese Goddess of Mercy, Kuan Im, and located on Ko Loy, an islet at the end of a 1500m causeway.

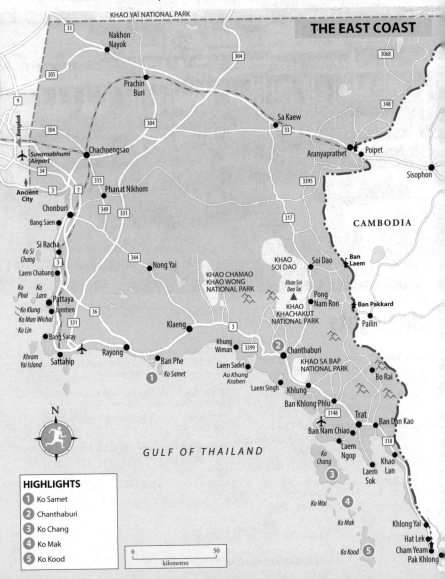

THE EAST COAST

HIGHLIGHTS
1. Ko Samet
2. Chanthaburi
3. Ko Chang
4. Ko Mak
5. Ko Kood

CROSSING THE CAMBODIAN BORDER VIA ARANYAPRATHET

The most commonly used overland crossing into **Cambodia** from Thailand is at **Poipet**, which lies just across the border from the Thai town of **Aranyaprathet (aka Aran)**, 210km due east of Bangkok. It's best to arm yourself in advance with an e-visa for Cambodia (see page 29) and to make the journey by regular public transport from Bangkok to Siem Reap and beyond. It's also possible to travel via Aranyaprathet and get a thirty-day visa on arrival at the border, though this can expose you to possible **scams**, including hustlers offering fake visas and rip-off currency exchange rates (it's not compulsory to buy riel before entering Cambodia, despite what some touts may say). Once you've walked across the border and entered Cambodia, it's about two hours in a taxi or bus to reach Siem Reap, 150km away. If you have the misfortune of getting stuck in Aranyaprathet, try the comfortable fan and a/c rooms at *Market Motel* at 105/30 Thanon Ratuthit (☎037 232302, ⊚aranyaprathethotel.com; fan B300, a/c B400).

From **Bangkok**, you can travel to Aranyaprathet Station, 4km from the border post, by **train** (2 daily; 6hr); you'll need to catch the 5.55am if you want to get across the border the same day. Return trains depart Aranyaprathet at 6.40am and 1.55pm (5hr 25min–6hr). Alternatively, take a **bus** from Bangkok's Northern (Mo Chit) Bus Terminal to Aranyaprathet (at least hourly; 4hr 30min), or a faster, more expensive a/c minibus from Victory Monument. If you have an e-visa, you can catch one of Baw Khaw Saw's public buses that run from Mo Chit via Aranyaprathet all the way to Siem Reap and Phom Penh. To reach Aranyaprathet from east-coast towns, take a bus or minibus from **Pattaya or Chanthaburi** to Aranyaprathet.

It's also possible to buy a **through ticket to Siem Reap** from Thanon Khao San in Bangkok (B350–600), but this option is dogged by scams, can take longer than doing it independently, and often uses clapped-out buses or even pick-ups on the Cambodian side, despite the promised "luxury bus".

4

ARRIVAL AND DEPARTURE   SI RACHA

BY BUS

Frequent buses pass through Si Racha on their journeys between Bangkok's Eastern (Ekamai) and Northern (Mo Chit) bus terminals, and Pattaya and Trat further east. They all drop off and pick up passengers near the huge Robinsons/Pacific Park shopping centre on Thanon Sukhumvit in Si Racha's town centre.

Destinations Bangkok (Eastern/Northern bus terminals; every 40min; 1hr 30min–2hr 30min); Chanthaburi (6 daily; 3hr 30min); Pattaya (every 20min; 30min); Trat (6 daily; 5hr).

BY TRAIN

Though a rail line connects Bangkok with Pattaya and Sattahip via Si Racha, it is served by just one slow, third-class, often late, train a day in each direction. The train station is on the far eastern edge of town, a tuk-tuk ride from the pier for Ko Si Chang.

Destinations Bangkok (daily; 3hr 30min); Pattaya (daily; 30min).

BY BOAT

Ferries to Ko Si Chang, which once left from Tha Ko Loy, now leave from Tha Jarin (Jarin pier), about 1km south of Tha Ko Loy on Chermchompon Soi 14, or 2.5km from Robinsons shopping centre; a motorbike taxi or tuk-tuk will cost you B40/B60. Boats run to Ko Si Chang between 7am and 8pm (hourly; 40–50min; B50).

ACCOMMODATION AND EATING

For **food**, Thanon Si Racha Nakhon 3 is a good place to browse, lined with restaurants and night-time food stalls, or there's an official night market by the day market and clocktower further south down Thanon Chermchompon.

City Hotel 6/126 Thanon Sukhumvit ☎038 322700, ⊚citysriracha.com. This high-rise, two hundred-room hotel, 300m south of Pacific Place, offers smart a/c digs, with a gym, a spa, a tennis court, Japanese and international restaurants and a pool on site. B2825

Mum Aroy 16/4 Soi Laemket, about 1km north of Ko Loy ☎081 110 4567. Ideal spot for a sunset seafood feast with views out over the gulf. Dishes range from a simple crab fried rice (B100) to elaborate lobster preparations. Daily 10am–11pm

Samchai Resort 3 Thanon Chermchompon, opposite Thanon Tessaban 1 ☎038 311800, ⊚facebook.com/samchairesort. A range of simply furnished but clean and comfortable fan and a/c rooms on a jetty jutting out over the atmospheric waterfront. Fan B320, a/c B500

Ko Si Chang

The unhurried pace and absence of consumer pressures make small, dry, rocky **KO SI CHANG** an engaging place to get away from it all for a day or two. Unlike most other east-coast destinations, it offers no real beach life – it's a populous, working island with a deep-sea port, rather than a tropical idyll – and there's little to do here but explore the craggy coastline by kayak or ramble up and down its steep, scrubby contours on foot or by motorbike. The island is famous as the location of one of Rama V's summer palaces, a few parts of which have been restored, and of a popular Chinese pilgrimage temple, as well as for its wild pigs and rare white squirrels, which live in the wooded patches inland.

Phra Chudadhut Palace

Hat Tha Wang • Tues–Sun 9am–5pm • Free

The most famous sight on the island is the former summer palace of Rama V, now known as **Phra Chudadhut Palace,** which occupies a large chunk of gently sloping land midway down the east coast, behind pebbly **Hat Tha Wang**. It's an enjoyable place to explore and can be reached on foot from the middle of Thanon Asadang in about half an hour.

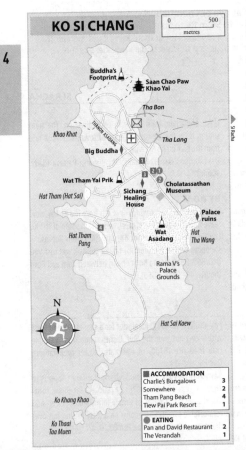

Built in the 1890s as a sort of health resort for sickly royals, the palace formed the heart of an extensive complex comprising homes for royal advisers, chalets for convalescents, quarters for royal concubines and administrative buildings. Within a few years, however, Rama V (King Chulalongkorn) was concerned about foreign incursions, particularly after the Franco-Siamese crisis of 1893, so in 1901 his golden teak palace was moved piece by piece to Bangkok, and reconstructed there as Vimanmek Palace; its foundations are still visible just south of the eye-catching Saphan Asadang pier. Following modern renovations, the elegant design of the palace grounds is apparent once more. They fan out around an elaborate labyrinth of fifty interlinked ponds and a maze of stone steps and balustrades that still cling to the shallow hillside. Close to the shore, four of the original Western-style **villas** have been reconstructed to house displays, of varying interest, on Chulalongkorn's relationship with Ko Si Chang; one of them also doubles as a weekend coffee shop. Inland, signs direct you up the hillside to the palace's unusual whitewashed shrine, **Wat Asadang**, whose circular walls are punctuated with Gothic stained-glass windows and surmounted by a chedi.

KO SI CHANG FESTIVALS

Ko Si Chang celebrates three particularly interesting festivals. **Songkhran** is marked from April 17 to 19 with sandcastle building, greasy-pole-climbing and kayak racing. At **Visakha Puja**, the full moon day in May when the Buddha's birth, death and enlightenment are honoured, islanders process to the old palace with hand-crafted Chinese lanterns. And on September 20, Ko Si Chang honours its royal patron **King Chulalongkorn**'s birthday with a sound and light show in the palace grounds and a beauty contest staged entirely in costumes from the Chulalongkorn era.

Hat Tham Pang and Ko Khang Khao

The main beach on the west coast, and the most popular one on the island, is **Hat Tham Pang**. It's a tiny patch of sand, backed by shoulder-to-shoulder umbrellas and deckchairs belonging to the basic beach restaurants; you can rent snorkelling equipment and kayaks here too. The best **snorkelling** spots are further south, around the tiny islands off Ko Si Chang's southern tip, particularly off the north coast of **Ko Khang Khao**, forty minutes by kayak from Hat Tham Pang.

Wat Tham Yai Prik

Accessible via a fork off Thanon Asadang opposite *Tiew Pai* (10min walk)

The **Wat Tham Yai Prik** temple and meditation centre is open to interested visitors and meditators, who can meditate in caves set into the mountain. Unusually, nuns as well as monks here wear brown (rather than white) and everyone participates in the upkeep of the splendid monastery: you can see some of the fruits of their labour in the extensive roadside orchard. Just west of the wat lies the pretty, rocky cove known as **Hat Tham** or **Hat Sai**, which is only really swimmable at low tide.

Khao Khat

On the northwest trajectory of the ring road, you'll pass beneath the gaze of a huge yellow Buddha before reaching the rocky northwest headland of **Khao Khat**, a few hundred metres further on. The uninterrupted panorama of open sea makes this a classic sunset spot, and there's a stairway leading down to the rocky shore.

Saan Chao Paw Khao Yai

The showy, multi-tiered Chinese temple of **Saan Chao Paw Khao Yai** (Shrine of the Father Spirit of the Great Hill) is stationed at the top of a steep flight of steps and commands a good view of the harbour and the mainland coast. Established here long before Rama V arrived on the island, the shrine was dedicated by Chinese seamen who saw a strange light coming out of one of the **caves** behind the modern-day temple. The caves, now full of religious statues and related paraphernalia, are visited by boatloads of Chinese pilgrims, particularly over Chinese New Year. Continue on up the cliffside to reach a small pagoda enshrining a **Buddha's Footprint**. A very long, very steep flights of stairs give access to the footprint from the main waterfront entrance to the Chinese temple, taking you past a cluster of monks' meditation cells, but there's also a steep paved road branching off the northern part of the ring road that motorbikes and samlors can climb. From the platform beside the footprint there are fantastic views looking south that take in both the east and west coasts of the island.

ARRIVAL AND INFORMATION   KO SI CHANG

By boat Ferries to Ko Si Chang leave from Tha Jarin in Si Racha (see page 379) from 6am to 8pm (hourly;   40–50min; B50), wending their way past the congestion of international cargo boats and Thai supply barges that anchor in the protected channel between the mainland and Ko Si Chang. On arrival, boats dock first at Tha Lang (also signed as Tateawavong Bridge) in the island's main settlement, with many then continuing to Tha Bon a short distance up the east coast. Some hotels and guesthouses offer free pick-ups if you inform them which ferry you are on. Otherwise, samlor drivers meet the boats and charge B50 to most accommodation, or B80 to Hat Tham Pang. Boats to the mainland leave Tha Lang between 6am and 7pm (hourly; 40–50min; B50 except for the 7pm ferry B60); the same boats depart Tha Bon 15min earlier.

Tourist information ⓦ ko-sichang.com, a useful website compiled by David at *Pan and David Restaurant* (see below), offers detailed coverage of the island.

GETTING AROUND

Both piers connect with Thanon Asadang, a small, concrete ring road on which you'll find the market, a bank and many shops. In town it's easy enough to walk from place to place, but to really enjoy what Ko Si Chang has to offer you'll need to either rent a motorbike or charter a samlor for a tour.

By motorbike Bikes can be rented from the pier or from *Charlie's Bungalows* for B300 a day.

By samlor The island's trademark samlors are driven by distinctive, elongated 1200cc motorbikes and virtually monopolise the roads, as there are barely any private cars; a quick tour of the main sights on the island will set you back around B250, and takes just over an hour.

ACCOMMODATION AND EATING

Though Ko Si Chang sees few Western visitors, there are now around 70 hotels and guesthouses that cater for weekenders from Bangkok, when rates are hiked up and booking ahead is advisable. There are plenty of cheap and cheerful eateries on Thanon Asadang.

Charlie's Bungalows Thanon Asadang, 2min walk south of Tiew Pai Park Resort in town ☎ 085 191 3863, ⓦ kohsichang.net; map p.380. A dozen or so attractive new bungalows, done out in a maritime theme around a small garden; all come with a/c, hot water, satellite TV and fridge. Prices go up a little at weekends. B1000

★ **Pan and David Restaurant** Thanon Asadang, 200m before the entrance to the old palace grounds ☎ 038 216 629, ⓦ ko-sichang.com; map p.380. The best restaurant on the island, run by a sociable and well-informed American expat and his Thai wife. The long and delicious menu includes authentically fiery Thai salads, tasty home-made fettuccine (B320 with porcini mushroom sauce), fillet steak, Thai curries (B180 with free-range chicken), and home-made fresh strawberry ice cream. Thurs–Tues 7.30am–9.30pm.

★ **Somewhere** Off Thanon Asadang, just south of Tha Lang ☎ 038 109 400, ⓦ somewherehotel.com; map p.380. This cute, boutique hotel with a maritime theme has just twenty spacious rooms, some with sea views from the upstairs balcony. There's a pool here too, and an excellent restaurant: The Verandah (see below). Breakfast included. B2500

Tham Pang Beach Hat Tham Pang ☎ 038 216 153, ⓦ tampangbeach.com; map p.380. Undergoing renovation at the time of writing, all rooms here have a/c and hot water bathrooms, though some rooms lack windows. The cheapest rooms are small for the price, and there's no breakfast included, but it's the only option if you want to be right on the beach. B1300

The Verandah At Somewhere Hotel, off Thanon Asadang ☎ 038 109 400 ⓦ somewherehotel.com; map p.380. The restaurant at this small resort serves some tasty pizzas and burgers as well as great Thai food. If you like spicy dishes, try the Southern Thai curry with salmon (B180). There's also a good range of wines and spirits and a cosy ambiance. Daily 6.30am–9.30pm.

Tiew Pai Park Resort Thanon Asadang, in town near Tha Lang ☎ 038 216 084, ⓦ tiewpai.net; map p.380. Very central and cheaper than the competition, this is most backpackers' first choice. Bungalows and rooms are crammed around a scruffy garden across the road from the restaurant and many don't have hot water; the best value are the en-suite fan bungalows, some of which have TV and fridge, and there are also some cheap single rooms with shared bathrooms (B200). No wi-fi. Fan B400, a/c B700

DIRECTORY

Massage The charming little Sichang Healing House (☎ 081 572 7840; Thurs–Tues 9am–6pm; ⓦ ko-sichang.com/spa_welcome.html), west off Thanon Asadang on the way to the old palace, offers Thai massage (B500 for 90min) and herbal treatments, as well as five-day massage courses (B6000), at its cute little garden retreat. They have a couple of rooms for rent too.

Pattaya

With its streets full of high-rise hotels and hustlers on every corner, **PATTAYA** is the epitome of exploitative tourism gone mad, but most of the two million annual visitors don't mind that the place looks like the Costa del Sol bathed in smog because what they are here for is sex. The city swarms with male and female **prostitutes**, spiced up by Thailand's largest population of *katoey* (transgender females), involved in sex work, and plane-loads of Western men flock here to enjoy their services in the rash of hostess bar-beers, go-go clubs and massage parlours for which "Patpong-on-Sea" is notorious. The signs trumpeting "Viagra for Sale" say it all. Pattaya also has the largest number of **gay**

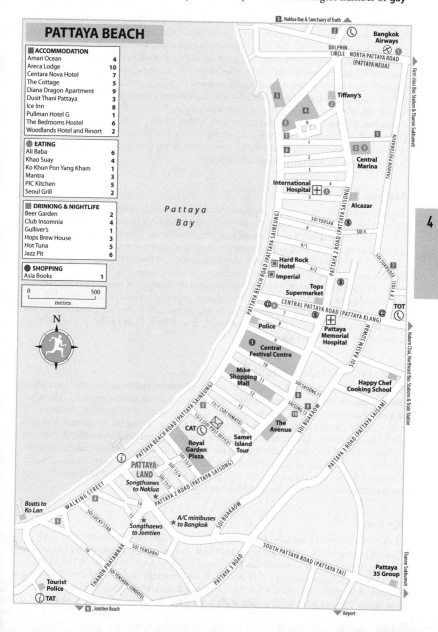

PATTAYA BEACH

ACCOMMODATION
Amari Ocean	4
Areca Lodge	10
Centara Nova Hotel	7
The Cottage	5
Diana Dragon Apartment	9
Dusit Thani Pattaya	3
Ice Inn	8
Pullman Hotel G	1
The Bedrooms Hostel	6
Woodlands Hotel and Resort	2

EATING
Ali Baba	6
Khao Suay	4
Ko Khun Pon Yang Kham	1
Mantra	3
PIC Kitchen	5
Seoul Grill	2

DRINKING & NIGHTLIFE
Beer Garden	2
Club Insomnia	4
Gulliver's	1
Hops Brew House	3
Hot Tuna	5
Jazz Pit	6

SHOPPING
Asia Books	1

0 ____ 500
metres

N

Pattaya Bay

Naklua Bay & Sanctuary of Truth

Bangkok Airways

DOLPHIN CIRCLE

NORTH PATTAYA ROAD (PATTAYA NEUA)

Tiffany's

THANON PHETRAKUN

Central Marina

International Hospital

SOI YODSAK

Alcazar

PATTAYA BEACH ROAD (PATTAYA SAINEUNG)

PATTAYA 2 ROAD (PATTAYA SAINEUNG)

SOI 4

SOI SUKRUDEE (SOI A.R.)

Hard Rock Hotel

Imperial

Tops Supermarket

CENTRAL PATTAYA ROAD (PATTAYA KLANG)

TOT

Police

Pattaya Memorial Hospital

Central Festival Centre

SOI KASEM SUWAN

Mike Shopping Mall

SOI SAISONG 11

SAISONG 13

Happy Chef Cooking School

The Avenue

SOI BUAKAOW

CAT

PATTAYA BEACH ROAD (PATTAYA SAINEUNG)

13/1 (SOI YAMATO)

13/2 (SOI POST OFFICE)

Royal Garden Plaza

Samet Island Tour

PATTAYA 3 ROAD (PATTAYA SAISAM)

PATTAYA-LAND

SOI 13/3

SOI 13/4

Songthaews to Naklua

PATTAYA 2 ROAD (PATTAYA SAISONG)

WALKING STREET

SOI LUCKY STAR

Boats to Ko Lan

Songthaews to Jomtien

A/C minibuses to Bangkok

SOI BUAKAOW

THANON PRATAMNAK

SOI YENSABAI

SOI YENSABAI CONDOTEL

PATTAYA 3 ROAD

SOUTH PATTAYA ROAD (PATTAYA TAI)

Pattaya 35 Group

Tourist Police

TAT

Jomtien Beach

Airport

First-class Bus Station & Thanon Sukhumvit

Nakorn Chai, Northeast Bus Stations & Train Station

Thanon Sukhumvit

4

services (targeted mainly at foreigners) in Thailand, with several exclusively gay hotels and an entire zone devoted to gay sex bars.

Pattaya's evolution into sin city began with the Vietnam War, when it got fat on selling sex to American servicemen. When the soldiers and sailors left in the mid-1970s, Western tourists were lured in to fill their places, and ex-servicemen soon returned to run the sort of joints they had once blown their dollars in. These days, at least half the bars and restaurants in Pattaya are Western-run. More recently, there has been an influx of criminal gangs from Germany, Russia and Japan, who reportedly find Pattaya a convenient centre for running their rackets in passport and credit-card fraud, as well as child pornography and prostitution; expat murders are a regular news item in the *Pattaya Mail*.

Local tourism authorities try hard to improve Pattaya's **image**, and with surprising success now entice families and older couples with a catalogue of more wholesome entertainments such as theme parks, golf courses, shopping plazas and year-round diving. Russian, Chinese and Korean holidaymakers seem particularly keen, and Cyrillic and Chinese scripts are now a common sight. A recent flush of more sophisticated boutique hotels and restaurants is also starting to bring in a younger Thai crowd, which has brightened the picture a little. But in truth the beach here is far from pristine – way outshone by Ko Samet just along the coast – so after-hours "entertainment" is still the primary inducement.

Pattaya Beach

At the heart of this ever-expanding adult playground is 4km-long **Pattaya Beach**, the noisiest, most unsightly zone of the resort, crowded with yachts and tour boats and fringed by a sliver of sand and a paved beachfront walkway. The densest glut of hotels, restaurants, bars, fast-food joints, souvenir shops and tour operators is halfway down Pattaya Beach Road (also signed as Pattaya Saineung), in **Central Pattaya** (Pattaya Klang), between sois 6 and 13, but after dark the action moves to the neon zone south of Soi 13/2. Here, in **South Pattaya**, and specifically along ultra-sleazy **Walking Street**, sex is peddled in hundreds of go-go bars, discos, massage parlours and open-sided bar-beers, and the hordes of visitors treat it as a tourist sideshow. The gay district is also here, in the lanes known as **Pattayaland** sois 1, 2 and 3 (or **Boyz Town**), but actually signed as sois 13/3, 13/4 and 13/5.

Jomtien Beach and Buddha Hill

South around the headland from South Pattaya, **Jomtien Beach** (sometimes spelt Chom Tian) is also fronted by enormous high-rises, many of them condominiums. Though the atmosphere here is not as frantic as in Pattaya, Jomtien also flounders under an excess of bar-beers and shops flogging tacky souvenirs and, like its neighbour, is forever under construction. The nicest stretch of sand is the shady **Dongtan Beach**, beyond the northern end of Jomtien Beach Road, which is also Pattaya's main gay beach, though used by all. The bulge of land behind Dongtan Beach, separating Jomtien from South Pattaya, is Khao Phra Tamnak, variously translated as **Buddha Hill** or **Pattaya Hill**, site of several posh hotels and the Pattaya Park waterpark and funfair.

Ko Lan

7km west of South Pattaya • Ferry from Bali Hai Pier at south end of Walking Street; 7 daily; B30 • ⓦ kohlarn.com

Pattaya's main beach might not be up to much, but things get considerably better at a few offshore islands, of which **Ko Lan**, just 4km long and 2km wide, is the most popular, attracting thousands of visitors each day. Several beaches on the west coast of the island boast powder-soft, white sand beaches and activities include glass-bottomed boat rides, banana boat rides, jetskis and parasailing. The last ferry returns to the mainland at 6pm, though it's also possible to arrange trips here and to other islands by speedboat; just ask at your resort.

Underwater World

Thanon Sukhumvit, just south of the Thep Prasit junction near Tesco Lotus, behind Jomtien Beach • Daily 9am–6pm • B500 • Ⓦ underwaterworldpattaya.com

If you've been disappointed with local reef life, the small and expensive but rather beautiful aquarium at **Underwater World** might make up for it, with its trio of long fibreglass tunnels that transport you through shallow rockpools to the ocean floor. There are touch pools and masses of reef fish, as well as a long roster of feeding times, detailed on the website.

Sanctuary of Truth (Wang Boran)

Off the west end of Soi 12, Thanon Naklua, close to the Garden Sea View hotel, beyond the north end of Pattaya Beach • Daily 8am–6pm • B500 • Ⓦ sanctuaryoftruth.com • From Central Pattaya take a Naklua-bound songthaew as far as Soi 12, then a motorbike taxi

The hugely ambitious **Sanctuary of Truth**, or **Wang Boran**, stands in a dramatic seaside spot behind imposing crenellated walls. Conceived by the man behind the Muang Boran

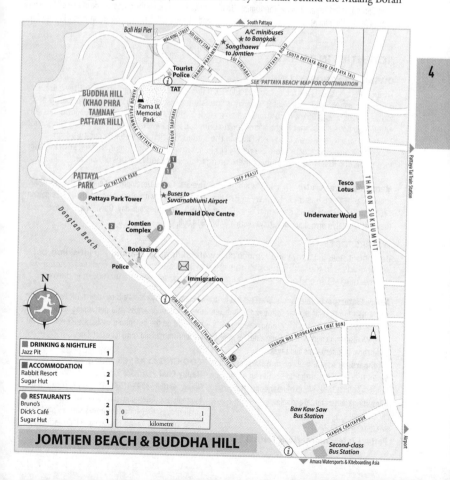

JOMTIEN BEACH & BUDDHA HILL

Ancient City complex near Bangkok (see page 132), it's a majestic 105m-high temple-palace built entirely of wood and designed to evoke the great ancient Khmer sanctuaries of Angkor. Though begun in 1981, it is ever-changing, its external walls covered in a growing gallery of beautiful, symbolic woodcarvings inspired by Cambodian, Chinese, Thai and Indian mythologies. Horse-drawn carriage and elephant rides are available in the grounds.

ARRIVAL AND DEPARTURE

PATTAYA

By plane Pattaya's U-Tapao Airport (☏038 245 595 ⓦutapao.com) is located at the naval base near Sattahip, about 25km south of the resort. Air Asia currently operates a cheap connecting bus service between the airport and downtown Pattaya; alternatively a taxi will cost you about B1000. You can also use Bangkok's Suvarnabhumi Airport (see page 132), which is linked to Pattaya by bus. It's served by Air Asia and Bangkok Airways flights. The Bangkok Airways office is at Fairtex Arcade, North Pattaya Road (☏038 412 382).
Destinations Chiang Mai (3 daily; 1hr 10min); Hat Yai (daily; 1hr 20min); Ko Samui (1–2 daily; 1hr); Phuket (2 daily; 1hr 35min); Udon Thani (2 daily; 1hr 10min); Ubon Ratchathani (daily; 1hr 20min).

By bus All first-class and VIP Bangkok buses, and some Suvarnabhumi Airport buses, arrive at and depart from the bus station on North Pattaya Road. Slower second-class Bangkok buses and some Suvarnabhumi Airport buses use the station on Thanon Chaiyapruk in Jomtien, and there are also airport buses from a terminal on Thanon Tabphaya in Jomtien. It's also possible to get to Pattaya direct from Isaan and the north: Nakorn Chai buses to and from Chiang Mai, Chiang Rai, Khorat and Ubon use a terminus on Thanon Sukhumvit, across from the Central Pattaya Road intersection (☏038 424871); other Isaan buses can be found at two terminals on the opposite side of Thanon Sukhumvit and at the first-class bus station on North Pattaya Road,

---

ACTIVITIES IN PATTAYA

DIVING AND SNORKELLING

Though Pattaya's reefs are far less spectacular than those along the Andaman coast, they can be dived year-round, and underwater visibility is consistent. Most **dive trips** focus on the group of "outer islands" about 25km from shore, which include Ko Rin, Ko Man Wichai and Ko Klung Badaan where you have a reasonable chance of seeing barracuda, moray eels and blue-spotted stingrays. There are also three rewarding wreck dives in the Samae San/Sattahip area. Be careful when choosing a dive operator as there are plenty of charlatans around. All tour agents sell **snorkelling** trips to nearby islands, the majority of them going to the reefs and beaches of **Ko Lan**.

Mermaid's Dive Centre Thanon Tabphaya in Jomtien, plus three branches elsewhere in Pattaya ☏038 303333, ⓦmermaidsdivecenter.com. One of the most reputable dive shops in Pattaya, with a PADI Five-Star Career Development Centre. It charges B3000 for two dives, with accompanying snorkellers paying B1000, and the four-day Open Water course costs B14,000.

WATERSPORTS

Beachfront stalls in Pattaya and Jomtien offer **waterskiing**, **parasailing** and **jet-skiing**, but you should avoid the last-mentioned: the jet-ski jockeys are notorious for finding scratches on the machine at the end of the rental and trying to charge an exorbitant amount in damages.

Amara Watersports Blue Lagoon Watersports Club, Soi 14 Naa Jomtien, at the far south end of Jomtien Beach ☏099 239 3642, ⓦamarawatersports.com. Windsurfing courses, rental and sales, as well as paddleboards, catamarans and kayaks.
Kiteboarding Asia Blue Lagoon Watersports Club, Soi 14 Naa Jomtien, at the far south end of Jomtien Beach ☏085 134 9588, ⓦbluelagoonpattaya.com. Kitesurfing courses, rental and sales.

MUSIC FESTIVAL
Pattaya International Music Festival Every year in March, Pattaya hosts a three-day music festival, with live bands from across Asia performing from 6pm to midnight on the beachfront esplanade. Check with TAT (ⓦtourismthailand.com) for exact dates.

COOKING CLASSES
Happy Chef 81/65 Soi 9, Nongpru, Thanon Pattaya Klang ☏080 809 4453, ⓦlearnthaicooking.net. Morning and afternoon classes (11am and 1pm) for small groups, preparing four dishes such as phat thai, green curry and kaeng phanaeng. B1000 including a recipe booklet.

4

which has songthaews that take you south along one-way Pattaya Beach Road (B20), returning along Pattaya 2 Road. Coming by bus from Si Racha, Rayong or Trat, you'll probably get dropped on Thanon Sukhumvit, the resort's eastern limit, from where songthaews will ferry you into town (B40). If heading on to these towns, you need to pick up your bus from one of the drops on Thanon Sukhumvit (easiest at the junctions with North, Central and South Pattaya roads).

Destinations Bangkok (Eastern/Northern bus terminals; every 30min; 2hr 30min–4hr); Bangkok (Southern Bus Terminal; every 2hr; 3hr 30min); Bangkok (Suvarnabhumi Airport; every 30min; 2hr); Chanthaburi (4 daily; 3hr); Chiang Mai (8 daily; 12–14hr); Chiang Rai (2 daily; 15–17hr); Khorat (5 daily; 5hr); Rayong (every 30min; 1hr 30min); Si Racha (every 20min; 30min); Trat (4 daily; 4hr 30min); Ubon Ratchathani (6 daily; 10–12hr).

By a/c minibus In Bangkok, hostels near Khao San Road can arrange an a/c minibus service to the beach near Walking Street for B400/person; drivers pick you up from your accommodation but may charge B100 to drop you off at your hotel or before the last stop. You can catch an a/c minibus to Bangkok's Victory Monument for B250 from several spots, including the east end of Central Pattaya Road

near Foodland and South Pattaya Road in front of the Family Mart near Krung Thai Bank. Any hotel can arrange a ticket on a shared a/c minibus to Suvarnabhumi Airport for around B250/person (or about B800/car for a metered taxi). There are also tourist minibus services to Ko Samet and Ko Chang (tickets can also be booked through most tour agents): Samet Island Tour on Soi Yamato (☎ 038 427277, ⊚ malibu-samet.com) runs to the Ban Phe pier (for Ko Samet; B300 including transfer and boat but not B200 national park fee); and Pattaya 35 Group, opposite Big C on South Pattaya Road (☎ 038 423447 ⊚ 35grouptour.com) goes to Ko Chang (B700 including ferry), via Ban Phe and Chanthaburi.

By train Pattaya is on a branch of the eastern rail line, and there's one slow train a day in each direction between the resort and Bangkok. Pattaya has two stations, both off the east side of Thanon Sukhumvit: the main one is about 500m north of the Central Pattaya Road intersection, while Pattaya Tai Station is in South Pattaya near the Thanon Thep Prasit junction. Songthaews (B30) wait at the main station to take passengers to Pattaya Beach Road; from Pattaya Tai Station a songthaew (B20) can take you along Thanon Thep Prasit to Jomtien Beach Road.

Destinations Bangkok (daily; 4hr); Si Racha (daily; 30min).

INFORMATION

Tourist information There are municipal tourist service booths (daily roughly 8.30am–4pm) on the beach at the mouth of Walking Street, at City Hall on North Pattaya Road, at the north end of Jomtien Beach Road and opposite Thanon Chaiyapruk on Jomtien Beach. Note that private tour companies also pose as "tourist information". The TAT office is inconveniently located at 609 Thanon Pratamnak between South Pattaya and Jomtien (daily 8.30am–4.30pm; ☎ 038 427667, ⊚ tatchon@tat.or.th).

GETTING AROUND

By songthaew Public songthaews – known locally as baht buses, and also available to charter – circulate continuously around the resort from dawn until at least 11pm. Most follow a standard anticlockwise route up Pattaya 2 Road as far as North Pattaya Road and back down Pattaya Beach Road, for a fixed fee of B10/person; others run along the main east–west arteries of North, Central and South Pattaya roads. Songthaews to Jomtien start from next to the school on the south side of the junction of Pattaya 2 Road and South Pattaya Road and cost B10–20. Songthaews to Naklua, beyond north Pattaya, start from the north side of the same junction and head up Pattaya 2 Road (also B10–20).

By mototaxi Drivers in red or green vests are everywhere and offer a very open-air ride from the centre of Pattaya Beach Road to Walking Street for about B50. Helmet not necessarily included; hold on to the rack behind you.

By motorbike Motorbike rental is available everywhere from B150/day, but beware of faulty vehicles, and of scams – sometimes rented bikes get stolen by touts keen to keep the customer's deposit, so you may want to use your own lock. Unpredictable drivers and a disregard for road rules makes Pattaya potentially dangerous for inexperienced riders, with frequent accidents and fatalities. Avoid wearing expensive-looking jewellery while riding a motorbike as ride-by snatchings sometimes occur.

By taxi

Metered taxis in Pattaya often don't stop when flagged on the street, never use their meters, and charge excessive rates. You're better off downloading the Grab app and using them instead.

By car Avis car rental (⊚ avisthailand.com) has an office inside the *Dusit Resort* (☎ 038 361627); many of the motorbike touts also rent out jeeps for about B1300/day.

ACCOMMODATION

The quietest and least sleazy end of town to stay in is **North Pattaya**, between Central Pattaya Road and North Pattaya Road (Thanon Hat Pattaya Neua) or just north

of here in Naklua. There's not much in the way of budget accommodation, apart from a few hostels offering dorm rooms.

4

PATTAYA BEACH AND NAKLUA

Amari Ocean 240 Pattaya Beach Road, North Pattaya ☎038 418418 ⓦamari.com/ocean-pattaya; map p.383. This long-standing, reliable, luxury hotel was adding two new wings at the time of writing, which will offer guests a wider range of facilities. The location is ideal, at the top end of Beach Road, and the hotel boasts Pattaya's top restaurant: *Mantra* (see below). B3400

Areca Lodge 198/21 Soi Saisong 13 (aka Soi Diana Inn), Central Pattaya ☎038 410123, ⓦarecalodge.com; map p.383. An unusually stylish place for Pattaya, with pleasantly furnished a/c rooms in three wings built around two swimming pools. Most rooms have balconies, and all have king beds and hot showers. Buffet breakfast included. B2100

Centara Nova Hotel Soi 12 (aka Soi A.R. or Soi Sukrudee), Central Pattaya Road ☎038 725999, ⓦcentarahotelsresorts.com/centara/nvp; map p.383. Central, quiet and welcoming boutique hotel, done out in a plush contemporary style that features a lot of burnished gold. There's a large, attractive pool fed by an artificial waterfall, a spa that uses Dead Sea mud and salt, and a fitness centre. Breakfast included. B1600

The Cottage Off Pattaya 2 Road, North Pattaya ☎038 425650, ⓦthecottagepattaya.com; map p.383. Good-value, simply furnished semi-detached brick bungalows, all with a/c, hot water, TV and fridge, pleasantly set among tall trees within a mature tropical garden away from the main road but opposite the Central Centre. Facilities include two small swimming pools. B1200

Diana Dragon Apartment 198/16 Soi Saisong 13 (aka Soi Diana Inn), Central Pattaya ☎038 423928, ⓦdianapattaya.co.th; map p.383. This long-running Pattaya institution has some of the cheapest doubles in town, just a few with fan and mostly a/c, and they're good value considering the competition: huge and quite light, with a breakfast included. Guests are left to their own devices, so expect a mild level of neighbour noise. Fan B400, a/c B750

Dusit Thani Pattaya 240/2 Pattaya Beach Road, North Pattaya ☎038 425611, ⓦdusit.com; map p.383. This luxury Thai chain hotel is one of only a few Beach Road hotels to be actually on the beach (the others are at the southern end). Sea-view rooms are worth paying extra for as the impressive panoramas take in the whole bay. Also on offer are two swimming pools, a spa and tennis courts. B2975

Ice Inn Corner of Saisong 12 and Pattaya 2 Road, Central Pattaya ☎038 720671, ⓦiceinnpattaya.com; map p.383. Cheap fan-cooled singles (B450) and reasonably priced a/c doubles in this small 28-room hotel behind a massage shop, a few metres from the busier bar-beer sois. Rooms are simple but are all en suite, making them some of the best value in town. B750

Pullman Hotel G 445/3 Moo 5, Wong Amat Beach, Thanon Pattaya-Naklua Soi 16 ☎038 411940-8, ⓦpullmanpattayahotelg.com; map p.383. Located on pretty Wong Amat Beach in Naklua, Hotel G is a chic, stylish hotel with two pools, a fitness centre and the relaxing Aisawan Spa. Rooms are equipped with all modern facilities and decorated in calming beige. Most rooms have balconies with sunset views. B4500

The Bedrooms Hostel 439/49 Pattaya Beach Road, near Soi 1 ☎063 395 5885, ⓦthebedroomshostelpattaya. com; map p.383. This smart hostel boasts a good location near the north end of Beach Road and a variety of rooms, including compact doubles, family bunk rooms (B2380) and well-equipped dormitories. All rooms share bathrooms. Double B1190, dorm B750

Woodlands Hotel and Resort 164 Thanon Pattaya-Naklua, North Pattaya ☎038 421707, ⓦwoodland-resort.com; map p.383. A quiet, unpretentious and welcoming family-friendly garden resort 100m north of the Dolphin Circle roundabout, and 400m from a scruffy but quiet thread of beach. The elegant, a/c rooms are in two storeys set round the pools and garden; the most expensive have direct access to the pool from ground-floor balconies. B3250

JOMTIEN AND BUDDHA HILL

★ **Rabbit Resort** Dongtan beachfront, Jomtien ☎038 251 730, ⓦrabbitresort.com; map p.385. Beautiful place that's the most appealing option in Jomtien and located on the nicest stretch of Dongtan Beach. Most accommodation is in teakwood cottages that are elegantly furnished with Thai fabrics and antiques and have garden-style bathrooms; there are also some "forest rooms" in a two-storey block. All are set around a tropical garden and pool just metres off the beach. Breakfast included. Rooms B4900, cottages B5900

Sugar Hut 391/18 Thanon Tabphaya, midway between South Pattaya and Jomtien ☎038 251686, ⓦsugar-hut. com; map p.385. The most characterful accommodation in Pattaya comprises a charming collection of Ayutthaya-style traditional wooden bungalows set in a fabulously profuse garden with three swimming pools, saunas and steam rooms. The bungalows are in tropical-chic style, with low beds, open-roofed shower rooms, mosquito nets and private verandas. There's a few eating options nearby, but you'll need your own transport for the 5min drive to Jomtien Beach Road or Pattaya Beach Road. B4500

EATING

In among the innumerable low-grade Western cafés that dominate Pattaya's **restaurant scene** are a few much classier joints serving good, sophisticated cuisine – at top-end prices. For the cheapest, most authentic Thai food, just head for the nearest of Pattaya's myriad building sites and you'll find street stalls catering to the construction-site workers.

PATTAYA BEACH

Ali Baba 1/13–14 Central Pattaya Road ☎038 361620 ⓦalibabarestaurantpattaya.com; map p.383. Look beyond the name and the wonderfully kitsch decor and waiters' uniforms, and you'll find some very good Indian food, which keeps many of Pattaya's visitors from the subcontinent happy. There's an authentically long menu of vegetarian dishes, featuring plenty of cheese and some interesting starters with okra; in addition, the butter chicken's a real winner (B280). Daily 11am–midnight.

Khao Suay Ground Floor, Central Marina, Pattaya 2 Road, North Pattaya; map p.383. A long menu of good modern Thai food (most mains B140–220) draws Thai families to this tiny café inside the shopping centre. The varied English menu includes *kaeng tai pla* (southern Thai fish stomach curry) and *nam prik pla thuu* (chilli relish with mackerel). The tasty one-meal rice dishes (B80) make for great solo dining. Daily 11am–9.45pm.

Ko Khun Pon Yang Kham North Pattaya Road, at Soi 6 ☎038 420571; map p.383. This garden restaurant offers Thailand's equivalent of wagyu beef, from pampered Pon Yang Kham cows that are bred (from French, Swiss and Thai breeds) and reared in Isaan. It's served northeastern-style too, so no chips or mustard, but it goes well with *som tam*, and the red wine is decent (B150/glass). B185 for a small but delicious portion of sirloin on a sizzling-hot plate. Daily 5.30pm–midnight.

★ **Mantra** Amari Orchid Hotel, Beach Road, North Pattaya ☎038 429591, ⓦmantra-pattaya.com; map p.383. Setting the standard unexpectedly high for Pattaya, this large, beautifully designed bar-restaurant creates an ambience somewhere between a contemporary Shanghai hotel and a maharaja's palace. Downstairs there's an open-plan view of the seven different, equally eclectic kitchens specializing in Japanese, Chinese, Indian, Mediterranean and Western food, grills and seafood. A meal might begin with a California maki roll (B520), supplemented with Hong Kong barbecued duck (B320), continue with lamb shanks in Merlot sauce (B820), and end with a baked mango and glutinous rice parcel with coconut ice cream (B350). The dress code is no shorts,

tank tops or sandals. Daily 6pm–1am; Sunday brunch 11am–3pm.

PIC Kitchen Soi 5, North Pattaya ☎038 428374, ⓦpic-kitchen.com; map p.383. Set in a simple, traditional, Thai house, this place serves up consistently delicious food, such as matsaman curry with chicken (B220). Daily 11am–10pm.

Seoul Grill The One Patio, next to Burger King, Pattaya 2 Road, North Pattaya ☎038 411982 ⓦthebimimbab. com; map p.383. Long streams of Korean visitors to Pattaya keep the dishes authentic at this clean, two-level spot with classics such as bibimbap (meat and vegetable rice bowls), hot pots and Korean barbecue. There are half a dozen other Korean and Japanese restaurants in the same outdoor plaza. Daily 11am–1pm.

JOMTIEN BEACH

Bruno's 306/63 Chateau Dale Plaza, Thanon Tabphaya, Jomtien ☎038 364600–1, ⓦbrunos-pattaya.com; map p.385. A local institution that's a favourite with expats celebrating special occasions. The food is upmarket, expensive and European – rack of lamb, sirloin steak, chocolate soufflé with passion fruit sauce – and there's a cellar of some 150 wines. Main dishes from B290. Daily noon–2.30pm & 6pm–late.

Dick's Café 413/129 Thanon Tabphaya, Jomtien ☎038 252417 ⓦdickscafe.com; map p.385. Located on Jomtien's Walking Street beside the Jomtien Complex, Dick's serves excellent Thai and Western food such as chicken breast with garlic rice (B250) in a cosy atmosphere. They also offer sandwiches and cakes, as well as a good range of imported wines and spirits. Daily 10am–1am.

Sugar Hut 391/18 Thanon Tabphaya, Jomtien; map p.385. Attached to the charming hotel of the same name (see page 388), this restaurant gives you the chance to soak up the ambience and enjoy the tropical gardens without shelling out for a bungalow. Meals are served in an open-sided *sala* and the menu is mainly classy Thai; recommendations include roast duck in red curry (B280). Live music from 7pm–11pm. Daily 8am–11pm.

DRINKING AND NIGHTLIFE

Pattaya's **nightlife** revolves around sex. It is, however, just about possible to have a night out without getting entangled in sleaze, at one of the growing number of hostess-free **bars** listed below, a few of which are surprisingly style-conscious. However you choose to spend your evening, be warned that Pattaya is notorious for female and *katoey* (transgender female) **pickpockets**, who target drunk men walking home in the early hours: while one "distracts" the victim from the front, the other extracts the wallet from behind.

Beer Garden Central Marina, Pattaya 2 Road, North

Pattaya; map p.383. Outdoor tables, draught beer and live music nightly (from about 8pm) from Thai singers and bands, doing mostly Thai pop and country. Also serves a full menu of Thai food (dishes from about B120), with Isaan and seafood specialities. Daily 5pm–2am.

Club Insomnia Walking Street, South Pattaya ☎038 711322 ⓦclubinsomniagroup.com; map p.383. Currently Pattaya's most popular dance club, where you can get you in the mood at the downstairs iBar before heading upstairs to party untill late. It gets very crowded at weekends, so watch out for pickpockets. Daily 6pm–4am.

4

Gulliver's Pattaya Beach Road, near Soi 1 ☎ 038 416680 ⓦ gulliverbangkok.com; map p.383. This large venue is more bar than restaurant – though there are plenty of tempting dishes on the menu – it's the place to go to watch sports on TV, have a game of pool, or just hang out people-watching while enjoying a cocktail (around B180) or pint of Guinness (B260). Choose between the spacious terrace and a/c interior. Daily 3pm–2am.

Hops Brew House Pattaya Beach Road, between sois 13/1 (Yamato) and 13/2 (Post Office), Central Pattaya ☎ 038 710653; map p.383. Cavernous and very popular a/c beer hall that brews its own beer, serves generous wood-fired pizzas and other Italian dishes, and stages live music nightly. Attracts a youngish crowd, including vacationing couples. Daily 2pm–1/2am.

Hot Tuna Walking Street, South Pattaya; map p.383. This open-sided bar hosts live music every night, with occasional appearances by Thai rock guitarist Lam Morrison. Most nights you'll hear covers of rock classics from bands like the Eagles and The Doors. Daily 6pm–3am.

Jazz Pit At the Sugar Hut Resort, 391/18 Thanon Tabphaya, Jomtien ☎ 038 364186; map p.383. Now moved from its location at PIC Kitchen, Pattaya's premier jazz bar is worth checking out in its new location, where Thai and Western musicians perform slick renditions of jazz classics. Weds–Mon 6pm–10pm.

ENTERTAINMENT

CINEMAS
There are several English-language screenings a day at the multiplexes.

Major Cineplex The Avenue shopping centre, Pattaya 2 Road, Central Pattaya ⓦ majorcineplex.com.

SF Cinema City Central Festival, Pattaya Beach Road, Central Pattaya ⓦ sfcinemacity.com.

KATOEY CABARETS
Tour groups – and families – constitute the main audience at Pattaya's *katoey* cabarets. Glamorous and highly professional, each theatre has a troupe of sixty or more transgender women who run through twenty musical-style numbers in fishnets and crinolines, ball gowns and leathers, against ever more lavish stage sets. Any tour agent can organize tickets or you can book at the venue.

Alcazar Opposite Soi 4 on Pattaya 2 Road in North Pattaya ⓦ alcazarthailand.com. From B600. Daily 5pm, 6.30pm, 8pm & 9.30pm.

Tiffany's North of Soi 1 on Pattaya 2 Road in North Pattaya ⓦ tiffany.cloudapp.net. Also hosts an annual international *katoey* beauty pageant over five days in March, Miss International Queen (ⓦ missinternationalqueen.com). From B800. Daily 6pm, 7.30pm & 9pm.

SHOPPING

Asia Books Floor 3, Central Festival Centre, between Pattaya Beach and Pattaya 2 Roads. Good selection of English-language books. Daily 11am–11pm; map p.383.

PATTAYA'S SEX INDUSTRY

Of the thousand-plus bars in Pattaya, the vast majority are staffed by women and men whose aim is to get bought for the night – depending on whom you believe, there are between six thousand and twenty thousand Thais (and quite a few Russians) working in Pattaya's **sex industry**; most depressing of all is that this workforce includes children as young as 10, despite fairly frequent high-profile paedophile arrests. The vast majority of Pattaya's bars are open-air **"bar-beers"**, which group themselves in neon clusters all over North, Central and South Pattaya so that there's barely a 500m stretch of road without a rowdy enclave. The setup is the same in all of them: from mid-afternoon the punters – usually lone males – sit on stools around a brashly lit circular bar, behind which the hostesses (and their high-end versions, the "coyotes") keep the drinks, bawdy chat and well-worn jokes flowing. Where prices aren't established, this is open to a well-known scam of demanding an inflated bill at the end, with threats if the client doesn't cough up.

Drinks are a lot more expensive in the bouncer-guarded **go-go bars** on Walking Street in South Pattaya, where near-naked hostesses serve the beer and live sex shows keep the boozers hooked through the night. The scene follows much the same pattern as in Patpong, Nana and Soi Cowboy in Bangkok, with the women dancing on a small stage in the hope they might be bought for the night – or the week. Go-go dancers, "modelling competitions", shower shows and striptease are also the mainstays of the **gay scene**, centred on Pattayaland Soi 3 (Soi 13/5), South Pattaya.

DIRECTORY

Emergencies For all emergencies, call the tourist police on ☎1155 (free, 24hr) or contact them at their office (☎038 429 371) beside TAT on Buddha Hill, between South Pattaya and Jomtien; in the evenings, they also set up a post at the north end of Walking Street.

Hospitals and dentists The best-equipped hospital is the private Bangkok–Pattaya Hospital (☎1719 or ☎038 259 999, ⍟bangkokpattayahospital.com) on Thanon Sukhumvit, about 400m north of the intersection with North Pattaya Road, which also has dental services.

Immigration office Soi 5, off Jomtien Beach Road, Jomtien (Daily 8.30am–4.30pm; ☎038 252751–4).

Ban Phe

The small coastal town of **BAN PHE**, which lies 17km east of Rayong, its provincial capital, and about 200km from Bangkok, is the port for Ko Samet. Several piers for Samet boats compete for attention here, along with minimarkets, internet centres and tour desks selling onward bus tickets and private transfers. Ban Phe's main street runs from west to east behind the seafront, passing in turn the Chok Krisda pier and the nearby Taruaphe pier, before petering out a few hundred metres later at the municipal pier, Tha Reua Tessaban.

ARRIVAL AND INFORMATION

BAN PHE

When the time comes to leave Ko Samet, you can book tickets for any of the following direct buses and minibuses from Ban Phe through your hotel on the island.

By bus There are direct a/c buses operated by Cherdchai between Bangkok's Eastern (Ekamai) Bus Terminal and Ban Phe; on departure from Ban Phe, you can easily find them near the municipal pier. Coming by bus from Chanthaburi or Trat, you'll be dropped at a T-junction on Highway 3, from where a songthaew or motorbike taxi will take you the remaining 2km to the Ban Phe piers. Rayong has a wider choice of buses, including services to Chiang Mai and Isaan; the Ban Phe piers are served by frequent songthaews (about 30min) from Rayong bus station.

Destinations Bangkok (14 daily; 3hr); Chanthaburi (from Highway 3; 6 daily; 1hr 30min); Trat (from Highway 3; 6 daily; 3hr).

By a/c minibus A/c minibuses run between many locations in Bangkok, including Thanon Khao San (3–4hr; B250), Victory Monument (about 3hr 30min; B200) and Suvarnabhumi Airport (about 3hr; B500), and Ban Phe. There are also services from Pattaya (see page 387) and Ko Chang (see page 405). On departure, you'll find numerous a/c minibus companies in Ban Phe, including some at the municipal pier and in the two sois opposite Taruaphe (including Pattaya and Ko Chang services), on either side of a 7-Eleven, and a frequent Victory Monument service runs from 200m west of the municipal pier.

By boat Frequent boats run from Ban Phe to Ko Samet, leaving from various piers – Tha Reua Tessaban has the widest choice. Details are given in our Ko Samet coverage (see below).

Tourist police At the municipal pier ☎038 611 227 or ☎1155.

ACCOMMODATION

Ban Phe Hostel In the lane next to the 7-Eleven opposite the Taruaphe pier ☎082 244 2241, ⍟hostelworld.com. This simple but clean hostel is a good choice for accommodation if you get stuck in Ban Phe, offering a couple of doubles and a couple of dorms, all with shared bathrooms. There's a communal area and bar for guests too. Doubles B400 dorms B200

Ko Samet

B200 national park admission fee

Blessed with the softest, squeakiest sand within weekending distance of Bangkok, the tiny island of **KO SAMET**, which measures just 6km from top to toe, is a favourite escape for Thais, expats and tourists. Its fourteen small but dazzlingly white beaches are breathtakingly beautiful, lapped by pale blue water and in places still shaded by coconut palms and occasional white-flowered cajeput (*samet*) trees, which gave the island its name and which are used to build boats. But they are also crowded – although on weekdays there's a lot more room to breathe and relax – and developed to full capacity with over fifty sprawling, albeit low-rise, bungalow developments, a disfiguring number of which pay scant attention to landscaping and rubbish disposal. It's a sobering state of affairs considering that much of the island's coastline has been protected as part of the Khao Laem Ya – Mu Ko Samet **national park** since 1981; all visitors to Ko Samet are required to pay the standard national park fee on arrival, and you should keep your ticket to show if you pass another checkpoint. Most hoteliers also pay rent to park authorities, but there's little evidence that this income has been used to improve the island's infrastructure.

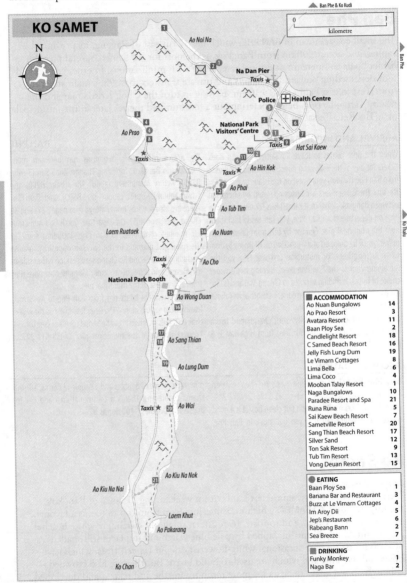

KO SAMET

Ban Phe & Ko Kudi

0   1
kilometre

Ban Phe

Ko Thalu

Ao Noi Na

Na Dan Pier
Taxis ★

Police ✚ **Health Centre**

**National Park
Visitors' Centre**

Ao Prao

Taxis ★

Taxis ★   Hat Sai Kaew

Ao Hin Kok

Taxis ★

Ao Phai

Ao Tub Tim

Laem Ruataek   Ao Nuan

Taxis ★   Ao Cho

National Park Booth

Ao Wong Duan

Ao Sang Thian

Ao Lung Dum

Taxis ★   Ao Wai

Ao Kiu Na Nok

Ao Kiu Na Nai

Laem Khut

Ao Pakarang

Ko Chan

■ ACCOMMODATION	
Ao Nuan Bungalows	14
Ao Prao Resort	3
Avatara Resort	11
Baan Ploy Sea	2
Candlelight Resort	18
C Samed Beach Resort	16
Jelly Fish Lung Dum	19
Le Vimarn Cottages	8
Lima Bella	6
Lima Coco	4
Mooban Talay Resort	1
Naga Bungalows	10
Paradee Resort and Spa	21
Runa Runa	5
Sai Kaew Beach Resort	7
Sametville Resort	20
Sang Thian Beach Resort	17
Silver Sand	12
Ton Sak Resort	9
Tub Tim Resort	13
Vong Deuan Resort	15

● EATING	
Baan Ploy Sea	1
Banana Bar and Restaurant	3
Buzz at Le Vimarn Cottages	4
Im Aroy Dii	5
Jep's Restaurant	6
Rabeang Bann	2
Sea Breeze	7

■ DRINKING	
Funky Monkey	1
Naga Bar	2

4

WATERSPORTS AND BOAT TRIPS ON SAMET

Samet has no decent coral reefs of its own, so you'll have to take a boat trip to the islands of Ko Kudi and Ko Thalu, off the northeast coast, to get good **snorkelling** (around B700 from most beaches) or **diving**. From the main beaches you can also organize **boat trips** around Samet itself (around B500), rent kayaks, jet skis and paddle boards, and arrange banana-boat rides and parasailing.

Samed Resorts Diving Centre Ao Prao ☎038 dive, and B17,000 for the four-day PADI Open Water 644100–3, ⊛samedresorts.com. B2000 for one course.

Samet's best **beaches** are along the **east coast**, where you'll find nearly all the bungalow resorts, though there's one rather exclusive beach on the west coast, and the north-coast shoreline retains a pleasing village ambience. Most islanders and many resort staff live in the northeast, near the island's main pier, in the ramshackle, badly drained village of **Na Dan**, which has small shops and cheap food stalls as well as Samet's only school, health centre and wat. Na Dan's high street, which runs from the pier down to Hat Sai Kaew, is paved, as are the island's other main routes – heading south down the island's forested central ridge, west to Ao Prao and along the northwest coast. Much of the **interior** is dense jungle, home to hornbills, gibbons and spectacular butterflies. The evergreen vegetation belies the fact that there are no rivers on this unusually dry island, which gets only scant rainfall in an average year. Lack of rain is another plus point for tourists, though it means water is a precious and expensive commodity as it has to be trucked in from the mainland.

The most backpacker-oriented beaches are east-coast **Ao Hin Kok**, **Ao Phai** and **Ao Tub Tim**, with Ao Hin Kok and Ao Phai both quite lively in the evenings; the travellers' vibe at nearby **Ao Nuan** is more alternative, with **Ao Sang Thian** and north-coast **Ao Noi Na** also worth investigating. **Hat Sai Kaew** and **Ao Wong Duan** are the busiest beaches on the east coast, dominated by upper-scale accommodation aimed at families, package tourists and Bangkok trendies. Samet's super-deluxe accommodation is on west-coast **Ao Prao** and southern beauty **Ao Kiu**.

Shops and stalls in Na Dan (which has a pharmacy) and on all the main beaches sell basic travellers' necessities. Many bungalows have **safety deposits** and it's worth making use of them: theft is an issue on Samet and there are occasional instances of drinks being spiked by freelance bar-girls, and punters waking next day without their valuables.

Na Dan and Hat Sai Kaew

From **NA DAN** pier, a ten-minute walk south along the high street brings you to **HAT SAI KAEW**, or Diamond Beach, named for its long and extraordinarily beautiful stretch of luxuriant sand, so soft and clean it squeaks underfoot – a result, apparently, of its unusually high silicon content. Unsurprisingly, it's the busiest beach on Samet, its shorefront packed with bungalows, restaurants, beachwear stalls, deckchairs and parasols, though the northern end is slightly more peaceful.

Ao Hin Kok

Separated from Hat Sai Kaew by a low promontory on which sits a mermaid statue (a reference to the early nineteenth-century poem, *Phra Abhai Mani*, by famous local poet Sunthorn Phu), **AO HIN KOK** is much smaller than its neighbour, and has more of a travellers' vibe. Just three sets of bungalows overlook the petite white-sand beach from the slope on the far side of the dirt road, and you can walk here from Na Dan in about fifteen minutes.

Ao Phai

Narrow but sparkling little **AO PHAI**, around the next headland from Ao Hin Kok, is Samet's party beach, where the shoreside *Silver Sand* bar and disco is known for its late-night dance music (with a strong gay presence at weekends). Not everyone has to join in though, as the bungalows on the fringes of the bay are far enough away for a good night's sleep. There's a minimarket on the beach, and you can walk to Na Dan pier in twenty minutes.

Ao Tub Tim

Also known as Ao Pudsa, **AO TUB TIM** is another cute white-sand bay sandwiched between rocky points, partly shaded with palms and backed by a wooded slope. It has just two bungalow operations and is only a short stroll from Ao Phai and the other beaches further north, and a half-hour hike from Na Dan pier.

Ao Nuan

Clamber up over the headland from Ao Tub Tim (which gives you a fine panorama over Hat Sai Kaew) to reach Samet's smallest and most laidback beach, the secluded **AO NUAN**, effectively the private domain of *Ao Nuan Bungalows* (see page 397). Because it's some way off the main track, the beach gets hardly any through-traffic and feels quiet and private. Although not brilliant for swimming, the rocky shore reveals a good patch of sand when the tide withdraws; the more consistent beach at Ao Tub Tim is only five minutes' walk to the north, and **Ao Cho**, which has some coral, is a five-minute walk south along the footpath.

Ao Wong Duan

The crescent-moon bay of **AO WONG DUAN**, a ten-minute walk round the next-but-one point from Ao Nuan, is Samet's second most popular beach after Hat Sai Kaew, but the mood is calmer and more family oriented while the water is still clear and the backdrop of trees gives plenty of shade. It offers some attractive upmarket accommodation; most guests are either Chinese and Russian package tourists, Pattaya overnighters, or weekending Bangkokians. Although the beach is fairly long and broad, the central shorefront is almost lost under a knot of tiny bars (many with irresistibly comfy armchairs) and tourist shops, and the main stretch of beach all but disappears at high tide. Facilities include minimarkets and ATMs.

Ao Sang Thian (Candlelight Beach) and Ao Lung Dum

A favourite with Thai students, who relish the beauty of its slightly wild setting, **AO SANG THIAN** ("Candlelight Beach") and contiguous Ao Lung Dum display almost none of the commerce of Wong Duan, a couple of minutes' walk over the hill, though the scenic shorefront is fronted by an unbroken line of bungalows. The narrow, white-sand coastline is dotted with wave-smoothed rocks and partitioned by larger outcrops that create several distinct bays; as it curves outwards to the south you get a great view of the island's east coast. At its southern end, Ao Sang Thian becomes **AO LUNG DUM**, and the various little bungalow outfits fringing the shore here are pretty similar.

Ao Wai

A fifteen-minute walk along the coast path from Lung Dum brings you to **AO WAI**, a very pretty white-sand bay, partially shaded and a good size considering it supports just one (large) **bungalow** operation, *Sametville Resort* (see page 397), which also spills across on to neighbouring little Ao Hin Kleang.

Ao Kiu

About a kilometre south of Ao Wai, the gorgeous little twin bays of **AO KIU** – Ao Kiu Na Nok on the east coast and Ao Kiu Na Nai on the west – are separated by just a few hundred metres of land. Both beaches are the domain of Samet's most exclusive hotel, the *Paradee Resort and Spa* (see page 397).

Ao Prao (Paradise Bay)

On the upper west coast, the rugged, rocky coastline only softens into beach once, at **AO PRAO**, also known as Paradise Bay, some 4km north of Ao Kiu Na Nai. This is Samet's most upmarket beach, dominated by two expensively elegant resorts, plus one slightly more affordable option, and nothing else to lower the tone. A paved road branches off to here from the main road heading south down the island, passing a large reservoir along the way. If staying on Ao Prao, your hotel will arrange boat transfers to Ban Phe on the mainland.

Ao Noi Na

West of Na Dan, the island's north coast – known simply as **AO NOI NA** even though it's not strictly a single bay – has a refreshingly normal village feel compared to the rest of Samet. There are an increasing number of places to stay along the narrow coastal road here, offering serene views across the water to the mainland hills behind Ban Phe, and just one white-sand beach of note at the far western end. Though this beach has been hogged by the luxurious *Mooban Talay Resort* (see page 398), it's not private and you can either walk there from Na Dan pier in about twenty-five minutes or ride by motorbike in five minutes, passing a good **restaurant** at Baan Ploy Sea (see page 398) en route.

ARRIVAL AND DEPARTURE   KO SAMET

The port of departure for Ko Samet is **Ban Phe** (see page 391). It helps to know where you are staying on your first night as this will determine your method of arrival; if you arrive without plans, you'll be besieged by touts and drivers looking for a commission. Once settled, all resorts, hotels and guest houses can help with onward travel, whether bus tickets to Bangkok or eastward travel towards Cambodia.

BY BOAT

RESORT BOATS

If you're staying in any of Samet's mid-range or expensive accommodation, ask the resort about boats when you book: many establishments have their own big boats or speedboats to ferry you direct from Ban Phe on reasonably priced shared transfers (usually at set times). Such transfers may be free, but a few resorts make their paid transfers compulsory. You might also want to look into the packages offered by many resorts, which is how most Thais travel to Ko Samet: as well as boats and accommodation, these might include things like dinners and massages.

PUBLIC BOATS

There are half a dozen competing piers in Ban Phe, offering a bewildering variety of speedboats and bigger, slower but much cheaper wooden boats; prices on the latter to Samet's main pier, Na Dan, are fixed (B50 one-way; 40min). Blue wooden boats direct to Ao Wong Duan are run by Malibu Travel (B70 one-way; 70min) from the Taruaphe pier. Watch out for rip-off touts in Ban Phe who try to sell boat tickets at inflated prices or falsely claim that visitors to Ko Samet have to buy a return boat ticket. The first boat from Ko Samet back to Ban Phe leaves Na Dan pier at 7am (from Ao Wong Duan at 8.30am, noon and 3.30pm), and in theory there's then an hourly service across to Ban Phe until 6pm, but if you have a plane to catch you should allow for boat no-shows and delays.

Tha Reua Tessaban The municipal pier at the east end of Ban Phe has a rather chaotic market hall of a dozen or so private booths which offer the widest choice of speedboats, as well as wooden boats (in high season, hourly to Na Dan, plus three daily to Ao Wong Duan for B70).

Chok Krisda About 500m west of Tha Reua Tessaban, this helpful pier (☎ 081 862 4067) offers speedboats (B1500/ boat to Na Dan; 15min) as well as wooden boats hourly to Na Dan (8am–6pm) and Ao Wong Duan (2 daily, 3 daily in the opposite direction; 70min; B70).

4

GETTING AROUND

A good way to explore the island is by walking south along the east-coast beaches and the narrow trails over headlands that connect them. This allows you to check out the mood of each beach and decide which is best for you. Now that the main roads are paved, it's also easy to explore by motorbike, though the sidetracks to beaches are bumpy and hazardous, so take care. Otherwise, there are shared taxis that run up and down the main road on the east coast, and waiting at stops marked on the map (see page 392).

By songthaew Fleets of green songthaews wait for fares at the Na Dan pier and half a dozen other stands around the island, as marked on our map (see page 392); they will also pick up from accommodation if you get staff to phone them, but rates are high. You'll generally be charged for chartering the whole vehicle (Na Dan pier to Ao Sang Thian B350; Ao Wong Duan to Hat Sai Kaew B200). Only if there's a large group of people travelling, for example when boats dock at Na Dan, will you get the "shared" rates (B20–B100/person, depending where you are going and how many passengers there are).

By motorbike Motorbikes are available for rent all over the island for B300–B500/day. Check that things like brakes and lights work OK as there are several steep hills to negotiate, and side tracks are treacherous.

ACCOMMODATION

The trend across the island is upmarket, and in high season you'll be hard pressed to secure an en-suite **bungalow** for under B800, though a few B400 dorm beds are available. All beaches get packed on weekends and national holidays, when booking ahead is advisable, though, unusually for Thailand, walk-in guests are often offered the best rates. Many bungalow managers raise their **prices** by sixty percent during peak periods and sometimes on weekends as well: the rates quoted here are typical weekday high-season rates. Keep in mind that on the far-flung beaches, your eating options are limited.

Choose between the poolside villas in the 'hip zone', rooms with balconies/terraces in the 'hub zone', or the deluxe cottages in the 'hide zone' on the quiet Laluna beach. Free daily yoga classes. $\overline{B6500}$

Ton Sak Resort Hat Sai Kaew ☎038 644314, ⓦtonsak. com; map p.392. The timbered cabins here are packed very close together, but the surrounding borders of shrubs add a little privacy, and few are more than 100m from the water. Interiors are comfortable if a little old-fashioned, and have a/c and modern hot-water bathrooms. It's worth paying a bit extra for deluxe rooms, away from the frantic beachfront. Breakfast included. $\overline{B2300}$

HAT SAI KAEW AND NA DAN

Much of the accommodation on Hat Sai Kaew is crammed uncomfortably close together and prices are high. Cheaper rooms are available at places like Runa Runa on the main street from Na Dan.

Lima Bella Na Dan ☎038 644222, ⓦlimaresort.co.th; map p.392. This little garden haven occupies a quiet heliconia-filled plot with its own pretty swimming pool, on the semicircular road that arcs round behind and to the east of Na Dan high street. Its 26 design-conscious a/c rooms all have hot water, fridges, TVs and daybeds; some have separate mezzanine bedrooms or living areas and many have bathtubs. The ambience is more intimate and private than most hotels on Samet and it's popular with families. Breakfast included. $\overline{B3000}$

Runa Runa On the west side of the main street from Na Dan to Hat Sai Kaew, about halfway along. ☎038 644306; map p.392. In the heart of the action and just a few minutes' walk from Na Dan pier, this hostel is a clean, cheap base if you're likely to be out most of the time. Smallish doubles and dorms with shared bathrooms, plus a small communal area. Double $\overline{B750}$ dorm $\overline{B500}$

Sai Kaew Beach Resort Hat Sai Kaew ☎038 644197, ⓦsameresorts.com; map p.392. This popular and highly efficient resort has over 150 a/c rooms with hot water, TV and fridge, most of them in distinctive and thoughtfully designed bungalows in bright primary colours.

AO HIN KOK

Avatara Resort Ao Hin Kok ☎038 644 112–3; map p.392. This stylish new resort has taken over the hillside formerly occupied by Jep's Bungalows, and perhaps more importantly, the hugely popular restaurant beachfront restaurant, which, for the moment at least, still bears Jep's name. A few of the old bungalows remain at the bottom of the hill, but the smart new rooms are in a block on the hillside, with a/c, hot water and efficient service. Bungalows $\overline{B1200}$, rooms $\overline{B3500}$

Naga Bungalows Ao Hin Kok ☎038 644035 ⓦnaga bungalows.com; map p.392. Long-running, basic resort, with a beachfront bar, a secondhand bookshop, and a currency exchange. Simple bamboo and wood huts are stacked in tiers up the slope, with decks, mosquito nets and shared bathrooms, as well as pricier concrete a/c rooms with their own adjacent hot-water bathroom. There is bar noise quite late and the compound's a bit scrappy, but the rooms are reasonably well maintained. Fan $\overline{B600}$, a/c $\overline{B1500}$

AO PHAI

Silver Sand Middle of Ao Phai ☎038 644300–1, ⓦsilversandsamed.com; map p.392. This party hub has a spread of well-turned-out rooms, including whitewashed chalets set around a pretty garden; they all come with safety boxes, verandas and good modern hot-water bathrooms, and some have polished wooden floors. An ideal base if you plan to party, as it's not far to stagger from the bar to bed. B2500

AO TUB TIM

Tub Tim Resort Ao Tub Tim ☎ 038 644 025–9, Ⓦtubtimresort.com; map p.392. The most popular place to stay on Ao Tub Tim is a sprawling, well-run resort with over a hundred handsome chalet-style wooden bungalows of various sizes and designs, all with classy modern furnishings and outdoor space, plus a good restaurant. The cheapest rooms are in a concrete block on the hill; they're a decent size and have a shared veranda. Breakfast is included in a/c rooms. Fan B600, a/c B2000

AO NUAN

★ **Ao Nuan Bungalows** Ao Nuan ☎ 038 644 334; map p.392. The octagonal restaurant and simple, idiosyncratic huts here hark back to a mellower, old-school island vibe, entirely removed from the commercialism and party-goers of the other beaches. The eleven sturdy timber huts are each built to a slightly different design and dotted across the tree-covered slope that drops down to the gorgeous, tiny bay, with a few hanging right over the beach, making it feel like just yours. Sharing bathrooms, the cheapest are large but spartan, with just a platform bed and a mosquito net; the most expensive boast a/c and hot water. What really makes this place, though, is the caring and competent family that run it. Wi-fi in restaurant area only. Fan B800, a/c B1500

AO WONG DUAN

Vong Deuan Resort Middle of Ao Wong Duan ☎ 091 234 7770, Ⓦvrresortkohsamed.com; map p.392. Ideally located in the middle of the beach, with attractive a/c bungalows in various designs set around a pretty tropical garden, including nice white cottages with thatched roofs, contemporary styled interiors and garden bathrooms (with hot showers). Service is efficient, attentive and hotel-like, which makes it a favourite with older guests. Breakfast included. B2700

C Samed Beach Resort Southern Ao Wong Duan ☎ 038 644260, Ⓦthecsamed.com; map p.392. Occupying a big chunk of the bay's southern end, this resort features over fifty rooms, all of them with safes and a/c. The spacious cottages are whitewashed timber huts built on stilts, with picture windows, decks and modern furnishings, divided into four types; standard, superior, seaview and beachfront, though interiors are all similar. There's also an attractive restaurant deck jutting out over the water, and kayaks and snorkelling equipment for rent. B2850

AO SANG THIAN

Candlelight Resort Ao Sang Thian ☎ 098 979 7910; map p.392. Simple wooden bungalows strung out in a long line, each one facing the water. All have a/c, hot showers and TVs but not much in terms of furnishings; there's no restaurant here either. One of the quietest spots on the island, on weekdays at least. B1200

Sang Thian Beach Resort Towards Ao Sang Thian's northern end ☎ 038 644 255, Ⓦsangthianbeachresort.com; map p.392. This efficiently-run complex, comprising a shop and an expansive waterfront restaurant area, stands in stark contrast to the minimalism of the neighbouring Candlelight Resort. It boasts tasteful a/c timber chalets built up the cliffside on a series of decks and steps – the decor is navy-and-white maritime chic. There's hot water, TVs and fridges, and views, mostly encompassing the sea, are above average for the area. B2500

AO LUNG DUM

Jelly Fish Lung Dum Ao Lung Dum ☎ 081 458 8430 or ☎ 081 652 8056; map p.392. Friendly spot under the bougainvillaea with a decent waterside restaurant. Most of the twenty bungalows with hot showers are right on the rocky shore, practically overhanging the water; a few cheaper rooms and bungalows at the back are also available. Fan B900, a/c B1300

AO WAI

★ **Sametville Resort** Ao Wai ☎ 038 651 681-2, Ⓦsametvilleresort.com; map p.392. This sizeable resort actually occupies two bays, both Ao Wai and Ao Hin Kleang; since Ao Wai is one of Samed's prettiest beaches, it gets full at weekends. There's a large swimming pool and bungalows of all kinds, all surrounded by greenery and plenty of different designs to choose from, including a cute converted boat; there's a detailed map of the resort on their website. Fortunately there's also a decent restaurant, as it's a bit of a walk to anywhere else. Fan B1400, a/c B2000

AO KIU

Paradee Resort and Spa Ao Kiu ☎ 038 644285-7, Ⓦwww.samedresorts.com; map p.392. Top of the range on Samet, a very luxurious five-star resort where each of the forty villas stretches over more than 100 square metres and most have their own small private pools. There's also an infinity-edged main pool, a spa and fitness centre, plus lots of nice little extras like DVD players, free kayaks and snorkelling equipment. B17,500

AO PRAO (PARADISE BAY)

Ao Prao Resort Ao Prao ☎ 038 644101, Ⓦwww.samedresorts.com; map p.392. Fifty luxurious wooden chalets and rooms set in a mature tropical garden that slopes down to the beach, all with a/c, TVs and mini-bars. There's an infinity pool, a dive centre, windsurfing and kayaking, among lots of watersports, and a picturesquely sited restaurant with a live band most evenings in high season. The resort runs a shuttle boat from Ban Phe three

4

times a day (11am, 1pm and 4pm; free for guests). B6850
Le Vimarn Cottages Ao Prao ☎ 038 644104, ⓦ www.
samedresorts.com; map p.392. The most indulgent
resort on this beach comprises charming, gorgeously
furnished cottages, a delightful spa and an infinity pool. Its
Buzz restaurant (see opposite) is highly regarded. B9,000
Lima Coco Ao Prao ☎ 038 644068, ⓦ limaresort.co.th;
map p.392. The youngest, trendiest and cheapest choice on
the beach, with a Bangkok contemporary chic look and lots of
white walls, brightly coloured cushions, day beds and decks.
Rooms are built close together in layers up the side of the hill,
so that most have some kind of a sea view. There's kayaks,
snorkels and sun beds for rent. Breakfast included. B3390

AO NOI NA
Baan Ploy Sea Ao Noi Na ☎ 02 438 9771–2, ⓦ www.
samedresorts.com; map p.392. Striking, brown

contemporary building with an orange infinity pool, where
bedrooms done out in dark wood and orange come with a/c,
rain showers, TV and fridge. Pricier options come with a sea-
view deck, and there's a good, relaxing seafood restaurant
(see below) on the beachfront. Breakfast and boat transfers
included. B4400
Mooban Talay Resort Northwestern Ao Noi Na ☎ 081
838 8682, ⓦ moobantalay.com; map p.392. At the far
northwest end of Noi Na bay is one of the classiest resorts on
the island, complete with its own pier. It's a secluded haven
at the end of the road, set under the trees on a gorgeous,
quiet white-sand beach. Accommodation is in large,
attractive a/c bungalows, all with platform beds, garden
bathrooms and outdoor seating: the priciest, seafront ones
have enormous decks, and there's a beachside pool and a
spa. Boat transfers and breakfast included. B3800

EATING

One of the wonders of Ko Samet is that just when you're
getting peckish while lazing on the beach, a grilled-chicken
or fresh-fruit vendor comes strolling by. As for eating in
restaurants, most resorts turn out reasonable food, so
many visitors tend not to wander far from their base, but
the following places are worth making the effort to get to.

rounder serves a great menu of authentic Thai dishes
(including popular *som tam* sets for B190), seafood, Indian
(with chicken biriyani for B190 and plenty of veggie dishes),
Italian and Mexican food at tables on the sand, set under trees
strung with fairy lights and given extra atmosphere by mellow
music. Also does cappuccino and cakes. Daily 7am–12.30am.

HAT SAI KAEW AND NA DAN
Banana Bar and Restaurant Na Dan high street,
opposite the police station; map p.392. Tiny, welcoming
establishment serving tastily authentic yellow, green and
red curries (B90), as well as *tom yam* and spicy salads. Daily
8am–10pm.
Im Aroy Dii Na Dan high street, 10m from the National
Park box on Hat Sai Kaew, on the west side of the road
(no English sign); map p.392. There's not much to this
basic but clean and bright restaurant, but its name, meaning
"Full, Delicious, Good", says it all: tasty, cheap dishes on rice
(from B60), as well as more interesting options such as squid
with salted egg and chicken with cashew nuts (both B140).
Fruit shakes and a cheery chef-owner, too. Daily 7am–9pm.
Rabeang Bann In front of Na Dan pier. ☎ 038 644063;
map p.392. Conveniently located if you're hungry on
arrival or need somewhere to relax while waiting for a
ferry to leave. They offer everything from rice soup (B70) to
burger and fries (B120) and ice creams. Daily 8am–9pm.

AO HIN KOK
★ **Jep's Restaurant** Ao Hin Kok ☎ 038 644 113; map
p.392. Now run by the Avatara Resort, this popular all-

AO PHAI
Sea Breeze At the north end of Ao Phai ☎ 038 644 124;
map p.392. Simple but satisfying seafood restaurant on
the beach, with a BBQ every evening from 6pm, as well as
dishes like seafood fried rice (B100). Wash it down with a
cold beer or fresh-fruit smoothie as you wiggle your toes in
the sand. Daily 8am–11pm

AO PRAO (PARADISE BAY)
Buzz at Le Vimarn Cottages Ao Prao ☎ 038 644 104,
ⓦ www.samedresorts.com; map p.392. Very refined
restaurant serving highly regarded Thai food, including a wide
choice of salads, dips and curries (from B290), in its chic modern
dining room and on the upstairs terrace. 10am–11pm.

AO NOI NA
Baan Ploy Sea Ao Noi Na ☎ 038 644 188–9; map
p.392. Seafood restaurant belonging to the resort of the
same name (see above), set in an impressive, open-sided
wooden building supported on tree trunks, with low tables,
sunken floors and axe cushions to recline on. The menu
includes lots of tempting dishes such as the prawn green
curry (B250). Daily 11am–9pm.

DRINKING

HAT SAI KAEW AND NA DAN
Funky Monkey Na Dan high street, just before the

National Parks checkpoint. ☎ 092 336 7843; map
p.392. A bustling bar in the evening, serving large beers

for B100, plus pizzas and all-day breakfasts. Worth checking out if you're heading into town. Daily 8.30am–11pm.

AO HIN KOK

Naga Bar Ao Hin Kok ☎ 038 644 035; map p.392. Great place for drinking, dancing, body painting and meeting world travellers. B52 shots, Red Bull buckets and various beers are on offer. No live music but a good soundtrack. Daily 4pm–midnight.

DIRECTORY

Banks There are ATMs at Na Dan pier, beside the Hat Sai Kaew national park office, and on all main beaches; the bigger resorts also change money, but at a poor rate.

Emergencies Ko Samet's health centre and police station (☎ 038 644 111) are on Na Dan high street, but for anything serious you should go to the Bangkok–Rayong hospital in Rayong (☎ 038 611 104, ✆ rayonghospital.net).

Post office On Ao Noi Na (see map p.000).

Chanthaburi

For over five hundred years, the seams of rock rich in sapphires and rubies that streak the hills of eastern Thailand have drawn prospectors and traders of all nationalities to the provincial capital of **CHANTHABURI**, 80km east of Ban Phe. Many of these hopefuls established permanent homes in the town, particularly the Shans from Myanmar, the Chinese and the Cambodians. Though the veins of precious stones have now been all but exhausted, Chanthaburi's reputation as a gem centre has continued to thrive and this is still one of the most famous places in Thailand to trade in gems (most of them now imported from Sri Lanka and elsewhere), not least because Chanthaburi is as respected a cutting centre as Bangkok, and Thai lapidaries are considered among the most skilled – and affordable – in the world. Chanthaburi is also an exceptionally fertile province, renowned for its abundance of orchards, particularly durian, rambutan and mangosteen, which are celebrated with an annual **fruit festival** in the town, held in May or June.

The town is becoming a popular weekend destination for Bangkokians looking to slow down the pace of life, usually by strolling along the atmospheric Chantaboon Waterfront, a wonderfully preserved and regenerated riverside lane, while the nearby cathedral and gem market provide added attractions. There are few Western faces to be seen here, but some appealing sleeping and eating options, making it a good spot to get off the beaten track for a while. The nearby Chanthaburi coastline is barely developed for tourism, though it's popular with Thai visitors for its quiet, shady beaches. Chanthaburi is also a major transit point for east-coast bus services and a handy terminus for buses to and from the northeast.

Chanthaboon Riverfront

Chanthaburi's most interesting neighbourhood is along Thanon Sukhaphiban, which runs for a kilometre beside the Chanthaburi River and is often referred to as the Chantaboon Riverfront. It's been zealously protected by the Chantaboon Waterfront Community, who have banded together to create a **Community Learning Centre** in the middle of the street with photos and information boards about the street's preservation, and who own shares in the delightful **Baan Luang Rajamaitri Historic Inn** (see below), which is part-museum, part-hotel, towards the north end of the street. The rest of the street is a wonderful mix of pastel-painted, colonial-style housefronts and traditional wooden shophouses, many displaying finely carved latticework, and trendy cafés. This district is also home to a large Catholic Vietnamese community, most of whom fled here in waves following religious persecution between the eighteenth century and the late 1970s. The earliest refugees constructed what is now, following several revamps, Thailand's largest cathedral, the **Cathedral of the Immaculate Conception**, located across the footbridge from the southern end of Thanon Sukhaphiban.

4

The gem dealers' quarter

The **gem dealers' quarter** is centred around Trok Kachang and Thanon Sri Chan (the latter signed in English as "Gem Street") and packed with dozens of gem shops. Most lie empty during the week, but on Fridays, Saturdays and Sundays they come alive as local dealers arrive to sift through mounds of tiny coloured stones and classify them for resale to the hundreds of buyers who drive down from Bangkok.

Taksin Park

Thanon Tha Chalaeb

Landscaped **Taksin Park** is the town's recreation area and memorial to King Taksin of Thonburi, the general who reunited Thailand between 1767 and 1782 after the sacking of Ayutthaya by the Burmese. Chanthaburi was the last Burmese bastion on the east coast – when Taksin took the town he effectively regained control of the whole country. The park's heroic bronze statue of Taksin is featured on the back of the B20 note.

ARRIVAL AND DEPARTURE   **CHANTHABURI TOWN**

By bus Chanthaburi bus station (☎039 311299) is on Thanon Saritdidech, about 750m northwest of the town centre and Thalat Nam Phu market. Some services are operated by regular buses, others by minibuses, and yet

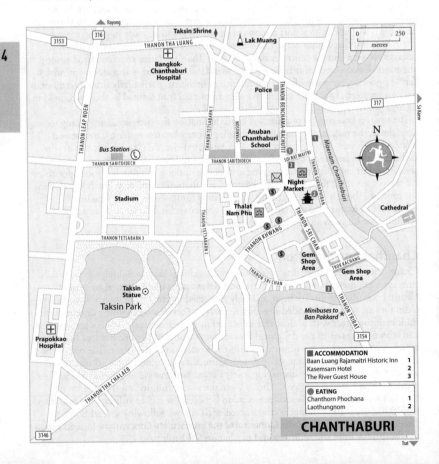

ACCOMMODATION
Baan Luang Rajamaitri Historic Inn	1
Kasemsarn Hotel	2
The River Guest House	3

EATING
Chanthorn Phochana	1
Laothungnom	2

CHANTHABURI

CROSSING TO CAMBODIA VIA CHANTHABURI PROVINCE

Most foreigners use the Aranyaprathet–Poipet crossing to get into **Cambodia** (see page 379), with access possible by bus via Chanthaburi. There are also two less used crossings in Chanthaburi province, giving access to the Cambodian town of Pailin, just east of the border. Daung Lem Border Crossing at **Ban Laem** is 88km northeast of Chanthaburi and the Phsa Prom border crossing is at **Ban Pakkard** (aka Chong Phakkat), 72km northeast of Chanthaburi. There's a minibus service in the morning from Chanthaburi (just south across the bridge from *The River Guest House*) to Ban Pakkard (1–2hr; B200) and one to Ban Laem (1–2hr; B200), that departs from south of the bridge. It's best to arm yourself in advance with an e-visa for Cambodia, but it's also possible to get a thirty-day visa on arrival at the border; if entering Thailand via this route you'll probably be obliged to show proof of onward travel from Thailand.

others by both regular buses and minibuses. There's a regular minibus service to Aranyaprathet via Sa Kaew (see page 379).

Destinations Aranyaprathet (every hour; 3hr); Bangkok (Eastern Bus Terminal; at least hourly; 4hr); Bangkok (Northern Bus Terminal; 9 daily; 4hr); Khorat (9 daily; 6hr); Laem Ngop (for Ko Chang; 3 daily; 2hr); Phitsanulok (2 daily; 11hr); Rayong (Every 40min; 2hr); Trat (hourly; 1hr 30min).

ACCOMMODATION

Baan Luang Rajamaitri Historic Inn 252 Thanon Sukhaphiban ☎ 088 843 4516. ⊕ baanluangrajamaitri. com; map p.400. If you've never slept in a museum, here's your chance. You'll need to book in advance, as it's very popular. There are just ten well-equipped rooms in this beautifully restored, 150-year-old house that is run by the Chantaboon Waterfront Community, with the ground made up of historical relics and a tranquil riverside terrace. B1550

Kasemsarn Hotel 98/1 Thanon Benchamarachutit ☎ 039 311 100, ⊕ hotelkasemsarn.com; map p.400. Unexpectedly contemporary hotel, whose comfortable a/c rooms, with hot showers, fridges and TVs, are built round a central atrium and done out in whitewash and dark wood; there is a smart coffee shop downstairs. Discounts frequently available. B1300

The River Guesthouse 3/5–8 Thanon Sri Chan ☎ 090 936 7499; map p.400. Recently refurbished, this traveller-oriented outfit offers good value. It's located on the edge of the gems quarter and features a breezy riverside terrace. The cheapest rooms are tiny and windowless and share hot-water bathrooms; it's worth forking out a bit more (B590) for a good-sized room, en-suite bathroom and view of the river. B500

EATING

Food stalls in Thalat Nam Phu wet market (open dawn to dusk) and at the informal night market off the riverside sois sell Vietnamese spring rolls (*cha gio*) with sweet sauce. Locally made Chanthaburi rice noodles (*sen Chan*) are popularly used in *phat thai* throughout Thailand, but in Chanthaburi they're also crucial to the local beef noodle soup, *kway tiaw neua liang*, whose dark broth is flavoured with pungent herbs and spices, including the cardamom that the Chanthaburi mountains are famous for. Thalat Nam Phu is also a popular place for fresh seafood, and several street stalls along Thanon Sukhaphiban sell local delicacies, both sweet and savoury.

★**Chanthorn Phochana** 102/5–8 Thanon Benchamarachutit; map p.400. By far the best of the town's restaurants is this spot opposite the *Kasemsarn Hotel*, for which Thai foodies make a beeline. As well as selling Chanthaburi delicacies as souvenirs, it serves regional dishes such as *lon puu* (a kind of salad dip with crab; B150) and *kway tiaw neua liang*, and a delicious range of spicy *yam* salads, Thai curries and stir-fries, many of them using local herbs and vegetables. Daily 9am–9pm.

Laothungnom 141 Thanon Sukhaphiban ☎ 087 611 3582; map p.400. A simple but smart café with wooden stools round tables, serving everything from rice soup (B50) to phat thai, chicken nuggets and Italian sodas. A good spot to pause for refreshment while exploring the Chantaboon riverfront. Daily 8am–8pm.

Coastal Chanthaburi

The barely developed **coastline** to the west of Chanthaburi is very pretty, popular with Thai visitors for its empty beaches and shady casuarina trees and worth exploring if you have your own transport.

YELLOW OIL

Trat is famous across Thailand for the **yellow herbal oil** mixture, *yaa luang*, invented by one of its residents, Mae Ang Ki, and used by Thais to treat many ailments: sniff it for travel sickness and blocked sinuses, or rub it on to relieve mosquito and sandfly bites, ease stomach cramps, or sterilize wounds. Ingredients include camphor and aloe vera. It's well worth investing in a lip-gloss-sized bottle of the stuff before heading off to the sandfly-plagued islands; you can buy it for about B70 and upwards at Trat market. There are now several imitations, but Mae Ang Ki's original product (Ⓦ somthawinyellowoil.com) has a tree logo to signify that it's made by royal appointment.

Hat Khung Wiman and Ao Khung Kraben

Just off Route 3399, about 30km southwest of Chanthaburi, or 80km east of Ban Phe, **HAT KHUNG WIMAN** is a quiet, shady, bronze-sand beach and has several places to stay. A couple of kilometres southeast of here and you're at the lip of **AO KHUNG KRABEN**, a deep, lagoon-like scoop of a bay that's occasionally visited by dugongs and is edged by dense mangrove forest. A wide swathe of this mangrove swamp is protected under a royal conservation project and crossed by a kilometre-long boardwalk; you can also rent double kayaks from a hut next to the observation tower for B150 an hour in the cool season and follow a signed riverine trail. Access is via Laem Sadet on the southern curve of the bay.

KKB (Khung Kraben Bay) Aquarium

Across the road from the mangrove project on Laem Sadet's beach road • Tues–Fri 8.30am–4.30pm, Sat & Sun 8.30am–5.30pm • Free

The impressively stocked **KKB Aquarium** is a royal initiative and displays a multicoloured variety of reef fish, some sea horses and a few larger marine creatures, with informative English signage. It's possible to walk here from Chao Lao Beach (3km), and as there's no public transport your only other option would be to drive.

ACCOMMODATION | KHUNG WIMAN

Al Medina Beach House Hat Khung Wiman ☏ 085 334 3555, Ⓦ almedinabeach.com. Nine very chic, Moroccan-inspired rooms, all with a/c, hot water and DVD players, some with rain showers and bathtubs. Bicycles and kayaks available. Breakfast included. B4950

★ **Faasai Resort** Khung Wiman ☏ 039 417404, Ⓦ faasai.com. This New Zealand–Thai owned, environmentally conscious resort is an ideal base from which to explore the coast. Its comfortable, family-friendly,

a/c bungalows sit in a tropical garden with views to the Cardamom mountains on the Cambodian border and there's a swimming pool and Wat Pho-trained massage therapists on site. Very unusually, the resort also has its own private little wetland conservation area, where you can sit bird-watching, swim in the natural spring pool or kayak along the rivulet. Hat Khung Wiman is 10min walk away and *Faasai* rents bicycles and kayaks, and organizes interesting local tours. B1600

Trat

The small and pleasantly unhurried provincial capital of **TRAT**, 68km southeast of Chanthaburi, is the perfect place to stock up on essentials, extend your visa, or simply take a break before striking out again. Most travellers who find themselves here are heading either for Ko Chang, for the outer islands, or for Cambodia, via the border at **Hat Lek**, 91km southeast of town. But Trat itself has its own distinctive, if understated, old-Thailand charm and there are lots of welcoming guesthouses to tempt you into staying longer.

Though there are no real sights in Trat, the historic neighbourhood down by Khlong Trat, where you'll find most of the guesthouses and traveller-oriented restaurants, is full of old wooden shophouses and narrow, atmospheric sois. The covered market in the heart of town is another fun place to wander. Out-of-town attractions that make enjoyable focuses for a leisurely cycle ride include the mangrove forest to the southeast near Ban Dan Kao, the ornate seventeenth-century **Wat Buppharam**, 2km west of Trat Department Store, and the nearby lake.

Mangrove forest

5.5km southeast of town

In the **mangrove forest** near Ban Dan Kao, a boardwalk with informative English signs takes you through the swamp; after dark it's a good place to see twinkling fireflies too. The boardwalk access is unsigned in English; to get here with your own transport, head east from Trat towards Ban Dan Kao and after about 5.4km you'll pass dolphin statues on your left – the track to the mangroves is about 100m further on, on the right (if you get to the estuary and road's end you've gone about 500m too far).

ARRIVAL AND DEPARTURE
TRAT

BY PLANE

Tiny Trat airport (☎039 525767–8), served by Bangkok Airways, is about 16km from the Ko Chang piers at Laem Ngop. There's an airport shuttle minibus direct to Ko Chang hotels for B500/person, including ferry ticket, and a/c minibuses to Trat town (run by Bangkok Limousine; ☎039 516005) are also B500/person, for a ride of less than 30min (though at least you'll be dropped off at your hotel).

Destinations Bangkok (3 daily; 50min).

BY BUS

All buses terminate at the bus station, 1.5km northeast of central Trat on Highway 318, from where songthaews shuttle passengers into the town centre (B30, or about B100 if chartered) or on to the departure points for the islands (see below). A/c minibuses to Bangkok's Victory Monument

4

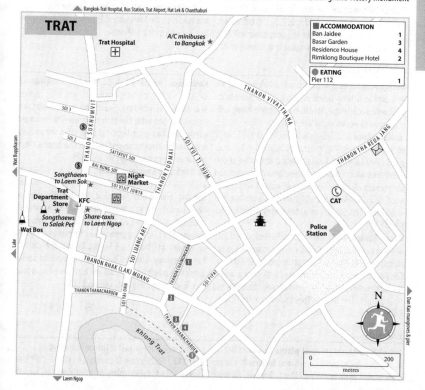

TRAT

▲ Bangkok-Trat Hospital, Bus Station, Trat Airport, Hat Lek & Chanthaburi

◼ ACCOMMODATION	
Ban Jaidee	1
Basar Garden	3
Residence House	4
Rimklong Boutique Hotel	2

● EATING	
Pier 112	1

Trat Hospital

A/c minibuses to Bangkok ★

THANON VIVATTHANA

SOI 3

THANON SUKHUMVIT

SOI 2

SATTAYUT SOI

RAI RUNG SOI

SOI VIJIT JUNYA

Songthaews to Laem Sok

Night Market

Trat Department Store

KFC

SOI YOT TI THUM

THANON TUD MAI

THANON THA REUA JANG

Songthaews to Salak Pet

Share-taxis to Laem Ngop

Wat Bos

CAT

SOI LUANG ART

Police Station

THANON CHAIMONGKON

THANON RHAK (LAK) MUANG

SOI PIPAI

THANON THANACHAROEN

SOI VIJAI

THANON THANAKCHAROEN

Khlong Trat

▲ Wat Buppharam

◀ Lake

▶ Dan Kao mangroves & pier

N

0   200

metres

▼ Laem Ngop

leave from the 7-Eleven just off Thanon Vivatthana, on the north side of town; there are also minibuses to Hat Lek from the bus station (see page 405).

Destinations Bangkok (Eastern Bus Terminal; 6 daily; 4hr 30min–6hr); Bangkok (Northern Bus Terminal; hourly; 4hr 30min); Bangkok (Suvarnabhumi Airport; 6 daily; 4hr 10min); Chanthaburi (hourly; 1hr 30min); Korat (6 daily; 7hr); Pattaya (6 daily; 4hr 30min); Rayong (6 daily; 3hr 30min); Si Racha (6 daily; 5hr).

BY BOAT
Details of boat services to Ko Chang, Ko Mak and Ko Kood are given in the relevant accounts. If you book your boat ticket through your guesthouse in Trat, they will help to arrange pick-up from the guesthouse. A useful reference for boat times is ⓦ kohchangferries.com.

VIA LAEM NGOP
All ferries to Ko Chang and some services to Ko Mak leave from one of two piers to the west of the small port town of Laem Ngop, 17km southwest of Trat (see map, p.403): Tha Thammachat and Tha Centrepoint for the Ko Chang car ferries, and Tha Krom Luang (Naval Monument Pier) for speedboats to Ko Mak. These piers are served by songthaew share-taxis from Trat's bus station and by songthaew and a/c minibus share-taxis from Thanon Sukhumvit in the town centre, costing B50/person or B250–300 if chartered; if sharing, allow 60–90min before your boat leaves for the share-taxi to fill up and get you to the pier.

VIA TRAT–SALAK PET SONGTHAEW
If you're going to the east coast of Ko Chang you can take a direct songthaew to Salak Pet (B200, including car ferry) from the temple compound behind *KFC* and Trat Department Store in Trat.

VIA LAEM SOK
Some boats to Ko Mak and nearly all boats to Ko Kood depart from Laem Sok, 30km south of Trat; boat tickets bought in Trat should include free transfers to Laem Sok, but there's also a Laem Sok songthaew service (at least hourly, 8am–1pm; 30–60min) that leaves from the town centre (see map, p.403).

INFORMATION
Tourist information The Trat and Ko Chang TAT office (daily 8.30am–4.30pm; ☎039 597259, ✉tattrat@tat. or.th) is out in Laem Ngop, but any guesthouse will help you out with information on transport to the islands or into Cambodia. Alternatively, drop by *Ban Jaidee Guest House* and ask Sergy, the knowledgeable French owner, who can help out with most travel queries.

ACCOMMODATION
Most **guesthouses** in Trat are small and friendly and are well used to fielding travellers' queries about the islands and Cambodia. All those listed here are within a 10min walk of the covered market on Soi Vijit Junya.

★ **Ban Jaidee** 67 Thanon Chaimongkon ☎039 520678 or ☎083 589 0839, ⓦhttps://bit.ly/2NtoH5s; map p.403. Very calm, good-value, inviting and rather stylish guesthouse with a pleasant seating area downstairs and just seven small, simple bedrooms. All rooms have polished wood floors, are decorated with quirky art, and share hot-water bathrooms. Staff are very knowledgeable and helpful. B300

Basar Garden 87 Thanon Thanacharoen ☎086 707 4688; map p.403. Decent-sized en-suite rooms in a lovely, atmospheric old wooden house at the greener end of town. Curtains and drapes made from faded batik sarongs add to the faintly bohemian ambience and all rooms have fans and mosquito nets. Free bicycles. They also offer cooking classes. B400

Residence House 87/1–2 Thanon Thanacharoen ☎039 510560, ⓦtrat-guesthouse.com; map p.403. Also known as Residang House, this is a comfortably appointed, good-value four-storey German–Thai-managed guesthouse. Rooms are large, light and clean and all have windows, thick mattresses and hot-water bathrooms; there are family rooms too. Fan B350, a/c B600

★ **Rimklong Boutique Hotel** 194 Thanon Lak Muang ☎081 861 7181, ⓦhttps://bit.ly/2ooI70x; map p.403. The five ground-floor rooms at this friendly, popular hotel are done out in a crisp contemporary style and well equipped: a/c, hot water, cable TV and fridge. Those on the side offer a bit more privacy than the two whose doors open right onto Thanon Lak Muang. There is also a nearly half-price single room (B600). The café in reception boasts a serious espresso machine, but you'll have to bring in your own food from outside for breakfast. B1100

EATING
Two of the best and cheapest **places to eat** in Trat are at the covered day market on Thanon Sukhumvit, and the night market (daily roughly 5–10pm), between Rai Rung Soi and Soi Vijit Junya, east of Thanon Sukhumvit.

Pier 112 132/2 Thanon Thanacharoen ☎082 469 1900; map p.403. A stylish eatery in a leafy garden, located

CROSSING THE CAMBODIAN BORDER VIA HAT LEK

Many travellers use the **Hat Lek–Koh Kong border crossing** for overland travel into Cambodia. You can arm yourself in advance with an **e-visa** for Cambodia (see page 29) and make the journey by regular public transport, but it's also possible to buy a package all the way through to Sihanoukville and Phnom Penh (around B600 through Ban Jaidee Guest House in Trat) and get a thirty-day visa on arrival at the border, though Cambodian officials have a reputation for extorting extra fees when issuing visas and for getting visitors to buy a health certificate, which is not required.

The only way to get to **Hat Lek** under your own steam is by minibus from Trat bus station, 91km northwest (roughly every 45min; 1hr–1hr 30min; B120). Hat Lek (on the Thai side) and Koh Kong (in Cambodia) are on opposite sides of the Dong Tong River estuary, but a bridge connects the two banks. Once through immigration, expensive tuk-tuks ferry you into **Koh Kong** town for onward transport to Sihanoukville and Phnom Penh or for guesthouses should you arrive too late for connections (mid-afternoon onwards). **Vans, buses and share-taxis** to Phnom Penh and Sihanoukville take around 4–5hr.

opposite Residence House, offering a range of Thai and Western dishes and several vegetarian options. Try the green curry with chicken (B100). There's also a good range of beers and cocktails. Daily 7.30am–10pm.

DIRECTORY

Emergencies Call the tourist police, who have a base at Laem Ngop, on ☎ 1155 (free, 24hr).

Hospital The best hospital is the private Bangkok–Trat Hospital (☎ 039 552 777, ⓦ bangkoktrathospital.com), part of the Bangkok Hospital group (not to be confused with the Trat Hospital), which has emergency facilities; it's on the Sukhumvit Highway, 1km north of the town centre.

Immigration office Located in Laem Ngop, 100m west of the TAT office (Mon–Fri 8.30am–4.30pm; ☎ 039 597 261).

Ko Chang

Edged with a chain of long, mostly white-sand beaches and dominated by a broad central spine of jungle-clad hills that rises sharply to over 700m, **KO CHANG** is developing fast but still feels green. It's Thailand's second-largest island, after Phuket, but unlike its bigger sister has no villages or tourist facilities within its steeply contoured and densely forested **interior**, just a few rivers, waterfalls and hiking trails that come under the auspices of the Mu Ko Chang National Park. Some of its marine environment is also protected, as the national park extends to over fifty other islands in the Ko Chang archipelago. Ko Chang's own coast, however, has seen major development over the past two decades, and the island is now well established as a mainstream destination, crowded with package tourists and the overspill from Pattaya, and suffering the inevitable inflated prices and inappropriate architecture. That said, it's still possible to find accommodation to suit most budgets, and though the beaches may be busy they're undeniably handsome, with plenty of inviting places to swim, stroll, or snooze under a palm tree.

At 30km north to south, Ko Chang has plenty of coast to explore. The western **beaches** are the prettiest and the most congested, with White Sand Beach (Hat Sai Khao) drawing the biggest crowds to its mainly upmarket and increasingly overpriced mid-range accommodation; smaller **Hat Kai Bae** is also busy. Most backpackers opt for so-called **Lonely Beach** (officially **Hat Tha Nam**), with its roadside village of travellers' accommodation and famous beachfront party scene; those in search of quiet choose the more laidback **Hat Khlong Phrao**, a long and lovely sweep of sand that caters to most pockets, or **Bang Bao**, which has a village on a jetty with fine views, and its quiet neighbouring beach, **Hat Khlong Kloi**. Every beach has **currency exchange** and most have **ATMs**, along with minimarkets, tour agents, dive shops, clothes stalls and souvenir shops. White Sand Beach and Hat Kai Bae have the densest concentrations of facilities.

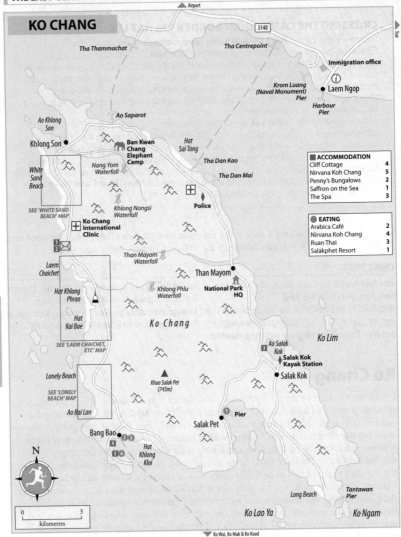

KO CHANG

Airport

Tha Thammachat

Tha Centrepoint

3148

Trat

Immigration office

(i)

Krom Luang
(Naval Monument)
Pier

Laem Ngop

Harbour
Pier

Ao Khlong
Son

Ao Saparot

Khlong Son

Ban Kwan
Chang
Elephant
Camp

Hat
Sai Tong

Tha Dan Kao

Tha Dan Mai

■ ACCOMMODATION	
Cliff Cottage	4
Nirvana Koh Chang	5
Penny's Bungalows	2
Saffron on the Sea	1
The Spa	3

White
Sand
Beach

Nang Yom
Waterfall

Khlong Nongsi
Waterfall

Police

Ko Chang
International
Clinic

SEE 'WHITE SAND
BEACH' MAP

● EATING	
Arabica Café	2
Nirvana Koh Chang	4
Ruan Thai	3
Salakphet Resort	1

Laem
Chaichet

Than Mayom
Waterfall

Than Mayom

Hat Khlong
Phrao

Khlong Phlu
Waterfall

National Park
HQ

Hat
Kai Bae

Ko Chang

Ko Lim

SEE 'LAEM CHAICHET,
ETC' MAP

Ao Salak
Kok

Salak Kok
Kayak Station

Lonely Beach

SEE 'LONELY
BEACH' MAP

Salak Kok

Khao Salak Pet
(743m)

Ao Bai Lan

Pier

Salak Pet

Bang Bao

Hat
Khlong
Kloi

N

Long Beach

Tantawan
Pier

Ko Lao Ya

Ko Ngam

0   3
kilometres

Ko Wai, Ko Mak & Ko Kood

During **peak season**, accommodation on every beach tends to fill up very quickly, so it's worth booking ahead. The island gets a lot quieter (and cheaper) from June to October, when heavy downpours and fierce storms can make life miserable, though sunny days are common too; be especially careful of riptides on all the beaches during the monsoon season.

Sandflies can be a problem on the southern beaches (see page 67); watch out also for **jellyfish**, which plague the west coast in April and May, and for **snakes**, including surprisingly common cobras, sunbathing on the overgrown paths into the interior. The other hazard is **theft** from rooms and bungalows: use your own padlock on bags (and doors where possible) or, better still, make use of hotel safety boxes. After a local eradication programme, Ko Chang is no longer considered to be a malaria-risk area by health authorities in the US and the UK.

KO KOOD

ARRIVAL AND DEPARTURE

KO CHANG

Access to Ko Chang from the **mainland** is by boat from the Laem Ngop coast, 17km southwest of Trat; details of transport to and from Laem Ngop are given on page 404. Tickets on tourist buses and minibuses to Ko Chang will often include the ferry crossing and transport to your hotel. During high season there are also boats to Ko Chang from Ko Mak and Ko Kood; a useful resource for island-hopping is ⊛kohchangferries.com. On Ko Chang, **songthaew share-taxis** meet boats at the Tha Dan Kao and Ao Saparot ferry piers and transport passengers to west-coast beaches (B50 to White Sand Beach, 25min; B100 to Lonely Beach, 1hr; B150 to Bang Bao, 1hr 15min). On departure, either wait for a songthaew on the main road or ask your accommodation to book one for you (for a small extra fee, usually B20). If you're heading to Ko Chang's east coast, you can make use of the songthaew to Salak Pet from central Trat (see page 404).

BY BOAT AND PLANE

Bangkok Airways (office in White Sand Beach, ☎039 551654) runs a shuttle-bus service from Ko Chang beaches via the ferry and on to Trat Airport (B500/person; see p.405).

BY BOAT VIA LAEM NGOP

The main Laem Ngop–Ko Chang boat services are operated by two different car ferry companies from two different piers. Fares are competitive and change frequently: expect to pay B80/person one-way, and about B120 for a vehicle. Centrepoint Ferry (☎039 538196) runs from Tha Centrepoint, 3km west of Laem Ngop, to Tha Dan Kao; and the more popular Ferry Ko Chang (☎039 518588 or ☎039 555188) runs from Tha Thammachat, 9km west of Laem Ngop, to Ao Saparot. Departures are from 6/6.30am–6/7pm, hourly in high season, every 2hr rest of year. There's plenty of long-distance transport direct to Laem Ngop, bypassing Trat town: a/c buses from Bangkok (5hr 15min–6hr), either from the Eastern (Ekamai) Bus Terminal, via Suvarnabhumi Airport and Chanthaburi (3–4 daily), or from Thanon Khao San and Hualamphong Station (2 daily);

and a/c minibuses from Bangkok's Victory Monument, Northern and Eastern bus terminals, Suvarnabhumi Airport and Thanon Khao San.

Destinations Tha Thammachat–Ao Saparot (25min); Tha Centrepoint–Tha Dan Kao (45min).

BY BOAT AND BUS FROM KO CHANG

Every hotel and guesthouse on Ko Chang offers all manner of bus and a/c minibus packages (including ferries) from the island to other popular tourist destinations – we've listed the key ones. Most (it's worth checking) will include pick-up from your hotel either by songthaew, if you're going by big bus from the mainland ports, or by the minibus itself, which will then board the ferry and take you all the way through.

Destinations Bangkok (big bus to Khao San Road B400, not including songthaew to the ferry; minibus to Khao San Road B700; minibus to Sukhumvit Road hotels B850; 5–6hr); Bangkok Suvarnabhumi Airport (big bus B450; minibus B850; about 5hr); Ko Samet (minibus and ferries B750; about 5hr); Pattaya (minibus B650; about 4hr 30min); Siem Reap (Cambodia, changing at the border; minibus B600; about 10hr).

BY BOAT VIA KO MAK AND KO KOOD

In high season, Bang Bao Boat (☎087 054 4300, ⊛kohchangbangbaoboat.com) runs wooden boats from Bang Bao on Ko Chang to *Koh Mak Resort* on Ao Suan Yai on Koh Mak (roughly Sept–June daily; 1hr 30min–2hr; B400), as well as speedboats to *Koh Mak Resort* (roughly Sept–June 2 daily; 1hr; B600) and on to the west coast of Ko Kood (about 1hr; B900 from Ko Chang). Prices include transfers to or from the west coast of Ko Chang. Several other companies run similar high-season inter-island speedboats, including Kai Bae and Leelawadee (⊛kohmakboat.com), who sail from Hat Kai Bae on Ko Chang, via *Makathanee Resort* on Ao Kao on Ko Mak, to the west coast of Ko Kood. Hotels on on Ko Chang, as well as guesthouses on Ko Mak and Ko Kood, will have current details.

GETTING AROUND

By songthaew A paved road runs nearly all the way round the island connecting all the beaches, served by plentiful, white songthaew share-taxis. They tend to charge according to how many passengers they have as well as the distance travelled (usually B50–150/person), but sometimes, especially on more remote beaches, you might have to wait until they fill up with enough passengers or the driver will ask you to charter the whole vehicle.

By motorbike or car You can rent motorbikes (from

B150) and cars (from B1000) on every beach, but the road is notoriously dangerous, with precipitously steep hills punctuated by sharp, unexpected hairpins, and many reckless, often drunk, drivers, so think twice if you're an inexperienced motorcyclist – accidents happen every day and fatalities are frequent.

By mountain bike Rental available at the bookshop just south of Ko Chang Gym in the VJ Plaza complex in Laem Chaichet (B150/day).

INFORMATION

Tourist information The widely distributed, detailed

free maps and quarterly Ko Chang guides published by

Whitesands Publications (w koh-chang-guide.com) are a handy source of information, and the website provides an accommodation-booking service, but for more intelligent insights and opinionated advice, check out w iamkohchang. com, compiled by a Ko Chang resident.

DIRECTORY

Clinic The private 24hr Ko Chang International Clinic (☎ 1719 or ☎ 039 551 555, w bangkoktrathospital.com) is located beyond the south end of White Sand Beach, 1km south of *Plaloma Cliff Resort*; it has emergency ambulances and a dental service and will transfer seriously ill patients to its parent Bangkok–Trat Hospital in Trat.

Post office On the main road beyond the southern end of White Sand Beach (Mon–Fri 10am–noon & 1–6pm, Sat 10am–1pm).

Tourist police At the north end of Hat Khlong Phrao (☎ 1155).

White Sand Beach (Hat Sai Khao)

Framed by a band of fine white sand at low tide, a fringe of casuarinas and palm trees and a backdrop of forested hills, **Hat Sai Khao**, more commonly referred to as **White Sand Beach**, is, at 2.5km long, the island's longest beach and its most commercial, with scores of mid-range and upmarket hotel and bungalow operations packed together along the shore, plus dozens of shops, travel agents, bars and restaurants lining the inland side of the road. The vibe is much more laidback and traveller-oriented at the far quieter northern end of the beach, however, beyond *KC Grande*, and this is where the most budget-priced accommodation squeezes in, some of it pleasingly characterful and nearly all of it enjoying its own sea view. An extra bonus is that the road is well out of earshot up here, and there's hardly any passing pedestrian traffic. There are some low-key beach **bars** up there too, and more along the shorefront in the central beach area – all of them quite different in feel from the rash of brash, Pattaya-style bar-beers inland from *Plaloma Cliff Resort* in southern Hat Sai Khao. Wherever you stay on White Sand Beach, be careful when swimming as the **currents** are very strong and there's no lifeguard service.

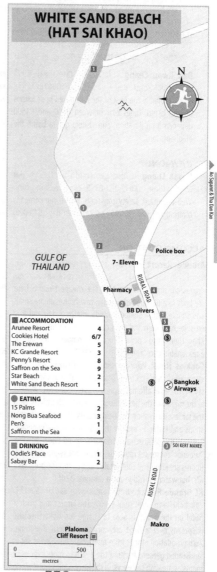

WHITE SAND BEACH (HAT SAI KHAO)

N

Ao Saparet & Tha Dan Kao

4

GULF OF THAILAND

Police box

7-Eleven

RURAL ROAD

Pharmacy

BB Divers

Bangkok Airways

SOI KERT MANEE

RURAL ROAD

Makro

Plaloma Cliff Resort

■ ACCOMMODATION	
Arunee Resort	4
Cookies Hotel	6/7
The Erewan	5
KC Grande Resort	3
Penny's Resort	8
Saffron on the Sea	9
Star Beach	2
White Sand Beach Resort	1

● EATING	
15 Palms	2
Nong Bua Seafood	3
Pen's	1
Saffron on the Sea	4

■ DRINKING	
Oodie's Place	1
Sabay Bar	2

0   500
metres

8, 9, 6, Ko Chang International Clinic, Post Office & Pearl Beach

KO CHANG ACTIVITIES

Your accommodation should be able to obtain tickets for most of the **activities** described below. There are **spas** at Ao Bai Lan (see page 416) and Ao Salak Kok (see page 418); you can also **snorkel** and **dive** in the archipelago (see page 411).

ELEPHANT CAMPS

Ko Chang or "Elephant Island" is named for its hilly profile rather than its indigenous pachyderms, but there are several **elephant camps** on the island that have brought in their own lumbering forest dwellers so that tourists can ride and help bathe them. Many people feel that riding elephants is unethical, because in order to be tame enough to be ridden, elephants are put through a cruel process that usually involves separation from their mothers, starvation, beating and sleep deprivation, among other methods. However, people have been riding elephants (and horses, for that matter) for centuries and are unlikely to stop now, so whether you decide to ride or not is up to you.

Ban Kwan Chang Khlong Son ☎ 081 919 3995 ⓦ facebook.com/ Ban-Kwan-Chang-100618275939 4224. Probably the best of the half dozen or so camps on the island. Rides cost between B800 and B1500 depending on duration, and visitors get to bathe the elephants too.

KAYAKING

Kayak Chang At Amari Emerald Cove Resort, Hat Khlong Phrao ☎ 097 182 8319, ⓦ kayakchang.com. Well-organized, safety-conscious, British-run company offering full-day (B3700) up to seven-day (B43,000)

expeditions around the archipelago, as well as three-day kayaking courses (B14,000). Return transport from your accommodation is included.

COOKING CLASSES

KaTi Culinary Cooking School Hat Khlong Phrao ☎ 039 557252, ⓦ facebook.com/katikhruathai. The amiable chef who runs the recommended *KaTi* restaurant (see page 414) teaches well-regarded cooking classes (Mon–Sat 11am; B1500, including recipe book and transfers as far as White Sand Beach and Hat Kai Bae).

ACCOMMODATION

Arunee Resort Just across the road from White Sand Beach ☎ 039 551075, ⓦ facebook.com/ aruneekohchang; map p.409. The cheapest rooms here are built in a partitioned wooden row-house; all are small and simple with a shared veranda, mattress, fan and tiny en-suite bathroom and are a good price for central Hat Sai Khao. There's also a newer block with compact, a/c rooms at a reasonable price. Fan B500 a/c B1500

Cookies Hotel White Sand Beach ☎ 081 861 4227, ⓦ cookieskohchang.com; map p.409. If you want hotel-style facilities at affordable prices this is a good option, right in the middle of the beach. Rooms are in two locations, with the far less interesting site being across the road, with only shops and traffic to look at through the picture windows. Better to pay B800 extra and go for a ground-floor, sea-view "superior" room, set round the shorefront swimming pool. Rooms are large and comfortable and all include breakfast, a/c, hot water, TV, fridge and a veranda. B2000

KC Grande Resort White Sand Beach ☎ 039 552 111, ⓦ kckohchang.com; map p.409. The largest and priciest hotel on the beach is able to charge top dollar because it spreads over a huge area of the northern shorefront. Accommodation ranges from rows of a/c bungalows set in landscaped gardens fronting the beach to more expensive rooms, some with sea views, in the three-storey hotel block.

WHITE SAND BEACH

Facilities are good and include a pool, a spa and a bar with live bands in the evening. Breakfast included. B4800

Penny's Resort Beyond the south end of White Sand Beach, down a lane behind the post office ☎ 039 551 122, ⓦ penny-thailand.com; map p.409. Welcoming, helpful, German-run place on what's sometimes called Pearl Beach (Hat Khai Mook), though it's just a rocky extension of Hat Sai Khao. On a compact, flowery plot around a lovely little pool (and a kids' pool too), the well-maintained bungalows and hotel-style rooms all have a/c, hot water, TV, fridge and a few decorative touches; the smaller, cheaper ones are near the sea. B1400

★ **Saffron on the Sea** Beyond the south end of White Sand Beach, three doors north of Penny's ☎ 039 551 253, ⓦ facebook.com/saffronontheseakohchang; map p.409. In a lovely, lush garden behind a very good restaurant (see page 413) are seven attractive, homely rooms with a/c, hot water, TV and fridge; the cheaper rooms have no sea view. Management is friendly and there are free kayaks for guests' use. B1200

Star Beach White Sand Beach ☎ 089 574 9486 ⓦ starbeach-kohchang.com; map p.409. Basic, cheerily painted plywood huts cling limpet-like to the rock-face here, just above the sand on the quiet, northern stretch of the beach. Rooms are very simple (no wi-fi) but are all en suite (some with hot showers) and enjoy high-level sea views and breezes. B500

The Erewan White Sand Beach ☎ 039 510 668 ⓦ erewankohchang.com; map p.409. This newish, medium-sized hotel across the road from the beach wins praise for its friendly and efficient staff, rooftop pool, great design and buffet breakfast. B4600

White Sand Beach Resort White Sand Beach ☎ 081 863 7737, ⓦ whitesandbeachkochang.com; map p.409. Spread across a long, attractive stretch of uncommercialized sand at the far north end of the beach, *White Sand* offers a big range of nicely spaced bungalows, many of them lapping up uninterrupted sea views. Interiors are fairly simple, but boast a/c, wooden floors, hot showers, TVs, fridges and a faintly contemporary style. If you're looking for a proper peaceful beach vibe and a little bit of affordable comfort, within a 10min walk of resort facilities, this is a good option. Arriving by songthaew, get off at the 7-Eleven beside *KC Grande* and phone for transport. Breakfast included. B1900

EATING AND DRINKING

15 Palms White Sand Beach ☎ 039 551 095, ⓦ 15palms. com; map p.409. One of the most popular of the row of restaurants that set their tables out on the sand, partly because of its nightly high-season fireshows and *katoey* shows on Tues & Sat. There's a barbecue every night (chicken kebab B295), plus Thai (seafood tom yam B155), Italian and Mexican à la carte, washed down with imported beers and lots of cocktails. Daily 8am–1am.

Nong Bua Seafood On the main road, White Sand Beach ☎ 039 551 595 ⓦ nongbuarestaurant.com; map p.409. Popular, bustling basic restaurant, serving noodle soups, fried noodles and fried rice with seafood (B70); other seafood dishes start at B150. Daily 7am–10pm.

Oodie's Place On the main road, White Sand Beach ⓦ facebook.com/oodies.place; map p.409. Ko Chang's most famous live-music venue, with live blues, rock, reggae and r'n'b played most nights, plus Thai food (from B80), pizzas (from B200) and French food (from B300). Daily 4pm–2am.

Pen's White Sand Beach; map p.409. Tiny beach restaurant in the northern bungalow cluster that serves

4

DIVING AND SNORKELLING IN THE KO CHANG ARCHIPELAGO

Because there's just one main tide a day in the inner Gulf, the **reefs** of the Ko Chang archipelago are much less colourful and varied than Andaman coast dive sites, and they can get very crowded, but they're rewarding enough to make a day-trip worthwhile. The main **dive and snorkel sites** are west of Ko Mak, in the national marine park around **Ko Rang** and its satellite islets. These range from beginners' reefs with lots of hard corals and anemones at depths of 4–6m, frequented by plenty of reef fish – including a resident ten-thousand-strong shoal of yellow fusiliers – and the occasional moray eel, to the more challenging 25m dive at the Pinnacles. There are also some technical wreck dives of Japanese boats from World War II and even some centuries-old Chinese trading ships. The coral around Ko Yuak, off Ko Chang's Hat Kai Bae, is mostly dead, though some operators still sell trips there.

DIVE SHOPS ON KO CHANG

The biggest concentration of **dive shops** is on Ko Chang, though there are also some on Ko Mak and Ko Kood (see pages 420 and 423 respectively). All dive shops on Ko Chang will organize pick-ups from any beach.

Waves permitting, Ko Chang operators run trips year-round, though during the **monsoon season** (June–Sept), visibility can be poor. **Prices** for local dive trips, with two tanks, are about B2900, or from B950 for accompanying **snorkellers**. Dive courses cost about B14,500 for the four-day Open Water, and B4500 for the one-day Discover Scuba introduction.

BB Divers Shops at Lonely Beach, Khlong Kloi Beach and White Sand Beach, main office in Bang Bao ☎ 086 129 2305 or ☎ 039 558040, ⓦ bbdivers.com. Belgian-run, environmentally minded PADI Five-Star IDC centre and certified Reef Check Facility which uses fishing boats (with sun decks) rather than speedboats.

SNORKELLING

From about November to May, several companies run dedicated **snorkelling trips** to reefs and islands around Ko Chang, Ko Wai and Ko Rang. Tickets are sold by tour agents on every beach and prices range from B600 to B1500, depending on the size of the boat (some take as many as a hundred people in high season) and the number of islands visited. In general the more islands "featured" (sailed past), the less time there is for snorkelling, though nearly all the actual snorkelling happens around **Ko Rang**.

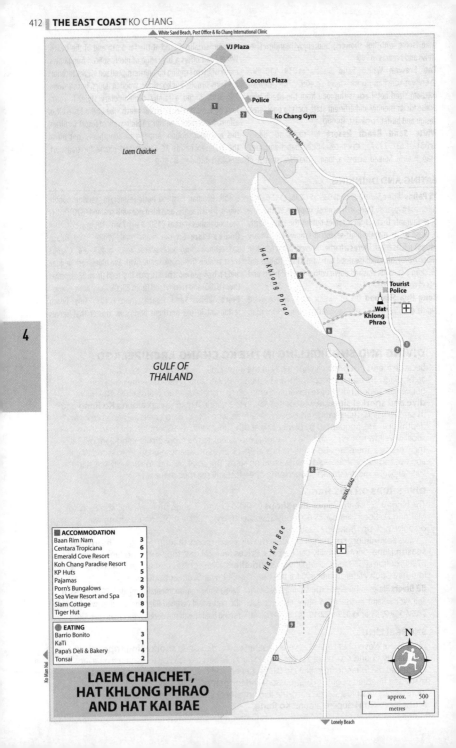

White Sand Beach, Post Office & Ko Chang International Clinic

VJ Plaza

Coconut Plaza

Police

Ko Chang Gym

Laem Chaichet

OMA ROAD

Tourist Police

Wat Khlong Phrao

Hat Khlong Phrao

GULF OF THAILAND

RURAL ROAD

Hat Kai Bae

Ko Man Nai

ACCOMMODATION

Baan Rim Nam	3
Centara Tropicana	6
Emerald Cove Resort	7
Koh Chang Paradise Resort	1
KP Huts	5
Pajamas	2
Porn's Bungalows	9
Sea View Resort and Spa	10
Siam Cottage	8
Tiger Hut	4

EATING

Barrio Bonito	3
KaTi	1
Papa's Deli & Bakery	4
Tonsai	2

LAEM CHAICHET, HAT KHLONG PHRAO AND HAT KAI BAE

N

0	approx.	500

metres

Lonely Beach

exceptionally good home-style Thai food at fairly cheap prices (B80–150 for curries), as well as Western breakfasts. Daily 8.30am–9.30pm.

Sabay Bar White Sand Beach ☎ 081 864 2074 ⓦ https://bit.ly/2NyadBc; map p.409. One of Ko Chang's longest-running institutions, where you can choose to sit in the chic a/c bar and watch the nightly live sets from the in-house cover band, or lounge on mats and cushions on the sand and listen in via the outdoor speakers. You pay for the pleasure,

however, as drinks are pricey. Also stages fire-juggling shows on the beach and full moon parties. Daily 6pm–2am.

Saffron on the Sea Beyond the south end of the beach, behind the post office three doors north of Penny's (see page 410) ☎ 039 551253; map p.409. On a pretty seafront deck, this restaurant is highly recommended for its Thai food, which doesn't stray too far from the usual suspects, such as deep-fried prawns with tamarind sauce (B350); also serves baguettes, wraps and pastas. Daily 8am–10pm.

Laem Chaichet and Hat Khlong Phrao

Four kilometres south of Hat Sai Khao, the scenic, rocky cape at **LAEM CHAICHET** curves round into sweeping, casuarina-fringed **HAT KHLONG PHRAO**, one of Ko Chang's nicest beaches, not least because it has yet to see the clutter and claustrophobic development of its neighbours. Most of the restaurants, bars and shops are way off the beach, along the roadside, with the shorefront left mainly to a decent spread of accommodation. Laem Chaichet protects an inlet and tiny harbour and offers beautiful views south across the bay and inland to the densely forested mountains. To the south, Hat Khlong Phrao begins with a nice 1km-long run of beach that's interrupted by a wide khlong, whose estuary is the site of some characterful stilt homes and seafood restaurants. You can rent a kayak from almost anywhere along the beach to explore the estuary, and after dark you could paddle upriver to see the fireflies twinkling in the khlongside *lamphu* trees. Beyond the estuary, the long southern beach is partly shaded by casuarinas and backed in places by a huge coconut grove that screens the shore from the road; it's quite a hike to the roadside shops and restaurants from here though, at least 1km along mostly unlit roads.

Both Chaichet and Khlong Phrao have roadside tourist villages with **ATMs**, minimarkets, tour agents, dive centres, shops and restaurants. The **tourist police** have a post here, and from the southern end of Khlong Phrao it's only a few hundred metres south to the start of the Kai Bae tourist village amenities.

Khlong Phlu Falls

2km east off the main road • B200

Upstream from Hat Khlong Phrao, the khlong that divides the beach in two tumbles into Ko Chang's most famous cascade, **Khlong Phlu Falls** (Nam Tok Khlong Phlu). Signs lead you inland to a car park and some hot-food stalls, where you pay your national park entry fee and walk the last five minutes to the 25m-high waterfall (best in the rainy season) that plunges into an invitingly clear pool defined by a ring of smooth rocks.

ACCOMMODATION   **LAEM CHAICHET AND HAT KHLONG PHRAO**

Baan Rim Nam Hat Khlong Phrao ☎ 087 005 8575, ⓦ iamkohchang.com; map p.412. Peaceful, scenic and unusual, this converted fishing family's house is built on stilts over the wide, attractive khlong at the end of a walkway through the mangroves. Run by the British author of the best Ko Chang website (see page 408), it has just five comfortable a/c rooms with good hot-water bathrooms, plus decks for soaking up views of the khlongside village, but no restaurant. You can borrow kayaks and it's a couple of minutes' walk to the beach, or 20min to the main Khlong Phrao facilities. B1000

Centara Tropicana Hat Khlong Phrao ☎ 039 557122 ⓦ centarahotelsresorts.com/centara/ckc; map p.412. This well-designed resort features rooms in two-storey blocks and thatched bungalows, all surrounded by a

profusion of tropical greenery. The spacious rooms are extremely comfortable. Facilities include a beachfront pool, kids' club and spa. B4700

Emerald Cove Resort Hat Khlong Phrao ☎ 039 552000, ⓦ emeraldcovekohchang.com; map p.412. Top-of-the-range hotel occupying a lovely, tranquil spot on the southern beach, complete with its own palm-shaded sandy terrace, spa and huge seafront swimming pool, with a palatial Jacuzzi. The rooms, in low-rise three-storey blocks set around the pool, tropical garden and lagoons, are in luxurious style, with wooden floors and balconies. B5000

Koh Chang Paradise Resort Laem Chaichet ☎ 039 551100–1, ⓦ kohchangparadise.com; map p.412. The biggest and most popular place to stay on the Chaichet end of the beach occupies a huge area between the road and the shore, so offers easy access to the beach as well as shops and restaurants. Its generously designed concrete bungalows have French windows and comfortable, hotel-style, a/c interiors. Some have private plunge pools and there's also a central swimming pool and a spa. B3820

KP Huts Hat Khlong Phrao ☎ 084 077 5995; map p.412. Though the 35 timber huts here are very simply furnished, they are attractively scattered through the broad, grassy shoreside coconut grove (about 1.5km from roadside amenities) with plenty of sea views. Even some of the cheapest options (with shared bathrooms) are right on the shore, and a few are raised high on stilts for an extra-seductive panorama; all of the en-suite huts have hot showers and some are designed for families. B500

Pajamas Hat Khlong Phrao ☎ 039 510789 ⓦ pajamaskohchang.com; map p.412. This neat hostel has super-clean dorms and doubles just 2min walk from Hat Khlong Phrao, with a common area for guests, laundry facilities, bicycle rental and the added bonus of a swimming pool. Dorm B600 double B2800

Tiger Hut Hat Khlong Phrao ☎ 084 109 9660; map p.412. One of the few budget-minded, old-school travellers' beach bungalows left on Ko Chang, occupying a sandy beachfront garden just south of the khlong and about 2km down a track from the main road. Recently renovated rooms (B900) are not such good value, but the older woven-bamboo and clapboard huts with mosquito nets and decent-sized bathrooms (some shared) are a good deal, and there's a restaurant deck and bar with pool table. B300

EATING AND DRINKING

KaTi On the main road, Hat Khlong Phrao ☎ 039 557252; map p.412. Restaurant and cookery school (see page 410) serving very tasty Thai food, slightly adapted for Western tastes, including lots of seafood, *matsaman* chicken curry (B220) and *laap* beef salad (B140), plus delicious home-made ice creams and Thai desserts. Mon–Sat 11am–10pm, Sun 6–10pm.

Tonsai On the main road, Hat Khlong Phrao ☎ 089 895 7229; map p.412. The atmosphere at this welcoming restaurant is pleasingly mellow with calm, polite staff, and the menu includes a delicious yellow curry with chicken and potatoes (B135), some interesting Thai dips and relishes, pastas, lots of vegetarian options and at least fifty cocktails. Daily 10am–7pm.

Hat Kai Bae

Narrow, pretty little **HAT KAI BAE** presents a classic picture of white sand, pale blue water and overhanging palms, but in places the shorefront is very slender indeed – and filled with bungalows – and the beach can disappear entirely at high tide. The beach is bisected by a khlong and rocky point, with most of the accommodation to the south. Seaward views from the southernmost end take in the tiny island of Ko Man Nai, whose sandy shores are easily reached by kayak, half an hour offshore from *Porn's Bungalows*. Kai Bae's roadside tourist village is busy and stretches a couple of kilometres. It's got plenty of shops, bars and restaurants, as well as ATMs, currency exchange and dive shops.

ACCOMMODATION   HAT KAI BAE

Porn's Bungalows Off the access road to Sea View, Hat Kai Bae ☎ 080 613 9266, ⓦ pornsbungalows-kohchang. com; map p.412. This budget accommodation option on Hat Kai Bae has scores of fan bungalows in various styles. The cheapest are concrete huts at the back at the south end; the most luxurious are spacious wooden cabins with hot showers and wraparound decks; all have fans. *Porn's* has two reception areas, at its northernmost and southernmost ends, and a two-storey restaurant in the middle. No reservations, so it's run on a first-come, first-served basis. B600

Sea View Resort and Spa Hat Kai Bae ☎ 039 552 888, ⓦ seaviewkohchang.com; map p.412. Swanky and huge beachfront hotel set in lawns and tropical flower gardens, which stretch around the steep headland at the south end of the beach and up to a lighthouse by the main road that shelters tables with good views at the *Lighthouse Restaurant*. A cable car joins up the resort's two swimming pools, pretty spa and its large, light and airy a/c rooms and cottages. B4600

Siam Cottage Hat Kai Bae ☎ 089 153 6664 ⓦ facebook. com/siamcottagekohchang; map p.412. With cheerily painted interiors, fans, partly outdoor bathrooms and decks, the 36 wooden bungalows (some with a/c) here face each other across a narrow but well-watered, flowery lot that runs down to the sea. There's a cute restaurant, as well as kayaks for rent (B100/hr). Fan B650, a/c B1050

EATING AND DRINKING

Papa's Deli & Bakery On the main road, Hat Kai Bae; map p.412. Hot pretzels, pizzas, croissants, baguettes and cakes emerge from this friendly German bakery, as well as the bread for some very tasty sandwiches (around B100).

If you're sitting in, you can also tuck into pastas and good espressos; to take away, there are imported cheeses and salamis, too. Daily 8am–7pm.

★ **Barrio Bonito** On the main road, Hat Kai Bae ☎ 080 092 8208 ⓦ barriobonito.com; map p.412. Mexican-run bar-restaurant serving excellent Mexican food such as nachos with minced beef (B220), as well as some more unusual dishes, such as ceviche (B250) washed down with Corona and lots of tequila cocktails. It's a very congenial place, a popular meeting spot in the evening with Latin sounds all the way. Daily 2pm–10.30pm.

Lonely Beach (Hat Tha Nam)

Hat Tha Nam – dubbed **LONELY BEACH** before it became Ko Chang's top place to party – is small and lively, with a shorefront that's occupied by increasingly expensive accommodation and a hinterland village, ten minutes' walk away, that's the most traveller-oriented on the island. It's at Lonely Beach, overlooking the rocks immediately south of the strand, and along the sandy sois that run inland to the main road, that most backpackers stay, in little bungalows and guesthouses squashed any old how beneath the remaining trees, with every other shop-shack offering tattoos or fruit smoothies. Despite the creeping concrete, creatively designed little wood and bamboo bar-restaurants abound, some of them offering chilled, low-key escapes from the loud dance music, all-night parties and buckets of vodka Red Bull that the beachfront places are notorious for.

Day and (especially) night, you should be extremely careful when swimming off Lonely Beach, particularly around *Siam Beach* at the northern end, as the steep shelf and dangerous current result in a sobering number of **drownings** every year, particularly during the monsoon season; do your swimming further south and don't go out at all when the waves are high. Also be careful with your belongings – many a drunken night sees cameras, phones and wallets pilfered unnoticed.

Among the roadside shops you'll find an **ATM**, dive centres, tour agents and motorbike rental and repair.

ACCOMMODATION
LONELY BEACH

Easy House Inland, up a side road opposite Kachapura Resort, Lonely Beach ☎ 082 951 5663, ⓦ https://bit.ly/2C1Fo6F; map p.415. Laidback place built around polished, dark-wood platforms. The old-style bungalows, decorated with murals and equipped with mosquito nets, fans and en-suite

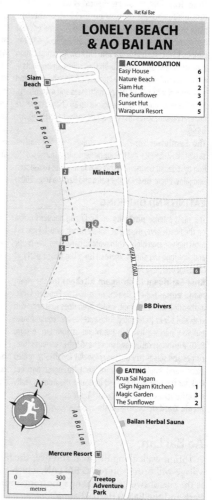

LONELY BEACH & AO BAI LAN

ACCOMMODATION	
Easy House	6
Nature Beach	1
Siam Hut	2
The Sunflower	3
Sunset Hut	4
Warapura Resort	5

EATING	
Krua Sai Ngam (Sign Ngam Kitchen)	1
Magic Garden	3
The Sunflower	2

bathrooms, are quite crowded together, but quiet and cheap. B500

Nature Beach Central Lonely Beach ☎081 803 8933 ⓦfacebook.com/NatureBeachKohChang; map p.415. Responsible for Lonely Beach's party reputation, this place's rooms, bar-restaurant (with built-in DJ station), swimming pool and the beach out front are all hugely popular. It occupies a prime location in the middle of the strand and is at the heart of the action (so if you prefer a quiet night's sleep, head elsewhere). Its recently renovated, air-conditioned bungalows range from attractive, polished-concrete en-suite abodes with verandas at the back by the road to bigger bungalows at the front with hot water and a partial sea view (B2000). B1200

Siam Hut Central Lonely Beach ☎086 609 7772, ⓦsiamhutkohchang.com; map p.415. The cheapest place to stay right on the beach, this classic traveller's rest has evening barbecues and movies, a dive school, a tattoo parlour, kayaks for rent and a 24hr kitchen. Accommodation consists of rows and rows of primitive, split-bamboo huts – eighty in total – all en suite (some with hot showers) and with little else but plank floors, mattresses and mozzie nets. As with many other budget lodgings on Ko Chang, there are no reservations, so it's first come, first served. Fan B480, a/c B560

The Sunflower Lonely Beach, inland on Soi Sunset ☎084 017 9960, ⓦthe-sunflower.com; map p.415. Run by a genial German and his Thai family, the two-dozen bungalows here are set under palm and banana trees 200m or so from the roadside village and equidistant from the rocky coast at *Sunset Hut*, a 5min walk south of the sandy beach. Choose between bamboo or wooden fan bungalows with mosquito nets and open-roofed bathrooms, and concrete bungalows with a/c and hot showers; all have good thick mattresses and are kept very clean. The restaurant is good (see below). Fan B500, a/c B800

Sunset Hut Lonely Beach, 5min walk south beyond Siam Hut, on the rocks ☎088 549 9942; map p.415. The concrete en-suite fan bungalows here have hot showers, proper beds and big windows, though no wi-fi and some share bathrooms. There are also some big a/c bungalows, but all are tightly packed together in rows running parallel to the shore. The seafront deck-restaurant and bar holds occasional parties. Though you can only swim here at high tide, it's a short walk to the sandy beach and just 400m inland to roadside shops and restaurants. Fan B500, a/c B800

Warapura Resort Lonely Beach, 2min walk south beyond Sunset Hut, on the rocks ☎089 696 0966, ⓦwarapuraresort.com; map p.415. Welcoming place with a good dose of Bangkok chic in its twenty gleaming white, balconied rooms and villas, a few of which are on the seafront; all have large bathrooms with hot rain showers, a/c, mini-bars, TVs and DVD players. "Cozy" rooms are especially stylish, with dark-wood furniture and a large indoor sitting area (B2400). Good-sized, attractive pool and breakfast included. B1870

EATING AND DRINKING

The most intense **partying** on Ko Chang happens down on the beach here, usually at *Nature Beach*, which kicks off most high-season nights with seafood barbecues, live music and fire-juggling shows; there's also a big beach party at *Siam Hut* on Friday nights.

Krua Sai Ngam (Sign Ngam Kitchen) On the main road, central Lonely Beach; map p.415. Popular, basic, authentic Isaan restaurant, which even does *som tam* with crab and *pla ra* (fermented fish sauce) – an acquired taste but very northeastern (on the menu as som tam e-sarn; B60). Also offers catfish and snakehead fish in various soups, curries and salads (try the *yam plaa duk foo*; B150), grilled chicken and simple dishes on rice (B60). No English sign, but look for the seafood displayed on ice at the front, directly opposite Soi Sunset. Daily noon–11.30pm.

Magic Garden On the main road, south of Lonely Beach ☎084 891 7637 ⓦmagicgardenresort.com; map p.415. This place serves excellent Thai and European dishes (mains around B100–B250), using homegrown vegetables wherever possible. There's also a well-stocked bar that stays open untill the early hours and features live music a couple of nights each week. It's very popular so reservations are recommended at peak eating times. Daily 8am–10pm.

The Sunflower Lonely Beach, inland on Soi Sunset ☎084 017 9960, ⓦthe-sunflower.com; map p.415. Friendly, laidback guesthouse restaurant dishing up very generous set breakfasts (B200), authentically spicy Thai curries (from B80), a wide choice of pricier Western food and German beer. Flop on to the axe cushions and soak up the cool sounds or watch a movie. Daily 7am–10pm.

Ao Bai Lan

A 15min walk along the road and over the hill from the southern end of Lonely Beach village will bring you to **AO BAI LAN**, which hasn't got much of a beach to speak of, but is the site of two of Ko Chang's most interesting attractions, the **Treetop Adventure Park** and the **Bailan Herbal Sauna**.

Treetop Adventure Park

South end of Ao Bai Lan • Daily 9am–5pm • B1250/half-day, including roundtrip transfer • ☎ 084 310 7600, ⓦ treetopadventurepark.com

If you're happy with heights and like a physical challenge, make an afternoon of it at **Treetop Adventure Park**, an enjoyable and professionally managed jungle activity centre where you get to swing through the trees on a series of trapezes, flying foxes, aerial skateboards, rope ladders and webs. Everyone gets a full safety harness and gloves and starts off with a training session before tackling the two adventure courses (or the special kids' one), which take around two hours in all, though there's no limit to repeat attempts.

Bailan Herbal Sauna

On the main road, Ao Bai Lan • Mon–Sat 3–9pm • Sauna B300, treatments from B100 • ☎ 084 464 4005, ⓦ herbalsaunabailan.com

Bailan Herbal Sauna is the perfect place to tease out any sore muscles. This charming, creatively designed US–Thai-run herbal steam sauna is an alternative little sanctuary of adobe buildings with glass-bottle windows, secluded within a patch of roadside forest. There's a sociable communal sauna, home-made DIY herbal treatments using fresh herbs from their own garden (kaffir lime for hair, white-mud for face and turmeric for skin), along with fresh juices and herbal teas.

Bang Bao

Almost at the end of the west-coast road, the southern harbour village of **BANG BAO**, much of it built on stilts off a 1km-long central jetty, is the departure point for boat trips and transfers to the outer islands and is also a popular place to stay. Though it has no beach of its own, you're within a short motorbike ride of both little-developed Hat Khlong Kloi, 2km to the east, and Lonely Beach, 5km up the coast. It's possible to stay on the jetty itself and tuck into seafood at one of its famous restaurants, but you'll probably have to fight your way through vanloads of day-trippers, who clog the narrow path along the jetty as they linger over the trinket shops, clothes stalls and dive shops.

4

ACCOMMODATION

BANG BAO

Cliff Cottage West side of Ao Bang Bao, next to Nirvana ☎ 080 823 5495, ⓦ cliff-cottage.com; map p.406. British-run resort with a nice deck restaurant on the west-facing cove, and kayaks and snorkels for rent. Choose between large, concrete rooms with air-con and hot water bathrooms, and "glamping" bell tents that aren't as glamorous as they sound but offer wide cliff-top views. Tents B650, rooms B850

★ **Nirvana Koh Chang** West side of Ao Bang Bao ☎ 039 510 611–3, ⓦ nirvanakohchang.com; map p.406. Secluded on a narrow neck of land across the bay to the west of the village, this boutique resort is a relaxed and lushly landscaped retreat with two pools; there's no real beach but they run free boats over to Hat Khlong Kloi twice a day. Accommodation is in a wide range of chic, Balinese-accented rooms and villas, some with direct sea views, and there's an attractive restaurant too (see below). Good à la carte breakfast included. B3000

EATING AND DRINKING

Arabica Café Opposite 7-Eleven, just before the start of Bang Bao jetty; map p.406. A leafy little café with cute fountains, serving up good espressos (B50), crepes (from 3pm) and sandwiches and Western breakfasts. Daily 8am–9pm.

Nirvana Koh Chang West side of Ao Bang Bao ☎ 039 510611–3, ⓦ nirvanakohchang.com; map p.406. Even if you're not staying at *Nirvana Koh Chang*, you can come and eat at *Tantra* restaurant, next to the pool, or drink at the panoramic, sunset-facing *Sun Deck*, which is reached by a cliffside boardwalk. Creatively furnished with woodcarvings

from the Indonesian archipelago, the restaurant serves a menu of contemporary Thai food such as panaeng curry. Most dishes will cost you between B150–B250. *Sun Deck* daily 4–7pm; *Tantra* daily 7–10pm.

Ruan Thai Bang Bao jetty ☎ 086 111 3435; map p.406. The best of several neighbouring restaurants, with a deck built on stilts off the west side of the jetty and fresh seafood awaiting its fate in tanks at the front. The fried rice with prawns is very good (B70), and there are plenty of fish, scallop and squid dishes too (B200–B400). Daily 8.30am–9pm.

Hat Khlong Kloi

The nearest swimmable beach to Bang Bao is long, sandy **Hat Khlong Kloi**, 2km east of the village and not far short of the end of the tarmac. It's backed by a lagoon and a long stretch of beach-scrub, but has great views from its small beach cafés and deckchairs. If you're coming by motorcycle, park up at the west end of the beach and walk, as the paved access road then takes a steep, tortuous route around the back of the beach.

ACCOMMODATION   **HAT KHLONG KLOI**

Klong Koi Cottage 100m from the west end of Hat Khlong Kloi ☎039 558169, ⓦfacebook.com/klongkloicottage. Friendly, popular spot on a nice stretch of beach, with deckchairs and umbrellas and great views of the bay and the offshore islands. The rather scruffy compound has small, thatched, fan-cooled, en-suite bungalows at the back, concrete ones at the front. The simple bar-restaurant hosts a nightly beach barbecue in the high season. Fan B800, a/c B1500

The east coast

The beaches along the mangrove-fringed **east coast** are less inviting than those in the west, but this side of Ko Chang is much less developed and makes for a fun day-trip; it's about 35km from Ao Khlong Son in the north to Salak Pet in the south.

Than Mayom

South of the piers at Ao Saparot and Tha Dan Kao, the east-coast road runs through long swathes of rubber and palm plantations, with jungle-clad hills to the west and bronze-coloured beaches to the east, passing the national park office and bungalows at **Than Mayom**, where signs direct you inland to the short but lovely Than Mayom falls with two calm pools to swim in, a 45-minute uphill hike away.

Salak Kok and Long Beach

Ao Salak Kok is a deep green bay hedged in with thick mangroves and wooden huts on stilts. To the south, it is at its most charming as the blue boats of the small fishing settlement of **SALAK KOK** bob into view. You can **rent kayaks** from the Salak Kok Kayak Station (B100/hr; run by the Koh Chang Discovery Club, a community tourism venture) to explore a marked route through the mangroves. From Salak Kok, the road continues to the tip of the southeastern headland where undeveloped **Hat Sai Yao**, or **LONG BEACH**, the prettiest white-sand beach on this coast, is good for swimming and has some coral close to shore. There are a few homestays and food stalls here for refuelling.

Salak Pet

The little fishing port of **SALAK PET**, on the south coast, is served by daily songthaews all the way from Trat town (see page 402). There are some white-knuckle moments on the way here, as the road hugs the coast, rewarding you with incredibly clear views of the sea and coast. Still a fairly quiet spot, the village of Salak Pet has a simple temple but is best known for its excellent **seafood restaurant**, *Salakphet Resort* (see below). While you are able to rent kayaks here, the port town is a glimpse into life on Ko Chang without the tourists, and you'll often find only the fishermen here to keep you company.

ACCOMMODATION AND EATING   **THE EAST COAST**

★**Salakphet Resort** Salak Pet ☎081 429 9983, ⓦkohchangsalakphet.com; map p.406. The bayside dining deck here offers fine views and seafood so good that people travel all the way from Trat just for lunch; crabs are a speciality – particularly stir-fried with black pepper, or with curry powder – but it's all fresh so the possibilities are infinite. Daily 8am–8pm.

The Spa Ao Salak Kok ☎083 115 6566, ⓦthespa kohchang.com; map p.406. This spa is a beautifully designed, upmarket wellness and detox retreat offering a variety of courses, such as a 'Clean-Me-Out' Fasting Detox programme of ten days and nine nights that costs B26,500 (accommodation not included). The a/c accommodation is set in a lovely mature tropical garden that runs down to the mangrove-ringed bay of western Ao Salak Kok. Breakfast included. They also offer daily meditation and yoga classes (8–10am) for B450/person, and healthy meals in the restaurant. B1630

Ko Wai

The tiny island of **KO WAI** (just 4 square kilometres) is located about 6km south of Ko Chang and is a popular destination for boat day-trips as its bays provide some of the best spots for snorkelling in the entire archipelago. In fact, you don't even need a mask or snorkel – just stand waist-deep in the water and watch shoals of fish swim around you and the colourful corals. Watch your step though, as some corals are razor-sharp. There are just a few resorts here, and the place is wonderfully peaceful when the tour groups are not around, so it's definitely worth staying overnight. However, almost everywhere closes during the rainy season (May – October). If an island with gorgeous beaches, no villages, shops, roads or cars, and limited electricity is your idea of heaven, Ko Wai is for you. Regular boats, both slow and fast, stop at one of the piers on the island, depending where people are staying, and it's easy to move on to Ko Mak and Ko Kood from here too.

ARRIVAL AND DEPARTURE

KO WAI

The only access to Ko Wai is by ferry – from Laem Ngop on the mainland, from Bang Bao or Kai Bae piers on Ko Chang, or from Ko Mak/Ko Kood. Check ⓦ kohchangferries.com for detailed timetables. Remember that most resorts close in the rainy season, and ferry service is intermittent.

VIA KO CHANG

From Bang Bao pier on Ko Chang there are three boats a day; a slow, wooden boat (9am; 1hr; B300) and speedboats (9am and noon; 30min; B400). From Kai Bae pier, there's one daily speedboat (9am; 30min; B400).

VIA LAEM NGOP

Slow, wooden boats run three times a week between Laem Ngop and Ko Wai, stopping at the pier by Pakarang Resort (2hr 30min; B300). Speed boats are operated by Leelawadee and Seatales companies, run three times a day (40min; B450).

VIA KO MAK OR KO KOOD

Speedboats operated by Bang Bao Boat or Kai Bae Hut Speedboats depart from Ko Kood (1hr 30min; B700) and Ko Mak (30min; B400) to Ko Chang, stopping at Ko Wai en route.

ACCOMMODATION

Ko Wai Pakarang Resort In the middle of the north coast ☏ 084 113 8946 ⓦ facebook.com/kohwai pakarang. The concrete bungalows here are not particularly attractive, but it's the only place on the north coast that stays open all year, has 24-hour electricity (from a noisy generator) and some a/c rooms. Fan B600, a/c B1500
Ko Wai Paradise On the west side of the north coast ☏ 061 424 1556 ⓦ https://bit.ly/2C2JV8Y. All bungalows here share bathrooms and come in two sizes: big or small. All are equipped with fans, mattresses and mosquito nets, and electricity is only from 6pm–midnight. There's a good restaurant and the snorkelling in the bay in front is fantastic, although it's often crowded with day-trippers in the afternoon. Closed May–October. B200

4

Ko Mak

Small, slow-paced, peaceful **KO MAK** (sometimes spelt "Maak") makes an idyllic, low-key alternative to Ko Chang, 20km to the northwest. Measuring just sixteen square kilometres, it's home to little more than four hundred people, divided into five main clans, who work together to keep the island free of hostess bars, jet skis, banana boats and the like, collaborating instead on making the island eco-friendly. A few narrow concrete roads crisscross the island, which is dominated by coconut and rubber plantations; elsewhere a network of red-earth tracks cuts through the trees. Ko Mak is shaped like a star, with fine white-sand beaches along the northwest coast at **Ao Suan Yai** and the southwest coast at **Ao Kao**, where most of the island's (predominantly mid-range and upper-bracket) tourist accommodation is concentrated. The two main beaches are just about within walking distance of each other, and other parts of the island are also fairly easy to explore on foot, or by mountain bike, motorbike or kayak. The best way to discover the empty, undeveloped beaches hidden along the north and eastern coasts, such as Ao Laem Son in the northeast corner, where there are no resorts, just a couple of simple shacks serving food and drinks, is on foot. The **reefs** of Ko Rang are also less than an hour's boat ride away so snorkelling and diving trips are quite popular. There is as yet no major commercial development on the island and **no bank or ATM**, though a few places accept credit cards and bungalows on both beaches will change money. There's a small clinic off the Ao Nid road, though for anything serious a speedboat will whisk you back to the mainland.

During the **rainy season** (mid-May–late Oct), choppy seas mean that boat services to Ko Mak are much reduced. Most Ko Mak accommodation stays open – and offers tempting discounts – but the smaller places often don't bother to staff their restaurants. Islanders say that it can be very pleasant during this "green season", though you may be unlucky and hit a relentlessly wet few days.

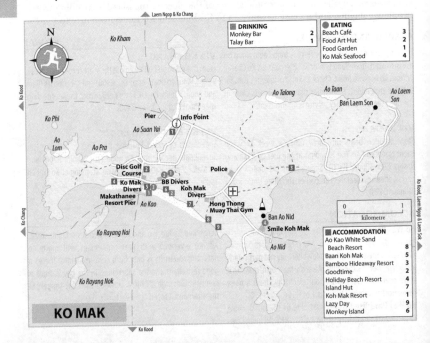

DRINKING

| Monkey Bar | 2 |
| Talay Bar | 1 |

EATING

Beach Café	3
Food Art Hut	2
Food Garden	1
Ko Mak Seafood	4

ACCOMMODATION

Ao Kao White Sand Beach Resort	8
Baan Koh Mak	5
Bamboo Hideaway Resort	3
Goodtime	2
Holiday Beach Resort	4
Island Hut	7
Koh Mak Resort	1
Lazy Day	9
Monkey Island	6

KO MAK

ACTIVITIES ON KO MAK

The reefs of Ko Rang (see page 411), part of the Ko Chang National Marine Park, are less than an hour's boat ride west of Ko Mak and are the island's main **diving and snorkelling** destination; they're the main focus of Ko Chang dive and snorkel boats too, so you won't be alone. You can also join a **cookery class**, practice **muay thai** or play **disc golf**.

BB Divers On the road to Ao Kao just west of Food Art Hut ☎ 092 602 2260 ⓦ bbdivers-koh-mak.com. Offers a Discover Scuba Diving course and one dive for B3000, two dives at Koh Rang for B3000 or snorkelling at Koh Rang for B1000; all include transfers.

Disc Golf Just south of Goodtime Resort; contact Pom at the Holiday Beach Resort for details ☎ 086 751 7668 ⓦ facebook.com/kohmakdiscgolf. Also known as 'frisbee golf', this relatively new sport is fun for all the family. Best in the late afternoon; a round of nine holes takes about an hour and costs B200.

Hong Thong Muay Thai On the road to Ao Kao just before the turning to Ao Nid. ☎ 081 711 1428 ⓦ facebook.com/muaythaikohmak. A good chance to combine relaxing with a physical work-out. All

equipment provided and instruction by professional Thai boxing teachers. One session B400 (10am or 4.30pm), 10 classes B3000.

Koh Mak Divers On the Ao Kao road just east of the pier, and also further east on the same road, behind the Ao Kao White Sand Beach Resort ☎ 083 297 7724, ⓦ kohmakdivers.com. British-run PADI centre that charges B2500 for two fun dives, B3500 for the beginners' one-day Discover Scuba Diving course and B790 for snorkellers, with transfers from your accommodation included.

Smile Koh Mak Next to Koh Mak Seafood restaurant at Ban Ao Nid ☎ 081 901 9972, ⓦ smilekohmak.com. 4hr cookery classes (10am–2pm; B1200, including a recipe book), with vegetarian options available.

4

Ao Kao

Ko Mak's longest beach is **AO KAO** on the southwest coast, a pretty arc of sand overhung with stooping palm trees and backed in places by mangroves. The beach is divided towards its southern end by a low rocky outcrop that's straddled by *Ao Kao White Sand Beach Resort*, with *Lazy Day Resort* occupying the strand beyond, while the long western beach is shared by a dozen other sets of bungalows, most of them around the pier at the *Makathanee Resort*. The roadside inland from the main accommodation area is where you'll find most of the restaurants and bars: if you're walking from the southern end, by far the easiest access is via the beach, tides permitting.

Ao Suan Yai and around

Long, curvy **AO SUAN YAI** is just as pretty a beach as Ao Kao; it only has a few resorts, but the sand is soft and white, the coconut palms lean seaward and the outlook is beautiful, with Ko Chang's hilly profile filling the horizon and Ko Kham and other islets in between. You'll need a bicycle or motorbike to access the variety of restaurants on the Ao Kao road.

ARRIVAL AND DEPARTURE   KO MAK

Check ⓦ kohmak.com or ⓦ kohchangferries.com for current routes and schedules for **boat services** from the mainland and the other islands. Boats arrive at one of Ko Mak's three **piers** – at *Koh Mak Resort* on Ao Suan Yai, at the *Makathanee Resort* on Ao Kao or at Ao Nid – and are usually met by a modest welcoming committee of accommodation staff offering free transport; similarly, if you book a room in advance, ask your resort for a free pick-up. When it comes to moving on, all hotels keep current boat schedules, can sell you a ticket and will take you to the pier. Slow boats to Laem Ngop cost B200 (8am; 3hr);

speedboats B450 (several departures daily; 50min).

VIA LAEM SOK

A year-round catamaran service sails to Ao Nid on Ko Mak from Laem Sok pier, 30km south of Trat (☎ 090 506 0020, ⓦ kohkoodcatamaran.com; daily; 50min; B400 including transfer to/from Trat bus station or downtown market). Some of the Laem Sok–Ko Kood high-season speedboats will call in at Ao Nid if they have enough customers (see page 427).

VIA LAEM NGOP

A year-round slow boat runs from the Krom Luang (Naval Monument) pier in Laem Ngop, some 20km southwest of Trat (3 weekly; 3hr; B300), to the Makathanee Resort pier on Ko Mak. From approximately October to May, Panan's speedboats also operate from this pier to *Ko Mak Resort* on Ao Suan Yai (2 daily; 45min–1hr; B450); the second of these is at 4pm, handy if you're arriving from Bangkok. A/c minibuses to Laem Ngop from Bangkok, for example, will sometimes only go as far as the Thammachat or Centrepoint Ko Chang piers, however – check exactly which piers are served when you buy your minibus ticket, or you may be able to pay the driver a little extra to go on to Krom Luang.

VIA KO CHANG OR KO KOOD

Boats run between Ko Chang, Ko Mak and Ko Kood in high season (see page 408).

INFORMATION

Tourist information Most resorts can arrange boat and bus tickets, motorbike or kayak rental and general information about the island. There's also a travel agent at *Makathanee Resort* (☎ 081 870 6287), by the pier on Ao Kao.

ⓦ kohmak.com is a useful, fairly comprehensive website about the island. At present there is no ATM on the island, so take cash with you.

GETTING AROUND

The island has narrow, paved roads connecting most parts, as well as rough dirt paths, but hardly any traffic, and most visitors rent a mountain bike or motorbike.

By taxi ☎ 089 752 5292 or ☎ 089 833 4474. 'Taxi' on Ko Mak means a songthaew, a pick-up truck with a bench seat on each side. B50/person; B100/person after 10pm;

minimum charge per vehicle B100.

By mountain bike or motorbike These (respectively B150/day and B200–300/day) can be rented through accommodation or from *Ko Mak Resort*'s Info Point; otherwise, *Food Art Hut* on Ao Kao (see opposite) has a particularly wide choice of bicycles, including kids' bikes.

ACCOMMODATION

AO KAO

Ao Kao White Sand Beach Resort Ao Kao ☎ 083 152 6564, ⓦ aokaoresort.com; map p.420. This welcoming, efficiently managed and lively set of upmarket bungalows occupies an attractive garden fronting the prettiest part of the beach. Its 25 large, comfortable, attractive timber bungalows come with a/c, hot showers and most have direct sea views. There are four restaurants and bars and lots of activities, including swimming, spa treatments, massage, Thai boxing, tennis, beach volleyball, yoga, a kids' trampoline, free kayaks and motorbikes for rent. Breakfast included. B4490

★ **Baan Koh Mak** Near the pier on Ao Kao ☎ 089 895 7592, ⓦ baan-koh-mak.com; map p.420. Arrayed around a clipped lawn, the eighteen bungalows at this chic and welcoming resort are modern, bright and comfortable, cutely done out in futuristically angular white, green and polished concrete, with a/c, hot water, small bedrooms and decent-sized bathrooms. There's a very good restaurant here too. B1890

Goodtime Ao Kao ☎ 039 501000, ⓦ goodtime-resort. com; map p.420. Luxurious, tasteful, Thai-style rooms and villas, all with a/c, hot water, TV, fridge, DVD player and use of a pool. They're located on higher ground inland from Ao Kao's *Makathanee Resort*, around a 15min walk from the beach. Room B1880, villa B5100

Holiday Beach Resort Ao Kao ☎ 086 751 7668, ⓦ holidaykohmak.com; map p.420. Friendly, well-maintained place, facing a large, beachside lawn with deckchairs and tables. White clapboard is the architectural style of choice here, either in small cottages with verandas and hammocks in the second row, or in large, attractive bungalows at the front. Kayaks, mountain bikes and motorbikes for rent. B1500

Island Hut Ao Kao ☎ 087 139 5537; map p.420. This little family-run place has the best-value and most idyllically sited accommodation on the beach, though not always the friendliest welcome. The two-dozen rough-hewn en-suite timber huts are more artfully designed than they might appear: most have cheery stripey doors and idiosyncratic driftwood artwork; all have fans, hanging space and their own deckchairs on decks or private sandy porches, but wi-fi in the restaurant area only. The cheapest share bathrooms, and there are a few a/c rooms with en-suite bathrooms too. Price depends on proximity to the narrow but pretty shore: the most expensive are at the water's edge and catch ocean breezes. Garden hut B250, beach hut B550, a/c B1200

Lazy Day Ao Kao ☎ 081 882 4002, ⓦ kohmaklazyday. com; map p.420. Civilized spot on a huge beachside lawn strewn with flowers and trees. As well as a/c, safes, hot showers and mini-bars (but no TVs, to preserve the quiet), the spacious, bright, mostly beachfront bungalows sport polished concrete floors, shining white walls and French windows out onto their balconies. Kayaks, bikes and motorbikes to rent. Breakfast included. B2700

Monkey Island Ao Kao ☎ 089 501 6030, ⓦ monkey islandkohmak.com; map p.420. There's a big range of bungalows here, all in timber and thatch, and a laidback, hippyish vibe. Top-end "Gorilla" seafront villas are huge, with a/c, hot water and the possibility of connecting villas; the large a/c "Chimpanzee" bungalows are also good, while some of the small "Ape" and "Baboon" options share bathrooms. There's also a kids' swimming pool, and a/c room rates include breakfast. Fan B400, a/c B1300

AO SUAN YAI AND AROUND

Bamboo Hideaway Resort A couple of kilometres east of Ao Suan Yai, accessed via tracks through the rubber plantations ☎039 501085, ⓦbamboohideaway.com; map p.420. An idiosyncratic haven, built almost entirely from lengths of polished bamboo. Its comfortable a/c rooms all have mosquito nets on the beds, hammocks and hot showers, and are connected by a raised walkway. Although the south coast is just a couple of minutes' walk downhill, Ao Suan Yai has the nearest decent beach. There's an attractive swimming pool on site, as well as a good restaurant. Breakfast included. Closed June–Sept. B1250

★ **Koh Mak Resort** Ao Suan Yai ☎089 600 9597, ⓦkohmakresort.com; map p.420. With no less than 1.5km of shoreline to play with, all of the bungalows here are beachfront (including the cheapest options, still with a/c and hot showers) and enjoy lovely panoramas from their verandas. There's a good-sized swimming pool as well as a kids' pool, a restaurant, a dessert bar, a shop and a helpful tour office. The resort also runs daily snorkelling trips to nearby Ko Kham. Breakfast included. B2800

EATING AND DRINKING

AO KAO

★ **Beach Café** At Baan Ko Mak, Ao Kao; map p.420. Coolly done out in black and white with some nice sofas, this restaurant serves exceptionally delicious Thai food, including good *tom kha* soups and a great *kaeng phanaeng* (both B92). Daily 8am–9.30pm.

Food Art Hut Opposite Monkey Island, Ao Kao; map p.420. Idiosyncratic all-rounder, offering ice cream, desserts, cakes and espressos, as well as Thai dishes and simple, passable Western food such as spaghetti bolognese (B140), breakfasts, pizzas and sandwiches. Daily 8am–3pm & 5–9pm.

Food Garden Opposite Monkey Island, Ao Kao; map p.420. This popular, cheap and enjoyable garden restaurant serves *phat thai*, various spicy salads and *matsaman* curries (B120), as well as seafood barbecues in the evening. Daily 10am–10pm.

Monkey Bar Monkey Island, Ao Kao; map p.420. Live music nightly, including jamming sessions, at this bar built around the beachfront trees. A good place to meet young travellers, if you can hear yourself over the music. Daily 9pm–midnight.

Talay Bar On the beach in front of Beach Café at Baan Ko Mak, Ao Kao; map p.420. Tables on the sand – with a fire show at 8pm – and great margaritas (B150) plus a long list of other cocktails. Mellow music and evening barbecues. Open in high season only. Evenings till late.

BAN AO NID

Ko Mak Seafood Just north of Ao Nid pier ☎089 833 4474; map p.420. Built out into the sea on stilts, with views of the bay, this restaurant is mostly true to its name, serving *phat thai* with fresh prawns (B80) and more complex dishes such as tasty squid with salted eggs (B200). (Don't get your hopes up about the advertised Ko Mak Museum next door, though – it's just a collection of old things in an old house.) Daily 10.30am–9pm.

Ko Kood

The fourth-largest island in Thailand, forested **KO KOOD** (also spelt Ko Kut and Ko Kud) is still a wild and largely uncommercialized island. Though it's known for its sparkling white sand and exceptionally clear turquoise water, particularly along the west coast, Ko Kood is as much a nature-lover's destination as a beach-bum's. Swathes of its shoreline are fringed by scrub and mangrove rather than broad sandy beaches, and those parts of the island not still covered in virgin tropical rainforest are filled with palm groves and rubber plantations. There are just a few paved roads, and most of the 25km-long island is penetrated only by sandy tracks and, in places, by navigable khlongs. All of this makes Ko Kood a surprisingly pleasant place to explore on foot (or kayak), especially as the cool season brings refreshing breezes most days. The interior is also graced with some huge, ancient trees and several waterfalls, the most famous of which is Nam Tok Khlong Chao, inland from Ao Khlong Chao.

Because of its relative lack of roads, Ko Kood was once the exclusive province of package tourists, but things have become much easier for independent travellers, with a choice of scheduled boat services from the mainland, as well as from Ko Chang and

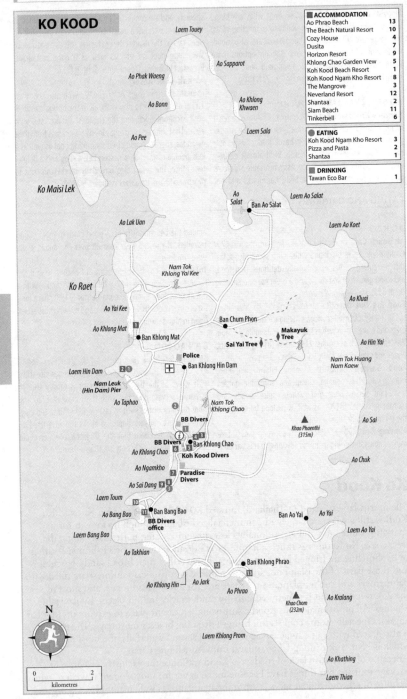

KO KOOD

Laem Touey

Ao Sapparot

Ao Phak Waeng

Ao Bonn

Ao Khlong Khwaen

Ao Pee

Laem Sala

Ko Maisi Lek

Ao Salat

Ban Ao Salat

Laem Ao Salat

Ao Lak Uan

Laem Ao Koet

Nam Tok Khlong Yai Kee

Ko Raet

Ao Kluai

Ao Yai Kee

Ban Chum Phon

Ao Khlong Mat

Makayuk Tree

Ban Khlong Mat

Sai Yai Tree

Ao Hin Yai

Police

Nam Tok Huang Nam Kaew

Laem Hin Dam

Ban Khlong Hin Dam

Nam Leuk (Hin Dam) Pier

Ao Taphao

Nam Tok Khlong Chao

Ao Sai

BB Divers

Khao Phaenthi (315m)

BB Divers

Ban Khlong Chao

Ao Khlong Chao

Koh Kood Divers

Ao Chuk

Ao Ngamkho

Paradise Divers

Ao Sai Dang

Laem Toum

The Beach Natural Resort

Ao Bang Bao

Ban Bang Bao

Ban Ao Yai

Ao Yai

BB Divers office

Laem Bang Bao

Laem Ao Yai

Ao Takhian

Ban Khlong Phrao

Ao Khlong Hin

Ao Jark

Ao Phrao

Khao Chom (232m)

Ao Kralang

N

Laem Khlong Prom

Ao Khathing

Laem Thian

0   2
kilometres

DIVING AND SNORKELLING OFF KO KOOD

Ko Kood's three **dive operators** charge around B3000 for two dives, with **snorkellers** paying B1000, and B14,500 for the four-day Open Water Diver course. You might prefer to opt for a local Ko Kood dive as the usual sites around Ko Rang (see page 411) are always packed with dive boats from Ko Chang and Ko Mak.

BB Divers On the main road at Ao Khlong Chao next to High Season Resort, and at Siam Beach Resort on Ao Bang Bao ☎ 082 220 6002, ⓦ bbdivers-koh-kood.com.
Koh Kood Divers On the main road at Ao Khlong Chao

near the junction with the road to Khlong Chao Falls ☎ 085 698 4122, ⓦ kohkooddivers.com.
Paradise Divers Opposite S-Resort on Ao Ngamkho ☎ 087 144 5945, ⓦ kohkood-paradisedivers.com.

Ko Mak, the emergence of some budget-minded guesthouses, and paved roads linking most beaches. The island is still pretty much a **one-season destination**, though, as rough seas mean that nearly all the boat services only operate from November through May. An increasing number of places are staying open year-round, however, and offer tempting discounts to those willing to chance the rains and the off-season quiet. There is some **malaria** on the island so be especially assiduous with repellent and nets if you are not taking prophylactics; there's a malaria-testing station in Ban Khlong Hin Dam.

Most of Ko Kood's fifteen hundred residents make their living from fishing and growing coconut palms and rubber trees. Many have Khmer blood in them, as the island population mushroomed at the turn of the twentieth century when Thais and Cambodians resident in nearby Cambodian territory fled French control.

The main settlements are **Ban Khlong Hin Dam**, just inland from the main Nam Leuk (Hin Dam) pier, **Ban Khlong Mat**, a natural harbour-inlet a few kilometres further north up the coast, the stilted fishing village of **Ban Ao Salat** across on the northeast coast and the fishing community of **Ban Ao Yai** on the southeast coast. On the southwest coast, several of the main beaches also have small villages. Of these, the obvious choices for budget travellers are **Ao Khlong Chao** and **Ao Ngamkho**, which both have a wide choice of accommodation and eating options and are within walking distance of each other; **Ao Bang Bao** also has several resorts and a beautiful beach but has no village and is more isolated. Seclusion is the thing on all the other west-coast beaches, most of which are the province of just one or two upmarket resorts.

Ao Khlong Chao

About 5km south of the main Nam Leuk (Hin Dam) pier on the west coast, **AO KHLONG CHAO** (pronounced "Jao") is a fun place to stay, boasting both a wide, sandy beach and the pretty 2km-long mangrove-lined Khlong Chao, which runs down from the famous Khlong Chao Falls. Close by and upstream of the road-bridge that spans the khlong, just 300m from the palm-fringed beach, is a cluster of little guesthouses, some of them built partially on stilts over the river, which offer the cheapest accommodation on the island. The beachfront is occupied by high-end resorts.

Nam Tok Khlong Chao (Khlong Chao Falls)

30min walk from Ao Khlong Chao, or kayak 20min upriver from the Khlong Chao bridge to the jetty near the falls, then walk for 10min; you can also drive to within 100m of the falls along a well-signed, paved road

The three-tiered **Nam Tok Khlong Chao** is a pretty if not exceptional waterfall that tumbles down into a large, refreshing pool that's perfect for a dip; it's quietest in the mornings, before the package groups arrive. The track continues beyond the falls through jungle for another few kilometres before terminating at a rubber plantation – if you walk the whole thing it's a pleasant and very quiet four-hour trip there and back, though watch out for snakes, especially cobras.

Ao Ngamkho

South of Ao Khlong Chao, the road goes over a headland and dips down to the tiny village at **AO NGAMKHO** and its beach, actually a series of pretty, miniature bays either side of a khlong and between rocky points, with quite rewarding snorkelling and plenty of fish at its southern end.

Ao Bang Bao

Beyond Ao Ngamkho, the road passes behind **AO BANG BAO**, with a side road leading a couple of kilometres down to the beach. This is one of Ko Kood's prettiest beaches, fronted by a longish sweep of bleach-white sand and deliciously clear turquoise water, plus the inevitable fringe of coconut palms, and embraced by a pair of protective promontories.

Ao Jark

On the main southbound road at the Ao Bang Bao turn-off, the main road turns eastward, while a turning south passes through coconut and rubber plantations on the way to **Ao Khlong Hin**, a wild little bay that's dominated by a small coconut-processing centre and is not really great for swimming. A few minutes further along this road, which hugs the coast so close here it gets washed by the waves at high tide, remote and breathtakingly lovely little **AO JARK** sits at the mouth of a wide, serene khlong and feels secluded and private.

Ao Phrao

The most southerly bay, **AO PHRAO**, is a long, stunning beach of white sand backed by densely planted palms and the slopes of Khao Chom; to get here, follow the main road eastwards from Ao Bang Bao. Behind Ao Phrao, the tiny fishing village of **Ban Khlong Phrao** occupies the mangrove-lined banks of Khlong Phrao (which extends another kilometre inland). There's a clinic here as well as a few small shops and hot-food stalls.

Ban Ao Yai

A 5km road that's very steep in places connects Ban Khlong Phrao with **Ban Ao Yai**, the southeast coast's main if rather lacklustre fishing village, built entirely on stilts and jetties around the shoreline of a natural harbour. Its main visitors are the crews of anchored fishing boats from Thailand and Cambodia, who come here for drink, supplies, karaoke and the rest.

Ban Khlong Hin Dam and around

The bays of northern Ko Kood, beyond Ao Khlong Chao, are even more thinly populated than the southwest coast, with just a few exclusive resorts hidden away. Inland is the island's administrative centre, **Ban Khlong Hin Dam**, 3.5km north of Ao Khlong Chao, site of a few shops, the hospital, police station, school and principal island temple. Ko Kood's main west-coast pier is a couple of kilometres to the west, at **Nam Leuk (Laem Hin Dam)**.

About 5km north of Ban Khlong Hin Dam, the small but appealing three-tiered waterfall **Nam Tok Khlong Yai Kee** is basically a miniature version of the famous Nam Tok Khlong Chao (see opposite) and rushes down into a good-sized pool that's ideal for swimming. It's accessible via a five-minute path that's very steep in places, but there are ropes at the crucial points.

Ban Ao Salat and around

The road northeast from Ban Khlong Hin Dam ends after 9km at the tiny stilt village, fishing community and port of **Ban Ao Salat**. Several of the wooden houses strung out along the jetty-promenade serve food and this is a great place for a fresh-seafood lunch, especially crab.

East off this road, in the mature rainforest near Ban Chum Phon, are a couple of locally famous ancient trees, thought to be between 200 and 500 years old, known to islanders as *makayuk and sai yai*. They're both 35m or more in height and surrounded by sprawling buttress roots and drip with lianas and epiphytes. They are signposted on opposite sides of a paved road that leads through rubber trees and rainforest, from where a short walk along forest trails leads to the enormous boles. Further east, this road leads to Nam Tok Huang Nam Kaew, another beautiful waterfall surrounded by rainforest.

ARRIVAL AND INFORMATION

KO KOOD

BY BOAT
All boat tickets to Ko Kood from the mainland should include transfers to the pier from Trat, though it's worth double-checking. Mainland and Ko Chang speedboats will drop off at and pick up from most of the west-coast accommodation. All Ko Kood hotels keep current time-tables and sell tickets.

FERRIES FROM THE MAINLAND
In all but the worst weather, Koh Kood Princess (⚏ 082 878 9900, ⚏ kohkoodprincess.com) runs a year-round boat service to Ko Kood from the Trat mainland, departing from Laem Sok, about 30km south of Trat, occasionally calling at Ao Nid on Ko Mak, and terminating at Ao Salat on the island's northeast coast (daily at 12.30pm; about 1hr 30min; B350 including transfers on Ko Kood). There is also a service operated by the Ko Kut Express, which sails from Laem Sok to Nam Leuk pier on Ko Kood's west coast (⚏ 084 524 4321, ⚏ kokutexpress.in.th; daily; 1hr 15min; B350). A third option, and the smoothest ride, is on the Boonsiri Catamaran (⚏ 085 921 0111 ⚏ boonsiriferry.com), which runs twice a day (10.45am and 2.20pm; 1hr 15min; B500).

SPEEDBOATS FROM THE MAINLAND
There are also several different companies offering high-season speedboat services between the Trat mainland and Ko Kood's western piers and beaches; these are faster and more expensive (up to 4 daily; about 1hr; B600) but can be wet and uncomfortable in all but the flattest seas. Schedules and mainland departure points vary, though most services depart from Laem Sok; ⚏ kohkoodferries.com is a useful resource.

VIA KO CHANG AND KO MAK
Boats run between Ko Chang, Ko Mak and Ko Kood in high season (see page 408). Speedboats from Ko Chang to Ko Kood (9am, 9.30am and 12.30pm; 1hr 45min; B900) can be caught at the stop-off at Ao Nid on Ko Mak (10am; 45–60min; B400) if there are enough takers.

Tourist information There's a municipal tourist information office on Ao Khlong Chao, just north of the bridge on the west side of the road, though it's often unattended (daily 8.30am–6pm).

4

GETTING AROUND

Exploring the southwest of the island on foot is both feasible and pleasant, and south of Ao Khlong Chao much of the route is shady. From Ao Khlong Chao to Ao Bang Bao takes about 40min; from Ao Bang Bao to Ao Jark is about 1hr, then another 20min to Ao Phrao.

By songthaew These can be chartered for around B1000/day.
By motorbike You can rent motorbikes through most guesthouses and resorts (from B250/day), but be warned that the mostly concrete west-coast road is narrow and steep, and badly rutted in places.

ACCOMMODATION

AO KHLONG CHAO
Cozy House On the south bank of the khlong, Ao Khlong Chao ⚏ 089 094 3650, ⚏ kohkoodcozy.com; map p.424. This travellers' haunt, with bungalows spread around a big, grassy area beside the khlong, has upgraded its accommodation, but the basic fan bungalows are a good

deal, and the a/c bungalows (B1200) are very spacious. Lots of facilities for backpackers, including free kayak use and motorbike rental. Fan B700 a/c B1000
Khlong Chao Garden View 100m south of the bridge, at the junction of the main road and the road to the waterfall, Ao Khlong Chao ⚏ 086 038 8420; map p.424.

Away from the khlong, this friendly place is set on a lawn dotted with ornamental trees beside the road. Choose between basic, fan-cooled huts with small bathrooms, and larger a/c bungalows with TVs. There's good food at the popular garden restaurant too – try the *kaeng phanaeng*. Fan B600, a/c B1000

★ **The Mangrove** On the south bank of the khlong, Ao Khlong Chao ☎089 936 2093, ⓦkohkood-mangrove. com; map p.424. The best of the khlongside options, with nice views of the water and sturdy wooden bungalows spaced around a well-tended lawn, dotted with pretty plants and trees. Interiors are modern and well furnished with TV and hot water. Free kayaks and motorbikes for rent. Includes breakfast. Fan B700, a/c B1500

Tinkerbell Ao Khlong Chao ☎081 813 0058, ⓦtinkerbellresort.com; map p.424. Stylishly designed and landscaped resort at the south end of the beach, which offers a difficult choice. For the same price (including breakfast), you can plump for either a bright, pastel-coloured villa with a/c, hot rain shower, fridge, TV, DVD player and large balcony right on the beach, or an equally attractive two-storey house in the second row, with a plunge pool and a separate large living room and toilet upstairs. There's a small swimming pool fed by an artificial waterfall. B9840

AO NGAMKHO

Dusita Ao Ngamkho ☎081 420 4861, ⓦdusitakohkood. com; map p.424. Occupying the lion's share of Ao Ngamkho, this resort zealously guards its private pier and grounds with 'Do Not Trespass' signs, guaranteeing privacy to its guests. There are just 16 thoughtfully designed a/c wooden cabins, some with nice pebbledash outdoor bathrooms, that all enjoy beautiful sea views and some shade among the manicured gardens and towering palms. Standard rooms are a bit small but family rooms are bright and spacious. B3090

Horizon Resort Ao Ngamkho ☎088 457 1551, ⓦhorizonresortkohkood.com; map p.424. The large, modern, a/c, hot-water wooden chalets here, some with outdoor bathrooms, sit on a flower-strewn slope atop the little rocky point at the southern end of the bay, with polished floorboards, panoramic sea views and easy access to swimming and snorkelling among the coral off the point. B2700

Koh Kood Ngam Kho Resort Ao Ngamkho ☎084 653 4644; ⓦfacebook.com/kohkoodngamkhoresort.com; map p.424. Set in a lovely location at the south end of Ao Ngamkho, this family-run, budget resort is a great place to base yourself, if only for the fantastic food in the restaurant (see page 429). Rooms range from small, fan-cooled rustic cabins on stilts to spacious a/c concrete bungalows. Be prepared for a noisy reception from the family dogs. Fan B800, a/c B1500

AO BANG BAO

The Beach Natural Resort Ao Bang Bao ☎084 717 0955, ⓦthebeachkohkood.com; map p.424. Though it doesn't actually sit on the nicest part of the beach, but behind a rocky area towards the northern end, this resort's diverse, thatched Balinese-style bungalows are tastefully furnished and have garden bathrooms; they're grouped quite closely together so most only offer glimpses of the sea. All have hot showers and a/c. Facilities include massage service and rental of kayaks. Breakfast included. B4900

Siam Beach Ao Bang Bao ☎081 907 1940, ⓦsiam beachresortkohkood.com; map p.424. This resort occupies almost all of the best part of the beach, sprawling across an extensive area, and is popular with budget travellers, though some bungalows are cramped tightly together. Its big, no-frills huts and bungalows on the seafront nearly all enjoy uninterrupted bay views. Some of the newer a/c rooms are in a less idyllic spot close to a khlong and back from the shore a bit, but they're cheaper than the beachside a/c options and have hot showers. Breakfast included in high season rates. Fan B1400, a/c B2200

AO JARK

Neverland Resort Ao Jark ☎081 762 6254, ⓦneverlandresort.com; map p.424. This remote resort is set among the palms between the limpid blue sea and the calm green khlong. It offers comfortable, balconied, log-clad a/c bungalows, some with hot showers, in a pretty garden, as well as fully equipped two-person tents, kayaks and snorkels. Breakfast included. Tents B500, bungalows B2000

AO PHRAO

Ao Phrao Beach Ao Phrao ☎081 429 7145, ⓦkokut. com; map p.424. Mainly but not exclusively package-oriented clusters of thatched and more expensive concrete a/c bungalows, all with hot showers and TVs; facilities include free kayaks and a karaoke room. Breakfast included. B2100

AROUND BAN KHLONG HIN DDAM

Koh Kood Beach Resort Ao Khlong Mat, about 2km northwest of Ban Khlong Hin Dam ☎081 908 8966, ⓦkohkoodbeachresorts.com; map p.424. This resort is set in loads of space on a sweeping, grassy slope above a lovely pool and a nice stretch of sandy beach. Rooms are of two types, all with a/c, outdoor hot showers, mini-bars, TVs, DVD players and sea views from their generous decks: high-roofed, thatched Balinese-style bungalows and slightly more expensive "Thai Twin Houses", very suitable for families, in which two rooms are connected to one terrace with a Jacuzzi. Guests get free rental of snorkels and kayaks. Breakfast included. B3900

★ **Shantaa** North end of Ao Taphao, about 2km west of Ban Khlong Hin Dam ☎ 081 566 0607, ⓦ shantaakohkood.com; map p.424. On a landscaped grassy rise, these beautifully designed villas have a/c and hot rain showers in attractive indoor-outdoor bathrooms. There are a couple of small beaches just a few steps away, and plenty of decks with sunloungers. There are no TVs in the rooms, in line with the owners' aspirations to make it an ecologically sound resort. The staff are extremely attentive and there's a great restaurant too. Breakfast included. B4900

EATING AND DRINKING

★ **Koh Kood Ngam Kho Resort** Ao Ngamkho T084 653 4644; map p.424. The restaurant of this unassuming resort has an extensive menu of Thai and international cuisine, all of which is tasty, but note the early closing time. Try the seafood tom yam (B180), it's fantastic. A visit in the daytime brings the added benefit of gorgeous views across the bay. Daily 7am–8pm.

Pizza and Pasta South side of Ban Khlong Hin Dam ☎ 083 297 2860, ⓦ pizzanpasta.info; map p.424. Genial Italian roadside restaurant serving a mean bolognese with home-made tagliatelle (B300), pizzas (B220), a few salads, pastries for breakfast and probably the best espresso on the island. Daily 9am–9pm.

Shantaa Ao Taphao ☎ 081 566 0607; map p.424. Not only does this resort do a great job of making its guests supremely comfortable, its restaurant also serves up delicious dishes such as mu cha muang (slow-steamed pork with sour leaves; B280) and stir-fried seafood with crispy Thai herbs (B290). It's worth heading here to eat even if you're not staying at the resort. Daily 11am–4pm & 5.30pm–8.30pm.

Tawan Eco Bar Ao Khlong Chao, about 500m north of the bridge ☎ 098 337 4223 ⓦ facebook.com/tawankohkood; map p.424. Small roadside bar in a wooden shack on stilts run by Jong, a friendly musician; live music every night. Daily 10am–1am.

DIRECTORY

Banks There are a couple of ATMs on Ko Kood. One is at Ao Khlong Chao, next to BB Divers, and the other is immediately south of the hospital.

Hospital Ban Khlong Hin Dam (☎ 089 603 8685).

Pharmacy The shop across from the hospital in Ban Khlong Hin Dam has a small pharmacy section and sells antihistamine tablets for bites from sandflies (see page 67), which can be legion on Ko Kood.

Police Ban Khlong Hin Dam (☎ 087 958 1991).

4

The northeast: Isaan

PHANOM RUNG, BURIRAM

5

The northeast: Isaan

Bordered by the Mekong River and Laos to the north and east, and Cambodia to the south, the tableland of northeast Thailand – known as Isaan, after the Hindu god of death and the northeast – comprises a third of the country's land area and is home to nearly a third of its population. This is the least-visited region of the kingdom, and the poorest: most Isaan residents are in debt, and many still earn less than the national minimum wage of B300 a day. Farming is the traditional livelihood here, despite relatively infertile soil (the friable sandstone contains few nutrients and retains little water), long periods of drought punctuated by downpours and intermittent bouts of flooding. As you'd expect, the landscape is mostly flat, but there are plenty of lively festivals and ancient temples to make a visit worth the effort.

Rather than the cities – which are chaotic, exhausting places, with little going for them apart from accommodation and onward transport – Isaan's prime destinations are its **Khmer ruins** and **national parks**. Five huge northeastern **festivals** also draw massive crowds: in May, Yasothon is the focus for the bawdy rocket festival; the end of June or beginning of July sees the equally raucous rainmaking festival of Phi Ta Kon in Dan Sai near Loei; in July, Ubon Ratchathani hosts an extravagant candle festival; in October, strange, pink fireballs float out of the Mekong near Nong Khai; while the flamboyant, though inevitably touristy, "elephant round-up" is staged in Surin in November.

It's rural life that really defines Isaan though, and you can learn a lot about the local residents by staying at one of the family-run **guesthouses** and **homestays** in the region. Locals call themselves khon isaan (Isaan people) to distinguish them from khon thai (Thai people) or khon lao (Lao people) across the border, and they speak a dialect that is distinct from other regions of the country.

If you make it this far you should endeavour to see at least one set of Isaan's Khmer ruins: those at **Phimai** are the most accessible, but it's well worth making the effort to visit **Phanom Rung** as well, which occupies a spectacular hilltop location. Relics of an even earlier age, prehistoric cliff-paintings also draw a few tourists eastwards to Pha Taem National Park beside the Mekong River near the little town of **Khong Chiam**.

Isaan's only mountain range of any significance divides the sleepy town of **Loei** from the central plains and offers some delightful walking, awesome scenery and the possibility of spotting unusual birds and flowers in the **national parks** that spread across its heights. Due north of Loei at **Chiang Khan**, the **Mekong River** begins its leisurely course around Isaan with a lush stretch where an array of resorts and guesthouses has opened up the river countryside to travellers. The powerful waterway acts as a natural boundary between Thailand and Laos, but it's no longer the forbidding barrier it once was; with Laos opening further border crossings to visitors, the river is becoming an increasingly important transport link.

At the eastern end of this upper stretch, the border town of **Nong Khai** is surrounded by wonderfully ornate temples, including the bizarre Sala Kaeo Kou. The grandest and most important religious site in the northeast, however, is **Wat Phra That Phanom**, way downstream beyond **Nakhon Phanom**, a town that affords some of the finest Isaan vistas.

In the 1960s, government schemes to introduce hardier crops set in motion a debt cycle that has forced farmers into monocultural cash-cropping to repay their loans for fertilizers, seeds and machinery. For many families, there's only one way off the treadmill: of the twenty-one million people who live in Isaan, around ten percent leave

Highlights

❶ Khao Yai National Park Easy and tough trails, lots of birds, gibbons and elephants, several waterfalls and night safaris. See page 435

❷ Khmer ruins Exquisite Angkor Wat-style temples at Phimai and Phanom Rung. See pages 444 and 458

❸ Silk A northeastern speciality, available all over the region but particularly around Khon Kaen. See page 458

❹ Yasothon rocket festival Bawdy rainmaking ritual involving ornate home-made rockets. See page 467

❺ Phu Kradung Towering table mountain, the most dramatic of the region's national parks. See page 481

❻ The Mekong The best stretch in Thailand for gentle exploration of the mighty riverscape is between Chiang Khan and Nong Khai. See page 484

❼ Wat Phu Tok Extraordinary meditation temple on a steep sandstone outcrop. See page 495

❽ Wat Phra That Phanom Isaan's most fascinating holy site, especially during the February pilgrimage. See page 498

HIGHLIGHTS ARE MARKED ON THE MAP ON PAGE 434

5

the area every year, most of them heading for Bangkok, where northeasterners make up the majority of the capital's lowest-paid workforce. Children and elderly parents remain in the villages, increasingly dependent on the money sent back every month from the metropolis and awaiting the annual visit in May, when migrant family members often return for a couple of months to help with the rice planting.

Brief history

Most northeasterners speak a dialect that's more comprehensible to residents of Vientiane than Bangkok, and Isaan's historic allegiances have tied it more closely to Laos and Cambodia than to Thailand. Between the eleventh and thirteenth centuries, the all-powerful **Khmers** covered the northeast in magnificent stone temple complexes, the remains of which constitute the region's most satisfying tourist attractions. During subsequent centuries the territories along the Mekong River changed hands numerous times, until the present border with Laos was set at the end of World War II. In the 1950s and 1960s, **Communist insurgents** played on the northeast's traditional ties with Laos; a movement to align Isaan with the Marxists of Laos gathered some force, and the Communist Party of Thailand, gaining sympathy among poverty-stricken northeastern farmers, established bases in the region. At about the same time, major US air bases for the **Vietnam War** were set up in Khorat, Ubon Ratchathani and Udon Thani, fuelling a sex industry that still exists in a downscaled form today. When the American military moved out, many northeastern women migrated to Bangkok, and today a large amount of prostitutes in the capital still come from Isaan.

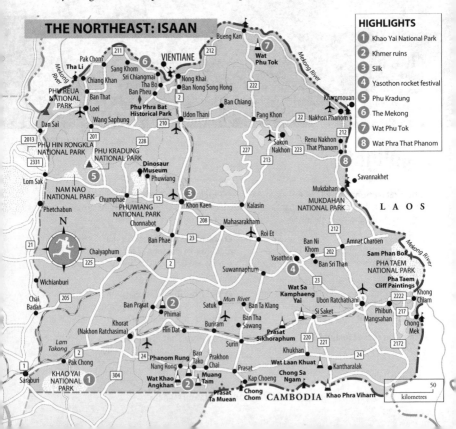

THE NORTHEAST: ISAAN

HIGHLIGHTS

1 Khao Yai National Park
2 Khmer ruins
3 Silk
4 Yasothon rocket festival
5 Phu Kradung
6 The Mekong
7 Wat Phu Tok
8 Wat Phra That Phanom

LAOS

CAMBODIA

0   50
kilometres

5

ISAAN'S BORDER CROSSINGS

Isaan has six major **border crossings into Laos** (see page 30), all but one (Bueng Kan–Paksan) of which issue Lao visas.

The most popular is at **Nong Khai**, a route that provides easy road access to the Lao capital, Vientiane; the others are Tha Li, Bueng Kan, Nakhon Phanom, Mukdahan and Chong Mek. If you want to avoid possible queues at the border, you can get a Lao visa in advance from the consulate in the central Isaan town of Khon Kaen. Here you'll also find a Vietnamese consulate issuing visas for Vietnam and a Chinese consulate issuing visas for China.

It's also possible to travel **overland between Isaan and Cambodia** (see page 29) through two different border crossings: via Chong Chom in Surin province to O'Smach, which has transport to Anlong Veng and then on to Siem Reap; and via Chong Sa Ngam in the Phusing district of Si Saket province to Choam in Anlong Veng.

ARRIVAL AND GETTING AROUND   **ISAAN**

All towns and cities in Isaan are connected by public transport, as are many of the larger villages, but compared to many other parts of the country, northeastern roads are fairly traffic-free, so hiring your own vehicle is also a good option.

By bus Many travellers approach Isaan from the north, either travelling directly from Chiang Mai to Loei, or going via Phitsanulok, in the northern reaches of the central plains, to Khon Kaen, but you can also take direct buses to Khorat from the east-coast towns of Pattaya, Rayong and Chanthaburi. All major northeastern centres have direct bus services from Bangkok.

By train Two rail lines cut through Isaan, terminating at Nong Khai and Ubon Ratchathani, providing useful connections with Bangkok and Ayutthaya.

By plane There are flights between Bangkok and several northeastern cities.

Khao Yai National Park

B400; vehicles B50 extra; daily 6am–6pm.

About 120km northeast of Bangkok, the cultivated lushness of the central plains gives way to the thickly forested Phanom Dangrek mountains. A 2166-square-kilometre chunk of this sculpted limestone range has been conserved as **KHAO YAI NATIONAL PARK**, the country's first national park to be established (in 1962) and one of its most popular. Spanning five distinct forest types and rising to a height of 1351m, the park sustains over three hundred bird and twenty large land-mammal species – hence its UNESCO accreditation as a World Heritage Site – and offers a plethora of waterfalls and several undemanding walking trails.

Rangers discourage visitors from exploring the outer reaches of the park unguided, partly for environmental reasons, but also because of trigger-happy **sandalwood poachers**. The highly prized sandalwood oil is extracted by making cuts in a mature aloewood tree and collecting chunks of oil-saturated wood; the oil now sells for B100,000 per litre. Sandalwood trees are indigenous to Khao Yai, and though oil collection does not usually kill the tree, it does weaken it. Guides can point out trees that have been cut in this way along the trails.

For many Thais, however, especially Bangkokians, Khao Yai is not so much a place for wildlife spotting as an easy weekend escape from the fumes. Some have second homes in the area, while others come for the golf and the soft-adventure activities, especially horseriding and off-road driving in ATVs, offered by popular "dude-ranch" resorts. The cooler climate here has also made Khao Yai one of Thailand's most productive areas for viticulture and dairy farming.

There's camping and basic accommodation in the park itself, and plenty more budget and luxury options just beyond the perimeter and in the nearby town of **Pak Chong**. It's quite easy to trek the park trails by yourself, but as some of Khao Yai's best waterfalls, caves and viewpoints are as much as 20km apart, a tour is well worthwhile. Try to avoid visiting at weekends and on public holidays, when it's always busy. Bring

5

KHAO YAI'S WILDLIFE

During the daytime you're bound to hear some of the local wildlife, even if you don't catch sight of it. Noisiest of all are the **white-handed (lar) gibbons**, which hoot and whoop from the tops of the tallest trees, and the bubbling trills of the **pileated (capped) gibbons**. Gibbons generally avoid contact with the ground, unlike the hard-to-miss **pig-tailed macaques**, many of which gather at favoured spots on the road through the park. **Hornbills** also create quite a racket, calling and flapping their enormous wings; Khao Yai harbours large flocks of four different hornbill species, which makes it one of the best observation sites in Southeast Asia. The great hornbill is particularly beautiful, with brilliant yellow and black undersides and a 2m wingspan; the magnificent oriental pied hornbill boasts less striking black and white colouring, but is more commonly seen at close range because it swoops down to catch fish, rats and reptiles. You might also see red-headed trogons, orange-breasted trogons, woodpeckers and Asian fairy-bluebirds, and, if you're very lucky, silver pheasants or Siamese firebacks, endemic only to Thailand and western Cambodia. From November to March Khao Yai hosts several species of **migrant birds**, including the dramatically coloured Siberian thrush and the orange-headed thrush.

A herd of around 200 Asian **elephants** lives in the park, and its members are often seen at night – it's the only place in Thailand where you have much chance of spotting wild elephants. Khao Yai was also once home to a few **tigers**, though none have been seen in the park since 2002. You're almost certain to spot **civets**, and you might come across a **slow loris**, while barking and sambar **deer** are less nervous after dark. **Wrinkle-lipped bats** assemble en masse at sunset, especially at the cave entrance next to Wat Tham Silathong, just outside the north (main) gate into the park, which every evening disgorges millions of them on their nightly forage.

binoculars if you have them and some warm clothes, as it gets cool at the higher altitudes, especially at night.

The park

Visitor centre (086 092 6529) daily 8am–6pm;

Several well-worn trails radiate from the area around the visitor centre and park headquarters at kilometre-stone 37, and a few more branch off from the roads that traverse the park; a few are signposted en route and some are colour-coded. The **visitor centre** provides brochures showing the more popular trails. Wear good boots, be prepared for some wading through rivers, and take a hat and plenty of water.

You won't spot much wildlife unless you know where to look, which is one reason to join a tour (see page 438), since the guides know which trees the hornbills perch on and where gibbons go to feed. If you don't want to join an organized tour, you can arrange a customised tour with a forest ranger (B500–B1,000), but you should set this up the day before. If you prefer to go it alone, the following trails are the most popular options.

Kong Kaew Nature Trail

The shortest and least taxing trail is the kilometre-long **Kong Kaew Nature Trail**, which starts just behind the visitor centre. It's paved all the way and takes just thirty minutes in each direction; if it's not too crowded, you could see gibbons, woodpeckers and kingfishers en route.

To Nong Pak Chee observation tower

Of the more adventurous hikes that begin from the park headquarters, the most popular runs from just uphill of the visitor centre restaurant to Nong Pak Chee observation tower in the west of the park. This is a fairly easy walk through forest and grassland that culminates at an observation tower built next to a lake. En route you'll hear white-handed gibbons in the tallest trees and might spot barking deer in the savanna. If you stay at the tower long enough you could see eagles soaring or needletails dive-bombing the lake; elephants and gaurs sometimes come to drink here, too. The walk takes about two and a half hours to the observation tower (4.5km), from where it's another 900m down a dirt track that meets the main road between kilometre-stones 35 and 36. From the road, you can walk or hitch back either to the headquarters (2km) or down to the checkpoint (12km) and then travel on to Pak Chong. If you just want to spend a few hours at the observation tower and forget the main part of the walk, stop beside the main road between kilometre-stones 35 and 36 (before reaching the park headquarters) and walk the kilometre down the access track to the tower.

Haew Suwat Falls and trail

Another good focus for walks is the area around **Haew Suwat Falls**, east of the visitor centre. These 25m-high falls are a great place for an invigorating shower, and featured in the 1999 film *The Beach*. To get to the falls from the park headquarters, either follow the 8km trail (allow 3–4 hours each way), or walk, drive or hitch the 6km road beyond the headquarters to Haew Suwat – it's a popular spot, so there should be plenty of cars. The **trail** begins on the Nature Trail behind the visitor centre, then veers off it, along a path marked with red flashes. En route to Haew Suwat you'll pass a turn-off to *Pha Kluai/Orchid* campsite and waterfall, 6.1km from the park headquarters (see below). Due to a series of deaths, swimming at Haew Suwat is no longer allowed.

To Pha Kluai/Orchid campsite

Day-trippers often do the short walk from Haew Suwat waterfall to **Pha Kluai/Orchid campsite**, which is paved most of the way and takes two hours at most (3.1km). You've a good chance of spotting gibbons and macaques along this route, as well as kingfishers and hornbills. The area around nearby Pha Kluai Falls is famous for its impressive variety of orchids.

ARRIVAL AND GETTING AROUND   KHAO YAI NATIONAL PARK

There are two access roads to the park – one from the south and another from the north – with checkpoints on both. Everyone travelling by public transport approaches the park from Pak Chong (see page 439), about 25km north of the northern entrance. Some tour companies, like Khao Yai Nature Life & Tours (see opposite), offer pick-up from the airport or hotels in Bangkok.

By shared songthaew The cheapest way to get to Khao Yai from Pak Chong is to take a public songthaew from outside the 7-Eleven shop, 200m west of the footbridge on the north side of the main road near Soi 21 (every 30min 6.30am–4pm, less frequently on Sun; 30min; B40). Public songthaews are not allowed to enter the park itself, so you'll be dropped at the park checkpoint, about 14km short of the

Khao Yai visitor centre, park headquarters and most popular trailheads. At the checkpoint (where you pay the national-park entrance fee), park rangers will flag down passing cars and get them to give you a ride up to the visitor centre; this is common practice here. The whole journey from Pak Chong to the visitor centre takes about 1hr.

Chartering a songthaew A quicker but pricier option is to charter a songthaew from Pak Chong: these count as private vehicles and are allowed inside the park. They can be chartered from the corner of Soi 19 in Pak Chong, and cost around B1000 for the ride from Pak Chong to Haew Suwat Falls, or about B2000 for a return trip, including several hours in the park.

Getting back Coming back from the park is often easier,

LEECHES

If hiking during or just after the rainy season you will almost certainly have some unsolicited encounters with **leeches**; mosquito repellent helps deter them, as do leech socks (canvas gaiters), available from the cafeteria complex opposite the visitor centre, or in the nearby accommodation office (they're also provided free if you join a tour). To get leeches off your skin, burn them with a cigarette or lighter, or douse them in salt; oily suntan lotion or insect repellent can make them lose their grip and fall off.

5

NIGHT SAFARIS

A much-touted park attraction is the hour-long **night safaris**, or "night-lightings", which take truckloads of tourists round Khao Yai's main roads in the hope of catching some interesting wildlife in the glare of the specially-fitted searchlights.

Night-time **sightings** often include deer and civets, and if you're very lucky you might see elephants too. Opinions differ on the quality of the experience: some find it thrilling to be out on the edges of the jungle after dark, others see it as rather a crass method of wildlife observation, especially at weekends, when the park can feel like a town centre, with four or five trucks following each other round and round the main roads.

All night-lightings are run by the **park rangers**, so tour operators sometimes join forces to hire a truck with ranger and searchlights. If you're on your own, you'll need to accompany one of these groups or pay for a truck yourself. The safaris depart the park headquarters **every night** at 7pm and 8pm (they can pick you up from the campsite if requested); trucks cost B500 to rent and can take up to ten people: book your place at the national park accommodation office, next to the visitor centre.

as day-trippers will usually give lifts all the way back to Pak Chong. Otherwise, hitch a ride as far as the checkpoint, or walk to it from the visitor centre – it's a pleasant 3–4hr walk along the fairly shaded park road, and you'll probably spot lots of birds and some macaques, gibbons and deer as well. At the checkpoint you can pick up a songthaew to Pak Chong: the last one usually leaves here at about 5pm. To get back to Pak Chong from one of the resorts on the road to the park, simply ask the owner to call one of the public

songthaews. You may have to wait a while, and pay a little extra for them coming to get you, but it still shouldn't be more than B100/person.

Motorbike rental Motorbikes can be hired from Petch Motors at 361/3 Thanon Mittraphap (044 280 248) in Pak Choing for B250–B300 a day.

Mountain bike rental You can rent mountain bikes from outside the visitor centre (B50/hr; B200/day).

INFORMATION AND TOURS

Tourist information The visitor centre (daily 8am–6pm), by the park office and main trailheads, offers maps and brochures.

Tours Khao Yai's tours are reasonably priced and cater primarily for independent tourists rather than big groups, though it's advisable to book in advance. But be warned: some unscrupulous operators charge exorbitant up-front fees for tours and then later ask customers to pay the park entry fee separately (including fees for the car, driver and/ or guide). As a result, we recommend only reputable outfits, all offering customized trips as well as their own version of the popular, undemanding one-and-a-half-day programme (around B1500/person, including the B400 park entry fee) which typically features a trip to a bat cave just outside the park at dusk, walks along one or two easy trails, a visit to Haew Suwat Falls and some after-dark wildlife spotting; it's usual, though not compulsory, to stay in the tour operator's own accommodation overnight. It's worth booking ahead, especially for overnight expeditions. Prices quoted are for a minimum of two trekkers. Note that it's also possible to hire a park ranger as your personal guide for the more remote trails (B500–B1,000); you can arrange this at the park headquarters the night before.

TOUR OPERATORS

Green Leaf Guest House and Tour Kilometre-stone 7.5

on the park road (call for free pick-up from Pak Chong) ☎044 365073 or ☎089 424 8809, ⓦgreenleaftour. com. At this family-run outfit treks are mostly led by owner Nine, who gets good reviews, particularly as a bird-spotter. Basic accommodation is available at the family guesthouse (see below).

Khao Yai Nature Life & Tours 3km west of Route 2090 (the turn-off is just south of Green Leaf Guest House) ☎096 565 5926, ⓦkhaoyainaturelifetours.com. This comfy resort offers a variety of programmes, including standard, one-and-a-half-day tours (B2900), one-day bird-watching tours (B7250, including Bangkok pick-up and drop-off) and tailor-made treks. "Eagle-eye" Tony is a highly accomplished bird-spotter and photographer. For details of their accommodation, see below.

Spice Roads ☎02 381 7490, ⓦspiceroads.com/ thailand/khao_yai. Upmarket bicycle tour of Khao Yai and its wineries, departing from Bangkok (two days B11,450/ person all-inclusive).

Wildlife Safari About 2km north of Pak Chong train station at 39 Thanon Pak Chong Subsanun, Nong Kaja (call to arrange free transport from Pak Chong) ☎088 359 1612, ⓔjayjungletrek@gmail.com. A good range of bespoke tours, including half-day trips (B300) for those on a tight schedule. Accommodation is in comfortable rooms (fan B400; a/c B650). Very kind and welcoming owners.

ACCOMMODATION AND EATING

You have several options when it comes to **accommodation** in Khao Yai, either in the park, or on the road that leads up to it. Alternatively, you could stay in Pak Chong (see p.442), 37km from the park's centre. If you decide to do a tour, it's usual to stay in the lodgings run by your tour guide. But be wary of places not listed here; plenty of people have been ripped off by unscrupulous outfits. There are restaurants beside the Visitors' Centre and the lodges in the park, though they tend to close by 7pm, and plenty of options along the road to the park.

IN THE PARK

If you're intending to do several days' independent exploring in the park, the most obvious places to stay are the national park lodges, dorms and tents in the heart of Khao Yai. The lodges have to be booked in advance at the Royal Forestry Department office in Bangkok (☎ 02 562 0760) or at ⓦ nps. dnp.go.th. Advance booking is not usually necessary if camping, but is advisable at weekends.

Lodges Spread across the park, these sleep two to thirty people (the latter in dorms). If you book in advance, you'll need to bring the receipt to the visitor centre accommodation office. On weekdays there's a thirty percent discount. B800

Camping Two-person tents can be rented at *Lam Takong* campsite, about 5km from the headquarters, and at *Pha Kluai Mai* campsite (aka *Orchid Camp*, very good for bird-spotting), about 4km east of the park headquarters, on the road to Haew Suwat falls. Equipment such as sleeping bags (B50), sleeping pads (B35) and pillows (B20) is available as well. You can pitch your own tent at either site for B30/person. B225

THE PARK ROAD

The 23km road that runs from Pak Chong up to the park checkpoint is dotted with luxurious hotels and resorts; most guests arrive by car, but Pak Chong transfers are usually available and the Pak Chong songthaew will also bring you here. Addresses are determined by the nearest kilometre-stone on Thanon Thanarat.

Balios Khao Yai At kilometre-stone 17 ☎ 044 365 971–5, ⓦ balioskhaoyai.com. Offers good-value upmarket accommodation in its large a/c rooms and has a swimming pool, mountain-bike rental, and two restaurants. Includes breakfast. B2973

Green Leaf Guest House and Tour 12.5km from Pak Chong, at kilometre-stone 7.5 ☎ 044 365073, ⓦ greenleaftour.com. One of the cheapest places to stay on the park road, this friendly, family-run outfit has twenty en-suite fan rooms (no hot water) behind its good, cheap restaurant; it also does guided treks into the national park (see above). B200

★ **Khao Yai Nature Life & Tours** 15km from Pak Chong, turn west just beyond kilometre-stone 7.5 ☎ 096 565 5926, ⓦ khaoyainaturelifetours.com. Run by a switched-on couple, this smart resort has a good selection of a/c rooms and villas set around two excellent outdoor pools. The best rooms have wooden floors and bed covers made from fine Thai silk. There's also a good restaurant. Breakfast included. B2500

Pak Chong

Whether you decide to see Khao Yai National Park on your own or as part of a tour, your first port of call is likely to be the town of **PAK CHONG**, 37km north of Khao Yai's visitor centre and major trailheads, and served by trains and buses. One of the four recommended Khao Yai tour leaders (see page 439) operates from Pak Chong, and there are plenty of places to stay in town too. The obvious drawback to basing yourself here is that it's about an hour's journey from the Khao Yai trailheads, but if you make an early start you can make use of the cheap public songthaew service.

ARRIVAL AND DEPARTURE

Thanon Tesaban cuts through central Pak Chong, and numerous small sois shoot off it: sois to the north are odd-numbered in ascending order from west to east (Soi 13–Soi 25) while those on the south side of the road have even numbers, from west to east (Soi 8–Soi 18). The heart of the town is on the north side, between the train station on Soi 15 and the footbridge a few hundred metres further east at Soi 21.

By train Pak Chong train station (☎ 044 311534) is on Soi 15, one short block north of Thanon Tesaban.

Destinations Ayutthaya (11 daily; 1hr 30min–2hr 30min); Bangkok (11 daily; 3hr 30min–4hr 45min); Khorat (11 daily; 1hr 15min–1hr 30min); Si Saket (8 daily; 4hr 20min–7hr 30min); Surin (10 daily; 3hr 10min–5hr 30min); Ubon Ratchathani (7 daily; 6hr 50min–8hr 40min); Udon Thani (1 daily; 6hr 30min).

By bus and minibus The bus station is towards the west end of town, one block south off the main road between sois 8 and 10. Some long-distance buses also stop in the town centre, beside the footbridge, while a/c minibuses to Bangkok and Khorat leave from offices on opposite sides of the road on Thanon Tesaban, just west of Soi 18.

Destinations Bangkok (hourly; 2–3hr); Khorat (every 20min; 1hr).

5

ACCOMMODATION AND EATING

There's a **day market** selling fresh fruit and vegetables in the centre of town, between the train station on Soi 15 and the footbridge a few hundred metres further east at Soi 21. You'll find a **supermarket** near here on the south side of the main road.

Ban Mai Chay Nam 21 Thanon Mittraphap ☎044 314 236, ☻banmaichaynam.com. Awesome old-style Thai restaurant stuffed with retro curios – from giant Spiderman figures to American gas pumps from the 1950s. It's often packed with Thai tourists, and the food is fresh and authentic. Dishes include a mean catfish salad (B150). Daily 9am–9pm.

Night Market The cheapest and most popular place to eat after dark, the night market sets up along the main road between Tesaban sois 17 and 19. Daily 6–10/11pm.

Pakchong Phubade Hotel 50m south of the train station down Tesaban Soi 15 ☎094 470 1122. Pak Chong's cheapest hotel with clean-ish, very basic rooms. A safe bet if you arrive late in the evening and need somewhere central to stay. Also offers a laundry service. Fan B400, a/c B550

Rim Tarn Inn 430 Thanon Mittraphap, 300m west of the bus station ☎044 313365–6, ☻rimtarninn.com. Smarter and more appealing than *Phubade*, this six-storey building has bright, comfortable a/c rooms, plus a pool and good restaurant. B1000

Veranda Restaurant behind the Rim Tarn Inn. ☎044 313 365–6. More relaxing than the nearby Ban Mai Chay Nam, this place enjoys lovely views of a shaded river from a raised terrace. Try the Chinese noodles, Hong-Kong style (B100). Tues–Sun 12pm–9pm.

DIRECTORY

ATMs There are several ATMs near the train station.
Hospital There's a branch of the Bangkok Hospital (☎044 316611) at 5/1 Thanon Mittraphap.
Post office On the corner of Soi 25 and Thanon Tesaban.

Khorat (Nakhon Ratchasima)

Beyond Pak Chong, Highway 2 and the rail line diverge to run either side of picturesque Lam Takong Reservoir, offering a last taste of undulating, forested terrain before reaching the largely barren Khorat plateau. They rejoin at **KHORAT** (officially known as **Nakhon Ratchasima**) – an abbreviation of its full name ("khon rat") – which is considered the gateway to the northeast.

If this is your first stop in Isaan, it's unlikely to be a pleasant introduction: Khorat is one of Thailand's most populous cities, its streets teem with traffic, and apart from the moat round the old city, there's nothing here you could call a genuine tourist attraction. On the plus side, Khorat is at the centre of a good transport network and is within striking distance of the **Khmer ruins** at Phimai, Phanomwan, Phanom Rung and Muang Tam, as well as the archeological remains of **Ban Prasat** and the pottery village at **Dan Kwian**. Aside from serving Bangkok and all the main centres within Isaan, Khorat's bus network extends south along Highway 304 to the east coast, enabling you to travel directly to Pattaya, Rayong and Chanthaburi without going through the capital.

Thao Suranari Monument

If you spend more than a couple of hours in the city you're bound to come across the landmark statue at the western gate of the old city walls. This is the much-revered **Thao Suranari ('Brave lady') Monument**, erected to commemorate the heroic actions of the wife of the deputy governor of Khorat, during an attack by the kingdom of Vientiane – capital of modern-day Laos – in 1826. Some chronicles say that Ya Mo (Grandma Mo), as she is affectionately known, organized a feast for the Lao army and enticed them to bed, where they were then slaughtered by the Thais; another tells how she and the other women of Khorat were carted off as prisoners to Vientiane, whereupon they attacked their guards with such ferocity that the Lao retreated out of fear that the whole Thai army had arrived. At any rate, Ya Mo saved the day and is still feted by the citizens of Khorat, who lay flowers at her feet, light incense at her shrine and even dance around it. From late March to early April, the town holds a week-long **festival** in her honour, with parades through the streets and the usual colourful trappings of Thai merry-making.

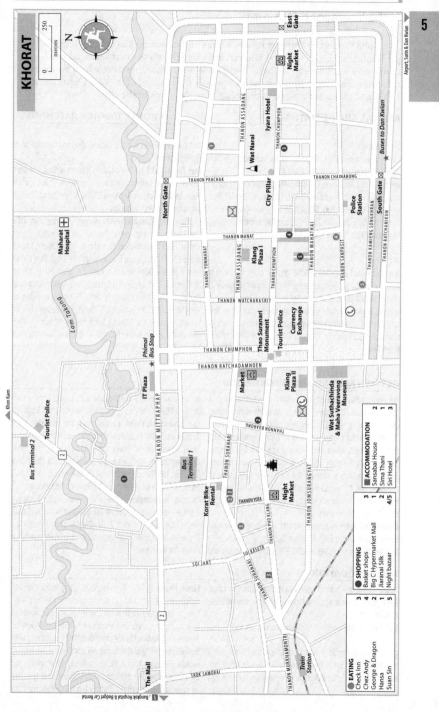

KHORAT

0 ——— 250
metres

N

EATING

Check Inn	3
Chez Andy	4
George & Dragon	2
Hansa	1
Suan Sin	5

SHOPPING

Basket shops	3
Big C Hypermarket Mall	1
Jiaranai Silk	2
Night bazaar	4/5

ACCOMMODATION

Sansabai House	2
Sima Thani	1
Siri Hotel	3

Maharat Hospital

Lam Tokong

Khon Kaen

Bus Terminal 2

Tourist Police

IT Plaza

Phimai Bus Stop

THANON MITTRAPHAP

Bus Terminal 1

Korat Bike Rental

THANON SURANARI

Night Market

THANON YOTA

SOI JANT

SOI KASERT

THANON SURANARI

THANON PHO KLANG

THANON JOMSURANGYAT

THANON MUKKHAMONTRI

TROK SAMORAI

Train Station

The Mall

North Gate

THANON PRACHAK

THANON YOMMARAT

THANON ASSADANG

THANON MANAT

Klang Plaza I

THANON CHUMPHON

THANON ASSADANG

THANON WATCHARASRIT

THANON CHUMPHON

THANON RATCHADAMNOEN

Market

Thao Suranari Monument

Tourist Police

Currency Exchange

Klang Plaza II

THANON BUARONG

Wat Suthachinda & Maha Veeravong Museum

Wat Narai

City Pillar

East Gate

Night Market

Iyara Hotel

THANON CHUMPHON

THANON CHAINARONG

South Gate

Police Station

THANON MAHATHAI

THANON SANPASIT

THANON KAMJENG SONGKHRAN

THANON RATCHANIKUN

Buses to Dan Kwian

5

Bangkok Hospital & Budget Car Rental

5

Maha Veeravong Museum

In the grounds of Wat Suthachinda, Thanon Ratchadamnoen • Wed–Sun 9am–4pm • B50

The **Maha Veeravong Museum** houses a small and unexceptional collection of predominantly Dvaravati- and Lopburi-style Buddha statues that belonged to a monk who was once the abbot of Wat Suthachinda (the grounds of which house the museum). The single-storey museum was built by Thailand's Fine Arts Department in 1954, and makes for a pleasant diversion from the chaos of the city.

ARRIVAL AND DEPARTURE
KHORAT (NAKHON RATCHASIMA)

BY TRAIN

The train station, on Thanon Mukkhamontri (📞044 242044), is served by city bus route #1.

Destinations Ayutthaya (11 daily; 4hr); Bangkok (11 daily; 4hr 30min–6hr 40min); Khon Kaen (1 daily; 3hr 20min); Pak Chong (11 daily; 1–2hr); Si Saket (8 daily; 4hr–5hr 30min); Surin (10 daily; 2hr–3hr 20min); Ubon Ratchathani (7 daily; 4hr–6hr 10min); Udon Thani (1 daily; 5hr).

BY BUS

Bus Terminal 2 (📞044 256006–9), the main terminal, is situated on the far northern edge of the city on Highway 2. It's the arrival and departure point for regular and a/c buses serving regional towns such as Pak Chong (for Khao Yai) and Phimai, as well as long-distance destinations such as Bangkok, Ban Tako (for Phanom Rung), Chiang Mai, Khon Kaen, Nong Khai, Pattaya, Rayong (for Ko Samet) and Surin. Traffic is chaotic in the city, so avoid choking in a tuk-tuk and take a cheaper a/c taxi instead (B40 to train station or nearby hotels).

Bus Terminal 1 (📞044 242899) is more centrally located just off Thanon Suranari, and also operates both fan and a/c buses to Bangkok, via Pak Tong Chai and Pak Chong, though departures are less frequent.

Destinations Bangkok (every 40min; 3–4hr); Ban Tako (for Phanom Rung; every 30min; 2hr); Buriram (every 30min; 3hr); Chanthaburi (8 daily; 6–8hr); Chiang Mai (7 daily; 12–14hr); Chiang Rai (4 daily; 14–16hr); Dan Kwian (every 30min; 30min); Khon Kaen (at least every 40min; 2hr 30min–3hr); Lopburi (10 daily; 3hr 30min); Nong Khai (hourly; 6hr); Pattaya (4 daily; 5hr); Phimai (every 30min; 1hr–1hr 30min); Phitsanulok (7 daily; 7hr); Rayong (for Ko Samet; 9 daily; 5hr 30min); Surin (every 40min; 3–4hr); Ubon Ratchathani (every hour; 5–7hr); Udon Thani (at least hourly; 3hr 30min–5hr).

GETTING AROUND AND INFORMATION

By songthaew and city bus Flat-fare songthaews (B8) and city buses (B8) travel most main roads within town. Expect to pay up to B15 for longer journeys to the city limits. The most useful routes – served by both songthaews and buses – are #2, which runs between the main TAT office in the west, via the train station, along Thanon Suranari and Thanon Assadang to beyond the *lak muang* (city pillar) in the east, and #3, which also runs right across the city, via Mahathai and Jomsurangyat roads, past the train station, to the TAT office in the west.

By tuk-tuk Easily flagged down off the main routes around town. Expect to pay B60–B100 for journeys of 1–2km.

By taxi Metered taxis (📞044 370 999) cruise the streets and are generally better value than tuk-tuks. Expect to pay a call-out fee of B30. Grab Cars (grab.com) also operate in Korat.

Car and motorbike rental Cars are available from Budget at 719/5 Thanon Mittraphap, outside Tesco Lotus 'Nom Neoy Bakery' (daily 8am–8pm; 📞044 341 654, 🌐budget.com). Motorbikes are available from Korat Bike Rental at 100 Thanon Suranari (daily 8am–6pm; 📞085 611 6615, 🌐koratbikerental.com), beginning at B300/day.

Tourist information The TAT office (daily 8.30am–4.30pm; 📞044 213 666, ✉tatsima@tat.or.th) is 1.6km west of the train station at 2102–2104 Thanon Mittraphap. The website whatsonkorat.com has some useful information about the town too.

ACCOMMODATION

Khorat has a few budget hotels that are reasonable value, but if you're planning to visit Phimai, consider staying there instead.

Sansabai House 335–337 Thanon Suranari 📞044 255 855, ✉sansabaikorat@yahoo.com; map p.441. Smart, good-value rooms in a central location. They have just a few fan rooms, but most are a/c, and they are often full. No breakfast included but there's a decent on-site café. Fan **B300**, a/c **B450**

Sima Thani 2112/2 Thanon Mittraphap, near the TAT office 📞044 213100, 🌐simathani.com; map p.441. One of the city's best hotels, with smart a/c rooms, a swimming pool, three restaurants and a babysitting service. There's a relaxed feel to the place despite its popularity with businesspeople, and the rooms are good value. It's located beside Highway 2 (the Bangkok–Nong Khai road), and buses from Bangkok or Khao Yai can drop you at the door en route to Bus Terminal 2, but it's too far to walk from the hotel to the town centre. B1200

Siri Hotel 688–690 Thanon Pho Klang ☎044 242831, ⓦsirihotelkorat.com; map p.441. Less than a 10min walk from the train station, the *Siri* is good value and makes an ideal base for exploring the town. Its carpeted and wood-panelled rooms are surprisingly quiet and spacious. B550

EATING AND DRINKING

The night bazaar on and around Thanon Manat includes a few hot-food stalls, but there's a bigger selection of **night-market**-style food stalls, with some streetside tables, about 800m further east near the *Iyara Hotel* on Thanon Chumphon. A smaller, more convenient grouping sets up about 400m east of *Siri Hotel* on the corner of Thanon Yota. Because of its sizeable contingent of expats, Khorat also offers the chance to satisfy foreign-food cravings. After dark, Westerners tend to head for the restaurants and bars along Thanon Suranari, while young Thais head for those along Thanon Yommarat.

Check Inn 423–425 Thanon Suranari ☎080 732 8536; map p.441. Popular among expats, this bar features a pool table, live music on weekend evenings, and a wide range of Thai (around B90) and Western (around B200) dishes. Mon–Sat 11am–midnight, Sun 3pm–midnight.

Chez Andy 5 Ban Kob Kaew ☎044 289 556, ⓦfacebook. com/andykorat.com; map p.441. This Swiss-run restaurant has a distinguished ambience and is famous for its Australian steaks (around B500–2200), but they also serve pizzas and some Swiss and Thai dishes. Daily 11am–11pm.

George & Dragon 361 Thanon Suranari ☎085 076 9708; map p.441. As you might guess from the name, this English-run pub offers a range of beers and comfort food, including a filling Full Monty breakfast (B200). There's also a pool table, friendly service and sports on TV. Daily 10am–midnight.

★ **Hansa** 266 Thanon Yommarat ☎044 269 108 ⓦfacebook.com/hansakorat; map p.441. Excellent place serving a wide range of Thai and fusion dishes such as grilled salmon with red curry (B250), on a breezy terrace or in the a/c interior. Low-key live music in the evenings and a selection of imported beers add to the appeal. Daily 5pm–midnight.

Suan Sin 163 Thanon Watcharasrit; map p.441. Simple place that's highly rated by locals for its tasty Isaan favourites, especially *laap* (spicy salad with minced meat) and *pla chon pao* (grilled fish). Most dishes B80–220. Daily 11am–8pm.

SHOPPING

Basket shops Thanon Chumphon; map p.441. Along Thanon Chumphon is a cluster of authentic basketware shops whose sticky-rice baskets, fish traps and rice winnowers make attractive souvenirs. Daily 8am–5pm.

Big C Hypermarket Mall Just off Thanon Mittraphap; map p.441. Your best bet for cheap music, DVDs and trainers. Daily 10am–10pm.

Jiaranai Silk 140/2 Thanon Pho Klang, on the corner with Thanon Buarong ☎044 243 819; map p.441.

Khorat is a good place to buy silk, much of which is produced in nearby Pak Tong Chai. This city-centre place has the best and most exclusive selection, while the specialist shops along Thanon Chumphon sell lengths of silk at reasonable prices. Mon–Sat 9.30am–5pm.

Night bazaar Thanon Manat and Thanon Mahathai; map p.441. This sets up at dusk every evening and deals mainly in bargain-priced fashions. Daily 6–10pm.

DIRECTORY

Hospitals Expats favour the private Bangkok Ratchasima Hospital (☎044 429 999), 1308/9 Thanon Mittraphap (Highway 2), near Tesco Lotus; the government Maharat Hospital (☎044 235000) is at 49 Thanon Changpuak on the north side of town.

Tourist police For all emergencies, call the tourist police (☎1155; free, 24hr), or contact them at one of their booths in town: their main office (☎044 3417 77–9) is opposite Bus Terminal 2 on Highway 2, and there's a more central booth beside the Thao Suranari Monument on Thanon Chumphon.

Dan Kwian

15km south of Khorat on Route 224 • Local bus #1307 (destination Chok Chai; every 30min; 30min) from Bus Terminal 2, or at Khorat's South Gate; get off as soon as you see the roadside pottery stalls

Some of the most popular household pottery in Thailand is produced by the potters of **DAN KWIAN**, a tiny village 15km south of Khorat. The local clay, dug from the banks of the Mun River, has a high iron content, which when fired in wood-burning kilns combines with ash to create the unglazed metallic finish characteristic of Dan Kwian pottery. The potters produce ceramic stoves for burning charcoal, water storage jars,

5

tiles, whimsical statues of cute, grinning kids and even life-sized statues of elephants and Spiderman. The workshops are spread along a few kilometres of the highway, so visiting by motorbike is a help.

Prasat Hin Phanom Wan

About 20km north of Khorat . Take a songthaew from Bus Terminal 2 to Ban Makha, then a motorbike taxi. With your own transport, follow Highway 2 northeast towards Khon Kaen and look for a signed turn to the right after about 14km, then continue straight for another 5km.

This well-preserved Khmer sanctuary, built during the 10th or 11th century, is surrounded by woodland and sees hardly any visitors, though it is well worth tracking down. It's like a small version of Phimai, with a central sanctuary of white sandstone and outer walls of laterite and pink sandstone. There are no carvings of note, but bags of atmosphere. Buddha images inside the sanctuary are draped in gold robes and surrounded by floral offerings. There's no admission fee and no signboards giving information; as it's so rarely visited, you're likely to have the place to yourself.

Ban Prasat

The quintessentially northeastern village of **BAN PRASAT**, north of Khorat, became a source of great interest to archeologists following the 1990s discovery of a series of **burial grounds** within its boundaries, some of which date back three thousand years. The skeletons and attendant artefacts have been well preserved in the mud, and many are now on display; the village has made extra efforts to entice tourists with low-key craft demonstrations and a homestay programme. It's also a pleasant village in its own right, a traditional community of stilt houses set beside the Tarn Prasat River.

There are currently three **excavation pits** open to the public, each clearly signed from the centre of the village and informatively labelled; pit number one is the most interesting. There's also a small museum (free; daily 8.30am–4.30pm) in the centre of the village. From the pits, archeologists have surmised that Ban Prasat was first inhabited in around 1000 BC and that its resident rice farmers traded with coastal people. Each pit contains bones and objects from different eras, buried at different depths.

Signs in the village direct you to local family-run projects, such as the household of **silk-weavers**, where you should be able to see several stages of the sericulture process (see page 458) and buy some cloth. Other village crafts include the weaving of floor mats from locally grown bulrushes, and the making of household brooms.

ARRIVAL AND ACCOMMODATION   BAN PRASAT

By bus Ban Prasat is 2km off Highway 2, 46km north of Khorat and 17km southwest of Phimai. Any Khorat–Phimai bus will drop you at the Highway 2 junction, from where motorbike taxis will ferry you to the village.

Accommodation There are no hotels or restaurants in the village, but there is a homestay programme (B400/person including two meals) giving visitors a chance to join in activities such as making baskets and farming; contact Khun Jarun at ☎ 081 725 0791.

Phimai

Hemmed in by its old city walls and encircled by tributaries of the Mun River, the small modern town of **PHIMAI**, 60km northeast of Khorat, is dominated by the charmingly restored Khmer temple complex of **Prasat Hin Phimai**. No one knows for sure when the prasat was built or for whom, but as a religious site it probably dates back to the reign of the Khmer king Suriyavarman I (1002–49), and parts of

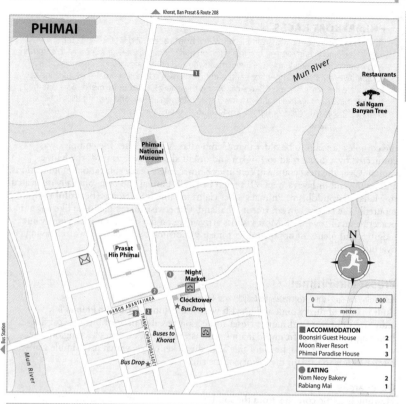

PHIMAI

Khorat, Ban Prasat & Route 208

Mun River

Restaurants

Sai Ngam
Banyan Tree

Phimai
National
Museum

N

Prasat
Hin Phimai

Night
Market

Clocktower
★ Bus Drop

THANON ANANTAJINDA

THANON CHOMSUDASADET

★ Buses to
Khorat

Bus Drop ★

Bus Station

Mun River

0 — 300
metres

■ ACCOMMODATION	
Boonsiri Guest House	2
Moon River Resort	1
Phimai Paradise House	3

● EATING	
Nom Neoy Bakery	2
Rabiang Mai	1

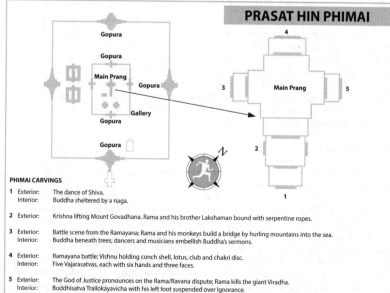

PRASAT HIN PHIMAI

Gopura

Gopura

Main Prang

Gopura

Gallery

Gopura

Gopura

4

3   Main Prang   5

2

1

N

PHIMAI CARVINGS

1 Exterior: The dance of Shiva.
   Interior: Buddha sheltered by a naga.

2 Exterior: Krishna lifting Mount Govadhana. Rama and his brother Lakshaman bound with serpentine ropes.

3 Exterior: Battle scene from the Ramayana; Rama and his monkeys build a bridge by hurling mountains into the sea.
   Interior: Buddha beneath trees; dancers and musicians embellish Buddha's sermons.

4 Exterior: Ramayana battle; Vishnu holding conch shell, lotus, club and chakri disc.
   Interior: Five Vajarasatvas, each with six hands and three faces.

5 Exterior: The God of Justice pronounces on the Rama/Ravana dispute; Rama kills the giant Viradha.
   Interior: Buddhisatva Trallokayavicha with his left foot suspended over Ignorance.

PHIMAI BOAT RACES

Phimai's biggest event of the year is its festival of **boat races**, held on the Mun's tributaries over a weekend in early November, in a tradition that's endured for over a century. In common with many other riverside towns, Phimai marks the end of the rainy season by holding fiercely competitive longboat competitions and putting on lavish parades of ornate barges done up to emulate the Royal Barges of Bangkok. During the festival, a **son et lumière** show is staged at the temple ruins for five nights in a row, usually starting at 7pm and costing B500; check with the Khorat TAT office for details (📞044 213666, ✉tatsima@tat.or.th).

the complex are said to be older than Cambodia's Angkor Wat. The complex was connected by a direct road to Angkor and oriented southeast, towards the Khmer capital. Over the next couple of centuries Khmer rulers made substantial modifications, and by the end of Jayavarman VII's reign in 1220, Phimai had been officially dedicated to Mahayana Buddhism. Phimai's other claim to fame is **Sai Ngam** (Beautiful Banyan), reputedly the largest banyan tree in Thailand. Otherwise there's plenty to like about its peaceful, small-town feel. Most visitors arrive here on day-trips, but with good-value lodgings and plenty of opportunities for early-morning bike rides, it's worth staying overnight.

Prasat Hin Phimai

Ruins Daily 7am–6pm • B100 • **Visitors' centre** Daily 8.30am–4.30pm • Free

Built mainly of dusky pink and greyish white sandstone, **Prasat Hin Phimai** is a seductive sight from a distance; closer inspection reveals a mass of intricate carvings. Entering the complex from the main southeastern gate, it's worth checking out the visitors' centre on the right-hand side after the ticket office, which uses simple wall-hung exhibits to explain the history of the site.

Outer areas

Heading into the complex from the southeastern gate, a staircase ornamented with classic naga (serpent) balustrades leads to a gopura in the **outer walls**, which are punctuated on either side by false balustraded windows – a bit of sculptural sleight-of-hand to jazz up the solid stonework without piercing the defences. A raised pathway bridges the space between these walls and the inner gallery that protects the prangs of the **inner sanctuary**. The minor prang to the right, made of laterite, is attributed to the twelfth-century Buddhist king Jayavarman VII, who engaged in a massive temple-building campaign. His statue is enshrined within; it's a copy of the much more impressive original, now housed in the Phimai National Museum. The pink sandstone prang to the left, connected to a Brahmin shrine where seven stone linga were found, was probably built around the same time.

The main prang

After more than twenty years of archeological detective work and painstaking reassembly, the towering white-sandstone **main prang** was restored to its original cruciform groundplan and conical shape in the 1960s, complete with an almost full set of carved lintels, pediments and antefixes, and capped with a stone lotus bud. The impressively detailed **carvings** around the outside of the prang depict predominantly Hindu themes. Shiva the Destroyer dances above the main entrance to the southeast antechamber: his destruction dance heralds the end of the world and the creation of a new order, a supremely potent image that warranted this position over the most important doorway. Inside, sedate Buddhist scenes give evidence of the conversion from Hindu to Buddhist faith, and the prasat's most important image, the Buddha sheltered by a seven-headed naga, sits atop a base that once supported a Hindu Shiva lingam.

5

Phimai National Museum

Thanon Tha Songkran, just northeast of Prasat Hin Phimai • Daily 9am–4pm • B100 • Ⓦ nationalmuseums.finearts.go.th • Walking distance from the ruins, though the Khorat–Phimai bus will stop outside the museum if requested

Much of the ancient carved stonework discovered at Phimai but not fitted back into the renovated structure can be seen at the **Phimai National Museum**, where it's easier to appreciate, being at eye level, well labelled and put in context. After a recent renovation, it is now one of the most impressive collections of Khmer carvings to be seen anywhere. The museum's *pièce de résistance* is the exceptionally fine sandstone statue of Jayavarman VII that was found in Phimai's laterite prang; seated and leaning slightly forward, he's lost his arms and part of his nose, but none of his grace and serenity. Elsewhere in the galleries, displays take you through the religious and cultural history of the Phimai region, featuring prehistoric items from Ban Prasat as well as some exquisite Buddha statues from more recent times.

Sai Ngam

2km northeast of the museum • Walk or rent a bicycle from one of the guesthouses (B50–B100/day) – locals will be able to point you in the right direction if you get lost en route

Sai Ngam is a banyan tree so enormous that it's reputed to cover an area about half the size of a football pitch (approximately 2300 square metres). It might look like a grove of small banyans, but Sai Ngam is in fact a single *Ficus bengalensis* whose branches have dropped vertically into the ground, taken root and spawned other branches, so growing further and further out from its central trunk. Banyan trees are believed to harbour animist spirits, and you can make merit here by releasing fish or turtles into the artificial lake that surrounds Sai Ngam. The tree is a popular recreation spot, and several restaurants have sprung up alongside it.

ARRIVAL AND GETTING AROUND

PHIMAI

By bus Phimai's bus station is inconveniently located 1.5km southwest of the ruins, on the bypass, but nearly everybody gets on and off in the town centre, either by the clock tower in the night-market area or in front of the museum. Regular bus #1305 runs direct to Phimai from Khorat's Bus Terminal 2, with a pick-up point near the Thanon Mittraphap/Ratchadamnoen junction (every 15min until 5.30pm, then sporadically until 10pm; 1hr 30min); the last return bus departs for Khorat at 7pm. The bus passes the turn-off to Ban Prasat, so if you get up early you can combine the two places on a day-trip from Khorat. If travelling from Khon Kaen, Udon Thani or Nong Khai, take any Khorat-bound bus along Highway 2 as far as the Phimai turn-off (Highway 206), then change onto the Khorat–Phimai service for the last 10km; the same strategy works in reverse.

By bicycle The best way to get around, although cycling isn't permitted inside the ruins. *Boonsiri Guest House* has bicycles for rent (B80/day). Aside from the ride out to Sai Ngam, the area just west of the ruins, beyond the post office, is especially atmospheric: many of the traditional wooden houses here double as workshops, and you'll often see householders weaving cane chairs in the shade beneath the buildings.

INFORMATION

Tourist information *Boonsiri Guest House* (see below) is an excellent source of local information.

Services There's a post office just west of Prasat Hin Phimai on Thanon Wonprang.

ACCOMMODATION AND EATING

If you fancy a meal with a view, head out to the string of basic **restaurants** just across from Sai Ngam. The **night market** sets up at dusk on the eastern stretch of Thanon Anantajinda, just southeast of the ruins.

Boonsiri Guest House Above a duck restaurant on Thanon Chomsudasadet ☎ 044 471159, Ⓦ boonsiri. net; map p.445. Central, family-run place offering clean dorms and en-suite rooms that are stylishly put together. The owners' cheery and knowledgeable son speaks great English, and can provide a map and tips for getting around Phimai. Dorm B150, fan double B350, a/c double B500

Moon River Resort Ban Sai Ngam, Pattana Soi 2 ☎ 085 633 7097, Ⓦ moon-river-resort-phimai.com; map p.445. Located by the river and near the museum, this rustic place offers a variety of rooms, some in traditional stilt houses in a rambling garden and some with balconies overlooking the river, which is good for swimming here. B600

5

Nom Neoy Bakery At the southeastern corner of the ruins. ☎ 089 948 5655; map p.445. A nice shady place to cool off with a cold frappe after wandering around the ruins; serves dishes like pork steaks (B100) and rice with green curry (B89) at lunchtime, but no evening meals. Daily 10am–5.30pm.

Phimai Paradise House 214 Moo 4, Thanon Chomsudasadet ☎ 044 471918, ⓦ phimaiparadisehotel; map p.445. Though the hotel of the same name has a pool, the rooms in this traditional wooden house are more atmospheric; they range from dorms with 4–6 beds (B200 per person) sharing bathrooms to spacious suites with canopied beds. Breakfast included. **B500**

Rabiang Mai Thanon Samairujee ☎ 081 760 9642; map p.445. Near the southeast corner of the historical park, this restaurant has a good range of Thai dishes and an English menu, though prices are a little higher than usual (B100–B200). Daily 5pm–midnight.

Phanom Rung and around

East of Khorat the plains roll on, and the landscape is dotted with 1000-year-old temple ruins that testify to the former extent of the Khmer kingdom. The most impressive of these, is **Prasat Hin Khao Phanom Rung**, although **Prasat Muang Tam** and **Wat Khao Angkhan** are also worth a visit. Built during the same period as Phimai, and for the same purpose, Phanom Rung and Muang Tam form two more links in the chain that once connected the Khmer capital of Angkor with the limits of its empire. Sited dramatically atop an extinct volcano, Phanom Rung has been beautifully restored, and the more recently renovated Muang Tam lies on the plains below. Wat Khao Angkhan, also located on an extinct volcano, features some *sema* (boundary) stones that date back to the eighth or ninth century, though the temple itself is quite modern. Early morning or late afternoon are the best times to visit, when the sites are less crowded.

Prasat Hin Khao Phanom Rung

Main complex Daily 6am–6pm • B100, joint ticket with Muang Tam B150 • **Tourist Information Centre** Daily 9am–4.30pm

Prasat Hin Phanom Rung is the finest example of Khmer architecture in Thailand, graced with innumerable exquisite carvings, its sandstone and laterite buildings designed to align with the sun at certain times of the year (see box below). As at most Khmer prasats, **building** here spanned several reigns, probably from the beginning of the tenth century to the early thirteenth. The heart of the temple was constructed in the mid-twelfth century, in early Angkorian style, and is attributed to local ruler Narendraditya and his son Hiranya. Narendraditya was a follower of the Shivaite cult, a sect which practised yoga and fire worship and used alcohol and sex in its rituals; carved depictions of all these practices decorate the temple. There are cheap food stalls outside the Gate 1 entrance and in its car park area, where the museum-like tourist information centre provides an outstanding introduction to the temple's construction, iconography and restoration.

The approach

The **approach** to the temple is the most dramatic aspect of the hilltop site. Symbolic of the journey from earth to the heavenly palace of the gods, the ascent to the inner compound is imbued with metaphorical import: by following the 200m-long avenue, paved in laterite and sandstone and flanked with lotus-bud pillars, you are walking to the ends of the earth. Ahead, the main prang, representing Mount Meru, home of the gods, looms large above the gallery walls, and is accessible only via the first of three **naga bridges**, a raised cruciform structure with sixteen five-headed naga balustrades. Once across the bridge, you have traversed the abyss between earth and heaven. A series of stairways ascends to the eastern entrance of the celestial home, first passing four small ponds, thought to have been used for ritual purification.

A second naga bridge crosses to the **east gopura**, entrance to the inner sanctuary, which is topped by a lintel carved with Indra (god of the east) sitting on a lion throne. The gopura is the main gateway through the **gallery**, which runs right round the inner

5

SPIRITUAL ALIGNMENT

Prasat Hin Phanom Rung is so perfectly built that on the morning or evening of four days each year (sunrise from 2–4 April and 8–10 September; sunset from 6–8 March and 5–7 October), you can stand at the westernmost gopura in the morning or the easternmost gopura in the evening, and see the sun rising or setting through all fifteen doors. These days are celebrated with huge parades all the way up the hill to the prasat – a tradition believed to go back eight hundred years.

compound and has been restored in part, with arched stone roofs, small chambers inside and false windows; real windows wouldn't have been strong enough to support such a heavy stone roof, so false ones, which retained the delicate pilasters but backed them with stone blocks, were an aesthetically acceptable compromise.

The main prang

Phanom Rung is surprisingly compact, the east gopura leading almost directly into the **main prang**, separated from it only by a final naga bridge. A dancing Shiva, nine of his ten arms intact, and a lintel carved with a relief of a **reclining Vishnu** preside over the eastern entrance to the prang. This depicts a common Hindu creation myth, known as "Reclining Vishnu Asleep on the Milky Sea of Eternity", in which Vishnu dreams up a new universe, and Brahma (the four-faced god perched on the lotus blossom that springs from Vishnu's navel) puts the dream into practice. This lintel had been stolen, but was returned in 1988 from the Art Institute of Chicago, culminating seventeen years of restoration work on this outstanding example of Khmer architecture.

On the pediment above this famous relief is a lively carving of **Shiva Nataraja**, or Shiva's Dance of Destruction, which shows him dancing on Mount Kailash in front of several other gods, including Ganesh, Brahma and Vishnu. The dance brings about the total destruction of the world and replaces it with a new epoch. Of the other figures decorating the prang, one of the most important is the lion head of Kala, also known as Kirtimukha, symbolic of both the lunar and the solar eclipse and – because he's able to "swallow" the sun – considered far superior to other planetary gods. Inside the prang kneels an almost life-size statue of Shiva's vehicle, the bull Nandi, behind which stands the all-powerful **Shiva lingam**, for which the prang was originally built; the stone channel that runs off the lingam and out of the north side of the prang was designed to catch the lustral water with which the sacred stone was bathed.

Two rough-hewn laterite libraries stand alongside the main prang, in the northeast and southeast corners, and there are also remains of two early tenth-century brick prangs just northeast of the main prang. The unfinished **prang noi** ("Little Prang") in the southwest corner now contains a stone Buddha footprint, which has become the focus of the merit-making at the annual April festivities, neatly linking ancient and modern religious practices.

Prasat Muang Tam

8km southeast of Phanom Rung • **Main complex** Daily 6am–6pm • B100, joint ticket with Phanom Rung B150 • **Tourist Information Centre and Film** Daily 9am–4.30pm • Free

Down on the plains, and accessed via a scenic minor road that cuts through a swathe of rice fields, the small but elegant temple complex of **Prasat Muang Tam** is sited behind a huge kilometre-long *baray* (Khmer reservoir), which was probably constructed at the same time as the main part of the temple, in the early eleventh century. Like Phanom Rung, Muang Tam was probably built in stages between the tenth and thirteenth centuries, and is based on the classic Khmer design of a central prang flanked by minor prangs and encircled by a gallery and four gopura. The history of Muang Tam is presented in brief at the Tourist Information Centre in the temple car park.

5

The ruins

The approach to Muang Tam is nothing like as grand as at Phanom Rung but, once through the main, eastern, gopura in the outside wall, it's a pretty scene, with the central gallery encircled by four **L-shaped ponds** – such important features that they are referred to in a contemporary inscription that states "this sanctuary is preserved by sacred water". The shape of the ponds gives the impression that the prasat is set within a moat that's been severed by the four entrance pathways at the cardinal points. Each pond is lined with laterite brick steps designed to enable easy access for priests drawing sacred water, and possibly also for devotees to cleanse themselves before entering the central sanctuary. The rims are constructed from sandstone blocks that form naga, the sacred water serpents.

The rectangular central **gallery** was probably roofed with timber (long since rotted away) and so could be punctuated with real windows, rather than the more load-bearing false versions that had to be used at Phanom Rung. Inside, the **five red-brick towers** of the inner sanctuary are arranged on a laterite platform, with three prangs in the front (eastern) row, and two behind. The main, central, prang has collapsed, leaving only its base, but the four other towers are merely decapitated and some have carved **lintels** intact. The lintel above the doorway of the front right tower is particularly lively in its depiction of the popular scene known as Ume Mahesvara (Uma and her consort Shiva riding the bull Nandi). There are interesting details in the temple complex, including recurrent motifs of foliage designs and Kala lion-faces, and figures of ascetics carved into the base of the doorway pillars on the eastern gopura of the outer wall.

Wat Khao Angkhan

Approx 20km west of Phanom Rung • Daily dawn to dusk; admission free.

While **Wat Khao Angkhan** receives far fewer visitors than Phanom Rung and Muang Tam, it's worth heading to the top of the extinct volcano on which this temple sits, both to admire its unusual combination of ancient and modern features, and to soak up the tranquil atmosphere, as there's rarely anyone here apart from a few monks. The first sight on reaching the top of the hill is a giant reclining Buddha, before you reach the main temple buildings and some fine views over the surrounding countryside. The temple incorporates a set of ancient sema stones that date back to the Dvaravati era (eighth to ninth century), and are so worn that the bas-reliefs on them (of the Buddha, lotus and stupa) have almost disappeared. The stones are now surrounded by a low wall surmounted by a line of sitting Buddha images draped in saffron robes. The ubosot, which stands inside this wall, was built in 1977 in a modern Khmer style and its interior features some rather whimsical murals of the life of the Buddha, though they are already deteriorating due to damp weather.

ARRIVAL AND DEPARTURE · PHANOM RUNG AND AROUND

Many people check out the ruins of Phanom Rung and Muang Tam on a **day-trip** from Khorat, though Nang Rong is much nearer and makes a more convenient base. There's public transport from Khorat or Nang Rong as far as the little town of **Ban Tako**, from where you'll need to take a motorbike taxi for the final few kilometres to the ruins. However, this works out quite expensive, so it makes more sense to arrange a tour through your hotel. There are three car parks and three entrances to the Phanom Rung complex: if you have your own transport, ignore the Gates 2 and 3 (west) entrances, signed off the access road, and carry on to the main, Gate 1 (east), entrance and car park – the drama of the site is lost if you explore it back-to-front; motorbike taxis should take you to the main entrance.

GETTING TO BAN TAKO

By bus Ban Tako is located on Highway 24 about 115km southeast of Khorat (about 2hr) and 83km southwest of Surin (about 1hr 30min). Frequent buses run from Khorat (via Nang Rong) and Surin; bus #274 travels between the two provincial capitals roughly every 30min.

BAN TAKO TO THE RUINS

By taxi or hitching From Ban Tako it's 12km south to

Phanom Rung and another 8km southeast along a side road to Muang Tam. There's no public transport to the ruins, so most people take a motorbike taxi here (B400–500/person) for the round trip to Phanom Rung, Muang Tam and back to Ban Tako.

NANG RONG TO THE RUINS
By bus Nang Rong is 14km west of Ban Tako on Highway 24 and served by the #274 and #563 bus routes from Khorat or Surin. For transport to the ruins at Phanom Rung and Muang Tam, either take the #274 bus to Ban Tako, then a motorbike taxi (see above); hire a motorbike taxi all the

way from Nang Rong (pricier than from Ban Tako), or rent a car or motorbike from *Phanmrung Puri Resort* or *P. Inter California Hostel*.

By rented car or motorbike If you want to visit Wat Khao Angkhan by yourself, visit Khun Wicha at *P. Inter California Hostel* (see below), who can provide a sketch map of the area; however, the route is not clearly signposted, so you might want to arrange a tour through your hotel.

By tour All hotels and guesthouses in Nang Rong and Khorat can arrange a day tour of Phanom Rung, Muang Tam and Wat Khao Angkhan; one-day tours of all three sites cost around B2500 per person for four people.

ACCOMMODATION

The nearest accommodation to Phanom Rung is in Nang Rong, 14km west of Ban Tako on Highway 24. There's little to see here, but there are few tourists and its quaint guesthouses are handy bases for a bit of temple exploring.

NANG RONG
★ Phanomrung Puri Resort 212 Thanon Prachantakhet ☎044 632 222, ☯phanomrungpuri. co.th. This comfortable resort constitutes Nang Rong's most luxurious place to stay and offers spacious, well-equipped

rooms, along with a swimming pool and decent restaurant, in a quiet location just north of the town centre. B1100
P. Inter California Hostel 59/9 Thanon Sangkakrit (call for pick-up from the bus station or main road) ☎081 808 3347. The comfortable rooms at this family-owned guesthouse have views across the surrounding countryside, and range from simple fan rooms to bigger, better furnished a/c rooms, with rates up to B600. Breakfast costs a little extra. Owner Khun Wicha is a mine of local information, and they have motorbikes for rent at B250/day. Fan B250, a/c B350

Buriram

Though Buriram Province is home to many famed Khmer sites such as Phanom Rung, the provincial capital has little to attract visitors, unless you happen to be a fan of football or Formula 1 motor racing. Buriram United FC is Thailand's most successful football team in recent years and play at the New I-Mobile Stadium (aka the Thunder Castle), which has a capacity of 32,600 (higher than the town's population). The club's success has largely been funded by owner Newin Chidchob, a wealthy politician, who also had the Chang International Circuit (CIC) built in 2014 to host Formula 1 races.

ARRIVAL AND DEPARTURE
BURIRAM

By train The train station (☎044 611 202) is located just north of the town centre.
Destinations Ayutthaya (10 daily; 5–6hr); Bangkok (10 daily; 6–8hr); Khorat (10 daily; 1hr 30min–2hr); Pak Chong (9 daily; 3–4hr); Si Saket (7 daily; 2hr–2hr 30min); Surin (10 daily; 45min–1hr); Ubon Ratchathani (7 daily; 3–4hr).

By bus The bus terminal (☎044 612 534) is on Thanon Bulamduan.
Destinations Bangkok (at least hourly; 5hr); Khorat (every 30min; 3hr); Nang Rong (every 30min; 40min); Surin (every hour; 1hr).

ACCOMMODATION AND EATING
Amari Buriram United 444 Moo 15, Thanon Buriram-Prakonchai ☎044 111444. ☯amari.com/buriram-united. Thailand's only football-themed hotel sits right next to the Thunder Castle, and boasts sixty spacious rooms and suites, all fitted with big TVs (for watching football, of course), pictures of football stars on the wall, a mini-football pitch, a pool and tennis courts. B1,350

Jimmy's Sports Café 479/20 Thanon Jira. ☎086 069 2044 ☯jimmysburiram.com. Where else do you eat while in a football-themed town but in a sports café? Jimmy's serves up Sunday roasts (B250), as well as lots of other Western favourites and a good range of Thai food too. There is, of course, sports on TV. Daily 9am–10pm

5

Surin and around

Best known for its much-hyped annual elephant round-up, the provincial capital of **SURIN**, around 50km east of Buriram and 175km east of Khorat, is an otherwise typical northeastern town, a reasonably comfortable place to absorb the easy-going pace of Isaan life. There's a handful of good, mid-range hotels in the centre and, as a bonus, there are some fantastic Khmer ruins in the vicinity. In fact, Surin has a stronger Khmer influence than any other town in Isaan, as attested by the lak muang (city pillar), which is purely

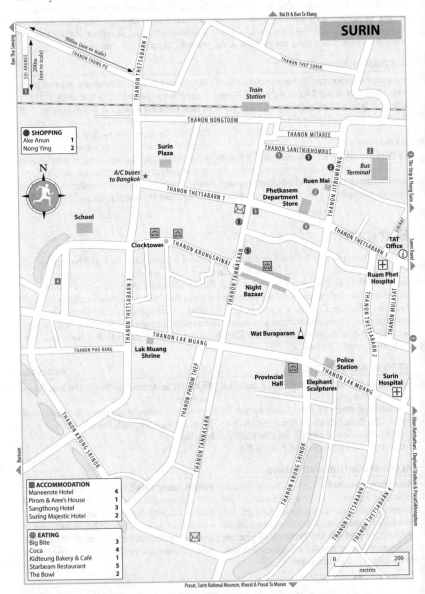

SURIN

● **SHOPPING**
Ake Anun	**1**
Nong Ying	**2**

■ **ACCOMMODATION**
Maneerote Hotel	**4**
Pirom & Aree's House	**1**
Sangthong Hotel	**3**
Suring Majestic Hotel	**2**

● **EATING**
Big Bite	**3**
Coca	**4**
Kidteung Bakery & Café	**1**
Starbeam Restaurant	**5**
The Bowl	**2**

Prasat, Surin National Museum, Khorat & Prasat Ta Muean ▼

5

> **SURIN ELEPHANT ROUND-UP**
>
> Surin's **elephant round-up**, held every year on the third weekend of November, is not so much a 'round-up' as a glorified elephant show. Many people see these shows as a form of cruelty, but the event attracts around forty thousand spectators to watch three hundred elephants enjoying a feast, playing football, engaging in tugs of war and parading in full battle garb. The weekend begins on Friday morning when locals set out long trestle tables filled with pineapples, bananas and sugar cane for the elephants to feast on, then on Saturday and Sunday, the elephants show off their skills in a show lasting around three hours. Accommodation rates soar at this time and advance booking is necessary. Note that however well controlled the elephants appear, you should always approach them with caution – in the past, frightened and taunted elephants have killed tourists. Tickets cost B500–1000 and can be booked through TAT, the provincial government website (W surin.go.th), or Saren Travel (see page 455), who can also arrange accommodation and transport if you contact them three months ahead; alternatively, you could join one of the overnight packages organized by Bangkok travel agencies.

Khmer in design. Many visitors pass through the city on their way to the village of Ban Tha Sawang, 10km away, where Thailand's most exclusive silk is produced.

Surin's elephant tie-in comes from the local Suay people, whose prowess with pachyderms is renowned and can be seen first-hand in the nearby village of **Ban Ta Klang**. Thais, Lao and Khmers make up the remainder of the population of Surin province; the Khmers have lived and worked in the region for over a thousand years, and their architectural legacy is still in evidence at the ruined temples of Ta Muean and Sikhoraphum. There's also **overland access between Thailand and Cambodia** via Surin province's Chong Chom checkpoint near Kap Choeng.

Ban Tha Sawang

10km northwest of Surin • Songthaews to Ban Tha Sawang leave regularly from near the clock tower on Thanon Krungsrinai

Some of Thailand's most exclusive silk is produced in the village of **BAN THA SAWANG**, which is just a short songthaew or bike ride from the town centre. The best months to visit are between November and June, when the women aren't required to work all day in the fields.

The **Tha Sawang fabric** is gold-brocade silk whose ancient designs are so intricate that it takes four weavers working simultaneously on a single loom a whole day to produce just 6cm. And while a standard everyday *mut mee* sarong might use five heddles (vertical frames of threads that determine the pattern) in its design, a Ban Tha Sawang sarong will use more than a thousand; not surprisingly, Ban Tha Sawang sarongs cost around B50,000 and must be ordered several months in advance. The Ban Tha Sawang Weaving Centre (daily 8.30am–5pm) houses around twenty looms, and visitors are welcome to observe the weavers at close quarters. There's a display area across the road where you can see some fine examples of brocade cloth. Several stalls in the village sell local silk, but not the Ban Tha Sawang brocades.

Ban Ta Klang

58km north of Surin • Local bus from Surin (hourly; 2hr); if driving, head north along Highway 214 for 36km, turn left at the village of Ban Nong Tad and continue for 22km • Centre for Elephant Studies daily 8.30am–4.30pm • Free • Elephant shows 10am & 2pm daily • B100

The quiet, ramshackle "elephant village" of **BAN TA KLANG** is the main settlement of the Suay people and the training centre for their elephants. One out of every two Ta Klang families owns its own elephant, occasionally using it as a Western farmer would a tractor, but otherwise treating it as a much-loved pet (see box opposite).

Ban Ta Klang's busy time, elephant-wise, is November, when the creatures and their mahouts prepare for the annual elephant show in Surin. In addition, every year on the

5

first weekend of November, the elephants compete in **swimming races**, held further up the Mun River in the town of Satuk, 30km west of Ta Klang. A more authentic local spectacle is the annual **monks' ordination ceremony**, which usually takes place in May in Ban Ta Klang as part of the preparations for the beginning of Buddhist Lent, when young men ride to the temple on ceremonially clad elephants.

The traditions of mahouts are documented, along with other elephant-related subjects, at the rather desultory **Centre for Elephant Studies** in the southern part of Ban Ta Klang village. To satisfy tourist curiosity, the centre also puts on elephant shows to coincide with the arrival of tour groups.

Prasat Ta Muean

78km south of Surin on the Cambodian border • Daily 8am–4pm • Free • No public transport; follow H214 south to H24, turn west, then south on H2397 and west on H224. Finally, at Ban Ta Miang, turn south on H2407

Atmospheric **Prasat Ta Muean** – comprising three laterite ruins – is so remote and hemmed in by dense vegetation that you can't help but feel like an intrepid explorer when you finally reach the site. The first of the three sites is a simple, laterite sanctuary snuggled in a shady glade, while the second consists of a gopura, mondop and prang, also of laterite, surrounded by a wall and with an adjacent pond. The last and biggest site, a few hundred metres further south and known as Prasat Ta Muean Thom, is much larger, consisting of three prangs and several other structures, some of laterite and others of sandstone, though few carvings remain. Unusually, like Phimai, the temple is oriented to the south rather than to the east, and the steep stairway which leads directly to Cambodia is heavily guarded by Thai military. In fact, visitors need to exchange their passports for visitors' passes on entering the site and reclaim them on leaving. Though it's in Surin province, it makes a convenient final destination on a day's exploration of Khmer temples between Nang Rong and Surin, after visiting Wat Khao Angkhan, Phanom Rung and Muang Tam (see page 448).

Prasat Sikhoraphum

Sikhoraphum, 30km northeast of Surin, just north of the H226 • Daily 8.30am–6pm • B50 • Regular buses between Surin and Si Saket stop at Sikhoraphum

Easily accessible and carefully maintained, Prasat Sikhoraphum consists of five prangs set on a laterite base, surrounded by a U-shaped moat and trim lawns. Built by King Suryavarman in the twelfth century, it boasts one of the most beautiful lintels in Thailand, depicting Shiva, Brahma, Ganesha and Vishnu, above the eastern entrance to the main prang. The temple runs a light-and-sound show to coincide with the Surin elephant round-up, and occasionally dancers practise a classical performance in the shade of an enormous bo tree at the entrance to the site.

ARRIVAL AND DEPARTURE   SURIN

By train The train station (☎ 044 511295) is on the northern edge of town.

Destinations Ayutthaya (10 daily; 5hr–7hr 30min);

Bangkok (10 daily; 6hr 30min–9hr 30min); Buriram (10 daily; 40–50min); Khorat (10 daily; 1hr 50min–3hr 10min); Pak Chong (10 daily; 3hr 10min–5hr); Si Saket (8 daily;

SURIN VILLAGE TOURS

One of the best reasons for coming to Surin, other than November's elephant round-up (see box above), is to take one of the excellent **local tours** (from B1700/person for a group of four) organized from *Pirom & Aree's House*. Pirom is a highly informed former social worker whose trips give tourists an unusual chance to catch glimpses of rural northeastern life as it's really lived. His village tours feature visits to local silk-weavers and basket-makers, as well as to Ban Ta Klang elephant trainers' village.

THE SUAY AND THE SURIN PROJECT

5

Traditionally regarded as the most expert hunters and trainers of elephants in Thailand, the **Suay tribe** (who call themselves 'Kuy') migrated to Isaan from Central Asia before the rise of the Khmers in the ninth century. It was the Suay who masterminded the use of elephants in the construction of the great Khmer temples, and a Suay chief who in 1760 helped recapture a runaway white elephant belonging to the king of Ayutthaya, earning the hereditary title "Lord of Surin". Surin was governed by members of the Suay tribe until Rama V's administrative reforms of 1907.

Now that elephants have been replaced almost entirely by modern machinery in the agricultural and logging industries, there's little demand for the Suay mahouts' skills as captors and trainers of wild elephants, or their traditional pre-hunting rituals involving sacred ropes, magic clothing and the keeping of certain taboos.

There are currently around two hundred elephants registered as living in Ban Ta Klang, and their mahouts are given subsidies for keeping them there. This discourages them from taking the elephants to Bangkok, where curious urbanites would have been charged for the pleasure of feeding the elephants or even walking under their trunk or belly for good luck (pregnant women who do this are supposedly guaranteed an easy birth). The downside is that there's very little for the elephants to do at the study centre, and they spend much of their time shackled up.

In a bid to give Surin's elephants a better life, the not-for-profit Elephant Nature Foundation has set up the **Surin Project** (W surinproject.org), which provides open spaces for elephants to roam in and teaches mahouts the benefits of ecotourism. At the time of writing, just twelve of the study centre's elephants were being cared for full-time at the project, with five more elephants at the centre on a part-time basis. It's possible to volunteer at the camp, and for B13,000 a week you can help to dig irrigation channels, build shelters and plant food for the animals. The rate includes food, accommodation and transport from Buriram, Bangkok or Chiang Mai (pick-ups every Mon).

1hr 15min–1hr 50min); Ubon Ratchathani (7 daily; 2hr 15min–3hr 20min).

By bus and minibus The bus terminal (☎044 511756) is off Thanon Jitbumrung. Minibuses from here run from Surin to Cambodia (see box below).

Destinations Bangkok (at least hourly; 7hr); Ban Ta Klang (hourly; 2hr); Buriram (hourly; 35–55min); Chiang Mai (6 daily; 12hr); Khorat (every 30min; 4–5hr); Khon Kaen (20 daily; 4hr–5hr 30min); Pattaya (12 daily; 8–10hr); Roi Et (hourly; 2–3hr); Si Saket (every 25min; 3hr–3hr 30min).

INFORMATION, TOURS AND GETTING AROUND

Tourist information There's a helpful TAT office (daily 8.30am–4.30pm; ☎044 514447–8, e tatsurin@tat.or.th) at 355/3–6 Thanon Thetsabarn 1, just east of the town centre, and the provincial government has a quite useful website (W surin.go.th), which includes booking forms for the elephant round-up.

Travel agency Saren Travel, 282/33 Thanon Ratphakdee (Mon–Sat 8am–6pm; ☎044 513 828, e sarentour@ hotmail.com; outside office hours ☎089 949 1185), sells air and train tickets and offers cars with/without driver (from B1800/day). They can also arrange day-trips to Phanom Rung, Muang Tam and Ban Ta Klang (B3200 for four people

sharing a car, excluding entry fees). A taxi from Chong Chom to Siem Reap (Cambodia) for B1500 per person is also available, as are elephant-show tickets. Elephant rides in Ban Ta Klang can be arranged too, for around B200/person.

Village tours At Pirom & Aree's House, at the far end of Soi Arunee off Thanon Thung Po ☎044 515140. Great opportunities to explore the villages around Surin with a friendly and very knowledgeable guide (see page 454).

Hospitals Ruam Phet Hospital, on the eastern arm of Thanon Thetsabarn 1 (☎044 513 638 & ☎044 513192); and the government-run Surin Hospital on Thanon Lak Muang (☎044 511 006 & ☎044 511757).

ACCOMMODATION

Except during the elephant round-up – when room rates in Surin rocket and **accommodation** is booked out weeks in advance – you'll have no trouble finding a place to stay.

★ **Maneerote Hotel** 11/1 Soi Poytungko, Thanon Krungsrinai ☎044 514 569; map p.452. It may be set a short way west of the centre, but rooms at the *Maneerote* are some of the best value in town. They are a good size and

bright, with marble floors and bathrooms, and each has its own balcony. There's a decent restaurant too. B450

Pirom & Aree's House At the far end of Soi Arunee, off Thanon Thung Po, 1.5km northwest of the train station ☎044 515140; map p.452. Surin's famously long-running guesthouse occupies a tranquil spot overlooking rice fields. The super-clean rooms in this modern take on

5

CROSSING THE CAMBODIAN BORDER VIA CHONG CHOM

There are a/c minivans (daily every 30min 6am–5.30pm; 2hr; B60) via Prasat to the **Chong Chom border pass**, 70km south of Surin. Cambodian visas are issued on arrival at the Chong Chom–O'Smach checkpoint (daily 7am–8pm; B1300), from where you can get transport to Anlong Veng and then on to Siem Reap, which is 150km from the border crossing (start negotiations for a taxi transfer to Siem Reap at B800/car, but expect to pay slightly more). There have been reports of people on visa runs being asked for more money by officials on the Cambodian side, especially if they try to return to Thailand on the same day.

Arriving **from Cambodia**, songthaews and motorbike taxis ferry travellers from the border checkpoint to the minibus stop for Prasat and Surin. For details on other overland routes into Cambodia, see page 29.

a traditional home are large and simply furnished with fans and shared bathrooms (no hot water), plus there are garden seating areas. The owners are incredibly friendly and welcoming, and can tell you everything you need to know about the local area. Good rates for singles. **B200**

Sangthong Hotel 279–281 Thanon Tannasarn ☎ 044 512099; map p.452. The best of the budget hotels, this place is friendly, good value and well run. All rooms are large and en suite, and some have a/c and TV. Fan **B150**, a/c **B350**

Surin Majestic Hotel 99 Thanon Jitbumrung, at the back of the bus station ☎ 044 713980, ⓦ surinmajestic. com; map p.452. A comfortable choice in the town centre, with smartly furnished rooms. All have a/c and TV plus a balcony overlooking the attractive, good-sized ground-floor swimming pool. **B1200**

EATING AND DRINKING

Aside from a reasonable range of local **restaurants**, Surin boasts a good-sized **night bazaar**, which occupies the eastern end of Thanon Krungsrinai and offers a tasty selection of local food (including roasted crickets and barbecued locusts in season), as well as stalls selling fashions and toys. Surin also has a surprisingly wild **nightlife** for a provincial town, with a clutch of seedy bars and discos around the neon-lit "Strip" east of the centre at the northern end of Thanon Sirirath and along Soi Kola, just north of the *Thong Tharin Hotel*.

Big Bite 60 Thanon Sirirat, in front of the Thong Tarin Hotel; map p.452. This welcoming, a/c restaurant serves a good range of Thai and Western dishes such as fish and chips (B280), as well as chilli dips and fresh fruit juices. Daily 10am–midnight.

Coca 128 Thanon Thetsabarn 1 (no English sign but it's easy to spot opposite and just east of the Phetkasem Department Store) ☎ 044 512 390; map p.452. A good range of Chinese and Thai dishes such as crispy catfish salad with mango and stewed duck feet with noodles (both

B100), served in a clean and welcoming setting. Daily 10am–10pm.

Kidteung Bakery & Café 28 Thanon Sanitnikhomrut, close to the junction with Thanon Tannasarn; map p.452. Breezy alfresco seating area draped in foliage and air-conditioned room inside. Serves delicious cakes and ice vanilla lattes (B55) to a mixed crowd, which includes local expats. Daily 7am–8pm.

Starbeam Restaurant 32/6 Soi Sraboran 2 ☎ 044 519 629, ⓦ facebook.com/starbeam.restaurant; map p.452. This simple restaurant is tricky to find, tucked away in a residential area, but it's worth tracking down for its fantastic range of food such as Mexican quesadillas (from B170), chicken madras (B185) and 'steak bomb' (B235). Daily 8am–9pm.

The Bowl 142 Thanon Jitbumrung ☎ 044 511 897; map p.452. Reasonably priced dishes such as chicken wings (B100) and beef steak (B200), as well as ice cream and cakes, in a clean and brightly lit environment. Daily 9am–10.30pm.

SHOPPING

Surin is famous for the variety of **silk weaves** produced here: there are seven hundred designs in Surin province alone, many of them of Cambodian origin, including the locally popular rhomboid pattern. In high season, there are usually several women selling their cloth around the Tannasarn–Krungsrinai intersection, and you can also visit local silk-weaving villages (see p.455).

Ake Anun 122–124 Thanon Sanitnikhomrut ☎ 044 511

441; map p.452. Sells ready-made *pha sin* (wrap-around skirts; B2500–3800), scarves, ties, jackets, and souvenirs such as silk elephants. Daily 8am–7.30pm.

Nong Ying 52 Thanon Jitbumrung ☎ 044 511 606; map p.452. A superb selection of silks as well as ready-made silk jackets, bags and accessories and axe pillows. Daily 8am–7pm.

5

SILK PRODUCTION

Most hand-woven **Thai silk** is produced by Isaan village women, some of whom oversee every aspect of sericulture, from the breeding of the silkworm to the dyeing of the fabric. Isaan's pre-eminence is partly due to its soils, which are particularly suitable for the growth of mulberry trees, the leaves of which are the **silkworms'** favoured diet. The cycle of production begins with the female silk-moth, which lives just a few days but lays around 300–500 microscopic eggs in that time. The eggs take about nine days to hatch into tiny silkworms, which are then kept in covered rattan trays and fed on mulberry leaves three or four times a day. The silkworms are such enthusiastic eaters that after three or four weeks they will have grown to about 6cm in length (around ten thousand times their original size), ready for the cocoon-building **pupal** stage.

The silkworm constructs its **cocoon** from a single white or yellow fibre that it secretes from its mouth at a rate of 12cm a minute, sealing the filaments with a gummy substance called sericin. The metamorphosis of the pupa into a moth can take anything from two to seven days, but the sericulturist must anticipate the moment when the new moth is about to break out in order to prevent the destruction of the precious fibre, which at this stage is often 900m long. At the crucial point the cocoon is dropped into boiling water, killing the moth (which is often eaten as a snack) and softening the sericin, so that the unbroken filament can be unravelled. The fibres from several cocoons are "reeled" into a single thread, and two or three threads are subsequently twisted or "thrown" into the yarn known as **raw silk** (broken threads from damaged cocoons are worked into a second-rate yarn called "spun silk"). In most cases, the next stage is the "de-gumming process", in which the raw silk is soaked to dissolve away the sericin, leaving it soft and semi-transparent. Extremely absorbent and finely textured, reeled silk is the perfect material for **dyeing**; most silk producers now use chemical dyes, though traditional vegetable dyes are making a bit of a comeback.

These days, it's not worth the bother for women who live near town to raise their own silkworms and spin their own thread as they can easily buy Japanese ready-to-weave silk in the market. **Japanese silk** is smoother than Thai silk but lasts only about seven years when woven into a sarong; hand-raised, raw Thai silk is rougher but lasts around forty years, and so is still favoured by women living in remote villages.

Once dyed (or bought), the silk is ready for **weaving**. This is generally done during slack agricultural periods, for example just after the rice is planted and again just after it's harvested. Looms are usually set up in the space under the house, in the sheltered area between the piles, and most are designed to produce a sarong of around 1m by 2m. Isaan weavers have many different weaving techniques and can create countless patterns, ranging from the simplest single-coloured plain weave for work shirts to exquisitely complex wedding sarongs that may take up to six weeks to complete. The most exclusive and intricate designs are those produced in Ban Tha Sawang (see page 453), costing tens of thousands of baht for a single sarong.

Khao Phra Viharn (Preah Vihear)

140km southwest of Ubon Ratchathani and 220km southeast of Surin • Closed at time of writing

Perched atop a 547m-high spur of the Dangrek mountains right on the Thai–Cambodian border, the ninth-to-twelfth-century Khmer ruins of **KHAO PHRA VIHARN** (or **Preah Vihear** to Cambodians) are as impressive as Phimai and Phanom Rung (see pages 444 and 448), but unfortunately the sanctuary has been inaccessible to visitors from the Thai side for many years due to a border dispute. It is also a difficult journey to get there from Surin or Ubon Ratchathani, but it might be worth checking with the TAT office in either town (see pages 455 and 462) to see if the situation has changed.

Si Saket

The quiet provincial capital of **SI SAKET** has no attractions in the municipal area, though it has a reasonable choice of hotels, a good night market and decent transport connections. The only reason to stay here is to check out a couple of quirky temples near town (Wat Sa Kamphaeng Yai and Wat Laan Khuat). It's also near the Cambodian border crossing at Chong Sa Ngam, though there's no public transport there.

Wat Sa Kamphaeng Yai

30km west of Si Saket, just south of H226 before the road crosses the railway (no English sign) • Daily 5.30am–6.30pm • Free • Bus from Si Saket (every 20min; 30min) or Surin (every 20min; 1hr 30min)

The temple compound at **Wat Sa Kamphaeng Yai** combines modern temple buildings with Khmer ruins which have been rather insensitively restored, using new bricks to replace sandstone blocks on the main prang, while two adjacent prangs have been almost entirely rebuilt of brick. There is some excellent detail on some of the lintels, though others have worn away. The most striking aspect of this temple, however, is its "Garden of Hell", behind the Khmer buildings and near the car park. The statues of people with enlarged heads, hands, eyes and sexual organs serve as a warning of the dangers of not following the Middle Way of Buddhism.

Wat Laan Khuat (Million Bottle Temple)

65km south of Si Saket • Daily dawn to dusk • Free • No public transport; follow H221 south from Si Saket, turn west on to H2111, cross H24 and the temple is on H2128 in Khun Han village

In the 1980s, the abbot at Wat Phra Maha Chedi Kaeo struck on the bright idea of decorating his temple with bottles to symbolize the clarity of purpose that all Buddhists seek. As a result, the buildings, pathways and balustrades here are now decorated with brown and green beer bottles and bottle tops – more than a million and a half of them. The result creates a striking sight, and has attracted a steady stream of visitors to see the temple, now known as **Wat Laan Khuat** – the million bottle temple.

ARRIVAL AND DEPARTURE · SI SAKET

By train Si Saket train station (☏ 045 611 525) is in the centre of the town.
Destinations: Bangkok (8 daily; 8–11hr); Khorat (8 daily; 3–4hr 30min); Surin (8 daily; 1hr 10min–2hr); Ubon Ratchatani (7 daily; 50min–1hr 10min).

By bus The bus station (☏ 045 612 500) is in the southern part of town.
Destinations: Bangkok (9 daily; 7–9hr); Surin (hourly; 3hr); Ubon Ratchathani (every 30min; 1hr–1hr 30min).

ACCOMMODATION AND EATING

As with most Thai towns, the **night market**, which sets up around a small plaza along the southern edge of the rail line, offers cheap and tasty eating options. However, the town also boasts sophisticated, air-conditioned restaurants that also offer evening entertainment, likw **Barco (see below)**.
Barco 1502/53 Thanon Khukhan ☏ 045 612 852, ⓦfacebook.com/barcocafe. This is a great spot to enjoy a pizza (from B255), German sausages (B295), tonkatsu with rice (B145) or a winged-bean salad (B95). Live entertainment from 7pm to 9pm most evenings. Daily 11.30am–10.30pm.

Boonsiri Boutique Hotel 1191/3 Thanon Vijitkakorn ☏045 622 222, ⓦboonsiriboutiquehotel.com. This pink place offers well-equipped rooms with cable TV, just a short walk from the station. The cheapest rooms are on the fourth floor, but there's no lift. B400
Gallery Design Hotel 1199 Thanon Ubon ☏045 611 999, ⓦhttps://bit.ly/2Ppdp2X. This smartly designed, business-oriented hotel with super efficient service comes as a bit of a surprise in a small provincial town like this. It offers 79 well-equipped rooms with complimentary snacks and a buffet breakfast included in the price. B1200

Ubon Ratchathani

The sprawling provincial capital of **UBON RATCHATHANI** (almost always referred to simply as Ubon – not to be confused with Udon, aka Udon Thani, to the north) holds little in the way of attractions beyond a couple of wats and a decent museum. Still, it's

5

more sedate than many northeastern cities, with plenty of opportunities for getting to grips with Isaan culture. There's a lively **walking street** on Thanon Sri Narong just east of Thung Si Muang Park on Friday to Sunday evenings (around 6pm–10pm). The best time to visit is at festival time (see page 461), but Ubon also makes a handy base for trips east to Khong Chiam and Sam Phan Bok, both beside the Mekong River, and the Lao border market at Chong Mek.

Thung Si Muang Park

Just south of Thanon Phalorangrit

Ubon's centrepiece is **Thung Si Muang Park** and its unmissable 22m-high **Candle Sculpture**, an enormous yellow-painted replica of the wax sculptures that star in the annual Candle Festival (see box above). This particular sculpture was inspired by a story written by King Bhumibol and features a boat with an enormous garuda

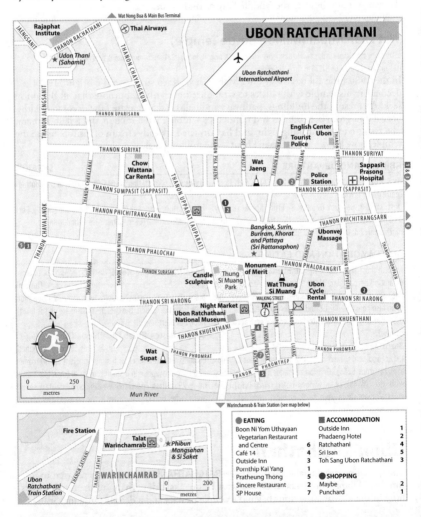

● EATING

Boon Ni Yom Uthayaan Vegetarian Restaurant and Centre	6
Café 14	4
Outside Inn	3
Pornthip Kai Yang	1
Pratheung Thong	5
Sincere Restaurant	2
SP House	7

■ ACCOMMODATION

Outside Inn	1
Phadaeng Hotel	2
Ratchathani	4
Sri Isan	5
Toh Sang Ubon Ratchathani	3

● SHOPPING

| Maybe | 2 |
| Punchard | 1 |

UBON FESTIVALS

If you're near Ubon in early July, you should definitely consider coming into town for the local **Asanha Puja** festivities, an auspicious Buddhist holiday celebrated all over Thailand to mark the beginning of Khao Pansa, the annual three-month Buddhist retreat. Ubon's version is the most spectacular in the country, famous for the majestic orange beeswax sculptures created by each of its temples, which are mounted on floats around enormous candles and paraded through the town – hence the tourist name for the celebrations, the **Ubon Candle Festival**. The sculptures are judged and then returned to the temple, where the candle is usually kept burning throughout the retreat period. The end of the retreat, **Awk Pansa** (early to mid–Oct), is also exuberantly celebrated with a procession of illuminated boats, each representing one of the city's temples, along the Mun River between Wat Suphat and the night market, as well as beauty contests, parades and lots of fireworks throughout the city, and *likay* theatre shows in Thung Si Muang Park. Traditional longboat races are staged on the river in the days following Awk Pansa.

---

figurehead that's ploughing past various figures who are apparently being devoured by sea monsters.

In the northeast corner of the park stands a far more unassuming memorial in the shape of a 3m-high obelisk. Known as the **Monument of Merit**, it was erected by a group of Allied POWs who wanted to show their gratitude to the people of Ubon for their support during World War II. Despite the real threat of punishment by the Japanese occupiers, between 1941 and 1943 Ubon citizens secretly donated food and clothes to the POWs imprisoned in a nearby camp.

Ubon Ratchathani National Museum

Thanon Khuenthani • Wed–Sun 9am–4pm • B100

Ubon Ratchathani National Museum was undergoing renovation at the time of this update, but is well worth a visit. It is designed around a central courtyard in a building constructed in 1918, which previously functioned as Ubon's City Hall. Re-opened as a national museum in 1989 by the Fine Arts Department, it offers a good overview of the history, geology and culture of southern Isaan, with well-labelled displays on everything from rock formations to folk crafts, such as the star-embroidered fabric that is a speciality of Ubon. There are also copies of the Pha Taem cliff paintings (see page 465) and a ninth-century representation of Ardhanarishvara, the union of Shiva and his consort Uma.

Wat Thung Si Muang

Entrance on Thanon Luang

Of the city's eight main wats, **Wat Thung Si Muang** is the most noteworthy, mainly for its unusually well-preserved teak library (*ho trai*) which is raised on stilts over a pond to keep book-devouring insects at bay. The murals in the bot, to the left of the library, have also survived remarkably well; their lively scenes of everyday life in the nineteenth century include local merit-making dances and musicians playing *khaen* pipes, as well as conventional portraits of city activities in Bangkok.

Wat Nong Bua

Thanon Thammawithi (west of Thanon Chayangkun, near the main bus terminal at the northern edge of town) • City songthaew #2 or #3 via Thanon Khuenthani

The modern **Wat Nong Bua** is modelled on the stupa at Bodh Gaya in India, scene of the Buddha's enlightenment; the white and gold replica is carved with scenes from the *Jataka* and contains a scaled-down version of the stupa covered in gold leaf. The

5

temple's wax carvers are some of the city's best – Wat Nong Bua often wins the award for best float in the annual Candle Festival (see page 461). Replicas of these floats are also on display in front of the ordination hall.

ARRIVAL AND DEPARTURE   UBON RATCHATHANI

BY PLANE
The airport (☎045 244 073) is just north of the town centre; a metered taxi to the town-centre hotels costs around B80 (☎045 265 999; call to ask for a pick-up). Thai Airways (⌨thaiairways.com) operates three flights a day between Ubon and Bangkok (1hr 5min), while budget airline Air Asia (⌨airasia.com) is cheaper and has three flights a day. Also cheap is Nok Air (⌨nokair.com), which operates seven flights a day between Bangkok and Ubon. Air Asia also runs two daily flights to Chiang Mai (1hr 30min).

BY TRAIN
Ubon's train station (☎045 312004) is in the suburb of Warinchamrab (Warin Chamrap), about 2km south across the Mun River from central Ubon. White city songthaew #2 meets all trains at Warinchamrab and takes passengers into central Ubon (B10), passing along Thanon Khuenthani, where several hotels and the TAT office are located.
Destinations Ayutthaya (7 daily; 7hr–10hr 40min); Bangkok (7 daily; 8hr 30min–12hr 15min); Buriram (7 daily; 2hr 30min–3hr 30min); Khorat (7 daily; 3hr 45min–6hr); Si Saket (7 daily; 40min–1hr); Surin (7 daily; 1hr 50min–2hr 40min).

BY BUS
Confusingly, several different companies run long-distance bus services in and out of Ubon, each with their own drop-off and pick-up points. Bus company depots are shown on our map (see page 460).
Main bus terminal Nearly all services pass through the

main terminal (☎045 314 299) on Thanon Chayangkun, on the northwest edge of town, which is served by city songthaews #2 and #3 from Warinchamrab via Thanon Khuenthani in central Ubon. The government Baw Khaw Saw bus company is based here and runs regular and a/c services to Bangkok, Buriram, Chiang Mai, Khorat, Si Saket, Surin and Yasothon, plus Pakse in Laos.
Nakhon Chai Air This nationwide private company (⌨nakhonchaiair.com) runs a/c services from its terminal opposite the main bus station. There's a non-stop service to Bangkok as well as routes to and from Chiang Mai, Chiang Rai and Rayong,
Sahamit A/c services (☎045 285 534) to Udon Thani run from the northwest of town, off Thanon Ratchathani.
Talat Warinchamrab Most local buses and songthaews to Phibun Mangsahan, as well as those to Si Saket, use this terminal near the marketplace in Warinchamrab, southeast of the river and served by city songthaews #1 (grey), #3 (pink) and #6 (pink) from Ubon. Minibuses to Khong Chiam (☎045 316 085) leave hourly until 5pm.
Destinations Bangkok (20 daily; 8hr 30min–10hr); Chiang Mai (6 daily; 14–15hr); Chong Mek (17 daily; 1hr); Khon Kaen (5 daily; 4hr 30min); Khong Chiam (hourly; 2–3hr); Khorat (at least 3 daily; 5hr); Mukdahan (every 30min; 2–3hr); Pakse (Laos; 2 daily; 2–3hr); Pattaya (10 daily; 12hr–13hr 30min); Phibun Mangsahan (every 25min; 1hr); Rayong (11 daily; 14hr); Si Saket (hourly; 1hr 30 min–2hr); Surin (at least 7 daily; 2hr 30min–3hr); Udon Thani (19 daily; 5–7hr); Yasothon (19 daily; 1hr 30min–2hr).

GETTING AROUND

By bike Some hotels like Outside Inn and Sri Isan hire bikes to guests for free. In the town centre, try Ubon Cycle Rental, 115 Thanon Sri Narong, east of the post office (☎062 954 9561; B20/hr or B100/24hr).
By motorbike or car Motorbikes (B250–1000/day) and cars (from B1500/day) can be rented from Chow Wattana (☎045 242202) at 269 Thanon Suriyat, and at the airport (☎081 967 5582). Avis (☎090 197 2263, ⌨avisthailand.

com) and Budget (☎045 240507, ⌨budget.co.th) car rental are also based at the airport.
By songthaew Numbered songthaews follow fixed routes in central Ubon and run a regular service (every 10–15min). Those of most use to visitors are mentioned in the text. TAT provides a map of routes.
By taxi Metered taxis (☎045 265 999) charge B35 flag fare and B20 per call. Grab Cars (grab.com) also operate in Ubon.

INFORMATION AND TOURS

Tourist information Staff at the TAT office (daily 8.30am–4.30pm; ☎045 243770, ✉tatubon@tat.or.th) at 264/1 Thanon Khuenthani can provide a helpful map of the city with songthaew routes marked and should be able to give information about the latest situation at Khao Phra Viharn.
Tours Sakda Travel World, 150/1 Thanon Kantaralak, Warinchamrab (☎081 879 8808, ⌨facebook.com/

sakdatour), offers guided tours around Isaan and into Laos, sells air tickets and offers car plus driver from B1800/day.
Massage Ubonvej Massage, 113 Thanon Thepyothi (☎045 260 345), provides a professional massage service, with lots of rooms and staff. Treat yourself to a 2-hour Thai massage (B250) or herbal ball massage (B420). Daily 10am–8pm.

BRUSH UP ON YOUR THAI IN UBON

If you find yourself in Ubon for more than a few days, and want to learn some **Thai**, check out English Center Ubon, where teacher Ooh offers a range of useful one-to-one courses.

English Center Ubon 388/5 Thanon Thepyothi ☎086 2460754, ✉englishcenterubon@hotmail.com. Rates start at B300/hr, but it's possible to get a discount for longer courses – 10hr course for B2900 or a 50hr course costs B13,500. Daily 9am–7pm.

ACCOMMODATION

Considering its remote location, Ubon's choice of hotels is surprisingly good, ranging from luxury options like the *Toh Sang* to the cozy bed and breakfast at the *Outside Inn*. Prices shoot up during the Candle Festival, when you'll need to book a room as far ahead as possible.

★ **Outside Inn** 11 Thanon Suriyat ☎088 581 2069, ⓦtheoutsideinnubon.com; map p.460. Located at the eastern end of Thanon Suriyat, this gem of a place offers great value, with just a handful of tastefully furnished rooms in a quiet location with a laidback vibe. Owners Brent and Tun go out of their way to guarantee guests a pleasant stay. They can advise and help out with travel arrangements, and also happen to run the best restaurant in town (see opposite). B650

Phadaeng Hotel 126 Thanon Pha Daeng, near Punchard crafts shop ☎045 254 600, ✉thephadaeng@gmail.com; map p.460. Clean, good-sized rooms in a quiet part of town, all with TV and a/c. Some have their own private balconies – although don't expect a great view. There's a rather bizarre "fine art gallery" on the ground floor, featuring prints of works by the likes of Da Vinci and Michelangelo, but it gives a splash of colour to the place. B500

Ratchathani 297 Thanon Khuenthani ☎045 244 388, ⓦtheratchathani.com; map p.460. This mid-range hotel has a great central location and a decent restaurant, but some rooms are smallish and dimly lit, so take a look before deciding. Avoid rooms out front as it can be noisy. B490

Sri Isan 62 Thanon Ratchabut ☎062 345 5144, ✉hotelsriisan@gmail.com; map p.460. This small, quite classy hotel enjoys a good location in Ubon's old quarter, just across from the market, and a mere 100m from the river. Its 33 small rooms (some with no window) are set around an open-roofed atrium and all have a/c and cable TV. B500

Toh Sang Ubon Ratchathani 251 Thanon Phalochai ☎045 245531, ⓦtohsang.com; map p.460. The poshest hotel in town, with comfortable a/c rooms and gorgeous suites (B2,500) in a peaceful but rather inconvenient location 1km west of Thanon Chayangkun or about 2km from TAT. It also houses one of the city's smartest restaurants, the *Pratheung Thong* (see opposite). Breakfast included. B1000

EATING

Ubon is a good place for sampling local Isaan specialities, either in a/c comfort at some of the **restaurants** listed below, or at one of the city's **night markets**: try the one on Thanon Ratchabut (north off Thanon Khuenthani) for chicken satay, *phat thai*, cheap fruit shakes, and fiery Isaan dishes.

Boon Ni Yom Uthayaan Vegetarian Restaurant and Centre Thanon Sri Narong; no English sign but its barn-like, open-sided wooden structure is unmistakeable; map p.460. Famous, canteen-style veggie place that's run by members of a Buddhist organization who grow, sell and cook their own produce. All sorts of meat substitutes and tasty veg and tofu dishes are on offer here at very cheap per-plate prices (B20–40). Breakfast and lunch only. Tues–Sun 6am–2pm.

Café 14 49/3 Thanon Pichitrangsan ☎045 260 398; map p.460. A classy restaurant with a choice of inside or outside dining, the latter on a shady wooden terrace. Specialities include morning glory and prawn salad (B145), and there's a good range of drinks as well. It's a popular spot in the evenings. Daily 6pm–midnight.

★ **Outside Inn** 11 Thanon Suriyat ☎088 581 2069, ⓦtheoutsideinnubon.com; map p.460. Delicious American, Mexican and Thai dishes served up by Tun, who has a real flair for creating unique dishes using locally sourced ingredients. Try one of the signature burgers (from B210), the burritos or home-made tacos, and don't miss the lip-smacking spicy dips. Reservations recommended. Daily 11am–2.30pm & 5–9pm.

Pornthip Kai Yang 136 Thanon Sumpasit, just east of Wat Jaeng, ☎089 720 8101; map p.460. This simple streetside restaurant, which also has an a/c dining room, is famous across town for its scrumptious barbecued chicken (*kai yang*) and papaya salad (*som tam*), for B80–150. Daily 7am–8pm.

Pratheung Thong Toh Sang Hotel, 251 Thanon Phalochai ☎045 245 531; map p.460. With its starched tablecloths and wide-ranging menu of Thai and Chinese dishes (B120–260), this restaurant oozes sophistication, and a pianist and singer serenade diners in the evening. Daily 6am–midnight.

Sincere Restaurant 126/1 Thanon Sumpasit ☎045

5

245061; map p.460. High-quality American steaks (fillet mignon B395) and baby clams (B200) served in an intimate little a/c restaurant just back from the main road by the police station. Mon–Sat 11am–10pm.

SP House 76–78 Thanon Ratchabut, ☎045 261 121;

map p.460. This simple a/c restaurant serves a great range of Thai food as well as sandwiches and cakes at cheap prices (shrimp salad B90; chicken with holy basil B60), plus a range of smoothies (B40). It's an ideal spot to cool off while exploring the town centre. Daily 9am–9pm.

SHOPPING

Silk, cotton and silverware are all good buys in Ubon. Both shops listed here specialize in fine-quality regional goods, like triangular axe pillows (*mawn khwaan*) and lengths of silk.

Maybe 124 Thanon Sri Narong ☎045 254 932; map p.460. This shop has a good selection of clothes made from the stripy rough cotton weaves peculiar to the Ubon area. Daily 8am–5pm.

★ **Punchard** 156/1 Thanon Pha Daeng ☎045 243 433; map p.460. *Punchard* is packed with stylish items such as cotton tableware and clothes made to local designs, as well as an appealing variety of home decor items upstairs. It's one of the best places in the northeast to shop for souvenirs or gifts. Thurs–Tues 9am–6pm.

DIRECTORY

Hospitals Sappasit Prasong Hospital (☎045 240 074), to the northeast of the town centre, has a 24hr emergency clinic.

Immigration office In the town of Chong Mek, 100km east of Ubon (Mon–Fri 8.30am–4.30pm; ☎045 485107).

Chong Mek is best accessed by bus (see page 462).

Tourist police For all emergencies, call the tourist police on ☎1155 (free) or contact them at their office on Thanon Sathit Nimankan, in Warin Chamrab ☎045 323 747.

Around Ubon

The area **around Ubon** is a good deal more interesting than the metropolitan hub, particularly if you venture eastwards towards the appealing Mekong riverside town of **Khong Chiam**, the prehistoric paintings at **Pha Taem** or the other-worldly landscape at **Sam Phan Bok**. There is also a crossing into Laos, and a border market, southeast of Ubon at **Chong Mek**.

Khong Chiam

The riverside village of **KHONG CHIAM** (pronounced Kong Jiem) is a popular destination for day-tripping Thais, who drive here from across Isaan to see the somewhat fancifully named "two-coloured river" for which the village is nationally renowned. Created by the merging of the muddy brown Mun with the muddy brown Mekong at the easternmost point of Thailand, the water is hardly an irresistible attraction (come in April to see the colour contrast at its most vivid), but the village itself has plenty of tranquil appeal. If you have your own transport, Khong Chiam combines well with visits to Chong Mek (just 27km away) and Kaeng Tana National Park.

TRIPS FROM KHONG CHIAM

Khong Chiam doesn't have many sights, but you can rent motorbikes (B250/day) or bicycles (B100/day) from *Ban Pak Mongkhon* and explore the quiet streets around the riverfront, or charter a **boat** for a trip to the "two-coloured river" (about B200) or up the Mekong River to see the Pha Taem cliff paintings (B800/boat per hour, depending on boat size; ask at your hotel). Otherwise you could charter a songthaew to **Pha Taem** from Khong Chiam (round trip about B1000); ask at the bus station.

Even though **Laos** is just a few hundred metres away from Khong Chiam, on the other bank of the Mekong, foreigners are not supposed to cross the border here, though you may be able to persuade boatmen to take you there and back for B200–B300/boat, with a quick stop at the bankside village of Ban Mai; the official border crossing is further downstream at Chong Mek.

Comprising little more than a collection of wooden houses and a few resorts, Khong Chiam feels like an island, with the Mun defining its southern limit and the Mekong its northern one. A concrete walkway runs along the banks of the Mekong, lined by predictable souvenir stalls and leading to the large *sala* that's built right over the confluence and affords uninterrupted views. Behind the *sala*, **Wat Khong Chiam** is a typically charming rural Thai temple and has an old wooden bell tower in its compound. Khong Chiam's other temple, the cliffside **Wat Tham Khu Ha Sawan**, located near the point where Route 2222 turns into Khong Chiam, is a striking white colour, with natural wood sculptures festooned with orchids in its grounds, and a huge Buddha image staring down on the villagers below.

ARRIVAL AND SERVICES
KHONG CHIAM

Khong Chiam is 30km northeast of **Phibun Mangsahan**, along Route 2222, and 75km from Ubon.

By minibus Minibuses terminate in front of the market at the west end of Thanon Kaewpradit, Khong Chiam's main drag. From Ubon, hourly minibuses (5am–6pm; 1hr 30min) run from the main bus terminal; the last bus back to Ubon leaves at 4pm. Two daily buses (departing Khong Chiam 7.30am and 4.30pm; 12hr) run between Khong Chiam and Bangkok (travelling via Yasothon).

Services There are a few banks and ATMs on Thanon Kaewpradit. The small pharmacy on Thanon Kaewpradit sells basic supplies.

ACCOMMODATION

Khong Chiam's **accommodation** options are relatively limited, and apart from a couple of exceptions, most places feel poor value compared to other parts of the northeast.

Ban Pak Mongkhon 595 Thanon Klaewpradit ☎045 351 352. A good budget alternative, just a few steps from the bus stop, offering decent a/c bungalows on the north side of the road, and fan rooms in a house on the south side of the road. Fan B250, a/c B400

Ban Rim Khong Resort 37 Thanon Kaewpradit ☎086 010 1637. Great-looking little resort with five timbered a/c chalets wreathed in bougainvillea and ranged round a lawn, plus these fabulous riverside ones (B1500, worth phoning ahead to reserve) with huge verandas overlooking the Mekong. The interiors are nothing special but all are spacious and have a/c, TVs and fridges, and there are discounts for stays of more than one night. B1000

Sibae Guest House 380 Moo 1 Ban Dankao, Thanon Radsadornbamroong; turn left off Thanon Klaewpradit just west of Tesco Lotus, then left again and it's on the left ☎045 351068, ✉watasinsibae@hotmail.com. A beautiful wooden house that has very clean (but very plain) rooms, the most luxurious of which have a/c, bathtubs, TVs and fridges. Friendly owner. Fan B200, a/c B400

Toh Sang Khongjiam Resort On the south bank of the Mun, about 3km east of Khong Chiam ☎045 351174, ⌨tohsang.com. Romantically located, upmarket resort where all rooms have balconies overlooking the river and are very comfortably, if a little kitschly, furnished. There's a swimming pool, table-tennis room, spa, bicycle and kayak rental, plus a couple of restaurants and boat trips to Pha Taem and other riverside sights. Check out their website for spa/resort package offers. With your own wheels, follow Highway 2134 south past Khong Chiam bus station, cross the river, take the first left and follow the signs. B4500

EATING

There's not much happening in Khong Chiam after dark, and restaurants tend to close early.

Araya On the Mekong in front of the district office. Two floating restaurants – *Araya* and nearby *Chonlada* – are the most popular places for Thai visitors to eat at lunch and dinner. Neither is signed in English, and there's little to choose between them; both serve fairly pricey menus of Thai–Chinese dishes (around B130 for basics) and, of course, plenty of fish. Daily 10am–8pm.

Rim Khong Next to the riverside bungalows at Ban Rim Khong Resort. Cheaper and less flashy than the other riverside restaurants (fried rice from B40), with better views, and friendly staff too. A good spot for a sunset beer. Daily 8am–9pm.

Tuk Tik Tham Mua 100m east of the bus station on Thanon Kaewpradit (no English sign or menu), just east of Tesco Lotus. Good local dishes at good cheap prices: spicy *som tam* (B35) and *laap* (B50) served with individual baskets of sticky rice. Daily 8am–7pm.

Pha Taem National Park

18km north of Khong Chiam • Daily 5am–6pm • B400 • To get here, head north out of town on H2173, continue northwest on H2134, then turn north on to H2112 for about 5km, where the park entrance is signposted to the east

5

CROSSING THE LAO BORDER VIA CHONG MEK

It is possible to get a Lao **visa** on arrival at Chong Mek **border crossing**; you'll be charged US$30–42, depending on your nationality, and will receive a thirty-day visa; you'll also need two passport photos (expect to pay an extra dollar if you turn up without photos). If you get an advance visa from Khon Kaen or elsewhere, it must specify Chong Mek as the entry point (see page 467).

Whichever option you choose, once at Chong Mek you first need to get the **Thai exit stamp** from the immigration office on the Thai side (daily 6am–8pm); you then need to walk through an underground tunnel to the Lao immigration office (daily 6am–8pm). Most people travel on the direct bus from Ubon to Pakse, which waits for passengers to complete formalities, though there's also a songthaew service there from Vang Tao, on the Lao side of the border. In reverse, you simply pay the Lao stamping fee (usually around B30/US$1) and get your Thai visa on arrival for free.

The main attraction in craggy **Pha Taem National Park**, which overlooks Laos and occupies an area of 340 square kilometres bordering the Mekong River, is the **Pha Taem cliff paintings**, though the park also features waterfalls, giant vines and weird rock formations. One of these clusters of odd-shaped rocks is at **Sao Chaliang**, which you pass just after entering the park. It's a group of mushroom-shaped sandstone rocks standing about 10m tall, which have been eroded by centuries of wind and rain and are well worth stopping to admire and photograph.

From Sao Chaliang the road continues to a car park, where there's a restaurant and visitor centre on top of the cliff by the Mekong River. To see the cliff paintings, follow the path from the car park to the left of the visitor centre, which runs down the cliff face and along a shelf in the rock. The bold, childlike paintings cover a 170m stretch of cliff face and are clear proof of the antiquity of the fertile Mekong valley, as they are believed to be between three thousand and four thousand years old – the work of rice-cultivating settlers who lived in huts rather than caves.

Protected from the elements by an overhang, the clearly discernible red-painted images (daubed from a mixture of soil, tree gum and fat) include alien-like forms, handprints and geometric designs as well as massive depictions of animals and enormous fish – possibly the prized catfish still occasionally caught in the Mekong. Try to avoid coming here on a weekend when the place gets swamped with tour buses, as the narrow path along the cliff gets very crowded. It's an especially popular spot at sunrise, this being the first place in Thailand to see the sun in the morning – a full eighteen minutes ahead of Phuket, the westernmost point.

If you continue along the path past the paintings, you'll eventually climb back up to the top of the cliff, via the viewpoint at Pha Mon, taking in fine views of the fertile Mekong valley floor and glimpses of hilly western Laos. It's just under 2km from Pha Mon back to the car park, along a signed trail across the rocky scrub.

ARRIVAL AND ACCOMMODATION   PHA TAEM NATIONAL PARK

By songthaew Aside from using your own wheels, the most practical way to reach the national park is by chartering a songthaew from Khong Chiam, 18km away (see opposite).

National park bungalows Sao Chaliang, ☎ 045 252 581. Book in advance via ⓦ nps.dnp.go.th. If you want to stay and catch the sunrise, you can rent bungalows and large two-person tents near the national park checkpoint at Sao Chaliang, about 2km before the car park. Tents B225, fan B1200, a/c B2000

Sam Phan Bok

120km northeast of Ubon and about 40km southeast of Khemmarat on H2112 • Nov–May only • No public transport; take H2050 northeast from Ubon, then go east on H2337, and finally south on H2112. Alternatively, head north on H2112 from Khong Chiam, but the road is in poor condition

Along 4350km between its source and the sea, the Mekong River creates some striking sights, such as whirlpools, rapids and temporary islands that disappear in the rainy season. One such sight is **Sam Phan Bok** (three thousand holes), an other-worldly landscape where erosion has created an area of thousands of circular pools that are exposed during the dry season when the level of the Mekong River drops by several metres. There's nothing to see during the wet season from June to October, but for the rest of the year you can wander across the bed of the receding river to marvel at the unique terrain that is caused by the erosive power of the rushing river on the soft sandstone. It makes a superb subject for abstract photographs, and the best light is early or late in the day. There are often longtail boats on hand to offer visitors a view of the pools along a few kilometres of the riverbank from the river itself; they charge around B500 for a 30min ride.

Chong Mek and the Lao border

The village of **CHONG MEK**, 44km east of Phibun Mangsahan at the Thai–Lao border, hosts a busy Thai–Lao market and is one of the legal border crossings for foreigners, with onward transport to Pakse.

Even if you're not planning to cross into Laos, the **border market** is good for a browse, especially at weekends when it's at its liveliest. The market on the Thai side of the border is full of Bangkok fashions, jeans and sarongs, but you'll also find traditional herbalists selling dried leaves and roots, lots of basketware sellers and plenty of restaurant shacks serving Thai and Lao dishes.

ARRIVAL AND DEPARTURE   **CHONG MEK**

By bus There are five daily buses between Chong Mek and Bangkok (10hr). Buses run twice a day (9.30am & 3.30pm; 3hr; B200) from Ubon Ratchathani's main bus station to Pakse in Laos, the easiest way to do the trip. Minibuses **also** run to Chong Mek from Ubon Ratchathani bus station (every 30min 7am–3.30pm; 1hr 30min). The bus station in Chong Mek is about 1km from the border, and motorbike taxis and tuk-tuks are on hand to take travellers there.

Yasothon and around

By the beginning of May, Isaan is desperate for rain; there may not have been a significant downpour for six months and the rice crops need to be planted. In northeastern folklore, rain is the fruit of sexual encounters between the gods, so at this time villagers all over Isaan hold the bawdy, merit-making **Bun Bang Fai rocket festival** to encourage the gods to get on with it. The largest and most public of these festivals takes place in the provincial capital of **YASOTHON**, 98km northwest of Ubon, on a weekend in mid-May (check with TAT for dates). Not only are the fireworks spectacular, but the rockets built to launch them are superbly crafted machines in themselves, beautifully decorated and carried proudly through the streets before blast-off. Up to 25kg of gunpowder may be packed into the 9m-long rockets and, in keeping with the fertility theme, performance is everything. Sexual innuendo, general flirtation and dirty jokes are essential components of Bun Bang Fai; rocket-builders compete to shoot their rockets the highest, and anyone whose missile fails to leave the ground gets coated in mud as a punishment.

At other times of the year, Yasothon has little to tempt tourists other than a handful of unremarkable wats and a few evocative old colonial-style shopfronts near **Wat Singh Tha** at the west end of Thanon Srisonthoon.

Ban Sri Than

21km east of Yasothon • Follow Route 202 northeast towards Amnat Charoen as far as kilometre-stone 18.5km, then turn south (right) off the highway for 3km; or take a songthaew (every 30min until noon) or bus (hourly throughout the day) to Ban Ni Khom on Route 202, then a motorbike taxi for the last 3km

5

The most interesting attraction in the surrounding area is the village of **BAN SRI THAN**, where nearly every household is employed in the making of the famous *mawn khwaan* triangular **axe pillows**. However, the scenes of sewing machines surrounded by heaps of cloth are not exactly photo contest winners, so it's really only worth a visit if you plan to buy the product. These pillows (*mawn*), so named because their shape supposedly resembles an axe-head (*khwaan*), have been used in traditional Thai homes for centuries, where it's normal to sit on the floor and lean against a densely stuffed *mawn khwaan*. It's possible to buy the cushions unstuffed so you can actually fit them in your luggage. The price depends on the number of triangular pods that make up the pillow and the number of attached cushions: in Ban Sri Than, a stand-alone ten-triangle pillow costs around B200, or B500–B700 with three attached cushions – about half of what it'll cost in Bangkok or Chiang Mai.

ARRIVAL AND DEPARTURE

By plane The nearest airports are in Roi Et (85km northwest) and in Ubon Ratchathani (100km southeast; see page 459). Nok Air operates two flights a day from Bangkok to Roi Et and seven flights a day to Ubon, while Air Asia has three flights a day to Roi Et and three flights a day to Ubon.

By bus Buses between Ubon and Khon Kaen stop at the bus

YASOTHON

station on Thanon Rattanakhet (21 daily; 3hr–3hr 30min from Khon Kaen, 1hr 30min–2hr from Ubon). Buses to and from Bangkok (9 daily; 8hr) use the same bus station.

Services Thanon Chaeng Sanit is where you'll find the post office and all the main banks, with ATMs and currency exchange facilities.

ACCOMMODATION

If you want to stay here during festival time, book your **hotel** well in advance and be prepared to pay double the normal prices quoted here. The liveliest place to **eat** is at the night market on Thanon Wareerachadet, which runs north off the central section of Thanon Chaeng Sanit.

★ **Green Park Grand** 209/12 Thanon Wareerachadet, just a block west of the bus station ☏ 045 7147 00–4, ⓦ https://bit.ly/2BN4t5w. The cheapest rooms in the building are great value, with bright, clean interiors and coffee-making facilities, while newer rooms in the main building (B900) are bigger and fancier. There's a fitness centre and swimming pool for guests' use, as well as helpful staff and a good restaurant. B450

JP Emerald 36 Thanon Prapa ☏ 045 714 455–6, ⓦ jpemerald.co.th. The *JP Emerald* has large, a/c rooms close to the provincial hall, though the place is a bit run-down and in need of a makeover. Breakfast costs an additional B150. B550

Khon Kaen

At Isaan's centre, **KHON KAEN** is the wealthiest and most sophisticated city in the northeast, seat of a highly respected university with over 30,000 students. There's a noticeably upbeat feel to the place, underlined by its apparently harmonious combination of traditional Isaan culture – huge markets and hordes of street vendors – with flashy shopping plazas and world-class hotels. Its location, 188km northeast of Khorat on the Bangkok–Nong Khai rail line and Highway 2, makes it a convenient resting point, even though a startling modern temple and the provincial museum are the only real sights in town. However, the wider province has some impressive prehistoric credentials, which you can get to grips with at Phuwiang's **dinosaur graveyard** (see page 473), within day-tripping distance of the city. Local silk is another draw; available year-round at outlets across the city, it gets special focus during the annual **Silk and Phuk Siao Festival** (usually Nov 29–Dec 10; check with TAT) when weavers from across the province congregate at the City Hall on Thanon Na Soon Rachakarn to display and sell their fabrics; this is also the chance to witness the moving *phuk siao* ceremony, a traditional friendship-deepening ritual involving the exchange of symbolic wrist strings. During the rest of the year, the foreigners staying in the city tend to be expat husbands of local women, businesspeople, university teachers and international students rather than tourists, though some travellers stop here for **Lao, Chinese and Vietnamese visas**, as these nations have consulates in Khon Kaen.

Wat Nongwaeng

Far southern end of Thanon Klang • 7am–5pm

Khon Kaen's most arresting sight is the enormous nine-tiered pagoda at **Wat Nongwaeng,** also known as Phra Mahathat Kaen Nakhon. Unmissable in its glittering livery of red, white and gold, this breathtakingly grand structure was the brainchild of the temple's famously charismatic and well-travelled abbot, Phra Wisuttikittisan.

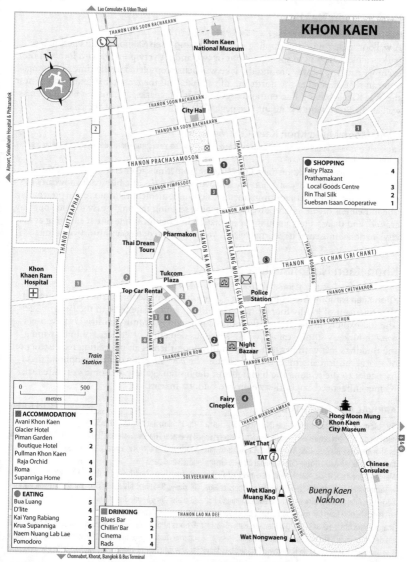

KHON KAEN

SHOPPING	
Fairy Plaza	4
Prathamakant Local Goods Centre	3
Rin Thai Silk	2
Suebsan Isaan Cooperative	1

ACCOMMODATION	
Avani Khon Kaen	1
Glacier Hotel	5
Piman Garden Boutique Hotel	2
Pullman Khon Kaen Raja Orchid	4
Roma	3
Supanniga Home	6

EATING	
Bua Luang	5
D'lite	4
Kai Yang Rabiang	2
Krua Supanniga	6
Naem Nuang Lab Lae	1
Pomodoro	3

DRINKING	
Blues Bar	3
Chillin' Bar	2
Cinema	1
Rads	4

5

The nine-tiered design is said to have been inspired by Myanmar's most sacred stupa, Shwedagon, but the gallery running around each tier is more Lao in style, and the crowning *that* (tower) is typically Thai. Though there has been a temple here since the early 19th century, the pagoda was completed in 1996 to commemorate the 200th anniversary of the province's founding and the Golden Jubilee of King Bhumibol's reign, and measures 50 metres on each side and is 80 metres high. Inside the pagoda, it's worth climbing the stairs in the northeast corner to admire the colourful murals depicting Isaan culture and the beautiful window carvings on each level, and to enjoy the panoramic view of the city and the lake, Bueng Kaen Nakhon, from the ninth tier.

Bueng Kaen Nakhon

In the southeast of town, 500m from the Fairy Plaza • Bike rental (evenings only) B60/hr

A walk or cycle round the rippling waters of **Bueng Kaen Nakhon** and its perimeter park is a pleasant way to spend an hour or two and it's very popular with locals in the evening. A new pathway around the lake was being completed at the time of writing. You can rent bicycles at the north end of the lake, and there are table-tennis tables near the Wat Klang Muang Kao entrance, several kids' playparks, and food stalls all over, as well as the **Bua Luang** restaurant (see page 472) at the north end of the lake.

Hong Moon Mung Khon Kaen City Museum

On the northern shore of Bueng Kaen Nakhon, across from the ornate Chinese temple in the utilitarian building beneath the outdoor amphitheatre • Tues–Sun 9am–5pm • B90

The **Hong Moon Mung Khon Kaen City Museum**, sometimes referred to as the "treasure hall", presents the history of Khon Kaen province in a series of tableaux. It showcases the region's rich cultural heritage, from the first signs of settlement right up to the present day. The museum is organized into five chronological sections, making it easy to find your way around, and there's a fair amount of explanation in English. While not as engaging as the city's national museum, it's worth a visit if you're interested in Isaan history or culture.

Khon Kaen National Museum

North of the centre at Thanon Lung Soon Rachakarn • Wed–Sun 9am–4pm • B100

Khon Kaen National Museum presents a digestible introduction to the region through an assortment of locally found artefacts, some of which date back to the Bronze Age. The star **exhibit** on the ground floor of the museum is a ninth-century Dvaravati-era *sema* (boundary stone), carved with a sensuous depiction of Princess Bhimba wiping the Buddha's feet with her hair. Also on this floor, there is an interesting reconstruction of a local musical ensemble centred around the *pong lang*, a wooden xylophone that's particular to the region. The highlights of the upstairs gallery are some exquisite little Khmer-influenced Lopburi-style bronze Buddha images.

ARRIVAL AND DEPARTURE

KHON KAEN

By plane Khon Kaen airport (☏043 468170), 10km northwest of the city centre, is served by Thai Smile (operated by Thai Airways), Air Asia, Lion Air and Nok Air flights to and from Bangkok. Air Asia also operate one flight a day to Chiang Mai, and one to Hat Yai. Hotel minibuses meet all flights – some hotels provide this service for free, others charge B80–100. Alternatively, pick up a metered taxi (around B80 to central hotels) from the road approaching the airport. The Thai Airways office (☏043 227701; Mon–Fri 8am–5pm) is inside the *Pullman Hotel* on Thanon Prachasamran.

Destinations Bangkok (21 daily; 55min); Chiang Mai (daily; 1hr 15min); Hat Yai (daily; 1hr 50min).

By train The train station (☏043 221 112) is to the southwest of the city centre, a short walk from downtown hotels and bars.

Destinations Ayutthaya (4 daily; 6hr 30min); Bangkok (4 daily; 8–10hr); Khorat (daily; 3hr 20min); Nong Khai (3 daily; 2hr 25min–3hr 30min); Udon Thani (4 daily; 1hr 50min–2hr 30min).

By bus Khon Kaen's bus services, including minibuses, now operate from the terminal to the south of the city centre at the junction of Thanon Mittraphap with the ring road

(☎043 471 563).

Destinations Bangkok (every 30min; 6–7hr); Chiang Mai (12 daily; 10–12hr); Khorat (every 30min; 3hr); Loei (every 30min; 4hr); Nong Khai (7 daily; 3hr 30min); Pattaya (4 daily; 9hr); Phitsanulok (12 daily; 5–6hr); Rayong (6 daily; 11hr); Sukhothai (daily; 6hr); Surin (hourly; 5hr 30min); Ubon Ratchathani (hourly; 4hr–4hr 30min); Udon Thani (every 30min; 2hr–2hr 30min).

GETTING AROUND

By songthaew Numbered and colour-coded songthaews ply the streets 6am–7pm, charging a fixed fare of B9–13. A useful map showing their routes is available at the bus station or at the TAT office.

By tuk-tuk A short tuk-tuk ride within the city should cost you B50–60.

By taxi Taxis tend to congregate near the *Pullman Hotel*, or call ☎043 465777. Ask for the meter to be switched on; short journeys within the city should cost B40–50. Grab (grab.com) also operates in Khon Kaen.

Car rental Avis (☎043 344313, ⓦavisthailand.com) and Budget (☎043 468220, ⓦbudget.co.th) both have desks at the airport. Cars with a driver (B1800/day, excluding fuel) are available at Top Car Rent (☎043 227448), just opposite the *Pullman Hotel* on Thanon Prachasamran. The service here is reliable, and the owners are able to plan customized trips around the northeast.

Motorbike rental Ask around at the bars near the *Pullman Hotel*, which can help arrange a daily rental for about B200/day.

INFORMATION AND TOURS

Tourist information The TAT office (daily 8.30am–4.30pm; ☎043 227714–5, ⓔtatkhkn@tat.or.th) is at 277/20–21 Thanon Klang Muang, at the northwest corner of Bueng Kaen Nakhon.

Tours and trips Thai Dream Tours (☎089 711 8331, ⓦthiadreamtours.com), at the *KK Centrum* hotel building, 33/49 Soi Supatheera, Thanon Si Chan, can arrange trips around the local area to places such as Chonnabot and Phuwiang National Park.

ACCOMMODATION

Khon Kaen has some of the best **accommodation** anywhere in the northeast, from all-out luxury to quirky and clean city hotels.

Avani Khon Kaen 999 Moo4, Thanon Prachasamosorn. ☎043 209888, ⓦavanihotels.com; map p.469. This new hotel, located roughly 1km outside of the city centre, offers stiff competition to the Pullman with its well-equipped rooms, choice of three restaurants, fitness room, spa and excellent service. B1500

Glacier Hotel 141 Thanon Prachasamran ☎043 334999, ⓦglacier-hotel.com; map p.469. A cool, crisply styled, seven-storey hotel that's vaguely themed around ice and snow (yes, there's a/c throughout). There are white pod chairs in the lobby, and the carpeted rooms have unusual touches like see-through glass walls separating the bathroom from the bedroom. There's also a small swimming pool. B1400

Piman Garden Boutique Hotel 6/110 Thanon Klang Muang ☎043 334 111, ⓦpimangardenhotel.com; map p.469. Though all rooms here are spacious and well equipped, it's worth paying a bit extra for the deluxe rooms (B1400), which are brighter than the superior rooms and also have balconies. Breakfast is included, staff are helpful and the location is very convenient. B1100

★**Pullman Khon Kaen Raja Orchid** 9/9 Thanon Prachasamran ☎043 913 333, ⓦpullmanhotels.com; map p.469. This gorgeously appointed, luxury high-rise hotel has extremely comfortable rooms, a swimming pool and spa, and plenty of bars and restaurants. It's shaped in the form of a giant *khaen*, the bamboo panpipes played in northeastern folk music. Significant discounts are often available, which makes it well worth splashing out on. B1755

Roma 50/2 Thanon Klang Muang ☎043 245888; map p.469. The best of several budget hotels in the city centre, the *Roma* is nothing special, but rooms are good value, the place is efficiently run and it has a central location. A/c rooms have a few features lacking in fan rooms, such as fridge, bathtub and padded headboards. Fan B230, a/c B500

★**Supanniga Home** 130/9 Thanon Potisarn ☎089 944 4880, ⓦsupannigahome.com; map p.469. It's well worth heading a couple of kilometres east of Khon Kaen's centre to discover this gorgeous property – just three luxurious villas, all with different design and character, set in a delightfully landscaped garden. It's a wonderful place to relax and enjoy nature, and the restaurant serves excellent Thai cuisine (see below), though it's best for those with their own transport as no buses go near. B4800

EATING, DRINKING AND ENTERTAINMENT

Khon Kaen has a reputation for very **spicy food**, particularly sausages, *sai krog isaan*, which are occasionally available with cubes of raw ginger, onion, lime and plenty of chilli sauce at stalls along Thanon Klang Muang around the *Roma Hotel*. In high season, these and other local favourites – such as pigs' trotters, roast duck and shellfish – can also be sampled at the stalls along the northern edge of lake Bueng Kaen Nakhon. Food stalls pop up across town at dusk, with a

5

particular concentration at the **night bazaar** on the eastern end of Thanon Ruen Rom. **Nightlife** is mainly focused along Thanon Prachasamran, behind the *Pullman Hotel*.

CAFÉS AND RESTAURANTS

Bua Luang At the north end of Bueng Kaen Nakhon ☎0043 222504 ⓦfacebook.com/bualuangkk; map p.469. Set at the northern end of the lake with a variety of different pavilion-style eating areas, this iconic restaurant offers good views, a fresh breeze and tasty Thai dishes, especially seafood. Try the steamed seafood pudding in coconut (B160) or the steamed seabass with chilli and lemon (B320), and wash it down with a cold beer or glass of wine. Daily 10am–11pm.

D'lite 348/17 Thanon Prachasamran, the lane immediately east of the Pullman Hotel ☎043 321124; map p.469. The place to come for stylishly presented Isaan dishes like long bean salad with crispy pork (B119). You can sit outside in the garden, which has soothing water features, or in the small a/c area. Daily 8am–10pm.

Kai Yang Rabiang Thanon Theparak ☎043 243413; map p.469. If you haven't yet tried the holy trinity of Isaan cuisine – grilled chicken, sticky rice and green papaya salad – then here's a good place to sample it. The setting is very simple, but the food, especially the chicken (B160 for a whole one) is superb. Daily 9am–3pm.

★ Krua Supanniga 130/9 Thanon Potisarn ☎089 944 4880; map p.469. The gourmet cuisine in this atmospheric restaurant, which is part of *Supanniga Home*, is beautifully prepared and presented, and makes a great place for a lazy lunch. It features some unusual dishes such as *mu cha muong* (slow steamed pork with sour leaves), and prices are very reasonable (B70–200). Reservations necessary as it is sometimes closed for private functions. Daily 11.30am–8.30pm.

Naem Nuang Lab Lae 61–67 Thanon Klang Muang ☎043 236296; map p.469. Set back from the east side of the main road just north of the *Roma*, this place can be tricky to find, but it's hugely popular with Thai visitors for its à la carte Vietnamese food plus some northeastern standards. Their eponymous speciality is *naem nuang*, Vietnamese spring rolls made with barbecued fermented pork sausage (B90–130 per set), which you assemble yourself from half a dozen or more ingredients of your choice, including lots of fresh coriander, mint, ginger, lemon rind, thin noodles and beansprouts. Daily 9am–9pm.

Pomodoro 348/16 Thanon Prachasamran ☎043 270464; map p.469. Next to *D'lite* on the lane to the east of the *Pullman Hotel*. A popular expat hangout serving good Italian pizzas, pastas and meat dishes. Most dishes are around B200–250, but portions are generous. Eat on the terrace or in the a/c interior. Daily 5–11pm.

BARS AND ENTERTAINMENT

Blues Bar Thanon Prachasamran, just west of the Pullman Hotel ☎085 477 5401 ⓦfacebook.com/bluesbarkhonkaen; map p.469. Very popular for its Western breakfasts as well as its pool tables, reasonably priced drinks and live music at weekends. Daily 9am–11pm

Chillin' Bar Just east of the Pullman Hotel driveway, off Thanon Prachasamran; map p.469. Popular little roadside hut serving strong drinks late into the night; one of several in the area. Daily 6pm–late.

Cinema Fairy Cineplex inside Fairy Plaza, between southern Thanon Na Muang and Klang Muang; map p.469. Tickets B80–120.

Rads 231/2 Thanon Prachasamran ☎043 225 988; map p.469. This one-stop entertainment complex has it all – restaurant and coffee shop, raucous rock and easy-listening live music venues, plus girls dancing on the bar. Coffees around B50, beers around B100. Daily 6pm–late.

SHOPPING

Khon Kaen's shops carry a wide range of regional **arts and crafts**, particularly high-quality Isaan **silk** of all designs and weaves. Itinerant vendors, who you'll sometimes see wandering the main streets with panniers stuffed full of silk and cotton lengths, also offer competitive prices. Usually they're gathered on Thanon Klang Muang around the *Roma Hotel*. On Saturday evenings from 5–11pm, there's a walking street along Thanon Soon Ratchakan, in front of City Hall, where vendors sell T-shirts, bags and other items, food stalls offer local treats and musicians entertain.

Fairy Plaza Between Na Muang and Klang Muang; map p.469. A huge modern mall with all the usual clothes, accessories and mobile phone concessions, plus fast food and a cinema (see opposite). Mon–Fri 10.30am–9.30pm, Sat & Sun 10am–9.30pm.

Prathamakant Local Goods Centre 79/2–3 Thanon Ruen Rom; map p.469. One of the best outlets in Khon Kaen, with a phenomenal selection of gorgeous *mut mee* cotton and silk weaves, as well as clothes, furnishings, triangular axe pillows (B500 for an unstuffed three-seater), *khaen* pipes and silver jewellery. Though it feels touristy, locals buy their home furnishings and dress fabrics here too. Mon–Sat 9am–8pm, Sun 9am–5pm.

Rin Thai Silk 410–412 Thanon Na Muang; map p.469. Stocks a smaller range of Isaan silk, but will tailor clothes too. Mon–Sat 8am–6.30pm, Sun 8am–5pm.

Suebsan Isaan Cooperative 21/2 Thanon Klang Muang; map p.469. Another fair-trade outlet for local craftspeople, which sells Isaan textiles, *mut mee* silks, cottons, basketware, herbal cosmetics, notebooks, purses, T-shirts, scarves and other traditional products. Mon–Sat 8am–5.30pm.

DIRECTORY

5

Consulates The Lao consulate (Mon–Fri 8am–noon & 1–4pm; ☎ 043 393 402) is located 8km north of the city centre at 512 Thanon Mittraphap, opposite Raja City. Thirty-day tourist visas for the trip over the border (see page 490) can be processed here on the spot; fees vary according to the applicant's nationality. The Vietnamese consulate (Mon–Fri 9–11.30am & 1.30–5pm; ☎ 043 242190, ⓦ vnconsulate-khonkaen.mofa.gov.vn) is at 65/6 Thanon Chataphadung, off Thanon Prachasamoson, and the Chinese Consulate (Mon–Fri 9am–12pm; ☎ 043 226873, ⓦ khonkaen.china-consulate.org) is at 142/44 Moo 2, Thanon Rob Bueng.

Hospitals Khon Kaen Ram Hospital (☎ 043 002002, ⓦ khonkaenram.com), on the far western end of Thanon Si Chan, is the main private hospital. The government Srinagarind Hospital (☎ 043 363714) is attached to Khon Kaen University, north of town on Highway 2.

Pharmacy Pharmakon, 104 Thanon Na Muang (☎ 043 237277; Mon–Sat 8.30am–6pm, Sun 8am–1pm).

Tourist police For all emergencies, call the tourist police on ☎ 1155 (free; 24hr).

Around Khon Kaen

The outer reaches of Khon Kaen province hold a couple of places that are worth exploring on **day-trips**. Chonnabot is a good place to see silk weavers at work, while Phuwiang National Park is most famous for dinosaur relics, a paleontological attraction with nine dig sites and its own museum.

Chonnabot

54km southwest of Khon Kaen • Any ordinary Khorat-bound bus to Ban Phae (every 30min), then a songthaew for the final 10km

Khon Kaen makes a reasonable base from which to explore the local silk-weaving centre of **CHONNABOT**. Traditionally a cottage industry, this small town's **silk production** (see page 458) has become centralized over the last few years, and weavers now gather in small workshops in town, each specializing in just one aspect of the process. You can walk in and watch the women (it's still exclusively women's work) at their wheels, looms or dye vats, and then buy from the vendors in the street out front. It's also worth heading 1km west of the town centre to the **Sala Mai Thai** (172 Thanon Changsanit, ☎ 043 286160; Mon–Fri 8am–5pm & Sat–Sun 9am–5pm), an exhibition centre displaying the various stages in the production of silk downstairs, and a variety of hand-woven silk in typical Isaan patterns upstairs. Look for the imposing building on the south side of the road as there's no English sign.

Phuwiang National Park and the Dinosaur Museum

Nai Muang sub-district, Amphur Phuwiang • ☎ 043 358073, ⓦ nps.dnp.go.th/parksdetail.php?id=61&name=PhuWiangNationalPark • **Park** daily 8am–6pm; B200 • **Museum** ☎ 043 438206, Wdmr.go.th; Tues–Sun 9am–5pm; B60

Khon Kaen hit the international headlines in 1976 when the oldest-ever fossil of a tyrannosaur **dinosaur** was unearthed in Phuwiang, about 90km northwest of Khon Kaen, which was made into a national park in 1991. Estimated to be 120 million years old, the fossil measures 6m from nose to tail and has been named *Siamotyrannus isanensis* – Siam for Thailand, and Isan after the northeastern region of Thailand. Before this find at Phuwiang, the oldest tyrannosaur fossils were the 65-million- to 80-million-year-old specimens from China, Mongolia and North America. These younger fossils are twice the size of the *Siamotyrannus*; the latter's age and size have therefore established the *Siamotyrannus* as the ancestor of the *Tyrannosaurus rex* and confirmed Asia as the place of origin of the tyrannosaur genus, which later evolved into various different species.

Many people, particularly children, find the state-of-the-art **Dinosaur Museum**, which is located just before the park entrance, more interesting than the park itself. The air-conditioned museum displays dinosaur bones, models of dinosaurs, including an animated one at the entrance, and many information boards explaining the age of the

5

dinosaurs and reasons they are thought to have become extinct. Also of great interest to children is the **Si Wiang Dinosaur Park**, located about halfway between Phuwiang and the national park, where there are concrete, life-sized models of many species of dinosaur. The park itself features several excavation sites that are spread over a wide area, and the trek to them all can be challenging for very young and very old visitors.

The fossil of the *Siamotyrannus isanensis* is displayed at **Site 9**, which is accessible via the 1.5km track that starts across the road from the visitor centre; from the car park at the end of the track, it's a 500m climb to the quarry. The fossil is an impressive sight for paleontologists, with large sections of the rib cage almost completely intact, but many visitors will wonder what all the fuss is about. **Site 1**, 900m south along a track from Site 9, contains the cream of the other finds, including two previously undiscovered species. The theropod *Siamosaurus suteethorni* (named after the paleontologist Warawut Suteethorn) is set apart from the other, carnivorous, theropods by its teeth, which seem as if they are unable to tear flesh; the 15–20m-long *Phuwiangosaurus sirindhornae* (named in honour of Thailand's Princess Royal) is thought to be a new species of sauropod.

ARRIVAL AND DEPARTURE	PHUWIANG NATIONAL PARK

By bus Non-a/c buses run from Khon Kaen to Phuwiang town (every 30min; about 1hr) – you then need to hire a motorbike taxi to the national park and back (about B300 return).

By car It's easier to rent your own wheels in Khon Kaen (see page 468) than to go by bus. To get to the park, head west out of Khon Kaen on Highway 12, following the signs for Chumpae as far as kilometre-stone 48, marked by a dinosaur statue. Turn right off the main road here, and continue for another 38km along Highway 2038, passing through the small town of Phuwiang, and follow signs for the national park.

ACCOMMODATION AND EATING

There are no bungalows available in the park, but tents are available to rent (B225; book online at ⓦnps.dnp.go.th).

There's a **restaurant** beside the visitor centre.

Udon Thani and around

The capital of an arid sugar-cane and rice-growing province, 137km north of Khon Kaen, **UDON THANI** was given an economic boost during the Vietnam War with the siting of a huge American military base nearby, and despite the American withdrawal in 1976, the town has maintained its rapid industrial and commercial development. Seen as charmless but economically important for many years, Udon has now started to attract more casual visitors, with the city's entertainment plaza and the relaxing Nong Prajak park providing the main focus for a couple of days in the city. By night, the area known as UD Town springs into life, with tourists and locals thronging the pedestrianized streets to eat, chatter and watch local dance troupes. Apart from these places, and the excavated Bronze Age settlement of **Ban Chiang** (see page 477), 50km to the east, there aren't many tourist attractions in the area, though **Phu Phra Bat Historical Park** (see page 494) is as easy to get to from here as from Nong Khai.

Nong Prajak Park

Just west of the TAT office • Bike rental B30–50/hr

Away from the racket of Udon's busier streets is **Nong Prajak Park**, a surprisingly quiet space set around a tranquil, fish-filled lake. Approaching from Thanon Thesa, on the eastern shore of the lake, it's possible to walk across a bridge to the central island. An alternative to feeding the fish (local women sell bags of food) is cycling around the lake's perimeter; bikes can be rented from its northeastern edge.

5

Red Lotus Sea

50km southeast of Udon • Boat ride B300

If you are a nature lover and happen to be in Udon between December and February, it's worth heading south of Udon to see this spectacular sight, though its name, talay bua daeng (red lotus sea) is something of a misnomer. It's a large lake that is smothered with pink water lilies during this period, peaking in late January to early February, though the blooms close before midday, so it needs to be a morning visit. Motorised, plastic boats with canopies holding up to ten people are on hand to take visitors on a 45min tour of the lake, offering great photo opportunities. Some boats stop at an island in the lake where there is a lookout tower offering views over the lake. To get there, head south on Highway 2, then turn east on Highway 2023 to Kumphawapi.

ARRIVAL AND DEPARTURE
UDON THANI

By plane The airport is located 3km southwest of the centre; a/c minibuses meet incoming flights. Thai Airways, Thai Lion Air, Bangkok Airways and Air Asia operate several flights a day from Bangkok to Udon Thani, while Nok Air currently runs three flights a day from Chiang Mai and Air Asia flies daily from Phuket. There are also direct a/c minibuses (B150–200) from the airport that head north to the Friendship Bridge and downtown Nong Khai.

Destinations Bangkok (26 daily; 1hr); Chiang Mai (3 daily; 1hr); Phuket (daily; 1hr 50min).

By train Udon's train station is on the east side of the centre, close to the night market.

Destinations Ayutthaya (4 daily; 7hr 30min–9hr 30min); Bangkok (4 daily; 10–12hr); Khon Kaen (4 daily; 1hr 35min–2hr 15min); Khorat (daily; 4hr 30min–5hr 30min); Nong Khai (3 daily; 40min–1hr).

By bus Buses pull in at a variety of locations, depending on where they've come from: Loei, Phitsanulok and Chiang Mai services use the terminal on the town's western bypass; Nong Khai buses are stationed at Talat Rangsina (Rangsina market, also used by Ban Pheu buses) on the north side of town; and Bangkok, Khorat, Khon Kaen, Nakhon Phanom and Ubon Ban Ratchathani services use the other main terminal on Thanon Sai Uthit, which also has a service direct to Vientiane, across the border in Laos, for those who have arranged their visa in advance.

Destinations Bangkok (every 30min; 9hr); Chiang Mai (10 daily; 11–13hr); Chiang Rai (10 daily; 12–14hr); Khon Kaen (every 30min; 1hr 30min–2hr); Khorat (hourly; 3hr 30min–5hr); Loei (every 30min; 3–4hr); Mukdahan (7 daily; 4hr–4hr 30min); Nakhon Phanom (every 30min; 5hr); Nong Khai (every 30min; 1–2hr); Phitsanulok (13 daily; 7hr); Rayong (7 daily; 12hr); Sakon Nakhon (every 20min; 3hr); That Phanom (7 daily; 4–5hr); Ubon Ratchathani (9 daily; 6hr); Vientiane (Laos; 8 daily; 1hr 30min).

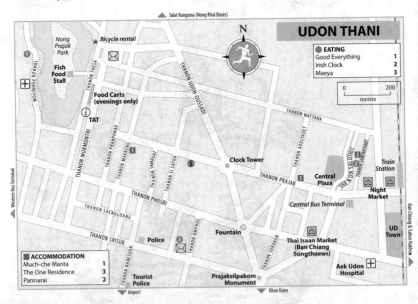

UDON THANI

EATING
Good Everything 1
Irish Clock 2
Maeya 3

ACCOMMODATION
Much-che Manta 1
The One Residence 3
Pannarai 2

GETTING AROUND AND INFORMATION

By songthaew Numbered songthaews ply set routes around town for B10/person (a map is available from TAT); among the more useful routes, #7 connects the central bus terminal with the western bus terminal on the western bypass, while #6 runs the length of Thanon Udon-Dussadi to Talat Rangsina (for buses to Nong Khai).

By tuk-tuk and samlor There are plenty of skylabs, Udon's version of tuk-tuks, for hire (about B70–100 for a medium-length journey). Samlors are cheaper still.

By taxi Taxis (☎080 010 1354) hang around the main bus terminal and Central Plaza, but they don't use their meters, so negotiate a fare before seting off. Grab Cars (grab.com) also operate in Udon and are cheaper.

Car rental Avis (☎042 244770, ⓦavisthailand.com) has a desk at the airport.

Tourist information Udon's TAT office (daily 8.30am–4.30pm; ☎042 325406–7, ⓔtatudon@tat.or.th) is at 16/5 Thanon Mukmontri on the southeast side of Nong Prajak, to the northwest of the centre. The Udon Thani Map (ⓦudonmap.com) website has lots of useful info about the town.

Services Aek Udon Hospital, 555/5 Thanon Phosri (☎042 342555, ⓦaekudon.com), south of the city centre, has international-standard facilities.

Shopping There's a walking street on Thanon Athibodi, just north of the TAT office, on Fridays and Saturday evenings from 5–11pm, but it's not as lively as similar markets in other towns.

ACCOMMODATION

Udon Thani has a good range of accommodation at all levels, from budget to luxury.

Much-che Manta 209-211 Thanon Makkeng ☎042 245222, ⓦmuch-chemanta.com; map p.476. This slick, modern hotel features well-equipped rooms (rain showers, cable TV and minibar) with a range of prices. The cheapest ("Cozy") are a bit cramped, though the biggest ("Fabulous"; B1600) are a good size, with king-sized beds and microwaves as well. A good breakfast is included. B900

★ **Pannarai** 19/8 Thanon Sampantamit ☎042 345111, ⓦthepannaraihotel.com; map p.476. Reliable, central hotel with helpful staff, a fitness centre and an inviting swimming pool. Rooms are big and well lit, with ceiling-to-floor windows. B1580

The One Residence 251/5 Thanon Prajak ☎042 244330, ⓦtheoneud.com; map p.476. With bright, clean rooms in a central location, this place is very popular and often full. Go for a room out back to avoid street noise. B600

EATING, DRINKING AND ENTERTAINMENT

In Udon the main **night market**, on the west side of the train station, is a good place to come for food and cut-price clothing, as is the evening market that sets up in front of Central Plaza. Just south of the train station is **UD Town**, a massive entertainment complex that is *the* commercial face of modern Udon Thani. After dark you'll find street entertainers, dance shows and stalls selling everything from indulgent perfumes to fruit shakes and spicy sausages. Thais and tourists pour into the restaurants, which range from Western fast-food joints to high-end noodle bars, giving the place a real buzz in the evenings. For cheaper eats, head to Thanon Thesa, where several simple bar-restaurants set out low-slung tables in the evening, alongside paint-your-own-pottery and massage stalls.

★ **Good Everything** 254/24 Thanon Prajak ☎042 245544; map p.476. This place opposite one of the entrances to Nong Prajak Park is a great find, and is well named. The ambience is very agreeable, with a choice of seating in a flower-filled garden or in the sparkling white interior. A range of Thai and Western dishes such as matsaman curry (B320) and sirloin steak (B490) is on offer, and both preparation and presentation are very impressive. Prices seem a bit steep but the quality warrants it. Daily 11am–10pm.

Irish Clock 19/5–6 Thanon Sampantamit ☎042 247450; map p.476. Located on the street known as "Farang Street" for its Western-oriented bars, the *Irish Clock* is the place to go for big Western breakfasts, imported beers such as Guinness (B240 a pint) and sports on TV. They also have some large rooms to rent (B750 per night). Daily 8.30am–11pm.

Maeya 79–81 Thanon Rachapatsadu ☎042 223 889; map p.476. On a quiet side street, covering three floors and frequented by a loyal clientele, *Maeya* is well worth tracking down. Its waiters are the best-dressed in town (starched shirts and bow ties), the menu covers a broad range of Thai and Western dishes, some with amusing names, such as pork babygue (read BBQ), and prices are very reasonable. Basic rice dishes from B69 and most main dishes around B120. Ice creams too. Daily 10am–10pm.

Ban Chiang

The excavated Bronze Age settlement of **BAN CHIANG**, 50km east of Udon Thani in sleepy farming country, was listed as a UNESCO World Heritage Site in 1992. It

5

CROSSING THE LAO BORDER VIA THA LI

It's possible to hop on a bus in Loei in the morning, exit the country at **Tha Li** by the Mekong River and hop off in **Luang Prabang** in the afternoon. Visa on arrival is available at the Thai–Lao Nam Heuang Friendship Bridge, and the immigration office is open from 8am to 6pm.

---

achieved worldwide fame in 1966, when a rich seam of archaeological remains was accidentally discovered: clay pots, uncovered in human graves alongside sophisticated **bronze** objects, were eventually dated to around 2000 BC, implying the same date for the bronze pieces. Ban Chiang has been hailed as the Southeast Asian vanguard of the Bronze Age, about three hundred years after Mesopotamia's discovery of the metal.

The village of Ban Chiang is unremarkable nowadays, although its fertile setting is attractive and the villagers, who still weave (and sell) especially rich and intricate lengths of silk and cotton *mut mee*, are noticeably friendly to visitors. The museum here, which focuses on the Bronze Age finds, is one of the region's most interesting. Though there are a few simple homestays and guesthouses in town, it's better to take in Ban Chiang on a day trip from Udon Thani.

National Museum

Towards the north of the village • Tues–Sun 9am–4pm • B150

The village's fine **National Museum** has managed to retain some of the choicest Bronze Age finds, which it fleshes out with a fascinating and thoughtful rundown of Ban Chiang culture, including its agriculture, pathology and burial rites. It also houses the country's best collection of characteristic late-period Ban Chiang clay pots, with their red whorled patterns on a buff background, which were used as funeral offerings – although not of prime historical significance, these pots have become an attractive emblem of Ban Chiang, and are freely adapted by local souvenir producers.

Excavation Site

In the grounds of Wat Pho Si Nai, on the east side of the village • Daily 8.30am–6pm • Same ticket as the museum

In the grounds of Wat Pho Si Nai, on the east side of the village, part of an early dig has been covered over and opened to the public. A **large burial pit** has been left exposed to show how and where artefacts were found, providing an interesting insight into the work of archaeologists here.

ARRIVAL AND GETTING AROUND   BAN CHIANG

By bus and samlor Catch a Sakon Nakhon-bound bus from the Thanon Sai Uthit terminal in Udon (1hr) to Nong Mek and then a tuk-tuk (about B100) for the last 10km or so from the main road to the village.

Getting around Bicycles are available from shops near the museum (around B50/day) for exploring the surrounding countryside, which looks particularly attractive during the rice-growing season (July–November).

Loei

Most visitors carry on from Udon Thani due north to Nong Khai, but making a detour via **LOEI**, 147km to the west, takes you within range of several towering national parks and sets you up for a lazy tour along the Mekong River. The capital of a province renowned for the unusual shapes of its stark, craggy mountains, Loei is also the crossroads of one of Thailand's least-tamed border regions, with all manner of illegal goods coming across from Laos. This trade may have been reined in – or perhaps spurred on – by the opening in 2008 of a 3km-long bridge across the Heuang River at Ban Nakaseng in Tha Li district, 80km northwest of Loei, to Sainyabuli province in Laos. Despite its frontier feel, the town, lying along the west bank of the small Loei River, is friendly and offers legitimate products of its own, such as sweet tamarind paste and pork sausages, which are for sale along Thanon Charoenrat, Loei's main street, and the adjacent Thanon Oua Aree. But Loei is really only useful as a transport hub and a base for the nearby national parks. The most popular are Phu Kradung National Park, which has some excellent walking trails, Nam Nao National Park, home to around a hundred different species of mammals, and Phu Reua National Park, which affords magnificent views over Laos.

ARRIVAL AND INFORMATION   LOEI

By air Both Nok Air and Air Asia currently operate two flights a day to and from Don Muang airport, Bangkok. Loei's airport is about 5km south of town on H201; a taxi into town should cost around B150.

By bus The bus terminal (📞042 811706) is on Thanon Maliwan, the main through north–south road (Highway 201), about 2.5km south of the centre. Two daily buses to Luang Prabang (📞042 811706) leave at 8am and 10am, arriving at 5pm and 7pm respectively, and cost B700. A tuk-tuk to the bus terminal costs around B60.

Destinations Bangkok (hourly; 9hr); Chiang Khan (every 30min; 1hr 15min); Chiang Mai (4 daily; 9–11hr); Khon Kaen (hourly; 3hr); Lom Sak (2 daily; 3hr); Luang Prabang (Laos; 2 daily; 9hr); Nong Khai (daily via Pak Chom; 6–7hr); Phitsanulok (3 daily; 4hr); Sang Khom (daily; 3hr); Udon Thani (every 30min; 3hr).

Tourist information The TAT office (daily 8.30am–4.30pm; 📞042 812812, ✉tatloei@tat.or.th), on Thanon Charoenrat, has information about the region's many national parks, including Phu Kradung and Phu Reua to the west.

Services The tourist police have an office on Thanon Maliwan (📞042 861164 or 📞1155).

Shopping On Saturday evenings from 4–10pm, Thanon Charoenrat in front of the TAT office is closed to traffic while the weekly walking street takes over.

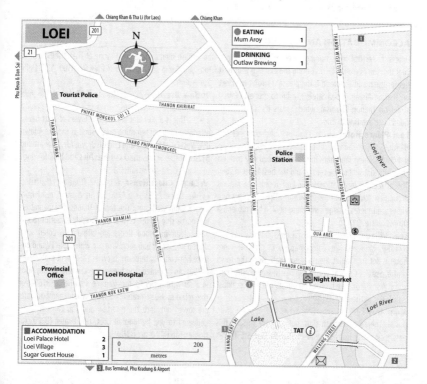

5

PHI TA KON

One reason to make a special trip to Loei province is to attend the unique rainmaking **festival of Phi Ta Kon**, or Bun Phra Wet, held over three days either at the end of June or the beginning of July (check ⓦtourismthailand.org near the time for exact dates) in the small town of **Dan Sai**, 80km to the southwest of the provincial capital. In order to encourage the heavens to open, townsfolk dress up as spirits in colourful patchwork rags and fierce, brightly painted masks (made from coconut palm fronds and the baskets used for steaming sticky rice), then rowdily parade the town's most sacred Buddha image round the streets while making fun of as many onlookers as they can, waving wooden phalluses about and generally having themselves a whale of a time. Top folk and country musicians from around Isaan perform in the evenings during Phi Ta Kon; the afternoon of the second day of the festival sees the firing off of dozens of bamboo rockets, while the third day is a much more solemn affair, with Buddhist sermons and a purification ceremony at Wat Phon Chai. The carnival can be visited in a day from Loei (ask at Loei's TAT office for transport details), though rooms are hard to come by at this time. The town's main permanent attraction is the **Dan Sai Folk Museum** at Wat Phon Chai on Thanon Kaew Asa, the town's high street (daily 8am–5pm; free), which shows the steps in building the masks, and has an impressive collection of vivid costumes and masks.

ACCOMMODATION
DAN SAI

Phunacome Resort 461 Moo 3, Ban Doen, 2km east of Dan Sai ⓣ042 892005–6, ⓦphunacomeresort.com. This laidback resort has a water buffalo theme, with many statues and a few real ones on the grounds. Choose between bungalows on stilts and rooms in a two-storey block; all are sumptuously furnished and enjoy great views. It's also a "green" resort, so it's smoke-free and the restaurant uses organic ingredients. If you're looking for luxury accommodation as a base for visiting Loei's national parks, this is your spot. B4200

ACCOMMODATION AND EATING

Unless it's festival time, finding a decent place to stay in Loei shouldn't be a problem. During the evening your best bet for Isaan and Thai food is the pleasant **night market** on Thanon Ahaan ('Food Street'), a broad, pedestrianized street off Thanon Chumsai, which wears its "Clean Food, Good Taste" signs with pride.

Loei Palace Hotel 167/4 Thanon Charoenrat ⓣ042 815668–73, ⓦmosaic-collection.com/loeipalace; map p.479. A shining landmark in the landscaped city park on the southeast side of the centre, and the best hotel in Loei. The attractive, international-standard rooms are ranged around an echoing, full-height atrium. They all enjoy fine views, and there's a large swimming pool, a hot tub and a fitness centre. B1250

Loei Village 17/62 Soi 3, Thanon Nokkaew. ⓣ042 811599. ⓦloeivillages.com; map p.479. This 45-room hotel is set in a quiet area a short walk from the town centre. Spacious rooms with deep mattresses on the beds and stylish decor. Free bicycles for guests' use and breakfast is included in the price. B1500

Mum Aroy 22/1 Thanon Sert Sri ⓣ042 833669; map p.479. There's no English sign, but it's easy to spot this eatery near the northern end of Thanon Sert Sri. There's an English menu and a good range of Thai dishes such as tom yam kung (B120) and stir-fries for B100–120. Daily 5pm–3am.

Outlaw Brewing 22/24 Thanon Sert Sri ⓣ096 695 8784, ⓦfacebook.com/outlawbrewingloei; map p.479. This is a pleasant surprise for lovers of craft beers, offering a range of tempting brews such as the Showdown IPA, West Coast Pale Ale and English Brown Ale, all at around B120 a bottle. Serves snacks such as fries and buffalo wings too. Daily 6pm–midnight.

★ **Sugar Guest House** 4/1 Soi 2, Thanon Wisuttitep ⓣ042 812982; map p.479. Set in a quiet residential area a 5min walk from the top of Thanon Charoenrat on the north side of the centre. The bright, colourful rooms with gleaming wood floors are either fan-cooled with shared hot-water bathrooms, or a/c with cable TV and en-suite hot-water bathrooms. Bicycles (B50) and motorbikes (B250) can be rented, and the owners can arrange day-trips in a car with driver to, for example, Phu Reua (B1600) or the relaxing Huay Krating (B500), where bamboo rafts are towed out onto the reservoir and you can eat lunch delivered to you by longtail boat. Good rates (B200) for singles. Fan B270, a/c B380

Phu Kradung National Park

80km south of Loei • Oct–May dawn–dusk • B400 • ☎ 042 810833–4, ⓦ nps.dnp.go.th

The most accessible and popular of the parks in Loei province, **PHU KRADUNG NATIONAL PARK** protects a grassy 1300m plateau whose temperate climate supports a number of tree, flower and bird species not normally found in Thailand. Walking trails crisscross much of sixty-square-kilometre Phu Kradung (Bell Mountain), and you could spend three days here exploring them fully – you'll need one night as a minimum, as the trip from Loei to the top of the plateau and back can't be done comfortably in a day. It was opened in 1962 as the country's second national park and is particularly busy at weekends and during national holidays, when the main headquarters up on the plateau is surrounded by a sea of tents.

The attractions of the mountain change with the seasons. October is muddy after the rains, but the waterfalls that tumble off the northwestern edge of the plateau are in full cascade and the main trail is green and shady. December brings out the maple leaves; by February the waterfalls have disappeared and the vegetation on the lower slopes has been burnt away. April is good for rhododendrons and wild roses, which in Thailand are only found at such high altitudes as this.

Among the park's **wildlife**, mammals such as elephants, sambar deer and gibbons can be seen very occasionally, but they generally confine themselves to the evergreen forest on the northern part of the plateau, which is out of bounds to visitors. In the temperate pines, oaks and beeches that dot the rest of the plateau you're more likely to spot resident **birds** such as jays, sultan tits and snowy-browed flycatchers if you're out walking in the early morning and evening.

The trails

The challenging main **trail** leads from the Sri Taan visitor centre, at the base of the mountain, 5.5km up the eastern side of Phu Kradung, passing occasional refreshment stalls, and becoming steeper and rockier on the last 1km, with wooden steps over the most difficult parts; most people take at least three hours, including rest stops. It's a good idea to hire a porter (around B30/kg) to carry your gear so that you can enjoy the surroundings on the walk. The main trail is occasionally closed for maintenance, when a parallel 4.5km trail is opened up in its place. At the end of the actual climb, the unbelievable view as your head peeps over the rim more than rewards the effort: flat as a playing field, the broad plateau is dotted with odd clumps of pine trees thinned by periodic lightning fires, which give it the appearance of a country park.

Several feeder trails fan out from here, including a 9.5km path along the precipitous southern edge that offers sweeping views of Dong Phaya Yen, the untidy range of mountains to the southwest that forms the unofficial border between the northeast and the central plains. Another trail heads along the eastern rim for 2.5km to Pha Nok An – also reached by a 2km path east from the main visitor centre – which looks down on neat rice fields and matchbox-like houses in the valley below, an outlook that's especially breathtaking at sunrise.

ARRIVAL AND INFORMATION

PHU KRADUNG NATIONAL PARK

By public transport To get to the park, take any bus from Loei to Khon Kaen (every 30min; 1hr 30min) or Khon Kaen to Loei (every 30min; 2hr 30min) and get off at the village of Phu Kradung, then hop on a songthaew for the remaining 5km to the Sri Taan visitor centre.

Tourist information The well-organized Sri Taan visitor

centre (daily Oct–May 8.30am–4.30pm) at the base of the plateau has a trail map. You can leave your gear at the visitor centre, or hire a porter to carry it to the top for you. The main visitor centre, which also gives out maps, is up on the plateau at Wang Kwang, 8km from the Sri Taan visitor centre.

ACCOMMODATION AND EATING

It's best to avoid going up and back down the mountain in one day, so try to stay here if you can. Beginning the

5

ascent after 2pm is not permitted. Simple restaurants at Wang Kwang rustle up inexpensive, tasty food from limited ingredients, so there's no need to bring your own provisions.

Sri Taan There are four national park bungalows at Sri Taan, with the added bonus of hot water. Each sleeps four people. These tend to take the overflow when accommodation on the mountain itself is full. B1200

Wang Kwang Up on the plateau at the main visitor centre, 8km from the Sri Taan visitor centre ⓦ nps.dnp.go.th. There are over twenty bungalows and rooms (mattresses only, no beds) sleeping four to twelve people here, most with hot-water bathrooms; at busy times it's best to reserve in advance. There are also fully equipped tents for rent, sleeping two people. Tents B250, rooms B900, bungalows B2400

Nam Nao National Park

160km south of Loei by road • Daily 6am–6pm • B200 • ☎ 056 729002 or ☎ 081 9626236, ⓦ nps.dnp.go.th

With its tallest peak reaching 1271m, **Nam Nao National Park** is easily visible among the undulating sandstone hills of the Phetchabun range. However, it remains a seldom-visited place, at least as far as tourists go, with plenty of wildlife and some good, challenging hikes.

At just under a thousand square kilometres, Nam Nao is home to a healthy wildlife population: around a hundred mammal species, including large animals such as forest elephant and banteng and a handful of tigers, and more-often-seen barking deer, gibbons and leaf monkeys, as well as over two hundred bird species. These creatures thrive in habitats ranging from tropical bamboo and banana stands to the dominant features of dry evergreen forest, grasslands, open forest and pine stands that look almost European.

Though the park was established in 1972, it remained a stronghold for guerrillas of the Communist Party of Thailand until the early 1980s and was long regarded as unsafe for visitors. Still much less visited than Phu Kradung (see page 481), it can provide a sense of real solitude. The range of wildlife here also benefited from a physical isolation that stopped abruptly in 1975, when Highway 12 was cut through the park and poachers could gain access more easily. However, as the park adjoins the Phu Khieo Wildlife Sanctuary, there is beneficial movement by some species between the two areas.

The trails

A good network of clearly marked circular forest **trails** begins near the **park headquarters**, ranging from a 1km nature trail that is often teeming with butterflies to a 6km track known for occasional elephant sightings; another 3.5km trail climbs through mixed deciduous forest to the Phu Kor outlook, with its sweeping views across to Phu Phajit.

Other trails can be accessed directly from **Highway 12**, most of them clearly signposted from the road: at kilometre-stone 39, a steep climb up 260 roughly hewn steps leads to the Tham Pha Hong viewpoint, a rocky outcrop offering stunning panoramas of the park; at kilometre-stone 49, there's a 4km nature trail taking in Suan Son Dang Bak viewpoint; and at kilometre-stone 67, a 700m trail leads to the beautiful Haew Sai waterfall, best seen during or immediately after the rainy season. Experienced hikers can reach the top of Phu Phajit along a rugged trail which begins from kilometre-stone 69; you need to hire a guide from the visitor centre (best booked in advance) for the steep six-hour climb.

ARRIVAL AND DEPARTURE

NAM NAO NATIONAL PARK

By bus Several buses a day run through the park at irregular times from the bus stations in Khon Kaen, Phitsanulok and Loei – all about 2–3hr journeys. The driver drops passengers off at the access road to the park headquarters.

By car The turn-off to the park headquarters is on Highway 12; look out for the sign at kilometre-stone 50, 147km west of Khon Kaen and 160km by road from Loei. The park entrance, where you'll be asked to pay, is 2km from the main road.

INFORMATION AND ACCOMMODATION

5

Tourist information Once you've paid the admission fee, walk or hitch the 2km down the road past the park HQ to the visitor centre, where you can pick up an English-language brochure that contains a rough sketch map of the park.

Accommodation There are a dozen or so bungalows and a campsite near the visitor centre. Stalls near the headquarters sell simple meals. Camping per person B30, four-person unit B1000

Phu Reua National Park

50km west of Loei • B200 • ☎ 088 509 5299, ⓦ nps.dnp.go.th

The 120-square-kilometre **PHU REUA NATIONAL PARK** gets the name "Boat Mountain" from its resemblance to an upturned sampan, with the sharp ridge of its hull running southeast to northwest. The highest point of the ridge, Yod Phu Reua (1365m), offers one of the most spectacular panoramas in Thailand: the land drops away sharply on the Laos side, allowing views over toy-town villages and the Heuang and Mekong rivers to countless green-ridged mountains spreading towards Luang Prabang. To the northwest rises Phu Soai Dao (2120m) on the Laos border; to the south are the Phetchabun mountains.

In the park itself, a day's worth of well-marked trails fans out over the mountain's meadows and pine and broad-leaved evergreen forests, taking in gardens of strange rock formations, orchids that flower year-round, the best sunrise viewpoint, Loan Noi, and, during and just after the rainy season, several waterfalls. The most spectacular **viewpoint**, Yod Phu Reua (Phu Reua Peak), is an easy 1km stroll or songthaew ride (B10) from the top of the summit road. The park's population of barking deer, wild pigs and pheasants has declined over recent years, but you may be lucky enough to spot one of 26 bird species, which include the crested serpent-eagle, green-billed malkoha, greater coucal, Asian fairy-bluebird, rufescent prinia and white-rumped munia, as well as several species of babbler, barbet, bulbul and drongo.

Warm clothes are essential on cool-season nights – the lowest temperature in Thailand (-4°C) was recorded here in 1981 – and even by day the mountain is usually cool and breezy.

ARRIVAL AND INFORMATION

PHU REUA NATIONAL PARK

The 9km paved road north from the village of Ban Phu Reua on Highway 21 to the summit means the park can get crowded at weekends, though during the week you'll probably have the place to yourself. The headquarters and Visitor Centre One are located 4km after the checkpoint on the summit road (where you'll pay the admission charge).

By bus and songthaew There's no organized public transport up the steep summit road – regular Lom Sak and Phitsanulok buses (3 daily; 1hr 30min) from Loei can drop you at the turn-off to the park on Highway 203, but then

you'll have to walk/hitch or charter a songthaew (around B700, including waiting time).

By bike The easiest way of accessing Phu Reua is probably to rent a motorbike at the *Sugar Guest House* in Loei (see page 480).

Tourist information Visitor Centre One is 4km after the entrance checkpoint, and has a trail map and a simple restaurant. Visitor Centre Two (Phuson), a 3km walk or 5.5km drive further up the mountain near Hin Sam Chan waterfall, boasts several restaurants and is at the heart of the mountain's network of paths.

ACCOMMODATION AND EATING

You can sleep in government-owned **bungalows** inside the park, which offer easy access to the trails. There are also plenty of private accommodation options, both on Highway 21 around Ban Phu Reua and on the summit road itself. *Phunacome Resort* in Dan Sai (see page 480) is about 40km southwest of the park. There are several **restaurants** and coffee shops along the main road in town.

Phupet Hill Resort 369 Moo 7, 800m up the summit

road ☎ 042 039853 or ☎ 081 320 2874. A small and friendly place with large, attractive rooms and chalets with hot water, a/c and TV. Fan B700, a/c B1500

Phu Rua Pochana Opposite the post office on Highway 21 ☎ 042 899159. A great place to enjoy a range of classic Thai dishes including spicy salads, stir-fried morning glory and prawns fried with ferns. Most main dishes B100–150. Daily 10am–10pm.

5

Phu Rua Resort 163 Moo 2, 2km towards Loei from the turn-off to the national park. ☎042 899048 📧 phuruaresort@hotmail.com. This ageing resort is a bit run-down but enjoys a great location, with views of a rushing stream from spacious balconies at the back of the resort. It also has a decent restaurant and helpful staff. B2000

Visitor Centre One There are six four- to six-berth national park bungalows with hot showers at Visitor Centre One. B2000–3000

Chiang Khan

A road runs beside the Mekong for 630km, linking the fast-growing border town of Mukdahan with **CHIANG KHAN**, a friendly town 55km north of Loei, which happily hasn't been entirely converted to concrete yet. Rows of shuttered wooden shophouses stretch out in a 2km ribbon parallel to the river, which for much of the year runs red with what locals call "the blood of the trees": rampant deforestation on the Lao side causes the rust-coloured topsoil to erode into the river. The town has only two streets – the main through-route (Highway 211), also known as **Thanon Sri Chiang Khan**, and **Thanon Chai Khong** on the waterfront – with a line of sois connecting them, numbered from west to east. Both streets are bordered by wooden shophouses, giving the town an air of Old Siam, and a new riverside promenade is an added attraction for the Bangkokians who flock here at weekends, particularly in the cool season. As well as soaking up the atmosphere along Thanon Chai Khong, which is closed to traffic from 5–10pm each evening, most visitors to Chiang Khan join a **boat trip** on the Mekong River. There's a cool vibe to the place, with entrepreneurial young Thais setting up quirky new gift shops and guesthouses all the time and there are a few interesting sights to see out of town.

Wat Tha Khaek

To get here, travel about 3km east of town along the main highway, then turn north towards the river

Wat Tha Khaek, a formerly ramshackle forest temple, has, on the back of millions of bahts' worth of donations from Thai tourists, embarked on an ambitious but slow-moving building programme in a bizarre mix of traditional and modern styles. The result is a temple that looks half finished, but if you grow weary of looking at the retro memorabilia that seems to clutter the main hotel street, it makes for a refreshing change.

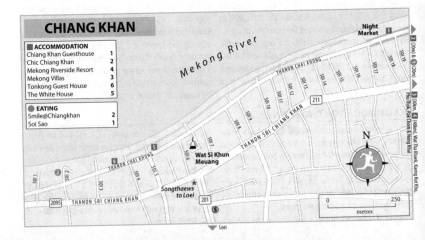

CHIANG KHAN

■ **ACCOMMODATION**
Chiang Khan Guesthouse	1
Chic Chiang Khan	2
Mekong Riverside Resort	4
Mekong Villas	3
Tonkong Guest House	6
The White House	5

● **EATING**
Smile@Chiangkhan	2
Soi Sao	1

> ## THE MAGNIFICENT MEKONG
> The **Mekong** is one of the great rivers of the world and the third longest in Asia, after the Yangtse and the Yellow rivers. From its source 4920m up on the east Tibetan plateau it roars down through China's Yunnan province – where it's known as Lancang Jiang, the "Turbulent River" – before snaking its way a little more peaceably between Myanmar and Laos, and then, by way of the so-called "Golden Triangle", as the border between Thailand and Laos. After a brief shimmy into rural Laos via Luang Prabang, the river reappears in Isaan to form 750km of the border between Thailand and Laos. From Laos it crosses Cambodia and continues south to Vietnam, where it splinters into the many arms of the Mekong Delta before flowing into the South China Sea, 4350km from where its journey began.

Kaeng Kut Khu

East of town, about 2km along a side road from Wat Tha Khaek • Boats B400/30min

A couple of kilometres east of Wat Tha Khaek, the river runs over rocks at a wide bend to form the modest rapids of **Kaeng Kut Khu**. Set against the forested hillside of imaginatively named Phu Yai (Big Mountain), it's a pretty enough spot, with small restaurants and souvenir shops shaded by trees on the river bank. If you're feeling brave, try the local speciality *kung ten*, or "dancing shrimp" – fresh shrimp served live with a lime juice and chilli sauce. Boats can be rented here for a pootle around the rapids – you can also get a boat here from Chiang Khan (see box opposite).

Phu Thok

Daily 5am–6pm • Head east from Chiang Khan on Highway 211, then just beyond the turn-off to Wat Tha Khaek and Kaeng Kut Khu to the north, turn south along 3km of rough paved road, before parking up (B20) and hopping on a songthaew (B25) for a last 2km to the summit

With your own transport you could continue your explorations to **Phu Thok**, an isolated hill topped by a communications mast to the south of town. From there, you'll be rewarded with splendid views of Chiang Khan, the Mekong and the striking patchwork of fields in the broad valley to the south. It's especially popular at sunrise in the cool season, when crowds of Thais come to look out over a sea of mist.

ARRIVAL AND GETTING AROUND
CHIANG KHAN

By bus and songthaew Big, slow songthaews (roughly every 30min) and buses from Loei (roughly hourly) stop at the west end of town near the main junction of Highway 201 (the road from Loei) and Highway 211.
Destinations Bangkok (6 daily; 9–11hr); Khorat (hourly; 7hr); Loei (hourly, plus frequent songthaews; 45min–1hr).

By bicycle and motorbike Most of Chiang Khan's guesthouses rent out bicycles (B50–100/day) and motorbikes (B200–250/day).

ACCOMMODATION

Truly budget accommodation is not easy to find in Chiang Khan as wealthy Thais tend to holiday here, which pushes prices up. Most guesthouses and hotels can arrange boat trips and bus tickets.

Chiang Khan Guesthouse 282 Thanon Chai Khong, near Soi 19 ☎042 033 282; map p.484. Chiang Khan's best budget option, offering fan and a/c rooms, plus a dorm in a friendly, well-kept old wooden house with wonky floorboards and a riverside balcony upstairs, where a couple of rooms have good river views. There are mosquito nets and some rooms share hot-water bathrooms. The owner, Mr Ong, knows a lot about the area, and also offers free coffee and bicycle rental to all guests. Dorm B150, fan B300, a/c B600

Chic Chiang Khan 290 Thanon Chai Khong, opposite soi 20 ☎089 900 9788, ⓦfacebook.com/chicchiangkhanhotel; map p.484. This modern, minimalist place has an ideal location at the eastern end of Thanon Chai Khong. Rooms are well-equipped, if a little on the small side. Some rooms have river views and there are free bicycles for guests to use. Breakfast at Soi Sao (opposite) is included. B1500

Mekong Riverside Resort and Camping 182 Moo 5, Huai Phichai, Pak Chom. About 48km northeast of Chiang Khan, 8km east of Pak Chom and 55km west of Sangkhom. ☎082 272 7472 ⓦmekongriverside.com; map p.484. This small, modern resort enjoys a peaceful location on the banks of the Mekong River, and is run by a knowledgeable American/Thai couple. The four rooms are well-designed and

5

BOAT TRIPS FROM CHIANG KHAN

Most guesthouses can arrange these tours, or variations of them, charging per boat. Alternatively go to the jetty in front of Wat Si Khun Muang and ask boat owners there.

Kaeng Kut Khu (See opposite). About B400/boat for a 30min ride.

Sunset on the Mekong The most basic of the boat trips, giving you the chance to see Chiang Khan from the water when the sunlight is at its best. B1000/boat, lasts around 1hr.

Upstream Upstream trips head west, gliding round a long, slow bend in the Mekong to the mouth of the Heuang River tributary, 20km from Chiang Khan, where the Mekong enters Thailand from Laos. There are fine views from Phra Yai, a 20m-tall golden Buddha standing on a hilltop at the confluence. Best undertaken in the afternoon, returning at sunset. B2500/boat, around 3hr.

have private balconies, while tents are also available for rent. Evening boat trips on the river cost B800 a boat for two people, and the kitchen serves up some delicious food. Perfect for an away-from-it-all escape. Tents B400, rooms B1590

★ **Mekong Villas** 96 Moo 6, Thanon Leab Mekong River, km 53, Ban Kok Pai, Pak Chom district (about 30km northeast of Chiang Khan and 15km west of Pak Chom) ☎089 810 0498, ⊛mekongvillas.com; map p.484. This dreamlike location with just three traditional Thai villas is part of the aptly named "Secret Retreats" group. Occupying a promontory with fabulous views of the Mekong, the villas are furnished with every luxury, including an infinity pool. The River House (B11,235) is the best of the three, with glorious views from its balcony. Ideal for a splurge such as a honeymoon. B3370

Tonkong Guesthouse 62/1 Thanon Chai Khong, between sois 3 & 4 ☎042 821879, ✉ben_jama@hotmail.com; map p.484. A good variety of bright, clean and airy rooms (though mattresses are rather thin), including an en-suite family room that sleeps six (B2000) and three simple rooms with fan and a shared bathroom. Owner Ben (female) runs a cooking course (B500) which includes a trip to the local market. Fan B400, a/c B600

The White House 112 Thanon Chai Khong, near Soi 5 ☎089 529 2698; map p.484. This spacious, colonial-style white mansion adorned with green shutters and hung with modern art has loads of character. Its four rooms have ensuite bathrooms, wooden floors and canopied beds, and breakfast is included in the price. There's also a pretty garden terrace and restaurant overlooking the river. B1500

EATING

One of the best places to eat is at the **night market**, which sets up along Thanon Chai Khong every night, with most stalls towards the eastern end, serving up everything from chicken on a stick to sweet, freshly made pancakes.

★ **Smile@Chiangkhan** 23/3 Moo 1, at the river end of Soi 2 ☎088 563 6377 ⊛facebook.com/SmileatChiangkhan; map p.484. This newish, two-storey restaurant offers fantastic river views from a terrace or air-conditioned interior, as well as dishes such as spicy

seafood stir-fry (B180). Smoothies (B65), beers and wine are available too, and service is good. Daily 11am–10pm.

Soi Sao At the river end of Soi 20, opposite Chic Chiang Khan Hotel ☎042 821 314; map p.484. A great spot for a cheap breakfast, serving up khao tom (rice soup, B30) and Indochina pan-fried eggs (B35) for breakfast, with a few curries and stir-fries served for lunch. Mon–Fri 6am–3pm, Sat–Sun 6am–9pm.

Sang Khom and around

The scenery downstream from Chiang Khan is still relatively wild, with just a couple of small towns dotted between the stretches of lush vegetation. Unfortunately there's no public transport along the river road between Chiang Khan and the otherwise forgettable town of Pak Chom, 41km downriver, so having your own wheels in this area is handy, if not vital. With the flexibility of a car or bike, a pleasant stopover on the much longer journey to Nong Khai is the peaceful town of **SANG KHOM**, about 60km east of Pak Chom, which has some basic amenities and a smile-inducing location by the water.

Than Tip Falls

3km south off Highway 211, just 14km west of Sang Khom

Than Tip Falls is well worth seeking out from May to November, though there's little water from December to April. The 20m-high waterfall splashes down into a rock pool overhung by jungle on three sides; from here, a steep stairway leads to a bigger waterfall that has a good pool for swimming, and if you can face the climb you can explore still higher levels.

Sang Khom

Staying in **SANG KHOM**, which straggles along the tree-shaded south bank of the Mekong about 60km east of Pak Chom, puts you in the heart of an especially lush stretch of the river within easy striking distance of several backroad villages and temples – a lovely guesthouse here offers bike rental and boat trips. It's becoming popular with Thai visitors as a quieter riverside alternative to Chiang Khan, and a few kitsch resorts have sprung up along the main road (Highway 211).

Wat Pha Tak Sua

2km southeast of Sangkhom. By road, follow Highway 211 east of Sangkhom for 12km, then turn right on to rural road 4028 and follow signs for another 8km

This hilltop temple had hardly any visitors until recently, when a U-shaped 'skywalk' was constructed with see-through walls and floor, jutting out from a cliff, allowing visitors superb views over the Mekong River and Laos from a considerable height. Since an appearance on Thai TV, it's now overrun, especially at weekends, with visitors, jostling to snap a selfie in this remote location.

Wat Hin Maak Peng

19km east of Sang Khom on Route 211

Overlooking a narrow section of the Mekong, **Wat Hin Maak Peng** is a famous meditation temple, popular with Thai pilgrims and rich donors. The long white boundary wall, huge modern buildings and extensive riverside gardens are evidence of the temple's prosperity, but its reputation is in fact based on the asceticism of the monks of the Thammayut sect, who keep themselves in strict poverty and allow only one meal a day to interrupt their meditation. The flood of merit-makers, however, proved too distracting for the founder of the wat, Luang Phu Thet, who before his death in 1994 decamped to the peace and quiet of Wat Tham Kham near Sakon Nakhon. Further east, between Tha Bo and Ban Nong Song Hong, the main route to Nong Khai passes Wat Phra That Bang Phuan (see page 494).

ARRIVAL AND INFORMATION

SANG KHOM AND AROUND

By bus Buses run between Sang Khom and Bangkok (2 daily; 10hr), Loei (1 daily via Pak Chom; 3hr) and Nong Khai (daily; 3–4hr). There's no bus station in Sang Khom; buses pull up in the middle of town a short walk from the guesthouse listed below. Than Tip Falls are best visited by rented motorbike, and for Wat Hin Maak Peng, take a bus bound for Nong Khai and ask to be dropped at the temple.

By boat Trips up the Mekong (B250/person for groups of 2–4) can be booked with *Bouy Guest House* in Sang Khom.

By motorbike You can rent motorbikes (B200/day) at *Bouy Guest House* in Sang Khom.

Banks Sang Khom has two banks and several ATMs.

ACCOMMODATION

★ **Bouy Guest House** 60/4 Moo 4 Sang Khom, by the river ☎042 441065, ✉toy_bgh@hotmail.com. The best of the accommodation in Sang Khom, enjoying a particularly choice location. The decent bamboo huts, some with fan and others a/c, have beautiful views out over the river and are set in a spacious, flower-strewn compound on a spit of land that's reached by a wooden bridge over a small tributary. The welcoming owners can arrange day-trips to Phu Phra Bat Historical Park (B800; see page 494); if that sounds too strenuous, you can settle for a massage (B250) or just relax in the hammocks strung from the veranda of each hut. Good Thai and Western food is available on a

5

deck overlooking the stream (most of it also in vegetarian versions). Fan B250, a/c B500

Ban Mai Rim Khong 211 Pha Tang, on the riverfront, about 1km east of Bouy Guest House ☎ 042 441560.

This pleasant, two-storey wooden building has good-sized, bright rooms and wonderful views of the Mekong River. There's also a coffee shop that serves meals as well. B600

Nong Khai

The major border town in Northern Isaan is **NONG KHAI**, an ethnically diverse town that's thrived since the construction of the **Thai-Australian Friendship Bridge** over the Mekong on the west side of town in 1994. Occupying a strategic position at the end of Highway 2 and the northeastern rail line, and just 24km from Vientiane, Nong Khai acts as a conduit for goods bought and sold by Thais and Lao, who are allowed to pass between the two cities freely for day-trips. Consequently, the covered souvenir market that sprawls to the east of the main pier, **Tha Sadet**, carries Lao silver, wood and cane items, as well as goods from as far afield as China, Korea and Russia, plus local basketware and silk.

As with most of the towns along this part of the Mekong, the thing to do in Nong Khai is just to take it easy, enjoying the **riverside atmosphere** and the peaceful settings of its guesthouses, which offer good value. Before you lapse into a relaxation-induced coma, though, **rent a bicycle** to explore the surrounding countryside, or make a **day-trip** out to see the impressive sculptures and rock formations in the surrounding countryside (see page 493).

Thanon Meechai

Nong Khai stretches for 4km along the south bank of the Mekong. Running from east to west, **Thanon Meechai** dominates activity; the main shops, banks and businesses are plumb in the middle around the post office. Although most of the old buildings have been replaced by concrete boxes, a few weather-beaten wooden houses remain, their attractive balconies, porticoes and slatted shutters showing the influence of colonial architecture, which was imported from across the river before the French were forced out of Laos in 1954.

Wat Pho Chai

Off the east end of Thanon Prajak

NONG KHAI

● SHOPPING
Hornbill Bookshop — 1
Village Weaver Crafts — 2

● EATING
Daeng Namnuang — 1
Dee Dee Pochana — 4
Mai's Restaurant — 5
Mut Mee Guest House — 3
Nam Tok Rim Khong — 2

■ ACCOMMODATION
Baan Sabai Rimkhong — 3
Janhom Apartment — 5
Mut Mee Guest House — 2
Pantawee Hotel — 6
Park & Pool Resort — 7
Ruan Thai Guest House — 1
Sawasdee Guest House — 4

Tourist office, Udon Thani, Route 211, Wat Phra That Bang Phuan & Phu Phra Bat Historical Park

5

NONG KHAI FESTIVALS

Nong Khai is an excellent place to celebrate any of the national or local Thai festivals, of which the strangest is the two-day festival of **Bang Fai Phaya Nak**. Every year on the full-moon night in October, silent and vapourless **naga fireballs** appear from the river – small, pink spheres that float vertically up to heights of as much as 300m, then disappear; in some years, several thousand appear, in others, just a handful. A tentative scientific theory proposes that the balls are a combination of methane and nitrogen from decomposed matter on the bottom of the river, which reach a certain temperature at that time of the year and are released, combusting in the presence of oxygen when they break the water's surface; romantics will prefer the local belief that the nagas or naks (serpents) of the river breathe out the fireballs to call the Buddha to return to earth at the end of Buddhist Lent. The festival coincides with Awk Phansa and the end of the longboat-racing season on the river. The fireballs have appeared as far afield as Sang Khom and Bueng Kan, but are generally most numerous around **Phon Phisai** and **Ban Nam Phe**, around 40km east of Nong Khai.

Among other festivals worth seeing in Nong Khai, the **Anou Saowari Festival** in mid-March includes a street parade and fair to celebrate the end of rebellions by the Haw minority in the 1880s. **Rocket festivals** take place in May to help bring on the rain season and provide water for crops, usually beginning after **Visaka Puja**, one of the three annual Puja festivals that takes place throughout Thailand. A **Candle Festival** takes place in July, when huge candles are paraded round the streets to commemorate the beginning of Buddhist Lent. In September, heats begin for the **Rowing Festival**, when up to 55 brightly dressed rowers paddle their dragon boats along the Mekong River, with the finals occurring just before the **Naga Fireballs Festival** in October. The streets come alive again in late October and early November for the **Chinese Dragon Festival**, and the national **Loy Krathong Festival**, also usually in November, which is particularly popular here as the Mekong River is an ideal place to launch a krathong. For more details and exact dates and of any of these festivals, contact the TAT or the staff at Mut Mee Guest House (see page 492).

The main temple of the region is **Wat Pho Chai**. The cruciform viharn, with its complex and elegant array of Lao tiers, shelters a venerated golden image, the Phra Sai Buddha, which is paraded around town and blessed with water during Songkhran. Prince Chakri, the future Rama I, is said to have looted the image from Vientiane, along with the Emerald Buddha, but the boat which was bringing back the Phra Sai overturned and sank in the Mekong. Later, the statue miraculously rose to the surface and the grateful people of Nong Khai built this great hangar of a viharn to house it, decorating the walls with murals of its miraculous journey. It's worth a visit for the Buddha's stagy setting, in front of a steep, flame-covered altar, dazzlingly lit from above and below. The solid gold head is so highly polished that you have to peer carefully to make out the Sukhothai influence in its haughty expression and beaked nose. The adjacent Po Chai Market is the town's biggest fresh market and worth a wander in the morning.

The riverside

The most pleasant place for a stroll is the **riverside area**. There's a pedestrianized promenade in the centre to the east of Tha Sadet, while things become more rustic and leafy around the fringes, which are often busy with people bathing, washing their clothes and fishing, especially in the early morning and evening.

Phra That Nong Khai

At the far eastern end of town

If you're lucky, you might catch sight of a sunken chedi at the far eastern end of town. **Phra That Nong Khai** (aka Phra That Klang Nam) slipped into the river during floods in 1847 and has since subsided so far that only the top of the chedi is visible in the dry season, though a replica, brightly illuminated at night, has been constructed on the adjacent bank.

5

CROSSING THE LAO BORDER VIA NONG KHAI

The crossing at Nong Khai is popular with tourists and relatively easy to use. Thais and Laos can cross the border via the ferry at Tha Sadet, but everyone else must use Nong Khai's **Thai-Australian Friendship Bridge** (daily 6am–10pm, although buses across the bridge stop at 8pm).

GETTING A VISA ON ARRIVAL

To get a **visa at the border**, take a tuk-tuk to the foot of the bridge (about B50 from the railway station), where you'll be stamped out of Thailand. You'll then need to take a bus (B20) across the span itself to the Laos immigration post, where you can get a thirty-day tourist visa for US$30–42 (depending on nationality; pay $1 extra if you arrive after 6pm), plus one photo. It's possible to pay in baht at the bridge, though it's over the odds at B1500 and upwards. From the Laos immigration post, you can catch a shared air-conditioned minibus (B100–150/person), tuk-tuk (about B300/vehicle) or infrequent bus (B30) to Vientiane, 24km away.

WITH A VISA

If you have already arranged a visa through a Lao embassy or consulate, you can head straight from Nong Khai into Laos. Six daily **buses** run all the way through to Vientiane from the bus station (B55, plus B5 to Thai immigration). The border is also accessible from further afield – there are direct buses from Bangkok, Udon Thani and Khon Kaen to Vientiane.

ARRIVAL AND DEPARTURE

NONG KHAI

By plane A/c minibuses (B150–200) from Udon Thani airport (see page 476) meet incoming flights from Bangkok and drop passengers at the Friendship Bridge or at their downtown hotels.

By train The station is 3km southwest of the centre near the Friendship Bridge. From Bangkok, you'll most likely be coming to Nong Khai by night train, arriving just after dawn. Tuk-tuks and motorbike taxis are on hand to run passengers into town.

Destinations Ayutthaya (3 daily; 9hr 30min–11hr); Bangkok (3 daily; 11–13hr); Khon Kaen (3 daily; 2hr

45min); Udon Thani (3 daily; 1hr).

By bus Day All buses pull in at the bus station on the east side of town off Thanon Prajak; Udon Thani buses make an extra stop at the corner of highways 233 and 212.

Destinations Bangkok (18 daily; 11hr); Bueng Kan (10 daily; 2hr); Chiang Mai (2 daily; 12hr); Khon Kaen (18 daily; 3hr 30min); Khorat (18 daily; 6hr 30min); Loei (daily via Pak Chom; 7hr); Nakhon Phanom (daily; 6hr); Rayong (14 daily; 12hr); Sang Khom (3 daily; 3–4hr); Udon Thani (every 30min; 1hr); Vientiane (Laos; 6 daily; 1hr).

GETTING AROUND

As everything in Nong Khai is so spread out, you might want to consider hopping on a **tuk-tuk** for getting around, or renting a bicycle or motorbike.

By tuk-tuk Around B40 for a short journey such as bus station to Tha Sadet, up to B60 for bus station to train station. The rates for these and other journeys are posted up in the bus station.

By bicycle and motorbike Nong Khai's flat terrain makes it ideal for exploring by bicycle. They are available at *Mut Mee*, *Ruan Thai* and *Sawasdee* guesthouses for around B50–100/day. Motorbikes (from B200/day) can be rented at Noui Motorcycle (☎081 975 4863) on Thanon Kaewworut in front of *Mut Mee Guesthouse*.

INFORMATION

Tourist office The TAT office, 1.5km south of the centre on the west side of Highway 2 (daily 8.30am–4.30pm; ☎042 421326, ✉tat_nongkhai@yahoo.com), has information about local homestays.

Massages Good, strong body and foot massages (B170/hr) can be had at Suan Sukapab (Healthy Garden), 623 Thanon Banterngjit (☎042 423323).

Police The tourist police are based on Thanon Prajak (☎042 460186 or ☎1155).

ACCOMMODATION

Baan Sabai Rimkhong 168 Thanon Rimkhong ☎042 413545, ✇baansabairimkhong.com; map p.488. If

you're looking for a room with a good view of the Mekong River, you won't find better than this. The cheapest rooms

5

have no view, but others (priced from B690–2000) have sweeping views and some have big balconies too. All rooms are a/c, equipped with modern furnishings and spotlessly clean. B490

Janhom Apartment 479 Soi Srichumchuen, Thanon Prajak ☎042 460293; map p.488. Located on a quiet soi, set against the wall of Wat Sri Chum Chuen and with a pleasant, shady sitting area at the front. Not really apartments, though they are available by the month, with substantial discounts, but large, clean, a/c rooms with armchairs, fridges, TVs and hot-water bathrooms. Breakfast is included. Some rooms are rather dim so take a look first. B400

★ **Mut Mee Guest House** 1111 Thanon Keawworut ☎042 460717, ⓦmutmee.com; map p.488. A huge range of well-kept rooms sprawl around a thatched, open-sided riverside restaurant at this magnet for travellers. Choose between ultra-basic single rooms (B200), clean twin rooms (some with shared bathrooms) or top-notch en-suite doubles with their own balconies and river views (B1650). With helpful, well-informed staff, it also offers yoga, meditation and massage sessions (high season only), as well as local information about bicycle tours and homestays. Julian, the English owner, has added loads of useful information about the area to the guesthouse's website. Fan B300, a/c B600

Pantawee Hotel 1049 Thanon Haisoke ☎042 411568, ⓦpantawee.com; map p.488. A comfortable, efficiently run, mid-range choice, with its cheapest, dimly lit rooms on the opposite side of the road. The clean a/c rooms come with hot-water bathrooms, TVs, DVD players, fridges and computers. There's also a small Jacuzzi pool, a spa and a 24hr restaurant. B620

★ **Park & Pool Resort** 163/1–3 Moo 3, Tambon Mechai, just east of the railway station ☎042 413 003, ⓦpark-poolresort.com; map p.488. This attractively landscaped compound has a real resort feel to it, with standard rooms in a colonial-style house, villas scattered around the grounds, lotus ponds, VIP rooms, a big swimming pool and good restaurant. Staff are extremely helpful. The only downside is that it's a bit of a trek to the town centre. B900

Ruan Thai Guest House 1126/2 Thanon Rimkhong ☎042 412 519; map p.488. A variety of large and small wooden houses in a quiet compound with attractive, well-maintained rooms, which range from smallish rooms with fan to standard rooms with a/c and family rooms. Fan B300, a/c B500

Sawasdee Guest House 402 Thanon Meechai ☎042 412 502, ⓦsawasdeeguesthouse.com; map p.488. A grand old wooden shophouse set around a pleasant courtyard, with helpful management. Rooms are either fan-cooled (try to avoid those overlooking the noisy main road) with shared bathrooms and hot showers available, or a/c with en-suite hot-water bathrooms. Fan B200, a/c B400

EATING AND DRINKING

Nong Khai is a great place to sample Isaan cuisine, as well as Vietnamese at *Daeng Namnuang*, the town's most famous **restaurant**. If you're counting the baht, head for the night-time **stalls** on Thanon Prajak, near the corner of Soi Chuenjit.

★ **Daeng Namnuang** 526–527 Thanon Rimkhong ☎042 411961; map p.488. Delicious, inexpensive Vietnamese food at this immaculately clean and popular place, with an a/c room and a lovely riverside terrace, though most Thais come for the take-away service. Specialities include *nam nuang* (roll-your-own Vietnamese spring rolls with grilled pork) and deep-fried prawns on sugar-cane skewers (3 for B130). Daily 8am–8pm.

Dee Dee Pochana 1155/9 Thanon Prajak ☎042 423 004; map p.488. This no-frills place is a classic Thai restaurant, serving all the usual staples like beef in oyster sauce (B120), as well as several Chinese and seafood dishes. Probably the fastest service in town. Daily 11am–2am.

Mai's Restaurant 11129/5 Thanon Nitipant ☎092 769 0376; map p.488. Located on a street with several bars, this unpretentious place serves up tasty fish and chips (B180) as well as curry and rice (about B140), with a choice of indoor or outdoor seating. Daily 11am–midnight.

★ **Mut Mee Guest House** 1111 Thanon Keawworut ☎042 460717; map p.488. You're spoilt for choice at this traveller's favourite, where the thatched pavilion is an ideal spot for a meeting of minds. Good Thai and Isaan dishes (around B80–100), particularly vegetarian versions, vie with tasty Western efforts (B200–250) including home-made apple pie. Daily 7am–10pm.

Nam Tok Rim Khong 1036 Thanon Rimkhong (no English sign); map p.488. Simple but popular and cheap restaurant in an old wooden building with an attractive terrace overlooking the river, specializing in *nam tok* (spicy hot beef salad, B70), as well as other Isaan delicacies such as *som tam*, dried beef and sausages. Daily 8am–8.30pm.

SHOPPING

Woven handicrafts are the main attraction here, shopping-wise. The northeastern method **mut mee** (literally "tied strings") involves tie-dyeing bundles of cotton thread before hand-weaving, which produces geometrical patterns on a coloured base. Tha Sadet market (7am–9pm), also known as the Indochina Market, which occupies a huge area by the Mekong River, has a selection of ready-made clothes, wall hangings, bags and axe pillows. On Saturday evenings (5–10pm), Thanon Rimkhong is closed to traffic between the pier and market for the weekly walking street.

Hornbill Bookshop On the narrow lane leading down to Mut Mee Guest House; map p.488. Stocks a reasonable selection of new and secondhand books in English. Mon–Sat 10am–7pm.

Village Weaver Crafts 1020 Thanon Prajak ☎ 042 422 651–3; map p.488. A superb selection of silk and cotton clothes, either off-the-peg or tailor-made. They also sell some lovely axe pillows, scarves and bags. Daily 8am–8pm.

Around Nong Khai

The most memorable sight around Nong Khai is **Sala Kaeo Kou**, also known as Wat Khaek, where you'll find dozens of curious sculptures. To the southwest of Nong Khai is **Wat Phra That Bang Phuan**, which offers some classic temple sightseeing, while the natural rock formations at **Phu Phra Bat Historical Park** and the spectacular temple **Wat Phu Tok** require much more effort and a full day out.

Sala Kaeo Kou (Wat Khaek)

5km east of Nong Khai • Daily 8am–6pm • B20 • About B150 return from Nong Khai in a tuk-tuk

By far the easiest and most popular day-trip out of Nong Khai is to **Sala Kaeo Kou**, a short hop to the east. The temple is best known for its bizarre sculpture garden; although at the time of writing, many of the sculptures had become blackened by pollution. Also known as Wat Khaek, it was founded by the late **Luang Phu Boonlua Surirat**, an unconventional Thai holy man who studied under a Hindu guru in Vietnam and preached in Laos until he was thrown out by the Communists in the 1970s. His charisma – those who drank water offered by him would, it was rumoured, give up all they owned to the temple – and heavy emphasis on morality attracted many followers among the farmers of Nong Khai. Luang Phu's popularity suffered, however, after his eleven-month spell in prison for insulting King Bhumibol, a crime alleged by jealous neighbours and probably without foundation; he died aged 72 in August 1996, a year after his release.

If you're heading over to Laos, the **Xiang Khouan** sculpture garden – Sala Kaeo Kou's precursor, 25km from downtown Vientiane on the Mekong River – shouldn't be missed; Luang Phu spent twenty years working on the sculptures there before his expulsion.

The sculpture garden

Arrayed with pretty flowers and plants, the **sculpture garden** bristles with Buddhist, Hindu and secular figures, all executed in concrete with imaginative abandon by unskilled followers under Luang Phu's direction. The religious statues, in particular, are radically modern. Characteristics that marked the Buddha out as a supernatural being – tight curls and a bump on the crown of the head called the *ushnisha* – are here transformed into beehives, and the *rashmis* on top (flames depicting the Buddha's fiery intellect) are depicted as long, sharp spikes. The largest statue in the garden shows the familiar story of the kindly naga king, Muchalinda, sheltering the Buddha, who is lost in meditation, from the heavy rain and floods: here the Buddha has shrunk in significance and the seven-headed snake has grown to 25m, with fierce, gaping fangs and long tongues.

CROSSING THE LAO BORDER VIA BUENG KAN

It's possible to cross from **Bueng Kan** to **Paksan** on the opposite side of the river in Laos (immigration office daily 8.30am–4.30pm), though there's no visa on arrival at this crossing. Take a tuk-tuk (around B100) to the ferry (B60), which leaves when it's got enough passengers, and then another tuk-tuk into Paksan. At the time of writing, plans were being made to build the fifth Thai-Lao Friendship Bridge across the Mekong River here within the next few years. From Paksan there are buses west to Vientiane or south to Savannakhet.

Many of the statues illustrate **Thai proverbs**. Near the entrance, an elephant surrounded by a pack of dogs symbolizes integrity, "as the elephant is indifferent to the barking dogs". The nearby serpent-tailed monster with the moon in his mouth – Rahoo, the cause of eclipses – serves as an injunction to oppose all obstacles, just as the people of Isaan and Laos used to ward off eclipses by banging drums and firing guns. In the corner furthest from the entrance, you enter the circle Circle of Life through a huge mouth representing the womb, inside which a hermit, a policeman, a monk, a rich man and a beggar, among others, represent different paths in life (for a detailed map of the Circle of Life sculpture, go to ⓦmutmee.com). A man with two wives is shown beating the older one because he is ensnared by the wishes of the younger one, and an old couple who have made the mistake of not having children now find they have only each other for comfort.

The disturbingly vacant, smiling faces of the garden Buddhas bear more than a passing resemblance to Luang Phu himself, photos of whom adorn the **temple building**, a huge white edifice with mosque-like domes.

Wat Phra That Bang Phuan

Ban Bang Phuan hamlet, around 22km southwest of Nong Khai on Highway 211 • Buses from Nong Khai to Pak Chom and Loei pass this way; depending on departure times it may be quicker to take an Udon-bound service 12km down Highway 2 to Ban Nong Song Hong, then change onto an Udon–Sri Chiangmai bus

More famous as the site of a now-concealed two-thousand-year-old Indian chedi than for its modern replacement, rural **Wat Phra That Bang Phuan** remains a highly revered place of pilgrimage.

The original **chedi** is supposed to have been built by disciples of the Buddha to hold 29 relics – pieces of breastbone – brought from India. A sixteenth-century king of Vientiane earned himself merit by building a tall Lao-style chedi over the top of the previous stupa; rain damage toppled this in 1970, but it was restored in 1977 to the fine, gleaming white edifice seen today. The unkempt but atmospheric compound also contains crumbling brick chedis, a naga pond and several Buddha images.

Phu Phra Bat Historical Park

61km southwest of Nong Khai, near Ban Pheu • Daily 8.30am–4.30pm • B100 • Information Centre daily 8.30am–4.30pm

Deep in the countryside, the wooded slopes around the village of **BAN PHEU** are dotted with strangely eroded sandstone formations, which have long exerted a mystical hold over people in the surrounding area. Local wisdom has it that the outcrops, many of which were converted into small temples from around the ninth century onwards, are either meteorites – believed to account for their burnt appearance – or, more likely, were caused by glacial erosion. Together with a stupa enshrining a Buddha footprint that is now an important pilgrimage site, especially during its annual festival in March, the rock formations have been linked up under the auspices of fifty-square-kilometre **Phu Phra Bat Historical Park**. The site was opened to the public in 1991 and is well-maintained by the Fine Arts Department.

The **information centre** by the park entrance contains fairly interesting displays on the red prehistoric paintings of animals, humans, hands and geometric patterns that are found on the rock formations, and on the tale of Ussa and Barot. Around the information centre, a well-signposted network of **paths** has been cleared from the thin forest to connect 25 of the outcrops, each of which has a helpful English-language information board attached. It would take a good five hours to explore the whole park on foot, but the most popular circuit, covering all the sights listed below, can be completed in an ambling two hours. There is little shade along the way and it can get very hot at midday, so start as early as possible and take some water, as well as a hat and/or an umbrella. Back at the car park beside the information centre, you'll find a decent restaurant and some good toilet facilities.

The outcrops

Among the most interesting of the outcrops are **Tham Wua** and **Tham Khon**, two natural shelters whose paintings of oxen and human stick figures suggest that the area was first settled by hunter-gatherers two to three thousand years ago. A legend that's well known in this part of Thailand and Laos accounts for the name of nearby **Kok Ma Thao Barot** (Prince Barot's Stable), a broad platform overhung by a huge slab of sandstone. A certain Princess Ussa, banished by her father to these slopes to be educated by a hermit, sent out an SOS that was answered by a dashing prince, Barot. The two fell in love and were married against the wishes of Ussa's father, prompting the king to challenge Barot to a distinctly oriental sort of duel: each would build a temple, and the last to finish would be beheaded. The king lost. Kok Ma Thao Barot is celebrated as the place where Barot kept his horse when he visited Ussa.

The furthest point of the circuit is the viewpoint at **Pha Sadej**, where the cliff drops away to give a lovely view across the green fields and forests of the Mekong valley to the distant mountains. More spectacular is **Hor Nang Ussa** (Ussa's Tower), a mushroom formed by a flat slab capping a 5m-high rock pillar. Under the cap of the mushroom, a shelter has been carved out and walled in on two sides. The *sema* found scattered around the site, and the square holes in which others would have been embedded, indicate that this was a shrine, probably during the ninth to eleventh centuries in the Dvaravati period. Nearby, a huge rock on a flimsy pivot miraculously balances itself against a tree at **Wat Por Ta** (the Father-in-Law's Temple); the walls and floor have been evenly carved out to form a vaguely rectangular shrine, with Dvaravati Buddha images dotted around.

Wat Phra Bat Bua Bok

The left fork shortly before the park entrance leads to **Wat Phra Bat Bua Bok**: a crude *that* built in imitation of Wat Phra That Phanom (see page 498), it's decorated with naive bas-reliefs of divinities and boggle-eyed monsters, which add to the atmosphere of simple, rustic piety. In a gloomy chamber in the tower's base, the only visible markings on the sandstone **Buddha footprint** show the Wheel of Law. Legend has it that the Buddha made the footprint here for a serpent that had asked to be ordained as a monk, but had been refused because it was not human. Higher up the slope, a smaller *that* perches on a hanging rock that seems to defy gravity.

ARRIVAL AND DEPARTURE   PHU PHRA BAT HISTORICAL PARK

By bus From Nong Khai, take the 7.15am bus to Ban Pheu; if you leave any later you won't have time to see the park properly, as the whole journey takes at least a couple of hours and the last bus back leaves at around 3.15pm. From Ban Pheu, it's another 14km west to the historical park; take a songthaew for the first 10km to the Ban Tiu intersection; from here a motorbike taxi will bring you the final 4km up to the main park entrance. If you are coming from Udon Thani, catch a bus from Talat Rangsina towards either Nam Som or Na Yung, which will drop you off at Ban Tiu.

Wat Phu Tok

The most compelling destination in the area to the east of Nong Khai is the extraordinary hilltop retreat of **Wat Phu Tok**. One of two sandstone outcrops that jut steeply out of the plain 35km southeast of Bueng Kan, Phu Tok has been transformed into a meditation wat, its fifty or so monks building their scattered huts on perches high above breathtaking cliffs. The outcrop comes into sight long before you get there, its sheer red face sandwiched between green vegetation on the lower slopes and tufts of trees on the narrow plateau above. As you get closer, the horizontal white lines across the cliffs reveal themselves to be painted wooden walkways, built to give the temple seven levels to represent the seven stages of enlightenment.

5

HOMESTAYS IN THE NORTHEAST

The lazy **villages** just downstream from Nong Khai and close to Mukdahan can be a welcome breath of fresh air after traipsing around Isaan's dusty cities. There's a good selection of welcoming **homestays** to bed down in, providing an opportunity to unwind and enjoy the slow pace of rural Isaan – and many rent out bikes and motorbikes for local exploration.

Homestay Ban Kham Pia Off Highway 212 between Bueng Kan and Nakhon Phanom, 7km southwest of Bung Khla, on the road running towards Phu Wua Wildlife Reserve ☏ 087 861 0601, ⓦ bunloedhuts. jimdo.com. Close to a reserve that's packed with wildlife, this homestay offers simple wooden bungalows, some with shared bathroom. See website for directions. B260

Thai House Isaan Around 60km southwest of Mukdahan, just off Highway 2042 ☏ 090 843 2970, ⓦ thaihouse-isaan.com. Set around an attractive northeastern-style building in a peaceful Phu Thai village, with a handful of a/c bungalows, a swimming pool and an apartment that has its own living room and karaoke machine. The owners can arrange tours lasting between a day and a week, ranging all over Isaan. Pick-ups available from Khon Kaen. B750

The ornamental garden

In an ornamental garden at the base, reflected in a small lake, an elegant, modern marble chedi commemorates **Phra Ajaan Juen**, the famous meditation master who founded the wat in 1968 and died in a plane crash ten years later while on his way to Bangkok to celebrate the queen's birthday. Within the chedi, the monk's books and other belongings, and diamond-like fragments of his bones, are preserved in a small shrine.

The ascent

The first part of the **ascent** of the outcrop takes you to the third level up a series of long, sometimes slippery, wooden staircases, so you'll need something sturdy on your feet. A choice of two routes – the left fork is more interesting – leads to the fifth and most important level, where the **Sala Yai** houses the temple's main Buddha image in an airy, dimly lit cavern. The artificial ledges that cut across the northeast face are not for the faint-hearted, but they are one way of getting to the dramatic northwest tip here on level five: on the other side of a deep crevice spanned by a wooden bridge, the monks have built an open-sided Buddha viharn under a huge anvil rock. This spot affords stunning **views** over a broad sweep of countryside and across to the second, uninhabited, outcrop. The flat top of the hill forms the seventh level, where you can wander along overgrown paths through thick forest. At times on the walkways you are walking above thin air, so it's not advisable to go up if you suffer from vertigo.

ARRIVAL AND DEPARTURE
WAT PHU TOK

Getting to Wat Phu Tok isn't easy – the location was chosen for its isolation, after all – but the journey out gives you a slice of life in remote countryside. The attached village sports a collection of simple **restaurants** and food stalls.

By motorbike or hired car The best option is to rent a motorbike and get a sketch map from *Mut Mee Guest House* (see page 492) or charter a car and driver in Nong Khai (B1500–2000) – leave early to make it there and back in a

day, allowing two hours to explore the temple.

By bus Going via public transport is a slog. Catch a bus from Nong Khai to Bueng Kan (hourly; 2hr); once there, you might be lucky enough to coincide with one of the occasional songthaews to Phu Tok via Ban Siwilai, 25km south on Route 222; otherwise, take one of the hourly buses to Siwilai and charter a motorized samlor (around B350) for the last 20km east to Phu Tok.

Nakhon Phanom

Beyond Bueng Kan, the river road rounds the hilly northeastern tip of Thailand before heading south through remote country with very few communities of any size. The Mekong can only be glimpsed occasionally until you reach **NAKHON PHANOM** ("City of Mountains"), a clean and prosperous town which affords the finest view of the river in northern Isaan, framed against the giant ant hills of the Lao mountains opposite.

The town makes a pleasant place to hang out, its quiet, broad streets lined with some grand old public buildings, colonial-style houses and creaking wooden shophouses. But most importantly for those with their sights set on Laos, the town is home to the third Thai-Lao Friendship Bridge, which opened to much fanfare in November 2011.

Walking around town, you'll see several lit-up boat shapes around the place, a reminder of Nakhon Phanom's best-known festival, the **illuminated boat procession**, which is held on the river every year at the end of the rainy season, usually in late October. Around fifty boats of up to 10m in length, adorned with elaborate lights and carrying offerings of food and flowers, are launched on the river in a spectacular display. The week-long celebrations – marking the end of the annual three-month Buddhist Rains Retreat – also feature colourful dragon-boat races along the Mekong, pitting Thai and Lao teams against each other.

Ho Chi Minh's House

3km southwest of Nakhon Phanom at Ban Na Chok (ask for directions at TAT) · **House** daily 8am–5pm · Free · **Museum** daily 8am–4pm · Free

The Vietnamese national hero, Ho Chi Minh, lived in Ban Na Chok in the late 1920s, when he was forced to go underground during the struggle for independence from France. His Vietnamese-style **wooden house** – terracotta roof tiles and no stilts – has been reconstructed, and there's a small museum nearby too, dedicated to the Vietnamese in Thailand. However, there's not much to see apart from some black-and-white photographs of Uncle Ho and a couple of trees he planted, so a visit here is really only recommended for Ho Chi Minh devotees; homestays in the village can be arranged through TAT (see below).

ARRIVAL AND INFORMATION

By plane You can fly to Nakhon Phanom from Bangkok with Air Asia (daily; 1hr 15min) or Nok Air (2 daily; 1hr 15min); a shuttle bus from the airport 15km west of town costs B100 per person.

By bus The main bus station is about 1km west of the centre off the north side of Highway 22.

Destinations Bangkok (24 daily; 12hr); Khon Kaen (5 daily; 5hr 30min); Mukdahan (every 25min; 2hr); Nong Khai (4 daily; 6hr); Thakhek (Laos; 8 daily; 1hr 30min); That Phanom (every 25min; 1hr); Ubon Ratchathani (11 daily; 5hr); Udon Thani (18 daily; 5hr).

NAKHON PHANOM

Tourist information TAT has an office in an impressive old mansion at 184/1 Thanon Suntorn Vichit, corner of Thanon Salaklang (daily 8.30am–4.30pm; ☏042 513490–1, ✉tatphnom@tat.or.th), 500m north of the pier for Laos; they also cover Mukdahan and Sakon Nakhon provinces.

Services There's a tourist police office on the riverfront just north of the *Fortune River View Hotel* (☏1155). On Friday and Saturday evenings (5–9pm), Thanon Sunthorn Wijit (the riverside road) is closed to traffic for two blocks north of the clock tower, and vendors set up stalls for a walking street.

ACCOMMODATION AND EATING

Thanon Fueng Nakhon, which runs west from the clock tower just north of the pier, has a choice of several simple places to **eat** and is a lively spot at night.

Chelsea Riverside Restaurant 123 Thanon Suntorn Vichit, north of the town centre ☏042 512 100

ⓦfacebook.com/chelseariversiderestaurant. This place ticks all the boxes: lovely river views, inside or outside eating, great Western dishes (especially the burgers; B190) and excellent Thai food such as phat thai (B75). They close for a few weeks in March and May. Daily 10am–10pm

---

BOAT TRIPS FROM NAKHON PHANOM

Even if you're not crossing the border, you can still appreciate the beautiful riverscape by joining one of the daily **boat trips** that depart from just south of the main pier at 5pm (B50; drinks available). Setting out as the sun begins to sink, they motor along between the banks nice and slowly, usually returning just before dark.

5

> ## CROSSING VIA THE THIRD THAI-LAO FRIENDSHIP BRIDGE
>
> The third **Thai-Lao friendship bridge** opened in late 2011 at a site 8km north of Nakhon Phanom's town centre. If you're heading for Laos, take a bus from Nakhon Phanom to Thakhek (daily 8am–5pm; B75) and complete immigration formalities on the bridge; Lao **visas** are available on arrival for US$30–42. There's also a passenger ferry that crosses the river, but this is for Thais and Lao only.

(Kitchen closes 8pm).

Fortune River View On Highway 212 towards the southern edge of town ☎042 522 333 ⓦfortunehotelgroup.com. This place is looking a bit run-down despite a recent refurbishment, but it's still one of the most reliable places in town, with an outdoor swimming pool and smart, tasteful riverside rooms that boast bathtubs. B1300

The River On Highway 212 about 2km south of the town centre ☎042 522 999, ⓦtherivernakhonphanom. com. This smart, newish hotel makes the most of Nakhon

Phanom's expansive river views. Comfortable beds with thick mattresses, modern furnishings and rain showers make for a comfy stay, and each room has a small balcony. There are bicycles (B20/hr, B60/day) and motorbikes (B250/day) for rent, and a shuttle bus to run guests into town. B790

Sri Thep Hotel 197 Thanon Sri Thep, 50m south of the main road (Highway 22), and one block west of the river ☎042 512 395. By far the friendliest budget choice, this Chinese-style hotel has tiled floors and solid wooden furniture in its clean, airy rooms. Fan B300, a/c B400

That Phanom

THAT PHANOM, a riverside village of weather-beaten wooden buildings, sprawls around Isaan's most important shrine, **Wat Phra That Phanom**. This far-northeastern corner of Thailand may seem like a strange location for one of the country's holiest sites, but the wat was built to serve both Thais and Lao, as evidenced by the ample boat-landing in the village. Plenty of Lao still come across the river for the fascinating Monday and Thursday morning waterfront **market**, bringing for sale such items as wild animal skins, black pigs and herbal medicines, alongside the usual fruit and veg.

Wat Phra That Phanom

Just off Highway 212, five blocks west from the Mekong

Popularly held to be one of the four sacred pillars of Thai religion (the other three are Chiang Mai's Wat Phra That Doi Suthep, Wat Mahathat in Nakhon Si Thammarat, and Wat Phra Phutthabat near Lopburi), **Wat Phra That Phanom** is a fascinating place of pilgrimage, especially at the time of the ten-day Phra That Phanom festival, usually in February, when thousands of people come to pay homage and enjoy themselves in the traditional holiday between harvesting and sowing; pilgrims believe that they must make the trip seven times during a full moon before they die.

The temple reputedly dates back to the eighth year after the death of the Buddha, when five local princes built a simple brick chedi to house bits of his breastbone. It's been restored or rebuilt seven times, most recently after it collapsed during a rainstorm in 1975; the latest incarnation is in the form of a Lao *that*, 57m high, modelled on the That Luang in Vientiane. From the river pier, a short ceremonial way leads under a Disneyesque **victory arch** erected by the Lao, through the temple gates to the present chedi, which, as is the custom, faces water and the rising sun.

The chedi

A brick-and-plaster structure covered with white paint and gold floral decorations, the **chedi** looks like nothing so much as a giant, ornate table leg turned upside down. From each of the four sides, an eye forming part of the traditional flame pattern stares down, and the whole thing is surmounted by an umbrella made of 16kg of gold, with precious gems and gold rings embedded in each tier. The chedi sits on a gleaming white marble platform, on which pilgrims say their prayers and leave every imaginable kind of offering to the relics. Look out for the **brick reliefs** in the shape of four-leaf clovers above three of the doorways in the base: on the northern side, Vishnu mounted on a garuda; on the western side, the four guardians of the earth putting offerings in the Buddha's alms bowl; and above the south door, a carving of the Buddha entering nirvana. At the corners of the chedi, brick plaques, carved in the tenth century but now heavily restored, tell the stories of the wat's princely founders.

ARRIVAL AND INFORMATION	THAT PHANOM

By bus The bus station is out to the west of the town centre, but all services from Nakhon Phanom and Mukdahan also stop in front of the temple; the Nakhon Phanom route is also covered by frequent songthaews, which gather to the north of the wat.

Destinations Bangkok (6 daily; 12hr); Mukdahan (every 25min; 1hr 20min); Nakhon Phanom (every 25min; 1hr); Ubon Ratchathani (hourly; 3–4hr); Udon Thani (6 daily; 4–5hr).

Banks There are several banks with ATMs on Thanon Chayangkun, near the wat.

ACCOMMODATION AND EATING	

Baan Ing Oon Guesthouse 19 Thanon Phanom Phanarak ☎ 042 540 111 ⓦ facebook.com/baaningoon. guesthouse.7. One of several welcoming guesthouses in That Phanom, this place features smallish but well-equipped rooms in a beautifully restored, French Indochinese-style house. It's just a block from the river and a 5min walk to the That. **B490**

Kritsada Rimkhong 90 Moo 2, Thanon Rim Khong ☎ 042 540088. On the riverside road about 1km north of the centre, opposite the hotel of the same name. The breezy

terrace of this restaurant, with expansive views across to Laos, is a good spot to enjoy a simple fried rice (B50) or a *tom yam* (spicy sour soup with shrimp; B150). Daily 8am–10pm.

That Phanom Riverview 258 Moo 2, Thanon Rim Khong ☎ 042 541555, ⓦ thatphanomriverviewhotel.com. This newish riverside hotel is the town's most comfortable place to stay, with good-sized, well-equipped rooms (work desks, cable TV) in an apartment-style complex, though few rooms actually have a view of the river. **B850**

Mukdahan

Fifty kilometres downriver of That Phanom, **MUKDAHAN** is the last stop on the Mekong trail before Highway 212 heads off inland to Ubon Ratchathani, 170km to the south. You may feel a long way from the comforts of Bangkok out here, but this is one of the fastest-developing Thai provinces, owing to increasing friendship between Laos and Thailand and the proximity of **Savannakhet**, the second-biggest Lao city, just across the water. Few farang visitors make it this far, though Mukdahan–Savannakhet is an officially sanctioned crossing to Laos, via the new bridge 7km north of town, and as the cranes dominating the skyline show, new hotels are springing up all the time.

Indochina Market

Daily 8am–6pm

The promenade overlooking Savannakhet is swamped by the daily **Indochina Market**, which is especially busy at weekends. On sale here are household goods and inexpensive ornaments, such as Vietnamese mother-of-pearl and Chinese ceramics, brought over from Laos; the market is also good for local fabrics like lengths of coarsely woven cotton in lovely muted colours, and expensive but very classy silks.

Mukdahan Tower

Thanon Samut Sakdarak • Daily 8am–6pm • B50

At the southern edge of town rises the 65m-high **Mukdahan Tower** (*Ho Kaeo Mukdahan*), a modern white edifice that looks somewhat out of place in the low-rise

5

CROSSING THE LAO BORDER VIA MUKDAHAN

Mukdahan–Savannakhet is an officially sanctioned **crossing** to Laos, via the second **Thai-Lao Friendship Bridge**, 7km north of town. Buses (12 daily 7.30am–7pm; B50) cross the bridge to **Savannakhet**, and it's possible to get a visa on arrival (US$30–42; see page 30 for further details).

outskirts. Built in 1996 to commemorate the fiftieth anniversary of the late King Bhumibol's accession to the throne, the tower houses an interesting array of historic artefacts from the Mukdahan area, including traditional Isaan costumes, pottery, coins, amulets, vicious-looking weaponry and fossils. The highlight, however, is the expansive view from the sixth floor – 50m high to reflect fifty years of Rama IX – over Mukdahan and the Mekong into Laos. On the smaller floor above is a much-revered, Sukhothai-style silver Buddha image, the Phra Phuttha Nawaming Mongkhon Mukdahan, fronted by the bone relics of famous monks in small glass containers.

ARRIVAL AND GETTING AROUND   MUKDAHAN

By bus Regular buses from That Phanom and Ubon Ratchathani stop at the bus terminal about 2km northwest of the centre on Highway 212. Songthaews shuttle between the bus station and Mukdahan Tower via the corner of Thanom Pitakpanomkhet, the main east–west street, and Thanon Samut Sakdarak, the main north–south street (B10–15/person).

Destinations Bangkok (20 daily; 10–11hr); Khon Kaen (every 30min; 4hr); Khorat (20 daily; 6hr); Nakhon Phanom (every 25min; 2hr); That Phanom (every 25min; 1hr 20min); Ubon Ratchathani (every 30min; 2–3hr).
By bicycle *Good Mook* café (see below) has mountain bikes for rent (B100/day).

ACCOMMODATION

Huanum 36 Thanon Samut Sakdarak at the corner of Thanon Song Nang Sathit, a block back from the pier ☎ 042 611137. There is a variety of rooms on offer at this budget hotel; fan rooms share cold-water bathrooms while a/c rooms have en-suite hot showers and TVs. Fan B200, a/c B350

Ploy Palace Hotel West of the centre at 40 Thanon Pitakpanomkhet ☎ 042 631111, ⓦ ploypalace.com. A grand edifice with a marbled lobby and tasteful bedrooms, this is probably the best of Mukdahan's big business hotels,

with good service, a rooftop restaurant with fine views and an outdoor swimming pool on the third floor. Rates include a buffet breakfast. B1180

Riverfront 22 Thanon Samranchaikhong, opposite the Indochina Market ☎ 042 633348, ⓦ riverfront mukdahan.com. The wood-fronted lobby of this place is right by the main river road. Superior rooms and suites (B1200–1800) have balconies that face Laos, and inside there are solid furnishings and cable TV. B850

EATING AND DRINKING

There's a lively, popular **night market** selling deep-fried insects and plenty of other Isaan specialities, four blocks back from the pier along Thanon Song Nang Sathit.

Good Mook 10 Thanon Song Nang Sathit ☎ 042 612091. Just a few steps west of the river, this classic travellers' café is a great find, with a laidback feel and cool sounds. They serve both Western and Thai dishes, such as *phat thai* and green curry, with prices ranging from B70–420. Tues–Sun

9am–10pm.

Wine Wild Why 11 Thanon Samranchaikhong ☎ 042 633122. This small restaurant, housed in a wooden building with a riverside terrace, has a short menu that includes Thai classics such as spicy soups, curries and spicy salads. Try the *kaeng liang kung* (B90), a peppery soup with lots of veggies and shrimp. Daily 11am–10pm.

Phu Pha Toep National Park

15km southeast of town • B200 • ☎ 089 619 7741, ⓦ nps.dnp.go.th

If you're tired of concrete Isaan towns, stretch your legs exploring the strange rock formations and beautiful waterfalls of **Phu Pha Toep National Park** (formerly known as Mukdahan National Park), which covers just 50 square kilometres. Just above the headquarters is a hillside of bizarre rocks, eroded into the shapes of toadstools, camels and crocodiles, which is great for scrambling around. The hillside also bears two remnants of the area's prehistory: the red finger-painting under one of the sandstone slabs is reckoned to be four thousand years old, while a small cage on the ground protects a 75-million-year-old fossil. Further up, the bare sandstone ridge seems to have been cut out of the surrounding forest by a giant lawnmower, but from October to December it's brought to life with a covering of grasses and wildflowers. A series of ladders leads up a cliff to the highest point, on a ridge at the western end of the park (a 2km walk from the headquarters), which affords a sweeping view over the rocks to the forests and paddies of Laos. Nearby, at least from July to November, is the park's most spectacular waterfall, Nam Tok Phu Tam Phra, a 30m drop through thick vegetation, and a cave in which villagers have enshrined scores of Buddha images.

ARRIVAL, ACCOMMODATION AND EATING   MUKDAHAN NATIONAL PARK

There are no restaurants in the park, just instant noodles for sale in a shop, so it's best to bring something with you.

By songthaew Regular songthaews from Mukdahan's bus terminal to Don Tan pass the turning for the park 14km out of town, from where it's a 1km walk uphill to the park headquarters.

Bungalow Near the headquarters. The park has just one standard-issue bungalow, sleeping six. It's also possible to camp here, with tents available for rent. Tent B300, bungalow B1800.

Southern Thailand: the Gulf coast

THONG NAI PAN YAI, KO PHA NGAN

Southern Thailand: the Gulf coast

Southern Thailand's gently undulating Gulf coast is famed above all for the Samui archipelago, three small, idyllic islands lying off the most prominent hump of the coastline. This is the country's most popular seaside venue for independent travellers, and a lazy stay in a beachfront bungalow is so seductive a prospect that most people overlook the attractions of the mainland, where the sheltered sandy beaches and warm clear water rival the top sunspots in most countries. Added to that you'll find scenery dominated by forested mountains that rise abruptly behind the coastal strip, and a sprinkling of fascinating historic sights.

The crumbling temples of ancient **Phetchaburi** are the first noteworthy sights you'll meet heading south out of Bangkok and fully justify a break in your journey. Beyond, the stretch of coast around **Cha-am** and **Hua Hin** is popular with weekending Thais escaping the capital and is crammed with condos, hotels and bars, not to mention a large population of foreign visitors. Far quieter and preferable are the beaches further south: the sophisticated little resort of **Pak Nam Pran**; golden-sand **Hat Phu Noi**, which is also the best base for exploring the karsts and caves of **Khao Sam Roi Yot National Park**; the welcoming town of **Prachuap Khiri Khan**, fronted by a lovely bay and flanked by an equally appealing beach; and laidback, lightly developed **Ban Krud**.

Of the islands, **Ko Samui** is the most naturally beautiful, with its long white-sand beaches and arching fringes of palm trees. The island's beauty has not gone unnoticed by tourist developers of course, and its varied spread of accommodation these days draws as many package tourists and second-homers as backpackers. In recent years the next island out, **Ko Pha Ngan**, has drawn increasing numbers of independent travellers away from its neighbour: its accommodation is generally simpler and cheaper than Ko Samui's, and it offers a few stunning beaches with a more laidback atmosphere. The island's southeastern headland, **Hat Rin**, has no fewer than three white-sand beaches to choose from, but now provides all the amenities the demanding backpacker could want, not to mention its notorious full moon parties. The furthest inhabited island of the archipelago, **Ko Tao**, has taken off as a **scuba-diving** centre, but despite a growing nightlife and restaurant scene, still has the feel of a small, rugged and isolated outcrop.

Tucked away beneath the islands, **Nakhon Si Thammarat**, the cultural capital of the south, is well worth a short detour from the main routes through the centre of the peninsula – it's a sophisticated city of grand old temples, delicious cuisine and distinctive handicrafts. With its small but significant Muslim population, and machine-gun dialect, Nakhon begins the transition into Thailand's deep south.

The Gulf coast has a slightly different **climate** from the Andaman coast and most of the rest of Thailand, being hit heavily by the northeast monsoon's rains, especially in November, when it's best to avoid this part of the country altogether. Most times during the rest of the year should see pleasant, if changeable, weather, with some effects of the southwest monsoon felt between May and October. Late December to April is the driest period, and is therefore the region's high season, which also includes July and August.

ARRIVAL AND GETTING AROUND   THE GULF COAST

The main arteries through this region are highways 4 (also known as the Phetkasem Highway, or usually Thanon Phetkasem when passing through towns) and 41, served by plentiful buses.

By plane The main airports in this region are on Ko Samui, at Chumphon, Surat Thani and Nakhon Si Thammarat, the last three providing, in combination with buses and boats, cheaper but slower competition for getting to the islands.

By train The railway from Bangkok connects all the mainland towns, including a branch line to Nakhon; nearly

SNORKELLING IN KO TAO

Highlights

❶ Phetchaburi Charming historic town, boasting several fine old working temples, as well as delicious traditional desserts. See page 507

❷ Pak Nam Pran Chic, artfully designed boutique hotels on a long, sandy beach, a popular weekend escape for design-conscious Bangkokians. See page 518

❸ Ang Thong National Marine Park A dramatic, unspoilt group of over forty remote islands, accessible on boat trips from Samui, Ko Pha Ngan or Tao. See page 549

❹ Full moon at Hat Rin, Ko Pha Ngan Party on, and on… See page 558

❺ Ao Thong Nai Pan on Ko Pha Ngan Beautiful, secluded bay with good accommodation. See page 560

❻ A boat-trip round Ko Tao Satisfying exploration and great snorkelling, especially off the unique causeway beaches of Ko Nang Yuan. See page 565

❼ Nakhon Si Thammarat Historic holy sites, intriguing shadow puppets, great-value accommodation and excellent cuisine. See page 572

❽ Krung Ching waterfall Walk past giant ferns and screeching monkeys to reach this spectacular drop. See page 578

HIGHLIGHTS ARE MARKED ON THE MAP ON PAGE 506

all services depart from Hualamphong Station, but a few slow trains use Thonburi Station.

By boat Daily boats run to all three main islands from two jumping-off points: Surat Thani, 650km from Bangkok, is close to Ko Samui and is generally more convenient for Ko Pha Ngan too, but if you're heading from Bangkok to Pha Ngan you might want to consider Chumphon, which is certainly the main port for Ko Tao.

Phetchaburi

6

Straddling the Phet River about 120km south of Bangkok, the provincial capital of **PHETCHABURI** (sometimes "Phetburi"; meaning "Diamond City") has been settled since at least the eleventh century, when the Khmers ruled the region. It was an important producer of salt, gathered from the nearby coastal salt pans, and rose to greater prominence in the seventeenth century as a trading post between the Andaman Sea ports and Ayutthaya. Despite periodic incursions from the Burmese, the town gained a reputation as a cultural centre – as the ornamentation of its older temples testifies – and after the new capital was established in Bangkok it became a favourite country retreat of Rama IV, who had a hilltop palace, **Phra Nakhon Khiri**, built here in the 1850s. Modern Phetchaburi is known for its limes and rose apples, but its main claim to fame is as one of Thailand's finest sweet-making centres, the essential ingredient for its assortment of *khanom* being the sugar extracted from the sweet-sapped palms that cover the province. This being very much a cottage industry, today's downtown Phetchaburi has lost relatively little of the ambience that so attracted Rama IV: the central riverside area is hemmed in by historic wats in varying states of disrepair, along with plenty of traditional wooden shophouses. The town's top three temples, described below, can be seen on a leisurely two-hour circular walk beginning from Chomrut Bridge, while Phetchaburi's other significant sight, the palace-museum at Phra Nakhon Khiri, is on a hill about 1km west of the bridge.

Despite the attractions of its old quarter, Phetchaburi gets few overnight visitors as most people see it on a day-trip from Bangkok, Hua Hin or Cha-am. The town sees more overnighters during the **Phra Nakhon Khiri Fair**, spread over at least a week usually in February, which features parades in historic costumes, cooking demonstrations and fireworks displays.

Wat Yai Suwannaram

Thanon Phongsuriya, about 700m east of Chomrut Bridge

Of all Phetchaburi's temples, the most attractive is the still-functioning seventeenth-century **Wat Yai Suwannaram**. The temple's fine old teak **sala** has elaborately carved doors, bearing a gash reputedly inflicted by the Burmese in 1760 as they plundered their way towards Ayutthaya. Across from the *sala* and hidden behind high, whitewashed walls stands the windowless Ayutthaya-style bot. The bot compound overlooks a pond, in the middle of which stands a small but well-preserved scripture library, or **ho trai**: such structures were built on stilts over water to prevent ants and other insects destroying the precious documents. Enter the walled compound from the south and make a clockwise tour of the cloisters filled with Buddha statues before entering the bot itself via the eastern doorway (if the door is locked, one of the monks will get the key for you). The **bot** is supported by intricately patterned red and gold pillars and contains a remarkable, if rather faded, set of murals, depicting Indra, Brahma and other lower-ranking divinities ranged in five rows of ascending importance. Once you've admired the interior, walk to the back of the bot, passing behind the central cluster of Buddha images, to find another Buddha image seated against the back wall: climb the steps in front of this statue to get a close-up of the left foot, which for some reason was cast with six toes.

6

Wat Kamphaeng Laeng

Thanon Phra Song, a 15min walk east and then south of Wat Yai

The five tumbledown prangs of **Wat Kamphaeng Laeng** mark out Phetchaburi as the likely southernmost outpost of the Khmer empire. Built probably in the thirteenth century to honour the Hindu deity Shiva and set out in a cruciform arrangement facing east, the laterite corncob-style prangs were later adapted for Buddhist use, as can be seen from the two that now house Buddha images. There has been some attempt to restore a few of the carvings and false balustraded windows, but these days worshippers congregate in the modern whitewashed wat behind these shrines, leaving the atmospheric and appealingly quaint collection of decaying prangs and casuarina topiary to chickens, stray dogs and the occasional tourist.

Wat Mahathat

Thanon Damnoen Kasem

Heading west along Thanon Phra Song from Wat Kamphaeng Laeng, across the river you can see the prangs of Phetchaburi's most fully restored and important temple, **Wat Mahathat**, long before you reach them. Boasting the "Mahathat" title only since 1954 – when the requisite Buddha relics were donated by the king – it was probably founded in the fourteenth century, but suffered badly at the hands of the Burmese. The five landmark prangs at its heart are adorned with stucco figures of mythical creatures, though these are nothing compared with those on the roofs of the main viharn and the bot. Instead of tapering off into the usual serpentine *chofa*, the gables are studded with miniature *thep* and *deva* figures (angels and gods), which add an almost mischievous vitality to the place. In a similar vein, a couple of gold-embossed crocodiles snarl above the entrance to the bot, and a caricature carving of a bespectacled man rubs shoulders with mythical giants in a relief around the base of the gold Buddha, housed in a separate mondop nearby.

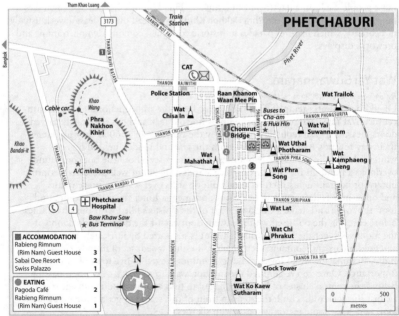

Khao Wang

Dominating Phetchaburi's western outskirts stands Rama IV's palace, a stew of mid-nineteenth-century Thai and European styles scattered over the crest of the hill known as **Khao Wang** ("Palace Hill"). During his day, the royal entourage would struggle its way up the steep brick path to the summit, but now there's a **cable car** (daily 8.30am–4.30pm; B200 including admission to the palace) which starts from the western flank of the hill off Highway 4; there's also a path up the eastern flank, starting near Thanon Rajwithi. If you do walk up the hill, be warned that hundreds of quite aggressive monkeys hang out at its base and on the path to the top.

Up top, the wooded hill is littered with wats, prangs, chedis, whitewashed gazebos and lots more, in an ill-assorted combination of architectural idioms – the prang-topped viharn, washed all over in burnt sienna, is particularly ungainly. Whenever the king came on an excursion here, he stayed in the airy summer house, **Phra Nakhon Khiri** (daily 8.30am–4pm; B150; visitors are asked to dress politely, covering knees and shoulders), with its Mediterranean-style shutters and verandas. Now a museum, it houses a moderately interesting collection of ceramics, furniture and other artefacts given to the royal family by foreign friends. Besides being cool and breezy, Khao Wang also proved to be a good stargazing spot, so Rama IV, a keen astronomer (see page 524), had an open-sided, glass-domed observatory built close to his sleeping quarters.

6

ARRIVAL AND DEPARTURE   PHETCHABURI

BY TRAIN

Phetchaburi station is on the north side of the town centre. Destinations Bangkok (Hualamphong Station 11 daily, Thonburi Station 2 daily; 2hr 45min–3hr 45min); Chumphon (11 daily; 4hr–6hr 30min); Hua Hin (13 daily; 1hr); Nakhon Pathom (13 daily; 1hr 30min–2hr); Nakhon Si Thammarat (2 daily; 12–13hr); Prachuap Khiri Khan (10 daily; 2–3hr); Ratchaburi (13 daily; 40min–1hr); Surat Thani (10 daily; 6hr 45min–9hr); Trang (2 daily; 13hr).

BY BUS

There's no longer a dedicated service between Bangkok and Phetchaburi, which is now served by through-buses on their way to or from Bangkok – all services between the capital and southern Thailand have to pass through the town on Highway 4.

Through-buses There's a small Baw Khaw Saw terminal on the east side of Highway 4 (Thanon Phetkasem), which

is where southbound through-buses will set you down or pick you up. Northbound through-buses on their way to Bangkok stop on the opposite side of the highway: ask to get off at "Sii Yaek Phetcharat", the crossroads of Highway 4 and Thanon Bandai-It by Phetcharat Hospital – otherwise you might be put off at the Big C Department Store about 5km south of town. Songthaews and motorbike taxis run between Highway 4 and the town centre.

From/to Cha-am and Hua Hin Local, roughly half-hourly buses from and to Cha-am (1hr 20min) and Hua Hin (1hr 50min) use the small terminal in the town centre, less than a 10min walk from Chomrut Bridge.

BY MINIBUS

Several companies, which all now congregate to the south of Khao Wang near Wat Tham Kaeo, offer licensed a/c minibuses to the Southern Bus Terminal in Bangkok, Ratchaburi, Nakhon Pathom, Kanchanaburi and Hua Hin.

GETTING AROUND

By samlor or songthaew Shared songthaews circulate round the town, but to see the major temples in a day and have sufficient energy left for climbing Khao Wang, you might want to hire a samlor or a songthaew for a couple of

hours, at about B100–200/hr, depending on distance.
By bicycle or motorbike You can rent bicycles (B100/day) and motorbikes (B100–250/day) from *Rabieng Rimnum Guest House*.

INFORMATION AND TOURS

Tourist information There's no TAT office in town, but *Rabieng Rimnum Guest House* is a good source of local information. It can also book day-trips and multi-day visits

to Kaeng Krachan National Park for hiking (two or three nights are good for trekking into the jungle), roughly from November to June or July.

6

SWEET PHETCHABURI

Almost half the shops in Phetchaburi stock the town's famous **khanom** (sweet snacks), as do many of the souvenir stalls crowding the base of Khao Wang and vendors at the day market on Thanon Matayawong. The most well-known local speciality is *maw kaeng* (best sampled from Raan Khanom Waan Mae Pin on the west side of Thanon Matayawong, just north of Phongsuriya), a baked sweet egg custard made with mung beans and coconut and sometimes flavoured with lotus seeds, durian or taro. Other Phetchaburi classics to look out for include *khanom taan*, small, steamed, saffron-coloured cakes made with local palm sugar, coconut and rice flour, and wrapped in banana-leaf cases; and *thong yot*, orange balls of palm sugar and baked egg yolk.

ACCOMMODATION

Rabieng Rimnum (Rim Nam) Guest House 1 Thanon Chisa-in, on the southwest corner of Chomrut Bridge ☎032 425707 or ☎089 919 7446; map p.508. Occupying a century-old house next to the Phet River and, less appealingly, a noisy main road, this popular, central guesthouse offers very simple rooms with shared, cold-water bathrooms, lots of local information and the best restaurant in town. Excellent rates for singles (B150). B240

Sabai Dee Resort 65 Thanon Khlong Kacheng ☎086 344 4418; map p.508. Centrally placed and friendly budget option opposite *Rabieng Rimnum*, with a small garden running

down to the river. If you don't mind sharing a bathroom, go for one of the large, white fan rooms with polished wooden floors in the bright, airy, mostly wooden main building, which are more characterful than the small, en-suite, a/c rooms and bamboo bungalows in the garden. B350

Swiss Palazzo Thanon Khiri Rataya ☎032 400 250, ✆swiss-palazzo.com; map p.508. Tastefully decorated in earth tones, this new boutique hotel has just four rooms, all with a/c, hot shower, TV, espresso machine and balcony. Below is a café that makes its own pasta and ice cream. Continental breakfast included. B1990

EATING

As well as for *khanom*, Phetchaburi is famous for savoury **khao chae**: originally a Mon dish designed to cool you down in the hot season, it consists of rice in chilled, flower-scented water served with delicate, fried side dishes, such as shredded Chinese radish and balls of shrimp paste, dried fish and palm sugar. It's available at the day market until sold out, usually around 3pm. There's a nice little **night market** on the small road parallel to and immediately west of Thanon Matayawong.

Pagoda Café Thanon Khlong Kacheng, opposite Wat Mahathat; map p.508. The cool industrial look of polished concrete and red bricks may be looking all-too-

familiar by now on your travels around Thailand, but the espresso coffees are very good, and they serve cakes and teas, too. Tues–Sun 9am–6pm.

Rabieng Rimnum (Rim Nam) Guest House 1 Thanon Chisa-in, on the southwest corner of Chomrut Bridge ☎032 425707 or ☎089 919 7446; map p.508. The town's best restaurant, an airy, wooden house with riverside tables, attached to the guesthouse of the same name. It offers a long and interesting menu of inexpensive Thai dishes, from banana-blossom salad (B80) to the tasty Phetchaburi speciality, sugar-palm fruit curry with prawns (B100) and is deservedly popular with local diners. Daily 8am–midnight.

Cha-am and around

Forever in the shadow of its more famous neighbour, Hua Hin, 25km to the south, the resort of **CHA-AM** is nevertheless very popular with Thais on short breaks, and it sports one or two package-holiday high-rises and Western-style restaurants for Europeans, too. Mostly, though, it's weekending families and partying student groups from Bangkok who eat and drink at the rows of umbrella-shaded tables and deckchairs on the sand, or brave the sea on banana boats or rubber tyres, the women clad modestly in T-shirts and shorts rather than bikinis. The long, straight beach here is pleasantly shaded, though rather gritty and very narrow at high tide, and the water is perfectly swimmable, if not pristine. During the week the pace of life in Cha-am is slow, and it's easy to find a solitary spot under the thick canopy of casuarinas, particularly at the northerly end of the beach, but that's rarely possible at weekends, when prices shoot up and traffic thickens considerably.

   Cha-am has a functional pocket of development around Thanon Phetkasem (Highway 4), close to the junction with Thanon Narathip, the main access road to the beach, 1km to the east. However, the 3km seaside promenade of Thanon Ruamchit is where you'll find most of the hotels, restaurants, a small tourist police station (corner of Thanon Narathip) and a few other tourist-oriented businesses; Thanon Ruamchit's sois are numbered according to whether they're north or south of Thanon Narathip.

Phra Ratchaniwet Marukhathaiyawan

10km south of Cha-am, off the road to Hua Hin, Highway 4 • Daily except Wed 8.30am–4.30pm (ticket office closes 4pm) • B30 • Dress politely (with shoulders and knees covered) as it's a former royal palace • Best accessed by private transport, but Cha-am–Hua Hin buses (roughly every 30min) stop within 2km of the palace at the sign for Rama VI Camp – just follow the road through the army compound

Set in beautiful grounds, the lustrous seaside palace of Rama VI, **Phra Ratchaniwet Marukhathaiyawan** (aka Mrigadayavan Palace), is rarely visited by foreigners, though it sees plenty of Thai visitors. Designed by an Italian architect, Ercole Manfredi, in a westernized Thai style, and completed in 1924, the entire, 400m-long complex of sixteen golden teak pavilions and connecting walkways is raised off the ground on over a thousand concrete columns, with a niche for water at the base of each to keep out ants. Commissioned by Rama VI, who'd been advised by his doctors to take the warm sea air for his rheumatoid arthritis, it's often referred to as "the palace of love and hope" as the king first visited with his pregnant queen, who later miscarried and was subsequently demoted to royal consort. After the king's death in 1925, the palace was abandoned to the corrosive sea air, until time-consuming restoration work began in the 1970s. During the current phase of works, scheduled to go on until 2024, the rooms upstairs are closed to visitors, but you can still wander the grounds and admire the architecture from below, a stylish composition of verandas and latticework painted in shades of cream and light blue. The king stayed in the central group of buildings, with the best sea view and a 50m-long elevated walkway to his private bathing pavilion, while the south wing contained the apartments of the royal consorts, with its own bathing pavilion connected by a walkway. You can look in on the spacious open hall on the ground floor of the north wing, hung with chandeliers and encircled by a first-floor balcony, which was once used as a meeting room and a theatre for the king to perform in his own plays. On the way back out towards Highway 4, towards the north end of the army camp, you can also explore a 300m boardwalk that's been laid over a mangrove swamp.

ARRIVAL AND DEPARTURE   CHA-AM

By train The station is a few blocks west of the main Phetkasem–Narathip junction.

Destinations Bangkok (Hualamphong Station 3 daily, Thonburi Station 2 daily; 3hr 30min–4hr 30min); Chumphon (3 daily; 5–7hr); Hua Hin (5 daily; 30min); Prachuap Khiri Khan (4 daily; 2hr).

By bus A handful of a/c minibus companies that run services to Bangkok's Southern Bus Terminal are based near the beach, including one on the south side of Thanon Narathip near the junction with Thanon Ruamchit that also serves Ratchaburi and Nakhon Pathom. However, these vehicles only depart when full, so for a wider choice of transport, you're better off heading to Highway 4, close to the junction with Thanon Narathip. Plenty of through-buses and the local, roughly half-hourly service between Hua Hin (35min) and Phetchaburi (1hr 20min) stop here, and there are several companies with desks on the pavement that operate a/c minibuses to Ratchaburi, Nakhon Pathom and Bangkok's Southern and Northern Bus Terminals and Don Muang Airport. Roong Reuang coaches from Hua Hin to Suvarnabhumi Airport or Pattaya will pick up passengers here, in front of the Government Savings Bank, just north of the crossroads (see page 515).

GETTING AROUND

By bicycle or motorbike A number of shops along the beachfront rent motorbikes as well as bicycles, tandems and even three- and four-person bikes.

INFORMATION

Tourist information The local TAT office (daily 8.30am–4.30pm; ☎032 471005–6, ✉tatphet@tat.or.th), which is on Highway 4 (west side) about 1km south of Thanon Narathip, covers the whole of Phetchaburi province, but can do little more than hand out a map of Cha-am, in Thai.

6

ACCOMMODATION

There are no obvious backpacker-oriented places in Cha-am; instead you'll find mainly small, mid-range hotels and guesthouses, concentrated on Thanon Ruamchit and the adjoining sois (with a concentration of budget places on Soi 1 North), and upmarket, out-of-town resorts, many on the road down to Hua Hin (covered on page 512). Many Cha-am hotels put their prices up on Saturdays and over bank-holiday weekends.

Golden Beach Cha-am Hotel Just south of Soi Cha-am North 8 at 208/14 Thanon Ruamchit ☎ 032 472 850–3, ⓦ goldenbeachchaam.com. Good-value twenty-storey hotel with a full-height atrium, an attractive, free-form swimming pool and gym, set back from the promenade. The large, nicely appointed rooms have a/c, hot water, mini-bars and TVs, as well as balconies, all with sea views. B1700

Nana North Beach North of Soi Cha-am North 10 towards the canal ☎ 032 471 357, ⓦ facebook.com/nananorthbeach. Huge range of well-kept accommodation with a/c, hot water, TVs and fridges, including two-bedroom houses (B2500) and bright, pretty, tiled rooms either in the main building on the front or down the quieter side alley. B950

Nirandorn 3 Just south of the Narathip junction on Thanon Ruamchit ☎ 032 470300. Clean, well-maintained hotel rooms and a few tightly packed, motel-style bungalows, decorated in crisp, modern whites and browns, with sofas, safes, a/c, TVs, fridges and hot water; all rooms in the hotel block are sea-facing, sporting balconies and deckchairs. There's also a small, attractive swimming pool. Room B700, bungalow B1000

So Sofitel 6km north of central Cha-am ☎ 032 709 555, ⓦ so-sofitel-huahin.com. Sleek, designer hideaway featuring a triumphal, white-marble staircase up to the lobby and a huge reflective pool as its centrepiece. The accommodation blocks have a striking cubic look but are very comfortable, while contemporary Thai food is served at the hotel's *White Oven restaurant*. There are two swimming pools (an active pool for families and an adult-only chill-out pool) and a luxurious spa. B4700

EATING AND DRINKING

The choice of **restaurants** in Cha-am is not a patch on the range you get in Hua Hin, but there should be enough Thai-style seafood to keep you satisfied, including at the dozens of deckchair-and-umbrella places on the beach.

Didine From the beachfront, take Soi Cha-am South 4, then turn left and right onto Soi Chao Lai ☎ 087 189 3864, ⓦ didine-chaam.com. One of the best places in Cha-am to get Western food, with a French chef and a long menu of tasty traditional favourites, such as beef bourguignon (B310), pizzas, pastas, salads and plenty of fish and seafood. Daily 5–10pm.

Krua Medsai North end of the beach, just after the canal ☎ 032 430 196. A very Thai institution, this huge, open-sided, thatched pavilion sits on the beach, with *luk thung* on the sound system, views down to Hua Hin and nice breezes off the sea. People flock here for the very good seafood, simply grilled or in dishes such as delicious stir-fried shrimp with acacia shoots (B250). Daily 10am–9.30pm.

O-Zone Thanon Ruamchit, north of Soi Cha-am North 7 ☎ 032 470 897. Popular bar-restaurant whose attractions include mellow live folk music early evening, followed from about 9pm by bands playing Thai and Western pop, and a menu that encompasses a few Western dishes such as pizza and steak, one-plate Thai dishes and more complex offerings such as miang kung sot (fresh prawns with wild betel leaves; B180). Daily 5pm–midnight.

Hua Hin

Thailand's oldest beach resort, **HUA HIN** used to be little more than an overgrown fishing village with one exceptionally grand hotel, but the arrival of mass tourism, high-rise hotels and farang-managed hostess bars has made a serious dent in its once idiosyncratic charm. With the far superior beaches of Ko Samui, Krabi and Ko Samet so close at hand, there's little to draw the dedicated sunseeker here. Hua Hin's most distinctive attractions are its distinctive squid-pier guesthouses and restaurants on Thanon Naretdamri, which are augmented by many other spots to enjoy fine seafood elsewhere in the resort, while at the other end of the scale the former *Railway Hotel* (now the *Centara Grand*) provides all the atmosphere you can afford. In addition, the town makes a convenient base for day-trips to Khao Sam Roi Yot National Park to the south and Pala-u Falls in Kaeng Krachan National Park to the west. Hua Hin also hosts the long-running annual Hua Hin International Jazz Festival, a free event on the beach featuring Thai and international musicians (ⓦ huahininterjazz.com).

Brief history

The **royal family** were Hua Hin's main visitors at the start of the twentieth century, but the place became more widely popular in the 1920s, when the opening of the Bangkok–Malaysia rail line made short excursions to the beach much more viable. The Victorian-style *Railway Hotel* was opened in 1922, originally as a necessary overnight stop on the three-day journey to Malaysia. At the same time Rama VI commissioned the nine-hole Royal Hua Hin Golf Course (now 18 holes; ☎032 512475) to the west of the station, and in 1926 Rama VII had his own summer palace, Klai Klangwon ("Far from Worries"), erected at the northern end of the beach. It was here, ironically, that Rama VII was staying in 1932 when the coup was launched in Bangkok against the system of absolute monarchy. Before his death in 2016, Rama IX stayed here as often as he could, which put the local police and military on their best behaviour. As a result, both Thais and expats consider Hua Hin a comparatively safe, hassle-free place to live and do business – hence the number of farang-oriented real-estate agencies in the area.

6

The central shorefront

The prettiest part of Hua Hin's 5km-long **beach** is the patch in front of and to the south of the *Centara Grand*, where the sand is at its softest and whitest. North of here the shore is crowded with tables and chairs belonging to a string of small restaurant shacks, beyond which the beach ends at a Chinese temple atop a flight of steps running down to Thanon Naretdamri. The coast to the north of the pagoda is dominated by the jetties and terraces of the squid-pier guesthouses and seafood restaurants, the hub of the original fishing village, which dates back to the early nineteenth century.

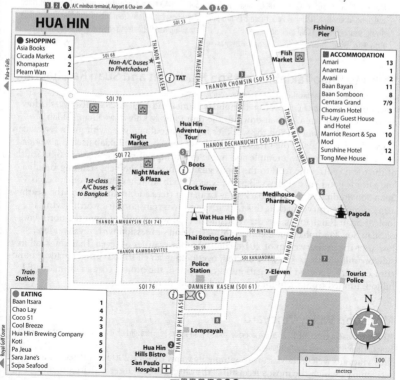

6

EXCURSIONS AND ACTIVITIES AROUND HUA HIN

A popular day-trip from Hua Hin is 63km west to the fifteen-tiered **Pala-u Waterfall**, situated close to the Burmese border and within **Kaeng Krachan National Park** (B300; ⓦnps.dnp. go.th). Though the falls themselves are hardly exceptional, the route there takes you through lush, hilly landscape and past innumerable pineapple plantations. There's no public transport to the falls, but every tour operator features them in its programme. To get there under your own steam, follow the signs from the west end of Thanon Chomsin along Highway 3218. Once inside the park you'll see hundreds of butterflies and may also catch sight of monitor lizards and six species of hornbill. A slippery and occasionally steep path follows the river through the fairly dense jungle up to the falls, passing the (numbered) tiers en route to the remote fifteenth level, though most people opt to stop at the third level, which has the first pool of any decent depth (full of fish but not that clear) and is a half-hour walk from the car park.

Hua Hin also offers excursions to Khao Sam Roi Yot National Park, Phetchaburi, Amphawa floating market and Kanchanaburi, not to mention the old summer palace of Phra Ratchaniwet Marukhathaiyawan just to the north (see page 511). In addition, a number of **activities** are available, such as cycling and kiteboarding.

TOUR OPERATORS

Hua Hin Adventure Tour 69/7 Thanon Naebkehat ☎032 530314, ⓦhuahinadventuretour.com. A huge range of tours, including Pala-u Falls (from B1700/ person), a boat trip in Kaeng Krachan National Park (from B2000), Khao Sam Roi Yot National Park (from B1700; including kayaking on Khao Daeng canal, from B2000), Phetchaburi (B1500), Amphawa Floating Market (B2000), sea cruises (B1800) and elephant watching in Kui Buri National Park (from B1900), plus diving, snorkelling and Thai cooking classes.

Hua Hin Bike Tours 15/120 Thanon Phetkasem ☎081 173 4469, ⓦhuahinbiketours.com. A variety of guided half-day (from B1450) and day rides (from B2950 including lunch), including transfers, as well as rental for B500/day and multi-day tours.

Kiteboarding Asia ☎081 591 4593, ⓦkite boardingasia.com. Kiteboarding courses and rental from three shops on the beach to the south of the *Centara Grand*, the first of which is between Soi 71 and Soi 73 (B4000 for a one-day course, B11,000 for three days; best conditions from Feb to mid-May); also offers stand-up paddleboarding courses and rental.

South to Khao Takiab, Suan Son Pradiphat and Suan Ratchaphak

Green songthaews run to Khao Takiab every 20min or so from central Thanon Sa Song

South of the *Centara Grand*, hotels, holiday homes and high-rise condos overshadow nearly the whole run of beach down to the promontory known as Khao Takiab (Chopstick Hill), but during the week it's fairly quiet along here, with just a few widely spaced food stalls along the broad, squeakily soft beach. **Khao Takiab** itself is a wooded outcrop surmounted by a temple and home to a troupe of monkeys, about 6km south of the town centre; the road to the top is guarded by a tall, golden, standing Buddha and affords good coastal views. Beyond Khao Takiab stretches another quiet beach, **Suan Son Pradiphat**, which is backed by casuarina trees and maintained by the nearby army camp. If you've made it this far with your own transport, it's worth having a look at Suan Ratchaphak, on the west side of Highway 4, inland from the north end of Suan Son Pradiphat, for a glimpse into Thailand's obsession with royalty. Here, just after the military coup of 2014, colossal bronze statues of seven Thai kings, all in suitably militaristic poses, were erected, overlooking an enormous army parade ground-cum-car park. Dogged by allegations of corruption, the project cost an estimated B1 billion, funded from the public purse and private donations.

Monsoon Valley Vineyard

45km west of Hua Hin ☎081 701 0222, ⓦmonsoonvalley.com • Shuttle service from Hua Hin Hills Bistro and Wine Cellar, next to Villa Market on Thanon Phetkasem (2 daily; B300 return)

This vineyard welcomes visitors to sample its wares (from B290 for a three-wine tasting set), among which the most successful is the Shiraz Rosé. Other activities include tours of the estate and vineyard by jeep, elephant or mountain bike; there's a restaurant with fine views from its terrace over the rows of vines to the broad, tranquil valley beyond.

ARRIVAL AND DEPARTURE

HUA HIN

There are currently no scheduled services to Hua Hin Airport.

BY TRAIN

All services between the south and Bangkok (mostly using Hualamphong, with a few stopping trains serving Thonburi station) stop at Hua Hin's photogenic 1920s station, a 10min walk west of the seafront.

Destinations Bangkok (Hualamphong 11 daily, Thonburi 2 daily; 3hr 30min–5hr); Padang Besar (for Malaysia; 1 daily; 13hr 40min); Chumphon (11 daily; 3hr 30min–5hr 20min); Nakhon Si Thammarat (2 daily; 12hr); Prachuap Khiri Khan (10 daily; 1hr 30min); Surat Thani (10 daily; 5hr 40min–8hr); Trang (2 daily; 12hr).

BY BUS

Baw Khaw Saw terminal Most government and private buses (including some through services on their way from Bangkok to points south) use the main Baw Khaw Saw terminal, which is well to the south of the centre, between Thanon Phetkasem sois 96 and 98, though some services will drop you off at the central clocktower (Wat Hua Hin) on their way in.

Destinations Chiang Mai (3 daily; 12–13hr); Chumphon (roughly hourly in the morning, fewer in the afternoon; 3hr 30min–4hr 30min); Krabi (2 daily; 9–10hr); Phuket (via Ranong; 5 daily; 9–10hr); Surat Thani (2 daily; 7–8hr).

From/to Bangkok's Southern Bus Terminal A/c buses (roughly every 2hr 30min; 4hr) to Bangkok's Southern Bus Terminal, stopping at Cha-am and Phetchaburi, leave from beside the *Siri Phetkasem* hotel on Thanon Sa Song.

From/to Bangkok's Suvarnabhumi Airport and Pattaya Roong Reuang (ⓦairporthuahinbus.com) operate coaches to and from Suvarnabhumi Airport (9 daily; 4hr) and Pattaya (1–2 daily; 5–6hr), from their base by the airport on the east side of Thanon Phetkasem, 6km north of the centre, which is linked to the clock tower by a non-stop shuttle van (B30).

Non-a/c Phetchaburi buses, via Cha-am From a spot north of TAT on Thanon Phetkasem opposite the Esso petrol station (roughly every 30min; 1hr 50min).

To the islands Lomprayah, with an office on Thanon Phetkasem south of Thanon Damnern Kasem (ⓣ032 533 739, ⓦlomprayah.com), runs a twice-daily bus and catamaran service (daily at 8.30am & 11.30pm) to Ko Tao (B1050), Ko Pha Ngan (B1300) and Ko Samui (B1400), via Chumphon.

BY MINIBUS

Several private, government-licensed companies based at a new terminal on Soi 51, just off Thanon Phetkasem, run a/c minibuses to and from many destinations in Bangkok, including the Southern and Northern Bus Terminals and Don Muang Airport, Kanchanaburi, Pranburi and Prachuap Khiri Khan.

BY BOAT TO PATTAYA

Ferries operated by Royal Passenger Liner (ⓣ087 905 2525) run once a day (2hr 30min; B1250) to the Bali Hai Pier in Pattaya from Soi Ao Hua Don 3, near Khao Takiab.

GETTING AROUND

By taxi service Hua Hin's taxi services include plentiful motorcycle taxis, samlors and pricy tuk-tuks.

By songthaew Shared songthaews of different colours operate several fixed routes in Hua Hin. Green ones run from the airport, 6km north of town, via Thanon Sa Song to Khao Takiab in the south. White songthaews head down Thanon Phetkasem from the railway station all the way to Soi 112 and Wat Huay Mongkol (daytime only). White ones with a red flash have two circular routes that both include a stretch on Thanon Phetkasem between Soi 94 and Soi 55 and Thanon Naebkehat, while the orange ones

also run up Thanon Phetkasem from Soi 94, via Thanon Sa Song, terminating at Makro hypermarket far to the north of town.

By car or motorbike Car rental outlets include Avis, on the north side of town at 15/112 Thanon Phetkasem, near Soi 29, who will deliver and collect anywhere in Hua Hin or Cha-am (ⓣ02 251 1131, ⓦavisthailand.com). Among the transport touts who rent out mopeds for B200/day on Thanon Damnern Kasem, try Khun Dennapa (ⓣ081 942 5615, ⓦden-carrental.com), who hangs out on the pavement in front of the *Sirin Hotel*, near the 7-Eleven.

INFORMATION

Tourist information The TAT office is on Thanon Phetkasem, just north of Thanon Chomsin (daily 8.30am–4.30pm; ⓣ032 513885). There's also a helpful municipal tourist information office (Mon–Fri 8.30am–4.30pm; ⓣ032 511047, ext 100) in the local government buildings on the corner of Thanon Damnern Kasem and Thanon

Phetkasem, with a satellite office just up Phetkasem at the clocktower (Mon–Fri 8.30am–7pm, Sat & Sun 9am–5pm).

Publications and websites Among Hua Hin's many English-language publications and maps, the *Hua Hin Pocket Guide*, a free, monthly booklet that includes an outline of the town's songthaew routes, is worth keeping an eye out for.

ACCOMMODATION

A night or two at the former *Railway Hotel* (now the *Centara Grand*) is reason in itself to visit Hua Hin, but there are plenty of other **places to stay**. The most unusual **guesthouses** are those built on the **squid piers** on Thanon Naretdamri, north of the pagoda, with rooms strung out along wooden jetties so you can hear, feel – and smell, especially at low tide – the sea beneath you, even if you can't afford a room with an actual sea view. Room rates at many places can drop significantly from Mondays to Thursdays, so don't be afraid to ask for a discount.

Amari 117/74 Thanon Takiab ☎ 032 616 600, ⓦ amari. com; map p.513. About 3km south of the centre on the road to Khao Takiab (with a free shuttle service to town), the *Amari* is set around a beautiful, 40m garden pool fed by fountains. The spacious rooms are elegantly contemporary with big walk-in showers, and there's a delightful spa, Breeze, offering innovative treatments to suit your mood, as well as a gym and a fun kids' club. It's not on the strand itself but has a beach club with a pool and restaurant a 5min walk (or a shuttle ride) away. **B3880**

★ **Anantara** 5km north of central Hua Hin on Thanon Phetkasem ☎ 032 520250, ⓦ anantara.com; map p.513. Set in effusive, beautifully designed tropical gardens, this is a lovely resort-style idyll, just out of town (with a regular shuttle service). Accommodation is in eight-room Thai-style pavilions, whose stylishly appointed rooms use plenty of red wood. The hotel has very good Italian, Thai and grill restaurants, two pools, a gorgeous spa, a cooking school, two tennis courts, a kids' club, free yoga classes and mountain bikes, and its own stretch of beach, with kayaks available. **B6730**

Avani About 8km north of central Hua Hin on Thanon Phetkasem ☎ 032 898 989, ⓦ minorhotels.com/avani; map p.513. Chic luxury hotel on a long, narrow plot of landscaped gardens with no less than three expansive swimming pools. Diverse rooms, including pool villas (some with Jacuzzis on their balconies) are done out in cool blond woods with splashes of green and blue. There's an attractive contemporary spa, a kids' club and a fine Italian beachfront restaurant. **B4470**

★ **Baan Bayan** 119 Thanon Petchkasem ☎ 032 533540–4, ⓦ baanbayan.com; map p.513. This very appealing boutique hotel has been sensitively renovated in keeping with the century-old Thai colonial-style villa at its heart, with polished teakwood floors, white clapboard walls, carved eaves and antique-style furniture. On the beachfront, there is a relaxing terrace café, together with separate kids' and adults' pools. Breakfast included. **B3780**

Baan Somboon 13/4 Soi Kaseam Sumphan, Thanon Damnern Kasem ☎ 032 511538, ⓦ facebook.com/ baansomboon; map p.513. Down a quiet but very central soi, this guesthouse divides between a lovely, old-fashioned house with polished teak floors, decorated with a melange of Thai antiques, woodcarvings and Western "old master"

prints, and a small annexe. Spruce, homely rooms come with small, hot-water bathrooms, fridges, TVs, fans and a/c (B100 discount if you can manage without the a/c), and there's a small garden crammed with plants, songbirds and a fish tank. **B800**

★ **Centara Grand** 1 Thanon Damnern Kasem ☎ 032 512 021–38, ⓦ centarahotelsresorts.com; map p.513. The original Thai "destination hotel", the main building is a classic of colonial-style architecture, boasting high ceilings, polished wood panelling, period furniture, wide sea-view balconies and a huge, landscaped garden full of topiary animals. Across the road, lush beachfront gardens shelter gorgeous, all-white clapboard villas, most with their own small marble pools, the rest with large outdoor Jacuzzis. With a total of four swimming pools, a lovely spa, tennis courts, a kids' club and a giant chessboard, you need never leave the grounds. You can even tuck into afternoon tea at *The Museum*, the original lobby, which now displays hotel memorabilia. **B7040**

Chomsin Hotel 130/4 Thanon Chomsin ☎ 032 515348 (bookable through ⓦ booking.com); map p.513. Handsome, sand-coloured, small hotel with a pleasant welcome, offering smart, bright, compact rooms in neutral colours with a few decorative touches and plenty of amenities: a/c, hot showers, cable TV, fridges and safes. Some have balconies from which you can glimpse the sea over the rooftops. **B1300**

Fu-Lay Guest House and Hotel 110/1 Thanon Naretdamri, guesthouse ☎ 032 513145, ⓦ fulayhuahin. net; hotel ☎ 032 513670, ⓦ fulayhuahin.com; map p.513. *Fu-Lay* is in two halves, with guesthouse rooms strung along a jetty and a/c hotel accommodation, some with sea-view balconies, in a low-rise block across the street. The jetty guesthouse is the most stylish of its kind in Hua Hin, offering attractively appointed a/c rooms with nice hot-water bathrooms (B1050), plus some cheap en-suite fan rooms (some with hot water) and a breezy seating area set right over the water, where you can enjoy breakfast. Fan **B550**, a/c **B950**

Marriott Resort & Spa 107/1 Thanon Phetkasem ☎ 032 904 666, ⓦ marriott.com; map p.513. Water features are at the heart of this lively new 300-room hotel. Children will love all the waterpark-like slides and fountains at the kids' and teen pools (not to mention the kids' club); there's also an adult pool, as well as a huge loop pool for exploring the gardens. Stylish rooms include subtle Thai elements in their contemporary design, and there's an excellent beachfront restaurant, Big Fish. **B6620**

Mod 116 Thanon Naretdamri ☎ 032 512296, ⓦ mod guesthouse.com; map p.513. A friendly and well-maintained little jetty guesthouse, where rooms are all shining white, with cable TV and small but attractive bathrooms, and come with either fan and cold water or a/c and hot. There's a nice, breezy, covered sea-view terrace at the end. Fan **B585**, a/c **B855**

SOI 67 GUESTHOUSES

About fifteen minutes' walk south down the beach from the *Centara Grand,* or 2km by road down Thanon Phetkasem, there's a little knot of accommodation on Soi 67. Here, facing each other across the short, narrow soi about 100m back from the beach, are a dozen little guesthouses, many Scandinavian–Thai run, which share a swimming pool; none comprises more than twenty rooms and most charge about B1000. They're very popular with older European couples, many of whom return for several months every winter, so booking is essential.

Sunshine Hotel Soi 67, off Thanon Phetkasem ☎032 515309, ✉sunshine.guesthouse.beach@gmail.com; map p.513. Typical Soi 67 guesthouse, with friendly staff and a wide variety of clean, well-maintained a/c rooms, most with small balconies, and all with hot water, cable TV and fridge. B800

Tong Mee House 1 Soi Ruam Phow, Thanon Naebkehat ☎032 530725, ⓦtongmeehousehuahin.com; map p.513. In a modern, five-storey block on a quiet soi, this friendly guesthouse offers great value: six small but neat rooms with a/c, hot water, fridges, TVs and small balconies, and an attractive "penthouse" double with a large, shaded roof terrace (B1000). B600

EATING AND DRINKING

Hua Hin is renowned for its **seafood**, and some of the best places to enjoy the local catch are the seafront and squid-pier restaurants along Thanon Naretdamri. Fish also features heavily at the large and lively **night market**, which sets up at sunset along Soi 72 (the western end of Thanon Dechanuchit). The biggest concentration of **bars** is in the network of sois between the *Hilton Hotel* and Wat Hua Hin, particularly along Soi Bintabat, Soi Kanjanomai and Thanon Poonsuk; most of these places are so-called "bar-beers", with lots of seating round the bar and hostesses dispensing beer and flirtation through the night.

Baan Itsara 7 Thanon Naebkehat, near Soi 10, north of Thanon Damrongrat (Phetkasem Soi 51) ☎032 530574; map p.513. Very good seafood in a traditional lime-green wooden house with simple tables on a seaside terrace. The speciality here is sweet basil sauce – which comes out something like pesto – with, for example, crab claws (B250), but the grilled mackerel and the seafood *laap* with land-lotus leaves are also delicious. Daily 11am–10pm.

Chao Lay 15 Thanon Naretdamri; map p.513. Hua Hin's most famous jetty restaurant is deservedly popular, serving up high-quality seafood from live tanks out front via a big open kitchen, including rock lobster, blue crab, scallops, cottonfish, mixed seafood hot plates and specialities such as the "prawn curry mousse" (*haw mok*). Most main dishes cost around B250–350. Daily 10am–10pm.

Coco 51 Soi 51, off the east side of Thanon Naebkehat ☎032 515597, ⓦcoco51.com; map p.513. Genteel, white-linen-tablecloth affair on a seductive beachfront terrace, where the menu splits evenly between Western and Thai food, including a few southern specialities. The chu chi curry with king prawns and lychees (B390) and the chicken in pandanus leaves are especially good, and there's live music every night (Sunday is Latino night). Daily 11am–10.30pm.

Cool Breeze 62 Thanon Naretdamri ☎032 531062, ⓦcoolbreezecafebar.com; map p.513. Either in the nice little garden at the back or amid the fresh, leafy decor inside an atmospheric old fisherman's house, you can tuck into some very tasty tapas (including plenty of vegetarian options) at this bar-café, which imports many of its ingredients from Spain. You can get a set of seven tapas for B995, and they also do baguettes, paella and other seafood and meat mains. Happy hour till 7pm includes 3-for-2 tapas and 2-for-1 sangria. Daily 11am until late.

Hua Hin Brewing Company Thanon Naretdamri; map p.513. Owned by the adjacent *Hilton,* this lively bar sports a nautical theme on its tiered streetside terraces and offers DJs, live bands, a pool table and TV sports. Daily 6pm–2am.

Koti Thanon Dechanuchit, corner of Thanon Phetkasem; map p.513. With pavement tables right on a prominent corner opposite the night market, this very simple Thai-Chinese restaurant rustles up justifiably famous *hoy jor* (deep-fried crab sausage; B200), which goes nicely with its tasty fried rice with salted fish (B80). Expect to queue for a table in the evening. Daily noon–4pm & 6–10pm.

Pa Jeua Thanon Naretdamri, opposite the Hilton Hua Hin. Famous roadside stall that sells Thailand's favourite dessert, delicious *khao niaw mamuang* (fresh mango with sticky rice and coconut milk), for B120. Daily 9.30am–2pm.

Sara Jane's 28/1 Thanon Poonsuk ☎032 532990; map p.513. This branch of an old Bangkok favourite provides authentic northeastern food, including *som tam* with raw salted crab (B95), delicious central Thai seafood dishes, as well as breakfasts, pizzas, pastas and other Western fare, in a lovely big garden shaded by trees. Daily 9.30am–1pm & 5.30–11pm.

★ **Sopa Seafood** Soi Mooban Takiab (a right fork off the main Khao Takiab road), near Lunar Hut Resort and opposite Soi Ao Hua Don 9 ☎081 880 7112; map

6

p.513. You won't regret the trek out to this excellent seafood restaurant, set on a wooden deck among banana trees, just inland from Khao Takiab. The poo nim phat phong karii (soft-shell crab fried in curry powder; B300) is exquisite and the plaa meuk det diaw (sun-dried squid; B200) is even better. Daily 9am–9pm (closed first Tues of the month).

ENTERTAINMENT

Thai Boxing Garden Down a small soi off Thanon Poonsuk ☎032 515 269, ⓦthaiboxinghuahin.com. Generally speaking, Tuesdays and Saturdays are fight nights (certainly in high season, sometimes taking a break in the off-season) at the Thai Boxing Garden with programmes starting at 9pm (B600–800); it's owned by local *muay thai* champion Khun Chop, who also runs Thai boxing classes every day (B400/hr for a one-to-one session).

SHOPPING

Asia Books Market Village shopping centre, Thanon Petchkasem near Soi 88/1 ☎098 494 1466; map p.513. Small branch of Thailand's main English-language bookstore chain. Daily 10.30am–9pm (until 10pm Fri & Sat).

Cicada Market Suan Sri, Thanon Takiab (near the Hyatt Regency, about 4km south of the Centara Grand) ⓦcicadamarket.com; map p.513. Modelled on Chiang Mai's walking streets, this weekend market features jewellery, cute accessories, lots of T-shirts and other clothes, artists' stalls and, of course, plenty of food, plus regular performances of all kinds in the amphitheatre. Fri & Sat 4–11pm, Sun 4–10pm.

Khomapastr 218 Thanon Phetkasem ☎032 511250, ⓦkhomapastrfabrics.com; map p.513. Famous outlet for *pha kiaw* (or *pha khomapastr*), brightly coloured, hand-printed cotton with lovely, swirling *kannok* patterns, usually with strong elements of gold – Khomapastr's founder, himself a prince, was inspired to start the business when rummaging through trunks of nineteenth-century royal clothing at Bangkok's National Museum in the 1940s. You can buy the cloth by the piece or metre, or made up into skirts, shirts, cushion covers and bags. Mon–Sat 9am–7pm, Sun 9am–5pm.

Plearn Wan Thanon Phetkasem, between sois 38 and 40 ⓦplearnwan.com; map p.513. Curious exercise in nostalgia and commercialism – the name "Enjoy the Past" says it all – that's been a raging success with Thais from all over the country. It's essentially a shopping mall, but in the vintage style of Thai-Chinese wooden shophouses, selling retro everything: *luk krung* CDs, old-fashioned toys, traditional coffee and desserts, ukuleles… Mon–Thurs & Sun 9am–9pm, Fri & Sat 9am–10pm.

DIRECTORY

Banks and exchange There are currency-exchange counters all over the resort, especially on Thanon Damnern Kasem and Thanon Naretdamri; most of the main bank branches with ATMs are on Thanon Phetkasem.

Hospital Bangkok Hospital, 888 Thanon Phetkasem, south of the centre near Soi 94 (☎032 616800, ⓦbangkokhospital.com/huahin).

Immigration office The place to go for extensions of tourist visas and tourist visa exemptions, and for re-entry permits at Bluport shopping centre, between sois 100 and 102, Thanon Petchkasem (Mon–Fri 10am–6pm).

Meditation English-medium courses in sitting and walking meditation, either weekly or week-long, with talks on Buddhism, at Wat Khao Santi, just off Soi 91, Thanon Phetkasem (free, donations welcome; ⓦmeditation inhuahin.org).

Pharmacy Several in the resort, including the helpful and well-stocked Medihouse (daily 9.30am–11pm), opposite the *Hilton* on Thanon Naretdamri.

Thai language Classes and private lessons at TLC, 83/14 Wongchomsin Building, Thanon Phetkasem (near Soi 63/1; ☎032 533428, ⓦthailanguagecentre.org).

Tourist police For all emergencies, call the tourist police on the free, 24hr phoneline (☎1155), or contact them at their office opposite the *Centara Grand* at the beachfront end of Thanon Damnern Kasem.

Pak Nam Pran

The stretch of coast between Hua Hin and Chumphon barely registers on most foreign tourists' radar, but many better-off Bangkokians have favourite beaches in this area, the nicest of which is sophisticated **PAK NAM PRAN** (aka Pranburi). Just 30km or so south of Hua Hin, Pak Nam Pran used to cater only for families who owned beach villas here, but in the past few years the shorefront homes have been joined by a growing number of enticing, if pricey, boutique hotels, and signs are there's more development to come. For now, facilities consist of just a few minimarkets, car-rental outlets and independent bars and restaurants, especially around the *Evason* hotel towards the northern end of the beach, plus the possibility of organizing day-trips to nearby Khao Sam Roi Yot National Park through hotel staff; there's also kiteboarding lessons and rental, as well as stand-up paddleboarding lessons, rental and tours, with Asian kiteboarding champion, Yoda (T 087 017 6428, W facebook.com/yodakiteschool), based at Preeburan Resort, about 2km south of the Evason.

As along much of the Gulf coast, the **beach** itself, also known as Hat Naresuan, is not exceptional (it has hardly any shade and is suffering from erosion in parts), but it is long, with fine sand, and nearly always empty, and you're quite likely to see dolphins playing within sight of the shore. The strand stretches south from Pak Nam Pran town at the mouth of the Pran River – which is known for its colourful fishing boats, specializing in squid – for around 7km to the headland at Khao Kalok ("Skull Mountain") and the tiny Thao Kosa Forest Park.

6

ARRIVAL AND DEPARTURE — PAK NAM PRAN

Easiest access is via the town of **Pranburi**, which straddles Highway 4 some 23km south of Hua Hin. There's no public transport from Pranburi to Pak Nam Pran beach, 10km or so away, but hotels can arrange transfers and any Pranburi songthaew driver will taxi you there. Because of this and because the hotels and restaurants are well spread out along the beach, it's best to have your own transport. Pranburi's main crossroads (Highway 4 and Thanon Ratbamrung) is at Talat Chaikaew – if making your own way, the easiest route is to turn east off Highway 4 here and take minor road 3168 down to the sea, picking up the relevant sign for your hotel.

FROM/TO PRANBURI

By train Pranburi's quaint old station is 4km east of the Highway 4 crossroads (Talat Chaikaew) towards the beach, off the north side of Route 3168.

Destinations Bangkok (Hualamphong 1 daily, Thonburi 2 daily; 5hr); Chumphon (2 daily; 4hr 30min); Prachuap Khiri Khan (3 daily; 1hr).

By bus As well as many through services to and from the south, Pranburi is served by a/c buses from Bangkok's Southern Bus Terminal and non-a/c buses from Thanon Sa Song in Hua Hin, which drop passengers close by the main Highway 4 crossroads at Talat Chaikaew.

Destinations Bangkok (every 30min; 3–4hr); Hua Hin (roughly every 30min; 30min).

By minibus A/c minibuses from Bangkok's Southern and Northern Bus Terminals generally stop at the Tesco Lotus supermarket on Highway 4 opposite Pranburi's City Hall, 2km north of Talat Chaikaew, but you could ask the driver to take you to your beach hotel for a little extra money.

ACCOMMODATION

Pak Nam Pran's charming boutique **accommodation** is its biggest draw. With influences ranging from Greece to the South Pacific, from Morocco to Scandinavia, the style tends to be more arty than five-star, though you will certainly be comfortable. Some hotels aren't suitable for kids owing to their multiple levels and unfenced flights of steps. Breakfast is generally included in the price of the room. During weekends in high season (Nov–May), hoteliers routinely put their prices up and you'll need to book ahead. The following are spread over a 2km stretch of the beachfront road, starting about 4km south of Pak Nam Pran town.

Aleenta Central Pak Nam Pran beach T 032 618333, W aleenta.com. This stunningly designed, eco-friendly hotel, divided between the Main Wing and the Frangipani Wing, 500m down the beach, offers gorgeous circular, thatched bungalows and very tasteful rooms and villas, most with uninterrupted sea views, decks and plunge pools. The feel is modernist chic, with elegantly understated local furnishings and huge windows, and iPods and wi-fi capability rather than TVs. There are pools in both wings and a spa, while the restaurant uses produce from its own organic farm. B5740

The Beach House Bungalows Northern Pak Nam Pran beach, set inland behind the Evason T 090 141 7208, W beach-housepranburi.com. Popular with kite-boarders, this friendly English-run resort offers half a dozen smart, polished-concrete bungalows, with a/c, hot showers, smart TVs and fridges, plus a family apartment, around a communal plunge pool. B800

Evason Northern Pak Nam Pran beach T 032 632111, W sixsenses.com/evason. The biggest and best-known hotel in Pak Nam Pran, but as accommodation is screened by graceful gardens, the feel is quite private and small-scale. Rooms are attractively cool and contemporary, with big balconies; for extra privacy, you could check into a super-luxe private-pool villa, a favourite choice of Thai film stars. Facilities include a huge pool, a spa, three restaurants, tennis courts and a kids' club with its own pool. Breakfast included. B5050

★ **Huaplee Lazy Beach** Central Pak Nam Pran beach T 032 630555, W huapleelazybeach.com. This exceptionally cute collection of six idiosyncratic white-cube beachfront rooms around a pretty lawn, as well as several nearby suites and villas, some with their own pools, is the work of the architect-interior designer owners. It's a characterful place of whimsical, marine-themed interiors done out with white-painted wood floors, blue-and-white colour schemes and funky shell and driftwood decor. The rooms are airy and bright but all have a/c, fridges and TVs; some have fantastic sea-view terraces. Breakfast included. B3500

EATING

Krua Jaew On the edge of Pak Nam Pran town, about 2km north of the Evason ☎ 032 631 302. The best of several neighbouring seafront restaurants, offering an enormous, mid-priced menu of mostly fish and seafood dishes, including the local speciality, deep-fried sun-dried squid (*pla meuk det diaw*; B200), excellent crab curry and seafood curry soufflé (*haw mok thalay*, on the menu as "steamed seafood with spicy and coconut milk"). Unsigned in English, but it's the first restaurant you'll come to heading up the beach road into Pak Nam Pran, on the left-hand side.

Daily roughly 10am–9pm.

Krua Sawatdikan Khao Kalok On the south side of Khao Kalok's rocky outcrop at the far southern end of Pak Nam Pran beach ☎ 086 701 8597. This simple shorefront restaurant has an extensive menu of very good seafood dishes (mostly B90–150) and great views of Khao Sam Roi Yot from its beach tables under the casuarinas; mosquitoes are a problem here though, so take repellent. Daily 11am–8pm, sometimes later (especially at weekends).

Khao Sam Roi Yot National Park

National park entry fee B200 • ☎ 032 821568, ⓦ nps.dnp.go.th

With a name that translates as "The Mountain with Three Hundred Peaks", **KHAO SAM ROI YOT NATIONAL PARK**, with its northern entrance 28km south of Pak Nam Pran beach or 63km from Hua Hin, encompasses a small but varied, mosquito-ridden coastal zone of just 98 square kilometres. The dramatic limestone crags after which it is named are the dominant feature, looming 600m above the Gulf waters and the forested interior, but perhaps more significant are the mud flats and freshwater marsh which attract and provide a breeding ground for thousands of migratory birds. **Bird-watching** at Thung Khao Sam Roi Yot swamp is a major draw, but the famously photogenic Phraya Nakhon Khiri cave is the focus of most day-trips, while a few decent trails and a couple of secluded beaches provide added interest.

Orientation in the park is fairly straightforward. One main inland road runs roughly north–south through it from the R3168 (the road from Pranburi's main junction to Pak Nam Pran), passing, in order: the 2km side road to **Hat Phu Noi**, a quiet, golden-sand beach that offers several resort alternatives to the park's accommodation and the chance to see dolphins in the cool season; the northern park checkpoint, 4km further on; the turn-offs for Ban Bang Pu (the jumping-off point for Tham Phraya Nakhon), Ban Khung Tanot (for Tham Sai) and Hat Sam Phraya (all to the east); then going over Khao Daeng canal, before looping westwards around the main massif, past the **park headquarters** (where park brochures and maps are available) and the southern checkpoint (14km from the northern checkpoint), to Highway 4 at kilometre-stone 286.5.

Tham Phraya Nakhon

B400 return per boat from Wat Bang Pu

Khao Sam Roi Yot's most visited attraction is the **Tham Phraya Nakhon** cave system, hidden high up on a cliffside above **Hat Laem Sala**, an unremarkable sandy bay with a national park visitor centre that's inaccessible to vehicles. The usual way to get to Hat Laem Sala is by a five-minute boat ride from the knot of food stalls behind Wat Bang Pu on the edge of **Ban Bang Pu** fishing village (6km from the northern checkpoint). It's also possible to walk over the headland from behind Wat Bang Pu to Hat Laem Sala, along a signed, but at times steep, 500m trail. From Hat Laem Sala, another taxing though shaded trail runs up the hillside to Tham Phraya Nakhon in around thirty minutes.

The huge twin **caves** are filled with stalactites and stalagmites and wreathed in lianas and gnarly trees, but their most dramatic features are the partially collapsed roofs, which allow the sunlight to stream in and illuminate the interiors, in particular beaming down in the late morning on the famous royal pavilion, Phra Thi Nang Khua Kharunhad, which was built in the second cave in 1890 in honour of Rama V.

Tham Sai

South of Tham Phraya Nakhon lies **Tham Sai**, a thoroughly dark and dank limestone cave, complete with stalactites, stalagmites and petrified waterfalls (electric lighting is switched on when there are enough visitors at weekends, but otherwise torches are available to rent). It's reached by a 20min trail from **Ban Khung Tanot** village (accessible by road, 8km on from the Ban Bang Pu turn-off).

6

Khao Daeng and around

Canal cruise B600 for up to six people • 089 903 1619

The next turning off the main road will take you down to **Hat Sam Phraya**, a quiet, kilometre-long beach with a national park visitor centre, while a little further on the road crosses mangrove-fringed **Khao Daeng canal**. From beside Wat Khao Daeng, on the west side of the main road here, you can charter a boat for a one-hour cruise that's best in the early morning or the late afternoon.

A couple of kilometres on, you can scramble up **Khao Daeng** itself, a 157m-high outcrop that offers good summit views over the coast, via a thirty-minute trail that begins near the park headquarters. The park's 45-minute **Mangrove Forest Nature Trail** also begins close to the headquarters leading through the swampy domiciles of monitor lizards and egrets, with the chance of encountering long-tailed (crab-eating) macaques.

Thung Khao Sam Roi Yot

Accessed not from the main park road, but by turning east off Highway 4, 200m north of kilometre-stone 276, and continuing for 9km

The park hosts up to three hundred species of **birds** and between September and November the mud flats are thick with migratory flocks from Siberia, China and northern Europe. To the west of Khao Sam Roi Yot lies Thailand's largest freshwater marsh, **Thung Khao Sam Roi Yot** (aka Beung Bua), near the village of Rong Jai (Rong Che). With open-sided shelters over the water, this is an excellent place for observing waders and songbirds, and is one of only two places in the country where the **purple heron** breeds.

ARRIVAL AND GETTING AROUND

KHAO SAM ROI YOT

Like most of Thailand's national parks, Khao Sam Roi Yot is hard to explore without your own **transport**, and its sights are spread too far apart to walk between.

By bicycle, motorbike or car All three are available at *Dolphin Bay Resort*, while motorbikes can be rented in Hua

Hin (which also has car rental) or Prachuap Khiri Khan.

With a tour The park can be visited on a one-day tour from Hua Hin, including cycling tours (see page 514), Pak Nam Pran or *Dolphin Bay Resort*.

ACCOMMODATION AND EATING

Given the limitations of the park accommodation, many people prefer to stay a few kilometres to the north at the long, pleasingly shaded beach of Hat Phu Noi.

IN THE PARK
National Park accommodation 032 821 568, nps. dnp.go.th. Bungalows (for 5–6 people, with hot showers; from B1200) are available at the headquarters and should be booked ahead. At Hat Laem Sala, there are tents to rent

(B180–230 per tent) and a restaurant, but the national park bungalows are currently unavailable. Hat Sam Phraya, a beach between Khao Daeng canal and Ban Khung Tanot, also has tents to rent and a restaurant. Camping is possible at Thung Khao Sam Roi Yot if you bring your own tent.

HAT PHU NOI
Brassiere Cozy Beach Bottom end of Hat Phu Noi 032 630555, brassierebeach.com. Under the same architect

owners as *Huaplee* at Pak Nam Pran (see p.523), *Brassiere Cozy Beach* gets its name from the two conical Nom Sao ("Breast") islands offshore and the mainland spirit house where fishermen leave bras for good luck, and contains rooms with playful monikers like "La Perla". That may sound a bit naff to some, but the hotel itself is the height of quirky chic, airy and light-filled, with a mostly white-and-blue colour scheme. Some rooms have their own small Jacuzzi and pool or an outdoor bathroom, and canoes and bicycles are available, as well as sailing and stand-up paddleboarding. Breakfast included; prices go up a little at weekends. B2500

Dolphin Bay Northern end of the beach ☎ 032 825190, ⓦ dolphinbayresort.com. Eco-conscious, family-focused resort just across the quiet road from the beach, offering comfortable a/c rooms, bungalows and family suites with fridges, hot water and TVs, large children's and adults' pools set in an attractive, palm-fringed lawn, plus a kids' playground. Pick-ups from Pranburi (B350) and Hua Hin (B700) can be arranged and there's plenty of things to do once you're here: transport to Tham Phraya Nakhon (B500) and Thung Khao Sam Roi Yot (B700), half-day tours to see wild elephants at Kuiburi National Park (from B950/person), boat trips to Tham Phraya Nakhon and local islands, plus kayak, catamaran and stand-up paddleboard rental. B1490

Prachuap Khiri Khan and around

Despite lacking any must-see attractions, the tiny, unfrequented provincial capital of **PRACHUAP KHIRI KHAN**, 67km south of Pranburi, makes a pleasant place to break any journey up or down the coast. Apart from pineapples – the province is the biggest producer in Thailand, with truckloads for sale all along Highway 4 – its greatest asset is its setting: a huge, palm-fringed, half-moon bay, dotted with colourful fishing boats and tipped by a rocky outcrop at the north end and by a small group of jungly islands to the south – the waterfront promenade in the town centre is great for a seafood lunch with a view. There's a lovely **beach** in the next bay to the south, Ao Manao, and generally Prachuap is a fine spot to settle into small-town Thai life.

The town is contained in a small grid of streets that runs just 250m east to west, between the sea and the train station – with Highway 4 about 2km west of the station – and around 1km north to south, from the Khao Chong Krajok hill at the northern end to the Wing 5 air-force base in the south. **Orientation** couldn't be simpler. The major central road across from the station to the pier is Thanon Kongkiat, while Highway 326, the main east–west access road to Highway 4, cuts across the north end of town, and there are four main north–south roads: Thanon Phitak Chat near the station, Thanon Salacheep, Thanon Susuek and the seafront road, Thanon Chai Thalay, which to the north of the pier becomes a **walking street** on Friday and Saturday evenings, selling food, clothes and handicrafts.

Khao Chong Krajok

The monkey-infested hill of **Khao Chong Krajok** is Prachuap's main sight: if you climb the 417 steps from Thanon Salacheep to the golden-spired chedi at the summit you get a great perspective on the scalloped coast below and west to the mountainous Burmese border, just 12km away.

Ao Manao

Inside Wing 5 air-force base (you usually need to sign in at the base checkpoint and may need to show your passport) • Head south down Thanon Salacheep (or down the promenade and turn right) to reach the checkpoint and continue for 2km through the base to the beach • Tuk-tuk to the beach around B80

At the far southern end of town, the long, clean, sandy beach at **Ao Manao** is the best place in the area for swimming and sunbathing, sheltered between pristine, tree-covered headlands. On weekdays you're likely to have the sand almost to yourself, but it's a very popular spot with Thai families on weekends when the stalls at the beachfront food centre do a roaring trade in the locally famous *som tam puu* (spicy

papaya salad with fresh crab), which you can eat at the deckchairs and tables under the thick canopy of pine trees on the beach. You can walk to the north end of the bay to the base of an outcrop known as Khao Lommuak, where a memorial commemorates the skirmish that took place here between Thai and Japanese forces in World War II.

King Mongkut Memorial Park of Science and Technology

12km south of town, on the beach at Wa Ko (Waghor) • Daily 9am–4pm, fish-feeding at 11am & 2pm (subject to change) • Aquarium B30 • ☎ 032 661103, ⊚ waghor.go.th • To get there, turn east off Highway 4 at kilometre-stone 335, or go through Ao Manao air-force base, bearing left along the coast all the way

The main feature of the **King Mongkut Memorial Park of Science and Technology** (also signed as Phra Chomklao Science Park) is the extensive and well-stocked **Waghor Aquarium**. Highlights include an underwater tunnel, touch pools and fish-feeding, and there are display boards and labels for most of the fish in English. It's nothing like as slick as Sea Life Ocean World in Bangkok, but then again it's less than a thirtieth of the price. About 500m south along the beach road, the park also contains an astronomy museum that's decidedly low-tech but with enough labels in English to maintain interest.

The park is thought to mark the spot where **Rama IV** came to observe a solar eclipse on August 18, 1868. Having predicted the eclipse's exact course, King Mongkut decided to publicize science among his subjects by mounting a large expedition, aiming specifically to quash their centuries-old fear that the sun was periodically swallowed by the dragon Rahoo, and more generally to rattle traditional notions of astrology and cosmology. To this end, he invited scientists all the way from France and the British governor of Singapore, and himself turned up with fifty elephants and all his court, including the astrologers – who, as the leader of the French expedition noted, "could hardly be blamed if they did not display much enthusiasm for the whole project". Unfortunately, both the king and his 15-year-old son contracted malaria at Waghor; Mongkut passed away in Bangkok on October 1, but Chulalongkorn survived to become Thailand's most venerated king, Rama V.

ARRIVAL AND DEPARTURE   PRACHUAP KHIRI KHAN

BY TRAIN

Most services on the Southern Line from Bangkok stop at the train station, which is just on the west side of the centre, at the western end of Thanon Kongkiat.

Destinations Bangkok (8 daily to Hualamphong, 2 to Thonburi; 5–7hr); Chumphon (9 daily; 2hr–3hr 30min); Nakhon Si Thammarat (2 daily; 10hr 30min); Surat Thani (8 daily; 4hr 30min–6hr); Trang (1 daily; 11hr).

BY BUS OR MINIBUS

Prachuap's bus terminal is out on Highway 4, north of Highway 326, the main access road to town. The number of long-distance bus services to and from the town centre is dwindling fast, with many people either heading out to the terminal to catch a through-bus (for points south, best in the morning or around midnight), or taking an a/c minibus from the centre.

Buses from/to Bangkok Pudtan Tour, on Thanon Phitak Chat just south of Thanon Kongkiat, runs a "first-class" a/c service to Bangkok's Southern Terminal (1 daily; 4hr 30min– 5hr), which stops at Pranburi, the Hua Hin bypass (Highway 37) and Phetchaburi.

A/c minibuses Several companies in the town centre offer a/c minibuses to Bangkok, including one near the start of Highway 326, just west of the Provincial Hall and the tourist office, which serves the Southern and Northern Bus Terminals, as well as Hua Hin. Around the corner, a short way down Thanon Phitak Chat, you'll find more a/c minibuses to Bangkok's Southern Bus Terminal. On Thanon Tessaban Bamrung (the road immediately north of Thanon Kongkiat), between Phitak Chat and Salacheep roads, you'll find services to Chumphon, which will stop on Highway 4 near Ban Krut.

INFORMATION AND GETTING AROUND

Tourist information There's a small but helpful municipal tourist information office (Mon–Fri 8.30am–4.30pm; ☎ 032 611491), where town maps are available, at the far northern end of town in a compound of provincial offices;

it's on the ground floor at the north end of a large modern building that faces the beachfront road across a car park.
Motorbike rental Motorbikes (B200–250/day) can be rented from *Sun Beach Guesthouse*.

ACCOMMODATION

Faa Chom Khleun Ao Manao ☎032 661088–9, ⓦaomanao.com. If you don't mind cosying up to the Thai military, this spruce air-force hotel on the Wing 5 base puts you right on the beach. All rooms have sea-view balconies, a/c, hot water, TV and fridge, and there's a large swimming pool. Breakfast included. B1240

Hadthong Hotel 21 Thanon Susuek, but also with an entrance just south of the pier on the beachfront road ☎032 601050, ⓦhadthong.com. Well-run, typical Thai provincial hotel, with comfortable rooms, many sporting balconies and peerless sea views, all with fridges, a/c, hot water and TVs – plus a 15m swimming pool overlooking the beach and snooker club. The cheapest rooms have mountain views, but it's only B100 more for a sea view. Breakfast included. B1100

House 73 73 Thanon Susuek, about 400m south of Thanon Kongkiat ☎086 046 3923, ⓦhomestay prachuap.blogspot.com. Striking modernist guesthouse with great views of the bay from its roof terrace and four a/c rooms which have been hand-painted in bold colours by the owners, taking inspiration from their favourite songs. B800

★ **Sun Beach Guesthouse** 160 Thanon Chai Thalay, 1km or so down the promenade from the pier ☎032 604770, ⓦsunbeachguesthouse.com. Run by a welcoming and helpful Thai–German couple, this palatial guesthouse is done out like a Mediterranean villa, with Corinthian columns and smart tiling everywhere. The bright, comfortable, mostly sky-blue rooms come with a/c, hot water, fridges, TVs and balconies, with prices varying according to the quality of the sea view. There's a seductive pool and whirlpool. B800

Thur Hostel 58 Thanon Chai Thalay, just south of Hadthong Hotel ☎096 047 5622, ⓦfacebook.com/ thurhostelprachuap. Newly opened, all-a/c hostel in an attractive white clapboard building with a sociable bar and pool table. Smart dorms have bunk beds and hot showers, while the private rooms range from twins with shared hot showers to en-suite doubles with large balconies overlooking the bay. There's a shared kitchen and bicycles for rent. Dorm B380, double B600

EATING AND DRINKING

Prachuap's famously good seafood is most cheaply sampled at the daytime food stalls at Ao Manao and at the town's lively and varied main **night market**, which sets up shop in the empty lot around the junction of Thanon Kongkiat and Thanon Phitak Chat.

Ma-prow 48 Thanon Chai Thalay, just south of Hadthong Hotel ☎092 667 2332. Mellow, rustic, airy restaurant overlooking the bay across the road (main courses around B150–200), which serves tasty squid with salted eggs and deep-fried spring rolls of crabmeat wrapped in tofu skin (hoy jor), as well as Western dishes including fish and chips. Daily 9am–9pm (last orders).

★ **Ploen Samut** South of the pier at 44 Thanon Chai Thalay, alongside the Hadthong Hotel ☎032 611115. The town's best restaurant has a pleasant, spacious courtyard facing the sea, and serves delicious pan-fried oysters, tasty crab claws and excellent *kaeng pa pla say* (silver whiting fish in country curry; B120) on its seafood-dominated menu. Daily 9.30am–10pm.

Rap Lom About 1km north of the centre, beyond Khao Chong Krajok and the adjacent bridge. Another locals' favourite for seafood, including a very good version of the regional speciality, *plaa meuk det diaw* (sun-dried squid; B170), but also offering some wild-boar dishes. On the landward side of the beach road, with views of the sea. Daily 10am–9pm.

Rome Seafood (MC Club House) Thanon Chai Thalay, just south of Thur Hostel. Excellent spot for a waterside drink and maybe a bite to eat, hung with motorcycle memorabilia and home to some of the friendliest bikers you're ever likely to meet. Daily 5/6pm until late.

Ban Krud

Graced with a tranquil, 5km sweep of white sand, pale-blue sea and swaying casuarinas, **BAN KRUD**, 70km south of Prachuap, supports a dozen or so fairly upmarket bungalow outfits and seafood restaurants along the central stretch of its shorefront road. About 1km inland from the main T-junction at the beach, the small, traditional village, which includes several ATMs, clusters around the train station. At the beach's northern end are a colourful fishing village that hosts a lively market on Thursday afternoons and a panoramic headland, **Khao Thongchai**, which is dominated by the 14m-high Phra Phut Kitti Sirichai Buddha image and its sparkling modern temple, **Wat Thang Sai**. Crowned with nine golden chedis, the temple displays an impressive fusion of traditional and contemporary features, including a series of charming modern stained-glass windows depicting Buddhist stories; reach it via a 1.5km-long road that spirals up from the

6

beachfront road. Other than a visit to the temple and possibly a snorkelling trip to Ko Thalu (from B400/person through, for example, *Bayview*), the main pastime in Ban Krud is sitting under the trees and enjoying a long seafood lunch or dinner.

ARRIVAL AND DEPARTURE BAN KRUD

By train Half a dozen services on the Southern Line from Bangkok stop at Ban Krud's tiny train station, where you should be able to find a motorbike taxi (with sidecar).
Destinations Bangkok (6 daily from Hualamphong, 1 from Thonburi; 5hr–7hr 30min); Chumphon (7 daily; 2hr); Nakhon Si Thammarat (1 daily; 9hr); Surat Thani (6 daily;

4hr–5hr 30min); Trang (1 daily; 10hr).
By bus Most southbound buses drop passengers on Highway 4, from where motorbike-and-sidecar taxis cover the 8km down to the beach; just one Bangkok–Bang Saphan a/c bus a day stops at Ban Krud itself.

ACCOMMODATION

Bayview North of the headland, 4km from Sala Thai on Hat Tangsai ☎ 032 695 566–7, ✆ bayviewbeachresort. com. Very welcoming, relaxed and shady spot on a long, quiet stretch of beach, with a swimming pool, a kids' pool and a lovely area for deckchairs under the beachside casuarinas. All the well-spaced, diverse bungalows boast a/c, fridges, TVs and hot water, and there's an excellent restaurant, free bicycles, and kayaks, motorbikes and cars to rent. Prices rise a little at weekends. Breakfast included. B1600

Sala Thai About 1km north of the central beachfront T-junction ☎ 032 695181, ✆ salathaibeachresort.com. Friendly resort where a wide variety of smart concrete bungalows and log cabins, all with a/c, hot water, fridge and TV, are spread around a spacious, pretty garden with lots of shady trees, just across the road from the beach; it also has a popular burger bar. Bikes and motorbikes for rent. Prices rise a little at weekends. Breakfast included. B1000

Chumphon

South Thailand officially starts at **CHUMPHON**, where the main highway splits into west- and east-coast branches, and inevitably the provincial capital saddles itself with the title "gateway to the south". Most tourists take this tag literally and use the town as nothing more than a transport interchange between the Bangkok train and boats to **Ko Tao, Pha Ngan and Samui**, so the town is well equipped to serve these passers-through, offering clued-up travel agents and efficient transport links. In truth, there's little call for exploring the fairly average beaches, islands and reefs around town when the varied and attractive strands of Ko Tao are just a short hop away.

ARRIVAL AND DEPARTURE CHUMPHON

BY PLANE
Nok Air flies to Chumphon from Bangkok's Don Muang Airport (2 daily; 1hr). It's possible to buy a combination ticket all the way from Bangkok through to Ko Tao with Nok, who also lay on a/c minibuses to Chumphon town for B200/person. At the time of writing, Air Asia were about to start a once-daily flight from Don Muang to Chumphon.

BY TRAIN
Chumphon train station is on the northwest edge of town, less than a 10min walk from most guesthouses and hotels.
Destinations Bangkok (10 daily to Hualamphong, 1 to Thonburi; 6hr 30min–9hr 30min); Padang Besar (for Malaysia; 1 daily; 9hr 30min); Nakhon Si Thammarat (2 daily; 7hr); Surat Thani (10 daily; 2hr 5min–4hr); Trang (2 daily; 7hr).

BY BUS OR MINIBUS
The government bus station is inconveniently located 11km west of town on Highway 41 (B150 on a motorbike taxi), though long-distance services will sometimes drop in town. There's a wide choice of destinations served by the bus station, but most that you're likely to be interested in are served by private, government-licensed a/c bus and minibus services based in town, departing from various locations (see map p.000). These include Suwanathee and Chokeanan Tour (✆ chokeanantour.com) buses to Bangkok, and Rungkit buses to Phuket, via Ranong and Khao Lak. Agents such as *Suda* and *Fame* (see page 527) can also fix you up with tourist a/c minibus tickets to Krabi, Ko Lanta and Khao Sok.
Destinations Bangkok (roughly hourly; 7–9hr); Hua Hin (roughly hourly; 3hr 30min–4hr 30min); Khao Lak (8 daily; 5–7hr); Nakhon Si Thammarat (8 daily; 5hr); Phuket (8

daily; 7–10hr); Prachuap Khiri Khan (every 45min; 3hr); Ranong (roughly hourly; 2hr 30min–3hr); Surat Thani (roughly hourly; 2hr 30min–4hr 30min).

BY BOAT

There are several different boat services from Chumphon to Ko Tao, Pha Ngan and Samui, tickets for all of which are sold by travel agents and guesthouses in town. Of these, the Songserm Express and the night boats are the most likely to be cancelled if the weather is very bad.

Lomprayah Catamaran Office at the train station ☏ 081 956 5644, ⓦ lomprayah.com. Daily 7am and 1.30pm from Ao Thung Makham Noi, 27km south of Chumphon, with a bus between pier and station costing B100 extra; 1hr 45min to Ko Tao (B600); around 3hr 45min to Ko Pha Ngan (B1000); around 4hr to Maenam, Ko Samui (B1100).

Songserm Office at the pier ☏ 077 506205, ⓦ songserm.

com. Daily 7am from Pak Nam, about 20km south of Chumphon, with transport to the pier from town included (pick-ups available from guesthouses and the station); 2hr 45min to Ko Tao (B500); around 5hr to Ko Pha Ngan (B800); around 6hr 15min to Na Thon, Ko Samui (B900).

Night boats to Ko Tao Cargo boats and car ferries of varying levels of comfort chug between Chumphon and Ko Tao overnight, taking about 6hr, some including transport to the pier from town in the ticket price, some not. Every night, except in the heaviest weather, at least one of these tubs will be running, though departure times may be affected by tides and storms; one of the more comfortable boats is the Porntaweesin (Tues, Thurs, Sat and Sun 11pm, from Tha Yang, about 15km south of Chumphon; ☏ 092 978 8302), charging B450, including transport from town and bunk beds, blankets and pillows in an a/c room.

INFORMATION AND TOURS

TAT office Down a short soi at 111 Thanon Tawee Sinka (daily 8.30am–4.30pm; ☏ 077 501831, ⓔ tatchumphon@ tat.or.th).

Suda Guest House Thanon Sala Daeng Soi 3 (aka Soi Bangkok Bank), 30m off Thanon Tha Tapao ☏ 080 144 2079 or ☏ 077 504366. The best source of information and fixer in town, offering a personal, unbiased service, is Suda at her

eponymous guesthouse. As well as tickets to Ko Tao, Suda offers discounted dive packages; bus and minibus tickets; twice-daily visa runs via Ranong to Myanmar (from B650; best in the morning); motorbike rental (B200–300/day); packages to Ko Chang (Ranong) and Ko Phayam; and local snorkelling and night-fishing trips.

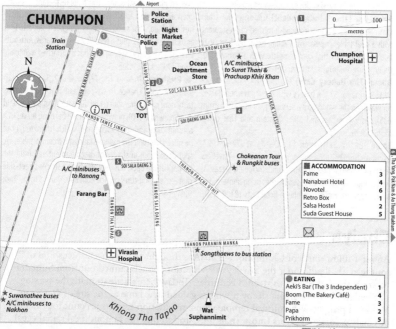

ACCOMMODATION

Fame 188/20–21 Thanon Sala Daeng ☎077 571077, ⓦchumphon-kohtao.com; map p.527. Above the restaurant and tour agency of the same name, this place has basic but good-sized and very clean rooms, with fans and hot water in either shared or en-suite bathrooms; the cheapest have mattresses on the floor. B150

Nanaburi Hotel 335/9 Thanon Pracha Uthit ☎077 503888, ⓦnanaburihotel.com; map p.527. Spread across two buildings in a quiet area set back from the main roads, the large rooms here have a pleasant, simple decor of wood and white paint and are equipped with a/c, hot showers, cable TV and fridges. B900

Novotel 15km southeast near Pak Nam ☎077 529529, ⓦnovotel-chumphon.com; map p.527. This low-rise luxury hotel on Paradornpab beach, done out in an unobtrusive Thai contemporary style, features spacious rooms with balconies and lots of dark wood, two restaurants, two swimming pools, a spa, a fitness centre, a nine-hole golf course and a kids' club and playground. Breakfast included. B2350

Retro Box About 1km east of the train station, just off Thanon Kromluang Chumphon on Soi 3 ☎077 510333, Wretroboxhotel.com; map p.527. Colourful a/c rooms with hot showers, TVs and fridges in salvaged shipping containers stacked up around an inviting swimming pool. The cheapest rooms only have enough space for bunk beds, while more expensive rooms have balconies, some of which give direct access to the pool. Light breakfast included. B690

Salsa Hostel Thanon Kromluang ☎077 505005, ⓦsalsahostel.com; map p.527. Welcoming hostel offering shining white, six- and seven-bed a/c dorms with modern bunk beds – with nice touches like individual reading lights – as well as a kitchen and rooftop terrace. Buffet breakfast included. Dorm B300

★ **Suda Guest House** Thanon Sala Daeng Soi 3 (aka Soi Bangkok Bank), 30m off Thanon Tha Tapao ☎080 144 2079 or ☎077 504366; map p.527. Chumphon's most welcoming homestay, offering clean, well-maintained rooms, some en suite but most with shared hot-water showers (two bedrooms to one bathroom), in the owner's modern house; the a/c can be switched on for an extra B100–150/room/night. Plenty of information available, B30 showers for passers-through and much more (see above). Phone for free transport from the train station (though not late at night). B250

EATING AND DRINKING

The cheapest place to eat is the **night market**, which sets up along both sides of Thanon Kromluang and is an enjoyable place to munch your way through a selection of fried noodles, barbecued chicken and sticky, coconut-laced sweets.

Aeki's Bar (The 3 Independent) Opposite the train station; map p.527. Rustic, wood-furnished bar-restaurant with a pool table, popular with young expat teachers, that doubles as a muay thai gym complete with a boxing ring. Daily 10am–midnight (kitchen closes at 10pm).

Boom (The Bakery Café) Thanon Tha Tapao ☎077 511523; map p.527. A bakery with a few pavement tables for watching the world go by, serving good espressos (from B35), tasty brownies and other Western and Thai cakes. Mon–Sat 8am–7pm.

Fame 188/20–21 Thanon Sala Daeng ☎077 571077, ⓦchumphon-kohtao.com; map p.527. Travellers' restaurant specializing in Italian food, including pizzas, as well as Indian dhal, loads of sandwiches using home-baked bread, espresso coffees and huge breakfasts (B100–150).

Daily 5am–9.30pm.

Papa Across from the train station on Thanon Kromluang ☎077 504504; map p.527. One of the liveliest places to eat dinner, this huge restaurant – mostly open-air, but with an a/c room – has an extensive menu of fresh seafood, Thai salads such as wingbean salad (B140) and Chinese dishes, plus a few Western standards. Also puts on live music every evening, and has an attached nightclub, Papa 2000. Daily 11am–3am.

★ **Prikhorm** Thanon Tha Tapao ☎077 570707; map p.527. A good chance to try southern Thai food such as tasty *nam phrik kung siap* (chilli dip with shrimp paste and dried prawns; B100), prawns and green *bai liang* leaves in a coconut curry and spicy *kaeng som*, which (thankfully) can be spiced to order. The main restaurant is a comfortable, a/c spot decked out in shades of green and entered from the car park at the back, but they also have a simple street-side canteen, serving curry on rice from B40. Daily 11am–9pm (last orders).

Chaiya

About 140km south of Chumphon, **CHAIYA** is thought to have been the capital of southern Thailand under the Srivijayan civilization, which fanned out from Sumatra between the eighth and thirteenth centuries. Today there's little to mark the passing of Srivijaya, but this small, sleepy town has gained new fame as the site of **Wat Suan Mokkh**, a progressively minded temple whose meditation retreats account for the bulk of Chaiya's foreign visitors (most Thais only stop to buy the famous local salted eggs).

Unless you're interested in one of the retreats, the town is best visited on a day-trip, either as a break in the journey south, or as an excursion from Surat Thani.

Wat Phra Boromathat

Western side of town, on the access road from Highway 41

The main sight in Chaiya is **Wat Phra Boromathat**, where the ninth-century chedi – one of very few surviving examples of Srivijayan architecture – is said to contain relics of the Buddha himself. Hidden away behind the viharn in a pretty, red-tiled cloister, the chedi looks like an oversized wedding cake surrounded by an ornamental moat. Its unusual square tiers are spiked with smaller chedis and decorated with gilt, in a style similar to the temples of central Java.

6

National Museum

On the eastern side of the temple • Wed–Sun 9am–4pm • B100

The **National Museum** is a bit of a disappointment. Although the Srivijaya period produced some of Thailand's finest sculpture, much of it discovered at Chaiya, the best pieces have been carted off to the National Museum in Bangkok. Replicas have been left in their stead, which are shown alongside fragments of some original statues, two intricately worked 2000-year-old bronze drums, found at Chaiya and Ko Samui, and various examples of Thai handicrafts. The best remaining pieces are a calm and elegant sixth- to seventh-century stone image of the Buddha meditating from Wat Phra Boromathat, and an equally serene head of a Buddha image, Ayutthayan-style in pink sandstone, from Wat Kaeo.

Wat Kaeo

On the south side of town

Heading towards the centre of Chaiya from Wat Phra Boromathat, you can reach this imposing ninth- or tenth-century brick chedi by taking the first paved road on the

---

MEDITATION RETREATS AT SUAN MOKKH

Meditation retreats are led by Western and Thai teachers over the first ten days of every month at the International Dharma Heritage (ⓦ suanmokkh-idh.org), a purpose-built compound 1km from the main temple at Wat Suan Mokkh. Large numbers of foreign travellers, both novices and experienced meditators, turn up for the retreats, which are intended as a challenging exercise in mental development – it's not an opportunity to relax and live at low cost for a few days. Conditions imitate the rigorous lifestyle of a *bhikkhu* (monk) as far as possible, each day beginning before dawn with meditation according to the Anapanasati method, which aims to achieve mindfulness by focusing on the breathing process. Although talks are given on Dharma (the doctrines of the Buddha – as interpreted by Buddhadasa Bhikkhu) and meditation technique, most of each day is spent practising Anapanasati in solitude. To aid concentration, participants maintain a rule of silence, broken only by daily chanting sessions, although supervisors are sometimes available for individual interviews if there are any questions or problems. Men and women are segregated into separate dormitory blocks and, like monks, are expected to help out with chores.

PRACTICALITIES

Turn up at Wat Suan Mokkh as early as possible (by 3pm at the latest) on the last day of the month to register (you can stay in Suan Mokkh the night before registration for free). The busiest period for the retreats is December–April, especially February and March. The fee is B2000 per person, which includes two vegetarian meals a day and accommodation in simple cells. Participants are required to hand in their mobile phones and tablets and are not allowed to leave the premises during the retreat – bring any supplies you think you might need (though there is a small, basic shop on site).

right, which brings you first to the restored base of the chedi at Wat Long, and then after 1km to **Wat Kaeo**, enclosed by a thick ring of trees. Here you can poke around the murky antechambers of the chedi, three of which house images of the Buddha subduing Mara.

Wat Suan Mokkh

6km south of Chaiya on Highway 41 • ⓦ suanmokkh.org • All buses between Surat Thani and Chumphon stop near the wat

The forest temple of **Wat Suan Mokkh** (Garden of Liberation) was founded by the abbot of Wat Phra Boromathat, **Buddhadasa Bhikkhu**, southern Thailand's most revered monk until his death in 1993 at the age of 87. His radical, back-to-basics philosophy, encompassing Christian, Zen and Taoist influences, lives on and continues to draw Thais from all over the country to the temple, as well as hundreds of foreigners. It's not necessary to sign up for one of the wat's **retreats** to enjoy the temple – you can simply drop by for a stroll through the wooded grounds.

The unusual layout of the wat is centred on the Golden Hill: scrambling up between trees and monks' huts, past the cremation site of Buddhadasa Bhikkhu, you'll reach a hushed clearing on top of the hill, which is the temple's holiest meeting place, a simple open-air platform decorated with images of the Buddha and the Wheel of Law. At the base of the hill, the outer walls of the Spiritual Theatre are lined with bas-reliefs, replicas of originals in India, which depict scenes from the life of the Buddha. Inside, every centimetre is covered with colourful didactic painting, executed by resident monks and visitors in a jumble of realistic and surrealistic styles.

ARRIVAL AND DEPARTURE   CHAIYA

By train The town lies on the main Southern Rail Line, served by trains (mostly overnight) from and to Bangkok's Hualamphong Station (8 daily; 8–11hr).

By bus Chaiya is 3km east of Highway 41, the main road down this section of the Gulf coast: buses running between Chumphon and Surat Thani will drop off (or pick up) on the highway, from where you can catch a motorbike taxi or blue songthaew into town.

By a/c minibus From Surat Thani's Talat Kaset II bus station, hourly a/c minibuses take 45min to reach Chaiya town centre.

Surat Thani

Uninspiring **SURAT THANI** ("City of the Good People"), 60km south of Chaiya, is generally worth visiting only as a jumping-off point for the Samui archipelago. Strung along the south bank of the Tapi River, with a busy port for rubber and coconuts near the river mouth, the town is experiencing rapid economic growth and paralyzing traffic jams. It might be worth a stay, however, when the Chak Phra Festival (see page 532) is on, or as a base for seeing the nearby historic town of Chaiya.

ARRIVAL AND DEPARTURE   SURAT THANI

Be aware that there have been reports of thefts from bags left in the luggage compartments of long-distance buses from Surat (keep your valuables with you); and of overcharging and **scams** by unregistered agents and touts selling tickets for minibus and bus services out of Surat, especially involving any kind of combination ticket, including those heading for Khao Sok National Park, Phuket, Krabi and Malaysia. To avoid the latter, either go direct to the relevant a/c minibus office at Talat Kaset II bus station (local offices are generally on the west side of the station, long-distance ones on the east side, and they all have to be authorized by the provincial office), or buy a bus ticket direct from the station.

BY PLANE

Arriving by air from Bangkok (currently Air Asia 7 daily, Nok Air 4 daily and Lion Air 4 daily from Don Muang, and Thai Smile 2 daily from Suvarnabhumi; 1hr 15min), Chiang Mai (Air Asia 2 daily; 2hr) or Kuala Lumpur (Malaysia, Air Asia 1 daily; 1hr 30min), you can take a B100 shuttle bus through Phantip (see page 531) for the 27km journey south from the airport into Surat Thani, while combination tickets through Lomprayah, for example, cost from B450 to Ko Samui, from B500 to Ko Pha Ngan and B950–1000 to Ko Tao. Avis (☎02 251 1131–2, ⍟avisthailand.com) and Budget (☎077 441166, ⍟budget.co.th) have outlets at the airport for car rental. Nok Air and Air Asia offer convenient flight-bus-boat through-tickets from Bangkok to Ko Samui and Ko Pha Ngan via Surat airport; Air Asia offer similar tickets to Ko Tao (though it's possible that these will stop when their Bangkok–Chumphon flights start). If you're flying out of Surat, you can most easily catch the airport shuttle bus from town at the Phantip office.

BY TRAIN

Arriving by train means arriving at Phunphin, 13km to the west, from where non-a/c buses run into Surat Thani, via the Baw Khaw Saw bus terminal, during daylight hours (in theory, every 15min, but more irregular than that). It's also possible to buy through-tickets to Ko Samui, Ko Pha Ngan and Ko Tao from a branch of Phantip Travel (see below) opposite the train station, including a connecting bus to the relevant pier. Buses heading out of Surat to Phang Nga and Phuket make a stop at Phunphin train station. You can book train tickets in Surat at Phantip travel agency, in front of Talat Kaset I at 293/6–8 Thanon Taladmai (☎077 272230, ⍟phantiptravel.com).

Destinations Bangkok (10 daily; 9–12hr); Padang Besar (for Malaysia; 1 daily; 7hr); Nakhon Si Thammarat (2 daily; 4hr 30min); Trang (2 daily; 4hr 30min).

BY BUS

Buses use three different terminals, two of which are on Thanon Taladmai in the centre of town: Talat Kaset I on the north side of the road (Phunphin, non-a/c Nakhon Si Thammarat and other local buses); and opposite at Talat Kaset II (most long-distance buses, including a/c services to Nakhon Si Thammarat; those for Phuket and Krabi have an office on the south side of Thanon Taladmai, opposite Phantip Travel). The Baw Khaw Saw terminal, 2km southwest of the centre on the road towards Phunphin, handles mostly Bangkok services. In addition, Phantip Travel (see page 531) runs many of its own a/c buses and minibuses to popular tourist destinations.

Destinations Bangkok (Southern Terminal; 20 daily; 9–12hr); Chumphon (roughly hourly; 3hr 30min–4hr 30min); Khao Lak (7 daily; 4hr); Khao Sok (7 daily; 2hr 30min); Krabi (every 30min; 3hr); Nakhon Si Thammarat (hourly; 2hr 30min–3hr); Phang Nga (6 daily; 3hr 30min); Phuket (every 40min; 5hr); Phunphin (irregular; 40min).

BY MINIBUS

A/c minibuses (to Chaiya, Chumphon, Ranong, Ratchabrapa Dam, Khao Sok, Phang Nga, Phuket, Krabi, Trang and Nakhon Si Thammarat) congregate around Talat Kaset II bus station, on the south side of Thanon Taladmai.

BOAT OPERATORS IN SURAT

Details of boats to Ko Samui, Ko Pha Ngan and Ko Tao, most of which leave from Don Sak pier, 68km east of Surat, are

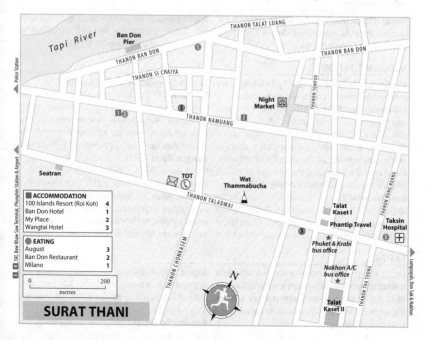

6

THE CHAK PHRA FESTIVAL

At the start of the eleventh lunar month (usually in October) the people of Surat Thani celebrate the end of Buddhist Lent with the **Chak Phra Festival** (Pulling the Buddha), which symbolizes the Buddha's return to earth after a monsoon season spent preaching to his mother in heaven. On the Tapi River, tugboats pull the town's principal Buddha image on a raft decorated with huge nagas, while on land sleigh-like floats bearing Buddha images and colourful flags and parasols are hauled across the countryside and through the streets. As the monks have been confined to their monasteries for three months, the end of Lent is also the time to give them generous offerings in the *kathin* ceremony, of which Surat Thani has its own version, called Thot Pha Pa, when the offerings are hung on tree branches planted in front of the houses before dawn. Longboat races, between teams from all over the south, are also held during the festival.

given in the account of each island – see pages 535, 553 and 565. Phunphin and the bus stations are teeming with touts, with transport waiting to escort you to their employer's boat service to the islands – they're generally reliable, but make sure you don't get talked onto the wrong boat. If you manage to avoid getting hustled, you can buy tickets direct from the boat operators or from Phantip travel agency (see page 531).

Lomprayah Tapi Pier, 5km northeast of the centre near the mouth of the Tapi River ☎081 893 3663, ⓦ lomprayah.com. Catamarans to Samui and Pha Ngan from Tapi Pier, and a passenger ferry to Samui and Pha Ngan from Don Sak, with their own connecting buses from Phunphin train station and the airport and connections on to Ko Tao via Ko Pha Ngan.

Seatran Thanon Taladmai, ☎077 950559, ⓦ seatranferry.com. Vehicle ferries to Samui (with their own connecting buses), from Don Sak.

Night boats The night boats to Samui, Pha Ngan and Tao, which are barely glorified cargo boats, line up during the day at Ban Don Pier in the centre of Surat; it's just a question of turning up and buying a ticket.

GETTING AROUND

By share-songthaew Small share-songthaews buzz around town, charging around B20/person for a short journey.

INFORMATION

Tourist information TAT's office is at the western end of town at 5 Thanon Taladmai (daily 8.30am–4.30pm; ☎077 288817–9, ⓔ tatsurat@tat.or.th).

Tourist police On the southern bypass near the junction with Thanon Srivichai, the westward continuation of Thanon Taladmai (☎1155 or ☎077 421281).

ACCOMMODATION

A lot of **accommodation** in Surat Thani is noisy, grotty and overpriced, but there are a few notable exceptions.

100 Islands Resort (Roi Koh) On the southern bypass near the tourist police and opposite Tesco Lotus ☎077 201 150–8, ⓦ 100islandsresort.com; map p.531. Though out of the centre, this place offers attractive, comfortable rooms with a/c, hot water, TVs and mini-bars, a small spa and a decent-sized, free-form pool set in a lush garden with a waterfall. Breakfast included. B900

Ban Don Hotel Above a restaurant at 268/2 Thanon Namuang ☎077 272167; map p.531. Most of the very clean rooms here, with en-suite bathrooms, TV and fans or a/c (some of the latter have hot showers), are set back from the noise of the main road. Fan B250, a/c B400

My Place 247/5 Thanon Namuang ☎077 272288, ⓦ myplacesurat.com; map p.531. A welcoming, modern Thai–Chinese hotel and café in the town centre with some bright splashes of colour and attractive floral motifs; the cheapest rooms have shared cold showers. Fan B199, a/c B490

Wangtai Hotel 1 Thanon Taladmai, on the western side of the centre by the TAT office ☎077 283020–5, ⓦ wangtaisurat.com; map p.531. Surat Thani's best upmarket option, and surprisingly good value, with over two hundred large, smart, recently refurbished rooms around a good-sized swimming pool, as well as fitness and massage rooms. Breakfast included. B1150

EATING

Besides the restaurants listed below, there's a large **night market** between Thanon Namuang and Thanon Ban Don, which displays an eye-catching range of dishes; a smaller offshoot by Ban Don pier offers less choice but is handy if you're taking a night boat.

August Thanon Taladmai; map p.531. Colourful café, decorated with cartoon murals, serving tuna sandwiches (B90), all-day breakfasts, espresso coffees and smoothies. Daily 7am–7pm.

Ban Don Restaurant 268/2 Thanon Namuang; map

p.531. Basic, bustling restaurant with plain, marble-topped tables, which serves large portions of tasty, inexpensive Thai and Chinese food – mostly noodle and rice dishes (around B50), but also green curry and *tom yam*. Daily 6am–4/5pm.

Milano Opposite the night-boat piers on Thanon

Ban Don ☎077 285633; map p.531. This place has an authentic oven turning out very tasty and reasonably priced pizzas (from B200), though its home-made pasta is not so successful. Also serves other Western main courses, Mexican dishes, sandwiches and espresso coffees. Daily 11am–10pm.

Ko Samui

Over a million visitors a year, ranging from globetrotting backpackers to suitcase-toting fortnighters, come to southern Thailand just for the beautiful beaches of **KO SAMUI**, 80km from Surat. At 15km across and down, Samui is generally large enough to cope with this diversity – except during the rush at Christmas and New Year – and the paradisal sands and clear blue seas have to a surprising extent kept their good looks, enhanced by a thick fringe of palm trees that gives a harvest of more than two million coconuts each month. However, development behind the beaches – which has brought the islanders far greater prosperity than the crop could ever provide – speeds along in a messy, haphazard fashion with little concern for the environment. At least there's a local bylaw limiting new construction to the height of a coconut palm (usually about three storeys), though this has not deterred either the luxury hotel

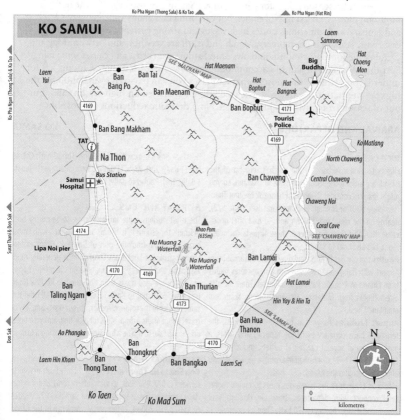

groups or the real-estate developers who have recently been throwing up estates of second homes for Thais and foreigners.

For most visitors, the days are spent indulging in a few watersports or just lying on the beach waiting for the next drinks-seller, hair-braider or masseur to come along. For something more active, you should not miss the almost supernatural beauty of the **Ang Thong National Marine Park** (see page 549), which comprises many of the eighty islands in the Samui archipelago. Otherwise, a day-trip by rented car or motorbike on the 50km round-island road will throw up plenty more fine beaches.

The island's most appealing strand, **Chaweng**, has seen the heaviest, most crowded development and is now the most expensive place to stay, though it does offer by far the best amenities and nightlife, ranging from tawdry bar-beers to cool beach clubs. Its slightly smaller neighbour, **Lamai**, lags a little behind in terms of looks and top-end development, but retains pockets of backpacker bungalow resorts. The other favourite for backpackers is **Maenam**, which, though less attractive again, is markedly quiet, with plenty of room to breathe between the beach and the round-island road. Adjacent **Bophut** is similar in appearance, but generally more sophisticated, with a cluster of boutique resorts, fine restaurants and a distinct Mediterranean feel in its congenial beachfront village, now dubbed "Fisherman's Village". **Choeng Mon**, set apart in Samui's northeast corner, offers something different again: the small, part-sandy, part-rocky bay is tranquil and pretty, the seafront between the handful of upmarket hotels is comparatively under-developed, and Chaweng's nightlife is within easy striking distance.

No particular **season** is best for coming to Ko Samui (see also page 9). The northeast monsoon blows heaviest in November, but can bring rain at any time between October and January, and sometimes causes high waves and strong currents, especially on the east coast. January is often breezy, March and April are very hot, and between May and October the southwest monsoon blows onto Samui's west coast and causes some rain.

At the lower end of Samui's **accommodation** scale, there are very few rooms left for under B500, while at the most upmarket places you can pay well over B5000 for the highest international standards. The prices listed are based on high-season rates, but out of season (roughly May, June, Oct & Nov) dramatic reductions are possible.

ARRIVAL AND DEPARTURE   KO SAMUI

BY PLANE
Flights to Samui Airport, in the northeastern tip of the island, are among the most expensive in Thailand, so you might want to consider flying from Bangkok to Surat Thani (see page 530) or Nakhon Si Thammarat (see page 572), nearby on the mainland; Nok Air and Air Asia offer good-value through-tickets via either of these airports, including flight, bus and boat to Samui.

Routes You can get to Ko Samui direct from Suvarnabhumi Airport with Bangkok Airways, which also operates flights from Chiang Mai, Krabi, Pattaya and Phuket. There are also direct flights from Malaysia, Singapore, Hong Kong and mainland China.

Airport facilities As well as bars and restaurants, the terminals have currency-exchange facilities and ATMs, post office and several car rental outlets, including Avis (☎02 251 1131–2, ⓦavisthailand.com) who will deliver and collect around the island.

Minibus transfers A/c minibuses meet incoming flights (and connect with departures, bookable through your accommodation), charging B120 to Na Thon for example.

Destinations Bangkok (25 daily; 1hr–1hr 30min); Chiang Mai (1 daily; 2hr); Krabi (1 daily; 55min); Pattaya (U-Tapao; 1 daily; 1hr); Phuket (6 daily; 50min).

BY BOAT AND BUS
The most obvious route for getting to Ko Samui by boat (45min–1hr 30min) is from Surat Thani, with most boats departing from the port of Don Sak, 68km east of town; catching a boat from Chumphon is generally more expensive and leaves you a long time on the often-choppy sea. There are also boats from Ko Samui to Ko Pha Ngan (see page 550) and to Ko Tao (see page 562); all offer the same service in the return direction. If your boat company or travel agent offers a drop-off at (or pick-up from) your hotel on Samui, take it: it'll be a lot cheaper than taking a taxi.

FROM SURAT THANI
Don Sak to Na Thon From Don Sak, hourly Seatran vehicle ferries (☎077 950 559, ⓦseatranferry.com) and a once-daily Lomprayah passenger ferry (on Samui ☎077 950028 or ☎077 950 700–4, ⓦlomprayah.com) run to the island

KO SAMUI ACTIVITIES

Samui has over a dozen scuba-diving companies, offering trips for divers and snorkellers and courses throughout the year, and there's a recompression chamber at Bangrak (☎077 427427, ⓦsssnetwork.com). Most trips for experienced divers, however, head for the waters around Ko Tao (see page 562); a day's outing costs around B4000–5500, but of course if you can make your own way to Ko Tao, you'll save money. Also on offer are plenty of spas, as well as meditation retreats, island tours, ziplines, kiteboarding and cooking and circus classes.

DIVE OPERATORS

Easy Divers Head office opposite Sandsea Resort, Lamai ☎077 231190, ⓦeasydivers-thailand.com. PADI Five-Star dive centre, with branches on Chaweng and Bangrak.

Planet Scuba Next to the Seatran pier on Bangrak ☎077 413050, ⓦplanetscuba.net.

SPAS

Banyan Tree Lamai ☎077 915 333, ⓦbanyantree. com. The beautiful spa at this luxury resort is home to Southeast Asia's only hydrotherapy spa, The Rainforest, in which you walk through around ten stations of hot, cold and massaging showers, jets, waterfalls and pools, as well as a sauna, steam room and ice fountain. Lasting an hour, it costs B1750 and can be combined with all manner of indulgent massage and beauty treatments.

Eranda Far north end of Chaweng ☎077 300323, ⓦerandaspa.com. Set on a waterfall- and flower-splashed hillside with a plunge pool, offering plenty of style (2hr Thai massage B2300).

Peace Tropical Spa On Route 4169 near the centre of Bophut beach ☎077 430199, ⓦpeacetropicalspa. com. Many types of massage, including a 2hr Thai massage for B1800, as well as body and facial treatments.

The Spa Resort Lamai ☎099 406 4503, ⓦthespa resorts.com. Everything from Thai massage (B450/ hr) for non-guests, to multi-day residential fasting and detox programmes. Also on offer are yoga and tea ceremonies, as well as in-house accommodation, either on the beach or in the hills above Lamai.

Tamarind Springs Lamai ☎085 926 4626, ⓦtamarindsprings.com. Set in a beautiful, secluded coconut grove just off the main road. A 90-minute session in its herbal steam caves, set between boulders by waterfall-fed plunge pools, plus a 2hr 30min Thai massage, for example, costs B5500; it also offers villas, a spa café and yoga holidays.

OTHER ACTIVITIES

Canopy Adventures ☎077 300340, ⓦcanopy adventuresthailand.com. A series of ziplines between treehouses and past waterfalls in the hills 4km above Maenam (2–3hr; B2200, including transfers).

The Hub Elysia Resort, east of the village T-junction in Bophut ☎077 430 317, ⓦelysiasamui.com. Classes in various types of yoga (B400/person), as well as meditation, according to a schedule posted on their website.

Kiteboarding Asia ☎083 643 1627, ⓦkite boardingasia.com. Instruction in kiteboarding (B4000 for one day), either from the beach south of Ban Hua Thanon or from Nathon, depending on the time of year, as well as rentals and stand-up paddleboarding.

Mr Ung's Magical Safari Tours ☎077 230114, ⓦungsafari.com. Day-trips that traverse the rough tracks of the mountainous interior to some spectacular viewpoints, as well as taking in Hin Yay Hin Ta, the Big Buddha and waterfall-swimming (from B1500 for a full day, including transfers and lunch).

Samui Circus Studio Coral Cove, south of Chaweng ☎087 881 0866, ⓦsamuicircus.com. Group and private circus classes, including juggling and clown skills, for adults and kids, from B300/person.

Samui Institute of Thai Culinary Arts (SITCA) Soi Colibri, opposite Centara Grand Resort in Chaweng ☎077 413172, ⓦsitca.com. This highly recommended outfit runs 2hr 30min cookery classes in the morning and afternoon (B1850), plus six- and twelve-day courses and fruit-carving classes. Closed Sun.

Wat Suan Mokkh meditation retreats ⓦdipab havan.weebly.com. Wat Suan Mokkh (see page 530) offers retreats from the 3rd to the 10th and the 20th to the 27th of each month at Dipabhavan, a hermitage in the hills above Lamai (full details on the website); pick-ups are laid on from *Utopia Resort*, north of the central crossroads in Lamai.

---

capital, Na Thon, all with their own connecting buses from Surat.

Don Sak to Lipa Noi Raja vehicle ferries run hourly between Don Sak and Lipa Noi, 8km south of Na Thon (☎02 276 8211–2, ⓦrajaferryport.com), some of which have their own connecting buses from Surat. From Lipa Noi,

you can catch an a/c minibus direct to the beaches (B200 to Chaweng, for example).

Surat Thani to Na Thon Lomprayah runs a catamaran to Na Thon from Tapi Pier (three daily), 5km northeast of central Surat near the mouth of the Tapi River. The night boat leaves Ban Don pier in Surat Thani itself for Na Thon at 11pm Mon–Sat, as long as it has enough cargo and passengers to make it worthwhile; tickets are sold at the pier on the day of departure.

Fares and journey times Ferries from Don Sak take about 1hr 30min to reach Samui, while the connecting Surat–Don Sak buses take 1hr–1hr 30min. The Lomprayah catamaran from Tapi Pier gets to Na Thon in 2hr. Seatran charges B230 from downtown Surat to Samui including connecting bus, while Phantip charges B280 from Phunphin train station. For transport from Surat Thani Airport, see page 530. Lomprayah's catamarans from Tapi Pier cost B600. The night boat takes 6hr and costs B400.

LONG-DISTANCE SERVICES

Ko Samui's government bus terminal (Baw Khaw Saw) is 2km south of Na Thon, just west off Route 4169 towards Samui Hospital (☎077 426354–5). It handles bus-and-boat services (via Don Sak and Lipa Noi), for example from Bangkok (8–11 daily; 12–13hr; mostly overnight, some from the Southern Bus Terminal, some from Mo Chit, some stopping at both), which cost from B508 on a basic a/c bus to B790 on a VIP bus – these are far preferable to the cheap deals offered by dodgy travel agents on Thanon Khao San, as the vehicles used on the latter services are often substandard and many thefts have been reported. The Baw Khaw Saw also sells through-tickets to Nakhon Si Thammarat, which combine the ferry to Don Sak either with a bus or an a/c minibus. Lomprayah also offers through-tickets from Bangkok, costing from B1400 (14hr 30min), including a VIP bus from its office on Thanon Ram Bhuttri in Banglamphu (☎02 629 2569–70), via Hua Hin, and a catamaran from Chumphon via Ko Tao and Ko Pha Ngan.

GETTING AROUND

BY SONGTHAEW

Songthaews, which congregate at the car park near the southerly pier in Na Thon, cover a variety of set routes during the daytime, either heading off clockwise or anticlockwise on Route 4169, to serve all the beaches; destinations are marked in English and typical fares are B80 to Maenam and B100 to Chaweng. In the evening, they tend to operate more like taxis and you'll have to negotiate a fare to get them to take you exactly where you want to go.

BY TAXI

Ko Samui sports dozens of a/c taxis. Although they all have meters, you'd be wasting your breath trying to persuade any driver to use his; instead, the quoted flat fares will take your breath away: B500 from Na Thon to Maenam, B1200 to Chaweng.

BY MOTORBIKE OR CAR

You can rent a motorbike for around B200 in Na Thon and on the main beaches. Dozens are killed on Samui's roads each year, so proceed with great caution, and wear a helmet – apart from any other consideration you can be landed with an on-the-spot B500 fine by police for not wearing one. In addition, thieves have been snatching bags from the front baskets of moving motorbikes on Samui, so keep yours on your person – or think about upgrading to a four-wheel drive (from around B800/day) or a car (available through companies such as Avis – see page 36).

INFORMATION

Tourist information The TAT office (daily 8.30am–noon & 1–4.30pm; ☎077 420504, ✉tat-samui@tat.or.th) is tucked away on an unnamed side road in Na Thon (north of the pier and inland from the post office). Here, and at many other places around Samui, you can pick up Siam Map Company's detailed map of the island.

Immigration office Soi 1, Maenam (Mon–Fri 8.30am–4.30pm; ☎077 421069).

Tourist police The tourist police are on the Route 4169 ring road between Bophut and Chaweng, north of Big C supermarket on the same side of the road (☎1155 or ☎077 430017–8).

Na Thon

The island capital, **NA THON**, at the top of the long western coast, is a frenetic small town which most travellers use only as a service station before hitting the sand: although all the main beaches now have currency-exchange facilities, ATMs, supermarkets, travel agents and clinics, and most of them have post offices, the tightest concentration of amenities is here. The town's layout is simple: the three piers come to land at the promenade, Thanon Chonvithi, which is paralleled first by narrow Thanon Ang Thong, then by Thanon Taweeratpakdee, aka Route 4169, the round-island road; the main cross-street is Thanon Na Amphoe, by the central pier. If you're driving yourself, note that there's a one-way system in the centre of town: south on Taweeratpakdee, north on Chonvithi.

ACCOMMODATION AND EATING

NA THON

Several stalls and small cafés purvey inexpensive Thai food around the market on Thanon Taweeratpakdee and on Thanon Chonvithi (including a lively night market by the piers).

Nathon Residence Thanon Taweeratpakdee next to Thanachart Bank ☎077 236081, bookable through ⓦexpedia.com. If you really need a place to stay in Na Thon, this is your best bet. A friendly, well-run establishment with plain but spotless tiled rooms with a/c, cable TV, fridges and en-suite, hot-water bathrooms – ask for a quiet room at the back. B650

★ **The Road Less Travelled** West side of Thanon Taweeratpakdee, just north of Thanon Na Amphoe. This is Samui's café of the moment, which is as sophisticated as anything that Bangkok might have to offer, and fetchingly done out with recycled wood and birdcage lampshades. It serves excellent espresso (and cold-brewed) coffees, using Arabica beans from northern Thailand, signature mixed juices, cocktails and all kinds of brunches including burritos (B220), as well as homemade chocolates, croissants and cakes. Tues–Sun 9.30/10am–6pm, until 8pm Fri & Sat.

6

DIRECTORY

Hospital The state hospital (☎077 421230–2) is 3km south of town off Route 4169.
Post office Towards the northern end of the promenade, just north of the central pier (Mon–Fri 8.30am–4.30pm,

Sat & Sun 9am–noon), with poste restante and packing services. International telephones upstairs (Mon–Fri 8.30am–4.30pm).

Maenam

MAENAM, 13km from Na Thon in the middle of the north coast, is Samui's most popular beach for budget travellers. Its exposed 4km-long bay is not the island's prettiest, being more of a broad dent in the coastline, and the sloping, yellow-sand beach is relatively narrow and slightly coarse by Samui's high standards. But Maenam features many of the cheapest bungalows on the island, unspoilt views of Ko Pha Ngan, and good swimming. Despite the recent opening of some upmarket developments on the shoreline and a golf course in the hills behind, this is still the quietest and most laidback of the major beaches. Though now heavily built up with multi-storey concrete shophouses (including several banks) and rows of small bars, the main road is set back far from the sea, connected to the beachside bungalows by an intricate maze of minor roads through the trees. At the midpoint of the bay, **Ban Maenam** is centred on a low-key road down to the fishing pier, which is flanked by cafés, bars, restaurants, travel agents and small boutiques. On Thursday evenings this becomes a pleasant **walking street** (modelled on those in Chiang Mai), with performances of traditional music and dance. On offer are lots of cheap clothes and some souvenirs, everything from bras to ukeleles, but what's most tempting is the panoply of food, both savoury and sweet, that locals cook up to sell.

ACCOMMODATION

MAENAM

★ **Four Seasons Resort** About 5km west of Maenam near Laem Yai ☎077 243000, ⓦfourseasons.com; map p.538. The top hotel in the Maenam area, this ultra-luxury spot has its own small beach and enjoys lovely views of Ko Pha Ngan and the setting sun. Each of the large, beautiful villas, designed for indoor-outdoor living in a subtle, modern but natural style, using brown and marine colours, has its own infinity-edge swimming pool; the resort lays on a wide range of other activities, from spa treatments to *muay thai* and tennis. B33,500
The Hammock Just east of the village ☎077 423815–6, ⓦhammocksamui.com; map p.538. Stylish, flashpacker resort with a small swimming pool surrounded by red beanbags and swings. Featuring beige- and white-

painted concrete and lots of dark wood, the rooms offer a/c, small hot-water bathrooms, minibars, TVs and DVD players; though crammed together in one- and two-storey rows on a small plot, they all have a small balcony or patio. Breakfast included. B2145

Harry's At the far western end, near Wat Na Phra Larn ☎077 447097, ⓦharrys-samui.com; map p.538. Popular, well-run place, set back about 200m from the beach amid a secluded and shady tropical garden. The public areas feature strong elements of traditional Thai architecture, less so in the bungalows, which are nevertheless clean and spacious, with a/c, hot water, TV, fridge and safe. There's also a decent-sized, free-form swimming pool and Jacuzzi. B1200

Lolita On the east side of Santiburi Resort ☎077 425134, ⓦlolitakohsamui.com; map p.538. Quiet, friendly and efficiently run resort in a beautiful, grassy garden on a long stretch of beach. A wide variety of large, wood and concrete bungalows, all with hot showers, cluster around a kitsch, circular bar-restaurant adorned with pink Corinthian columns, and come with fans (at the back), or with a/c and fridges on the beach. Fan B800, a/c B1700

Maenam Resort 500m west of the village, just beyond Santiburi Resort ☎077 247286–7, ⓦmaenamresort. com; map p.538. A welcoming, tranquil resort (no TVs) in tidy, shady grounds, with an especially long stretch of beach. The large bungalows, with verandas, hot water, fridges and a/c, offer good-value comfort. B1930

Moonhut On the east side of the village ☎077 425 247, ⓦmoonhutsamui.com; map p.538. Welcoming English-run place on a large, sandy, shady plot, with a lively restaurant and beach bar, and colourful, substantial and very clean bungalows; all have verandas, mosquito screens, wall fans and en-suite bathrooms, and some have hot water and a/c. Kayaking, waterskiing and stand-up paddleboarding available. Fan B650, a/c B1300

New Lapaz Villa Down a 1km access road, east of the village centre but just west of the post office ☎077 425 296, ⓦnewlapaz.com; map p.538. Enjoying plenty of shade, the lush, spacious grounds here shelter a small swimming pool and fifty recently renovated bungalows on stilts, with verandas, a/c, TVs, fridges and hot showers, many in bright pastel colours. Their "Superior Seaview" rooms offer good value for a beachfront pad (B1800). Breakfast included. B1400

Treehouse Silent Beach At the eastern end of the bay ☎062 240 4305, ⓦtree-house.org; map p.538. This long-running place has been recently reborn as a new-school hippy resort, combining the tagline "Follow the Flowers" with super-fast wi-fi. The colourful bungalows are quite close together, but feature hot showers and hammocks on their verandas; the shaggy thatched roofs of the beachfront bungalows (B800) are especially appealing. The cheapest offerings are bamboo huts with shared bathrooms. Fan B350, a/c B1100

EATING AND DRINKING

Angela's Bakery Almost opposite the police station on the main through-road, east of the pier ☎077 961952, ⓦfacebook.com/angelasbakerycafe; map p.538. American-style, a/c diner with comfortable booths, offering great breakfasts and a wide choice of sandwiches (chicken and avocado B150), salads, soups and Western main courses, as well as home-made cakes and apple pie. Daily 8am–3pm.

Haad Bang Po About 5km west of Maenam, at the far west end of Ban Bang Po; map p.538. The last of a string of locally popular seafood restaurants, this rough-hewn, sand-between-your-toes affair enjoys pretty views of Ko Pha Ngan. You'll need to go off-menu and practise your Thai a little to get the best out of it, but the superb khai jiaw haw mok thalay, (seafood coconut-milk curry omelette served with shrimp paste chilli dip and vegetables; B150), fully justifies the effort. Other available southern Thai favourites that are not on the English-language menu include kaeng som (fiery yellow curry), kaeng liang (peppery soup) and seasonal het loop, a kind of sea cucumber. Daily 10am–10pm.

Ko Seng On the road parallel to and just east of the pier road ☎077 425365; map p.538. This locally famous seafood restaurant, simply decorated apart from the chunky wooden tables and chairs, has featured apart from the chunky wooden tables and chairs, has featured on national TV. Buy your fish and seafood according to weight, splash out on the crab and king prawn specialities, or plump for noodles (B120) or dishes such as fish and fish roe curry with

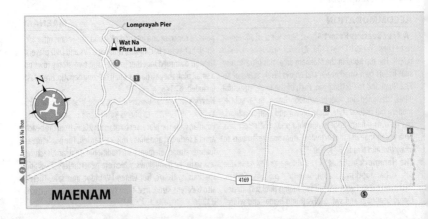

tamarind paste (*kaeng som plaa*; B350), which can be spiced to order. Daily 10am–9pm.

Sunshine Gourmet At the west end of the bay, signposted on a lane that runs east from Wat Na Phra Larn; map p.538. Popular, clean and friendly spot that does a bit of everything, from cappuccinos and breakfasts, through sandwiches, to Thai and international, especially German, main courses. Daily 8am–10pm.

Bophut

The next bay east is **BOPHUT**, which has a similar look to Maenam but shows a marked difference in atmosphere and facilities, with a noticeable Mediterranean influence. The quiet, 2km-long beach attracts a mix of young and old travellers, as well as families, and **Ban Bophut**, now tagged "**Fisherman's Village**", at the east end of the bay, is well geared to meet their needs, with a sprinkling of boutique hotels and banks, ATMs, scuba-diving outlets, travel agents and minimarts. While through traffic sticks to Route 4171 towards the airport and Route 4169 to Chaweng, which is now lined with hypermarkets and multiplex cinemas, development of the village has been reasonably sensitive, preserving many of its old wooden shophouses on the two narrow, largely car-free streets that meet at a T-junction next to the small pier. At night, in sharp contrast to Chaweng's frenetic beach road, it's a fine place for a promenade, with a concentration of good upmarket restaurants and low-key farang-run bars, particularly to the west of the T-junction; on Friday evenings, the village hosts a **walking street**, very similar to Maenam's Thursday affair (see page 537). The nicest part of the beach itself is at the west end of the bay, towards *Zazen* resort, but again the sand is slightly coarse by Samui's standards. With several branches along the beach, including in front of *Free House Bungalows*, Orange Wave offers all manner of watersports, including jet skis and stand-up paddleboards (☏ 080 525 0650, ✆ orangewave-watersports.com).

ACCOMMODATION   **BOPHUT**

Most establishments here are spaced out at regular intervals along the length of the beach, though a handful of small, stylish, good-value boutique hotels cluster together in Ban Bophut itself.

★ **Anantara** West of the village on the main road ☏ 077 428300, ✆ anantara.com. Luxury hotel with attentive service in the style of an opulent oriental palace. The balconied rooms are arrayed round lush gardens and ponds that are lit at night with flaming torches, and there's an attractive infinity-edge swimming pool on the beachfront and a central bar and restaurant, specializing in contemporary Australian cuisine. A very attractive spa, a kids' club and a huge range of activities, from yoga and cocktail mixing classes to tennis and watersports, round out the picture. Breakfast included. B8010

Cactus Access from the highway, west Bophut ☏ 077 245565, ✆ cactus-bungalow.com. Ochre cottages with attractive bed platforms, large French windows and stylish, earth-tone bathrooms stand in two shady rows, running down to the inviting beachfront restaurant with a wood-

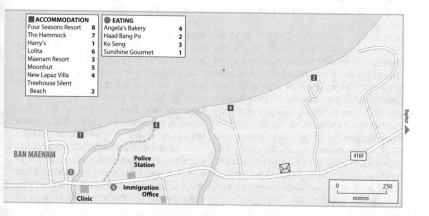

ACCOMMODATION		EATING	
Four Seasons Resort	8	Angela's Bakery	4
The Hammock	7	Haad Bang Po	2
Harry's	1	Ko Seng	3
Lolita	6	Sunshine Gourmet	1
Maenam Resort	3		
Moonhut	5		
New Lapaz Villa	4		
Treehouse Silent Beach	2		

BAN MAENAM

Police Station

Immigration Office

Clinic

4169

Bophut

0   250
metres

6

fired pizza oven. Choose either fan and cold shower or a/c and hot shower. Fan B800, a/c B1350

Cocooning East of the village T-junction, opposite The Waterfront ☎085 781 4107, ⊚cocooninghotel.com. Small, good-value hotel set back from the beach, with compact but well-equipped rooms (a/c, hot shower, fridge, safe, DVD player) in a bright and breezy contemporary style; the English owner is a mine of local information. B1300

★ **Free House** West of the village ☎077 427517. On a quiet plot that's shaded by a thick canopy of trees, running back from the popular beachfront bar-restaurant, the tasteful en-suite bungalows here are well designed and maintained, with plenty of natural light. Made either of white-painted concrete or slatted dark wood, they feature mosquito nets, hammocks, hot showers and verandas. Fan B700, a/c B1500

Hansar At the west end of the village ☎077 245511, ⊚hansarsamui.com. You'll be surprised how spacious this hotel feels, with its long beachfront and just 74 low-rise rooms (all with huge shower areas and sea views from their big balconies), set around gardens and a pool. The stylish decor is a riot of geometry in brown and beige – unvarnished wood, bamboo, marble and granite – and there's a spa, gym and luxury restaurant, *H Bistro*, with ingredients flown in from around the world. Breakfast included. B7300

Juzz'a Pizza East of the village T-junction ☎077 332512–3. Above a good restaurant (see below), four small but smart rooms, well equipped with comfy beds, a/c, hot showers, fridges, cable TV and DVD players. Two rooms have no view, while the other two have beachside terraces with great views. B1200

The Lodge Towards the western end of the village ☎077 425337, ⊚lodgesamui.com. Small, three-storey, beachfront hotel with immaculately clean and tastefully decorated modern rooms, all with balconies looking over the water, and boasting a/c, ceiling fan, mini-bar, satellite TV, plus marble bathrooms with tubs to soak in. There's a seafront bar downstairs where you can get breakfast. Now also offers a few simple rooms with a/c, fridge and hot showers in an annexe (B550). B2680

Us Hostel Off Route 4169 at the east end of Bophut ☎095 427 1525, ⊚facebook.com/ushostelsamui. Friendly, new hostel with smart bunks in a/c recycled shipping containers, hot showers, an attractive pool and wooden chill-out decks scattered with beanbags. Dorm B380, double B1000

The Waterfront East of the village T-junction ☎077 427165, ⊚thewaterfrontbophut.com. English-run boutique hotel, sociable and family-friendly, with a small swimming pool in a grassy garden. All of the tastefully decorated rooms and bungalows have a/c, hot water, mini-bars, safes, cable TV, DVD players and views of the sea. Minimum stay 2 nights. Free airport pick-ups and drop-offs; breakfast included in the price. B3120

Zazen At the far west end of the beach ☎077 425085, ⊚samuizazen.com. Stylish bungalows and villas clustered round a cute pool and kids' pool, furnished with Thai and other Asian objets d'art, as well as satellite TV, DVD player, mini-bar and daybed; all sport a tropical-style open-air bathroom with rain shower. Other facilities at this eco-friendly resort include a spa, a Thai-Mediterranean restaurant that hosts Thai dancing (Thurs & Sun) and a Western restaurant offering classic afternoon tea, cooking classes, and free kayaks and bicycles. Breakfast included. B6540

EATING AND DRINKING

Café 69 On Highway 4169 west of the traffic lights, opposite The Wharf community mall ☎081 978 1945. This plush roadside restaurant conjures up creative fusion dishes that really work, such as green curry roti pie with mango (B229) and black squid-ink spaghetti with salmon laap. Mon–Sat 1–10pm.

Enjoy Just west of the village T-junction ☎081 485 7112, ⊚enjoybeach-hotel-samui.com. At this very friendly, French-run hotel, the café-restaurant is a great spot for a breakfast of croissants and coffee on the lovely, breezy seafront terrace. Later in the day, it serves French specialities such as tournedos of charolais beef with pepper sauce (B490), lots of tempting Western desserts and a decent selection of wine and brandy. Daily 8am–10.30pm.

Happy Elephant West of the village T-junction ☎077 427 222. This long-standing restaurant offers a good choice of mostly Thai food, including a few less mainstream dishes such as pork *nam tok* (B260) and lots of seafood, which is displayed out front and priced by weight. Service is friendly and there's an attractive beachside terrace. Daily 11am–10pm.

Juzz'a Pizza East of the village T-junction ☎077 332 512–3. Friendly, small, elegant restaurant with a beachside terrace, serving excellent, authentic pizzas (from B260), with vegetarian and seafood options, as well as pastas, sandwiches and Thai and Western main courses. Tues–Sun noon–10pm.

Ninja Crepes Far east end of the bay, on the road towards Bangrak. In a beachfront location with nice tables on a terrace by the sea, this is a popular option for cheap, decent-quality Western and Thai meals along with breakfasts and sweet and savoury crepes. Main dishes around B80. Daily 9am–8pm.

Ristorante alla Baia Just west of the village T-junction, next to Enjoy ☎077 332647. Run by an Italian who is passionate about his food and has come up with a well-designed menu of standard but authentic dishes, such as *scaloppine al vino bianco* (pork or chicken fillets in white wine; B370), using meat imported from Argentina. Also on offer are pizzas, pasta and seafood, with the catch of the day displayed outside. With white tablecloths and plants, lots of wrought iron and a terrace on the beach, you could almost be sitting by the Adriatic. Daily noon–10.30pm.

The Shack Grill West of the village T-junction ☎087 264 6994, ⓦtheshackgrillsamui.com. Small, pricey spot, run by an ebullient New Yorker, and focused on the large, open grill at the front of the restaurant: here all manner of local seafood and imported meats priced by weight, such as Wagyu beef tenderloin (B1800/200g) and New Zealand lamb, are cooked to your liking. Delicious apple pie and decent house wine. Daily 5.30–11pm.

Bangrak

Beyond the sharp headland with its sweep of coral reefs lies **BANGRAK**, sometimes called **Big Buddha Beach** after the colossus that gazes sternly down on the sun worshippers from its island in the bay. The beach is no great shakes, especially during the northeast monsoon, when the sea retreats and leaves a slippery mud flat, but Bangrak still manages to attract the watersports crowd, and every Sunday locals and expats descend for the Sunday Sessions at Secret Garden Beach Resort on the main beach road (☎077 332661, ⓦsecretgardensamui.com), with barbecues, drinks and live music from around 7pm. Generally, however, it's hard to recommend staying on Bangrak, as the resorts are squeezed together in a narrow, noisy strip between busy Route 4171 and the shore, next to the busy inter-island piers and underneath the airport flight path.

Built in 1972, the **Big Buddha** (*Phra Yai*) is certainly big and works hard at being a tourist attraction, but is no beauty. A short causeway at the eastern end of the bay leads across to a messy clump of souvenir shops and food stalls in front of the temple, catering to day-tripping Thais as well as foreigners. Ceremonial dragon-steps then bring you up to the covered terrace around the Big Buddha, from where there's a fine view of the sweeping north coast. Look out for the B10 rice-dispensing machine, which allows you symbolically to give alms to the monks at any time of the day.

Choeng Mon

After Bangrak comes the high-kicking boot of Samui's **northeastern cape**, with its small, rocky coves overlooking Ko Pha Ngan and connected by narrow lanes. Songthaews run along Route 4171 to the largest and most beautiful bay, **Choeng Mon**, whose white sandy beach is lined with casuarina trees that provide shade for the bungalows and upmarket resorts. Choeng Mon is now popular enough to support small supermarkets, travel agents, a post office and a bank, but on the whole it remains relatively laidback.

ACCOMMODATION   **CHOENG MON**

Imperial Boat House Beach Resort Central Choeng Mon ☎077 425041–52, ⓦmelia.com. Named after the two-storey rice barges that have been converted into suites in the grounds, the *Boat House* also offers good-value luxury rooms with balconies in more prosaic modern buildings, often filled by package tours. As well as a beachside boat-shaped pool, there's a garden pool with attached kids' pool, a spa, kayaks and table tennis. B4030

Island View Tucked in on the east side of the Boat House Hotel ☎083 221 2450, ⓦislandviewsamui.com. Smart, good-value rooms and chalets with a/c, hot water, TV and fridge, in a lively compound that crams in a super-market and a beachfront bar-restaurant that specializes in southern Thai food, as well as a massage *sala* and jet-skis on the beach. B1350

Ô Soleil West of the Boat House Hotel ☎077 425232, ⓦosoleilbungalow.com. Lovely, orderly, Belgian-run place in a tranquil, pretty garden dotted with ponds. Among the well-built, clean bungalows, the cheapest are fan-cooled, with cold showers, at the back, while the elegant beachside restaurant has a nice shaded deck area and serves six hundred cocktails. Fan B600, a/c B1100

Sea Dance Resort Just south of Choeng Mon on Hanuman Bay ☎077 426621, ⓦseadanceresort.com (bookable through ⓦsecret-retreats.com). You'll get a warm welcome at this relaxing resort, which has a cute little spa and a free-form pool on the tranquil, part-sandy, part-rocky bay. The villas, many of which have their own plunge pools on lawns surrounded by hedges, are luxurious, with touches of rustic chic in their thatched canopies and bamboo furniture. Breakfast included. B5400

★ Tongsai Bay North side of Choeng Mon ☎077

245480, ⊚ tongsaibay.co.th. Easy-going, environmentally aware establishment with excellent service. The luxurious rooms, red-tiled cottages and palatial villas (some with their own pool) command beautiful views over the huge, picturesque grounds, the private beach and two swimming pools. In addition they nearly all sport second bathtubs on their secluded open-air terraces, and some also have outdoor, four-poster beds with mosquito nets if you want to sleep under the stars. There's also an array of very fine restaurants and a delightful spa. Breakfast included. B10,500

Chaweng

For looks alone, none of the other beaches can match **CHAWENG**, with its broad, gently sloping strip of white sand sandwiched between the limpid blue sea and a line of palm trees. Such beauty has not escaped attention of course, which means, on the plus side, that Chaweng can provide just about anything the active beach bum demands, from thumping nightlife to ubiquitous and diverse watersports. The negative angle is that the new developments are ever more cramped and expensive, while building work behind the palm trees and repairs to the over-commercialized main beach road are always in progress.

North Chaweng

The 6km bay is framed between the small island of Ko Matlang at the north end and the 300m-high headland above Coral Cove in the south. From **Ko Matlang**, where the waters provide some decent snorkelling, an often exposed coral reef slices southwest across to the mainland, marking out a shallow lagoon and **North Chaweng**. This S-shaped part of the beach is comparatively peaceful, though it has some ugly pockets of development; at low tide it becomes a wide, inviting playground, and from October to January the reef shelters it from the northeast winds.

Central Chaweng and Chaweng Noi

South of the reef, the idyllic shoreline of **Central Chaweng** stretches for 2km in a dead-straight line, the ugly, traffic-clogged and seemingly endless strip of amenities on the parallel main drag largely concealed behind the tree line and the resorts. Around a low promontory is **Chaweng Noi**, a little curving beach in a rocky bay, which is comparatively quiet in its northern part, away from the road. Well inland of Central Chaweng, the round-island road, Route 4169, passes through the original village of **Ban Chaweng**.

Coral Cove

South of Chaweng, the road climbs past **Coral Cove**, a tiny, isolated beach of coarse sand hemmed in by high rocks, with some good coral for snorkelling. It's well worth making the trip to *Vikasa Resort*'s restaurant, at the tip of the headland dividing Chaweng from Lamai, for a jaw-dropping view over Chaweng and Choeng Mon to the peaks of Ko Pha Ngan.

ACCOMMODATION   CHAWENG

Over fifty **bungalow resorts** and **hotels** at Chaweng are squeezed into thin strips running back from the beachfront at right angles. The cheapest digs here, however, are set back from the beach and are generally little more than functional.

NORTH CHAWENG

Amari North Chaweng ⊕077 300 306–9, ⊚amari. com; map p.543. Congenial, eco-friendly luxury hotel that's unpretentious and good value. Cheery and spacious contemporary accommodation, stretching back across the road from the beach, includes family-friendly duplexes, and there are two elegant restaurants, including *Prego* (see page 545), a full-service spa, a gym, a kids' club and two free-form swimming pools with kids' pools. B5085

Anantara Lawana North Chaweng ⊕077 960333, ⊚anantara.com; map p.543. The design of this recently renovated luxury hotel was inspired by Chinese merchants' houses in Thailand in the last century, which gives a pleasing retro feel to the spacious rooms, most of which have indoor-outdoor bathrooms. Much of the accommodation is in two-storey houses, in which the ground-floor room has a plunge pool and the first-floor room a terrace; other villas either have their own pools or share semi-private ones. There's also a main, semi-circular pool, of course, down by the beach, as well as an excellent spa, a good concierge service and fine restaurants, including *Tree Tops*, where you eat in romantic, open-sided treehouses. Breakfast included. **B8630**

Chaweng Regent At the bottom end of North Chaweng ☎ 077 300 500, ⓦ chawengregent.com; map p.543. Reliable, well-run, luxury place offering elegant bungalows and low-rise rooms with private terraces and all mod cons, around lotus ponds, two large pools with kids' pools, a fitness centre and spa. **B5500**

★ **Coral Bay Resort** At the far north end of North Chaweng ☎ 077 234 555, ⓦ coralbay.net; map p.543. A charming, eco-friendly vision of how Chaweng might have developed – if only there'd been more space. In quiet, delightful, ten-acre gardens with over 500 species of plants, the huge, thatched villas have been thoughtfully and tastefully designed with local woods, bamboo and coconut; all have extensive verandas and waterfall showers. There's an attractive free-form pool and a good beachside bar-restaurant. Breakfast included. **B6850**

Tango Beach Resort North Chaweng ☎ 077 300451, ⓦ tangobeachsamui.com; map p.543. This helpful and welcoming place has a modern Thai style that sets it apart from most of Samui's farang-oriented hotels: a variety of cutesy, colourful, well-equipped rooms are separated by a small, shady pool and a wooden boardwalk that runs down to the beach, where the Lazy Wave restaurant offers Thai cooking classes. **B2200**

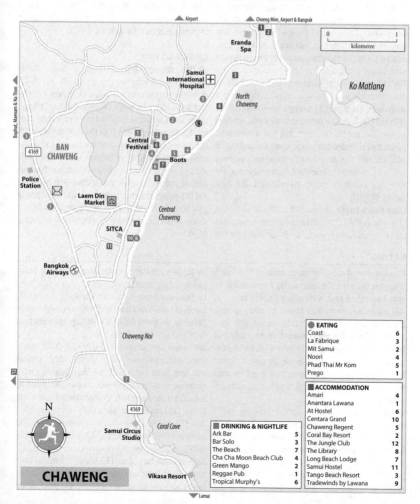

EATING
Coast	6
La Fabrique	3
Mit Samui	2
Noori	4
Phad Thai Mr Kom	5
Prego	1

ACCOMMODATION
Amari	4
Anantara Lawana	1
At Hostel	6
Centara Grand	10
Chaweng Regent	5
Coral Bay Resort	2
The Jungle Club	12
The Library	8
Long Beach Lodge	7
Samui Hostel	11
Tango Beach Resort	3
Tradewinds by Lawana	9

DRINKING & NIGHTLIFE
Ark Bar	5
Bar Solo	3
The Beach	7
Cha Cha Moon Beach Club	4
Green Mango	2
Reggae Pub	1
Tropical Murphy's	6

CHAWENG

CENTRAL CHAWENG

At Hostel North end of Central Chaweng, between Central Festival shopping centre and the main beach road ☎077 332 555, ⓦathostelsamui.com; map p.543. In the heart of the party zone, just down from Soi Green Mango, this new hostel has shining-white mixed/female dorms containing anything up to eighteen bunk beds with individual curtains, as well as a bright red swimming pool and a lively bar. **Dorm** B450

Centara Grand Central Chaweng ☎077 230500, ⓦcentarahotelsresorts.com; map p.543. Modelled on the first Thai "destination hotel", the *Railway Hotel* in Hua Hin (now also a *Centara Grand* – see page 516), this place has added a smart contemporary finish to its graceful, low-rise, colonial-style architecture. All the rooms and their broad balconies face the sea across the broad immaculate gardens of hedgerows, palm trees and lawns, which also shelter a huge, free-form pool. The hotel lays on varied daily programmes of activities for both adults and kids, not to mention plenty of watersports, and there's a lovely spa and a fine bar-restaurant, *Coast* (see below). B8360

The Library Central Chaweng ☎077 422767–8, ⓦthelibrarysamui.com; map p.543. High-concept design hotel, based around a shining white library of books, DVDs and CDs. The idea is continued in the rooms, which all feature iMacs and Blu-ray players, and have a sleek, cubic theme; they're divided into suites (downstairs) and studios with balconies (upstairs). There's a blood-red swimming pool, a fitness centre, a beachfront terrace restaurant, *The Page*, and a roadside cocktail bar-restaurant, The Drink Gallery. B13,200

Long Beach Lodge Towards the north end of Central Chaweng ☎077 422162, ⓦlongbeachsamui.com; map p.543. An unusually spacious, sandy compound for this part of the beach, with plenty of shade. All the orderly, clean bungalows and rooms are a decent size and have hot water, fridge, TV and a/c. Service is friendly, and breakfast is included in the price. B1500

Samui Hostel South end of Chaweng, beyond the Centara Grand Hotel ☎085 922 9426, ⓦfacebook.com/samuihostelthailand; map p.543543. On a side road off the main beach road near the Mercure Hotel, this neat, welcoming hostel has fan or a/c six- to twelve-bed mixed dorms, as well as a/c doubles or twins with hot showers, TVs and fridges. **Dorm** B200, **double** B600

Tradewinds by Lawana Central Chaweng ☎077 414294, ⓦtradewindsbylawana.com; map p.543. A cheerful, well-run place of characterful, colourfully painted bungalows and rooms (all with a/c, hot water, mini-bar, cable TV and balcony), with plenty of room to breathe in colourful tropical gardens that run down to a beachfront swimming pool. Breakfast included. B3625

CHAWENG NOI

★ **The Jungle Club** 2km up a steep, partly paved road behind Chaweng Noi ☎081 891 8263, ⓦjungleclubsamui.com; map p.543. Breezy, French–Thai antidote to Chaweng's commercial clutter: a huge, grassy, shady plot with a small pool on the edge of the slope to catch the towering views of Ko Pha Ngan and beyond. A chic bar-restaurant has been built into the rocks, while the accommodation – nearly all thatched, with mosquito nets and fans – includes wooden huts with cold-water indoor-outdoor bathrooms, concrete bungalows with hot water and DVD players and a two-bedroom a/c villa with a private pool. Minimum stay three nights for selected rooms. Offers a shuttle service from the beach – contact directly for details. B800

EATING

Chaweng offers all manner of foreign **cuisines**, from French to Russian, much of it of dubious quality. Among all this, it's quite hard to find good, reasonably priced Thai food – as well as the places recommended below, it's worth exploring the cheap and cheerful food stalls, popular with local workers, at **Laem Din night market**, on the middle road between Central Chaweng and Highway 4169. On Saturday evenings, the walking street in the car park of Central Festival, a shopping centre between the lake and the main beach road, serves plenty of food, as well as souvenirs and clothes.

Coast Centara Grand Hotel, Central Chaweng ☎077 230500, ⓦcoast-beach-club.com; map p.543. Cool, beachclub-like bar-restaurant with swing chairs, sunken booths in the sand and lots of beachfront to make the most of the sea views. The focus of the well-designed menu is on excellent seafood and grills, but you'll also find pizzas (B420), tapas, and meat and cheese platters. A DJ and fire-jugglers entertain over the Monday evening beach barbecue. Daily noon–11pm.

La Fabrique Route 4169, Ban Chaweng; map p.543. Branch of Lamai's excellent French café-patisserie, handily placed by the traffic lights at Chaweng's main junction. Daily (except Wed) 8.30am–5pm.

Mit Samui Ban Chaweng road ☎089 727 2034, ⓦmit-samui-restaurant.com; map p.543. Very popular with both locals and tourists, this large, bustling, simple restaurant specializes in pick-your-own seafood (priced by weight), but also serves tasty stir-fried squid with salted egg (B200), satay and fresh fruit juices. Daily 11am–midnight.

Noori Opposite Chaweng Buri Resort towards the north end of Central Chaweng, just up from McDonald's ☎077 300757, ⓦnooriindiasamui.com; map p.543. Superior Indian food (around B200/dish) in relatively basic surroundings, including all the old favourites such as chicken tikka masala, as well as over twenty types of bread, plenty of seafood and vegetarian options and Indian desserts. Also offers Indian cooking classes. Daily 11am–11.30pm.

Phad Thai Mr Kom Route 4169, Ban Chaweng; map p.543. You'll get an energetic welcome at this basic little restaurant, where you can tuck into tasty phat thai with your choice of extras (from B60). It's in Buffalo Market, an open-air food mall (also serving som tam, rice porridge, Japanese and pasta) that's popular with Thais. Mon–Sat 11.30am–11pm.

★ **Prego** Amari Palm Reef Hotel, North Chaweng ⓣ077 300317, ⓦprego-samui.com; map p.543. Excellent, chic restaurant that would stand on its own two feet in Milan, the head chef's home town. The varied menu of contemporary rustic Italian dishes includes good *antipasti*, pizzas from a proper wood-fired oven, handmade pastas and top-notch risottos, with many ingredients flown in from Italy, and there's a very good selection of wines. Booking advised in high season. Daily noon–midnight.

6

DRINKING AND NIGHTLIFE

Avoiding the raucous hostess bars and English-themed pubs on the main through road, the best place to **drink** is on the beach: at night dozens of resorts and dedicated bars lay out candlelit tables on the sand, especially towards the north end of Central Chaweng and on North Chaweng.

Ark Bar North end of Central Chaweng ⓦark-bar.com; map p.543. Hosts very popular beach parties on Wed & Fri, with international and Thai house DJs, a swim-up pool bar and fire shows. Daily 2pm–2am.

Bar Solo North end of Central Chaweng, on the main road just north of Green Mango ⓦfacebook.com/solobarsamui; map p.543. One of the bars of the moment, whose black-and-white industrial look is matched by tech house on the sound system, with international DJs like Goldie occasionally flying in. Diversions include a pool table, and there's a great streetside patio out the front for people-watching. Daily 6pm–2am.

★ **The Beach** Chaweng Noi, south of the Sheraton (not to be confused with The Beach Bar at the Impiana Resort just to the south) ⓦfacebook.com/thebeachbarsamui; map p.543. Big, chic, new, indoor-outdoor beach bar with plenty of room along the sand for beanbags and mats. The best of Thai and international techno and house DJs, including the likes of Nakadia, get to work on a top-quality sound system. Daily 10am–1am.

Cha Cha Moon Beach Club North end of Central Chaweng, next to Ark Bar ⓦfacebook.com/chachamoonbeachclub; map p.543. Stylish beach bar with daybeds on the sand and Thai and international DJs spinning house and techno, especially for the weekly climax of full, black and half-moon parties. Daily roughly 3pm–2am.

Green Mango North end of Central Chaweng ⓦfacebook.com/thegreenmangoclub; map p.543. Long-standing dance venue, in a huge shed that combines an industrial look with that of a tropical greenhouse. Now with its own alley, Soi Green Mango, lined with other vibrant bars and clubs. Daily roughly 9pm–2am.

Reggae Pub Inland from Central Chaweng across the lake ⓣ077 422331–3; map p.543. Chaweng's oldest nightclub is a venerable Samui institution – with a memorabilia shop to prove it. It does time now as an unpretentious, good-time, party venue, with some nice lakeside tables, pool tables, big-screen sports and live bands every night. Daily 7pm–2am.

Tropical Murphy's Opposite McDonald's in Central Chaweng ⓣ077 413614, ⓦtropicalmurphys.com; map p.543. One theme pub that is worth singling out: with draught Guinness, Kilkenny and Hoegaarden, a huge range of big-screen sports, pool tables and decent food, *Murphy's* has turned itself into a popular landmark and meeting place. Daily 9am–1am.

DIRECTORY

Airlines Bangkok Airways, south end of Ban Chaweng on Route 4169 ⓣ077 601300.

Hospital The private Samui International Hospital in North Chaweng (ⓣ077 300394–5, ⓦsih.co.th) provides 24hr ambulance and emergency services, a dental clinic and travel inoculations.

Pharmacy Boots has several convenient branches in Central Chaweng, including one just up the road from *Tropical Murphy's* pub (ⓣ077 413724; daily 10am–11pm).

Lamai

LAMAI is like a second city to Chaweng's capital, not quite as developed and much less frenetic, while lacking the latter's wide range of chic hotels, restaurants and nightclubs. Development is concentrated into a farang toytown of tawdry open-air hostess bars and Western restaurants that has grown up behind the centre of the beach, interspersed with supermarkets, clinics, banks, ATMs and travel agents; on Sunday evenings, the area to the east of the market hosts a **walking street** similar to the one in Maenam on Thursday. Running roughly north to south for 4km, the white, palm-fringed beach itself is still a picture, and generally quieter than Chaweng, with far less in the way of watersports – it's quite easy to get away from it all by staying at the peaceful extremities of the bay, where the backpackers' resorts are preferable to Chaweng's functional guesthouses. At the northern end, the spur of land that hooks eastward into the sea is perhaps the prettiest spot and is beginning to attract some upmarket development: it has more rocks than sand, but the shallow sea behind the coral reef is protected from the high seas of November, December and January.

The original village of **Ban Lamai**, set well back on Route 4169, remains surprisingly aloof, and its wat contains a small museum of ceramics, agricultural tools and other everyday objects. Most visitors get more of a buzz from **Hin Yay** (Grandmother Rock) and **Hin Ta** (Grandfather Rock), small rock formations on the bay's southern

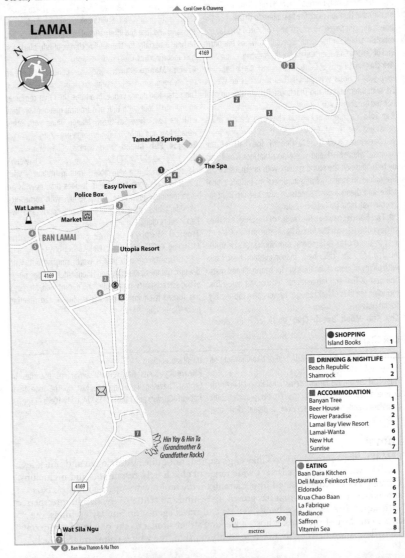

LAMAI

Coral Cove & Chaweng

4169

Tamarind Springs

The Spa

Easy Divers

Police Box

Wat Lamai

Market

BAN LAMAI

Utopia Resort

4169

Hin Yay & Hin Ta
(Grandmother &
Grandfather Rocks)

4169

Wat Sila Ngu

, Ban Hua Thanon & Na Thon

0   500
metres

● **SHOPPING**
Island Books   1

■ **DRINKING & NIGHTLIFE**
Beach Republic   1
Shamrock   2

■ **ACCOMMODATION**
Banyan Tree   1
Beer House   5
Flower Paradise   2
Lamai Bay View Resort   3
Lamai-Wanta   6
New Hut   4
Sunrise   7

● **EATING**
Baan Dara Kitchen   4
Deli Maxx Feinkost Restaurant   3
Eldorado   6
Krua Chao Baan   7
La Fabrique   5
Radiance   2
Saffron   1
Vitamin Sea   8

promontory, which never fail to raise a giggle with their resemblance to the male and female sexual organs.

ACCOMMODATION

Lamai's **accommodation** is generally less cramped and slightly better value than Chaweng's, though it presents far fewer choices at the top end of the market. Budget accommodation is concentrated around the beach's northern and southern ends. Lamai supports two famous spa resorts, Tamarind Springs and The Spa Resort (see page 535).

Banyan Tree On the bay's northern headland ☎077 915333, ⓦ banyantree.com; map p.546. Occupying a steep-sided, landscaped valley, with towering views of Chaweng from the lobby bar, *Banyan Tree* provides the height of luxury in its beautiful, stilted pool villas: lofty living rooms, walk-in wardrobes, possibly the biggest big-head showers in Thailand and landscaped pools. Electric buggies will ferry you down to the spa, the main swimming pool, kids' pool and private cove with a good stretch of beach, where plenty of watersports are on offer. B25,520

Beer House In the central section of the northern part of the beach ☎077 256591, ⓦ beerhousebungalow.com; map p.546. Appealing bungalows with fans, hot showers, verandas and hammocks in a lush, shaded compound – try to bag one of the four on the beachfront, which are only B50 extra. Double B600

Flower Paradise On the bay's northern headland ☎077 270675, ⓦ samuiroestiland.com; map p.546. Just a short walk from the beach, a friendly, well-run German–Swiss place in a small but beautiful garden. All the attractive, well-tended bungalows of varying sizes have verandas and hot water, and there's a good restaurant, *Röstiland* (closed Sun), specializing in the eponymous hash browns. Fan B400, a/c B800

Lamai Bay View Resort On the bay's northern headland ☎077 458778–9, ⓦ bayviewsamui.com; map

p.546. Neat, stylish bungalows with verandas, mini-bars and hot-water bathrooms in an extensive, flower-bedecked, grassy compound; the poshest come with a/c and cable TV. Offers a friendly, German–Thai welcome, kayaking and great sunset views of the beach from the attractive restaurant. Fan B1650, a/c B1750

Lamai-Wanta East of the central crossroads ☎077 424550, ⓦ lamaiwanta.com; map p.546. Welcoming, well-placed hotel with a seductive beachfront swimming pool and a good restaurant. Set around trim lawns, the seventy large, bright rooms and villas are decorated in white and dark wood in a restrained Thai style, with terracotta floor tiles and a few splashes of colour; all have a/c, TVs, mini-bars, safes and hot water. Discounts for longer stays. B2800

New Hut Beer House's eastern neighbour on the northern part of the beach ☎077 230437, ⓦ newhutbungalow.com; map p.546. These bungalows are tightly packed and luridly coloured but they're right on the beach and there's a good restaurant attached. The cheapest are rustic A-frames with nothing more than a mattress, fan and mosquito net, sharing cold-water bathrooms, while the more expensive en suites come with a/c. Fan B400, a/c B600

Sunrise On the Hin Yay Hin Ta access road ☎077 424433, ⓦ sunrisebungalow.com; map p.546. Welcoming and clued-up establishment on the far southern end of the beach, with a decent restaurant, a gym and snorkels to rent. In a quiet, shady garden amid coconut palms, choose between clean fan rooms with cold or hot showers and larger a/c bungalows with hot water, cable TV and fridge. Fan B600, a/c B1600

EATING AND DRINKING

Besides the **restaurants** recommended below, there's a **market** of cheap takeaway food stalls and simple restaurants inland just off Highway 4169 (east of Tesco Lotus supermarket) that's popular with locals for lunch and dinner (closes around 8 or 9pm). Apart from a few bar-restaurants on the beach near *Lamai-Wanta*, Lamai's **nightlife** is all within spitting distance of the central crossroads.

Baan Dara Kitchen Highway 4169, Ban Lamai; map p.546. A locals' favourite right beside the entrance to Wat Lamai, this simple but attractive restaurant serves cheap and very tasty noodle soup with pork (B70), dim sum, *phat thai*, green curry and espressos made with organic coffee beans. Daily 8am–6pm.

Beach Republic On the bay's northern headland ☎077 458100, ⓦ beachrepublic.com; map p.546. Although it features accommodation and a spa, this chic beach club

is best known for its restaurant and bar, arrayed around two pools and a Jacuzzi, with plenty of loungers and day-beds and fine views of the bay. Among sandwiches, global tapas, pasta and pizza, the very good beer-battered fish and chips (B420) on the daytime menu stand out. Weekly events include two DJ sets on weekend afternoons, "Soulful Saturdays" and "Sunday Sessions" with a special Sunday brunch. Restaurant daily 7–10.30am & 11am–10.30pm.

Deli Maxx Feinkost Restaurant North of the central crossroads, near Highway 4169 ☎077 419010; map p.546. At this popular little bar-restaurant, you can tuck into a wide selection of Western, mostly German, food, including plenty of sausages, wiener schnitzel (B240) and good steaks and pizzas, and wash it all down with German beer. Tues–Sun 6pm–2am.

Eldorado Just west of the central crossroads ☎094

6

409 0614, ⓦfacebook.com/eldorado.lamai; map p.546. Highly recommended friendly, good-value Swedish restaurant, serving a few Thai and Swedish favourites including meatballs, salads, steaks, pizzas and other international main courses. All-you-can-eat barbecue on Wednesday (B290). Mon–Sat 3pm–midnight.

Krua Chao Baan Highway 4169, about 1km south of Hin Yay Hin Ta ☎077 418589; map p.546. With a cute little garden and scenic seafront terraces between the road and the sea, this well-regarded restaurant concentrates on seafood (mostly sold by weight) and serves a few southern Thai dishes such as *kaeng som kung* ("sour prawn curry"; B150). Daily 10am–10pm.

★ **La Fabrique** Route 4169, just south of the temple in Lamai village; map p.546546. Authentic French patisserie-café, a civilized retreat from the busy road. Breakfast sets, superb custard cakes, sweet and savoury crepes, quiches (B85), omelettes, pizzas, salads and sandwiches. Daily 6.30am–8pm.

Radiance The Spa Resort, at the far north end of the beach; map p.546. Excellent, casual beachside restaurant, serving a huge range of vegetarian Thai and international (including Mexican) dishes, plus raw and vegan food, as well as plenty of meat and marine offerings. The veggie "ginger nuts" stir-fry (B140) and *som tam* with spicy Thai sausage (B125) are excellent. A long menu of "longevity

drinks"– juices, smoothies and shakes – includes a delicious lime juice with honey. Daily 6am–10.30pm (last orders).

Saffron Banyan Tree (see page 547); map p.546. Feast your eyes on the views over the restaurant's private inlet – the rest of Samui might as well not be there – and on the artistic presentations of its imaginative Thai haute cuisine. The foundation is central Thai cooking, with seafood featuring heavily, but there are one or two nods to regional flavours: the northeastern nam tok with Australian tenderloin is excellent (B520), while the northern curry noodle soup, khao soi, here comes with salmon and its roe (B790). Daily 6–11pm.

Shamrock North of the central crossroads ⓦthesamui shamrock.com; map p.546. Popular, friendly Irish bar with lots of TV sports, which also hosts lively cover bands every evening and serves Guinness, Magner's cider and Kilkenny bitter (all on draught). Daily 9am–2.30am.

★ **Vitamin Sea** On Highway 4169 in Ban Hua Thanon, 50m north of the dogleg in the road and about 2km south of Hin Yay Hin Ta ⓦthesamuishamrock.com; map p.546. Genial, Belgian-run bar-restaurant on a lovely, breezy terrace right over the beach, artfully done out in white, aquamarine and recycled wood. The coq au vin is very tasty (B320), but the real stars are the chips it comes with, thick cut and double-fried. Mon–Sat 11am–11pm (kitchen closes 9.30pm).

SHOPPING

Island Books On Highway 4169, opposite Beer House bungalows ☎061 193 2132, ⓦisland-books-samui. com; map p.546. Samui's best secondhand bookshop for buying, selling, renting or trading, with its stock of tens of thousands of books mostly detailed on the website. Daily 9am–7pm.

The south and west coasts

Lacking the long, attractive beaches of the more famous resorts, the **south and west coasts** have much less to offer in the way of accommodation, though there are one or two interesting spots that are worth heading for on a round-island tour. If you happen to be here in November, the west coast's flat, unexceptional beaches might make a calm alternative when the northeast winds buffet the other side of the island.

Ko Taen and Ko Mad Sum

The two small islands of **Ko Taen** and **Ko Mad Sum**, a short way off the south coast, offer some of Samui's best snorkelling, especially around Ko Taen. TK Tour in Ban Thongkrut (☎077 334052–3, ⓦtktoursamui.com) goes to both islands on a four- to five-hour boat trip, costing B1300 per person (B1500 with kayaking, or with a quick look at Ko Si Ko Ha, the heavily guarded islands to the west where sea gypsies gather swifts' nests for bird's-nest soup – see page 671), including pick-up from your accommodation, snorkelling equipment and lunch. Island Hoppers World (☎081 361 5605, ⓦislandhoppersworld.com) offers snorkelling day-trips to Ko Taen (B1490, including pick-up from your accommodation, all equipment and lunch), as well as overnight trips, staying in bungalows on the island. Both TK and Island Hoppers World also offer sunset snorkelling trips to Ko Taen and trips to the mainland coast near Khanom to see pink dolphins.

Na Muang Falls

About 5km inland of **Ban Hua Thanon**, near **Ban Thurian**, the **Na Muang Falls** make a popular outing as they're not far off the round-island road (each of the two main falls has its own signposted kilometre-long paved access road off Route 4169). The lower fall splashes and sprays down a 20m wall of rock into a large pool, while Na Muang 2, upstream, is a more spectacular, shaded cascade. However, don't expect to appreciate the sparkling scenery in tranquillity, as the falls are now on most package tour itineraries, surrounded by water slides, zip lines and elephant camps.

Ang Thong National Marine Park

Closed Nov & most of Dec • Park entry fee B300 • Park headquarters ☎ 077 280222 or ☎ 077 286025, ⊛ nps.dnp.go.th (look for "Mu Ko Ang Thong" – mu ko means "archipelago")

Even if you don't get your buns off the beach for the rest of your stay on Samui or Pha Ngan, it's worth taking at least a day out to visit the beautiful **Ang Thong National Marine Park**, a lush, dense group of 42 small islands strewn like dragons' teeth over the deep-blue Gulf of Thailand, 30km or so west of Samui. Once a haven for pirate junks, then a Royal Thai Navy training base, the islands and their white-sand beaches and virgin rainforest are now preserved under the aegis of the National Parks Department. Erosion of the soft limestone has dug caves and chiselled out fantastic shapes that are variously said to resemble seals, a rhinoceros, a Buddha image and even the temple complex at Angkor.

The surrounding waters are home to dolphins, wary of humans because local fishermen catch them for their meat, and *pla thu* (short-bodied mackerel), part of the national staple diet, which gather in huge numbers between February and April to spawn around the islands. On land, long-tailed macaques, leopard cats, wild pigs, sea otters, squirrels, monitor lizards and pythons are found, as well as dusky langurs, which, because they have no natural enemies here, are unusually friendly and easy to spot. Around forty bird species have had confirmed sightings, including the white-rumped shama, noted for its singing, the brahminy kite, black baza, little heron, Eurasian woodcock, several species of pigeon, kingfisher and wagtail, as well as common and hill mynah; in addition, island caves shelter swiftlets, whose homes are stolen for bird's-nest soup (see page 671).

Ko Wua Talab

The largest landmass in the group is **Ko Wua Talab** (Sleeping Cow Island), where the park headquarters shelter in a hollow behind the small beach. From there, you can climb to the island's peak to gawp at the panorama, which is especially fine at sunrise and sunset: in the distance, Ko Samui, Ko Pha Ngan and the mainland; nearer at hand, the jagged edges of the surrounding archipelago; and below the peak, a secret cove on the western side and an almost sheer drop to the clear blue sea to the east. It's a fairly tricky 500m trail, with some scrambling including a patch of sharp rocks at the summit (allow about 2hr return at a comfortable pace with a break at the top; bring walking sandals or shoes). Another climb from the beach (allow about 1hr return) leads to **Tham Buabok**, a cave set high in the cliff-face. Some of the stalactites and stalagmites are said to resemble lotuses, hence the cave's appellation, "Waving Lotus". If you're visiting in September, look out for the white, violet-dotted petals of **Ang Thong lady's slipper orchids** among the rocks and cliffs, an endemic species found only on the archipelago.

Ko Mae Ko

The park's name, Ang Thong ("Golden Bowl"), comes from a landlocked saltwater lake, 250m in diameter, on **Ko Mae Ko** to the north of Ko Wua Talab, which was the inspiration for the setting of the bestselling novel and film, *The Beach*. Steep steps (allow 30min return) lead from the beach to the rim of the cliff wall that encircles the lake, affording another stunning view of the archipelago and of the shallow, blue-green water below, which is connected to the sea by an impassable natural underground tunnel.

ARRIVAL AND DEPARTURE — ANG THONG

There are no scheduled boats to Ang Thong, only organized **day-trips**, which can be booked through your accommodation or a travel agent. If you do want to stay, you can go over on a boat-trip ticket, through Highway for example – it's valid for a return on a later day.

FROM KO SAMUI

Blue Stars ☎ 077 300615 or ☎ 077 413884, ⓦ bluestars. info. If you want to make the most of the park's beautiful scenery of strange rock formations and hidden caves, take a dedicated kayaking trip with Blue Stars. For a one-day trip, taking in the lake at Ko Mae Ko, snorkelling at Ko Thai Plao in the northern part of the park and kayaking at both islands, it charges B2500 (in a group of two people), including pick-up from your accommodation and boat from Na Thon over to the park, buffet lunch and snorkelling gear.

Highway ☎ 077 421290 or ☎ 081 843 1533, ⓦ highseatour.com. The main operator, whose big boats leave Na Thon every day at 8.30am, returning at 4.30–5pm. In between, there's a two-and-a-half-hour stop to explore Ko Wua Talab (just enough time to climb to the viewpoint and have a quick swim – or possibly visit the cave – so don't dally), lunch on the boat, some cruising through the archipelago, a visit to the viewpoint over the lake on Ko Mae Ko and some time for snorkelling. Tickets cost B1100/person (or B1650 with kayaking), including pick-up from your accommodation.

The Dive Academy ☎ 092 464 3264, ⓦ thedive academysamui.com. This highly recommended dive school on Bophut offers small-group snorkelling day-trips to Ang Thong in a speedboat (B4000, including pick-up from your accommodation, snorkelling with good masks and fins, optional kayaking, lunch and national park entrance fee), with a high ratio of experienced guides to customers, taking in Ko Mae Ko but not Ko Wua Talab.

FROM KO PHA NGAN

Similar day-trips to those from Samui are available on Pha Ngan, and they include transfers from the main beaches, lunch and snorkelling. If you want to do a dedicated kayaking trip with Blue Stars (see above), the first Lomprayah catamaran from Thong Sala will get you over to Nathon pier on Samui just in time for their boat departure.

Orion ☎ 081 894 5076, ⓦ phanganboattrips.com. Recommended, well-organized day-trips in a wooden cruiser, costing B2000, or B2200 with kayaking (including national park entrance fee, light breakfast, a good buffet lunch, snacks, fruit and soft drinks), taking in Ko Mae Ko and Ko Wua Talab.

FROM KO TAO

Island Travel (see page 568). Weekly, small-group day-trips in a speedboat, costing B3600 for snorkellers, B5100 for divers (including pick-up from your accommodation, national park entrance fee, all equipment, lunch, snacks, fruit and soft drinks), taking in Ko Mae Ko.

GETTING AROUND

Boat and kayak rental For getting around the archipelago from Ko Wua Talab, it's possible to charter a motorboat or rent a kayak from marine park staff at headquarters, who also rent out snorkelling gear; the archipelago's waters are heavily sedimented from the Tapi River and too shallow for really good coral, but the best of it is off Ko Thai Plao, in the north of the park.

ACCOMMODATION AND EATING

National park bungalows At park headquarters on Ko Wua Talab ☎ 077 280222 or ☎ 077 286025, ⓦ nps. dnp.go.th. Simple two- to eight-berth bungalows and a restaurant, in a sheltered grassy glade behind the main beach. B500

Camping At park headquarters on Ko Wua Talab and on Ko Samsao. Two-person tents can be rented for around B250 a night from headquarters.

Ko Pha Ngan

In recent years, backpackers have tended to move over to Ko Samui's fun-loving little sibling, **KO PHA NGAN**, 20km to the north, which still has a comparatively simple atmosphere, mostly because the poor road system is an impediment to the developers. With a dense jungle covering its inland mountains and rugged granite outcrops

along the coast, Pha Ngan lacks the huge, gently sweeping beaches for which Samui is famous, but it does have plenty of coral to explore and some beautiful, sheltered bays. If you're seeking total isolation, trek out to **Hat Khuat (Bottle Beach)** on the north coast or the half-dozen pristine beaches on the east coast; **Thong Nai Pan**, at the top of the east coast, is not quite as remote, and offers a wide range of amenities and accommodation; while on the long neck of land at the southeast corner, **Hat Rin**, a pilgrimage site for ravers, is a thoroughly commercialized backpackers' resort in a gorgeous setting.

Much of Pha Ngan's development has plonked itself on the south and west sides along the only coastal roads on the island, which fan out from **Thong Sala**, the capital. The long, straight south coast is lined with bungalows, especially around **Ban Tai** and **Ban Khai**, to take the overspill from nearby Hat Rin, but it's hard to recommend staying here, as the beaches are mediocre by Thai standards, and the coral reef that hugs the length of the shoreline gets in the way of swimming. The west coast, however, offers several handsome sandy bays with great sunset views, notably **Hat Yao** and **Hat Salad**.

Pha Ngan's **bungalows** all now have running water and electricity, and plenty of places offer air conditioning, though there is only a handful of real luxury hotels. The three hundred-plus resorts generally have more space to spread out than on Ko Samui, and the cost of living is lower. The **prices** given on the following pages are standard for most of the year (though on Hat Rin they vary with the phases of the moon), but in slack periods you'll be offered discounts (possible, roughly, in May, June, Oct & Nov),

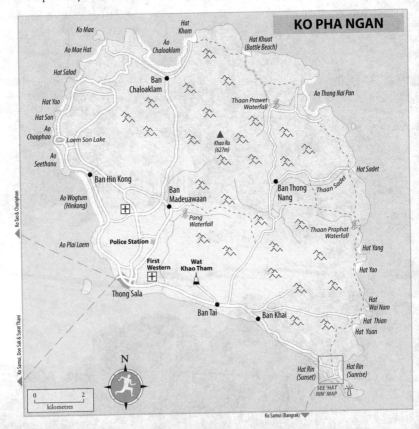

KO PHA NGAN ACTIVITIES

The most popular activities on Ko Pha Ngan are trips to Ang Thong National Marine Park (see page 549) and **snorkelling trips**, typically encompassing Hat Salad, Mae Hat, Hat Khom and Bottle Beach, and sometimes Thong Nai Pan and Thaan Sadet, which can be arranged at most travel agents and bungalow resorts around the island (around B900/person, including simple lunch and snorkelling equipment, sometimes with the option of kayaking too). The island isn't a great base for **scuba diving**: getting to the best sites around Ko Tao involves time-consuming and expensive voyages, and there aren't as many dive companies here as on Ko Samui or Ko Tao. Other **activities** include learning to cook Thai food, bicycle tours, yoga, wakeboarding and kiteboarding. Many of Pha Ngan's activities are available through the booking site ⓦbackpackersthailandtravel.com.

Agama Yoga North of Thong Sala, with several bases around Ao Seethanu ☎089 233 0217, ⓦagamayoga.com. Yoga drop-in classes and retreats.

Kiteboarding Asia Lime and Soda Resort, just east of Thong Sala ☎080 600 0573, ⓦkiteboardingasia.com. Kiteboarding classes and rental; the action moves to Ao Chaloaklam during the northeast monsoon (roughly Nov to mid-Jan).

Eco Nature Tour ☎062 421 4244, ⓦfacebook.com/phanganisland2017. A well-received programme of half- and one-day tours that might take in elephant trekking, snorkelling, zip lining, Thai boxing, archery, Pang Waterfall and boating to Bottle Beach; free pick-ups from most parts of the island.

Jungle Gym Hat Rin ☎077 375115, ⓦjunglegymandecolodge.com. Gym offering Thai boxing classes and yoga.

Lotus Diving Dive resort on Ao Chaloaklam ☎077 374142, ⓦlotusdiving.com. SSI centre, which offers frequent courses and trips to Ang Thong National Marine Park, Southwest Pinnacle and Sail Rock (see page 567), halfway between Pha Ngan and Tao.

My Wok and Me Ao Chaloaklam ☎087 893 3804, ⓦfacebook.com/pages/My-Wok-and-Me/14699 9882047571. Highly recommended cooking classes, including a trip to the local food market; vegetarian menu available.

Phangan Bicycle Tours Thong Sala ☎064 053 4112, ⓦphanganbicycletours.com. Danish-run half-day sightseeing tours on well-maintained bikes, either in the morning or early evening, including a family option with kids' seats, trailers and bikes available.

Siam Healing Centre Thong Sala ☎089 965 8752, ⓦsiamhealing.com. Have a Thai massage, learn how to massage or drop in for a yoga class.

Wake Up Ao Chaloaklam ☎087 283 6755, ⓦwakeupwakeboarding.com. Wakeboarding in the sheltered bay here (best Feb–Nov).

and at the very busiest times (especially Dec & Jan) Pha Ngan's bungalow owners are canny enough to raise the stakes. **Nightlife** is concentrated at Hat Rin, climaxing every month in a wild **full moon party** on the beach; several smaller outdoor parties have now got in on the act, all at Ban Tai on the south coast: the **Half Moon Festival** (twice monthly, about a week before and after the full moon; ⓦhalfmoonfestival.com) and the monthly **Black Moon Culture** (ⓦblackmoon-culture.com) have now been joined by the Waterfall Party (two days before and two days after each full moon; ⓦfacebook.com/waterfallparty) and Jungle Experience (one day before each full moon; ⓦjungle-experience.com). Meanwhile, 5 Senses Thailand (ⓦfacebook.com/5sensesfest) held its first twelve-day festival in early February 2018, featuring dozens of international house and techno DJs at diverse locations across the island, day and night.

ARRIVAL AND DEPARTURE
KO PHA NGAN

The most obvious way of getting to Ko Pha Ngan is on a boat from the **Surat Thani** area, but there are also boats from Chumphon (see page 526). Nok Air and Air Asia offer combination flight-bus-boat tickets from Bangkok's Don Muang Airport via Surat Thani and Nakhon Si Thammarat airports.

FROM SURAT THANI OR DON SAK
Surat Thani to Thong Sala Boat services fluctuate according to demand, but the longest-established is the night boat from Ban Don pier in Surat Thani to Thong Sala, which leaves at 11pm Mon–Sat (☎077 284928 or ☎081 326 8973; 7hr; B400); in the opposite direction, the night boat departs from Thong Sala at 10pm. Tickets are available from the pier on the day of departure, but note that sometimes these boats don't depart if they haven't got enough takers to make it worth their while, especially in the rainy season. In addition, there are three Lomprayah catamaran services a day from Tapi Pier, 5km northeast

of central Surat (2hr 30min; B700; on Pha Ngan ☎ 077 423761–2, ⓦ lomprayah.com).

Don Sak to Thong Sala There are one Lomprayah passenger ferry and six Raja vehicle ferries a day (on Pha Ngan ☎ 077 377452–3, ⓦ rajaferryport.com) from Don Sak, 68km east of Surat Thani, most of which have connecting buses to the pier from Surat, with a total journey time of around 4hr (from B350).

FROM BANGKOK

Bus packages From Bangkok bus packages similar to those for getting to Ko Samui are available, notably government buses from the Southern Terminal (first-class a/c 2 daily B585; VIP 1 daily B910; 13hr–15hr 30min). Leaving Pha Ngan, you can catch these buses from the Raja Ferry pier in Thong Sala (☎ 077 238507 or ☎ 077 238762). Lomprayah also offers through-tickets from Bangkok, costing B1300 (2 daily; 12hr), including a VIP bus from its office on Thanon Ram Bhuttri in Banglamphu (☎ 02 629 2569–70), via Hua Hin, and a catamaran from Chumphon via Ko Tao.

FROM KO SAMUI

To Thong Sala Three Lomprayah catamarans a day do the 30min trip from Na Thon on Ko Samui to Thong Sala (B300; at

Na Thon ☎ 077 950028, on Ko Pha Ngan ☎ 077 423761–2). Three Seatran Discovery boats a day (B300; at Bangrak ☎ 077 954171, on Pha Ngan ☎ 077 953056; ⓦ seatrandiscovery. com) and three Lomprayah boats a day (B250; at Bangrak ☎ 077 953084), both from the east end of Bangrak, and two Lomprayah catamarans from Maenam (B300; at Maenam ☎ 077 950700–4) call in at Thong Sala after 30min.

To Hat Rin and the east coast From the centre of Bangrak, the *Haad Rin Queen* crosses four times a day to Hat Rin in under an hour. Times have remained constant over the years, with extra services operated around the full moon: from Bangrak 10.30am, 1pm, 4pm & 6.30pm, from Hat Rin 9.30am, 11.40am, 2.30pm & 5.30pm (B200; on Samui ☎ 077 484668, on Pha Ngan ☎ 077 375113; ⓦ haadrinqueen.com). If there are enough takers and the weather's good enough – generally reliable between roughly Jan and Oct – one small boat a day crosses from the pier in Ban Maenam at noon to Hat Rin, before sailing up Ko Pha Ngan's east coast, via Hat Thian and Hat Sadet, to Thong Nai Pan; tickets to Hat Sadet, for example, cost B350.

FROM KO TAO

There are boats from Ko Tao to Ko Pha Ngan (see page 565); all offer the same service in the return direction.

INFORMATION

Tourist information There's no TAT office on Ko Pha Ngan, but a free, widely available booklet, *Phangan Info*, provides regularly updated information about the island with maps, and has a website (ⓦ phangan.info) and an app, on which you can book accommodation.

Thong Sala

Like the capital of Samui, **THONG SALA** is a port of entrance and little more, where the incoming ferries, especially around noon, are met by touts sent to escort travellers to bungalows elsewhere on the island. Seatran and Lomprayah share a pier, while a short way to the north, the Raja Ferry pier gives onto the town's dusty main street, which is flanked by banks, supermarkets, travel agents, a day market and a night market. Branching off south is the old main street, which on Saturday evenings becomes a "Walking Street" weekly market, selling clothes, crafts and food. Songthaews, jeeps and air-conditioned minibuses to the rest of the island congregate by the pier heads.

GETTING AROUND

THONG SALA

By motorbike or jeep Motorbikes (B150–200/day) and jeeps (B800–1000/day) can be rented from many places on the main road to the piers.

ACCOMMODATION AND EATING

Charu Bay Villas On the beach about 2km east of the Thong Sala piers on the road to Ban Tai ☎ 084 242 2299, ⓦ charubayvillas.com. Luxurious studios and villas, featuring lots of polished concrete in a colourful, contemporary style, with self-catering facilities and a shared swimming pool among many thoughtful amenities. Minimum stay two nights. B2000

Nira's Home Bakery South along the waterfront from the main street, opposite the Seatran pier ☎ 077 377 524 or ☎ 086 595 0636. Very pleasant, long-running café offering "quick meals to catch the boat": all-day breakfasts, espressos, juices, shakes, bakery goods such as quiche lorraine and deli sandwiches. Daily 7am–7pm; closed on the 10th of every month.

Goodtime Beach Backpackers About 2km east of the Thong Sala piers on the road to Ban Tai ☎ 077 377 165,

Ⓦgoodtimethailand.com. If you really need to stay near Thong Sala, head for this new hostel on the beach, which offers a swimming pool and a wide variety of dorm rooms (some of them beachfront), private rooms, bungalows and even a treehouse, all with hot showers. Dorms B275, doubles B800

DIRECTORY

Cinema Moonlight Cinema, on the east side of town at the start of the Ban Chaloaklam road (B150; Ⓣ093 638 5051, Ⓦfacebook.com/moonlightphangan), shows films every evening (except Monday) in a lovely garden setting, accompanied by popcorn, seasonal smoothies and vegan, gluten-free food.

Hospitals The island's basic main hospital (Ⓣ077 377034) lies 3km north of town, on the inland road towards Mae Hat. This has recently been joined by several small private hospitals, including First Western on the Ban Tai road on the east side of town, about 1km from the post office (Ⓣ077 377474, Ⓦfirstwesternhospital.healthcare). There's also an island-wide 24hr emergency rescue service, staffed by volunteers (Ⓣ077 377500).

Police The main station is 2km up the Ban Chaloaklam road (Ⓣ077 377501 or Ⓣ077 377114), and there's a tourist police office at the main pier in Thong Sala (Ⓣ1155).

Post office About 500m southeast of the piers on the old main street (Mon–Fri 8.30am–4.30pm, Sat 9am–noon).

6

Pang (Phaeng) Waterfall

Than Sadet–Ko Pha Ngan National Park, 4km northeast of Thong Sala off the road to Chaloaklam • Free admission • Take a Chaloaklam-bound songthaew as far as Ban Madeuawaan, from where it's a 1km signposted walk east

From most places on the island, it's fairly easy to get to the grandiosely termed Than Sadet–Ko Pha Ngan National Park, which contains **Pang (Phaeng) Waterfall**, Pha Ngan's biggest drop. The park headquarters are northeast of Thong Sala off the main road to Chaloaklam. From here, the main fall – bouncing down in stages over the hard, grey stone – is a steep 250m walk up a forest path. The trail then continues for 300m to a stunning viewpoint overlooking the south and west of the island.

Hat Rin

HAT RIN is firmly established as the major party venue in Southeast Asia, especially in the peak seasons of August, December and January, but it's most famous for its year-round **full moon parties** – something like *Apocalypse Now* without the war. Hat Rin's compact geography is ideally suited to an intense party town: it occupies the flat neck of Pha Ngan's southeast headland, which is so narrow that the resort comprises two back-to-back beaches, joined by transverse roads at the north and south ends.

The eastern beach, usually referred to as **Sunrise**, or Hat Rin Nok (Outer Hat Rin), is what originally drew visitors here, a classic curve of fine white sand between two rocky slopes; there's still some coral off the southern slope to explore, though the water is far from limpid these days. This beach is the centre of Hat Rin's action, with a solid line of bars, restaurants and bungalows tucked under the palm trees.

Sunset beach, or Hat Rin Nai (Inner Hat Rin), which for much of the year is littered with flotsam, looks ordinary by comparison but has plenty of quieter accommodation. Bandon International Hospital, a large private hospital on Ko Samui, runs a clinic here, on the southern transverse near the pier (Ⓣ077 375471). Unfortunately, development between the beaches does no justice to the setting: it's ugly, cramped and chaotic, with new low-rise concrete shophouses thrown up at any old angle. Businesses here are concentrated around **Chicken Corner** (where the southern transverse road meets the road along the back of Sunrise), named after the legendary, Israeli-style chicken schnitzel sandwiches at Mama's round-the-clock café; they include supermarkets, plenty of ATMs and bank currency-exchange booths, as well as outlets for more outré services such as bikini waxing and Playstation rental. Half-hearted attempts to tart up the large body of water in the middle of the headland with a few park benches and lights have been undermined by all-too-accurate signposts pointing to "Hat Rin Swamp".

6

ARRIVAL AND DEPARTURE
HAT RIN

By songthaew or minibus Songthaews and a/c minibuses run between Thong Sala and Hat Rin (B100 during the day, more at night); in Hat Rin, you can find them or their touts at the pier, Chicken Corner or near the police box.

By boat The easiest approach to Hat Rin, if you're coming from Ko Samui, or even Surat Thani, is on the boat from Bangrak on Samui's north coast (see page 554): four boats a day cross to the pier on Sunset beach in under an hour.

GETTING AROUND

By jeep or motorbike Plenty of places on Hat Rin rent motorbikes (around B250 for 24hr) and a few have jeeps (about B1000/day). There have been lots of reports, however, of travellers being charged exorbitant amounts if they bring the vehicle back with even the most minor damage – at the very least, check the vehicle over very carefully before renting and ask if you can leave cash instead of your passport as a deposit. Sun Cliff (see page 557), which has an office just off the southern transverse, is a reliable place for motorbikes, and won't try this scam. The section of road between Hat Rin and Ban Khai is paved but winding and precipitous – take care if you're driving yourself.

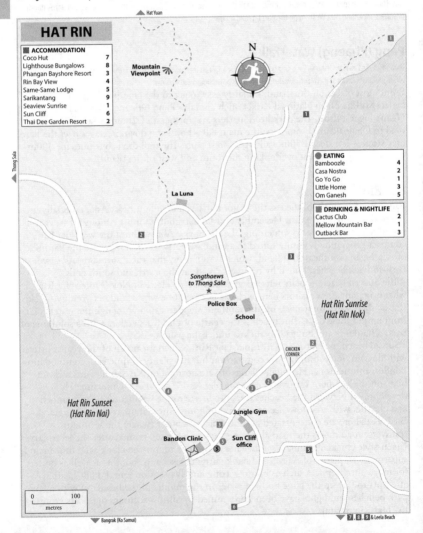

HAT RIN

ACCOMMODATION
Coco Hut	7
Lighthouse Bungalows	8
Phangan Bayshore Resort	3
Rin Bay View	4
Same-Same Lodge	5
Sarikantang	9
Seaview Sunrise	1
Sun Cliff	6
Thai Dee Garden Resort	2

EATING
Bamboozle	4
Casa Nostra	2
Go Yo Go	1
Little Home	3
Om Ganesh	5

DRINKING & NIGHTLIFE
Cactus Club	2
Mellow Mountain Bar	1
Outback Bar	3

Hat Yuan

Mountain Viewpoint

Thong Sala

La Luna

Songthaews to Thong Sala

Police Box

School

Hat Rin Sunrise (Hat Rin Nok)

CHICKEN CORNER

Hat Rin Sunset (Hat Rin Nai)

Jungle Gym

Bandon Clinic

Sun Cliff office

0   100
metres

Bangrak (Ko Samui)

7, 8, 9 & Leela Beach

ACCOMMODATION

Staying on **Sunrise** is often expensive and noisy, though you should have more luck towards the north end of the beach. On **Sunset**, the twenty or more resorts are squeezed together in orderly rows, and are especially quiet and inexpensive between April and June and in October. Many visitors choose to stay on the **headland** to the south of the main beaches, especially at white-sand, palm-fringed **Leela Beach** on the west side of the promontory, which is a twenty-minute walk along a well-signposted route from Chicken Corner. At any of the places out here your bungalow is likely to have more peace and space and better views, leaving you a torchlit walk to the night-time action.

Coco Hut Leela Beach ☎077 375 368–9, ⓦcocohut. com; map p.556. On a clean, quiet stretch of beach, this lively, efficiently run place is smart and attractive, with some traditional southern Thai elements in the architecture. On offer is a wide variety of upscale accommodation, from wooden bungalows with a/c, hot showers, minibars, TVs and DVDs, to beachfront villas with plunge pools, as well as two pools and an adobe-style spa. Free pick-up from Hat Rin. Breakfast included. B4460

Lighthouse Bungalows On the far southwestern tip of the headland ☎098 014 4930, ⓦfacebook.com/ lighthouse.bungalows; map p.556. At this friendly haven about 30min walk from Chicken Corner, wooden and concrete en-suite bungalows, sturdily built to withstand the wind on a boulder-strewn slope and backed by trail-filled jungle, are priced according to size and comfort; all have good-sized balconies with hammocks. The restaurant food is varied and tasty, and they host regular DJ parties. Currently reached by a wooden walkway over the rocky shoreline, though they may be forced by the authorities to replace this with a track over the hills. Fan B600, a/c B1800

Phangan Bayshore Resort In the middle of Sunrise ☎077 375 224, ⓦphanganbayshore.com; map p.556. Hat Rin's first upmarket resort, a well-ordered, slightly institutional place, boasting 80m of beachfront that's party central at full moon time. There's a large, shamrock-shaped pool and a wide variety of close-knit bungalows and rooms with a/c, hot water, TV, safety box and minibar, on a green lawn shaded with palms. Around the full moon, as well as a minimum stay of five nights, there's a big hike in prices. B2600

Rin Bay View Near the pier on Sunset ☎077 375188; map p.556. A good-value, friendly option in a tightly squeezed central location, occupying a narrow strip of land running down to a small, beachfront, infinity-edge pool, ornamented with flowers and trees. The a/c rooms with hot showers, TVs, fridges, safety boxes and balconies are a decent size and generally well maintained and clean. B1000

Same-Same Lodge Above the south end of Sunrise at the start of the road to Leela Beach ☎077 375 200, ⓦsame-same.com; map p.556. Sociable Danish-run spot set above a popular, often raucous, bar-restaurant that hosts lively full moon warm-up parties. The clean, colourful and decent-sized rooms come with fan and cold showers or a/c and hot water; there are also tightly packed a/c dorms. Free safety boxes. Dorms B500, fan doubles B550, a/c doubles B850

Sarikantang Leela Beach ☎077 375 055–6, ⓦsarikantang.com; map p.556. Boutique resort with two swimming pools (one with a kids' pool), a beachside spa and a good measure of style. Accommodation ranges from bungalows with a/c, TVs, minibars, verandas, hammocks and hot-water bathrooms to villas with DVD players, iPod docks, separate living rooms and outdoor Jacuzzis. Free kayaks, cooking classes and kids' activities; free pick-ups from Sunset pier and shuttles to downtown Hat Rin. Breakfast included. B2500

Seaview Sunrise Northern end of Sunrise ☎077 375160, ⓦseaviewsunrise.com; map p.556. On a big plot of shady, flower-strewn land at the quieter end of the beach, this clean, friendly, orderly old-timer with a good restaurant offers over forty bungalows and rooms. The bungalows on the beachfront are all fan-cooled with hot showers. Further back are a/c versions, as well as the cheapest rooms with cold showers. Kayaks for rent. Comparatively small price rise at full moon. Minimum stay 2 nights (5 at full moon). Fan B500, a/c B900

Sun Cliff High up on the tree-lined slope above the south end of Sunset ☎077 375134 or ☎077 375463, ⓔrsvnsuncliff@hotmail.com; map p.556. Friendly, spacious place with great views of the south coast and Ko Samui, especially from its heart-shaped pool by the restaurant. Among a wide range of bungalows that are a bit rough around the edges, you'll find some quirky architectural features such as rock-built bathrooms and fountains; some have huge decks for partying. A/c rooms all have hot showers, fridges and TVs. The cheapest options are rooms out on the road by the front office. Fan B400, a/c B600

Thai Dee Garden Resort Northern transverse ☎098 701 8898; map p.556. Pleasant staff and a range of smart concrete and white clapboard bungalows, on a broad, grassy slope strewn with trees and plants and set back from the road. Choose either fan and cold water or a/c and hot. A likely spot to have rooms free at full moon, although, as well as a minimum stay of five nights, there's a big hike in prices. Fan B400, a/c B650

EATING

Bamboozle Off the southern transverse, near Sunset pier ☎085 471 4211; map p.556. Among a wide variety of tasty Mexican food here, the chicken fajitas with all the trimmings (B250) are especially good. Also offers pizzas and

6

FULL MOON PARTIES: A SURVIVOR'S GUIDE

Even if you're not the type to coat yourself in day-glo and dance till dawn, a **full moon party** at Hat Rin is certainly a sight to see, and the atmosphere created by thousands of folk mashing it up on a beautiful, moon-bathed beach, lit up by fireworks and fire-jugglers, is quite a buzz. If you're planning to get in on the action, first of all you'll need to check exactly when the party is: when the full moon coincides with an important **Buddhist festival**, the party is moved one night away to avoid a clash; check out ⓦfullmoon.phangan.info for details. There's also a big party at Hat Rin on Christmas Day, and a massive one on New Year's Eve. Party-goers not staying on Hat Rin are charged an admission fee of B100. On the nights around the full moon, foam, pool and all sorts of other parties are organized.

On full moon night, *Paradise*, at the very southern end of Sunrise, styles itself as the main party **venue**, sometimes bringing in big-name international DJs. However, the mayhem spreads along most of Sunrise, fuelled by hastily erected drinks stalls and around a dozen major **sound systems**. Next morning, as the beach party winds down, *Back Yard* hosts the afterparty, with the best of the previous night's DJs; it's up the hill behind the south end of Sunrise off the path to Leela Beach.

Drug-related horror stories are common currency in Hat Rin, and some of them are even true: dodgy MDMA, *ya baa* (Burmese-manufactured methamphetamines), Ice (crystal meth), magic mushrooms and all manner of other concoctions put several farangs a month into hospital for psychiatric treatment. The local authorities have started clamping down on the trade in earnest, setting up a permanent police box at Hat Rin (with a temporary tourist police office nearby for the full moon), instigating regular roadblocks and bungalow and personal searches, paying dealers, bungalow and restaurant owners to inform on travellers to whom they've sold drugs, and drafting in scores of police (both uniformed and plain-clothes) on full moon nights. It doesn't seem to have dampened the fun, only made travellers a lot more circumspect. Not only that but the "bucket" sellers on Sunrise Beach replace brand-name spirits with dodgy, illegal, home-brewed alcohol, which often contain harmful substances that will give you more of a hangover than you bargained for.

Other **tips** for surviving the full moon are mostly common sense: leave your valuables in your resort's safe – it's a bad night for bungalow break-ins – and don't take a bag out with you; keep an eye on your drink to make sure it's not spiked; watch out for broken bottles and anchors on the beach; and do not go swimming while under the influence – there have been several deaths by drowning at previous full moon parties. There have also been several reports of sexual assaults on women – don't walk or take a taxi home alone – of muggings and of unprovoked, late-night gang attacks in Hat Rin, especially around full moon night.

ACCOMMODATION AND TRANSPORT

Hat Rin now has around five thousand **rooms** – some of them hastily converted dorms that open at party time, charging B600–1000 per person – but on full moon nights up to thirty thousand revellers may turn up. Unless you're prepared to forget about sleep altogether, you should book well in advance (booking sites such as ⓦbackpackersthailandtravel.com offer multi-day full moon, half moon and New Year's Eve packages) or arrive several days early to bag a room, as resort owners specify a minimum stay of three–five nights (in some places up to ten nights, especially over the Christmas and New Year's Eve parties). Alternatively, you can take the Had Rin Queen over from Bangrak on Ko Samui and back in the morning, or hitch up with one of the many **party boats** (about B1000 return per person) organized through guesthouses and restaurants on Ko Samui, especially at Bangrak and Bophut, which leave in the evening and return in the early hours until around dawn, though they're sometimes dangerously overcrowded. There's also transport by boat or car from all the other beaches on Pha Ngan; at nearby Ban Tai, there are also dorms to take the overflow.

a short menu of tapas. Sprawl on an axe cushion in the tree-shaded courtyard, play a bit of pool or swing in a hammock. Daily roughly 4pm–after midnight.

Casa Nostra On the southern transverse ☏094 881 0421; map p.556. Tiny Italian café-restaurant which prepares great pastas – try the spaghetti bolognese (B220) or go for one of the day's specials – pizzas, espresso coffee, salads and plenty of other dishes for vegetarians, washed down with Italian wines and spirits. 3/4–11pm, closed most Sundays.

Go Yo Go On the southern transverse; map p.556. Chi-chi Italian-run gelateria, serving delicious frozen yoghurt, crepes, waffles and cocktails. An espresso and a slice of their torta della nonna (cashew and vanilla tart; B160) makes a great breakfast. Daily 10.30am–2am.

Little Home On the southern transverse; map p.556. This well-organized, basic restaurant is your best bet for cheap Thai food in Hat Rin, serving staples such as *phat thai*

(B70), chicken and cashew nuts and green, red and yellow curries, plus Western breakfasts and homemade yoghurt. Daily 10.30am–10.30pm.

Om Ganesh On the southern transverse near the pier ☎086 063 2903; map p.556. Relaxing Indian restaurant with good thalis (from B160), biryanis, plenty of veggie dishes and breads, Indian breakfasts and cheerful service. Free deliveries. Daily 10am–11.30pm.

NIGHTLIFE

Cactus Club South end of Sunrise; map p.556. Centrally placed open-air dance hall that pumps out mostly radio-friendly dance music onto low-slung candlelit tables and mats on the beach. Evenings till late.

Mellow Mountain Bar North end of Sunrise; map p.556. Made for chilling, this trippy hangout occupies a great position up in the rocks, with floor cushions, hammocks and peerless views of the beach. Closed by the

authorities for supposed "encroachment" issues at the time of writing, but likely to have reopened with a bang by the time you read this. Evenings till late.

Outback Bar On the southern transverse; map p.556. Lively meeting place with a "no trance" music policy, free pool tables, big-screen sports, a selection of bottled ciders and well-received English breakfasts, cottage pies and the like. Daily 11am–late.

Hat Yuan, Hat Thian and Hat Sadet

North of Hat Rin, there are no roads along the rocky, exposed east coast, which stretches as far as **Ao Thong Nai Pan**, the only substantial centre of development. First up are the adjoining small, sandy bays of **HAT YUAN** and **HAT THIAN**, which have established a reputation as a quieter alternative to Hat Rin. A rough track has recently been bulldozed from Ban Khai, and the bays now sport about a dozen bungalow outfits between them.

Steep, remote **HAT SADET**, about 8km as the crow flies from Hat Rin, has a handful of bungalow operations, sited here because of their proximity to **Thaan Sadet**, a boulder-strewn brook that runs out into the sea. The spot was popularized by various kings of Thailand – Rama V visited no fewer than fourteen times – who came here to walk, swim and vandalize the huge boulders by carving their initials on them; the river water is now considered sacred and is transported to Bangkok for important royal ceremonies. A paved road runs through the woods above and parallel to Thaan Sadet to connect with the road from Thong Sala to Ao Thong Nai Pan.

If you're feeling intrepid, you could try hiking along this stretch of coast, which in theory is paralleled by a steep, 15km trail, though it's reported to be overgrown in many places. With decent navigational skills, the leg between Hat Rin, starting from near *La Luna Bungalows*, and Hat Yuan should certainly be manageable (about 2hr), aided by green dot and white arrow markers.

ARRIVAL AND DEPARTURE   HAT YUAN, HAT THIAN, HAT SADET

By boat A daily, seasonal boat runs via the east coast beaches from Hat Rin to Thong Nai Pan, having started its voyage across at Maenam on Ko Samui (see page 554).

Otherwise there are ample longtails at Hat Rin that will take you up the coast – around B150/person to Hat Yuan, for example.

ACCOMMODATION

HAT YUAN

Barcelona ☎077 375113, ⓦbarcelonakpg.com. Good, relaxing budget choice, with great views and decent accommodation, mostly in colourful, stilted bungalows running up the steep hillside from the beach, equipped with fans, mosquito nets, balconies and hot showers. **B700**

Pariya ☎081 737 3883, ⓦpariyahaadyuan.com. The most luxurious resort in the vicinity of Hat Rin comprises forty spacious octagonal villas, some with their own private Jacuzzi pool, and half-a-dozen much smaller rooms, all with lots of polished concrete, rain showers, bathtubs and large verandas, set on a steep slope running down to the beach.

6

There's a free-form pool and kids' pool and a spa. Breakfast included. **B3125**

HAT THIAN

★ **The Sanctuary** ⓣ081 271 3614, ⓦthesanctuary thailand.com. This magical fairyland, connected by a labyrinth of paths, offers a huge range of basic and luxury en-suite bungalows, as well as dorm accommodation (B350), built into the lush promontory. It also hosts all-inclusive yoga and detox courses, and has a spa that does massage, facials and beauty treatments. The beautiful timber restaurant serves up good vegetarian meals, seafood and home-made bread and cakes. The cheaper accommodation is not bookable in advance, but you can phone up on the morning of your planned arrival and they'll hold a spot for you until later in the afternoon. **B950**

HAT SADET

Mai Pen Rai ⓣ093 959 8073, ⓦthansadet.com. The main operation on Hat Sadet, with its own reggae bar, this welcoming spot has a huge variety of attractive bungalows with airy bathrooms, fans and hammocks (some with big upstairs terraces), either on the beach at the stream mouth or scattered around the rocks for good views. A jeep taxi leaves Thong Sala for the resort every day at 1pm (B200/person). **B580**

Ao Thong Nai Pan

AO THONG NAI PAN is a beautiful, semicircular bay backed by steep, green hills, which looks as if it's been bitten out of the island's northeast corner by a gap-toothed giant, leaving a tall hump of land (occupied by *Panviman Resort*) dividing the bay into two parts: **Thong Nai Pan Noi** to the north, **Thong Nai Pan Yai** to the south. With lovely, fine, white sand, the longer, more indented Thong Nai Pan Yai has marginally the better beach, but both halves of the bay are sheltered and deep enough for swimming. A paved road winds its way for 13km over the steep mountains from Ban Tai on the south coast to Thong Nai Pan, but once you get here you'll find most of the basic amenities you'll need: travel agents, dive outfits, ATMs, supermarkets and clinics.

ARRIVAL AND DEPARTURE **AO THONG NAI PAN**

By jeep Jeeps connect with incoming and outgoing boats at Thong Sala every day (B300/person).
By boat One seasonal boat a day runs via the east coast

beaches from Hat Rin to Thong Nai Pan, having started its voyage across at Maenam on Ko Samui (see page 554).

ACCOMMODATION AND EATING

★ **Anantara Rasananda** Thong Nai Pan Noi ⓣ077 956 660, ⓦanantara.com. Congenial and chic luxury hideaway, with speedboat transfers from Samui. Accommodation is in sixty spacious, contemporary villas and suites, all with their own plunge pool, most with indoor-outdoor bathrooms. There's also a main, infinity-edge swimming pool, which forms the central hub of the resort, along with a sociable bar, a beach bistro and a Japanese teppanyaki restaurant. The very good spa stretches up the hillside behind, with a steam room built into the rocks. Other activities include kayaking, cooking and yoga classes. **B12,810**
Baan Panburi Village Southern end of Thong Nai Pan Yai ⓣ077 445075. Two rows of well-designed bungalows with verandas and deckchairs run down a slope dotted with wicker hammocks, either side of a small, artificial waterfall. Choose between old-style, thatched, wood-and-bamboo huts with mosquito nets, fans and cold showers, and large, wooden, a/c affairs with hot water and tiled floors. Fan **B600**, a/c **B1400**
Longtail Beach Resort At the far southern end of Thong Nai Pan Yai ⓣ077 445018, ⓦlongtailbeachresort.com. In four quiet, leafy rows on either side of two long strips of lawn that run down to the attractive beachfront restaurant,

spa and small swimming pool, these diverse, mostly wooden, partly thatched bungalows are well designed and maintained; all have verandas, hammocks and hot showers, and for most of them, you can choose whether to pay extra for a/c or not. Fan **B850**, a/c **B1000**
Sand in My Shoes Northern end of Thong Nai Pan Noi ⓣ087 429 4949, ⓦfacebook.com/sandinmyshoes kohphangan. One of the destinations of the moment on Pha Ngan, this chic bar-restaurant-pizzeria on the beach has recently added a handful of stylish and luxurious guest rooms, kitted out with platform beds, balconies and geometric objets d'art – with more bedrooms planned. Good breakfast included. **B5040**
★ **Siam House** About 100m from the beach towards the main road, behind Dreamland Resort, Thong Nai Pan Yai ⓦfacebook.com/dolphinbarandcafe. Run by the former proprietors of Dolphin Resort, this mellow café-bar is set in a lovely, open-sided, two-storey house with a garden and lotus pond (and now boasts a beach bar annexe nearby). It serves great coffee and breakfasts, salads and other Western lunches (mains from around B100), as well as barbecues on Tues and Fri evenings. Daily 8.30am–2pm, plus Tues & Fri 6.30–11pm.

The north coast

The largest indent on the **north coast**, Ao Chaloaklam, has long been a famous R&R spot for fishermen from all over the Gulf of Thailand, with sometimes as many as a hundred trawlers littering the broad and sheltered bay. As a tourist destination, it has little to recommend it – save that its village, **Ban Chaloaklam**, can easily be reached from Thong Sala, 10km away, by songthaew (B150) along a paved road – but the small, quiet beaches to the east, Hat Khom and Hat Khuat, have much more to offer.

Hat Khom

Dramatically tucked in under Ao Chaloaklam's eastern headland is the tiny cove of **HAT KHOM**. Linked to the outside world by a partly paved road, it offers an attractive strip of white sand backed by shady trees, good coral close to the beach for snorkelling and plenty of seclusion.

6

Hat Khuat (Bottle Beach)

If the sea is not too rough, longtail boats run several times a day for most of the year from Ban Chaloaklam (east of the fishing pier; B100/person or about B600/boat) to isolated **HAT KHUAT** (**BOTTLE BEACH**), the best of the beaches on the north coast, sitting between steep, jungle-clad hills in a perfect cup of a bay that's good for swimming. You could also walk there along a testing trail from Hat Khom in around ninety minutes.

ACCOMMODATION AND EATING   **THE NORTH COAST**

Caffè della Moca (Cucina Italiana) Ban Chaloaklam ☎ 086 470 4253. Run by a friendly, enthusiastic native of Rimini, this simple, authentic Italian restaurant towards the west end of the village offers tables on the sand and great pizzas (around B200), home-made gnocchi, lasagne and tiramisu. 5pm–late; closed Wed.

Haad Khuad Resort Hat Khuat ☎ 077 445153–4, ⊛ haadkhuadresort.com. Well-organized spot in the middle of the bay, offering deluxe rooms in a two-storey hotel block with view-filled French windows, a/c, hot water, TV, mini-bars and breakfast included. Also has a choice of wooden or concrete fan bungalows and rooms with cold showers on the beachfront and in the garden. Kayaks available. Daily transfers from Thong Sala (B400/person). Fan B500, a/c B1500

Smile Resort Western end of Hat Khuat ☎ 085 429 4995. Set on a rocky slope strewn with flowers and trees on the western side of the beach, with fun owners and a sociable bar-restaurant area. The attractive, bamboo-clad, en-suite bungalows come with wall fans and mosquito nets. B520

The west coast

Pha Ngan's **west coast** has attracted about the same amount of development as the forgettable south coast, but the landscape here is more attractive and varied, broken up into a series of long sandy inlets with good sunset views over the islands of the Ang Thong National Marine Park to the west. Most of the bays, however, are sheltered by reefs which can keep the sea too shallow for a decent swim, especially between May and October.

Ao Chaophao and Hat Yao

Just north of the small, pretty bay of **AO CHAOPHAO** lies the west coast's main beach, **HAT YAO**, a long, gently curved strip of fine sand. It's gradually and justifiably becoming busier and more popular, with several stand-alone bars, diving outfits, a 7-Eleven supermarket, a pharmacy, ATMs and jeep and bike rental, as well as a nonstop line of bungalows.

Hat Salad

To the north of Hat Yao, **HAT SALAD** is another pretty bay, sheltered and sandy, with good snorkelling off the northern tip. On the access road behind the beach is a rather untidy service village of shops, travel agents, and bike and jeep rental outlets. Take your pick from a dozen or so bungalow outfits.

Ao Mae Hat

On the island's northwest corner, **AO MAE HAT** is good for swimming and snorkelling among the coral that lines the sandy causeway to the tiny islet of Ko Maa. The broad, coarse-sand bay supports several bungalow resorts.

ARRIVAL AND GETTING AROUND

By motorbike or jeep There's a paved coastal road up as far as Hat Salad, where it loops inland to meet the main inland road from Thong Sala via the hospital to Ao Mae Hat.

THE WEST COAST

By songthaew Songthaews from Thong Sala serve all of the beaches on the west coast, charging B200–300/person to go as far as Ao Mae Hat, for example.

ACCOMMODATION

AO SEETHANU

Loy Fa ☎077 377 319, ⓦloyfanaturalresort.com. Well-run, friendly, flower-strewn place that commands good views from its perch on the steep southern cape of otherwise nondescript Ao Seethanu. There's good snorkelling and swimming from its private beach below, as well as two saltwater pools. Smart bungalows are scattered around the hilltop and the slope down on the beach, and come with large verandas, a/c, hot water, mini-bar, TV and DVD player. Breakfast and transfers from Thong Sala included. B2450

AO CHAOPHAO

★ **Seaflower** ☎077 349 090, ⓦseaflowerbungalows. com. Quiet, congenial spot, set in a lush, shady garden, with good veggie and non-veggie food and nice touches like an annual sandcastle-building competition. Bright, en-suite, a/c bungalows with their own hot-water bathrooms vary in price according to their size, age and distance from the beach. Even cheaper rooms have marble-tiled floors and bathrooms and big balcony seating areas. Free pick-ups from Thong Sala with 24hr notice. Minimum stay two nights. B1200

HAT YAO

Long Bay Resort ☎077 349 057–9, ⓦlongbay-resort. com. Hat Yao's nicest upmarket spot boasts a long stretch of beach and spacious gardens towards the north end of the bay. Choose between small but smart bungalows ("Garden Huts") and a range of large cottages, all with verandas, a/c and hot water. There's an attractive, free-form swimming pool with kids' pool and kayaks and snorkels to rent. Transfer from Thong Sala and breakfast included. B1800

Shiralea ☎077 349 217, ⓦshiralea.com. On a broad, grassy bank beneath coconut trees set back from the north end of the beach, the spacious, very attractive thatched bungalows here all come with hot water and verandas with hammocks, and there's a seductive pool with a pool bar, smart a/c dormitories, a games room and a sociable atmosphere. Dorms B270, fan doubles B640, a/c B1180

HAT SALAD

★ **Salad Hut** ☎077 349246, ⓦsaladhut.com. Among the dozen or so bungalow outfits here, this congenial, family-friendly and well-run old-timer stands out. Behind a small, infinity-edge swimming pool, in a shady, colourful garden, are stylish bungalows done out in dark woods, red and white, with day beds with axe cushions and hammocks on their large verandas, as well as larger villas and family rooms. All come with hot water, mini-bar and TV, and a cooked breakfast at the chic bar-restaurant is included. Library, pool table and snorkel and kayak rental. Fan B2200, a/c B2500

AO MAE HAT

Wang Sai Resort Ao Mae Hat ☎077 374238, ⓦwangsairesort.com. Popular, friendly spot by a shady creek at the south end of the bay. On a huge plot of land, most of the en-suite bungalows are set back from the beach, including the cheapest options, with fans and cold showers, which are set on a slope with great sunset views. The best and most expensive are across the creek on the beach, all with a/c, fridge and hot water, some with TV. On-site dive school and kayaks and snorkels for rent. Fan B1200, a/c B1600

Ko Tao

KO TAO (Turtle Island) is so named because its outline resembles a turtle nose-diving towards Ko Pha Ngan, 40km to the south. The rugged shell of the turtle, to the east, is crenellated with secluded coves, where one or two bungalows hide among the rocks and there's good snorkelling. On the western side, the turtle's underbelly is a long curve of classic beach, **Hat Sai Ree**, facing **Ko Nang Yuan**, a beautiful Y-shaped group of islands offshore, also known as Ko Hang Tao (Turtle's Tail Island). The 21 square kilometres of granite in between are topped by dense forest on the higher slopes and dotted with huge boulders that look as if they await some Easter Island sculptor. It's fun to spend a couple of days exploring the network of rough trails, after which you'll probably know all 2200 of the island's inhabitants. Ko Tao is now best known as a venue for **scuba-diving courses**, with a wide variety of dive sites in close proximity.

The island is the last and most remote of the archipelago that continues the line of Surat Thani's mountains into the sea. It served as a jail for political prisoners from 1933 to 1947, then was settled by a family from Ko Pha Ngan. Now, there are around 150 sets of **bungalows** for visitors, just about enough to cope during the peak seasons of

6

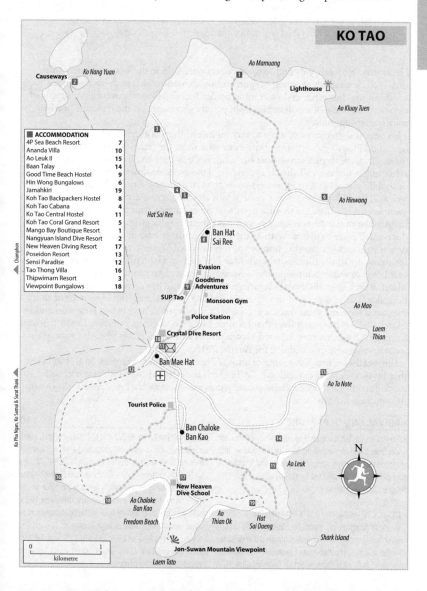

KO TAO

■ ACCOMMODATION	
4P Sea Beach Resort	7
Ananda Villa	10
Ao Leuk II	15
Baan Talay	14
Good Time Beach Hostel	9
Hin Wong Bungalows	6
Jamahkiri	19
Koh Tao Backpackers Hostel	8
Koh Tao Cabana	4
Ko Tao Central Hostel	11
Koh Tao Coral Grand Resort	5
Mango Bay Boutique Resort	1
Nangyuan Island Dive Resort	2
New Heaven Diving Resort	17
Poseidon Resort	13
Sensi Paradise	12
Tao Thong Villa	16
Thipwimarn Resort	3
Viewpoint Bungalows	18

6

ECO TAO

With so many divers and other visitors coming to this tiny island, the pressures on the environment, both above and below the waterline, are immense. Coral nurseries have been started around Ko Tao, as well as more than half a dozen artificial reefs, which allow divers to practise their skills without damaging coral. You might want to ask your dive operator if they get involved in regular beach and dive-site clean-ups and coral monitoring programmes, but much of what visitors can do to help is common sense: avoiding littering, recycling where possible and turning down plastic bags when you're shopping. The island suffers from a scarcity of water, with occasional droughts during the hot season after a poor rainy season, so conserve water whenever possible. In the sea, the main rule is not to touch the coral, which may mean avoiding snorkelling when the water is low from April to September – if in doubt, ask locally for advice, be careful and go out at high tide. Don't take away dead shells, and don't buy coral or shell jewellery.

December to March, July and August, concentrated along the west and south sides; they include a rapidly growing number of upscale resorts with such luxuries as air conditioning, hot water and swimming pools. There's a limited government supply of electricity, so some of it still comes from private generators on the remotest beaches, usually evenings only.

If you're just arriving and want to stay on one of the less accessible beaches, it might be a good idea to go with one of the touts who meet the ferries at **Mae Hat**, the island's main village, with pick-up or boat on hand, since at least you'll know their bungalows aren't full; otherwise call ahead, as even the remotest bungalows now have landlines or mobile phones and most owners come to market once a day (pick-ups are either free or B50–150/person). Some resorts with attached scuba-diving operations have been known to refuse guests who don't sign up for diving trips or courses; on the other hand, most of the dive companies now have their own lodgings, available free or at a discounted price to divers. With a year-round customer base of divers – and resident dive instructors – a growing number of sophisticated Western **restaurants** and **bars** are springing up all the time, notably in Mae Hat and on Hat Sai Ree. For nightlife, your best bet is to watch out for posters advertising weekly and monthly parties around the island, which keep the crowds rotating; women should be careful getting back to their bungalow late at night and should avoid walking home alone. The biggest event to hit the island in many years was the eco-friendly Tao Festival, held over a long weekend in March 2017 ⓦtaofestival.live) that featured DJs such as Gilles Peterson, Kevin Yost and Santiago Salazar, rappers Arrested Development and visual artists like Alex Face; the second instalment is scheduled for August 2018.

The **weather** is much the same as on Pha Ngan and Samui (see page 534), but being that bit further off the mainland, Ko Tao feels the effect of the southwest monsoon more: June to October can have strong winds and rain, with a lot of debris blown onto the windward coasts.

ARRIVAL AND DEPARTURE
KO TAO

All boats to Ko Tao dock at Mae Hat. Boat services and prices may fluctuate according to demand, and in high season extra boats may appear. Voyages to and from Ko Tao may occasionally be affected by the weather at any time between June and January.

FROM CHUMPHON AND BANGKOK
The main jumping-off point for boats to Ko Tao is Chumphon (see page 526), which is connected to Bangkok by train and bus. The two main Chumphon–Ko Tao boat companies both offer through-tickets from Bangkok; with

Lomprayah (on Ko Tao ⓣ077 456176, ⓦlomprayah.com), for example, this costs B1100, including a VIP bus from its office on Thanon Ram Bhuttri (ⓣ02 629 2569–70), via Hua Hin. It's better to buy a Bangkok–Tao through-ticket direct from the boat company's website or office in the capital rather than from a travel agency, otherwise you're unlikely to get your money back if the boat turns out to be full, which is possible in high season, or is cancelled because of very bad weather. Both Nok Air and Air Asia offer flight-bus-boat combination tickets to Ko Tao from Bangkok's Don Muang Airport.

FROM KO PHA NGAN AND KO SAMUI

Two main companies operate daily scheduled boats between Thong Sala on Ko Pha Ngan and Ko Tao: Lomprayah (see opposite; 3 daily; around 1hr 15min; B500–600) and Seatran (on Ko Tao ☎077 953057, ⓦseatrandiscovery.com; 3 daily; around 1hr 30min; B450). Lomprayah offer services either from Maenam (2 daily) or Na Thon (1 daily) on Ko Samui, while all the Seatran boats originate at Bangrak (total journey time to Ko Tao on all services about 1hr 45min–2hr 30min; B600–700).

FROM SURAT THANI

With Lomprayah If you're coming from Surat Thani, you could for example take Lomprayah's catamaran service from Tapi Pier, about 5km northeast of Surat centre (2 daily; total journey time from Surat about 4–5hr; B800–900).

With the night boat There are night boats from Ban Don pier in Surat Thani town, departing at 10pm (in theory, 1–2 daily, though they don't always run; 8hr; B500); in the opposite direction, this leaves Ko Tao at 9pm; book at the piers.

6

GETTING AROUND

You can **get around** easily enough on foot, but there are roads of sorts now to most of the resorts, though some are still very rough, steep tracks, suitable for 4WD only.

By pick-up taxi Pick-ups (starting from B100/person to Chaloke Ban Kao, for example, depending on how many people are going; rates are higher at night, or for a 4WD to somewhere more remote) are available in Mae Hat.

By motorbike As on Ko Phangan, there have been lots of reports of travellers being charged exorbitant amounts if they bring their rented motorbike back with even the most minor damage – avoid the outfits immediately

in front of the main pier in Mae Hat, and rent from your bungalow or someone reliable like Island Travel (Koh Tao Scooters, ⓦkohtaoscooters.com), who offer environmentally friendly bikes from B200/day (insurance and drop-offs/pick-ups around the island available; leave your passport or a deposit). If you can, resist the temptation to rent a quad bike, or ATV – not only do they have a disproportionate number of accidents, but they're also very polluting.

By mountain bike Mountain bikes can be rented for B150/day from Evasion on Hat Sai Ree (see page 569).

INFORMATION

There isn't a TAT office on Ko Tao, but the regularly updated and widely available free booklet, *Koh Tao Info*, is a useful source of information, along with its associated website,

ⓦkohtao-online.com. This is now in competition with ⓦkohtaocompleteguide.com, though its hard-copy format is more difficult to find.

Mae Hat and around

MAE HAT, a small, lively village and port in a pleasant, beachfront setting, boasts the lion's share of the island's amenities. A paved high street heads straight up the hill from the main pier, paralleled by another paved road just to the north heading up the hill from the Seatran pier and another to the south heading inland from the Songserm pier, with a narrower front street running at right angles, parallel to the seafront. Three of the ferry companies each have their own pier, Lomprayah and Songserm to the south of the main one, Seatran to the north.

ACCOMMODATION   MAE HAT AND AROUND

Ananda Villa North end of the village, on the beach ☎077 456478, ⓦanandavilla.com; map p.563. Cute, well-designed and maintained a/c rooms in a two-storey block, sporting French windows that give onto balconies with wooden balustrades. Inside, silks and other decorative touches set off the dark-wood furniture; facilities include large, hot-water bathrooms, DVD players and fridges. Also has some a/c wooden bungalows in the garden (B1200) and fan rooms in a beachside single-storey block that are tiny but boast hot showers. Fan <u>B600</u>, a/c <u>B1800</u>

BOAT TOURS AND SNORKELLING ON KO TAO

Some dive companies will take along **snorkellers**, usually on their afternoon trips, when they visit the shallower sites, but your best bet for snorkelling is probably a round-island **boat tour**. Available through your bungalow or at Island Travel (see page 568) in Mae Hat for example (from B600/person for a day-trip, including lunch, equipment and pick-ups and drop-offs, or around B2000 to hire your own longtail boat for the day), these take in snorkelling at Ao Thian Ok (aka Shark Bay), Ao Leuk, Ao Hinwong, Ao Mamuang and the beautiful Japanese Gardens off Ko Nang Yuan, but you'll have to pay the B100 entrance fee if you set foot on the island to climb up to the viewpoint.

Ko Tao Central Hostel On the Seatran road in Ban Mae Hat ☎077 456925, ⓦkohtaohostel.com; map p.563563. English-run hostel – look for the London Underground logo – encompassing the Island Travel agency (where reception is) and The Reef Sports Bar and Restaurant. Smart, partitioned dorm beds with a/c and hot showers. Discounts for guests at many outlets around the island. Dorm B340

Sensi Paradise On the lower slopes of the headland just south of the village ☎077 456244, ⓦsensi paradiseresort.com; map p.563. Charming resort in flower-covered grounds, offering a pretty beachside restaurant, an attractive free-form pool and some of the best upmarket accommodation on the island: well-designed Thai-style cottages, family houses and villas made of polished red wood with mini-bars and a/c, most with hot showers and some with large terraces and open-air bathrooms. Transfer from the pier and breakfast included. B3300

Tao Thong Villa Cape Jeda Gang ☎077 456078; map p.563. Sturdy, en-suite bungalows dotted around the rocky outcrop of Cape Jeda Gang and the slope behind, with a breezy restaurant above the tiny, grassy isthmus with two small beaches in between. Plenty of shady seclusion, great views and good snorkelling and swimming. About 1hr walk south of Mae Hat, or get there by pick-up or boat taxi. Fan B500, a/c B1600

EATING AND DRINKING

Cappuccino 100m from the pier, up the high street on the left ☎077 456 870. French-run café and bakery that does a mean pain au chocolat, plus gourmet sandwiches on homemade bread, burgers and panini. Daily 7am–6pm.

The Factory About 1km up the Ao Leuk road ☎098 718 6712, ⓦfacebook.com/thefactorykohtao. Trek

DIVING OFF KO TAO

Some of the best **dive sites** in Thailand are found off Ko Tao, which is blessed with outstandingly clear (visibility is up to 35m), safe and relatively deep water, studded with underwater pinnacles close in to shore, as well as sheltered bays for beginners to practice. On top of that, there's a kaleidoscopic array of coral species and other marine life – you may be lucky enough to encounter whale sharks, barracudas, leatherback turtles and pilot whales – and a couple of popular wreck-diving sites. Diving is possible at any time of year, with sheltered sites on one or other side of the island in any **season** – the changeover from southwest to northeast monsoon in November is the worst time, while **visibility** is best from April to July, in September (usually best of all) and October. Dive courses on Ko Tao are particularly heavily subscribed in the days after the full moon party on Ko Pha Ngan, when it would be worth booking in advance. Ko Tao supports several evacuation centres, clinics that specialize in diving medicine, while the nearest recompression chamber is on Ko Samui, ninety minutes away by speedboat (see page 535).

DIVE COMPANIES, COURSES AND TRIPS

Ko Tao has about fifty **dive companies**, making this the largest dive-training centre in the world. Most of the companies are staffed by Westerners and based at Mae Hat, Hat Sai Ree or Ao Chaloke Ban Kao. You'll generally be offered discounted or free accommodation while you're diving but ask exactly how long it's for (three or four nights for an Openwater course), where it is and what it's like. **Operators** on Ko Tao include Crystal (☎077 456106, ⓦcrystaldive.com), a large, lively, sociable PADI Five-Star Career Development Centre based on the north side of Mae Hat just beyond Ananda Villa, with two swimming pools, three big boats and a speedboat, offering courses in small groups in dozens of languages, plus a wide choice of good accommodation in three resorts on the north side of Mae Hat. At the other end of the scale are schools that are small, personal and laidback (though with no compromising on safety) such as New Heaven in the centre of Ao Chaloke Ban Kao (☎077 457045, ⓦnewheavendiveschool.com), which takes a maximum of four people per course or dive trip. Both of these companies have a strong commitment to marine conservation (also check out the website of Crystal's marine conservation partner, ⓦecokohtao.com, which features internships and gap-year programmes) and run reef conservation and research programmes for qualified divers among many other activities. You'll find further advice on choosing a dive company in Basics (see page 53).

By far the most popular **course**, PADI's four-day "Openwater" for beginners, costs around B9800 in high season with a reputable dive centre. One-day introductions to diving are also available for B2000, as is the full menu of PADI courses, up to "Instructor".

For **qualified divers**, one dive typically costs B1000, a ten-dive package B7000, with ten- to fifteen-percent discounts if you bring your own gear. Among a wide range of specialities, Crystal (see above) offers wreck diving, nitrox and underwater photography and videography courses.

out to this cool, industrial-looking café during the day for their great all-day vegetarian and vegan brunches such as eggs benedict (B160), healthy drinks and espresso coffees. Come back after dark for one of their club nights, including a "Sunday Service" of underground tech house, featuring international DJs. Tues–Sun 8am–5pm.

★ **Kakureya** Up a small hill on the southeast side of the village, off the south side of the road that heads inland from the Songserm pier ☎087 936 2160, ⓦfacebook.com/kakureyatao. Small, relaxing and thoroughly authentic Japanese restaurant with nice sunset views, serving some of the best food on the island, including appetizer tasting sets, salmon and tuna sashimi and lots of other fish dishes, home-smoked ham and noodles. Asahi beer on draught and a good choice of sake. Usually closed part of June and Nov – check on the Facebook page. Daily 4–10pm.

Moov On the southeast side of the village, on the south side of the road that heads inland from the Songserm pier ☎063 083 5537, ⓦfacebook.com/moovinn. Chilled-out, artsy bar with a lovely big garden, providing alternative nightlife events, which can mean anything from Latin parties and drum and bass DJs to movie nights. Also has a hostel if you really want to get lost in Tao's alternative scene. Daily 8.30am–late.

★ **Whitening** 200m south of the main pier down the front street ☎077 456199. Congenial, mellow and chic bar-restaurant with a great deck and relaxing beach tables and beanbags overlooking the bay, all in white. It dishes up some very tasty Thai food, such as green curries (B140), and more creative, pricier Western food, as well as lunchtime sandwiches, evening seafood barbecues and good cocktails. Daily 11am–midnight.

6

MAIN DIVE SITES

Ko Nang Yuan Surrounded by a variety of sites, with assorted hard and soft corals and an abundance of fish: the Nang Yuan Pinnacle (aka Red Rock), a granite pinnacle with boulder swim-throughs, morays and reef sharks; Green Rock, a maze of boulder swim-throughs, caves and canyons, featuring stingrays and occasional reef sharks; Twins, two rock formations covered in corals and sponges, with a colourful coral garden as a backdrop; and the Japanese Gardens, on the east side of the sand causeway, which get their name from the hundreds of hard and soft coral formations here and are good for beginners and popular among snorkellers.

White Rock (Hin Khao) Between Hat Sai Ree and Ko Nang Yuan, where sarcophyton leather coral turns the granite boulders white when seen from the surface; also wire, antipatharian and colourful soft corals, and gorgonian sea fans. Plenty of fish, including titan triggerfish, butterfly fish, angelfish, clown fish and morays.

Shark Island Large granite boulders with acropora, wire and bushy antipatharian corals, sea whips, gorgonian sea fans and barrel sponges. Reef fish include angelfish, triggerfish and barracuda; leopard and reef sharks may be found as well as occasional whale sharks.

Hinwong Pinnacle At Ao Hinwong; generally for experienced divers, often with strong currents. Similar scenery to White Rock, over a larger area, with beautiful soft coral at 30m depth. A wide range of fish, including blue-spotted fantail stingrays, sweetlips pufferfish and boxfish, as well as hawksbill turtles.

Chumphon or **Northwest Pinnacle** A granite pinnacle for experienced divers, starting 14m underwater and dropping off to over 36m, its top covered in anemones; surrounded by several smaller formations and offering the possibility of exceptional visibility. Barrel sponges, tree and antipatharian corals at deeper levels; a wide variety of fish, in large numbers, attract local fishermen; barracudas, batfish, whale sharks (seasonal) and huge groupers.

Southwest Pinnacle One of the top sites in terms of visibility, scenery and marine life for experienced divers. A huge pyramid-like pinnacle rising to 6m below the surface, its upper part covered in anemones, with smaller pinnacles around; at lower levels, granite boulders, barrel sponges, sea whips, bushy antipatharian and tree corals. Big groupers, snappers and barracudas; occasionally, large rays, leopard and sand sharks, swordfish, finback whales and whale sharks.

Sail Rock (Hin Bai) Midway between Ko Tao and Ko Pha Ngan, emerging from the sand at a depth of 40m and rising 15m above the sea's surface. Visibility of up to 30m, and an amazing 10m underwater chimney (vertical swim-through). Antipatharian corals, both bushes and whips, and carpets of anemones. Large groupers, snappers and fusiliers, blue-ringed angelfish, batfish, kingfish, juvenile clown sweetlips and barracuda; the most likely spot in the area for sighting whale sharks year round.

6

DIRECTORY

Banks Thanachart (Siam City Bank), up the high street on the left, with an ATM.

Health Mae Hat shelters a small government hospital (halfway up the high street, turn right; ☎ 077 456490), plus several private clinics and pharmacies. Ko Tao now has a 24hr volunteer emergency response team, equipped with pick-ups and speedboats (☎ 087 979 0191, ☎ 077 456031 or ☎ 1669).

Police The tourist police (☎ 1155 or ☎ 077 430 018) are based a short way out on the Ao Chaloke Ban Kao road, about 1km from the main pier, while the main police station is a 5min walk north of Mat Hat, on the narrow road towards

Hat Sai Ree (☎ 077 456 631 or ☎ 077 456 098).

Post office At the top of the Seatran road (parallel to and north of the high street), near the start of the main paved road to Ban Hat Sai Ree (Mon–Fri 9am–noon & 1–5pm, Sat 9am–noon).

Travel agent Reliable, English-run Island Travel on the Seatran road (parallel to and north of the high street; ☎ 077 456769, ⓦ islandtravelkohtao.com) offers all kinds of transport tickets, tours and activities on the island and visa services, as well as renting out good motorbikes and having a useful website.

Hat Sai Ree

To the north of Mae Hat, beyond a small promontory, you'll find **Hat Sai Ree**, Ko Tao's only long beach. The strip of white sand stretches for 2km in a gentle curve, backed by a smattering of coconut palms and scores of bungalow resorts. Around the northerly end of the beach spreads **BAN HAT SAI REE**, a burgeoning village of supermarkets, clinics, pharmacies, travel agents, currency-exchange booths, ATMs, restaurants and bars. A narrow, mostly paved track runs along the back of the beach between Mae Hat and Ban Hat Sai Ree, paralleled by the main road further inland.

ACCOMMODATION   HAT SAI REE

★ **4P Sea Beach Resort** North end of Ban Hat Sai Ree ☎ 077 456116; map p.563. This popular old-timer (formerly Blue Wind) offers a variety of well-kept, en-suite rooms and bungalows scattered about a shady compound, most of which have been recently reconstructed in an appealing southern Thai style, with clapboard walls and nice balcony furniture, some with four-poster beds and mosquito nets. Fan B700, a/c B1800

Good Time Beach Hostel South end of Hat Sai Ree ☎ 061 461 0933, ⓦ goodtimethailand.com; map p.563. Sociable hostel run by the island's adventure specialists (see page 569), who offer weekly booze cruises too. Smart, well-equipped private rooms and six- to ten-person dorms, some with balconies on the beach, have a/c and hot showers. Dorms B500, doubles B1600

Koh Tao Backpackers Hostel Ban Hat Sai Ree, inland from Silver Sands Resort ☎ 088 447 7921, ⓦ kohtaobackpackers.com; map p.563. Functional, four- and eight-bed dorms with a/c and hot showers in a small, concrete building set back from the beach. Free use of the adjacent pool of affiliated dive company Davy Jones' Locker, which has its own bar-restaurant. Dorm B300

Koh Tao Cabana Far north end of beach ☎ 089 698 2266, ⓦ kohtaocabana.com; map p.563. Welcoming,

eco-friendly, rustic-chic luxury resort and spa, with a long beach frontage backed by elegant day beds and a waterfall-fed swimming pool. Most of the a/c accommodation is in thatched rooms with open-air bathrooms, including round, adobe-style villas up the slope behind the beach and stilted cottages on the headland, some with fantastic views and some with private pools. Breakfast included. B5000

Koh Tao Coral Grand Resort North of Ban Hat Sai Ree ☎ 077 456431, ⓦ kohtaocoral.com; map p.563. Welcoming luxury beachfront development with a dive school, where the sandstone-pink octagonal cottages with polished coconut-wood floors and large, attractive bathrooms gather – some a little tightly – around a pretty, Y-shaped pool; all have balconies, hot water, TV and a/c. Round-trip pier transfers and breakfast included. B2500

Thipwimarn Resort North of Hat Sai Ree, opposite Ko Nang Yuan ☎ 077 456409, ⓦ thipwimarnresort.com; map p.563. Stylish, eco-friendly, upscale spot with a spa, which tumbles down a steep slope, past an elevated, infinity-edge swimming pool, to its own small beach. Dotted around the hillside, smart, thatched, whitewashed villas, most with hot water, enjoy a fair measure of seclusion, satellite TV, DVD players, mini-bars and fine sunset views. Breakfast included. Fan B2000, a/c B2200

EATING AND DRINKING

Choppers On the main transverse road down to the beach ☎ 077 456641, ⓦ choppers-kohtao.com. Popular, well-run, full-service Aussie bar, with good food, plenty of imported bottled and draught beers, live bands on

weekday nights and no fewer than seventeen screens for TV sports (with schedules posted on its website). Plenty of offers on drink, including happy hours 4–7pm. Daily 9am–late.

HAT SAI REE ACTIVITIES

Goodtime Adventures, towards the southern end of the beach (☏ 087 275 3604, ⓦ gtadventures. com), offer **rock-climbing** and **abseiling**, as well as beginner and advanced flying trapeze lessons. Just north of here, Evasion (☏ 062 665 2860, ⓦ evasionkohtao.com) do bouldering, guided hiking trips, wakeboarding and kitesurfing lessons and rental. SUP Tao (☏ 093 348 7661) at Maya Beach Club further towards the southern end of the beach offer stand-up paddleboarding, while drop-in **yoga** classes are held at 4P Sea Beach Resort towards the north end of the beach (1–2 daily; ☏ 084 440 6755, ⓦ shambhalayogakohtao.com). Monsoon Gym, on the main road behind the south end of Hat Sai Ree (☏ 086 271 2212, ⓦ monsoongym.com), is a well-equipped gym and muay thai fight camp (with dorm beds available for committed pugilists).

Fizz Beach Lounge On the beach at Silver Sands Resort ☏ 095 069 0350, ⓦ facebook.com/fizz.beachlounge. Chic beach lounge, where you can sink into the trademark green beanbags, sip great cocktails and bask in glorious sunsets. The DJ roster includes Soul Heaven on Saturdays and regular appearances by international names, and the Thai and Western food's good, too. Daily noon–1am (sometimes opening at 4pm in low season).

★ **The Gallery** On the east side of central Ban Hat Sai Ree, 50m down the Ao Hin Wong/Ao Mao road on the right ☏ 077 456547, ⓦ thegallerykohtao.com. This classy restaurant, with an attached wine and cocktail lounge and a photographic gallery, serves carefully sourced wines and

excellent food from inherited family recipes (main courses start at B170), including its signature dish, seafood and chicken curry soufflé served in a young coconut (haw mok), superb prawn cakes and Thai desserts. Worth making a reservation in high season. Daily noon–11pm.

Lotus Bar On the beach near New Heaven Café. Raucous, very popular late-night haunt for drinking and dancing, with fire and tightrope shows. Evenings until very late.

New Heaven Café On the beach road on the south side of the village centre. Stylish, mostly organic spot offering great home-baked breads and cakes, as well as all-day Western breakfasts (around B100), sandwiches, salads, ice cream, espressos and juices. Daily 7.30am–5.30pm.

Ko Nang Yuan

One kilometre off the northwest of Ko Tao, **KO NANG YUAN**, a close-knit group of three tiny islands, provides the most spectacular beach scenery in these parts, thanks to the causeway of fine white sand that joins up the islands. You can climb up to the mountain viewpoint on the northernmost island, and swim off the east side of the causeway to snorkel over the Japanese Gardens, which feature hundreds of hard and soft coral formations. However, there's little chance of having the place to yourself, as the island swarms with day-trippers and their boats: try to get there in the early morning, if you can.

ARRIVAL AND DEPARTURE   KO NANG YUAN

By boat Boats from the Lomprayah pier in Mae Hat, just south of the main pier, run back and forth (departing 10.30am, returning at 1.30pm & 4.30pm; B200 return), and there are other, irregular services from Hat Sai Ree; Ko Nang Yuan features on all round-island boat trips, too. Note that rules to protect the environment here include banning all visitors from bringing cans, plastic bottles and fins with them, and day-trippers are charged B100 to land on the island.

ACCOMMODATION AND EATING

Nangyuan Island Dive Resort ☏ 086 312 7128, ⓦ nangyuan.com; map p.563. The decor at this resort is not much to write home about, but it makes the most of its beautiful location – which you'll be able to enjoy in some peace after the day-trippers have gone– spreading its a/c bungalows, all with en-suite hot showers, TVs and fridges, over all three islands. There's also a restaurant, a coffee shop and an on-site dive shop. Transfers from and to Mae Hat and breakfast included. B2500

The north and east coasts

Ao Mamuang (Mango Bay), the lone bay on the **north coast**, is a beautiful, tree-clad bowl, whose shallow reef is a popular stop on snorkelling day-trips and on beginners' dive trips, though there's little in the way of a beach. The attractive bar-restaurant of *Mango Bay Boutique Resort* spreads its large deck over the rocks here.

The sheltered inlets of the **east coast**, most of them containing one or two sets of bungalows, can be reached by boat, pick-up or 4WD. The most northerly habitation here is at **Ao Hinwong**, a deeply recessed, limpid bay strewn with large boulders and great coral reefs, which has a particularly remote, almost desolate, air.

In the middle of the coast, the dramatic tiered promontory of Laem Thian shelters on its south side a tiny beach and a colourful reef, which stretches down towards the east coast's most developed bay, **Ao Ta Note**, with half a dozen resorts and a mostly paved road from Mae Hat. Ta Note's horseshoe inlet is sprinkled with boulders and plenty of coarse sand, with excellent snorkelling just north of the bay's mouth.

The last bay carved out of the turtle's shell, **Ao Leuk**, has a well-recessed beach and water that's deep enough for good swimming and snorkelling, featuring hard and soft coral gardens. Snorkels are available to rent at the beachfront bar.

ACCOMMODATION THE NORTH AND EAST COASTS

AO MAMUANG
Mango Bay Boutique Resort ☎02 107 1409, ⓦmangobayboutiqueresort.com; map p.563. At this remote resort, the well-appointed, thatched bungalows on stilts are scattered across a rocky slope; all come with hot water, a/c, minibars, TVs and balconies and some have huge verandas. Snorkels and kayaks available for rent. Transfers from Mae Hat and breakfast included. B2780

AO HINWONG
Hin Wong Bungalows ☎077 456006 or ☎081 229 4810; map p.563. The oldest of this bay's small handful of resorts is welcoming and quiet, providing good en-suite accommodation on a steep, grassy slope above the rocks, in wooden huts with mosquito nets, hammocks, large, cold-water bathrooms and great views. It has a beach bar and restaurant and rents out kayaks and snorkels. Discounts for longer stays. B600

AO TA NOTE
Poseidon Resort ☎077 456734, ⓦposeidontao. atspace.com; map p.563. At this friendly, mellow resort, the basic fan bungalows with en-suite cold showers,

balconies and hammocks are set back a little from the sands on the flower-strewn, rocky slopes. The beachfront restaurant has a nice big deck and there are kayaks and snorkels for rent. B800

AO LEUK
Ao Leuk II ☎077 456779, ⓦaowleuk2.net; map p.563. Large bungalows and family rooms, with big balconies, panoramic windows, fans and hot showers, on the bay's southern cape. If there happens to be no room here, don't worry – the same friendly family own two other resorts in the bay (including some cheaper, cold-shower bungalows), its taxis and the beachfront bar. Breakfast included. B1600
★**Baan Talay** ☎077 457045, ⓦbaantalaykohtao. com; map p.563. Sustainable, secluded retreat owned by New Heaven Dive School (see page 566), with great views from its hillside location that slopes down to the north side of the bay. Stylish bungalows on stilts sport big verandas, mosquito nets on the beds and hot showers; the cheaper hardwood "huts" have shaggy thatched roofs and indoor-outdoor bathrooms. Yoga courses and kayaks for rent. Free transfers from Mae Hat pier. Fan B1200, a/c B2500

The south coast

The southeast corner of the island sticks out in a long, thin mole of land, which points towards Shark Island, a colourful diving and snorkelling site just offshore; the headland shelters the sandy beach of **Hat Sai Daeng** on one side if the wind's coming from the northeast, or the rocky cove on the other side if it's blowing from the southwest. Beyond quiet, sandy **Ao Thian Ok**, the next bay along on the south coast, the deep indent of **Ao Chaloke Ban Kao** is protected from the worst of both monsoons, and consequently has seen a fair amount of development, with several dive resorts taking advantage of the large, sheltered, shallow bay, which sometimes gets muddy at low tide. Behind the beach are clinics, ATMs, supermarkets, bike

rental shops, bars and restaurants. At New Heaven dive school (see page 566), drop-in **yoga** classes are held once or twice a day (not Mondays) on a veranda overlooking the bay.

On the east side of Ao Chaloke Ban Kao, carved out of the Laem Tato headland, the idyllic white sand of **Freedom Beach** is a secluded palm-lined spot with a beach bar; it's reached by walking through *Taatoh Freedom Beach Bungalows*. A fifteen-minute walk above the bungalows, the last stretch up a steep hillside, will bring you to **Jon-Suwan Mountain Viewpoint**, which affords fantastic views, especially at sunset, over the neighbouring bays of Chaloke Ban Kao and Thian Ok and across to Ko Pha Ngan and Ko Samui.

ACCOMMODATION AND EATING   THE SOUTH COAST

HAT SAI DAENG AND AO THIAN OK
Jamahkiri ☎077 456 400, ⊛jamahkiri.com; map p.563. The remote, rocky coastline between Sai Daeng and Thian Ok provides the spectacular location for this luxurious resort. There's a panoramic bar-restaurant, a full-service spa, a dive centre and a lovely swimming pool, as well as opulent, secluded rooms and bungalows, in a chic mix of Thai and Western design, with great sea views. Free transfers from Mae Hat and free boat transfers to sandy Ao Thian Ok. Breakfast included. B6110

AO CHALOKE BAN KAO
New Heaven Diving Resort On the main road near the centre of the beach, attached to New Heaven Dive School (see page 566) ☎077 457 045, ⊛newheavendiveschool. com; map p.563. Friendly, eco-conscious resort offering stylish, balconied private rooms, some with a/c and hot water, and a/c dorms with well-equipped, curtained-off bunk beds, as well as a small swimming pool overlooking the bay. There's also a lovely little café-restaurant by the pool, Koppee, serving everything from espresso coffees to Thai main courses. Dorms B350, fan doubles B800, a/c doubles B1800
Viewpoint Bungalows ☎091 823 3444, ⊛viewpoint resortkohtao.com; map p.563. Run by a friendly bunch, these distinctive bungalows sprawl along the western side of the bay and around the leafy headland beyond, with a seafront free-form pool and great sunset views; architect-designed in chic Balinese style, they boast indoor-outdoor bathrooms, lovely polished hardwood floors, mosquito nets and attractive verandas. There are also half a dozen tasty villas with their own infinity-edge pools (from B10,000). Breakfast included. B3050

Nakhon Si Thammarat

NAKHON SI THAMMARAT, the south's second-largest town, occupies a blind spot in the eyes of most tourists, whose focus is fixed on Ko Samui, 100km to the north. Nakhon's neglect is unfortunate, for it's an absorbing place: the south's major pilgrimage site and home to a huge army base, it's relaxed, self-confident and sophisticated, well known for its excellent cuisine and traditional **handicrafts**. The stores on Thanon Thachang are especially good for local nielloware (*kruang tom*), household items and jewellery, elegantly patterned in gold or silver, often on black, and *yan lipao*, sturdy basketware made from intricately woven fern stems of different colours. Nakhon is also the best place in the country to see how Thai **shadow plays** work, at Suchart Subsin's workshop, and the main jumping-off point for towering **Khao Luang National Park** and its beautiful waterfall, **Krung Ching** (see page 578).

Orientation in Nakhon is simple, though the layout of the town is puzzling at first sight: it runs in a straight line for 7km from north to south and is rarely more than a few hundred metres wide; originally this was a long sand dune dotted with fresh-water wells and flanked by low, marshy ground. The modern centre for businesses and shops sits at the north end around the landmark **Tha Wang intersection**, where Thanon Neramit meets Thanon Ratchadamnoen. To the south, centred on the elegant, traditional mosque on Thanon Karom, lies the old Muslim quarter; south again is the start of the old city walls, of which few remains can be seen, and the historic centre, with the town's main places of interest now set in a leafy residential area.

FESTIVALS IN NAKHON

Known as *muang phra*, the "city of monks", Nakhon is still the religious capital of the south, and the main centre for **festivals**. The most important of these are the **Tamboon Deuan Sip**, held during the waning of the moon in the tenth lunar month (either Sept or Oct), and the **Hae Pha Kheun That**, which is held several times a year, but most importantly on Makha Puja, the full moon of the third lunar month, usually February, and on Visakha Puja, the full moon of the sixth lunar month, usually May (see page 47). The purpose of Tamboon Deuan Sip is to pay homage to dead relatives and friends; it is believed that during this fifteen-day period all *pret* – ancestors who have been damned to hell – are allowed out to visit the world, and so their relatives perform a merit-making ceremony in the temples, presenting offerings from the first harvest to ease their suffering. A huge ten-day fair takes place at Thung Talaat park on the north side of town at this time, as well as processions, shadow plays and other theatrical performances. The Hae Pha Khun That also attracts people from all over the south, to pay homage to the relics of the Buddha at Wat Mahathat. The centrepiece of this ceremony is the Pha Phra Bot, a strip of yellow cloth many hundreds of metres long, which is carried in a spectacular procession around the chedi. Meanwhile, Nakhon is still a centre of Brahminism, which plays an important part in Thai royal ceremonials. During Songkhran (the Thai New Year in April), Buddhism and Brahminism both have their moment in the sun: the Phra Buddha Sihing image is paraded through the streets and blessed with lustral water; and at the Hindu shrine of Phra Isuan on Thanon Ratchadamnoen, the Giant Swing ceremony has recently been revived – two Brahmins swing up to grab a bag of gold coins from a tree, in honour of Shiva (in Thai, Phra Isuan) and Vishnu (in Thai, Phra Narai).

Brief history

Nakhon Si Thammarat seems to have been part of the shadowy early kingdom of Tambralinga, and was well placed for trade with China and southern India (via an overland route from the port of Trang, on the Andaman Sea) from at least the early centuries AD. The first local event that can be dated with any reliability occurred in 1001 AD, when Tambralinga asserted its independence from the regional powers of Srivijaya and Angkor by sending its own tribute mission to China. From the twelfth century, Nakhon had significant contacts with Sri Lanka, including a major rebuilding of the prestigious Buddha-relic chedi at Wat Mahathat in the Lankan style; in the following century, Sri Lankan monks from Nakhon are said to have helped spread the Theravada form of Buddhism to Sukhothai, the major new Thai city-state to the north.

By the sixteenth century, Nakhon Si Thammarat had come under the control of Ayutthaya, which sent out governors to rule this rich and important region, in place of native princes. In the same century, trading links began with the Portuguese, who were followed by the Dutch, the English and the French; Nakhon – which was generally known to the Westerners by its Malay name, Ligor, to Thais as Lakhon – could offer local pepper, tin and hides. After the Burmese destruction of Ayutthaya and its treasures in 1767, the town played an important part in the cultural rebirth of the nation, sending its copy of the Tripitaka (the Buddhist scriptures) to King Taksin's new capital at Thonburi to be transcribed, as all the kingdom's copies had been lost.

Wat Mahathat

Main entrance faces Thanon Ratchadamnoen, about 2km south of the modern centre

Missing out **Wat Mahathat** would be like going to Rome and not visiting St Peter's, for the Buddha relics in the vast chedi make this the south's most important shrine. In the courtyard inside the temple cloisters, row upon row of smaller chedis, spiked like bayonets, surround the main chedi, the 60m-tall **Phra Boromathat**. This huge, stubby Sri Lankan bell supports a slender, ringed spire, which is in turn topped by a shiny pinnacle said to be covered in 600kg of gold. According to the chronicles, tooth

6

relics of the Buddha were brought here from Sri Lanka over two thousand years ago by an Indian prince and princess and enshrined in a chedi. It's undergone plenty of face-lifts since then: two earlier Srivijayan versions, models of which stand outside the entrance to the cloisters, are encased in the present twelfth-century chedi. The most recent restoration work, funded by donations from all over Thailand, rescued it from collapse, although it still seems to be leaning dangerously to the southeast. Worshippers head for the north side's vast enclosed stairway, framed by lions and giants, which they liberally decorate with gold leaf to add to the shrine's radiance and gain some merit. At the base of the stairway, look out for two delicate gilded reliefs showing the "Great Retirement", as the Buddha leaves his palace and family on horseback to become an ascetic; and for the two magnificent, Ayutthaya-period doors depicting Vishnu and Brahma.

Viharn Phra Kien Museum
Extends north from the chedi • Hours irregular, but usually daily 8.30am–4pm • Free

An Aladdin's cave of bric-a-brac, the **Viharn Phra Kien Museum** is said to house fifty thousand artefacts donated by worshippers, ranging from ships made out of seashells to gold and silver models of the Bodhi Tree. At the entrance to the museum, you'll pass the Phra Puay, an image of the Buddha giving a gesture of reassurance. Women pray to the image when they want to have children, and the lucky ones return to give thanks and leave photos of their chubby progeny.

Viharn Luang
Outside the cloister to the south

Raised on elegant slanting columns, the eighteenth-century **Viharn Luang** (actually a bot, surrounded by eight *sema* stones) is a beautiful example of Ayutthayan architecture. Beyond the pediment, with its gilded figure of Vishnu on his traditional elephant mount Erawan, you'll find that the interior is austere at ground level, but the red coffered ceiling shines with carved and gilded stars and lotus blooms. In the spacious grounds around the viharn, cheerful, inexpensive stalls peddle local handicrafts such as shadow puppets, bronzeware and basketware.

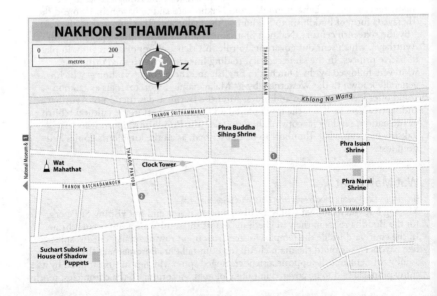

NAKHON SI THAMMARAT

The National Museum

Thanon Ratchadamnoen, a 10min walk south from Wat Mahathat • Wed–Sun 9am–noon & 1–4pm • B150

The **National Museum** houses a small but diverse collection, mostly of artefacts from southern Thailand. In the prehistory room **downstairs**, look out for the two impressive ceremonial bronze kettledrums dating from the fifth century BC; they were beaten in rainmaking rituals and one of them is topped with chunky frogs (the local frogs are said to be the biggest in Thailand and a prized delicacy). Also on the ground floor are some interesting Hindu finds, including several stone lingams from the seventh to ninth centuries AD and later bronze statues of Ganesh, the elephant-headed god of wisdom and the arts. Look out especially for a vivacious, well-preserved bronze of Shiva here, dancing within a ring of fire on the body of a dwarf demon, who holds a cobra symbolizing stupidity. Among the collections of ceramics **upstairs**, you can't miss the seat panel from Rama V's barge, a dazzling example of the nielloware for which Nakhon is famous – the delicate animals and landscapes have been etched onto a layer of gold which covers the silver base, and then picked out by inlaying a black alloy into the background. The nearby exhibition on local wisdom includes interesting displays on Buddhist ordinations and weddings, and on *manohra*, the southern Thai dramatic dance form.

Suchart Subsin's House of Shadow Puppets

Ban Nang Thalung Suchart Subsin, 110/18 Soi 3, Thanon Si Thammasok, a 10min walk east of Wat Mahathat • Daily 8am–5pm • Free • ☎ 075 346394

The best possible introduction to *nang thalung*, southern Thailand's **shadow puppet theatre**, is to head for the atmospheric compound of the late Suchart Subsin, a designated National Artist who was one of the south's leading exponents of *nang thalung* until his death in 2015. His sons and former apprentices have now succeeded him as puppeteers and have kept their workshop open to the public. There's a small museum of puppets from Thailand, Indonesia and Cambodia dating back as far as the eighteenth century, and, especially if you phone in advance, they'll usually be able to show you a few scenes from a shadow play in the small theatre (by donation,

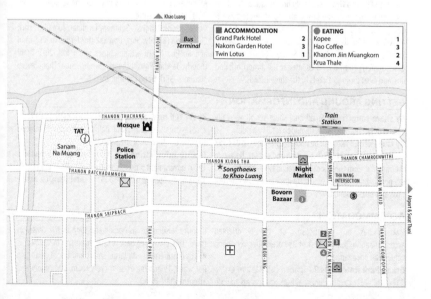

6

about B50/person). You can also see the intricate process of making the leather puppets and can buy the finished products as souvenirs: puppets sold here are of much better quality and design than those usually found on southern Thailand's souvenir stalls.

The Phra Buddha Sihing shrine

In the provincial administration complex on Thanon Ratchadamnoen • Mon–Fri 8.30am–4.30pm • Free

Magically created in Sri Lanka in the second century, the **Phra Buddha Sihing** statue was, according to legend, sent by ship to the king of Sukhothai in the thirteenth century, but the vessel sank and the image miraculously floated on a plank to Nakhon. Two other images, one in the National Museum in Bangkok, one in Wat Phra Singh in Chiang Mai, claim to be the authentic Phra Buddha Sihing, but none of the three is in the Sri Lankan style, and all three may have originated as replacements for a lost original. Although similar to the other two in size and shape, the image in Nakhon, dated between the thirteenth and sixteenth centuries, has a style unique to this area, distinguished by the heavily pleated flap of its robe over the left shoulder, a beaky nose and harsh features, which sit uneasily on the short, corpulent body. The statue's plumpness has given the style the name *khanom tom*, after a kind of coconut and rice pudding. The much-revered image is sheltered by a delicate, golden five-tiered parasol, and housed in an attractive, 100-year-old, Ayutthaya-style shrine.

ARRIVAL AND DEPARTURE   NAKHON SI THAMMARAT

BY PLANE

The airport (☎075 369540–2), served daily by Nok Air, Lion Air and Air Asia from Bangkok's Don Muang Airport (12 daily; 1hr 10min), is about 20km northwest of the city off the Surat Thani road. From here, taxis charge around B250 to take you into Nakhon (B1500 to Don Sak, for ferries to Ko Samui and Ko Pha Ngan) while big hotels such as the *Twin Lotus* offer airport shuttle buses; an airport bus to town is being considered – check with the TAT office. Nok Air and Air Asia offer flight-and-boat through-tickets to Ko Samui, Ko Pha Ngan and Ko Tao, and Seatran (☎077 950559, ⓦseatranferry.com) have a counter at the airport offering bus-and-boat through-tickets to the three islands.

BY TRAIN

The train station is very central and sits at the end of a branch off the main southern line from Bangkok (2 daily; 15hr 30min–16hr 30min).

BY BUS AND A/C MINIBUS

All buses and a/c minibuses now use the terminal on the west side of the centre.

Destinations Bangkok (Southern Terminal; 20 daily; 13hr); Chumphon (8 daily; 5hr); Don Sak (for ferries to Ko Samui and Ko Pha Ngan; a/c minibuses when full; 2hr); Krabi (hourly; 3–4hr); Phuket (hourly; 5–6hr); Surat Thani (every 30min; 2–3hr); Trang (hourly; 2hr).

GETTING AROUND AND INFORMATION

By share-songthaew Small blue share-songthaews ply up and down Thanon Ratchadamnoen for B10 a ride.
By taxi Metered taxis can be booked by phone (☎077 357 888) and hang out at the bus station and airport. Be aware though, that from these locations you may well have a hard job persuading them to switch their meters on. Motorbike taxis also buzz around town.

By rented car Avis, based at the airport (☎02 251 1131–2, ⓦavisthailand.com), will deliver and collect vehicles anywhere in Nakhon Si Thammarat.
Tourist information TAT has an office in a restored 1920s government officers' club on Sanam Na Muang (daily 8.30am–4.30pm; ☎075 346 515–6, ⓔtatnksri@tat.or.th).

ACCOMMODATION

Nakhon has no guesthouses or traveller-oriented accommodation, but the best of its hotels offer very good value in all price ranges.
Grand Park Hotel 1204/79 Thanon Pak Nakhon ☎075 317 666–75, ⓦgrandparknakhon.com; map p.574.

If you're looking for an upmarket option in the centre of town, this place, set back a little from the busy road, is worth considering – it's large, smart and bright, with a/c, hot water, TV and mini-bar in every room, and cheery and attentive staff. **B700**

SHADOW PUPPETS

Found throughout southern Asia, **shadow puppets** are one of the oldest forms of theatre, featuring in Buddhist literature as early as 400 BC. The art form seems to have come from India, via Java, to Thailand, where it's called *nang*, meaning "hide": the puppets are made from the skins of water buffalo or cows, which are softened in water, then pounded until almost transparent, before being carved and painted to represent the characters of the play. The puppets are then manipulated on bamboo rods in front of a bright light, to project their image onto a large white screen, while the story is narrated to the audience.

The grander version of the art, **nang yai** – "big hide", so called because the figures are life-size – deals only with the *Ramayana* story (see page 88). It's known to have been part of the entertainment at official ceremonies in the Ayutthayan period, but has now almost died out. The more populist version, **nang thalung** – *thalung* is probably a shortening of the town name, Phatthalung (which is just down the road from Nakhon), where this version of the art form is said to have originated – is also in decline now: performances are generally limited to temple festivals, marriages, funerals and ordinations, lasting usually from 9pm to dawn. As well as working the 60cm-high *nang thalung* puppets, the puppet master narrates the story, impersonates the characters, chants and cracks jokes to the accompaniment of flutes, fiddles and percussion instruments. Not surprisingly, in view of this virtuoso semi-improvised display, puppet masters are esteemed as possessed geniuses by their public.

At big festivals, companies often perform the *Ramayana*, sometimes in competition with each other; at smaller events they put on more down-to-earth stories, with stock characters such as the jokers Yor Thong, an angry man with a pot belly and a sword, and Kaew Kop, a man with a frog's head. Yogi, a wizard and teacher, is thought to protect the puppet master and his company from evil spirits with his magic, so he is always the first puppet on at the beginning of every performance.

In an attempt to halt their decline as a form of popular entertainment, the puppet companies are now incorporating modern instruments and characters in modern dress into their shows, and are boosting the love element in their stories. They're fighting a battle they can't win against television and cinemas, although at least the debt owed to shadow puppets has been acknowledged – *nang* has become the Thai word for "movie".

★**Nakorn Garden Hotel** 1/4 Thanon Pak Nakhon ☎075 313 333; map p.574. A rustic but comfortable haven in two three-storey, red-brick buildings overlooking a big tree-shaded courtyard. The large, attractive rooms are looking a bit tired now but come with a/c, hot water, cable TV and mini-bar. B445

Twin Lotus About 3km southeast of the centre at 97/8 Thanon Patanakarn Kukwang ☎075 323 777, ⊕twinlotushotel.net; map p.574. Gets pride of place in Nakhon – though not for its location; sports Thai and Chinese restaurants, a beer garden, a small spa, a large, attractive outdoor swimming pool, a sauna and a fitness centre. Breakfast and round-trip airport transfers included with Superior rooms (B1500). B800

EATING AND DRINKING

Nakhon is a great place for inexpensive food, not least at the busy, colourful **night market** on Thanon Chamroenwithi.

Kopee Thanon Nang Ngam ☎089 4319 999; map p.574. This faithful and attractive re-creation of an old Chinese-style, southern Thai coffee shop, with marble-topped tables, wooden shutters and ceiling fans, is famous nationwide and serves southern dishes such as khua kling (a dry curry of minced pork, served on rice; B40), khao mok kai (a kind of chicken biryani) and sweet and savoury roti pancakes, all washed down with traditional, cloth-filtered coffee (kopii). Daily 6.30am–11pm.

Hao Coffee In the Bovorn Bazaar, Thanon Ratchadamnoen; map p.574. Popular place in a quiet courtyard, modelled on an old Chinese-style coffee shop and packed full of ageing lamps, clocks and other antiques. Offers a wide selection of inexpensive Thai dishes, a few Western breakfasts, teas, juices and espresso coffees (from B35), including delicious iced cappuccinos. Daily 7am–4pm.

Khanom Jiin Muangkorn 23 Thanon Panyom, near Wat Mahathat ☎075 342 615; map p.574. Justly famous, inexpensive indoor-outdoor restaurant dishing up one of the local specialities, *khanom jiin*, rice noodles topped with hot, sweet or fishy sauce served with *pak ruam*, a platter of crispy raw vegetables. Daily 8am–3.30pm.

★**Krua Thale** Thanon Pak Nakhon, opposite the Nakorn Garden Hotel; map p.574. The town's best restaurant, renowned among locals for its excellent, varied and inexpensive seafood. Plain and very clean, with an open kitchen and the day's catch displayed out front, and relaxing patio tables and an a/c room at the back. Recommended dishes include a very good *yam plaa duk foo*, shredded and deep-fried catfish with a mango salad dip (B120), whole baked fish and king prawns (priced by weight and delicious with tamarind sauce), and *hoy maleang poo op mordin*, large green mussels in a delicious herb soup containing lemon grass, basil and mint. Daily 4–10pm (last orders 9pm).

Khao Luang National Park

Headquarters to the south of the summit near Karom Waterfall • National park admission fee B200 • ☎ 075 300 494, ⓦ nps.dnp.go.th

Rising to the west of Nakhon Si Thammarat and temptingly visible from all over town is 1835m-high **Khao Luang**, southern Thailand's highest mountain. A huge **national park** encompasses Khao Luang's jagged green peaks, beautiful streams with numerous waterfalls, tropical rainforest and fruit orchards. The mountain is also the source of the Tapi River, one of the peninsula's main waterways, which flows into the Gulf of Thailand at Surat Thani. **Fauna** here include macaques, musk deer, civets and binturongs, as well as more difficult-to-see Malayan tapirs, serows, tigers, panthers and clouded leopards, plus over two hundred bird species. There's an astonishing diversity of **flora** too, notably rhododendrons and begonias, dense mosses, ferns and lichens, plus more than three hundred species of both ground-growing and epiphytic orchids, some of which are unique to the park.

The best **time to visit** is after the rainy season, from January onwards, when there should still be a decent flow in the waterfalls, but the trails will be dry and the leeches not so bad. However, the park's most distinguishing feature for visitors is probably its difficulty of **access**: main roads run around the 570-square-kilometre park with spurs into some of the waterfalls, but there are no roads across the park and very sparse public transport along the spur roads. The Ban Khiriwong Visitor Service Centre (☎075 533113 or ☎075 533 370) can arrange **treks** to the peak roughly between January and July, beginning at Ban Khiriwong, a village famous for its organic orchards and crafts on the southeast side of the park, and including two nights camping on the mountain, meals and guides, as well as homestays in the village. Otherwise only **Krung Ching Waterfall**, one of Thailand's most spectacular, really justifies the hassle of getting to the park.

Krung Ching Waterfall

A trip to **Krung Ching**, a nine-tier waterfall on the north side of the park, makes for a highly satisfying day out with a **nature trail** taking you through dense, steamy jungle to the most beautiful, third, tier. Starting at the Krung Ching park office, which lies 13km south of Ban Huai Phan, this shady, mostly paved, 4km trail is very steep in parts, so you should allow four hours at least there and back. On the way you'll pass giant ferns, including a variety known as *maha sadam*, the largest fern in the world, gnarled banyan trees, forests of mangosteen and beautiful, thick stands of bamboo. You're bound to see colourful birds and insects, but you may well only hear macaques and other mammals. At the end, a long, stepped descent brings you to a perfectly positioned wooden platform with fantastic views of the 40m fall, which used to appear on the back of thousand-baht notes; here you can see how, shrouded in thick spray, it earns its Thai name, Fon Saen Ha, meaning "hundreds of thousands of rainfalls".

ARRIVAL AND DEPARTURE   **KHAO LUANG**

By songthaew Irregular songthaews on the main roads around the park and to Ban Khiriwong congregate on Thanon Klong Tha in Nakhon. None of them is scheduled to go to Krung Ching — you'd have to catch one to the T-junction (saam yaek) at Ban Na Leng in Nopphitam district (about 1hr), then change to another songthaew for the last 25km or so to the falls.

By car Rental cars are available from Avis (see page 36). The easiest way to get to Krung Ching from Nakhon with your own transport is to head north on Highway 401 towards Surat Thani, turning west at Tha Sala on to Highway 4140, then north again at Ban Na Leng in Nopphitam district on to Highway 4186, before heading south from Ban Huai Phan on Highway 4188, the spur road to the Krung Ching park office, a total journey of about 70km.

ACCOMMODATION AND EATING

National park accommodation ☎ 075 460463, ⌨ dnp.go.th. Two- to twenty-person bungalows, most with hot water and fridges, are available at the Krung Ching park office. There's also a campsite. Bungalows <u>B600</u>

National park canteen There's a basic canteen near the Krung Ching park office, where food needs to be ordered in advance.

6

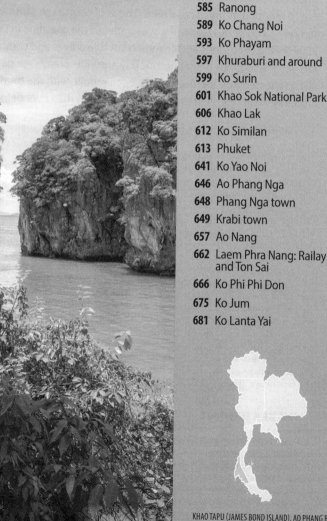

Southern Thailand: the Andaman coast

KHAO TAPU (JAMES BOND ISLAND), AO PHANG BAY

Southern Thailand: the Andaman coast

As Highway 4 switches from the east flank of the Thailand peninsula to the Andaman coast it enters a markedly different country: nourished by rain nearly all the year round, the vegetation down here is lushly tropical, with forests reaching up to 80m in height, and massive rubber, palm-oil and coconut plantations replacing the rice and sugar-cane fields of central Thailand. Sheer limestone crags spike every horizon and the translucent Andaman Sea laps the most dazzlingly beautiful islands in the country, not to mention its finest coral reefs. This is of course the same sea whose terrifyingly powerful tsunami waves battered the coastline in December 2004, killing thousands and changing countless lives and communities forever. The legacies of that horrific day are widespread (see page 608), but all the affected holiday resorts have been rebuilt, with the tourist dollar now arguably more crucial to the region's well-being than ever before.

The **cultural mix** along the Andaman coast is also different from central Thailand. Many southern Thais are Muslim, with a heritage that connects them to Malaysia and beyond. This is also the traditional province of nomadic *chao ley*, or sea gypsies, many of whom have now settled but still work as boat captains and fishermen. The commercial fishing industry, on the other hand, is mostly staffed by immigrants – legal and not – from neighbouring Myanmar, just a few kilometres away along the northern Andaman coast.

The attractions of the northern Andaman coast are often ignored in the race down to the high-profile honeypots around Phuket and Krabi, but there are many quiet gems up here, beginning with the low-key little sister islands of **Ko Chang Noi** (quite different from its larger, more famous east-coast namesake) and the fast-developing **Ko Phayam**, where the hammocks and paraffin lamps still offer an old-style travellers' vibe that's harder to find further south. Snorkellers and divers are drawn in their hundreds to the reefs of the remote National Park island chains of **Ko Surin** and **Ko Similan**, with many choosing to base themselves at the mainland beach resort of **Khao Lak**, though homestay programmes around **Khuraburi** offer an interesting alternative. Inland, it's all about the jungle – with twenty-first-century amenities – at the enjoyable **Khao Sok National Park**, where accommodation is on rafts on the lake and in treehouses beneath the limestone crags.

Phuket, Thailand's largest island, is the region's major resort destination for families, package tourists and novice divers; its dining, shopping and entertainment facilities are second to none, but the high-rises and hectic consumerism dilute the Thai-ness of the experience. There's Thai life in spades across on the quiet rural island of **Ko Yao Noi**,

---

THE KRA ISTHMUS

Thailand's Andaman coast begins at **Kraburi**, where, at kilometre-stone 545 (the distance from Bangkok), a signpost welcomes you to the **Kra Isthmus**, the narrowest part of peninsular Thailand. Just 44km separates the Gulf of Thailand from the Andaman Sea's Chan River estuary, and Burmese border, here. Though a seemingly obvious short cut for shipping traffic between the Indian Ocean and the South China Sea, avoiding the 1500km detour via the Strait of Malacca, the much-discussed **Kra Canal** project has yet to be realized, despite being on the table for over three hundred years.

SINO-PORTUGUESE ARCHITECTURE IN PHUKET OLD TOWN

Highlights

❶ **Island idylls** Tranquillity rules on the uncommercial islands of Ko Phayam, Ko Yao Noi and Ko Jum. See pages 593, 641 and 675

❷ **Khao Sok National Park** Sleep in a jungle treehouse or on a lake amid spectacular karst scenery, and wake to the sound of hooting gibbons. See page 601

❸ **Ko Similan** Remote island chain offering the finest snorkelling and diving, and easily accessible on day-trips and live-aboards. See page 612

❹ **Sea-canoeing in Ao Phang Nga** The perfect way to explore the limestone karsts and hidden lagoons of this spectacular bay. See page 615

❺ **Phuket Town** Handsome Sino-Portuguese architecture and some of the most interesting sleeping, eating and drinking options on the island. See page 617

❻ **Rock-climbing** Even novices can get a bird's-eye view of the Railay peninsula's fabulous coastal scenery. See page 664

❼ **Ko Lanta Yai** The "island of long beaches", with an atmospheric old town, offers an appealing choice of relaxing mid-range facilities. See page 679

HIGHLIGHTS ARE MARKED ON THE MAP ON PAGE 584

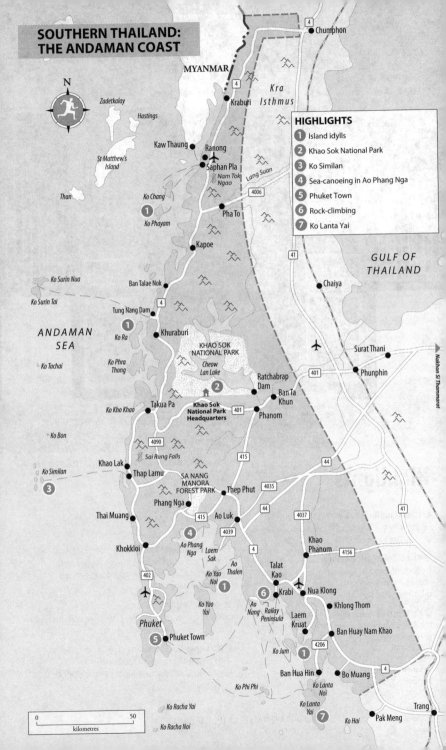

SOUTHERN THAILAND: THE ANDAMAN COAST

MYANMAR

Kra Isthmus

GULF OF THAILAND

ANDAMAN SEA

HIGHLIGHTS

1. Island idylls
2. Khao Sok National Park
3. Ko Similan
4. Sea-canoeing in Ao Phang Nga
5. Phuket Town
6. Rock-climbing
7. Ko Lanta Yai

Zadetkalay

Hastings

St Matthew's Island

Than

Kaw Thaung

Ranong

Saphan Pla

Nam Tok Ngao

Kraburi

Long Suan

4

4

4006

Chumphon

Ko Chang

Pha To

Ko Phayam

Kapoe

Chaiya

Ko Surin Nua

Ban Talae Nok

Ko Surin Tai

Tung Nang Dam

Khuraburi

4

Ko Ra

Ko Tachai

Ko Phra Thong

KHAO SOK NATIONAL PARK

Cheow Lan Lake

Ratchabrap Dam

Ban Ta Khun

Surat Thani

Phunphin

401

Khao Sok National Park Headquarters

Phanom

Takua Pa

Ko Kho Khao

401

Ko Bon

4090

Sai Rung Falls

415

415

44

Khao Lak

Ko Similan

Thap Lamu

SA NANG MANORA FOREST PARK

Thep Phut

4035

44

4037

41

Phang Nga

Thai Muang

415

Ao Luk

Khao Phanom

4156

Khokkloi

Ao Phang Nga

4039

Laem Sak

Ao Thalen

4

Talat Kao

402

Ko Yao Noi

Krabi

Nua Klong

Khlong Thom

Ko Yao Yai

Ao Nang

Railay Peninsula

Laem Kruat

Ban Huay Nam Khao

Phuket

Ko Jum

4206

Phuket Town

Ban Hua Hin

Bo Muang

4

Ko Phi Phi

Ko Lanta Noi

Trang

Ko Racha Yai

Ko Lanta Yai

Ko Racha Noi

Pak Meng

Ko Hai

Nakhon Si Thammarat

N

0   50
kilometres

scenically located within the spectacular bay of **Ao Phang Nga**, whose scattered karst islets are one of the country's top natural wonders, best appreciated from a sea-canoe. The Andaman coast's second hub is **Krabi** province, rightly famous for its turquoise seas and dramatic islands. Flashiest of these is the flawed but still handsome **Ko Phi Phi**, with its great diving, gorgeous beaches and high-octane nightlife. Mainland and mainstream **Ao Nang** can't really compete, but is at least close to the majestic cliffs and superb rock-climbing of the **Railay** peninsula at **Laem Phra Nang**. Offshore again, there's horizon-gazing aplenty at mellow **Ko Jum** and the choice of half a dozen luxuriously long beaches, and plentiful resort facilities, at **Ko Lanta Yai**.

Unlike the Gulf coast, the Andaman coast is hit by the **southwest monsoon**, which usually generally lasts from the end of May until at least the middle of October. During this period, heavy rain and high seas render some of the outer islands inaccessible, but conditions aren't usually severe enough to ruin a holiday on the other islands, or on the mainland, and you'll get tempting discounts on accommodation. Some bungalows at the smaller resorts shut down entirely during low season (highlighted in the text), but most beaches keep at least one place open, and some dive shops lead expeditions year-round.

7

ARRIVAL AND DEPARTURE
THE ANDAMAN COAST

There is no rail line down the Andaman coast, but many travellers take the **train** from Bangkok to the Gulf coast's transport hub Surat Thani and then nip across by bus. There are also plenty of direct **buses** that travel south from the capital overnight. The fastest option is to arrive by **plane**: both Phuket and Krabi have international airports, and there's a domestic airport at Trang, not far from Ko Lanta in the deep south.

Ranong

Despite being the soggiest town in the country, with over 5000mm of rain a year, **RANONG** has a pleasing buzz about it, fuelled by its mix of Burmese, Thai, Chinese and Malay inhabitants. It's a prosperous town, the lucrative nineteenth-century tin-mining concessions now replaced by a thriving fishing industry centred on the port of Saphan Pla, 5km southwest of town, and its scores of fishing boats and fish-processing factories staffed mainly by notoriously poorly treated Burmese workers. As with most border areas, there's also said to be a flourishing illegal trade in amphetamines, guns and labour, not to mention the inevitable tensions over international fishing rights, which sometimes end in shoot-outs, though the closest encounter you're likely to have will be in the pages of the *Bangkok Post*. Thai tourists have been coming here for years, to savour the health-giving properties of the local spring water, but foreign travellers have only quite recently discovered it as a useful departure point for the alluring nearby little islands of **Ko Chang Noi** and **Ko Phayam**. The other reason to stop off in Ranong is to make a visa run to the Burmese town of **Kaw Thaung**, but double check with local travel agents (or come equipped with a 60-day Thai tourist visa), as immigration attitudes toward visa runs keep changing, and you may have trouble re-entering Thailand.

A stroll along Ranong's main road, **Thanon Ruangrat**, brings its history and geography to mind. The handsome, if faded, shopfront architecture bears many of the hallmarks of nineteenth-century Sino-Portuguese design (see page 619), with its arched "five-foot" walkways shading pedestrians, pastel paintwork and shuttered windows. Chinese goods fill many of the shops – this is a good place to stock up on cheap clothes too – and many signs are written in the town's three main languages: Thai, Chinese and curly Burmese script.

First Governor's House

West off Thanon Ruangrat on the northern edge of town • Daily 9am–4.30pm • Free

Ranong's history is closely associated with its most famous son, Khaw Soo Cheang, a poor Hokkien Chinese emigrant turned tin baron who became the first governor of

Ranong province in 1854; he is still so esteemed that politicians continue to pay public homage at his grave, and his descendants bear the respected aristocratic surname "na Ranong" ("of Ranong"). Little now remains of Khaw Soo Cheang's house, but in its grounds stands a Khaw clan house and small museum, the **First Governor's House** (Nai Khai Ranong), containing interesting photos of the governor.

The geothermal springs

Raksawarin Park, about 3km east of the Thanon Ruangrat market • **Raksawarin Hot Springs** daily 7am–9pm • free; Tinidee pools B40, or B60 including transfer from Tinidee Hotel (see page 588) • **Siam Hot Spa Ranong** daily noon–9pm • treatments from B200 ☎ 077 813551–4, ⊕ siamhotsparanong.com • Accessible on red songthaew #2 from the market or by motorbike taxi

It can be fun to follow the crowds of domestic tourists who flock to Ranong's famously pure **geothermal springs** for its stress-relieving and supposed medicinal properties. The springs are the focus of forested Raksawarin Park, which is set in a narrow, lush river valley, surrounded by restaurants and souvenir shops. At the park's Raksawarin Hot Springs, you can bathe or paddle in either the open-access, public mineral spa pools or the better-appointed and deeper, Jacuzzi-type spa pools, which are run by the *Tinidee Hotel*. Alternatively, you may opt to relax on the heated floor of the elephant-adorned pavilion behind the pools or take a leisurely soak at the indoor Siam Hot Spa Ranong across the road, which offers public and private Jacuzzi pools, private bathrooms and inexpensive massage and steam treatments.

RANONG

■ ACCOMMODATION
The B	1
Kiwi Orchid Guesthouse	5
Luang Poj	2
Sino Mansion	3
Tinidee Hotel	4

● EATING
209 Kafe	1
Pon's Place	2

ARRIVAL AND DEPARTURE

By plane Budget airline Nok Air (⊕nokair.com) flies from Bangkok's Don Mueang airport (2 daily; 1hr 30min) to Ranong airport, 20km south of town on Highway 4. *Pon's Place* (⊕081 597 4549, ⊕ponplace-ranong.com) has a tours booth at the airport and can also arrange a transfer into town or the Saphan Pla pier for B200–300/person. You can also wait on the highway outside of the terminal for a songthaew (B25) into town.

By bus or minibus Most Andaman-coast buses travelling between Bangkok or Chumphon and Khuraburi, Takua Pa or Phuket stop briefly at Ranong's bus station on Highway 4 (Thanon Phetkasem), 1km southeast of the central market. If coming from Khao Sok or Surat Thani, you'll usually need to change buses at Takua Pa, though there is also an a/c minibus service from and to Surat Thani (hourly 6am–5pm; 3hr). There are direct buses operated by Rungkit from Chumphon (4 daily; 2–3hr), as well as faster a/c minibuses (hourly 6am–5pm; 2hr; B150), so from Bangkok it's often more comfortable to take a night train to Chumphon and then change on to a bus or minibus. Alternatively, Chokeanan and New Mittour run VIP buses from opposite Wat Bowoniwes and the Siam Commercial Bank in Banglamphu, via the Southern Bus Terminal, to Chumphon's Thanon Tha Muang. Rungkit buses to Chumphon and Phuket and the a/c minibuses operate out of Ranong Bus Station.

Destinations: Bangkok (7 daily; 9hr); Chumphon (hourly 7am–5pm; 2–3hr); Hat Yay (3 daily; 7hr); Hua Hin (3 daily; 5hr 30min); Khao Lak (5 daily; 3hr 45min); Khuraburi (4 daily; 2hr); Krabi (2 daily; 5hr); Phang Nga (4 daily; 4hr); Phuket (via Khao Lak; 4 daily; 5–7hr); Surat Thani (10 daily; 4hr); Takua Pa (4 daily; 3hr).

By boat to the islands via Saphan Pla Boats to Ko Chang Noi (see page 589) and Ko Phayam (see page 593) leave from Ranong's port at Saphan Pla, 5km southwest of the town centre and served by songthaews (see below) or by share-taxi from *Pon's Place* (B50). Songthaews drop passengers on the main road through Saphan Pla, from where it's a 500m walk south to the Islands Pier, while share-taxis take you to the pier itself, and also wait around for passengers when boats return from the islands.

Destinations: Ko Chang Noi (3 longtail boats daily; 1hr–1hr 30min; 200B); Ko Phayam (up to 10 speedboats daily; 45min; 350B).

GETTING AROUND AND INFORMATION

By songthaew Songthaews shuttle across and around Ranong, starting from the Thanon Ruangrat market, close to the town-centre hotels. Many have their destinations written in English on the side, and most charge around B15 per ride. Several songthaews pass Ranong bus station, including the #2 (red), which runs to the Thanon Ruangrat hotels and day market, and the #6 (blue), which starts at the day market and heads on to the port area at Saphan Pla, 5km to the southwest (for boats to Ko Chang Noi, Ko Phayam and Kaw Thaung); red #3 songthaew runs direct from the market on Thanon Ruangrat to the Saphan Pla port area.

Car and bike rental *Pon's Place*, 129 Thanon Ruangrat (daily 7.30am–9pm; ⊕081 597 4549, ⊕ponplace-ranong. com), rents bicycles (80B/day), motorbikes (200B/day manual and 250B/day automatic) and cars (1200B/day).

Tourist information The best source of tourist information in town is the ever helpful Pon at *Pon's Place* restaurant and tour agency, 129 Thanon Ruangrat (daily 7.30am–9pm; ⊕081 597 4549, ⊕ponplace-ranong.com; also a booth at Ranong airport), where you can also organize a visa run to Myanmar and back (1300b), arrange tours of the local area, book accommodation on Ko Chang Noi and Ko Phayam, and buy air, bus and minibus tickets, as well as train tickets from Chumphon or Surat Thani. There's a branch of Smiling Seahorse Diving along Thanon Ruangrat (⊕086 0110614; ⊕thesmilingseahorse.com).

ACCOMMODATION

The B 295/2 Thanon Ruangrat ⊕077 823111, ⊕facebook. com/thebranong; map p.586. Ranong's classiest boutique hotel offers immaculate, spacious en-suite rooms with industrial chic design and rainwater showers. Rooms are set over three floors that alternate between bright-coloured door frames and darker, shabby-chic furnishings. Breakfast and free bicycle rental is included, and the annexed bistro is a great place to check out some local live bands. **B1200**

Kiwi Orchid Guesthouse 96/19–20 Moo 1, off Thanon Phetkasem ⊕081 6910404, ⊕kiwiorchid@hotmail. com; map p.586. A run-down place right next to the bus terminal, but the fan rooms are surprisingly quiet and comfortable, and the affable owner always ready to give useful advice on what to do in the area and how to get around. Shared bathrooms are a little grimy, but the hostel makes a handy transit to plan your next move with other budget travellers over a beer in the restaurant, which serves good vegetarian dishes (from B80). **B300**

Luang Poj 225 Thanon Ruangrat ⊕077 833377, ⊕luangpoj@gmail.com; map p.586. Appealing conversion of a Sino-Portuguese shophouse, maintaining its polished wooden floors, which styles itself as a "boutique hostel" though there are no dorms. The smart, attractive bedrooms come with attractive murals: heavy sleepers who like to be in the thick of the action will like the two fan rooms with wooden shutters facing the street; others may prefer to opt for the same priced, windowless a/c options. Hot showers are shared and there's a restaurant upstairs. **B600**

7

7

INTO MYANMAR: KAWTHAUNG (KO SONG)

The southernmost tip of Myanmar – known as **Kawthaung** in Burmese, Ko Song in Thai, and Victoria Point when it was a British colony – lies just a few kilometres west of Ranong across the gaping Chan River estuary and is easily reached by longtail boat from Saphan Pla fishing port just outside Ranong town centre when the crossing is open (daily 8am–6pm). Kawthuang can be used as an entry point for travelling in Myanmar (you'll need to arrange an eVisa at least three days in advance; see ⓦ evisa.moip.gov.mm), though its position in the far south doesn't make it the most convenient option; most people, however, choose to use this crossing for a visa run. Note that immigration regulations are subject to change and have become stricter recently, so it is advisable to check the present situation before you make the journey (see page 29).

You can either try the visa run independently, as described below, or you can make use of one of the all-inclusive **"visa run" services** advertised all over town, including at *Pon's Place* (B1300 including visa; see page 589). Most visa-run operators use the Saphan Pla route, but they can also book you on the faster, more luxurious **Andaman Club boat** (6 daily 7am–4pm, later boats available for those staying overnight; 20min each way; B1500 including visa), which departs from the Andaman Club pier 5km north of Ranong's town centre and travels to and from the swanky *Andaman Club* hotel (ⓦ andamanclub.com), casino and duty-free complex, located on a tiny island in Burmese waters just south of Kawthaung.

Boats to Kawthaung leave from the so-called Burmese Pier (go through the PTT petrol station on the main road) in the port of Saphan Pla, 5km southwest of town and served by songthaews from Ranong market (B15) – the blue #6 goes via the bus station but the red #3 is more direct. Thai exit formalities are done at the pier (daily 8am–6pm), after which longtail boats take you to Kawthaung (B300–400 return per boat, or B50 one-way on shared boat – pay at the end; 30min each way) and **Burmese immigration**. Don't get off the boat at the mid-way checkpoint hut. Here you pay US$10 (or B500) for a pass that should entitle you to stay in Kawthaung for a week but forbids travel further than 8km inland. Note that Myanmar time is thirty minutes behind Thailand time, and that to get back into Thailand you'll have to be at the immigration office in Saphan Pla before it closes at 6pm. Thai money is perfectly acceptable in Kawthaung.

There's nothing much to do in **Kawthaung** itself, but it has quite a different vibe to Thai towns. As you arrive at the quay, the market, immigration office and tiny town centre lie before you, while over to your right, about twenty minutes' walk away, you can't miss the hilltop **Pyi Taw Aye Pagoda**, surmounted by a huge reclining Buddha and a ring of smaller ones. Once you've explored the covered market behind the quay and picked your way through the piles of tin trunks and sacks of rice that crowd the surrounding streets, all that remains is to take a coffee break in one of the quayside pastry shops.

★ **Sino Mansion** 28/8 Thanon Ruangrat ☏ 077 985 988; ⓦ facebook.com/baansino; map p.586. Set 50m back from the road behind a small market, this beautifully refurbished, white-tinted mansion is an atmospheric throwback to Ranong's Sino-Portuguese legacy. Peranakan-style floor tiles and Neoclassical columns make for a good introduction to two floors of immaculate en suite rooms; there's also an inviting lounge and restaurant. Breakfast costs B100 extra. B890

Tinidee Hotel 41/144 Thanon Tha Muang ☏ 077 835240, ⓦ tinideeranong.com; map p.586. The top digs in town are at this welcoming, good-value high-rise hotel, a 10min walk from the market, which fully lives up to its name ("It's good here"). The large, bright a/c rooms are tastefully furnished and all come with mini-bars, TVs and bathtubs fed by the local mineral water; there's also a spa and an attractive swimming pool and Jacuzzi. B1560

EATING

Ranong's ethnic diversity ensures a tasty range of eating options, and a stroll up Thanon Ruangrat takes you past Muslim food stalls and Chinese pastry shops as well as a small but typically Thai night market. A bigger night market convenes at dusk just east of the CAT phone office off Thanon Phoem.

209 Kafe 209 Thanon Ruangrat ☏ 089 2125205 ⓦ bit. ly/2AWsmm4; map p.586. Housed in a former barbershop, this narrow yet cosy café and sweet shop uses its original fittings to great choreographic effect. It bristles with young locals and expatriates, who come here for the fresh fruit smoothies (B40), ice creams (from B45) and home-made

cakes (B80). Wed–Mon 10am–7pm, closed Tue.
Pon's Place 129 Thanon Ruangrat ☎081 597 4549;
map p.586. This nice little restaurant, which is decorated
with orchids, is the obvious place for farang-style breakfast

(French toast B55) with traditional Thai coffee, free wi-fi and
as much local information as you care to gather. It also offers
sandwiches and standard Thai dishes, including plenty of
seafood and some veggie options. Daily 7.30am–9pm.

Ko Chang Noi

Not to be confused with the much larger Ko Chang off Thailand's east coast (see page 405), Ranong's **KO CHANG NOI** is a forested little island about 5km offshore, whose car-free, ATM-free, ultra laidback, roll-your-own vibe more than compensates for the less-than-perfect beaches. The pace of life here is very slow, encouraging long stays, and for the relatively small number of tourists who make it to the island the emphasis is strongly on kicking back and chilling out – bring your own hammock and you'll fit right in. Those in search of livelier scenes head across the water to sister-island Ko Phayam (see page 593). Most islanders make their living from fishing and from the rubber, palm and cashew nut plantations that dominate the flatter patches of the interior. The beaches are connected by tracks through the trees and there are only sporadic, self-generated supplies of electricity for a few hours each evening.

The best of Ko Chang Noi's beaches are on the west coast, and of these the longest, nicest and most popular is **Ao Yai**. The tiny bays to the north and south mostly hold just one set of bungalows each and are good for getting away from it all, though access to Ao Yai is easy enough if you don't mind the hike. About halfway between the west and east coasts, a crossroads bisects Ko Chang Noi's only **village**, a tiny settlement that is home to most of the islanders and holds just a few shops, restaurants and a clinic.

Nearly all the bungalows on Ko Chang Noi **close** down from about late April or early May until mid-to-late October, when the island is subjected to very heavy rain, the beaches fill with flotsam, paths become dangerously slippery and food supplies dwindle with no ice available to keep things fresh. Many bungalow staff relocate to the mainland for this period, so you should phone ahead to check first if you're thinking of heading out here.

Ao Yai (Long Beach) and Ao Daddaeng

Effectively divided in two by a *khlong* (canal) and the stumps of a long wooden pier, **Ao Yai**, or **Long Beach**, enjoys a fine view of the brooding silhouette of Myanmar's St Matthew's Island, which dominates the western horizon. The 800m-long stretch of Ao Yai that runs north from the *khlong* is the most attractive on the island, nice and wide even at high tide, and especially good for kids. South of the *khlong*, the beach is very narrow at high tide, but when the water goes out you have to walk a longish distance to find any depth. Further south still, around a rocky headland, tiny secluded gold-sand **Ao Daddaeng** (Tadang) is sandwiched between massive boulders and holds just a few bungalows: reach it via a five-minute footpath from behind Tadang Bay Bungalows.

Most longtail boats from Ranong will moor directly in front of your resort of choice on Ao Yay. Alternatively, a narrow concrete road connects central Ao Yai with the mangrove-filled little harbour on the east coast, stretching for a distance of around 3km that can be walked in under an hour. The western end of the road begins beside the island's only temple, **Wat Pah Ko Chang**, whose bot and monks' quarters are partially hidden among the trees beside the beach, with a sign that asks tourists to dress modestly when in the area and not to swim or sunbathe in front of it.

Northern Ko Chang Noi

North of Ao Yai, the crenellated coast reveals a series of tiny bays occupied by just one set of bungalows apiece. The gritty gold-sand beaches are secluded and feel quite

---

ACTIVITIES ON KO CHANG NOI

Going for walks (and not minding getting lost) is the most popular activity on this large, traffic-free island, but several resorts, including *Koh Chang Resort*, run **fishing, snorkelling and camping trips** to Ko Kham, which is famed for its beautiful beaches and reefs, and to Ko Phayam. For **divers**, Ko Chang Noi is particularly well placed for the sites in the Mergui Archipelago across the border in Myanmar, while the top local dive sites in Thailand are Ko Surin, Ko Bon, Ko Tachai, Ko Similan and Richelieu Rock.

Aladdin Dive Safari Cashew Resort, Ao Yai, and at the Islands Pier in Saphan Pla ☎087 278 6908, ⓦaladdindivesafari.com. This German–Dutch-run dive shop teaches PADI diving courses and runs a huge selection of live-aboards that take in all the local dive sites (from B14,900 for three days excluding equipment and national park fees).

Om Tao North of Cashew Resort, Ao Yai ☎085 470 9312, ⓦomtao.net. Morning yoga classes and t'ai chi in season.

---

remote, accessible only via a track through forest and rubber plantations. Even if you don't want to base yourself up here, you can do an enjoyable **loop** around the northern bays in well under three hours from Ao Yai. Alternatively, you could make use of the Ranong boats, which charge about B50 for any hop up or down the west coast.

Following **the track** inland from just north of Om Tao, a 10min walk north brings you to the top of the first of several hills and the barbed-wire perimeters of a military camp, established here to monitor activity along the (maritime) Thai–Myanmar border. A further 10min walk will bring you to the aptly named *Nice View* restaurant and bungalows: perched atop an outcrop with glorious panoramas over the unfolding little bays and islets beyond, this is a perfect spot to break for lunch or a drink. It's another twenty minutes to *Sea Eagle* (you need to go via the beach at *Hornbill* before returning inland), the last of the northern bay bungalows, beyond which a 10min walk up and over the next hill takes you to the edge of the northeast-facing Morgan fishing village, an unprepossessing place complete with incongruous Christian church. This is **Ao Ko**, which is linked by road to the east coast's rainy-season pier, and also to Ao Yai.

Southern Ko Chang Noi

Ao Siad, at the southern end of the island, is even more isolated than the north coast and makes a good focus for a day-walk, or a source of extra secluded accommodation options. It's sometimes known as **Ao Lek**, though the real **Ao Lek** is the mangrove-lined bay fifteen minutes' walk to the northeast, on the other coast. From Ao Daddaeng, a clear path takes you south, in about an hour, to **Ao Kai Tao**, a pretty beach and site of the national park ranger station. From here, the route then follows an indistinct path across the saddle between two hills and along a creek bed to reach east-coast Ao Lek (this takes another hour), after which it's fifteen minutes south to Ao Siad. Retracing your steps to Ao Lek to start with, it's then about 5km (2hr) to the crossroads in the village.

ARRIVAL AND INFORMATION | KO CHANG NOI

Cashew Resort can arrange bus tickets.

BY BOAT
To/from Ranong From early November to late April, there are two guaranteed daily boat departures to Ko Chang Noi from Saphan Pla's Islands Pier (9.30am & 2pm; 1hr 30min; B200), which stop at most resorts on the west coast. Note that these services are sometimes cancelled in the rainy season. Ask your resort or at *Pon's Place* in Ranong (see page 589) for the latest schedules.

To/from Ko Phayam The only option is to hop onto one of the speedboats that travel from Ranong to Ko Phayam, which stop at Ko Chang Noi's east coast pier on demand. Ask your resort to call ahead and book you a seat, which will cost between B270 and B350. If arriving from Ko Phayam, you should be able to arrange a pick-up from the pier through your resort; otherwise, it's B100 on a motorcycle taxi or a simple 3km walk to Ao Yai. A charter between the two islands costs about B2000 per boat.
Tourist information For general information on the island see ⓦkohchang-ranong.com.

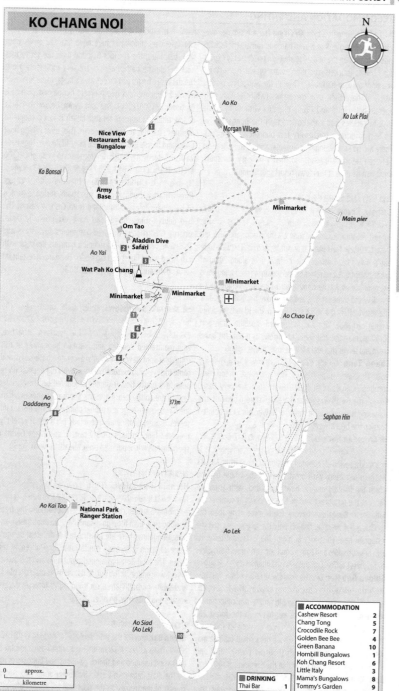

KO CHANG NOI

N

Ao Ko

Morgan Village

Ko Luk Plai

Nice View
Restaurant &
Bungalow

1

Ko Bonsai

Army
Base

Minimarket

Main pier

7

Om Tao

2

Aladdin Dive
Safari

3

Wat Pah Ko Chang

Ao Yai

Minimarket

Minimarket

Minimarket

1

Ao Chao Ley

4

5

6

7

Ao Daddaeng

8

373m

Saphan Hin

Ao Kai Tao

National Park
Ranger Station

Ao Lek

9

*Ao Siad
(Ao Lek)*

10

0	approx.	1

kilometre

■ **ACCOMMODATION**
Cashew Resort	2
Chang Tong	5
Crocodile Rock	7
Golden Bee Bee	4
Green Banana	10
Hornbill Bungalows	1
Koh Chang Resort	6
Little Italy	3
Mama's Bungalows	8
Tommy's Garden	9

■ **DRINKING**
Thai Bar	1

ACCOMMODATION AND EATING

Most of the bungalows on Ko Chang Noi are simple, old-school wooden-plank or woven bamboo constructions with mosquito nets on the beds; you shouldn't necessarily expect flush toilets (buckets and dippers are provided), curtains or a door on your bathroom. Though the bungalow resorts nearly all have their own generators (which usually only operate between 6 and 10pm, together with wi-fi), some stick to candles and paraffin lamps in the bungalows so it's best to bring a torch; very few bungalows have fans. There are no stand-alone restaurants, and as the distances between resorts are long and there's no easy transport, most visitors dine at their own resort's restaurant.

AO YAI (LONG BEACH)

Cashew Resort ☎081 4584530 or ☎081 485 6002, ✉cashew_resort@hotmail.com; map p.591. The longest-running accommodation on the island, and also the largest, *Cashew* feels like a tiny village, with its forty en-suite bungalows spread among the cashew trees along 700m of prime beachfront, and returnees personalizing their bungalows like mini homes. All the wood or brick bungalows enjoy both a sea view and some privacy, and some have big glass windows. The resort offers the most facilities on the island, including foreign exchange, Visa and MasterCard capability, transport bookings, massage and books to borrow. Its restaurant bakes bread and serves Thai and a few German dishes. **B500**

Chang Tong ☎089 875 3353, ✉aoy_changthong@hotmail.com; map p.591. The cheapest wood and bamboo bungalows at this friendly spot are very basic, though they're all en suite and are well spaced beneath the shoreside trees; pay a bit more for newer, better appointed ones on the beachfront. **B350**

★**Crocodile Rock** ☎081 370 1434 or ☎087 040 8087, ⊕facebook.com/CrocodileRockBungalows; map p.591. In a shady, secluded, elevated position at the start of Ao Yai's southern headland, with great views of the whole bay, on which the friendly owners have capitalized, with attractive decks at the restaurant and picture windows in some of the bathrooms. Bungalows have a touch more style than the Ko Chang Noi average, though only the larger ones and the restaurant have electricity at night. The restaurant bakes its own bread, cookies and banana muffins, and serves fresh juices and espresso coffee. Computer-based internet access. **B400**

Golden Bee Bee On the middle section of Ao Yai, just after the bridge over the khlong ☎085 795 3955, ⊕bit.ly/2oeGLG0; map p.591. Simple family-run collection of wooden en-suite bungalows, set between the forest and the sea. The restaurant serves good portions of the usual Thai curries and fish dishes. Those on a small budget may also camp out on the beach (B50 per pitch). Wi-fi only available in the restaurant and in the evenings. **B300**

Koh Chang Resort ☎081 896 1839, ⊕kohchangandaman.net; map p.591. Occupying a fabulous spot high on the rocks right over the water, the best of the en-suite wooden bungalows here have fine sea views from their balconies; the cheaper bamboo ones are set further back beside the path. Interiors are very rudimentary but the decks are huge, and there's also a large, more luxurious family bungalow, and two concrete bungalows with fans (between B1500/2000). You can swim below the rocks at low tide, or the more reliable beach is just a couple of minutes' scramble to south or north. They offer fishing boat tours, and there's the very chilled, fairy-lit *Air Bar*. They have wi-fi and electricity, which run from 8am to midnight. **B200**

Little Italy ☎084 851 2760, ✉daniel060863@yahoo.it; map p.591. This tiny Italian–Thai-run outfit has just three attractive bungalows set in a shady, secluded garden of paperbark trees 100m inland from *Cashew Resort*. The two double-storey bungalows have exceptionally clean, smartly tiled papaya-coloured bathrooms downstairs and Thai-style bamboo-walled sleeping quarters upstairs, with varnished wood floors and big decks. The garden restaurant serves deliciously authentic pastas. **B350**

AO DADDAENG

★**Mama's Bungalows** 5min walk south over the headland from Ao Yai, on Ao Daddaeng ☎087 276 7784, ⊕bit.ly/2of66zo; map p.591. The fourteen attractive, well-maintained wooden and bamboo bungalows at this congenial spot have colourfully decorated bathrooms and come in several sizes, some of them with big decks. They're built in a pretty flower garden staggered up the hillside; several are on the beach and the uppermost ones overlook the bay from the edge of a rubber plantation. The restaurant serves espresso coffee and generous portions of carefully prepared food, including tasty tzatziki and many German specialities. Very popular, so book ahead. No wi-fi. **B250**

NORTHERN BAYS

Hornbill Bungalows North around two headlands from Ao Yai, about a 35min walk ☎089 590 6008, ✉66_hornbill@hotmail.com; map p.591. Set among the trees fronting their own little gold-sand bay, the unobtrusive en-suite bungalows here are constructed to different designs, some of them extremely comfortable, and all enjoy sea views. The food here has a good reputation and the owner is very welcoming. It lives up to its name, as majestic black-and-white hornbills are a common sight. Internet access, kayaks and boat trips on offer. **B350**

SOUTHERN BAYS

Green Banana On the southern end of Ao Siad ☎081 728 5147; map p.591. A pirate-themed, ultra-basic complex of driftwood bamboo and thatch pavilions and bungalows run by Thai Rastafarians in a secluded corner of Ao Siad. Rooms consist of mattresses on the floor and mosquito nets, with simple shared toilets. Located right on an attractive, long stretch of beach. No internet connection. B300

Tommy's Garden On the western corner of Ao Siad ☎ 093 710 8966, ✆facebook.com/Tommysgardenbungalow; map p.591. Perched on a forested slope overlooking the

secluded bay at the western end of Ao Siad, these rustic hillside bungalows are as basic as they can be (including squat toilets), but enjoy beautiful sunset views over a secluded bay with decent swimming. For a bit more (B450), the beach front bungalows are no less spartan but more spacious. B300

DRINKING

Thai Bar In the middle section of Ao Yai, between the bridge over the khlong and Golden Bee ☎ 093 151 2833; map p.591. A local attempt to make Ao Yai a little less sleepy, Thai Bar attracts a crowd thanks to its jolly driftwood

and bamboo bar set right on the beach and shaded by low trees. Come for beers and cocktails (B80), occasional free fish barbecues, table football and live music. Daily 3pm until late.

Ko Phayam

Like it or not, in recent years the diminutive kangaroo-shaped island of **KO PHAYAM** has not only surfaced on the tourist radar, but it's also become a hit with Thai tourists, who now come in droves to enjoy its first Maldives-style (and price) five-star resort, *Blue Sky*. Things are set to change even more drastically: at the time of writing, unlimited electric supply cables from the mainland were about to be connected, meaning that a breath of modernity threatens to overturn the island's chilled and low-key reputation. Regardless, Ko Phayam still offers fine white-sand beaches and coral reefs, and is home to around five hundred people, most of whom either make their living from prawn, squid and crab fishing, or from growing cashew nuts, *sator* beans, coconut palms and rubber trees. Most islanders live in Ko Phayam's only **village**, behind the pier on the northeast coast, which connects to other corners of the island via a network of concrete roads and a few rutted tracks. The bays either side of the village have a couple of nice places to stay, but the main beaches and accommodation centres are on the west coast, at **Ao Yai** and **Ao Kao Kwai**. A motorbike taxi service covers all routes, but no journey is very long as the island measures just 10km by 5km at its widest point.

Ko Phayam has a much livelier, younger and more developed feel than neighbouring Ko Chang Noi (see page 589), underlined by a low-key beach-bar scene – all hand-painted signs and driftwood sculptures – and the presence of a significant number of foreigners who choose to spend six or more months here every year. Some expats even take up the **rainy-season** challenge, staying on through the downpours and rough seas that lash the island from June to October, but a number of bungalows close down during this time and staff take refuge in Ranong. It's important to mention that, even though they are currently lined with rows of bungalows and small resorts, both Ao Yai and Ao Kao Kwai have been reclaimed by the Thai government as forest reserves. At present, nobody really knows what this means for the future of tourism on Ko Phayam. For the moment, the place is definitely thriving – for better or for worse.

The village and around

The tiny cluster of homes and shops that constitute Ko Phayam's only **village** is connected to the pier via a strip lined with tourist facilities and boat ticket stalls. There are a few little general stores here, plus several restaurants and a **clinic**. A little way north up the shoreline stands the island **temple**, with its circular *viharn* resting on a huge concrete lotus flower at the end of its own pier.

Ao Yai

Ko Phayam's main beach is the 3km-long **AO YAI** on the southwest coast, a wide and handsome sweep of powdery white sand backed by an unbroken line of casuarina trees, which curves quite deeply at its northern and southern ends into rocky outcrops that offer some snorkelling possibilities. The shore is pounded by decent waves that are fun for boogie-boarding and pretty safe; the sunsets are quite spectacular too. For the moment Ao Yai's bungalow operations are mostly widely spaced along the shoreline, and much of the forest behind the beach is still intact. You're more than likely to see – and hear – some of the resident black-and-white hornbills at dawn and dusk, along with many white-bellied sea eagles, and sightings of crab-eating macaques are also common.

Ao Kao Kwai and around

The northwest coast is scalloped into **AO KAO KWAI**, a name that's pronounced locally as **Ao Kao Fai** and translates as **Buffalo Horn Bay**; from the cliffside midway along the bay you can see how the two halves of the beach curve out into buffalo-like horns. The southern half of Ao Kao Kwai is subject to both very low and very high tides, which makes it unreliable for swimming, but the northern stretch is exceptionally pretty, secluded between outcrops with decent swimming at any tide, and none of the big

7

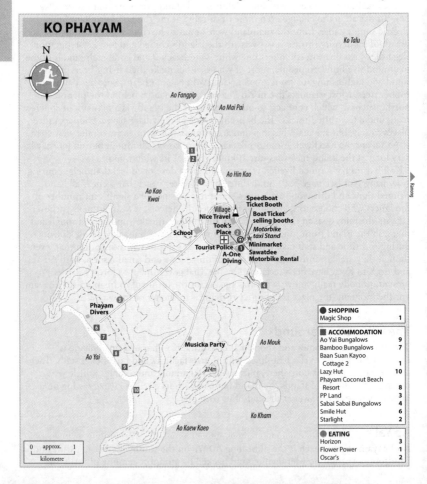

KO PHAYAM

Ko Talu

N

Ao Fangpip

Ao Mai Pai

Ao Hin Kao

Ao Kao Kwai

1
2

1
3

Ranong

Speedboat Ticket Booth
Village
Nice Travel
Took's Place
School
Tourist Police
A-One Diving
Boat Ticket selling booths
Motorbike taxi Stand
Minimarket
Sawatdee Motorbike Rental
@
2
1

4

Phayam Divers
3

6
7
8
Ao Yai
9
224m
Musicka Party
Ao Mouk

10

Ko Kham

Ao Kaew Kaeo

0   approx.   1
kilometre

● SHOPPING
Magic Shop   1

■ ACCOMMODATION
Ao Yai Bungalows   9
Bamboo Bungalows   7
Baan Suan Kayoo
  Cottage 2   1
Lazy Hut   10
Phayam Coconut Beach
  Resort   8
PP Land   3
Sabai Sabai Bungalows   4
Smile Hut   6
Starlight   2

● EATING
Horizon   3
Flower Power   1
Oscar's   2

ACTIVITIES ON KO PHAYAM

Most bungalows can arrange **fishing** and **snorkelling** day-trips, while *Oscar's* in the village takes people **wakeboarding** in the bay. The **dive companies** teach PADI courses and run live-aboards to Ko Surin, Richelieu Rock, Ko Tachai, Ko Bon and Ko Similan (from about B16,000 for three days, plus B600 per day for equipment rental).

A-One Diving In the village ✆ 081 891 5510, ⓦ a-one-diving.com. Also does live-aboards to Burma Banks and the Mergui archipelago across the Burmese border.

Phayam Divers Phayam Lodge, Ao Yai ✆ 095 665 3915, ⓦ phayamlodge.com. One-day trips to Ko Surin or Richelieu Rock for B4900 (plus equipment rental and national park fee).

waves that characterize Ao Yai. It is also the best spot on the island to see the famed glowing-pink sunsets.

From the northern end of Ao Kao Kwai, a 30min walk brings you to the pretty little sandy beach at **Ao Fangpip** (also spelt Ao Kwang Pib), which is the best spot on the island for snorkelling. There's also some snorkellable reef at **Ao Hin Kao** on the northeast coast.

ARRIVAL AND DEPARTURE
KO PHAYAM

Took's Place, north of the pier-head in the village (✆ 093 713 8380), sells bus, train, airline and boat tickets, including direct transfers to Ko Phangan (see page 550), Ko Samui (see page 533) and Ko Tao (see page 562). Nearby **Oscar's** (✆ 084 842 5070; see below) also sells transport tickets and charters speedboats to other islands. Most bungalows sell boat tickets, and some sell bus tickets, too.

BY BOAT

Motorbikes meet incoming boats at the main pier on the northwest coast.

To/from Ranong From November to May there are two daily slow boats to Ko Phayam from the Taikak pier, about 2km south of Saphan Pla (see page 587), and 5km south of Ranong town centre (10am & 3pm, returning from the island at 11.30am & 1.30pm; 2hr; B200). There are also two express boats (9am & 1pm; 1hr 30m; B250), as well as up to ten speedboat services a day (45min; B350). During the rainy season, services are reduced; *Pon's Place* in Ranong (see page 589) keeps the latest timetables.

To/from Ko Chang Noi The only way of travelling between Ko Phayam and Ko Chang Noi is by taking one of the speed boats to Ranong (B350 – the full price of a one-way ticket), which will stop on demand at Ko Chang Noi's east coast pier (see page 590 for arrival details). A charter between the two islands costs about B2000 per boat.

GETTING AROUND

Many travellers heading into the village from one of the beaches opt to walk at least one way: from Ao Yai's *Smile Hut* it's an enjoyable 7km stroll along the narrow concrete road that cuts through the cashew plantations. It takes less than an hour to walk from southern Ao Kao Kwai to the village.

Motorbike taxis Motorbike taxis can be booked directly at the pier; a ride between the village and the beaches costs about B100 depending on distance (there are no cars on the island).

Motorbike rental You can rent your own motorbike for about B250 through resorts on the beaches and outlets in the village next to the pier, such as the recommended Sawatdee Motorbike Rental (✆ 083 187 7887, ✉ supachai338@hotmail.com).

Bike rental Ask at your resort or in the village.

INFORMATION

Took's Place ✆ 093 713 8380, daily 8.30am–7pm, and **Starlight** ✆ 098 013 5301, daily 8.30am–6pm. Both are located in the village, change money and offer Visa cash advances (charging 4 percent), as there are no ATMs on the island. They can arrange boat hire and fishing tours, book onward flights, bus and train tickets.

Oscar's Bar In the village ✆ 084 842 5070. A good source of island information and tickets; also changes money at good rates.

ACCOMMODATION

Most bungalows only provide electricity from around 6 to 11pm and the cheapest rooms often don't have a fan. Unless otherwise stated, all bungalows open year-round, and offer worthwhile discounts in low season.

THE VILLAGE AREA

Most people choose to stay at the west-coast beach centres, but there are a couple of nice little hideaways within easy reach of the village and its facilities.

PP Land ☎ 081 678 4310, ⊛ ppland-heavenbeach.com; map p.594. Fronting a small beach about a 10min walk north from the village, this Belgian–Thai place, with an organic garden, is a cut above most places to stay on the island. Its tasteful, green-painted shaggy thatched bungalows line the beach and boast pretty furnishings, polished wood floors inside and out, nice bathrooms, and big comfy decks. They don't accept children under 15 so as to maintain the quiet atmosphere – children are more than welcome at their sister property *Heaven Beach Arts Resort*, in Ao Kao Kwai. There's an attractive swimming pool, plus 24-hour electricity. B900

Sabai Sabai Bungalows 5min walk south of the pier ☎ 087 895 4653, ⊛ sabai-bungalows.com; map p.594. Once a feel-good backpacker dig, *Sabai Sabai* still dominates the secluded little beach, but has upgraded facilities and prices to keep up with the island's development. The sea-breeze-catching wooden bungalows, some with 24hr electricity, come in en-suite (B800) and shared bathroom varieties. There's also a gracious lounge with wi-fi, sunset yoga sessions (B200), and occasional movie-nights. Motorbikes, bicycles, kayaks and snorkels available. B500

AO YAI

Ao Yai Bungalows ☎ 083 389 8688 or ☎ 084 061 3283, ⊛ aowyaibungalows.com; map p.594. Established by a French–Thai couple, this was the first set of bungalows on the island and remains one of the most popular, although prices have gone up considerably. The 26 good-quality en-suite bungalows are dotted around an extensive garden of flowers, fruit trees and palms and come in various styles: the cheapest wooden or thatched bamboo affairs come with mosquito nets but no fans, while the most expensive are built with concrete and have hot showers. Snorkels and kayaks available to rent. B800

Bamboo Bungalows Southern end of Ao Yai ☎ 077 820012, ⊛ bamboo-bungalows.com; map p.594. Ao Yai's liveliest accommodation is Israeli–Thai managed and very traveller-savvy, offering snorkels, kayaks, surf- and boogie-boards, currency exchange and an internet connection. Its en-suite bungalows are set under the trees in a well-tended flower garden and range from luxuriously large chalets with pretty furnishings to shell-studded concrete bungalows and a choice of bamboo and wood huts with mosquito nets, all with fan. Electricity is 24hr in high season, but more limited in low season. B550

★ **Lazy Hut** Southern end of Ao Yai ☎ 093 668 7619, ⊛ facebook.com/lazyhutthailandkohphayam; map p.594. The most attractive bungalows on Ao Yai are sheltered by a row of tall trees and fronted by inviting sunbeds that spill onto the beachfront. Completely built from dark bamboo, the bungalows feature plush beds with mosquito nets, large en-suite bathrooms and breezy verandas. Wi-fi is available at the restaurant, which serves Thai and international cuisines. B500

Phayam Coconut Beach Resort Central Ao Yai ☎ 089 920 8145; map p.594. Occupying a great spot in the centre of the bay and run by a Ko Phayam family, the 27 good-value bungalows here are of a high standard, each set in its own tiny garden. Accommodation ranges from small bamboo en-suite huts through larger wood or bamboo versions to big concrete or clapboard air-conditioned bungalows at the top end (up to B2500). Closed during the worst of the rainy season. B500

Smile Hut Northern side of Ao Yai ☎ 081 515 0856, ⊛ smilehutthai.com; map p.594. Like *Bamboo*, this is a very popular choice with travellers. The split-bamboo and wooden huts with mosquito nets are simple but en suite and are spread among the shorefront trees, with the slightly cheaper versions set one row behind. Wi-fi is available only in the evening, and they have kayaks. B500

AO KAO KWAI

Baan Suan Kayoo Cottage 2 Northern end of Ao Kao Kwai ☎ 063 970 8794, ⊛ bit.ly/2yTTD6J; map p.594. This cluster of simple en-suite bungalows on stilts is a good budget option, set on a shady forest slope and next to a small stream. It's a 1min walk from the northernmost end of the beach, where there's a restaurant with wi-fi and strategically positioned loungers. B300

★ **Starlight** Northern end of Ao Kao Kwai ☎ 081 978 5301, ⊛ facebook.com/starlightresortkophayam; map p.594. Dominating a stretch of beach with arguably the best sunset views in Ao Kao Kwai, the American-run *Starlight* offers a series of attractive beachfront bungalows (B1500) and cheaper, smaller rooms in a concrete block set further back from the sea. There's a good-sized beach-facing swimming pool, and a restaurant that, besides the obvious Western breakfast sets and Thai mains, is the only sushi bar on the island. B800

EATING

THE VILLAGE

Oscar's Just north of the pier ☎ 084 842 5070; map p.594. Offers breakfasts, including home-baked bread, Thai standards such as *tom yam kung* (B90), pizzas, Indian curries, shepherd's pie (B190) and other English favourites, but is most famous for its partially open air bar, which is a fun, relaxed focal point of the expat social scene. Daily 7am–late.

AO YAI

Horizon Just inland on the Ao Yai road; map p.594. Congenial outdoor restaurant for very tasty Thai food, all of it offered vegetarian, with the option of adding meat: a toothsome *matsaman* curry with carrot, pumpkin and potatoes costs B70, and you can add chicken for B20. Also does a few Western main courses, sandwiches, a wide choice of breakfasts, Thai desserts, and all kinds of teas, juices and lassis. Nov–May daily 7/8am–8/9pm; June–Oct daily 7/8am–sunset (closed when it rains).

AO KAO KWAI

★ **Flower Power** On the northern end of Ao Kao Kwai road ☎096 430 4260, ⓦfacebook.com/flowerpowerphayam; map p.594. Besides good value bungalows, this Italian-run jungle resort has a spacious restaurant serving authentic Italian and Burmese food. It's one of the few vegan-friendly eateries on the island, and the menu heavily relies on their own organic produce, including tomatoes, courgettes and basil. Try the delicious thin-crust pizzas (from B170), pastas (from B100) and large-sized bruschettas (from B70). Wash them all down with the house's homemade *limoncello*, whisky and chocolate creams. Open all year round. Daily 8am–9pm.

DRINKING

There's not a massive scene Ko Phayam, although several laid-back little beach-bars, including the long-running *Rasta Baby* on Ao Yai and the *Hippie Bar* on Ao Kao Kwai, put on fire shows and occasional parties. On Saturdays, the *Musicka Parties* bring people together in a forest clearing more or less halfway along the paved path to Ao Yai.

SHOPPING

THE VILLAGE

Magic Shop Just opposite Took's Place on the village main road ☎081 678 4310; map p.594. A good selection of locally produced soap bars, skincare products, jewellery and beads, plus a bakery that sells the famed local nuts. Daily 7am–6pm.

Khuraburi and around

The small town of **KHURABURI**, 110km south of Ranong on Highway 4, is the main departure point for the magnificent national park island chain of Ko Surin. Much closer to Khuraburi are the islands of **Ko Ra** and **Ko Phra Thong**, which offer empty beaches and decent snorkelling and bird-watching, or there's the chance to participate in typical village life at **homestays** in mainland coastal communities.

Khuraburi's commercial heart is a 500m strip of shops and businesses either side of Highway 4. Most travellers use the town just as a staging post en route to or from the Surin islands: the main pier for boats to the islands is just 7.5km away, and Khuraburi's tour agents sell boat tickets and offer transport to the pier. Though lacking in famous attractions, the local area is nonetheless scenic, both offshore and inland: with an afternoon or more to spare, you could either rent a motorbike, mountain bike or kayak to explore it independently, or charter a motorbike taxi or longtail boat.

Ko Ra

Hilly, forested **Ko Ra** (measuring about 10km north to south and 3km across) sits just off Khuraburi pier's mangrove-lined estuary and is graced with intact rainforest full of towering trees, hornbills and wild, empty beaches. The island is home to some two dozen *chao ley* people (see page 600), but at the time of writing, there was no accommodation available, and visiting was only possible by chartering boats for day-trips (about B1500).

Ko Phra Thong

Immediately to the south of Ko Ra, just 1km or so off the Khuraburi coast, **Ko Phra Thong** (Golden Buddha Island) also has some lovely beaches, the nicest of which, on the

7

ANDAMAN DISCOVERIES HOMESTAY PROGRAMME

Khuraburi is the headquarters of the community-based tourism initiative Andaman Discoveries (☏ 087 917 7165, ⌨ andamandiscoveries.com), which runs a recommended **day-trip and homestay programme** in several local villages, as well as interesting trips to Ko Surin (see page 599). It was established after the tsunami to help the area's many devastated fishing communities get back on their feet and has since developed a range of stimulating one- to seven-day packages (from B1600 per person per day) featuring all sorts of village jobs and activities, from soap-making and batik design to cashew nut-farming and roof-thatching. The office is just east off the highway (south of the bus station), up the soi beside the police box, across from the post office.

west coast, is 10km long and blessed with fine gold sand. This is the site of the *Horizon Beach Bungalows* and of the British-run Blue Guru Dive Centre (☏ 080 144 0551, ⌨ blue-guru.org). The resort offers kayaking, trekking and yoga, while Blue Guru runs all manner of snorkelling tours, PADI courses, dive trips and live-aboards to Ko Tachai, Ko Surin, Richelieu Rock and into Myanmar. Blue Guru's owners also organize longtail tours of the island's mangroves and maintain a website to promote the island, ⌨ kohphrathong. com, which includes information about homestays and budget bungalows.

ARRIVAL AND DEPARTURE

KHURABURI AND AROUND

KHURABURI

By bus Services between Phuket and Ranong and Phuket and Chumpon stop at the bus station, which is just off the east side of Highway 4 in the centre of town. Some long-distance through buses only stop on the highway.

Destinations: Chumpon (5 daily; 3hr 20min); Khao Lak (10 daily; 1hr 45min); Phuket (10 daily via Khao Lak; 3hr 30min); Ranong (10 daily; 3hr); Takua Pa (10 daily; 1hr).

KO RA

By boat A longtail transfer from the pier at Khuraburi costs B1000 (on demamd; 20min).

KO PHRA THONG

By boat A longtail transfer to your resort from the pier at Khuraburi (the only way to get to Ko Phra Thong) costs B1800 (90min) and B1700 (90min; must be pre-booked with Blue Guru Dive Centre).

GETTING AROUND

KHURABURI

Bike and motorbike rental Tom & Am Tour, who have their office on the west side of the main road in the town centre and maintain a desk in the bus station in high season

(☏ 086 272 0588, ✉ tom_am01@hotmail.com, ⌨ bit. ly/2Dd7SHc), rent bicycles, motorbikes and cars. *Boon Piya Resort* (see below) also rent motorbikes.

ACCOMMODATION

KHURABURI

Boon Piya Resort 100m north of the bus station, on the same side of the main road ☏ 076 491 969. Well-appointed, if rather tightly packed, motel-style concrete bungalows in a tree-strewn courtyard set just back off the road. All have a/c and powerful hot showers; they're the usual choice of sales reps and NGOs. **B650**

Tararin Resort On the south bank of the river towards the northern end of town, about 200m north of the bus station ☏ 061 183 8101. This rustic-style place next to the riverside has fifteen en-suite bungalows, the best of which are on stilts and sit in the river, with small balconies. The row of shabbier concrete rooms across the courtyard is

less attractive, but still pretty good value for the price. Fan **B300**, a/c **B350**

KO PHRA THONG

Golden Buddha Beach Resort ☏ 081 892 2208, ⌨ goldenbuddharesort.com. Tasteful complex of 25 individually decorated wooden Thai-style homes of varying price, sleeping two to six, with a spa and clubhouse. It feels like you have the island and beach to yourself here, and this tranquillity is why most choose Ko Phra Thong over other islands. Prices are for two (including breakfast) and drop significantly in low season (late Oct–mid-Dec). Closed May–Oct. **B2700**

EATING AND DRINKING

KHURABURI

The morning market (daily from 5am) across from *Boon Piya* is the place to stock up on food for the Surin islands.

Kosak Seafood Along Highway 4 in the central part of town, across the road from Tararin Resort ☎ 081 079

9442. Popular place to eat tasty seafood dishes like *pla nueng manaw* (steamed fish with spicy lime sauce, B300) or simpler Thai staples such as fried noodles and rice (B60). Daily 10.30am–10pm.

Ko Surin

Mu Ko Surin National Park, about 60km offshore • Nov–April • B500 entry fee, B300 child, valid for 5 days • ⓦ dnp.go.th

Unusually shallow reefs, a palette of awesomely clear turquoise waters and dazzling white sands, and dense forests of lofty dipterocarps combine to make the islands of **Ko Surin** one of the most popular destinations in south Thailand. However, Ko Surin's most famous feature, its spectacular and diverse coral lying in fields just below the surface at the perfect depth for snorkelling, was severely bleached by a sudden rise in sea temperature in early 2010. Four of the most popular reefs are still closed to visitors, though half a dozen other sites that were less severely affected by the bleaching remain open; the national park is still a good spot for snorkellers, with plenty of fish to see, but it will take many years for the reefs to recover.

Ko Surin is very much an outdoors experience, with the bulk of accommodation in national park tents, no commerce on the islands at all, and twice-daily snorkelling the main activity. Several tour operators run snorkelling day-trips from Khuraburi, and there are diving trips too, most of which also take in nearby Richelieu Rock, considered to be Thailand's top dive site (see page 635), but independent travel is also recommended. Because the islands are so far out at sea, Ko Surin is closed to visitors from roughly May to October, when monsoon weather renders the 60km trip a potentially suicidal undertaking.

Surin Nua and Surin Tai

The most easily explored of the reefs are those off the two main islands in the group, Ko Surin Nua (north) and Ko Surin Tai (south), which are separated only by a narrow channel. **Surin Nua**, slightly the larger at about 5km across, holds the national park headquarters, visitor centre and park accommodation.

Across the channel, **Surin Tai** is the long-established home of a community of **Moken** *chao ley* (see page 600), who are no longer allowed to fish in national park waters but make their living mostly as longtail boatmen for snorkellers staying on Surin Nua. Their recent history has been an unhappy one: not only were their settlements destroyed in the 2004 tsunami, but the aid and outside intervention that followed has changed the community forever, amalgamating two villages, building new homes too close together and introducing various modern-day vices; on top of that, tourist numbers are down since the coral bleaching in 2010. In **Ao Bon** village is a visitor centre built by Bangkok's Chulalongkorn University with English display boards, where you can hire a Moken guide to lead you on a nature trail around the village; don't go just in your swimwear, but take a sarong for modesty's sake. You can also make a positive contribution by buying one of the woven pandanus-leaf souvenirs or wooden model boats the villagers make; donations of toothpaste and clothes would also be appreciated. One of the Moken traditions that does persist is the new year celebration that's held every April, during Songkhran, when *chao ley* from nearby islands (including those in Burmese waters) congregate here and, among other rites, release several hundred turtles into the sea, a symbol of longevity.

7

THE CHAO LEY: MOKEN AND URAK LAWOY

Sometimes called sea gypsies, the **chao ley** or *chao nam* ("people of the sea" or "water people") have been living off the seas around the west coast of the Malay peninsula for hundreds of years. Some still pursue a traditional nomadic existence, living in self-contained houseboats known as **kabang**, but many have now made permanent homes in Andaman coast settlements in Thailand, Myanmar and Malaysia. Dark-skinned and sometimes with an auburn tinge to their hair, the *chao ley* of the Andaman Sea are thought to number around five thousand, divided into five groups, with distinct lifestyles and dialects.

Of the different groups, the **Urak Lawoy**, who have settled on the islands of Ko Lanta, Ko Jum, Ko Phi Phi, Phuket and Ko Lipe, are the most integrated into Thai society. They came north to Thailand from Malaysia around two hundred years ago (having possibly migrated from the Nicobar Islands in the Indian Ocean some two centuries prior) and are known as *Thai Mai*, or "New Thai". Thailand's Urak Lawoy have been recognized as Thai citizens since the 1960s, when the late Queen Mother granted them five family names, thereby enabling them to possess ID cards and go to school. Many work on coconut plantations or as fishermen, while others continue in the more traditional *chao ley* **occupations** of hunting for pearls and seashells on the ocean floor, attaching stones to their waists to dive to depths of 60m with only an air-hose connecting them to the surface; sometimes they fish in this way too, taking down enormous nets into which they herd the fish as they walk along the sea bed. Their agility and courage make them good bird's-nesters as well (see page 671).

The **Moken** of Thailand's Ko Surin islands and Myanmar's Mergui archipelago probably came originally from Myanmar and are the most traditional of the *chao ley* communities. Some still lead remote, itinerant lives, and most are unregistered as Thai citizens, owning no land or property, but dependent on fresh water and beaches to collect shells and sea slugs to sell to Thai traders. They have extensive knowledge of the plants that grow in the remaining jungles on Thailand's west-coast islands, using eighty different species for food alone, and thirty for medicinal purposes.

The *chao ley* are **animists**, with a strong connection both to the natural spirits of island and sea and to their own ancestral spirits. On some beaches they set up totem poles as a contact point between the spirits, their ancestors and their shaman. The sea gypsies have a rich **musical heritage** too. The Moken do not use any instruments as such, making do with found objects for percussion; the Urak Lawoy, on the other hand, due to their closer proximity to the Thai and Malay cultures, are excellent violin- and drum-players. During community entertainments, such as the Urak Lawoy's twice-yearly full moon **festivals** on Ko Lanta (see page 679), the male musicians form a semicircle around the old women, who dance and sing about the sea, the jungle and their families.

Building a new boat is the ultimate expression of what it is to be a *chao ley*, and tradition holds that every newly married couple has a *kabang* built for them. But the complex art of constructing a seaworthy home from a single tree trunk, and the way of life it represents, is disappearing. In Thailand, where **assimilation** is actively promoted by the government, the truly nomadic flotillas have become increasingly marginalized, and the number of undeveloped islands they can visit unhindered gets smaller year by year. The 2004 tsunami further threatened their cultural integrity: when the waves destroyed the Moken's boats and homes on Ko Surin, they were obliged to take refuge on the mainland, where some were encouraged by missionaries to convert from their animist religion. Though the Moken have since returned to the Surin islands, inappropriate donations and the merging of two villages have exacerbated family rivalries and caused divisions that may prove lethal to their traditional way of life.

ARRIVAL AND GETTING AROUND

By boat There are no public boats to Ko Surin, but if you want to stay on the islands, it's perfectly possible to come over on one of the tour boats from Khuraburi and return on another day.

By longtail Once on the islands, there's an efficient system of boat hire: Moken longtails depart twice a day from the national park campsites to the different reefs and Ao Bon village and charge B150/person for half-day (snorkel sets cost B80/day). You can also charter your own longtail (maximum fifteen people) for B1500/B3000 per half-day/day.

TOURS

Most visitors either do **snorkelling day-trips** to the islands from Khuraburi or opt for **dive trips** or live-aboards out of Ko Phra Thong, Khao Lak, Phuket, Ranong, Ko Chang Noi or Ko Phayam. . During the season, speedboat snorkelling trips to Ko Surin depart most days from Khuraburi pier, 7.5km northwest of Khuraburi town; big, slow, wooden boats (2–3hr; B1300 return) only run at weekends and on national holidays for large groups of Thai tourists.

Andaman Discoveries Khuraburi (see page 598), ⓦ andamandiscoveries.com. Four-day trips, with two nights on Ko Surin, focusing on learning about Moken life, including guided forest, village and snorkelling tours and cooking classes (B14,000).

Blue Guru Dive Centre Ko Phra Thong (see page 597) ⓦ surinislands.com. Upmarket day-trips on a dive cruiser or speedboat, including "gourmet lunch", for snorkelling (from B3300 including national park fee); transfers from Khuraburi hotels included. Also offers multi-day live-aboard trips to Surin from Khao Lak (4D/4N from B22500 plus B1800 for national park fees).

Boon Piya Resort Khuraburi (see page 598). Sells boat tickets and packages, including discounts on national park bungalows on weekdays.

Tom & Am Tour Office on the west side of the main road in Khuraburi town centre, but they also maintain a desk in the bus station in high season ☎ 086 272 0588, ✉ tom_am01@yahoo.co.th. Speedboats to Ko Surin (1hr 15min–2hr), departing the pier at 8.30am, leaving the islands at about 2pm; B1650 return including transfers. They also rent tents (B50–100/day), bedding sets (B20/day), snorkel sets (B50/day) and fins (B50/day) for Ko Surin (all cheaper than national park prices).

ACCOMMODATION

All island accommodation is on Surin Nua and is provided by the national park. Both campsites have bathrooms, lockers (B100/day) and dining rooms where meals are served at fixed times three times a day (B100–250); many people take their own supplies from Khuraburi instead. Bungalows need to be booked in advance either through the national parks websites (ⓦ dnp.go.th or ⓦ thaiforestbooking.com) or at the Khuraburi pier office (☎ 076 472145–6), but tents should be available on spec except during public holidays and long weekends.

Ao Chong Khad On the beach here, near the park headquarters and pier, you have the choice between en-suite national park bungalows (for two people) and either renting a national park tent or pitching your own (available for rent in Khuraburi); bedding sets cost B60/day. No wi-fi. Camping pitches B80, tents B300, bungalows B2000

Ao Mai Ngam Home to the nicer campsite, with tents (B300–450/day) and pitches (B80/day) but no bungalows, and reached via a 2km trail from headquarters or by longtail. No wi-fi. Pitches B80, tents B300

Khao Sok National Park

ⓘ 077 395139, ⓦ khaosok.com · B300, B150 for children up to 14 years old, payable at the checkpoint at headquarters and valid for 24hr; you'll have to pay again at Cheow Lan Lake if you arrive more than 24hr later

Most of the Andaman coast's highlights are, unsurprisingly, along the shoreline, but the stunning jungle-clad karsts of **KHAO SOK NATIONAL PARK** are well worth heading inland for. Located about halfway between the southern peninsula's two coasts and easily accessible from Khao Lak, Phuket and Surat Thani, the park has become a popular stop on the travellers' route, offering a number of easy trails, a bit of amateur spelunking and some scenic rafthouse accommodation on Cheow Lan Lake. Much of the park, which protects the watershed of the Sok River and rises to a peak of nearly 1000m, is carpeted in impenetrable rainforest, home to gaurs, leopard cats and tigers among others – and up to 155 species of bird. The limestone crags that dominate almost every vista both on and away from the lake are breathtaking, never more so than in the early morning: waking up to the sound of hooting gibbons and the sight of thick white mist curling around the karst formations is an experience not quickly forgotten.

The park has two centres: the **tourist village** that has grown up around the park headquarters and trailheads, which offers all essential services, including an **ATM** at Morning Mist Minimarket and currency exchange at Khao Sok Track & Trail; and the dam, 65km further east, at the head of **Cheow Lan Lake**. Most visitors stay in the tourist village and organize their lake trips from there, but it's also feasible to do one or more nights at the lake first. Take plenty of water when hiking as Khao Sok is notoriously humid.

The trails

Seven of the park's nine attractions (waterfalls, pools, gorges and viewpoints) branch off the clearly signed main **trail** that runs west of the park headquarters and visitor centre, along the Sok River. The first 3.5km constitute the **interpretative trail** described in *Waterfalls and Gibbon Calls* (see page 604), an unexceptional ninety-minute one-way trail along a broad, road-like track. Most people continue along the river to **Ton Kloi waterfall**, 7km from headquarters (allow 3hr each way), which flows year-round and tumbles into a pool that's good for swimming. En route, signs point to **Bang Liap Nam waterfall** (4.5km from headquarters), which is a straightforward hike; and **Tan Sawan waterfall** (6km from headquarters), which involves wading along a river bed for the final kilometre and should not be attempted during the rainy season. The trail to the

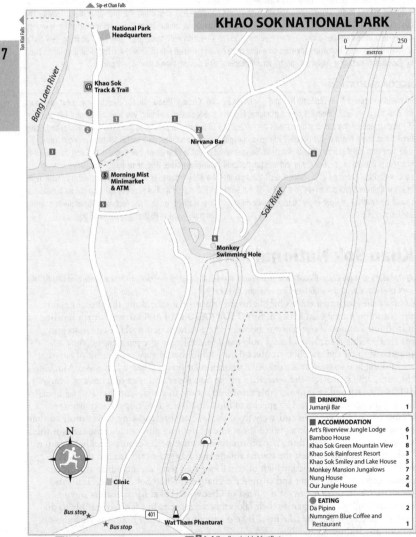

KHAO SOK NATIONAL PARK

0 ——— 250
metres

Sip-et Chan Falls

National Park Headquarters

Bang Laen River

Ton Kloi Falls

@ Khao Sok Track & Trail

Nirvana Bar

$ Morning Mist Minimarket & ATM

Sok River

Monkey Swimming Hole

N

Clinic

Bus stop
Bus stop

401

Wat Tham Phanturat

Takua Pa

Ban Ta Khun, Cheow Lan Lake & Surat Thani

DRINKING
Jumanji Bar ... 1

ACCOMMODATION
Art's Riverview Jungle Lodge ... 6
Bamboo House ... 1
Khao Sok Green Mountain View ... 8
Khao Sok Rainforest Resort ... 3
Khao Sok Smiley and Lake House ... 5
Monkey Mansion Jungalows ... 7
Nung House ... 2
Our Jungle House ... 4

EATING
Da Pipino ... 2
Numngern Blue Coffee and Restaurant ... 1

GUIDED TREKS AND TOURS OF KHAO SOK

PARK TREKS AND NIGHT SAFARIS

The vast majority of visitors choose to join a **guided trek** at some point during their stay in the park. Though the trails are waymarked and easy to navigate alone, the guided experience alerts you to details you'd certainly miss on your own – the claw marks left by a sun-bear scaling a tree in search of honey, for example, or the medicinal plants used for malarial fevers and stomach upsets – and is both fun and inexpensive; prices are fixed but exclude the national park entrance fee.

The usual **day trek** (B700–900) goes to Ton Kloi waterfall, and from about December to March there's also a special route (B700) that takes in the blooming of the world's second-biggest flower, the **rafflesia kerrii meier**, a rather unprepossessing brown, cabbage-like plant whose enormous russet-coloured petals unfurl to a diameter of up to 80cm; it's also known as "stinking corpse lily" because it gives off a smell like rotting flesh.

After-dinner **night safaris** along the main park trails (B700, excluding park entrance fee, for 2–4hr) are also popular, not least because they're good for spotting civets, mouse deer and slow lorises and, if you're exceptionally lucky, elephants and clouded leopards as well – more likely on darker nights away from the full moon.

You get to stay out in the jungle on the **overnight camping trips** (about B2500), usually around Tan Sawan falls.

Reputable and long-serving **guides** include those booked through *Bamboo House*, *Nung House* and *Khao Sok Rainforest Resort* and at Khao Sok Track & Trail (☎081 958 0629, ⓦkhaosoktrackandtrail.com).

Any guesthouse can also arrange a two-hour visit to the **elephant sanctuary** (B1200) and fix you up with equipment and transfers for **tubing** and **canoeing** trips along the Sok River (from B350/800).

CHEOW LAN LAKE TOURS

Most Khao Sok guesthouses can organize tours to Cheow Lan Lake, but all rely on the floating lake house accommodation managed by Khao Sok Smiley (☎089 871 5744, ⓦkhaosoksmiley. com), which also has headquarters (and tree houses, see below) in the tourist village. It makes sense to just arrange your tour directly with them. Charges are B1500 for a day-trip to the lake and around B2500 for two-day, one-night trips; the fee include four meals, trekking and a morning boat cruise, but excludes park entry fees. It's also possible to simply turn up at the dam and hire a boat for a day-trip for around B2000.

7

rather spectacular eleven-tiered **Sip-et Chan waterfall**, which shoots off north from the park headquarters and follows the course of the Bang Laen River, is no longer much used and can be quite indistinct. Though the falls are only 4km from headquarters, there's a fair bit of climbing on the way, plus half a dozen river crossings, so you should allow three hours each way.

Cheow Lan Lake

65km from national park headquarters

Dubbed Thailand's Guilin because of its photogenic karst islands, forested inlets and mist-clad mountains encircling jade-coloured waters similar to those sprouting around China's world-famous village, the vast 28km-long **Cheow Lan Lake** (also known as **Ratchabrapa Dam** reservoir) is Khao Sok's most famous feature and the most popular destination for guided tours. It was created in 1987 when the Khlong Saeng River was dammed to power a new hydroelectricity plant, and its forested shores and hundred-plus islands now harbour abundant bird life, as well as some primates, most easily spotted in the very early morning. Tours generally combine a trip on the lake with a wade through the nearby flooded cave system and a night on a floating rafthouse. The lake can only be explored by longtail boat tour, arranged either from Khao Sok or from Ratchabrapa Dam.

For many people, the highlight of their lake excursion is the adventurous three-hour trek to and through the 800m-long horseshoe-shaped **Nam Talu cave**, a five-minute boat ride from the national park rafthouses, or about an hour's boat ride from the dam. The **trek** is not for everyone, however, as the cave section entails an hour-long wade through the river that hollowed out this tunnel: it's slippery underfoot and pitch black and there will be at least one 20m section where you have to swim. When the river level is high there will be longer swims. Never attempt the cave without an authorized park guide and heed any closure signs posted because of high water levels and strong currents; in October 2007 a flash flood caused nine fatalities here and the park authorities are now stricter. Wear sandals with decent grip and request (or take) your own torch.

Part of the appeal of a night in a rafthouse on Cheow Lan Lake is the **dawn safari** the next morning, when you've a good chance of seeing langurs, macaques and gibbons on the lakeshore; some tours include this option, or you can usually borrow a kayak from your accommodation and paddle around the shore yourself.

ARRIVAL AND DEPARTURE   KHAO SOK NATIONAL PARK

Khao Sok National Park headquarters, its tourist village and Cheow Lan Lake are all north off Highway 401, which is served by frequent **buses**: all services between the junction town of **Takua Pa**, 40km south of Khuraburi, and Surat Thani come this way, including some Surat Thani services to and from Khao Lak and Phuket. Coming from Bangkok, Hua Hin or Chumphon, take a Surat Thani-bound bus as far as the Highway 401 junction, about 20km before Surat Thani, and change onto one for Takua Pa.

Nang (2hr 30min), Ranong (4hr), Surat Thani's Talat Kaset II via the train station at Phunphin (1hr 45min), Ko Chang Noi (4hr 45min), Ko Lanta (4hr), Ko Phayam (4hr 30min), Ko Samui (3hr), Pha Nga (3hr), Trang (4hr 30min), Hat Yay (8hr) and even across the southern border into Malaysia.

Bus destinations: Bangkok (via Surat Thani, Hua Hin and Petchaburi; daily; 11hr); Khao Lak (9 daily; 1hr 30min); Surat Thani (hourly; 1–2hr); Takua Pa (9 daily; 50min).

CHEOW LAN LAKE

Access to the lake is via the town of Ban Ta Khun, 50km east of Khao Sok on Route 401, from where it's 12km north to the dam. Many travellers book their tour of the lake from their Khao Sok accommodation, in which case all transport is included, but if coming from Surat Thani or Phang Nga, you could do the lake first. There's a regular minibus service from Talat Kaset II in Surat Thani, via Phunphin train station, to Cheow Lan Lake (about every 2hr; 1hr), or you could take a Surat Thani–Takua Pa bus, alight at Ban Ta Khun and get a motorbike taxi to the dam.

PARK HEADQUARTERS

The access road to the tourist village and trailheads is at kilometre-stone 109 on Highway 401, where guesthouse staff meet bus passengers and offer free lifts to their accommodation, the furthest of which is about 3km from the main road.

Khao Sok Track & Trail in the tourist village (☎ 081 958 0629, ⊛ khaosoktrackandtrail.com) sells bus (including a VIP bus to Bangkok, via Surat Thani), boat, plane and train tickets, as well as tickets for a/c minibuses to multiple destinations including Chiang Mai (12hr), Krabi (2hr), Ao

INFORMATION

Map The checkpoint office at headquarters supplies a small sketch map of the park and trails.
Guidebooks The best introduction to Khao Sok is the

guidebook *Waterfalls and Gibbon Calls* by Thom Henley, which is available at some Khao Sok minimarkets and bungalows.

ACCOMMODATION

PARK HEADQUARTERS

The bulk of the budget accommodation is scenically sited beneath the karsts near the park headquarters, but despite the edge-of-the-rainforest location, it can get noisy of an evening, with the sound systems at some backpacker bars pitched against the chattering of the cicadas. Every guesthouse offers its own park and lake trips, so it is worth talking to the park guides before booking a trip. Around here, "treehouses" means bungalows built on very tall stilts among the trees, rather than actually in the trees.

★ **Art's Riverview Jungle Lodge** ☎ 081 489 8489 or ☎ 090 167 6818, ⊛ artsriverviewlodge.com; map p.602. Popular place nicely located away from the main fray next to a good swimming hole, surrounded by jungle. The cheaper bungalows are spacious, tastefully designed wooden affairs, with shutters and a deck, while the deluxe versions (B2500) are bigger still and attractively furnished, some with red-brick outdoor bathrooms and waterfall-style showers. All rooms have fans and mosquito nets, wi-fi is available at the lobby area, and breakfast is included. They offer free pick-ups from the highway junction (advance booking required). B1000

Bamboo House 📞 081 787 7484, 📧 bamboohouse. khaosok@gmail.com; map p.602. Set in a grassy orchard, this was one of the first guesthouses in the park and is run by welcoming members of the park warden's family. The simple, stilted, en-suite wooden huts with mosquito nets here are the cheapest in this part of the park and there are also pebble-dashed concrete versions, a couple of treehouse-style bungalows and large, wooden affairs with hot showers and balconies on stilts right over the river (B800). B300

Khao Sok Green Mountain View 1500m north up a mostly paved road from Highway 401, just east of the km 106 marker 📞 087 263 2481, 🌐 khaosok-greenmountainview.com; map p.602. This is a great budget option if you want a remote location, situated as it is in a very quiet spot far from almost everyone else. The seven good-quality bamboo and wood bungalows of varying sizes are all en suite and have some nice touches, with pretty open-roofed bathrooms, fans, mosquito nets, decks and hammocks. They sit on the edge of a rubber plantation on the other side of the karsts from the main accommodation area. There's free transport to the park village or you can walk to *Our Jungle House* across the river in 15min and on to the park headquarters in another 25. B300

Khao Sok Rainforest Resort 📞 064 224 9654, 🌐 khaosokrainforest.com; map p.602. This welcoming place has some spectacularly sited mountain view bungalows that are set high on a jungle slope and affording unsurpassed karst views, plus a/c treehouses (B2500) and a/c riverside bungalows (B2000). Interiors are decent enough though lacking style, and wi-fi is only available at the restaurant, where breakfast (included in rate) is served. B1500

Khao Sok Smiley and Lake House 📞 089 871 5744, 🌐 khaosoksmiley.com; map p.602. Set beyond a not-so-attractive restaurant and lounge, these two rows of concrete bungalows (B500) and wooden treehouses have fairly basic toilets and facilities, but are overall good value – especially the latter, with their spacious verandas backed by lush vegetation. They are also the main tour operator for Cheow Lan lake (see page 603), where they manage prettier floating raft houses. B300

★**Monkey Mansion Jungalows** 🌐 facebook.com/ khaosokjungalows; map p.602. This Thai–German-run, tree-covered wooden house is a perfect spot for both backpackers and families. There's a welcoming veranda with a vegan-friendly restaurant that's perfect for chilling out and offers luggage storage and book-exchange facilities. The different types of en-suite bungalows – some bamboo-walled, others made of wood and concrete – all have mosquito nets and are set around an attractive stone and wood garden next to a pond filled with carp. When available, the family rooms can also function as dorms (B200) for walk-in guests. B450

Nung House 📞 077 380 723 and 086 283 31037, 🌐 nunghouse.com; map p.602. Friendly place run by the park warden's son and his family, with eighteen very good huts set around an attractive grassy garden full of rambutan trees. Choose between simple but sturdy bamboo and wood constructions with en-suite facilities, brick and concrete bungalows, and treehouses. The *Nirvana Bar* (next door) is a good spot to meet other travellers and have a few drinks. B300

Our Jungle House 📞 081 417 0546, 🌐 khaosok accommodation.com; map p.602. Peaceful, upmarket riverside option, a 20min walk from park headquarters, secluded in lush rainforest where you might spot hornbills and several species of monkey. Choose between airy, well-designed, wood and bamboo bungalows and treehouses (B2900); all have fans and mosquito nets and most are on the river bank, which has a small beach. B950

CHEOW LAN LAKE

On overnight tours to the lake (see page 603), accommodation is either in tents in the jungle or at rafthouses on the lake. There are both private and national park rafthouses moored at various scenic spots around the lake shore, mostly around an hour's boat ride from the dam. All rafthouse huts are rudimentary bamboo structures with nets and mattresses, offering fabulous lake views from your pillow. If you've arranged your own boat transport, you can stay at any of the lake's rafthouses for B600 per person, including meals. Accommodation packages that include boat transfers from the dam and a cave tour cost around B2500 with *Khao Sok Smiley and Lake House* (📞 089 871 5744, 🌐 khaosoksmiley.com). *Jungle Yoga* runs yoga, meditation and massage retreats at the remote *Praiwan* rafthouses from December to April (🌐 jungleyoga.com).

EATING

There are just a couple of places that might tempt you away from your guesthouse restaurant in the tourist village near park headquarters.

PARK HEADQUARTERS

Da Pipino map p.602. Homely, rustic, not to say scruffy, Italian restaurant, strewn with lovely plants in a scenic spot by the river. The menu runs to seafood antipasti, decent fettuccine bolognese (B195), a few Italian main courses and a wide range of tasty handmade pizzas. Daily noon–10pm.

Numngern Blue Coffee and Restaurant Towards the end of the village road, close to park headquarters 📞 083 391 3391; map p.602. Simple yet cosy restaurant serving good brews and a menu of hearty, mostly vegetarian Thai dishes, such as *ma khu yao kraug gang* (curry sauce with eggplant and tofu, B90) and *pad med ma muang* (stir-fried cashew nut with mushrooms, tofu and onion, B90). Daily 8am–9pm.

7

DRINKING

PARK HEADQUARTERS

Jumanji Bar Next to Nung House; map p.602. Pure reggae-style, bamboo bar that earns a few extra points thanks to its nice location in a quiet spot, with low driftwood tables surrounded by trees. Most cocktails, including mojitos and Singapore slings, cost B150. Daily 8am–9pm.

Khao Lak

Handily located just an hour north of Phuket International Airport, and some 30km south of Takua Pa, **KHAO LAK** has established itself as a thriving, mid-market beach resort with plentiful opportunities for diving and snorkelling, easy access to the supreme national park reefs of Ko Similan and a style that is determinedly unseedy. It lacks sophistication and is mostly a bit pricey for backpackers – aside from a handful of very well-run hostels – but is ideal for families and extremely popular with European tourists. High season here runs from November to April, when the weather and the swimming are at their best and the Similan Islands are open to the public; during the rest of the year, Khao Lak quietens down a lot – and becomes much cheaper too.

The area usually referred to as Khao Lak is in fact a string of beaches west off Highway 4. **Khao Lak** proper is the southernmost and least developed, 5km from the most commercial part of the resort, **Nang Thong** (aka Bang La On), which throngs with shops, restaurants, dive centres and countless places to stay, both on the beachfront and inland from Highway 4. North again about 3km (5min by taxi or a 45min walk up the beach) is lower-key, slightly more youthful **Bang Niang**, a lovely long stretch of golden sand that's backed by a developing tourist village whose network of sois is away from the highway and feels more enticing than its neighbour. Removed from all this commerce, **Laem Pakarang**, 12km further up the coast, a headland and popular sunset-watching spot that gives onto 11km Hat Pakweeb (Hat Bang Sak), is where you find the area's best accommodation.

There is, thankfully, little obvious evidence these days of the area's devastating experience during the December 2004 **tsunami**, when the undersea earthquake off Sumatra sent a series of murderous waves on to Khao Lak's shores (and the rest of the Andaman coast), vaporizing almost every shorefront home and hotel here and killing thousands. Nang Thong quickly became the centre of a huge reconstruction effort, with thousands of volunteers arriving to help, and rebuilding was mostly completed within a couple of years, though for many survivors recovery will probably take a lifetime.

Police Boat Memorial

Bang Niang

Inland from the highway – and accessible from it across a field and a bridge – a **beached police boat** has become a memorial to the extraordinary power of the tsunami waves. It was propelled up here, 2km inland, while patrolling the waters in front of *La Flora* resort, where Princess Ubolrat and her children, one of whom perished in the disaster, were staying. To the right there's an overpriced (daily 9am–9pm; B300) **Tsunami Memorial Museum**, which essentially offers a room with pictures and data remembering the devastating effects the catastrophe had on the region.

Ban Nam Khem Memorial

13km north of Laem Pakarang up Highway 4, then left for a signposted 3km

The main local tsunami memorial is on the beach at **Ban Nam Khem**, the worst-hit village in Thailand, where half of the four thousand inhabitants died in the waves, as described in Erich Krauss's *Wave of Destruction* (see page 779). Built by the

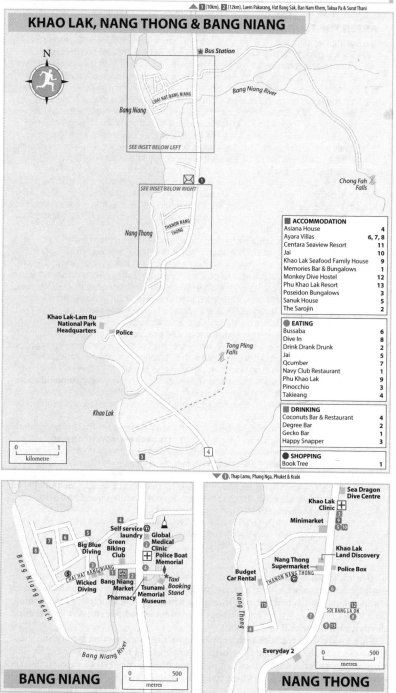

1 (10km), 2 (12km), Laem Pakarang, Hat Bang Sak, Ban Nam Khem, Takua Pa & Surat Thani

KHAO LAK, NANG THONG & BANG NIANG

N

★ Bus Station

CHAI HAT BANG NIANG

Bang Niang River

Bang Niang

SEE INSET BELOW LEFT

SEE INSET BELOW RIGHT

Chong Fah
Falls

Nang Thong

THANON NANG THONG

7

Khao Lak-Lam Ru
National Park
Headquarters   Police

Tong Pling
Falls

Khao Lak

0   1
kilometre

4

1, Thap Lamu, Phang Nga, Phuket & Krabi

■ ACCOMMODATION
Asiana House	4
Ayara Villas	6, 7, 8
Centara Seaview Resort	11
Jai	10
Khao Lak Seafood Family House	9
Memories Bar & Bungalows	1
Monkey Dive Hostel	12
Phu Khao Lak Resort	13
Poseidon Bungalows	3
Sanuk House	5
The Sarojin	2

● EATING
Bussaba	6
Dive In	8
Drink Drank Drunk	2
Jai	5
Qcumber	7
Navy Club Restaurant	1
Phu Khao Lak	9
Pinocchio	3
Takieang	4

■ DRINKING
Coconuts Bar & Restaurant	4
Degree Bar	2
Gecko Bar	1
Happy Snapper	3

● SHOPPING
Book Tree	1

BANG NIANG

Self service
laundry Global
Green Medical
Biking Clinic
Club Police Boat
Memorial

Big Blue
Diving

Bang
Niang
Beach

CHAI HAT BANG NIANG

Wicked Bang Niang
Diving Market

Taxi
Booking
Stand

Tsunami
Memorial
Museum

Pharmacy

Bang Niang River

0   500
metres

NANG THONG

Sea Dragon
Dive Centre

Khao Lak
Clinic

Minimarket

Khao Lak
Land Discovery

Nang Thong
Supermarket Police Box

Budget
Car Rental

THANON NANG THONG

Nang Thong

SOI BANG LA ON

Everyday 2

0   500
metres

AFTER THE TSUNAMI

The **Boxing Day tsunami** hit Thailand's Andaman coast just after 9.30am on December 26, 2004. The first place to suffer significant damage was Phuket, and the next two hours saw village after resort get battered or decimated by the towering waves thundering in from the Sumatra fault line, 1000km away. The entire coastline from Ranong to Satun was affected, but not all of it with the same intensity: the worst-hit province was Phang Nga, where 4200 people were recorded dead or missing, many of them in the resort of Khao Lak; over 2000 suffered a similar fate on Ko Phi Phi; and more than 900 died on the beaches of Phuket, especially on Patong and Kamala. There were 8212 fatalities in all, a third of them holidaymakers. Another 6000 people were made homeless and some 150,000 lost their jobs, mostly in the tourism and fishing industries. By the end of that day, nearly a quarter of a million people in a dozen countries around the Indian Ocean had lost their lives in the worst natural disaster in recorded history.

Many homes, shops and hotels were quite swiftly rebuilt, but the emotional and social **legacy** of the tsunami endures and most residents along the Andaman coast have a story of terror and bereavement to tell. It's no surprise that many survivors are now afraid of the sea: fearing ghosts, some longtail boatmen won't motor solo past where villages once stood, and hundreds of hotel staff have since sought new jobs in the northern city of Chiang Mai, as far from the sea as they could go.

Immediately after the tsunami, many were surprised when then prime minister Thaksin Shinawatra declined offers of **aid** from foreign governments. But help poured in instead from the Thai government and from royal foundations and local and foreign NGOs and individuals. Of the many **projects** established to help support and rebuild affected communities, the majority have now completed their task; others have evolved into longer-term NGO ventures, including an English-teaching programme in Khao Lak (see page 70), and the community-based tourism company Andaman Discoveries in Khuraburi (see page 598).

Generosity and altruism were not the only responses to the disaster, however. Almost every tsunami-affected community talks of **dishonourable practice** and **corruption**, experiences which have caused bitterness and rifts. Many allegations concern donated money and goods being held back by the local leaders charged with distributing them, and in some cases big business interests muscled in on land deemed "ownerless" because the paperwork had been lost to the waves. Most small businesses had no insurance, and government **compensation** was inconsistently awarded and invariably lacking. In a country where most family enterprises scrape by season to season, it's sobering to contemplate the number of tsunami victims who simply picked up and started over.

Determined not to be caught unawares again, in the unlikely event of Thailand being struck by a second tsunami, the government has created a **tsunami early-warning system** that relays public announcements from towers all the way down the Andaman coast. They have also mapped out evacuation routes, flagged by innumerable "Tsunami Hazard Zone" signs in all the big resorts. For their part, Phuket authorities have remodelled stretches of Ao Patong's beachfront as a building-free zone, creating a park that doubles as a tsunami **memorial**. Krabi officials now require all new buildings to be constructed at least 30m inland from a high-tide boundary, and they even forbid the use of sunloungers below that point. In Khao Lak, a beached police boat (see page 606) has become an eloquent memorial: it rests where it was hurtled by the wave, 2km inland, on the other side of the highway.

Thai army, it's an evocative installation: you walk down a path between a curling, 4m-high, concrete "wave" and a grassy bank, representing the land, on which plaques commemorate individual victims. Through a window in the concrete wave, a fishing boat looms over you – this "miracle boat" was swept inland but stopped just short of devastating a house and its occupants.

While you're out here, it's worth popping in on the **Saori weaving factory and shop** (Mon–Sat), on the left about 1km further up Highway 4 from the Ban Nam Khem turn-off, towards the northern end of Ban Bang Muang village. It's a regeneration and occupational therapy project, where you can watch the women weaving and buy some lovely scarves.

ARRIVAL AND DEPARTURE

By plane Khao Lak is just 70km north of Phuket airport (1hr; B1700–2200 by taxi; see page 616).

By bus and minibus All buses running from Phuket to Takua Pa and Ranong (and vice versa) pass through Khao Lak and can drop you anywhere along Highway 4; coming from Krabi or Phang Nga, you'll generally need to change buses in Khokkloi, from Khao Sok, in Takua Pa. On departure, you can flag down most buses on the main road, but the Bangkok services use a bus station at the far north end of Bang Niang. There are also a/c tourist minibuses that run at least daily to Surat Thani (via Khokkloi, not Khao Sok; 4hr), Krabi/Ao Nang (3hr/3hr 30min)

and Trang (change in Krabi; 5hr 30min). Bus and a/c minibus tickets can be booked through a number of travel agents, including Khao Lak Land Discovery in Nang Thong (☎076 485411, ⌨ khaolaklanddiscovery.com), who also offer transfers to and from Phuket Airport (B600/person or B1500/minibus). Destinations: Bangkok (3 daily; 12hr); Phuket (20 daily; 2hr 30min); Ranong (8 daily; 2hr 30min–3hr); Takua Pa (18 daily; 30min).

By boat Boats to the Similans depart from the pier at Thap Lamu, which is 6km south of Nang Thong, then 5km west off Highway 4 (see page 613).

GETTING AROUND

By songthaew A few public songthaews shuttle between Nang Thong and Bang Niang (where they have a base in front of the market), mostly by day, charging B20–50, but largely they act as private taxis instead and charge more

than B100.

Motorbike and car rental Many hotels rent motorbikes, and rental cars are available through tour operators.

7

ACCOMMODATION

LAEM PAKARANG

★ **Memories Bar & Bungalows** About 10km north of Khao Lak and 2km inland off Highway 4, at the end of a dirt-road marked by a surfboard ☎08 97292251, ⌨ memoriesbar-khaolak.com; map p.607. Even though

it attracts well-heeled customers from nearby resorts, this established surf-school turned hip beach restaurant is a perfect, under the radar, traveller hangout. Set on 300 metres of pristine beach right before the cape's headland, it's blessed by Khao Lak's best waves and sunset views.

DIVING AND SNORKELLING AROUND KHAO LAK

Khao Lak is the closest and most convenient departure point for **diving and snorkelling trips** to the awesome national park islands of **Ko Similan** (see page 612), which can be reached in three to four hours on a live-aboard or other large boat or in two hours in a less comfortable speedboat. The islands are currently only open from approximately October to May and all divers have to pay a one-off national park fee of B400 plus a B200-a-day diving fee, usually on top of dive-trip prices. **Local Khao Lak dives** are generally possible year-round, especially the highly rated **wreck** of a tin-mining boat near Bang Sak, which is especially rich in marine life such as ghost pipefish, moray eels, scorpion fish, nudibranchs and yellow-tail barracuda. All Khao Lak dive shops also teach PADI **dive courses**, with the last two days of the Open Water course often done on location in the Similans; for advice on choosing a dive shop see "Basics" (see page 53).

Big Blue Diving Along Bang Niang's main tourist road ☎076 485544, ⌨ bigbluedivingkhaolak.com. Established PADI Centre that specializes in 4D/4N live-aboard trips to the Similans, on a big dive boat (from B31,500) and day-trips to several dive sites, including Richelieu Rock (from B4,800). Their PADI courses cost B16,200.

Sea Dragon Dive Center Nang Thong ☎076 485420, ⌨ seadragondivecenter.com. Highly recommended PADI Five-Star Instructor Development Centre which has three live-aboard boats – including budget and deluxe options – running frequent three-day trips to the Similans and Ko Bon (from B10,900 including equipment), and

four-day trips to the Similans, Surin islands, Ko Bon, Ko Tachai and Richelieu Rock (from B19,600). No national park fees are included here. Snorkellers get about one-third off. Also offers local wreck and other dives (starting from B2000, not including equipment, for a two-tank dive) and PADI dive courses: the four-day Open Water is B10,500, or B15,000 with one day-trip diving the Similans.

Wicked Diving Along Bang Niang's main tourist road ☎076 468868, ⌨ wickeddiving.com/wd-locations/khao-lak/. A reliable company offering six-day live-aboard diving trips to the Similans and Richelieu Rock (US$995, includes fees), discover scuba, Open Water courses and fun dives.

7

Accommodation is in a cluster of simple, yet well-manned and clean, thatched-bamboo bungalows with floor mattresses and mosquito nets, set right on the seafront. The shared toilets are very clean, and the staff make you feel like you are part of the family. There's no wi-fi and food is a little on the costly side, at around B250 for a meal. **B500**

The Sarojin 12km north of Khao Lak ☎076 427905, ⓦthesarojin.com; map p.607. With a staff-to-guest ratio of two to one and a style and attitude that exudes understated, unpretentious class, this is the top place to stay around Khao Lak. The 56 sleek, tastefully simple rooms are discreetly sited around the wide beachfront garden and stunning square turquoise swimming pool. It's an obvious honeymoon choice, with a policy of no under-10s, a range of excursions designed for two, and private candlelit tables for dinner on the beach or at a nearby waterfall. There are complimentary non-motorized watersports and mountain bikes, and a spa. All-day breakfast with sparkling wine included. Special promotions often available. **B12,000**

BANG NIANG

Asiana House Tucked along a backroad connecting the highway to the beachside ☎081 577 1921, ⓔasianahouse@hotmail.co.th; map p.607. These eight delightful en-suite rooms and mini-apartments come in pastel hues, with wooden floors and bed-stands. They are within easy walking distance of the beach and most of Bang Niang's facilities, yet offer a more secluded atmosphere as they are housed in concrete bungalows at the back of a private Thai home. Breakfast included. **B1500**

Ayara Villas ☎076 486478–9, ⓦayara-villas.com; map p.607. An attractive upper-mid-range option, spread over three different compounds with two swimming pools. At the top end are beachfront villas right on the sand; many others are terraced bungalows just a few metres from the sea, and the rest are in a three-storey building, with ground-floor rooms enjoying direct pool access. The a/c interiors are nicely furnished with dark wood in contemporary style and all have kitchenettes. Breakfast included. **B5000**

Sanuk House ☎083 390 3229, ⓦsanukresort.com; map p.607. Dinky little Swiss-managed group of five comfortable and spacious brick bungalows in a small garden with a heart-shaped whirlpool, just 100m from the beach. Popular with German-speaking and long-term tourists. Bungalows come with a/c, hot showers, fridges and kitchenettes. **B1600**

NANG THONG

Centara Seaview Resort On Nang Thong's southern beachfront ☎076 429800 ⓦcentarahotelsresorts.com; map p.607. A good choice for families or those looking for peace and a bit of luxury. Rooms are located in two-storey beachfront wing set around a swimming pool facing the sea, or in a large building beyond the access road. There is ample

parking space and wi-fi in all rooms. Continental breakfast is included in the rate and is served around the pool. **B5,500**

Jai ☎076 485390, ⓔjai_bungalow@hotmail.com; map p.607. A busy, family-run place that offers some of the cheapest accommodation in Khao Lak. The good-quality, decent-sized, en-suite concrete bungalows are set around a lawn dotted with trees behind the popular restaurant, quite close to the highway and about 600m from the beach; a/c options have hot showers and fridges. Fan **B450**, a/c **B650**

Khao Lak Seafood Family House Soi Noen Thong ☎076 485318, ⓦkhaolakseafood.com; map p.607. The large, good-quality bungalows here are set well back from the road in a garden behind the eponymous restaurant. The fan ones are especially good value for Khao Lak: roomy and nicely designed with good, hot-water bathrooms; a/c rooms in a couple of two-storey blocks are also available. It's a family business and very popular with returning guests and long stayers. Fan **B600**, a/c **B1200**

★ **Monkey Dive Hostel** At the southern end of Nhang Thong's main highway ☎082 424 9257 and 081 956 5654 ⓦmonkeydivekhaolak.com; map p.607. Possibly the best backpacker option in Khao Lak, this new, industrial chic hostel has a huge, comfortable common area with TV and beanbags that is a great place to socialise. The immaculate dorms have charging stations, LED lights and free lockers (bring your own padlock though). There's also a series of smart private rooms with futon-styled beds (B500) on wooden mezzanines, each with interesting trivia on a different sea creature etched on the pastel-coloured walls. The weekly barbecues (held on Saturdays) are cheap (B35 per skewer) and a great way to meet new people. **B350**

Phu Khao Lak Resort ☎076 485141; map p.607. There is a luxurious amount of space at this well-run place, where the thirty large, spotlessly clean bungalows sit prettily amid a grassy park-style coconut plantation. Fan rooms have tiled floors and most have hot-water bathrooms; a/c ones have picture windows and quite stylish interiors. There's a swimming pool and a good restaurant. About 500m walk from the beach. Fan **B800**, a/c **B1800**

KHAO LAK

Poseidon Bungalows 7km south of central Nang Thong ☎087 895 9204, ⓦsimilantour.com; map p.607. Surrounded by rubber plantations and set above a sandy shore of wave-smoothed rocks just north of the Thai navy's private beach, this Swedish–Thai-run guesthouse is both a quiet place to hang out for a few days and a long-established organizer of snorkelling expeditions to the Similan islands (see page 609). All fifteen bungalows are en suite and fan cooled, with generous amounts of space, hot showers and balconies, some enjoying sea views. There's also motorbike rental available. Get off the bus at the *Poseidon* sign between kilometre-stones 53 and 54, then phone for a pick-up or walk 1km. **B950**

KHAO LAK DAY-TRIPS AND OTHER ACTIVITIES

Aside from diving and snorkelling trips (see page 609), there are several other attractions within day-tripping distance of Khao Lak, including a number of local **waterfalls**. Of these, Sai Rung (Rainbow Falls), about 16km north of Nang Thong in Bang Sak, is the most satisfying. Others include Tong Pling, across from the *Merlin* resort in Khao Lak; Nam Tok Lumphi, about 20km south of Khao Lak; and Chong Fah Falls, located less than 5km east of Bang Niang, but subject to a B200 entry fee because it's part of Khao Lak–Lam Ru National Park (⊛dnp.go.th). The national park's headquarters is on the headland between Nang Thong and Khao Lak beaches, and about 1km south of it, you can easily walk down to a quiet, pretty sandy cove – look for a sign saying "small sandy beach" on the west side of the main road, opposite a layby.

Everyday 2 Restaurant South end of Nang Thong ☎085 299 0410. Morning Thai cooking courses for B1200, including pick-ups.

The Green Biking Club Bang Niang ☎076 443211, ⊛facebook.com/greenbikingclub. Runs interesting guided mountain-bike trips around rural and coastal Khao Lak (from B2400 for half a day).

Khao Lak Land Discovery Nang Thong ☎076 485411, ⊛khaolaklanddiscovery.com. One of the best and most reputable, though not the cheapest, local tour operators, whose day-trips include dolphin-spotting sunset cruises (B2500), elephant-riding and bathing (B1900) and trekking and canoeing in Khao Sok National Park and Cheow Lan Lake (B750).

EATING

BANG NIANG

Drink Drank Drunk Right across the road from Bang Niang Market's entrance ☎076 671466 ⊛facebook.com/khaolakdrinkdrankdrunk; map p.607. Almost hidden between two hotels, this Italian–Thai-run open-air wine restaurant (B120 per glass) dishes up good seafood platters and brick-oven baked pizzas (from B240), as well as some interesting fusion dishes, such as the calzone *phat thai* (B290). Daily 12pm–10pm.

Pinocchio ☎076 443079; map p.607. Home-made pasta, decent pizza made in a wood-fired oven (around B300), a few Italian meat main courses and lots of seafood, topped off with tiramisu and other home-made desserts. Look for the white picket fence and fairy lights. Daily 1–11pm.

Takieang map p.607. Wooden roadside restaurant that's gone slightly upmarket, offering authentic Thai food, including good *tom yum kung* (B150), banana-flower salad (B120) and exceptional seafood hotplates (B270). Daily noon–10pm.

NANG THONG

Bussaba map p.607. Welcoming bistro with a long menu of Thai food, including seafood and fish priced by weight and some slightly more unusual dishes such as shrimp green curry with roti bread (B189). Also does sandwiches and a few other Western choices, and good espressos. Daily 1.30–11pm.

★ **Dive In** Khao Lak Banana resort, Soi Bang La On; map p.607. Owner and chef Sunny cooks up a storm here and is a favourite with expats, locals and returning tourists. Highlights include a deliciously aromatic *matsaman* curry (B90), *khanom jiin* Phuket-style noodles with fish and red curry, and deep-fried fish topped with mango. The Western menu runs to home-made cakes and bread, breakfasts and espressos. Free wi-fi. Daily 6.30am–11pm.

Jai map p.607. This lofty, open-sided, roadside restaurant is deservedly popular for its hearty, often fiery curries in good-sized portions (B120), including *kaeng phanaeng* and *matsaman*, seafood and *tom yam kung*. Also does a few Thai desserts and Western breakfasts. Daily 8.30am–10pm.

Phu Khao Lak ⊛phukhaolak.com; map p.607. Well-known and good-value restaurant attached to the bungalows of the same name serving exceptionally good Thai food from a picture menu that stretches to over a hundred dishes. Everything from red, yellow and green curries (B140–170) to seafood platters. Daily 7am–10pm.

Qcumber Along the southern end of Nhang Thong's main highway ☎063 994 2211 ⊛facebook.com/qcumbersaladbar; map p.607. This little café has a hip vibe with plenty of paintings on the walls, naked light-bulbs and an eclectic menu that ranges from healthy (and pricey) Thai mains such as *pat thai* with tofu and bean sprouts (B149), to Western-style salad and vegetarian mains (from B90). They also offer Thai cooking classes (9am–12pm Tue, Thurs & Sat; B1500/person).11am–9pm, closed Wed.

THAP LAMU

Navy Club Restaurant On the right by the pier, 11km southwest of Nang Thong ☎081 648 8656; map p.607. It's worth the trip out here for some authentic Thai food and the freshest seafood, at prices lower than in Khao Lak itself. Specialities include soft-shell crab, white snapper, pomfret (B35/100g), king prawns and squid, and there are dozens of Thai salads (B80). The restaurant is unprepossessing, but you could phone ahead to book a table on the terrace overlooking the harbour. Daily 10am–10pm.

7

DRINKING

BANG NIANG

Degree Bar At the entrance of Khao Niau Road; map p.607. With its wooden tables, water-buffalo skulls and folksy, Thai-country vibe, this welcoming and local bar-cum-restaurant is a fun place to listen to live bands, from 10pm every night, playing Thai and Western pop. It's cheap too. Daily 9pm–2am.

Gecko Bar ☎081 41544167, ⓦbit.ly/2BOb51X; map p.607. This small and cosy snooker bar, festooned with global football memorabilia and beer banners is popular among the foreign instructors who work at the local dive centres. Beers (B80) and spirits (B100) come cheap and the friendly owners love to challenge their guests to a game of table football. Daily 7pm–2am.

NANG THONG

Coconuts Bar and Restaurant On Nang Thong's beach southern headland, next to Suwan Resort ☎061 401 5637 or 061 401 5636 ⓦfacebook.com/coconutsnangthong; map p.607. This feel-good beachside bistro is casual enough to hang out in with friends whilst tucking your toes in the sand, but also sees a steady flow of higher-end resort clientele. Pricewise, however, there's something for everyone, from fish and chips and spaghetti (both B160), to grilled seafood mixed platters (B900). Happy hour is actually five hours – from 3 to 8pm every day – and beers cost B160 during this time. Daily 7am–10pm.

Happy Snapper ⓦfacebook.com/HappySnapperBar; map p.607. Khao Lak's most famous dive-staff hangout is chilled and pleasant, with a folksy lounge ambience and a drinks menu of over one hundred cocktails. There's a live band every night, from around 10.30pm, except on Sundays, when there is a chill-out DJ. Expect the occasional open-mic session too. Daily 8.30pm–1am.

SHOPPING

Nang Thong offers plenty of shopping, mainly for clothes, souvenirs and handicrafts, with countless tailors and opticians too. Bang Niang has a popular street market in the soi, parallel to the main bar and accommodation strip (Mon, Wed, Thurs and Sat; 10am–10pm)

Book Tree Far north end of Nang Thong; map p.607. Sells plenty of new and second-hand books plus magazines, newspapers and art cards, and also serves good coffee. Daily 9am–9pm.

Ko Similan

Mu Ko Similan National Park • B400, valid for 5 days if staying within the national park • Closed May to Oct

Rated as one of the world's best spots for both above-water and underwater beauty, the eleven islands at the heart of the **Mu Ko Similan National Park** are among the most exciting **diving** destinations in Thailand. Massive granite boulders set magnificently against turquoise waters give the islands their distinctive character, but it's the 30m visibility that draws the divers. The 5000-year-old reefs are said to be the oldest in Thailand, so there's an enormous diversity of species, and the underwater scenery is nothing short of overwhelming: the reefs teem with coral fish, and you'll also see turtles, manta rays, moray eels, jacks, reef sharks, sea snakes, red grouper and quite possibly white-tip sharks, barracuda, giant lobster and enormous tuna.

The **islands** lie 64km off the mainland and include the eponymous Ko Similan chain of nine islands as well as two more northerly islands, Ko Bon and Ko Tachai, which are both favoured haunts of manta rays and whale sharks and are halfway between the Similan chain and the islands of Ko Surin. The Similans are numbered north–south from nine to one and are often referred to by number: Ko Ba Ngu (9), Ko Similan (8), Ko Payoo (7), Ko Hin Posar (aka Ko Hok; 6), Ko Ha (5), Ko Miang (4), Ko Pahyan (3), Ko Pahyang (2) and Ko Hu Yong (1). The national park headquarters and accommodation is on Ko Miang and there's also a campsite and restaurant on Ko Similan. Ko Similan is the largest island in the chain, blessed with a beautiful, fine white-sand bay and impressive boulders and traversed by two nature trails; Ko Miang has two pretty beaches, twenty minutes' walk apart, and three nature trails; Ko Hu Yong has an exceptionally long white-sand bay but access is restricted by the Thai navy as **turtles** lay their eggs there from November to February.

Such beauty has not gone unnoticed and the islands are extremely popular with day-trippers from Phuket and Khao Lak, as well as with divers and snorkellers on longer live-aboard trips. This has caused inevitable congestion and environmental problems and the Similan reefs have been damaged in places by anchors and by the local practice of using dynamite in fishing. National parks authorities have responded by banning fishermen and enforcing strict regulations for tourist boats, including **closing the islands** during the monsoon season, from May to October.

ARRIVAL AND GETTING AROUND
KO SIMILAN

Independent travellers wanting to stay on the island for a few days can usually use the snorkelling tour boats for transfers (about B900 one-way). There are also plenty of live-aboard diving or snorkelling trips to the islands, the best and cheapest of which run out of Khao Lak (see page 609).

Snorkelling tours Most travel agents in Khao Lak, Phuket and Phang Nga sell snorkelling packages to Ko Similan, usually as day-trips featuring at least four island stops (from B3500 including national park fees); two-day, one-night (B5800 staying in tents), and three-day, two-night (B7200) packages, staying on Ko Miang, are also available. The majority of these trips carry quite large groups and use fast boats that depart from Thap Lamu pier, about

11km southwest of Khao Lak's Nang Thong, 90km north of Phuket town, at about 8.30am and get to the islands in under two hours. They depart the islands at around 3pm. Companies offering this service, all of which offer pick-ups in Khao Lak and Phuket, include Seastar (☎076 485595, ⓦseastarandaman.net) and Green Andaman Travel (☎076 485598, ⓦgreenandamantravel.net), both of which have offices at the Thap Lamu pier; and Khao Lak Land Discovery in Nang Thong (☎076 485411, ⓦkhaolaklanddiscovery.com).

Getting around If travelling independently, you'll need to use Ko Similan longtail boats to travel between the islands and to explore different reefs: prices are fixed and cost around B200 per person one-way.

ACCOMMODATION AND EATING

Limited accommodation is available on **Ko Miang**, in the shape of national park rooms and bungalows (fan B1000, a/c B2000) and tents (B450), and there's a campsite on **Ko Similan** too; both islands also have a restaurant. Accommodation should be booked ahead, either at the

national parks office 500m east of Thap Lamu pier (☎076 453272) or online (ⓦdnp.go.th or ⓦthaiforestbooking.com), as facilities can get crowded with tour groups, especially on weekends and holidays.

Phuket

Thailand's largest island and a province in its own right, **PHUKET** (pronounced "Poo-ket") has been a prosperous region since the nineteenth century, when Chinese merchants got in on its tin-mining and sea-borne trade, before turning to the rubber industry. It remains the wealthiest province in Thailand, with the highest per-capita income, but what mints the money nowadays is **tourism**: with an annual influx of visitors that tops five million, Phuket ranks second in popularity only to Pattaya, and the package-tour traffic – particularly from Russia – has wrought its usual transformations. Thoughtless tourist developments have scarred much of the island, and the trend is upmarket, with few budget possibilities (expect to shell out up to twice what you'd pay on the mainland for accommodation and food, and sometimes more than double for transport, which is a particular headache on Phuket). However, many of the beaches are still strikingly handsome, resort facilities are second to none, and the offshore snorkelling and diving are exceptional. Away from the tourist hubs, many inland neighbourhoods are clustered round the local mosque – 35 percent of Phuketians are **Muslim**, and there are said to be more mosques on the island than Buddhist temples; though the atmosphere is generally as easy-going as elsewhere in Thailand, it's especially important to dress with some modesty outside the main resorts, and not to sunbathe topless on any of the beaches.

Phuket's capital, Muang Phuket, or **Phuket town**, is on the southeast coast, 42km south of the Sarasin Bridge causeway to the mainland. Though it's the most

7

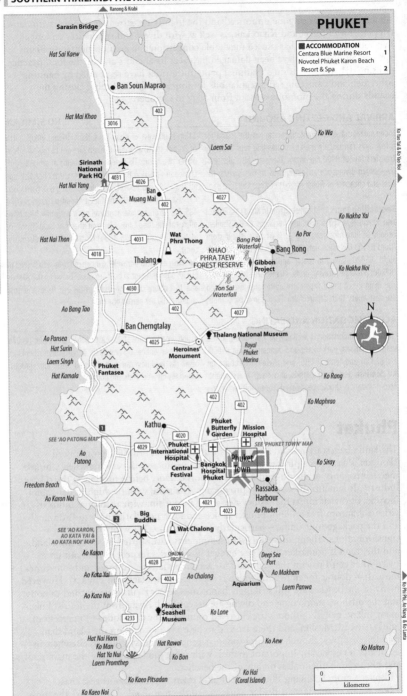

PHUKET DAY-TRIPS AND OTHER ACTIVITIES

Bookings for most of the following **Phuket day-trips and activities** can be made through any tour agent and should include return transport from your hotel (though not for the cooking classes). In addition to the trips listed below, diving is also available (see page 634). Other **sights** worth checking out, especially for kids, include the Phuket Butterfly Garden and Insect World in Phuket town (see page 620), the Aquarium on Laem Panwa (see page 639), the Shell Museum in Rawai (see page 638), the Big Buddha near Chalong (see page 638) and the Gibbon Rehabilitation Project near Thalang (see page 640). Avoid any tour that features Ko Siray (Ko Sireh), the island across the narrow channel from Phuket town, which merely encourages tour-bus passengers to gawp at Phuket's largest and longest-established indigenous *chao ley* community (see page 600).

Bicycle touring Full- and half-day guided mountain-bike rides into Phuket's rural hinterlands and to Ko Yao Noi, as well as multi-day rides around Phang Nga Bay, with Action Holidays Phuket (☎076 263575, ⓦbiketoursthailand. com; full day with transfers from B3200).

Kiteboarding One- (B4000) and three-day courses (B11,000) at Hat Nai Yang and Ao Chalong (depending on the season) are offered by Kiteboarding Asia (☎081 591 4594, ⓦkitephuket.com).

Mini-golf If you just need a little time off from the beach or to entertain kids, head for the eighteen-hole Dino Park mini-golf (daily 10am–midnight; B240; ⓦdinopark. com), next to *Marina Phuket Resort* on the headland between Ao Karon and Ao Kata, which is part of a pseudo-prehistoric theme park comprising a dinosaur restaurant and an erupting "volcano" (evenings only).

Sea-canoeing There are dozens of companies offering canoeing and kayaking in Phuket, but the two with the best reputations are John Gray's Sea Canoe (☎076 254505–7, ⓦjohngray-seacanoe.com), who offer afternoon and evening trips around the spectacular limestone karsts of Ao Phang Nga (B3950 includes transfers), as well as multi-day and self-paddle trips; and Paddle Asia (☎076 241519, ⓦpaddleasia.com), who run day-trips to Ao Phang Nga (B4300 includes transfers) and multi-day trips, which can include Khao Sok National Park and other adventure activities.

Surfing The rainy season (roughly May–Oct) is the best time for surfing off Phuket's west coast; courses (B1500 for a 90min private lesson) and board rental are available from Phuket Surf on Ao Kata Yai (☎087 889 7308, ⓦphuketsurf.com).

Thai cookery courses Most famously, every Sat and Sun morning at *The Boathouse* hotel on Ao Kata Yai (B2200; ☎076 330015, ⓦboathouse-phuket.com); but also at the *Holiday Inn Phuket*, 86/11 Thanon Thavee Wong, Patong (Wed, Sat & Sun 10am; B2575; ☎076 340608, ⓦphuket.holiday-inn.com); and the *Blue Elephant Restaurant*, 96 Thanon Krabi, Phuket town (B2800 for a half-day class; daily 8.30am & 1.30pm; ☎076 354355, ⓦblueelephantcookingschool.com/phuket).

7

culturally stimulating place on Phuket, most visitors pass straight through the town on their way to the **west coast**, where three resorts corner the bulk of the trade: high-rise **Ao Patong**, the most developed and expensive, with an increasingly seedy nightlife; the slightly nicer, if unexceptional, **Ao Karon**; and adjacent **Ao Kata**, the smallest of the trio. If you're after a more peaceful spot, aim for the 17km-long national park beach of **Hat Mai Khao**, its more developed neighbour **Hat Nai Yang**, or one of the smaller alternatives at **Hat Nai Thon** or **Hat Kamala**. Most of the other west-coast beaches are dominated by just a few upmarket hotels, specifically **Hat Nai Harn**, **Ao Pansea** and **Ao Bang Tao**; the southern and eastern beaches are better for seafood than swimming.

As with the rest of the Andaman coast, the sea around Phuket is at its least inviting during the **monsoon**, from June to October, when the west-coast beaches in particular become quite rough and windswept. At any time of year, beware the strong **undertow** and heed any red warning flags; there are dozens of fatalities in the water each year, but there is currently no official lifeguard service on the island. Some stretches of Phuket's coast were very badly damaged by the December 2004 **tsunami** (see page 608), which caused significant loss of life and destroyed a lot of property. Reconstruction was swift, however, and a first-time visitor to the island is now unlikely to notice any major post-tsunami effect.

BY PLANE

Phuket International Airport (📞076 327230–79) is near the northern tip of the island, between Hat Mai Khao and Hat Nai Yang, 32km northwest of Phuket town. It has ATMs, currency exchange, a post office, a Bangkok Hospital clinic, hotel booking and travel agency counters plus a left-luggage service (daily 6am–10pm; B80 per item per day). There are scores of international flights into Phuket, including several direct services from Australia. Between them, Thai Airways, Air Asia, Bangkok Airways, Orient Thai, Thai Lion Air and Nok Air run around thirty domestic flights a day between Bangkok and Phuket, while Bangkok Airways and Air Asia fly from Chiang Mai, Air Asia flies from Udon Thani and Bangkok Airways connects Phuket with Pattaya and Ko Samui.

Onward transport The orange airport bus (📞080 4655666, 🌐airportbusphuket.com; B100; 1hr 20min) runs every 90min to/from the bus station in Phuket town, via Thalang, with an inconvenient 2hr 30min wait after the 4pm bus from the airport and after the 8am bus from the bus station; as it doesn't serve the beaches, you'll need to change on to the songthaews in town to reach those. Travel agents in and outside the arrivals hall run a/c minibuses that seat ten but is it up to passengers to rustle up other people if they wish to share the costs to Phuket town (B1100), Rassada Harbour pier (B1400), Patong (B1400) and Kata (B1600). Outside the arrivals hall at the south end of the building, you'll find booths for set-rate taxis to Phuket town (B450), Patong (B650) and Kata (B750), which includes a B100 airport charge. On departure from the beaches, most people use taxis organized by their hotel – about B500 for the hour's ride from Patong or Karon. If you're landing at the airport and want to catch a bus north, you can save going into Phuket town by getting a taxi or the airport bus to Ban Muang Mai, about 6km southeast of the airport on Highway 402, where you can pick up your northbound bus.

Destinations: Bangkok (30 daily; 1hr 20min); Chiang Mai (3 daily; 2hr); Ko Samui (2–5 daily; 50min); Pattaya/U-Tapao (daily; 1hr 35min); Udon Thani (1 daily; 2hr).

BY BUS AND MINIBUS

A pink songthaew from bay 12 of Bus Station 2 shuttles to/from Bus Station 1 (B10; every 30min until 7pm; 30min).

Bus Station 1 The "old" Baw Khaw Saw bus station, Bus Station 1, is off the eastern end of Thanon Phang Nga in Phuket town. It's a 10min walk or a short tuk-tuk ride to the town's central hotel area. On the west side of the bus station, licensed private companies offer a/c minibuses to Krabi, Ko Lanta, Surat Thani, Nakhon Si Thammarat, Trang and Hat Yai. Songthaews to the beaches depart from here and continue to the market area, so are another option for getting to the Old Town.

Destinations: Khao Lak (20 daily; 2hr 30min); Khao Sok (4 daily; 3–4hr); Takua Pa (20 daily; 2hr 30min–3hr); Phang Nga (at least hourly; 2hr 30min).

Bus Station 2 The "new" Phuket Bus Station 2, 4km north of Phuket town, is now the main station for long-distance destinations, and also has minibuses. Most a/c buses from Bangkok's Southern Bus Terminal to Phuket make the journey overnight, departing from mid-afternoon onwards. There's no train service to Phuket, but you could book an overnight sleeper train to Surat Thani, about 290km east of Phuket, and take one of the regular buses from there to Phuket Bus Station 2 (about 5hr).

Destinations: Bangkok (21 daily; 12hr); Chiang Mai (1 daily; 18hr); Chumphon (4 daily; 5hr); Hat Yai (43 daily; 6hr); Khuraburi (hourly; 3hr); Ko Lanta (8 daily; 6hr); Ko Samui (daily; 6hr); Krabi town (11 daily; 4hr); Nakhon Si Thammarat (17 daily; 6hr); Phang Nga Town (54 daily; 1hr); Ranong (3 daily; 4hr); Satun (8 daily; 6hr); Surat Thani (17 daily; 4hr); Trang (17 daily; 5hr30min).

BY BOAT

If you're coming to/from Phuket from Ko Lanta or Ao Nang in Krabi province, the quickest and most scenic option is to take the boat. Most hotels can arrange trips that include minivan transfers to the harbour. Infrequent songthaews run between Phuket town's Thanon Ranong market and the pier at Bang Rong, via the Heroines' Monument (about 1hr; B50). A taxi to Bang Rong from town or the main beaches costs about B500, from Phuket airport B450, or about B260 if you can cajole the driver into turning his meter on; the taxi service at Bang Rong pier charges B500 to the airport, B800 to Patong.

To/from Ko Phi Phi During peak season, up to three ferries a day, plus a speedboat or two, make the trip to and from Ko Phi Phi, docking at Rassada Harbour on Phuket's east coast; during low season, there's at least one ferry a day in both directions.

To/from Ko Yao Noi Boats from Ko Yao Noi and the high-season speedboat service from Ao Nang via Ko Yao Noi terminate at Bang Rong on Phuket's northeast coast.

To/from Ko Lanta Travellers from Sala Dan on Ko Lanta (Nov–May only) may have to change boats at Ao Nang or Ko Phi Phi to get to Phuket's Rassada Harbour.

To/from Ao Nang Ferries go to Rassada Harbour; the speedboat service from Ao Nang via Ko Yao Noi terminates at Bang Rong.

Onward transport from Rassada Harbour Shared a/c minibuses meet the ferries at Rassada Harbour and charge B50 per person for transfers to Phuket town hotels, B150 to Patong and B200 to the airport; taxis charge B500–600 per car to the major west-coast beaches or the airport (leave plenty of extra time if you have a flight to catch as boats are notoriously tardy).

Onward transport from Bang Rong Infrequent songthaews shuttle between Bang Rong and Phuket town (about 1hr; B40), while taxis charge B500–800 to the airport or the west-coast beaches.

Destinations: Ao Nang (Nov–May 2 daily; 2hr); Ko Lanta Yai (Nov–May several daily; 4hr 30min); Ko Phi Phi Don (several daily; 2hr); Ko Yao Noi (roughly hourly; 40min–1hr 10min).

GETTING AROUND

Getting around the island is a nightmare: on the one hand, tuk-tuks and taxis know that they have a captive audience and charge through the nose; on the other, Phuket has often steep and winding roads, with quite a few hairpin bends – if you do decide to drive yourself, stay alert. There is a system of public songthaews (supplemented by buses) radiating out from Phuket town, but to get from one beach to another by this method you nearly always have to go back into town. For transport within resorts, the cheapest option is to make use of the public songthaews where possible, or to hail a motorbike taxi where available (B30–100).

By songthaew Songthaews run regularly throughout the day (when they have a full complement of passengers) from Thanon Ranong at the market in the centre of Phuket town to the coast and beaches and cost B25–45.

By tuk-tuk or taxi Tuk-tuks and taxis do travel directly between major beaches, but are notoriously overpriced (there are almost no metered taxis on the island), charging at least B150 from Kata to Karon or B300 between Patong and Karon and often doubling their prices after dark – they have been known to ask for B1000 to go from Patong to Karon at night. Phuket TAT (see page 620) issues a list of price guidelines but you'll have to bargain hard to get near the quoted prices.

Motorbike rental Many tourists rent their own motorbike or moped, which are widely available (from B300/day), but be warned that there is a very sobering average of ten thousand motorbike injuries a year on Phuket, and about a hundred fatalities; it makes sense to obey the compulsory helmet law, which is anyway strictly enforced in most areas of Phuket, with flouters subject to a B500 fine.

Car rental At the airport, there are offices of Avis (☏ 02 251 1131/2, ⊛ avisthailand.com) and Budget (☏ 1 800 283 438, ⊛ budget.co.th), who also have a branch on Patong (see page 628); both charge from around B1200/day.

INFORMATION

On the web There's a wide-ranging website about Phuket, ⊛ phuket.com, which is particularly good for discounted accommodation.

Guidebooks For a detailed historical and cultural guide to the island, it's hard to better Oliver Hargreave's impressive *Exploring Phuket & Phi Phi* (Within Books).

Tourist office Phuket's TAT office is in Phuket Town (see page 620) and has a small number of displays with photos on the history of Phuket Town but little else.

DIRECTORY

Dentists At Phuket International Hospital and Bangkok Hospital Phuket (see below).

Hospitals Phuket International Hospital (☏ 076 249400, emergencies ☏ 076 210935, ⊛ phuketinternationalhospital. com), north of Central Festival shopping centre on Highway 402, just west of Phuket town, is considered to have Phuket's best facilities, including an emergency department and an ambulance service. Reputable alternatives include Bangkok Hospital Phuket, on the northwestern edge of Phuket town just off Thanon Yaowarat at 2/1 Thanon Hongyok Uthis (☏ 076 254425, ⊛ phukethospital.com), and the Mission Hospital (aka Phuket Adventist Hospital), on the northern outskirts at 4/1 Thanon Thepkasatri (☏ 076 237220–6, emergencies ☏ 076 237227, ⊛ missionhospitalphuket.com).

Immigration office At the southern end of Thanon Phuket, in the suburb of Saphan Hin, Phuket town (☏ 076 221905, ⊛ phuketimmigration.go.th; Mon–Fri 8.30am–noon & 1–4.30pm), plus an information centre in Patong (see p.629).

Tourist police For all emergencies, contact the tourist police, either on the free, 24hr phone line (☏ 1155), at their main office at 327 Thanon Yaowarat in Phuket town (☏ 076 223891, ⊛ phukettouristpolice.go.th), or at their branch in Patong (see page 631).

Phuket Town

Though it has plenty of hotels and restaurants, **PHUKET TOWN** (Muang Phuket) stands distinct from the tailor-made tourist settlements along the beaches as a place of tangible history and culture. Most visitors hang about just long enough to jump on a beach-bound songthaew, but you may find yourself returning for a welcome dose of real life; there's plenty to engage you in a stroll through the small but atmospherically restored heart of the Old Town, along with many idiosyncratic cafés and art shops, several notable restaurants and some good handicraft shops. The town works well as an overnight transit point between the islands and the bus stations or airport, but is also worth considering as a base for exploring the island, with more interesting and affordable accommodation, eating and drinking options than the beaches, but linked to them by regular songthaews.

The Old Town

Between Thanon Dibuk and Thanon Rat Sada ⓦ lestariheritage.net/phuket

Phuket town's most interesting features are clustered together in the **Old Town** conservation zone, a grid of streets between Thanon Dibuk and Thanon Rat Sada whose colonial-style **Sino-Portuguese shophouses** (see below) date back to the nineteenth century, the former homes of emigrant Chinese merchants from Penang, Singapore and Melaka. Indeed, modern-day residents have put a lot of effort into restoring these handsome old neighbourhoods, and with plenty of mural art, budget traveller accommodation and hip streetside cafés, the Old Town truly resembles the two aforementioned Unesco-protected Malaysian towns. The Phuket Old Town Foundation helps to publish the excellent free

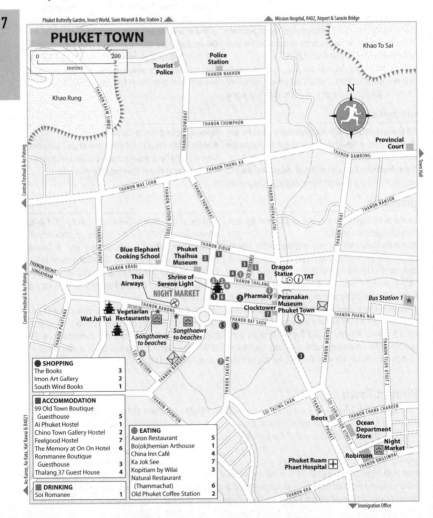

PHUKET TOWN

Phuket Butterfly Garden, Insect World, Siam Niramit & Bus Station 2 ▲

▲ Mission Hospital, R402, Airport & Sarasin Bridge

Khao To Sai

0 — 200
metres

Police Station

Tourist Police

THANON NAKHON

N

Khao Rung

THANON KAEW SIMBU

THANON YAOWARAT

THANON CHUMPHON

Provincial Court

THANON DAMRONG

Town Hall

THANON THUNG KA

THANON MAE LUAN

THANON SATORN (SOI)

THANON YAOWARAJ

THANON THEPKASATTRI

THANON SUTHAT

THANON NANSON

Central Festival & Ao Patong

THANON PATHIPAT

THANON KRABI

Blue Elephant Cooking School

Phuket Thaihua Museum

THANON DIBUK

SOI ROMANEE

Dragon Statue

ⓘ TAT

THANON VICHIT SONGKHRAM

Thai Airways

Shrine of Serene Light

THANON THALANG

Central Festival & Ao Patong

THANON PHATTANA

NIGHT MARKET

THANON RANONG

Wat Jui Tui

Vegetarian Restaurants

Pharmacy

Peranakan Museum
Phuket Town

Bus Station 1 ★

THANON PHANG NGA

Clocktower

Songthaews to beaches

Songthaews to beaches

THANON RAT SADA

THANON MONTRI

THANON TILOK UTHIT 2

SOI PHUTORN

THANON BANGKOK

THANON TAKUA PA

Ao Kamm, Ao Kata, Hat Rawai & R4021

THANON POONPON

SOI TALING CHAN

THANON SOI SIRIN TILOK UTHIT 1

Boots

THANON CHANA CHAROEN

Ocean Department Store

THANON SOI SIRIN TILOK UTHIT 1
THANON PHUKET

Night Market

Phuket Ruam Phaet Hospital ✚

Robinson

THANON ONGSIMPAI

THANON KRA

Immigration Office ▼

● SHOPPING

The Books	3
Imon Art Gallery	2
South Wind Books	1

■ ACCOMMODATION

99 Old Town Boutique Guesthouse	5
Ai Phuket Hostel	1
Chino Town Gallery Hostel	2
Feelgood Hostel	7
The Memory at On On Hotel	6
Rommanee Boutique Guesthouse	3
Thalang 37 Guest House	4

■ DRINKING

| Soi Romanee | 1 |

● EATING

Aaron Restaurant	5
Bo(ok)hemian Arthouse	1
China Inn Café	4
Ka Jok See	7
Kopitiam by Wilai	3
Natural Restaurant (Thammachat)	6
Old Phuket Coffee Station	2

7

PHUKET TOWN SINO-PORTUGUESE ARCHITECTURE

As Chinese immigrant merchants got rich on tin-mining profits they started building homes, the vast majority of which are eminently practical terraced **shophouses** at the heart of the merchant district. Phuket's Old Town retains south Thailand's finest examples, some of which are open to the public, but there are also intact, if less well-conserved, shophouse neighbourhoods in many other southern cities, including Ranong and Takua Pa.

Shophouse design followed a standard prototype favoured by the mixed-race Chinese–Malay ("Baba-Nyonya") and Straits Chinese immigrants from Penang, Melaka and other parts of the Malay Peninsula. It's a style now widely dubbed **Sino-Portuguese** because Melakan architecture of the time was itself strongly influenced by the territory's Portuguese former colonists, though it also incorporates traits from Dutch and Anglo-Indian colonial architecture. Although some features have evolved with changing fashions the basic look is still recognizably mid-nineteenth century.

Because streetside space was at a premium, shophouses were always long and thin, with narrow frontages, recessed entrances and connecting porches that linked up all the way down the block to make shady, arched colonnades known as **five-foot walkways**, ideal to protect pedestrians and shoppers from the tropical sun and rain. The front room was (and often still is) the business premises, leaving the rest of the two- or three-storey building for living. A light well behind the front room encouraged natural ventilation and sometimes fed a small courtyard garden at its base, and the household shrine would always occupy a prominent and auspicious position. Outside, the hallmark features that make the neighbourhoods so striking today include pastel-painted **louvred windows** that might be arched or rectangular and perhaps topped by a pretty glass fantail, lacquered and inlaid wooden doors, fancy gold-leaf fretwork, detailed **stucco mouldings** and perhaps Neoclassical pilasters.

Phuket Town Treasure Map, available all over the Old Town, and also stages the **Old Town Festival** just before Chinese New Year (sometime between Jan & March).

Some of the Old Town's most elegant buildings line the western arm of **Thanon Thalang**, where a dozen signboards – including at *Thalang Guest House* at no. 37 (see page 621) and outside the *China Inn Café* at no. 20 (see page 621) – highlight the special features worth an upward or sideways glance: pastel-coloured doors and shutters, elaborate stucco mouldings, ornate wooden doors, and the distinctively arched "five-foot walkways" that link them. Further east along Thanon Thalang there's more of an Islamic emphasis, with many old-style shops selling fabric and dressmaking accessories, including lots of good-value sarongs from Malaysia and Indonesia. The road's former red-light alley, **Soi Romanee**, has also been given a major multicoloured face-lift and these days buzzes come sundown with arty accommodation options, little bars and red lanterns, while on nearby **Thanon Dibuk** the doors and window shutters of *Dibuk Restaurant* at no. 69 display intricate wooden and gold-leaf fretwork. You'll find other renovated Sino-Portuguese buildings on **Thanon Yaowarat**, and on **Thanon Ranong** (where the Thai Airways office occupies a fine old mansion), **Thanon Phang Nga** (especially the *On On Hotel*) and **Thanon Damrong**, whose town hall, just east of the Provincial Court, stood in for Phnom Penh's US embassy in the film *The Killing Fields*.

Peranakan Museum Phuket Town

Corner of Phang Nga Road and Phuket Road • Tue–Sun 9am–4.30pm • Free • ⓦ peranakan-phuket-museum.business.site/

Phuket Town's latest museum celebrates the islands' links to Peranakan Chinese culture. The experience is quite modest, and there aren't many explanations beyond a short video on the second floor. The collection of textiles and original furniture is pretty impressive though, and the helpful staff are happy to show visitors around.

Phuket Thaihua Museum

28 Thanon Krabi • Daily 9am–5pm • B200 + B200 for cameras • ⓦ phuket.com/attractions/phuket-thai-hua-museum.htm

The **Phuket Thaihua Museum** is housed in a 1930s Neoclassical former school – complete with grand columns, stucco decoration, shuttered windows and

NGAN KIN JEH: THE VEGETARIAN FESTIVAL

For nine days, usually in October or November, at the start of the ninth lunar month (see Ⓦphuketvegetarian.com for exact dates), the celebrations for **Ngan Kin Jeh** – the Vegetarian Festival – set the streets of Phuket town buzzing with processions, theatre shows and food stalls, culminating in the unnerving spectacle of men and women parading about with steel rods pierced through their cheeks and tongues. The festival marks the beginning of **Taoist Lent**, a month-long period of purification observed by devout Chinese all over the world, but celebrated most ostentatiously in Phuket, by devotees of the island's five Chinese temples. After six days' abstention from meat (hence the festival's name), alcohol and sex, the white-clad worshippers flock to their local temple, where drum rhythms help induce a trance state in which they become possessed by spirits. As proof of their new-found transcendence of the physical world they skewer themselves with any available sharp instrument – fishing rods and car wing-mirrors have done service in the past – before walking over red-hot coals or up ladders of swords as further testament to their otherworldliness. In the meantime, there's singing and dancing and almost continuous firework displays, with the grandest festivities held at Wat Jui Tui on Thanon Ranong in Phuket town.

The ceremony dates back to the mid-nineteenth century, when a travelling Chinese opera company turned up on the island to entertain emigrant Chinese working in the tin mines. They had been there almost a year when suddenly the whole troupe – together with a number of the miners – came down with a life-endangering fever. Realizing that they'd neglected their gods, the actors performed elaborate rites and kept to a vegetarian diet, and most were soon cured. The festival has been held ever since, though the self-mortification rites are a later modification, possibly of Hindu origin.

central light well. Some of the old school desks are still *in situ*, but the focus of the museum's excellent displays, videos and historic photos is on the role and traditions of Phuket's main immigrant groups, namely the Chinese and mixed-race Baba-Nyonya (Malay–Chinese) communities who arrived to work in the island's burgeoning tin-mining industry.

San Jao Saeng Tham (Shrine of Serene Light)

Accessed via a soi through the narrow archway next to South Wind Books on Thanon Phang Nga • Daily 8.30am–noon & 1.30–5.30pm

The spiritual heritage of Phuket's Chinese immigrants is kept very much alive by their descendants, notably in the extraordinary spectacle of the annual Vegetarian Festival (see box above). They also maintain many shrines around town, including **San Jao Saeng Tham**, the tiny **Shrine of Serene Light**, whose roof is decorated with intensely coloured ceramic figurines of dragons, carp and sages in bright blues, greens and reds.

Phuket Butterfly Garden and Insect World

2km beyond the northern end of Thanon Yaowarat at 71/6 Soi Paneang in Ban Sam Kong • Daily 9am–5pm • B300 • Ⓣ076 210861, Ⓦphuket.com/attractions/phuket-butterfly-garden.htm • A tuk-tuk from the town centre should cost around B200 return

Kids usually enjoy the **Phuket Butterfly Garden and Insect World**, whose thousands of butterflies of some twenty indigenous species flit around the prettily landscaped grounds; there's also a silk museum documenting the amazingly industrious short life of the silkworm, plus scorpions, tarantulas and other notorious creepy-crawlies.

ARRIVAL AND INFORMATION
PHUKET TOWN

By songthaew Songthaews (supplemented by buses) run regularly throughout the day from the market on Thanon Ranong in the town centre to all the main beaches and cost B25–45. Return songthaews can finish as early as 4pm so check before you go.

Tourist information The TAT office is at 63 Thanon Thalang (daily 8.30am–4.30pm; Ⓣ076 212213, Ⓔtatphket@tat.or.th), and has a small number of displays with photos on the history of Phuket Town and unique souvenirs but little else.

Travel agent The travel desk in the lobby of *The Memory at On On Hotel* on Thanon Phang Nga (Ⓣ076 216161), is a helpful agent, good for all kinds of transport bookings, including cheap boat tickets, as well as activities and day-trips.

ACCOMMODATION

★ **99 Old Town Boutique Guesthouse** 99 Thanon Talang ☏081 797 4311, ⓦ99oldtownguesthouse. com; map p.618. Atmospheric renovation of an original Sino-Portuguese shophouse, which retains original blinds, shutters and wooden partitions, set along lantern-lit corridors paved with crimson and golden tiles. The rooms, all with hanging LED screens and industrial chic en-suite bathrooms, may be a bit small, but the curtained bed-frames and dark-wooden flooring really help preserve the building's heritage. B890

Ai Phuket Hostel 88 88 Thanon Yaowarat ☏076 212881, ⓦaiphukethostel.com; map p.618. Funky and friendly hostel that looks better beyond the reception and tour desk, where dark-wood floorboards lead to two storeys of rooms and a cosy garden. The dorms have no windows but are spotless and come with plush mattress and lockers. The few grey-hued, luminous and attractive doubles are a step up in price but better value. There is free wi-fi and a coin-operated laundry machine for guests. Dorms B250, doubles B900

Chino Town Gallery Hostel Thanon Yaowarat ☏086 941 8783, ⓦchinotownphuket.com; map p.618. A very good budget option with a spacious dark wooden floored a/c dorm filled with single beds, each with individual reading lights and electric sockets, and a few compact yet surprisingly smart rooms (some en-suite) with Peranakan Chinese motifs on the floor tiles. Dorms B200, doubles B590

Feelgood Hostel 92 Thanon Phang Nga ☏095 4273846, ⓦfeelgoodhostel.com; map p.618. As the name suggests, this hostel has a friendly atmosphere, tempting travellers to stay longer than planned. The spotless dorms have two rows of bunkbeds with privacy curtains and are set in a spacious wooden-floored loft. Potted plants spruce up the industrial chic shared bathrooms. There's free wi-fi and coffee too; even a simple breakfast is included in the price. Couples can stay in the one en-suite private room (B800). B280

The Memory at On On Hotel 19 Thanon Phang Nga ☏076 363700, ⓦthememoryhotel.com; map p.618. This stunningly renovated, colonial-style 1920s building no longer caters to budget travellers, but it's still a very atmospheric option to enjoy the Old Town's heritage charms. The doubles have a/c and en suite bathrooms, plus there's a tour agent on site. B1600

Rommanee Boutique Guesthouse 15 Soi Rommanee T089 7289871, ⓦtherommanee.com/rommaneeboutique/; map p.618. Artistic flourishes abound in the seven rooms, which feel more luxurious than their price tag may suggest. Rustic mirrors, designer furniture, high ceilings and plush bedding make for a comfortable stay in this renovated 80-year-old building. All come with en suite, a/c and a simple breakfast. The café downstairs has international brews (from B55), home-made pastries, and is a relaxed spot to mingle with other travellers. B1200

Thalang 37 Guest House 37 Thanon Thalang ☏076 214225, ⓦfacebook.com/thalangguesthouse37; map p.618. Housed in a 1940s, Sino-Portuguese, wood-floored shophouse in one of the Old Town's most attractive streets, this place is fairly simple but full of character, traveller-friendly and good value. The twelve fan and a/c rooms are large and en suite – the best of them are up on the rooftop, affording unusual panoramic views. It's very popular, so it's best to book ahead; rates include a simple breakfast. Fan B400, a/c B500

EATING

Phuket town has the largest concentration of good Thai food on the island, well worth making the trip here for. Unlike Thais in most other parts of the country, Phuketians like to breakfast on noodles rather than rice; spindly white *khanom jiin* noodles, made with rice-flour and ladled over with one of several different fiery, soupy curry sauces, are a local speciality and served at some of the restaurants listed below. You can try snacks such as fresh hot tofu and sticky rice at the night market, which starts by the beach songthaews on Thanon Ranong. Over half a dozen simple Thai vegetarian restaurants display tasty look-and-pick mock-meat curries and cold veg dishes with rice for B30–60 on Thanon Ranong and Soi Puthorn, west of Wat Jui Tui. They are open from the early morning till nearly midnight.

Aaron Restaurant Thanon Talang, ☏098 016 6562; map p.618. This hole-in-the-wall coffee shop dishes up delicious Malay-style *rotis*, pulled and baked to perfection on a metal table right before your eyes. They also have beef soup and authentic *khaoyam pattani* (a tossed rice salad with fresh vegetables, typical of south Thailand). A meal will set you back about B100. Daily 6.30am–5pm

Bo(ok)hemian Arthouse 61 Thanon Thalang, ☏096 524223; map p.618. Artsy little bookstore and hangout for cappuccinos (B60), free wi-fi, DVD rental and occasional film screenings. Mon–Fri 9am–7pm, Sat & Sun 9am–8.30pm.

China Inn Café 20 Thanon Thalang ☏081 979 8258, ⓦfacebook.com/chinainnphuket; map p.618. This beautifully renovated heritage house and courtyard garden would be reason enough to stop by for a meal, but the menu is also enticing, proffering Thai dishes such as *phat thai* (B210) and spicy salads like the inspired pomelo, coconut and prawn (B290), as well as a few Western, mostly Italian, dishes. Streetside, the gallery shop displays Asian antiques, textiles and lacquerware. Tue–Sun 10.30am–6.30pm, closed Mondays.

Ka Jok See 26 Thanon Takuapa ☏076 217903; map p.618. A Phuket institution, housed in a charmingly

7

7

restored traditional shophouse (unsigned), this place serves fabulous Thai food on a pricey set menu (B2000) and fosters a fun, sociable atmosphere – after meals, tables are literally set against the walls by the staff, who attempt to coax everyone into dancing. Mains are sophisticated and beautifully presented – their *goong sarong*, individual shrimps bound in a crisp-noodle wrap, is famous island-wide. Reservations are essential. Daily 7.30pm–late.

Kopitiam by Wilai 14 & 18 Thanon Thalang ☎ 83 6069776; map p.618. Eating at the dark-wood tables while surrounded by vintage Chinese scrolls and typewriters can transport you into the rustic world of old Phuket Town. The extensive Thai menu includes Phuket-style grilled pork with Chinese herbs (B125), and even Peranakan Chinese *hokkien mee* and *bak kut the* (B130); be sure to try the delicious passionfruit juice (B50). Mon–Sat 11am–10pm.

★ **Natural Restaurant (Thammachat)** 62/5 Soi Putorn ☎076 224287, ☻naturalrestaurantphuket.com; map p.618. There are plenty of reasons to linger over a casual dinner at this rambling, hugely popular restaurant, not least the two hundred different choices on the menu, and the affordable prices (main dishes around B150). Highlights include fried sea bass with chilli paste, fried chicken with Muslim herbs, soft-shelled crab with garlic and pepper, and spicy Phuket bean salad. Daily 10.30am–11.30pm.

Old Phuket Coffee Station 72/1 Thanon Yaowarat, ☎099 475 6846; map p.618. Hip bistro in an old mansion, all furnished in Old World style, including an impressive wall of vintage radios and assorted memorabilia that fills up every corner. The coffee (B60) is good and they also serve staple Thai fried-rice and noodle dishes (from B130). Daily 9am–8pm.

DRINKING

Soi Romanee map p.618. This artfully restored, plant-strewn soi connecting Dibuk and Thalang roads shows off its handsome pastel paintwork and stuccoed Old Town facades with half a dozen little café-bars whose seating spills out on to the pavement for ultimate architectural appreciation. Try *Glasnost* for live music, particularly jazz, and its bohemian atmosphere. Most places serve classic Thai dishes and beers and get going 6–10pm, staying open slightly later Nov–April.

ENTERTAINMENT

Siam Niramit Phuket North of town off Thanon Chalerm Prakiat ☎076 335000, ☻siamniramit.com. An offshoot of the Siam Niramit Bangkok extravaganza, this 70min show presents a tourist-oriented rendering of traditional Thai theatre, in a high-tech spectacular of fantastic costumes and huge chorus numbers, enlivened by acrobatics and flashy special effects. Tickets from B1500. Mon & Wed–Sun 8.30pm.

SHOPPING

The two most fruitful shopping roads for handicrafts and antiques are Thanon Yaowarat and Thanon Rat Sada, while the shops on eastern Thanon Thalang keep a phenomenal range of well-priced sarongs, mostly of Burmese, Malaysian and Indonesian designs. *Art and Culture South*, a useful, free, quarterly booklet that's available at TAT and other outlets, details shops and galleries in the town and around. For retro enamelware and gifts, visit the shop attached to the *Rommanee Classic* hotel.

The Books Thanon Phuket; map p.618. Decent selection of new English-language books and magazines, with a coffee corner and internet access. Daily 10am–9pm.

Imon Art Gallery Thanon Phang Nga, ☎086 961 8968 ☻bit.ly/2Bvmgth; map p.618. An impressive collection of woodcut prints and arty postcards by local artist Monthian. Daily 9am–7.30pm.

South Wind Books Thanon Phang Nga, ☎089 724 2136; map p.618. Big, sprawling range of secondhand books. Mon–Sat 9am–5pm, Sun 10am–3pm.

Hat Mai Khao

Phuket's longest and quietest beach, the 17km **HAT MAI KHAO**, unfurls along the island's upper northwest coast, beginning some 3km south of the Sarasin Bridge causeway and ending just north of the airport (34km from Phuket town). It's a beautiful piece of casuarina- and palm-shaded coastline, minimally developed and protected in part as **Sirinath National Park** because of the few giant marine turtles that lay their eggs here between October and February.

ARRIVAL AND DEPARTURE   HAT MAI KHAO

It's possible to get here on foot via the adjacent beaches; otherwise, the beach is reachable with your own transport

or a taxi, which is the most practical way.

ACCOMMODATION

Accommodation on Hat Mai Khao is predominantly five-star: an enclave of half a dozen luxury hotels is elegantly spaced behind the sloping shoreline towards the north end of the beach, accessed by an all-but-private road that is not served by any public transport. Most of the resorts have a swimming pool as the undertow here can be fierce and unpredictable.

★ **Anantara Phuket Villas** ☎076 336100–9, ⓦphuket.anantara.com. Set amid stylishly landscaped grounds and lagoons, all the secluded villas here have their own plunge pool, outdoor bath and garden *sala*, while the luxurious interiors feature antique furniture, lots of dark wood, dressing rooms and espresso machines. There's an impressive selection of free activities, including sailing and yoga, a kids' club, a beautiful spa and excellent seafood at the stylish restaurant, *Sea Fire Salt*. Rates are sometimes reduced by more than half in low season; check the website for regular promotions. B15,500

Mai Khao Beach Bungalows Next door to the Holiday Inn ☎081 895 1233, ⓦmaikhaobeach.wordpress. com. Six simple en-suite bungalows sit in spacious, grassy grounds just behind the shore beneath coconut palms hung with hammocks. There's a restaurant and motorbike rental here too, but not much else. Easiest access to *Mai Khao Beach Bungalows* is by bus to or from Phuket town: ask to be dropped at Thachatchai police box, 4km away on Highway 402, from where you can phone the bungalows for a pick-up. Closed Augest, sometimes longer, during the rainy season; you have to pay more for hot water. Fan B1000, a/c B1500

Sala Phuket ☎076 338888, ⓦsalahospitality.com/ phuket. The sharp, Sino-modern architecture of the villa compounds here – all done out in cool creams and silver, with colour-coordinated planting and the occasional lacquered screen – attract mainly couples, especially honeymooners, who enjoy the style and privacy, especially of the pool villas. There's an enticing open-air seafront lounging area here too, with deliciously squishy sofas, plus a rooftop terrace, a spa and three swimming pools. Breakfast included. B10,000

Hat Nai Yang

The long, curved sweep of **HAT NAI YANG**, 5km south of Hat Mai Khao and 30km north of Phuket town, is partly under the protection of Sirinath National Park and has only fairly low-key development. In the plentiful shade cast by the feathery casuarinas and cajeput trees that run most of the length of the bay stand more than a dozen small seafood restaurants, and a small, low-rise tourist village of travel agents, a few accommodation options, ATMs, a massage pavilion, internet and dive shops. The beach is clean and good for swimming at the southern end, and there's a reasonable, shallow **reef** about 1km offshore (10min by longtail boat) from the Sirinath National Park headquarters, which is a fifteen-minute walk north of the tourist village (if you're driving yourself to Hat Nai Yang, when the main access road hits the beach, turn left for the tourist village, right for the national park).

ARRIVAL AND DEPARTURE   HAT NAI YANG

By taxi Hat Nai Yang is just 2km south of the airport, about B200 by taxi.

By songthaew An infrequent songthaew service (B40; 1hr 45min) runs between Phuket town and Hat Nai Yang.

ACCOMMODATION

Discovery Beach Resort ☎081 6939359, ✉discovery-phuket@hotmail.com. Set inside a beachfront mansion that doesn't look too attractive from the roadside, the spacious en-suite rooms here have wooden floors, a/c, TV and most importantly, are right on the beach, behind a line of trees. The family rooms for four people (B2200) are great value for this area. B1500

The Slate ☎ 076 327006, ⓦtheslatephuket.com. Luxurious rooms and villas look onto attractively landscaped plantation-style gardens that run down to the southern end of the beachfront road; facilities include a meandering lagoon-like saltwater swimming pool, a dive shop, an inventively programmed activities centre, a spa and a kids' club. Interiors are designed to evoke Phuket's tin-mining history, with metallic colour schemes, polished cement floors and a penchant for industrial art, but the look is softened by very comfortable furniture, generous balconies and plenty of greenery. B10,000

EATING

The tourist village in Nai Yang is locally famous for its small shorefront restaurants that serve mostly barbecued seafood (and the odd wood-fired pizza), on mats under the trees and at tables on the sand, which are candlelit and exceptionally tranquil at night.

The Beach Restaurant On the northern end of the

beach ☎088 7612310, ✉kio.thebeach@gmail.com. One of several little beach bars in the tourist village, that besides being a cool, relaxed place for a drink in its low-slung track-side chairs on the beach, has a good selection of Thai rice and noodle curries (from B170). Happy hour(s) between 3–5pm & 10–11pm. Daily noon–1am.

Black Ginger The Slate ☎076 327006, ⊕facebook. com/BlackGingerRestaurant. For a really top-notch romantic dinner, you can't beat the intimate, black-painted, award-winning *sala* here, accessible only by boat. Highlights from the classy menu (from B300) include the Phuket lobster with red coconut curry, fresh Vietnamese-style rice flour pancakes stuffed with shrimps, coriander and other herbs, and local *kaeng leuang* (yellow curry with fish fillet; B900). Reservations advisable. Daily 6.30–11pm.

Hat Nai Thon

The next bay south down the coast from Hat Nai Yang is the small but perfectly formed 500m-long gold-sand **HAT NAI THON**, backed by pristine viridian hills and with good snorkelling at reefs a short longtail ride offshore. Shops, hotels and restaurants line the inland side of its narrow little shorefront road, but there's still a low-key, village-like atmosphere here. 1km up the hill, along road 4018 is the turn off to **BANANA BEACH**, a secluded cove accessible only by foot, that sees few visitors despite its stunning location at the bottom of a viridian slope.

ARRIVAL AND DEPARTURE   HAT NAI THON

Most visitors rent their own transport as songthaews don't make the detour from the highway and taxis are thin on the ground.

ACCOMMODATION

Andaman White Beach Resort About 2km south of Hat Nai Thon over the southern headland ☎076 316300, ⊕andamanwhitebeach.com. Occupying secluded cliff-side land that runs down to a gorgeous little private bay of white sand and turquoise water (sometimes known as Hat Nai Thon Noia), this resort offers luxurious rooms and villas with unsurpassed views, including some designed for families, plus a 40m swimming pool and a spa. B7200

Naithonburi Beach Resort ☎076 318700, ⊕naithonburi.com. Huge resort, with over two hundred posh a/c rooms in a U-shaped complex enclosing an enormous pool, some of them with direct pool access, though it doesn't dominate the bay. B2800

EATING

Tycoon Ting Across the road from the northern end of the beach ☎076 602286. High-class, industrial chic glass and concrete restaurant with a *sala* filled with white furniture, at affordable prices. It's a perfect option for wine and cocktails, or Western-Thai fusion dishes, including fried minced pork with fish cake (B200), pastas (from B220) and stir-fried chicken with cashew nut (B190). Daily 11am–11pm.

Ao Bang Tao

Re-landscaped from a former tin-mining concession to encompass lagoons, parkland and Phuket's best eighteen-hole golf course, **AO BANG TAO** is dominated by the vast, upscale *Laguna Phuket*, a gated "integrated resort" of seven luxury hotels on an impressive 8km shorefront. It's a world away from the thrust and hustle of Patong and a popular choice for families, with no need to leave the *Laguna* village, though beware of the undertow off the coast here, which confines many guests to the hotel pools. There's free transport between the seven hotels, which between them offer a huge range of leisure and sports facilities, as well as a shopping centre.

ARRIVAL AND ACCOMMODATION   AO BANG TAO

Half-hourly **songthaews** (B25; 1hr 15min) cover the 24km from Phuket town to Ao Bang Tao during the day, or there are resort shuttle **buses** and on-site **car** rental.

Laguna Phuket ☎076 362300, ⊕lagunaphuket. com. The main website sometimes has discounted rates at *Laguna*'s seven hotels, while the family-oriented

Best Western Allamanda Laguna (📞076 324050, 📧allamandaphuket.com), comprising 150 apartment-style suites with kitchenette and separate living area, has the cheapest rates in the complex. Haunt of high society and sports stars, the exclusive *Banyan Tree Phuket* (📞076 372400, 🌐banyantree.com/en/thailand/phuket) offers lavish villas in private gardens, many with private pools, and the gloriously indulgent, award-winning, Banyan Tree spa. Best Western B6000, Banyan Tree B21,930

Hat Surin and Ao Pansea

South around Laem Son headland from Ao Bang Tao, handsome little **HAT SURIN** is a favourite weekend getaway for sophisticated Phuketians and a big draw for expats, who inhabit the ever-expanding forest of condo developments inland from the small, pretty beach. The shorefront gets very crowded, however, packed with sunloungers and beach restaurants, so it can be hard to appreciate the setting. Eating and shopping facilities cater to the upmarket clientele, and beachfront dining and drinking is the main pastime. Things are much quieter on Hat Surin's northern bay, **AO PANSEA**, which is divided from the main beach by a rocky promontory.

ARRIVAL AND DEPARTURE HAT SURIN AND AO PANSEA

By songthaew Songthaews travel the 24km between Phuket town and Hat Surin approximately every half-hour during the day and cost B35.

ACCOMMODATION

Benyada Lodge 103 Thanon Hat Surin 📞076 271261, 🌐benyadalodge-phuket.com. Just across the small park from the beach, this thirty-room lodge with high standards of service is well maintained in a crisp, bright contemporary style, with the addition of a rooftop pool and bar-restaurant. The spacious a/c rooms all have hot showers, TV and fridge. Breakfast included. B2800

EATING

Taste 📞087 886 6401, 🌐tastebargrill.com. This sophisticated seafront restaurant is known for its great seafood, such as steamed red snapper fillet with a lemon and butter sauce (B490), but also serves international mains, from Italian gorgonzola-garnished flatbreads (B225) to Mexican tostadas (B345). Tues–Sun 3.30pm–midnight.

Twin Brothers 📞089 7231874, 🌐bit.ly/2zqjSlt. The eponymous local twins pair a spectacular location under the palm trees on the sand with down-to-earth prices for their Thai seafood dishes (white snapper B100/100g) and Western food. Daily 8am–10pm.

Hat Kamala and Laem Singh

With its cheerfully painted houses and absence of high-rises, the small, village-like tourist development at **HAT KAMALA** is low-key and mid-market, sandwiched between the beach and the predominantly Muslim town of Ban Kamala, about 300m west of the main Patong–Surin road, 6km north of Patong and 26km northwest of Phuket town. Accommodation, shops, restaurants and other tourist services are mostly clustered either side of shoreside Thanon Rim Had (also spelt Rim Hat) which, despite its limited choice, is a much pleasanter place to browse than the big resorts. The beach gets prettier and quieter the further north you go, away from Thanon Rim Had, with restaurant shacks renting sunloungers along most of its course. A stretch of this area is backed by the Muslim cemetery, so it's particularly important to respect local sensibilities and avoid going topless.

Kamala was very badly hit by the 2004 **tsunami**, which killed many residents and wiped out the beachfront school, the temple and countless homes and businesses. Though extensive rebuilding has extinguished most of the physical scars, a copper sculpture in the park opposite *Print Kamala* bears witness to the devastation, and a volunteer English-teaching programme at the school, Phuket Has Been Good to Us (see page 70), aims to continue rebuilding some of the young lives affected.

About 1km northeast of Hat Kamala, a couple of steep paths lead west off the main Patong–Surin road down to **Laem Singh** cape, a pretty little sandy cove whose picturesque combination of turquoise water and smooth granite boulders makes it one of Phuket's finest. It's good for swimming and very secluded, plus there's a decent patch of shade throughout the day.

ARRIVAL AND DEPARTURE HAT KAMALA AND LAEM SINGH

By songthaew The cheapest way to get to Hat Kamala is by songthaew from Phuket town (about every 30min during the day, 1hr 15min; B40).

ACCOMMODATION

Hat Kamala is popular with long-stay tourists, and several hotels offer rooms with kitchenettes; there's also a preponderance of small-scale places.

Baan Kamala Fantasea Hostel On the soi parallel to the beachside road, ☎076 279053, ⓦbaankamalaphuket.com. It would be a mistake to dismiss this guesthouse for its tacky nautical theme, which is visible from the street. But get past the boat-shaped reception desk and bar, through charming pastel-coloured corridors dotted with potted plants and both the dorms and doubles will prove to be some of the best value in the area. Dorms have plush beds and sparkling clean common bathrooms, while the more expensive private rooms (some with little balconies and all en suite) are much better equipped than you might think for the price. Dorms B450, Doubles B2000

Benjamin Resort 83 Thanon Rim Had, opposite the school at the southerly end of the beachfront road ☎084 1906848, ✉benjaminresort@hotmail.com. Set right on the beach and about the cheapest deal in Kamala, this block of 37 a/c rooms has seen better days but couldn't be closer to the sea. Although views are obstructed from all but the most expensive rooms (B800), the spacious interiors are almost identical and all have a balcony, fridge, TV and hot water. There's no wi-fi and breakfast is an additional B99. B500

Kamala Dreams 74/1 Thanon Rim Had ☎076 279131, ⓦkamalabeach.net. Epitomising all the best things about Kamala, this is a really nice, small hotel set right on the shore, in the middle of the tourist village and above its annexed seafood restaurant. Its eighteen rooms are large and furnished in contemporary style, and all have a/c, TVs, a kitchenette and a large balcony overlooking the pool and the sea. B2300

★ **Layalina** 75 Thanon Kamala ☎076 385944, ⓦlayalinahotel.com. This gem of a mid-range hotel has breezy wooden partitions and a beachfront café. A central staircase gives way to two floors of large rooms that use their wooden fittings to great effect. The en-suite bathrooms have Jacuzzi-style bathtubs, and the large windows on the ground floor give access to a small yet pretty sea-facing swimming pool. There's also a private sunbathing deck on the rooftop; breakfast is included. B4000

Swissotel Resort Phuket Kamala North of Kamala beach, on the way to Hat Surin ☎076 303000, ⓦswissotel.com/phuket. Attractive mini apartment-style rooms in several concrete blocks shaded by tall palm trees, all set around the resort's centrepiece: an attractive, huge swimming pool with its own water slide and wooden bridges connecting the different wings. The poolside bar plays techno tunes well into the night. Continental buffet breakfast included. B4275

EATING, DRINKING AND ENTERTAINMENT

Most people eat and drink on the beach, especially at the restaurant shacks and bars that pretty much line the shore all the way north from opposite *Print Kamala*; seafood is the big seller here, and you can bury your feet in the sand.

Le Café Lafayette On the soi parallel to the beachside road, ☎099 4017017, ⓦfacebook.com/lafayettefrenchbakery. Cosy industrial chic building that opens onto an inner courtyard filled with potted plants, offering a quiet break from the hustle and bustle of the beachfront. Coffees (from B70) are strong, the fresh-fruit smoothies (B130) refreshing, whilst the eclectic cakes (such as delicious Mango Charlotte, B120) attract plenty of expats and European tourists looking to step back into their comfort zones. Daily 7.30am–7.30pm.

Duck Spicy Thanon Kamala near corner with Thanon Rim Had. Spicy really means spicy here, so be careful what you ask for from the extensive, authentic Thai menu. The place itself is not fancy, but it makes a welcome dose of reality to eat dishes such as duck and mint salad (B120) with the locals, away from the resorts. Daily 8am–10pm.

Phuket FantaSea About 1km northeast of Hat Kamala off the main Patong–Surin road ☎076 385111, ⓦphuket-fantasea.com. The enjoyable, hi-tech mega-spectacular, "Fantasy of a Kingdom, Cultural Illusion Show", is staged at the enormous FantaSea entertainments complex, featuring seventy minutes of high-wire trapeze acts, acrobatics, pyrotechnics, illusionists, comedy and traditional dance – plus a depressing baby elephant circus. B1800 or B2200 including the unexciting pre-show dinner. Mon–Wed & Fri–Sun 9pm.

7

Ao Patong

The busiest and most popular of all Phuket's beaches, **AO PATONG** – 5km south of Ao Kamala and 15km west of Phuket town – is vastly overdeveloped and hard to recommend. A congestion of high-rise hotels, tour agents and souvenir shops disfigures the beachfront road, tireless and tiresome touts are everywhere, and hostess bars and strip joints dominate the nightlife, attracting an increasing number of single Western men to the most active scene between Bangkok and Hat Yai. On the plus side, the broad, 3km-long beach offers good sand and plenty of shade beneath the parasols and there are hundreds of shops and bars plus a surprising number of good restaurants to keep you busy after dark.

ARRIVAL AND GETTING AROUND

By songthaew Songthaews from Phuket town (approx every 15min, 6am–6pm; 30min; B30) approach Patong from the northeast, driving south along one-way Thanon Raja Uthit Song Roi Phi (Thanon Raja Uthit 200 Phi) then circling back north along beachfront Thanon Thavee Wong (also one-way) via the *Patong Merlin*, where they wait to pick up passengers for the return trip.

Vehicle rental National car rental (☎076 340608, ⓦnationalcarthailand.com) has a desk inside the *Holiday*

Inn, the local Budget agent is at the nearby *Patong Merlin* (☎076 292389, ⓦbudget.co.th); beware of renting jeeps and motorbikes from transport touts on Thanon Thavee Wong as scams abound.

Tours and activities Most of the tour agents have offices on the southern stretch of Thanon Thavee Wong, offering a number of day-trips and activities (see box, p.618); this is also where you'll find many of the dive operators (see box, pp.636–637).

ACCOMMODATION

Regardless of its seediness, Patong offers something for every budget. Overall, upper-end hotels are reasonable value.

The Album 29 Thanon Sawatdirak ☎076 297023, ⓦthealbumhotel.com; map p.629. Tiny urban-chic boutique inn, where the 22 carefully designed a/c rooms all have a flat-screen TV, DVD player and a petite balcony. There's a small Jacuzzi pool on the fourth-floor roof terrace; rates include continental breakfast and high tea. Discounts of up to fifty percent are available online. B6000

Bearpacker 140 Thanon Thavee Wong ☎076 685118, ⓔbearpackerhostel@gmail.com; map p.629. Four-storey backpacker hostel, decorated with blue-and-white cartoonish bears and packed to the gills. Featuring sparkling clean a/c dorms with plush bedding, reading lights and individual lockers (bring your own padlock, or pay B50). Also has a rooftop restaurant with a tiny Jacuzzi pool. Free coffee and tea is served from 8 to 10am. B500

★**Centara Blue Marine Resort and Spa** 290/1 Prabaramee Road ☎076 370400, ⓦcentarahotels resorts.com/centara/cmp/; map p.629. Dominating the hillside just north of Ao Patong, this Thai chain hotel retains all the quiet and calm the beach is missing. Most rooms are in concrete blocks facing the bay. There's an Olympic-size swimming pool, and the inclusive continental breakfast is above average. Free shuttles transfer guests to Patong Beach several times a day. B4452

Hemingway's 179/95–8 Soi Saen Sabai ☎076 540895, ⓦpatonghemingways.com; map p.629. Smart, modern, a/c rooms done out in dark wood, black and red, with small, hot-water bathrooms, TVs and fridges. Wicker chairs and old-

fashioned ceiling fans downstairs are all that conjure up the ghost of Ernest Hemingway, but the big plus-point of this place is the small rooftop pool, Jacuzzi and bar with views of the surrounding hills. Breakfast is B200 extra. B1800

Holiday Inn Phuket 52 Thanon Thavee Wong ☎076 370200, ⓦphuket.holidayinnresorts.com; map p.629. Well-run, innovative, upmarket chain hotel that offers smart, contemporary rooms just across the road from the beach, and fosters an informal, unpretentious atmosphere. The poshest Busakorn villa rooms have their own interconnected pools and there are several restaurants and an interesting programme of daily activities. The hotel makes a big effort to be family-friendly, with special suites for children, an all-day kids' club and a teens' club and two children's pools. Also offers wheelchair-accessible rooms. Breakfast included. B4788

Lupta Hostel 138 Thanon Thavee Wong, across the road from Rip Curl's shop ☎076 602462, ⓦluptahostel.com; map p.629. Attractive apartment that has been converted into a chic hostel with a common area filled with beanbags, four- and eight-person dorms with plush bedding, privacy curtains, and one room for three people (B1200). The shared toilets are squeaky clean and there's a washing machine for guests' use. Free wi-fi and flow of hot drinks provided. B450

Novotel Phuket Resort Thanon Phra Barami/Thanon Hat Kalim ☎076 342777, ⓦnovotelphuket.com; map p.629. Luxurious and relaxing chain hotel built on the hillside above Kalim Bay, the quieter, northern end of the resort, a 10min walk or a free shuttle ride to Patong's main beach and shops, but very close to some of the best restaurants. Occupying sloping landscaped tropical gardens

and offering exceptional high-level sea views, it's especially popular with families as it offers heaps of activities plus a multi-level swimming pool. Large discounts online. **B5270**
Seahorse Guesthouse 189/7 Rat U Thit 200 Pee Road ☎091 826 1817, ⓦseahorsephuket.com; map p.629. Sociable hostel tucked away in a quiet soi, yet not far from

Thanon Bangla's action and the beach. Dorms and shared bathrooms are functional and clean, there's motorbike rental (B350/day); a simple toast and coffee breakfast is B50 extra. The few private doubles have en-suite toilets and small balconies. Dorms **B250** Doubles **B1000**
Shamrock Park Inn Above The Deli supermarket, 31

7

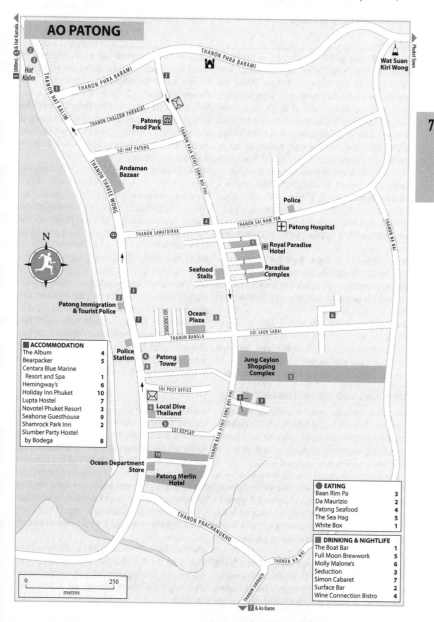

AO PATONG

Wat Suan Kiri Wong

Patong Food Park

Andaman Bazaar

Police

Patong Hospital

Royal Paradise Hotel

Seafood Stalls

Paradise Complex

Patong Immigration & Tourist Police

Ocean Plaza

Police Station

Patong Tower

Jung Ceylon Shopping Complex

Local Dive Thailand

Ocean Department Store

Patong Merlin Hotel

THANON PHRA BARAMI
THANON HAT KALIM
THANON CHALERM PHRAKIAT
SOI HAT PATONG
THANON THAVEE WONG
THANON SAWATDIRAK
THANON SAI NAM YEN
THANON RAJA U THIT SONG ROI PHI
THANON BANGLA
SOI SAEN SABAI
SOI POST OFFICE
SOI KEPSAP
SOI CROCODILE
THANON PRACHANUKHO
THANON NA NAI
THANON SIRIRACH

N

ACCOMMODATION
The Album	4
Bearpacker	5
Centara Blue Marine Resort and Spa	1
Hemingway's	6
Holiday Inn Phuket	10
Lupta Hostel	7
Novotel Phuket Resort	3
Seahorse Guesthouse	9
Shamrock Park Inn	2
Slumber Party Hostel by Bodega	8

EATING
Baan Rim Pa	3
Da Maurizio	2
Patong Seafood	4
The Sea Hag	5
White Box	1

DRINKING & NIGHTLIFE
The Boat Bar	1
Full Moon Brewwork	5
Molly Malone's	6
Seduction	3
Simon Cabaret	7
Surface Bar	2
Wine Connection Bistro	4

0   250
metres

& Ao Karon

Thanon Raja Uthit Song Roi Phi ☎076 340991; map p.629. Friendly, good-value three-storey hotel at the northern end of the resort with large, pleasant, well-maintained and cheerily painted a/c rooms, all with TVs, fridges and safety boxes. Ask for a room on the north side of the building: they're cooler, have balconies and are away from the noise of the adjacent Irish bar. B800

Slumber Party Hostel by Bodega 189/3 Rat U Thit 200

Pee Road ☎076 602 191, ⓦslumberpartyhostels.com/locations/phuket; map p.629. With a hall that looks like the entrance of a fraternity house and a name that says it all, this is the perfect place for the young party crowd. Beside pub crawls and plenty of social activities, the dorm rooms, each with their own en-suite bathroom, are sparkling clean and equipped with everything today's backpacker has come to expect. Dorms B500

EATING

Much of the food on Patong is dire, but in among the disastrous little cafés advertising everything from Hungarian to Swedish "home cooking" you'll find a few genuinely reputable, long-running, upmarket favourites; reservations are recommended at all the places listed here. For well-priced Thai fast food, there are the regional speciality stalls at the *Food Haven* food centre in Jung Ceylon, the *Patong Food Park* night market that sets up around 5pm towards the northern end of Thanon Raja Uthit Song Roi Phi, and the row of seafood stall-restaurants further south, opposite the *Royal Paradise Hotel* complex.

★ **Baan Rim Pa** Across from the Novotel on Thanon Hat Kalim ☎076 340789, ⓦbaanrimpa.com; map p.629. One of Phuket's most famous fine-dining restaurants, this is an elegant spot that's beautifully set in a teak building on a clifftop overlooking the bay, with tables also on its sea-view terrace. Known for its classic "Royal Thai" cuisine (mains from about B350), including banana blossom salad, creamy duck curry and fried tiger prawns with tamarind sauce, as well as for its wine cellar. Live jazz every night in the *Piano Bar*. Daily noon–midnight.

Da Maurizio Across from the Novotel on Thanon Hat Kalim ☎076 344079, ⓦbaanrimpa.com/italian-restaurant; map p.629. Superior Italian restaurant in a stunning location set over the rocks beside the sea. Serves authentic antipasti and home-made pasta such as

pappardelle with scallops and crab in a spicy tomato sauce, Phuket lobsters and other great seafood, and a good wine list. Main dishes from B450. Daily noon–midnight.

Patong Seafood 98/2 Thanon Thavee Wong ☎081 691 5298; map p.629. Established Thai restaurant on the main beach strip, decked out in wood and specialising in seafood and Western staples. The prices are pretty good for the location: Thai noodles start at B150, pastas at B220, and seafood goes by the kilo. Daily 11am–midnight.

★ **The Sea Hag** Down Soi Dr Wattana (Soi Permpong 3), on the southern side of Patong Beach ☎076 341111, ⓦseahag-patong.com; map p.629. The same chef has been cooking great seafood here for two decades and this is where expat hoteliers come here for a good Patong feed. Fish and seafood cooked any number of Thai-style ways for B200–400. Daily noon–4pm & 6pm–midnight.

White Box Thanon Hat Kalim, 1.5km north of the Novotel ☎076 346271, ⓦwhitebox.co.th; map p.629. This chic, sophisticated waterside restaurant and bar, strikingly designed as a modernist cube with panoramic picture windows, is a magnet for visiting celebs and style-conscious expats. The very expensive menu (mains from B520) mixes Thai and Mediterranean flavours – sea-bass fillet with truffles, grilled hazelnut and vegetables (B850), or red curry with roasted duck – and the rooftop sofas are ideal for a pre- or post-dinner drink. Daily 11am–11.30pm.

DRINKING AND ENTERTAINMENT

After dark, everyone heads to pedestrianised Thanon Bangla for their own taste of Patong's notorious **nightlife** and the road teems with a cross section of Phuket tourists, from elderly couples and young parents with strollers, to glammed-up girlfriends and groups of lads. One of the big draws is Thanon Bangla's Soi Crocodile, better known as Soi Katoey, where barely clad transgender women dance and pout on podiums at the mouth of the soi and charge for photos with tourists. But the real action happens further down the many bar-filled sois shooting off Thanon Bangla, where open-air bar-beers and neon-lit go-go clubs packed with strippers and goggle-eyed punters pulsate through the night. The pick-up trade pervades most bars in Patong, and though many of these joints are welcoming enough to couples and female tourists, there are a few alternatives listed below, for anyone not in that kind of mood. The **gay**

entertainment district is concentrated around the Paradise Complex, a network of small sois and dozens of bar-beers in front of *Royal Paradise Hotel* on Thanon Raja Uthit Song Roi Phi: see ⓦgaypatong.com for events listings, including dates for the annual Gay Pride festival, which has recently been held in late April. If you're looking for something else to do with yourself (or your kids) in the evening, check out the *katoey* (transsexual) Simon Cabaret, or the spectacular show at nearby Phuket FantaSea (see page 627). The Jung Ceylon shopping centre has a seven-screen **cinema**, SF Cinema City.

The Boat Bar Soi 5, Paradise Complex, off Thanon Raja Uthit Song Roi Phi ⓦboatbar.com; map p.629. Long-running, very popular gay bar and disco, with two cabaret shows nightly, at around midnight and 1.30am. Daily 9pm–late.

Full Moon Brewwork Port Zone (next to the replica junk), Jung Ceylon shopping centre, Thanon Raja Uthit Song Roi Phi ☎ 076 366 753, ⓦ fullmoonbrewwork. com; map p.629. The best of this microbrewery's offerings is their dark ale, a decent bitter that might appease homesick Brits, and there's good food, too, including *tom yam kung* (B180) and bangers and mash. Live music upstairs (Mon, Wed & Fri–Sat 7.30–10pm). Daily 11am–midnight.

Molly Malone's 94/1 Thanon Thavee Wong ☎ 076 292771; map p.629. Genial Thai–Irish pub chain next to *McDonald's* that serves draught Guinness and Kilkenny, shows international sports TV, stages live bands playing pub rock from 9.30pm and has pool tables, a small beer garden and no overt hostess presence. Daily 10am–2am.

Seduction Soi Happy, off Thanon Bangla ⓦ seduction disco.com; map p.629. A favourite dance venue for partying couples and others not looking for freelance company, this four-storey bar and club has fairly classy lounge areas, hi-tech lighting and Euro dance, and occasionally brings in big-name international DJs. Free until midnight, B300–500 thereafter. Touts outside give useful discount vouchers but avoid the short-lived, diluted-drinks package on the door. Daily 10pm–4am.

Simon Cabaret 8 Thanon Sirirach, south end of Patong ☎ 076 3420 114–6, ⓦ phuket-simoncabaret.com; map p.629. Famously flamboyant extravaganza starring a troupe of *katoey* (transsexuals). It's all very Hollywood – a little bit risqué but not at all sleazy – and popular with tour groups and families. Daily 6pm, 7.45pm & 9.30pm.

Surface Bar Top floor, La Flora Resort Patong, 39 Thanon Thavee Wong ☎ 076 344 241 ⓦ laflorapatong. com/surface_bar.html; map p.629. The perfect place for a sophisticated sundowner, enjoyed from the comfort of enormous sofas on the hotel's wide rooftop terrace. Expansive ocean views and a sea breeze as well. Daily 5pm–midnight.

Wine Connection Bistro First floor of Banana Walk shopping mall, 124/11 Thanon Thavee Wong ☎ 076 510 622, ⓦ wineconnection.co.th; map p.629. Imported international wines, from New Zealand to Italy and South Africa (from B500 per glass), served on a pleasant terrace with a sea view, right in the centre of Patong, yet without any hint of seediness. Daily 10am–12pm.

DIRECTORY

Immigration The tiny Patong branch (information only) of Phuket's immigration office is next to *Surface Bar* on Thanon Thavee Wong (☎ 076 340 477; Mon–Fri 10am–noon & 1–3pm).

Post office Thanon Thavee Wong (daily 9am–7pm).

Shopping Though you can't move for shops in downtown Patong, by far the best, and least hectic, place to browse is Jung Ceylon on Thanon Raja Uthit Song Roi Phi (daily 11am–10pm; ⓦ jungceylon.com), an enormous shopping centre, whose refreshingly tasteful and spacious design includes fountains and plaza seating plus countless shops and restaurants. There are branches of Robinsons Department Store and, on the ground floor at the front end, Boots the Chemist and Asia Books (for English-language books, magazines and newspapers), plus the That's Siam Thai handicrafts emporium in the basement.

Tourist police In front of the immigration office on Thanon Thavee Wong (☎ 076 340244 or ☎ 1155).

Ao Karon

AO KARON, Phuket's second resort, after Patong, is very much a middle-of-the-road destination. Far less lively, or congested, than Patong, but more commercial and less individual than the smaller beaches, it's the domain of affordable guesthouses and package-tour hotels and appeals chiefly to mid-budget tourists, many of them from Scandinavia and Russia. The 2.5km-long **beach** is graced with squeaky soft golden sand and is completely free of developments, though there's very little natural shade; an embankment screens most of the southern half of the beach from the road running alongside, but north of the *Hilton* the road is more often in view and parts of the shore back on to lagoons and wasteland. Karon's main **shopping and eating areas**, with all the usual resort facilities, are grouped around the *Centara Karon Resort* on the northern curve of Thanon Patak; along and around Thanon Luang Pho Chuain, location of the Karon Plaza enclave of accommodation, restaurants and bars; and along Thanon Taina (sometimes referred to as Kata Centre).

The **undertow** off Ao Karon is treacherously strong during the monsoon season from June to October, so you should heed the warning signs and flags and ask for local advice – fatalities are not uncommon. The tiny bay just north of Ao Karon – known as **Karon Noi** or Relax Bay – is almost exclusively patronized by guests of the *Le Meridien* hotel, but non-guests are quite welcome to swim and sunbathe here.

ARRIVAL AND DEPARTURE

AO KARON

By songthaew Ao Karon is 5km south of Patong and 20km southwest of Phuket town. Most songthaews from Phuket town (approx every 20min; 30min; B40) arrive in Karon via Thanon Patak, hitting the beach at the northern end of Ao Karon and then driving south along beachfront Thanon

Karon, continuing over the headland as far as *Kata Beach Resort* on Ao Kata Yai. To catch a songthaew back into town, just stand on the other side of the road and flag one down. Transport touts throughout the resort rent motorbikes and jeeps.

ACCOMMODATION

★**Casa Brazil** 9 Soi 1, Thanon Luang Pho Chuain ☎076 396317, ⍟phukethomestay.com; map p.632. Appealingly arty little hotel, designed in Santa Fe style, with adobe-look walls, earth-toned paintwork, and funky decor and furnishings. The 21 rooms are comfortable, with hot showers, fridges and TVs, and nearly all have a/c.

Choose rooms at the back for a rare green and peaceful view of Karon's hilly backdrop, best enjoyed from the French windows and private balconies. Rates include breakfast. Fan B1200, a/c B1400

Centara Grand Beach Resort 683 Thanon Patak ☎076 201234, ⍟centarahotelsresorts.com/centaragrand/

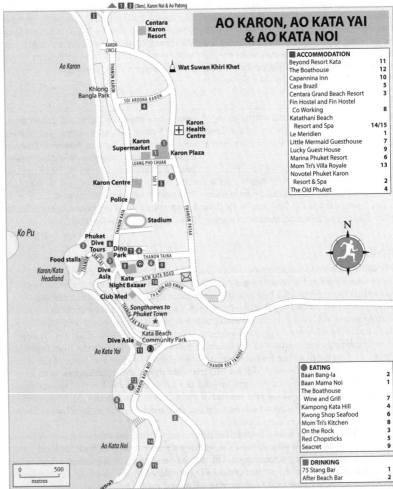

▲ **1**, **2** (3km), Karon Noi & Ao Patong

AO KARON, AO KATA YAI & AO KATA NOI

3 Centara Karon Resort

Ao Karon

KARON CIRCLE

THANON KARON

✝ Wat Suwan Khiri Khet

Khlong Bangla Park

SOI AROONA KARON **4**

✚ Karon Health Centre

Karon Supermarket **1**

LUANG PHO CHUAN

Karon Plaza

Karon Centre

SOI 1

5 **2**

Police

THANON KATA

Stadium

THANON PATAK

Ko Pu

Phuket Dive Tours **3**

Dino Park **7** **4**

THANON TAINA

Food stalls

Dive Asia **8** @ **6** **9**

Karon/Kata Headland

Kata Night Bazaar

NEW KATA ROAD

THANON KED KWAN **10**

Club Med ◆

Songthaews to Phuket Town

THANON PAK BANG

★ Kata Beach Community Park

Dive Asia

11 💲

Ao Kata Yai

THANON KOK TANODE

N

▶ Phuket Town

THANON KATA NOI

12

7

6

13

2

Ao Kata Noi

14

0 ——— 500
metres

9 **15**

▼ Hat Nai Harn

7

cpbr/; map p.632. Huge, low-rise, beachfront luxury hotel, which very loosely echoes Phuket's Sino-Portuguese architecture, all in different shades of pink. It's particularly good for children, with two kids' clubs, a kids' pool, a free-form main pool and a "Lazy River", an artificial river that runs under bridges and under tunnels for exploration on inner tubes. There's an adults-only pool too, and grown-ups can also enjoy kayaking, windsurfing, tennis, the spa and a long menu of other activities. Large discounts on their website. B10,500

Le Meridien Ao Karon Noi (also known as Relax Bay), north of Ao Karon ☎076 370100, ⓦlemeridien.com; map p.632. This huge hotel complex has the tiny bay all to itself and boasts an amazing breadth of facilities, including ten restaurants and bars, two lagoon-style swimming pools (with islands), a spa, squash and tennis courts, free non-motorized watersports and private woods. It's a good choice for kids, with reliable babysitting services and a kids' club. Breakfast included. B8500

Lucky Guest House 110/44–45 Thanon Taina, Kata Centre ☎076 330572, ⓔluckyguesthousekata@ hotmail.com; map p.632. Good-value place offering unusually large, bright en-suite rooms in a low-rise block (the best have balconies) and some rather plain but very clean semi-detached bungalows on land further back; set back a bit down a small soi, this guesthouse has a refreshing sense of space that's at a premium on this road packed with shops, bars and restaurants. Fan B600, a/c B900

Marina Phuket Resort 47 Thanon Karon, far southern end of Ao Karon, on the Karon/Kata headland ☎076 330625, ⓦmarinaphuket.com; map p.632. Enjoying both a very central location, backing on to the beach, just steps from restaurants and shops, and a luxuriously spacious and secluded tropical garden in a former coconut plantation, this is a good upper-end choice. Garden View cottages are old-fashioned and plain, but Jungle View versions are very appealing – and there's a pool and the prettily located On the Rock restaurant. Breakfast included; book through their website for free dinner and airport transfer. B7290

Novotel Phuket Karon Resort & Spa 568 Patak Road ☎076 358 666, ⓦnovotelphuketkaron.com; map p.632. One of the latest offerings from the chain is set 1.5km north of the beach but makes up for the distance with a central free-form swimming pool. Around it, there are several blocks of excellent and modern rooms, including some with private plunge pools. There's a spa centre and a Western–Thai fusion restaurant. A continental buffet breakfast is included. B4380

The Old Phuket Soi Aroona Karon, 192/36 Thanon Karon ☎076 396353–6, ⓦtheoldphuket.com; map p.632. The Sino wing at this attractive, peacefully secluded, heritage-conscious hotel is designed to evoke Sino-Portuguese shophouse architecture. Its rooms are both pretty and modern, with coloured glass window panels and East Indies-style wooden doors. Furnishings in the more expensive Serene Wing are much more contemporary and minimalist and many of its rooms have direct access to the lagoon-like pool. B7000

EATING

Karon's choice of restaurants is underwhelming, lacking either the big-name restaurants of Patong or Kata, or the authenticity of Phuket town. Though go-go bars haven't arrived yet, clusters of outdoor bar-beers with hostess service are popping up at a depressing rate.

Baan Bang-la 6 Soi Patak, off Thanon Patak ☎81 968 5878; map p.632. The seafood here has a good reputation and there are also pasta dishes and pizzas – made in a brick oven by an Italian *pizzaiolo* – on the menu too. Dining is mostly alfresco in Thai *salas* set around a pretty little garden. Mains B180–300. Daily 6pm–late.

Baan Mama Noi Karon Plaza, next door but one to Pineapple Guesthouse on a lane off Thanon Patak ☎091 889 2381; map p.632. Expats, dive staff and Italian tourists fill this place at lunch and dinnertime, savouring the home-from-home taste of the excellent, mid-priced,

Italian food, such as spaghetti bolognese (B150). Daily 9.30am–10pm.

Kwong Shop Seafood 114 Thanon Taina, ☎076 3285201; map p.632. Unassuming but very popular, friendly family-run institution sporting gingham tablecloths that's famous for its well-priced fresh fish (all B40/100g) and seafood cooked to order. Daily 8am–midnight.

On the Rock In the grounds of Marina Phuket Resort, Kata/Karon headland ☎076 330625, ⓦmarinaphuket.com/restaurants; map p.632. Occupying a fine spot above the rocks at the southern end of Ao Karon, this open-air restaurant serves especially good baskets of grilled and deep-fried seafood, such as lobster gratin (B1500), baked mussels and mixed seafood satay. Especially romantic at night. Main dishes from B350. Daily 12am–12pm.

DRINKING

75 Stang Bar Karon Plaza, up a lane off Thanon Luang Pho Chuain, near Thanon Patak ☎085 471 5759 ⓦfacebook.com/75StangReggaeBar; map p.632. Amongst the sports bars and rooms for rent in Karon Plaza, there are a couple of art bars run by locals, including this invitingly bohemian outdoor place. It's a charming mess of driftwood and found objects, where the only things that seem to have been bought new are the red, gold and green stools, which match the reggae bands on stage on most nights. Drinks are cheap. Daily 1pm–2am.

Ao Kata Yai and Ao Kata Noi

Broad, curving **AO KATA YAI** (Big Kata Bay) is only a few minutes' drive around the headland from Karon (17km from Phuket town), but both prettier and safer for swimming, thanks to the protective rocky promontories at either end. It's also a good distance from the main road. The northern stretch of Kata Yai is overlooked by the unobtrusive buildings of the *Club Med* resort, and the southern by *Kata Beach Resort*: in between, the soft sand is busy with sunloungers and the occasional drink and fruit stall. The rest of the accommodation, and the bulk of the tourist village, with its restaurants, bars, tour operators and many shops, fans out eastwards from the walled *Club Med* compound, up to the main road, Thanon Patak.

Beyond the southern headland, **AO KATA NOI**'s (Little Kata Bay) smaller white-sand bay feels secluded, being at the end of a no-through road, but is very popular and filled with loungers and parasols. Kata Noi has its own low-key but rather charmless cluster of businesses, including an ATM and minimarket, though it's dominated by the various sections of the enormous *Katathani* hotel; public access to the beach is down to the right just beyond the hotel's Thani wing.

ARRIVAL AND DEPARTURE   **AO KATA YAI AND AO KATA NOI**

By songthaew Most songthaews from Phuket go first to Karon, then drive south past *Club Med* and terminate beside *Kata Beach Resort* on the headland between Kata Yai and Kata Noi (B30; returning songthaews depart approx every 20min 5am–4.30pm). To get to Kata Noi, continue walking over the hill (around 20min), or take a tuk-tuk for about B200.

DIVING AND SNORKELLING OFF PHUKET

The reefs and islands within sailing distance of Phuket rate among the most spectacular in the world, and **diving and snorkelling** trips are both good value and hugely popular. Many trips operate year-round, though some of the more remote islands and reefs become too dangerous to reach during part or all of the monsoon season, roughly June to October.

DIVE SHOPS AND TRIPS

All the dive **shops** listed below are established and accredited PADI Five-Star Instructor or Career Development Centres; they teach courses, organize dive trips and rent equipment. Advice on choosing a dive shop and other general diving information can be found in "Basics" (see page 53). Expect to pay around B4000 for a one-day introductory **diving course**, and B16,000 for the four-day Open Water course, including equipment. **Day-trips** to the closest of the dive sites listed below, including at least two dives, cost around B4900, while multi-day **live-aboard** cruises to the more distant top-rated reefs of Ko Similan and Ko Surin, Hin Daeng and Hin Muang, and the Mergui archipelago can cost as much as B33,000 for four days, including sixteen dives and full board but excluding equipment and national park fees.

There are **recompression chambers** at Phuket International Hospital in Phuket town (see page 617), and at Vachira Hospital, Soi Wachira, Thanon Yaowarat, Phuket town (☎076 211114, ⓦvachiraphuket.go.th).

Dive Asia 23/6 Thanon Karon, Kata/Karon headland, Ao Karon, and 1/21 Patbang Rd, Ao Kata ☎081 894 8588, ⓦdiveasia.com.
Local Dive Thailand A small office close to McDonald's, Ao Patong ☎062 2262354, ⓦlocal divethailand.com.
Phuket Dive Tours Laem Sai Road, Ao Kata ☎087 0225356, ⓦphuketdivetours.com.

SNORKELLING TRIPS

The most popular snorkelling destination from Phuket is **Ko Phi Phi** (see p000). All travel agents sell mass-market day-trips there, on huge ferries with capacities of a hundred plus; prices average B3800 and include snorkelling stops at Phi Phi Leh and Phi Phi Don, snorkel rental and a seafood lunch. Smaller speedboat trips to Ko Phi Phi are usually worth the extra money to avoid the big groups; those run by Offspray Leisure (B3500; ☎076 281375, ⓦoffsprayleisure.com) get good reviews, and they also run speedboat snorkel trips to **Ko Racha Yai** (B3500). Day-trip packages to the remote but beautiful **Ko Similan** islands start from B6900 (see page 612). Many of the

ACCOMMODATION

Beyond Resort Kata Thanon Kata, Kata Yai ☎076 330530–4, ⓦkatagroup.com/kata-beach/home/; map p.632. Recently re-branded, this huge 275-room, four-storey hotel occupies a great spot right on Kata Yai's white-sand beach. It has a seafront restaurant, two swimming pools, a palm-shaded seaside garden, a spa and a dive shop. Some of the attractive, balconied, wooden-floored rooms have direct pool access, whilst some have sea views. Continental breakfast included. B5500

The Boathouse 182 Thanon Kok Tanode, Kata Yai ☎076 330015–7, ⓦboathouse-phuket.com; map p.632. Exclusive contemporary beachfront boutique hotel, with just 38 elegantly furnished seafront rooms, a reputation for classy service and a top-notch restaurant. There's a pool, a spa and weekend cooking classes (see page 615). Advance booking essential. B12,600

Capannina Inn The Beach Centre, "New Kata Road", Kata Yai ☎076 284450, ⓦphuket-capannina-inn.com; map p.632. Smart, modern, large bedrooms and well-equipped bathrooms, with a/c, cable TV, hot water, fridges and espresso machines. Guests have the use of an attractive, shared, garden pool in front. It's set in a newer development of shops and hotels, a 5min walk from the beach –there's a free tuk-tuk to the beach and the restaurant. Continental breakfast included. B1800

★ **Fin Hostel** and **Fin Hostel Co Working** 100/20 Kata Night Plaza, Kata Yai ☎ 088 753 1162 ⓦfinhostelphuket.com; map p.632. Facing each other on a busy corner of Kata Yai's village area, these two surfer-friendly hostels have squeaky clean a/c dorm rooms featuring reading lights and charging stations. Toilets are luxurious for the category and look swanky with their bare walls, naked light bulbs and potted plants. Fin also has some en-suite doubles, a kitchen for guest use and a rooftop swimming pool. *Fin Co Working* has capsule pods for couples at a bargain B450 and two halls dotted with computer stations on the ground floor that – as the name suggests – serve as working space for digital nomads. They are free for guests, but they can be also rented for B100/hour. Dorms B400, Doubles B2000

7

dive companies listed welcome snorkellers on board their day-trips, and sometimes on the live-aboards (from two days/one night B15,000) too, for a discount of about thirty percent.

ANDAMAN COAST DIVE AND SNORKEL SITES

Anemone Reef About 22km east of Phuket. Submerged reef of soft coral and sea anemones starting about 5m deep. Lots of fish, including leopard sharks, tuna and barracuda. Usually combined with a dive at nearby Shark Point. Unsuitable for snorkellers.

Burma Banks About 250km northwest of Phuket; only accessible on live-aboards. A series of submerged "banks", well away from any landmass and very close to the Burmese border. Only worth the trip for its sharks. Visibility up to 25m.

Hin Daeng and **Hin Muang** 56km southwest of Ko Lanta. Hin Daeng is an exceptional reef wall, named after the red soft corals that cover the rocks, with visibility up to 30m. One hundred metres away, Hin Muang also drops to 50m and is good for stingrays, manta rays, whale sharks and silvertip sharks. Visibility up to 50m. Because of the depth and the current, both places are considered too risky for novice divers who have logged fewer than twenty dives. Unsuitable for snorkellers.

King Cruiser Near Shark Point, between Phuket and Ko Phi Phi. Dubbed the *Thai Tanic*, this became a wreck dive in May 1997, when a tourist ferry sank on its way to Ko Phi Phi. Visibility up to 20m, but hopeless for snorkellers because of the depth, and collapsed sections make it dangerous for any but the most experienced divers.

Ko Phi Phi 48km east of Phuket's Ao Chalong (see page 638). Visibility up to 30m. The most popular destination for Phuket divers and snorkellers. Spectacular drop-offs; good chance of seeing whale sharks.

Ko Racha Noi and **Ko Racha Yai** About 33km and 28km south of Phuket's Ao Chalong respectively. Visibility up to 40m. Racha Yai (aka Raya Yai) is good for beginners and for snorkellers; at the more challenging Racha Noi there's a good chance of seeing manta rays, eagle rays and whale sharks.

Ko Rok Nok and **Ko Rok Nai** 100km southeast of Phuket, south of Ko Lanta (see page 679). Visibility up to 18m. Shallow reefs that are excellent for snorkelling.

Ko Similan 96km northwest of Phuket; easiest access from Khao Lak (see page 606). One of the world's top diving spots. Visibility up to 30m. Leopard sharks, whale sharks and manta rays, plus caves and gorges.

Ko Surin 174km northwest of Phuket; easiest access from Khuraburi (see page 597). Shallow reefs of soft and hard corals that are good for snorkelling.

Richelieu Rock Just east of Ko Surin, close to Burmese waters. A sunken pinnacle that's famous for its whale sharks. Considered by many to be Thailand's top dive spot.

Shark Point (Hin Mu Sang) 24km east of Phuket's Laem Panwa. Protected as a marine sanctuary. Visibility up to 10m. Notable for soft corals, sea fans and leopard sharks. Often combined with the *King Cruiser* dive and/or Anemone Reef; unrewarding for snorkellers.

Katathani Beach Resort and Spa 14 Thanon Kata Noi, Kata Noi ☎076 318 350, ⓦkatathani.com; map p.632. The various wings and offshoots of the enormous and luxurious *Katathani* now occupy almost the entire shoreline of small, secluded Kata Noi. The beachfront all-suite Thani wing has the prime position, with the narrow lawn dropping seamlessly onto the white sand; all rooms here have seaview balconies. Across the effectively private, no-through road, the cheaper, garden-view Bhuri wing has a distinctively contemporary, pastel-coloured look and its rooms too are very deluxe. There's daily shuttle service to town and to Patong. The hotel has six restaurants, six swimming pools and a spa, plus an arm-long menu of activities and a kids' club. Breakfast included. **B14,000**

Little Mermaid Guesthouse 126 Thaina Road, Kata Yai ☎076 330873, ⓦfacebook.com/littlemermaid guesthouserestaurant; map p.632. Spacious en-suite rooms above a popular Thai bar. Most of the rooms have certainly seen better days but are still kept very clean and are good value for the price, considering there's wi-fi, a/c and hot water. Paying a bit extra will get you a window with courtyard view (B840). **B790**

Mom Tri's Villa Royale 12 Thanon Kata Noi, Kata Noi ☎076 333569, ⓦvillaroyalephuket.com; map p.632. Luxurious suites, richly decorated with fine textiles and teak, a renowned restaurant, an excellent spa and two saltwater and one freshwater pools, all set in landscaped tropical gardens with fine views above Kata Noi. **B18,100**

EATING

The Boathouse Wine and Grill Thanon Kok Tanode, Kata Yai ☎076 330015–7, ⓦboathouse-phuket.com; map p.632. One of the best-known restaurants on Phuket – not least for its famously extensive, award-winning wine list – where the skills of the French chef are best sampled on four-course Thai or French tasting menus (just over B1800, or B3300 with paired wines). The beachside terrace and dining room, decorated with nautical touches and attached to the boutique hotel of the same name, enjoy fine sunset views, and there are cooking classes here every weekend (see box, page 615). Reservations recommended. Daily 11am–11pm.

Kampong Kata Hill 12 Patak Road, on the slope right above the Little Mermaid, ☎076 330 103 ⓦfacebook. com/kampongkatahill; map p.632. Atmospheric Thai and seafood restaurant decked out like a timeless Asian temple, with all the quirky statues, potted tropical plants, teakwood and faux architecture. It is touristy, but it pulls off the concept pretty well. There are Western-style starters and salads, but the king prawns and lobster platters steal the show. A meal for two will set you back around B1500. Daily 4pm–11pm.

Mom Tri's Kitchen Mom Tri's Villa Royale, 12 Thanon Kata Noi, Kata Noi ☎076 333569, ⓦmomtriphuket. com; map p.632. Highly regarded luxury restaurant, offering Thai and European fine dining, in dishes such as veal parmigiana and jumbo prawns in red curry. Mains from B590. Reservations recommended. Daily 6.30am–11.30pm.

Red Chopsticks Next to the Marina Hotel, ☎ 098 015 0519; map p.632. The Kata outlet of this Thai franchise, a part of the Marina Hotel, features a well-choreographed dining room, the ceiling of which is covered with thatched lamps, nets and other northern Thai memorabilia. The usual local staples, such as fried chicken with cashew nuts and fried red curry, come in big portions here and start at B199. Daily 10am–10pm.

★ **Seacret** Katathani Beach Resort and Spa, 14 Thanon Kata Noi, Kata Noi ☎076 330124–6, ⓦkatathani. com; map p.632. Excellent Phuket and southern Thai cuisine, such as the classic dried-shrimp relish, *nam prik kung siap*, *pla thawt khamin* (deep-fried fish with turmeric and pineapple relish; B290) and *muu hong* (stewed pork belly with cinnamon). All this and an attractive, open-air setting by the swimming pool, with the best tables on a deck under fairy-lit trees by the beach. Daily 11am–5pm & 6–10.30pm.

DRINKING

After Beach Bar 44 Thanon Kata, up the hill past Andaman Cannacia Resort, ☎ 089 594 7475, ⓦbit. ly/2q8cZGi; map p.632. Long-running, rustic reggae-style bar set on top of a hill. The wooden deck offers great views over Kata's coast; highly recommended for a romantic sundowner (from B100). Daily 12pm–9pm.

Hat Nai Harn

The favourite beach of the many expats who live in nearby Rawai, **HAT NAI HARN**, 18km southwest of Phuket town, is an exceptionally beautiful curved bay of white sand backed by a stand of casuarinas and plenty of food stalls but only minimal development. It does get crowded with Russian tourists, parasols and loungers, however, and during the monsoon the waves here are huge.

ARRIVAL AND DEPARTURE

By songthaew Songthaews from Phuket town (approx every 30min; 45min; B40) go to Nai Harn, via Rawai, with the last one returning at an early 4pm.

HAT NAI HARN

ACCOMMODATION

All Seasons Naiharn Phuket ☎076 289327, ⌨allseasons-naiharn-phuket.com. Run by the French Accor group, this well-sited hotel offers contemporary-styled rooms with ocean or garden view, five restaurants and bars, a spa, a kids' club and a decent-sized pool. It's just over the narrow road from the shore, next door to *Royal Phuket Yacht Club* (under lengthy renovations). **B2950**

EATING

Rock Salt ☎076 380200, ✉rocksalt@thenaiharn.com. Expensive restaurant that's part of *The Naiharn Resort*, on a stunning location over the northern end of the beach. The oyster and *fruit de mer* plates don't come cheap (from B1750), but they definitely make an impression. They also have tasty pasta dishes (from B450) and tandoori chicken and *naan* bread (B550). Daily 12.30pm–10pm

★**Trattoria del Buongustaio** ☎087 467 2554, ⌨trattoriabuongustaio.ilmiosito.net. This Italian-run restaurant offers gorgeous views of the bay from a lovely balcony above the rocks on the northern headland and is reachable via the paved road through *The Naiharn Resort*. The full menu covers a wide choice of starters and meat and especially seafood main courses, plus risottos and pastas such as delicious seafood ravioli with sage and butter (B370). Daily noon–12.30am; the kitchen closes at 11pm, while the downstairs lounge bar closes at 2am.

Hat Ya Nui and Laem Promthep

Follow the coastal road 2km south around the lumpy headland from Hat Nai Harn and you reach the tiny roadside beach of **Hat Ya Nui**, which gets a surprising number of visitors despite being so small and right next to the admittedly quiet road. There are coral reefs very close to shore, though the currents are strong, and kayaks and sunloungers for rent.

The rugged, wind-blasted, grassy flanked headland of **Laem Promthep**, 1km beyond Hat Ya Nui, marks Phuket's southernmost tip, jutting dramatically – and photogenically – into the deep blue of the Andaman Sea. The cape is one of the island's top beauty spots, and at sunset busloads of tour groups get shipped in to admire the spectacle; Thais pay their respects at the Hindu shrine here, offering elephant figurines in honour of the enshrined four-headed god Brahma and his elephant mount, Erawan. You can escape the crowds by following the trail along the ridge and down to the rocks just above the water.

ARRIVAL

Songthaews to and from Nai Harn pass through Rawai, so to explore both places, you could catch a songthaew from Phuket town to Nai Harn (approx every 30min; 45min;

HAT YA NUI AND LAEM PROMTHEP

B40), then walk up and around the promontory in a couple of hours, to pick up another songthaew back to town from Rawai (see below).

ACCOMMODATION

Nai Ya Beach Bungalow 99 Moo 6 Tumbon Rawai, a few hundred metres along Soi Naya off Road 4233 ☎076 288676, ⌨naiyabeachbungalow.com. Two hundred metres uphill from Ya Nui beach towards the cape, this friendly and pleasant place has attractive, sturdy, thatched-roofed bamboo bungalows with fans, en-suite cold showers and verandas. They're nicely shaded by cashew nut trees and bougainvillaea and enjoys high-level sea views. Closed May–Oct. **B990**

EATING AND DRINKING

Yanui Restaurant ☎087 2808937, ✉nuk-yanui@hotmail.com. Casual bamboo and driftwood eatery under an umbrella of tree branches that stretches right across from the beach. They serve juicy pastas (from B160) and fish (B350), and it's a chilled spot for a fruit smoothie or a sundowner (from B150). Daily 8am–9pm

Hat Rawai

Phuket's southernmost beach, **HAT RAWAI**, was the first to be exploited for tourist purposes, but, half a century on, the hoteliers have moved to the far more appealing sands of Kata and Karon, leaving Rawai to its former inhabitants, the Urak Lawoy *chao ley* (see page 600), and to an expanding expat population. Most visitors are here for the many alfresco **seafood restaurants** along Thanon Viset's beachside promenade.

Phuket Seashell Museum

1500m north of the beach on Highway 4024 • Daily 8am–5.30pm • B200

Aside from its seafront restaurants, Rawai's chief attraction is the **Phuket Seashell Museum**, which displays some two thousand species of shell, including 380-million-year-old fossils, giant clams and a 140-carat gold pearl.

ARRIVAL HAT RAWAI

By songthaew Songthaews from Phuket town pass through Rawai (approx every 30min, 35min; B30) on their way to and from Nai Harn.

ACCOMMODATION

Sandy House 62 Moo 6 Viset Road, tucked at the upper end of a soi parallel to the beach; turn left about one hundred metres down the alley straight opposite from Nikita ☎085 8880821, ✉peachmaker_yib@hotmail.com. Sparkling clean en-suite rooms with a/c and mini balconies with chairs and tables, set in a Thai home shaded by a lush garden. There's free wi-fi, motorbike rental and free bicycles for guests; breakfast costs B100 extra. Prices are slashed in low season, popular with long-term visitors. **B950**

EATING

Nikita's Towards the northern end of the promenade ☎076 288703, ⌨nikitas-phuket.com. A standout among the many expat-favoured bar-restaurants in the area, not least for the horizon-gazing potential from its peaceful tables on the sand (candlelit at night). Pizzas from a wood-fired oven (from B240) feature on its Thai and Western menu, alongside well-priced cocktails, wines by the glass and espresso coffees. Daily 10am–2am at the latest, kitchen closes 11pm.

Salaloy Opposite Nikita's, towards the northern end of the promenade ☎076 613740. The best and most famous of Rawai's restaurants, whose highlights include *pla thawt khamin* (fried fish with turmeric) and omelette topped with baby oysters (B110); it has some lovely outdoor tables right on the shorefront under the casuarinas. Daily 10am–9.30pm.

Ao Chalong, Laem Panwa and around

North of Rawai, the sizeable offshore island of Ko Lone protects the broad sweep of **AO CHALONG**, where many a Chinese fortune was made from the huge quantities of tin mined in the bay. These days, Ao Chalong is the main departure point for dive excursions and snorkelling and fishing trips, which mostly leave from Chalong Pier, east of the bottle-neck roundabout known as Chalong Circle, or Chalong Ha Yaek.

Wat Chalong

8km southwest of Phuket town, on Thanon Chao Fa Nok, aka Route 4022 • Phuket–Karon songthaews pass the entrance

For islanders, Chalong is important as the site of **Wat Chalong**, Phuket's loveliest and most famous temple, which enshrines the statue of revered monk Luang Pho Saem, who helped resolve a violent rebellion by migrant Chinese tin miners in 1876. Elsewhere in the temple compound, the Phra Mahathat chedi is believed to contain a relic of the Buddha.

Big Buddha of Phuket

Access is via the very steep and winding 6km Soi Jao Fa 51, signed west off Thanon Chao Fa Nok (Route 422), 2km south of Wat Chalong, or 1km north of Chalong Circle • ⌨mingmongkolphuket.com

With your own transport, a visit to Wat Chalong combines well with a pilgrimage to the modern-day **Big Buddha of Phuket** (officially Phra Phuttha Mingmongkol

Eaknakakeeree), a towering 45m statue atop the aptly named Khao Nakkerd hill, which dominates many island vistas, including from Kata Yai to the southwest, and is easily spotted from aeroplane windows. Made of concrete but faced with glistening white-marble tiles, the eastward-looking Buddha boasts enormous proportions: sitting on a lotus flower that's nearly 25m across with individual hair curls measuring almost 1m each. Views from the base of the statue extend east over Ao Chalong to hilly Ko Lone beyond, while western panoramas take in Kata Noi; it's a popular sunset-viewing spot.

Phuket Aquarium

Laem Panwa, 10km south of Phuket town • Daily 8.30am–4.30pm, feeding show Sat & Sun 11am • B180 • ⓦ phuketaquarium.org • Songthaews leave from the market in Phuket town (B30), the last one returning at about 3.30pm

Ao Chalong tapers off eastwards into **Laem Panwa**, at the tip of which you'll find the **Phuket Aquarium**. Run by the island's Marine Biological Centre, it's not a bad primer for what you might see on a reef and has walk-through tunnels, a sea-turtle pool and a shark-feeding show.

ARRIVAL   AO CHALONG

By songthaew Songthaews to Ao Chalong from Phuket town charge B30.

ACCOMMODATION

Shanti Lodge Soi Bangrae, 1500m south down Thanon Chao Fa Nok from Wat Chalong; the Phuket–Karon songthaew can drop you close by ☎076 280233, ⓦ shantilodge.com. Though there's no special reason to stay on this part of the island, you might make an exception for this place. It's set in a relaxing garden and is home to a saltwater swimming pool, book exchange and vegetarian restaurant. There are fan and a/c doubles, with or without private hot-water bathrooms – some of which are wheelchair accessible – and family rooms. Discounts are offered for long stays. Fan B750, a/c B850

EATING

Kan Eang @ Pier Ao Chalong ☎076 381212, ⓦ kaneang-pier.com. Classy, long-running restaurant, which is handily, and scenically, sited on a 200m frontage at the mouth of Chalong Pier. The big draw here is the seafood, the best of it barbecued old-style on burning coconut husks (from B1200/kg); deep-fried seaweed with shrimps and chilli sauce is also good, and the *haw mok* (fish curry steamed in a banana leaf) is exceptional. Sister restaurant *Kan Eang Seafood*, north up the beach (☎076 381323, ⓦ phuket-seafood.com), enjoys a similarly good reputation and offers free pick-ups. Daily 10.30am–11pm.

Thalang and around

There's not a great deal for tourists in the northeast of Phuket island around the district town of **THALANG**, but you're quite likely to pass the landmark **Heroines' Monument**, which stands in the centre of the Tha Rua junction, 12km north of Phuket town on Highway 402. The monument commemorates the repulse of the Burmese army by the widow of the governor of Phuket and her sister in 1785; together they rallied the island's womenfolk who, legend has it, frightened the Burmese away by cutting their hair short and rolling up banana leaves to look like musket barrels – a victory that's celebrated every March 13 to 15 with a monks' ordination ceremony and processions.

Peranakan Phuket Museum

On Route 402, in the Garden Mall complex opposite Home Pro • Daily 9am–6pm • B300 • ☎076 313556 • ⓦ peranakanphuketmuseum.com

Opened in 2017, the **Peranakan Phuket Museum** is dedicated to Phuket's Peranakan heritage. The upstairs exhibit features outfits, furniture and original Peranakan homeware, the stories of which are all explained by knowledgeable English-speaking guides. Downstairs, in a huge hall choreographed like an old Sino-Portuguese town, the experience is much more commercial: visitors can dress up in traditional Peranakan clothes and have their pictures taken in a studio, buy jewellery, or sample Peranakan-style coffee and dishes at the *Yaya Kitchen* restaurant and *Pinana Café* (both Daily 9am–6pm).

Thalang National Museum

On Route 4027, 200m east of the Heroines' Monument • Wed–Sun 9am–4pm • B30 • All mainland-bound traffic and all songthaews between Phuket and Hat Surin and Hat Nai Yang pass the monument

As the only official introduction to Phuket's rich and intriguing history, **Thalang National Museum** doesn't really match up to the task, but taken in conjunction with the privately funded Thaihua Museum in Phuket town (see page 619), the picture starts to flesh out. Displays include some interesting exhibits on the local tin and rubber industries, accounts of some of the more colourful folkloric traditions and photos of the masochistic feats of the Vegetarian Festival (see page 620).

Wat Phra Thong

Just beyond the crossroads in Thalang town, 8km north of the Heroines' Monument

Wat Phra Thong is one of Phuket's most revered temples on account of the power of the Buddha statue it enshrines. The solid gold image is half-buried and no one dares dig it up for fear of a curse that has struck down excavators in the past. After the wat was built around the statue, the image was encased in plaster to deter would-be robbers.

Khao Phra Taew Forest Reserve

Visitor centre 3km east of the crossroads in Thalang town • B200

Several paths cross the small hilly enclave of **Khao Phra Taew Forest Reserve**, leading you through the forest habitat of macaques and wild boar, but the most popular features of the park are the Gibbon Rehabilitation Project and the Ton Sai and Bang Pae waterfalls, which combine well as a day-trip or on a tour (see page 615). You can get drinks and snacks at the food stall next to the Rehabilitation Centre, and the route to the waterfalls is signed from here.

The Gibbon Rehabilitation Project

10km northeast of the Heroines' Monument, off Route 4027 • Daily 9am–3.30pm • Ⓦ gibbonproject.org • Songthaews from Phuket town, more frequent in the morning, will take you most of the way: ask to be dropped off at Bang Pae (a 40min drive from town) and then follow the signed track for about 1km to get to the project centre

Phuket's forests used to resound with the whooping calls of indigenous white-handed lar gibbons (see page 755), but they make such charismatic pets that they were poached to extinction on the island by the mid-1980s. The lar is now an endangered species, and in 1992 it became illegal in Thailand to keep them as pets, to sell them or to kill them. Despite this, you'll come across a depressing number of pet gibbons on Phuket, kept in chains by bar and hotel owners as entertainment for their customers. The **Gibbon Rehabilitation Centre** aims to reverse this by rescuing pet gibbons and then re-socializing and re-educating them for the wild before finally releasing them back into the forests. It is not unusual for gibbons to be severely traumatized by their experience as pets: not only will they have been taken forcibly from their mothers, but they may also have been abused by their owners.

Visitors are welcome at the project, which is centred in the forests of Khao Phra Taew Forest Reserve, protected as a "non-hunting area", close to Bang Pae waterfall, but because the whole point of the rehab project is to minimize the gibbons' contact with humans, you can only admire the creatures from afar. There's a small exhibition here on the aims of the project, and the well-informed volunteer guides will fill you in on the details of each case and on the idiosyncratic habits of the lar gibbon. The website has details on how you can become a **project volunteer**, adopt a gibbon, or make a donation.

Bang Pae and Ton Sai waterfalls

If you follow the track along the river from the Gibbon Project, you'll soon arrive at **Bang Pae Falls**, a popular picnic and bathing spot, ten to fifteen minutes' walk away.

Continue on the track south for another 2.8km (about 1hr 30min on foot) and you should reach **Ton Sai Falls**: though not a difficult climb, the route is unsigned and indistinct, and is steep in places and rough underfoot. There are plenty of opportunities for cool dips in the river en route. Once at Ton Sai you can either walk back down to the access road to the Khao Phra Taew Forest Reserve visitor centre and try to hitch a ride back home, or return the way you came.

Ko Yao Noi

Located in an idyllic spot in Phang Nga bay, almost equidistant from Phuket, Phang Nga and Krabi, the island of **KO YAO NOI** enjoys magnificent maritime views from almost every angle and makes a refreshingly tranquil getaway. Measuring about 12km at its longest point, it's home to some four thousand islanders, the vast majority of them Muslim, who earn their living from rubber and coconut plantations, fishing and shrimp-farming. Tourism is increasing as visitors keep trickling from nearby Andaman Coast hotspots, lured by Ko Yao Noi's famed rural ambience and lack of commercial pressures. In reality, several high-end resorts have popped up along the coastline and the beaches lack the wow factor of more sparkling nearby sands. Nonetheless, there's decent swimming off the east coast at high tide, and at low tide too in a few places, and plenty of potential for kayaking, rock-climbing and other activities.

Most tourists stay on the east side, which has the bulk of the accommodation, at **Hat Tha Khao**, **Hat Khlong Jaak (Long Beach)**, **Hat Pasai** and **Laem Sai**. Exploring the interior is a particular pleasure, either via the barely trafficked round-island road as it runs through tiny villages and the island's diminutive town, **Ban Tha Khai**, or via the trails that crisscross the forested interior, where you've a good chance of encountering monkeys as well as cobras and even pythons, not to mention plenty of birds, including majestic oriental pied hornbills.

Hat Tha Kao and Hat Sai Taew

The most northerly of the main eastern beaches is **HAT THA KAO**, site of a small village, **BAN THA KAO**, with a couple of shops and restaurants, an ATM, the pier for boats to and from Krabi and a cluster of accommodation. It's not an attractive beach itself, barely swimmable, but is the closest point to Ko Yao's nicest beach, so-called **Temple Beach** or **Hat Sai Taew**, 2km away, whose pretty, gold-sand shore is great for swimming at any tide. However, it's backed by private land that belongs to the Dhammakaya Foundation, a populist Buddhist sect, and is unsigned and a bit tricky to find. From Tha Kao pier, head inland and take the first right behind the shops, walk alongside the khlong and its sheltered marina, over the bridge, then via the faint trail over the hill to the beach. Alternatively, you can kayak there from the pier.

Hat Khlong Jaak (Long Beach)

A couple of kilometres south of Hat Tha Kao, **HAT KHLONG JAAK**, more commonly referred to as **Long Beach**, is the site of the longest-running and best-known tourist accommodation and the liveliest places to eat and drink. The beach is indeed long, around 1500m from the northern end to *Sabai Corner* on the southern headland. Much of it is rocky and all but unswimmable at low tide, except in front of *Koyao Island Resort*, the smoothest stretch. The seaward views are glorious from every angle, however, taking in the many lovely islets of eastern Ao Phang Nga.

Hat Pasai and Laem Sai

A minute's walk south from *Sabai Corner* on Hat Khlong Jaak and you're on **HAT PASAI**, a rather pretty little beach, with some shade, several resorts and a few simple beach restaurants with tables under the casuarinas at the south end.

Beyond Hat Pasai, tiny **HAT LAEM SAI** is often known simply as **Hat Lom'Lae**, after the appealing Thai–Canadian *Lom'Lae Beach Resort*, which sits on the shore (see page 645).

A few hundred metres west from the *Lom'Lae* turn-off, about 3km from Tha Kai, another side-road takes you down towards **Tha Laem Sai** (Laem Sai pier), along a coast that has no real beach but is scenically dotted with houses on stilts, fishing platforms, dozens of longtails and some inviting views of Ko Yao Noi's larger twin, Ko Yao Yai, just across the channel. At the tip of the peninsula stands a good

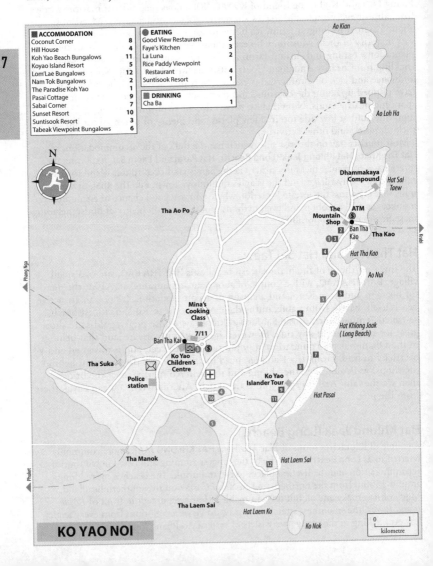

■ ACCOMMODATION	
Coconut Corner	8
Hill House	4
Koh Yao Beach Bungalows	11
Koyao Island Resort	5
Lom'Lae Bungalows	12
Nam Tok Bungalows	2
The Paradise Koh Yao	1
Pasai Cottage	9
Sabai Corner	7
Sunset Resort	10
Suntisook Resort	3
Tabeak Viewpoint Bungalows	6

● EATING	
Good View Restaurant	5
Faye's Kitchen	3
La Luna	2
Rice Paddy Viewpoint Restaurant	4
Suntisook Resort	1

■ DRINKING	
Cha Ba	1

KO YAO NOI

seafood restaurant (see p.647), and there's a nice little beach 300m east further around the rocks.

Ban Tha Kai and north

The island's commercial and administrative centre is **BAN THA KAI**, inland from the main piers on the southwest coast. This is where you'll find the post office, banks, hospital, police station, obligatory 7-Eleven shop with ATM, as well as several internet centres, the main market and several roti stalls.

Visitors are very much encouraged to drop by the **Ko Yao Children's Community Centre** (☎087 929 4320, ⓦkoyao-ccc.com), at the western end of town, an NGO that aims to help improve the English-language, arts, handicraft and computer skills of island children and adults, as well as organising regular beach clean-ups.

The road running **north from Tha Kai**'s 7-Eleven is particularly scenic, taking you through several hamlets with their mosques and latex-pressing mangles, and past rice fields and their resident buffaloes, framed by mangroves in the middle distance, sea eagles hovering overhead, and the rounded hills of nearby islands in the background. At a junction about 3km from Tha Khai, the northbound road soon turns into a rough track leading to the beautiful beach at **AO LOH HA**, while veering right will take you over the hill and down to Tha Kao on the east coast, about 4km away.

7

ARRIVAL AND DEPARTURE

KO YAO NOI

There are three mainland departure points for **boats** to Ko Yao Noi – from Phuket, Krabi's Ao Thalen, and Phang Nga – plus services from Ao Nang. On Ko Yao Noi, shared songthaew **taxis** meet all arriving boats and charge up to B100 per person (depending on distance) for transfers to accommodation, or B150 if chartered for a single traveller. In high season, private speedboats depart to Railay, Ko Jum, Ko Lanta, Ko Kradan, Ko Mook, Trang's Haad Yao pier, Ko Bulon Lae and Ko Lipe. They all leave at 9am, doing multiple stops at different islands/piers. Book tickets a day in advance at **The Pier Restaurant** (☎089 728 0740) on the main junction in front of Ban Tha Khao's jetty .

To/from Phi Phi From November to April there's a daily direct speedboat service from Ko Yao Noi's Manor Pier to Phi Phi's Tonsai, leaving at 9.00 am (50min; B1500). It returns from Ko Phi Phi at 3.00pm. You must book ahead with *Sun Smile Tours* (☎ 099 479 1410 or 093 698 1911, ⓦ fivestartravelandtours.com/product-category/sun-smile-tours).

To/from Phuket The most common route is from Bang Rong on Phuket's northeast coast to Tha Manok on Ko Yao Noi's southwest coast, which is covered by four longtail boats (1hr 10min; B150) and at least seven speedboats a day (40min; B200), with the last service at around 5pm.

Returning to Bang Rong, boats depart Tha Manok every hour or so until 5.40pm.

To/from Ao Thalen Most of the Krabi province boats leave from Ao Thalen, 33km northwest of Krabi town, and arrive at the Tha Kao pier on Ko Yao Noi's northeast coast. There are about ten services a day, via longtail boat (1hr; B150) or speedboat (30min; B200), the last leaving at 4pm from Ko Yao Noi, and between 4.30 and 5pm from Thalen. In Thalen, an infrequent songthaew service to Krabi Town runs until 2.30pm. A taxi will cost around B700. You can also drive yourself and park cars and motorbikes (B100/50 per night) overnight

To/from Ao Nang In high season, speedboat services connect Ao Nang's Hat Nopparat Thara with Ko Yao Noi once a day (45min; B650, including pick-ups in the Krabi area). They leave Tha Manok pier at 3.30pm and Noppharattara pier in Ao Nang at 11am.

To/from Phang Nga The most scenic journey to Ko Yao Noi is the daily (Mon–Sat) service from Phang Nga, which takes you through the heart of Ao Phang Nga, passing close by the stilt-house island of Ko Panyi (see page 646). It departs the Phang Nga bay pier at Tha Dan, 9km south of Phang Nga town, at 1pm and returns from Tha Suka on Ko Yao Noi at 7.30am (90min; B200); songthaews connect Phang Nga town with the pier.

GETTING AROUND AND INFORMATION

Getting around Songthaew taxis are easily arranged and many hotels can organize motorbike (B200–350/day) and bicycle (B150) rental. Several shops at Ban Tha Khao's pier also offer motorbike rental.

Tourist information ⓦ kohyaotravel.com and ⓦ koyaonoi. com have good information on ferry time tables, resorts and available tours. There are ATMs in front of the Mountain Shop in Ban Tha Khao and at the 7-Eleven in Ban Tha Kai.

KO YAO NOI ACTIVITIES

KAYAKING AND SNORKELLING

Kayaking around the coast is a very enjoyable pastime, and the dozens of tiny islands visible from eastern shorelines make enticing destinations for experienced paddlers; kayaks can be rented through Ko Yao Noi hotels for about B400 per day. Try **Pasai Kayak** (☎08640164713; limited English spoken), located on the north side of Pasai Beach. Just about every hotel and travel agent sells kayaking and snorkelling trips to Ko Hong and other islands in Ao Phang Nga.

DIVING

Koh Yao Diver Lom'Lae Resort, Laem Sai ☎089 92 72871 or 089 868 8642, ��kohyaodiver.com. Diving trips and courses on the island are the speciality of Koh Yao Diver, where two local dives cost B4000, two dives at the reefs around Phi Phi in a longtail B7200 and the Open Water course is B16,700.

ROCK-CLIMBING

Ko Yao Noi is fast becoming a respected destination for **rock-climbers**, who appreciate the fresh sites and uncrowded routes compared to the hectic scene at nearby Ton Sai and Railay. There are over 150 bolted routes on the island, from beginner level to advanced (5 to 8A), established by the American and Thai climbers who run The Mountain Shop in Ban Tha Kao. Many routes are over water and accessible only by boat, or at the least via a hike off the dirt track to *Paradise* hotel.

The Mountain Shop In a house, set 50m along the road to the right of Ban Tha Kao's main jetty junction ⓔthemountainshopadventures@gmail. com, ⓦfacebook.com/mountainshopadventures. For beginners, prices start from B2500 for a half-day's course, with multi-day courses also available; there are guides and rental gear for experienced climbers.

OTHER CLASSES AND ACTIVITIES

Lam Sai Hotel Laem Sai ⓦphuket-krabi-muaythai. com. B600 for a two-hour Thai boxing class or B10,000 for a week of classes.

Mina's Cooking Classes 500m from Ban Tha Kai's roundabout ☎087 887 3161, ⓦminas-cooking-classes.com. Three-hour classes in chef Mina's beautiful Thai wooden home, starting at 10.30am and 3.30pm. B1800/person up to six people, or B2500 for individual one to one lessons.

Ulmer's Nature Lodge Hat Tha Kao ☎087 3879475, ⓦthailandyogaretreats.com. Daily drop-in yoga classes (B600), plus diverse workshops and retreats (4D/3N from B5,600).

ACCOMMODATION

HAT THA KAO

Nam Tok Bungalows ☎087 292 1102; map p.642. Set back from the beach around a khlong, a 5min walk south from the Tha Kao ferry pier, this ultra laidback set of bungalows is one of the cheapest places to stay on the island. The budget options are comfortable bamboo and wood huts, with cute bathrooms and hammocks on the deck, encircling a small garden full of flowers and a fish pond; the more luxurious ones have hot water. *They sometimes organize* camping trips to Ko Pak Bia (from B2400 per boat). Fan B550, a/c B1700

Hill House 10min walk south from the Tha Kao ferry pier ☎089 875 5486; map p.642. Set back from the beach around a khlong, this handful of attractive terraced wooden bungalows offer good views over the bay. All rooms have en-suite bathrooms, fridges, deckchairs and hammocks you'll hardly want to leave. B1100

★ **Suntisook Resort** ☎089 781 6456, ⓦkohyaotravel.

com/suntisook; map p.642. Genial, well-organized place where the bungalows are nicely spaced around a garden and come with TVs, fridges and good, hot-water bathrooms. They're all a bit different but each has a deck and a hammock and some have a/c and three beds. Motorbikes, mountain bikes and kayaks for rent. a/c B1800

HAT KHLONG JAAK (LONG BEACH)

Koyao Island Resort ☎076 597474, ⓦkoyao.com; map p.642. This lovely, stylish resort occupies the best part of the beach and comprises just eighteen chic, thatched, mostly fan-cooled cottage compounds, all of them with separate living areas, huge bathrooms with open-air showers, and sliding doors that give access to the spacious garden and its fine bay views. There's a swimming pool and spa, and if you book directly on their website, free use of mountain bikes and kayaks. Breakfast included. B12,000

★**Sabai Corner** ☎081 892 1827, ⌨sabaicorner bungalows.com; map p.642. Occupying Long Beach's rocky southern headland, this long-established, laidback little Italian–Thai outfit has eleven thoughtfully designed wooden bungalows, all with fans, nets and rustic bathrooms, plus decks and hammocks. They're dotted along a rise between the road and the beach, under cashew and jackfruit trees. There's a good restaurant, serving home-made bread and yoghurt, plus Italian and Thai food, and kayak hire on site. B1000

Tabeak Viewpoint Bungalows ☎089 590 4182, ⌨kohyaotravel.com/hotel.htm; map p.642. Two hundred metres inland, on a cross-island track, this Japanese–Thai place has large, well-outfitted, fan-cooled, wood and bamboo bungalows, all with hot showers, polished wood floors and French windows and balconies that give commanding views of the islands. The Thai owner is a community policeman and enthusiastic fisherman, and an excellent source of island information. B800

HAT PASAI

Coconut Corner ☎076 454221, ⌨bit.ly/2DCl34e; map p.642. Offering some of the cheapest and most traveller-friendly accommodation on the island, in simple en-suite bungalows set around a small garden just across the road from the northern end of Hat Pasai beach. It's just a few minutes' walk from *Pyramid Bar* on Long Beach and has bicycle and motorbike rental. B600

Koh Yao Beach Bungalows ☎076 454213, ⌨kohyao beach.com; map p.642. Clean, well-kept bungalows around a pretty, well-tended lawn, across the main road from the south end of the beach. The fan bungalows are thatched, with mosquito nets, cold-water bathrooms and TVs; a/c options are big and smart with hot showers. Fan B800, a/c B1500

Pasai Cottage ☎089 240 8326, ⌨pasaicottage. blogspot.com; map p.642. The ten bamboo cottages here, just across from Pasai's beach but set back from the road, have unexpectedly tasteful interiors, folding glass doors and prettily tiled bathrooms. B1200

LAEM SAI

★**Lom'Lae Beach Resort** ☎076 597486, ⌨lomlae. com; map p.642. Beautiful, secluded haven, backed by rice fields and rubber plantations and enjoying stunning bay views from its palm-fringed beach and grassy garden. The attractive, airy, wooden, fan-cooled bungalows are thatched and widely spaced, and have sliding doors, fridges and kitchenettes, as well as hammocks to make the most of the views. Some have additional upstairs loft beds, and there are two-bedroom family houses as well. Kayaks, two bikes or a motorbike is included in the price and there's a dive shop. B3500

Sunset Resort Along the uphill road leading to rice paddy ☎082 331 6581, ⌨lamsaivillagehotel.com; map p.642. A few bungalows set in a garden high on the hill-slope that dominates the southern side of the island. Some rooms are simpler than others, but all are en suite and have cosy verandas. There's a restaurant with sunset views. Fan B500, a/c B1200

AO LOH HA

The Paradise Koh Yao ☎076 584450, ⌨paradise-kohyao.com; map p.642. Set on a lovely but isolated beach, these large, deluxe, thatched, a/c rooms and villas all have plenty of outdoor space and semi-outdoor bathrooms, some with private Jacuzzis. There's a huge pool, a spa, kayaks and yoga classes. Breakfast included. B7,600

EATING AND DRINKING

There's a lively nightmarket on Ban Thai Kao's pier, perfect for cheap barbecued fish, rice flour pancakes and mingling with the locals.

HAT THA KAO

Suntisook Resort ☎089 781 6456, ⌨kohyaotravel. com/suntisook; map p.642. Charming restaurant serving a long menu of Thai food, including fish (according to market price) and a good, generous chicken *matsaman* curry, as well as spaghetti, mashed potato and Western breakfasts. Daily 7.30am–9pm.

HAT KHLONG JAAK (LONG BEACH)

★**Cha Ba** ☎ 087 266 1404 ⌨facebook.com/chabacafe; map p.642. Thai–Swiss run organic vegetarian café that doubles up as a wine shop and secondhand bookstore. It serves vegan-friendly food, including zesty paninis (from B140), vegan burgers (B200) and pastas (from B180). The restaurant is a joyful open-air affair, full of driftwood and recycled boat parts that have been turned into tables, whilst the wine bar has its own intimate terrace, where the island's residents come to chatter at night. Daily 9am–5pm.

La Luna ☎084 629 1550, ⌨lalunakohyao.com; map p.642. Congenial, Italian-owned bar-restaurant in a garden setting with hammocks. On offer are homemade pastas, including very tasty tagliatelle with cream and prosciutto (B230), proper pizzas (around B250), Italian desserts and lots of cocktails. Call for free delivery to your resort. Daily 2pm –late, although the kitchen closes at 9.30/10pm.

LAEM SAI

Good View Restaurant On the main road between Tha Manok and Hat Laem Ko ☎089 290 5407, ⌨bit. ly/2DD495F; map p.642. Named after its attractive palm-fringed beach location, set before a quiet bay that is perfect for sundowners (from B120) and romantic dinners (try the barbecue prawns, B250), this seafood restaurant's outdoor terrace is a popular spot to spending an evening. Daily 11am–12pm

Rice Paddy Viewpoint Restaurant On top of a hill overlooking Tha Manok and Tha Laem Sai ☏ 076 410 233, ⓦ ricepaddy.website; map p.642. Lovable organic café and ice cream parlour with wooden tables spilling on a cliff-top and unmatched views over the island's southern beaches. They serve a range of international cuisines, from hummus (B120) to overpriced Thai mains like chicken *pat thai* (B180). But the views and friendly atmosphere, especially at sunset, just about make up for the price hike.

Booking is recommended in high season. Tue–Sun 1pm–late, Mon 4pm–late, closed Mon between April and October.

BAN THA KAI

Faye's Kitchen At the village's roundabout ☏ 084 645 8963 ⓦ facebook.com/fayeskohyao; map p.642. This welcoming vegan-friendly, foreign-owned restaurant has a warm wooden décor and dishes up hearty pastas (from B180), burgers and sandwiches (from B260) and Thai food. They serve a good selection of cocktails (from B190) and beers (B110). Daily 9am–10pm.

7 Ao Phang Nga

National Park admission B300 • ⓦ dnp.go.th

Protected from the ravages of the Andaman Sea by Phuket, **AO PHANG NGA** has a seascape both bizarre and beautiful. Covering some four hundred square kilometres of coast between Phuket and Krabi, the mangrove-edged bay is spiked with limestone karst formations up to 300m in height, jungle-clad and craggily profiled. This is Thailand's own version of Vietnam's world-famous Ha Long Bay, reminiscent too of Guilin's scenery in China, and much of it is now preserved as **national park**. The bay is thought to have been formed about twelve thousand years ago when a dramatic rise in sea level flooded the summits of mountain ranges, which over millions of years had been eroded by an acidic mixture of atmospheric carbon dioxide and rainwater. Some of these karst islands have been further eroded in such a way that they are now hollow, hiding secret lagoons or *hongs* that can only be accessed at certain tides and only by kayak. The main *hong* islands are in the **western** and **eastern** bay areas – to the west or east of Ko Yao Noi, which sits roughly midway between Phuket and Krabi. But the most famous scenery is in the **central bay** area, which boasts the biggest concentration of karst islands, and the weirdest rock formations.

The central bay

On tours of the **central bay**, the standard itinerary follows a circular or figure-of-eight route, passing extraordinary karst silhouettes that change character with the shifting light – in the eerie glow of an early morning mist it can be a breathtaking experience. Some of the formations have nicknames suggested by their weird outlines – like **Khao Machu** (**Marju**), which translates as "Pekinese Rock". Others have titles derived from other attributes – **Tham Nak** (or Nark, meaning Naga Cave) gets its name from the serpentine stalagmites inside; **Ko Thalu** (Pierced Cave) has a tunnel through it; and a close inspection of **Khao Kien** (Painting Rock) reveals a cliff wall decorated with paintings of elephants, monkeys, fish, crabs and hunting weapons, believed to be between three thousand and five thousand years old.

Ao Phang Nga's most celebrated features, however, earned their tag from a movie: the cleft **Khao Ping Gan** (Leaning Rock) and its tapered outcrop **Khao Tapu** (Nail Rock) are better known as **James Bond Island**, having starred as Scaramanga's hideaway in *The Man with the Golden Gun*. Every boat stops off here so tourists can pose in front of the iconic rock – whose narrowing base is a good example of how wave action is shaping the bay – and the island crawls with seashell and trinket vendors.

The central bay's other major attraction is **Ko Panyi**, a Muslim village built almost entirely on stilts around the rock that supports the mosque. Nearly all boat tours stop here for lunch, so you're best off avoiding the pricey seafood restaurants around the

> ## THE HONGS
>
> **Hongs** are the *pièce de résistance* of Ao Phang Nga: invisible to any passing vessel, these secret tidal lagoons are enclosed within the core of seemingly impenetrable limestone outcrops, accessible via murky tunnels that can only be navigated at certain tides in kayaks small enough to slip beneath and between low-lying rocky overhangs. Like the karsts themselves, the *hongs* have taken millions of years to form, with the softer limestone hollowed out from above by the wind and the rain, and from the side by the pounding waves. Eventually, when the two hollows met, the heart of the karst was able to fill with water via the wave-eroded passageway at sea level, creating a lagoon. The world inside these roofless hollows is an extraordinary one, protected from the open bay by a ring of cliff faces hung with vertiginous prehistoric-looking gardens of upside-down cycads, twisted bonsai palms and tangled ferns. And as the tide withdraws, the *hong's* resident creatures emerge to forage on the muddy floor, among them fiddler crabs, mudskippers, dusky langurs and crab-eating macaques, with white-bellied sea eagles often hovering overhead.

jetty, and heading instead towards the islanders' food stalls near the mosque. You can enjoy a more tranquil Ko Panyi experience by joining one of the overnight tours from Phang Nga town (see page 648), which include an evening meal and guesthouse accommodation on the island – and the chance to watch the sun set and rise over the bay; you can also rent a kayak from the jetty and go exploring yourself.

At some point on your central-bay tour you should pass several small brick **kilns** on the edge of a mangrove swamp, which were once used for producing charcoal from mangrove wood. You'll also be ferried beneath **Tham Lod**, a photogenic archway roofed with stalactites that opens onto spectacular limestone and mangrove vistas.

The western bay: Ko Panak and Ko Hong

The main attraction of **the western bay** is **Ko Panak**, whose limestone cliffs hide secret tunnels to no fewer than five different **hongs** within its hollowed heart. These are probably Ao Phang Nga's most spectacular hidden worlds, the pitch-black tunnel approaches infested by bats and the bright, roofless *hongs* an entire other world, draped in hanging gardens of lianas and miniature screw pines and busy with cicadas and the occasional family of crab-eating macaques. Western-bay tours also usually take in nearby **Ko Hong** (different from the Ko Hong in the eastern bay), whose exterior walls are coated with red, yellow and orange encrusting sponges, oyster shells and chitons (560-million-year-old slipper-shaped shells), which all make good camouflage for the scuttling red, blue and black crabs. Ko Hong's interior passageways light up with bioluminescent plankton in the dark and lead to a series of cave-lagoons.

The eastern bay: Ko Hong, Ao Thalen and Ao Luk

The principal *hong* island in the **eastern bay**, known both as **Ko Hong** and **Ko Lao Bileh**, lies about midway between Krabi's Hat Klong Muang beach and the southeast coast of Ko Yao Noi. The island is fringed by white-sand beaches and exceptionally clear aquamarine waters that make it a popular snorkelling destination. The island's actual *hong* lacks the drama of Ao Phang Nga's best *hongs* because it's not fully enclosed or accessed via dark tunnels as at Ko Panak, but it is pretty, full of starfish, and tidal, so can only be explored at certain times.

The eastern bay's other big attractions are the mangrove-fringed inlets along the mainland coast between Krabi and Phang Nga, particularly around **Ao Luk** and **Ao Thalen** (sometimes Ao Talin or Talane), though the latter can get very crowded with tour groups. Trips around here take you through complex networks of channels that weave through the mangrove swamps, between fissures in the limestone cliffs, beneath karst outcrops and into the occasional cave. Many of these passageways are *hongs*, isolated havens that might be up to 2km long, all but cut off from the main bay and accessible only at certain tides. The **Ban Bor Tor** (or Ban Bho Tho) area of Ao Luk bay is especially known for **Tham Lod**, a long tunnel hung with stalactites whose entrance is obscured by vines, and for nearby **Tham Phi Hua Toe**, whose walls display around a hundred prehistoric cave paintings, as well as some interestingly twisted stalactite formations.

TOURS OF THE BAY
AO PHANG NGA

By sea canoe The most rewarding, and generally the most expensive, option for exploring Ao Phang Nga is to join a sea-canoeing trip (either guided or self-paddle), which enables you both to explore inside the *hongs* and to see at close quarters the extraordinary ecosystems around and inside the karst islands. Most sea-canoeing tours use large support boats carrying groups of up to thirty people. They can be arranged from any resort in Phuket, or through the specialist operators John Gray's Sea Canoe and Paddle Asia (see page 615); at Khao Lak, for example through Khao Lak Land Discovery (see page 611); at all Krabi beaches and

islands and in Krabi town (see page 649), and on Ko Yao Noi (see page 641). The itinerary is usually determined by your departure point, with Phuket trips focusing on the western bay and Krabi tours concentrating on the eastern half.

By tour boat Most tours of the central bay are either in large tour boats booked out of Phuket or Krabi, which generally feature snorkelling and beach stops rather than kayaking, or in inexpensive, small-group longtail boats that depart from Phang Nga town (see page 648), as well as from Phuket and Ko Yao Noi. All the main areas of the bay are extremely popular so don't expect a solitary experience.

Phang Nga town

Friendly if unexciting little **PHANG NGA TOWN**, beautifully located under looming limestone cliffs edged with palm groves midway between Phuket and Krabi, serves mainly as a point from which to organize budget longtail trips around the spectacular karst islands of Ao Phang Nga (see page 646). But there are also several caves and waterfalls nearby, accessible on cheap tours run by Phang Nga tour operators.

ARRIVAL AND INFORMATION
PHANG NGA TOWN

By bus Phang Nga has good bus connections, but its bus station is inconveniently located around 7km south of town, along Highway 415. Some guesthouses can help with pick-ups and drop-offs, if contacted in advance, or a taxi into town will cost around B120. If you're heading to Khao Sok National Park headquarters (see page 601), it's usually fastest to take a Surat Thani bus and change in Phanom. Some of the services to Bangkok's Southern Bus Terminal continue to Mo Chit station on the north side of the city.
Destinations: Bangkok (5 daily; 13hr); Ko Samui (daily; 6hr); Krabi (hourly; 1hr 30min–2hr); Phuket (at least

hourly; 1hr 30min–2hr 30min); Ranong (5 daily; 3hr); Satun (3 daily; 8hr); Surat Thani (every 2hr; 4hr); Takua Pa (hourly; 1hr); Trang (every 1hr; 6hr).

By boat The pier for boats around Ao Phang Nga, and to Ko Yao Noi (daily; 90min), is at Tha Dan, 9km south of town and served by songthaews that pass on Thanon Phetkasem (B25).

Tourist information The TAT information office for Phang Nga is inconveniently located 2km south of the town on Highway 4 (daily 8.30am–4.30pm; ☎076 411586). You will find the tour desk at *Thaweesuk Hotel* (see below) more helpful.

ACCOMMODATION

Phang Nga's best hotels are all clustered in the northeastern end of Thanon Phetkasem (Highway 4).

Baan Phang Nga 100/2 Thanon Phetkasem (on the left-hand side) ☎076 413276 and 095 9456546, ⓦfacebook.com/BaanPhangnga. Friendly guesthouse and bakery above a café that was being renovated at the time of writing. The a/c rooms have TVs, small, hot-water bathrooms and a few touches of kitsch contemporary décor. There's a simple local art gallery and souvenir shop on the ground floor too. B650

★**Thaweesuk Hotel** 77 Thanon Phetkasem (near

Krung Thai Bank) ☎ 076 412100 or 094 316 6053 ⓦthaweesukhotel.com. Recently renovated and catering to budget travellers, this is an exquisite old-style mansion built by a Penang architect. The spacious reception and lounge has a small café that's good to relax in with a book, and the *Sayan Tour* desk (see above) for unbiased local information. Up a wooden staircase are well-maintained and very clean and bright fan rooms, a couple of huge a/c options (B800) and a rooftop terrace. Breakfast, which is prepared with fresh fruit from the manager's garden, is B80 extra. B500

The Sleep 144 Thanon Phetkasem (in front of a small

TOURS FROM PHANG NGA TOWN

AO PHANG NGA

The most popular budget tours of Ao Phang Nga (see page 646) are the **longtail boat trips** run by local tour operators who offer almost identical itineraries. The recommended Sayan Tour (☎076 430348, ⓦ sayantour.com) operates from the lobby of *Thaweesuk Hotel*. They offer half-day tours of the bay (daily at about 8.30am & 2pm; 3–4hr) costing B950 per person (including national park fee; minimum four people), as well as full-day trips, which cost B1250, including lunch and national park fee. Take the 8.30am tour to avoid seeing the bay at its most crowded. All tours include a chance to swim in the bay, and most offer the option of an hour's canoeing around Ko Thalu as well, for an extra B500.

All tour operators also offer the chance to **stay** overnight at their own guesthouse on **Ko Panyi**. This can be tacked onto the half- or full-day tour for an extra B500; dinner, accommodation and breakfast are included in the price.

LOCAL SIGHTS AROUND PHANG NGA TOWN

You can arrange trips (B600) to **Tham Phung Chang**, or **Elephant Belly Cave**, a natural 1200m-long tunnel through the massive 800m-high wooded cliff that towers over the Provincial Hall, about 4km west of the town centre. With a bit of imagination, the cliff's outline resembles a kneeling elephant, and the hollow interior is, of course, its belly. You can travel through the elephant's belly to the other side of the cliff and back on a two-hour excursion that involves wading, rafting and canoeing along the freshwater stream, Khlong Tham, that has eroded the channel. There are also tours (from B500) that take in several other local caves, plus **Sa Nang Manora Forest Park**, which has hiking trails through thick, impressive rainforest and several waterfalls with swimmable pools, 9km north of the town centre.

A 2km walk west from the *Thaweesuk Hotel* brings yyou to the quirky garden of **Wat Tham Ta Pan**, which is filled with macabre life-sized statues depicting the Naraka, the Buddhist hell. Enter through the open-mouthed, neon-lit guardian stone dragon.

7

mosque and Ibank) ☎076 411828 ⓦ the-sleep-phang-nga-th.book.direct. A brand-new boutique hostel with an open front porch filled with wooden tables, and a few floors of good value en-suite a/c rooms with plush beds and modern décor. Breakfast is not included, but coffee is free for guests. ‖B600‖

EATING

Duang Thanon Phetkasem, a couple of doors away from Baan Phang Nga Guesthouse (a tiny sticker shows the name in English). Locals rate this simple but friendly restaurant with a few outdoor tables as the best in town; it's been going thirty years and serves a good squid salad (*yam pla meuk*; B200), as well as rice and noodle dishes for about B80. Daily 10.30am–1pm.

Kafeh Thanon Phetkasem (no English sign). For a great Thai breakfast, go left down Phetkasem about 200m past *Thaweesuk Hotel* to find this hugely popular dessert shop on the left. Fill your tray with assorted Thai *khanom* – banana-leaf parcels of sticky rice laced with sweet coconut milk and stuffed with banana, mango or other delights – at about B10 apiece, then order from the selection of hot and cold coffees and watch Thai breakfast TV with everyone else. Daily 6am–6pm.

Krabi town

The estuarine town of **KRABI** is both provincial capital and major hub for onward travel to some of the region's most popular islands and beaches, including Ko Phi Phi, Ko Lanta, Ao Nang, Klong Muang and Laem Phra Nang (Railay). So efficient are the transport links that you don't really need to stop here, but it also makes an appealing base, strung out along the west bank of the Krabi estuary, with mangrove-lined shorelines to the east, craggy limestone outcrops on every horizon, and plenty of guesthouses. The beaches of **Ao Nang** (see p.657) and **Railay** (see p.663) are both within 45 minutes of town, and other nearby attractions include the **mangrove swamps** and

> ## MANGROVE TOURS
>
> A boat trip through the eerily scenic **mangrove**-lined channels of the Krabi estuary is a fun way to gain a different perspective on the area. As well as a close-up view of the weird creatures that inhabit the swamps (see box, p.653), you'll get to visit a riverside cave or two. **Tours** are best organized directly with the longtail boatmen who hang around Krabi's two piers and the surrounding streets (B300–500/boat/hr) but can also be arranged through most tour agents.
>
> The estuary's most famous features are the twin limestone outcrops known as **Khao Kanab Nam**, which rise a hundred metres above the water from opposite sides of the Krabi River near the *Maritime Park and Spa Resort* and are so distinctive that they've become the symbol of Krabi. One of the twin karsts hides caves, which can be explored – many skeletons have been found here over the centuries, thought to be those of immigrants who got stranded by a flood before reaching the mainland. You can also choose to visit the Muslim island of Ko Klang (see p.653).

7

villagey **Ko Klang** peninsula across the estuary, the dramatically sited Tiger Cave Temple at **Wat Tham Seua** and **Khao Phanom Bencha National Park**. A number of organized **day-trips in the Krabi area**, including snorkelling and kayaking excursions, are available (see box, p.658).

Krabi town has no unmissable sights but is small enough for a pleasant stroll around its main landmarks by day and excellent street food markets by night. Its chief attraction is its setting, and a good way to appreciate this is to follow the paved **riverside walkway** down to the fishing port, about 800m south of Tha Chao Fa; several hotels capitalise on the views here, across to mangrove-ringed Ko Klang, and towards the southern end the walkway borders the municipal Thara Park.

Inland, in the centre of town, you can't fail to notice the bizarre sculptures of hulking **anthropoid apes** clutching two sets of traffic lights apiece at the Thanon Maharat/Soi 10 crossroads. They are meant to represent Krabi's most famous ancestors, the tailless *Siamopithecus oceanus*, whose forty-million-year-old remains were found in a lignite mine in the south of the province and are believed by scientists to be among the earliest examples worldwide of the ape-to-human evolutionary process.

Wat Kaew Korawaram

West off Thanon Maharat • Free

It's hard to miss the striking white walls of the minimalist modern bot at the town-centre temple, **Wat Kaew Korawaram** (Grovaram), approached via a grand naga staircase. The interior murals depict traditional scenes, including *Jataka* episodes from the lives of the Buddha, but are spiced up with some modern twists – including warring hairy foreigners on either side of the door.

Ko Klang

Across the river from Krabi town • Frequent shared longtails from Tha Chao Fa (B20; 10min) and Tha Thara Park (B20; 3min; bicycles carried); longtail charter also possible (B60–100)

Most of Krabi's longtail boatmen come from **Ko Klang**, the mangrove-encircled peninsula just across the channel from Tha Chao Fa and Tha Thara Park. On a two-hour mangrove tour, you can choose to stop off on the peninsula for a visit, or you can go there yourself, on one of the public longtail **boats** that shuttle across from Krabi town throughout the day. You can also stay in Ban Ko Klang as part of a **homestay** programme, which can be booked locally through Krabi Friendly Tour or in advance as part of a package with Tell Tale Travel (@ telltaletravel.co.uk).

The predominantly Muslim peninsula is home to three small **villages** housing a total of around four thousand people, most of whom earn their living from tourism and fishing. Seafood restaurants have sprung up at the pier and can give free mini tours of their fish farms. The island is no great beauty but therein lies its charm, offering the chance to experience a little of typical southern Thai life, which is a highlight of staying in Krabi Town. You can swim off Ko Klang's long, wild southwestern **beach**, from where you also get an excellent view of the distinctive profiles of all the famous local **islands** – Laem Phra Nang (30min boat ride away), Ko Poda (45min), Bamboo Island, Ko Phi Phi (2hr) and Ko Jum; any Ko Klang boatman will take you to the beach for the same price as from Krabi town. Wandering around the village on foot is equally fascinating.

Wat Tham Seua

10km northeast of Krabi town, about 2km north of Highway 4 • Minibuses (100B) leave Krabi Town for the temple every two hours from 7am to 5pm, collecting passengers at most guesthouses. Return trips to Krabi Town depart from the temple between 10am and 7.30pm.

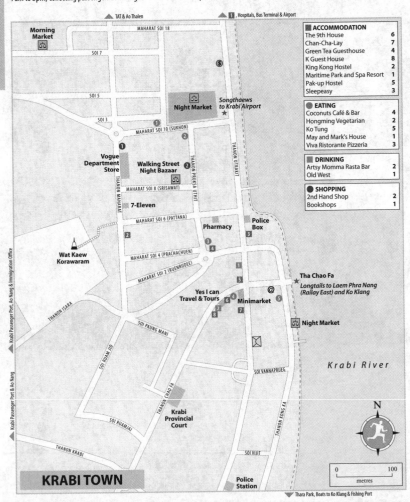

ACCOMMODATION

The 9th House	6
Chan-Cha-Lay	7
Green Tea Guesthouse	4
K Guest House	8
King Kong Hostel	2
Maritime Park and Spa Resort	1
Pak-up Hostel	5
Sleepeasy	3

EATING

Coconuts Café & Bar	4
Hongming Vegetarian	2
Ko Tung	5
May and Mark's House	1
Viva Ristorante Pizzeria	3

DRINKING

Artsy Momma Rasta Bar	2
Old West	1

SHOPPING

2nd Hand Shop	2
Bookshops	1

KRABI TOWN

LIFE IN A MANGROVE SWAMP

Mangrove swamps are at their creepiest at low tide, when their aerial roots are fully exposed to form gnarled and knotted archways above the muddy banks. Not only are these roots essential parts of the tree's breathing apparatus, they also reclaim land for future mangroves, trapping and accumulating water-borne debris into which the metre-long mangrove seedlings can fall. In this way, mangrove swamps also fulfil a vital ecological function: stabilizing shifting mud and protecting coastlines from erosion and the impact of tropical storms.

Mangrove swamp mud harbours some interesting creatures too, like the instantly recognizable **fiddler crab**, named after the male's single outsized reddish claw, which it brandishes for communication and defence purposes; the claw is so powerful it could open a can of baked beans. If you keep your eyes peeled you should be able to make out a few **mudskippers**. These specially adapted fish can absorb atmospheric oxygen through their skins as long as they keep their outsides damp, which is why they spend so much time slithering around in the sludge; they move in tiny hops by flicking their tails, aided by their extra-strong pectoral fins. You might well also come across **kingfishers** and white-bellied **sea eagles**, or even a **crab-eating macaque**.

Though the Krabi mangroves have not escaped the **environmentally damaging** attentions of invasive industry, or the cutting down of the bigger trees to make commercial charcoal, around fifteen percent of the Andaman coastline is still fringed with mangrove forest, the healthiest concentration of this rich, complex ecosystem in Thailand.

7

Spectacularly situated amid limestone cliffs within a tropical forest, **Wat Tham Seua** (Tiger Cave Temple) is a famous meditation temple of caves, wooded trails and panoramic viewpoints. As it's a working monastery, visitors are required to wear respectable dress (no shorts or sleeveless tops for men or women).

Wat Tham Seua's abbot is a renowned teacher of Vipassana meditation, and some of his educational tools are displayed in the main **bot**, on the left under the cliff overhang, in the main temple compound. Though these close-up photos of human entrails and internal organs may seem shockingly unorthodox, they are there as reminders of the impermanence of the body, a fundamental tenet of Buddhist philosophy; the human skulls and skeletons dotted around the rest of the compound serve the same purpose. Beyond the bot, follow the path past the nuns' quarters to reach the pair of steep **staircases** that scale the 600m-high cliffside. The first staircase is long (1272 steps) and very steep, and takes about an hour to climb, but the vista from the summit is quite spectacular, affording fabulous views over the limestone outcrops and out to the islands beyond. Watch out for the monkeys: they are high skilled at stealing food and valuables, so try to avoid carrying unnecessary items and any plastic bags. There's a large seated Buddha image and chedi at the top, and a few monks' cells hidden among the trees. The second staircase, next to the large statue of the Chinese Goddess of Mercy, Kuan Im, takes you on a less arduous route down into a deep dell encircled by high limestone walls. Here the monks have built themselves self-sufficient meditation cells (*kuti*) in and around the rocky crannies, linked by paths through the lush ravine: if you continue along the main path you'll eventually find yourself back where you began, at the foot of the staircase. The valley is home to squirrels and monkeys as well as a pair of remarkable trees with overground **buttress roots** over 10m high.

ARRIVAL AND DEPARTURE

KRABI TOWN

You can buy bus, a/c minibus, boat, train and air tickets, including combination bus and train tickets, to Bangkok via Surat Thani and through-tickets to Ko Samui and Ko Pha Ngan, from clued-up, helpful Krabi Friendly Tour & Travel, 9/3 Thanon Chao Fa (☎075 612558).

BY PLANE

Krabi airport (☎075 636541–2, ⊛krabiairport.org) is just off Highway 4, 18km east of Krabi town, 35km from Ao Nang. It's served by many international flights and by domestic flights from Bangkok with Thai Airways, Bangkok Airways, Nok Air, Thai Lion Air and Air Asia, from Chiang Mai with Air Asia and from Ko Samui with Bangkok Airways. An airport shuttle bus (hourly; B150 per person) runs to Krabi town, stopping at Krabi Provincial Court, or there are fixed-price taxis at B350 per car to Krabi town and port. Frequent songthaews (20min; B40) from the airport depart on the main road 400m from the terminal and drop passengers anywhere along Thanon Utrakit; but to the airport drop you off at departures, leaving from north Thanon Utrakit in Krabi Town. Car rental is also available (see opposite).

Destinations: Bangkok (up to 15 daily; 1hr 20min); Chiang Mai (2 daily; 2hr); Ko Samui (1 daily; 50min).

BY BUS

Numerous long-distance buses run to Krabi's bus terminal, which is 5km north of the town centre in the suburb of Talat Kao, beside Highway 4. Frequent red songthaews (B20) shuttle between the town centre (where they do a little circuit to pick up passengers, starting from the 7-Eleven on Thanon Maharat or *Pak-up Hostel* on Thanon Utrakit) and the bus station. Between 6am and 6.30pm, white songthaews to Ao Nang depart from Krabi bus terminal roughly every 15 minutes.

To/from Bangkok A/c and VIP buses between Bangkok's Southern Bus Terminal and Krabi depart mainly in the late afternoon or evening, arriving at the other end in the early morning. Think twice before taking a private bus direct from Thanon Khao San (see p.136).

By a/c minibus Private a/c minibus services (all roughly hourly) run from Krabi to Surat Thani, Nakhon Si Thammarat, Trang and Ko Lanta (see map, p.652). Aimed specifically at tourists, in competition with the boats, the Lanta service will pick up from hotels in Krabi and charges B250–350, depending on which beach you want to be dropped off at on Ko Lanta Yai. From the Talat Kao bus terminal, you can also catch an a/c minibus that originates on Lanta to Phuket airport/town (roughly every 2hr; 2–3hr; B400/350 bookable through Krabi hotels and travel agents).

Bus destinations: Bangkok (12 daily; 12hr); Hat Yai (hourly from 7am to 5pm; 4–5hr); Khao Sok (every 2 hours from 7.30am to 4pm; 4–5hr); Ko Lanta (hourly from 7am to 5pm; 2–3hr); Nakhon Si Thammarat (at least hourly; 3hr); Phang Nga (every 30min; 2hr); Phuket Town Bus Station 2 (at least hourly; 3hr); Ranong (2 daily; 5hr); Satun (4 daily; 5hr); Surat Thani (hourly from 7.30am to 4.30pm; 2hr); Takua Pa (4 daily; 3hr 30min–4hr 30min); Trang (hourly until 5pm; 2–3hr); Satun (4 daily; 4hr).

BY TRAIN AND BUS

A more comfortable alternative to taking a bus from Bangkok is to catch an overnight train from the capital to Surat Thani or Trang, and then change on to one of the frequent a/c buses or minibuses to Krabi (hourly; 2hr).

BY BOAT

Ferries to Ko Phi Phi, Ko Lanta and Ko Jum leave from Krabi Passenger Port (sometimes referred to as Tha Khlong Jilad; ☎075 620052), a couple of kilometres southwest of Krabi town centre. Ferry tickets bought from tour operators in town should include a free transfer to Krabi Passenger Port, but there are also red songthaews that do a circuit of the town centre before heading out to the port. Songthaews from Krabi town connect with most boats, leaving about an hour before from the morning market on Maharat Soi 7, passing the 7-Eleven on Thanon Maharat and Talat Kao bus terminal.

Ko Jum Boats leave year-round from the Laem Kruat pier, about 40km south of Krabi Town. Catch the yellow and blue songthaew (B100) from the Siam Bank, near the piers and the 7-Eleven.

Ko Phi Phi Ferries to Ko Phi Phi from Krabi Passenger Port

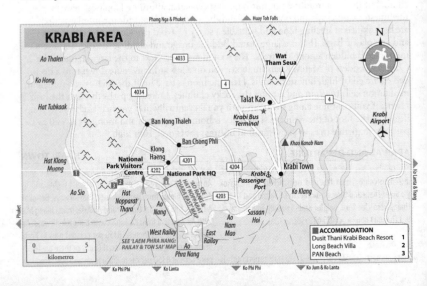

KRABI AREA

Phang Nga & Phuket

Huay Toh Falls

Ao Thalen

Ko Hong

Hat Tubkaak

4033

4034

Wat Tham Seua

4

Talat Kao

Krabi Bus Terminal

Khao Kanab Nam

4

Krabi Airport

Ban Nong Thaleh

Ban Chong Phli

Klong Haeng

4201

Hat Klong Muang

National Park Visitors' Centre

4202

National Park HQ

4204

Krabi Passenger Port

Krabi Town

Ko Klang

Ao Sio

Hat Nopparat Thara

Ao Nang

4203

Susaan Hoi

Ao Nam Mao

West Railay

East Railay

SEE 'LAEM PHRA NANG: RAILAY & TON SAI' MAP

Ao Phra Nang

SEE 'AO NOPPARAT THARA–EAST RAILAY' MAP

0   5
kilometres

Phuket

Ko Lanta & Trang

Ko Phi Phi   Ko Lanta   Ko Phi Phi   Ko Jum & Ko Lanta

■ ACCOMMODATION	
Dusit Thani Krabi Beach Resort	1
Long Beach Villa	2
PAN Beach	3

depart four times daily in high season and at least twice daily in low season (2hr; B350–400).

Ko Lanta Yai Going by a/c minibus to Ko Lanta (see above) is more popular these days, but there's still one ferry a day from Krabi Passenger Port, via Ko Jum (B350; 2hr), in peak season (roughly mid-Nov to mid-April 11.30am; 2hr 30min; B400).

Ko Phi Phi Ferries to Ko Phi Phi from Krabi depart three times daily (five times on weekends; 2hr; B480).

Ko Yao Noi In addition to boats from Ao Nang, there are services from the pier at Ao Thalen, 33km northwest of Krabi town to Ko Yao Noi (see page 641).

Laem Phra Nang (East Railay) Longtail boats for East Railay on Laem Phra Nang (45min; B1500/boat or B150/ person if there are 8–10 passengers) leave on demand from the town-centre pier at Tha Chao Fa on Thanon Kong Ka.

Ko Yao Noi As well as boats from Ao Nang, there are services from the pier at Ao Thalen, 33km northwest of Krabi town, to Ko Yao Noi (see p.643).

Destinations: Ko Jum (roughly mid-Nov to mid-April daily; 1hr 30min–2hr); Ko Lanta Yai (roughly mid-Nov to mid-April daily; 2hr 30min); Ko Phi Phi Don (2–4 daily; 2hr); Ko Yao Noi (from Ao Thalen; 6–7 daily; 1hr).

GETTING AROUND

By songthaew Most of the public songthaew services to local beaches, towns and attractions circulate around town before heading out, making stops outside the 7-Eleven just south of the Soi 8 intersection on Thanon Maharat and along Thanon Utrakit; most run at least twice an hour from dawn till noon, and then less frequently until dusk. For getting around town, the most useful are probably the red songthaews that run between Tesco Lotus, out on Highway 4 beyond the Wat Tham Seua turn-off, and Krabi Passenger

Port. White songthaews start at Talat Kao bus terminal and do a spin around town before heading out to Ao Nang (B50 daytime, B60 after 6pm).

By car or motorbike Budget (☏ 075 636171, ⊚ budget. co.th) and Avis (☏ 089 969 8676, ⊚ avisthailand.com) have desks at the airport. Most accommodation offer rental motorbikes.

By bicycle *Pak-up Hostel* (see p.656) rents mountain bikes for B150/day.

INFORMATION AND TOURS

Tourist information Krabi's unhelpful TAT office (daily 8.30am–4.30pm; ☏ 075 612812, ⊚ tatkrabi@tat.or.th) is inconveniently located 2km north of the centre on Thanon Maharat.

Books If you're spending some time in this region, it's worth buying a copy of *Krabi: Caught in the Spell – A Guide to Thailand's Enchanted Province*, expat environmentalist

Thom Henley's lively and opinionated book about Krabi people, islands and traditions (see p.781).

Tour agents Yes I can Travel & Tour on Thanon Chao Fa (☏ 098 194 4532, ⊚ sweet_rose001@hotmail.com) has many day-trip options (see page 660) and sells bus, flight and train tickets.

ACCOMMODATION

★ **The 9th House** 9/9 Thanon Chao Fa ☏ 075 656485, ⊚ facebook.com/the9house9; map p.652. Eight spacious en-suite rooms with wall windows and small balconies set on the upper storeys of a well-kept Thai home. It's smack in the middle of the action, yet retains a homely, secluded vibe that appeals to both couples and families. B1300

★ **Chan-Cha-Lay** 55 Thanon Utrakit ☏ 075 620952; map p.652. With its stylish blue-and-white theme throughout, funky bathrooms, white-painted wooden furniture and blue shutters, this is the most charming and arty place to stay in Krabi. The en suites in the garden come with fan or a/c and are by far the nicest option, further from the street; quieter rooms in the main building share bathrooms and some don't have windows. Fan B500, a/c B800

Green Tea Guesthouse 4 Issara Road, ☏ 075 630 609; map p.652. A veritable cheapie run by a friendly Thai family on the first floor of a traditional corner house. It has twins and doubles with basic shared bathrooms, with attractive wooden floors and walls that are a throwback to a bygone era of budget travel in Thailand. B200

K Guest House 15–25 Thanon Chao Fa ☏ 075 623166, ⊚ kguesthouse@yahoo.com; map p.652. Deservedly popular and well run, in a peaceful but central spot, this long, timber-clad row house has bedrooms with wooden floors, panelled walls, streetside balconies and hot showers – ask for a more attractive upstairs room. Also offers some cheaper shabby rooms with windows onto the hall and shared bathroom downstairs and at the back. Fan B400, a/c B600

King Kong Hostel 44 Maharaj Road right opposite Wat Kaew's entrance, ☏ 075 623 199; map p.652. Sparkling new central hostel with a hair salon in the lobby and clean and comfortable dorms, immaculate shared toilets and a few rooms that are perhaps a bit too cramped for the price. Dorm B300 Doubles B650

Maritime Park and Spa Resort 2km north of town off Thanon Utrakit ☏ 075 620028–35, ⊚ maritime parkandspa.com; map p.652. Beautifully located upper-end hotel, set beside the limestone karsts and mangroves of the Krabi River. Rooms are a little old-fashioned but large and comfortable and have fine views over the extensive

7

landscaped grounds and lake. There's a big pool and a spa, and shuttles into Krabi town and Ao Nang. Good-value packages sometimes available on their website. Breakfast included. **B2600**

Pak-up Hostel 87 Thanon Utrakit ☏075 611955, ⓦpakuphostel; map p.652. Colourful, modern hostel in a short tower block on probably Krabi's busiest corner, with smart ten-bed a/c dorms and two private doubles. This is the place backpackers come to be sociable, with lots of common areas, beer pong tournaments, a rooftop bar and an adjacent garden bar. Dorm **B360**, double **B1500**

Sleepeasy 248 Thanon Utrakit ☏089 2870163, ⓦsleepeasykrabi.com; map p.652. This central Thai–British run guesthouse offers dorms, doubles, triples and family rooms, all with shared and very clean bathrooms, in three storeys, topped by a sociable rooftop bar with views over the river. There's free tea, coffee, and fresh fruit for guests. Double **B700**

EATING

Krabi offers plenty of traveller-oriented restaurants but there's also inexpensive local-style dining at the night markets on riverside Thanon Kong Ka and on Maharat Soi 10. The Walking Street night bazaar on Soi 8 (Fri, Sat & Sun 5–10pm) also brims with excellent food stalls, as well as an entertainment stage and trinket and craft stalls.

Coconuts Café and Bar Thanon Chao Fa ☏094 6978 999, ⓦbit.ly/2GjUSkI; map p.652. This welcoming bistro serves fresh coffee (from B50), healthy smoothies and breakfast sets – try the bargain granola, yogurt and muesli bowls (B80). It packs quite a crowd of travellers who come here to indulge in some European comforts, such as hot dogs made with original English Cumberland sausages (B60) and fast wi-fi. Daily 7am–4pm & 6pm–10pm

Hongming Vegetarian 83 Thanon Pruksa Uthit ☏075 621 273; map p.652. A relaxed local spot to get a mix of Thai greens in one dish, even if you aren't vegetarian. The bain-maries are loaded with soy-meat and veg dishes such as matsaman curry and aubergine tofu bake. Two choices on rice is a thrifty B35. Mon–Sat 7am–5pm.

★ **Ko Tung** 66 Thanon Maharat, about 2km north of town centre towards the bus station ☏075 656 822; map p.652. Though it looks nothing much, this little Thai restaurant is always packed with locals savouring the excellent, good-value, southern-style seafood. Special highlights include the sweet mussels (hawy wan), baked crab, and mushroom, long bean and shrimp yam salads. Most dishes B80–100. Mon–Sat 11am–10pm.

May and Mark's House Soi 2, Thanon Maharat, ☏075 612 562, ⓦfacebook.com/MayAndMarkHouse; map p.652. Early hours, home-baked bread (like real sourdough), fresh coffee (B50) and full-English fry-ups make this a popular spot for breakfast. Also does tacos, sandwiches, cheese and tuna melts (B180), pizzas (B200) and Thai, German and vegetarian food. Daily 7am–9pm.

Viva Ristorante Pizzeria 29 Thanon Pruksa Uthit, ☏089 220 4796; map p.652. Genuine Italian-owned joint serving home-made pastas and ravioli (from B160), thin crispy pizzas (from B200), and some imported beers from Belgium and Germany. Daily 11am–11pm.

DRINKING

Artsy Momma Rasta Bar Thanon Chao Fa, ☏061 806 6652; map p.652. This hole-in-the-wall, driftwood and bamboo reggae-style bar draws a decent crowd thanks to occasional live music and its cheap drinks: beers are B80 and cocktails start at B120. Daily 2pm–1am.

Old West Thanon Utrakit, ☏089 195 8575, ⓦbit.ly/2DGRmmZ; map p.652. All bare wood and Wild West photos, with racks of imported spirits behind the long bar. The top-notch sound system churns out wall-to-wall rock music and there are a couple of pool tables. Daily 4pm–4am.

SHOPPING

2nd Hand Shop Thanon Pruksa Uthit, ☏ 075 815343; map p.652. Everything from books to bikes to furniture at pre-loved prices. Daily 10am–9pm.

Bookshops Pakarang on Thanon Utrakit; map p.652. Buys and sells secondhand books, as well as selling handicrafts and espresso coffees. Daily 8am–9pm.

DIRECTORY

Hospitals Krabi Hospital is about 1km north of the town centre at 325 Thanon Utrakit (☏075 611202) and also has dental facilities, but the better hospital is considered to be the private Muslim hospital, Jariyatham Ruam Phet Hospital (☏075 611223), which is about 3km north of town at 514 Thanon Utrakit and has English-speaking staff.

Immigration office In the compound of government offices on the way to Krabi Passenger Port (Mon–Fri 8.30am–4.30pm; ☏075 611097).

Police For all emergencies, call the tourist police on the free, 24hr phone line ☏1155, or contact the local branch of the tourist police in Ao Nang on ☏075 637208.

Ao Nang

AO NANG (sometimes confusingly signed as Ao Phra Nang), 22km west of Krabi town, is a busy, continually expanding, rather faceless mainland resort that mainly caters for mid-budget and package-holiday tourists. Although it lacks the fine beaches of the nearby Railay peninsula (an easy 10min boat ride away), it is less claustrophobic, and has a much greater choice of restaurants and bars, masses of shopping (mostly beachwear, DVDs and souvenirs), plus a wealth of dive shops, day-tripping and snorkelling possibilities and other typical resort facilities. Adjacent **Hat Nopparat Thara**, part of which comes under the protection of a national marine park, is prettier, and divided into two separate beaches by a khlong. The uncrowded, 2km-long **eastern beach** is effectively linked to Ao Nang by a conurbation of accommodation and shops, but the **western beach**, sometimes known as **Hat Ton Son**, across the khlong, is an altogether quieter and more beautiful little enclave, accessible only via longtail or a circuitous back road. Fifteen kilometres' drive west of Ao Nang, **Hat Klong Muang** is no great shakes as a beach but does have some attractive four- and five-star accommodation.

Central Ao Nang and Ao Phai Plong

Ao Nang's central beach is unexceptional and busy with longtail traffic, though it's backed by a pleasantly landscaped promenade. The nicer stretch is east beyond *Ao Nang Villa Resort*, accessed by the pavement that takes you all the way along the shore to the appropriately named *Last Café*, a very pleasant spot for a shady drink. Follow the wooden walkway from beyond *The Last Café* and scale the steps up and over the headland to reach, in about ten minutes, the beach at diminutive **Ao Phai Plong**, which is the sole province of the luxurious *Centara Grand* hotel.

Hat Nopparat Thara east

Immediately west of Ao Nang, beyond the headland occupied by *Krabi Resort* but reached by simply following the road (on foot or in one of the frequent Krabi-bound songthaews), **Hat Nopparat Thara east** is long and pretty, with the road running along a landscaped promenade behind it. Its eastern hinterland is developing fast with hotels and restaurants, but the other end, close to the T-junction with Route 4202, is

---

DIVING FROM AO NANG

Ao Nang is Krabi's main centre for **dive shops**, with a dozen or more outlets, the most reputable of which include Kon-Tiki (☎075 637826, ⓦkontiki-thailand.com) and Poseidon (☎075 637263, ⓦposeidon-diving.com); they have a price agreement for PADI courses, but Poseidon is cheaper for dive trips. Diving with Ao Nang operators is possible year-round, with some dive staff claiming that off-season diving is more rewarding, not least because the sites are much less crowded.

Most one-day **dive trips** head for the area round Ko Phi Phi (from B2700 including two tanks; B1700 for snorkellers with Poseidon) and often include dives at Shark Point and the "King Cruiser" wreck dive (see page 635); the Ko Ha island group, near Ko Lanta, is also popular but more expensive (see page 685).

Two dives in the Ao Nang area – at Ko Poda and Ko Yawasam – cost B2800–3200 (B11500 for snorkellers with Poseidon). PADI dive courses cost B4900 for the introductory Discover Scuba day, or B14,900 for the Open Water.

The nearest recompression chambers are on Phuket; check to see that your dive operator is insured to use one of them. General information on diving in Thailand can be found in Basics (see page 53).

the site of the Hat Nopparat Thara–Mu Ko Phi Phi **national park headquarters** and accommodation. Here too is the **tsunami memorial**, *Hold Me Close* by Louise Bourgeois (2005), a roofless, wood-slatted corncob structure in disrepair enclosing two pairs of hands, joined, prayer like and pleading, extending from a lumpy sea.

At low tide it's almost impossible to swim on this beach, but the sands come alive with thousands of starfish and hermit crabs, and the view out towards the islands is glorious; you can walk to the nearest outcrop at low water.

The **national park visitor centre** is at the end of the beach, beside the khlong and its sheltered marina and jetty, Tha Nopparat Thara, which is the departure point for Ao Nang ferry services to Phuket, Phi Phi and Ko Lanta, as well as for longtails to the western beach. The visitor centre's car park is famous for its **seafood restaurants**, and Krabi residents also like to picnic under the shorefront casuarina trees here.

Hat Nopparat Thara west

Hat Nopparat Thara west has a quite different atmosphere from its eastern counterpart: just a handful of small bungalow hotels and a few private residences share its long swathe of peaceful casuarina- and palm-shaded shoreline, making it a great place to escape the crowds and commerce of other Krabi beaches. The views of the karst islands are magnificent, though swimming here is also tide-dependent. Without your own transport you can only get here by longtail across the narrow but deep khlong beside the national park visitor's centre, but with a car or bike you can arrive via the very quiet back road that snakes through the mangroves from the Klong Muang road to the edge of the bungalow properties.

ARRIVAL AND DEPARTURE   AO NANG

Ao Nang has no proper transport terminals of its own so most long-distance journeys entail going **via Krabi town** (see p.655), though tour services on every corner of Ao Nang can arrange direct a/c minivans to the same destinations with convenient hotel transfers, such as to Phuket town (B300). Taxis from Krabi to Ao Nang charge about B500. From the **airport** (see p.654), a shuttle bus runs to Ao Nang

for B200, while taxis charge B600–900 to Ao Nang and Klong Muang.

By songthaew The cheapest onward connection from Krabi to Ao Nang is by white songthaew, which run regularly throughout the day from Krabi town centre and bus station (generally every 10min; 45min; B50 daytime, B60 after dark) and pass Hat Nopparat Thara east en route. Alight at

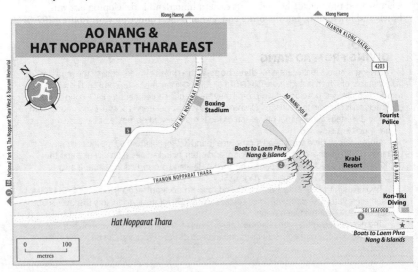

AO NANG & HAT NOPPARAT THARA EAST

the Nopparat Thara national park T-Junction and car park for longtails across the narrow khlong to the western beach (B100) or, with your own transport, follow the Klong Muang road until signs direct you off it. There's also a songthaew service from Krabi town to Hat Klong Muang.

By boat In addition to the ferries listed below, longtails to Laem Phra Nang (see p.663) and boats to Ko Yao Noi (see p.643) are also available; the latter include a daily, high-season Green Planet speedboat (book through any tour agent) that continues to Bang Rong in Phuket (B1200 from Ao Nang). There are once-daily ferry services from Tha Nopparat Thara west, near the national park visitors' centre, to Ko Phi Phi Don (2hr 30min; B450) and to Phuket (3hr; B700), both year-round in theory although they sometimes don't run in the monsoon season; and to Ko Lanta (2hr 30min; B550) and Ko Yao Noi (3hr; B650) from roughly November to May. Transfers from Ao Nang hotels are included in the ticket price.

GETTING AROUND AND SERVICES

Getting around The Krabi songthaews (see above) are useful for nipping between Ao Nang, Hat Nopparat Thara and town, and motorcycle taxis with sidecars buzz around Ao Nang and Hat Nopparat Thara. Motorbikes and jeeps are available for rent throughout the resort; and there are kayaks on the beach in front of *The Last Café* at the far eastern end of Ao Nang (B100–150/hr), from where, in calm seas, it's an easy 15min paddle to Ao Phai Plong or about 45min to Ao Ton Sai and West Railay.

Tourist police On the main road between Ao Nang and Hat Nopparat Thara (☎075 637208).

7

ACCOMMODATION

During high season, it's hard to get a double room for under B600 in Ao Nang, though the many backpacker dorms remain good value. For a simple bungalow on the beach you need to go to Hat Nopparat Thara west. Mid- and upper-end accommodation is plentiful throughout and of a high standard; you can usually get decent discounts through online booking agents. Prices across the board drop by up to fifty percent during the rainy season (May–Oct).

AO PHAI PLONG
Centara Grand Beach Resort Ao Phai Plong, east end of Ao Nang ☎075 637789, ⊛centarahotelsresorts. com; map p.658. Ao Nang's top hotel has the secluded sandy bay of Ao Phai Plong all to itself and is connected by longtail boat to the shops and restaurants of Ao Nang or free speedboat shuttle to Hat Nopparat Thara east. Designed to sit almost seamlessly against the forested crags behind, there's a lovely green feel here and seaward vistas are also beautiful. Nearly all rooms in the four-storey hotel buildings and detached villas have sea views. Interiors are modern and generous with sun-balconies and shaded outdoor daybeds. There's a big pool, a diving and watersports centre, kids' club, gym and spa. `B7000`

CENTRAL AO NANG
Ao Nang Eco Inn Moo 5 Thanon Ao Nang, ☎075 695184, ⊛aonang-ecoinn.com; map p.658. Compact and functional boutique guesthouse with better rooms than

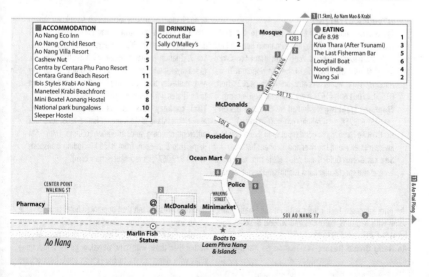

ACTIVITIES AROUND KRABI, AO NANG AND LAEM PHRA NANG

Any tour agent in Krabi town, Ao Nang, Klong Muang or Railay can set you up on these **snorkelling day-trips** and other **activities**; prices usually include transport from your accommodation. Diving (see p.657) and rock-climbing (see p.664) are also available.

SNORKELLING DAY-TRIPS

By far the most popular organized outings from Krabi, Ao Nang and Laem Phra Nang are the **snorkelling trips** to nearby islands. The main **islands** in question are Ko Poda, Ko Tub and Chicken Island, all of them less than half an hour's longtail ride from Ao Nang or Railay. There are various permutations, offered by numerous companies, including the number of islands you visit (usually three, four or five) and whether you go in a longtail boat, a larger wooden boat or speedboat; prices start as low as B450 for a longtail trip to three islands, including packed lunch and snorkel set. In all cases you should be prepared to share the experience with dozens, even hundreds, of others, because pretty much everyone congregates at the same spots. It's a lot more fun than it sounds though – so long as you're not expecting a solitary experience.

It's also possible to organize your own boat trip with the **longtail boatmen** on Ao Nang waterfront, leaving earlier to beat some of the crowds. Their prices are fixed, but don't include park entry fees, snorkelling equipment or lunch: for the return trip to either Ko Poda, Ko Tub or Chicken Island (8am–4pm), they charge B300 per person, minimum six people; for Ko Hong (see p.649) it's B2800 per boat per full day, for Bamboo Island, near Ko Phi Phi (see p.667), B3800 per boat per full day. Krabi town is quite a bit further away so its boatmen charge B1800–2300 for the three main islands.

From some angles, one of the pinnacles on **Chicken Island** does indeed look like the scrawny neck and beaky head of a chicken. There's decent snorkelling off its coast, with a fair range of reef fish and quite a lot of giant clams, though most of the reef is either bleached or dead. Its dazzlingly white-sand northeastern shore, which has a food stall, toilets and kayak rental, is connected to the islets of **Ko Tup** by a sandbank, which is walkable at low tide – quite a striking sight as you arrive to see other visitors seemingly walking on water. Nearby **Ko Poda**, which sits directly in front of the Ao Nang beachfront, is encircled by lovely white-sand beaches and clear turquoise water. There's a restaurant here and plenty of shade under the casuarina trees, so this is the typical lunch stop; sandwich-selling boats dock here too. Though you might get three hundred people lunching on the shore here at any one time, it's big enough to cope. Some itineraries also feature **Ao Phra Nang** and its cave, on the Laem Phra Nang (Railay) peninsula (see p.664), and this is the one to avoid unless you enjoy scrambling for your metre of sand on this overrun little bay.

OTHER ACTIVITIES

Cycle rides Half- and full-day rides into the Krabi countryside, or to Ko Klang, Khao Phanom Bencha falls or Khlong Tom's Emerald Pool, with Krabi Eco Cycle, based about 2km inland from the Hat Nopparat Thara National Park visitors' centre on Route 4202 (from B1500; ☎081 607 4162, ⊛krabiecocycle.com).

Elephant trekking Nosey Parker's Elephant Trekking (☎075 612258, ⊛krabidir.com/noseyparkers), 7km north of Ao Nang, has a good reputation. From B800 for an hour's trek along the river and elephant bathing.

Sea canoeing Guided and self-paddle trips take place around the spectacular karst islands and secret lagoons of Ao Phang Nga, usually focusing on Ao Luk, Ao Thalen and Ko Hong in the eastern bay (see p.649). Dozens of companies offer this, including Sea Kayak Krabi, Soi 2, Thanon Maharat, Krabi town (☎075 630270, ⊛seakayak-krabi.com), who offer a multitude of day and multi-day trips, charging B1500 for a full-day trip to Ao Thalen, for example.

Thai cookery lessons Ya's Thai Cookery School, about 4km inland of Ao Nang off Route 4203, runs four different morning and afternoon courses (Mon–Sat 9am–1pm & 2–6pm; from B1200 including transport; ☎081 979 0677, ⊛yacookeryschool.com).

the price suggests. Each comes with en-suite bathrooms, some with bathtubs, balconies and writing desks. A light breakfast is included. B1300

Ao Nang Orchid Resort 141 Thanon Ao Nang ☎075 638426–8, ⊛aonangorchid-resort.com; map p.658.

This medium-sized but well-appointed hotel is good value for Ao Nang. Choose from rooms in the hotel wing, where the nicest overlook the pool and karst mountains beyond (rather than those with "city" views), or go for stand-alone villas with direct access to the lagoon pool. Interiors are chic and attractive, and the rooms and bungalows all have decks. B3300

Ao Nang Villa Resort 113 Thanon Ao Nang ☎075 637 271–4, ⓦaonangvilla.com; map p.658. A very popular hotel and spa whose grounds run down to the beachfront walkway. The upscale, a/c rooms are contained within several low-rise wings, a few of them enjoying a sea view, but most overlooking the garden or the bigger of the resort's two pools. Breakfast included. B5200

Centra by Centara Phu Pano Resort Off a side road 1.5km north of Ao Nang, ☎ 075 607 888, ⓦcentarahotelsresorts.com/centra/cpp; map p.658. Set in a quiet location facing Ao Nang's limestone peaks, this new hotel has comfortable en-suite rooms and mini-apartments for families that come with bunk beds. There's a picturesque swimming pool next to the restaurant; continental breakfast costs an additional B400. B2550

Ibis Styles Krabi Ao Nang 725 Moo 2, Thanon Ao Nang, opposite a mosque ☎026 592888, ⓦibis.com; map p.658. Being further away from the beach has its benefits with the karst cliffs and wild trees shielding the pool and kids' playground here, offering an oasis of good-value rooms. Rooms are comfortable and a/c, with TV and large safes. The beach is just a 20min walk away past the Ao Nang shops and good street food, or there's a shuttle bus. Breakfast included. B2500

Mini Boxtel Aonang Hostel Off Thanon Ao Nang, ☎086 9046613, ⓦminiboxtel.com; map p.658. Tucked in a corner off the main road, this female-only a/c dorm has twelve cosy individual pods with plush beds, duvets, power sockets and privacy curtains. Mixed groups can rent the whole space, and the downstairs café, *Lion & Shark*, serves a great breakfast (included). B550

★ **Sleeper Hostel** 350 Thanon Ao Nang, ☎075 695531, ⓦsleeperhostel.com; map p.658. This dorm-only hostel is loved by travellers for its several storeys of mixed and female dorms. The shared toilets have naked lightbulbs, potted plants and red privacy curtains. The front desk can organize cheap bus-and-boat tickets to most Thai islands, and there's a list of fun daily activities that include pub crawls (B450), sunset kayaking (B490) and rock climbing (B900). B300

HAT NOPPARAT THARA EAST

Cashew Nut Soi Hat Nopparat Thara 13 ☎081 081 8095, ⓦcashewnutbungalows.com; map p.658. Good, sturdy en-suite brick and concrete bungalows with fan or a/c and hot showers ranged around a peaceful garden full of

cashew trees, just 5min walk from Hat Nopparat Thara east. Family-run, welcoming and peaceful. Fan B600, a/c B800

Maneetel Krabi Beachfront 225 Moo 3 Noppharattara Beach, ☎ 06 534 86225, ⓦfacebook.com/ ManeetelKrabiBeachfront; map p.658. Sleek boutique hotel that marries industrial chic touches, including bare rough walls and naked bulbs, together with Arabic motifs in the bed stands and room furnishings. There's also an outdoor pool and breakfast included. B2200

National park bungalows Beside the national park headquarters on Thanon Nopparat Thara east ☎075 637 200, ⓦdnp.go.th; map p.658. Fan-cooled, en-suite bungalows, 2km from Ao Nang's main facilities but just across the road from a nice stretch of beach and a 5min walk from the seafood restaurants near the visitors' centre. B1000

HAT NOPPARAT THARA WEST

Long Beach Villa 600m west from the khlong ☎087 465 6680, ⓦlongbeachvilla.com; map p.654. Set round a grassy, tree-strewn lawn next to a secluded beach, the main offerings at this place are attractive wood-and-bamboo bungalows with fans, mosquito nets and en-suite bathrooms; it also has large, concrete eight-person family bungalows with two bathrooms and four bunk beds, with fan (B4500). Electricity at night only and wi-fi only in restaurant. Informal cooking classes, snorkelling trips and reasonably priced pick-ups. B2500

PAN Beach At the westernmost end of the beach, about 700m walk from the khlong ☎089 866 4373, ⓦpanbeachkrabi.com; map p.654. Sturdy, simply furnished wooden bungalows in two sizes and styles (non a/c is B800), each with screened windows, fans and bathrooms, set just back from the shore around a lawn. Also has motorbikes and cars for rent, and organizes local boat trips. Electricity at night only. Free pick-ups in the morning from Ao Nang. B1200

HAT KLONG MUANG

Dusit Thani Krabi Beach Resort ☎075 628000, ⓦdusit.com/dusitthani/krabibeachresort; map p.654. The top-notch *Dusit Thani* was built among the mangroves and alongside a khlong; the result is refreshingly green and cool – and full of birdsong. The sandy shore – the nicest in Klong Muang – just a few steps away, accessible via a series of wooden walkways. Rooms are large, sleek and very comfortable; there are two beachfront pools, a spa and a variety of restaurants to choose from. Breakfast is included. B11,050

EATING

At weekends, locals flock to the **seafood restaurants** in the national park visitors' centre car park on Hat Nopparat Thara, or buy fried chicken from nearby stalls and picnic on mats under the shorefront trees.

CENTRAL AO NANG

Café 8.98 143/7–8 Moo 2, ☎075 656 980, ⓦcafe898. com; map p.658. Smart Western-style all-day café that attracts a good crowd thanks to its hearty breakfast and

7

7

brunch sets (from B180), pastries and waffles (from B55), and strong Arabica roasted coffee beans. Daily 7am–11pm.

The Last Fisherman Bar Soi Ao Nang 17, ⓦfacebook. com/thelastfisherman; map p.658. On the sand at the far east end of the beach, serving simple Thai food and a huge range of sandwiches for lunch, but most famous for its evening barbecues (from B500), which come with baked potatoes, corn-on-the-cob, salads and desserts. Daily 11.30am–4.30pm & 6pm–midnight.

Longtail Boat Soi Seafood ☎075 638093, ⓦfacebook. com/longtailboatrestaurant; map p.658. A mix of Thai and Italian dishes, including lasagne, pastas, plenty of fish and seafood, which is displayed on ice and in tanks at the entrance. A meal will set you back around B600. Daily 2.30–11pm.

Noori India 245/5 Moo 2 Ao Nang Beach, opposite Sally O Malley's, ☎081 396 0283, ⓦnooriindiakrabi. com; map p.658. This Indian restaurant, located on Ao Nang's main strip, is a good choice for vegetarian food such as paneer pakora plates (B180) and baigan bartha (sauteed

eggplant with tomatoes and onions; B150), and also serves meat – try the yummy lamb sheek kebab (B350). Daily 11am–11pm.

HAT NOPPARAT THARA EAST

Krua Thara (After Tsunami) National park visitors' centre car park, ☎091 825 9252; map p.658. Hugely popular with locals, expats and visiting Thais for its reasonably priced fresh seafood (mostly sold by weight), but also serves northeastern salads, rice and noodle dishes (around B80) and excellent espresso coffees. Daily 11am–10pm.

★ **Wang Sai** Beside the bridge at the eastern end of Thanon Nopparat Thara ☎075 638128; map p.658. Good sunset views from its beachfront tables, an enormous range of seafood and lots of southern Thai specialities. The hearty haw mok thalay (on the menu as "steam seafood curry sauce"; B200) is excellent, stuffed with all kinds of fish and seafood, or you can get seafood fried rice for just B80. Daily 10.30am–10pm.

DRINKING

The bar scene is mainly focused around **Center Point Walking Street**, a U-shaped passageway behind the beachfront shops that's packed with rock, reggae and all-sorts bars, including Krabi's first pole-dancing club.

Coconut Bar Along Thanon Ao Nang, about 200m from the beach, ☎095 418 7095, ⓦbit.ly/2nrP2WP; map p.658. A step up in the reggae-bar category, this venue

has welcoming wooden interiors, a proper stage for live bands, fire shows, and B100 Happy hour on all cocktails between 5.30 and 8pm. Daily 12pm–late.

Sally O'Malley's Up a small soi off the promenade, ⓦbit. ly/2Gu99LL; map p.658. Friendly, Irish-themed pub with a long bar, regular live bands and a pool table. Kilkenny bitter, Guinness and cider are all on draught. Daily 11am–1/2am.

Laem Phra Nang: Railay and Ton Sai

Seen from the close quarters of a longtail boat, the combination of sheer limestone cliffs, pure white sand and emerald waters around the **LAEM PHRA NANG** peninsula is spectacular – and would be even more so without the hundreds of other admirers gathered on its four beaches. The peninsula (often known simply as **Railay**) is effectively a tiny island, embraced by impenetrable limestone massifs that make road access impossible – but do offer excellent, world-famous **rock-climbing**; transport is by boat only, from Krabi town or, most commonly, from nearby Ao Nang. It has four beaches within ten minutes' walk of each other: **Ao Phra Nang** (walkable via East Railay) graces the southwestern edge, and is flanked by **East and West Railay**, just 500m apart; **Ao Ton Sai** is beyond West Railay, on the other side of a rocky promontory. Almost every patch of buildable land fronting East and West Railay has been taken over by bungalow resorts, and development is creeping up the cliffsides and into the forest behind. But at least high-rises don't feature, and much of the construction is hidden among trees or set amid prettily landscaped gardens. Accommodation is at a premium and not cheap, so the scene on West and East Railay, and Ao Phra Nang, is predominantly holidaymakers on short breaks rather than backpackers. The opposite is true on adjacent Ao Ton Sai, Krabi's main travellers' hub and the heart of the rock-climbing scene.

West Railay

The loveliest and most popular beach on the cape is **WEST RAILAY**, with its gorgeous white sand, crystal-clear water and impressive karst scenery at every turn. The best of the peninsula's bungalow hotels front this shoreline, and longtail boats from Ao Nang pull in here too, so it gets crowded.

East Railay

Follow any of the paved tracks inland, through the resort developments, and within a few minutes you reach **EAST RAILAY** on the other coast, lined with mangrove swamps and a muddy shore that make it unsuitable for swimming; boats from Krabi town dock here. There's more variety in accommodation choices and prices here, although its mostly an uncomfortable mix of uninspired, low-grade developments and unsubtle bars with names like *Skunk* and *Stone*. Depressingly, much of East Railay's hinterland is despoiled by trash and building rubble, but inland it's another story, with a majestic amphitheatre of forested karst turrets just ten minutes' walk away, on the back route to Ao Ton Sai.

Ao Phra Nang

Head to the far south end of East Railay's shoreline to pick up the path to the diminutive, cliff-bound beach at **AO PHRA NANG** (also called **Hat Tham Phra Nang**).

7

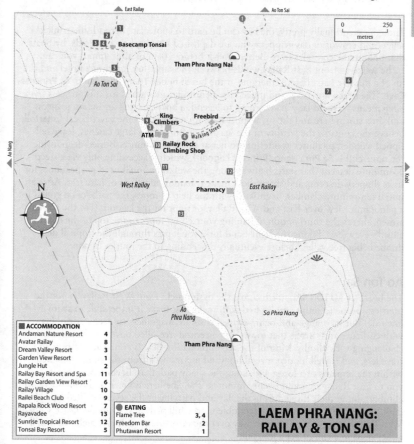

ACCOMMODATION	
Andaman Nature Resort	4
Avatar Railay	8
Dream Valley Resort	3
Garden View Resort	1
Jungle Hut	2
Railay Bay Resort and Spa	11
Railay Garden View Resort	6
Railay Village	10
Railei Beach Club	9
Rapala Rock Wood Resort	7
Rayavadee	13
Sunrise Tropical Resort	12
Tonsai Bay Resort	5

EATING	
Flame Tree	3, 4
Freedom Bar	2
Phutawan Resort	1

LAEM PHRA NANG:
RAILAY & TON SAI

ROCK-CLIMBING AND KAYAKING ON LAEM PHRA NANG

Ton Sai and Railay are Thailand's biggest **rock-climbing** centres, attracting thousands of experienced and novice climbers every year to the peninsula's seven hundred bolted routes, which range in difficulty from 5a to 8c (see ⓦrailay.com for a full rundown). Of the many climbing **schools** that rent out equipment and lead guided climbs, the most established include King Climbers on Walking Street on West Railay (☎075 662096, ⓦrailay.com/railay/climbing/climbing_king_climbers.shtml) and Basecamp Tonsai on Ton Sai (☎081 149 9745, ⓦbasecamptonsai.com). A typical half-day introduction costs B1800, a full day B2800, while B6000 will get you a three-day course, learning all rope skills; equipment can be rented for about B2400 per day for two people from Railay Rock Climbing Shop (☎081 7972517) on West Railay's Walking Street. If you don't need instruction, the locally published and regularly updated guidebooks, Basecamp Tonsai's *Rock Climbing in Thailand and Laos* and King Climbers' Thailand *Route Guide Book*, will give you all the route information you need. Unaided over-water climbing on cliffs and outcrops out at sea, known as **deep-water soloing**, with no ropes, bolts or partner, is also becoming a big thing around here and can be arranged through most climbing schools for about B1000.

   Kayaking around this area is also very rewarding – you can get to Ao Nang in less than an hour; kayaks cost B200 per hour to rent, for example on the beach in front of *Flame Tree* restaurant on West Railay. **Freebird** (☎ 061 953 9913, ⓦgofreebird.com) rents paddle boards (B250/hour) and organizes floating yoga classes (B600 minimum four people) and two-hour long guided night tours of the bay at 6pm (B1700/person).

Though exceptionally pretty, the bay can be hard to appreciate beneath the trinket sellers and crowds of day-trippers who are deposited here in their hundreds, by boats that pollute the coastal waters. Better to visit before 10am or after 4pm if you can.

The walkway from East Railay winds between the super-lux *Rayavadee* hotel and the lip of a massive karst before emerging at the beach beside **Tham Phra Nang**, or **Princess Cave**. The beach and cave, and indeed the peninsula, are named for this princess (*phra nang* means "revered lady"): according to legend, a boat carrying an Indian princess sank in a storm here and the royal spirit took up residence in the cave. Local fisherfolk believe she controls the fertility of the sea and, to encourage large catches, leave red-tipped wooden phalluses as offerings to her at the cave entrance. Buried deep inside the same cliff is **Sa Phra Nang** (**Princess Lagoon**), which is accessible only via a steep 45-minute descent that starts halfway along the walkway. You'll need proper shoes for it, as slippery descents and sharp rocks make it hard in flip-flops or bare feet. After an initial ten-minute clamber, negotiated with the help of ropes, the path forks: go left for a panoramic view over East and West Railay, or right for the lagoon. (For the strong-armed, there's the third option of hauling yourself up ropes to the top of the cliff for a bird's-eye view.) Taking the right-hand fork, you'll pass through the tropical dell dubbed "big tree valley" before eventually descending to the murky lagoon.

Ao Ton Sai

The beach at **AO TON SAI**, north across the oyster rocks from West Railay, is not the prettiest, prone to murk and littered with rocks that make it impossible to swim at low tide. But its orange-and-ochre-striped cliffs are magnificently scenic, dripping with curlicues and turrets that tower over a central tree-filled bowl and host scores of challenging rock climbs. Most of the accommodation here is aimed at climbers and travellers, and is well hidden several hundred metres back from the shore, scattered within the remains of a forest and along the shady path that, beyond *Sai Tong*, takes you to East Railay in about twenty minutes. The vibe here is green and comradely, with climbers doing their thing during the day and partying at the several chilled bars after dark. At low tide, you can easily scramble up the hill path next to *Railay Beach Club* on West Railay, or you can pick your way over the razor-sharp rocks. At high tide you'll either need to swim or get a longtail.

ARRIVAL AND DEPARTURE

Laem Phra Nang is only accessible by **boat**.

To/from Krabi town Longtail boats to Laem Phra Nang depart from the Krabi riverfront (45min; B200/person, minimum eight people, or around B18000 when chartered), leaving throughout the day as soon as they fill up. Depending on the tide, all Krabi boats land on or off East Railay, so you may have to wade; they do run during the rainy season, but the waves make it a nerve-wracking experience, so you're advised to go via Ao Nang instead. Coming back, contact a travel agent or your guesthouse on Laem Phra Nang about the half a dozen timed departures a day.

To/from Ao Nang and beyond Ao Nang is much closer than Krabi town to Laem Phra Nang, and shared longtails run from the beachfront here to West Railay, Ao Phra Nang

LAEM PHRA NANG

and Ao Ton Sai when full (10min; B100 until 6pm, B150 after dark; minimum eight people; return tickets are open, allowing return from any of the three beaches). There are several longtail boat stations with ticket booths, including one at the Hat Nopparat Thara national park visitor centre, all charging the same price; the one at the eastern end of the beachfront road is the most popular, so you'll probably have the shortest wait for the boat to fill up here. Expect to get your legs wet wading out to the songthaew on both beaches. During high season there should also be daily ferries from Ao Nang via West Railay to Ko Phi Phi (9.45am; 2hr 30min; B450), Ko Lanta (10.30am; 2hr; B600), and Phuket (3.15pm year-round, plus a 10.30am speedboat in high season; 2hr; B650); if not, you'll need to travel via Ao Nang.

GETTING AROUND AND SERVICES

Getting around Shared longtail boats between Ao Ton Sai and West Railay cost B50 per person (minimum four people).

ATM Several in the resort, including nearly opposite *Flame Tree* restaurant.

ACCOMMODATION

Because demand is so high, from November to March it's often hard to get a room on spec on West or East Railay, though you should have more luck on Ao Ton Sai.

WEST RAILAY

Railay Bay Resort and Spa ☎ 075 819 401–3, ⊛ krabi-railaybay.com; map p.663. There's a huge range of rooms and bungalows here, in a shady coconut grove that runs down to both East and West Railay, plus two swimming pools and a spa. The pick of the bunch are the very large beachfront suites, which have marble bathrooms with Jacuzzi tubs and great sea views from their verandas. B4800
Railay Village ☎ 075 819412–3, ⊛ railayvillagekrabi.com; map p.663. Occupying very pretty gardens in between the two beaches, with nowhere more than 300m from the West Railay shore, the style here is elegant tropical, in whitewashed Jacuzzi villas (B7500) and pool-access hotel rooms, all roofed in low-impact wooden tiles, with wooden floors and Thai furnishings completing the look. There are two pools and a spa. Breakfast included. B6000
Railei Beach Club ☎ 086 685 9359, ⊛ raileibeachclub.com; map p.663. Unusual compound of charming, mostly fan-cooled private houses, built of wood in idiosyncratic Thai style and rented out by their owners. One- to four-bed houses are available, all well-spaced, and there are a couple of cheaper private rooms; most have kitchen. The compound is only minimally screened from the beach, so seafront houses get good views but may lack privacy and bear the brunt of the noisy longtail traffic. Minimum stays of three nights, rising to seven from mid-Dec to mid-Jan. B2900

AO PHRA NANG

Rayavadee ☎ 075 620740, ⊛ rayavadee.com; map

p.663. The supremely elegant two-storey spiral-shaped pavilions here, some set in enclosed gardens, some with whirlpools, are set in a beautifully landscaped, eco-friendly compound with lotus ponds that borders all three beaches. Facilities include a pool with a kids' pool, a spa, a squash court and tennis courts, a gym and two restaurants. Breakfast is included. B17,550

EAST RAILAY

Avatar Railay ☎ 075 818 333, ⊛ avatarrailay.com; map p.663. A collection of modern and spacious rooms and villas set right below the karsts and in two concrete blocks, separated by a long, attractive swimming pool. The pool villas have direct access to the water from their balconies, and there's a restaurant and a cocktail bar. Breakfast is included. B2500
★ **Railay Garden View Resort** ☎ 085 888 5143, ⊛ railaygardenview.com; map p.663. This place really stands out for its simple rustic-chic style, great high-level views over the mangroves and sea beyond, and green surrounds in a garden of jackfruit, banana and papaya trees. The fan-cooled bungalows, built from good-quality split bamboo, are widely spaced and on stilts, with colour-washed cold-water bathrooms, wooden-floored bedrooms and decks, and plenty of triangular cushions for lounging. The drawback is that it's up a steep stairway beyond the far north end of East Railay, accessed via a short walkway beyond *The Last Bar*, about 15min walk from West Railay. Breakfast included. B1450
Rapala Rock Wood Resort ☎ 083 703 5006, ⊛ facebook.com/RAPALARailay; map p.663. Climb a steep flight of stairs to reach the thirty rough-hewn, fan-cooled timber and brick huts here, which are among the

cheapest on Railay, set around a scruffy, breezy garden high above the beach, with some enjoying dramatic karst views from their verandas. There's also a nice communal deck among the treetops, and a friendly restaurant that serves Indian food and bakes its own tasty biscuits and bread. Walk-ins only and no wi-fi. B500

★ **Sunrise Tropical Resort** ☎075 819418–20, Ⓦsunrisetropical.com; map p.663. The most stylish of the affordable hotels on the cape offers just forty rooms, most in elegantly designed a/c bungalows, and some in a couple of two-storey buildings, all with Thai furnishings and generously spacious living areas, set around a landscaped tropical garden with a pool and spa. Doubles B4500, villas B5800

AO TON SAI

Andaman Nature Resort ☎081 979 6050, Ⓦbit.ly/2GyKB4n; map p.663. Wooden bungalows fan out in the jungle behind the large stilted restaurant of this long-standing and good value budget option. Rooms are basic, with mosquito nets and en-suite bathrooms, and the friendly staff try hard to make guests feel like family. B400

Dream Valley Resort ☎075 819810–2, Ⓦdreamvalleykrabi.com; map p.663. The ninety bungalows here are ranged discreetly among the trees, running far back towards the cliff-face, offering a range of good-

quality accommodation in various categories, from wooden bungalows with fans, mosquito screens and bathrooms through to a/c villas with hot showers, the best of which are the premier accommodation on Ao Ton Sai. Breakfast included. B2500

Garden View Resort ☎085 793 7449; map p.663. Set amongst Ao Ton Sai's bars, the simple yet spacious en-suite rooms here are all set in a concrete block, which is removed from the main road. Rooms have small porches facing a well-kept hillside garden, making it easy to relax and forget about the crowds. B500

Jungle Hut ☎062 118 5289, Ⓦfacebook.com/Junglehut.Tonsai; map p.663. Rustic en-suite wooden bungalows with fan and mosquito nets catering to backpackers. Located next to the popular Chill Out Bar, which plays dance music well into the night. B500

Tonsai Bay Resort ☎075 695599, Ⓦtonsaibaykrabi.com; map p.663. With its large, widely spaced and plain but comfortable bungalows and rooms, this is one of the top places to stay on Ao Ton Sai. The detached and semi-detached bungalows (B2700) boast huge glass windows and big decks from which to soak up the pretty location in a grove of trees set back from the shore, and all have a/c, hot shower, satellite TV, fridge and safety box. Breakfast included. B2600

EATING AND DRINKING

There's no shortage of traveller-style bars on Laem Phra Nang, especially at the north end of East Railay and on the beach at Ton Sai, with their fire-juggling, driftwood furniture, chillums and occasional parties.

WEST RAILAY

Flame Tree On the seafront ☎088 819 9221, Ⓦbit.ly/2E2s162; map p.663. This sprawling, laidback, semi-outdoor place has a more varied menu than most of the restaurants on Laem Phra Nang, including cashew nut salad (B175), some southern Thai dishes, mushroom sauce steak (B395), pasta, sandwiches, a variety of breakfasts and espresso coffees. Daily 6.30am–10.30pm.

EAST RAILAY

Phutawan Resort map p.663. Quietly located in the middle of the spectacular cliff-lined basin on the track to Ton Sai, a 10min walk from both East and West Railay, the restaurant here offers fine views and good food, mostly seafood and Thai curries, and largely in the reasonable B120–150 range. Daily 7.30am–10pm.

AO TON SAI

Freedom Bar Ⓦfacebook.com/freedombar.tonsai; map p.663. The unmissable beachfront location makes *Freedom Bar* a popular spot to enjoy a cocktail or two (from B150) or a beer (from B70). Daily 10am–12pm.

Ko Phi Phi Don

About 40km south of Krabi, the island of **KO PHI PHI DON** looks breathtakingly handsome as you approach from the sea, its classic arcs of pure white sand framed by dramatic cliffs and lapped by water that's a mouthwatering shade of turquoise. A flat sandy isthmus connects the hilly east and west halves of the island, scalloped into the much-photographed symmetrical double bays of Ao Ton Sai and Ao Loh Dalum. The vast majority of the tourist accommodation is squashed in here, as is the island's wild nightlife, with just a few alternatives scattered along eastern coasts. Phi Phi's few indigenous islanders mostly live in the northeast.

Such beauty, however, belies the island's turbulent recent history. By the early 1990s, Phi Phi's reputation as a tropical idyll was bringing unfeasibly huge crowds of

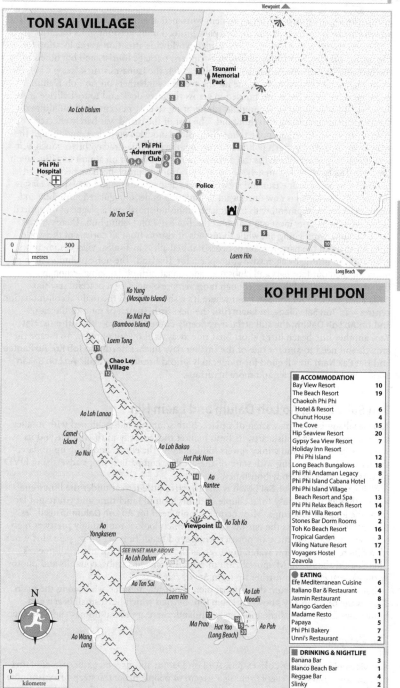

TON SAI VILLAGE

Viewpoint

Tsunami Memorial Park

Ao Loh Dalum

Phi Phi Adventure Club

Phi Phi Hospital

Police

Ao Ton Sai

Laem Hin

0 — 300
metres

Long Beach

7

KO PHI PHI DON

Ko Yung (Mosquito Island)

Ko Mai Pai (Bamboo Island)

Laem Tong

Chao Ley Village

Ao Loh Lanaa

Camel Island

Ao Nui

Ao Loh Bakao

Hat Pak Nam

Ao Rantee

Ao Yongkasem

Viewpoint

Ao Toh Ko

SEE INSET MAP ABOVE
Ao Loh Dalum

Ao Ton Sai

Laem Hin

Ao Loh Moodii

N

Ma Prao

Hat Yao (Long Beach)

Ao Poh

Ao Wang Long

0 — 1
kilometre

Ko Phi Phi Leh

ACCOMMODATION
Bay View Resort	10
The Beach Resort	19
Chaokoh Phi Phi Hotel & Resort	6
Chunut House	4
The Cove	15
Hip Seaview Resort	20
Gypsy Sea View Resort	7
Holiday Inn Resort Phi Phi Island	12
Long Beach Bungalows	18
Phi Phi Andaman Legacy	8
Phi Phi Island Cabana Hotel	5
Phi Phi Island Village Beach Resort and Spa	13
Phi Phi Relax Beach Resort	14
Phi Phi Villa Resort	9
Stones Bar Dorm Rooms	2
Toh Ko Beach Resort	16
Tropical Garden	3
Viking Nature Resort	17
Voyagers Hostel	1
Zeavola	11

● EATING
Efe Mediterranean Cuisine	6
Italiano Bar & Restaurant	4
Jasmin Restaurant	8
Mango Garden	3
Madame Resto	1
Papaya	5
Phi Phi Bakery	7
Unni's Restaurant	2

■ DRINKING & NIGHTLIFE
Banana Bar	3
Blanco Beach Bar	1
Reggae Bar	4
Slinky	2

backpackers to its shores, and the problem worsened after uninhabited little sister island **Ko Phi Phi Leh** – under national marine park protection on account of its lucrative bird's-nest business (see box, p.673) – gained worldwide attention as the location for the movie *The Beach* in 1999, adding day-trippers, package tourists and big hotels to the mix on Phi Phi Don. Then, in December 2004, the **tsunami** struck (see p.610). As a 5m-high wave crashed in from the north, over the sunbathers on Ao Loh Dalum, a 3m-high wave from the south hurtled in across the ferry dock and tourist village at Ao Ton Sai. The waves met in the middle, obliterating seventy percent of all buildings on the sandy flats and killing two thousand. The rest of the island was barely affected.

Volunteers and donations poured in to help the island back on its feet, and though the rebuild was dogged by much political wrangling, the Phi Phi of today thrives much as it ever did, firmly re-established as the destination to be ticked off on almost any itinerary in southern Thailand. Unfortunately, few of the pre-tsunami **problems** have been properly resolved – in part because tsunami survivors were desperate to make a new start as fast as they could. The island is now once again floundering under unregulated, unsightly and unsustainable development, with inadequate rubbish disposal and a plague of overpriced accommodation, at its most acute around the Ton Sai–Loh Dalum hub. There's always more building work going on, while thousands of visitors from all corners of the world fight for space in the narrow maze of pedestrianized alleys in Ton Sai village, sometimes generating an unusually aggressive atmosphere for Thailand. The noise pollution from the untrammelled outdoor bars and clubs is an additional turn-off for some – though it is a fun place to party, and there are enough more remote escapes for a peaceful stay too.

All boats dock in **Ao Ton Sai**, from where it's a short walk to the main accommodation centres – in **Ton Sai village**, at **Laem Hin**, the next little stretch of sand to the east, and on **Ao Loh Dalum**, the still attractive, deeply curved bay across the isthmus. **Hat Yao**, another fine beach just a short boat ride away, is also very popular. To escape the crowds you need to aim for one of the smaller bays further north: **Ao Toh Ko**, **Ao Rantee** and **Hat Pak Nam** are all good for moderately priced breakaways, while **Ao Loh Bakao** and **Laem Tong** are pricier and more luxurious.

Ton Sai village, Ao Loh Dalum and Laem Hin

Ton Sai village is a hectic warren of a place, both strangely old-fashioned with its alley traffic of bicycles and pushcarts, its fresh market tucked away in the middle and its squalid shanty town and stinky sewers hidden along the edges, and bang up to date, the narrow lanes bursting with state-of-the-art dive companies, shops advertising DVD players for rent and trendy boutiques.

West of the pier, **Ao Ton Sai** beach is an attractive little retreat under the limestone karsts, though it gets busy for a couple of hours around lunchtime and you're not far from the longtail moorings. Most people simply head for **Ao Loh Dalum** instead, less than 300m north across the narrow isthmus, which looks astonishingly pretty at high tide, with its glorious curve of powder-white sand beautifully set off by pale blue water; it's a different story at low water, however, as the tide goes out for many kilometres. There's a tiny Tsunami Memorial Park of carefully tended shrubs, epitaphs and photos at the eastern end, a bit further up from *Stones Bar*.

East along the coast from the Ton Sai pier, about ten minutes' walk along the main alley, is the promontory known as **Laem Hin**, beyond which lies a small beach and bungalows that enjoy a little more space. Inland, there are island homes and a mosque.

The viewpoint

B30

The **viewpoint** that overlooks eastern Ao Loh Dalum affords a magnificent panorama over the twin bays and every evening a stream of people make the steep fifteen-minute climb up the steps for sunset shots; early morning is also photogenic, and the shop at

PHI PHI ACTIVITIES

SNORKELLING

There's some great **snorkelling** around Phi Phi's shallow fringing reefs, most rewardingly at strikingly beautiful **Ko Mai Pai (Bamboo Island)**, off Phi Phi Don's northeast coast, where much of the reef lies close to the surface, and at nearby **Ko Yung (Mosquito Island)**, with its spectacular, steep-sided drop. Phi Phi Don has its own worthwhile reefs too, including at west-coast **Ao Yongkasem**, within kayaking distance of Loh Dalum, but **Ao Maya** on Phi Phi Leh is more famous, and a lot more crowded (see page 670).

Outings are easily arranged as part of an **organized tour** (B500–800 including equipment) or by **hiring your own longtail** boatman (B1500/3000 per boat per half/full day), the latter far preferable to the largest tour boats, whose groups of forty-plus trippers inundate the reefs. **Overnight camping trips** to Ao Maya are a neat way of avoiding the crowds, offering late-afternoon snorkelling, and possibly kayaking, rounded off with a beach barbecue.

DIVING

Offering visibility touching 30m, a great diversity of healthy hard and soft corals, and potential encounters with white-tip sharks, moray eels and stingrays, the diving around Ko Phi Phi is the best in the area and the usual destination of dive boats from Ao Nang and Phuket. Highlights include the gorgonian sea fans, barracudas, manta rays and even whale sharks at **Ko Bidah Nok** and **Ko Bidah Nai**, the mass of leopard sharks at **Hin Bidah**, and the *King Cruiser* **wreck** (see page 635).

There are at least twenty dive shops on Phi Phi, the majority of them in Ton Sai. Note that it's considered risky for a novice diver with fewer than twenty dives to dive at Hin Daeng and Hin Muang (see page 635), due to the depth and the current; reputable dive shops will only take Advanced Divers there. There are also small dive centres on Hat Yao, Ao Loh Bakao and Laem Tong.

Prices for **day-trips** including two tanks, equipment and lunch start at B2500, while the four-day PADI Open Water **course** costs B13,800. Check that your dive operator is insured to use one of the recompression chambers on Phuket (see page 617).

ROCK-CLIMBING

The main **rock-climbing** area is just to the west of Ao Ton Sai, and includes the Ton Sai Tower and the Drinking Wall, with thirty routes from grades 5 to 7a. A newer attraction is **deep-water soloing**, unaided climbing on cliffs and outcrops over the sea.

OPERATORS

Maya Bay Tours East of Ao Ton Sai pier, Ko Phi Phi Don, on the fourth north–south alley ⓦ mayabaytours.com. Overnight camping on Phi Phi Leh for B3500.
Phi Phi Adventure Club East of Ao Ton Sai pier, Ko Phi Phi Don, on the fourth north–south alley ☎ 081 895 1334, ⓦ diving-in-thailand.net. Responsible, small-group dive trips, courses and snorkelling trips ("with sharks guaranteed"; 3hr; B1100).
Phi Phi Scuba Diving Centre East of the pier, on the fourth north–south alley ⓦ ppscuba.com. The largest operator on the island.

Spidermonkey Next to Princess Divers on the route to the east end of Loh Dalum ☎ 087 881 2450, ⓦ spidermonkeyphiphi.com/climbing. Climbing instruction (from B1200 for half a day), guide service and equipment rental. Also runs snorkelling (on Phi Phi Leh) and climbing day-trips (B2000).
Viking Divers East of the pier, on the fourth north–south alley ⓦ vikingdiversthailand.com. Phi Phi Diving Association member.

the "Topview" summit, set within a pretty tropical garden, serves coffee as well as cold drinks. There are good, free views just metres before the viewpoint entrance and from the restaurant patio halfway up. From the viewpoint, you can descend the rocky and at times almost sheer paths to the trio of little east-coast bays at Ao Toh Ko, Ao Rantee (Lanti) and Hat Pak Nam, each of which takes about thirty minutes.

Hat Yao (Long Beach)

With its fine white sand and large reefs packed with polychromatic marine life just 20m offshore, **HAT YAO** (Long Beach) is considered the best of Phi Phi's main beaches, but it's lined with hotels so gets very busy. UK-run Long Beach Divers (ⓦlongbeachdivers.com) here runs all the same **dive** trips and courses as shops in the village and offers discounted stays at *Long Beach Bungalows* (see page 673) for dive students.

Longtail **boats** do the ten-minute shuttle between Hat Yao and Ao Ton Sai (B100/person, or B150 after dark), but at low tide it's also possible to **walk** between the two in half an hour, via the coast in front of *Bay View Resort* on Laem Hin and then via *Viking*. The island's single **road** follows an inland route to *The Beach Resort* from *The Rock* junction in the village, passing the post-tsunami housing project and Water Hill reservoir en route; it's a hot, hilly and unshaded forty-minute walk.

Ao Toh Ko, Hat Rantee and Hat Pak Nam

Travellers wanting to escape the crowds around Ton Sai and Hat Yao without spending a fortune head for the trio of little bays midway along the east coast: **AO TOH KO** and adjacent **AO RANTEE** (Lanti) and **HAT PAK NAM**. You can reach the bays inland, via steep forest trails that run from the Viewpoint above Ao Loh Dalum (see page 668) in half an hour, while you can walk from Ao Toh Ko to Ao Rantee in five minutes at low tide. Rantee is probably the pick of the three, a palm- and casuarina-fringed white-sand bay, with great snorkelling at the reef right off the beach.

Ao Loh Bakao and Laem Tong

Far removed from the hustle of Ao Ton Sai and its environs, the beautiful, secluded northern beaches at Ao Loh Bakao and Laem Tong are the domain of just a few upscale resorts. *Phi Phi Island Village Beach Resort and Spa* (see page 673) has the gorgeous 800m-long white-sand beach and turquoise waters of **AO LOH BAKAO** all to itself. If you tire of these sands, and the hotel's four restaurants, there's a cluster of reasonably priced local restaurants behind the resort, and you can walk to the long, semi-circular beach at **Ao Loh Lanaa**, across on the west coast, in ten minutes, or to Laem Tong in half an hour.

Almost right at Phi Phi's northernmost tip, **LAEM TONG** is busier and more commercial than Loh Bakao, with several upmarket resorts and stand-alone restaurants along its white-sand shores, and views across to nearby Bamboo and Mosquito islands. The beach is home to a group of Urak Lawoy *chao ley* "sea gypsies" (see box, p.602), whose village is next to the *Holiday Inn*; all longtail boat tours and transfers are run by Laem Tong's *chao ley* cooperative.

Ko Phi Phi Leh

B400

More rugged than its twin, Ko Phi Phi Don, and a quarter the size, **KO PHI PHI LEH** is the number one day-tripping destination from Phi Phi Don, twenty minutes north, and a feature of snorkelling tours out of Phuket and Ao Nang (the national park admission fee is only levied if you set foot on the island, but not if you only snorkel offshore). It is very scenic indeed, and world famous, following its starring role in the film *The Beach*, so expect huge crowds, a plethora of discarded polystyrene lunch boxes, and a fair bit of damage to the reefs from the carelessly dropped anchors of tourist and fishing boats. The best way to appreciate the island is probably on one of the overnight camping and snorkelling trips from Phi Phi Don (see page 669).

Most idyllic of all the island's bays, and the most famous backdrop of the film *The Beach*, is **Ao Maya** (or Maya Bay) on the southwest coast, where the water is still and very clear. However, be prepared to potentially share it with the hundreds of tourists that visit daily during high season. At the time of writing however, Ao Maya was closed to boat access between June and September 2018 to prevent further damage to its coral. It is not currently clear if these mesasure will be repeated annually, or how many daily visitors will be permitted in the future.

Ao Phi Leh, an almost completely enclosed east-coast lagoon of breathtakingly turquoise water, is also beautiful. Nearby, the **Viking Cave** gets its misleading name from the scratchy wall paintings of Chinese junks inside, but more interesting than this 400-year-old graffiti is the **bird's-nesting** that goes on here (see page 671): rickety bamboo scaffolding extends hundreds of metres up to the roof of the cave, where intrepid *chao ley* harvesters spend the day scraping the unfeasibly valuable nests made by tiny sea swifts off the rockface, for export to specialist Chinese restaurants all over the world.

ARRIVAL AND DEPARTURE   KO PHI PHI DON

Tour agents in Phuket, Ao Nang, Krabi town and Ko Lanta all organize snorkelling day-trips to Phi Phi Don and Phi Phi Leh. Touts and bungalow staff always meet the ferries at the pier in Ton Sai; if you've pre-booked accommodation your luggage will usually be transported in a handcart. There is a waste management fee of B20 in cash on arrival; and a left-luggage booth (B50/piece).

To/from Phuket Large, crowded ferries leave from Rassada Harbour (see page 616) in Phuket to Ko Phi Phi Don three times daily (11am, 1.30pm & 3pm; 2hr; B400). Andaman Wave Master (Ⓦ andamanwaveferry. com; 8.30am, 12.30pm & 1.30pm; 2hr) has three daily departures in high season, calling in at Ao Ton Sai (B750), and continuing up the west coast to Laem Tong (B800 single), where the resorts send out longtail boats to pick up guests from the ship. A daily speedboat also runs from Rassada to Phi Phi (which continues to Ko Lanta), but it costs B1500 for the 50min journey.

To/from Krabi From Krabi Passenger Port, there are boats to Phi Phi daily year-round, with at least four a day in high season (2hr; B400). You can also reach Phi Phi by once-daily ferries from Ao Nang, via West Railay (2hr 30min; B450), which are year-round in theory though they sometimes don't run in the monsoon season.

To/from Ko Lanta Yai From Ban Sala Dan on Ko Lanta Yai, there are two daily departures to Ko Phi Phi in high season (8am & 1pm; 1hr 30min; B450).

To/from Ko Jum In high season a daily ferry runs to Ko Jum (2pm; 2hr; B600). Private charters can be arranged for B2000–2500 at the pier or through travel agents in Ton Sai village.

GETTING AROUND

It's possible to **walk** along the paths across the steep and at times rugged interior. There are only a few short motorbike tracks and one road, from the back of Ton Sai village to *The Beach Resort* on Long Beach, which takes around forty minutes on foot.

By boat From Ao Ton Sai, east of the main pier, you can catch a longtail to any of the other beaches, which range in price from B100 per person (minimum two people) to Hat Yao, to B1000 per boat to Laem Tong; prices often double after dark. The Andaman Wave Master ferry (see above) and a smaller shuttle boat each run twice a day between Ton Sai and the east-coast bays as far as Laem Tong (both B200).

BIRD'S-NESTING

Prized for its aphrodisiac and energizing qualities, **bird's-nest soup** is such a delicacy in Taiwan, Singapore and Hong Kong that ludicrous sums of money change hands for a dish whose basic ingredients are tiny twigs glued together with bird's spit. Collecting these nests is a lucrative but life-endangering business: sea swifts (known as edible-nest swiftlets) build their nests in rock crevices hundreds of metres above sea level, often on sheer cliff-faces or in cavernous hollowed-out karst. **Nest-building** begins in January and the harvesting season usually lasts from February to May, during which time the female swiftlet builds three nests on the same spot, none of them more than 12cm across, by secreting an unbroken thread of saliva, which she winds round as if making a coil pot. **Gatherers** will only steal the first two nests made by each bird, allowing the bird to build a final nest and raise her chicks in peace. Gathering the nests demands faultless agility and balance, skills that seem to come naturally to the *chao ley* (see page 600), whose six-man teams bring about four hundred nests down the perilous bamboo scaffolds each day, weighing about 4kg in total. At a market rate of up to $2000 per kilo, so much money is at stake that a government franchise must be granted before any collecting commences, and armed guards often protect the sites at night. The *chao ley* seek spiritual protection from the dangers of the job by making offerings to the spirits of the cliff or cave at the beginning of the season; in the Viking Cave, they place buffalo flesh, horns and tails at the foot of one of the stalagmites.

You could also get about by kayak (B700 per day from in front of *Slinky Bar* on Ao Loh Dalum), which is the perfect way to explore the limestone cliffs and secluded bays, without the roar of an accompanying longtail or cruise ship.

ACCOMMODATION

As demand for accommodation frequently outstrips supply on Phi Phi, if you haven't made a reservation, it's worth using the agents' booking service at the pier head, where pictures and – genuine – room prices for hotels in all categories are posted for easy browsing; staff then call ahead to secure your room, and might even carry your bag there. Be warned though that rooms are very expensive on Phi Phi, and often poorly maintained. We've quoted rates for high season, which runs from November to April, but most places slap on a thirty- to fifty-percent surcharge during Christmas and New Year and, conversely, will discount up to fifty percent in quiet periods between May and October.

TON SAI VILLAGE AND AO LOH DALUM

Ton Sai hotels are the least good value on the island and almost none, however expensive, is out of earshot of the thumping all-night beats cranked up by the various bars and clubs; bring some heavy-duty earplugs if you're not planning to party every night.

★ **Chaokoh Phi Phi Hotel & Resort** 350m walk to the right of Tonsai pier, ⓦ chaokohphiphihotel.com; map p.667. Despite being walking distance from Tonsai pier, this collection of spacious en-suite deluxe rooms complements its quiet location by blending futuristic design with simple carved wooden panels and beams. Some suites have sea-facing balconies and bathtubs, whilst there's a small swimming pool set in a private garden. Breakfast is included and served at the beach-facing restaurant. B4000

Chunut House Turn right at The Rock and walk for about 5min back towards Laem Hin ☎075 601227, ⓦ chunuthouse.com; map p.667. Very welcoming, relaxing place in a leafy, sloping garden, in a relatively quiet location. Big, stylish, thatched cottages come with a/c, flat-screen TVs, mini-bars and spacious, attractive, hot-water bathrooms. Breakfast included. B2600

Phi Phi Island Cabana Hotel West of the pier on Ton Sai ☎075 601 170–7, ⓦ phiphi-cabana.com; map p.667. The views from the contemporary a/c rooms at this large, imposing hotel are breathtakingly lovely. Most look out across the scoop of Ao Loh Dalum and its framing cliffs, and ground-floor ones have direct access to the sand. There's a huge infinity pool and a spa, and two restaurants; the Beach Terrace is ideal for a romantic evening. On the negative side, the hotel lacks atmosphere, and some rooms are affected by late-night club noise. B5000

Stones Bar Dorm Rooms A 5min walk down the right side of Ao Loh Dalum, past Slinky's and Chillout Bar, ☎094 803 1539, ⓦ stonesbardorm.weebly.com; map p.667. Sociable dorm-only hostel with a popular beachfront bar. There are over thirty a/c bunk beds split

over two floors, with three en-suite bathrooms per room and secure access via key card. It's not the quietest choice for sleeping, but guests come here to enjoy the party vibe and the superb beach location. B500

Tropical Garden Beyond the turn-off for the path to the viewpoint ☎081 729 1436, ⓦ thailandphiphi.com; map p.667. Here you'll find a wide variety of rooms and good-sized rough-timber bungalows, which are mostly built on stilts up the side of an outcrop. The better ones have a breezy veranda (though not much of a view) and there's a refreshing amount of greenery around, plus a small pool, despite being surrounded by other accommodation. Fan B900, a/c B1700

Voyagers Hostel Opposite the tsunami shelter, ⓦ bit.ly/2BoEkb8; map p.667. Revered by travellers for its central yet quiet location, and the enthusiasm and care bestowed upon all guests by the manager, Yui. The two a/c dorm rooms and shared bathrooms are clean, yet cramped with bunk beds; overall, you'll get a good night's sleep here. B500

LAEM HIN

Bay View Resort ☎075 601127, ⓦ phiphibayview.com; map p.667. The draw at the seventy large, a/c bungalows here is their prime location: they're set high on the cliffside at the far eastern end of Laem Hin beach, strung out along the ridge almost as far as Hat Yao. All have massive windows and decks to enjoy the great views and there's a pool here too. Be prepared for lots of steps though. Breakfast included. B3900

Gypsy Sea View Resort About 150m down the track between the mosque and Phi Phi Andaman Legacy ☎075 601044, ⓦ gypsyseaview.com; map p.667. The forty spacious and colourful en-suite rooms here all have a/c, LED TVs and face a good-sized swimming pool, flanked by sunbeds. It's just minutes from the action, yet has an air of seclusion. Breakfast is included. B3000

Phi Phi Andaman Legacy ☎075 601106, ⓦ ppandamanlegacy.com; map p.667. Set in a secluded enclosure just a few metres back from the beach, the rather old-fashioned bungalows here are arranged in a square around a large lawn and small central swimming pool, while the 36 more modern rooms occupy a three-storey hotel building at the back. All rooms are a/c and come with TVs, hot water, fridges and safety boxes. Breakfast included. B2500

Phi Phi Villa Resort ☎075 601100, ⓦ phiphivillaresort.com; map p.667. The best of the many options at this outfit are the huge a/c family cottages occupying the front section of the prettily landscaped garden, near the pool. Also available are smaller bungalows and stylish newer rooms in an annexe set back from the beach, all with a/c, hot water, fridge and TV. Breakfast included. B3200

LONG BEACH (HAT YAO)

The Beach Resort ☎075 819206, ⓦphiphithebeach. com; map p.667. One of poshest option son Hat Yao, this place has a throng of large, timber-clad chalets built on stilts up the hillside, with the tallest, most deluxe ones enjoying commanding views of Phi Phi Leh. Interiors are fairly upscale, with a/c and liberal use of wood for flooring and wall panels. There's also a small beachfront pool, a restaurant and a dive centre. B6300

Hip Seaview Resort ☎095 851 4000, ⓦfacebook.com/ HIPseaview; map p.667. Dominating the azure waters of Shark Point, this resort is a good choice away from the hustle and bustle, but still just a short boat ride (B100), or a 30min walk, from the main jetty and next to two of Phi Phi's best beaches. The a/c rooms have sleek minimal designs and en-suite bathrooms, with cosy outdoor porches boasting lounge sofas. A good breakfast selection is included. B3500

Long Beach Bungalows ☎086 470 8984, ⓔlong beach@gmail.com; map p.667. The first choice of most budget travellers, this relatively cheap, well-located and long-running option has dozens of tightly packed huts for rent, ranging from simple, clean bamboo huts with fans, mosquito nets and cold-water bathrooms, to smart beach-front cottages with hot water. Wi-fi is patchy. B1500

Viking Nature Resort ☎075 819399, ⓦvikingnature resort.com; map p.667. Tucked away on and above two private little coves just west of Hat Yao, with easy access via a rocky path, this is a very stylish take on classic Thai beach-bungalow architecture. It's nearly all wood and bamboo here, with no a/c, but interiors are styled with Asian boho-chic artefacts. The most glamorous accommodation is in the enormous, high-level, one- to four-bedroom "Makmai" tree houses, with their massive living-room decks overlooking the bay. There's a stylish lounge and dining area on the beach; kayaks and snorkels are available. B2000

AO TOH KO

Toh Ko Beach Resort ☎081 537 0528, ⓦtohkobeach resort.com; map p.667. Only accessible by longtail boat or jungle trek, this is the place to stay if you want to get away from Tonsai's parties and modern comforts. The accommodation, which is in en-suite, thatched bamboo huts or a/c concrete bungalows (some right on the sand), is quite basic. The common area, with mats right on the beach, is very charming though. They organize two free boat transfers daily; the other option is an expensive charter from the main port after sunset. Wi-fi only works in the common room and electricity is only switched on after 6pm. Fan B2000, a/c B2500

EATING

Ton Sai has the widest selection of cuisines on the island, but there are good beachfront restaurants, aside from the resorts on Laem Tong.

HAT RANTEE

The Cove ☎087 474 7770, ⓦthecovephiphi.com; map p.667. Choose between the very good value en-suite garden, ocean or cliff-view bamboo-decked villas and bungalows, all facing Rantee Bay and easy swimming distance from a good snorkelling spot. All rooms are spacious, with hot rain showers, private balconies and sun beds. There's also a sea-facing restaurant; breakfast is included. B3000

HAT PAK NAM

Phi Phi Relax Beach Resort ☎094 756536, ⓦphiphi relaxresort.com; map p.667. Rustic but comfortable and very welcoming accommodation, in 51 attractive, en-suite wood and bamboo bungalows, set in rows in among the beachfront trees. Kayaks available and there's pick-ups from the pier twice a day (B150 per person). Advanced online bookings get worthwhile discounts. B1900

AO LOH BAKAO

Phi Phi Island Village Beach Resort and Spa ☎075 628999, ⓦphiphiislandvillage.com; map p.667. This plush, a/c resort on a lovely beach is a popular honeymoon spot, and a great location for anyone looking for a quiet, comfortable break. The thatched, split-bamboo bungalows and pool villas are mostly designed in traditional Thai style and furnished with character and elegance. There's a large pool and a spa in the prettily landscaped tropical gardens, as well as a dive centre. B14,000

LAEM TONG

Holiday Inn Resort Phi Phi Island ☎075 627300, ⓦphiphiisland.holidayinnresorts.com; map p.667. The *Holiday Inn* enjoys nearly a kilometre of beachfront at the southern end of the bay, but its 120 deluxe a/c bungalows and spacious, balconied, sea-view rooms are nicely hidden by the shoreline trees and sit in graceful gardens of tidy lawns and flowering shrubs. There's a popular sunset bar at the top of the ridge, two swimming pools, a dive centre, a massage pavilion and tennis courts, plus cooking classes, free kayaks and snorkelling equipment are available. B10,000

Zeavola ☎075 627000, ⓦzeavola.com; map p.667. High-end resort made up of beautiful Asian teakwood suites and villas with glass walls, all set in hibiscus-lined gardens just minutes from the beach. The plush king-sized beds, bamboo blinds that open on private verandas with loungers, and indoor or outdoor showers with aromatic bath products are a great set up to get away from it all. Breakfast included. B12,000

TON SAI VILLAGE

Efe Mediterranean Cuisine East of the pier, off the fourth north–south alley, on the main route north, ☎095

7

150 4434, ⓦfacebook.com/eferestaurant; map p.667. A favourite Turkish and Mediterranean spot, specialisoing in grilled kebabs, hummus and lamb kofte, burgers and pizzas, served in a cosy, small *sala* with an intimate outdoor patio (mains from B170–700). Tue–Sun 12pm–10pm.

Italiano Bar & Restaurant On the main alley running east from the pier, ☏075 601 065, ⓦitalianorestaurantphiphi.com; map p.667. Italian, Western and Thai food, all served in an attractive wooden-decked sala topped by a bamboo and thatch-roofed umbrella. The brick oven bakes excellent crispy pizzas (from B200), which pair well with the imported cold cuts and other authentic Italian mains. Daily 11am–11pm.

Mango Garden On the main alley running east from the pier, ☏095 250 3954, ⓦfacebook.com/the mangogarden; map p.667. Vegan-friendly, breakfast and dessert bistro for serious aficionados of the sticky fruit. Try the mango or banana-topped waffles (B140). Serves delicious smoothies (from B90) and hearty breakfast toast sets (B110). Daily 7am–10pm.

Madame Resto East of the pier, off the fourth north–south alley, on the main route heading towards the beach; map p.667. Deservedly popular for its curries – *phanaeng, matsaman*, green and red – mostly B80. Also offers thin-crust pizzas and a decent vegetarian selection, as well as Western breakfasts and espresso coffees. Daily 8am–11pm.

Papaya East of the pier, just off the fourth north–south alley, ☏087 280 1719; map p.667. One of the best of several village-style kitchens whose authentic and reasonably cheap Thai standards, including noodle soups, *phat thai*, fried rice dishes and fiery curries (B150), make it very popular with locals and dive staff. Infact it's so popular that a sister restaurant, *Papaya 2*, opened one block away. Daily 9am–10pm.

Phi Phi Bakery On the main alley running east from the pier, ☏075 601 017, ⓦfacebook.com/phiphibakery; map p.667. This place, and *Patcharee Bakery*, square up to each other across the narrow alley, vying for the breakfast trade. Croissants – plain, chocolate (B30), almond or savoury – are the thing here, washed down with espresso coffees. There are also pastas and pizzas, and vegetarian-friendly meals. Daily 7am–5pm.

Unni's Restaurant East of the pier, off the fourth north–south alley, on the main route north, ☏091 837 5931, ⓦfacebook.com/unnis.phiphi; map p.667. Beloved bistro, popular for its homemade breakfast bagels, Greek salads, pastas, burritos, nachos, and indulgent cocktails – think Baileys, cream, chocolate and espresso. Mains from B140. Daily 8am–11pm.

LAEM TONG

Jasmin Restaurant On the beach, ☏086 277 0959; map p.667. Run by a *chao ley* family, this simple beachfront restaurant impresses with larger-than-life portions of fiery Thai food, best enjoyed with an ice-cold beer, whilst tucking your toes in the sand. Part of the earnings go to support the local school. Daily 8am–11pm.

NIGHTLIFE AND ENTERTAINMENT

TON SAI VILLAGE AND AO LOH DALUM

Concentrated on the beach at Loh Dalum, Ton Sai nightlife is young and drunken, involving endless buckets of SangSom Thai rum and Red Bull, dance music played until dawn, and fire-juggling shows on the beach. Most of the bars offer a pretty similar formula, so it's often the one-off events and happy hours that make the difference.

Banana Bar East of the pier, off the fourth north–south alley, on the main route heading towards the beach, ☏087 330 6540, ⓦfacebook.com/BananaBarPhiPhi; map p.667. Tonsai's only rooftop bar is spread on multiple levels and removed from the beach's techno cannonade. Start the evening with tasty Tex-Mex food (from B250) and a free movie (daily at 7pm). Later, the bar turns into the usual dance floor, but with neon paint, UV lights and a wider range of music, it beats the competition. Daily 11am–1am.

Blanco Beach Bar On the beach at the east end of Loh Dalum, ⓦblancobeachbarkohphiphi.com; map p.667. Part of a hostel of the same name, it's not for everyone, but it is where most of the under-35 action is. Their boat parties (B2000, including entry fee to Maya Bay and free flow of drinks; Tblancoboatparty.com) are a fun and inexpensive way to get around Phi Phi's main sights, although you may not remember it the next day. Daily, open roughly 10am–3am.

Reggae Bar East of the pier, off the fourth north–south alley, on the main route heading towards The Rock; map p.667. A Phi Phi institution in the heart of the village that's been running for years in various incarnations. These days it arranges regular amateur *muay thai* bouts in its boxing ring at around 9pm – "beat up your friend and win free buckets" – and has pool tables and a bar around the sides. There's even reggae karaoke. Daily roughly 10am–1am.

Slinky Towards the east end of Loh Dalum, where the left fork just before The Rock hits the beach; map p.667. The messy, throbbing heart of Phi Phi nightlife, with a booming sound system, fire shows, and buckets and buckets of booze. Daily 6pm–late.

DIRECTORY

ATMs and exchange Plenty of machines in Ton Sai village, including next to the Siam Commercial Bank exchange counter (daily 9am–8.30pm), on the main alley running east of the pier.

Hospital Phi Phi Hospital (☎075 622151 or ☎081 270 4481), at the western end of Ao Ton Sai.

Police As well as a police station (☎075 611177) on the main alley running east of the Ao Ton Sai pier, out towards Laem Hin, there's a tourist policeman on Phi Phi (☎1155).

Ko Jum

Situated halfway between Krabi and Ko Lanta Yai, **KO JUM** (whose northern half is known as **Ko Pu**) is the sort of laidback spot that people come to for a couple of days, then can't bring themselves to leave. Though there's plenty of accommodation on the island, there's nothing more than a handful of beach bars for evening entertainment, and little to do during the day except try out the half-dozen west-coast beaches. The beaches may not be pristine and are in some places unswimmably rocky at low tide, but they're mostly long and wild, and all but empty of people. Nights are also low-key: it's paraffin lamps and starlight after about 11pm (or earlier) at those places that are off the main grid, and many don't even provide fans as island breezes are sufficiently cooling.

The island is home to around three thousand people, the majority of them Muslim, though there are also communities of *chao ley* sea gypsies on Ko Jum (see page 600), as well as Buddhists. The main village is **Ban Ko Jum**, on the island's southeastern tip, comprising a few local shops and small restaurants, one of the island's three piers for boats to and from Laem Kruat on the mainland, and a beachfront school. It's about 1km from the village to the southern end of the island's most popular beach, the appropriately named **Long Beach**. Long Beach is connected to **Golden Pearl Beach**, which sits just south of **Ban Ting Rai**, the middle-island village that's about halfway down the west coast and about 1km north of **Mutu Pier**, with the most boats to Laem Kruat. North of Ban Ting Rai, a trio of smaller, increasingly remote beaches at **Ao Si**, **Ao Ting Rai**, and **Ao Luboa** completes the picture. The island's third village, **Ban Ko Pu**, occupies the northeastern tip, about 5km beyond Ban Ting Rai, and has another Laem Kruat ferry pier. Many islanders refer to the north of the island, from Ban Ting Rai upwards, as Ko Pu, and define only the south as Ko Jum. Much of the north is made inaccessible by the breastbone of forested hills, whose highest peak (422m) is Khao Ko Pu.

Very high winds and heavy seas mean that Ko Jum becomes an acquired taste from May through October, so nearly all accommodation and restaurants **close** for that period: the few exceptions are highlighted in the text.

Long Beach and Golden Pearl Beach

LONG BEACH (sometimes known as **Andaman Beach**) is the main backpackers' beach and is indeed long – at around 2.5km – with large chunks of the shoreline still uncultivated, backed by trees and wilderness, and well beyond sight of the island road. From *New Bungalow* towards the southern end it's a twenty-minute walk into Ban Ko Jum village.

ACTIVITIES ON KO JUM

Most bungalows can organize **day-trips**, as will tour agencies in Ban Ko Jum, for example to Ko Phi Phi, Bamboo Island and Mosquito Island (about B3500–4000/boat), or around Ko Jum (B2500/boat). Many offer guided hikes up **Khao Ko Pu** (about B1000, including lunch). Ko Jum Divers, at *Ko Jum Beach Villas* at the north end of Long Beach (☎082 273 7603, ⊛kohjum-divers.com), run daily **dive** trips to Ko Phi Phi (B3900 for two dives), with snorkellers welcome (B1900), and diving courses on offer (fun dive B4600; Open Water B14,200).Koh Jum Explorer (☎086 477 7731 or 088 267 0966) organizes 3-hour long kayaking, kayak-fishing and biking trips at 9am and 2pm (B800/person). Baan Tiew (☎095 429 1717 ⊛bantiew.com) offers batik-painting and three different cooking classes (B1500/person, minimum 2 people).

At its northern end, Long Beach segues into **GOLDEN PEARL BEACH**, which is about a 15min walk north up the beach from *Bo Daeng*, 5km by road from Ban Ko Jum and 1km south of Ban Ting Rai. Like Long Beach, it also has only a few bungalow outfits along its curving shoreline, though these are close by the island road.

Ao Si

Around the rocky headland from Golden Pearl Beach, accessible in ten minutes at low tide or quite a bit further by road, long and beautifully uncluttered **AO SI** is good for swimming. There are a few places to stay, and a big troupe of monkeys makes its home here too. A ten-minute walk through the rubber trees from the uppermost of *Ao Si Bungalows* brings you to Magic Beach, just south of Ao Ting Rai.

Ban Ting Rai, Khao Ko Pu and Ao Ting Rai

The road begins to climb as soon as you leave Golden Pearl Beach, taking you up through the ribbon-like village of **Ban Ting Rai**, pretty with bougainvillaea and wooden houses, and the location of a few small restaurants and noodle shops. At 422m, **Khao Ko Pu**, which rises in the distance, is the island's highest mountain and home to macaques that sometimes

7

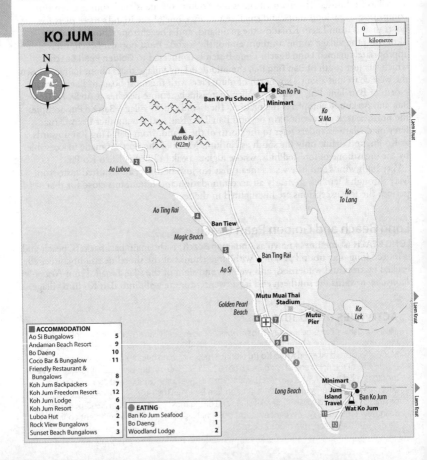

KO JUM

0   1
kilometre

N

Ban Ko Pu School
Ban Ko Pu
Minimart
Ko Si Ma

Khao Ko Pu (422m)

Ao Luboa

Ko To Lang

Ao Ting Rai

Ban Tiew

Magic Beach

Ban Ting Rai

Ao Si

Mutu Muai Thai Stadium

Golden Pearl Beach

Mutu Pier

Ko Lek

Minimart
Jum Island Travel
Ban Ko Jum
Wat Ko Jum

Long Beach

Laem Kruat
Laem Kruat
Laem Kruat

■ ACCOMMODATION

Ao Si Bungalows	5
Andaman Beach Resort	9
Bo Daeng	10
Coco Bar & Bungalow	11
Friendly Restaurant & Bungalows	8
Koh Jum Backpackers	7
Koh Jum Freedom Resort	12
Koh Jum Lodge	6
Koh Jum Resort	4
Luboa Hut	2
Rock View Bungalows	1
Sunset Beach Bungalows	3

● EATING

Ban Ko Jum Seafood	3
Bo Daeng	1
Woodland Lodge	2

come down to forage on the rocks around the northern beaches; guided treks up the eastern flank to the summit take about an hour and reward you with fine 360-degree panoramas encompassing the entire island, the mainland and the outer islands.

The little bay of **AO TING RAI**, sometimes known as **Hat Kidon**, has some nice places to stay and good snorkelling off its shore, with a reef to explore and plenty of fish. At low tide it's too rocky for swimming; you'll need either to pick your way over the rocks, rent a kayak, or walk south 500m along the coastal road, to get to the little sandy crescent known as **Magic Beach**, which is swimmable at any tide. You can walk to Ao Ting Rai from Ao Si in about twenty minutes along the coast road.

Ao Luboa

Ko Jum's peaceful northernmost beach, **AO LUBOA**, feels remote. It's accessed chiefly by a loop in the main island road that circles the northeastern slopes of Khao Ko Pu and terminates at the north end of the bay, though the steeply undulating coast road from Ao Ting Rai can also be walked (about 45min from *Koh Jum Resort*). Like Ao Ting Rai, Ao Luboa's shorefront reef gets exposed at low tide, making it impossible to swim, though at high water things are fine and it's anyway a supremely quiet, laidback beach with just a few bungalows.

7

ARRIVAL AND DEPARTURE

KO JUM

To/from Krabi & Ko Lanta During high season, usual access to Ko Jum is via the Krabi–Ko Lanta ferry (daily; 1hr 30min from Krabi, currently leaving at 11.30am, or about 45min from Ko Lanta, currently leaving at 8.30am; B400 including transfer to pier). Some bungalows, like Andaman Beach Resort, send longtails out to meet the ferries as they make two stops off the west coast: coming from Krabi, stop one is for the northern "*Ko Pu*" bungalows (on Ao Ting Rai and Ao Luboa), and the second, "*Ko Jum*", stop is for bungalows on *Ao Si, Golden Pearl* and *Long Beach*.
There is also a daily 9am (30min; B700) speedboat service to Ko Lanta by Muk-Anda Travel (☎82 278 5137, ⊛bit.ly/2GwTLyh), which also has boats to Phuket, Phi Phi and the deep south islands (see below). Advance booking necessary.Coming from Krabi town, you need to take a blue songthaew, passing the airport, either all the way through to Laem Kruat (B100) or changing in Nua Klong. Service is from 7am to about 3pm.
To/from Ko Phi Phi Muk-Anda runs a daily speedboat from Ko Jum to Tonsai beach at 9am (1hr; B800). Reserve a day before through your hotel.
To/from Laem Kruat From Laem Kruat, in the dry season five daily boats depart to Ban Ko Pu (45min–1hr; B100) about every two hours from 11.30am; likewise, there are five daily services to Mutu — the most used pier and the closest to most accommodation — from 10am to 5pm. At time of

research, there seemed to be no direct services to Ban Ko Jum. At Mutu, if you haven't arranged a motorbike taxi with sidecar to transfer you to your resort (about B100/person), touts will offer taxi services or motorbike rental (from B200/day). You can also walk 15minutes to the main road, where *Koh Jum Backpackers* is the closest place to rent your own wheels.
From Mutu pier, about seven boats per day return to Laem Kruat starting at 6.30am. The last service leaves at 2.30pm and should be well-timed to connect with the last blue songthaew departure to Krabi town — which passes by the airport, Tesco Lotus, Big C and the bus station. In the rainy season you have to travel to Ko Jum by minibus on transport ferries, conveniently never having to change transport. An increasing number of visitors now use this route year-round; some bungalow operators, for example, offer transfers from Krabi airport using this route (about B800/car to Laem Kruat), which continues to Ko Jum.
To/from Phuket During high season, Muk-Anda Travel runs a daily speedboat from Ko Jum to Phuket's Rassada Harbour at 2.30pm (30min; B1900).
To/from the deep south islands Muk-Anda Travel runs a daily speedboat from Ko Jum to Ko Lipe at 9am (4hr 30min; B2500) in high season. It also stops at Ko Ngai (1hr 30min; B1400), Ko Mook (2hr; B1600), Ko Kradan (2hr 20min; B1800) and Ko Bulon Lae (3hr 30min; B2500).

GETTING AROUND AND SERVICES

Getting around Most bungalows can arrange kayak (about B700/day) and motorbike (about B350/day) rental, while *Bo Daeng* has mountain bikes (B150/day; see below). The main island road is slowly being paved north from Ban Ko Jum, but the track on the west side of Khao Ko Pu remains a bumpy nightmare.
Tourist information For a comprehensive guide to life on the island and pictures of all the bungalow operations, see

⊛kohjumonline.com.
Clinic The island medical centre is on the road near *Ko Jum Lodge*, beyond the southern edge of Ban Ting Rai.
Exchange There's no ATM on the island, so it's best to bring all the cash you'll need with you. At a pinch, you can change money at Jum Island Travel (T081 797 7397), next to the pier in Ban Ko Jum, at expensive rates.

ACCOMMODATION

LONG BEACH

Andaman Beach Resort ☎081 476 3689 or 089 724 1544, ⊛facebook.com/andamanbeachresortkohjum; map p.676. You can't miss the steeply roofed concrete bungalows at this friendly, well-run place, painted like gingerbread houses in shocking pink, yellow and other "lucky" colours. Set in a pleasant garden filled with lucky-charm Chinese-style little statues, and even a giant golden *naga*, the rooms are all bright, clean and en suite, with mosquito screens and terraces, and are priced according to size and proximity to the beach (rising to B3000 for a big, a/c, beachfront pad with hot water and breakfast). Their restaurant, where free Wi-fi is available, opens from 7.30am to 10pm and has good and reasonably priced Thai and Western dishes. B300

Bo Daeng ☎081 494 8760; map p.676. This funky, ultra-cheap and ultra-basic (no wi-fi and open-roofed shared showers encased by just four low corrugated iron walls) travellers' classic is run by a famously welcoming charismatic island *chao ley* family and has legendary food. The rudimentary bamboo huts come with or without private bathrooms, but all have nets and electricity during the evening. Open all year. B300

Coco Bar & Bungalow On the southern end of Long Beach, further north from Koh Jum Freedom Resort ☎081 895 6768, ⊛cocokohjum.com; map p.676. Clustered around a pretty beach-facing bar (open daily from 7.30am until late), surrounded by casuarinas and low wooden tables, the bungalows here are simple yet well equipped, with spacious verandahs strewn with hammocks, plush mattresses and mosquito nets. Breakfast is served at the bar and costs about B150 extra. B900

★ **Friendly Restaurant & Bungalows** Along the tarred road between the main coastal road and Andaman Beach Resort ☎088 8209901, ⊛facebook.com/friendlyrestaurant.kohjum; map p.676. Just five beautiful en-suite darkwood bungalows on low stilts set in a garden full of colourful flowers, a 5min walk from the beach. The rooms are spacious and clean; across the road, the restaurant dishes up some hearty Thai and Western dishes (from B100). Breakfast is included. B900

Koh Jum Freedom Resort At the southernmost point of the island ☎086 239 8075, ⊛kohjumfreedomhut.com; map p.676. This popular and rustic cluster of budget bamboo huts recently received a plush makeover. The sea-facing, en-suite bungalows and two treehouses have a/c, floor tiles, dark wooden bed-frames with sturdy mattresses, thick mosquito nets, and breezy front verandahs. Wi-fi is only available at their bar-restaurant. B1800

GOLDEN PEARL BEACH

Koh Jum Backpackers A few metres from the turnoff to Mutu Pier ☎087 461 7175, ✉kohjumhostel@gmail.com; map p.676. The island's first bona fide hostel occupies a large white-tiled room inside of a Thai home, with just a few bunk beds and plenty of empty space. There are a couple a/c en-suite doubles (B850), motorbike (B300) and bicycle (B100) rental. Shared toilets are clean, and it's a 15min walk from the Mutu pier. B250

Koh Jum Lodge ☎089 921 1621, ⊛kohjumlodge.com; map p.676. This French–Thai place is one of the most upscale resorts on the island, with nineteen thatched wooden chalets designed in charming rustic-chic style. Thoughtfully constructed to make the most of the island breezes, they have doors onto the veranda to avoid the need for a/c, plus low beds and elegantly simple furniture. The resort has a small pool, a TV and DVD area, a massage service and a restaurant. Minimum stay four nights, seven in peak season. Closed in low season. Breakfast included. B4500

AO SI

Ao Si Bungalows ☎081 747 2664, ⊛kohjumonline.com/aosi.html; map p.676. On Ao Si's northern headland, the woven-bamboo, en-suite bungalows here are built on piles up the side of the cliff and have wrap-around verandas for soaking up the commanding views of the bay and the southern half of the island. No wi-fi. B500

AO TING RAI

Koh Jum Resort ☎061 235 1332, ⊛kohjumresort.com; map p.676. Upmarket resort set amongst well-manicured tropical gardens on a rocky slope that hugs one of Ting Rai's best stretches of coast. The thatched-bamboo spacious bungalows and teak villas – all en suite – are set on stilts and have perfect verandas to soak the sunset views. There's also an infinity pool and a restaurant. Breakfast is included; book online for discounts of up to 40%. B7000

AO LUBOA

Luboa Hut ☎081 388 9241, ⊛luboahut.com; map p.676. Friendly establishment with ten en-suite bamboo and wooden bungalows, all recently renovated, with sea views from their verandas in a well-shaded spot under shoreside trees; many of them are roomy and good quality, some have extra beds or sofas and all have mosquito nets. The owners offer free kayaks and cooking classes. 30% discounts off season. B500

★ **Sunset Beach Bungalows** After a rocky headland on the central part of the beach ☎085 797 1602, ⊛sunsetbeachbungalow.com; map p.676. A leftover of Ko Jum's former self, set below huge trees and in metres from the water, as if it were a forlorn village of thatched-bamboo huts, most sharing bathrooms. The two tree-houses, literally built in the canopy overhead, tower above a relaxed reggae-style restaurant tstrewn with hammocks.

A few concrete bungalows (B700) have en-suite toilets and offer more comfort, but all rooms are fan only. There's a well-stocked bar, a snooker table, and the friendly owner fills the place with good vibes. On a good day, Phi Phi island is visible from the bar. B300

NORTHERN SHORE

Rock View Bungalows Down a signposted slope on Ko Jum's northernmost headland ☎095 916 1530 ⓦfacebook.com/rockviewterrace; map p.676. With Ko Jum's increasing development, it's no surprise that new places are starting to pop all over the coastline. Recently opened *Rock View Bungalows* chose a great spot above a secluded bay to set their bar-restaurant (with free wi-fi, and Thai mains from B80), a delightful white wooden platform perched on rocks, just metres from the waves. Right behind the vegetation are a few treehouses on stilts, and three slightly more expensive en-suite bungalows (B1100), that are sheltered by jungle and among the quieter accommodation on the island. B500

EATING AND DRINKING

LONG BEACH

★ **Bo Daeng** map p.676. For an outstanding Thai meal, at some of the cheapest prices on the island (around B100), you should join the (sometimes lengthy) queue here, whose highlights include baked fish, vegetable tempura (B90) and a southern yellow curry (B90), plus Thai desserts, home-baked bread and coconut shakes. Daily 7.30am–9pm.

Woodland Lodge map p.676. Delicious curries – try the Indian curry with prawns (B200) – plenty of choice for vegetarians, including tasty vegetable tempura (B90), plus Western food, including breakfast and fish and chips. Daily roughly 7am–8.30/9pm.

BAN KO JUM

Ban Ko Jum Seafood ☎081 893 6380 ⓦfacebook.com/kohjumseafood; map p.676. The big name in the village is this very popular and very good restaurant, whose tables occupy a scenically sited jetty near the pier and enjoy fine views across the mangrove channel. Among its big menu of fresh seafood cooked any number of ways (B150–400), the juicy fat prawns barbecued with honey are a standout, and their crab and lobster dishes are famous too. Standards such as *phat thai* (B150) are here too. Daily 9am–10pm.

Ko Lanta Yai

Although **KO LANTA YAI** can't quite compete with Phi Phi's stupendous scenery, the thickly forested 25km-long island has the longest beaches in the Krabi area – and plenty of them. There's decent snorkelling and diving nearby, plus caves to explore, kayaking and other watersports, so many tourists base themselves here for their entire holiday fortnight. The island is especially popular with families, in part because of the local laws that have so far prevented jet-skis, beachfront parasols and girlie bars from turning it into another Phuket, though there's now a long line of resorts stretching along the west coast. Lanta is also rapidly being colonised by Scandinavian expats and tourists, with villa homes and associated businesses all over the place. The majority of Ko Lanta Yai's ten thousand indigenous residents are mixed-blood descendants of Muslim Chinese–Malay or animist *chao ley* ("sea gypsy") peoples (see page 600), most of whom supported themselves by fishing and cultivating the land before the tourist boom brought new jobs, and challenges.

One of those challenges is that the **tourist season** is quite short, with the weather and seas at their calmest and safest from November to April; the main ferries don't run outside that period, and some hotels close, though most do stay open and offer huge

---

LANTA FESTIVALS

Every March, Ko Lanta Yai celebrates its rich ethnic heritage at the **Laanta Lanta Festival** (*laanta* meaning roughly "eye-dazzling"), which is held over five days in Lanta Old Town and features both traditional and modern music and entertainments, countless specialist food stalls, and crafts for sale. Traditional *chao ley* rituals are celebrated on Ko Lanta twice a year, on the full moons of the sixth and eleventh lunar months – usually June and Oct/Nov (see below). Meanwhile, the Chinese shrine in Lanta Old Town is the focus of the island's version of the **Vegetarian Festival** (see p.623), which involves processions, cultural performances and walking on hot coals.

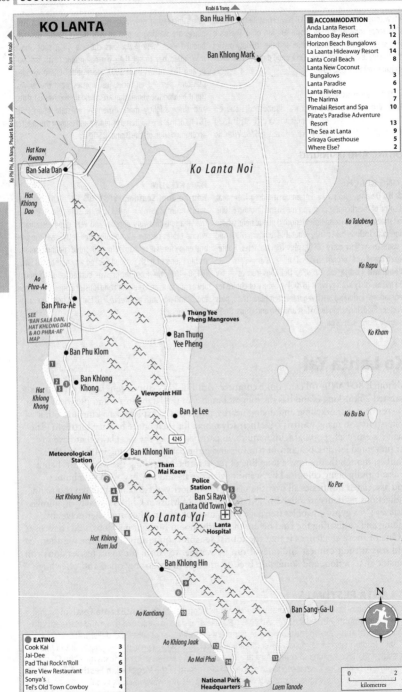

KO LANTA

Krabi & Trang

Ban Hua Hin

Ban Khlong Mark

Ko Jum & Krabi

Ko Phi Phi, Ao Nang, Phuket & Ko Lipe

7

Hat Kaw
Kwang

Ban Sala Dan

Ko Lanta Noi

Hat
Khlong
Dao

Ko Talabeng

Ko Rapu

Ao
Phra-Ae

Ban Phra-Ae

SEE
'BAN SALA DAN,
HAT KHLONG DAO
& AO PHRA-AE'
MAP

Thung Yee
Pheng Mangroves

Ban Thung
Yee Pheng

Ko Kham

Ban Phu Klom

Hat
Khlong
Khong

Ban Khlong
Khong

Viewpoint Hill

Ban Je Lee

Ko Bu Bu

4245

Ban Khlong Nin

Meteorological
Station

Tham
Mai Kaew

Hat Khlong Nin

Police
Station

Ban Si Raya
(Lanta Old Town)

Ko Por

Ko Lanta Yai

Lanta
Hospital

Hat Khlong
Nam Jud

Klongson Pier (for Trang)

Ban Khlong Hin

Ban Sang-Ga-U

N

Ao Kantiang

Ao Khlong Jaak

Ao Mai Phai

National Park
Headquarters

Laem Tanode

0   2
kilometres

ACCOMMODATION

Anda Lanta Resort	11
Bamboo Bay Resort	12
Horizon Beach Bungalows	4
La Laanta Hideaway Resort	14
Lanta Coral Beach	8
Lanta New Coconut Bungalows	3
Lanta Paradise	6
Lanta Riviera	1
The Narima	7
Pimalai Resort and Spa	10
Pirate's Paradise Adventure Resort	13
The Sea at Lanta	9
Sriraya Guesthouse	5
Where Else?	2

EATING

Cook Kai	3
Jai-Dee	2
Pad Thai Rock'n'Roll	6
Rare View Restaurant	5
Sonya's	1
Tel's Old Town Cowboy	4

discounts. The short money-making window, however, means that accommodation prices on Ko Lanta fluctuate more wildly than many other south Thailand destinations.

The local *chao ley* name for Ko Lanta Yai is *Pulao Satak*, "Island of Long Beaches", an apt description of the string of beaches along the **west coast**, each separated by rocky points and strung out at quite wide intervals. Broadly speaking, the busiest and most mainstream beaches are in the north, within easy reach of the port at **Ban Sala Dan**: **Hat Khlong Dao** is the family beach and **Ao Phra-Ae** the longer and more beautiful. The middle section has variable sands but some interesting, artsy places to stay, at **Hat Khlong Khong**, **Hat Khlong Nin** and **Hat Khlong Nam Jud**. Southerly **Ao Kantiang** is reliable for swimming year-round and currently marks the end of the made road; beyond here **Ao Khlong Jaak** and **Ao Mai Phai** are a little harder to get to and so feel more remote. Lanta Yai's mangrove-fringed **east coast** has no real tourist development but is both good for kayaking and culturally interesting because of the traditional homes in **Lanta Old Town**. North across the narrow channel from the port at Ban Sala Dan, Lanta Yai's sister island of **Ko Lanta Noi** has Ko Lanta's administrative offices and several small villages but no tourist accommodation. The rest of the Ko Lanta archipelago, which comprises over fifty little islands, is mostly uninhabited.

Ban Sala Dan

During high season, boats from Krabi, Phi Phi and Ko Lipe arrive at the T-shaped fishing port and tourist village of **BAN SALA DAN** (see page 687), on the northernmost tip of Ko Lanta Yai. Pretty much everything you'll need is here, from beachwear shops and minimarkets to banks with currency exchange and ATMs, tour agents and dive shops. The old part of the village, strung out along the north-facing shorefront, retains its charming old wooden houses built on piles over the water, many of which have been turned into attractive restaurants.

Hat Khlong Dao

Long and gently curving **HAT KHLONG DAO** is known as "the family beach", both for its plentiful mid-range accommodation, and for its generous sweep of flat sandy shoreline that's safe for swimming and embraced by protective headlands; there's good snorkelling at the far northwestern end of the beach, off the

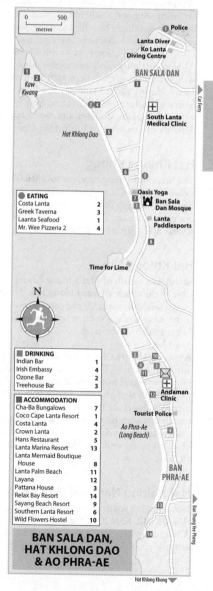

EATING

Costa Lanta	2
Greek Taverna	3
Laanta Seafood	1
Mr. Wee Pizzeria 2	4

DRINKING

Indian Bar	1
Irish Embassy	4
Ozone Bar	2
Treehouse Bar	3

ACCOMMODATION

Cha-Ba Bungalows	7
Coco Cape Lanta Resort	1
Costa Lanta	4
Crown Lanta	2
Hans Restaurant	5
Lanta Marina Resort	13
Lanta Mermaid Boutique House	8
Lanta Palm Beach	11
Layana	12
Pattana House	3
Relax Bay Resort	14
Sayang Beach Resort	9
Southern Lanta Resort	6
Wild Flowers Hostel	10

BAN SALA DAN, HAT KHLONG DAO & AO PHRA-AE

tiny Kaw Kwang peninsula. Despite being developed to capacity, Khlong Dao is broad enough never to feel overcrowded, the sunsets can be magnificent, and the whole beach is framed by a dramatic hilly backdrop. Though Ban Sala Dan is close by, the beach supports plenty of its own minimarkets and transport outlets, both shoreside and along the main road.

Ao Phra-Ae (Long Beach)

With its lovely long parade of soft, white sand, calm and crystal-clear water that's good for swimming and shady fringe of casuarina trees, **AO PHRA-AE** (also known as **Long Beach**) is strikingly beautiful and the best of Lanta's many long beaches. There's a little more variety and character among the accommodation options here than at Khlong Dao, a couple of kilometres to the north, and quite a development of shops, with ATMs, restaurants and tour agents along the main road. The main stretch of the beach is divided from the southern rocky extremity by a shallow, easily wadeable khlong; *Lanta Marina Resort* marks the southern reaches of the beach and is about half an hour's walk along the beach from *Sayang* at the northern end. Phra-Ae's budget enclave, with plenty of guesthouses, driftwood bars and a feelgood vibe is clustered along a network of sandy tracks behind the *Ozone Bar*.

Hat Khlong Khong

The luxuriously long beach at **HAT KHLONG KHONG**, 2km south of Ao Phra-Ae's *Relax Bay Resort*, is peppered with rocks and in most parts only really swimmable at high tide, though the snorkelling is good. Another big draw is the traveller-oriented bungalows, among the most creatively designed places to stay on the island. There are several funky little beach bars.

Hat Khlong Nin

About 4km south of Hat Khlong Khong the road forks at kilometre-stone 13, at the edge of the village of **Ban Khlong Nin**. The left-hand, east-bound arm runs across to Ko Lanta Yai's east coast, via the caves and viewpoint (see page 684). The right-hand fork is the route to the southern beaches and continues southwards along the west coast for 14km to the southern tip.

Just beyond the junction, the little enclave of bungalows, restaurants, bars and tour agents at **HAT KHLONG NIN** lends this beach more of a village atmosphere than the northern beaches. The beach itself is lovely, long and sandy and good for swimming, though the road runs close alongside it. There are several reasonably priced places to stay here, with the cheapest beds in some hotels located in separate little garden compounds on the inland side of the road, and a low-key collection of shoreside bar-restaurants with plenty of character and mellow vibes.

There are minimarkets, ATMs and a clinic at the Ban Khlong Nin junction, and from here you could walk the 3km to the Tham Mai Kaew caves from Khlong Nin in about an hour.

Hat Khlong Nam Jud (Nui Beach)

Just over 1km south of Hat Khlong Nin, the road passes the two tiny little bays known as **HAT KHLONG NAM JUD**. The northerly one is the domain of *The Narima* (see page 689). A brief scramble around the rocky point to the south, the next tiny cove is rocky in parts but enjoys a swimmable beach and is home to *Lanta Coral Beach* (see page 689).

YOGA AND COOKING CLASSES ON LANTA

YOGA

During high season there are **yoga** classes at *Cha-Ba* bungalows on Khlong Dao (⊛cha-babbungalows.com; also meditation classes and yoga and meditation retreats), but the most famous teacher is now at *Oasis Yoga* on Hat Khlong Dao (⊛oasisyoga-lanta.com).

THAI COOKING CLASSES

Five-hour **cooking** classes (B2000) are offered by Time for Lime, at the south end of Hat Khlong Dao (☎075 684590, ⊛timeforlime.net).

Ao Kantiang

The secluded cove of **AO KANTIANG**, some 7km beyond Hat Khlong Nam Jud, is an impressively long curve, backed by jungle-clad hillsides and dominated by one luxury hotel, which keeps the southern half of the beach in pristine condition. Unusually for Lanta, the bay is protected enough to be good for swimming year-round, and there's some coral at the northern end; snorkelling and fishing trips are easily arranged. The small but lively roadside village covers most necessities, including tours, onward transport, motorbike rental and internet access.

Ao Khlong Jaak and Ao Mai Phai

The road beyond Ao Kantiang to Lanta's southern tip, about 4km away, is steeply undulating but slowly being paved. The next bay south of Kantiang is **AO KHLONG JAAK**, site of some accommodation including the lively *Anda Lanta Resort* (see page 689). Though it's not much more than a trickle, the **waterfall** inland from Ao Khlong Jaak can be reached from the bay by walking along the course of the stream for about two hours. South around the next headland, western Lanta plays its final card in the shape of handsome white-sand **AO MAI PHAI**, a peaceful getaway because of its remote position. There's good coral close to shore here, but this makes it too rocky for low-tide swimming, when you'll need to kayak or walk up to Ao Khlong Jaak instead.

Tham Mai Kaew caves

3km southeast of the Khlong Nin junction • 2hr tours Mon–Thurs, Sat & Sun 9am–4pm, Fri 8–10am & 1.30–4pm • B300, including national park entry fee and head torch • ☎089 288 8954 • A motorcycle taxi costs about B200 each way from Khlong Dao or Ao Phra-Ae

The myriad chambers at **Tham Mai Kaew caves**, some of which you can only just crawl into, are Ko Lanta's biggest inland attraction. They are filled with stalactites and interesting rock formations, and there's a creepy cave pool too, as well as the inevitable bats. Tours of the cave are given by the local family who first properly explored the cave system in the 1980s; as well as the standard tour they sometimes offer longer cave tours and overnight jungle treks. Most of Thailand's countless caves are underwhelming and certainly not worth B300, but this is one of the better ones: among its star features are crystallized waterfalls, fossils and ammonites embedded in the cave walls and overhangs, stalagmites and stalactites young and old and a tangible sense of there being endless passageways to explore. Set aside three hours for getting into and out of the caves and use sensible shoes and clothes you're happy to get dirty. In the rainy season there may well be some wading involved, together with the option of a dip in the wet-season-only lagoon.

Viewpoint Hill

3km beyond the turn-off to the Tham Mai Kaew caves • Café daily 8am–8pm

Beyond the turn-off to the caves, the eastbound road drops down over the central spine of hills and you pass Viewpoint café, where nearly everyone stops for a drink and a gawp at the stunning panorama. The **view over the east coast** is glorious, encompassing the southeast coast of mangrove-fringed Ko Lanta Noi, dozens of islets – including Ko Bubu and Ko Por – adrift in the milky blue sea, and the hilly profile of the mainland along the horizon.

SNORKELLING TRIPS AND WATERSPORTS ON LANTA

SNORKELLING TRIPS

The best and most popular **snorkelling** is at the islands of **Ko Rok Nai** and **Ko Rok Nok**, 47km south of Ko Lanta; these forested twins are graced with stunning white-sand beaches and accessible waterfalls and separated by a narrow channel full of fabulous shallow reefs. Also hugely popular is the "**four island**" snorkelling trip that takes in the much nearer islands off Trang – the enclosed emerald lagoon on **Ko Mook** (see page 703), plus nearby **Ko Hai** (Ko Ngai), **Ko Ma** and **Ko Kradan** – but these sites can get very crowded. Another option is the day-trip to **Phi Phi Don**, Phi Phi Leh and Bamboo Island (see page 669). The trips cost around B1300 in a speedboat or B900 in a big boat, including lunch, snorkelling equipment and national park entry fee. For a smaller, more personal experience, contact Sun Island Tours or Freedom Adventures.

DIVING

The **reefs** around Ko Lanta are quieter and in some cases more pristine than those round Phi Phi and Phuket, and excellent for seeing whale sharks. The **diving season** runs from November to April, though a few dive shops continue to run successful trips from May to August. All dive boats depart from Ban Sala Dan, and nearly all dive courses are taught either in Sala Dan or on Hat Khlong Dao, though there are dive shops on every beach.

Some of Lanta's best **dive sites** are located between Ko Lanta and Ko Phi Phi, including the soft coral at **Ko Bidah**, where you get lots of leopard sharks, barracuda and tuna. West and south of Lanta, the **Ko Ha** island group offers four different dives on each of its five islands, including steep drop-offs and an "underwater cathedral" and other caves; visibility is often very good. Much further south, about 56km from Ko Lanta, are **Hin Daeng** and **Hin Muang** (see page 635).

The nearest recompression chambers are located on Phuket (see page 617); check to see that your dive operator is insured to use one of them (see page 53).

KAYAKING

There are several rewarding **kayaking** destinations, rich in mangroves and caves, around Ko Lanta Yai's east coast and around Ko Lanta Noi and its eastern islands, including **Ko Talabeng** and **Ko Bubu**; a few companies also offer kayak-snorkel trips to the four islands described above.

OPERATORS

Easy Day Thailand ☎062 245 1224, ⊛easyday thailand.com/koh-lanta/koh-lanta-tours. Kayaking trips to Ko Talabeng for B1300.

Freedom Adventures ☎084 910 9132, ⊛freedom-adventures.net. A variety of snorkelling day-trips, as well as all-inclusive overnight camping trips on Ko Rok and Ko Kradan (2D/1N B3200 including meals, camping and snorkelling gear).

Ko Lanta Diving Centre On the main road into Ban Sala Dan ☎075 668 065, ⊛kolantadivingcenter. com. German-run outfit charging B3000 plus B600 National Park fees for two dives, including equipment, B1500 for accompanying snorkellers and B14,500 for the Open Water course.

Lanta Diver On the main road into Ban Sala Dan ☎075 684 208, ⊛lantadiver.com. Swedish-owned,

PADI Five-Star Instructor Development Centre charging from B3300 for two dives, excluding equipment, and B14,400 for the Open Water course.

Lanta Paddlesports On the main road in Hat Khlong Dao and on several beaches ☎082 278 8055, ⊛bit.ly/2nAI95C. Paddleboard lessons, rental and tours, as well as windsurfing, kayaking, surfing and snorkelling trips.

Pirate Kings Tour & Travel ☎091 0369669, ⊛bit. ly/2nzLGjL. One of the main operators of four-island snorkelling trips, which can be booked through any agent on Ko Lanta.

Sun Island Tours ☎086 001 6138, ⊛lantalongtail. com. Various longtail trips to the four islands, around Ko Lanta, and to Lanta's eastern islands (where there's also an overnight camping option), which come very highly rated and cost B1500, excluding national park fees.

7

Lanta Old Town (Ban Si Raya)

The seductively atmospheric little waterfront settlement of **LANTA OLD TOWN**, officially known as **Ban Si Raya**, is Ko Lanta's oldest town. It began life as a sheltered staging post for ships and served as the island's administrative capital from 1901 to 1998. The government offices have since moved to Ko Lanta Noi, and Ban Sala Dan has assumed the role of harbour, island gateway and commercial hub, so Ban Si Raya has been left much as it was a century ago, with its historic charm intact. There's little more to the Old Town than its peaceful main street, which runs right along the coast parallel to Route 4245 and is lined with traditional, hundred-year-old sea- and wind-blasted wooden homes and shops, many of them constructed on stilted jetties over the sea, their first-floor overhangs shading the pavements and plant-filled doorways. The Chinese shrine midway down the street is evidence of the town's cultural mix: Ban Si Raya is home to a long-established Buddhist Chinese–Thai community as well as to Muslims and, in its southern neighbourhood, communities of animist Urak Lawoy *chao ley* ("sea gypsies").

The **Urak Lawoy** *chao ley* (see page 600) are thought to have been Ko Lanta's first inhabitants, perhaps as long as five hundred years ago, living along the shoreline during the monsoon season and setting off along the coast again when the winds abated. They have now settled permanently in their own villages on the island, including at **Ban Sang-Ga-U**, 4km to the south of Lanta Old Town; other Urak Lawoy living elsewhere in the Andaman Sea, around Trang and beyond, consider Ko Lanta their capital and will always stop at Sang-Ga-U when making a journey. One of the accessible elements of Urak Lawoy culture is their **music**, an interesting fusion of far-flung influences, featuring violins (from the Dutch East Indies), drums (from Persia) and gongs (from China), as well as singing, dancing and ritual elements. A good time to hear their music is at one of their twice-yearly three-day full-moon **festivals**, or at the Laanta Lanta Festival (see page 679).

As an additional incentive to linger among the wooden architecture of the main street, there are several **shops** selling batik sarongs and souvenirs, plus the charming Hammock House (✆jumbohammock.com), whose amazing range of hammocks includes ones woven by people of the endangered Mrabri tribe of northern Thailand (see page 325).

Koh Lanta Community Museum

Across the small grassy park from the pier and parking lot · Daily 9am–3pm · B40

There's an attempt to introduce the cultures of Ban Si Raya's three distinct but peaceable communities at the **Koh Lanta Community Museum**, which is housed in the attractive 1901 wooden building that used to serve as the local district office. Archive photos and one or two English-language captions describe the main occupations for the communities, including fishing and making charcoal from mangrove wood.

Thung Yee Pheng mangroves

About 1km north of the junction of Route 4245 and the road across from Ao Phra-Ae, take the right turn for a couple of hundred metres · Daily 8am–4pm · B20

This community tourism project allows you to take a short, not very compelling stroll along a 200m boardwalk out into the **mangrove swamps** that line Ko Lanta Yai's east coast. More interesting are the one-hour longtail tours available here (B1000/person, including guide), and you can also hire a two-person kayak to have a look around (B500/2hr, B300 extra for a guide).

ARRIVAL AND DEPARTURE   **KO LANTA YAI**

The principal mainland gateways to Ko Lanta are Krabi, Phuket and Trang, all of which have good long-distance bus services, and **airports**. Trang also has a train station. Flight and minibus through-tickets from Don Muang Airport in Bangkok are offered by Air Asia, Thai Smile, Thai Lion Air, via Krabi Airport; and by Nok Air, via Trang Airport. In high season, joint tickets can get you directly to Baan Sala Dan.

By boat In high season ferries and speedboats to Ko Lanta Yai depart from Krabi (via Ko Jum, B480, 2hr); from Ko Jum (B800, 45min); from Phuket (ferry via Ko Phi Phi, B950, 4hr; direct speedboats B1500, 2hr); from Ko Phi Phi (B450, 1hr; speedboats B800, 30min); and from Ao Nang via West Railay (B580, 2hr15min). There are also high-season services to Ko Lanta from the Trang islands and Ko Lipe (B1700, 2hr 30min), with connections to Langkawi in Malaysia. All of these ferries dock at Ban Sala Dan and are met by bungalow touts who usually transport you to the beach of your choice for free. If you need to use the motorbike sidecar taxi service instead, be warned that drivers will try and charge arrivals way over the normal fares; walk 250m from the pier head to the main road to get a ride at more reasonable rates. Speedboats run between Ban Si Raya at Lanta Old Town and Klongson pier in Trang (3 daily; 30min; B480), which you can book through your resort or Lanta Info (☎ 081 979 7947; ✉ nong@lantainfo.com).

Destinations: Ao Nang, via West Railay (daily; 2hr 30min); Ko Phi Phi Don (2 daily; 1hr 30min); Krabi, via Ko Jum (daily; 2hr 30min); Phuket (1–2 daily; 4hr 30min).

By road The alternative to the ferries is the overland route to Ko Lanta Yai – essential during the rainy season but increasingly popular at any time of year. Access is via Ban Hua Hin on the mainland, 75km south of Krabi, from where a small ferry crosses to Ban Khlong Mark on Ko Lanta Noi, after which there's a 7km drive across to Lanta Noi's southwest tip, then a bridge over the narrow channel to the car-ferry port on Ko Lanta Yai's northeastern coast; the ferry runs approximately every 20min from about 7am to 10pm (B100 per car, plus B20 per passenger). This is the route used by a/c minibuses from Krabi town (hourly; 2hr; B250–400 depending on which beach you get dropped at, terminates in Lanta Old Town); from Phuket (9 daily; 5hr; B500); from Trang (roughly hourly; 3hr; B300); and by anyone bringing their own vehicle. From Lanta, the Krabi minibuses will make stops at Krabi bus station, airport and then town; on arrival, you'll need to call ☎ 081 606 3591 to ask them to pick you up at the airport. There's also a daily bus between Ban Hua Hin and Bangkok's Mo Chit bus terminal (12hr), fed by a/c minibuses to and from Ko Lanta Yai, such as the Krabi town minibuses (hourly; 30–50min depending on your pick-up point on Ko Lanta Yai), which any hotel can arrange.

7

GETTING AROUND AND INFORMATION

There's no public transport on the island, but motorbikes are widely available for rent and there are jeeps too.

By share-taxi and songthaew A fleet of motorbike sidecar share-taxis, with drivers in numbered vests, and a few white songthaews operate out of Ban Sala Dan and will go pretty much anywhere on the island, though they usually need to be phoned (by staff at hotels or restaurants) for pick-ups from anywhere outside Sala Dan. Lanta has its share of scamming taxi-drivers, so bear in mind the following approximate per-person rates for rides out of Sala

Dan: B40 to Hat Khlong Dao, B60 to Ao Phra-Ae, B90 to Hat Khlong Kong, or about B50 between the above; B200 to Ao Mai Phai.

Tourist Information The free handbook **Lanta Pocket Guide** (download it at ⊛ lantapocketguide.com or pick a copy on the island; published quarterly) has the latest information on transport and activities, with an updated list of operators and hotels. **Love Lanta** (⊛ lovelanta.com) distributes a handy nightlife and accommodation pocket map.

ACCOMMODATION

Ko Lanta Yai is extremely popular during high season (Nov–Feb), when it's worth either booking your first night's accommodation in advance or taking up the suggestions of the bungalow touts who ride the boats from the mainland. A confirmed booking also means you should get free transport from the port to your hotel. **Accommodation pricing** on Ko Lanta is disconcertingly flexible and alters according to the number of tourists on the island: bungalow rates can double between mid-December and mid-January (and some resorts extend their "peak season" to include the whole of January and February), while during the rainy season (May–Oct) rates are vastly discounted.

HAT KHLONG DAO

There are a couple of budget-oriented places to stay on Hat Khlong Dao, but the emphasis is on accommodation for families and others looking for a/c comfort.

Cha-Ba Bungalows ☎ 075 684 823, ⊛ cha-babungalows. com; map p.681. There's plenty of kitsch creativity at this welcoming, idiosyncratic complex of bungalows, set among model dinosaurs and Flintstone boulders. The tightly packed bungalows are simple and flimsy, but cute, decorated with loud retro-look fabrics and wallpapers. Fan ones come with hot showers, while the a/c ones also have TVs, fridges and free breakfasts. Fan B1300, a/c B2000

Coco Cape Lanta Resort ☎ 062 954 1527, ⊛ cococape resort.com; map p.681. Perched on the northwesternmost tip of the cape, the 35 sea-facing en-suite rooms mix bright colours with industrial chic furnishings. There's also one swanky islet-facing honeymoon suite (B4900) and large family rooms (B4300). Set amidst plenty of greenery, the swimming pool, bar and restaurant tempt guests into not leaving the premises. Breakfast included. B2500

Costa Lanta ☎ 075 684630, ⊛ costalanta.com; map

7

p.681. You're either going to love or hate this ultra-brutal minimalist grouping of 22 polished-grey concrete boxes, each bungalow consisting of an unadorned bedroom all in grey and white with a mosquito net, a similarly styled bathroom with rain shower and a large terrace. The bamboo cottages are equally minimalist, but warmer thanks to the wood and nice verandas. They're all set in a broad garden bisected by khlongs, with a big, sleek pool and a striking bar-restaurant. Breakfast included. Rooms B7100 Cottages B4800

Crown Lanta ☎075 626999, ⓦcrownlanta.com; map p.681. Upmarket, German-managed resort on the island's very northwestern tip, where crown motifs feature heavily on the rooftops. The hotel divides into two zones: standard (with very large balconies) and pool-access rooms near the lobby; up on the hill, villas and another free-form pool, plus a panoramic restaurant, a spa and steps down to a part-sandy, part-rocky private beach. B8400

Hans Restaurant ☎075 684152, ⓦkrabidir.com/hansrestaurant; map p.681. One of the cheapest places on this beach, with over twenty huts ranged along a narrow, scruffy strip of garden behind the shorefront restaurant, next to the *Royal Lanta* resort in the heart of the beach. Choose between very simple, rickety bamboo bungalows with mosquito nets and bathrooms, and slightly better-furnished wooden versions (from B1300). Open in high season only. B700

★ **Lanta Mermaid Boutique House** ☎075 684364, ⓦlantamermaid.com; map p.681. This three-storey house, set across the road from the beach, hides a sparkling-clean, high-end yet affordable boutique hotel. Rooms, all with balconies and en-suite bathrooms, have either mountain or sea views, and glamorous wooden tiles that emphasise space and comfort. Breakfast included. B3500

Pattana House On the road between Kaw Kang cape and Ban Sala Dan, ☎098 674 9122; map p.681. Almost hidden behind a small café, these rooms and little bungalows set around a stone courtyard are some of the best value in northern Lanta. Preferred for long-term stays (from B7000 per month), they are mostly en suite, with large beds and wall windows. Breakfast is B100 extra. B200

Southern Lanta Resort ☎075 684175–7, ⓦsouthernlanta.com; map p.681. One of the biggest hotels on the beach, offering dozens of very spacious a/c bungalows set at decent intervals around a garden of shrubs, clipped hedges and shady trees. There's a good-sized swimming pool, too. Popular with families and package tourists. Breakfast included. B2000

AO PHRA-AE (LONG BEACH)

★ **Lanta Marina Resort** ☎075 684168, ⓦlantamarina.com; map p.681. At the far southern end of Ao Phra-Ae by a rocky point, this friendly place has 23 shaggily thatched wood-and-split-bamboo bungalows, connected by wooden walkways, which circle a very pretty lawn and

flower garden. All the huts have nice beds, well-designed bathrooms, high palm-leaf roofs and fans, and the larger, more expensive ones on the beach have hot showers. B800

Lanta Palm Beach ☎075 684406, ⓦlantapalmbeachresort.com; map p.681. A busy, clean, central and popular spot within stumbling distance of several beach bars. The concrete bungalows and large, bright cottages sit back from the shore a little, within a garden of neat clipped hedges, and come with a/c and hot water. Has internet access and a dive centre. Breakfast included. B3000

★ **Layana** ☎075 607100, ⓦlayanaresort.com; map p.681. Located plumb in the middle of the beautiful beach, this is currently the top spot on Ao Phra-Ae and one of the best and most liked on the whole island, not least for its calm ambience (the hotel has a no-under-18s policy) and attentive service. Its 44 a/c rooms occupy chunky, two-storey villas designed in modern-Thai style and set around a tidy beachfront garden of lawns and mature shrubs. There's a gorgeous shorefront saltwater infinity pool, a spa and plenty of activities and day-trips. Breakfast included. The rack rate is one third higher than the internet rate listed here. B15,100

Relax Bay Resort ☎075 684194, ⓦrelaxbay.com; map p.681. On a tiny bay south around the next rocky point (and quite a hike) from *Lanta Marina*, the style of this French-managed place is affordable rustic chic. Accommodation is in forty tastefully simple thatched bungalows, all with large sea-view decks. Also has a luxury safari-style tent on a large deck with a chic outdoor bathroom. There's a pool, a dive centre and yoga classes during high season. Breakfast included. Fan B2150, a/c B5300

Sayang Beach Resort ☎075 684 156, ⓦsayangbeachresort.com; map p.681. Welcoming, family-run place whose thirty a/c bungalows are nicely spaced beneath the palm trees in the expansive shorefront grounds. Some bungalows are designed for families and there's also a beachfront suite. Prices include buffet breakfasts and there's a very good restaurant here too. Daily free transfers to Sala Dan. B2000

★ **Wild Flowers Hostel** Opposite Treehouse Bar, ☎094 258 2597, ⓦfacebook.com/wildflowershostel; map p.681. With well-manicured gardens and a sociable bamboo and driftwood bar, this Italian-run 70s-themed hostel is a notch above the rest of Long Beach's budget accommodation. The a/c dorms, set in a cosy bungalow strewn with floor pillows and bamboo carpets, have plush beds, wooden bed stands, and clean shared bathrooms. Paying a little more will get you a private cosy en-suite. Breakfast is included. Dorms B300 Doubles B900

HAT KHLONG KHONG

Lanta New Coconut Bungalows ☎081 537 7590, ⓦlantanewcoconut.com; map p.680. Attractive collection of bungalows flanked by coconut trees and set next to an azure free-form swimming pool. Most bungalows are wooden and en-suite, with plush double beds, TVs and pleasing wooden furnishings. There's a restaurant that serves Thai food; a simple breakfast is included. B1000

Lanta Riviera ☎ 075 667043, ⓦ lantariviera.net; map p.680. There are rows and rows of good, standard-issue, comfortably furnished fan and a/c concrete bungalows here, plus a few rooms in a two-storey building, set among shady beds of shrubs and flowers at the far northern end of the beach. Many of the rooms sleep three so it's popular with families. Also has a pool and Jacuzzi near the shore. Fan B800, a/c B1360

Where Else? ☎ 075 667 173, ⓦ whereelselanta.com; map p.680. This charming collection of bungalows has a laidback vibe and lots of personality, and *their Feeling Bar* also makes it a bit lively. The artfully and individually designed bamboo and coconut-wood bungalows all have fans, mosquito nets, hammocks and open-air bathrooms filled with plants, and there are shell mobiles, driftwood sculptures and pot plants all over the place. The pricier bungalows are larger and nearer the sea, and some even have bamboo sunroofs and turrets. B600

HAT KHLONG NIN

★ **Horizon Beach Bungalows** ☎ 087 626 4493, ⓦ lantahorizon.com; map p.680. A well-executed mix of sociable traveller-oriented hangout and mid-range guesthouse, *Horizon* is artfully decked out in wood and stone. Sun loungers and little tables spill out on to the beach. Rooms vary from good value budget doubles with exceptionally clean shared bathrooms, to pricier en-suites, and family bungalows (B3800). The restaurant dishes up quality Thai meals; the beach bar has live bands and fire shows. B500

Lanta Paradise ☎ 075 662569, ⓦ lantaparadise beachresort.com; map p.680. Though the shorefront concrete bungalows at this friendly spot are packed uncomfortably close together, they feel spacious inside and are well maintained; they lack style and are plain, but are all a/c with hot showers, and there's a pool here too. Breakfast included. B1800

HAT KHLONG NAM JUD (NUI BEACH)

Lanta Coral Beach ☎ 088 761 2428, ⓦ lantacoralresort. com; map p.680. Friendly resort with a lovely, lofty restaurant – especially nice at sunset – up on the rocky point. The twenty good-sized, plain but very clean en-suite bamboo and concrete huts here are scattered over a lawn among the palms (some of which are hung with hammocks); the concrete options, whether fan or a/c, boast hot showers. Fan B500, a/c B1200

The Narima ☎ 075 662668, ⓦ narima-lanta.com; map p.680. Very quiet but welcoming, elegantly designed, environmentally conscious resort of 32 posh but unadorned thatch-roofed bamboo bungalows set in three rows in a palm-filled garden. The bungalows all have polished wood floors, verandas with sea view, hot showers and fans as

well as a/c (but no TV or wi-fi, just paid internet); there's also a three-tiered pool (with kids' level) and a dive centre, and staff rent out jeeps, motorbikes and mountain bikes. Breakfast included. B2700

AO KANTIANG

Pimalai Resort and Spa ☎ 075 607999, ⓦ www. pimalai.com; map p.680. One of Ko Lanta's poshest hotels, at the southern end of Ao Kantiang, spreading over such an extensive area that guests are shuttled around in golf buggies. All rooms are luxuriously and elegantly designed in contemporary style, and there's a delightful spa, two infinity-edge swimming pools, a dive centre and lots of other watersports, tennis courts and free bicycles. However, only the more expensive accommodation gets a sea view (the pool villas and walled beach villas are particularly stunning). In high season, guests are usually transferred direct to the resort by boat, landing at the *Pimalai*'s private floating jetty. Breakfast is included. B14,500

The Sea at Lanta At the beginning of Ao Kantiang's tourist village, ☎ 075 665158, ⓦ facebook.com/thesea atlantahotel; map p.680. This ultra-modern two-storey hotel on the hillside may not look like much value from the outside, but inside has smart en-suite a/c rooms. Some have sea views; all boast large bathrooms, plush beds, windows and LED TVs. There's also motorbike rental (B300) and a tour desk. B1000

AO KHLONG JAAK

Anda Lanta Resort ☎ 075 665018, ⓦ andalanta. com; map p.680. Lively, buzzing resort that offers well-furnished, well-maintained a/c bungalows and rooms (all with hot showers, balconies and DVD players), set around the shorefront garden and swimming pool. It's popular with families and has free kayaks and plenty of day-tripping options. B5500

AO MAI PHAI

Bamboo Bay Resort ☎ 075 665023, ⓦ bamboobay. net; map p.680. At the northern end of the bay, this welcoming and very popular Thai–Danish resort offers 21 concrete bungalows with hot showers, stepped up the cliffside above the headland. Nearly all have great sea views and interiors are spacious and of a high standard. Its *pièce de résistance* is its idyllically sited deck restaurant and bar, which jut out over the rocks just above the water. Wi-fi barely works and only near the restaurant. Fan B1800

La Laanta Hideaway Resort ☎ 075 665066, ⓦ lalaanta.com; map p.680. Luxurious bolthole at the far southern end, which is very well liked for its attentive staff and chic, thatched, wooden-floored villas – all with a/c, hot showers, DVD players and low beds – built to a cosy, village-style layout, around two pools and a beachfront garden. Breakfast included. B2800

7

LANTA OLD TOWN (BAN SI RAYA)

★ **Sriraya Guesthouse** 77 Moo 2 ☎075 697045 or 082 536 1781; map p.680. Beautiful conversion of a 100-year-old Sino-Portuguese shophouse, featuring wooden floors, original beams and creaking staircases. The good value fan rooms mix the house's original charm with modern plush beds, while the few a/c rooms (B1000) have en-suite bathrooms and large windows. There's a relaxing wooden veranda over the sea at the back, and a kitchen available for guests' use. **B500**

BAN-SANG-GA-U

Pirate's Paradise Adventure Resort At the end of Ban-Sang-Ga-U's paved road, ☎099 315 6993, ⓦfacebook.com/Piratesparadiseresort; map p.680. Good value en-suite wooden bungalows under a sloping green hill next to Lanta's southeastern tip. The sea-facing, free-form swimming pool is right above a reef with good snorkelling and only 1km from the national park, where staff organize kayaking trips. Their *Pirasta Bar* is an ideal spot for sundowners and parties. **B1000**

EATING

BAN SALA DAN

Many charming old wooden houses built on piles over the water have been turned into attractive jetty restaurants, perfect for whiling away a breezy hour with views of marine activity.

Laanta Seafood ☎075 684 016, ⓦbit.ly/2nLMmSS; map p.681. The oldest restaurant in town and the most highly rated – its seafood, displayed on ice at the front, is great, including *haw mok thalay* (curried seafood soufflé; B140) and local dishes such as *nam prik kung siab*, smoked prawn dip with vegetables. Daily 11am–10pm.

HAT KHLONG DAO

Restaurant tables fill the shoreline in the evening, illuminated with fairy lights and lanterns, which lends a nice mellow atmosphere. The formula is very similar at most of them, with fresh seafood barbecues the main attraction during the season. Clusters of little beach bars serve cocktails on deckchairs and cushions, often with chill-out music and a campfire to gather round.

Costa Lanta ☎075 684630 (see page 687); map p.681. The most sophisticated venue on the beach is a great place for a sundowner, with sea-view daybeds, plump bolsters, cool sounds and lemon-grass martinis. The food, however, doesn't match up to its hefty price tag. Daily 11am–midnight.

AO PHRA-AE (LONG BEACH)

Most of Ao Phra-Ae's most interesting restaurants are along the main road.

★ **Greek Taverna** ☎083 521 6613, ⓦbit.ly/2FDb3IG; map p.681. The authentic Greek food served here is popular and comes in big portions. There's a wide choice of vegetarian and non-vegetarian dishes, all served with delicious pitas. A meal will set you back around B800. Daily 10am–10pm

Mr. Wee Pizzeria 2 On the beachfront, ☎098 618 4378; map p.681. A simple beach restaurant with tables spilling out on to the sand, ideal for a romantic but casual sunset dinner. The pizzas (from B200) are crunchy and well-baked; there's also Swedish food (from B250), burgers (B150) and Thai mains (B100/150). Daily 8am–12pm.

HAT KHLONG KHONG

Sonya's On the main road, just north of 7-Eleven, ☎075 667 055, ⓦfacebook.com/sonyahomekohlanta; map p.680. Very popular, cheap, garden restaurant with free wi-fi (and pay computers), where you can "build your own" pasta from a wide choice of pastas, sauces, meats and extras. Also has a big selection of Thai food (from B75), Western breakfasts and teas, as well as sandwiches and espresso coffees. Daily 8.30am–9.30pm.

HAT KHLONG NIN

A dozen or so mellow little beachfront bar-restaurants make inviting places to while away a few hours, day or night, with mats and cushions on the sand, tables under the shade of the spiky shoreside pandanus trees, and appropriately chilled sounds.

Cook Kai ☎087 461 8598, ⓦcookkairestaurant.com; map p.680. Friendly restaurant hung with shell mobiles and lamps, dishing up hearty portions of all the Thai classics, plus famous hotplate dishes such as sizzling squid with garlic and pepper (B190) and a few Western dishes including breakfast. Daily 7.30am–10.30pm.

Jai-Dee North end of the beach, squeezed between the road and the beach, ☎088 832 2664, ⓦbit.ly/2DUzBAI; map p.680. Bar-restaurant with a lovely shady deck and hammocks, internet access and free wi-fi, and a good menu of Thai curries and sandwiches (bacon B80), fresh coffee and breakfasts. Daily 9am–late, kitchen closes 9pm.

AO KANTIANG

Pad Thai Rock'n'Roll ☎080 784 8729 ⓦfacebook.com/phadthairock77; map p.680. The bass player of a Thai rock band dishes up simple yet zesty Thai food in this cosy café, furnished with musical memorabilia and boasting beautiful sea views. The *phat thai* (B90/120), green curry (B150) and fresh fruit smoothies (B80) are highly recommended. Daily 11am–4pm & 6pm–9pm.

LANTA OLD TOWN (BAN SI RAYA)

★ **Rare View Restaurant** ☎087 191 3353; map p.680. Shophouse converted into a seafood restaurant, with a modern indoor *sala* and an attractive long, wooden veranda that extends over the water. Try the steamed prawn in butter and garlic sauce (B280), fried soft crabs in yellow curry (B300), or just grab a cup of coffee (B60) and enjoy the views of Ko Lanta's eastern islets from the two swings perched at the back. Daily 8am–9pm.

Tel's Old Town Cowboy ⓦbit.ly/2nw3c9e; map p.680. Decked out like a Wild West saloon with swinging doors, this long shophouse may try a little too hard, but draws a crowd thanks to the wide selection of beers and whiskey shots (from B90). Open during the high season only. Daily 12pm–12am.

DRINKING

HAT KHLONG DAO
Clusters of little beach bars serve cocktails on deckchairs and cushions, often with chill-out music and a campfire to gather round.

Indian Bar Three doors south of Cha-Ba Bungalows; map p.681. One of the most genial bars on the beach, where the host, dressed as a Hollywood-style American Indian, makes a mean cocktail and does good fire-juggling shows. Claims to open 24hr.

AO PHRA-AE (LONG BEACH)
The cluster of guesthouses and driftwood bars beyond the beach attract a steady flow of backpackers and youngsters with their dance music and cheap beers.

Irish Embassy On the main road near the centre of the bay, ☎089 472 0464, ⓦirishembassylanta.com; map p.681. Very friendly Irish bar, serving a good selection of beers and comfort food such as fish and chips (B220). Also host quiz nights and live bands. Daily 4pm–1am.

Treehouse Bar In front of Wild Flowers Hostel along the beach road, ☎098 765 4321, ⓦfacebook.com/Treehouselanta; map p.681. The quintessential Long Beach party bar, perched on wooden stilts and set just off the main stretch of beach. It's all made in driftwood, with a dancefloor literally set into the thicket. It's very popular on Wednesdays and Sundays, when bands and DJs perform. Daily roughly 4pm–3am.

Ozone Bar On the beach, ☎084 060 6244, ⓦfacebook.com/ozonebar; map p.681. One of the most famous bars on the beach, especially for its weekly DJ parties (currently Thurs), which usually draw a lively crowd. Daily roughly 11am–late.

DIRECTORY

Banks and ATMs Several banks and ATMs in Ban Sala Dan, and there are ATMs beside the road at most of the beaches and in Lanta Old Town, but there are no ATMs or shops at the very southern tip at Ao Mai Phai.

Hospitals Nearly every beach has a clinic; **South Lanta Medical Clinic** has branches in Saladan (☎075 656134) and Hat Klong Khong (☎075 656843), while the rather basic island hospital is in Lanta Old Town (☎075 697017). However, for anything serious you'll need to go to Phuket.

Post offices At the south end of Hat Khlong Dao and in Lanta Old Town.

Post offices At the south end of Hat Khlong Dao and in Lanta Old Town.

Tourist police On the main road in Ao Phra-Ae (Long Beach; ☎1155).

Travel agent A helpful, clued-up travel agent is Otto Lanta Tour at *Otto Bungalows* on Hat Khlong Nin (☎083 634 8882, @ottolantatour@gmail.com; see p.689), who sell plane, train and bus tickets, as well as booking tours and accommodation.

7

The deep south

KO LIPE

The deep south

The frontier between Thailand and Malaysia carves across the peninsula six degrees north of the equator, but the cultures of the two countries shade into each other much further north. According to official divisions, the southern Thais – the Thai Pak Tai – begin around Chumphon, and as you move further down the peninsula into Thailand's deep south you'll see ever more sarongs, yashmaks and towering mosques, and hear with increasing frequency a staccato dialect that baffles many Thais. Here too, you'll come across caged singing doves outside many houses, as well as strange-looking areas spiked with tall metal poles, on which the cages are hung during regular cooing competitions; and you'll spot huge, hump-backed Brahma bulls on the back of pick-up trucks, on their way to bullfights (in the Thai version, beast is pitted against beast, and the first to back off is the loser).

In Trang and Phatthalung provinces, the Muslim population is generally accepted as being Thai, but the inhabitants of the southernmost provinces – Satun, Pattani, Yala, Narathiwat and most of Songkhla – are ethnically more akin to the Malays: most of the 1.5 million followers of Islam here speak a dialect of Malay and write Jawi, an old modification of Arabic script to reflect Malay pronunciation. To add to the ethnic confusion, the region has a large urban population of Chinese, whose comparative wealth makes them stand out sharply from the Muslim farmers and fishermen.

The touristic interest in the deep south is currently all over on the beautiful **west coast**, where sheer limestone outcrops, pristine sands and fish-laden coral stretch down to the Malaysian border. Along Trang's **mainland coast**, there's a 30km stretch of attractive beaches, dotted with mangroves and impressive caves that can be explored by sea canoe, but the real draw down here is the offshore **islands**, which offer gorgeous panoramas and beaches, great snorkelling and small clusters of resorts. Apart from the tiny and remote but overcrowded honeypot of Ko Lipe, the other islands remain less developed, and scheduled boat services offer the intriguing possibility of **island-hopping** your way down from Phuket as far as Penang in Malaysia without setting foot on the peninsula. Yet, by going east from Trang, travellers find a slice of authentic rural Thailand at the lesser-visited **Thale Noi** (see page 715) protected wetland near Phattalung or decent beaches and Sino-Portuguese heritage at **Songkhla**, 30km northeast of **Hat Yai** (see page 716).

ARRIVAL AND GETTING AROUND

As well as the usual bus services, the area covered in this chapter is served by **flights** and **trains** to Trang (see page 697), as well as by **boats** between the islands (see page 702) and from the mainland to the islands.

By share-taxi The deep south has traditionally been the territory of share-taxis, which connect certain towns for about twice the fare of ordinary buses. They leave when full, which usually means six passengers — charter the whole car if you're in a hurry.

By minivan A/c minibuses cover the same routes as share-

taxis, but at lower prices. You'll have a seat to yourself, and services usually run from major bus stations to a rough timetable. However, in town centres, they tend to leave as soon as they're full.

By train Hat Yay is the deep south's major train hub, with several northbound trains to the Gulf coast and Bangkok, together with the unreliable southbound services to Sungai Kolok. Trang also has two convenient evening services to Bangkok.

Brief history

The central area of the Malay peninsula first entered Thai history when it came under the sway of Sukhothai, probably around the beginning of the fourteenth century. Islam

CRAB-EATING MACAQUE, KO TARUTAO NATIONAL MARINE PARK

Highlights

❶ Ko Hai A variety of good resorts for all budgets and gorgeous views of the karst islands to the east, especially at sunset. See page 701

❷ Tham Morakhot Ko Mook's Emerald Cave, with its inland beach of powdery sand at the base of an awesome natural chimney, is best visited by kayak or chartered longtail boat. See page 703

❸ Ko Kradan Remote island with a long, white, east-facing strand, crystal-clear waters, a reef for snorkellers to explore and a few diverse resorts. See page 704

❹ Thale Noi Boat hop amidst lotus flowers in Thailand's biggest, yet undiscovered, waterfowl reserve. See page 715

❺ Ko Tarutao Huge national park island with mangroves, limestone caves and jungle tracks to investigate, and the most unspoilt beaches in the area along its 26km west coast. See page 708

❻ Hat Pattaya Though far from undiscovered, Ko Lipe's main beach is a beautiful crescent of white sand as fine as flour that squeaks as you walk along it. See page 711

HIGHLIGHTS ARE MARKED ON THE MAP ON PAGE 696

was introduced to the area by the end of that century, by which time Ayutthaya was taking a firmer grip on the peninsula. **Songkhla** and **Pattani** then rose to be the major cities, prospering on the goods passed through the two ports across the peninsula to avoid the pirates in the Straits of Malacca between Malaysia and Sumatra. More closely tied to the Muslim Malay states to the south, the Sultanate of Pattani began to **rebel** against the power of Ayutthaya in the sixteenth century, but the fight for self-determination only weakened Pattani's strength. The town's last rebellious fling was in 1902, after which it was definitively and brutally absorbed into the Thai kingdom, while its allies, Kedah, Kelantan and Trengganu, were transferred into the suzerainty of the British in Malaysia.

During World War II the **Communist Party of Malaya** made its home in the jungle around the Thai border to fight the occupying Japanese. After the war they turned their guns against the British colonialists, but having been excluded from power after independence, descended into general banditry and racketeering around Betong. The Thai authorities eventually succeeded in breaking up the bandit gangs in 1989 through a combination of pardons and bribes, but the stability of the region soon faced disruption from another source, a rise in Islamic militancy.

The troubles: 2004 to the present

Armed resistance to the Thai state by **Muslim separatists** had fluctuated at a relatively low level since the 1960s, but in early 2004 the violence escalated dramatically. Since

TRAVEL WARNING

Because of the ongoing **violence** in the deep south (see below), Western governments are currently advising their citizens **not to travel** to or through Pattani, Yala, Narathiwat and Songkhla provinces unless essential; following on from this, check if your insurance company covers travel in the affected areas. The four provinces encompass the city and transport hub of **Hat Yai** and several of the main border crossings to Malaysia: by rail from Hat Yai (and Bangkok) to Butterworth (near Penang in Malaysia) via Padang Besar and to Sungai Kolok; and by road from Hat Yai to Sadao, from Yala via Betong, and down the east coast to Kota Bharu. In practice, however, crossing from Hat Yay into Malaysia by train is a very popular and generally safe route used daily by many international travellers.

On the contrary, avoid the routes to Sungai Kolok, Betong and Kota Bharu as they pass through particularly volatile territory, with **martial law** declared in Pattani, Yala and Narathiwat provinces; however, martial law is only in effect in certain districts of Songkhla province, and not in Hat Yai itself.

The provinces of **Trang** and **Satun** are not affected, and it's also possible to continue overland to Malaysia via Satun: by air-conditioned minibus from Satun to Kangar, or by ferry from Thammalang to the Malaysian island of Langkawi (see page 715); or by boat from Ko Lipe to Langkawi (see page 711). For up-to-the-minute advice, consult your government travel advisory (see page 63).

then, there have been hundreds of deaths on both sides in the troubles: the insurgents have targeted Buddhist monks, police, soldiers, teachers and other civil servants, as well as attacking a train on the Hat Yai–Sungai Kolok line and setting off bombs in marketplaces, near tourist hotels and bars and at Hat Yai airport. Increasingly, they have attacked other Muslims who are seen to be too sympathetic to the Thai state.

Often writing the militants off as bandits, the authorities have stirred up hatred – and undermined moderate Muslim voices – by reacting violently, notably in crushing protests at Tak Bai and the much-revered Krue Se Mosque in Pattani in 2004, in which a total of over two hundred alleged insurgents died. In 2005, the government announced a **serious state of emergency** in Pattani, Yala and Narathiwat provinces, and imposed **martial law** here and in southern parts of Songkhla province. This, however, has exacerbated economic and unemployment problems in what is Thailand's poorest region.

A large part of the problem is that a wide variety of shadowy groups – with names like the Pattani Islamic Mujahideen, the Barisan Revolusi Nasional-Coordinate and Runda Kumpulan Kecil – are operating against the government, generally working in small cells at village level without central control. Rather than religious issues, the most likely causes of their militancy are ethnic grievances. However, it's unclear exactly who they are or what they want, and, faced with such shifting sands, so far all attempts to broker a ceasefire have failed.

Trang town

TRANG (also known as Taptieng) is a popular jumping-off point for travellers drawn south from the crowded sands of Krabi to the pristine beaches and islands of the nearby coast. The town, which prospers on rubber, oil palms, fisheries and low-key tourism, is a sociable place whose wide, clean streets are dotted with crumbling, wooden-shuttered houses. In the evening, the streets are festooned with colourful lights and, from Thursday to Sunday, the central square in front of the station hosts a lively market, while during the day, many of the town's Chinese inhabitants hang out in the cafés, drinking the local filtered coffee. Trang's Chinese population makes the **Vegetarian Festival** in October or November almost as frenetic as Phuket's (see page 620). You can also take a day-trip to nearby **Kantang**, 25km south of town with its well-preserved old train station.

ARRIVAL AND DEPARTURE

By plane Air Asia and Nok Air run daily flights between Bangkok and Trang airport (1hr 30min), which is 3km south of town. On arrival, a/c minibuses bring passengers downtown (B100/person), while on departure, you can charter a tuk-tuk or taxi (about B300/two people).

By train Two overnight trains from Bangkok (15–16hr) use a branch of the southern line to Trang and return to the capital at 1.30pm and 5.25pm. A daily third-class service (10.36am; 15min; B20) also runs to Kantang.

By bus Buses arrive at and depart from the new bus terminal on Thanon Phattalung (Highway 4), opposite Robinson department store, about 3km northeast of the centre, including an a/c bus service between Satun and Phuket four times daily. Shared songthaews (B20) shuttle between here and the train station.

Destinations Bangkok (5 daily; 12hr); Krabi (roughly every 30min; 2hr); Phuket (hourly; 5hr).

By minibus A/c minibuses to Pak Meng, Ban Chao Mai, Satun (via Langu), Ko Lanta (including drop-offs as far south as Hat Klong Nin; 6 daily; 3hr), Krabi, Nakhon Si Thammarat, Phattalung, Songkhla, Surat Thani and Hat Yai also use the new bus terminal on Thanon Phattalung. In high season, travel agents such as Trang Island Hopping Tour can arrange through tickets to Ko Lipe (B700–750), Ko Tarutao and Ko Bulon Lae (both B650), including an a/c minibus to Pak Bara (departing 9am) and the boat trip.

By share-taxi Share-taxis for Pak Bara, Satun and Krabi congregate at the old bus station on Thanon Huay Yod, on the north side of town (about 500m north of the junction with Thanon Wisetkul).

GETTING AROUND

By rental car Avis (☎ 02 251 1131–2, ⊛avisthailand. com) and Budget (☎075 572159, ⊛budget.co.th), both at the airport.

By motorbike Motorbikes can be rented at *Sri Trang Hotel* (see below), on Thanon Rama VI (B250/day).

INFORMATION AND TOURS

Tourist information TAT office on Thanon Huay Yod (daily 8.30am–4.30pm; ☎075 211 058) is located out of town, but Green House Coffee (see below), just east of the clock tower, distributes free city maps and information.

Tourist police Thanon Phattalung (Highway 4), about 2km northeast of the centre ☎075 211903 or ☎1155.

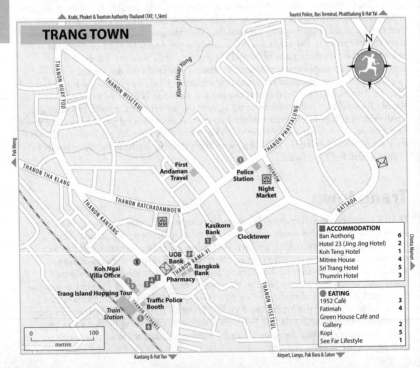

▮ ACCOMMODATION	
Ban Aothong	6
Hotel 23 (Jing Jing Hotel)	2
Koh Teng Hotel	1
Mitree House	4
Sri Trang Hotel	5
Thumrin Hotel	3

● EATING	
1952 Café	3
Fatimah	4
Green House Café and Gallery	2
Kopi	5
See Far Lifestyle	1

Travel agents The best travel agent in town is Trang Island Hopping Tour, with a desk at Fatimah, directly opposite the station at 28/2 Thanon Sathanee (☎082 804 0583, ⓦtrang-all-tour.com, ✉trangalltour@gmail.com). They offer one-day boat trips around the islands (B750 excluding the B200 national park entry fee) and day-trips and camping trips to Ko Rok (B3800 for 3D/2N), and inland excursions to waterfalls and caves (B1200), as well as trekking, bird-watching, rafting and kayaking.

ACCOMMODATION

Ban Aothong 25/28–31 Thanon Sathanee ☎075 290 192, ⓦfacebook.com/banaothongandmyfriend; map p.698. An overblown facade of multi-tiered roofs and gables announces this upmarket guesthouse, with its chunky wooden furniture, half-tester beds and rather kitsch decor. "Standard" double rooms are compact, some with no window, while the slightly pricier "superior" twins have more space, though the bathrooms are still small; all have a/c, hot showers, fridges and cable TV. B700

★ **Hotel 23 (Jing Jing Hotel)** 77–79 Thanon Rama VI, ☎075 218 077, ⓦfacebook.com/hotel23trang; map p.698. This affordable boutique hotel packs six spacious rooms that integrate modern plush beds and cute rattan furniture with the building's original wooden features. Bathrooms are clean and shared, but some of the a/c rooms (B500) come with private showers. Free coffee and tea for all guests is supplied. B300

Koh Teng Hotel 77–79 Thanon Rama VI ☎075 218622 or ☎075 218148; map p.698. This characterful 1940s Chinese hotel is a little battered and dusty but offers large, mostly clean, basic en-suite rooms with cold showers, some with cable TV and a/c, above a popular restaurant and coffee shop that serves southern Thai and Chinese food and Western breakfasts. Fan B200, a/c B360

Mitree House 6–8 Thanon Sathani, ☎075 212292, ⓦfacebook.com/mitreehouse; map p.698. Interesting mid-range choice opposite the train station, with a series of clean and white-tinted rooms (those with windows feel much less claustrophobic) spread over two wooden-decked floors tucked behind a spacious lounge-cum-reception. Breakfast is included. B750

Sri Trang Hotel 22 Thanon Sathanee ☎075 218122, ⓦsritranghotel.com; map p.698. Welcoming, thoroughly updated 1950s hotel offering spacious a/c rooms with some colourful decorative touches, hot water, cable TV, DVD players and fridges above a cool little café. B550

Thumrin Hotel Thanon Rama VI ☎075 211011–4, ⓦthumrin.co.th; map p.698. Good-value, very central hotel offering international-standard facilities – a/c, hot water, TV, mini-bar – in a high-rise block above its popular bakery-cum-coffee shop. B700

EATING AND DRINKING

Trang's streets are dotted with dozens of traditional cafés, which serve up gallons of **kopi** (local filtered coffee) accompanied by various tidbits and light meals. Most famous of these is the local speciality, **muu yaang**, delicious charcoal-grilled pork, which is generally eaten for breakfast. There's an excellent weekend **night market** in front of the train station, and, near Centrepoint shopping mall, the hipper **Chinta Market,** which features an upmarket food court, souvenir stalls, and live music.

1952 Café Opposite the train station on Thanon Sathanee, ☎089 114 4777, ⓦwww.facebook.com/nineteenfiftytwocafeattrang; map p.698. Annexed to Sri Trang Hotel, this contemporary-styled cafe is the place to get Western comfort foods. There are burgers (from B190), pizzas (from B200), chicken wings (B100), Thai mains and a good selection of drinks and coffee. Daily 8am–9pm.

Fatimah Opposite the train station on Thanon Sathanee, ☎086 5942083, ⓦwww.facebook.com/FatimahHalalRestaurant; map p.698. Simple Thai and Malay-style halal restaurant that's especially popular in the evenings. Buffet of southern curries, tasty *phat thai* (B40), fried rice and noodles (B40), *kopi* and tea. Tues–Sun roughly 8.30am–9pm.

★ **Green House Café and Gallery** 148/1 Rama VI, 15m east of the clocktower ☎075 218411, ⓦfacebook.com/greenhouseattrang; map p.698. Congenial hip café that bakes delicious cakes and wholemeal wheat breads, serves all-day brunch, and brews strong coffee in an arty, sociable sala. The manager, Dear, speaks great English and is happy to share her local knowledge with customers and travellers. Daily 10am–10pm.

Kopi Next to the train station at 25/25–26 Thanon Sathanee ☎075 214225; map p.698. Very popular, updated traditional café: *kopi* with dim sum and main courses (fried rice B50), or espresso, various teas and Western breakfasts. Daily 7am–5pm.

See Far Lifestyle 37 Thanon Phattalung (right by the entrance to Soi 3) ☎075 210139; map p.698. Good, inexpensive restaurant with a varied menu of carefully prepared dishes, specialising in healthy cuisine, vegetarian and local food, such as *tom som plakapong*, a light, refreshing soup of sea bass, mushrooms and cumin, and *kao yook* (B150), a Chinese-style dish of steamed pork with taro found only in Trang. Daily 10.30am–8.30pm.

8

The Trang coast

From Pak Meng, 40km due west of Trang town, down to the mouth of the Trang River runs a 30km-long stretch of lovely beaches, broken only by dramatic limestone outcrops. A paved road roughly parallels this stretch of coast, but otherwise there's surprisingly little development, as the shoreline is technically part of Hat Chao Mai National Park.

Pak Meng and Hat Chang Lang

Although it has a fine outlook to the headlands and islands to the west (with regular boats to the biggest, Ko Hai), the beach at **PAK MENG** is not the most attractive on the coast, becoming a rather muddy strip of sand at low tide. At other times, however, it offers quiet, calm swimming, and there's always the possibility of a meal at one of the many tree-shaded food stalls and restaurants that line the back of the beach.

Immediately south of Pak Meng's beach is the white sand of **Hat Chang Lang**, famous for its oysters, which shelters at its north end the finest luxury hotel in the province, *Anantara Si Kao*.

Hat Chao Mai National Park HQ

The turning for the headquarters is 3km on from Hat Chang Lang • B200 • ☎ 075 213260, ⓦ dnp.go.th

Hat Chao Mai National Park covers 230 square kilometres, including parts of Ko Mook and Ko Kradan, but the park admission fee is only rigidly enforced if you visit its headquarters. From the HQ a short trail leads to the south end of the beach and a viewpoint partway up a karst pinnacle, from which you can see Ko Mook and occasionally dugongs in the bay below. At headquarters there's a simple café as well as accommodation.

Hat Yong Ling and Hat Yao

About 5km south of the national park HQ, beyond Kuantunku, the pier for Ko Mook, is **Hat Yong Ling**. This quiet and attractive convex beach, which shelters a national park ranger station (entry B200), is probably the nicest along this stretch of coast, with a large cave which you can swim into at high tide or walk into at low tide. Immediately beyond comes **Hat Yao**, which is free, runs in a broad 5km white-sand strip, and is backed by casuarina trees and some simple restaurants.

Ban Chao Mai

At the south end of Hat Yao is **BAN CHAO MAI** (also called **Ban Hat Yao**), a straggle of houses on stilts, which exists on fishing, especially for crabs. From the harbour, boats run regularly across to Ko Libong, and this is the mainland ferry stop on Tigerline's Lanta–Lipe route. Also on offer are trips by longtail and canoe through the mangroves to the nearby cave of **Tham Chao Mai** (daily 8am–5pm), which shelters impressively huge rock pillars and a natural theatre, its stage framed by rock curtains – contact Bang Wit (☎ 087 463 7628), who speaks English, or ask around in the village for him.

ARRIVAL AND GETTING AROUND · THE TRANG COAST

Air-conditioned **minibuses**, departing roughly hourly but leaving early if already full, run from the bus station in Trang to Pak Meng (45min), as well as via Hat Yao to Ban Chao Mai (1hr), but if you want to explore the whole coastline, you'll need to rent a **motorbike** or **car** in Trang (see page 698).

ACCOMMODATION AND EATING

PAK MENG

Lay Trang Boutique ☎089 4744423, ⓦfacebook.com/laytrangboutique/. The nicest place to stay and eat at Pak Meng, a stone's throw from the pier at the far north end of the beach. Ranged around a large, peaceful garden with lawns and orchids set back from the beach, its bright concrete chalets with huge bathrooms and smart brick rooms come with verandas, hot showers, a/c and TV. Its welcoming, reasonably priced restaurant is nationally famous for its seafood, including *nam prik kung siap* (dried shrimp relish) and *kaeng som* soup with sea bass. B1500

HAT CHANG LANG

★ **Anantara Si Kao** ☎075 205888, ⓦanantara.com. The finest luxury hotel in the province, where the low-rise blocks of stylish bedrooms and pool suites, all with large balconies, are set behind a line of casuarina trees. Facilities encompass a beautiful, large pool, Italian and international restaurants, a kids' club, a fitness centre and a spa. Watersports on offer include diving, kayaking and sailing, and there's plenty of other activities, notably cooking and Thai-language lessons and some interesting local tours. The hotel also has its own beach club and restaurant on the main strand on Ko Kradan (see page 704), reached by daily boat transfer. Breakfast included. B9000

HAT CHAO MAI NATIONAL PARK HQ

National park bungalows ⓦdnp.go.th. Fan-cooled, en-suite bungalows and rooms, most with refrigerators, for two to six people, set under the casuarinas at the back of the sandy beach, and a simple café. B1000

The Trang and Satun islands

Generally blessed with blinding white beaches, great coral and amazing marine life, the islands off the coast of **Trang** and **Satun** provinces have managed, mostly with just a handful of resorts on each, to cling onto some of that illusory desert-island atmosphere which better-known places like Phuket and Samui lost long ago. Indeed, islands such as **Ko Hai** and **Ko Kradan** support no permanent settlements other than the bungalow concerns, while on **Ko Tarutao** and **Ko Adang** in the far south, the peace and quiet is maintained by the national parks department; at the other end of the scale, however, nearby **Ko Lipe** boasts over fifty resorts, as well as a substantial *chao ley* village (see page 600).

    Accommodation on the islands, much of which is mid-priced, is now often fully booked at the very busiest times. Most of the resorts open year-round, though in practice many can't be reached out of season (roughly June–Oct) due to treacherous seas. It's sensible to get in touch ahead of time to check whether the resort you're interested in is open or has vacancies, and in many cases to arrange transfers from agents in Trang town.

Ko Hai (Ko Ngai)

KO HAI (also known as **KO NGAI**), 16km southwest of Pak Meng, is the most developed of the Trang islands, though it's still decidedly low-key and much quieter than Ko Lipe down in Satun. The island's action, such as it is, centres on the east coast, where half a dozen resorts enjoy a dreamy panorama of jagged limestone outcrops, whose crags glow pink and blue against the setting sun, stretching across the sea to the mainland behind. The gently sloping beach of fine, white sand here runs unbroken for over 2km (though at low tide, swimming is not so good at the northern end, which is scattered with dead coral), and there's some good snorkelling in the shallow, clear water off the island's southeastern tip.

ARRIVAL AND DEPARTURE   **KO HAI**

If you're planning to **fly** into Trang or Krabi airports, contact your resort in advance about transfers. There are also plenty of island-hopping options (see above). Hat Chao Mai National Park maintains a booth at Pak Meng pier, where visitors to Ko Hai will usually be charged B200 entrance fee; hang on to your ticket as this should also cover you if you take a trip to Ko Mook's Emerald Cave.

By ferry In high season a ferry leaves Pak Meng pier

at 12pm (45min–1hr; B350), returning from Ko Hai at 10am; longtail boats come out to meet the ferries and shuttle passengers to the various resorts up and down the beach. Travel agents in Trang offer a/c minivan and boat combination tickets for B500. In high season, speedboats connect Ko Hai all the way to Ko Lipe, with stops at Ko Mook, Ko Kradan and Ko Tarutao.

By chartered longtail If you miss the ferries, you can charter a longtail boat for around B1500, for example through *Coco Cottage* (see below).

ACCOMMODATION

★**Coco Cottage** Towards the northern end of the beach ☎089 724 9225, �ⓦcoco-cottage.com. Charming, helpful and family-friendly resort in a grassy palm grove, where most of the chic, thatched, a/c wooden bungalows (both detached and semi-detached) sport verandas and well-designed bathrooms, with outdoor bamboo hot showers, wooden basins and indoor toilets. Also has a stylish beach bar and a very good restaurant that serves creative Thai food, Thai desserts and espresso coffees. Breakfast included. B2500

Ko Hai Seafood Near the centre of the beach, north of Koh Ngai Villa ☎095 014 1853. Large, well-built, thatched, woven-bamboo bungalows with wall fans, mosquito screens and cold-water bathrooms, in a single row facing the beach across a nice lawn. B1500

Mayalay Beach Resort Near the centre of the main beach, south of Koh Ngai Villa ☎081 894 3585, ⓦmayalaybeachresort.com. Welcoming place with nineteen deluxe, a/c, woven-bamboo bungalows with thatched roofs, day beds, fridges and capacious hot-water bathrooms. Often open all year round. Breakfast included. B3000

Sea Camp Hostel North end of the beach, ⓦbit.ly/2sMSm3y. Basic but charming mixed dorm with mosquito nets, literally on the sand with no flooring, and facing its own private part of beach. Ideal for backpackers and nature lovers. B600

Thanya South end of the beach ☎075 206967, ⓦkohngaithanyaresort.com. A large, very attractive beachside swimming pool with Jacuzzis, set on a spacious lawn, is the main draw here. As well as a/c, hot water and fridges, the dark-wooden villas feature verandas, big French windows and lots of polished teak, while the restaurant has a varied menu of Thai food, including some interesting seafood dishes. Breakfast included. B3600

Thapwarin Resort Towards the northern end of the main beach, north of Coco Cottage ☎081 894 3585, ⓦthapwarin.com. Welcoming, shady resort, where you can choose between well-appointed bamboo and rattan cottages with semi-outdoor bathrooms, and large, very smart, beachfront wooden bungalows; all are thatched and have a/c, mini-bars and hot showers (more expensive stilted villas, with bedrooms upstairs and living area downstairs, are also planned). There's a massage spa, beach bar and good restaurant, serving Thai and Western food, including seafood barbecues in the evening. Breakfast included. B3800

ISLAND-HOPPING AND TOURS

Access to the Trang and Satun islands from their nearest mainland ports is described in the individual island accounts, but what sets this area apart are the enticing opportunities for **island-hopping**, thanks to regular boat services in the tourist season between Ko Lanta and Ko Lipe, or even between Phuket and Langkawi in Malaysia, which can be booked through any travel agent in the area. (Several companies on Ko Lanta that organize day-trips by speedboat to Ko Hai, Ko Mook and Ko Kradan will drop you off at any of the islands, but the cost will be about the same as with Bundhaya Speedboat, Satun Pakbara Speedboat Club and Tigerline detailed below.) If you just fancy a day exploring some of the islands, any travel agent in Trang can book you on a **boat trip** (roughly mid-Oct to mid-May only) to Ko Kradan for snorkelling, the Emerald Cave on Ko Mook, and other small nearby islands for snorkelling, for around B750/person including packed lunch and soft drinks (excluding the B200 national park fee).

Bundhaya Speedboat ☎074 783111, ⓦbundhaya speedboat.com. Speedboats between Lanta and Lipe (1 daily; about 4hr; B1900) via Ko Hai, Hat Farang on Ko Mook and Ko Bulon Lae. Onward, same-day connections to Langkawi, and to Ko Phi Phi and Phuket.

Satun Pakbara Speedboat Club ☎081 959 2094, ⓦspcthailand.com. Speedboats between Lanta and Lipe (1 daily; about 4hr; B1900) via Ko Hai, Hat Farang on Ko Mook, Ko Kradan and Ko Bulon Lae. Onward, same-day connections between Lipe and Langkawi, and between Lanta and Ko Phi Phi and Phuket.

Tigerline ☎098 016 8181, ⓦtigerlinetravel.com. Ferries between Phuket and Langkawi (1 daily; about 9hr; B3500), via Ko Phi Phi, Ko Lanta, Ko Hai, Hat Farang on Ko Mook (with longtail transfers to Ko Kradan), Ban Chao Mai on the mainland (usually with a change of boat) and Ko Lipe. Hai–Lipe, for example, costs B1600.

KO HAI ACTIVITIES

You can rent **snorkelling equipment** and **kayaks** at most of the resorts. All the resorts offer **boat trips** (B1800/boat, maximum six people, at *Ko Hai Seafood*, for example) that take in the Emerald Cave on Ko Mook, nearby islands such as Ko Cheuak and Ko Waen and some snorkelling off Ko Hai.

Towards the southern end of the beach, *Fantasy Resort* has a well-organized **dive shop**, the German-run Ko Hai Divers, which specialises in small-group trips and PADI courses (☎ 080 545 5012, ⊛ kohaidivers.com; Nov–April).

Ko Mook

KO MOOK, about 8km southeast of Ko Hai, supports a comparatively busy fishing village on its eastern side, around which – apart from the sandbar that runs out to the very pricey *Sivalai Resort* – most of the beaches are disappointing, reduced to dirty mud flats when the tide goes out. However, across on the island's west coast lies beautiful **Hat Farang**, with gently shelving white sand, crystal-clear water that's good for swimming and snorkelling, and gorgeous sunsets.

Tham Morakhot

Part of Hat Chao Mai National Park • Open mid-Nov to mid-May • B200 admission fee if the park rangers are around

The island's main source of renown is **Tham Morakhot**, the stunning "Emerald Cave" north of Hat Farang on the west coast, which can only be visited by boat, but shouldn't be missed. An 80m swim through the cave – 10m or so of which is in pitch darkness – brings you to a *hong* (see page 647) with an **inland beach** of powdery sand open to the sky, at the base of a spectacular natural chimney whose walls are coated with dripping vegetation. Chartering your own longtail from the boatmen's co-operative on Hat Farang (B1000/boat, maximum four people; the boatman will swim with you to guide you through the cave) is preferable to taking one of the big day-trip boats that originate on Lanta or Pak Meng: if you time it right, you'll get the inland beach all to yourself, an experience not to be forgotten. (The boatmen also offer combined trips to Tham Morakhot, Ko Kradan and Ko Cheuak for B2500/boat.) It's also easy enough to **kayak** there from Hat Farang (from B200/hr from *Sawaddee*), and at low tide you can paddle right through to the inland beach: buoys mark the cave entrance, from where a tunnel heads straight back into the rock; about halfway along, there's a small, right-hand kink in the tunnel which will plunge you briefly into darkness, but you should soon be able to see light ahead from the *hong*. Mid-afternoon is often a good time to paddle off on this trip, after the tour boats have left and providing the tide is right.

ARRIVAL AND DEPARTURE
KO MOOK

In addition to the services mentioned below, there are plenty of island-hopping options (see page 702).

By Boat A year-round minibus leaves Trang station at 11.30am, connecting to the local ferry at Kuan Thung Khu pier, 8km south of Pak Meng (B250 all included). Ferries disembark at the main Ko Mook jetty, off Ao Kham, a 30min walk or B50–100 motorbike-taxi ride over to Hat Farang.

Travel agents in Trang can also organise minibus-and-boat packages to Hat Farang, which costs about B350, including a 30min longtail ride direct to the beach. In high season, speedboats depart from Hat Farang hopping all the way south to Ko Lipe (B1400), stopping at other islands en route. There are also direct services to Phi Phi (B1600) and Phuket (B2400) via Ko Lanta (B900).

ACCOMMODATION

Had Farang Bungalows ☎ 087 884 4785, ⊛ facebook.com/hadfarang. The eighteen bungalows and rooms at this friendly place are simple, yet clean and with wood and bamboo furnishing and mosquito nets. Nearly all are en suite with their own verandas and the restaurant is very good. Fan B400, a/c B1000

Ko Mook Hostel 400m from the boat pier, ☎ 089 724 4456, ⊛ facebook.com/Kohmookhostelfanpage. This single-storey blue building, the cheapest option on the island, has three (a/c female, a/c mixed and fan mixed) six and ten-bed dorms. The clean bunk beds are equipped with wooden dividers, privacy curtains and reading lights, and

8

the shared bathrooms are kept clean. There's free coffee and tea, and an in-house bakery-cum-coffee-shop that makes for a perfect breakfast spot. **B380**

Ko Mook Riviera Beach Resort ☎087 885 7815, ⊚ riviera-resorts.com. On the south-facing shore of the sandbar that ends at *Sivalai Resort*, the bright, concrete bungalows at this sustainable, eco-friendly resort all have mosquito-screened French windows directly facing the sea, as well as a/c, satellite TV and DVD player. Bicycles, kayaks and trips to the Emerald Cave and neighbouring islands available. Breakfast and dinner included. **B3000**

★ **Mountain View Resort** A 3min walk inland from Charlie's Beach, ☎ 065 053 3077 ⊚ .facebook.com/moutainviewresortkohmook. A collection of Thai-style bungalows set in a well-tended, shady garden just minutes away from the beach. All rooms are en suite, some are graciously decked out in thatched bamboo, and all have serene wooden verandas. Breakfast is included. **B1300**

Ko Kradan

About 6km to the southwest of Ko Mook, **KO KRADAN** is the remotest of the inhabited islands off Trang, and one of the most beautiful, with crystal-clear waters. On this slender, 4km-long triangle of thick jungle, the **main beach** is a long strand of steeply sloping, powdery sand on the east coast, with fine views of Ko Mook, Ko Libong and the karst-strewn mainland, and an offshore reef to the north with a great variety of hard coral; such beauty, however, has not escaped the attention of the day-trip boats from Ko Lanta, who turn the beach into a lunchtime picnic ground most days in high season. From a short way north of the *Anantara* beach club (see page 701), which is located towards the south end of this beach, a path across the island will bring you after about fifteen minutes to **Sunset Beach**, another lovely stretch of fine, white sand in a cove; a branch off this path at *Paradise Lost* leads to a beach on the short south coast, which enjoys good reef snorkelling (also about 15min from the *Anantara* beach club).

ARRIVAL AND DEPARTURE   KO KRADAN

By minibus-and-longtail transfer Agencies such as Trang Island Hopping Tour (see page 699) can arrange minibus-and-longtail transfers from Trang town, via Kuan Thung Khu pier (twice daily in season; B450). There are also plenty of island-hopping options (see page 702).

ACCOMMODATION

Kalume ☎093 650 0841, ⊚ kalumekradan.com. Eco-friendly Italian-run resort on the beach next to *Seven Seas*, with small, basic, thatched bamboo huts with mosquito nets, fans and en-suite bathrooms and smart, large, wooden bungalows with French windows and nice verandas. Good Italian food at the bar-restaurant. **B1500**

Paradise Lost ☎089 587 2409; for further information, go to ⊚ kokradan.wordpress.com. In the middle of the island, roughly halfway along the path to *Sunset Beach*, is Kradan's best-value accommodation, run by an American and his dogs. Set in a grassy, palm-shaded grove, it offers simple, clean, thatched rattan bungalows with mosquito nets, fans and shared bathrooms or larger, en-suite, wooden affairs (some with hot showers), kayaks, snorkels and good Thai and Western food. **B700**

Seven Seas ☎075 203389–90, ⊚ sevenseasresorts. com. By far the best of several resorts on the east coast, *Seven Seas* adds a surprising splash of contemporary luxury to this remote spot. Behind a small, black, infinity-edge pool, the large bungalows, villas and rooms with outdoor warm-water bathrooms are stylishly done out in greys and whites, and sport a/c, fridges, TVs and DVD players. There's a spa and a dive shop, and breakfast is included. **B9300**

Ko Libong

The largest of the Trang islands with a population of six thousand, **KO LIBONG** lies 10km southeast of Ko Mook, opposite Ban Chao Mai on the mainland. Less visited than its northern neighbours, it's known mostly for its wildlife, although it has its fair share of golden beaches too. Libong is one of the most significant remaining refuges in Thailand of the **dugong**, a large marine mammal similar to the manatee, which feeds on sea grasses growing on the sea floor – the sea-grass meadow around Libong is reckoned to be the largest in Southeast Asia. Sadly, dugongs are now an endangered

KO LIBONG ACTIVITIES

Libong Beach Resort runs **boat trips** to see the dugongs for B1500 per boat. To this you can add on a visit to the bird sanctuary (B1800 in total), plus a cruise around the island (B2000 in total). The resorts can also organize trips to the Emerald Cave on Ko Mook. For **diving**, ask at *Libong Beach Resort*: Yat, a dive master who works on Ko Hai, can usually arrange trips from his home island of Libong.

species, traditionally hunted for their blubber (used as fuel) and meat, and increasingly affected by fishing practices such as scooping, and by coastal pollution, which destroys their source of food. The dugong has now been adopted as one of fifteen "reserved animals" of Thailand and is the official mascot of Trang province.

Libong is also well known for its migratory **birds**, which stop off here on their way south from Siberia, drawn by the island's food-rich mud flats (now protected by the Libong Archipelago Sanctuary, which covers the eastern third of the island). For those seriously interested in ornithology, the best time to come is during March and April, when you can expect to see brown-winged kingfishers, masked finfoots and even the rare black-necked stork, not seen elsewhere on the Thai–Malay peninsula.

The island's handful of resorts occupies a long, thin strip of golden sand at the fishing village of **Ban Lan Khao** on the southwestern coast. At low tide here, the sea retreats for hundreds of metres, exposing rock pools that are great for splashing about in but not so good for a dip.

ARRIVAL AND DEPARTURE
KO LIBONG

By public longtail Public longtails depart daily year-round from Ban Chao Mai (see page 700) when full (most frequent in the morning and around lunchtime; B50/person), arriving 20min later at Ban Phrao on Ko Libong's north side. From here motorbike taxis (B100) transport you to Ban Lan Khao.

In high season, Tigerline speedboats (ⓦtigerlinetravel.com) stop at Hat Yao on Ko Libong and can take you to/from Phi Phi, Phuket, Ko Lanta, Ko Hai, Ko Mook, Ko Kradan, Ko Lipe and Langkawi in Malaysia.

By private transfer You can arrange a direct boat transfer from Ban Chao Mai through *Libong Beach Resort* for B1000/boat.

ACCOMMODATION

Libong Beach Resort ☎075 225205, ⓦlibong-beach.com. Friendly resort on the north side of Ban Lan Khao with a wide variety of accommodation set amid lawns and flowers, ranging from small, en-suite concrete and wood bungalows at the back to spacious, bright, stilted, wooden cabins with a/c and nice decks on the beachfront (B2500). Kayak and motorbike rental are available. Fan B1000, a/c B1500

Libong Relax Beach Resort ☎091 825 4886, ⓦlibongrelax.com. Located on an attractive stretch of the beach, all of the bungalows here face directly onto the sea across a narrow, tree-lined lawn and sport some attractive Thai decorative touches. The "Pavilions" have Thai-style roofs, picture windows and large verandas, while the "Cottages" are more functional with smaller verandas; upgrading to a/c also snags you a hot shower. There's a massage hut and the resort can arrange island tours on a motorcycle with a sidecar. Fan B1400, a/c B2000

Ko Sukorn

A good way south of the other Trang islands, low-lying, ATM-free **KO SUKORN** lacks the white-sand beaches and beautiful coral of its neighbours but makes up for it with its friendly inhabitants and laidback ambience; for a glimpse of how the Muslim islanders live and work, this is a good place to come.

The lush interior is mainly given over to rubber plantations, interspersed with rice paddies, banana and coconut palms; the island also produces famously delicious watermelons, which are plentiful in March and April. Hat Talo Yai, the main **beach** – 500m of gently shelving brown sand, backed by coconut palms – runs along the southwestern shore.

KO SUKORN BOAT TRIPS AND OTHER ACTIVITIES

Boat excursions arranged through the resorts include trips out to the islands of Ko Lao Liang and Ko Takieng, which are part of the Mu Ko Phetra National Marine Park, for some excellent snorkelling. These run nearly every day from November to May; at other times of year, the sea is sometimes calm enough but you're usually restricted to fishing trips – and to looking round the island itself, which, at thirty square kilometres, is a good size for exploring. Yataa Island Resort has a handy map that marks all the sights, including the three villages and seafood market, and offers motorbikes (B250/half-day) and mountain bikes (B150/half-day) for rent.

ARRIVAL AND DEPARTURE   KO SUKORN

Transfers from Trang A songthaew-and-boat transfer to Ko Sukorn (B300/person), via the public ferry from Laem Ta Sae, can be arranged through any travel agent in Trang, leaving daily at 11.30am and taking about two and a half hours, or you can arrange a private transfer through the resorts for about B2000 all-in.

Inter-island transfers *Yataa Island Resort* can organize pricey longtail-boat transfers to or from any of the nearby islands.

ACCOMMODATION

Ko Sukorn Cabana ☎089 724 2326, ⊛sukorncabana. com. This friendly and peaceful place offers stilted, a/c bungalows with attractive bathrooms and large, well-appointed log cabins on a secluded beach to the north of Hat Talo Yai. Kayaks and motorbikes are also available. Breakfast included. B1000

Yataa Island Resort (Sukorn Beach Bungalows) ☎089 647 5550, ⊛sukornisland.yataaresort.com.

Low-key, quiet resort under new management, where the attractively decorated bungalows and different categories of rooms – all a/c and with en-suite hot showers – are set around a lush garden dotted with deckchairs and umbrellas, and there's a small swimming pool and a good restaurant. At the resort, you can also get a good massage, and you're free to paddle around in kayaks. Breakfast included. B1400

8

Ko Bulon Lae

The scenery at tiny **KO BULON LAE**, 20km west of Pak Bara in Satun province, isn't as beautiful as that generally found in Ko Tarutao National Park just to the south, but it's not at all bad: a 2km strip of fine white sand runs the length of the casuarina-lined east coast, where the two main resorts can be found (open roughly from Nov to April or mid-May), while *chao ley* fishermen make their ramshackle homes in the tight coves of the rest of the island. A reef of curiously shaped hard coral closely parallels the eastern beach, while **White Rock** to the south of the island has beautifully coloured soft coral and equally dazzling fish.

ARRIVAL AND DEPARTURE   KO BULON LAE

From/to Pak Bara Boats for Ko Bulon Lae currently leave Pak Bara daily at about 12.30pm (about 1hr; B450). As there's no pier on Bulon Lae, boat arrivals are met by longtails to transfer visitors to shore at School Beach (B50). Boats return from Bulon Lae to Pak Bara at around 9.30am. There are also island-hopping options (see page 702).

KO LAO LIANG

The beautiful twin islets of **Ko Lao Liang**, with their white-sand beaches, abundant corals and dramatic rock faces, lie to the west of Ko Sukorn and are part of the Mu Ko Phetra National Park. They're deserted apart from a single adventure-sport camp, *Lao Liang Resort* (☎084 304 4077, ⊛facebook.com/LaoLiangResort; open Nov to April; B1500). All-in costs at the resort comprise camping in deluxe tents on the beach, three meals, including seafood barbecues, and snorkelling gear; kayak rental, rock-climbing, bouldering and snorkelling tours are extra. The resort offers transfers from Trang for B1600 per person return.

ACCOMMODATION

Bulone ☎ 081 897 9084 or ☎ 086 960 0468, ⊕ bulone-resort.net. Friendly, very popular spot in a huge grassy compound under the casuarinas at the north end of the main beach. Airy, en-suite bungalows on stilts come with large verandas and most have a/c, while the restaurant features plenty of vegetarian options and a small selection of tasty Italian favourites. Breakfast included. B3000

Pansand ☎ 081 693 3667, ⊕ pansand-resort.com; Trang office at First Andaman Travel on Thanon Wisetkul. The oldest and largest resort on the island, on the east-coast beach, where large, smart, peaceful cottages come with verandas, fans, mosquito screens, cold-water bathrooms and plenty of room to breathe. On the beach side of the shady, well-tended grounds, there's a sociable restaurant serving up good seafood and other Thai dishes; boat trips and snorkelling gear are also available. Breakfast included. B1700

Ko Tarutao National Marine Park

B200 admission fee • ⊕ dnp.go.th

The unspoilt **KO TARUTAO NATIONAL MARINE PARK** is probably the most beautiful of all Thailand's accessible beach destinations. Occupying 1400 square kilometres of the Andaman Sea in Satun province, the park covers 51 mostly uninhabited islands. Site of the park headquarters, the main island, **Ko Tarutao**, offers a variety of government-issue accommodation and things to do, while **Ko Adang** to the west is much more low-key and a springboard to some excellent snorkelling. The port of **Pak Bara** is the main jumping-off point for the park and houses a **national park visitor centre** (☎ 074 783485), next to the pier, where you can gather information and book a room on Tarutao or Adang before boarding your boat.

The park's forests and seas support an incredible variety of **fauna**: langurs, crab-eating macaques and wild pigs are common on the islands, which also shelter several unique subspecies of squirrel, tree shrew and lesser mouse deer; among the hundred-plus bird species found here, reef egrets and hornbills are regularly seen, while white-bellied sea eagles, frigate birds and pied imperial pigeons are more rarely encountered; and the park is the habitat of about 25 percent of the world's tropical fish species, as well as dugongs, sperm whales, dolphins and a dwindling population of turtles.

The park amenities on Adang, though not on Tarutao, are officially closed to tourists in the monsoon season from mid-May to mid-November (the exact dates vary from year to year). Accommodation is especially likely to get full around the three New Years (Thai, Chinese and Western), when it's best to book national park rooms in advance (see page 39).

Ko Tarutao

The largest of the national park's islands, **KO TARUTAO** offers the greatest natural variety: mountains covered in semi-evergreen rainforest rise steeply to a high point of 700m; limestone caves and mangrove swamps dot the shoreline; and the west coast is lined

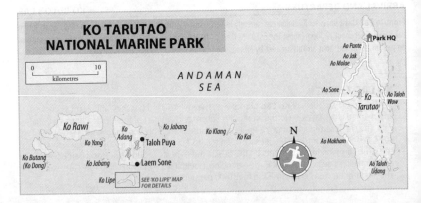

TRANSPORT TO AND FROM PAK BARA

The main port for Bulon Lae, Tarutao and Lipe is **PAK BARA**, towards the north end of Satun province. **From Trang**, you can book minibus-and-boat packages to all three islands and there are direct share-taxis to Pak Bara (see page 698); otherwise you'll need to take a Satun-bound bus (2hr–2hr 30min) to the inland town of **Langu** (also served by buses from Phuket via Krabi to Satun) and change there to a red songthaew for the 10km hop to the port. There are also direct a/c minibuses **from Hat Yai** (see page 716) Talad Kaset station, while **from Satun**, frequent buses and a/c minibuses make the 50km trip to Langu, where you'll have to change onto a songthaew.

with perfect beaches for most of its 26km length. For a different perspective on Ko Tarutao, John Gray's Sea Canoe in Phuket runs multi-day **sea-kayaking** trips that include trips round the island (☏ 076 254505–6, ⊛ johngray-seacanoe.com).

The west coast

At **Ao Pante**, site of the **park headquarters**, you'll find the only shop on the island, selling basic supplies, as well as a visitor centre. Behind the settlement, the steep, half-hour climb to **To-Boo cliff** is a must, especially at sunset, for the view of the surrounding islands and the crocodile's-head cape at the north end of the bay. A fun ninety-minute trip by boat (B400/boat; contact the visitor centre to book) or kayak can also be made near Ao Pante, up the canal which leads 2km inland from the pier, through a bird-filled mangrove swamp, to **Crocodile Cave** – where you're unlikely to see any of the big snappers, reported sightings being highly dubious.

A half-hour walk south from Ao Pante brings you to the two quiet bays of **Ao Jak** and **Ao Molae**, fringed by coconut palms and filled with fine white sand. Beyond the next headland (a 2hr walk from Ao Pante) lies **Ao Sone** (which gets its name from the casuarina trees that fringe the beach), where a pretty freshwater stream runs past the ranger station at the north end of the bay, a good place for peaceful camping. The main part of the bay is a 3km sweep of flawless sand, with a one-hour trail leading up to **Lu Du Waterfall** at the north end, a ninety-minute trail to **Lo Po Waterfall** in the middle and a **mangrove swamp** at the far south end.

The east coast

On the east side of the island, **Ao Taloh Wow** is a rocky bay with a ranger station, shop and campsite, connected to Ao Pante by a 12km-long road through old rubber plantations and evergreen forest. Beyond Taloh Wow, a 16km-long trail cuts through the forest to **Ao Taloh Udang**, a sandy bay on the south side where you can pitch a tent. Here the remnants of a penal colony for political prisoners are just visible: the royalist plotters of two failed coup attempts against the recently established constitutional regime – including the author of the first English-Thai dictionary – were imprisoned here in the 1930s before returning to high government posts. The ordinary convicts, who used to be imprisoned here and at Ao Taloh Wow, had a much harsher time, and during World War II, when supplies from the mainland dried up, prisoners and guards ganged together to turn to piracy. This turned into a lucrative business, which was not suppressed until 1946 when the Thai government asked the British in Malaysia to send in three hundred troops. Pirates and smugglers still occasionally hide out in the Tarutao archipelago, but the main problem now is illegal trawlers fishing in national park waters.

ARRIVAL AND DEPARTURE
KO TARUTAO

From Pak Bara and Ko Lipe The speedboat services between Pak Bara and Ko Lipe (see page 711) will usually call in at Ko Tarutao if requested; Tarutao is about 30min from Pak Bara (B450) and 1hr from Lipe (B450). Boats drop passengers off at Ao Pante on Tarutao; the pier at Ao Pante is sometimes inaccessible at low tide, when longtails (B50) shuttle people to shore.

8

> ## SNORKELLING TRIPS AROUND KO ADANG
> You can charter **longtail boats** (and rent snorkels and masks, for B50/day) through the rangers for excellent snorkelling trips to nearby islands such as Ko Rawi and Ko Jabang (around B1500–2500 for up to ten people, depending on how far you want to go).

GETTING AROUND

By truck The visitor centre can arrange transport by road, usually in an open truck, to several of the island's beaches, charging B50/person one-way to Ao Molae, around B400 per vehicle to Ao Sone and B600 per vehicle to Ao Taloh Wow.

By boat Transfers to the same places by boat cost at least twice as much, though you may be tempted by a round-island boat trip for B3000.

By kayak or mountain bike Kayaks and mountain bikes are available at headquarters.

ACCOMMODATION

National park accommodation At park headquarters, the rooms and bungalows (sleeping four people, or available as twin rooms), which are spread over a large, quiet park behind the beach, are for the main part national park standard issue with cold-water bathrooms, but there are also some basic mattress-on-floor four-person rooms in longhouses, sharing bathrooms, as well as a restaurant. There are also bungalows containing en-suite twin rooms and a small restaurant at Ao Molae. HQ B500, Ao Molae B600

Camping There are campsites at Ao Pante, Ao Molae and Ao Taloh Wow. Two-person tents can be rented from Ao Pante for B150/night (plus B50/person for bedding).

Ko Adang

At **KO ADANG**, a wild, rugged island covered in tropical rainforest 40km west of Ko Tarutao, the park station with its accommodation and restaurant is at **Laem Sone** on the southern shore, where the beach is steep and narrow and backed by a thick canopy of pines. The half-hour climb to **Sha-do** cliff on the steep slope above Laem Sone gives good views over Ko Lipe to the south, while about 2km west along the coast from the park station, a twenty-minute trail leads inland to the small **Pirate Waterfall**.

ARRIVAL AND DEPARTURE   KO ADANG

By boat To get to Ko Adang, take any boat to Ko Lipe (see page 711), from where a longtail transfer to Adang will cost B100–200/person.

ACCOMMODATION

National park accommodation At the park station at Laem Sone, there are rooms in bamboo longhouses sleeping three, bungalows of various sizes (2–6 people), and two/ three-person tents can be rented (B225/night plus B50/person for bedding). Rooms B300, bungalows B600

Ko Lipe

Home to a population of around a thousand *chao ley*, tiny **KO LIPE**, 2km south of Ko Adang, is something of a frontier maverick, attracting ever more travellers with one dazzling beach, over fifty private bungalow resorts and a rough-and-ready atmosphere. It's technically a part of Ko Tarutao National Marine Park, but the authorities seem to have given up on the island and don't collect an admission fee from visitors. A small, flat triangle, Lipe is covered in coconut plantations and supports a school and a health centre in the village on the eastern side. By rights, such a settlement should never have been allowed to develop within the national park boundaries, but the *chao ley* on Lipe are well entrenched: Satun's governor forced the community to move here from Phuket and Ko Lanta between the world wars, to reinforce the island's Thai character and prevent the British rulers of Malaya from laying claim to it.

More recently, a huge, diverse influx of tourists – Westerners, Thais, Chinese and Malaysians, families and backpackers – has been enticed here by the gorgeous beach of **Hat Pattaya**, a shining crescent of squeaky-soft white sand with an offshore reef to explore on its eastern side, as well as by the relaxed, anything-goes atmosphere and mellow nightlife. Many of Lipe's *chao ley* have now sold their beachfront land to Thai–Chinese speculators from the mainland, who have increased the island's capacity to over two thousand guest rooms; with the money earned, the *chao ley* have bought the scores of longtail boats that clog up the bay at Hat Pattaya. Lipe's main drag is **Walking Street**, a paved path lined with tourist businesses between the eastern end of Hat Pattaya and the south end of the village, which lies on east-facing **Sunrise**, an exposed, largely featureless beach that gives access to some good snorkelling around Ko Gra; a few other narrow roads also radiate out from the village. A track runs from *Pattaya Song Resort* at the west end of Pattaya across to **Sunset** beach, a shady, attractive spot with good views of Ko Adang, in around ten minutes.

ARRIVAL AND DEPARTURE
KO LIPE

As well as being one of the hubs for island-hopping boats (see page 702), Ko Lipe is served by **speedboats** from Pak Bara in the north of Satun province and from the Malaysian island of Langkawi. However, services to Lipe seem to change by the year, due to competition between the boat companies and local politicking; in the past, there have been boats from Thammalang near Satun town (see page 715), which may or may not resurface; for up-to-date **transport information**, contact Koh Lipe Thailand (see below). There is no pier on Lipe, so boats usually anchor at a platform off Hat Pattaya, where they're met by **longtails** (B50–100/person to any beach on Lipe); sometimes speedboats will just run ashore at Pattaya, leaving you to jump off onto the beach; in low season, all boats tend to stop at Sunrise Beach, where there's shelter from the southwest monsoon, leaving you with a longtail trip to any of the beaches.

Via Pak Bara Several companies run speedboats (plus occasional ferries) between Pak Bara (see page 709) and Ko Lipe in high season (usually at 11.30am & 3.30pm; 1hr 30min; B750). In the rainy season, there's at least one crossing a day, usually heading out at 11.30am.

Via Langkawi Boats operate between Ko Lipe and Langkawi, the large Malaysian island to the southeast, several times a day in high season (1hr; B1000–1400). During the season, a Thai immigration post is set up at the far east end of Lipe's Hat Pattaya to cover this route.

INFORMATION

Koh Lipe Thailand The best travel agent and source of information on the island is Koh Lipe Thailand (Boi's Travel; ☎089 464 5854 or ☎081 541 4489, ⓦkohlipethailand.com or ⓦthaibeachtravellers.com), which currently has two outlets on Walking Street between Hat Pattaya and the village, with the main, year-round one hard by the beach (the second, seasonal, shop, further inland towards *Pooh's*, has a book exchange). On offer are all manner of

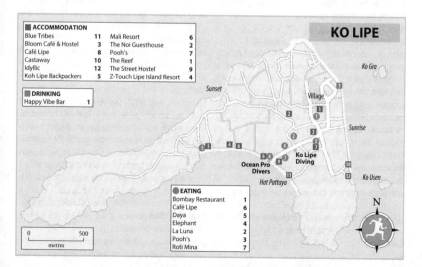

■ **ACCOMMODATION**
Blue Tribes	11
Bloom Café & Hostel	3
Café Lipe	8
Castaway	10
Idyllic	12
Koh Lipe Backpackers	5
Mali Resort	6
The Noi Guesthouse	2
Pooh's	7
The Reef	1
The Street Hostel	9
Z-Touch Lipe Island Resort	4

■ **DRINKING**
Happy Vibe Bar	1

● **EATING**
Bombay Restaurant	1
Café Lipe	6
Daya	5
Elephant	4
La Luna	2
Pooh's	3
Roti Mina	7

KO LIPE

SNORKELLING AND DIVING AROUND KO LIPE

The prime **diving and snorkelling sites** near Ko Lipe are around Ko Adang, Ko Rawi and Ko Dong, just to the north and west in Ko Tarutao National Marine Park, where encounters with reef and even whale sharks, dolphins and stingrays are not uncommon. Further afield to the south, advanced divers head for Eight Mile Rock, a pinnacle that rises to about 14m from the surface, with soft corals, mantas, leopard and whale sharks. A handful of dive shops operate on Lipe, and there are dozens of places offering snorkelling day-trips on *chao ley* longtail boats; snorkellers are liable to pay the park admission fee of B200, though some longtail captains will try to dodge the park rangers.

Koh Lipe Thailand See below. This travel agent offers snorkelling day-trips to the best sites around the islands on the west side of Ko Adang for B550–650/person, including lunch and full snorkelling equipment, or a sunset trip for B450.

Ko Lipe Diving On Walking Street between Sunrise and Hat Pattaya ☎087 622 6204, ⌨kolipediving. com. Well-regarded SSI dive centre offering daily trips (B2800 for two dives) and SSI courses (B14,500 for the

Open Water; for PADI add B1500). Also runs snorkelling trips (B1000).

Ocean Pro Divers On Pattaya beach, just east of the main pier ☎089 733 8068, ⌨oceanprodivers. com. Five-Star PADI centre offering daily trips (B3000, including equipment rental and National Marine Park diving fees, for two dives) and PADI courses (B14,500 for the Open Water). Also offers diving and accommodation packages for divers.

transport tickets (including a/c minibuses in high season to Penang and other popular mainland destinations) plus accommodation bookings (including on the websites).
Currency exchange There are currently no ATMs on Ko

Lipe (the nearest is in Pak Bara), but Koh Lipe Thailand, for instance, offers currency exchange and cash advances.
Tourist police Behind the immigration post at the far east end of Hat Pattaya ☎1155.

ACCOMMODATION

The majority of Lipe's bungalows are on **Hat Pattaya**, the prettiest but most crowded and expensive beach on the island. There are a bunch of resorts on **Sunset** beach on the northwest side, while twenty or so have set up shop on **Sunrise**, on the east side near the village. If you turn up on the island and are struggling to find a vacant room, head for one of the Koh Lipe Thailand offices on Walking Street for booking assistance (see opposite).

Blue Tribes East end of Hat Pattaya ☎080 546 9464, ⌨bluetribeslipe.com; map p.711. Congenial, Italian-run resort and restaurant with very spacious, well-spread and well-designed bungalows and rooms, either in lovely dark wood or in thatched white concrete, sporting large, attractive tiled bathrooms with hot showers, fans, mosquito nets and large verandas; some are two-storey with a balcony and chill-out room/extra bedroom upstairs. Closed mid-May to July. B1700

★ **Bloom Café & Hostel** On the eastern end of Walking Street, ☎095 440 2288, ⌨facebook.com/ bloom.cafe.hostel; map p.711. Right in the midst of the action, this cosy boutique hostel has eight-bed dorms and some attractive black-tinged private rooms (B1100), all with plush mattresses, dark-wooden bed stands and floor tiles. The immaculate and chic shared bathrooms have rain showers. The cafe downstairs is a popular travellers hangout and serves some of Lipe's best brews. B600

Café Lipe West of Walking Street, central Pattaya ☎086 969 9472, ⌨cafe-lipe.com; map p.711. Eco-

conscious, solar-powered place in a great location, offering large, old-style bamboo bungalows that are nicely spaced out under a thick canopy of teak and fruit trees. Each has a partly outdoor, cold-water bathroom, fan and mosquito net. Three-night minimum stay. B1000

★ **Castaway** Sunrise ☎083 138 7472, ⌨castaway-resorts.com; map p.711. Airy, thatched, mostly two-storey bungalows featuring well-equipped bathrooms with cold rain showers, ceiling fans, big decks, hammocks and a certain amount of style, mostly bestowed by the distinctive red Indonesian hardwood that they're made from. On a sandy patch with a dive shop, a mellow, multi-tiered bar-restaurant and a massage spa; kayaks and snorkels for rent. B2700

Idyllic South end of Sunrise ☎074 750399, ⌨idyllic resort.com; map p.711. This welcoming "concept resort" comes as a big surprise out here in Thailand's far maritime corner, with its angular contemporary architecture in white, grey and wood. Set in an attractive garden, the minimalist rooms boast huge windows, a/c, hot outdoor rain showers, mini-bars and nice touches such as sun hats for guests' use. There are two pools – one infinity-edged and beachside, with a swim-up bar, the other with a Jacuzzi – as well as kayaks and other watersports. Breakfast included. B6000

Koh Lipe Backpackers West end of Hat Pattaya, ⌨kohlipebackpackers.com; map p.711. Part of Davy Jones' Locker diving centre (free stays with included with a PADI course), this place offers two eight-bed dorms in plain concrete rooms with thick mattresses, hot showers and lockers, as well as plain, a/c double bedrooms with en-suite hot-water bathrooms. Wi-fi is only available in the lobby. Dorms B500, doubles B1200

Mali Resort Towards the west end of Hat Pattaya ☎077 033020, ⊛maliresorts.com/koh-lipe/pattaya-beach; map p.711. At this shady, well-appointed luxury resort, go for one of the Balinese bungalows if you can (from B6800), thatched, dark-wood affairs with big French windows, sizeable verandas and open-air bathrooms, which are spread out around a lovely lawn and beach bar. Breakfast included. B4300

The Noi Guesthouse ☎094 495 4953, ⊛facebook. com/noiguesthouse; map p.711711. Comfortable en-suite rooms with naked walls and wooden furnishings. Most rooms have little balconies facing the road that are set over the annexed restaurant, where guest can enjoy the rich included breakfast. The friendly staff are more than happy to pick up guests from the docks. B2000

Pooh's On Walking Street between Sunrise and Hat Pattaya ☎074 750345, ⊛facebook.com/poohbar kohlipe; map p.711. Well inland behind the popular restaurant, but a good, functional choice if you get stuck for somewhere to stay. The eight, concrete single-storey rooms have small terraces, a/c, hot showers and TVs, and there's a dive centre. Breakfast included. B1800

The Reef In the village, ☎82 733 7034, ⊛thereef kohlipe.com; map p.711. Boutique guesthouse with a range of homely, spacious a/c rooms, ranging from smart budget singles (B950), to charming family suites with wooden mezzanines (B2400) or cosy, large wooden balconies (B3000). It's a quieter option, slightly removed from the action, but still within walking distance of all the main beaches. Breakfast included. B1400

The Street Hostel On Walking Street, ☎099 125 9146, ⊛thestreethostels.com; map p.711. Housed in a metallic net-covered building that opens with an arty loft filled with wooden frames, hanging bulbs and industrial chic furniture, this is a comfortable, clean and modern hostel. The white-tinged a/c rooms have private pods – some with double beds for couples (B1000) – equipped with privacy curtains, plugs and reading lights. The shared bathrooms are squeaky clean; there's free coffee and tea and a fridge for guests' house. B600

Z-Touch Lipe Island Resort On the West end of Hat Pattaya, ☎086 292 8204, ⊛ztouchresort.com; map p.711. Clustered around gardens that face a relatively boat-free stretch of beach, the rooms, villas and cottages here have en-suite bathrooms and spacious verandas. There's an inviting free-form swimming pool; breakfast is included. B2800

8

EATING AND DRINKING

There are a couple of beach bars on Sunset, but the east end of Pattaya has the biggest concentration, with low candlelit tables and cushions sprawled on the sand, fire shows and names like *Peace and Love*.

Bombay Restaurant On Walking Street, ☎094 810 1872, ⊛bit.ly/2FvFaCT; map p.711. Authentic Indian food served with care and attention by the affable owner. The naan bread is particularly good, and a meal will set you back around B400. Daily 10am–10pm.

Café Lipe West of Walking Street, central Pattaya (see page 712); map p.711. Behind a thick screen of foliage this resort restaurant serves up decent veggie choices among its inexpensive Thai dishes, sandwiches and espressos, as well as home-made bread, fruit juices and muesli. Daily 7am–5pm.

Daya West end of Hat Pattaya (see page 712); map p.711. One of the most popular of half a dozen restaurants that lay out candlelit tables and seafood barbecues on the beach at night. It also offers a long menu of mostly Thai dishes, such as prawn tempura (B160), lots of tofu options for vegetarians, Thai desserts and Western breakfasts. Daily 7am–11pm.

Elephant Walking Street, 100m inland from Pattaya ☎088 046 8234, ⊛facebook.com/ElephantKohLipe; map p.711. Mellow restaurant and secondhand bookshop, where you can tuck into delicious chicken sandwiches (B180) and burgers made with Australian beef, as well as salads, breakfasts and espressos. Daily 8am–8pm.

Happy Vibe Bar On Sunrise beach, ☎084 807 3781, ⊛bit.ly/2F8ilaS; map p.711. Welcoming Dutch-owned thatch-and-bamboo beach bar festooned with hand-painted driftwood signs. They serve cocktails (from B150), coffee and fresh fruit shakes (B120). There's a cosy upstairs veranda, and wooden tables and loungers spilling out on to the sand – a good reminder of Lipe's low-key yesterdays. Daily 10am–late.

La Luna ☎082 286 1910, ⊛facebook.com/laluna kohlipe; map p.711. An appreciated Italian restaurant set in the hotel of the same name, with an attractive wooden-decked sala and bar. Pizzas (from B200) are crunchy, and the ravioli, bruschettas and tiramisu taste authentic. A meal will set you back around B1000. Daily 6pm–11pm.

Pooh's On Walking Street between Sunrise and Hat Pattaya (see page 712), ☎087 392 3838, ⊛facebook.com/ poohbarkohlipe; map p.711. This well-run and welcoming bar-restaurant-bakery is a long-standing institution and a popular hive of activity, with nightly movies. Offers tasty Thai food, including chicken with cashew nuts (B150) and vegetarian dishes, as well as sandwiches, cakes, evening barbecues, DJs and live music, plus a wide choice of breakfasts and espresso coffees. Daily roughly 8.30am–10.45pm.

Roti Mina Walking Street, about 50m inland from Hat Pattaya on the right-hand side ☎081 397 7018; map p.711. Serves all manner of outlandish roti pancakes – raisin and cheese roti, anyone? – as well as the more familiar roti with curry (B100) and banana roti. Also does some classic southern and central Thai dishes. Daily 7am–10pm.

Satun town

Nestling in the last wedge of Thailand's west coast, the remote town of **SATUN** is served by just one road, Highway 406, which approaches through forbidding karst outcrops. Set in a green valley bordered by limestone hills, the town is leafy and relaxing but not especially interesting, except during its small version of the Vegetarian Festival (see page 620) and its International Kite Festival at the end of February. There's little reason to come here apart from the boat service to and from Langkawi in Malaysia.

National Museum

Soi 5, Thanon Satun Thani, on the north side of the centre • Wed–Sun 9am–4pm • B30

The **National Museum** has a memorable setting in the graceful **Kuden Mansion**, which was built in British colonial style, with some Thai and Malay features, by craftsmen from Penang, and inaugurated in 1902 as the Satun governor's official residence. The exhibits and audiovisuals in English have a distinctive anthropological tone, but are diverting enough, notably concerning Thai Muslims, the *chao ley* on Ko Lipe, and the **Sakai**, a dwindling band of nomadic hunter-gatherers who still live in the jungle of southern Thailand.

ARRIVAL AND DEPARTURE   **SATUN TOWN**

By bus Satun's bus station is far to the southeast of the centre on the bypass, but Trang buses usually do a tour of the town centre, stopping, for example, near *On's* on Thanon

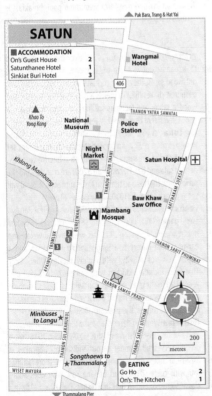

SATUN

ACCOMMODATION	
On's Guest House	2
Satunthanee Hotel	1
Sinkiat Buri Hotel	3

Pak Bara, Trang & Hat Yai

Wangmai Hotel

406

Khao To Yong Kong

National Museum

THANON YATRA SAWATAL

Police Station

Night Market

Satun Hospital ✚

Khlong Mambang

THANON SATUN THANI

Baw Khaw Saw Office

HATTHAKAM SUEKSA

BUREEWANIT

Mambang Mosque

THANON SARIT PHUMINAT

APAIWILA, TRIMKLIR

THANON SAMAK PRADIT

N

Minibuses to Langu ★

THANON SULAKANUKUL

THANON SARIT UTITHAM

0   200
metres

Songthaews to ★ Thammalang

WISET MAYURA

● EATING
Go Ho   2
On's: The Kitchen   1

▼ Thammalang Pier

Bureewanit; incoming buses from Phuket via Krabi, Trang and Langu will set you down on Thanon Satun Thani by the *Wangmai* hotel; and you can book long-distance tickets in advance at the central Baw Khaw Saw office on Thanon Hatthakam Sueksa (for the long journey to Bangkok, it's worth shelling out a bit extra for the VIP buses that depart around 3–4pm).

Destinations Bangkok (4 daily; 16hr); Phuket (4 daily; 8hr); Trang (hourly; 2hr 30min–3hr).

By minibus A/c minibuses to Langu congregate on Thanon Sulakanukul.

By ferry There are ferries from nearby Thammalang pier to Langkawi in Malaysia (see box below).

GETTING AROUND

By motorbike or car On Kongnual (see below) offers motorbike (B250–300/day) and car rental (B1000–1500/day).

INFORMATION

On Kongnual 36 Thanon Bureewanit ☎074 724133 or ☎081 097 9783, ✉onmarch13@ hotmail.com. From her restaurant, *On's: The Kitchen*, On Kongnual dispenses helpful tourist information and sells all kinds of transport tickets.

ACCOMMODATION

On's Guest House 36 Thanon Bureewanit ☎074 724133 or ☎081 097 9783, ✉onmarch13@hotmail. com; map p.714. A variety of rooms in two opposite modern, Sino-Portuguese-style buildings with wooden shutters and coloured-glass windows, one above *On's: The Kitchen*. There's a fan-cooled dorm but most have a/c, fridges and satellite TV; bathrooms with hot

CROSSING INTO MALAYSIA FROM SATUN

Two or three ferry boats a day cross from Thammalang to the Malaysian island of **Langkawi** (☎074 725294, ⓦlangkawi-ferry.com; 1hr 15min; B300). The journey from Satun town to Thammalang is covered by orange songthaews (roughly every 30min; B40) from near the 7-Eleven supermarket on Thanon Sulakanukul, as well as chartered tuk-tuks (B150) and motorcycle taxis (B60–70).

It's also possible to take an a/c minibus to Malaysia's **Kangar** (which has bus connections to Penang and Kuala Lumpur) through the Wang Kelian border and Thale Ban National Park (B400; 1 daily in the morning; about 2hr) – contact On Kongnual (see above) to book tickets.

showers are shared but plentiful. Dorms B300, doubles B500
Satunthanee Hotel Thanon Satun Thani ☎074 711010; map p.714. This centrally placed, good-value, traditional Chinese hotel offers battered but clean rooms with small bathrooms and TVs, though it suffers from noise from the road and the mosque. Fan B300, a/c B400

Sinkiat Buri Hotel 50 Thanon Apainuratrumluk ☎074 721055–8, ⓦsinkiathotel.com; map p.714. Higher-end hotel in Satun, offering large bedrooms in a minimalist style with lots of dark wood, a/c, rain showers, fridges, flat-screen TVs and good views over the surrounding countryside from the upper floors. Breakfast included. B1500

EATING AND DRINKING

Satun has a slim choice of restaurants, but for a meal in the evening you can't do much better than the lively and popular night market, north of the centre on the west side of Thanon Satun Thani.
Go Ho Thanon Saman Pradit, opposite the Chinese temple ☎074 711018; map p.714. A cheap, busy, friendly restaurant with leafy pavement tables that serves tasty Thai and Chinese food, including plenty of seafood (according to market price), salads and southern specialities such as *kaeng som* (B120). Mon–Sat 3pm–midnight.

On's: The Kitchen 36 Thanon Bureewanit ☎074 724133 or ☎081 097 9783; map p.714. Very tasty Thai food, including southern specialities, some interesting fish dishes and handy set menus, such as green curry with prawn patties (*thawt man kung*) and rice for B120. Also offers a wide array of Western food, including good breakfasts, jacket potatoes, pies and espresso coffees. (On's bar, a couple of doors away, *The Living Room*, stays open late, depending on customers.) Daily 8am–10pm.

Phattalung

The friendly town of **Phattalung**, strewn below the looming limestone boulder housing the **Tham Malai Caves**, sees very few visitors despite its excellent sites. The caves, a 2.5km walk north of the train station along Apaiborirak Soi 1 and up a steep staircase, are creepy and filled with bats, but the main draw here is the stunning lotus-filled **Thale Noi**, 16km to the northeast. The smallest extension of Songkhla Lake is Thailand's biggest waterfowl reserve, supporting more than 180 species of protected local and migratory birds. Boats can be chartered (RM500/hour) in Baan Thale Noi, but with your own vehicle, you can drive along scenic backroads towards the **Pak Pra Canal**, where local fishermen still use stilted Chinese fishing nets (*yor yak* in Thai).

ARRIVAL AND DEPARTURE

PHATTALUNG

By train Phattalung is on the main Northern line, with at least five daily sleeper trains to Bangkok (15hr), and five daily to Hat Yai (3hr).
By bus The bus station is inconveniently located 6km out of the centre off Route 41 (B40 one-way by motorbike taxi from the train station). From here, minivans travel to

Baan Thale Noi roughly every 30 minutes (B70). All services dwindle after 6pm.
Destinations Bangkok (at least 7 daily; 13hr); Hat Yai (every 15min; 3hr); Phuket (at least 6 daily, with stops in Trang and Krabi; 6/7hr); Songkhla (hourly; 2hr); Surat Thani (half-hourly; 3hr30min); Trang (half-hourly; 1hr).

ACCOMMODATION

Phattalung Thai Hotel 14 Dissarasakarin Rd, ☎074 611636. The cheapest option in town has old yet clean en-suite rooms with televisions and large windows, some with

a/c (B500), and is in easy walking distance from the train station. B300

Hat Yai & Songkhla

Regardless of the volatile situation in the south (see page 696), travelling to **HAT YAI**, the biggest city in the region and a major transport axis, is possible and relatively safe; check up-to-date information before setting off though. Besides a lively night market and the shopping streets around central thoroughfare Thanon Sanehanusorn, the Phra Maha Chedi Tripob Trimongkol, set on a hilltop in the south of town and better-known as the **Stainless Steel Temple**, is worth a visit for its unique futuristic design, especially when illuminated after sunset. It's about B300 in a taxi, including a short wait. For beaches and a livelier atmosphere, you are better off moving to **SONGKHLA**, 30km northeast of Hat Yai.

Songkhla

Set on a narrow peninsula separating the Gulf of Thailand from the coastal lake of the same name, breezy **Songkhla**, with accessible beaches and a Sino-Portuguese Old Town, makes for a rewarding stop. The main beach, **Samilla**, has a popular **Golden Mermaid Statue** perched on the easternmost tip of the cape. Swimming is possible, but **Chalathat Beach** directly to the south is quieter. The atmospheric **Old Town** extends around the **City Pillar Shrine**, on the eastern side of Songkhla's peninsula. Nakhorn Nok, Nakhorn Nai and Nang Ngam roads are filled with street art and relaxed shop house cafés where Chinese-Thais dish up the best of their town's mixed culinary heritage.

ARRIVAL AND DEPARTURE

HAT YAI

Travel agency The helpful Cathay Tour (93/1 Thanon Niphat Uthit 2, ☎ 074 235044, ⊚ cathaytourthailand. com), a travel agency on the ground floor of the guesthouse of the same name, handles onward flight, bus, share-taxi, a/c minibus and ferry bookings, both within Thailand and into Malaysia, as well as offering car and motorbike rental.

By plane About 5km south of town, Hat Yai airport is connected to the downtown area by a/c minibuses (B80) and has Avis (☎ 02 251 1131, ⊚ avisthailand.com) and Budget (☎ 074 227268, ⊚ budget.co.th) car rental desks.

By train The train station is on the west side of the centre at the end of Thanon Thamnoon Vithi, and has useful late afternoon departures to Bangkok, stopping in Surat Thani, Chumpon and Hua Hin.

By bus or minibus Hat Yai bus terminal is southeast of the centre on Thanon Kanchanawanit, while the a/c minibus terminal at Talat Kaset is about 5km west of town, both leaving you with a songthaew ride to the centre. Minibuses for Songkhla depart from the main bus terminal and the clock tower until about 7pm and cost B30, returning from the Anuban Songkhla School on Ramwithi Road, just south of Songkhla's clock tower.

INFORMATION

Tourist information The TAT office is at 1/1 Soi 2, Thanon Niphat Uthit 3 (daily 8.30am–4.30pm; ☎ 074 243747, ⊚ tatsgkhl@tat.or.th).

Tourist police Thanon Niphat Uthit 3, near the TAT office ☎ 074 246733 or ☎ 1155.

ACCOMMODATION

Baan Nai Nakhon Boutique Hotel 166 Nang Ngam Rd, Songkhla, ☎ 095 438 9323, ⊚ facebook.

THANON PETCHKASEM

THANON DUANGCHAN

HAT YAI

0   200
metres

Air-con Minibus Terminal, Airport & Highway 4

THANON RATAKARN

THANON PRACHATHIPAT

Food stalls

THANON SAENG CHAN

THANON PARADON

Central Shopping Mall

THANON SANEHANUSORN

Railway Police

THANON THAMNOON VITHI

THANON SHE UTHIT

ATM

Odeon Shopping Mall

Train Station

THANON NIPHAT UTHIT 1

THANON NIPHAT UTHIT 2

THANON NIPHAT UTHIT 3

THANON KIMPRADIT

Central Festival Shopping mall, Asean Night Market (3.2 km) & Stainless Steel Temple (6km)

Robinson

THANON ROTHAI

THANON MANASRUDEE

THANON NIPHAT UTHIT 1

Thai Airways

PREEDAROM

Khlong Toei

THANON NIYOM ROT

N

THANON PADUNGPAKDEE

■ **ACCOMMODATION**
Ban Naai Nakhon Boutique Hotel	1
Centara Hotel	2
The Train Hotel	3

Tourist Police   (i) **TAT**

▼ Bus Terminal

CROSSING INTO MALAYSIA FROM HAT YAI

Two daily trains leave Hat Yai station at 7.30am and 13.05pm to Padang Basar KTM station in Malaysia (☎603 2267 1200, ⊛ktmb.com.my/ktmb_ui; 30min; B70), where there is an immigration checkpoint. Malaysian trains proceed to Butterworth (for Penang; RM10.20), departing roughly hourly from 6am to 9.30pm; at least five high-speed trains also leave daily to Kuala Lumpur (4/5hr; from RM56).

You can also reach Padang Besar using local buses (roughly every 30min; B30) and a/c minivans (B100): both leave from Hat Yai's train station or the clock tower and will drop you opposite the Thai immigration checkpoint. From there, it's a 500m walk to the Malaysian border, which is about 300m to the left of Padang Besar's train station.

As another option, direct a/c minibuses to Penang (several daily; 5hr; B500/700) can be booked from most travel agents in Hat Yai's Thanon Sanehanusorn, and use the Sadao/Bukit Kayu Hitam border, connecting to Malaysia's North-South Expressway E1.

com/baannainakhon; map p.716. Absorb Songkhla's old town vibe in these dark crimson-tinged, Sino-Thai inspired wooden floored rooms, equipped with plush queen beds, handmade quilts, and en-suite bathrooms with rain showers. Breakfast included. B1500

Centara Hotel 3 Thanon Sanehanusorn ☎074 352222, ⊛centarahotelsresorts.com; map p.716. Luxury hotel in a central location next to the Central Department Store, featuring contemporary-styled rooms with a spa, fitness centre, sauna, swimming pool and Thai, Chinese and Japanese food at its several restaurants. B3000

The Train Hotel Hat Yay Railway Station ☎074 221 133–35, ⊛bit.ly/2HNFuh1; map p.716. Modern bunk bed dorms and spacious, smart en-suite rooms located inside of Hat Yai station, right next to the ticket booth. It's cleaner than most nearby budget hotels and convenient for early departures, but it gets noisy when trains come and go late at night or early in the morning. Dorms B300 Doubles B700

8

MEDITATING BUDDHA, WAT YAI SUWANNARAM, PHETCHABURI

Contexts

History

As long as forty thousand years ago, Thailand was inhabited by hunter-gatherers who lived in semi-permanent settlements and used tools made of wood, bamboo and stone. By the end of the last Ice Age, around ten thousand years ago, these groups had become farmers, keeping chickens, pigs and cattle, and – as evidenced by the seeds and plant husks which have been discovered in caves in northern Thailand – cultivating rice and beans. This drift into an agricultural society gave rise to further technological developments: the earliest pottery found in Thailand has been dated to 6800 BC, while the recent excavations at Ban Chiang in the northeast have shown that bronze was being worked at least as early as 2000 BC. By two thousand years ago, the peoples of Southeast Asia had settled in small villages, among which there was regular communication and trade, but they had split into several broad families, differentiated by language and culture. At this time, the ancestors of the Thais, speaking proto-Thai languages, were still far away in southern China, whereas Thailand itself was inhabited by Austroasiatic speakers, among whom the Mon were to establish the region's first distinctive civilization, Dvaravati.

Dvaravati and Srivijaya

The history of **Dvaravati** is ill-defined to say the least, but the name is applied to a distinctive culture complex which shared the **Mon** language and **Theravada Buddhism**. This form of religion may have entered Thailand during the third century BC, when the Indian emperor, Ashoka, is said to have sent missionaries to Suvarnabhumi, "land of gold", which seems to correspond roughly to mainland Southeast Asia.

From the discovery of monastery boundary stones (*sema*), clay votive tablets and Indian-influenced Buddhist sculpture, it's clear that Dvaravati was an extensive and prosperous Buddhist civilization that had its greatest flourishing between the sixth and ninth centuries AD. No strong evidence has turned up, however, for the existence of a single capital – rather than an empire, Dvaravati seems to have been a collection of city-states. Nakhon Pathom, Lopburi, Si Thep and Muang Sema were among the most important Dvaravati sites, and their concentration around the Chao Phraya valley would seem to show that they gained much of their prosperity, and maintained religious and cultural contacts with India, via the **trade route** from the Indian Ocean over the Three Pagodas Pass.

Although they passed on aspects of their heavily Indianized art, religion and government to later rulers of Thailand, these Mon city-states were politically fragile

6800 BC	3rd century BC	6th–9th centuries AD
Date of earliest pottery found in Thailand	Theravada Buddhism probably first enters Thailand	Dvaravati civilization flourishes

and from the ninth century onwards succumbed to the domination of the invading Khmers from Cambodia. One northern outpost, the state of **Haripunjaya**, centred on Lamphun, which had been set up on the trade route with southern China, maintained its independence until the thirteenth century.

Meanwhile, to the south of Dvaravati, the shadowy Indianized state of Lankasuka had grown up in the second century, centred on Ligor (now Nakhon Si Thammarat) and covering an area of the Malay peninsula which included the important trade crossings at Chaiya and Trang. In the eighth century, it came under the control of **Srivijaya**, a Mahayana Buddhist city-state on Sumatra, which had strong ties with India and a complex but uneasy relationship with neighbouring Java. Thriving on seaborne trade between Persia and China, Srivijaya extended its influence as far north as Chaiya, its regional capital, where discoveries of temple remains and some of the finest stone and bronze statues ever produced in Thailand have borne witness to the cultural vitality of this crossroads empire. In the tenth century the northern part of Lankasuka, under the name **Tambralinga**, regained a measure of independence, although it seems still to have come under the influence of Srivijaya as well as owing some form of allegiance to Dvaravati. By the beginning of the eleventh century, however, peninsular Thailand had come under the sway of the Khmer empire, with a Cambodian prince ruling over a community of Khmer settlers and soldiers at Tambralinga.

The Khmers

The history of central Southeast Asia comes into sharper focus with the emergence of the **Khmers**, vigorous empire-builders whose political history can be pieced together from the numerous stone inscriptions they left. The Khmers of **Chenla** – to the north of Cambodia – seized power in the latter half of the sixth century during a period of economic decline in the area. Chenla's rise to power was knocked back by a punitive expedition conducted by the Srivijaya empire in the eighth century, but was reconsolidated during the watershed reign of **Jayavarman II** (802–50), who succeeded in conquering the whole of Kambuja, an area which roughly corresponds to modern-day Cambodia. In order to establish the authority of his monarchy and of his country, Jayavarman II had himself initiated as a *chakravartin*, or universal ruler, the living embodiment of the **devaraja**, the divine essence of kingship – a concept which was adopted by later Thai rulers. Taking as the symbol of his authority the phallic lingam, the king was thus identified with the god Shiva, although the Khmer concept of kingship and thus the religious mix of the state as a whole was not confined to Hinduism: elements of ancestor worship were also included, and Mahayana Buddhism gradually increased its hold over the next four centuries.

It was Jayavarman II who moved the Khmer capital to **Angkor** in northern Cambodia, which he and later kings, especially after the eleventh century, embellished with a series of prodigiously beautiful temples. Jayavarman II also recognized the advantages of the lakes around Angkor for irrigating rice fields and providing fish, and thus for feeding a large population. His successors developed this idea and gave the state a sound economic core with a remarkably complex system of **reservoirs** (*baray*) and water channels, which were copied and adapted in later Thai cities.

In the ninth and tenth centuries, Jayavarman II and his imperialistic successors, especially **Yasovarman I** (889–900), confirmed Angkor as the major power in Southeast

8th century	802–50	Late 9th century
Srivijaya gains sway over southern Thailand	Reign of Khmer king Jayavarman II, founder of Angkor	Khmers begin to push into Thailand

Asia. They pushed into Vietnam, Laos and southern China, as well as into northeastern Thailand, where the Khmers left dozens of Angkor-style temple complexes, as seen today at Prasat Phanom Rung and Prasat Hin Phimai. To the west and northwest, Angkor took control over central Thailand, with its most important outpost at Lopburi, and even established a strong presence to the south on the Malay peninsula. As a result of this expansion, the Khmers were masters of the most important trade routes between India and China, and indeed nearly every communications link in the region, from which they were able to derive huge income and strength.

The reign of **Jayavarman VII** (1181–1219), a Mahayana Buddhist who firmly believed in his royal destiny as a *bodhisattva*, sowed the seeds of Angkor's downfall. Nearly half of all the surviving great religious monuments of the empire were erected under his supervision, but the ambitious scale of these building projects and the upkeep they demanded – some 300,000 priests and temple servants of 20,000 shrines consumed 38,000 tonnes of rice per year – along with a series of wars against Vietnam, exhausted the economy.

In subsequent reigns, much of the life-giving irrigation system around Angkor turned into malarial swamp through neglect, and the rise of the more democratic creed of Theravada Buddhism undermined the divine authority which the Khmer kings had derived from the hierarchical Mahayana creed. As a result of all these factors, the Khmers were in no position to resist the onslaught between the thirteenth and fifteenth centuries of the vibrant new force in Southeast Asia, the Thais.

The earliest Thais

The earliest traceable history of the **Thai people** picks them up in southern China around the fifth century AD, when they were squeezed by Chinese and Vietnamese expansionism into sparsely inhabited northeastern Laos and neighbouring areas. The first entry of a significant number of Thais onto what is now Thailand's soil seems to have happened in the region of Chiang Saen, where it appears that some time after the seventh century the Thais formed a state in an area then known as **Yonok**. A development which can be more accurately dated and which had immense cultural significance was the spread of Theravada Buddhism to Yonok via Dvaravati around the end of the tenth century, which served not only to unify the Thais but also to link them to Mon civilization and give them a sense of belonging to the community of Buddhists.

The Thais' political development was also assisted by **Nan-chao**, a well-organized military state comprising a huge variety of ethnic groups, which established itself as a major player on the southern fringes of the Chinese empire from the beginning of the eighth century. As far as can be gathered, Nan-chao permitted the rise of Thai *muang* or small principalities on its periphery, especially in the area immediately to the south known as **Sipsong Panna**.

Thai infiltration continued until, by the end of the twelfth century, they seem to have formed the majority of the population in Thailand, then under the control of the Khmer empire. The Khmers' main outpost, at Lopburi, was by then regarded as the administrative capital of a land called "Syam" (possibly from the Sanskrit *syam*, meaning swarthy) – a mid-twelfth-century bas-relief at Angkor Wat, portraying the troops of Lopburi preceded by a large group of self-confident Syam Kuk mercenaries, shows that the Thais were becoming a force to be reckoned with.

Mid-12th century	1181–1219	1238
Bas-relief at Angkor Wat depicting Thai mercenaries, a new force to be reckoned with in the region	Reign of Jayavarman VII, perhaps the greatest and certainly the most ambitious of the Khmer kings	The Thais seize the Khmer outpost of Sukhothai

Sukhothai

By the middle of the thirteenth century, the Thais, thanks largely to the decline of Angkor and the inspiring effect of Theravada Buddhism, were poised on the verge of autonomous power. The final catalyst was the invasion by Qubilai Khan's Mongol armies of China and Nan-chao, which began around 1215 and was completed in the 1250s. Demanding that the whole world should acknowledge the primacy of the Great Khan, the Mongols set their hearts on the "pacification" of the "barbarians" to the south of China, which obliged the Thais to form a broad powerbase to meet the threat.

The founding of the first Thai kingdom at **Sukhothai**, now popularly viewed as the cornerstone of the country's development, was in fact a small-scale piece of opportunism which almost fell at the first hurdle. At some time around 1238, the princes of two small Thai principalities in the upper Chao Phraya valley joined forces to capture the main Khmer outpost in the region at Sukhothai. One of the princes, **Intradit**, was crowned king, but for the first forty years Sukhothai remained merely a local power, whose existence was threatened by the ambitions of neighbouring princes. When attacked by the ruler of Mae Sot, Intradit's army was only saved by the grand entrance of Sukhothai's most dynamic leader: the king's 19-year-old son, Rama, held his ground and pushed forward to defeat the opposing commander, earning himself the name **Ramkhamhaeng**, "Rama the Bold".

When Ramkhamhaeng came to the throne around 1278, he saw the south as his most promising avenue for expansion and, copying the formidable military organization of the Mongols, established control over much of the Chao Phraya valley. Over the next twenty years, largely by diplomacy rather than military action, Ramkhamhaeng gained the submission of most of modern-day Thailand; local rulers entered into a complex system of tribute-giving and protection – the political system that persisted in Thailand until the end of the nineteenth century – either through the pressure of the Sukhothai king's personal connections or out of recognition of his superior military strength and moral prestige. To the east, Ramkhamhaeng extended his sphere of influence as far as Vientiane in Laos; by marrying his daughter to a Mon ruler to the west, he obtained the allegiance of parts of southern Burma; and to the south his vassals stretched down the peninsula at least as far as Nakhon Si Thammarat. To the north, Sukhothai concluded an alliance with the parallel Thai states of Lanna and Phayao in 1287 for mutual protection against the Mongols – though it appears that Ramkhamhaeng managed to pinch several *muang* on their eastern periphery as tribute states.

Meanwhile **Lopburi**, which had wrested itself free from Angkor some time in the middle of the thirteenth century, was able to keep its independence and its control of the eastern side of the Chao Phraya valley. Having been first a major cultural and religious centre for the Mon, then the Khmers' provincial capital, and now a state dominated by migrating Thais, Lopburi was a strong and vibrant place mixing the best of the three cultures, as evidenced by the numerous original works of art produced at this time.

Although Sukhothai extended Thai influence over a vast area, its greatest contribution to the Thais' development was at home, in cultural and political matters. A famous **inscription** by Ramkhamhaeng, now housed in the Bangkok National Museum, describes a prosperous era of benevolent rule: "In the time of King Ramkhamhaeng this land of Sukhothai is thriving. There is fish in the water and rice in the fields ... [The King] has hung a bell in the opening of the gate over there: if any commoner has a grievance

1278	1281	1287
Ramkhamhaeng "the Bold" comes to the throne of Sukhothai	With the conquest of the Dvaravati outpost of Haripunjaya, King Mengrai unifies the north as the Thai state of Lanna	Alliance between the Thai states of Sukhothai, Lanna and Phayao

which sickens his belly and gripes his heart … he goes and strikes the bell … [and King Ramkhamhaeng] questions the man, examines the case, and decides it justly for him." Although this plainly smacks of self-promotion, it seems to contain at least a kernel of truth: in deliberate contrast to the Khmer god-kings, Ramkhamhaeng styled himself as a **dhammaraja**, a king who ruled justly according to Theravada Buddhist doctrine and made himself accessible to his people. To honour the state religion, the city's temples were lavishly endowed: as original as Sukhothai's political systems were its religious **architecture and sculpture**, which, though bound to borrow from existing Khmer and Sri Lankan styles, show the greatest leap of creativity at any stage in the history of art in Thailand. A further sign of the Thais' new self-confidence was the invention of a new **script** to make their tonal language understood by the non-Thai inhabitants of the land.

All this was achieved in a remarkably short period of time. After the death of Ramkhamhaeng around 1299, his successors took their Buddhism so seriously that they neglected affairs of state, and by 1320 Sukhothai had regressed to being a kingdom of only local significance.

Lanna

Almost simultaneous with the birth of Sukhothai was the establishment of a less momentous but longer-lasting kingdom to the north, called **Lanna**. Its founding father was **Mengrai**, chief of Ngon Yang, a small principality on the banks of the Mekong near modern-day Chiang Saen. Around 1259 he set out to unify the squabbling Thai principalities of the region, first building a strategically placed city at Chiang Rai in 1262, and then forging alliances with Ngam Muang, the Thai king of Phayao, and with Ramkhamhaeng of Sukhothai.

In 1281, after ten years of guileful preparations, Mengrai conquered the Mon kingdom of Haripunjaya based at Lamphun, and was now master of northern Thailand. Taking advice from Ngam Muang and Ramkhamhaeng, in 1292 he selected a site for an impressive new capital of Lanna at **Chiang Mai**, which remains the centre of the north to the present day. Mengrai concluded further alliances in Burma and Laos, making him strong enough to successfully resist further Mongol attacks, although he was eventually obliged to bow to the superiority of the Mongols by sending them small tributes from 1312 onwards. When Mengrai died after a sixty-year reign in 1317, supposedly struck by a bolt of lightning, he had built up an extensive and powerful kingdom. But although he began a tradition of humane, reasonable laws, probably borrowed from the Mons, he had found little time to set up sound political and administrative institutions. His death severely destabilized Lanna, which quickly shrank in size and influence.

It was only in the reign of **Ku Na** (1355–85) that Lanna's development regained momentum. A well-educated and effective ruler, Ku Na enticed the venerable monk Sumana, from Sukhothai, to establish an ascetic Sri Lankan sect in Lanna in 1369. Sumana brought a number of Buddha images with him, inspiring a new school of art that flourished for over a century, but more importantly his sect became a cultural force that had a profound unifying effect on the kingdom. The influence of Buddhism was further strengthened under **Tilok** (1441–87), who built many great monuments at Chiang Mai and cast huge numbers of bronze seated Buddhas in the style of the central image at Bodh Gaya in India, the scene of the Buddha's enlightenment. Tilok,

1299	1317	1351
With the death of Ramkhamhaeng, Sukhothai begins its decline	Mengrai dies after being struck by lightning	Ramathibodi founds Ayutthaya

however, is best remembered as a great warrior, who spent most of his reign resisting the advances of Ayutthaya, by now the strongest Thai kingdom.

Under continuing pressure both from Ayutthaya and from Burma, Lanna went into rapid decline in the second quarter of the sixteenth century. For a short period after 1546, Chiang Mai came under the control of Setthathirat, the king of Lan Sang (Laos), but, unable to cope with Lanna's warring factions, he then abdicated, purloining the talismanic Emerald Buddha for his own capital at Luang Prabang. In 1558, Burma decisively captured Chiang Mai, and the Mengrai dynasty came to an end. For most of the next two centuries, the Burmese maintained control through a succession of puppet rulers, and Lanna again became much as it had been before Mengrai, little more than a chain of competing principalities.

Ayutthaya

While Lanna was fighting for its place as a marginalized kingdom, from the fourteenth century onwards the seeds of a full-blown Thai nation were being sown to the south at **Ayutthaya**. The city of Ayutthaya itself was founded on its present site in 1351 by U Thong ("Golden Cradle") of Lopburi. Taking the title **Ramathibodi**, he soon united the principalities of the lower Chao Phraya valley, which had formed the western provinces of the Khmer empire. When he recruited his bureaucracy from the urban elite of Lopburi, Ramathibodi set the **style of government** at Ayutthaya – the elaborate etiquette, language and rituals of Angkor were adopted, and, most importantly, the conception of the ruler as *devaraja*. The king became sacred and remote, an object of awe and dread, with none of the accessibility of the kings of Sukhothai: when he processed through the town, ordinary people were forbidden to look at him and had to be silent while he passed. This hierarchical system also provided the state with much-needed manpower, as all freemen were obliged to give up six months of each year to the Crown either on public works or military service.

The site chosen by Ramathibodi turned out to be the best in the region for an international port, and so began Ayutthaya's rise to prosperity, based on its ability to exploit the upswing in **trade** in the middle of the fourteenth century along the routes between India and China. Flushed with economic success, Ramathibodi's successors were able to expand their control over the ailing states in the region. After a long period of subjugation, Sukhothai became a province of the kingdom of Ayutthaya in 1438, six years after Boromraja II had powerfully demonstrated Ayutthaya's pre-eminence by capturing the once-mighty Angkor, enslaving large numbers of its subjects and looting the Khmer royal regalia. (The Cambodian royal family were forced to abandon the palace and to found a new capital near Phnom Penh.)

Although a century of nearly continuous warfare against Lanna was less decisive, success generally bred success, and Ayutthaya's increasing wealth through trade brought ever greater power over its neighbouring states. To streamline the functioning of his unwieldy empire, **Trailok** (1448–88) found it necessary to make reforms to its administration. His **Law of Civil Hierarchy** formally entrenched the inequality of Ayutthayan society, defining the status of every individual by assigning him or her an imaginary number of rice fields – for example, 25 for an ordinary freeman and 10,000 for the highest ministers of state. Trailok's legacy is found in today's unofficial but fiendishly complex status system, by which everyone in Thailand knows their place.

1432	1477	1511
Ayutthaya captures and loots Angkor	The eighth world council of Theravada Buddhism is held in Chiang Mai	The first Western power, Portugal, begins trading with Ayutthaya

Ramathibodi II (1491–1529), almost at a loss as to what to do with his enormous wealth, undertook an extensive programme of public works. In the 1490s he built several major religious monuments, and between 1500 and 1503 cast the largest standing metal image of the Buddha ever known, the Phra Si Sanphet, which gave its name to the temple of the royal palace. By 1540, Ayutthaya had established control over most of the area of modern-day Thailand.

Burmese wars and European trade

In the sixteenth century recurring tensions with Burma led **Chakkraphat** (1548–69) to improve his army and build brick ramparts around the capital. This was to no avail however: in 1568 the Burmese besieged Ayutthaya with a huge army, said by later accounts to have consisted of 1,400,000 men. The Thais held out until August 8, 1569, when treachery within their own ranks helped the Burmese break through the defences. The Burmese looted the city, took thousands of prisoners and installed a vassal king to keep control.

The decisive character who broke the Burmese stranglehold twenty years later and re-established Ayutthaya's economic growth was **Naresuan** (1590–1605), who defied the Burmese by amassing a large army. The enemy sent a punitive expedition, which was conclusively defeated at Nong Sarai near modern-day Suphanburi on January 18, 1593, Naresuan himself turning the battle by killing the Burmese crown prince. Historians have praised Naresuan for his personal bravery and his dynamic leadership, although the chronicles of the time record a strong streak of tyranny – in his fifteen years as king he had eighty thousand people killed, excluding the victims of war. A favoured means of punishment was to slice off pieces of the offender's flesh, which he was then made to eat in the king's presence.

The period following Naresuan's reign was characterized by a more sophisticated engagement in **foreign trade**. In 1511 the Portuguese had become the first Western power to trade with Ayutthaya, and Naresuan himself concluded a treaty with Spain in 1598; relations with Holland and England were initiated in 1608 and 1612 respectively. For most of the seventeenth century, European merchants flocked to Thailand, not only to buy Thai products, but also to gain access to Chinese and Japanese goods on sale there. The role of foreigners at Ayutthaya reached its peak under **Narai** (1656–88), but he overstepped the mark in cultivating close links with Louis XIV of France, who secretly harboured the notion of converting Ayutthaya to Christianity. On Narai's death, relations with Westerners were cut back.

Despite this reduction of trade and prolonged civil strife over the succession to the throne whenever a king died – then, as now, there wasn't a fixed principle of primogeniture – Ayutthaya continued to flourish for much of the eighteenth century. The reign of **Borommakot** (1733–58) was particularly prosperous, producing many works of drama and poetry. Furthermore, Thai Buddhism had by then achieved such prestige that Sri Lanka, from where the Thais had originally imported their form of religion in the thirteenth century, requested Thai aid in restoring their monastic orders in 1751.

However, immediately after the death of Borommakot the rumbling in the Burmese jungle to the north began to make itself heard again. Alaunghpaya of Burma, apparently a blindly aggressive country bumpkin, first recaptured the south of his

1558	1569	1590–1605
The Burmese decisively capture Chiang Mai	The Burmese take Ayutthaya and install a vassal king	Reign of the warrior king Naresuan, who sends the Burmese packing

country from the Mon, and then turned his attentions to Ayutthaya. A siege in 1760 was unsuccessful, with Alaungphaya dying of wounds sustained there, but the scene was set. In February 1766 the Burmese descended upon Ayutthaya for the last time. The Thais held out for over a year, during which they were afflicted by famine, epidemics and a terrible fire that destroyed ten thousand houses. Finally, in **April 1767**, the walls were breached and the city taken. The Burmese razed everything to the ground and tens of thousands of prisoners were led off to Burma, including most of the royal family. The king, Suriyamarin, is said to have escaped from the city in a boat and starved to death ten days later. As one observer has said, the Burmese laid waste to Ayutthaya "in such a savage manner that it is hard to imagine that they shared the same religion with the Siamese". The city was abandoned to the jungle, but with remarkable speed the Thais regrouped and established a new seat of power, further down the Chao Phraya River at Bangkok.

The early Bangkok empire

As the bulk of the Burmese army was obliged by war with China to withdraw almost immediately, Thailand was left to descend into banditry. Out of this lawless mess several centres of power arose, the most significant being at Chanthaburi, commanded by **Phraya Taksin**. A charismatic, brave and able general who had been unfairly blamed for a failed counterattack against the Burmese at Ayutthaya, Taksin had anticipated the fall of the besieged city and quietly slipped away with a force of five hundred men. In June 1767 he took control of the east-coast strip around Chanthaburi and very rapidly expanded his power across central Thailand.

Blessed with the financial backing of the Chinese trading community, to whom he was connected through his father, Taksin was crowned king in December 1768 at his new capital of Thonburi, on the opposite bank of the river from modern-day Bangkok. One by one the new king defeated his rivals, and within two years he had restored all of Ayutthaya's territories. More remarkably, by the end of the next decade Taksin had outdone his Ayutthayan predecessors by bringing Lanna, Cambodia and much of Laos under his sway. During this period of expansionism, Taksin left most of the fighting to Thong Duang, an ambitious soldier and descendant of an Ayutthayan noble family, who became the *chakri*, the military commander, and took the title **Chao Phraya Chakri**.

However, by 1779 all was not well with the king. Being an outsider, who had risen from an ordinary family on the fringes of society, Taksin became paranoid about plots against him, a delusion that drove him to imprison and torture even his wife and sons. At the same time he sank into religious excesses, demanding that the monkhood worship him as a god. By March 1782, public outrage at his sadism and dangerously irrational behaviour had reached such fervour that he was ousted in a coup.

Chao Phraya Chakri was invited to take power and had Taksin executed. In accordance with ancient etiquette, this had to be done without royal blood touching the earth: the king was duly wrapped in a black velvet sack and struck on the back of the neck with a sandalwood club. (Popular tradition has it that even this form of execution was too much: an unfortunate substitute got the velvet sack treatment, while Taksin was whisked away to a palace in the hills near Nakhon Si Thammarat, where he is said to have lived until 1825.)

1767	1768	1782–1809
Ayutthaya is razed to the ground by the Burmese	Taksin crowned king at the new capital, Thonburi	Reign of Rama I, founder of the current Chakri dynasty

Rama I

With the support of the Ayutthayan aristocracy, Chakri – reigning as **Rama I** (1782–1809) – set about consolidating the Thai kingdom. His first act was to move the capital across the river to Bangkok, a better defensive position against any Burmese attack from the west. Borrowing from the layout of Ayutthaya, he built a new royal palace and impressive monasteries, and enshrined in the palace wat the Emerald Buddha, which he had snatched back during his campaigns in Laos.

As all the state records had disappeared in the destruction of Ayutthaya, religious and legal texts had to be written afresh and historical chronicles reconstituted – with some very sketchy guesswork. The monkhood was in such a state of crisis that it was widely held that moral decay had been partly responsible for Ayutthaya's downfall. Within a month of becoming king, Rama I issued a series of religious laws and made appointments to the leadership of the monkhood, to restore discipline and confidence after the excesses of Taksin's reign. Many works of drama and poetry had also been lost in the sacking of Ayutthaya, so Rama I set about rebuilding the Thais' literary heritage, at the same time attempting to make it more cosmopolitan and populist. His main contribution was the *Ramakien*, a dramatic version of the Indian epic *Ramayana*, which is said to have been set to verse by the king himself – with a little help from his courtiers – in 1797. Heavily adapted to its Thai setting, the *Ramakien* served as an affirmation of the new monarchy and its divine links, and has since become the national epic.

In the early part of Rama I's reign, the Burmese reopened hostilities on several occasions, the biggest attempted invasion coming in 1785, but the emphatic manner in which the Thais repulsed them only served to knit together the young kingdom. Trade with China revived, and the king addressed the besetting problem of manpower by ordering every man to be tattooed with the name of his master and his town, so that avoiding royal service became almost impossible. On a more general note, Rama I put the style of government in Thailand on a modern footing: while retaining many of the features of a *devaraja*, he shared more responsibility with his courtiers, as a first among equals.

Rama II and Rama III

The peaceful accession of his son as **Rama II** (1809–24) signalled the establishment of the **Chakri dynasty**, which is still in place today. This Second Reign was a quiet interlude, best remembered as a fertile period for Thai literature. The king, himself one of the great Thai poets, gathered round him a group of writers including the famous Sunthorn Phu, who produced scores of masterly love poems, travel accounts and narrative songs.

In contrast, **Rama III** (1824–51) actively discouraged literary development – probably in reaction against his father – and was a vigorous defender of conservative values. To this end, he embarked on an extraordinary redevelopment of Wat Pho, the oldest temple in Bangkok. Hundreds of educational inscriptions and mural paintings, on all manner of secular and religious subjects, were put on show, apparently to preserve traditional culture against the rapid change which the king saw corroding the country. In foreign affairs, Rama III faced a serious threat from the vassal states of Laos, who in 1827 sent an invading army from Vientiane, which got as far as Saraburi, only three days' march from Bangkok. The king's response was savage: having repelled the initial

1782	1809–24	1824–51
A grandiose new capital, Bangkok, is established, modelled on Ayutthaya	The Chakri dynasty is consolidated with the reign of Rama II	Rama III's reign

invasion, he ordered his army to destroy everything in Vientiane apart from Buddhist temples and to forcibly resettle huge numbers of Lao in Isaan. In 1834, the king went to war in Cambodia, in a tug of war with Vietnam for control of the land in between; after fourteen years of indecisive warfare, Cambodia lay devastated but in much the same servile position – as one Vietnamese emperor described it, "an independent country that is slave of two".

More significant in the long run was the danger posed by the increase in Western influence that began in the Third Reign. As early as 1825, the Thais were sufficiently alarmed at British colonialism to strengthen Bangkok's defences by stretching a great iron chain across the mouth of the Chao Phraya River, to which every blacksmith in the area had to donate a certain number of links. In 1826 Rama III was obliged to sign a limited trade agreement with the British, the **Burney Treaty**, by which the Thais won some political security in return for reducing their taxes on goods passing through Bangkok. British and American missions in 1850 unsuccessfully demanded more radical concessions, but by this time Rama III was seriously ill, and it was left to his far-sighted and progressive successors to reach a decisive accommodation with the Western powers.

Mongkut and Chulalongkorn

Rama IV (1851–68), commonly known to foreigners as **Mongkut** (in Thai, *Phra Chom Klao*), had been a Buddhist monk for 27 years when he succeeded his brother. But far from leading a cloistered life, Mongkut had travelled widely throughout Thailand, had maintained scholarly contacts with French and American missionaries and, like most of the country's new generation of leaders, had taken an interest in Western learning, studying English, Latin and the sciences. He had also turned his mind to the condition of Buddhism in Thailand, which seemed to him to have descended into little more than popular superstition; indeed, after a study of the Buddhist scriptures in Pali, he was horrified to find that Thai ordinations were probably invalid. So in the late 1830s he set up the rigorously fundamentalist Thammayut sect (the "Order Adhering to the Teachings of the Buddha") and as abbot of the order he oversaw the training of a generation of scholarly leaders for Thai Buddhism from his base at Bangkok's Wat Bowonniwet, which became a major centre of Western learning and is still sponsored by the royal family.

When his kingship faced its first major test, in the form of a threatening British mission in 1855 led by **Sir John Bowring**, the Governor of Hong Kong, Mongkut dealt with it confidently. Realizing that Thailand was unable to resist the military might of the British, the king reduced import and export taxes, allowed British subjects to live and own land in Thailand and granted them freedom of trade. Of the **government monopolies**, which had long been the mainstay of the Thai economy, only that on opium was retained. After making up the loss in revenue through internal taxation, Mongkut quickly made it known that he would welcome diplomatic contacts from other Western countries: within a decade, agreements similar to the Bowring Treaty had been signed with France, the US and a score of other nations. Thus by skilful diplomacy the king avoided a close relationship with only one power, which could easily have led to Thailand's annexation.

1826	1851–68	1855
The signing of the Burney Treaty, a trade agreement with Britain	Reign of Rama IV (Mongkut)	The Bowring Treaty exacts further trade concessions for the British

While all around the colonial powers were carving up Southeast Asia among themselves, Thailand suffered nothing more than the weakening of its influence over Cambodia, which in 1863 the French brought under their protection. As a result of the open-door policy, foreign trade boomed, financing the redevelopment of Bangkok's waterfront and, for the first time, the building of paved roads. However, Mongkut ran out of time for instituting the far-reaching domestic reforms which he saw were needed to drag Thailand into the modern world.

The modernization of Thailand

Mongkut's son, **Chulalongkorn**, took the throne as Rama V (1868–1910) at the age of only 15, but he was well prepared by an education which mixed traditional Thai and modern Western elements – provided by Mrs Anna Leonowens, subject of *The King and I*. When Chulalongkorn reached his majority after a five-year regency, he set to work on the reforms envisaged by his father. One of his first acts was to scrap the custom by which subjects were required to prostrate themselves in the presence of the king, which he followed up in 1874 with a series of decrees announcing the gradual abolition of slavery. The speed of his financial and administrative reforms, however, proved too much for the "**Ancients**" (*hua boran*), the old guard of ministers and officials inherited from his father. Their opposition culminated in the Front Palace Crisis of 1875, when a show of military strength almost plunged the country into civil war, and, although Chulalongkorn skilfully defused the crisis, many of his reforms had to be quietly shelved for the time being.

An important administrative reform that did go through, necessitated by the threat of colonial expansionism, concerned the former kingdom of Lanna. British exploitation of teak had recently spread into northern Thailand from neighbouring Burma, so in 1874 Chulalongkorn sent a commissioner to Chiang Mai to keep an eye on the prince of Chiang Mai and make sure that he avoided any collision with the British. The commissioner was gradually able to limit the power of the princes and to begin to integrate the region into the kingdom.

In the 1880s prospects for reform brightened as many of the "Ancients" died or retired. This allowed Chulalongkorn to **restructure the government** to meet the country's needs: the Royal Audit Office made possible the proper control of revenue and finance; the Department of the Army became the nucleus of a modern armed services; and a host of other departments was set up, for justice, education, public health and the like. To fill these new positions, the king appointed many of his younger brothers, who had all received a modern education, while scores of foreign technicians and advisers were brought in to help with everything from foreign affairs to rail lines.

Throughout this period, however, the Western powers maintained their pressure on the region. The most serious threat to Thai sovereignty was the **Franco–Siamese Crisis** of 1893, which culminated in the French, based in Vietnam, sending gunboats up the Chao Phraya River to Bangkok. Flouting numerous international laws, France claimed control over Laos and made other outrageous demands, which Chulalongkorn had no option but to concede. In 1907 Thailand was also forced to acknowledge French control over Cambodia, and in 1909 three Malay states fell to the British (while Thailand retained a fourth Muslim state, Pattani). In order to preserve its independence, the country ceded control over huge areas of tributary states and

1863	1868–1910	1874
The French bring Cambodia under their protection	Reign of Rama V (Chulalongkorn)	Beginning of the abolition of slavery in Thailand

forwent huge sums of tax revenue. But from the end of the Fifth Reign, the frontiers were fixed as they are today.

By the time of the king's death in 1910, Thailand could not yet be called a modern nation-state – Bangkok still did not have complete control over the outermost regions, and corruption and nepotism were grave problems, for example. However, Chulalongkorn had made remarkable advances, and, almost from scratch, had established the political institutions to cope with twentieth-century development.

The end of absolute monarchy

Chulalongkorn was succeeded by a flamboyant, British-educated prince, **Vajiravudh**, who was crowned Rama VI (1910–25). The new king found it difficult to shake the dominance of his father's appointees in the government, who formed an extremely narrow elite, comprised almost entirely of members of Chulalongkorn's family. In an attempt to build up a personal following, Vajiravudh created, in May 1911, the **Wild Tigers**, a nationwide paramilitary corps recruited widely from the civil service. However, in 1912 a group of young army lieutenants, disillusioned by the absolute monarchy and upset at the downgrading of the regular army in favour of the Wild Tigers, plotted a **coup**. The conspirators were easily broken up before any trouble began, but this was something new in Thai history: the country was used to in-fighting among the royal family, but not to military intrigue from men from comparatively ordinary backgrounds.

Vajiravudh's response to the coup was a series of modernizing **reforms**, including the introduction of compulsory primary education and an attempt to better the status of women by supporting monogamy in place of the widespread practice of polygamy. His huge output of writings invariably encouraged people to live as modern Westerners, and he brought large numbers of commoners into high positions in government. Nonetheless, he would not relinquish his strong opposition to constitutional democracy.

When **World War I** broke out in 1914, the Thais were generally sympathetic to the Germans out of resentment over their loss of territory to the French and British. The king, however, was in favour of neutrality, until the US entered the war in 1917, when Thailand followed the expedient policy of joining the winning side and sent an expeditionary force of 1300 men to France in June 1918. The goodwill earned by this gesture enabled the Thais, between 1920 and 1926, to negotiate away the unequal treaties that had been imposed on them by the Western powers. Foreigners on Thai soil were no longer exempted from Thai laws, and the Thais were allowed to set reasonable rates of import and export taxes.

Prajadhipok

Vajiravudh's extravagant lifestyle – during his reign, royal expenditure amounted to as much as ten percent of the state budget – left severe financial problems for his successor. Vajiravudh died without leaving a son, and as three better-placed contenders to the Crown all died in the 1920s, **Prajadhipok** – the seventy-sixth child and last son of Chulalongkorn – was catapulted to the throne as Rama VII (1925–35). Young and inexperienced, he responded to the country's crisis by creating a Supreme Council of State, seen by many as a return to Chulalongkorn's absolutist "government by princes".

1893	1910–25	1912
Gunboats up the Chao Phraya: the Franco–Siamese Crisis obliges Thailand to give up its claims to Laos and Cambodia	Reign of Rama VI (Vajiravudh)	The first of many coup attempts in modern Thailand

Prajadhipok himself seems to have been in favour of constitutional government, but the weakness of his personality and the opposition of the old guard in the Supreme Council prevented him from introducing it. Meanwhile a vigorous community of Western-educated intellectuals had emerged in the lower echelons of the bureaucracy, who were increasingly dissatisfied with the injustices of monarchical government. The final shock to the Thai system came with the Great Depression, which from 1930 onwards ravaged the economy. On June 24, 1932, a small group of middle-ranking officials, led by a lawyer, Pridi Phanomyong, and an army major, Luang Phibunsongkhram, staged a **coup** with only a handful of troops. Prajadhipok weakly submitted to the conspirators, or "Promoters", and 150 years of absolute monarchy in Bangkok came to a sudden end. The king was sidelined to a position of symbolic significance and in 1935 he abdicated in favour of his 10-year-old nephew, **Ananda**, then a schoolboy living in Switzerland.

To the 1957 coup

The success of the 1932 coup was in large measure attributable to the army officers who gave the conspirators credibility, and it was they who were to dominate the constitutional regimes that followed. The Promoters' first worry was that the French or British might attempt to restore the monarchy to full power. To deflect such intervention, they appointed a government under a provisional constitution and espoused a wide range of liberal Western-type reforms, including freedom of the press and social equality, few of which ever saw the light of day.

The regime's first crisis came early in 1933 when **Pridi Phanomyong**, by now leader of the government's civilian faction, put forward a socialist economic plan based on the nationalization of land and labour. The proposal was denounced as communistic by the military, Pridi was forced into temporary exile and an anti-communist law was passed. Then, in October, a royalist coup was mounted which brought the kingdom close to civil war. After intense fighting, the rebels were defeated by Lieutenant-Colonel **Luang Phibunsongkhram** (or Phibun), so strengthening the government and bringing Phibun to the fore as the leading light of the military faction.

Pridi was rehabilitated in 1934 and remained powerful and popular, especially among the intelligentsia, but it was Phibun who became prime minister after the decisive **elections of 1938**, presiding over a cabinet dominated by military men. Phibun encouraged a wave of nationalistic feeling with such measures as the official institution of the name Thailand in 1939 – Siam, it was argued, was a name bestowed by external forces, and the new title made it clear that the country belonged to the Thais rather than the economically dominant Chinese. This latter sentiment was reinforced with a series of harsh laws against the Chinese, who faced discriminatory taxes on income and commerce.

World War II

The outbreak of **World War II** gave the Thais the chance to avenge the humiliation of the 1893 Franco–Siamese Crisis. When France was occupied by Germany in June 1940, Phibun seized the opportunity to invade western Cambodia and the area of Laos lying to the west of the Mekong River. In the following year, however, the threat of a Japanese attack on Thailand loomed. On December 8, 1941, almost at the same

1925–35	1932	1935–46
Reign of Rama VII (Prajadhipok)	A coup brings the end of the absolute monarchy and introduces Thailand's first constitution	Reign of Rama VIII (Ananda), mostly in absentia

time as the assault on Pearl Harbor, the Japanese invaded the country at nine points, most of them along the east coast of the peninsula. The Thais at first resisted for a few hours, but realizing that the position was hopeless, Phibun quickly ordered a ceasefire. Meanwhile, the British sent a force from Malaysia to try to stop the Japanese at Songkhla, but were held up in a fight with Thai border police. The Japanese had time to establish themselves, before pushing down the peninsula to take Singapore.

The Thai government concluded a military alliance with Japan and declared war against the US and Great Britain in January 1942, probably in the belief that the Japanese would win the war. However, the Thai minister in Washington, Seni Pramoj, refused to deliver the declaration of war against the US and, in cooperation with the Americans, began organizing a resistance movement called **Seri Thai**. Pridi, now acting as regent to the young king, furtively coordinated the movement under the noses of the occupying Japanese, smuggling in American agents and housing them in a European prison camp in Bangkok.

By 1944 Japan's final defeat looked likely, and Phibun, who had been most closely associated with them, was forced to resign by the National Assembly in July. A civilian, Khuang Aphaiwong, was chosen as prime minister, while Seri Thai became well established in the government under the control of Pridi. At the end of the war, Thailand was forced to restore the annexed Cambodian and Lao provinces to French Indochina, but American support prevented the British from imposing heavy punishments for the alliance with Japan.

Postwar upheavals

With the fading of the military, the election of January 1946 was for the first time contested by organized political parties, resulting in Pridi becoming prime minister. A new constitution was drafted and the outlook for democratic, civilian government seemed bright.

Hopes were shattered, however, on June 9, 1946, when King Ananda was found dead in his bed, with a bullet wound in his forehead. Three palace servants were tried and executed, but the murder has never been satisfactorily explained. Public opinion attached at least indirect responsibility for the killing to Pridi, who had in the past shown anti-royalist feeling. He resigned as prime minister, and in April 1948 the military made a decisive return: playing on the threat of communism, with Pridi pictured as a Red bogeyman, Phibun took over the premiership.

After the bloody suppression of two attempted coups in favour of Pridi, the main feature of Phibun's second regime was its heavy involvement with the US. As communism developed its hold in the region, with the takeover of China in 1949 and the French defeat in Indochina in 1954, the US increasingly viewed Thailand as a bulwark against the Red menace. Between 1951 and 1957, when its annual state budget was only about $200 million a year, Thailand received a total $149 million in American economic aid and $222 million in military aid. This strengthened Phibun's dictatorship, while enabling leading military figures to divert American money and other funds into their own pockets.

In 1955, his position threatened by two rival generals, Phibun experienced a sudden conversion to the cause of democracy. He narrowly won a general election in 1957, but only by blatant vote-rigging and coercion. Although there's a strong tradition

1939	1941	1946
The country's name is changed from Siam to the more nationalistic Thailand	The Japanese invade, and Thailand forms an alliance with them	Rama VIII is mysteriously shot dead; his brother, Rama IX (Bhumibol), accedes

of foul play in Thai elections, this is remembered as the dirtiest ever: after vehement public outcry, **General Sarit**, the commander-in-chief of the army, overthrew the new government in September 1957.

To the present day

Believing that Thailand would prosper best under a unifying authority – an ideology that still has plenty of supporters today – Sarit set about re-establishing the monarchy as the head of the social hierarchy and the source of legitimacy for the government. Ananda's successor, **King Bhumibol** (Rama IX), was pushed into an active role while Sarit ruthlessly silenced critics and pressed ahead with a plan for economic development. These policies achieved a large measure of stability and prosperity at home, although from 1960 onwards the international situation worsened. With the Marxist Pathet Lao making considerable advances in Laos, and Cambodia's ruler, Prince Sihanouk, drawing into closer relations with China, Sarit turned again to the US. The Americans obliged by sharply increasing military aid and by stationing troops in Thailand.

The Vietnam War

Sarit died in 1963, whereupon the military succession passed to **General Thanom**, closely aided by his deputy prime minister, **General Praphas**. Neither man had anything of Sarit's charisma and during a decade in power they followed his political philosophies largely unchanged. Their most pressing problem was the resumption of open hostilities between North and South Vietnam in the early 1960s – the **Vietnam War**. Both Laos and Cambodia became involved on the side of the communists by allowing the North Vietnamese to supply their troops in the south along the Ho Chi Minh Trail, which passed through southern Laos and northeastern Cambodia. The Thais, with the backing of the US, quietly began to conduct military operations in Laos, to which North Vietnam and China responded by supporting anti-government insurgency in Thailand.

The more the Thais felt threatened by the spread of communism, the more they looked to the Americans for help – by 1968 around 45,000 US military personnel were on Thai soil, which became the base for US bombing raids against North Vietnam and Laos, and for covert operations into Laos and beyond.

The effects of the **American presence in Thailand** were profound. The economy swelled with dollars, and hundreds of thousands of Thais became reliant on the Americans for a living, with a consequent proliferation of corruption and prostitution. What's more, the sudden exposure to Western culture led many to question traditional Thai values and the political status quo.

The democracy movement and civil unrest

At the same time, poor farmers were becoming disillusioned with their lot, and during the 1960s many turned against the Bangkok government. At the end of 1964, the **Communist Party of Thailand** and other groups formed a **broad left coalition** that soon had the support of several thousand insurgents in remote areas of the northeast. By 1967, the problem had spread to Chiang Rai and Nan provinces, and a separate

1957–63	**1973**	**1976**
Successful coup-maker and military strongman, General Sarit, brings Thailand ever closer to the US	Bloody student demonstrations bring the downfall of Sarit's successor, General Thanom	The brutal suppression of further student demos ushers the military back in

threat had arisen in southern Thailand, involving **Muslim dissidents** and the Chinese-dominated **Communist Party of Malaya**.

Thanom was now facing a major security crisis, especially as the war in Vietnam was going badly. In 1969 he held elections which produced a majority for the government party but, still worried about national stability, the general got cold feet. In November 1971 he reimposed repressive military rule, under a triumvirate of himself, his son Colonel Narong and Praphas, who became known as the "Three Tyrants". However, the 1969 experiment with democracy had heightened expectations of power-sharing among the middle classes, especially in the universities. **Student demonstrations** began in June 1973, and in October as many as 500,000 people turned out at Thammasat University in Bangkok to demand a new constitution. King Bhumibol intervened with apparent success, and indeed the demonstrators were starting to disperse on the morning of October 14, when the police tried to control the flow of people away. Tensions quickly mounted and soon a full-scale riot was under way, during which over 350 people were reported killed. The army, however, refused to provide enough troops to control the situation, and later the same day, Thanom, Narong and Praphas were forced to resign and leave the country.

In a new climate of openness, **Kukrit Pramoj** (see page 126) managed to form a coalition of seventeen elected parties and secured a promise of US withdrawal from Thailand, but his government was riven with feuding. Meanwhile, the king and much of the middle class, alarmed at the unchecked radicalism of the students, began to support new, often violent, right-wing organizations. In October 1976, the students demonstrated again, protesting against the return of Thanom to Thailand to become a monk at Wat Bowonniwet. Supported by elements of the military and the government, the police and reactionary students launched a massive assault on Thammasat University. On October 6, hundreds of students were brutally beaten, scores were lynched and some even burnt alive; the military took control and suspended the constitution.

General Prem

Soon after, the military-appointed prime minister, **Thanin Kraivichien**, imposed rigid censorship and forced dissidents to undergo anti-communist indoctrination, but his measures seem to have been too repressive even for the military, who forced him to resign in October 1977. General Kriangsak Chomanand took over, and began to break up the insurgency with shrewd offers of amnesty. His power base was weak, however, and although Kriangsak won the elections of 1979, he was displaced in February 1980 by **General Prem Tinsulanonda**, who was backed by a broad parliamentary coalition.

Untainted by corruption, Prem achieved widespread support, including that of the monarchy. Parliamentary elections in 1983 returned the military to power and legitimized Prem's rule. Overseeing a period of strong foreign investment and rapid economic growth, the general maintained the premiership until 1988, with a unique mixture of dictatorship and democracy sometimes called **Premocracy**: although never standing for parliament himself, Prem was asked by the legislature after every election to become prime minister. He eventually stepped down (though he remains a powerful privy councillor) because, he said, it was time for the country's leader to be chosen from among its elected representatives.

1980–88	1991	1992
Period of Premocracy, General Prem's hybrid of military rule and democracy	The military launch a coup, protesting the corruption of the recently democratically elected government	Mass demonstrations lead to bloodshed – and the return of democracy

The 1992 demonstrations and the 1997 constitution

The new prime minister was indeed an elected MP, **Chatichai Choonhavan**, a retired general with a long civilian career in public office. He pursued a vigorous policy of economic development, but this fostered widespread corruption, in which members of the government were often implicated. Following an economic downturn and Chatichai's attempts to downgrade the political role of the military, the armed forces staged a bloodless **coup** on February 23, 1991, led by Supreme Commander Sunthorn and General Suchinda, the army commander-in-chief, who became premier.

When Suchinda reneged on promises to make democratic amendments to the constitution, hundreds of thousands of ordinary Thais poured onto the streets around Bangkok's Democracy Monument in **mass demonstrations** between May 17 and 20, 1992. Hopelessly misjudging the mood of the country, Suchinda brutally crushed the protests, leaving hundreds dead or injured. Having justified the massacre on the grounds that he was protecting the king from communist agitators, Suchinda was forced to resign when King Bhumibol expressed his disapproval in a ticking-off that was broadcast on world television.

Elections were held in September, with the **Democrat Party**, led by Chuan Leekpai, a noted upholder of democracy and the rule of law, emerging victorious. Chuan was succeeded in turn by Banharn Silpa-archa – nicknamed by the local press "the walking ATM", a reference to his reputation for buying votes – and General Chavalit Yongchaiyudh. The most significant positive event of the latter's tenure was the approval of a **new constitution** in 1997. Drawn up by an independent drafting assembly, its main points included: direct elections to the senate, rather than appointment of senators by the prime minister; acceptance of the right of assembly as the basis of a democratic society and guarantees of individual rights and freedoms; greater public accountability; and increased popular participation in local administration. The eventual aim of the new charter was to end the traditional system of patronage, vested interests and vote buying.

Tom yam kung: the 1997 economic crisis

In February 1997 foreign-exchange dealers began to mount speculative attacks on the **baht**, alarmed at the size of Thailand's private foreign debt – 250 billion baht in the unproductive property sector alone, much of it accrued through the proliferation of prestigious skyscrapers in Bangkok. Chavalit's government defended the pegged exchange rate, spending $23 billion of the country's formerly healthy foreign-exchange reserves, but at the beginning of July was forced to give up the ghost – the baht was floated and soon went into freefall. Thailand was obliged to seek help from the **IMF**, which in August put together a $17-billion **rescue package**, coupled with severe austerity measures.

In November, the inept Chavalit was replaced by Chuan Leekpai, who immediately took a hard line in following the IMF's advice, which involved maintaining cripplingly high interest rates to protect the baht and slashing government budgets. Although this played well abroad, at home the government encountered increasing hostility from its newly impoverished citizens – the downturn struck with such speed and severity that it was dubbed the **tom yam kung crisis**, after the searingly hot Thai soup. Chuan's tough stance paid off, however, with the baht stabilizing and inflation falling back.

1997	**1997**	**2001**
A landmark new constitution aims to end corruption and guarantee individual rights and freedoms	Tom yam kung: Thailand is ravaged by economic crisis	Thaksin Shinawatra, loved and hated in roughly equal measure, wins the general election

Thaksin

The general election of January 2001 was the first to be held under the 1997 constitution, which was intended to take vote-buying out of politics. However, this election coincided with the emergence of a new party, **Thai Rak Thai** ("Thai Loves Thai"), formed by one of Thailand's wealthiest men, **Thaksin Shinawatra**, an ex-policeman who had made a personal fortune from government telecommunications concessions.

Thaksin duly won the election, but instead of moving towards greater democracy, as envisaged by the new constitution, he began to apply commercial and legal pressure to try to silence critics in the media and parliament. As his standing became more firmly entrenched, he rejected constitutional reforms designed to rein in his power – famously declaring that "democracy is only a tool" for achieving other goals.

Thaksin did, however, maintain his reputation as a reformer by carrying through nearly all of his election promises. He issued a three-year loan moratorium for perennially indebted farmers and set up a one-million-baht development fund for each of the country's seventy thousand villages. To improve public health access, a standard charge of B30 per hospital visit was introduced nationwide.

Despite a sharp escalation of violence in the Islamic southern provinces in early 2004 (see page 696), Thaksin breezed through the February 2005 election, becoming the first prime minister in Thai history to win an outright majority at the polls but causing alarm among a wide spectrum of Thailand's elites. When Thaksin's relatives sold their shares in the family's Shin Corporation in January 2006 for $1.7 billion, without paying tax, tens of thousands of mostly middle-class Thais flocked to Bangkok to take part in protracted demonstrations, under the umbrella of the **People's Alliance for Democracy** (**PAD**). After further allegations of corruption and cronyism, in September Thaksin, while on official business in the United States, was ousted by a military **coup**.

... and the spectre of Thaksin

Thaksin set up home in London, but his supporters, now the People's Power Party (PPP), won the December 2007 general election. In response, the PAD – its nationalist and royalist credentials and its trademark **yellow shirts** (the colour of the king) now firmly established – restarted its mass protests.

Matters came to a head in November and December 2008: the PAD seized and closed down Bangkok's Suvarnabhumi airport; the ruling People's Power Party was declared illegal by the courts; and **Pheu Thai**, the PPP's swift reincarnation, found itself unable to form a new coalition government. Instead, led by the Eton- and Oxford-educated **Abhisit Vejjajiva**, the Democrat Party jumped into bed with the Bhumjaithai Party, formerly staunch supporters of Thaksin, to take the helm.

This in turn prompted Thaksin's supporters – now **red-shirted** and organized into the **UDD** (United Front for Democracy against Dictatorship) – to hold mass protest meetings. In March 2009, Thaksin claimed by video broadcast that Privy Council President, Prem Tinsulanonda, had masterminded the 2006 coup and Abhisit's appointment as prime minister, and called for the overthrow of the *amat* (elite).

Amid a clampdown by the Democrat government on free speech, including heavy-handed use of Article 112, the *lèse majesté* law, much more violent protests took place early the following year. Calling on Abhisit to hold new elections, thousands of red shirts set up a heavily defended camp around the **Ratchaprasong** intersection in central

2004	2006	2010
The violence in the Islamic southern provinces sharply escalates	While in the US, Thaksin is ousted in a military coup and goes into exile	Red-shirted supporters of Thaksin set up a month-long protest camp in Bangkok, before being dispersed by force

Bangkok in early April. On May 19, Abhisit sent in the army to break up the camp by force; altogether 91 people died on both sides in the two months of protests.

Mass popular support for Thaksin, however, did not wane, and in the general election of May 2011, Pheu Thai – now led by his younger sister, **Yingluck Shinawatra** – romped home with an absolute majority.

Thailand's first woman prime minister, Yingluck proposed an amnesty bill for all those involved in the political turmoils of the last ten years, which would have included wiping out Thaksin's corruption convictions, thus allowing him to return to Thailand. However, in late 2013 this prompted further mass protests on the streets of Bangkok: led by Suthep Thaugsuban, who resigned his seat as a Democrat Party MP, thousands of nationalists – no longer wearing yellow shirts, but now blowing whistles as their trademark – occupied large areas of the city centre for several months, in an attempt to provoke the military into staging a coup. In May 2014, this duly happened, and was Thailand's twelfth successful **coup d'état** in the period of constitutional monarchy since 1932 (not to mention seven failed attempts). The army chief, **General Prayut Chan-ocha**, installed himself as prime minister, at the head of a military junta known as the National Council for Peace and Order (NCPO).

All political gatherings and activities have been banned, politicians, journalists, academics and activists have been imprisoned or have fled abroad and censorship of the media and social media has been greatly tightened (which in turn has fostered broad self-censorship). General elections were initially promised for 2015, but have been postponed repeatedly; the latest proposal is for February 2019, but at the time of writing that too seems about to slip.

In October 2016, the much-revered King Bhumibol passed away, to be succeeded by his 64-year-old son Vajiralongkorn, who spends much of his time in Germany. A year-long nationwide period of mourning followed, until the funeral was held in October 2017; a date for King Vajiralongkorn's coronation has not yet been set. The new king seems to favour a return to old ways and intervened in the drafting of the new constitution (Thailand's twentieth charter since 1932) to take direct control of the immense holdings of the Crown Property Bureau (the equivalent of the Royal Household). This constitution also reduces the power of elected politicians while bolstering the power of the military, with provisions for a strong appointed Senate of 250 members and for a prime minister who is not an elected representative. In 2017, Yingluck Shinawatra fled abroad just before she was sentenced to five years in prison for negligence.

2011	2014	2016
Thaksin's sister, Yingluck, wins the general election with an outright majority	Thailand's twelfth military coup since 1932	The much-loved Rama IX dies, and is succeeded by Maha Vajiralongkorn (Rama X)

Religion: Thai Buddhism

Over 85 percent of Thais consider themselves Theravada Buddhists, followers of the teachings of a holy man usually referred to as the Buddha (Enlightened One), though more precisely known as Gautama Buddha to distinguish him from lesser-known Buddhas who preceded him. Theravada Buddhism is one of the two main schools of Buddhism practised in Asia, and in Thailand it has absorbed an eclectic assortment of animist and Hindu elements.

Islam is the biggest of the minority religions in Thailand, practised by between five and ten percent of the population. Most Muslims live in the south, especially in the deep-south provinces of Yala, Pattani and Narithiwat, along the Malaysian border, whose populations are over eighty percent Muslim. The separatist violence in this region (see page 696) has caused great tension between local Buddhist and Muslim communities, which have traditionally co-existed peacefully; it has not, however, obviously affected inter-faith relationships elsewhere in Thailand. The rest of the Thai population comprises Mahayana Buddhists, Hindus, Sikhs, Christians and animists.

The Buddha: his life and beliefs

Gautama Buddha was born as **Prince Gautama Siddhartha** in Nepal, in the seventh century BC according to the calculations for the Thai calendar, though scholars now think it may have been a century or two later. At his birth, astrologers predicted that he would become either a famous king or a celebrated holy man, depending on which path he chose. Much preferring the former, the prince's father forbade the boy from leaving the palace grounds, and set about educating Gautama in all aspects of the high life. Most statues of the Buddha depict him with elongated earlobes, which is a reference to this early pampered existence, when he would have worn heavy precious stones in his ears.

The prince married and became a father, but at the age of 29 he flouted his father's authority and sneaked out into the world beyond the palace. On this fateful trip he encountered successively an old man, a sick man, a corpse and a hermit, and thus for the first time was made aware that pain and suffering were intrinsic to human life. Contemplation seemed the only means of discovering why this was so – and therefore Gautama decided to leave the palace and become a **Hindu ascetic**.

For several years he wandered the countryside leading a life of self-denial and self-mortification, but failed to come any closer to the answer. Eventually concluding that the best course of action must be to follow a "Middle Way" – neither indulgent nor overly ascetic – Gautama sat down beneath the famous riverside bodhi tree at **Bodh Gaya** in India, facing the rising sun, to **meditate** until he achieved enlightenment. For 49 days he sat cross-legged in the "lotus position", contemplating the causes of suffering and wrestling with temptations that materialized to distract him. Most of these were sent by **Mara**, the Evil One, who was finally subdued when Gautama summoned the earth goddess **Mae Toranee** by pointing the fingers of his right hand at the ground – the gesture known as **Calling the Earth to Witness**, or *Bhumisparsa Mudra*, which has been immortalized by thousands of Thai sculptors. Mae Toranee wrung torrents of water from her hair and engulfed Mara's demonic emissaries in a flood, an episode that's also commonly reproduced, especially in temple murals.

Temptations dealt with, Gautama soon came to attain **enlightenment** and so become a Buddha. As the place of his enlightenment, the **bodhi tree** (*bodhi* means "enlightenment" in Sanskrit and Pali; it's sometimes also known as the bo tree, in Thai *ton po*) has assumed special significance for Buddhists: not only does it appear in many

Buddhist paintings, but there's often a real bodhi tree (*Ficus religiosa*, or sacred fig) planted in temple compounds as well. In addition, the bot is nearly always built facing either a body of water or facing east (preferably both).

The Buddha preached his **first sermon** in the deer park at Sarnath in India, where he characterized his doctrine, or **Dharma**, as a wheel. From this episode comes the early Buddhist symbol the **Dharmachakra**, known as the Wheel of Law, which is often accompanied by a statue of a deer. Thais celebrate this first sermon with a public holiday in July known as **Asanha Puja**. On another occasion 1250 people spontaneously gathered to hear the Buddha speak, an event remembered in Thailand as **Makha Puja** and marked by a public holiday in February.

For the next forty-odd years the Buddha travelled the region converting non believers and performing miracles. One rainy season he even ascended into the **Tavatimsa heaven** (Heaven of the 33 Gods) to visit his mother and to preach the doctrine to her. His descent from this heaven is quite a common theme of paintings and sculptures, and the **Standing Buddha** pose of numerous Buddha statues comes from this story.

The Buddha "died" at the age of eighty on the banks of a river at Kusinari in India – an event often dated to 543 BC, which is why the **Thai calendar** is 543 years out of synch with the Western one, so that the year 2019 AD becomes 2562 BE (Buddhist Era). Lying on his side, propping up his head on his hand, the Buddha passed into **Nirvana** (giving rise to another classic pose, the **Reclining Buddha**), the unimaginable state of nothingness which knows no suffering and from which there is no reincarnation. Buddhists believe that the day the Buddha entered Nirvana was the same date on which he was born and on which he achieved enlightenment, a triply significant day that Thais honour with the **Visakha Puja** festival in May.

Buddhists believe that Gautama Buddha was the five-hundredth incarnation of a single being: the stories of these five hundred lives, collectively known as the **Jataka**, provide the inspiration for much Thai art. Hindus also accept Gautama Buddha into their pantheon, perceiving him as the ninth manifestation of their god Vishnu.

The spread of Buddhism

After the Buddha entered Nirvana, his **doctrine** spread relatively quickly across India, and probably was first promulgated in Thailand in about the third century BC, when the Indian emperor Ashoka (in Thai, Asoke) sent out missionaries. His teachings, the *Tripitaka*, were written down in the Pali language – a then-vernacular derivative of Sanskrit – in a form that became known as **Theravada**, or "The Doctrine of the Elders".

By the beginning of the first millennium, a new movement called **Mahayana** (Great Vehicle) had emerged within the Theravada school, attempting to make Buddhism more accessible by introducing a pantheon of **bodhisattva**, or Buddhist saints, who, although they had achieved enlightenment, postponed entering Nirvana in order to inspire the populace. Mahayana Buddhism spread north into China, Korea, Vietnam and Japan, also entering southern Thailand via the Srivijayan empire around the eighth century and parts of Khmer Cambodia in about the eleventh century. Meanwhile, Theravada Buddhism (which the Mahayanists disparagingly renamed "Hinayana" or "Lesser Vehicle") established itself most significantly in Sri Lanka, northern and central Thailand and Burma.

Buddhist doctrine and practice

Central to Theravada Buddhism is a belief in **karma** – broadly speaking, the belief that every action has a consequence – and **reincarnation**, along with an understanding that craving is at the root of human suffering. The ultimate aim for a Buddhist is to get off the cycle of perpetual reincarnation and suffering and instead to enter the blissful state of non-being that is **Nirvana**. This enlightened state can take many lifetimes to achieve so the more realistic goal for most is to be reborn slightly higher up the karmic ladder each time. As Thai Buddhists see it, animals are at the bottom of the karmic scale and monks at the top, with women on a lower rung than men.

Living a good life, specifically a life of "pure intention", creates good karma and Buddhist doctrine focuses a great deal on how to achieve this. Psychology and an understanding of human weaknesses play a big part. Key is the concept of *dukka* or **suffering**, which holds that craving is the root cause of all suffering or, to put it simplistically, human unhappiness is caused by the unquenchable dissatisfaction experienced when one's sensual, spiritual or material desires are not met. The concepts concerning suffering and craving are known as the **Four Noble Truths** of Buddhism. The route to enlightenment depends on a person being sufficiently detached from earthly desires so that *dukka* can't take hold. One acknowledges that the physical world is impermanent and ever changing, and that all things – including the self – are therefore not worth craving. A Buddhist works towards this realization by following the **Eightfold Path**, or **Middle Way**, that is by developing a set of highly moral personal qualities such as "right speech", "right action" and "right mindfulness". Meditation is particularly helpful in this.

A devout Thai Buddhist commits to the **five basic precepts**, namely not to kill or steal, to refrain from sexual misconduct and incorrect speech (lies, gossip and abuse) and to eschew intoxicating liquor and drugs. There are **three extra precepts** for special *wan phra* holy days and for those laypeople including foreign students who study meditation at Thai temples: no eating after noon, no entertainment (including TV and music) and no sleeping on a soft bed; in addition, the no-sexual-misconduct precept turns into no sex at all.

Making merit

Merit-making in popular Thai Buddhism has become slightly skewed, so that some people act on the assumption that they'll climb the karmic ladder faster if they make bigger and better offerings to the temple and its monks. However, it is of course the purity of the intention behind one's **merit-making** (*tham buun*) that's fundamental.

Merit can be made in many ways, from giving a monk his breakfast to attending a Buddhist service or donating money and gifts to the neighbourhood temple, and most **festivals** are essentially communal merit-making opportunities. Between the big festivals, the most common days for making merit and visiting the temple are **wan phra** (holy days), which are determined by the phase of the moon and occur four times a month. The simplest **offering** inside a temple consists of lotus buds, candles and three incense sticks (representing the three gems of Buddhism – the Buddha himself, the Dharma or doctrine, and the monkhood). One of the more bizarre but common merit-making activities involves **releasing caged birds**: worshippers buy tiny finches from vendors at wat compounds and, by liberating them from their cage, prove their Buddhist compassion towards all living things. The fact that the birds were free until netted earlier that morning doesn't seem to detract from the ritual. In riverside and seaside wats, fish or even baby turtles are released instead.

For an insightful introduction to the philosophy and practice of Thai Buddhism, see ⓦthaibuddhism.net. A number of Thai temples welcome foreign students of Buddhism and meditation (see page 52).

The monkhood

It's the duty of Thailand's 200,000-strong **Sangha** (monkhood) to set an example to the Theravada Buddhist community by living a life as close to the Middle Way as possible and by preaching the Dharma to the people. The life of a monk (*bhikkhu*) is governed by 227 precepts that include celibacy and the rejection of all personal possessions except gifts.

Each day begins with an alms round in the neighbourhood so that the laity can donate food and thereby gain themselves merit, and then is chiefly spent in meditation, chanting, teaching and study. As the most respected members of any community, monks act as teachers, counsellors and arbiters in local disputes, and sometimes become spokesmen for villagers' rights. They also perform rituals at cremations, weddings and other events, such as the launching of a new business or even the purchase of a new car. Many young boys from poor families find themselves almost obliged to become either a *dek wat* (temple boy) or a **novice monk** because that's the only way they can get accommodation, food and, crucially, an education. This is provided free in exchange for duties around the wat, and novices are required to adhere to ten rather than 227 Buddhist precepts.

Monkhood doesn't have to be for life: a man may leave the Sangha three times without stigma, and in fact every Thai male (including royalty) is expected to **enter the monkhood** for a short period, ideally between leaving school and marrying, as a rite of passage into adulthood. Thai government departments and some private companies grant their employees paid leave for their time as a monk, but the custom is in decline as young men increasingly have to consider the effect their absence may have on their career prospects. Instead, many men now enter the monkhood for a brief period after the death of a parent, to make merit both for the deceased and for the rest of the family. The most popular time for temporary ordination is the three-month Buddhist retreat period – **Pansa**, sometimes referred to as "Buddhist Lent" – which begins in July and lasts for the duration of the rainy season. (The monks' confinement is said to originate from the earliest years of Buddhist history, when farmers complained that perambulating monks were squashing their sprouting rice crops.)

Monks in contemporary society

Some monks extend their role as village spokesmen to become influential activists: Wat Tham Krabok near Lopburi and Wat Nong Sam Pran in Kanchanaburi are among a growing number of temples that have established themselves as successful drug rehabilitation centres; monks at Wat Phra Bat Nam Pu in Lopburi run a hospice for people with HIV/AIDS as well as a famously hard-hitting AIDS-awareness museum; monks at Wat Phai Lom near Bangkok have developed the country's largest breeding colony of Asian open-billed storks; while the monks at Wat Pa Luang Ta Bua Yannasampanno in Kanchanaburi hit the headlines for the wrong reasons with their controversial, now closed tiger sanctuary. Other monks, such as the famous Luang Pho Khoon of Wat Ban Rai in Nakhon Ratchasima province, who died in 2015 aged 91, have acquired such a reputation for giving wise counsel and bringing good fortune to their followers that they have become national gurus and their temples now generate great wealth through the production of specially blessed amulets and photographs.

Though the increasing involvement of many monks in the secular world has not met with unanimous approval, far more disappointing to the laity are those monks who **flout the precepts** of the Sangha by succumbing to the temptations of a consumer society, flaunting Raybans, Rolexes and Mercedes (in some cases actually bought with temple funds), chain-smoking and flirting, even making pocket money from predicting lottery results and practising faith-healing. With so much national pride and integrity riding on the sanctity of the Sangha, any whiff of a deeper scandal is bound to strike deep into the national psyche. Cases of monks involved in drug dealing, gun running, even rape and murder have prompted a stream of editorials on the state of the Sangha and the collapse of spiritual values at the heart of Thai society. The inclusivity of the monkhood – which is open to just about any male who wants to join – has been highlighted as a particularly vulnerable aspect, not least because donning saffron robes has always been an accepted way for criminals, reformed or otherwise, to repent of their past deeds.

Interestingly, back in the late 1980s, the influential monk Phra Bodhirak (Photirak) was defrocked after criticizing what he saw as a tide of decadence infecting Thai

Buddhism. He now preaches his ascetic code of anti-materialism through his breakaway **Santi Asoke** sect, famous across the country for its cheap vegetarian restaurants, its philosophy of self-sufficiency and for the simple blue farmers' shirts worn by many of its followers.

Women and the monkhood

Although the Theravada Buddhist hierarchy in some countries permits the ordination of **female monks**, or *bhikkhuni*, the Thai Sangha does not. Instead, Thai women are officially only allowed to become **nuns**, or *mae chii*, shaving their heads, donning white robes and keeping eight rather than 227 precepts. Their status is lower than that of the monks and they are chiefly occupied with temple upkeep rather than conducting religious ceremonies.

However, the progressives are becoming more vocal, and in 2002 a Thai woman became the first of several to break with the Buddhist authorities and get **ordained** as a novice *bhikkhuni* on Thai soil. Thailand's Sangha Council, however, still recognizes neither her ordination nor the temple, Watra Songdhammakalyani in Nakhon Pathom, where the ordination took place. The Watra (rather than Wat) is run by another Thai *bhikkhuni*, Dhammananda Bhikkhuni, the author of several books in English about **women and Buddhism** and of an informative website, ⓦ thaibhikkhunis.org.

Hindu deities and animist spirits

The complicated history of the area now known as Thailand has made Thai Buddhism a confusingly syncretic faith, as you'll realize when you enter a Buddhist temple compound to be confronted by a statue of a Hindu deity. While regular Buddhist merit-making insures a Thai for the next life, there are certain **Hindu gods and animist spirits** that many Thais – sophisticated Bangkokians and illiterate farmers alike – also cultivate for help with more immediate problems; and as often as not it's a Buddhist monk who is called in to exorcize a malevolent spirit. Even the Buddhist King Bhumibol employs Brahmin priests and astrologers to determine auspicious days and officiate at certain royal ceremonies and, like his royal predecessors of the Chakri dynasty, he also associates himself with the Hindu god Vishnu by assuming the title Rama IX – Rama, hero of the Hindu epic the *Ramayana*, having been Vishnu's seventh manifestation on earth.

If a Thai wants help in achieving a short-term goal, like passing an exam, becoming pregnant or winning the lottery, he or she will quite likely turn to the **Hindu pantheon**, visiting an enshrined statue of Brahma, Vishnu, Shiva or Ganesh, and making offerings of flowers, incense and maybe food. If the outcome is favourable, the devotee will probably come back to show thanks, bringing more offerings and maybe even hiring a dance troupe to perform a celebratory *lakhon chatri*. Built in honour of Brahma, Bangkok's Erawan Shrine is the most famous place of Hindu-inspired worship in the country.

Spirits and spirit houses

Whereas Hindu deities tend to be benevolent, **spirits** (or *phi*) are not nearly as reliable and need to be mollified more frequently. They come in hundreds of varieties, some more malign than others, and inhabit everything from trees, rivers and caves to public buildings and private homes – even taking over people if they feel like it.

So that these *phi* don't pester human inhabitants, each building has a special **spirit house** (*saan phra phum*) in its vicinity, as a dwelling for spirits ousted by the building's construction. Usually raised on a short column to set it at or above eye level, the spirit house must occupy an auspicious location – not, for example, in the shadow of the main building. It's generally about the size of a dolls' house and designed to look like a wat or a traditional Thai house, but its ornamentation is supposed to reflect the status of the humans' building, so if that building is enlarged or refurbished, the spirit house should be improved accordingly. And as architects become increasingly bold in their designs, so modernist spirit houses are also beginning to appear, especially in Bangkok where an eye-catching new skyscraper might be graced by a spirit house of glass or polished concrete. **Figurines** representing the relevant guardian spirit and his aides are sometimes put inside, and daily offerings of incense, lighted candles and garlands of jasmine are placed alongside them to keep the *phi* happy – a disgruntled spirit is a dangerous spirit, liable to cause sickness, accidents and even death. As with any religious building or icon in Thailand, an unwanted or crumbling spirit house should never be dismantled or destroyed, which is why you'll often see damaged spirit houses placed around the base of a sacred banyan tree, where they are able to rest in peace.

Art and architecture

Aside from pockets of Hindu-inspired statuary and architecture, the vast majority of historical Thai culture takes its inspiration from Theravada Buddhism, and, though the country does have some excellent museums, to understand fully the evolution of Thai art you have to visit its temples. Artists, sculptors and architects have tended to see their work as a way of making spiritual merit rather than as a means of self-expression or self-promotion, so pre-twentieth-century Thai art history is all about evolving styles rather than individual artists. This section is designed to help make sense of the most common aspects of Thai art and architecture at their various stages of development.

The wat

Buddhist temple complexes, or **wats**, are central to nearly every community in Thailand and, as the main expressions of public architecture and art over the centuries, are likely to loom large in visitors' experiences of the country, too. Wat architecture has evolved in diverse ways, but the names and purposes of the main buildings have stayed constant in Thailand for some fifteen centuries.

Some **general design features** of Thai temples are also distinctive. The Khmers, who had ruled much of the country long before the Thais came onto the scene, built their temples to a cosmological plan, with concentric layers representing earth, oceans and heavens, rising to a central high point (Phanom Rung near Surin is a stunning example of this). Remnants of this layout persisted in Thai temples, including boundary walls – which are sometimes combined with a moat – and the multi-tiered roofs of so many wat buildings.

Furthermore, the Thais come from a tradition of building in wood rather than stone or brick, hence the leaning walls and long, curving roofs that give wats their elegant, tapering lines. On top of this, wat architects have long been preoccupied with light, the symbol of Buddhist wisdom and clarity, covering their buildings with gilt, filigree and vividly coloured glass mosaics.

The bot

The most important wat building is the **bot** (sometimes known as the *ubosot*), where monks are ordained. It usually stands at the heart of the compound, but lay people are rarely allowed inside. There's only one bot in any wat complex, and often the only way you'll be able to distinguish it from other temple buildings is by the eight **sema** or boundary stones which always surround it. Positioned at the four corners of the bot and at the cardinal points of the compass, these *sema* define the consecrated ground and usually look something like upright gravestones, though they can take many forms. They are often carved all over with symbolic Buddhist scenes or ideograms, and sometimes are even protected within miniature shrines of their own. One of the best *sema* collections is housed in the National Museum of Khon Kaen, in the northeast.

The viharn

Often almost identical in appearance to the bot, the **viharn** or assembly hall is the building you are most likely to enter, as it usually contains the wat's principal Buddha image, and sometimes two or three minor images as well. Large wats may have several viharns, while strict meditation wats, which don't deal with the laity, may not have one at all.

The chedi

Upon the Buddha's death, disciples from all over Asia laid claim to his relics, enshrining them in specially constructed towers, known as **chedis** in Thailand. In later centuries, chedis have also become repositories for the ashes of royalty or important monks – and anyone else who could afford to have one built. Each chedi's three main components reflect a traditional symbolism. In theory, the chedi base should be divided into three layers to represent hell, earth and heaven. Above this, the dome usually contains the cube-shaped reliquary, known as a *harmika* after the Sanskrit term for the Buddha's seat of meditation. Crowning the structure, the spire is graded into 33 rings, one for each of the 33 Buddhist heavens.

The mondop and ho trai

Less common wat buildings include the square **mondop**, usually built with a complex, cruciform roof, which houses either a Buddha statue or footprint, or holy texts. One of the most spectacular examples, with an ornate green-and-gold roof and huge doors encrusted with mother-of-pearl, shelters Thailand's holiest footprint of the Buddha, at Wat Phra Phutthabat near Lopburi.

The **ho trai**, or scripture library, is generally constructed on stilts, sometimes over a pond, to protect against termites and fire. You can see particularly good examples of traditional *ho trai* at Wat Rakhang in Bangkok, at Wat Phra Singh in Chiang Mai and at Wat Yai Suwannaram in Phetchaburi.

Buddhist iconography

In the early days of Buddhism, image-making was considered inadequate to convey the faith's abstract philosophies, so the only approved iconography comprised doctrinal **symbols** such as the *Dharmachakra* (Wheel of Law, also known as Wheel of Doctrine or Wheel of Life; see page 739). Gradually these symbols were displaced by **images of the Buddha**, construed chiefly as physical embodiments of the Buddha's teachings rather than as portraits of the man. Sculptors took their guidance from the Pali texts, which ordained the Buddha's most common postures (*asanha*) and gestures (*mudra*).

All three-dimensional Buddha images are objects of reverence, but some are more esteemed than others. Some are alleged to have reacted in a particular way to unusual events, others have performed miracles, or are simply admired for their beauty, their phenomenal size or even their material value – if made of solid gold or jade, for

---

POSTURES AND GESTURES OF THE BUDDHA

Of the **four postures** – sitting, standing, walking and reclining – the **seated Buddha**, which represents him in meditation, is the most common in Thailand. A popular variation shows the Buddha seated on a coiled serpent, protected by the serpent's hood: a reference to the story about the Buddha meditating during the rainy season, when a serpent offered to raise him off the wet ground and shelter him from the storms. The **reclining** pose symbolizes the Buddha entering Nirvana at his death, while the **standing** and **walking** images both represent his descent from heaven.

The most common **hand gestures** include:

Dhyana Mudra (Meditation), in which the hands rest on the lap, palms upwards.

Bhumisparsa Mudra (Calling the Earth to Witness, a reference to the Buddha resisting temptation), with the left hand upturned in the lap and the right-hand fingers resting on the right knee and pointing to the earth (see page 738).

Vitarkha Mudra (Teaching), with one or both hands held at chest height with the thumb and forefinger touching.

Abhaya Mudra (Dispelling Fear), showing the right hand (occasionally both hands) raised in a flat-palmed "stop" gesture.

example. Most Thais are familiar with these exceptional images, all of which have been given special names, always prefixed by the honorific "Phra", and many of which have spawned thousands of miniaturized copies in the form of amulets. Pilgrimages are made to see the most famous originals.

It was in the Sukhothai era that the craze for producing **Buddha footprints** really took off. Harking back to the time when images were allusive rather than representative, these footprints were generally moulded from stucco to depict the 108 auspicious signs or *lakshanas* (which included references to the sixteen Buddhist heavens, the traditional four great continents and seven great rivers and lakes) and housed in a special mondop. Few of the Sukhothai footprints remain, but Ayutthaya- and Ratanakosin-era examples are found all over the country, the most famous being Phra Phutthabat near Lopburi, the object of pilgrimages throughout the year. The feet of the famous Reclining Buddha in Bangkok's Wat Pho are also inscribed with the 108 *lakshanas*, beautifully depicted in mother-of-pearl inlay.

Hindu iconography

Hindu images tend to be a lot livelier than Buddhist ones; there are countless gods to choose from and many have mischievous personalities and multiple inventive incarnations. In Hindu philosophy any object can be viewed as the temporal residence, embodiment or symbol of the deity so you get abstract representations such as the phallic lingam (pillar) for Shiva, as well as figurative images. Though pure Hinduism receded from Thailand with the collapse of the Khmer empire, Buddhist Thais have incorporated some Hindu and Brahmin concepts into the national belief system and have continued to create statues of the three chief Hindu deities – Brahma, Vishnu and Shiva – as well as using many mythological creatures in modern designs.

The Hindu Trinity

Vishnu has always been a favourite: in his role of "Preserver" he embodies the status quo, representing both stability and the notion of altruistic love. He is most often depicted as the deity, but has ten manifestations in all, of which **Rama** (number seven) is by far the most popular in Thailand. The epitome of ideal manhood, Rama is the superhero of the epic story the *Ramayana* – in Thai, the *Ramakien* (see page 88) – and appears in storytelling reliefs and murals in every Hindu temple in Thailand; in painted portraits you can usually recognize him by his green face. Manifestation number eight is **Krishna**, more widely known than Rama in the West, but slightly less common in Thailand. Krishna is usually characterized as a flirtatious, flute-playing, blue-skinned cowherd, but he is also a crucial figure in the lengthy moral epic poem, the *Mahabharata*. Confusingly, Vishnu's ninth avatar is the **Buddha** – a manifestation adopted many centuries ago to minimize defection to the Buddhist faith. When represented as **the deity**, Vishnu is generally shown sporting a crown and four arms, his hands holding a conch shell (whose music wards off demons), a discus (used as a weapon), a club (symbolizing the power of nature and time), and a lotus (symbol of joyful flowering and renewal). He is often depicted astride a **garuda**, a half-man, half-bird. Even without Vishnu on its back, the garuda is a very important beast: a symbol of strength, it's often shown "supporting" temple buildings.

Statues and representations of **Brahma** (the Creator) are rare. He too has four arms, but holds no objects; he has four faces (sometimes painted red), is generally borne by a goose-like creature called a *hamsa*, and is associated with the direction north.

Shiva (the Destroyer) is the most volatile member of the pantheon. He stands for extreme behaviour, for beginnings and endings, as enacted in his frenzied Dance of Destruction, and for fertility, and is a symbol of great energy and power. His godlike form typically has four, eight or ten arms, sometimes holding a trident (representing creation, protection and destruction) and a drum (to beat the rhythm of creation). In his most famous role, as **Nataraja**, or Lord of the Dance, he is usually shown in stylized standing position with legs bent into a balletic position, and the full complement of arms outstretched above his head. Three stripes on a figure's forehead also indicate Shiva, or one of his followers. In abstract form, he is represented by a **lingam** (once found at the heart of every Khmer temple in the northeast). Primarily a symbol of energy and godly power, the lingam also embodies fertility, particularly when set upright in a vulva-shaped vessel known as a **yoni**. The yoni doubles as a receptacle for the holy water that worshippers pour over the lingam.

Lesser gods

Close associates of Shiva include **Parvati**, his wife, and **Ganesh**, his elephant-headed son. As the god of knowledge and overcomer of obstacles (in the path of learning), Ganesh is used as the symbol of the Fine Arts Department, so his image features on all entrance tickets to national museums and historical parks.

The royal, three-headed elephant, **Erawan**, usually only appears as the favourite mount of the god **Indra**, the king of the gods, with specific power over the elements (particularly rain) and over the east. Other **Hindu gods of direction**, which are commonly found on the appropriate antefix in Khmer temples, include **Yama** on a buffalo (south); **Varuna** on a naga (mythical serpent) or a *hamsa* (west); Brahma (north); and **Isaana** on a bull (northeast).

Lesser mythological figures, which originated as Hindu symbols but feature frequently in wats and other Buddhist contexts, include the **yaksha** giants who ward off evil spirits (like the enormous freestanding ones guarding Bangkok's Wat Phra Kaeo); the graceful half-woman, half-bird **kinnari**; and the ubiquitous **naga**, or serpent king of the underworld, often with as many as seven heads, whose reptilian body most frequently appears as staircase balustrades in Hindu and Buddhist temples.

The schools

In the 1920s art historians and academics began compiling a classification system for Thai art and architecture that was modelled along the lines of the country's historical periods; these are the guidelines followed below. The following brief overview starts in the sixth century, when Buddhism began to take a hold on the country; few examples of art from before that time have survived, and there are no known, earlier architectural relics.

Dvaravati (sixth to eleventh centuries)

Centred around Nakhon Pathom, U Thong and Lopburi in the Chao Phraya basin and in the smaller northern enclave of Haripunjaya (modern-day Lamphun), the **Dvaravati** civilization was populated by Mon-speaking Theravada Buddhists who were strongly influenced by Indian culture.

The only known surviving Dvaravati-era **building** is the pyramidal laterite chedi at Lamphun's Wat Chama Thevi, but the national museums in Bangkok, Nakhon Pathom and Lamphun house quite extensive collections of Buddha **images** from that period. To make the best of the poor-quality limestone at their disposal, Dvaravati sculptors made their Buddhas quite stocky, cleverly dressing the figures in a sheet-like drape that dropped down to ankle level from each raised wrist, forming a U-shaped hemline – a style which they used when casting in bronze as well. Where the faces have survived, they are strikingly naturalistic, distinguished by their thick lips, flattened noses and wide cheekbones.

Nakhon Pathom, thought to have been a target of Buddhist missionaries from India since before the first century AD, has also yielded many **dharmachakra**, originating in the period when the Buddha could not be directly represented. These metre-high carved stone wheels symbolize the cycles of life and reincarnation, and in Dvaravati examples are often accompanied by a small statue of a deer, which refers to the Buddha preaching his first sermon in a deer park.

Srivijaya (eighth to thirteenth centuries)

While Dvaravati's Theravada Buddhists were influencing the central plains and, to a limited extent, areas further to the north, southern Thailand was paying allegiance to the Mahayana Buddhists of the **Srivijayan** civilization. Mahayanists believe that those who have achieved enlightenment – known as **bodhisattva** – should postpone their entry into Nirvana in order to help others along the way, and depictions of these saint-like beings were the mainstay of Srivijayan art.

The finest Srivijayan *bodhisattva* statues were cast in bronze and are among the most graceful and sinuous ever produced in Thailand. Many are lavishly adorned, and some were even bedecked in real jewels when first made. By far the most popular *bodhisattva* subject was **Avalokitesvara**, worshipped as compassion incarnate. Generally shown with four or more arms and with an animal skin over the left shoulder or tied at the waist, Avalokitesvara is also sometimes depicted with his torso covered in tiny Buddha images. Bangkok's National Museum holds the most beautiful Avalokitesvara, the Bodhisattva Padmapani found in Chaiya, but there's a good sandstone example *in situ* at Prasat Muang Singh near Kanchanaburi.

The most typical intact example of a Srivijayan **temple** is the heavily restored Javanese-style chedi at Chaiya's Wat Phra Boromathat, with its highly ornamented, stepped chedi featuring mini-chedis at each corner.

Khmer and Lopburi (tenth to fourteenth centuries)

By the end of the ninth century the **Khmers** of Cambodia were starting to expand from their capital at Angkor into the Dvaravati states, bringing with them the Hindu faith and the cult of the god-king (*devaraja*). They built hundreds of imposing stone **sanctuaries** across their newly acquired territory, most notably within southern Isaan, at Phimai, Phanom Rung and Khao Phra Viharn.

Each magnificent castle-temple – known in Khmer as a **prasat** – was constructed primarily as a shrine for a Shiva lingam, the phallic representation of the god Shiva. They followed a similar pattern, centred on at least one pyramidal or corncob-shaped tower, or **prang**, which represented Mount Meru (the gods' heavenly abode) and housed the lingam. Prangs were surrounded by concentric rectangular **galleries**, whose **gopura** (entrance chambers) at the cardinal points were usually approached by staircases flanked with **naga balustrades**; in Khmer temples, nagas generally appear as symbolic bridges between the human world and that of the gods. Most compounds enclosed ponds between their outer and inner walls, and many were surrounded by a network of moats and **reservoirs**: historians attribute the Khmers' political success in part to their skill in designing highly efficient irrigation systems.

Exuberant **carvings** ornamented almost every surface of the prasat. Usually gouged from sandstone, but frequently moulded in stucco, they depict Hindu deities, incarnations and stories, especially episodes from the *Ramayana*. Towards the end of the twelfth century, the Khmer leadership became Mahayana Buddhist, commissioning Buddhist carvings to be installed alongside the Hindu ones, and often replacing the Shiva lingam with a Buddha or *bodhisattva* image.

The temples built in the former Theravada Buddhist principality of **Lopburi** during the Khmer period are much smaller than those in Isaan; the triple-pranged temple of Phra Prang Sam Yot is typical. Broad-faced and muscular, the classic Lopburi-era Buddha **statue** wears a diadem or ornamental headband – a nod to the Khmers' ideological fusion of earthly and heavenly power – and the *ushnisha* (the sign of enlightenment) becomes distinctly conical rather than a mere bump on the head. Early Lopburi Buddhas also come garlanded with necklaces and ornamental belts. As you'd expect, Lopburi National Museum houses a good selection.

Sukhothai (thirteenth to fifteenth centuries)

Capitalizing on the Khmers' weakening hold over central Thailand, two Thai generals established the first major Thai kingdom in **Sukhothai** in 1238, and over the next two hundred years its citizens produced some of Thailand's most refined art.

Sukhothai's artistic reputation rests above all on its **sculpture**. More sinuous even than the Srivijayan images, Sukhothai Buddhas tend towards elegant androgyny, with slim oval faces and slender curvaceous bodies usually clad in a plain, skintight robe that fastens with a tassel close to the navel. The sculptors favoured the seated pose, with hands in the *Bhumisparsa Mudra*, most expertly executed in the Phra Buddha Chinnarat image, now housed in Phitsanulok's Wat Si Ratana Mahathat (replicated at Bangkok's Wat Benjamabophit) and in the enormous Phra Sri Sakyamuni, now enshrined in Bangkok's Wat Suthat. They were also the first to represent the **walking Buddha**, a supremely graceful figure with his right leg poised to move forwards and his left arm in the *Vitarkha Mudra*, as seen at Sukhothai's Wat Sra Si.

Rather than pull down the sacred prangs of their predecessors, Sukhothai builders added bots, viharns and chedis to the existing structures, as well as conceiving quite separate **temple complexes**. Their viharns and bots are the earliest halls of worship still standing in Thailand (the Khmers didn't go in for large public assemblies), but in most cases only the stone pillars and their platforms remain, the wooden roofs having long since disintegrated. The best examples can be seen in the historical parks at Sukhothai, Si Satchanalai and Kamphaeng Phet.

Most of the **chedis** are in much better shape. Many were modelled on the Sri Lankan bell-shaped reliquary tower (symbolizing the Buddha's teachings ringing out far and wide), often set atop a one- or two-tiered square base surrounded by elephant buttresses; Si Satchanalai's Wat Chang Lom is a good example. The architects also devised the **lotus-bud chedi**, a slender tower topped with a tapered finial that was to become a hallmark of the Sukhothai era; in Sukhothai both Wat Mahathat and Wat Trapang Ngoen display classic examples.

Ancient Sukhothai is also renowned for the skill of its potters, who produced **ceramic ware** known as Sawankhalok, after the name of one of the nearby kiln towns. Most museum ceramics collections are dominated by Sawankhalok ware, which is distinguished by its grey-green celadon glazes and by the fish and chrysanthemum motifs used to decorate bowls and plates; there's a dedicated Sawankhalok museum in Sukhothai.

Lanna (thirteenth to sixteenth centuries)

Meanwhile, to the north of Sukhothai, the independent Theravada Buddhist kingdom of **Lanna** was flourishing. Its art styles – known interchangeably as **Chiang Saen** and Lanna – built on the Dvaravati heritage of Haripunjaya, copying direct from Indian sources and incorporating Sukhothai and Sri Lankan ideas from the south.

The earliest surviving Lanna **monument** is the Dvaravati-style Chedi Si Liam at Wiang Kum Kam near Chiang Mai, built to the pyramidal form characteristic of Mon builders. Also in Chiang Mai, Wat Jet Yot replicates the temple built at Bodh Gaya in India to commemorate the seven sites where the Buddha meditated in the first seven weeks after attaining enlightenment.

Lanna **sculpture** also drew some inspiration from Bodh Gaya, echoing the plumpness of the Buddha image, and its broad shoulders and prominent hair curls. The later works are slimmer, probably as a result of Sukhothai influence, and one of the most famous examples of this type is the Phra Singh Buddha, enshrined in Chiang Mai's Wat Phra Singh. Other good illustrations of both styles are housed in Chiang Mai's National Museum.

Ayutthaya (fourteenth to eighteenth centuries)

From 1351 Thailand's central plains came under the thrall of a new power centred on **Ayutthaya** and ruled by a former prince of Lopburi. Over the next four centuries, the Ayutthayan capital became one of the most prosperous and ostentatious cities in Asia, its rulers commissioning some four hundred grand wats as symbols of their wealth and power. Though essentially Theravada Buddhists, the kings also adopted some Hindu and Brahmin beliefs from the Khmers – most significantly the concept of *devaraja* or god-kingship, whereby the monarch became a mediator between the people and the Hindu gods. The religious buildings and sculptures of this era reflected this new composite ideology, both by fusing the architectural styles inherited from the Khmers and from Sukhothai and by dressing their Buddhas to look like regents.

Retaining the concentric layout of the typical Khmer **temple complex**, Ayutthayan builders refined and elongated the prang into a **corncob-shaped tower**, rounding it off at the top and introducing vertical incisions around its circumference. As a spire they often added a bronze thunderbolt, and into niches within the prang walls they placed Buddha images. In Ayutthaya itself, the ruined complexes of Wat Phra Mahathat and Wat Ratburana both include these corncob prangs, but the most famous example is Bangkok's Wat Arun, which, though built during the subsequent Bangkok period, is a classic Ayutthayan structure.

Ayutthaya's architects also adapted the Sri Lankan **chedi** favoured by their Sukhothai predecessors, stretching the bell-shaped base and tapering it into a very graceful conical spire, as at Wat Phra Si Sanphet in Ayutthaya. The **viharns** of this era are characterized by walls pierced by slit-like windows, designed to foster a mysterious atmosphere by limiting the amount of light inside the building. As with all of Ayutthaya's buildings, few viharns survived the brutal 1767 sacking, with the notable exception of Wat Na Phra Mane. Phitsanulok's Wat Phra Si Ratana Mahathat was built to a similar plan – and in Phetchaburi, Wat Yai Suwannaram has no windows at all.

From Sukhothai's Buddha **sculptures** the Ayutthayans copied the soft oval face, adding an earthlier demeanour to the features and imbuing them with a hauteur in tune with the *devaraja* ideology. Early Ayutthayan statues wear crowns to associate kingship with Buddhahood; as the court became ever more lavish, so these figures became increasingly adorned, until – as in the monumental bronze at Wat Na Phra Mane – they appeared in earrings, armlets, anklets, bandoliers and coronets. The artists justified these luscious portraits of the Buddha – who was, after all, supposed to have given up worldly possessions – by pointing to an episode when the Buddha transformed himself into a well-dressed nobleman to gain the ear of a proud emperor, whereupon he scolded the man into entering the monkhood.

While a couple of wats in Sukhothai show hints of painted decoration, religious **painting** in Thailand really dates from the Ayutthayan era. Unfortunately most of Ayutthaya's own paintings were destroyed in 1767, but several temples elsewhere have well-preserved murals, in particular Wat Yai Suwannaram in Phetchaburi. By all accounts typical of late seventeenth-century painting, the Phetchaburi murals depict rows of *thep*, or divinities, paying homage to the Buddha, in scenes presented without shadow or perspective, and mainly executed in dark reds and cream.

Ratanakosin (eighteenth century to the 1930s)

When **Bangkok** emerged as Ayutthaya's successor in 1782, the new capital's founder was determined to revive the old city's grandeur, and the **Ratanakosin** (or Bangkok) period began by aping what the Ayutthayans had done. Since then neither wat architecture nor religious sculpture has evolved much further.

The first Ratanakosin **building** was the bot of Bangkok's Wat Phra Kaeo, built to enshrine the Emerald Buddha. Designed to a typical Ayutthayan plan, it's coated in glittering mirrors and gold leaf, with roofs ranged in multiple tiers and tiled in green and orange. To this day, most newly built bots and viharns follow a more economical version of this paradigm, whitewashing the outside walls but decorating the pediment in gilded ornaments and mosaics of coloured glass. Tiered temple roofs still taper off into the slender bird-like finials called *chofa*, and naga staircases – a Khmer feature inherited by Ayutthaya – have become almost obligatory. The result is that modern wats are often almost indistinguishable from each other, though Bangkok does have a few exceptions, including Wat Benjamabophit, which uses marble cladding for its walls and incorporates Victorian-style stained-glass windows, and Wat Rajabophit, which is covered all over in Chinese ceramics. The most dramatic chedi of the Ratanokosin era was constructed in the mid-nineteenth century in Nakhon Pathom to the original Sri Lankan style, but minus the elephant buttresses found in Sukhothai.

Early Ratanakosin sculptors produced adorned **Buddha images** very much in the Ayutthayan vein. The obsession with size, first apparent in the Sukhothai period, has since plumbed new depths, with graceless concrete statues up to 60m high becoming the norm, often painted brown or a dull yellow. Most small images are cast from or patterned on older models, mostly Sukhothai or Ayutthayan in origin.

Painting has fared much better, with the *Ramayana* murals in Bangkok's Wat Phra Kaeo a shining example of how Ayutthayan techniques and traditional subject matters could be adapted into something fantastic, imaginative and beautiful.

Contemporary

Following the democratization of Thailand in the 1930s, artists increasingly became recognized as individuals, and took to signing their work for the first time. In 1933 the first school of fine art (now Bangkok's Silpakorn University) was established under the Italian sculptor **Corrado Feroci** (later Silpa Bhirasri), designer of the capital's Democracy Monument and, as the new generation experimented with secular themes and styles adapted from the West, Thai art began to look a lot more "**modern**". As for subject matter, the leading artistic preoccupation of the past eighty years has been Thailand's spiritual heritage and its role in contemporary society. Since 1985, a number of Thailand's more established contemporary artists have earned the title **National Artist**, an honour that's bestowed annually on notable artists working in all disciplines, including fine art, performing arts, film and literature.

The artists

One of the first modern artists to adapt traditional styles and themes was **Angkarn Kalayanapongsa** (1926–2012), an early recipient of the title National Artist. He was employed as a temple muralist and many of his paintings, some of which are on show in Bangkok's National Gallery, reflect this experience, typically featuring casts of two-dimensional Ayutthayan-style figures and flying *thep* in a surreal setting laced with Buddhist symbols and nods to contemporary culture.

Taking this fusion a step further, one-time cinema billboard artist, now National Artist **Chalermchai Kositpipat** (b. 1955) specializes in temple murals with a modern, controversial, twist. Outside Thailand his most famous work enlivens the interior walls of London's Wat Buddhapadipa with strong colours and startling imagery. At home, his most famous project is the unconventional and highly ornate all-white Wat Rong Khun in his native Chiang Rai province (see page 356).

ART GALLERIES AND EXHIBITIONS

Bangkok has a near-monopoly on Thailand's **art galleries**. While the permanent collections at the capital's National Gallery (see page 97) are disappointing, regular exhibitions of more challenging contemporary work appear at the huge, ambitious **Bangkok Art and Cultural Centre** (see page 119); the main art school, Silpakorn University Art Centre (see page 93); the Queen's Gallery (see page 105); and at smaller gallery spaces around the city. The excellent *Bangkok Art Map* (𝕨 facebook.com/bangkokartmap) carries exhibition listings. Large-scale art museums in the provinces include the Contemporary Thai Art Centre, part of Silpakorn University's secondary campus in Nakhon Pathom (see page 179), and Chiang Mai University Art Museum (see page 285). For a preview of works by Thailand's best modern artists, visit the virtual Rama IX Art Museum at 𝕨 rama9art.org.

Aiming for the more secular environments of the gallery and the private home, National Artist **Pichai Nirand** (b. 1936) rejects the traditional mural style and makes more selective choices of Buddhist imagery, appropriating religious objects and icons and reinterpreting their significance. He's particularly well known for his fine-detail canvases of Buddha footprints, many of which can be seen in Bangkok galleries and public spaces.

National Artist **Pratuang Emjaroen** (b. 1935) is famous for his social commentary, as epitomized by his huge and powerful canvas *Dharma and Adharma; The Days of Disaster*, which he painted in response to the vicious clashes between the military and students in 1973. It picture depicts severed limbs, screaming faces and bloody gun barrels amid shadowy images of the Buddha's face, a spiked *dharmachakra* and other religious symbols.

Prolific traditionalist **Chakrabhand Posayakrit** (b. 1943) is also inspired by Thailand's Buddhist culture; he is famously proud of his country's cultural heritage, which infuses much of his work and has led to him being honoured as a National Artist. He is best known for his series of 33 *Life of the Buddha* paintings, and for his portraits, including many depicting members of the Thai royal family.

More controversial, and more of a household name, especially since the opening of his Baan Dam museum in Chiang Rai (see page 356), National Artist **Thawan Duchanee** (1939–2014) tended to examine the spiritual tensions of modern life. His surreal juxtaposition of religious icons with fantastical Bosch-like characters and explicitly sexual images prompted a group of outraged students to slash ten of his early paintings in 1971 – an unprecedented reaction to a work of Thai art. Nevertheless, Thawan continued to produce allegorical investigations into the individual's struggles against the obstacles that dog the Middle Way, prominent among them lust and violence.

Complacency is not a criticism that could be levelled at **Vasan Sitthiket** (b. 1957), one of Thailand's most outspoken and iconoclastic artists, whose uncompromising pictures are shown at – and still occasionally banned from – large and small galleries around the capital. A persistent crusader against the hypocrisies of establishment figures such as monks, politicians, CEOs and military leaders, Vasan's is one of the loudest and most aggressive political voices on the contemporary art scene, expressed on canvas, in multimedia works and in performance art.

Equally confrontational is fellow Biennale exhibitor, the photographer, performance artist and social activist **Manit Sriwanichpoom** (b. 1961). Manit is best known for his "Pink Man" series of photographs in which he places a Thai man (his collaborator Sompong Thawee), dressed in a flashy pink suit and pushing a pink shopping trolley, into different scenes and situations in Thailand and elsewhere. The Pink Man represents thoughtless, dangerous consumerism and his backdrop might be an impoverished hill-tribe village (*Pink Man on Tour*; 1998), or black-and-white shots from the political violence of 1973, 1976 and 1992 (*Horror in Pink*; 2001).

Women artists tend to be less high profile in Thailand, but in 2007 **Pinaree Sanpitak** (b. 1961) became the first female recipient of the annual Silpathorn Awards for established artists. Pinaree is known for her interest in gender issues and for her recurrent use of a female iconography in the form of vessels and mounds, often exploring the overlap with Buddhist stupa imagery. She works mainly in multimedia; her "Vessels and Mounds" show of 2001, for example, featured installations of huge, breast-shaped floor cushions, candles and bowls.

Among the younger faces on the Thai art scene, **Thaweesak Srithongdee** (b. 1970) blends surrealism and pop culture with the erotic and the figurative, to cartoonlike effect. He is preoccupied with popular culture, as is **Jirapat Tatsanasomboon** (b. 1971), whose work plays around with superheroes and cultural icons from East and West, pitting the *Ramayana*'s monkey king, Hanuman, against Spiderman in *Hanuman vs Spiderman*, and fusing mythologies in *The Transformation of Sita (after Botticelli)*. Alex Face (born Patcharapol Tangruen, 1982) is one of Thailand's first collectable street artists, employing plenty of wit and humour in his usually indirect political commentary.

Flora, fauna and environmental issues

Spanning some 1650km north to south, Thailand lies in the heart of Southeast Asia's tropical zone, its northernmost region just a few degrees south of the Tropic of Cancer, its southern border running less than seven degrees north of the Equator. As with other tropical regions, Thailand's climate is characterized by high humidity and even higher temperatures, a fertile combination which nourishes a huge diversity of flora and fauna in a vast range of habitats, from mixed deciduous and dry dipterocarp forests in the mountainous north to wet tropical rainforests in the steamy south. At least six percent of the world's vascular plants are found here, with over fifteen thousand species so far recorded.

The best places to appreciate Thailand's biodiversity are its national parks, the most accessible of which include Khao Yai in the northeast, Doi Inthanon and Doi Suthep in the north, and Khao Sam Roi Yot, Khao Sok and Ko Tarutao in the south. General practical information on national parks is given in Basics (see page 54).

The geography of Thailand

Thailand has a **tropical monsoon climate**. Most rain is brought from the Indian Ocean by the southwest monsoon from May to October, the so-called rainy season. From November to February the northeast monsoon brings a much cooler and drier climate from China: the cold, dry season. However, this northeastern monsoon hits the peninsular east coast after crossing the South China Sea, loading up with moist air and therefore bringing this region's rainiest season in November.

Agriculture plays a significant role in Thailand's economy, and some forty percent of Thais live off the land or the sea. Waterlogged rice paddies characterize the central plains; cassava, tapioca and eucalyptus are grown as cash crops on the scrubby plateau of the northeast; and rubber and palm-oil plantations dominate the commercial land use of the south. Dotted along Thailand's coastline are mangrove swamps and palm forests.

Mixed deciduous and dry dipterocarp forests

An estimated 65 percent of Thailand's forests are **deciduous**, sometimes referred to as monsoon forest because they have to survive periods of up to six months with minimal rainfall, so the trees shed their leaves to conserve water. Deciduous forests are often light and open, with canopies of 10–40m and dense undergrowth. They are dominated by trees of the **Dipterocarpaceae** family, a group of tropical hardwoods prized for their timber and, in places, their resin. **Teak** was also once common in northern deciduous forests, but its solid, unwarpable timber is so sought after that nearly all the teak forests have been felled. Since teak trees take around two hundred years to mature, logging them was banned in Thailand in 1989 and these days most of Thailand's teak comes in from Myanmar.

Bamboo thrives in a monsoon climate, shooting up at a remarkable rate during the wet season, usually in soils too poor for other species; it often predominates in secondary forests, where logging or clearing has previously taken place. The smooth, hollow stem characteristic of all varieties of bamboo is a fantastically adaptable material, used by the Thais for constructing everything from outside walls to chairs to water pipes (in hill-tribe villages) and musical instruments; and the bamboo shoot is common in Thai–Chinese cuisine.

Tropical rainforests

Thailand's **tropical rainforests** occur in areas of high and prolonged rainfall in the southern peninsula, most accessibly in the national parks of Khao Sok, Tarutao and Khao Luang. Some areas contain as many as two hundred species of tree within just a couple of acres. Characteristic of a tropical rainforest is the multi-layered series of **canopies**. The uppermost storey sometimes reaches 60m, and these towering trees often have enormous buttressed roots for support; beneath this, the dense canopy of 25–35m is often festooned with climbers and epiphytes such as ferns, lianas, mosses and orchids; then comes an uneven layer 5–10m high consisting of palms, rattans, shrubs and small trees. The forest floor in tropical rainforests tends to be relatively open and free of dense undergrowth, owing to the intense filtering of light by the upper three layers. Again, members of the *Dipterocarpaceae* family are dominant, playing an important role as nesting sites for hornbills, as lookout posts for gibbons – and as timber.

Semi-evergreen and montane forests

Semi-evergreen forests are the halfway house between tropical rainforests and dry deciduous forests and include all lowland and submontane evergreen forests from the plains to about 1000m. They thrive in regions with distinctly seasonal rainfall and fine examples can be found at Khao Yai and Kaeng Krachan national parks, and all along the Burmese border, all of which are potentially good places to observe large mammals, including elephants, gaurs, tigers and bears.

Above 1000m, the canopy of tall trees gives way to hardy **evergreen montane forest** growth such as oaks, chestnuts and laurels, many with twisted trunks and comparatively small leaves. Frequent rainfall means plenty of moss and a dense undergrowth of epiphytes, rhododendrons and tree ferns. Good examples can be seen in Doi Inthanon and Phu Kradung national parks, and in parts of Doi Suthep and Khao Yai national parks.

Mangrove swamps and coastal forests

Mangrove swamps are an important habitat for a wide variety of marine life (including two hundred species of bird, seventy species of fish and fifty types of crab) but, as with much of Thailand's inland forest, they have been significantly degraded by encroachment and large-scale prawn farming. Huge swathes of Thailand's littoral used to be fringed with mangrove swamps, but now they are mainly found only along the west peninsular coast, between Ranong and Satun, though Chanthaburi's Ao Khung Kraben is a notable east-coast exception. On Phuket, the Thachatchai Nature Trail leads you on a guided tour through a patch of mangrove swamp, but an even better way of **exploring the swamps** is to paddle a kayak through the mangrove-clogged inlets and island-lagoons of Ao Phang Nga. Not only do mangrove swamps harbour a rich and important ecosystem of their own, but they also help prevent coastal erosion; in certain areas of the tsunami-hit Andaman coast intact mangrove forest absorbed some of the waves' impact, protecting land and homes from even worse damage.

Nipa palms share the mangrove's penchant for brackish water, and these stubby-stemmed palm trees grow in abundance in the south, though commercial plantations are now replacing the natural colonies. Like most other species of palm indigenous to Thailand, the nipa is a versatile plant that's exploited to the full: alcohol is distilled from its sugary sap, and its fronds are woven into roofs (especially for beach huts and village homes), sticky-rice baskets and chair-backs.

The hardy **coconut palm** is also very tolerant of salty, sandy soil, and is equally useful. On islands such as Ko Kood, it's the backbone of the local economy, with millions of coconuts harvested every month for their milk, their oil-producing meat (copra), and their fibrous husks or coir (used for making ropes, matting, brushes and mattress stuffing); the palm fronds are woven into roof thatching and baskets, and the wood has an attractive grain.

Casuarinas (also known as she-oaks or ironwoods) also flourish in sandy soils and are common on beaches throughout Thailand; fast-growing and tall (up to 20m), they are quite often planted as wind breaks. Though its feathery profile makes it look like a pine, it's actually made up of tiny twigs, not needles.

The wildlife

Thailand lies in an exceptionally rich "transition zone" of the Indo-Malayan realm, its forests, mountains and national parks attracting wildlife from both Indochina and Indonesia. In all, Thailand is home to three hundred species of mammal (37 of which are considered to be endangered or vulnerable), while 982 species of bird have been recorded here (49 of them globally threatened).

Mammals

In the major national parks such as Khao Yai, Doi Inthanon and Khao Sok, the animals you're most likely to encounter are **primates**, particularly macaques and gibbons. The latter spend much of their time foraging for food in the forest canopy, while the former often descend closer to the ground to rest and to socialize.

The gibbons are responsible for the distinctive hooting that echoes through the forests. Chief noise-maker is the **white-handed** or **lar gibbon**, a beige- or black-bodied, white-faced animal whose cute appearance, intelligence and dexterity unfortunately make it a popular pet. The poaching and maltreatment of lar gibbons has become so severe that several organizations are now dedicated to protecting them (see page 759).

Similarly chatty, macaques hang out in gangs of twenty or more. The **long-tailed** or **crab-eating macaque** lives in the lowlands, near rivers, lakes and coasts as at Ao Phang Nga, Krabi, Ko Tarutao, Ang Thong and Khao Sam Roi Yot. It eats not only crabs, but mussels, other small animals and fruit, transporting and storing food in its big cheek pouch when swimming and diving. The **pig-tailed macaque**, named after its short curly tail, excels at scaling the tall trees of Erawan, Khao Yai, Doi Inthanon and other national parks, a skill which has resulted in many of the males being captured and trained to pick coconuts.

Much more elusive is the **Indochinese tiger**, which lives under constant threat from both poachers and the destruction of its habitat by logging interests, which together have reduced the current population to probably fewer than one hundred; for now Khao Yai and Khao Sok are the two likeliest places for sightings. The medium-sized arboreal **clouded leopard** is also on the endangered list, and is hard to spot anyway as it only comes out to feed on birds and monkeys under cover of darkness, rarely venturing out in moonlight, let alone daylight.

The shy, nocturnal **tapir**, an ungulate with three-toed hind legs and four-toed front ones, lives deep in the forest of peninsular Thailand but is occasionally spotted in daylight. A relative of both the horse and the rhino, it's the size of a pony, with a stubby trunk-like snout and distinctive two-tone colouring to confuse predators: its front half and all four legs are black, its rear half is white.

It's thought there are now as few as two thousand wild **elephants** left in Thailand: small-eared Asian elephants found mainly in Khao Yai and Khao Sok national parks (see page 759).

Birds

Because of its location at the zoogeographical crossroads of Southeast Asia, Thailand boasts a huge diversity of **bird** species. The forests of continental Thailand are home to many of the same birds that inhabit India, Myanmar and Indochina, while the mountains of the north share species with the Himalayas and Tibet, and the

THE GECKO

Whether you're staying on a beach, in a national park or in a town, chances are you'll be sharing your room with a few **geckos**. These pale green tropical lizards, which are harmless to humans and usually measure a cute four to ten centimetres in length, mostly appear at night, high up on walls and ceilings, where they feed on insects. Because the undersides of their flat toes are covered with hundreds of microscopic hairs that catch at the tiniest of irregularities, geckos are able to scale almost any surface, including glass, which is why you usually see them in strange, gravity-defying positions. The largest and most vociferous gecko is known as the **tokay** in Thai, named after the disconcertingly loud sound it makes. *Tokays* can grow to an alarming 35cm, but are welcomed by most householders, as they devour insects and mice; Thais also consider it auspicious if a baby is born within earshot of a crowing *tokay*.

peninsular forests are home to birds found also in Malaysia and Indonesia. Khao Yai and Khao Nor Chuchi are prime year-round sites for bird-spotting, and, during the dry season, Doi Inthanon is a good place for flycatchers and warblers, while Khao Sam Roi Yot and Thale Noi Waterbird Park are rewarding areas to see migrant waders and waterfowl. For exhaustive information on specific **bird-watching** locations throughout Thailand see ⓦthaibirding.com; for guided birding tours contact Thailand Bird Watching (ⓦthailandbirdwatching.com); bird-watching guidebooks are listed in Books (see page 781).

There are twelve species of **hornbill** in Thailand, all majestic with massive, powerful wings (the flapping of which can be heard over long distances) and huge beaks surmounted by bizarre horny casques. Khao Yai is one of the easiest places to spot the plain black-and-white **oriental pied hornbill** and the flashier **great hornbill**, whose monochromic body and head are broken up with jaunty splashes of yellow; the little islands of Ko Phayam and Ko Chang in Ranong province also have many resident oriental pied hornbills.

The shyness of the gorgeous **pitta** makes a sighting all the more rewarding. Usually seen hopping around on the floor of evergreen forests, especially in Doi Inthanon, Doi Suthep and Khao Yai, these plump little birds – varieties of which include the **rusty-naped**, the **blue** and the **eared** – have dazzling markings in iridescent reds, yellows, blues and blacks. The one pitta you might see outside a rainforest is the **blue-winged** pitta, which occasionally migrates to drier bamboo forests. Thailand is also home to the extremely rare **Gurney's pitta**, found only in Khlong Thom National Park, in Krabi province.

Members of the pheasant family can be just as shy as the pittas, and are similarly striking. The black-and-white-chevron-marked **silver pheasant** and the **green peafowl** are particularly fine birds, and the commonly seen **red jungle fowl** is the ancestor to all domestic chickens.

Thailand's **rice fields** attract a host of different birds including the various species of **munia**, a chubby relative of the finch, whose chunky, conical beak is ideally suited to cracking unripened rice seeds. **Egrets** and **herons** also frequent the fields, wading through the waterlogged furrows or perching on the backs of water buffaloes and pecking at cattle insects, while from November to April, thousands of **Asian open-billed storks** descend on agricultural land as well, building nests in sugar-palm trees and bamboos and feeding on pira snails.

Coastal areas also attract storks, egrets and herons, and Thale Noi Waterbird Park and the mud flats of Khao Sam Roi Yot are breeding grounds for the large, long-necked **purple heron**. The magnificent **white-bellied sea eagle** haunts the Thai coast, nesting in the forbidding crags around Krabi, Ao Phang Nga and Ko Tarutao and preying on fish and sea snakes. The tiny **edible nest swiftlet** makes its eponymous nest – the major ingredient of the luxury food, bird's-nest soup – in the limestone crags, too (see page 671).

Snakes

Thailand is home to around 175 different species and subspecies of **snake**, 56 of them dangerously venomous. Death by snakebite is not common, however, but all hospitals should keep a stock of serum, produced at the Snake Farm in Bangkok (see page 122).

Found everywhere and highly venomous, the 2m, nocturnal, yellow-and-black-striped **banded krait** is one to avoid, as is the shorter but equally venomous **Thai** or **monocled cobra**, which lurks in low-lying humid areas and close to human habitation and sports a distinctive "eye" mark on its hood. The other most widespread venomous snake is the 60cm **Malayan pit viper**, which has an unnerving ability to camouflage its pinky-brown and black-marked body. Non-venomous, but typically measuring an amazing 7.5m (maximum 10m) and with a top weight of 140kg, the **reticulated python** frequents human habitation all over Thailand and feeds on rats, pigs, cats and dogs, strangling them to death; it will do the same to humans if provoked.

Marine species

The Indian Ocean (Andaman Sea) and the South China Sea (Gulf of Thailand) together play host to over 850 species of open-water fish, more than one hundred species of reef fish and some 250 species of hard coral. Forty percent of Thailand's coral reef is protected within **national marine parks**, and these offer the best snorkelling and diving, particularly around Ko Similan, Ko Surin and Ko Tarutao (see page 53).

Coral

Coral reefs are living organisms composed of a huge variety of marine life forms, but the foundation of every reef is its ostensibly inanimate **stony coral** – hard constructions such as boulder, mushroom, bushy staghorn and brain coral. Stony coral is composed of colonies of polyps – minuscule invertebrates which feed on plankton, depend on algae and direct sunlight for photosynthesis, and extract calcium carbonate (limestone) from sea water in order to reproduce. The polyps use this calcium carbonate to build new skeletons outside their bodies (an asexual reproductive process known as budding), and this is how a reef is formed. It's an extraordinarily slow process, with colony growth averaging somewhere between 5mm and 30mm a year.

The fleshy plant-like **soft coral**, such as dead man's fingers and elephant's ear, generally establishes itself on and around these banks of stony coral, swaying with the currents and using tentacles to trap microorganisms. Soft coral is also composed of polyps, but a variety with flaccid internal skeletons built from protein rather than calcium. **Horny coral**, like sea whips and intricate sea fans, looks like a cross between the stony and the soft varieties, while **sea anemones** have the most obvious, and venomous, tentacles of any member of the coral family, using them to trap fish and other large prey.

Fish and turtles

The algae and plankton that accumulate around coral colonies attract a huge variety of **reef fish**. Most are small, with vibrant colours that serve as camouflage against the coral, and flattened bodies and broad tails for easy manoeuvring around the reef.

Among the most easily recognizable is the **emperor angel fish**, which boasts spectacular horizontal stripes in bright blue and orange, and an orange tail. The bizarrely shaped **moorish idol** trails a pennant fin from its dorsal fin and has a pronounced snout and dramatic black, yellow and white bands of colour; the ovoid **powder-blue surgeon fish** has a light blue body, a bright yellow dorsal fin and a white "chinstrap". The commonly spotted **long-nosed butterfly fish** is named for the butterfly-like movements of its yellow-banded silver body as it darts in and out of crevices looking for food. The bright orange **clown fish**, whose thick white stripes make it resemble a clown's ruff, is more properly known as the anemone fish because of its mutually protective relationship with the sea anemone, near which it can usually be sighted.

Some reef fish, among them the ubiquitous turquoise and purple **parrot fish**, eat coral. With the help of a bird-like beak, which is in fact several teeth fused together, the parrot fish scrapes away at the coral and then grinds the fragments down with another set of back teeth – a practice reputedly responsible for the erosion of a great deal of Thailand's reef. The magnificent mauve and burgundy **crown-of-thorns starfish**, named for its "arms" covered in highly venomous spines, also feeds on coral, laying waste to as much as fifty square centimetres of stony coral in a 24-hour period.

Larger, less frequent visitors to Thailand's offshore reefs include the **moray eel**, whose elongated jaws of viciously pointed teeth make it a deadly predator, and the similarly equipped **barracuda**, the world's fastest-swimming fish. **Sharks** are quite common off the reefs, where it's also sometimes possible to swim with a **manta ray**, whose extraordinary flatness, strange wing-like fins and massive size – up to 6m across and weighing some 1600kg – make it an astonishing presence. **Turtles** sometimes paddle around reef waters, too, but all four local species – leatherback, Olive Ridley, green and hawksbill – are fast becoming endangered in Thailand.

Environmental issues

Thailand's rapid economic growth has had a significant effect on its environment. Huge new infrastructure projects, an explosion in real-estate developments and the constantly expanding tourist industry have all played a part, and the effects of the subsequent **deforestation** and pollution have been felt nationwide. Such was the devastation caused by floods and mud slides in Surat Thani in 1988 that the government banned commercial logging the following year, though land continues to be denuded for other purposes. There is also the endemic problem of "influence" so that when a big shot wants to clear a previously pristine area for a new property development, for example, it is virtually impossible for a lowly provincial civil servant to reject their plan, or money.

Flooding has always been a feature of the Thai environment, crucial to the fertility of its soil, and its worst effects are obviated by the stilted design of the traditional Thai house. However, there is now an almost annual inundation in certain riverside town centres, and of roads and railways, particularly along the Gulf coast; 2011 saw especially severe floods, when towns in the Central Plains, including the World Heritage Site of Ayutthaya and many suburbs of Bangkok, were under metres of water for weeks on end. And in recent times, far more dangerous **flash floods** have recurred with depressing frequency, most dramatically around the northern town of Pai in 2005, where many homes and guesthouses were washed away. The link between deforestation and floods is disputed, though encroaching cement and tarmac on Thai flood plains surely play a part, as does the clogging of exit channels by garbage and other pollutants, and of course climate change.

Reefs and shorelines

A number of Thailand's **coral reefs** – some of which are thought to be around 450 million years old – are being destroyed by factors attributable to tourism, most significantly the pollution generated by coastal hotels with inadequate sewage systems. Longtail boats that anchor on reefs, souvenirs made from coral, and the use of harpoon guns by irresponsible dive leaders all have a cumulative effect, dwarfed however by the local practice of using dynamite to gather fish, including reef fish for sale to aquariums.

The 2004 **tsunami** also caused significant damage to coastal and marine environments the length of the Andaman coast. Reefs close to shore were crushed by debris (furniture, machinery, even cars) and buried under displaced soil; the sea was temporarily polluted by extensive damage to sewage systems; and tracts of shorefront farmland were rendered unusable by salt water. In 2010, a mass **coral bleaching** event occurred in all of the world's oceans, damaging especially shallow-water reefs in Thailand, such as Ko Surin's;

the event was caused by sudden, steep rises in sea temperatures, and has been interpreted as dramatic evidence of the effects of climate change.

National parks

Although Thailand has since the 1970s been protecting some of its natural resources within **national parks**, these have long been caught between commercial and conservationist aims, an issue which the government addressed in 2002 by establishing a new National Park, Wildlife and Plant Conservation Department (DNP; ⓦnps.dnp.go.th), separate from the Royal Forestry Department and its parent Ministry of Agriculture.

With 140 national parks and marine parks across the country, as well as various other protected zones, over thirteen percent of the country is now, in theory at least, protected from encroachment and hunting (a high proportion compared to other nations, such as Japan at 6.5 percent, and the US at 10.5 percent).

However, the **touristification** of certain national parks endures; Ko Phi Phi and Ko Samet in particular have both suffered irreversible environmental damage as a direct result of the number of overnight visitors they receive. While most people understand that the role of the national parks is to conserve vulnerable and precious resources, the dramatic hike in entrance fees payable by foreign visitors to national parks – from B20 up to B200 in 2000 and up again to B400 or B500 for a few special parks – was greeted with cynicism and anger, not least because there is often little sign of anything tangible being done on site with the money.

Elephant trekking and the wildlife trade

Despite the efforts of local and international conservation and wildlife-protection organizations, **animal rights** issues often meet with a confused response in Thailand. The muddled thinking behind the launch of the Chiang Mai Night Safari park was typical: not only was this commercial animal park erected on land appropriated from a national park, but early publicity trumpeted the fact that meat from many of the exotic animals kept in the park – including tigers, lions and elephants – would be available in the park's restaurant. Negative comment soon quashed that, but exotic meats from endangered animals are served, albeit clandestinely, all over Thailand.

Some of Thailand's many **zoos**, such as those in Bangkok and Chiang Mai, are legitimate, reasonably decent places, but a number of the country's other private

---

WILDLIFE CHARITIES AND VOLUNTEER PROJECTS

The Golden Triangle Asian Elephant Foundation Anantara Resort, Sop Ruak, Chiang Rai ⓦhelpingelephants.org. Elephant welfare is the primary concern at this well-regarded elephant camp, which offers elephant activities at local hotels. Profits support the foundation's elephant rescue centre. See page 368.

Elephant Nature Park Near Chiang Mai ⓦelephantnaturepark.org. Famous conservation-education centre and sanctuary for elephants that's open to pre-booked visitors, overnight guests and volunteers. See page 350.

Gibbon Rehabilitation Project Phuket ⓦgibbonproject.org. & ⓦwarthai.org. Resocializes abused pet gibbons before releasing them back into the forests. Visitors and volunteers welcome. See page 640.

Highland Farm Gibbon Sanctuary Near Mae Sot ⓦgibbonathighlandfarm.org. Day-trippers and serious, self-motivated long-term volunteers are welcome at this haven caring for injured and abandoned gibbons. See page 260.

Wild Animal Rescue Foundation of Thailand (WAR) ⓦwarthai.org. A campaigning organization that runs animal rescue sanctuaries, hospitals and research centres in various locations across Thailand and is open to unskilled paying volunteers.

wildlife theme parks and zoos – particularly those specializing in tigers and crocodiles – have more dubious purposes and some have been targeted by international animal welfare organizations such as Born Free.

There is also increasing concern about the **ethics of elephant trekking**, a fast-growing and lucrative arm of the tourist industry that some consider has got out of hand. What began as a canny way for elephants to earn their (very expensive) keep, after the 1989 ban on logging rendered most working elephants unemployed, is now endangering Southeast Asia's dwindling population of wild elephants as more and more are captured for the trekking trade (see page 314). Burmese elephants are particularly vulnerable and reportedly get smuggled across the border in significant numbers. In addition, welfare standards at these elephant trekking centres vary enormously. On the positive front, there's an increasing number of **animal sanctuaries** working to look after abused and endangered animals, especially elephants and gibbons (see page 759), which operate both as safe havens and as educational visitor attractions.

The wildlife trade

Though Thailand signed the Convention on the International Trade in Endangered Species – **CITES** – in 1983, and hosted the annual CITES conference in 2004, the trading of threatened animals and animal products continues.

Most of the trade in **endangered species** is focused along the borders with Cambodia and Myanmar, where Thai middle-merchants can apparently easily acquire any number of creatures. Some will be sold as pets and to zoos, while others are destined for dining tables and medicine cabinets. **Tiger** body-parts are especially lucrative and mostly end up on the black markets of China, Korea, Taiwan and Hong Kong, where bones, skin, teeth, whiskers and penis are prized for their "medicinal" properties; it's thought that much of Thailand's dwindling tiger population ends up this way. **Bear** paws and gall bladders are considered to have similar potency and are a star feature, along with other endangered species, at certain clandestine restaurants in Thailand catering to "gourmet" tourists from China and Korea; the traditional custom of slicing paws off a living bear and enhancing gall-bladder flavour by taking it from an animal that is literally scared to death make this practice particularly vile. The Burmese border market at Thachilek near Mae Sai is a notorious outlet for tiger and bear body-parts, while Chatuchak Weekend Market in Bangkok has long had a thriving trade in live animals – everything from hornbills to slow loris – despite occasional crackdowns.

Music

Music is an important part of Thai culture, whether related to Buddhist activities in the local temple (still a focal point for many communities), animist rituals, Brahmanic ceremonies or the wide range of popular song styles. While local forms of Thai popular music such as *luk thung* and *mor lam* remain very popular and distinctively Thai in character, a lively, ever-changing rock, indie, DJ/clubbing and underground scene is also fast developing.

The classical tradition

Thai classical dance and music can be traced back to stone engravings from the Sukhothai period (thirteenth to fifteenth centuries), which show ensembles of musicians playing traditional instruments, called **piphat**. The *piphat* ensembles include many percussion instruments, rather like Indonesian gamelan – gong circles, xylophones and drums – plus a raucous oboe called the *pinai*. The music was developed to accompany classical dance-drama (*khon* or *lakhon*) or shadow-puppet theatre (*nang*): a shadow-puppet show is depicted in the magnificent *Ramayana* murals at Wat Phra Kaeo in Bangkok's Grand Palace complex.

Piphat music sounds strange to Western ears as the seven equal notes of the Thai scale fall between the cracks of the piano keyboard. But heard in the right environment – in a temple, at a dance performance or at a Thai boxing match – it can be entrancing. As there is no notation, everything is memorized. And, as in all Thai music, elements have been assimilated over the years from diverse sources, and synthesized into something new. Check out any of the international albums by the Prasit Thawon Ensemble (Prasit was a National Artist).

Despite the country's rapid westernization, Thai classical music has been undergoing something of a revival in the past few years, partly as a result of royal patronage. There have been recent experiments, too, at blending Thai classical and Western styles – often jazz or rock – led by groups like **Kangsadan** and **Fong Naam**. **Boy Thai** followed their lead, albeit with a more pop-oriented sound, and had some mainstream success with two albums. One of the two *ranat* (xylophone) playing brothers from Boy Thai, Narongrit Tosa-nga, now has his own contemporary jazz band: **Khun-In Jazz of Siam**. The 2004 biopic *Homrong* (*The Overture*) features a character called Khun-In (played by Narongrit) who duels on the *ranat* against Thailand's greatest classical musician, Luang Pradit Phairoh.

There are dance and classical music **performances** in Bangkok at the Sala Chalermkrung Theatre, the National Theatre and the Thailand Cultural Centre (see page 164), and you may also come across some more lacklustre examples at the Erawan Shrine on Thanon Rama I and the *lak muang* shrine in front of the Grand Palace, where people give thanks to deities by paying for the temple musicians and dancers to go through a routine. A number of Bangkok restaurants also feature music and dance shows for tourists: look out for Bruce Gaston of Fong Naam at the *Tawandang German Brewery* (see page 162), and **Duriyapraneet**, the latter being the country's longest-established classical band.

Folk music

Thailand's folk music is called **phleng pheun bahn**, and different styles are found in the country's four distinct regions (central, north, northeast and south). Despite Thailand's rush to modernity, numerous folk styles are still enthusiastically played, from the hill-tribe New Year dances in the far north to the *saw* (a kind of three-stringed violin) and *fon lep* (fingernail dance) of Chiang Mai, from the all-night singing jousts of northeastern *lam klawn*, to the haunting Muslim vocals of *likay huuluu* in the deep south.

Most Thais are familiar with the exciting central folk styles like *lam tad*, *phleng choi* and *phleng I-saw*, which often feature raunchy verbal jousting between male and female singers. Styles like these and the ever-popular *mor lam* from the northeast (see page 765) are incorporated into modern popular styles such as *luk thung* (see page 764).

One notable folk style to have grown in popularity in recent years is the up-tempo and danceable northeastern instrumental style known as **pong lang** (a wooden xylophone that is attached vertically to a tree and was originally used to keep birds off crops). *Pong lang* is ancient, predating Indian–Thai culture, and was updated by National Artist Pleung Chairaasamee in the 1970s. A few years ago, **Pong-Lang Sa-Orn** emerged with an action-packed comedy show that propelled the band to national fame, million-selling albums and movies.

The best place to see *pong lang* is upcountry, especially in Kalasin province in central Isaan in the dry season between November and March. Folk music also features prominently at the major festivals (see page 47) held in the northeastern cities of Khon Kaen, Ubon Ratchathani and Udon Thani, particularly during Songkhran (April), the Bun Bang Fai rocket festival (May), and the Asanha Puja candle festival (July). Generally, any national holiday or religious festival is a good time to look out for folk music, in any region.

Popular styles

Thailand is the second-biggest Southeast Asian music market after Indonesia, and Bangkok is a major and increasingly important regional hub for pop music and popular culture.

Western orchestration for Thai melodies was introduced in the 1920s and 1930s and this led to the development of *phleng Thai sakon*, or "international Thai music", in the form of big band and swing, country and western, Hollywood film music, rock'n'roll, and so on. In the early days, two distinctive Thai genres developed: *phleng luk krung*, a romantic ballad form, popularized by Thailand's most beloved composer and bandleader Euah Sunthornsanan and his Suntharaporn band; and *phleng luk thung* (country music). **Luk krung**, with its clearly enunciated singing style and romantic fantasies, was long associated with the rich strata of Bangkok society (*krung* comes from Krung Thep, the Thai name for the capital); it's the kind of music that is played by state organs such as Radio Thailand. However, it was largely transformed during the 1960s by the popularity of Western stars like Cliff Richard; as musicians started to mimic the new Western music, a new term was coined, *wong shadow* (*wong* meaning group, *shadow* from the British group The Shadows).

String

The term **string** came into use as Thai-language pop music rapidly developed in the economic boom times of the 1980s. *String* encompasses ballads, rock and alternative, indie, disco, techno/house, J-Pop and K-Pop (Japan and Korea), heavy metal, reggae, ska, rap and underground; whatever trend is popular internationally is picked up and put into the Thai cultural blender. Currently popular are all things Korean – boy bands, girl bands, fashion styles and haircuts, teen TV shows, soap operas, food and comics.

Megastars such as veteran **Thongchai "Bird" Macintyre** generally record on either of the two major labels, GMM Grammy and RS. Grammy, which controls more than half the market, has an umbrella of labels that release everything from popster **Bie The Star** to *luk thung* star "Got" Chakrapand Arbkornburi. Their most famous Thai rock act of recent years, though, the talented brothers **Asanee and Wasan** (**Chotikul**), have now set up their own label, Music Union, to produce a new generation.

The Thai alternative rock scene developed in the mid-1990s with the emergence, on the then-indie Bakery label (now part of Sony Music Entertainment), of **Modern Dog**, whose last album *Ting Nong Noy* (2008) swept various Thai rock awards. Bakery helped kick-start indie rock and rap with the mercurial **Joey Boy**, who later moved to GMM Grammy. **Loso** developed into the most popular rock band, with leader **Sek Loso** enjoying a serious solo career and iconic status, but over the last few years his main starring role has been on the gossip pages because of his rehab and marital problems.

Recently, more Western and Asian musicians have joined their Thai counterparts – as with electro-clash band **Futon** (Thai–Japanese–Western). And no list of current Thai pop stars and rockers would be complete without mentioning **Ebola** (metal plus rap), **Bodyslam** (heavy rock), **Thaitanium** (hip-hop from US-raised Thais), **Tattoo Colour** (indie rock), **Cocktail** (soft rock) and singer-songwriters **Palmy** and **Stamp**.

Thailand, and in particular Bangkok, is developing its own musical identity, partly as a result of many high-profile **festivals**, such as the Pattaya Music Festival in March, which showcases Asian bands and Cat EXPO in Bangkok in November for indie bands, and partly because of the explosion of new genres and the emergence of a busy underground and **live scene**. You'll find Thai, foreign and mixed bands and DJs playing in Bangkok's many clubs and bars, and dynamic scenes in Chiang Mai, Khorat and Ko Samui.

Campuses such as Ramkhamhaeng University are good places to get information on upcoming **events**, as are radio stations (especially Cat Radio on ⓦthisiscat.com). Bangkok is the best place to catch gigs – check out ⓦbk.asia-city.com for listings.

Songs for Life and reggae

Another important genre is **phleng pheua chiwit**, or "**Songs for Life**", which started as a kind of progressive rock in the early 1970s, with bands like **Caravan** (no relation to the British songsters) blending *phleng pheun bahn* (folk songs) with Western folk and rock. Caravan were at the forefront of the left-wing campaign for democracy with songs like *Khon Kap Khwai* (*Human with Buffaloes*):

Greed eats our labour and divides people into classes
The rice farmers fall to the bottom
Insulted as backward and ignorant brutes
With one important and sure thing: death.

Although an elected government survived from 1973 to 1976, the military returned soon after, and Caravan, like many of the student activists, went into hiding in the jungle. There they performed to villagers and hill-tribe people and gave the occasional concert. When the government offered an amnesty in 1979, most of the students, and Caravan too, disillusioned with the Communist Party's support for the Khmer Rouge in Cambodia, returned to normal life.

In the 1980s a new group emerged to carry on Caravan's work, **Carabao**. The band split up in 1988 but has had many reunions and reincarnations since; their influence is still strong, with leader Ad Carabao still in the limelight but now more as a businessman hawking his "energy" drink, Carabao Daeng, via the band's gigs and nasty nationalistic TV ad campaigns. However, despite the bloody street riots of 1992 (in protest at the then military-installed government) once again bringing Songs for Life artists out to support the pro-democracy protests, since the 1980s the strong social activism of Caravan's early years has generally been replaced by more individual and personal themes. The current top act is fresh-faced singer-songwriter **Pongsit Kamphee**, whose earnest approach and rise through the ranks (he was reportedly once a stagehand for Caravan) have garnered him a sizeable following.

Musically, the genre has developed little over the years, remaining strongly rooted in Western folk-rock styles. Recently, however, this has begun to change as musicians have belatedly discovered that **reggae** riddims work well with Songs for Life vocals; perhaps they were inspired by **T-Bone**, for so long the only reggae band in the kingdom. Best of this new sub-genre is Southerner **Job** of the **Job 2 Do** band, while the best classic Marley-style reggae band is the **Srirajah Rockers**.

Songs for Life fans should check out CD stalls at Bangkok's Chatuchak Weekend Market, several of which specialize in this genre.

Luk thung

Go to one of the huge **luk thung** shows held in a temple or local stadium on the outskirts of Bangkok, or to any temple fair in the countryside, and you'll hear one of the great undiscovered popular musics of Asia. The shows, amid the bright lights, food stalls and fairground games, last several hours and involve dozens of dancers and costume changes. In contrast with *luk krung*, *luk thung* (literally, "child of the field") has always been associated with the rural and urban poor, and because of this has gained nationwide popularity over the past forty years.

According to *luk thung* DJ Jenpope Jobkrabuanwan, the term was first coined by Jamnong Rangsitkhun in 1964, but the first song in the style was *Oh Jao Sao Chao Rai* (Oh, the Vegetable Grower's Bride), recorded in 1937, and the genre's first big singer, **Kamrot Samboonanon**, emerged in the mid-1940s. Originally called *phleng talat* (market songs) or *phleng chiwit* (songs of life), the style blended together folk songs, central Thai classical music and Thai folk dances. Malay strings and fiddles were added in the 1950s, as were Latin brass and rhythms like the cha-cha-cha and mambo (Asian tours by Xavier Cugat influenced many Asian pop styles during the 1950s), as well as elements from Hollywood movie music and "yodelling" country and western vocal styles from the likes of Gene Autry and Hank Williams. In 1952, a new singer, **Suraphon Sombatjalern**, made his debut with a song entitled *Nam Ta Lao Wiang* (Tears of the Vientiane Girl) and became the undisputed king of the style until his untimely murder (for serious womanizing, rumour has it) in 1967. Suraphon helped develop the music into a mature form, and was known as the "King" of the genre, along with his Queen, sweet-voiced Pongsri Woranut.

Today, *luk thung* is a mix of Thai folk music and traditional entertainment forms like *likay* (travelling popular theatre), as well as a range of Western styles. There are certainly some strong musical affinities with other regional pop styles like Indonesian *dangdut* and Japanese *enka*, but what is distinctly Thai – quite apart from the spectacular live shows – are the singing styles and the content of the lyrics. Vocal styles are full of heavy ornamentation (*luk khor*) and sustained notes (*auen* or "note-bending"). A singer must have a wide vocal range, as the late *luk thung* megastar **Pumpuang Duangjan** explained: "Making the *luk thung* sound is difficult, you must handle the high and low notes well. And because the emotional content is stronger than in *luk krung*, you must also be able to create a strongly charged atmosphere."

Pumpuang had the kind of voice that turns the spine to jelly. She rose to prominence during the late 1970s, joining **Sayan Sanya** as the biggest male and female names in the business. Like Suraphon Sombatjalern, both came from the rural peasantry, making identification with themes and stories that related directly to the audience much easier. Songs narrate mini-novellas, based around typical characters like the lorry driver, peasant lad or girl, poor farmer, prostitute or maid; and the themes are those of going away to the big city, infidelity, grief, tragedy and sexual pleasure. Interestingly, it is not always the lyrics that carry the sexual charge of the song (and if lyrics are deemed too risqué by the authorities the song will be subject to strict censorship) but rather the vocal style and the stage presentation, which can be very bawdy indeed.

With the advent of TV and the rise in popularity of *string*, the number of large upcountry *luk thung* shows has declined. It's not easy, said Pumpuang, to tour with over a hundred staff, including the dancers in the *hang kruang* (chorus). "We play for over four hours, but *string* bands, with only a few staff members, play a paltry two hours!" Her response to the advent of *string* and the increasing importance of promotional videos was to develop a dance-floor-oriented sound – **electronic luk thung** (**Grand X** had already experimented with *luk thung* and disco a few years earlier). Few *luk thung* singers are capable of this, but Pumpuang had the vocal range to tackle both ballad forms and the up-tempo dance numbers. Her musical diversification increased her popularity enormously, and when she died in 1992, aged only 31, up to 200,000 people, ranging from royalty to the rural poor, made their way to her funeral in her home town of Suphanburi (look out for the major biopic, *Pumpuang*, made in 2011).

Pumpuang's death pushed ongoing political problems (the 1992 coup) off the front pages of newspapers, a situation that was repeated in 2008 when **Yodrak Salakjai** died. Yodrak was the most recorded *luk thung* star of all time, with some three thousand songs and five hundred albums to his credit.

After Pumpuang's death, the top *luk thung* slot was occupied by "**Got**" **Chakrapand Arbkornburi**, whose switch from pop to full-time *luk thung* brought many younger listeners to the style, while the reigning female singer was **Sunaree Ratchasima**, but she has been superseded by the perkier **Arpaporn Nakornsawan** and, more recently, by Ying Lee and Tai Orathai. **Mike Piromporn**, originally a *mor lam* man, became Got's main challenger, but both now have to give way to Phai Phongsathon. Bangkok's first 24-hour *luk thung* radio station, Luk Thung FM (now Rak Thai FM, at 90 FM), was launched in 1997, and it's even cool for the middle class to like *luk thung* these days. There is some truth, however, in the criticism that some new *luk thung* stars are being artificially manufactured just like their pop and rock counterparts, and there's a tendency to rate a pretty face over vocal expertise.

For many years, *luk thung* was sung by performers from the Suphanburi area in the central plains, but more regional voices are being heard in the genre now, with northeasterners now outnumbering these singers. A slightly faster rhythm, *luk thung Isaan*, has been developed, initially by "**Khru**" (**Teacher**) **Saleh Kunavudh** in the 1980s. The south, too, has its own *luk thung* star, in the enormously popular **Ekachai Srivichai**.

As well as at temple fairs, fairs at district offices in provincial capitals, national holiday events and New Year celebrations are the best places to catch *luk thung* shows.

Mor lam

Mor lam is the folk style from the poor, dry northeastern region of Isaan, an area famed for droughts, spicy food, good boxers and great music. Over the past 25 years, the modern pop form of this style has risen dramatically. Traditionally, a *mor lam* is a master of the *lam* singing style (sung in the Isaan dialect, which is actually Lao), and is accompanied by the *khaen* (bamboo mouth organ), the *phin* (two- to four-string guitar) and *ching* (small temple cymbals). Modern **mor lam** developed from *mor lam klawn*, a narrative form where all-night singing jousts are held between male and female singers, and from *mor lam soeng*, the group-dance form. Both still play an important part in many social events like weddings, births and deaths, festivals and temple fairs. A *mor lam* may sing intricate fixed-metre Lao epic poems or may relate current affairs in a spontaneous rap. In the large groups, Western instruments like guitar (replacing the *phin*) and synthesizer (for the *khaen*) are used.

The style came to national prominence more than thirty years ago, when a female *mor lam* singer, **Banyen Rakgan**, appeared on national TV. In the early 1980s the music was heard not only in Isaan but also in the growing slums of Bangkok, as rural migrants poured into the capital in search of work. By the end of the decade, stars like **Jintara Poonlarp** (with her hit song *Isaan Woman Far From Home*) and **Pornsak Songsaeng** could command the same sell-out concerts as their *luk thung* counterparts. Jintara remains one of the biggest stars, and her shows mix both *luk thung* and *lam*; **Siriporn Ampaiporn**, whose strong vocals burst upon the *lam* scene with the monster-selling *Bor Rak Si Dam* album, mainly records *luk thung* these days.

The format of a *mor lam* **performance** is similar to that of *luk thung* shows – lots of dancers in wild costumes, comedy skits and a large backing orchestra – as is the subject matter. The music is definitely hot, especially if you see it live, when bands will often play through the night, never missing the groove for a minute, driven on by the relentless *phin* and *khaen* playing. To some people, the fast plucking style of the *phin* gives a West African or Celtic tinge; the *khaen* has a rich sound – over a bass drone players improvise around the melody, while at the same time vamping the basic rhythm. Male and female singers rotate or duet humorous love songs, which often start with one of the *mor khaen* setting up the beat. They sing about topical issues, bits of news, crack lewd jokes or make fun of the audience – all very tongue-in-cheek.

Musically, however, *mor lam* and *luk thung* are very different; *mor lam* has a much faster, relentless rhythm and the vocal delivery is rapid-fire, rather like a rap. You'll immediately recognize a *mor lam* song with its introductory wailing moan "*Oh la naw*", meaning "fortune". *Mor lam* artists, brought up bilingually, can easily switch from *luk thung* to *mor lam*, but *luk thung* artists, who often only speak the national central Thai dialect, cannot branch out so easily.

In the 1990s, *mor lam* musicians headed off the challenge of increasingly popular *string* bands by creating **mor lam sing**, a turbo-charged modern version of *mor lam klawn* played by small electric combos. The number of large touring *luk thung* or *mor lam* shows has declined in recent years, owing to high overheads, TV entertainment and the popularity of *string* bands, so *mor lam sing* satisfies the need for local music with a modern edge.

Mor lam sing was followed quickly by a more rock-oriented *mor lam* sound (this is a little similar to Grand X in the 1980s, which played a mix of rock and *luk thung*), led by funky little combos like **Rocksadert** and **Rock Saleang**, actually much better live than on recordings, although the latter had a hilarious hit in 2006 with *Motorcy Hoy*. Mor lam got a shot in the arm in 2012 with the formation of The Paradise Bangkok Molam International Band by DJs Chris Menist and Maft Sai of Zudrungma Records (see below), who also play percussion. Fronted by veteran khaen and phin players, the band has gone on to play at Glastonbury and other international festivals.

Kantrum: Thai–Cambodian pop

"Isaan *neua* (north) has *mor lam*, Isaan *tai* (south) has *kantrum*," sings **Darkie**, the first star of **kantrum**, Thai–Cambodian pop, in his song *Isaan Tai Samakkhi* (Southern Isaan Unity). His music is a very specific offshoot, from the southern part of Isaan, where Thai–Cambodians mix with ethnic Lao and Thais. So far *kantrum* is only popular in Isaan in Thailand but it has spread over the border to nearby Cambodian towns like Siem Reap where the style is known as Khmer Ler or Khmer Surin.

Modern *kantrum* has developed from Cambodian folk and classical music, played in a small group consisting of fiddle, small hand-drums and *khrab* (pieces of hardwood bashed together rather like claves). This traditional style is now quite hard to find in Thailand; thirty years ago, musicians started to electrify the music, using both traditional and Western instruments. Shunning the synthesizer preferred by his competitors such as **Khong Khoi**, Oh-Yot and Samanchai, Darkie added the wailing fiddle centre-stage and cranked up the rhythms (*kantrum* has a harder beat than even *mor lam*). In 1997, he broke new ground with *Darkie Rock II: Buk Jah*, the first *kantrum* crossover album to have success in the mainstream pop market. Sadly, in 2001, Darkie died aged 35, but a new generation of *kantrum* stars emerged, led by **Songsaeng Lungluangchai**, who has recorded several excellent albums of Darkie covers.

Discography

In Bangkok, ask the vendors at the day and night markets about **CDs**, or the stores on Thanon Charoen Krung (New Road) or at Saturday evening's Klong Thom market (in the small sois behind Thanon Charoen Krung, between Plaplachai and

Mahachak intersections). Most major *luk thung* or *mor lam* artists release an album every three months, which is often given an artist's series number. Old-style recordings of Suraphon Sombatjalern and the like can be found on through Mae Mai Pleng Thai (⑩maemaiplengthai.com), while DJ Siam, nearby on Soi 7, Siam Square, is good for Thai indie and pop (⑩facebook.com/djsiambangkok.com). Look out for the intriguingly diverse output of Zudrangma Records (⑩zudrangmarecords.com): they've released compilations of old *luk thung* and *mor lam* on their own label, and it's well worth browsing their record store, next door to *WTF* (see page 162), just off Soi 51, Thanon Sukhumvit; they have also opened a nearby bar, Studio Lam, and run awesome club nights, where you might find *mor lam* mixed with Jamaican dancehall.

In addition, several **DVDs** are well worth seeking out: Jeremy Marre's episode on music in Thailand, *Two Faces of Thailand: A Musical Portrait* (Shanachie, US), from his award-winning *Beats of the Heart* music-TV documentary series; *Homrong* (see page 761); and *Mon Rak Transistor* (see page 768).

CLASSICAL

Fong Naam *The Hang Hong Suite.* A good introduction to the vivacious and glittering sound of classical Thai music, this CD includes some upbeat funeral music and parodies of the musical languages of neighbouring cultures. *The Sleeping Angel* is also a splendid recording.

Lai Muang Ensemble *The Spirit of Lanna: Music from the North of Thailand.* Top-quality recording, featuring multi-instrumentalist Somboon Kawichai on the *peejum* (bamboo pipes) and the eerie-sounding *pin pia*, a chest-resonated oboe.

The Prasit Thawon Ensemble *Thai Classical Music.* Brilliant playing (and outstanding recording quality) from some of Thailand's best performers, mainly of *piphat* style. Includes the overture *Homrong Sornthong* and, on *Cherd Chin*, some scintillating dialogues between different instruments.

FOLK MUSIC

David Fanshawe *Music From Thailand and Laos: Southeast Asia Recordings.* Excellent range of folk music from different regions of both countries.

Various *Sea Gypsies of the Andaman Sea.* The traditional music of nomadic Moken (*chao ley*) fisherfolk in southern Thailand, mostly recorded in the Surin islands.

Various *Thailand: Musiques et Chants des Peuples du Triangle d'Or.* Recordings of the traditional music of Thailand's main hill-tribe groups by the French label, Globe Music: Hmong, Lisu, Lahu, Yao, Akha and Karen, as well as Shan (Thai Yai).

THAI SAKON

Euah Sunthornsanan *Chabab Derm* ("Old Songs") Vols 1–5, 6–10. Modern Thai music was popularized by the late master Euah. Some of the most popular Thai songs ever were performed by the Suntharaporn band and a bevy of singers.

STRING AND SONGS FOR LIFE

Carabao *Made in Thailand* and *Ameri-koi.* Two classic albums from the Songs for Life giants. *Made in Thailand* was right in tune with the times and targeted social problems like consumerism, the sex trade and a failing education system. *Ameri-koi* (*Greedy America*) is even more nationalistic than the previous one, but it also hits out at Thai migrant workers exploited by labour brokers.

Futon *Never Mind the Botox.* Electro-clash with a punk attitude from the kingdom's favourite underground band.

Excellent cover of Iggy Pop's *I Wanna Be Your Dog.*

Loso/Sek Loso The best compilation of Loso's music is the 2001 release *The Red* album, while the solo work of Sek Loso is best captured on the same year's *Black & White* and live on *10 Years Rock Volumes 1 & 2.*

Modern Dog *Modern Dog.* This album of alternative rock marked an important change of direction for the Thai rock scene. Also see albums *Love Me Love My Life, That Song* and their most recent, *Ting Nong Noy.*

LUK THUNG

If you can't find any of the albums below, go for a compilation of past albums, usually under a title like *Ruam Hits* (*Mixed Hits*).

"Got" Chakrapand Arbkornburi *12 Years of Grammy Gold.* Packed with slow ballads, this is one for the ladies from *luk thung*'s heartthrob.

Pumpuang Duangjan In Thailand, the best of many albums to go for is *Pumpuang Lai Por Sor* ("Pumpuang's Many Eras"). Her early spine-tingling hits can be found on several compilations from Bangkok Cassette (Mae Mai Pleng

Thai), some recorded when she was known as Nampung Petsupan (Honey Diamond from Suphanburi).

Sayan Sanya *Sayan Tao Thong* ("Sayan Golden Star"). Classic 1970s *luk thung* featuring the "honey-voiced" master. As Yodrak said, "Women cry when he [Sayan] sings."

Suraphon Sombatjalern *Ruam Phleng* ("Mixed Songs") Vols 1–4. Greatest hits by the king of *luk thung*. Great voice, great songs, great backing – Siamese soul.

Various *Mon Rak Transistor* ("A Transistor Love Story"). From the hit movie about a young country boy who tries to make it in the big city as a *luk thung* singer. Includes Suraphon's wonderful theme song, *Mai Leum* ("Don't Forget").

Various *The Rough Guide to the Music of Thailand*. Good review of *mor lam* and *luk thung*, despite confusing liner notes, elephants, and the odd pop group.

MOR LAM/NORTHEASTERN MUSIC

Chalard Songserm *Rhythms of I-Sarn Vols 1 & 2*. Top-quality album from National Artist Chalard, *khaen* maestro Sombat Simlao and a band of great musicians, covering many styles of Lao music in the region. Sombat's train-sounding *khaen* solo is a standout.

Isan Slété *Songs and Music from North East Thailand*. Excellent selection of traditional *mor lam*. Vocal and instrumental numbers, played by a band of master musicians.

Jintara Poonlarp *Ruam Hit 19 Pii Tawng Chut*. Nineteen years at the top on two killer volumes. Vol. 1 features haunting *mor lam*.

Various *Instrumental Music of Northeast Thailand*. Wonderful Japanese collection of *pong lang* and related instrumental northeastern styles. Lively and fun.

Various *The Paradise Bangkok Molam International Band 21st Century Molam & Planet Lam*. Rousing albums from 2014 and 2016, featuring Kammao Perdtanon on the lute-like *phin* and Sawai Kaewsombat on the *khaen* pipes.

Various, featuring Chaweewan Damnoen *Mor Lam Singing of Northeast Thailand*. Female *mor lam* National Artist, Chaweewan, headlines this fine Japanese collection of many *lam* styles. Most *mor lam klawn* narrative and dance styles, even spirit-possession rituals, are included.

KANTRUM

Darkie *Darkie, Rock II: Buk Jah*. The first-ever *kantrum* crossover album achieved nation-wide stardom for the King of Kantrum. Darkie's booming voice moves from rap-like delivery to moans and wails, shadowed closely by the fiddle

and some funky riddims. Unmissable.

Songsaeng Lungluangchai *Songsaeng Kantrum Rock: Chut Ta Don Duay*. Keyboardless, rootsy sound. Look out for his tribute album to Darkie, *Kantrum Rock*.

John Clewley (Adapted from *The Rough Guide to World Music*)

The hill tribes

Originating in various parts of China and Southeast Asia, the hill tribes are sometimes termed Fourth World people, in that they are migrants who continue to migrate without regard for established national boundaries. Most arrived in Thailand during the last century, and many of the hill peoples are still found in other parts of Southeast Asia – in Vietnam, for example, where the French used the *montagnards* ("mountain dwellers") in their fight against communism. Since 1975, a large percentage of the one million refugees that Thailand has accepted from Myanmar, Laos and Cambodia has been hill-tribe people. Some, however, have been around for much longer, like the Lawa, who are thought to have been the first settlers in northern Thailand, though these days they have largely been assimilated into mainstream Thai culture.

Called **chao khao** (mountain people) by the Thais, the tribes are mostly pre-literate societies, whose sophisticated systems of customs, laws and beliefs aim to harmonize relationships between individuals and their environment. In recent years their ancient culture has come under threat, faced with the effects of population growth and the ensuing competition for land, discrimination and exploitation by lowland Thais, and tourism. However, the integrity of their way of life is as yet largely undamaged, and what follows is the briefest of introductions to an immensely complex subject. If you want to learn more, visit the Highland People Discovery Museum in Chiang Mai (see page 282) or the Hill Tribe Museum in Chiang Rai (see page 355) before setting out on a trek.

Agriculture

Although the hill tribes keep some livestock, such as pigs, poultry and elephants, the base of their economy is **swidden agriculture** (slash-and-burn), a crude form of shifting cultivation also practised by many Thai lowland farmers. At the beginning of the season an area of jungle is cleared and burned, producing ash to fertilize rice, corn, chillies and other vegetables, which are replanted in succeeding years until the soil's nutrients are exhausted. This system is sustainable with a low population density, which allows the jungle time to recover before it is used again. However, with the increase in population over recent decades, ever greater areas are being exhausted, and the decreasing forest cover is leading to erosion and microclimatic change.

As a result, many villages took up the large-scale production of **opium** to supplement the traditional subsistence crops, though the Thai government has now largely eradicated opium production in the north. However, the cash crops which have been introduced in its place have often led to further environmental damage, as these low-profit crops require larger areas of cultivation, and thus greater deforestation. Furthermore, the water supplies have become polluted with chemical pesticides, and although more environmentally sensitive agricultural techniques are being introduced, they have yet to achieve widespread acceptance.

Religion and festivals

Although some tribes have taken up Buddhism and others – especially among the Karen, Mien and Lahu – have been converted by Christian missionaries bringing the incentives of education and modern medicine, the hill tribes are predominantly **animists**. In this belief system, all natural objects are inhabited by spirits which, along with the tribe's ancestor spirits and the supreme divine spirit, must be propitiated to prevent harm to the family or village. Most villages have one or more religious leaders, which may include a priest who looks after the ritual life of the community, and at least one shaman who has the power to mediate with the spirits and prescribe what has to be done to keep them happy. If a member of the community is sick, for example, the shaman will be consulted to determine what action has insulted which spirit, and will then carry out the correct sacrifice.

The most important festival, celebrated by all the tribes, is at **New Year**, when whole communities take part in dancing, music and rituals particular to each tribe: Hmong boys and girls, for instance, take part in a courting ritual at this time, while playing catch with a ball. The New Year festivals are not held on fixed dates, but at various times during the cool-season slack period in the agricultural cycle from January to March.

Costumes and handicrafts

The most conspicuous characteristics of the hill tribes are their exquisitely crafted **costumes** and adornments, the styles and colours of which are particular to each group. Although many men and children now adopt Western clothes for everyday wear, with boys in particular more often running around in long shorts and T-shirts with logos, many women and girls still wear the traditional attire. It's the women who make the clothes too – some still spin their own cotton, though many Hmong, Lisu and Mien women are prosperous enough to buy materials from itinerant traders. Other distinctive hill-tribe artefacts – tools, jewellery, weapons and musical instruments – are the domain of the men, and specialist **blacksmiths** and **silversmiths** have such high status that some attract business from villages many kilometres away. Jewellery, the chief outward proof of a family's wealth, is displayed most obviously by Lisu women at the New Year festivals, and is commonly made from silver melted down from Indian and Burmese coins, though brass, copper and aluminium are also used.

Clothing and **handicrafts** were not regarded as marketable products until the early 1980s, when cooperatives were set up to manufacture and market these goods, which are now big business in the shops of Thailand. The hill tribes' deep-dyed coarse cloth, embroidered with simple geometric patterns in bright colours, has become popular among middle-class Thais as well as farang visitors. Mien material, dyed indigo or black with bright snowflake embroidery, is on sale in many shops, as is the simple but very distinctive Akha work – coarse black cotton, with triangular patterns of stitching and small fabric patches in rainbow colours, usually made up into bags and hats. The Hmong's much more sophisticated **embroidery** and **appliqué**, added to jacket lapels and cuffs and skirt hems, is also widely seen.

Besides clothing, the hill tribes' other handicrafts, such as knives and wooden or bamboo musical pipes, have found a market among farangs, the most saleable product being the intricate engraving work of their silversmiths, especially in the form of chunky bracelets. For a sizeable minority of villages, handicrafts now provide the security of a steady income to supplement what they make from farming.

The main tribes

Within the small geographical area of northern Thailand there are at least ten different hill tribes, many of them divided into distinct subgroups – the following are the main seven, listed in order of population and under their own names, rather than the sometimes derogatory names used by Thais. Beyond the broad similarities outlined above, this section sketches their differences in terms of history, economy and religion, and describes elements of dress by which they can be distinguished.

Karen

The **Karen** (called Kaliang or Yang in Thai) form by far the largest hill-tribe group in Thailand with a population of about 500,000, and are the second oldest after the Lawa, having begun to arrive here from Burma and China in the seventeenth century. The Thai Karen, many of them refugees from Burma (see box, page 261), mostly live in a broad tract of land west of Chiang Mai, which stretches along the border from Mae Hong Son province all the way down to Kanchanaburi, with scattered pockets in Chiang Mai, Chiang Rai and Phayao provinces.

The Karen traditionally practise a system of **rotating cultivation** – ecologically far more sensitive than slash-and-burn – in the valleys of this region and on low hills. Their houses, very similar to those of lowland Thais, are small (they do not live in extended family groups), built on stilts and made of bamboo or teak; they're often surrounded by fruit gardens and neat fences. As well as farming their own land, the Karen often hire out their labour to Thais and other hill tribes, and keep a variety of livestock including elephants, which used to be employed in the teak trade but are now often found giving rides to trekking parties.

Unmarried Karen women wear loose white or undyed V-necked shift dresses, often decorated with grass seeds at the seams. Some subgroups decorate them more elaborately, Sgaw girls with a woven red or pink band above the waist, and Pwo girls with woven red patterns in the lower half of the shift. Married women wear blouses and skirts in bold colours, predominantly red or blue. Men generally wear blue, baggy trousers with red or blue shirts, a simplified version of the women's blouse.

Hmong

Called the Meo ("barbarians") by the Thais, the **Hmong** ("free people") originated in central China or Mongolia and are now found widely in northern Thailand. There are two subgroups: the **Blue Hmong**, who live around and to the west of Chiang Mai; and the **White Hmong**, who are found to the east. Their overall population in Thailand is about 110,000, making them the second-largest hill-tribe group.

Of all the hill tribes, the Hmong have been the quickest to move away from subsistence farming. In the past, Hmong people were more involved in opium production than most other tribes in Thailand, though now many have eagerly embraced the newer cash crops. Hmong clothing has become much in demand in Thailand, and Hmong women will often be seen at markets throughout the country selling their handicrafts. The women, in fact, are expected to do most of the work on the land and in the home.

Hmong **villages** are usually built at high altitudes, below the crest of a protecting hill. Although wealthier families sometimes build the more comfortable Thai-style houses, most stick to the traditional house, with its dirt floor and a roof descending almost to ground level. They live together in extended families, with two or more bedrooms and a large guest platform.

The Blue Hmong dress in especially striking **clothes**. The women wear intricately embroidered pleated skirts decorated with parallel horizontal bands of red, pink, blue and white; their jackets are of black satin, with wide orange and yellow embroidered cuffs and lapels. White Hmong women wear black baggy trousers and simple jackets with blue cuffs. Men of both groups generally wear baggy black trousers with colourful sashes round the waist, and embroidered jackets closing over the chest with a button at the left shoulder. All the Hmong are famous for their chunky **silver jewellery**, which the women wear every day, the men only on special occasions: they believe silver binds a person's spirits together, and wear a heavy neck-ring to keep the spirits weighed down in the body.

Lahu

The **Lahu**, who originated in the Tibetan highlands, migrated to southern China, Burma and Laos centuries ago; only since the end of the nineteenth century did they begin to come into Thailand from northern Burma. They're called Muser – from the Burmese word for "hunter" – by the Thais, because many of the first Lahu to reach northern Thailand were professional hunters. With a population of about 80,000, they are the third-largest hill-tribe group: most of their settlements are concentrated close to the Burmese border, in Chiang Rai, northern Chiang Mai and Mae Hong Son provinces, but families and villages change locations frequently. The Lahu language has become a *lingua franca* among the hill tribes, since the Lahu often hire out their labour. About one-third of Lahu have been converted to Christianity (through exposure in colonial Burma), and many have abandoned their traditional way of life as a result. The remaining animist Lahu believe in a village guardian spirit, who is often worshipped at a central temple that is surrounded by banners and streamers of white and yellow flags. Village houses are built on high stilts with walls of bamboo or wooden planks, thatched with grass. While subsistence farming is still common, sustainable agriculture – plantations of orchards, tea or coffee – is becoming more prevalent, and cash crops such as corn and cotton have taken the place of opium.

Some Lahu women wear a distinctive black cloak with diagonal white stripes, decorated in bold red and yellow at the top of the sleeve, but traditional costume has been supplanted by the Thai shirt and sarong among many Lahu groups. The tribe is famous for its richly embroidered **yaam** (shoulder bags), which are widely available in Chiang Mai.

Akha

The poorest of the hill tribes, the **Akha** (Kaw or Eekaw in Thai) migrated from Tibet over two thousand years ago to Yunnan in China, where at some stage they had an organized state and kept written chronicles of their history – these chronicles, like the Akha written language, are now lost. From the 1910s the tribe began to settle in Thailand and is found in four provinces – Chiang Rai, Chiang Mai, Lampang and Phrae – with a population of nearly 50,000 in about 250 villages. A large Akha population still lives in Yunnan and there are communities in neighbouring Laos as well as in Myanmar.

The Akha are less open to change than the other hill tribes, and have maintained their old agricultural methods of **shifting cultivation**. The Akha's form of animism – *Akhazang*, "the way of life of the Akha" – has also survived in uncompromised form. As well as spirits in the natural world, *Akhazang* encompasses the worship of ancestor spirits: some Akha can recite the names of over sixty generations of forebears.

Every Akha village is entered through ceremonial **gates** decorated with carvings depicting human activities and attributes – even cars and aeroplanes – to indicate to the spirit world that beyond here only humans should pass. To touch any of these carvings, or to show any lack of respect to them, is punishable by fines or sacrifices. The gates are rebuilt every year, so many villages have a series of gates, the older ones in a state of disintegration. Another characteristic of Akha villages is a giant **swing** (also replaced each year), and used every August or early September in a swinging festival.

Akha **houses** are recognizable by their low stilts and steeply pitched roofs, though some may use higher stilts to reflect higher status. Even more distinctive is the elaborate **headgear** which women wear all day; it frames the entire face and usually features white beads interspersed with silver coins, topped with plumes of red taffeta and framed by dangling, hollow silver balls and other jewellery or strings of beads. The rest of their heavy costume is made up of decorated tube-shaped ankle-to-knee leggings, an above-the-knee black skirt with a white beaded centrepiece, and a loose-fitting black jacket with heavily embroidered cuffs and lapels.

Mien

The **Mien** (called Yao in Thai) consider themselves the aristocrats of the hill tribes. Originating in central China, they began migrating southward more than two thousand years ago to southern China, Vietnam, Laos and Thailand. In Thailand today the Mien are widely scattered throughout the north, with concentrations around Nan, Phayao and Chiang Rai, and a population of about 40,000. They are the only hill tribe to have a written language, and a codified religion based on medieval Chinese Taoism, although in recent years there have been many Mien converts to Christianity and Buddhism. In general, the Mien strike a balance between integration into Thai life and maintenance of their separate cultural base. Many earn extra cash by selling exquisite embroidery and religious scrolls, painted in bold Chinese style.

Mien villages are not especially distinctive: their houses are usually built of wooden planks on a dirt floor, with a guest platform of bamboo in the communal living area. The **clothes** of the women, however, are instantly recognizable: long black jackets with glamorous-looking stole-like lapels of bright scarlet wool, heavily embroidered loose trousers in intricate designs which can take up to two years to complete, and a similarly embroidered black turban. The caps of babies are also very beautiful, richly embroidered with red or pink pom-poms. On special occasions, like weddings, women and children wear silver neck-rings, with silver chains decorated with silver ornaments extending down the back, and even their turbans are crossed with lengths of silver. A Mien woman's wedding headdress is quite extraordinary, a carefully constructed platform with arched supports that are covered with red fabric and heirlooms of embroidered cloth. Two burgundy-coloured fringes create side curtains obscuring her face, and the only concession to modernity is the black insulating tape that holds the structure to her head.

Lisu

The **Lisu** (Lisaw in Thai), who originated in eastern Tibet, first arrived in Thailand in 1921 and are found mostly in the west, particularly between Chiang Mai and Mae Hong Son, but also in western Chiang Rai, Chiang Mai and Phayao provinces, with a population of around 30,000. Whereas the other hill tribes are led by the village headman or shaman, the Lisu are organized into patriarchal clans which have authority over many villages, and their strong sense of clan rivalry often results in public violence.

The Lisu live in extended families at moderate to high altitudes, in houses built on the ground, with dirt floors and bamboo walls. Both men and women dress colourfully; the women wear a blue or green parti-coloured knee-length tunic, split up the sides to the waist, with a wide black belt and blue or green pants. At New Year, the women don dazzling outfits, including waistcoats and belts of intricately fashioned silver and turbans with multi-coloured pom-poms and streamers; traditionally, the men wear green, pink or yellow baggy trousers and a blue jacket.

Lawa

The history of the **Lawa** people (Lua in Thai) is poorly understood, but it seems very likely that they have inhabited Thailand since at least the eighth century; they were certainly here when the Thais arrived around eight hundred years ago. The Lawa people are found only in Thailand; they believe that they migrated from Cambodia and linguistically they are certainly closely related to Mon-Khmer, but some archeologists think that their origins lie in Micronesia, which they left perhaps two thousand years back.

This lengthy cohabitation with the Thais has produced large-scale integration, so that most Lawa villages are indistinguishable from Thai settlements and most Lawa speak Thai as their first language. However, in an area of about 500 square kilometres between Hot, Mae Sariang and Mae Hong Son, the Lawa still live a largely traditional life, although even here the majority have adopted Buddhism and Thai-style houses. The basis of their economy is subsistence agriculture, with rice grown on terraces according to a sophisticated rotation system. Those identified as Lawa number just over ten thousand.

Unmarried Lawa women wear distinctive strings of orange and yellow beads, loose white blouses edged with pink, and tight skirts in parallel bands of blue, black, yellow and pink. After marriage, these brightly coloured clothes are replaced with a long fawn dress, but the beads are still worn. All the women wear their hair tied in a turban, and the men wear light-coloured baggy pants and tunics or, more commonly, Western clothes.

Film

Until recently, Thai cinema was almost impenetrable to the outside world. But the West began to take notice in 2000, when films such as *Iron Ladies*, *Tears of the Black Tiger* and later *The Legend of Suriyothai* showed that Thai directors had the style and wit to entertain non-Thai-speaking audiences. Many larger-budget Thai films are now released outside Thailand and with English subtitles.

A brief history

Thailand's first **cinema** was built in 1905 in Bangkok, behind Wat Tuk on Thanon Charoen Krung, and for a couple of decades screened only short, silent films from America, Europe and Japan. Though nothing remains of the earliest film-theatres, the renovated Art Deco Sala Chalermkrung, which was built in 1933 in Bangkok's Chinatown, is still in use today as a venue for live theatre and the occasional screening.

The **first home-grown film**, *Chok Sawng Chan* (*Double Luck*), made by the Wasuwat brothers of the Bangkok Film Company, didn't emerge until 1927, and it was another five years before *Long Thang* (*Going Astray*), the first Thai film with sound, followed.

During the 1920s, a few foreign film companies came to Thailand to film the local culture and wildlife. One early classic from this period is *Chang* (1927; available on video), which tells the simple story, in documentary style, of a family who live on the edge of the forest in Nan province. *Chang's* American directors Merian Cooper and Ernest B. Schoedsack later drew on their experiences in the Thai jungle for their 1933 classic, *King Kong*.

Though Thai film-making continued throughout the 1930s and 1940s, it was virtually suspended during World War II, before re-emerging with a flourish in the 1950s. The 1950s, 1960s and 1970s were golden years for the production of large numbers of hastily made but hugely popular low-budget escapist films, mainly action melodramas featuring stereotypical characters, gangsters and corny love interest. Many of these films starred **Mitr Chaibancha**, Thailand's greatest-ever film star. He played the handsome hero in 265

POSTERS AND BILLBOARDS

Until the 1990s, domestic and foreign films were always promoted in Thailand with **original Thai artwork**, especially commissioned to hang as billboards and to be reproduced on posters. The artists who produced them really poured their hearts into these images, interpreting the film in their own style and always including an extraordinary amount of detail, usually as montage. Unlike the films themselves, Thai film posters were rarely subject to any censorship and as a result they were often far more eye-catchingly graphic and explicit than Western artwork for the same films. Posters for horror films (always very big in Thailand) depicted particularly gruesome, blood-drenched images, while ads for the (illegal) screenings of soft-porn movies often displayed a surprising amount of naked flesh.

Locally produced posters are still used to advertise films in Thailand, but for over a decade now they have featured photographic images instead of original artwork. However, there's still a chance to admire the exuberant creativity of Thai cinema art because many provincial cinemas continue to employ local artists to produce their own **billboard** paintings every week. Look for these giant works of art above cinema doors, at key locations around town, and on the sides of the megaphone trucks that circulate around town screeching out the times and plot lines of the next show. Within seven days they will have been dismantled, reduced to a pile of planks and painted over with the artwork for next week's film.

REVIEWS AND MORE

For reviews and archive stories on all aspects of Thai cinema, see ⓦ thaicinema.org, the website of leading Thai film critic Anchalee Chaiworaporn, or Wise Kwai's Thai Film Journal (ⓦ thaifilmjournal.blogspot.com).

films, in many of them performing opposite former beauty queen **Petchara Chaowarat**. Of the 165 movies they made together, their most famous was *Mon Rak Luk Thung* (*Enchanting Countryside*, 1969), a folk-musical about life and love in the countryside that played continuously in Bangkok for six months and later spawned a bestselling soundtrack album. Every Thai adult of a certain age can recall the days when Mitr co-starred with Petchara, and when Mitr fell to a dramatic death in 1970 – during a stunt involving a rope ladder suspended from a helicopter – it caused nationwide mourning. He was cremated at Wat Thepsirin in Bangkok (off Thanon Luang in Chinatown), where photos of the cremation ceremony and the crowds of fans who attended are still on display. Though non-Thai speakers are denied the pleasure of seeing Mitr and Petchara in action, you can get a good idea of the general tone of their films from the 2000 hit *Tears of the Black Tiger* (see page 777), which affectionately parodies the films of this period.

The 1970s and 1980s

For many years after Mitr's death, Thai cinema continued to be dominated by action melodramas, though a notable exception was *Khao Cheu Karn* (*His Name is Karn*), the first Thai film to tackle corruption in the civil service – it was released in 1973, not long before mass student demonstrations led to the ousting of the military government, and was made by Chatri Chalerm Yukol, who went on to direct the 2001 epic *The Legend of Suriyothai* (see page 777). The other standout film of the 1970s is *Phlae Khao* (*The Old Scar*, 1977), in which director Cherd Songsri uses traditional rural Thailand as a potent setting for a tragic romance that ends with the heroine's death.

With competition from television and large numbers of imported Hollywood films, Thai film production dwindled during the 1980s, but in 1984 the **Thai National Film Archive** was set up to preserve not only Thai films but also many of the wonderful posters used to promote them. A rare gem from the 1980s is Yuttana Mukdasanit's coming-of-age drama *Butterflies and Flowers* (*Pee Sua Lae Dok Mai,* 1986), which is set in a Muslim community in southern Thailand and looks at the pressures on a poor teenager who ends up smuggling rice across the nearby Malaysian border. The film won an award at the Hawaii International Film Festival.

By the 1990s, the Thai film industry was in a rather sorry state and the few films still produced were mainly trite melodramas aimed at an undiscerning teenage audience. But everything started to change for the better in 1997.

Modern Thai cinema

The rebirth of the Thai film industry started in 1997 with the release of Pen-Ek Ratanaruang's *Fun Bar Karaoke* and Nonzee Nimibutr's *Daeng Bireley and the Young Gangsters*. Fuelled by a **new wave** of talented directors and writers, including Nonzee and Pen-Ek, this resurgence has seen Thai films benefiting from larger budgets and achieving international acclaim. The new breed of Thai film-makers has moved away from traditional action melodramas and soap operas to create films that are more imaginative and stylish. With a new emphasis on production values, they also look very good, yet it is the fresh, distinctly Thai flavour that most charms Western audiences, a style summed up by one Thai film commentator as "neo-unrealist", and by another as being influenced by the popular *likay* genre of bawdy, over-the-top Thai street-theatre, where actors use song and dance as well as speech to tell their story.

Directors of the new wave

Daeng Bireley and the Young Gangsters (*2499 Antaphan Krong Muang*) was the surprise hit of 1997; **Nonzee Nimibutr** showed in this story of 1950s gangsters that he was able to appeal to the international festival circuit as well as local cinema-goers. He followed it up with the even more successful *Nang Nak* in 1999, giving the big-budget treatment to a traditional nineteenth-century Thai ghost story about a woman who dies while in labour, along with her unborn child. In *Jan Dara* (2001), the 1930s story of a young man who despises his womanizing stepfather, yet eventually becomes just such a person, Nonzee pushed the envelope of what was acceptable in Thai cinema by including scenes of rape and lesbianism that would not have been permitted a decade earlier. *Queens of Langkasuka* (*Puen Yai Jom Salad*, 2008) saw him turning to the more conservative genre of historical action fantasy, complete with sumptuous costumes, pirates, sea gypsies and sorcerers, while his latest, *Distortion* (2012), is a psycho-thriller, full of stylized gore.

In a wry tale of messages received from beyond the grave, **Pen-Ek Ratanaruang**'s first film *Fun Bar Karaoke* (1997) looked at how the lives of modern middle-class Thais are still affected by traditional superstitions. His next film *6ixtynin9* (*Ruang Talok 69*, 1999) was a fast-paced thriller set during the Asian financial crisis, with a down-on-her-luck woman stumbling upon a hoard of money. Pen-Ek followed this with *Mon Rak Transistor: A Transistor Love Story* (2003), a bitter-sweet love story about a naïve boy from the country with ambitions to be a *luk thung* singer. It's full of charm and the popular soundtrack is available on CD (see page 768). Pen-Ek's *Last Life in the Universe* (2003) is a much darker, more melancholy affair, following two very different personalities – a suicidal Japanese man and a Thai girl – who are brought together in grief. In *Ploy* (2007), a jet-lagged night in a Bangkok hotel sees the marriage of an expat Thai couple unravel, with sex scenes deemed too explicit by Thai censors. Pen-Ek's latest fiction, *Headshot* (*Fon Tok Kheun Faa*, literally "Rain Falling up to the Sky"; 2011), which tells of a hitman who wakes up from a coma seeing the world upside down, is a noirish thriller with a satirical political edge. He followed this up with a controversial documentary on Thailand's recent political history, *Paradoxocracy* (*Prachathipathai*; 2013).

The scriptwriter on Nonzee's *Daeng Bireley* and *Nang Nak* was Wisit Sasanatieng, who, in 2000, directed **Tears of the Black Tiger** (*Fah Talai Jone*). This gentle send-up of the old Thai action films of the 1960s and 1970s uses exaggerated acting styles and irresistible comic-book colours to tell the story of handsome bandit Dum and his love for upper-class Rumpoey. Writer-director Wisit grew up watching the spaghetti westerns of Sergio Leone and includes more than a few passing references to those films. His **Citizen Dog** (*Mah Nakorn*, 2004) is an even more surreal colour-saturated satire, both comic and pointed, about a country boy looking for work and romance in Bangkok.

Blockbusters at home and abroad

Among other high-profile international successes, the warm and off-beat comedy **Iron Ladies** (*Satri Lek*, 2000) charts the often hilarious true-life adventures of a Lampang volleyball team made up of transsexuals and transvestites. **Beautiful Boxer** (2003) fashions a sensitive, insightful biopic out of a similar subject – the true story of transvestite *muay thai* champion Nong Toom who fights in order to win money for sex-change surgery. **Bangkok Dangerous** (*Krung Thep Antharai*, 2000) is a riveting John Woo-style thriller directed by brothers Oxide and Danny Pang; both a brutal tale about a deaf hitman and the story of his love affair with a girl innocent of his occupation, it features several scenes shot in the streets of Bangkok.

The visually stunning historical blockbuster **The Legend of Suriyothai** (2001) tells the true story of a sixteenth-century queen of the Ayutthayan court who gave her life defending her husband during a Burmese invasion. Keen to give international appeal to this complex portrait of court intrigue and rather partisan take on Thai-Burmese relations, director Chatrichalerm Yukol brought in Francis Ford Coppola to edit a shortened version for Western audiences. He followed it with the most expensive Thai film to date, at a reported cost of B700 million, **The Legend of King Naresuan** (*Tamnan Somdej Phra Naresuan*, 2007), telling the story of King Naresuan, a national hero who ruled Thailand from Ayutthaya in the sixteenth century. Capturing a strong nationalist and royalist mood in certain sections of Thai society, the film was turned into a series, with the sixth and final episode coming out in 2015, followed by two (and counting) separate TV series, by the same director about the same subject. Garnering the bizarre "P" rating in the new Thai film classification system (meaning that a film has to be promoted, and all Thais are encouraged to watch it, because of its supposed cultural merit), the third and fourth episodes in the series were the two top-grossing films of 2011. The series was shot at the purpose-built Prommitr Film Studios just outside Kanchanaburi, whose period sets are now open to the public.

Prachya Pinkaew's martial arts action flick **Ong Bak** (2003) was such a huge box-office hit around the world that its star **Tony Jaa** – who performed all his own extraordinary stunts – was appointed Cultural Ambassador for Thailand. Director and star teamed up again in the similarly testosterone-fuelled **Tom Yum Goong** (2005), in which Tony Jaa's fight skills lead him to Australia on the trail of a stolen elephant. Two prequels to *Ong Bak* have been made up to now, and one sequel to *Tom Yum Goong*.

At the other end of the spectrum, Thai art house also went international with the success of **Apichatpong Weerasethakul**'s challenging **Tropical Malady** (*Sud Pralad*, 2004), which won the Jury Prize at Cannes in 2004. Part gay romance, part trippy jungle ghost story, it was for some a pioneering experiment in Thai storytelling, to others an inaccessible bore. His *Syndromes and a Century* (*Sang Sattawat*, 2006) was Thailand's first film to be entered in competition at the Venice Film Festival but failed to impress the Thai censors who, among other reasons, banned it for its depiction of a guitar-playing Buddhist monk. Apichatpong responded by joining a protest against the introduction of a new, reactionary film-ratings system, but to no avail. His *Uncle Boonmee (who can Recall his Past Lives)*, a dreamy, quasi-realist exploration of Thai belief in *phii* (spirits), won the Palme d'Or at Cannes in 2010 but achieved only a limited release back in Thailand, while 2015's Cemetery of Splendour presents a mysterious epidemic of sleeping sickness among a group of soldiers as a metaphor for the ills of Thai society. Other experimental directors to look out for include **Thanska Pansittivorakul**, **Kongdej Jaturanrasamee** and **Thanwarin Sukhaphisit**.

Neil Pettigrew

Books

We have included publishers' details for books that may be hard to find outside Thailand, though some of them can be ordered online through ⑩dcothai.com, which sells e-books on ⑩ebooks.dco.co.th. Other titles should be available worldwide. Titles marked ★ are particularly recommended. There's a good selection of Thai novels and short stories in translation, available to buy as e-books, on ⑩thaifiction.com.

TRAVELOGUES

Carl Bock *Temples and Elephants* (Orchid Press, Bangkok). Nineteenth-century account of a rough journey from Bangkok to the far north, dotted with vivid descriptions of rural life and court ceremonial.

Karen Connelly *Touch the Dragon*. Evocative and humorous journal of an impressionable Canadian teenager, sent on an exchange programme to Den Chai in northern Thailand for a year.

Charles Nicholl *Borderlines*. Entertaining adventures and dangerous romance in the "Golden Triangle" form the core of this slightly hackneyed traveller's tale, interwoven with stimulating and well-informed cultural diversions.

James O'Reilly and Larry Habegger (eds) *Travelers'* *Tales: Thailand*. Absorbing anthology of contemporary writings about Thailand, by Thailand experts, social commentators, travel writers and first-time visitors.

Steve Van Beek *Slithering South* (Wind and Water, Hong Kong). An expat writer tells how he single-handedly paddled his wooden boat down the entire 1100km course of the Chao Phraya River, and reveals a side of Thailand that's rarely written about in English.

Tom Vater *Beyond the Pancake Trench: Road Tales from the Wild East*. Adventures, insights and encounters on the margins of twenty-first-century Thailand. Also covers Cambodia, Laos, Vietnam and India.

CULTURE AND SOCIETY

Michael Carrithers *The Buddha: A Very Short Introduction*. Accessible account of the life of the Buddha, and the development and significance of his thought.

★ **Philip Cornwel-Smith and John Goss** *Very Thai*. Why do Thais decant their soft drinks into plastic bags, and how does one sniff-kiss? Answers and insights aplenty in this intriguingly observant, fully illustrated guide to contemporary Thai culture. In a similar vein is *Very Bangkok*.

James Eckardt *Bangkok People*. The collected articles of a renowned expat journalist, whose encounters with a varied cast of Bangkokians – from construction-site workers and street vendors to boxers and political candidates – add texture and context to the city.

Sandra Gregory with Michael Tierney *Forget You Had a Daughter: Doing Time in the "Bangkok Hilton" – Sandra Gregory's Story*. The frank and shocking account of a young British woman's term in Bangkok's notorious Lard Yao prison after being caught trying to smuggle 89g of heroin out of Thailand.

Roger Jones *Culture Smart! Thailand*. Handy little primer on Thailand's social and cultural mores, with plenty of refreshingly up-to-date insights.

★ **Erich Krauss** *Wave of Destruction: One Thai Village and Its Battle with the Tsunami*. A sad and often shocking, clear-eyed account of what Ban Nam Khem went through before, during and after the tsunami. Fills in many gaps left unanswered by news reports at the time.

Elaine and Paul Lewis *Peoples of the Golden Triangle*. Hefty, exhaustive work illustrated with excellent photographs, describing every aspect of hill-tribe life.

Father Joe Maier *Welcome to the Bangkok Slaughterhouse: The Battle for Human Dignity in Bangkok's Bleakest Slums* and *The Open Gate of Mercy*. Catholic priest Father Joe shares the stories of some of the Bangkok street kids and slum-dwellers that his charitable foundation has been supporting since 1972 (see page 59).

Trilok Chandra Majupuria *Erawan Shrine and Brahma Worship in Thailand* (Tecpress, Bangkok). The most concise introduction to the complexities of Thai religion, with a much wider scope than the title implies.

Cleo Odzer *Patpong Sisters*. An American anthropologist's funny and touching account of her life with the prostitutes and bar girls of Bangkok's notorious red-light district.

★ **Phra Peter Pannapadipo** *Little Angels: The Real-Life Stories of Twelve Thai Novice Monks*. A dozen young boys, many of them from desperate backgrounds, tell the often poignant stories of why they became novice monks. For some, funding from the Students Education Trust (see page 59) has changed their lives.

Phra Peter Pannapadipo *Phra Farang: An English Monk in Thailand*. Behind the scenes in a Thai monastery: the frank, funny and illuminating account of a UK-born former businessman's life as a Thai monk.

★ **Pasuk Phongpaichit and Sungsidh Piriyarangsan** *Corruption and Democracy in Thailand*. Fascinating academic study, revealing the nuts and bolts of corruption in Thailand and its links with all levels of political life, and suggesting a route to a stronger society. Their sequel, a study of Thailand's illegal economy, *Guns, Girls, Gambling, Ganja*, co-written with Nualnoi Treerat, makes equally eye-opening and depressing reading.

Denis Segaller *Thai Ways*. Fascinating collection of short pieces on Thai customs and traditions written by a long-term English resident of Bangkok.

Pira Sudham *People of Esarn*. Wry and touching, potted life stories of villagers who live in, leave and return to the poverty-stricken northeast, compiled by a northeastern lad turned author.

Phil Thornton *Restless Souls: Rebels, Refugees, Medics and Misfits on the Thai–Burma Border*. An Australian journalist brings to light the terrible and complicated plight of the Karen, thousands of whom live as refugees in and around his adopted town of Mae Sot on the Thai–Myanmar border.

Richard Totman *The Third Sex: Kathoey – Thailand's Ladyboys*. As several *kathoey* share their life stories with him, social scientist Totman examines their place in modern Thai society and explores the theory, supported by Buddhist philosophy, that *kathoey* are members of a third sex whose transgendered make-up is predetermined from birth.

Tom Vater and Aroon Thaewchatturat *Sacred Skin*. Fascinating, beautifully photographed exploration of Thailand's spirit tattoos, *sak yant*.

William Warren *Living in Thailand*. Luscious gallery of traditional houses, with an emphasis on the homes of Thailand's rich and famous; seductively photographed by Luca Invernizzi Tettoni.

Daniel Ziv and Guy Sharett *Bangkok Inside Out*. This A–Z of Bangkok quirks and cultural substrates is full of slick photography and sparky observations but was deemed offensive by Thailand's Ministry of Culture, so some Thai bookshops won't stock it.

HISTORY

Anna Leonowens *The English Governess at the Siamese Court*. The mendacious memoirs of the nineteenth-century English governess that inspired the infamous Yul Brynner film *The King and I*; low on accuracy, high on inside-palace gossip.

Chang Noi *Jungle Book: Thailand's Politics, Moral Panic and Plunder 1996–2008* (Silkworm Books, Chiang Mai). A fascinating, often humorous, selection of columns about Thailand's political and social jungle, by "Little Elephant", an anonymous foreign resident, which first appeared in *The Nation* newspaper.

Michael Smithies *Old Bangkok*. Brief, anecdotal history of the capital's early development, emphasizing what remains to be seen of bygone Bangkok.

John Stewart *To the River Kwai: Two Journeys – 1943, 1979*. A survivor of the horrific World War II POW camps along the River Kwai returns to the region, interlacing his wartime reminiscences with observations on how he feels 36 years later.

William Warren *Jim Thompson: the Legendary American of Thailand*. The engrossing biography of the ex-intelligence agent, art collector and Thai silk magnate whose disappearance in Malaysia in 1967 has never been satisfactorily resolved.

Thongchai Winichakul *Siam Mapped*. Intriguing, seminal account of how Rama V, under pressure on his borders from Britain and France at the turn of the twentieth century, in effect colonized his own country, which was then a loose hierarchy of city-states.

★ **David K. Wyatt** *Thailand: A Short History*. An excellent treatment, scholarly but highly readable, with a good eye for witty, telling details. Good chapters on the story of the Thais before they reached what's now Thailand, and on more recent developments. The same author's *Siam in Mind* (Silkworm Books, Chiang Mai) is a wide-ranging and intriguing collection of sketches and short reflections that point towards an intellectual history of Thailand.

ART, ARCHITECTURE AND FILM

Jean Boisselier *The Heritage of Thai Sculpture*. Expensive but accessible, seminal tome by influential French art historian.

★ **Susan Conway** *Thai Textiles*. A fascinating, richly illustrated work which draws on sculptures and temple murals to trace the evolution of Thai weaving techniques and costume styles, and to examine the functional and ceremonial uses of textiles.

★ **Sumet Jumsai** *Naga: Cultural Origins in Siam and the West Pacific*. Wide-ranging discussion of water symbols in Thailand and other parts of Asia, offering a stimulating mix of art, architecture, mythology and cosmology.

Bastian Meiresonne (ed) *Thai Cinema* (⚙asiexpo.com). Anthology of twenty short essays on Thai cinema up to 2006, published to accompany a film festival in France, including pieces on art house, shorts and censorship. In French and English.

Steven Pettifor *Flavours: Thai Contemporary Art*. Takes up the baton from Poshyananda (see below) to look at the newly invigorated art scene in Thailand from 1992 to 2004, with profiles of 23 leading lights, including painters, multimedia and performance artists.

★ **Apinan Poshyananda** *Modern Art In Thailand*. Excellent introduction which extends up to the early 1990s, with very readable discussions on dozens of individual artists, and lots of colour plates.

Dome Sukwong and Sawasdi Suwannapak *A Century of Thai Cinema*. Full-colour history of the Thai film industry and the promotional artwork (billboards, posters, magazines and cigarette cards) associated with it.

★ **Steve Van Beek** *The Arts of Thailand*. Lavishly produced and perfectly pitched introduction to the history of Thai architecture, sculpture and painting, with superb photographs by Luca Invernizzi Tettoni.

William Warren and Luca Invernizzi Tettoni *Arts and Crafts of Thailand*. Good-value large-format paper-back, setting the wealth of Thai arts and crafts in cultural context, with plenty of attractive illustrations and colour photographs.

NATURAL HISTORY AND ECOLOGY

Ashley J. Boyd and Collin Piprell *Diving in Thailand*. A thorough guide to 84 dive sites, plus general introductory sections on Thailand's marine life, conservation and photography tips.

★ **Boonsong Lekagul and Philip D. Round** *Guide to the Birds of Thailand*. Unparalleled illustrated guide to Thailand's birds. Worth scouring secondhand sellers for.

Craig Robson *A Field Guide to the Birds of Thailand*. Expert and beautifully illustrated guide to Thailand's top. bird species, with locator maps.

Eric Valli and Diane Summers *The Shadow Hunters*. Beautifully photographed photo-essay on the bird's-nest collectors of southern Thailand, with whom the authors spent over a year, together scaling the phenomenal heights of the sheer limestone walls.

LITERATURE

Alastair Dingwall (ed) *Traveller's Literary Companion: Southeast Asia*. A useful though rather dry reference, with a large section on Thailand, including a book list, well-chosen extracts, biographical details of authors and other literary notes.

M.L. Manich Jumsai *Thai Ramayana* (Chalermnit, Bangkok). Slightly stilted, abridged prose translation of King Rama I's version of the epic Hindu narrative, full of gleeful descriptions of bizarre mythological characters and supernatural battles. Essential reading for a full appreciation of Thai painting, carving and classical dance.

★ **Chart Korbjitti** *The Judgement* (Howling Books). Sobering modern-day tragedy about a good-hearted Thai villager who is ostracized by his hypocritical neighbours. Contains lots of interesting details on village life and traditions, and thought-provoking passages on the stifling conservatism of rural communities. Winner of the S.E.A. Write Award in 1982.

★ **Rattawut Lapcharoensap** *Sightseeing*. This outstanding debut collection of short stories by a young Thai-born author now living overseas highlights big, pertinent themes – cruelty, corruption, racism, pride – in its neighbourhood tales of randy teenagers, bullyboys, a child's friendship with a Cambodian refugee, a young man who uses family influence to dodge the draft.

Nitaya Masavisut (ed) *The S.E.A. Write Anthology of Thai Short Stories and Poems* (Silkworm Books, Chiang Mai). Interesting medley of short stories and poems by Thai writers who have won Southeast Asian Writers' Awards, providing a good introduction to the contemporary literary scene.

Kukrit Pramoj *Si Phaendin: Four Reigns* (Silkworm Books, Chiang Mai). A kind of historical romance spanning the four reigns of Ramas V to VIII (1892–1946). Written by former prime minister Kukrit Pramoj, the story has become a modern classic in Thailand, made into films, plays and TV dramas, with heroine Ploi as the archetypal feminine role model.

S.P. Somtow *Jasmine Nights*. An engaging and humorous rites-of-passage tale, of an upper-class boy learning what it is to be Thai. *Dragon's Fin Soup and Other Modern Siamese Fables* is an imaginative and entertaining collection of often supernatural short stories, focusing on the collision of East and West.

★ **Khamsing Srinawk** *The Politician and Other Stories*. A collection of brilliantly satiric short stories, full of pithy moral observation and biting irony, which capture the vulnerability of peasant farmers in the north and northeast, as they try to come to grips with the modern world. Written by an insider from a peasant family, who was educated at Chulalongkorn University, became a hero of the left, and joined the communist insurgents after the 1976 clampdown.

Atsiri Thammachoat *Of Time and Tide* (Thai Modern Classics). Set in a fishing village near Hua Hin, this poetically written novella looks at how Thailand's fishing industry is changing, charting the effects on its fisherfolk and their communities.

Klaus Wenk *Thai Literature – An Introduction* (White Lotus, Bangkok). Dry, but useful, short overview of the last seven hundred years by a noted German scholar, with plenty of extracts.

THAILAND IN FOREIGN LITERATURE

Dean Barrett *Kingdom of Make-Believe*. Despite the clichéd ingredients – the Patpong go-go bar scene, opium smuggling in the Golden Triangle, Vietnam veterans – this novel about a return to Thailand following a twenty-year absence turns out to be a rewardingly multi-dimensional take on the farang experience.

★ **Mischa Berlinski** *Fieldwork*. Anthropology versus evangelism, a battle played out over an imaginary hill tribe in the hills of Chiang Rai by a fascinating cast of characters, as wrily and vividly told by its narrator.

Botan *Letters from Thailand*. Probably the best introduction to the Chinese community in Bangkok, presented in the form of letters written over a twenty-year period by a Chinese emigrant to his mother. Branded as both anti-Chinese and anti-Thai, this 1969 prize-winning book is now mandatory reading in school social studies' classes.

Pierre Boulle *The Bridge Over the River Kwai*. The World War II novel that inspired the David Lean movie and kicked off the Kanchanaburi tourist industry.

John Burdett *Bangkok 8*. Riveting Bangkok thriller that takes in Buddhism, plastic surgery, police corruption, the *yaa baa* drugs trade, hookers, jade smuggling and the spirit world.

Alex Garland *The Beach*. Gripping cult thriller (later made into a film, shot partly on Ko Phi Phi Leh) that uses a Thai setting to explore the way in which travellers' ceaseless quest for "undiscovered" utopias inevitably leads to them despoiling the idyll.

Andrew Hicks *Thai Girl*. A British backpacker falls for a reticent young beach masseuse on Ko Samet but struggles with age-old cross-cultural confusion in this sensitive attempt at a different kind of expat novel.

Michel Houellebecq *Platform*. Sex tourism in Thailand provides the nucleus of this brilliantly provocative (some would say offensive) novel, in which Houellebecq presents a ferocious critique of Western decadence and cultural colonialism, and of radical Islam too.

Christopher G. Moore *God of Darkness*. Thailand's best-selling expat novelist sets his most intriguing thriller during the economic crisis of 1997 and includes plenty of meat on endemic corruption and the desperate struggle for power within family and society.

Darin Strauss *Chang & Eng*. An intriguing, imagined autobiography of the famous nineteenth-century Siamese twins (see page 183), from their impoverished Thai childhood via the freak shows of New York and London to married life in small-town North Carolina. Unfortunately marred by lazy research and a confused grasp of Thai geography and culture.

FOOD AND COOKERY

Vatcharin Bhumichitr *The Taste of Thailand*. Another glossy introduction to this eminently photogenic country, this time through its food. The author runs a Thai restaurant in London and provides background colour as well as about 150 recipes adapted for Western kitchens.

Jacqueline M. Piper *Fruits of South-East Asia*. An exploration of the bounteous fruits of the region, tracing their role in cooking, medicine, handicrafts and rituals. Well illustrated with photos, watercolours and early botanical drawings.

★ **David Thompson** *Thai Food* and *Thai Street Food*. Comprehensive, impeccably researched celebrations of the cuisine with hundreds of recipes, by the owner of the first Thai restaurant ever to earn a Michelin star.

TRAVEL GUIDES

Oliver Hargreave *Exploring Phuket & Phi Phi: From Tin to Tourism*. Fascinating, thoroughly researched guide to the Andaman coast's big touristic honeypots; especially good on Phuket's history.

★ **Thom Henley** *Krabi: Caught in the Spell – A Guide to Thailand's Enchanted Province* (Thai Nature Education, Phuket). Highly readable features and observations on the attractions and people of south Thailand's most beautiful region, written by an expat environmentalist.

Dawn F. Rooney *Ancient Sukhothai*. Lively and beautifully photographed full-colour guide to the ruins of the northern plains: Sukhothai, Si Satchanalai and Kamphaeng Phet.

William Warren *Bangkok*. An engaging portrait of the unwieldy capital, weaving together anecdotes and character sketches from Bangkok's past and present.

Language

Thai belongs to one of the oldest families of languages in the world, Austro-Thai, and is radically different from most of the other tongues of Southeast Asia. Being tonal, Thai is very difficult for Westerners to master, but by building up from a small core of set phrases, you should soon have enough to get by. Most Thais who deal with tourists speak some English, but once you stray off the beaten track you'll probably need at least a little Thai. Anywhere you go, you'll impress and get better treatment if you at least make an effort to speak a few words.

Distinct dialects are spoken in the north, the northeast and the south, which can increase the difficulty of comprehending what's said to you. **Thai script** is even more of a problem to Westerners, with 44 consonants and 32 vowels. However, street signs in touristed areas are nearly always written in Roman script as well as Thai, and in other circumstances you're better off asking than trying to unscramble the swirling mess of letters and accents. For more information on transliteration into Roman script, see the box in this book's introduction.

Paiboon Publishing's (ⓦ paiboonpublishing.com) *Thai-English, English-Thai Dictionary* (also available as an app) lists words in phonetic Thai as well as Thai script, with audio recordings for each word.

The best **teach-yourself course** is the expensive *Linguaphone Thai* (including eight CDs and an alphabet book), which also has a shorter, cheaper beginner-level *PDQ* version (with four CDs or available as a downloadable coursebook and audio files). *Thai for Beginners* by Benjawan Poomsan Becker (book with CDs or app; Paiboon Publishing) is a cheaper, more manageable textbook and is especially good for getting to grips with the Thai writing system. For a more traditional textbook, try Stuart Campbell and Chuan Shaweevongse's *The Fundamentals of the Thai Language*, which is comprehensive, though hard going. The **website** ⓦ thai-language.com is an amazing free resource, featuring a searchable dictionary with over seventy thousand entries, complete with Thai script and audio clips, plus lessons and forums; you can also browse and buy Thai language books and learning materials. There are also plenty of **language classes** available in Thailand (see page 70).

Pronunciation

Mastering **tones** is probably the most difficult part of learning Thai. Five different tones are used – low, middle, high, falling, and rising – by which the meaning of a single syllable can be altered in five different ways. Thus, using four of the five tones, you can make a sentence from just one syllable: "mái mài mâi maˇi" meaning "New wood burns, doesn't it?" As well as the natural difficulty in becoming attuned to speaking and listening to these different tones, Western efforts are complicated by our habit of denoting the overall meaning of a sentence by modulating our tones – for example, turning a statement into a question through a shift of stress and tone. Listen to native Thai speakers and you'll soon begin to pick up the different approach to tone.

The pitch of each tone is gauged in relation to your vocal range when speaking, but they should all lie within a narrow band, separated by gaps just big enough to differentiate them. The **low tones** (syllables marked `) **middle tones** (unmarked syllables), and **high tones** (syllables marked ´) should each be pronounced evenly and with no inflection. The **falling tone** (syllables marked ^) is spoken with an obvious drop in pitch, as if you were sharply emphasizing a word in English. The **rising tone** (marked ˇ) is pronounced as if you were asking an exaggerated question in English.

As well as the unfamiliar tones, you'll find that, despite the best efforts of the transliterators, there is no precise English equivalent to many **vowel and consonant sounds** in the Thai language. The lists below give a simplified idea of pronunciation.

VOWELS

a as in dad	**eu** as in sir, but heavily nasalized
aa has no precise equivalent, but is pronounced as it looks, with the vowel elongated	**i** as in tip
	ii as in feet
ae as in there	**o** as in knock
ai as in buy	**oe** as in hurt, but more closed
ao as in now	**oh** as in toe
aw as in awe	**u** as in loot
ay as in pay	**uu** as in pool
e as in pen	

CONSONANTS

r as in rip, but with the tongue flapped quickly against the palate – in everyday speech, it's often pronounced like "l"	**th** as in time
	k is unaspirated and unvoiced, and closer to "g"
	p is also unaspirated and unvoiced, and closer to "b"
kh as in keep	**t** is also unaspirated and unvoiced, and closer to "d"
ph as in put	

GENERAL WORDS AND PHRASES

GREETINGS AND BASIC PHRASES

When you speak to a stranger in Thailand, you should generally end your sentence in *khráp* if you're a man, *khâ* if you're a woman – these untranslatable politening syllables will gain goodwill, and are nearly always used after *sawàt dii* (hello/goodbye) and *khàwp khun* (thank you). *Khráp* and *khâ* are also often used to answer "yes" to a question, though the most common way is to repeat the verb of the question (precede it with *mâi* for "no"). *Châi* (yes) and *mâi châi* (no) are less frequently used than their English equivalents.

Hello sawàt dii

Where are you going? pai năi? (not always meant literally, but used as a general greeting)

I'm out having fun/I'm travelling pai thîaw (answer to pai năi, almost indefinable pleasantry)

Goodbye sawàt dii/la kàwn

Good luck/cheers chôhk dii

Excuse me khăw thâwt

Thank you khàwp khun

It's nothing/it doesn't matter mâi pen rai

How are you? sabai dii reŭ?

I'm fine sabai dii

What's your name? khun chêu arai?

My name is... phŏm (men)/diichăn (women) chêu...

I come from... phŏm/diichăn maa jàak...

I don't understand mâi khâo jai

Do you speak English? khun phûut phasăa angkrìt dâi măi?

Do you have...? mii...măi?

Is...possible? ...dâi măi?

Can you help me? chûay phŏm/ diichăn dâi măi?

(I) want... ao...

(I) would like to... yàak jà...

(I) like... châwp...

What is this called in Thai? níi phasăa thai rîak wâa arai?

GETTING AROUND

Where is the...? ...yùu thîi năi?

How far? klai thâo rai?

I would like to go to... yàak jà pai...

Where have you been? pai năi maa?

Where is this bus going? rót níi pai năi?

When will the bus leave? rót jà àwk mêua rai?

What time does the bus arrive in...? rót theŭng... kìi mohng?

Stop here jàwt thîi níi

here thîi níi

there/over there thîi nâan/thîi nôhn

right khwăa

left sái

straight trong

north neŭa

south tâi

east tawan àwk

west tawan tòk

near/far klâi/klai
street thanŏn
train station sathàanii rót fai
bus station sathàanii rót mae
airport sanăam bin
ticket tŭa
hotel rohng raem
post office praisanii
restaurant raan ahăan
shop raan
market talàat
hospital rohng pha-yaabaan
motorbike rót mohtoesai
taxi rót táksîi
boat reua
bicycle jàkràyaan

ACCOMMODATION AND SHOPPING

How much is...? ...thâo rai/kìi bàat?
I don't want a plastic bag, thanks mâi ao thŭng khráp/
khâ
How much is a room here per night? hăwng thîi nîi
kheun lá thâo rai?
Do you have a cheaperroom? mii hâwng thùuk kwàa
măi?
Can I/we look at the room? duu hâwng dâi măi?
I/We'll stay two nights jà yùu săwng kheun
Can you reduce the price? lót raakhaa dâi măi?
Can I store my bag here? fàak krapăo wái thîi nîi dâi
măi?
cheap/expensive thùuk/phaeng
air-con room hăwng ae
ordinary room hăwng thammadaa
telephone thohrásàp
laundry sák phâa
blanket phâa hòm
fan phát lom

GENERAL ADJECTIVES

alone khon diaw
another ìik...nèung
bad mâi dii
big yài
clean sa-àat
closed pìt
cold (object) yen
cold (person or weather) năo
delicious aròi
difficult yâak
dirty sokaprok
easy ngâi
fun sanùk
hot (temperature) ráwn
hot (spicy) phèt

hungry hiŭ khâo
ill mâi sabai
open pòet
pretty sŭay
small lek
thirsty hiŭ nám
tired nèu-ay
very mâak

GENERAL NOUNS

Nouns have no plurals or genders, and don't require an
article.
bathroom/toilet hăwng nám
boyfriend or girlfriend faen
food ahăan
foreigner fàràng
friend phêuan
money ngoen
water/liquid nám

GENERAL VERBS

Thai verbs do not conjugate at all, and also often double
up as nouns and adjectives, which means that foreigners'
most unidiomatic attempts to construct sentences are often
readily understood.
come maa
do tham
eat kin/thaan khâo
give hâi
go pai
sit nâng
sleep nawn làp
walk doen pai

NUMBERS

zero sŭun
one nèung
two săwng
three săam
four sìi
five hâa
six hòk
seven jèt
eight pàet
nine kâo
ten sìp
eleven sìp èt
twelve, thirteen... sìp săwng, sìp săam...
twenty yîi sìp/yiip
twenty-one yîi sìp èt
twenty-two, twenty-three... yîi sìp săwng, yîi sìp
săam...
thirty, forty, etc săam sìp, sìi sìp...
one hundred, two hundred... nèung rói, săwng rói...

one thousand nèung phan
ten thousand nèung mèun
one hundred thousand nèung săen
one million nèung lăan

TIME

The most common system for telling the time, as outlined below, is actually a confusing mix of several different systems. The State Railway and government officials use the 24-hour clock (9am is *kâo naalikaa*, 10am *sìp naalikaa*, and so on), which is always worth trying if you get stuck.

1–5am tii nèung–tii hâa
6–11am hòk mohng cháo–sìp èt mohng cháo
noon thîang
1pm bài mohng
2–4pm bài săwng mohng– bài sìi mohng
5–6pm hâa mohng yen– hòk mohng yen
7–11pm nèung thûm–hâa thûm
midnight thîang kheun
What time is it? kìi mohng láew?
How many hours? kìi chûa mohng?
How long? naan thâo rai?
minute naathii
hour chûa mohng

day wan
week aathít
month deuan
year pii
today wan níi
tomorrow phrûng níi
yesterday mêua wan níi
now diăw níi
next week aathít nâa
last week aathít kàwn
morning cháo
afternoon bài
evening yen
night kheun

DAYS

Sunday wan aathít
Monday wan jan
Tuesday wan angkhaan
Wednesday wan phút
Thursday wan pháréuhàt
Friday wan sùk
Saturday wan săo

FOOD AND DRINK

BASIC INGREDIENTS

kài chicken
mŭu pork
néua beef, meat
pèt duck
ahăan thalay seafood
plaa fish
plaa dùk catfish
plaa mèuk squid
kûng prawn, shrimp
hŏy shellfish
hŏy nang rom oyster
puu crab
khài egg
phàk vegetables

VEGETABLES

makĕua aubergine
makĕua thêt tomato
nàw mái bamboo shoots
tùa ngâwk bean sprouts
phrík chilli
man faràng potato
man faràng thâwt chips
taeng kwaa cucumber
phrík yùak green pepper
krathiam garlic

hèt mushroom
tùa peas, beans or lentils
tôn hŏrm spring onions

NOODLES

ba mìi egg noodles
kwáy tiăw (sên yaì/sên lék) white rice noodles (wide/ thin)
khanŏm jiin nám yaa noodles topped with fish curry
kwáy tiăw/ba mìi haêng rice noodle/egg noodles fried with egg, small pieces of meat and a few vegetables
kwáy tiăw/bamìi nám (mŭu) rice noodle/egg noodle soup, made with chicken broth (and pork balls)
kwáy tiăw/ba mìi rât nâ (mŭu) rice noodles/egg noodles fried in gravy-like sauce with vegetables (and pork slices)
mìi kràwp crisp fried egg noodles with small pieces of meat and a few vegetables
phàt thai thin noodles fried with egg, bean sprouts and tofu, topped with ground peanuts
phàt siyú wide or thin noodles fried with soy sauce, egg and meat

RICE

khâo rice
khâo man kài slices of chicken served over marinated rice

khâo mǔu daeng red pork with rice

khâo nâ kài/pèt chicken/duck served with sauce over rice

khâo niăw sticky rice

khâo phàt fried rice

khâo kaeng curry over rice

khâo tôm rice soup (usually for breakfast)

CURRIES AND SOUPS

kaeng phèt hot, red curry

kaeng phánaeng thick, savoury curry

kaeng khîaw wan green curry

kaeng mátsàman rich Muslim-style curry, usually with beef and potatoes

kaeng karìi mild, Indian-style curry

hàw mòk thalay seafood curry soufflé

kaeng liang peppery vegetable soup

kaeng sôm tamarind soup

tôm khà kài chicken, coconut and galangal soup

tôm yam kûng hot and sour prawn soup

kaeng jèut mild soup with vegetables and usually pork

SALADS

lâap spicy ground meat salad

nám tòk grilled beef or pork salad

sôm tam spicy papaya salad

yam hua plee banana flower salad

yam néua grilled beef salad

yam plaa mèuk squid salad

yam sôm oh pomelo salad

yam plaa dùk foo crispy fried catfish salad

yam thùa phuu wing-bean salad

yam wun sen noodle and pork salad

OTHER DISHES

hâwy thâwt omelette stuffed with mussels

kài phàt bai kraprao chicken fried with holy basil leaves

kài phàt nàw mái chicken with bamboo shoots

kài phàt mét mámûang chicken with cashew nuts

kài phàt khîng chicken with ginger

kài yâang grilled chicken

khài yát sài omelette with pork and vegetables

kûng chúp paêng thâwt prawns fried in batter

mǔu prîaw wǎan sweet and sour pork

néua phàt krathiam phrík thai beef fried with garlic and pepper

néua phàt nám man hâwy beef in oyster sauce

phàt phàk bûng fai daeng morning glory fried in garlic and bean sauce

phàt phàk ruam stir-fried vegetables

pàw pía spring rolls

plaa nêung páe sá whole fish steamed with vegetables and ginger

plaa rât phrík whole fish cooked with chillies

plaa thâwt fried whole fish

sàté satay

thâwt man plaa fish cake

THAI DESSERTS (KHANǑM)

khanǒm beuang small crispy pancake folded over with coconut cream and strands of sweet egg inside

khâo lăam sticky rice, coconut cream and black beans cooked and served in bamboo tubes

khâo niăw daeng sticky red rice mixed with coconut cream

khâo niăw thúrian/mámûang sticky rice mixed with coconut cream and durian/mango

klûay khàek fried banana

lûk taan chêum sweet palm kernels served in syrup

sǎngkhayaaa coconut custard

tàkôh squares of transparent jelly (jello) topped with coconut cream

DRINKS (KHREÛANG DEÙM)

bia beer

chaa ráwn hot tea

chaa yen iced tea

kaafae ráwn hot coffee

kâew glass

khúat bottle

mâekhǒng (or anglicized Mekong) Thai brand-name rice whisky

klûay pan banana shake

nám mánao/sôm fresh, bottled or fizzy lemon/orange juice

nám plào drinking water (boiled or filtered)

nám sǒdaa soda water

nám taan sugar

kleua salt

nám yen cold water

nom jeùd milk

ohlíang iced black coffee

thûay cup

ORDERING

I am vegetarian/vegan **Phǒm (male)/diichǎn (female) kin ahǎan mangsàwirát/jeh**

Can I see the menu? **Khǎw dùu menu nóy?**

I would like… **Khǎw…**

with/without… **Sài/mâi sài…**

Can I have the bill please? **Khǎw check bin?**

Glossary

Amphoe District.

Amphoe muang Provincial capital.

Ao Bay.

Apsara Female deity.

Avalokitesvara Bodhisattva representing compassion.

Avatar Earthly manifestation of a deity.

Ban Village or house.

Bang Village by a river or the sea.

Bencharong Polychromatic ceramics made in China for the Thai market.

Bhumisparsa mudra Most common gesture of Buddha images; symbolizes the Buddha's victory over temptation.

Bodhisattva In Mahayana Buddhism, an enlightened being who postpones his or her entry into Nirvana.

Bot Main sanctuary of a Buddhist temple.

Brahma One of the Hindu trinity – "The Creator". Usually depicted with four faces and four arms.

Celadon Porcelain with grey-green glaze.

Changwat Province.

Chao ley/chao nam "Sea gypsies" – nomadic fisherfolk of south Thailand.

Chedi Reliquary tower in Buddhist temple.

Chofa Finial on temple roof.

Deva Mythical deity.

Devaraja God-king.

Dharma The teachings or doctrine of the Buddha.

Dharmachakra Buddhist Wheel of Law (also known as Wheel of Doctrine or Wheel of Life).

Doi Mountain.

Erawan Mythical three-headed elephant; Indra's vehicle.

Farang Foreigner/foreign.

Ganesh Hindu elephant-headed deity, remover of obstacles and god of knowledge.

Garuda Mythical Hindu creature – half man, half bird; Vishnu's vehicle.

Gopura Entrance pavilion to temple precinct (especially Khmer).

Hamsa Sacred mythical goose; Brahma's vehicle.

Hanuman Monkey god and chief of the monkey army in the *Ramayana*; ally of Rama.

Hat Beach.

Hin Stone.

Hinayana Pejorative term for Theravada school of Buddhism, literally "Lesser Vehicle".

Ho trai A scripture library.

Indra Hindu king of the gods and, in Buddhism, devotee of the Buddha; usually carries a thunderbolt.

Isaan Northeast Thailand.

Jataka Stories of the Buddha's five hundred lives.

Khaen Reed and wood pipe; the characteristic musical instrument of Isaan.

Khao Hill, mountain.

Khlong Canal.

Khon Classical dance-drama.

Kinnari Mythical creature – half woman, half bird.

Kirtimukha Very powerful deity depicted as a lion-head.

Ko Island.

Ku The Lao word for prang; a tower in a temple complex.

Laem Headland or cape.

Lakhon Classical dance-drama.

Lak muang City pillar; revered home for the city's guardian spirit.

Lakshaman/Phra Lak Rama's younger brother.

Lakshana Auspicious signs or "marks of greatness" displayed by the Buddha.

Lanna Northern Thai kingdom that lasted from the thirteenth to the sixteenth century.

Likay Popular folk theatre.

Longyi Burmese sarong.

Luang Pho Abbot or especially revered monk.

Maenam River.

Mahathat Chedi containing relics of the Buddha.

Mahayana School of Buddhism now practised mainly in China, Japan and Korea; literally "the Great Vehicle".

Mara The Evil One; tempter of the Buddha.

Mawn khwaan Traditional triangular or "axe-head" pillow.

Meru/Sineru Mythical mountain at the centre of Hindu and Buddhist cosmologies.

Mondop Small, square temple building to house minor images or religious texts.

Moo/muu Neighbourhood.

Muang City or town.

Muay thai Thai boxing.

Mudra Symbolic gesture of the Buddha.

Mut mee Tie-dyed cotton or silk.

Naga Mythical dragon-headed serpent in Buddhism and Hinduism.

Nakhon Honorific title for a city.

Nam Water.

Nam tok Waterfall.

Nang thalung Shadow-puppet entertainment, found in southern Thailand.

Nielloware Engraved metalwork.

Nirvana Final liberation from the cycle of rebirths; state of non-being to which Buddhists aspire.

Pak Tai Southern Thailand.

Pali Language of ancient India; the script of the original Buddhist scriptures.

Pha sin Woman's sarong.

Phi Animist spirit.

Phra Honorific term – literally "excellent".

Phu Mountain.

Prang Central tower in a Khmer temple.

Prasat Khmer temple complex or central shrine.

Rama/Phra Ram Human manifestation of Hindu deity Vishnu; hero of the *Ramayana*.

Ramakien Thai version of the *Ramayana*.

Ramayana Hindu epic of good versus evil: chief characters include Rama, Sita, Ravana, Hanuman.

Ravana see Totsagan.

Reua hang yao Longtail boat.

Rishi Ascetic hermit.

Rot ae/rot tua Air-conditioned bus.

Rot thammadaa Ordinary bus.

Sala Meeting hall, pavilion, bus stop – or any open-sided structure.

Samlor Three-wheeled passenger tricycle.

Sanskrit Sacred language of Hinduism; also used in Buddhism.

Sanuk Fun.

Sema Boundary stone to mark consecrated ground within temple complex.

Shiva One of the Hindu trinity – "The Destroyer".

Shiva lingam Phallic representation of Shiva.

Soi Lane or side road.

Songkhran Thai New Year.

Songthaew Public transport pick-up vehicle; means "two rows", after its two facing benches.

Takraw Game played with a rattan ball.

Talat Market.

Talat nam Floating market.

Talat yen Night market.

Tambon Subdistrict.

Tavatimsa Buddhist heaven.

Tha Pier.

Thale Sea or lake.

Tham Cave.

Thanon Road.

That Chedi.

Thep A divinity.

Theravada Main school of Buddhist thought in Thailand; also known as Hinayana.

Totsagan Rama's evil rival in the *Ramayana*; also known as Ravana.

Tripitaka Buddhist scriptures.

Trok Alley.

Tuk-tuk Motorized three-wheeled taxi.

Uma Shiva's consort.

Ushnisha Cranial protuberance on Buddha images, signifying an enlightened being.

Viharn Temple assembly hall for the laity; usually contains the principal Buddha image.

Vipassana Buddhist meditation technique; literally "insight".

Vishnu One of the Hindu trinity – "The Preserver". Usually shown with four arms, holding a disc, a conch, a lotus and a club.

Wai Thai greeting expressed by a prayer-like gesture with the hands.

Wang Palace.

Wat Temple.

Wiang Fortified town.

Yaksha Mythical giant.

Yantra Magical combination of numbers and letters, used to ward off danger.

Small print and index

A ROUGH GUIDE TO ROUGH GUIDES

Published in 1982, the first Rough Guide – to Greece – was a student scheme that became a publishing phenomenon. Mark Ellingham, a recent graduate in English from Bristol University, had been travelling in Greece the previous summer and couldn't find the right guidebook. With a small group of friends he wrote his own guide, combining a contemporary, journalistic style with a thoroughly practical approach to travellers' needs.

The immediate success of the book spawned a series that rapidly covered dozens of destinations. And, in addition to impecunious backpackers, Rough Guides soon acquired a much broader readership that relished the guides' wit and inquisitiveness as much as their enthusiastic, critical approach and value-for-money ethos. These days, Rough Guides include recommendations from budget to luxury and cover more than 120 destinations around the globe, from Amsterdam to Zanzibar, all regularly updated by our team of roaming writers.

Browse all our latest guides, read inspirational features and book your trip at **roughguides.com**.

Rough Guide credits

Editor(s): Tom Fleming and Rachel Mills
Cartography: Katie Bennett
Managing editor: Rachel Lawrence
Picture editor: Michelle Bhatia

Cover photo research: Aude Vauconsant
Senior DTP coordinator: Dan May
Head of DTP and Pre-Press: Rebeka Davies

Publishing information

Tenth edition 2018

Distribution

UK, Ireland and Europe
Apa Publications (UK) Ltd; sales@roughguides.com
United States and Canada
Ingram Publisher Services; ips@ingramcontent.com
Australia and New Zealand
Woodslane; info@woodslane.com.au
Southeast Asia
Apa Publications (SN) Pte; sales@roughguides.com
Worldwide
Apa Publications (UK) Ltd; sales@roughguides.com
Special Sales, Content Licensing and CoPublishing
Rough Guides can be purchased in bulk quantities
at discounted prices. We can create special editions,
personalised jackets and corporate imprints tailored to
your needs. sales@roughguides.com.

roughguides.com
Printed in Poland by Pozkal
A catalogue record for this book is available from the
British Library
The publishers and authors have done their best to ensure
the accuracy and currency of all the information in **The
Rough Guide to Thailand**, however, they can accept
no responsibility for any loss, injury, or inconvenience
sustained by any traveller as a result of information or
advice contained in the guide.

Help us update

We've gone to a lot of effort to ensure that the tenth
edition of **The Rough Guide to Thailand** is accurate
and up-to-date. However, things change – places get
"discovered", opening hours are notoriously fickle,
restaurants and rooms raise prices or lower standards. If
you feel we've got it wrong or left something out, we'd like
to know, and if you can remember the address, the price,
the hours, the phone number, so much the better.

Please send your comments with the subject
line "**Rough Guide Thailand Update**" to mail@
uk.roughguides.com. We'll credit all contributions and
send a copy of the next edition (or any other Rough Guide
if you prefer) for the very best emails.

Acknowledgements

Ron Emmons thanks to Chumsaeng Na Ayutthaya (Chiang Khan), Benjaporn Sombatmaithai (Surin), Payungsak Inchai
(Ubon Ratchathani), Brent and Tun Fenneman (Ubon Ratchathani), Siraphat Thongsiri (Khao Yai National Park), Julian
Wright (Nong Khai), the staff at TAT Udon Thani, Pattaraporn Paisoon and Patcharat Noiwanna (Loei), Pattaraporn
Buaprommee (Khon Kaen), David Knapp (Ko Si Chang), Wanpen Chanthariya (Pattaya), Thanyaporn Thirawat (Pattaya),
Maneenuch Assavanichakorn (Ko Chang) and Alessandro Orsi (Ko Kood).

Marco Ferarrese thanks to Andy Turner who commissioned me on this guide, Georgia Stephens who picked it up when
he left, and Tom Fleming who edited it. A special thanks with hugs goes to my wife Kit Yeng Chan, who offered her car,
was my co-pilot, and a perfect moral booster during this umpteenth research trip. At last, a strong heads up to all the
people who helped me out in a way or another during the different legs of the research trip, in particular Maneenuch
Assavanichakorn at Centara.

Paul Gray thanks to Anne Bachmann, Mike Barraclough, Lucy Ridout, Josep Marti Romero and Ron Emmons; Marion
Walsh in Bangkok; Evelien in Kanchanaburi; Tan and Michel in Sukhothai; Fhu and Ung in Nan; Kung in Chiang Khong;
Suda in Chumphon; and Tuppadit Thaiarry and all the staff at Avis. Big thanks to Gade and Stella, who make everything
possible.

Photo credits
(Key: t-top; c-centre; b-bottom; l-left; r-right)

ABOUT THE AUTHORS

Ron Emmons (Ⓦronemmons.com) has been based in Chiang Mai, Thailand, since the late 1980s. He has contributed to several editions of *The Rough Guide to Vietnam* and *The Rough Guide to Thailand*, and has updated guidebooks to Southeast Asian destinations for National Geographic, Frommer's and DK Books. His travel articles and images regularly appear in international publications.

Marco Ferrarese (Ⓦmarcoferrarese.com and Ⓦmonkeyrockworld.com) first came to Thailand in 2007 to escape a frigid Chinese winter, and has kept visiting the country's well-trodden and plain obscure corners from his home base of Penang, Malaysia. Besides writing for Rough Guides, he covers Southeast Asia, the Indian subcontinent and the Middle East for a number of international publications that include Travel + Leisure Southeast Asia, Nikkei Asian Review, The Guardian, BBC Travel, Adventure.com and many regional in-flight magazines.

Paul Gray After twenty years of toing and froing, Paul settled down in Thailand. He is author of *The Rough Guide to Bangkok*, and co-author of *The Rough Guide to Thailand's Beaches and Islands*, as well as *The Rough Guide to Ireland*, and has edited and contributed to many other guidebooks, including an update of his native Northeast for *The Rough Guide to England*.

Index

Map symbols

The symbols below are used on maps throughout the book

	International boundary	ⓘ	Tourist information	🐘	Wildlife park
	Provincial boundary	✉	Post office	⌒	Arch
	Chapter division boundary	☎	Telephone office	⌂	Park HQ
	Expressway	@	Internet access	⊠	Gate/entrance
	Pedestrian road	Ⓢ	Bank/ATM		Swimming
	Road	E	Embassy/consulate		Museum
	One-way street	✚	Hospital/clinic	⊙	Statue
	Steps		Market	∴	Ruins/archeological site
	Unpaved road		Landmark hotel		Temple
	Path	◎	Landmark restaurant		Mosque
	Railway	◆	Point of interest		Hindu temple
	Ferry route	⬆	Border crossing		Chinese temple/pagoda
	Wall	▲	Peak		Church
●---●	Cable car & station	⌃⌃	Mountains		Building
✈	International airport	⌒	Cave		Stadium
✗	Domestic airport		Waterfall		Christian cemetery
★	Transport stop		Spring		Swamps/marshes
⊗	Airline office		Lighthouse		Park/forest
⚓	Port		Viewpoint		Beach

Listings key

▨	Accommodation
●	Eating
▨	Drinking/nightlife
●	Shopping

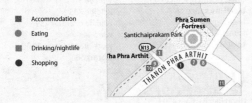